NEW PERSPECTIVES ON

Microsoft® Word 2010

COMPREHENSIVE

Important Information About This Printing
This printing of this book was approved to meet the official standards for the Microsoft Office Specialist Word 2010 Expert exam. This printing includes a new Appendix A that provides:

- Information on Microsoft Office Specialist certification
- Coverage of additional skills related to the exam that are not covered in the main tutorials of this text
- A table that lists the skills for the exam and identifies where each is covered in the text

The information about the Microsoft Office Specialist exams on page ii is also new to this printing. Otherwise, the book contains the exact page-for-page content of previous printings.

What is the Microsoft® Office Specialist Program?

The Microsoft Office Specialist Program enables candidates to show that they have something exceptional to offer—proven expertise in certain Microsoft programs. Recognized by businesses and schools around the world, over 4 million certifications have been obtained in over 100 different countries. The Microsoft Office Specialist Program is the only Microsoft-approved certification program of its kind.

What is the Microsoft Office Specialist Certification?

The Microsoft Office Specialist certification validates through the use of exams that you have obtained specific skill sets within the applicable Microsoft Office programs and other Microsoft programs included in the Microsoft Office Specialist Program. The candidate can choose which exam(s) they want to take according to which skills they want to validate.

The available Microsoft Office Specialist Program exams include*:

- Using Windows Vista®
- Using Microsoft® Office Word 2007
- Using Microsoft® Office Word 2007 – Expert
- Using Microsoft® Office Excel® 2007
- Using Microsoft® Office Excel® 2007 – Expert
- Using Microsoft® Office PowerPoint® 2007
- Using Microsoft® Office Access® 2007
- Using Microsoft® Office Outlook® 2007
- Using Microsoft SharePoint® 2007

The Microsoft Office Specialist Program 2010 exams will include*:

- Microsoft Word 2010
- Microsoft Word 2010 Expert
- Microsoft Excel® 2010
- Microsoft Excel® 2010 Expert
- Microsoft PowerPoint® 2010
- Microsoft Access® 2010
- Microsoft Outlook® 2010
- Microsoft SharePoint® 2010

What does the Microsoft Office Specialist Approved Courseware logo represent?

The logo indicates that this courseware has been approved by Microsoft to cover the course objectives that will be included in the relevant exam. It also means that after utilizing this courseware, you may be better prepared to pass the exams required to become a certified Microsoft Office Specialist.

For more information:

To learn more about Microsoft Office Specialist exams, visit www.microsoft.com/learning/msbc

To learn about other Microsoft approved courseware from Cengage Learning, visit www.cengagebrain.com

The availability of Microsoft Office Specialist certification exams varies by Microsoft program, program version and language. Visit www.microsoft.com/learning for exam availability.

NEW PERSPECTIVES ON

Microsoft® Word 2010

COMPREHENSIVE

S. Scott Zimmerman
Brigham Young University

Beverly B. Zimmerman
Brigham Young University

Ann Shaffer
Katherine T. Pinard

Australia • Brazil • Japan • Korea • Mexico • Singapore • Spain • United Kingdom • United States

New Perspectives on Microsoft Word 2010, Comprehensive

Vice President, Publisher: Nicole Jones Pinard

Executive Editor: Marie L. Lee

Associate Acquisitions Editor: Brandi Shailer

Senior Product Manager: Kathy Finnegan

Product Manager: Leigh Hefferon

Associate Product Manager: Julia Leroux-Lindsey

Editorial Assistant: Jacqueline Lacaire

Director of Marketing: Cheryl Costantini

Senior Marketing Manager: Ryan DeGrote

Marketing Coordinator: Kristen Panciocco

Developmental Editor: Kim T. M. Crowley

Senior Content Project Manager: Jill Braiewa

Content Project Manager: Jennifer Feltri

Composition: GEX Publishing Services

Art Director: Marissa Falco

Text Designer: Althea Chen

Cover Designer: Roycroft Design

Cover Art: © Veer Incorporated

Copyeditor: Michael Beckett

Proofreader: Kathy Orrino

Indexer: Alexandra Nickerson

For product information and technology assistance, contact us at
Cengage Learning Customer & Sales Support, 1-800-354-9706

For permission to use material from this text or product, submit all requests online at **www.cengage.com/permissions**
Further permissions questions can be emailed to
permissionrequest@cengage.com

Library of Congress Control Number: 2010935967

ISBN-13: 978-0-538-74892-6

ISBN-10: 0-538-74892-3

Course Technology
20 Channel Center Street
Boston, MA 02210
USA

Cengage Learning is a leading provider of customized learning solutions with office locations around the globe, including Singapore, the United Kingdom, Australia, Mexico, Brazil, and Japan. Locate your local office at:
international.cengage.com/global

Cengage Learning products are represented in Canada by Nelson Education, Ltd.

To learn more about Course Technology, visit **www.cengage.com/course technology**

To learn more about Cengage Learning, visit **www.cengage.com.**

Purchase any of our products at your local college store or at our preferred online store
www.cengagebrain.com

Printed in the United States of America
2 3 4 5 6 7 16 15 14 13 12 11

Preface

The New Perspectives Series' critical-thinking, problem-solving approach is the ideal way to prepare students to transcend point-and-click skills and take advantage of all that Microsoft Office 2010 has to offer.

In developing the New Perspectives Series, our goal was to create books that give students the software concepts and practical skills they need to succeed beyond the classroom. We've updated our proven case-based pedagogy with more practical content to make learning skills more meaningful to students.

With the New Perspectives Series, students understand *why* they are learning *what* they are learning, and are fully prepared to apply their skills to real-life situations.

"The scenarios in this text provide real-life lessons that engage students while they're learning software skills. The hands-on, project-based assessments immerse students in diverse and interesting situations in which they can apply what they've learned."

—Brian Ameling
Limestone College

About This Book

This book provides complete coverage of Microsoft Word 2010, and includes the following:

- Detailed, hands-on instruction of Word 2010, including creating, editing, and formatting documents; creating MLA-style research papers; working with tables; desktop publishing; performing a mail merge; collaborating with others; working with macros; and creating forms
- Expanded coverage of using themes, styles, style sets, and templates to create professional-looking documents
- Exploration of new features in Word 2010, including working in Backstage view, using the Navigation pane, editing photos, using the Document Translator, and sharing files on SkyDrive

New for this edition!

- Each session begins with a Visual Overview, a new two-page spread that includes colorful, enlarged screenshots with numerous callouts and key term definitions, giving students a comprehensive preview of the topics covered in the session, as well as a handy study guide.
- New ProSkills boxes provide guidance for how to use the software in real-world, professional situations, and related ProSkills exercises integrate the technology skills students learn with one or more of the following soft skills: decision making, problem solving, teamwork, verbal communication, and written communication.
- Important steps are highlighted in yellow with attached margin notes to help students pay attention to completing the steps correctly and avoid time-consuming rework.

System Requirements

This book assumes a typical installation of Microsoft Word 2010 and Microsoft Windows 7 Ultimate using an Aero theme. (You can also complete the material in this text using another version of Windows 7, such as Home Premium, or earlier versions of the Windows operating system. You will see only minor differences in how some windows look.) The browser used for any steps that require a browser is Internet Explorer 8.

"The clear step-by-step instructions, real-world data files, and helpful figures make New Perspectives texts excellent for courses taught in the classroom, the hybrid/blended format, or entirely online."
—Sylvia Amito'elau
Coastline Community College

The New Perspectives Approach

Context
Each tutorial begins with a problem presented in a "real-world" case that is meaningful to students. The case sets the scene to help students understand what they will do in the tutorial.

Hands-on Approach
Each tutorial is divided into manageable sessions that combine reading and hands-on, step-by-step work. Colorful screenshots help guide students through the steps. **Trouble?** tips anticipate common mistakes or problems to help students stay on track and continue with the tutorial.

VISUAL OVERVIEW

Visual Overviews
New for this edition! Each session begins with a Visual Overview, a new two-page spread that includes colorful, enlarged screenshots with numerous callouts and key term definitions, giving students a comprehensive preview of the topics covered in the session, as well as a handy study guide.

PROSKILLS

ProSkills Boxes and Exercises
New for this edition! ProSkills boxes provide guidance for how to use the software in real-world, professional situations, and related ProSkills exercises integrate the technology skills students learn with one or more of the following soft skills: decision making, problem solving, teamwork, verbal communication, and written communication.

KEY STEP

Key Steps
New for this edition! Important steps are highlighted in yellow with attached margin notes to help students pay close attention to completing the steps correctly and avoid time-consuming rework.

INSIGHT

InSight Boxes
InSight boxes offer expert advice and best practices to help students achieve a deeper understanding of the concepts behind the software features and skills.

TIP

Margin Tips
Margin Tips provide helpful hints and shortcuts for more efficient use of the software. The Tips appear in the margin at key points throughout each tutorial, giving students extra information when and where they need it.

REVIEW
APPLY

Assessment
Retention is a key component to learning. At the end of each session, a series of Quick Check questions helps students test their understanding of the material before moving on. Engaging end-of-tutorial Review Assignments and Case Problems have always been a hallmark feature of the New Perspectives Series. Colorful bars and brief descriptions accompany the exercises, making it easy to understand both the goal and level of challenge a particular assignment holds.

REFERENCE
TASK REFERENCE
GLOSSARY/INDEX

Reference
Within each tutorial, Reference boxes appear before a set of steps to provide a succinct summary and preview of how to perform a task. In addition, a complete Task Reference at the back of the book provides quick access to information on how to carry out common tasks. Finally, each book includes a combination Glossary/Index to promote easy reference of material.

www.cengage.com/ct/newperspectives

Our Complete System of Instruction

BRIEF
INTRODUCTORY
COMPREHENSIVE

Coverage To Meet Your Needs

Whether you're looking for just a small amount of coverage or enough to fill a semester-long class, we can provide you with a textbook that meets your needs.

- Brief books typically cover the essential skills in just 2 to 4 tutorials.
- Introductory books build and expand on those skills and contain an average of 5 to 8 tutorials.
- Comprehensive books are great for a full-semester class, and contain 9 to 12+ tutorials.

So if the book you're holding does not provide the right amount of coverage for you, there's probably another offering available. Go to our Web site or contact your Course Technology sales representative to find out what else we offer.

CourseCasts – Learning on the Go. Always available...always relevant.

Want to keep up with the latest technology trends relevant to you? Visit our site to find a library of podcasts, CourseCasts, featuring a "CourseCast of the Week," and download them to your mp3 player at http://coursecasts.course.com.

Our fast-paced world is driven by technology. You know because you're an active participant—always on the go, always keeping up with technological trends, and always learning new ways to embrace technology to power your life.

Ken Baldauf, host of CourseCasts, is a faculty member of the Florida State University Computer Science Department where he is responsible for teaching technology classes to thousands of FSU students each year. Ken is an expert in the latest technology trends; he gathers and sorts through the most pertinent news and information for CourseCasts so your students can spend their time enjoying technology, rather than trying to figure it out. Open or close your lecture with a discussion based on the latest CourseCast.

Visit us at http://coursecasts.course.com to learn on the go!

Instructor Resources

We offer more than just a book. We have all the tools you need to enhance your lectures, check students' work, and generate exams in a new, easier-to-use and completely revised package. This book's Instructor's Manual, ExamView testbank, PowerPoint presentations, data files, solution files, figure files, and a sample syllabus are all available on a single CD-ROM or for downloading at http://www.cengage.com/coursetechnology.

SAM: Skills Assessment Manager

SAM is designed to help bring students from the classroom to the real world. It allows students to train and test on important computer skills in an active, hands-on environment.

SAM's easy-to-use system includes powerful interactive exams, training, and projects on the most commonly used Microsoft Office applications. SAM simulates the Office application environment, allowing students to demonstrate their knowledge and think through the skills by performing real-world tasks, such as bolding text or setting up slide transitions. Add in live-in-the-application projects, and students are on their way to truly learning and applying skills to business-centric documents.

Designed to be used with the New Perspectives Series, SAM includes handy page references, so students can print helpful study guides that match the New Perspectives textbooks used in class. For instructors, SAM also includes robust scheduling and reporting features.

WebTUTOR™

Content for Online Learning

Course Technology has partnered with the leading distance learning solution providers and class-management platforms today. To access this material, visit www.cengage.com/webtutor and search for your title. Instructor resources include the following: additional case projects, sample syllabi, PowerPoint presentations, and more. For students to access this material, they must have purchased a WebTutor PIN-code specific to this title and your campus platform. The resources for students might include (based on instructor preferences): topic reviews, review questions, practice tests, and more. For additional information, please contact your sales representative.

Acknowledgments

Tremendous thanks to Kim Crowley, the world's best developmental editor, who deserves a Nobel prize in thoroughness, accuracy, patience and overall excellence. She's also very nice. Many thanks, too, to the amazing Kathy Finnegan, the hardest working product manager in the publishing business. For all their help and support, we are extremely grateful to the whole New Perspectives team, including Marie Lee, Executive Editor; Brandi Shailer, Associate Acquisitions Editor; Leigh Hefferon, Product Manager; Julia Leroux-Lindsey, Associate Product Manager; and Jacqueline Lacaire, Editorial Assistant. Thanks to Jill Braiewa, Senior Content Project Manager, who oversaw the million details involved in transforming the manuscript into the final book, all the while making it look easy. As always, we relied on the ace Manuscript Quality Assurance testers at Course Technology, who provided detailed comments on every tutorial. Many thanks to Christian Kunciw, MQA Supervisor, and to the following MQA testers: John Freitas, Green Pen Quality Assurance, Susan Pedicini, Danielle Shaw, Marianne Snow, and Teresa Storch.

Finally, we are extremely grateful to our reviewers, who provided valuable insights into the needs of their students: Brian Ameling, Limestone College; Christopher Cheske, Lakeshore Technical College; Kristen Hockman, University of Missouri–Columbia; Ahmed Kamel, Concordia College; Karen O'Connor, Cerro Coso Community College; Kelly Swain, Humber College; Karen Toreson, Shoreline Community College; Bradley West, Sinclair Community College; Raymond Yu, Douglas College; and Violet Zhang, George Brown College.

– Scott Zimmerman
– Beverly Zimmerman
– Ann Shaffer
– Katherine T. Pinard

BRIEF CONTENTS

TABLE OF CONTENTS

WORD LEVEL II TUTORIALS

WORD LEVEL III TUTORIALS

Tutorial 8 Customizing Word and Automating Your Work

Tutorial 9 Creating Online Forms Using Advanced Table Techniques

WINDOWS

Managing Your Files

Organizing Files and Folders with Windows 7

OBJECTIVES

- Develop file management strategies
- Explore files, folders, and libraries
- Create, name, copy, move, and delete folders
- Name, copy, move, and delete files
- Work with compressed files

Case | *Distance Learning Company*

The Distance Learning Company specializes in distance-learning courses for people who want to gain new skills and stay competitive in the job market. Distance learning is formalized education that typically takes place using a computer and the Internet, replacing normal classroom interaction with modern communications technology. The head of the Customer Service Department, Shannon Connell, interacts with the Distance Learning Company's clients on the phone and from her computer. Shannon, like all other employees, is required to learn the basics of managing files on her computer.

In this tutorial, you'll work with Shannon to devise a strategy for managing files. You'll learn how Windows 7 organizes files and folders, and you'll examine Windows 7 file management tools. You'll create folders and organize files within them. You'll also explore options for working with compressed files.

STARTING DATA FILES

Tutorial	Review	Case1
Flyer.docx	Album.pptx	Art-Agenda.docx
Map.png	Bills.xlsx	Art-Eval.docx
Members.htm	Brochure.docx	Art-Notes.docx
Paris.jpg	Budget.xlsx	Garden.jpg
Proposal.docx	Photo.jpg	Inv01.xlsx
Resume.docx	Plan.xlsx	Inv02.xlsx
Rome.jpg	Receipt.xlsx	Inv03.xlsx
Stationery.docx	Sales.xlsx	Sculpture.jpg

VISUAL OVERVIEW

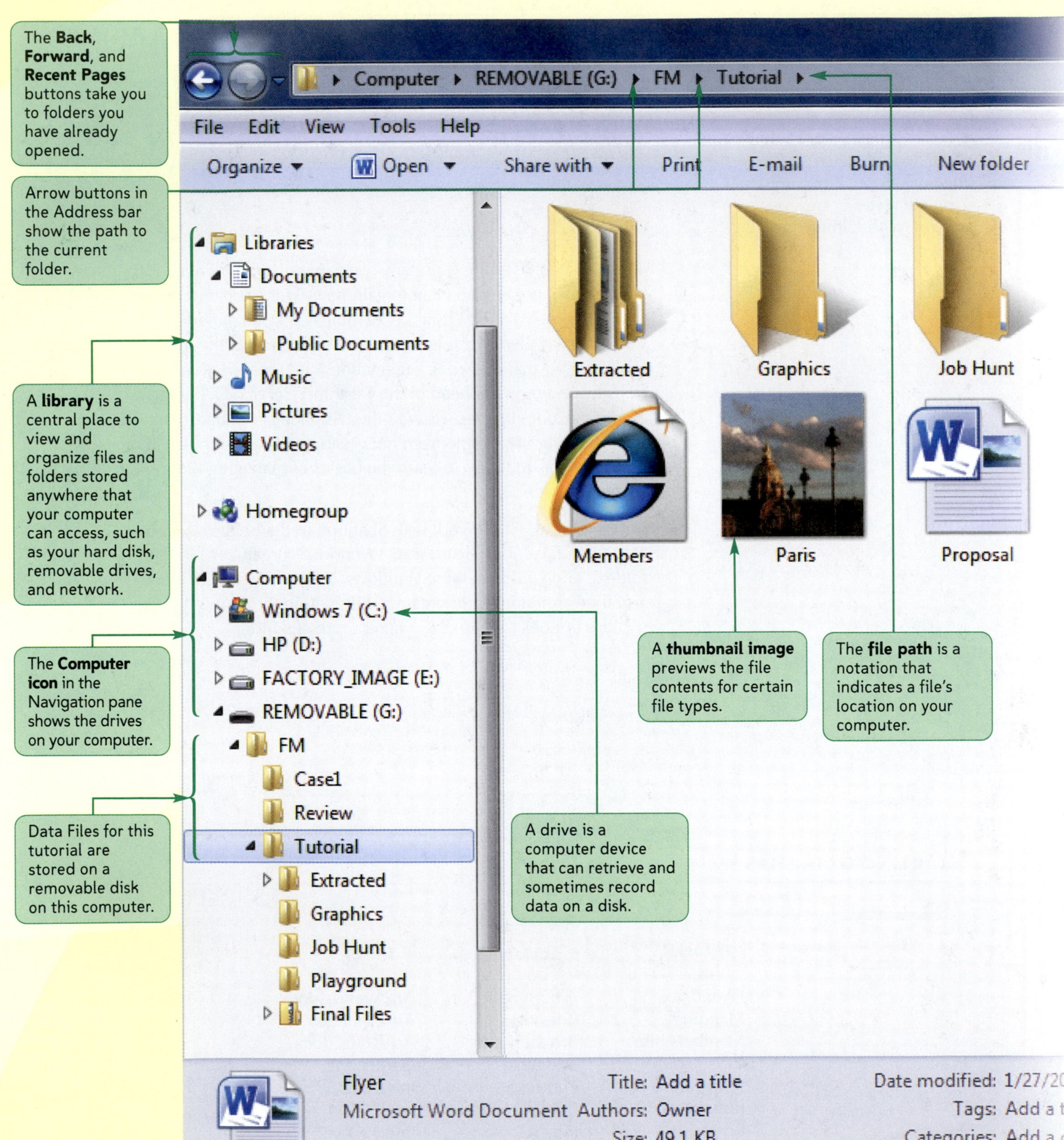

The **Back**, **Forward**, and **Recent Pages** buttons take you to folders you have already opened.
Arrow buttons in the Address bar show the path to the current folder.
A **library** is a central place to view and organize files and folders stored anywhere that your computer can access, such as your hard disk, removable drives, and network.
The **Computer icon** in the Navigation pane shows the drives on your computer.
Data Files for this tutorial are stored on a removable disk on this computer.
A drive is a computer device that can retrieve and sometimes record data on a disk.
A **thumbnail image** previews the file contents for certain file types.
The **file path** is a notation that indicates a file's location on your computer.
Computer ▸ REMOVABLE (G:) ▸ FM ▸ Tutorial ▸
File Edit View Tools Help
Organize Open Share with Print E-mail Burn New folder
Libraries
Documents
My Documents
Public Documents
Music
Pictures
Videos
Homegroup
Computer
Windows 7 (C:)
HP (D:)
FACTORY_IMAGE (E:)
REMOVABLE (G:)
FM
Case1
Review
Tutorial
Extracted
Graphics
Job Hunt
Playground
Final Files
Extracted
Graphics
Job Hunt
Members
Paris
Proposal
Flyer
Microsoft Word Document
Title: Add a title
Authors: Owner
Size: 49.1 KB
Date modified: 1/27/201
Tags: Add a ta
Categories: Add a ca

FILES IN A FOLDER WINDOW

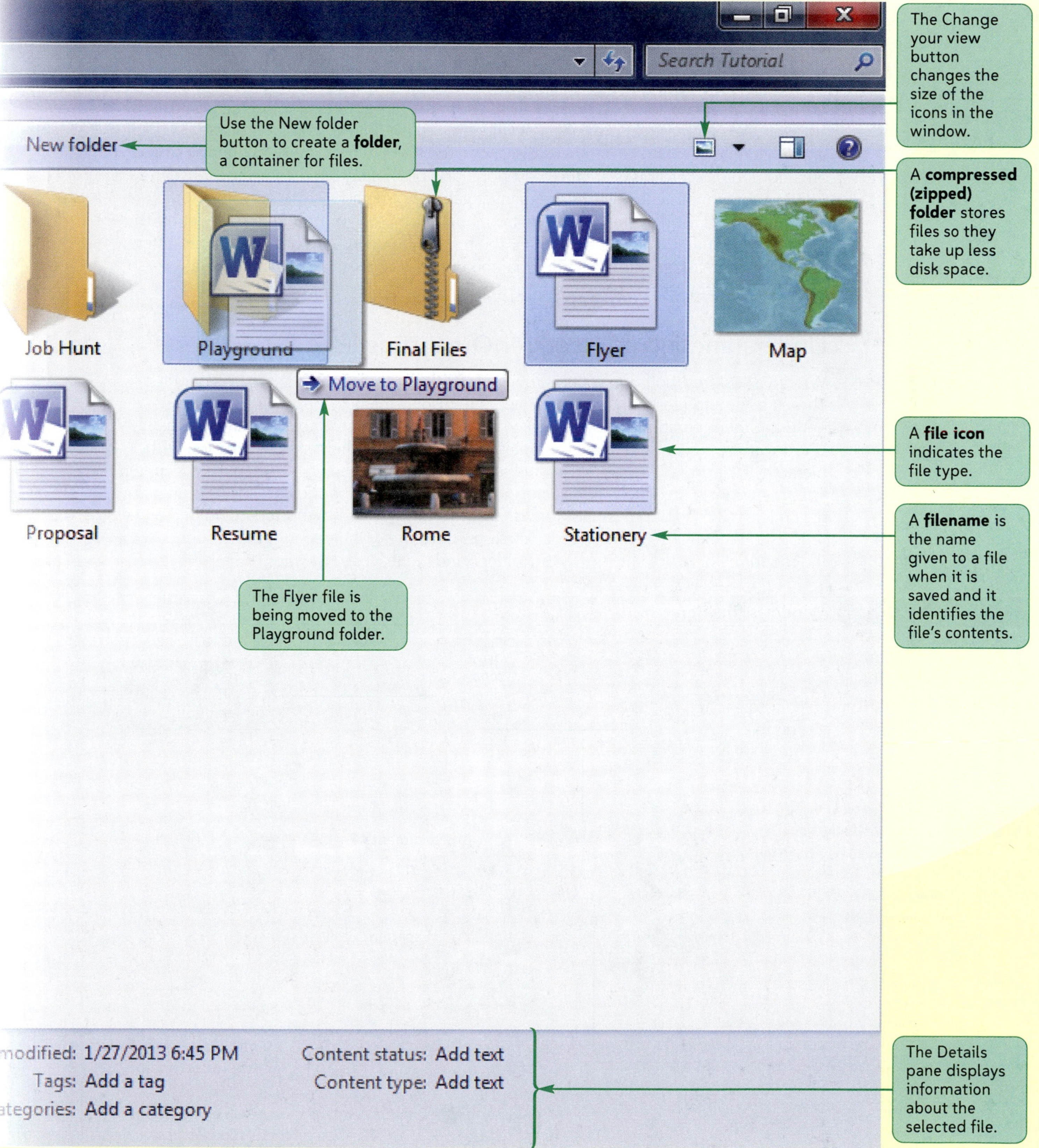

Search Tutorial
New folder
Use the New folder button to create a **folder**, a container for files.
The Change your view button changes the size of the icons in the window.
A **compressed (zipped) folder** stores files so they take up less disk space.
Job Hunt
Playground
Final Files
Flyer
Map
Move to Playground
Proposal
Resume
Rome
Stationery
A **file icon** indicates the file type.
A **filename** is the name given to a file when it is saved and it identifies the file's contents.
The Flyer file is being moved to the Playground folder.
modified: 1/27/2013 6:45 PM
Tags: Add a tag
ategories: Add a category
Content status: Add text
Content type: Add text
The Details pane displays information about the selected file.

Organizing Files and Folders

Knowing how to save, locate, and organize computer files makes you more productive when you are working with a computer. A **file**, often referred to as a document, is a collection of data that has a name and is stored on a computer. After you create a file, you can open it, edit its contents, print it, and save it again—usually using the same program you used to create it. You organize files by storing them in folders. You need to organize files so that you can find them easily and work efficiently.

A computer can store folders and files on different types of disks, ranging from removable media—such as USB drives (also called USB flash drives), compact discs (CDs), and digital video discs (DVDs)—to **hard disks**, or fixed disks, which are permanently stored on a computer. Hard disks are the most popular type of computer storage because they provide an economical way to store many gigabytes of data.

A computer distinguishes one drive from another by assigning each a drive letter. The hard disk is usually assigned to drive C. The remaining drives can have any other letters, but are usually assigned in the order that the drives were installed on the computer—so your USB drive might be drive D or drive G.

Understanding the Need for Organizing Files and Folders

Windows 7 stores thousands of files in many folders on the hard disk of your computer. These are system files that Windows 7 needs to display the desktop, use drives, and perform other operating system tasks. To ensure system stability and to find files quickly, Windows 7 organizes the folders and files in a hierarchy, or **file system**. At the top of the hierarchy, Windows 7 stores folders and files that it needs when you turn on the computer. This location is called the **root directory**, and is usually drive C (the hard disk). The term *root* refers to a popular metaphor for visualizing a file system—an upside-down tree, which reflects the file hierarchy that Windows 7 uses. In Figure 1, the tree trunk corresponds to the root directory, the branches to the folders, and the leaves to the files.

Figure 1 Windows file hierarchy

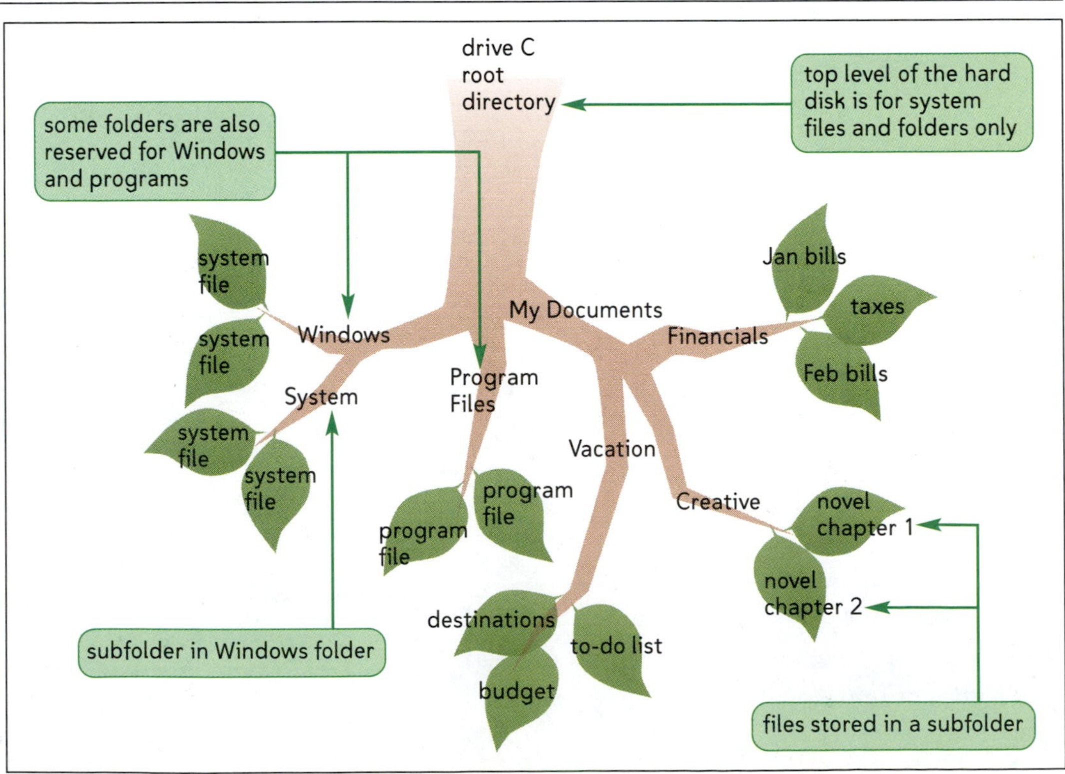

Note that some folders contain other folders. An effectively organized computer contains a few folders in the root directory, and those folders contain other folders, also called **subfolders**.

The root directory, or top level, of the hard disk is for system files and folders only—you should not store your own work here because it could interfere with Windows or a program. (If you are working in a computer lab, you might not be allowed to access the root directory.)

Do not delete or move any files or folders from the root directory of the hard disk—doing so could disrupt the system so that you can't run or start the computer. In fact, you should not reorganize or change any folder that contains installed software because Windows 7 expects to find the files for specific programs within certain folders. If you reorganize or change these folders, Windows 7 cannot locate and start the programs stored in that folder. Likewise, you should not make changes to the folder (usually named Windows) that contains the Windows 7 operating system.

Developing Strategies for Organizing Files and Folders

The type of disk you use to store files determines how you organize those files. Figure 2 shows how you could organize your files on a hard disk if you were taking a full semester of distance-learning classes. To duplicate this organization, you would open the main folder for your documents, create four folders—one each for the Basic Accounting, Computer Concepts, Management Skills II, and Professional Writing courses—and then store the writing assignments you complete in the Professional Writing folder.

Figure 2 **Organizing folders and files on a hard disk**

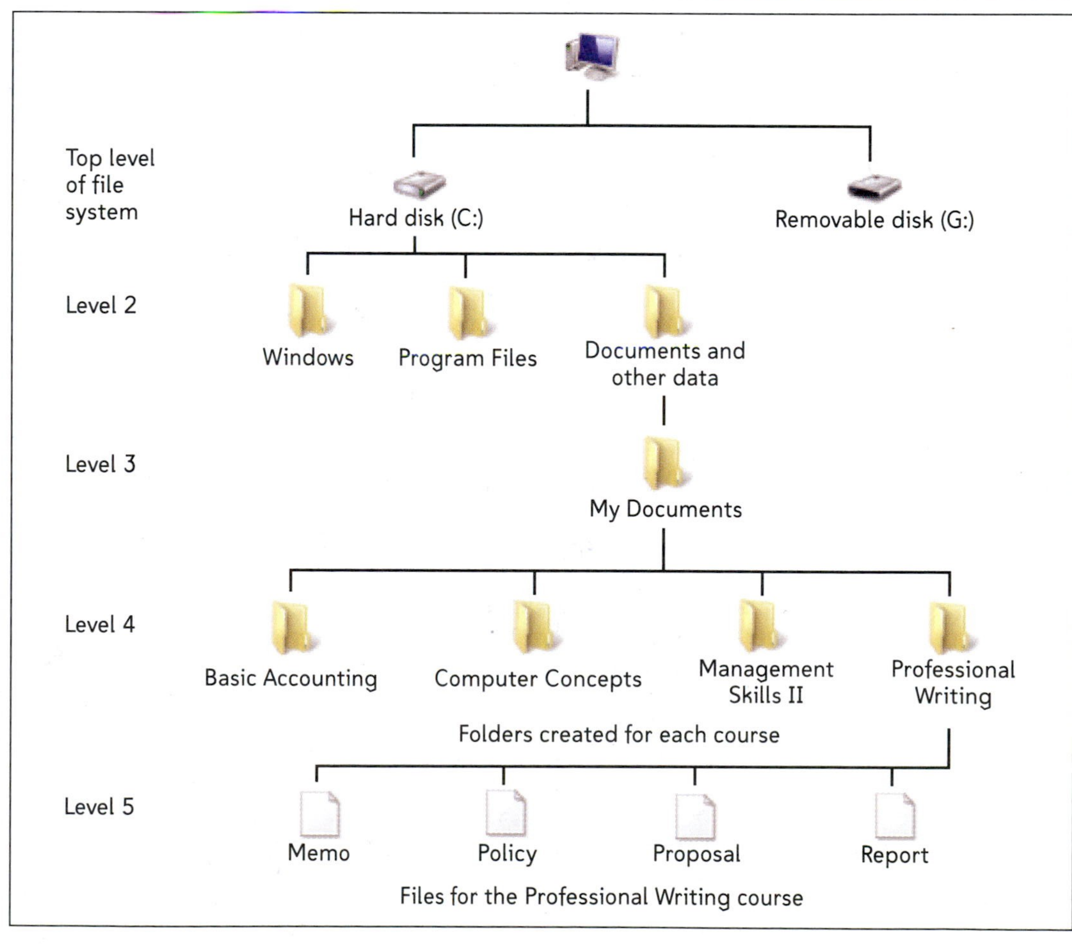

If you store your files on removable media, such as a USB drive or rewritable CD, you can use a simpler organization because you do not have to account for system files. In general, the larger the medium, the more levels of folders you should use because large media can store more files, and, therefore, need better organization. For example, if you are organizing your files on a USB drive, you could create folders in the top level of the USB drive for each general category of documents you store—one each for Courses, Creative, Financials, and Vacation. The Courses folder could then include one folder for each course, and each of those folders could contain the appropriate files.

INSIGHT

Duplicating Your Folder Organization

If you work on two computers, such as one computer at an office or school and another computer at home, you can duplicate the folders you use on both computers to simplify transferring files from one computer to another. For example, if you have four folders in your My Documents folder on your work computer, you would create these same four folders on your removable medium as well as in the My Documents folder of your home computer. If you change a file on the hard disk of your home computer, you can copy the most recent version of the file to the corresponding folder on your removable disk so the file is available when you are at work. You also then have a **backup**, or duplicate copy, of important files.

Exploring Files, Folders, and Libraries

Windows 7 provides two tools for exploring the files and folders on your computer—Windows Explorer and the Computer window. Both display the contents of your computer, using icons to represent drives, folders, and files. However, by default, each presents a slightly different view of your computer. **Windows Explorer** opens to show the contents of the Windows default libraries, making it easy to find the files you work with often, such as documents and pictures. The **Computer window** shows the drives on your computer and makes it easy to perform system tasks, such as viewing system information. You can use either tool to open a **folder window** that displays the files and subfolders in a folder.

Folder windows are divided into two sections, called panes. The left pane is the Navigation pane, which contains icons and links to locations you use often. The right pane lists the contents of your folders and other locations. If you select a folder in the Navigation pane, the contents of that folder appear in the right pane. To display the hierarchy of the folders and other locations on your computer, you select the Computer icon in the Navigation pane, and then select the icon for a drive, such as Local Disk (C:) or Removable Disk (G:). You can then open and explore folders on that drive.

TIP

Move the mouse pointer into the Navigation pane to display the expand and collapse icons.

If the Navigation pane showed all the folders on your computer at once, it could be a very long list. Instead, you open drives and folders only when you want to see what they contain. If a folder contains undisplayed subfolders, an expand icon ▷ appears to the left of the folder icon. (The same is true for drives.) To view the folders contained in an object, you click the expand icon. A collapse icon ◢ then appears next to the folder icon; click the collapse icon to hide the folder's subfolders. To view the files contained in a folder, you click the folder icon, and the files appear in the right pane. See Figure 3.

Figure 3 **Viewing files in a folder window**

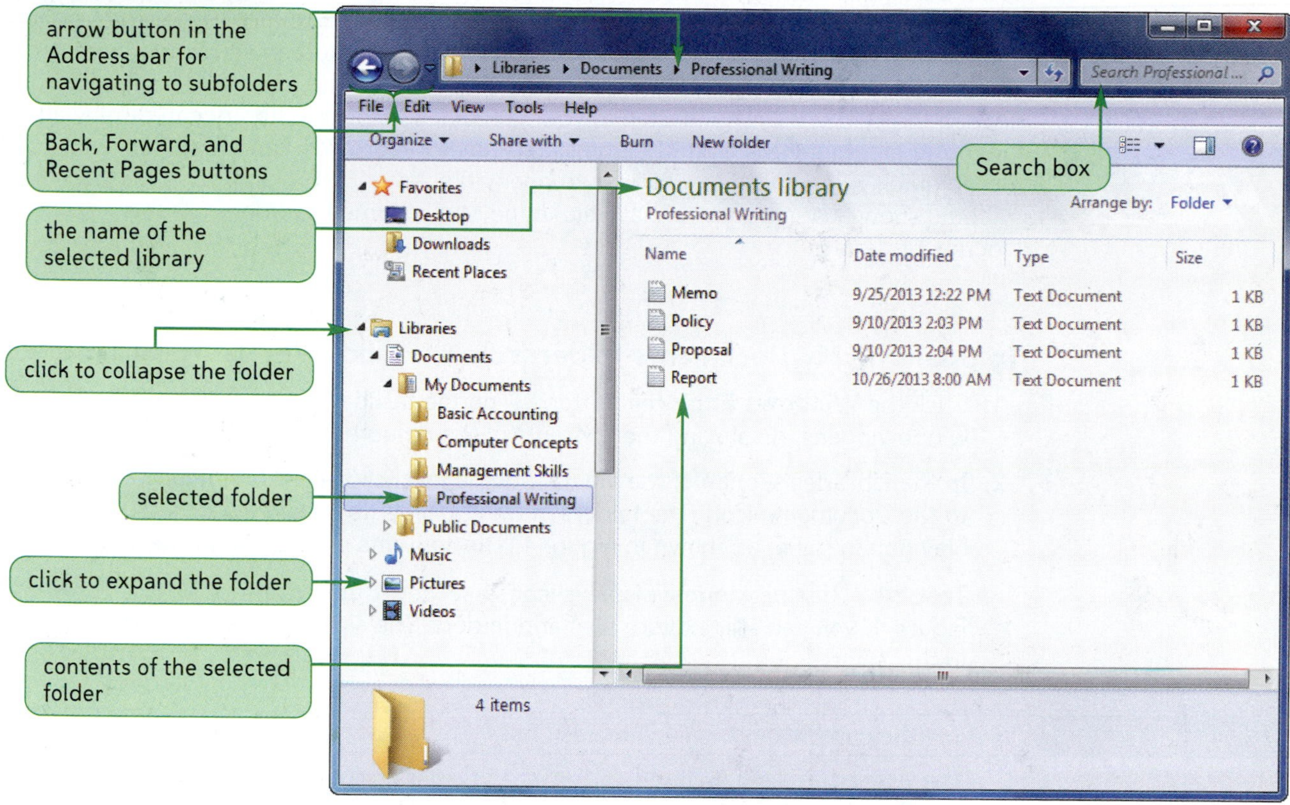

Using the Navigation pane helps you explore your computer and orients you to your current location. As you move, copy, delete, and perform other tasks with the files in the right pane of a folder window, you can refer to the Navigation pane to see how your changes affect the overall organization.

In addition to using the Navigation pane, you can use folder windows and many dialog boxes to explore your computer in the following ways:

- Opening drives and folders in the right pane: To view the contents of a drive or folder, double-click the drive or folder icon in the right pane of a folder window.
- Using the Address bar: Use the Address bar to navigate to a different folder. The Address bar displays your current folder as a series of locations separated by arrows. Click a folder name or an arrow button to navigate to a different location.
- Clicking the Back, Forward, and Recent Pages buttons: Use the Back, Forward, and Recent Pages buttons to navigate to other folders you have already opened. After you change folders, use the Back button to return to the original folder or click the Recent Pages button to navigate to a location you've visited recently.
- Using the Search box: To find a file or folder stored in the current folder or its subfolders, type a word or phrase in the Search box. The search begins as soon as you start typing. Windows finds files based on text in the filename, text within the file, and other characteristics of the file, such as tags (descriptive words or phrases you add to your files) or the author.

Using Libraries and Folders

When you open Windows Explorer, it shows the contents of the Windows built-in libraries by default. A library displays similar types of files together, no matter where they are stored. In contrast, a folder stores files in a specific location, such as in the Professional Writing subfolder of the My Documents folder on the Local Disk (C:) drive. When you want to open the Report file stored in the Professional Writing folder, you must navigate to the Local Disk (C:) drive, then the My Documents folder, and finally the Professional Writing folder. A library makes it easier to access similar types of files. For example, you might store some music files in the My Music folder and others in a folder named Albums on your hard disk. You might also store music files in a Tunes folder on a USB drive. If the USB drive is connected to your computer, the Music library can display all the music files in the My Music, Albums, and Tunes folders. You can then arrange the files to quickly find the ones you want to open and play.

You'll show Shannon how to navigate to the My Documents folder from the Documents library.

To open the My Documents folder from the Documents library:

1. Click the **Windows Explorer** button on the taskbar. The Windows Explorer window opens, displaying the contents of the default libraries.
2. In the Libraries section of the Navigation pane, click the **expand** icon next to the Documents icon. The folders in the Documents library appear in the Navigation pane, as shown in Figure 4. The contents of your computer will differ.

   Trouble? If your window displays icons in a view different from the one shown in Figure 4, you can still explore files and folders. The same is true for all the figures in this tutorial.

Figure 4 Viewing the contents of the Documents library

TIP

By default, the Documents library shows all the documents located in the My Documents folder.

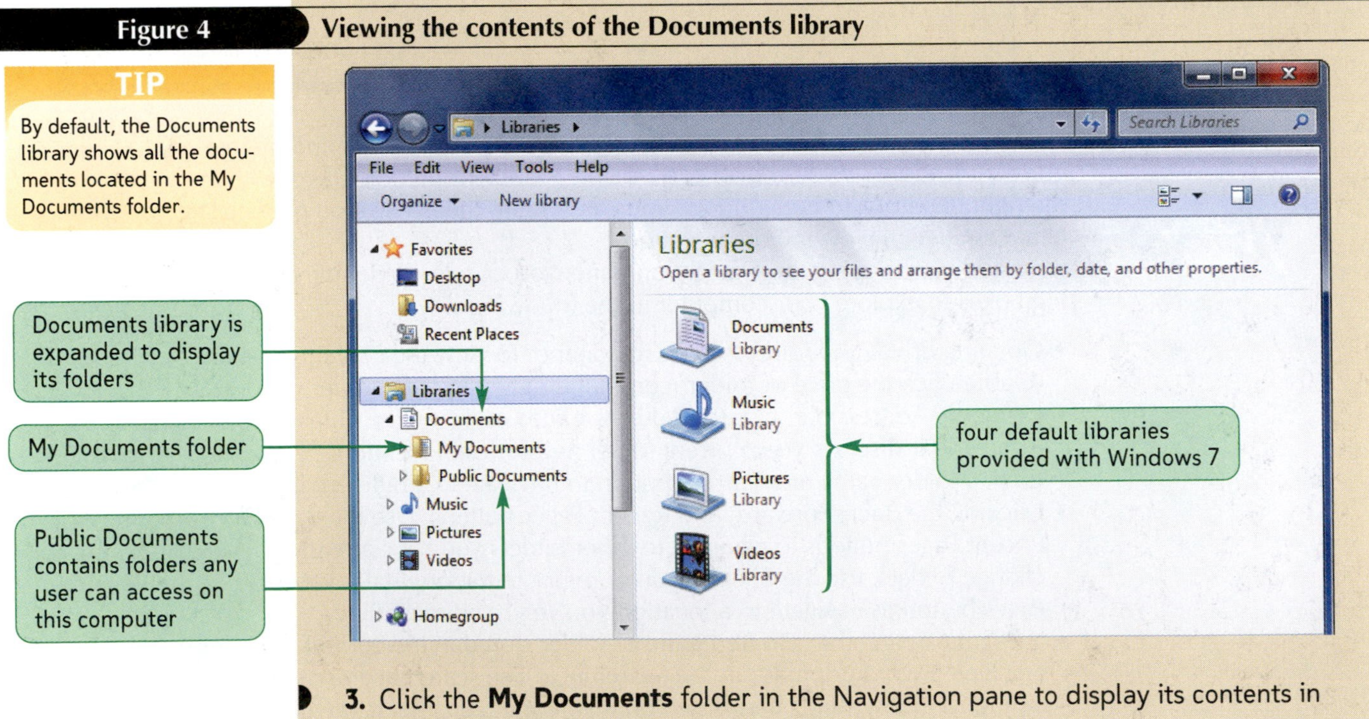

3. Click the **My Documents** folder in the Navigation pane to display its contents in the right pane.

Navigating to Your Data Files

To navigate to the files you want, it helps to know the file path, which leads you through the file and folder organization to your file. For example, the Map file is stored in the Tutorial subfolder of the FM folder. If you are working on a USB drive, for example, the path to this file might be as follows:

G:\FM\Tutorial\Map.png

This path has four parts, and each part is separated by a backslash (\ ):

- G: The drive name; for example, drive G might be the name for the USB drive. (If this file were stored on the hard disk, the drive name would be C.)
- FM: The top-level folder on drive G
- Tutorial: A subfolder in the FM folder
- Map.png: The full filename, including the file extension

If someone tells you to find the file G:\FM\Tutorial\Map.png, you know you must navigate to your USB drive, open the FM folder, and then open the Tutorial folder to find the Map file.

You can use any folder window to navigate to the Data Files you need for the rest of this tutorial. In the following steps, the Data Files are stored on drive G, a USB drive. If necessary, substitute the appropriate drive on your system when you perform the steps.

To navigate to your Data Files:

1. Make sure your computer can access your Data Files for this tutorial. For example, if you are using a USB drive, insert the drive into the USB port.

   Trouble? If you don't have the starting Data Files, you need to get them before you can proceed. Your instructor will either give you the Data Files or ask you to obtain them from a specified location (such as a network drive). In either case, make a backup copy of the Data Files before you start so that you will have the original files available in case you need to start over. If you have any questions about the Data Files, see your instructor or technical support person for assistance.

2. In the open folder window, click the **expand** icon ▷ next to the Computer icon to display the drives on your computer, if necessary.
3. Click the **expand** icon ▷ next to the drive containing your Data Files, such as Removable Disk (G:). A list appears below the drive name showing the folders on that drive.
4. If the list of folders does not include the FM folder, continue clicking the **expand** icon ▷ to navigate to the folder that contains the FM folder.
5. Click the **expand** icon ▷ next to the FM folder, and then click the **FM** folder. Its contents appear in the Navigation pane and in the right pane of the folder window. The FM folder contains the Case1, Review, and Tutorial folders, as shown in Figure 5. The other folders on your system might vary.

Figure 5 Navigating to the FM folder

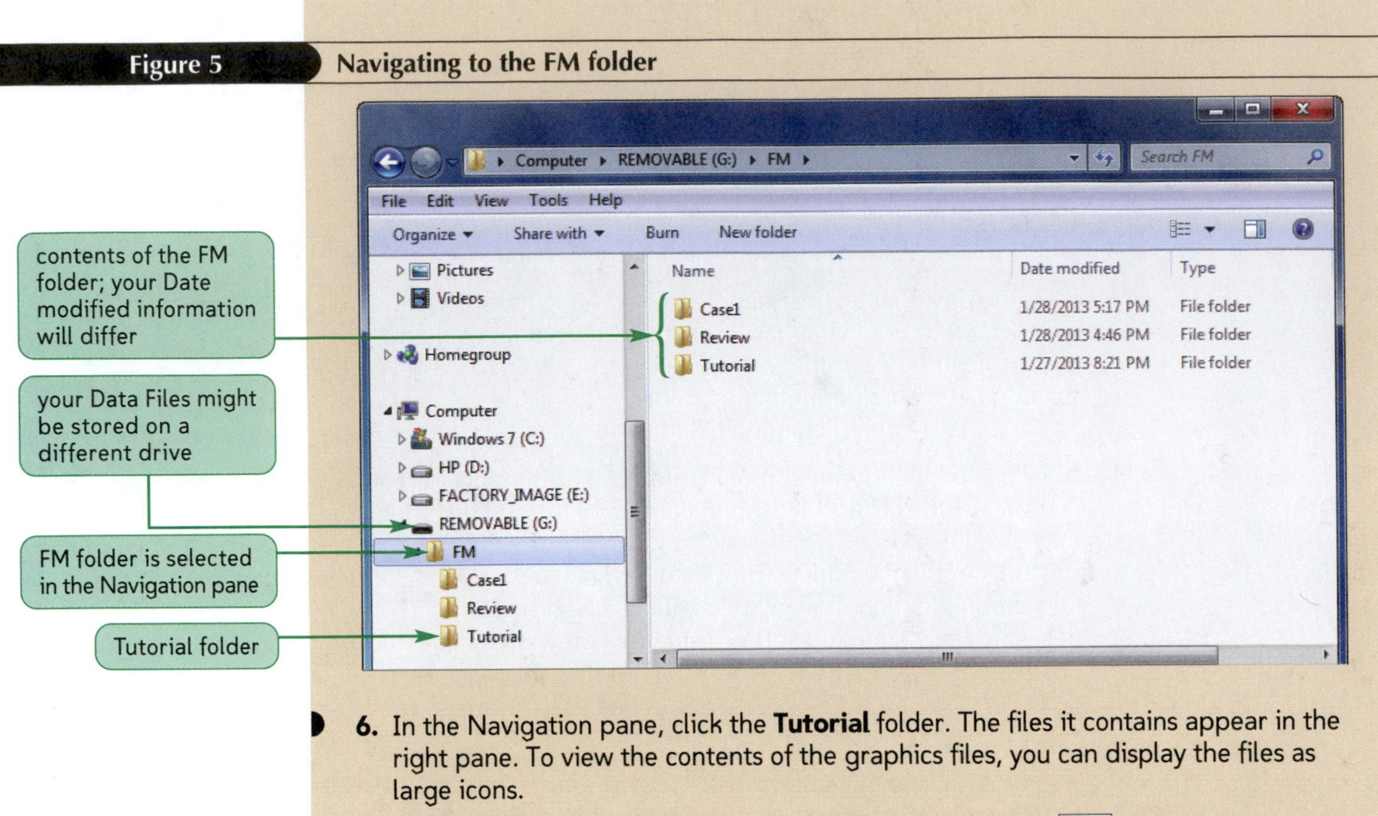

6. In the Navigation pane, click the **Tutorial** folder. The files it contains appear in the right pane. To view the contents of the graphics files, you can display the files as large icons.
7. If necessary, click the **Change your view button arrow** 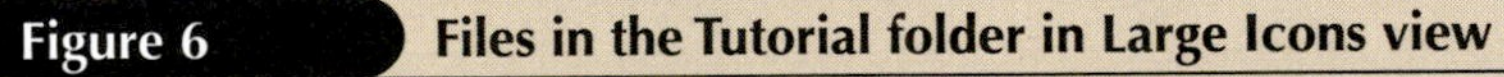 on the toolbar, and then click **Large Icons**. The files appear in Large Icons view in the folder window. See Figure 6.

Figure 6 Files in the Tutorial folder in Large Icons view

TIP

If you change the view of one folder, other folders continue to display files in the default Details view.

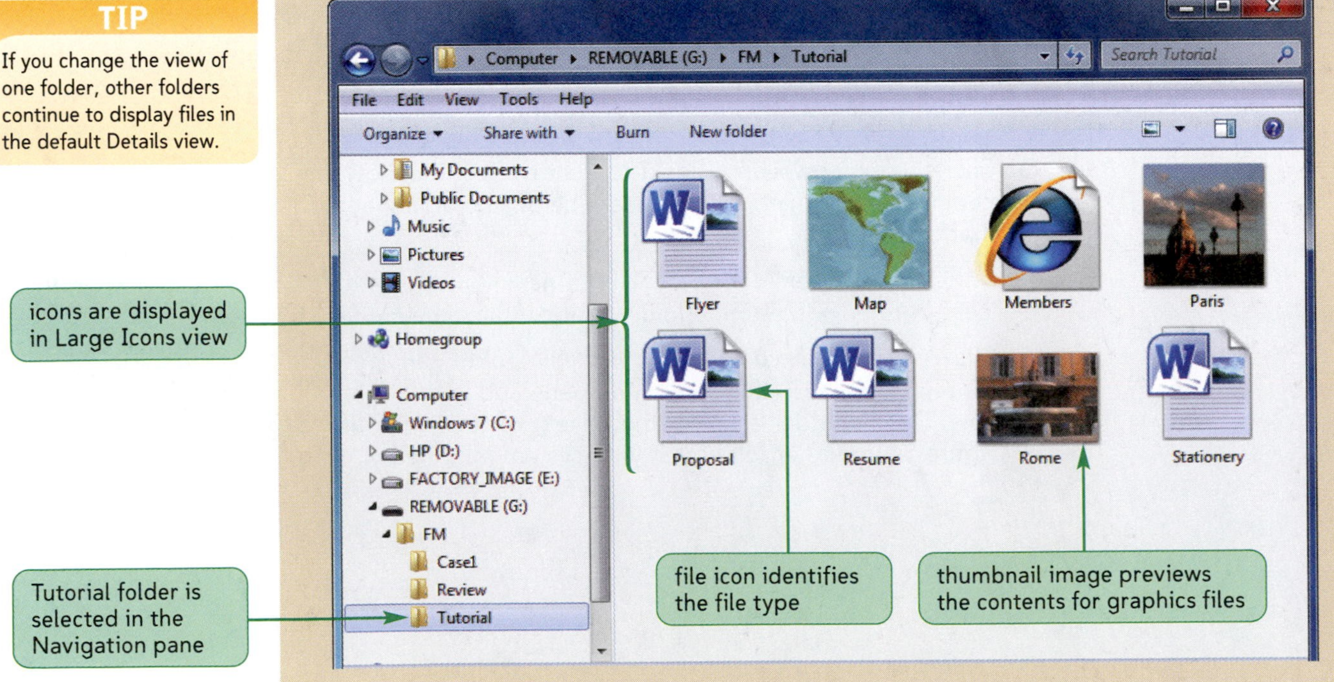

The file icons in your window depend on the programs installed on your computer, so they might be different from the ones shown in Figure 6.

Managing Folders and Files

After you devise a plan for storing your files, you are ready to get organized by creating folders that will hold your files. For this tutorial, you'll create folders in the Tutorial folder. When you are working on your own computer, you usually create folders within the My Documents folder and other standard folders, such as My Music and My Pictures.

Examine the files shown in Figure 6 again and determine which files seem to belong together. Map, Paris, and Rome are all graphics files containing pictures or photos. The Resume and Stationery files were created for a summer job hunt. The other files were created for a neighborhood association trying to update a playground.

One way to organize these files is to create three folders—one for graphics, one for the job hunt files, and another for the playground files. When you create a folder, you give it a name, preferably one that describes its contents. A folder name can have up to 255 characters, except / \ : * ? " < > or |. Considering these conventions, you could create three folders as follows:

- Graphics folder: Map, Paris, and Rome files
- Job Hunt folder: Resume and Stationery files
- Playground folder: Flyer, Proposal, and Members files

INSIGHT

Guidelines for Creating Folders

- Keep folder names short and familiar: Long names can be cut off in a folder window, so use names that are short but clear. Choose names that will be meaningful later, such as project names or course numbers.
- Develop standards for naming folders: Use a consistent naming scheme that is clear to you, such as one that uses a project name as the name of the main folder, and includes step numbers in each subfolder name, such as 01Plan, 02Approvals, 03Prelim, and so on.
- Create subfolders to organize files: If a file listing in a folder window is so long that you must scroll the window, consider organizing those files into subfolders.

Creating Folders

You've already seen folder icons in the windows you've examined. Now, you'll show Shannon how to create folders in the Tutorial folder.

REFERENCE

Creating a Folder in a Folder Window

- In the Navigation pane, click the drive or folder in which you want to create a folder.
- Click New folder on the toolbar.
- Type a name for the folder, and then press the Enter key.

or

- Right-click a folder in the Navigation pane or right-click a blank area in the folder window, point to New, and then click Folder.
- Type a name for the folder, and then press the Enter key.

You'll create the Graphics, Job Hunt, and Playground folders in your Tutorial folder.

To create folders in a folder window:

1. Click the **New folder** button on the toolbar. A folder icon with the label *New folder* appears in the right pane. See Figure 7.

Figure 7 Creating a folder in the Tutorial folder

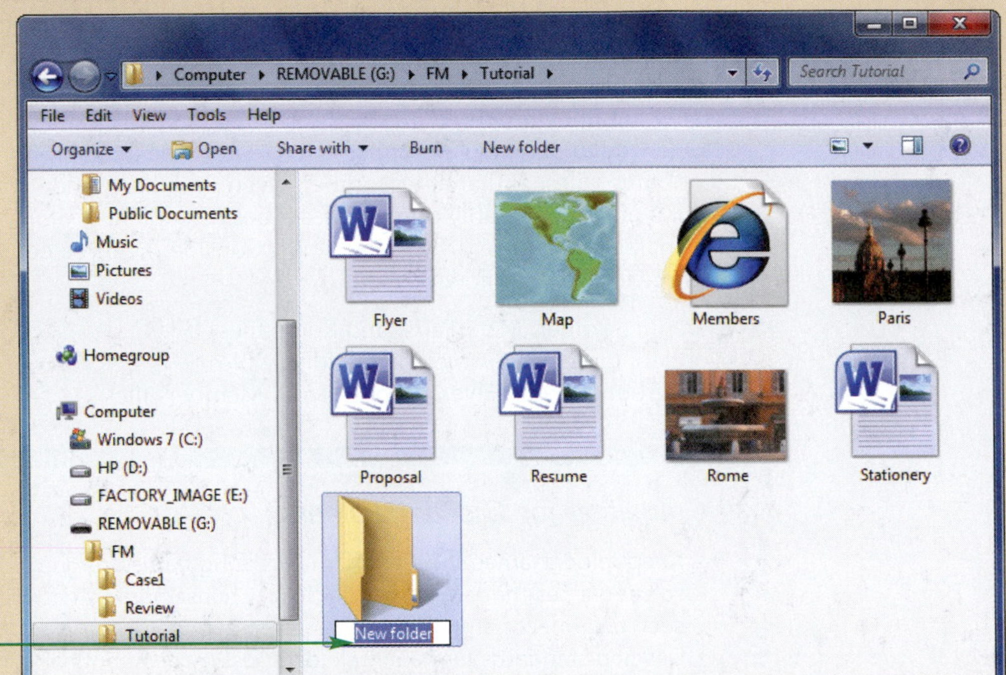

Trouble? If the *New folder* name is not selected, right-click the new folder, click Rename, and then continue with Step 2.

Windows 7 uses *New folder* as a placeholder, and selects the text so that you can replace it with the name you want.

2. Type **Graphics** as the folder name, and then press the **Enter** key. The new folder is named Graphics and is the selected item in the right pane. You'll create a second folder using a shortcut menu.
3. Right-click a blank area near the Graphics folder, point to **New** on the shortcut menu, and then click **Folder**. A folder icon with the label *New folder* appears in the right pane with the *New folder* text selected.
4. Type **Job Hunt** as the name of the new folder, and then press the **Enter** key.
5. Using the toolbar or the shortcut menu, create a folder named **Playground**. The Tutorial folder contains three new subfolders.

Moving and Copying Files and Folders

If you want to place a file into a folder from another location, you can move the file or copy it. **Moving** a file removes it from its current location and places it in a new location you specify. **Copying** also places the file in a new location that you specify, but does not remove it from its current location. Windows 7 provides several techniques for moving and copying files, which you can also use to move and copy folders.

REFERENCE

Moving a File or Folder in a Folder Window

- Right-click and drag the file or folder you want to move to the destination folder.
- Click Move here on the shortcut menu.

or

- Right-click the file or folder you want to move, and then click Cut on the shortcut menu. (You can also click the file or folder and then press the Ctrl+X keys.)
- Navigate to and right-click the destination folder, and then click Paste on the shortcut menu. (You can also click the destination folder and then press the Ctrl+V keys.)

Next, you'll move the Flyer, Proposal, and Members files to the Playground folder.

To move a file using the right mouse button:

1. Point to the **Flyer** file in the right pane, and then press and hold the *right* mouse button.
2. With the right mouse button still pressed down, drag the **Flyer** file to the **Playground** folder. When the *Move to Playground* ScreenTip appears, release the button. A shortcut menu opens.
3. With the left mouse button, click **Move here** on the shortcut menu. The Flyer file is removed from the main Tutorial folder and stored in the Playground subfolder.

   Trouble? If you release the mouse button before dragging the Flyer file to the Playground folder, the shortcut menu opens, letting you move the file to a different folder. Press the Esc key to close the shortcut menu without moving the file, and then repeat Steps 1–3.
4. In the right pane, double-click the **Playground** folder. The Flyer file is in the Playground folder.
5. In the left pane, click the **Tutorial** folder to see its contents. The Tutorial folder no longer contains the Flyer file.

The advantage of moving a file or folder by dragging with the right mouse button is that you can efficiently complete your work with one action. However, this technique requires polished mouse skills so that you can drag the file comfortably. Another way to move files and folders is to use the **Clipboard**, a temporary storage area for files and information that you have copied or moved from one place and plan to use somewhere else. You can select a file and use the Cut or Copy commands to temporarily store the file on the Clipboard, and then use the Paste command to insert the file elsewhere. Although using the Clipboard takes more steps, some users find it easier than dragging with the right mouse button.

You'll move the Resume file to the Job Hunt folder next by using the Clipboard.

To move files using the Clipboard:

1. Right-click the **Resume** file, and then click **Cut** on the shortcut menu. Although the file icon is still displayed in the folder window, Windows 7 removes the Resume file from the Tutorial folder and stores it on the Clipboard.
2. In the right pane, right-click the **Job Hunt** folder, and then click **Paste** on the shortcut menu. Windows 7 pastes the Resume file from the Clipboard to the Job Hunt folder. The Resume file icon no longer appears in the folder window.

3. In the right pane, double-click the **Job Hunt** folder to display its contents. The Job Hunt folder now contains the Resume file.

   Next, you'll move the Stationery file from the Tutorial folder to the Job Hunt folder.

TIP

To use keyboard shortcuts to move files, click the file you want to move, press Ctrl+X to cut the file, navigate to a new location, and then press Ctrl+V to paste the file.

4. Click the **Back** button on the Address bar to return to the Tutorial folder, right-click the **Stationery** file in the folder window, and then click **Cut** on the shortcut menu.
5. Right-click the **Job Hunt** folder, and then click **Paste** on the shortcut menu.
6. Click the **Forward** button on the Address bar to return to the Job Hunt folder. It now contains the Resume and Stationery files. See Figure 8.

Figure 8 **Moving files**

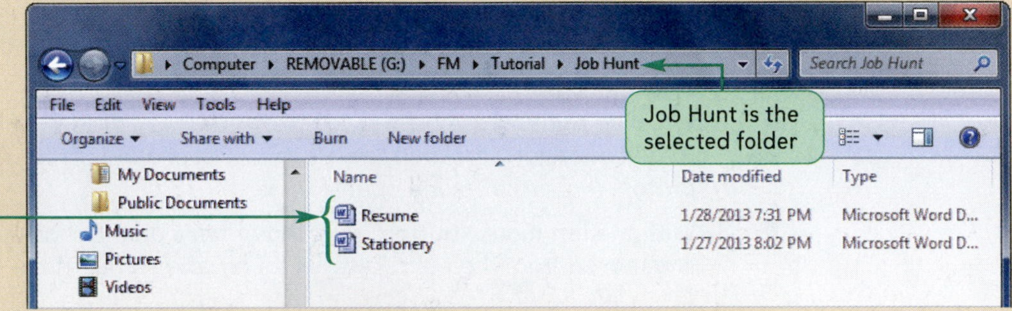

7. Click the **Back** button to return to the Tutorial folder.

You can also copy a file using the same techniques as when you move a file—by dragging with the right mouse button or by using the Clipboard. You can copy more than one file at the same time by selecting all the files you want to copy, and then clicking them as a group. To select files that are listed together in a window, click the first file in the list, hold down the Shift key, click the last file in the list, and then release the Shift key. To select files that are not listed together, click one file, hold down the Ctrl key, click the other files, and then release the Ctrl key.

REFERENCE

Copying a File or Folder in a Folder Window

- Right-click and drag the file or folder you want to move to the destination folder.
- Click Copy here on the shortcut menu.

or

- Right-click the file or folder you want to copy, and then click Copy on the shortcut menu. (You can also click the file or folder and then press the Ctrl+C keys.)
- Navigate to and right-click the destination folder, and then click Paste on the shortcut menu. (You can also click the destination folder and then press the Ctrl+V keys.)

You'll copy the three graphics files from the Tutorial folder to the Graphics folder now.

To copy files using the shortcut menu:

1. In the Tutorial window, click the **Map** file.
2. Hold down the **Ctrl** key, click the **Paris** file, click the **Rome** file, and then release the **Ctrl** key. Three files are selected in the Tutorial window.
3. Right-click a selected file, and then click **Copy** on the shortcut menu.
4. Right-click the **Graphics** folder, and then click **Paste** on the shortcut menu. Windows copies the three files to the Graphics folder.

Now you can use a different technique to copy the Proposal and Members files to the Playground folder.

To copy two files by right-dragging:

1. Click the background of the folder window to remove the selection from the three files, hold down the **Ctrl** key, click the **Members** file, click the **Proposal** file, and then release the **Ctrl** key. The two files are selected in the Tutorial window.
2. Point to a selected file, and then press and hold the *right* mouse button.
3. With the right mouse button still pressed down, drag the **Members** and **Proposal** files to the **Playground** folder, and then release the mouse button. A shortcut menu opens.
4. With the left mouse button, click **Copy here** on the shortcut menu to copy the files to the Playground subfolder.

You can move and copy folders in the same way that you move and copy files. When you do, you move or copy all the files contained in the folder.

PROSKILLS

Decision Making: Determining Where to Store Files

When you create and save files on your computer's hard disk, you should store them in subfolders. The top level of the hard disk is off-limits for your files because they could interfere with system files. If you are working on your own computer, store your files within the My Documents folder, which is where many programs save your files by default. When you use a computer on the job, your employer might assign a main folder to you for storing your work. In either case, if you simply store all your files in one folder, you will soon have trouble finding the files you want. Instead, you should create subfolders within a main folder to separate files in a way that makes sense for you.

Even if you store most of your files on removable media, such as USB drives, you still need to organize those files into folders and subfolders. Before you start creating folders, whether on a hard disk or removable disk, you need to plan the organization you will use.

Naming and Renaming Files

As you work with files, pay attention to filenames—they provide important information about the file, including its contents and purpose. A filename such as Car Sales.docx has three parts:

- Main part of the filename: The name you provide when you create a file, and the name you associate with a file

- Dot: The period (.) that separates the main part of the filename from the file extension
- File extension: Usually three or four characters that follow the dot in the filename

The main part of a filename can have up to 255 characters—this gives you plenty of room to name your file accurately enough so that you'll know the contents of the file just by looking at the filename. You can use spaces and certain punctuation symbols in your filenames. Like folder names, however, filenames cannot contain the symbols \ / ? : * " < > | because these characters have special meaning in Windows 7.

A filename might display an **extension**—three or more characters following a dot—to help you identify files. For example, in the filename Car Sales.docx, the extension *docx* identifies the file as one created by Microsoft Office Word, a word-processing program. You might also have a file called Car Sales.jpg—the *jpg* extension identifies the file as one created in a graphics program, such as Paint. Though the main parts of these filenames are identical, their extensions distinguish them as different files. You usually do not need to add extensions to your filenames because the program that you use to create the file adds the file extension automatically. Also, although Windows 7 keeps track of extensions, not all computers are set to display them.

Be sure to give your files and folders meaningful names that help you remember their purpose and contents. You can easily rename a file or folder by using the Rename command on the file's shortcut menu.

INSIGHT

Guidelines for Naming Files

The following are a few suggestions for naming your files:

- Use common names: Avoid cryptic names that might make sense now, but could cause confusion later, such as nonstandard abbreviations or imprecise names like Stuff2013.
- Don't change the file extension: When renaming a file, don't change the file extension. If you do, Windows might not be able to find a program that can open it.
- Find a comfortable balance between too short and too long: Use filenames that are long enough to be meaningful, but short enough to read easily on the screen.

Next, you'll rename the Flyer file to give it a more descriptive name.

To rename the Flyer file:

1. In the Tutorial folder window, double-click the **Playground** folder to open it.
2. Right-click the **Flyer** file, and then click **Rename** on the shortcut menu. The filename is highlighted and a box appears around it.
3. Type **Raffle Flyer**, and then press the **Enter** key. The file now appears with the new name.

   Trouble? If you make a mistake while typing and you haven't pressed the Enter key yet, press the Backspace key until you delete the mistake, and then complete Step 3. If you've already pressed the Enter key, repeat Steps 2 and 3 to rename the file again.

   Trouble? If your computer is set to display file extensions, a message might appear asking if you are sure you want to change the file extension. Click the No button, right-click the Flyer file, click Rename on the shortcut menu, type *Raffle Flyer*, and then press the Enter key.

All the files in the Tutorial folder are now stored in appropriate subfolders. You can streamline the organization of the Tutorial folder by deleting the duplicate files you no longer need.

Deleting Files and Folders

TIP

A file deleted from removable media, such as a USB drive, does not go into the Recycle Bin. Instead, it is deleted when Windows 7 removes its icon, and cannot be recovered.

You should periodically delete files and folders you no longer need so that your main folders and disks don't get cluttered. In a folder window, you delete a file or folder by deleting its icon. When you delete a file from a hard disk, Windows 7 removes the file from the folder but stores the file contents in the Recycle Bin. The **Recycle Bin** is an area on your hard disk that holds deleted files until you remove them permanently; an icon on the desktop allows you easy access to the Recycle Bin. When you delete a folder from the hard disk, the folder and all of its files are stored in the Recycle Bin. If you change your mind and want to retrieve a file or folder deleted from your hard disk, you can use the Recycle Bin to recover it and return it to its original location. However, after you empty the Recycle Bin, you can no longer recover the files it contained.

Shannon reminds you that because you copied the Map, Paris, Proposal, Members, and Rome files to the Graphics and Playground folders, you can safely delete the original files in the Tutorial folder. As with moving, copying, and renaming files and folders, you can delete a file or folder in many ways, including using a shortcut menu.

To delete files in the Tutorial folder:

1. Use any technique you've learned to navigate to and open the **Tutorial** folder.
2. Click the **first file** in the file list, hold down the **Shift** key, click the **last file** in the file list, and then release the **Shift** key. All the files in the Tutorial folder are now selected. None of the subfolders should be selected.
3. Right-click the selected files, and then click **Delete** on the shortcut menu. Windows 7 asks if you're sure you want to delete these files.

   Make sure you have copied the selected files to the Graphics folder before completing this step.
4. Click the **Yes** button to confirm that you want to delete five files.

So far, you've moved, copied, renamed, and deleted files, but you haven't viewed any of their contents. To view file contents, you can preview or open the file. When you double-click a file in a folder window, Windows 7 starts the associated program and opens the file. To preview the file contents, you can select the file in a folder window, and then click the Show the preview pane button on the toolbar to open the Preview pane, if necessary.

Working with Compressed Files

If you transfer files from one location to another, such as from your hard disk to a removable disk or vice versa, or from one computer to another via e-mail, you can store the files in a compressed (zipped) folder so that they take up less disk space. You can then transfer the files more quickly. When you create a compressed folder, Windows 7 displays a zipper on the folder icon.

You compress a folder so that the files it contains use less space on the disk. Compare two folders—a folder named Photos that contains about 8.6 MB of files, and a compressed folder containing the same files but requiring only 6.5 MB of disk space. In this case, the compressed files use about 25 percent less disk space than the uncompressed files.

You can create a compressed folder using the Send to Compressed (zipped) folder command on the shortcut menu of one or more selected files or folders. Then you can compress additional files or folders by dragging them into the compressed folder. You can open a file directly from a compressed folder, although you cannot modify the file. To edit and save a compressed file, you must extract it first. When you **extract** a file, you create an uncompressed copy of the file in a folder you specify. The original file remains in the compressed folder.

If a different compression program, such as WinZip, has been installed on your computer, the Send to Compressed (zipped) folder command might not appear on the shortcut menu. Instead, it might be replaced by the name of your compression program. In this case, refer to your compression program's Help system for instructions on working with compressed files.

Shannon suggests that you compress the files and folders in the Tutorial folder so you can more quickly transfer them to another location.

To compress the folders and files in the Tutorial folder:

1. Select all the folders in the Tutorial folder, right-click the selected folders, point to **Send to**, and then click **Compressed (zipped) folder**. After a few moments, a new compressed folder with a zipper icon appears in the Tutorial window.

   Trouble? If the Compressed (zipped) folder command does not appear on the Send to submenu of the shortcut menu, this means that a different compression program is probably installed on your computer. Click a blank area of the Tutorial window to close the shortcut menu, and then read but do not perform the remaining steps.

2. Type **Final Files** and then press the **Enter** key to rename the compressed folder. See Figure 9.

   Trouble? If the filename is not selected after you create the compressed folder, right-click the compressed folder, click Rename on the shortcut menu, and then complete Step 2.

Figure 9 Creating a compressed folder

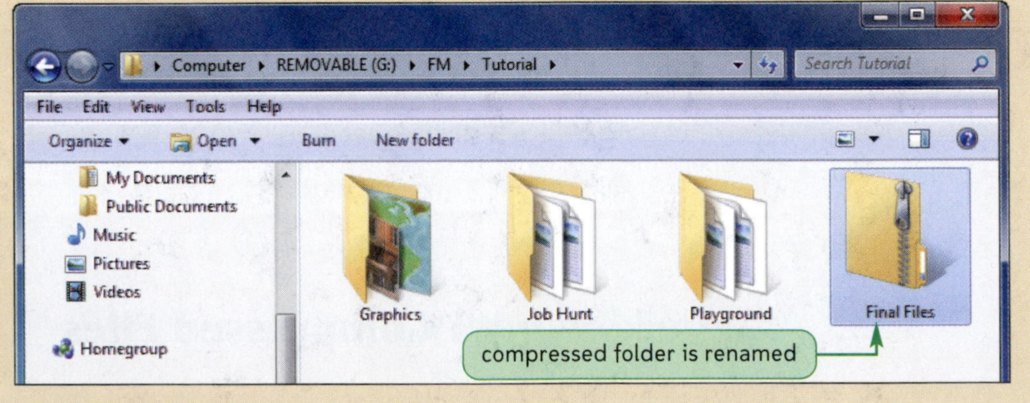

When you compress the folders in the Tutorial folder, the original folders remain in the Tutorial folder—only copies are stored in the new compressed folder.

You open a compressed folder by double-clicking it. You can then move and copy files and folders in a compressed folder, although you cannot rename them. When you extract files, Windows 7 uncompresses and copies them to a location that you specify, preserving the files in their folders as appropriate.

To extract the compressed files:

1. Right-click the **Final Files** compressed folder, and then click **Extract All** on the shortcut menu. The Extract Compressed (Zipped) Folders dialog box opens.
2. Press the **End** key to deselect the path in the text box, press the **Backspace** key as many times as necessary to delete *Final Files*, and then type **Extracted**. The final three parts of the path in the text box should be *\FM\Tutorial\Extracted*. See Figure 10.

Figure 10 Extracting compressed files

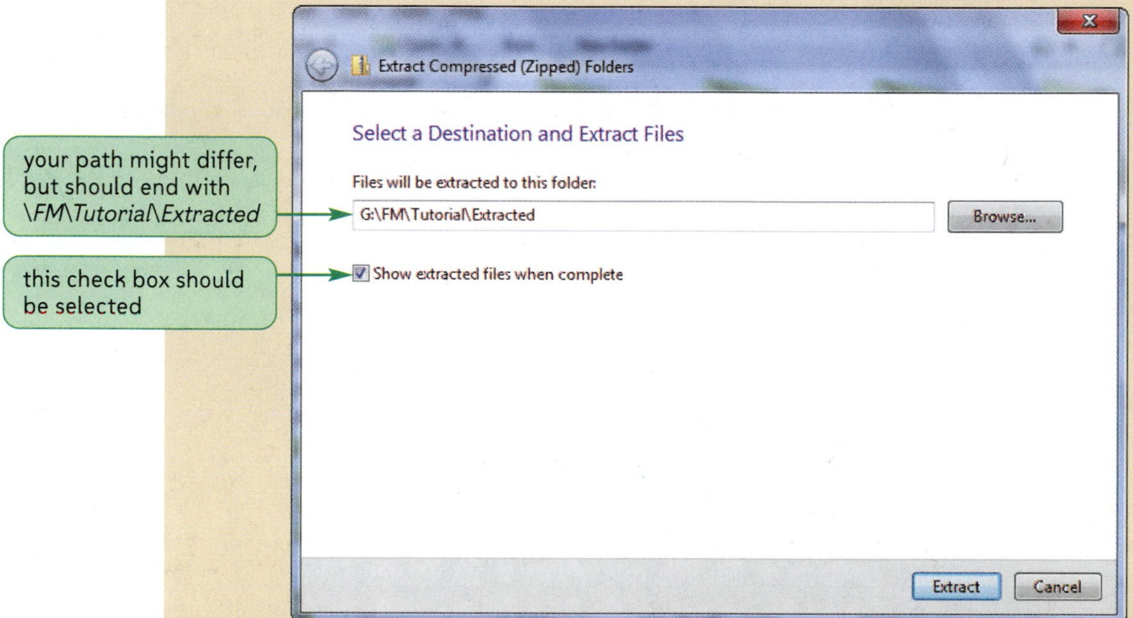

3. Make sure the **Show extracted files when complete** check box is checked, and then click the **Extract** button. The Extracted folder opens, showing the Graphics, Job Hunt, and Playground folders.
4. Open each folder to make sure it contains the files you worked with in this tutorial.
5. Close all open windows.

REVIEW

Quick Check

1. What do you call a named collection of data stored on a disk?
2. The letter *C* is typically used for the ______________ drive of a computer.
3. The term ______________ refers to any window that displays the contents of a folder.
4. Describe the difference between the left and right panes of the Windows Explorer window.
5. What does the file path tell you?
6. True or False. The advantage of moving a file or folder by dragging with the right mouse button is that you can efficiently complete your work with one action.
7. What does a filename indicate?
8. Is a file deleted from a compressed folder when you extract it?

Practice the skills you learned in the tutorial.

PRACTICE

Review Assignments

For a list of Data Files in the Review folder, see page FM 1.

Complete the following steps, recording your answers to any questions:

1. Use a folder window as necessary to find the following information:
   - Where are you supposed to store the files you use in the Review Assignments for this tutorial?
   - Describe the method you will use to navigate to the location where you save your files for this book.
   - Do you need to follow any special guidelines or conventions when naming the files you save for this book? For example, should all the filenames start with your course number or tutorial number? If so, describe the conventions.
   - When you are instructed to open a file for this book, what location are you supposed to use?
   - Describe the method you will use to navigate to this location.
2. Use a folder window to navigate to and open the **FM\Review folder** provided with your Data Files.
3. In the Review folder, create three folders: **Business**, **Marketing**, and **Project**.
4. Move the **Bills**, **Budget**, **Plan**, **Receipt**, and **Sales** files from the Review folder to the Business folder.
5. Move the **Brochure** file to the Marketing folder.
6. Copy the remaining files to the Project folder.
7. Delete the files in the Review folder (do *not* delete any folders).
8. Rename the Photo file in the Project folder as **Pond**.
9. Create a compressed (zipped) folder in the Review folder named **Final Review** that contains all the files and folders in the Review folder.
10. Extract the contents of the Final Review folder to a new folder named **Extracted**. (*Hint*: The file path will end with *\FM\Review\Extracted*.)
11. Locate all copies of the Budget file in the subfolders of the Review folder. In which locations did you find this file?
12. Close all open windows.
13. Submit the results of the preceding steps to your instructor, either in printed or electronic form, as requested.

Use your skills to manage files and folders for an arts organization.

APPLY

Case Problem 1

For a list of Data Files in the Case1 folder, see page FM 1.

Jefferson Street Fine Arts Center Rae Wysnewski owns the Jefferson Street Fine Arts Center (JSFAC) in Pittsburgh, and offers classes and gallery, studio, and practice space for young artists, musicians, and dancers. Rae opened JSFAC two years ago, and this year the center has a record enrollment in its classes. She hires you to teach a painting class and to show her how to manage her files on her new Windows 7 computer. Complete the following steps:

1. In the FM\Case1 folder in your Data Files, create two folders: **Invoices** and **Art Class**.
2. Move the **Inv01**, **Inv02**, and **Inv03** files from the Case1 folder to the Invoices folder.
3. In the Invoices folder, rename the Inv01 file as **Jan**, the Inv02 file as **Feb**, and the Inv03 file as **March**.
4. Move the three text documents from the Case1 folder to the Art Class folder. Rename the three documents, using shorter but still descriptive names.

5. Copy the remaining files in the Case1 folder to the Art Class folder.
6. Switch to Details view, if necessary, and then answer the following questions:
   - What is the largest file in the Art Class folder?
   - How many files in the Art Class folder are JPEG images?
7. Delete the Garden and Sculpture files from the Case1 folder.
8. Open the Recycle Bin folder by double-clicking the Recycle Bin icon on the desktop. Do the Garden and Sculpture files appear in the Recycle Bin folder? Explain why or why not. Close the Recycle Bin window.
9. Make a copy of the Art Class folder in the Case1 folder. The duplicate folder appears as Art Class – Copy. Rename the Art Class – Copy folder as **Images**.
10. Delete the text files from the Images folder.
11. Delete the Garden and Sculpture files from the Art Class folder.
12. Close all open windows, and then submit the results of the preceding steps to your instructor, either in printed or electronic form, as requested.

Use your skills to manage files for a social service organization.

CHALLENGE

Case Problem 2

There are no Data Files needed for this Case Problem.

First Call Outreach Victor Crillo is the director of a social service organization named First Call Outreach in Toledo, Ohio. Its mission is to connect people who need help from local and state agencies to the appropriate service. Victor has a dedicated staff, but they are all relatively new to Windows 7. Because of this, they often have trouble finding files that they have saved on their hard disks. He asks you to demonstrate how to find files in Windows 7. Complete the following:

EXPLORE

1. Windows 7 Help and Support includes topics that explain how to search for files on a disk without looking through all the folders. Click the Start button, click Help and Support, and then use one of the following methods to locate topics on searching for files:
   - In the Windows Help and Support window, click the Learn about Windows Basics link. Click the Working with files and folders link.
   - In the Windows Help and Support window, click the Browse Help topics link. (If necessary, click the Home icon first, and then click the Browse Help topics link.) Click the Files, folders, and libraries link, and then click Working with files and folders.
   - In the Search Help box, type **searching for files**, and then press the Enter key. Click the Working with files and folders link.

EXPLORE

2. In the *In this article* section, click Finding files. Read the topic and click any *See also* or *For more information* links, if necessary, to provide the following information:
   a. Where is the Search box located?
   b. Do you need to type the entire filename to find the file?
   c. What does it mean to filter the view?

EXPLORE

3. Use the Windows 7 Help and Support window to locate topics related to using libraries. Read the topics to answer the following questions:
   a. What are the names of the four default libraries?
   b. When you move, copy, or save files in the Pictures library, in what folder are they actually stored?
   c. What can you click to play all the music files in the Music library?
4. Submit the results of the preceding steps to your instructor, either in printed or electronic form, as requested.

ASSESS

SAM: Skills Assessment Manager

For current SAM information, including versions and content details, visit SAM Central (http://samcentral.course.com). If you have a SAM user profile, you may have access to hands-on instruction, practice, and assessment of the skills covered in this tutorial. Since various versions of SAM are supported throughout the life of this text, check with your instructor for the correct instructions and URL/Web site for accessing assignments.

ENDING DATA FILES

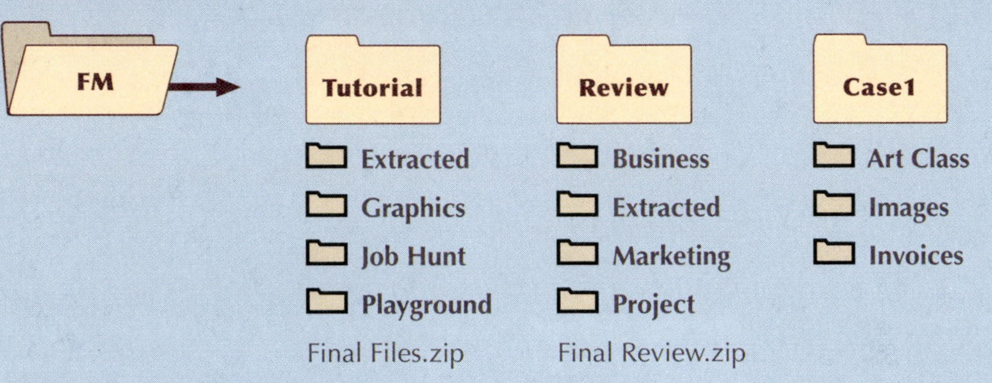

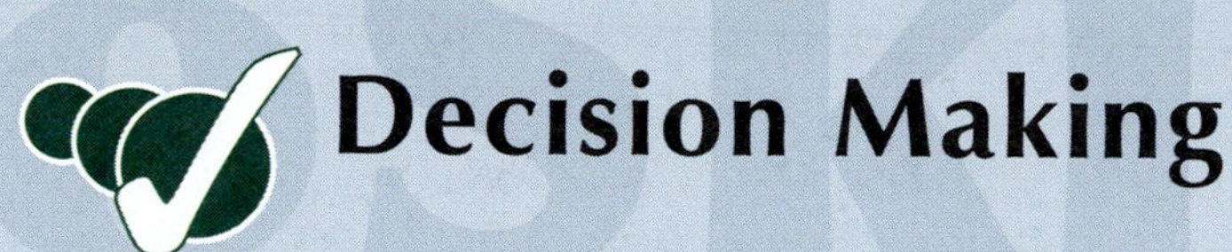

Choosing the Most Efficient Organization for Your Computer Files

Decision making is choosing the best option from many possible alternatives. The alternative you select is your decision. When making a decision, you typically complete the following steps:

1. Gather information.
2. Make predictions.
3. Select the best alternative.
4. Prepare an action plan.
5. Perform tasks and monitor results.
6. Verify the accuracy of the decision.

If you are involved in making a complex decision that affects many people, you perform all six steps in the process. If you are making a simpler decision that does not affect many people, you can perform only those steps that relate to your decision.

Gather Information and Select the Best Alternative

Start by gathering information to identify your alternatives. For example, when organizing your files, you could store most of your work on your computer hard disk or on removable media, such as a USB drive or an external hard drive. Ask questions that quantify information, or use numbers to compare the alternatives. For example, how much space do you need for your files? In how many locations do you need to access the files? How often do you work with your files?

Next, ask questions that compare the qualities of the alternatives. For example, is one alternative easier to perform or maintain than another? After testing each alternative by asking both types of questions, one alternative should emerge as the best choice for you. If one option does not seem like the best alternative, continue comparing alternatives by listing the pros and cons of each.

Prepare an Action Plan

After you make a decision, prepare an action plan by identifying the steps you need to perform to put the decision into practice. One way to do this is to work backward from your final goal. If you are determining how best to manage your computer files, your final goal might be a set of folders and files organized so that you can find any file quickly. Start by listing the tasks you need to perform to meet your goal. Be as specific as possible to avoid confusion later. For example, instead of listing *Create folders* as a task, identify each folder and subfolder by name and indicate which files or types of files each folder should contain.

Next, estimate how long each task will take, and assign the task to someone. For simple decisions, you assign most tasks to yourself. If you need to use outside resources, include those in the action plan. For example, if you decide to store your files on USB drives, include a step to purchase the drives you need. If someone else needs to approve any of your tasks, be sure to include that step in the action plan. If appropriate, the action plan can also track your budget. For example, you could track expenses for a new hard disk or backup media.

ProSkills

Complete the Tasks and Monitor the Results

After you prepare an action plan and receive any necessary approvals, perform the tasks outlined in the plan. For example, create or rename the folders you identified in your action plan, and then move existing files into each folder. As you perform each step, mark its status as complete or pending, for example.

When you complete all the tasks in the action plan, monitor the results. For example, after reorganizing your files, did you meet your goal of being able to quickly find any file when you need it? If so, continue to follow your plan as you add files and folders to your computer. If not, return to your plan and determine where you could improve it.

PROSKILLS

Organize Your Files

Now that you have reviewed the fundamentals of managing files, organize the files and folders you use for course work or for other projects on your own computer. Be sure to follow the guidelines presented in this tutorial for developing an organization strategy, creating folders, naming files, and moving, copying, deleting, and compressing files. To manage your own files, complete the following tasks:

1. Use a program such as Word, WordPad, or Notepad to create a plan for organizing your files. List the types of files you work with, and then determine whether you want to store them on your hard disk or on removable media. Then sketch the folders and subfolders you will use to manage these files. If you choose a hard disk as your storage medium, make sure you plan to store your work files and folders in a subfolder of the Documents folder.
2. Use Windows Explorer or the Computer window to navigate to your files. Determine which tool you prefer for managing files, if you have a preference.
3. Create or rename the main folders you want to use for your files. Then create or rename the subfolders you will use.
4. Move and copy files to the appropriate folders according to your plan, and rename and delete files as necessary.
5. Create a backup copy of your work files by creating a compressed file and then copying the compressed file to a removable disk, such as a USB flash drive.
6. Submit your finished plan to your instructor, either in printed or electronic form, as requested.

OFFICE

Getting Started with Microsoft Office 2010

Preparing a Meeting Agenda

OBJECTIVES

- Explore the programs in Microsoft Office
- Start programs and switch between them
- Explore common window elements
- Minimize, maximize, and restore windows
- Use the Ribbon, tabs, and buttons
- Use the contextual tabs, the Mini toolbar, and shortcut menus
- Save, close, and open a file
- Learn how to share files using SkyDrive
- Use the Help system
- Preview and print a file
- Exit programs

Case | *Recycled Palette*

Recycled Palette, a company in Oregon founded by Ean Nogella in 2006, sells 100 percent recycled latex paint to both individuals and businesses in the area. The high-quality recycled paint is filtered to industry standards and tested for performance and environmental safety. The paint is available in both 1 gallon cans and 5 gallon pails, and comes in colors ranging from white to shades of brown, blue, green, and red. The demand for affordable recycled paint has been growing each year. Ean and all his employees use Microsoft Office 2010, which provides everyone in the company with the power and flexibility to store a variety of information, create consistent files, and share data. In this tutorial, you'll review how the company's employees use Microsoft Office 2010.

STARTING DATA FILES

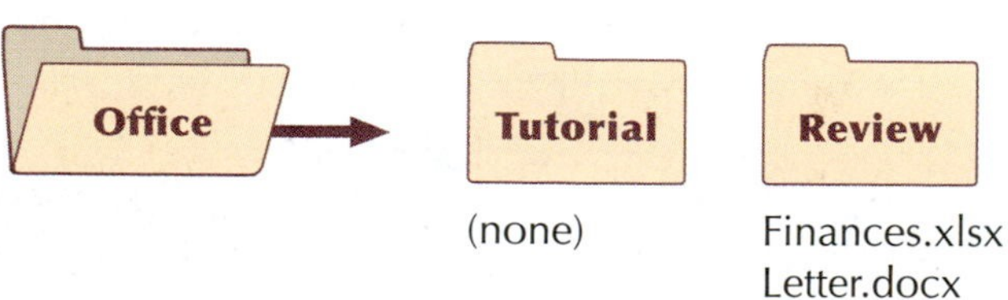

(none)

Finances.xlsx
Letter.docx

VISUAL OVERVIEW

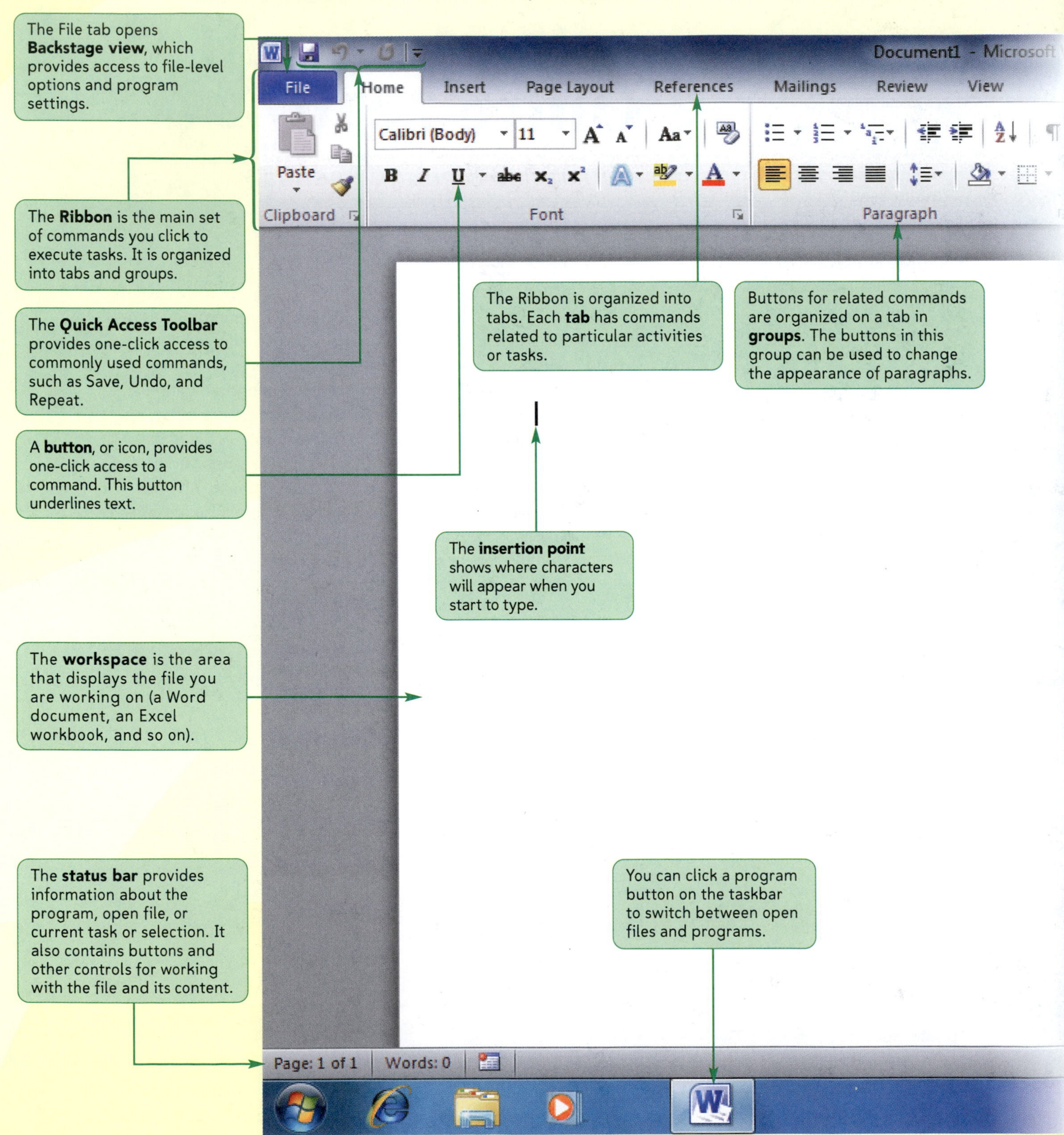

The File tab opens **Backstage view**, which provides access to file-level options and program settings.
The **Ribbon** is the main set of commands you click to execute tasks. It is organized into tabs and groups.
The **Quick Access Toolbar** provides one-click access to commonly used commands, such as Save, Undo, and Repeat.
A **button**, or icon, provides one-click access to a command. This button underlines text.
The Ribbon is organized into tabs. Each **tab** has commands related to particular activities or tasks.
Buttons for related commands are organized on a tab in **groups**. The buttons in this group can be used to change the appearance of paragraphs.
The **insertion point** shows where characters will appear when you start to type.
The **workspace** is the area that displays the file you are working on (a Word document, an Excel workbook, and so on).
The **status bar** provides information about the program, open file, or current task or selection. It also contains buttons and other controls for working with the file and its content.
You can click a program button on the taskbar to switch between open files and programs.
Document1 - Microsoft
File
Home
Insert
Page Layout
References
Mailings
Review
View
Calibri (Body)
11
Paste
Clipboard
Font
Paragraph
Page: 1 of 1
Words: 0

COMMON WINDOW ELEMENTS

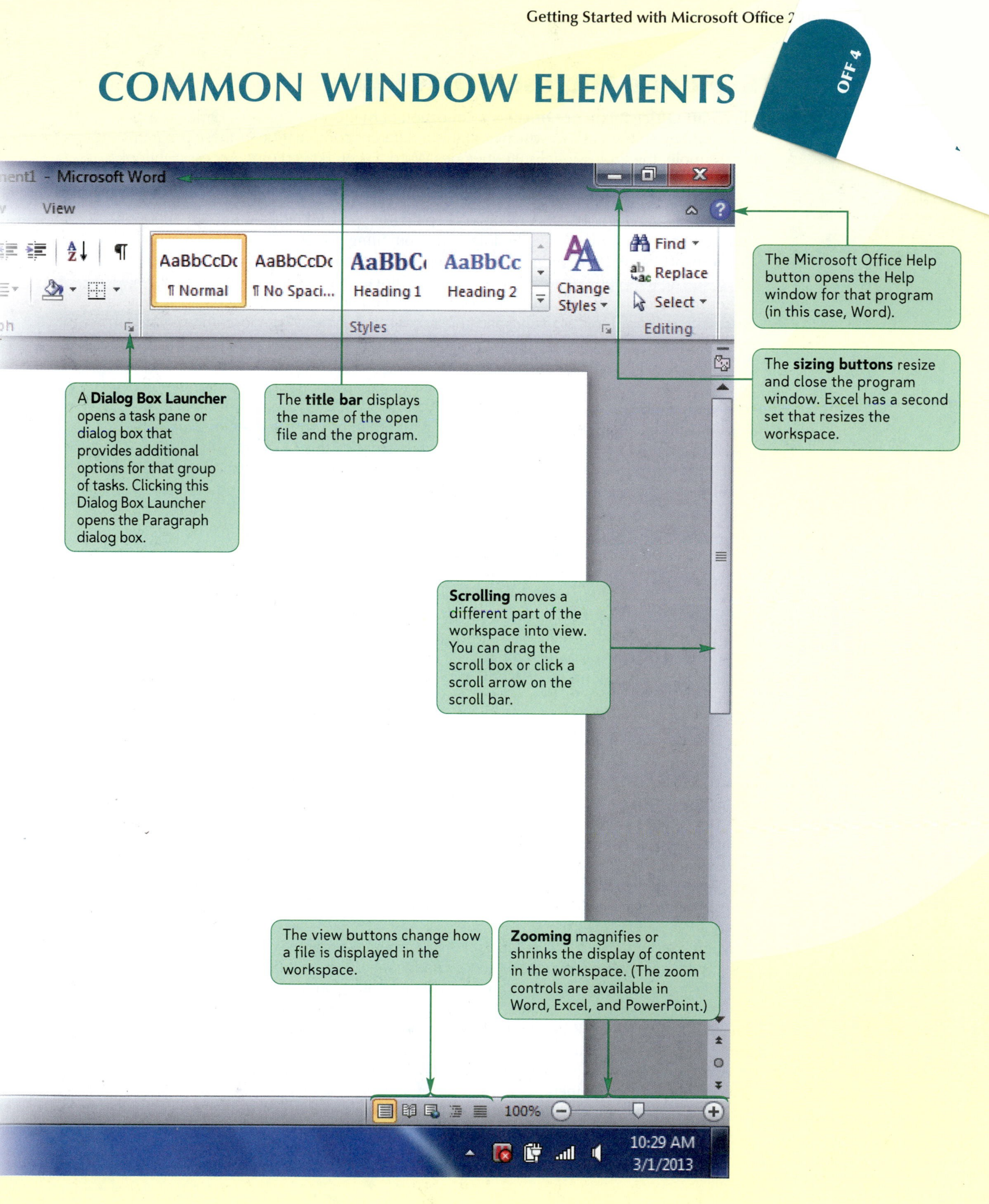

ment1 - Microsoft Word
View
AaBbCcDc
¶ Normal
AaBbCcDc
¶ No Spaci...
AaBbC
Heading 1
AaBbCc
Heading 2
Change Styles
Find
Replace
Select
Styles
Editing
The Microsoft Office Help button opens the Help window for that program (in this case, Word).
The **sizing buttons** resize and close the program window. Excel has a second set that resizes the workspace.
A **Dialog Box Launcher** opens a task pane or dialog box that provides additional options for that group of tasks. Clicking this Dialog Box Launcher opens the Paragraph dialog box.
The **title bar** displays the name of the open file and the program.
Scrolling moves a different part of the workspace into view. You can drag the scroll box or click a scroll arrow on the scroll bar.
The view buttons change how a file is displayed in the workspace.
Zooming magnifies or shrinks the display of content in the workspace. (The zoom controls are available in Word, Excel, and PowerPoint.)
100%
10:29 AM
3/1/2013

Exploring Microsoft Office 2010

TIP

For additional information about the available suites, go to the Microsoft Web site.

Microsoft Office 2010, or **Office**, is a collection of Microsoft programs. Office is available in many suites, each of which contains a different combination of these programs. For example, the Professional suite includes Word, Excel, PowerPoint, Access, Outlook, Publisher, and OneNote. Other suites are available and can include more or fewer programs. Each Office program contains valuable tools to help you accomplish many tasks, such as composing reports, analyzing data, preparing presentations, compiling information, sending email, planning schedules, and compiling notes.

Microsoft Word 2010, or **Word**, is a computer program you use to enter, edit, and format text. The files you create in Word are called **documents**, although many people use the term *document* to refer to any file created on a computer. Word, often called a word-processing program, offers many special features that help you compose and update all types of documents, ranging from letters and newsletters to reports, brochures, faxes, and even books, in attractive and readable formats. You can also use Word to create, insert, and position figures, tables, and other graphics to enhance the look of your documents. For example, the Recycled Palette employees create business letters using Word.

Microsoft Excel 2010, or **Excel**, is a computer program you use to enter, calculate, analyze, and present numerical data. You can do some of this in Word with tables, but Excel provides many more tools for recording and formatting numbers as well as performing calculations. The graphics capabilities in Excel also enable you to display data visually. You might, for example, generate a pie chart or a bar chart to help people quickly see the significance of and the connections between information. The files you create in Excel are called **workbooks** (commonly referred to as spreadsheets), and Excel is often called a spreadsheet program. The Recycled Palette accounting department uses a line chart in an Excel workbook to visually track the company's financial performance.

Microsoft Access 2010, or **Access**, is a computer program used to enter, maintain, and retrieve related information (or data) in a format known as a database. The files you create in Access are called **databases**, and Access is often referred to as a database or relational database program. With Access, you can create forms to make data entry easier, and you can create professional reports to improve the readability of your data. The Recycled Palette operations department tracks the company's inventory in an Access database.

Microsoft PowerPoint 2010, or **PowerPoint**, is a computer program you use to create a collection of slides that can contain text, charts, pictures, sound, movies, multimedia, and so on. The files you create in PowerPoint are called **presentations**, and PowerPoint is often called a presentation graphics program. You can show these presentations on your computer monitor, project them onto a screen as a slide show, print them, share them over the Internet, or display them on the Web. You can also use PowerPoint to generate presentation-related documents such as audience handouts, outlines, and speakers' notes. The Recycled Palette marketing department uses a PowerPoint slide presentation to promote its paints.

Microsoft Outlook 2010, or **Outlook**, is a computer program you use to send, receive, and organize email; plan your schedule; arrange meetings; organize contacts; create a to-do list; and record notes. You can also use Outlook to print schedules, task lists, phone directories, and other documents. Outlook is often referred to as an information management program. The Recycled Palette staff members use Outlook to send and receive email, plan their schedules, and create to-do lists.

Although each Office program individually is a strong tool, their potential is even greater when used together.

PROSKILLS

Teamwork: Integrating Office Programs

One of the main advantages of Office is **integration**, the ability to share information between programs. Integration ensures consistency and accuracy, and it saves time because you don't have to reenter the same information in several Office programs. It also means that team members can effortlessly share Office files. Team members can create files based on their skills and information that can be used by others as needed. The staff at Recycled Palette uses the integration features of Office every day, as described in the following examples:

- The accounting department created an Excel bar chart on fourth-quarter results for the previous two years, and inserted it into the quarterly financial report created in Word. The Word report includes a hyperlink that employees can click to open the Excel workbook and view the original data.
- The operations department included an Excel pie chart of sales percentages by paint colors on a PowerPoint slide, which is part of a presentation to stockholders.
- The marketing department produced a mailing to promote its recycled paints to local contractors and designers by combining a form letter created in Word with an Access database that stores the names and addresses of these potential customers.
- A sales representative merged the upcoming promotion letter that the marketing department created in Word with an Outlook contact list containing the names and addresses of prospective customers.

Even these few examples of how information from one Office program can be integrated with another illustrate how integration can save time and effort. Each team member can focus on creating files in the program best suited to convey the information he or she is responsible for. Yet, everyone can share the files, using them as needed for their specific purpose.

Starting Office Programs

You can start any Office program from the Start menu on the taskbar. As soon as the program starts, you can immediately begin to create new files or work with existing ones.

REFERENCE

Starting an Office Program

- On the taskbar, click the Start button.
- On the Start menu, click All Programs, click Microsoft Office, and then click the name of the program to start.

or

- Click the name of the program to start in the left pane of the Start menu.

You'll start Word using the Start button.

To start Word and open a new, blank document:

1. Make sure your computer is on and the Windows desktop appears on your screen.

   Trouble? If your screen varies slightly from those shown in the figures, your computer might be set up differently. The figures in this book were created while running Windows 7 with the Aero feature turned on, but how your screen looks depends on the version of Windows you are using, the resolution of your screen, and other settings.

2. On the taskbar, click the **Start** button, and then click **All Programs** to display the All Programs list.

3. Click **Microsoft Office**, and then point to **Microsoft Word 2010**. Depending on how your computer is set up, your desktop and menu might contain different icons and commands. See Figure 1.

Figure 1 Start menu with All Programs list displayed

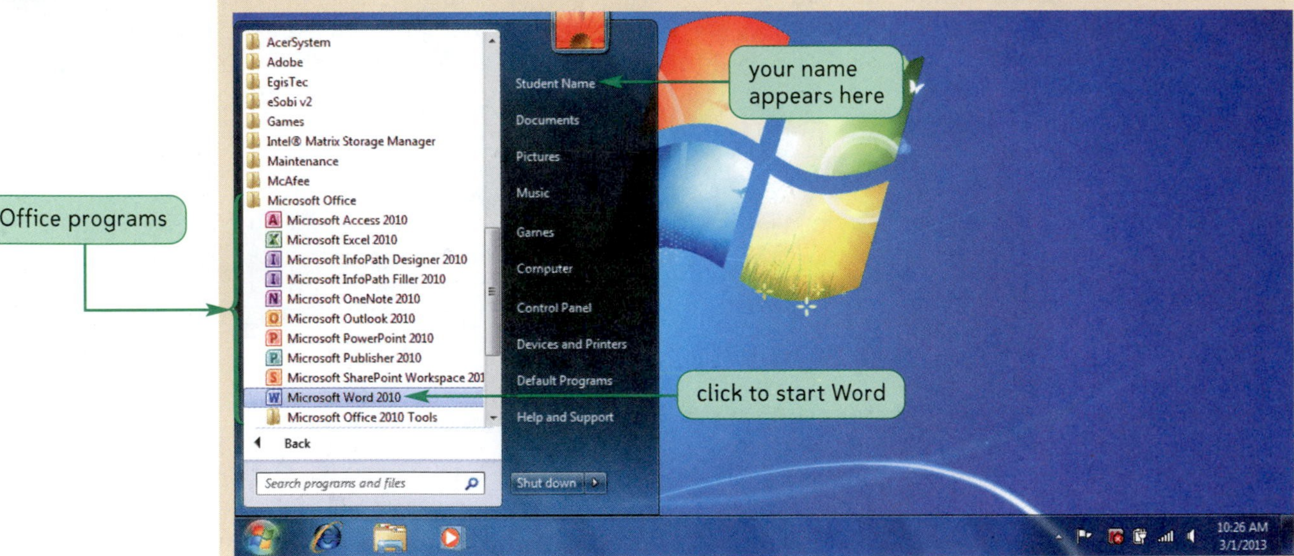

   Trouble? If you don't see Microsoft Office on the All Programs list, point to Microsoft Word 2010 on the All Programs menu. If you still don't see Microsoft Word 2010, ask your instructor or technical support person for help.

4. Click **Microsoft Word 2010**. Word starts and a new, blank document opens. Refer to the Visual Overview to review the common program window elements.

   Trouble? If the Word window doesn't fill your entire screen as shown in the Visual Overview, the window is not maximized, or expanded to its full size. You'll maximize the window shortly.

You can have more than one Office program open at once. You'll use this same method to start Excel and open a new, blank workbook.

To start Excel and open a new, blank workbook:

1. On the taskbar, click the **Start** button, click **All Programs** to display the All Programs list, and then click **Microsoft Office**.

   Trouble? If you don't see Microsoft Office on the All Programs list, point to Microsoft Excel 2010 on the All Programs list. If you still don't see Microsoft Excel 2010, ask your instructor or technical support person for help.

2. Click **Microsoft Excel 2010**. Excel starts and a new, blank workbook opens. See Figure 2.

Figure 2 New, blank Excel workbook

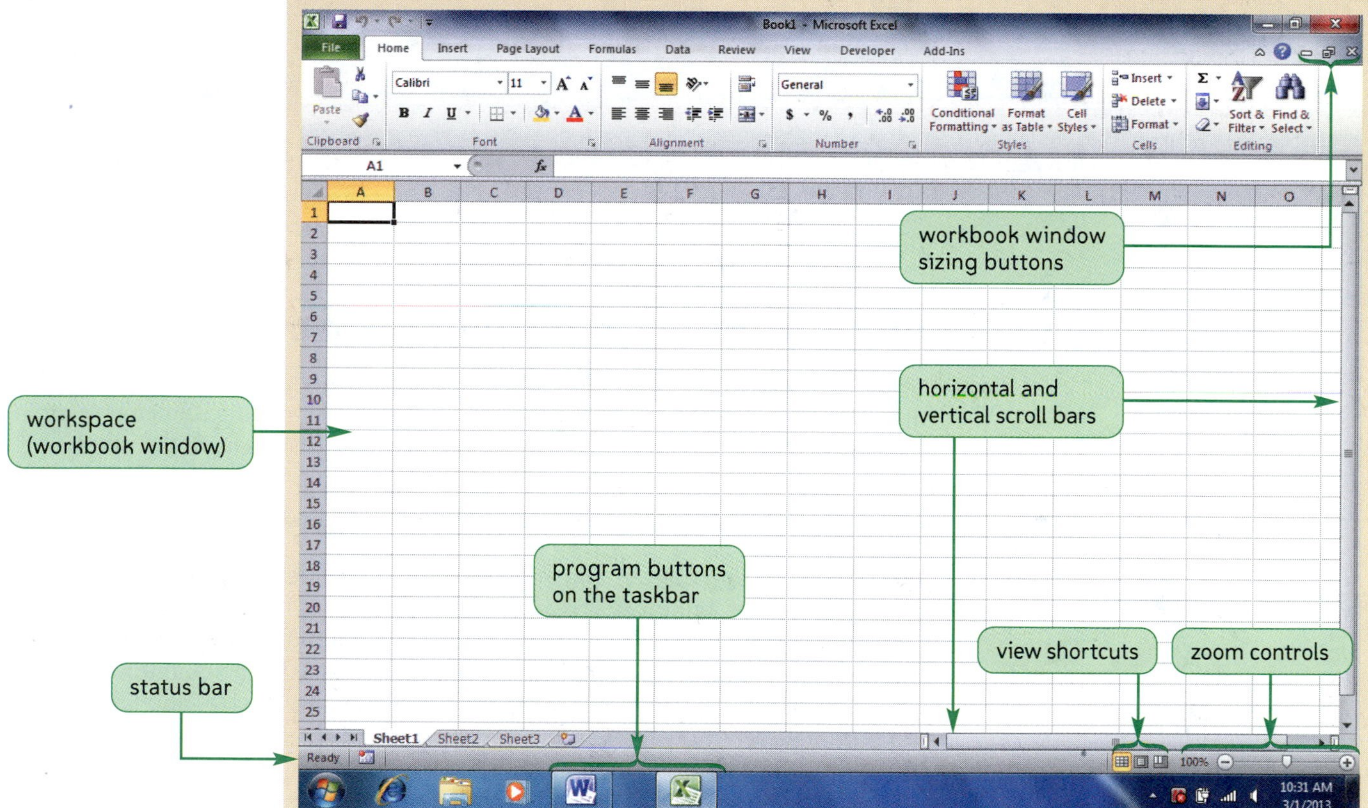

Trouble? If the Excel window doesn't fill your entire screen, the window is not maximized, or expanded to its full size. You'll maximize the window shortly.

Switching Between Open Programs and Files

Two programs are running at the same time—Word and Excel. The taskbar contains buttons for both programs. When you have two or more programs running or two files within the same program open, you can click the program buttons on the taskbar to switch from one program or file to another. When you point to a program button, a thumbnail (or small picture) of each open file in that program is displayed. You can then click the thumbnail of the file you want to make active. The employees at Recycled Palette often work in several programs and files at once.

To switch between the open Word and Excel files:

1. On the taskbar, point to the **Microsoft Word** program button. A thumbnail of the open Word document appears. See Figure 3.

Figure 3 Thumbnail of the open Word document

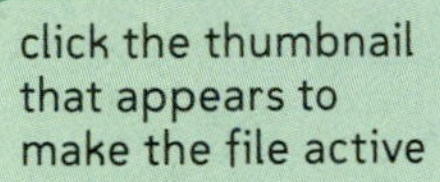

click the thumbnail that appears to make the file active

2. Click the **Document1 - Microsoft Word** thumbnail. The active program switches from Excel to Word.

Exploring Common Window Elements

As you can see, many elements in both the Word and Excel program windows are the same. In fact, most Office programs have these same elements. Because these elements are the same in each program, after you've learned one program, it's easy to learn the others.

Resizing the Program Window and Workspace

TIP

Excel has two sets of sizing buttons. The top set controls the program window and the bottom set controls the workspace.

There are three different sizing buttons that appear on the right side of a program window's title bar. The Minimize button, which is the left button, hides a window so that only its program button is visible on the taskbar. The middle button changes name and function depending on the status of the window—the Maximize button expands the window to the full screen size or to the program window size, and the Restore Down button returns the window to a predefined size. The Close button, on the right, exits the program or closes the file.

The sizing buttons give you the flexibility to arrange the program and file windows to best fit your needs. Most often, you'll want to maximize the program window and workspace to take advantage of the full screen size you have available. If you have several files open, you might want to restore down their windows so that you can see more than one window at a time, or you might want to minimize programs or files you are not working on at the moment.

To resize the windows and workspaces:

1. On the Word title bar, click the **Minimize** button. The Word program window is reduced to a taskbar button. The Excel program window is visible again.
2. On the Excel title bar, click the **Maximize** button to expand the Excel program window to fill the screen, if necessary.

3. In the bottom set of Excel sizing buttons, click the **Restore Window** button. The workspace is resized smaller than the full program window. See Figure 4.

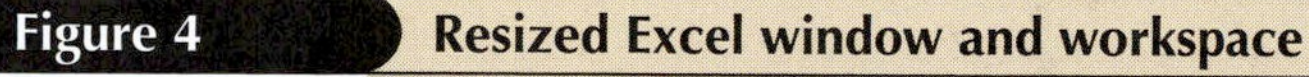

Figure 4 Resized Excel window and workspace

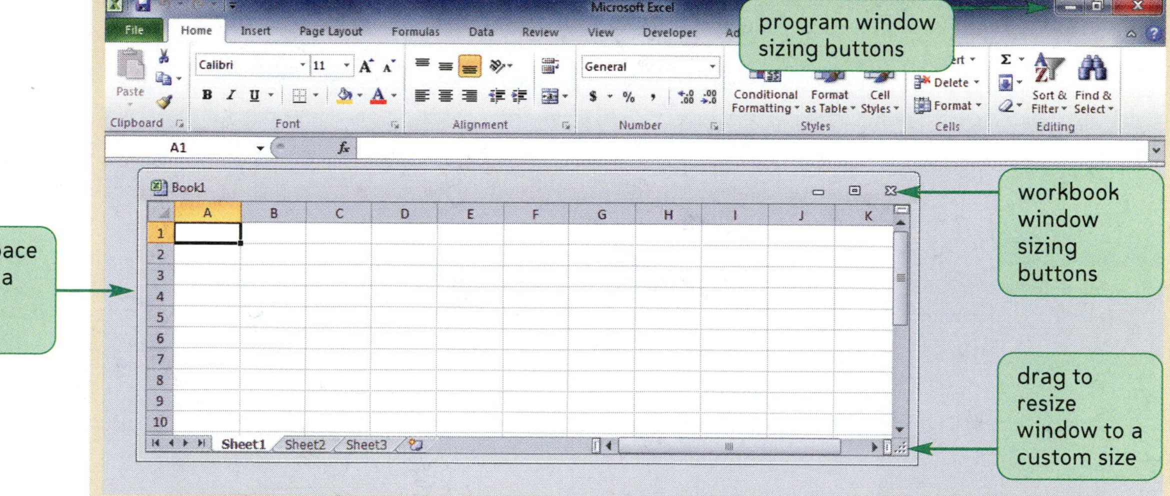

4. On the workbook window, click the **Maximize** button. The workspace expands to fill the program window.
5. On the taskbar, click the **Microsoft Word** program button. The Word program window returns to its previous size.
6. On the Word title bar, click the **Maximize** button if necessary to expand the Word program to fill the screen.

Switching Views

TIP

You can quickly switch between views using the view buttons on the status bar or options on the View tab on the Ribbon.

Each program has a variety of views, or ways to display the file in the workspace. For example, Word has five views: Print Layout, Full Screen Reading, Web Layout, Outline, and Draft. The content of the file doesn't change from view to view, although the presentation of the content does. In Word, for example, Print Layout view shows how the document would appear as a printed page, whereas Web Layout view shows how the document would appear as a Web page. You'll change views in later tutorials.

Zooming and Scrolling

You can zoom in to get a closer look at the content of an open document, worksheet, slide, or database report. Likewise, you can zoom out to see more of the content at a smaller size. You can select a specific percentage or size based on your file. The zoom percentage can range from 10 percent to 400 percent (Excel and PowerPoint) or 500 percent (Word). The figures shown in these tutorials show the workspace zoomed in to enhance readability. Zooming can shift part of the workspace out of view. To change which area of the workspace is visible in the program window, you can use the scroll bars. A scroll bar has arrow buttons that you can click to shift the workspace a small amount in the specified direction and a scroll box that you can drag to shift the workspace a larger amount in the direction you drag. Depending on the program and zoom level, you might see a vertical scroll bar, a horizontal scroll bar, or both.

To zoom and scroll in Word and Excel:

1. On the Word status bar, drag the **Zoom slider** to the left until the percentage is **10%**. The document is reduced to its smallest size, which makes the entire page visible but unreadable. See Figure 5.

Figure 5 Word zoom level set to 10%

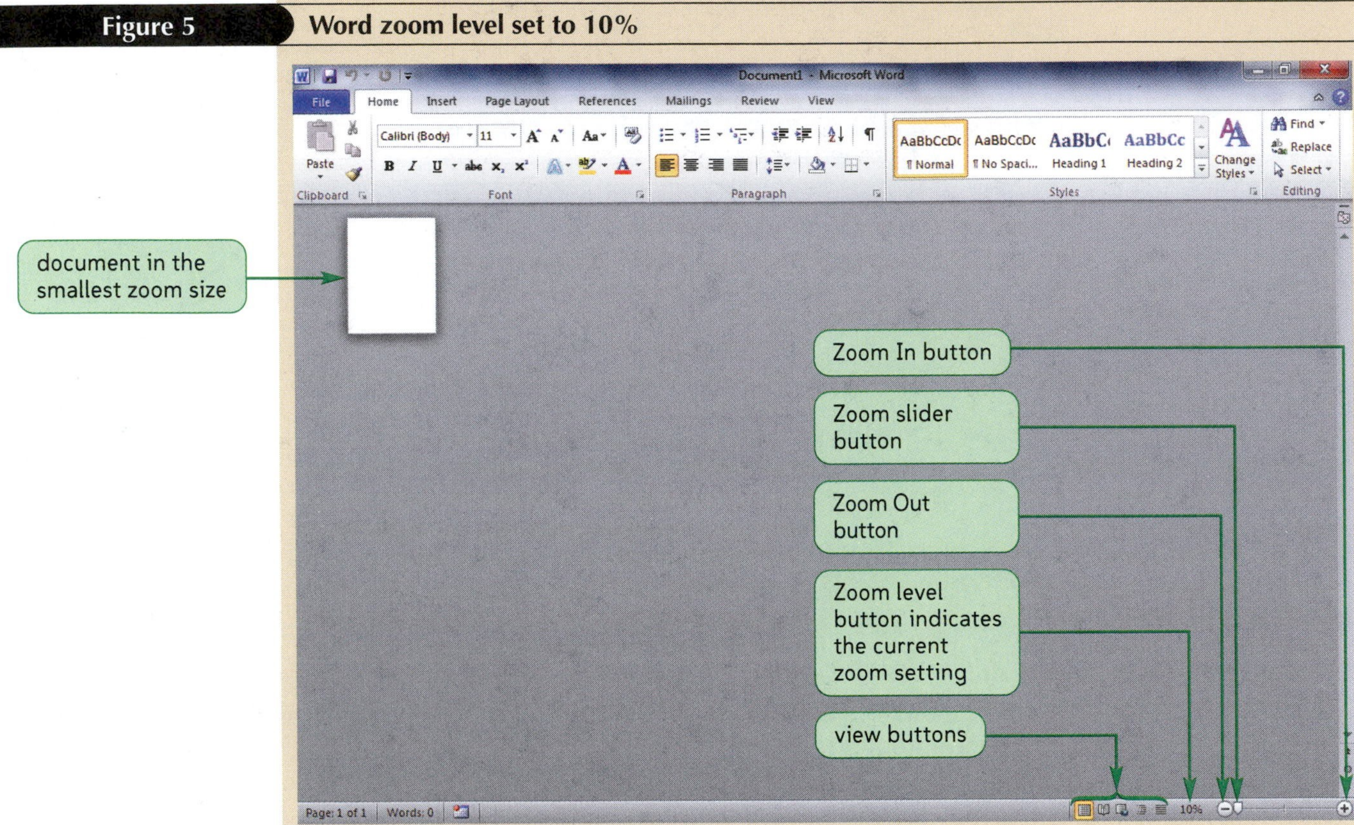

2. On the Word status bar, click the **Zoom level** button 10%. The Zoom dialog box opens. See Figure 6.

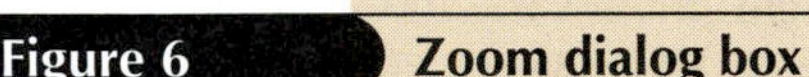
Figure 6 Zoom dialog box

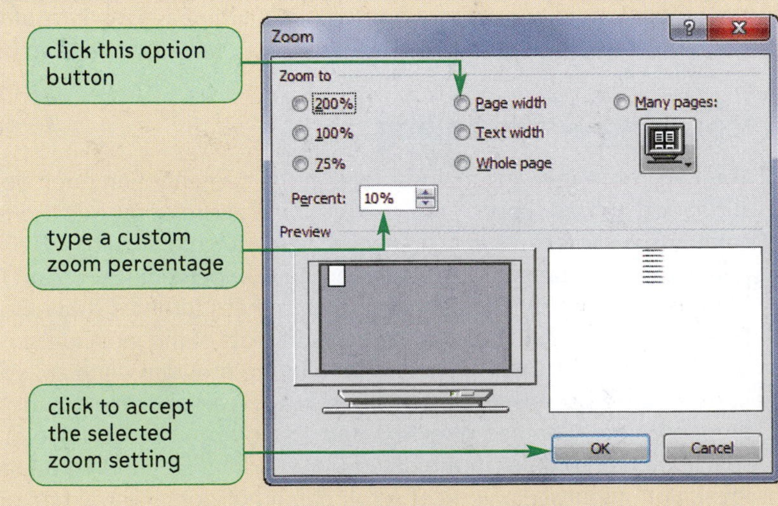

3. Click the **Page width** option button, and then click the **OK** button. The Word document is magnified to its page width, which matches how the Word figures appear in the tutorials.
4. On the taskbar, click the **Microsoft Excel** program button. The Excel program window is displayed.
5. On the status bar, click the **Zoom In** button twice. The worksheet is magnified to 120%, which is the zoom level that matches the Excel figures shown in the tutorials.
6. On the horizontal scroll bar, click the **right arrow** button twice. The worksheet shifts two columns to the right. Columns A and B (labeled by letter at the top of the columns) shift out of view and two other columns shift into view.
7. On the horizontal scroll bar, drag the **scroll box** all the way to the left. The worksheet shifts left to display columns A and B again.
8. On the taskbar, click the **Microsoft Word** program button. The Word program window is displayed.

Using the Ribbon

TIP

To view more workspace, click the Minimize the Ribbon button, located below the sizing buttons, to reduce the Ribbon to a single line. Click the Expand the Ribbon button to redisplay the full Ribbon.

Although the tabs on the Ribbon differ from program to program, each program has two tabs in common. The first tab on the Ribbon, the File tab, opens Backstage view. Backstage view provides access to file-level features, such as creating new files, opening existing files, saving files, printing files, and closing files, as well as the most common program options. The second tab in each program—called the Home tab—contains the commands for the most frequently performed activities, including cutting and pasting, changing fonts, and using editing tools. In addition, the Insert, Review, and View tabs appear on the Ribbon in all Office programs except Access, although the commands they include might differ from program to program. Other tabs are program specific, such as the Design tab in PowerPoint and the Datasheet Tools tab in Access.

To use the Ribbon tabs:

1. In Word, point to the **Insert** tab on the Ribbon. The Insert tab is highlighted, though the Home tab with the options for using the Clipboard and formatting text remains visible.
2. Click the **Insert** tab. The Insert tab is displayed on the Ribbon. This tab provides access to all the options for adding objects such as shapes, pages, tables, illustrations, text, and symbols to a document. See Figure 7.

Figure 7 Insert tab on the Ribbon in Word

Insert tab selected

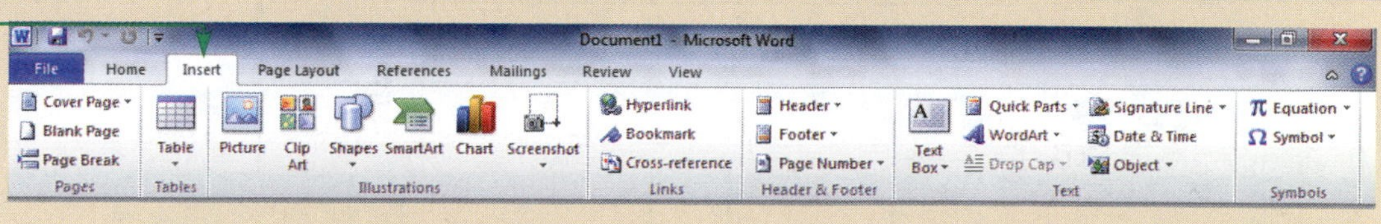

3. Click the **Home** tab. The Home tab options appear on the Ribbon.

Clicking Buttons

> **TIP**
>
> You can point to a button on the Ribbon to display a ScreenTip with that button's name and a brief description of what the button does when you click it.

For the most part, when you click a button, something happens in the file. For example, the Clipboard group on the Home tab includes the Cut, Copy, Paste, and Format Painter buttons, which you can click to move or copy text, objects, and formatting.

Buttons can be **toggles**: one click turns the feature on and the next click turns the feature off. While the feature is on, the button remains colored or highlighted. For example, on the Home tab in Word, the Show/Hide ¶ button in the Paragraph group displays the nonprinting characters when toggled on and hides them when toggled off.

Some buttons have two parts: a button that accesses a command, and an arrow that opens a menu of all the commands or options available for that task. For example, the Paste button in the Clipboard group on the Home tab includes the Paste command and an arrow to access all the Paste commands and options. To select one of these commands or options, you click the button arrow and then click the command or option.

> **INSIGHT**
>
> *How Buttons and Groups Appear on the Ribbon*
>
> The buttons and groups on the Ribbon change based on your monitor size, your screen resolution, and the size of the program window. With smaller monitors, lower screen resolutions, and reduced program windows, buttons can appear as icons without labels and a group can be condensed into a button that you click to display the group options. The figures in these tutorials were created using a screen resolution of 1024 × 768 and, unless otherwise specified, the program and workspace windows are maximized. If you are using a different screen resolution or window size, the buttons on the Ribbon might show more or fewer button names, and some groups might be reduced to a button.

You'll type text in the Word document, and then use the buttons on the Ribbon.

To use buttons on the Ribbon:

1. Type **Meeting Agenda** and then press the **Enter** key. The text appears in the first line of the document and the insertion point moves to the second line.

   Trouble? If you make a typing error, press the Backspace key to delete the incorrect letters, and then retype the text.

2. In the Paragraph group on the Home tab, click the **Show/Hide ¶** button ¶. The nonprinting characters appear in the document, and the Show/Hide ¶ button remains toggled on. See Figure 8.

> **TIP**
>
> The **default** (original setting) for the Show/Hide ¶ button is for the button to be toggled off.

Figure 8 Button toggled on

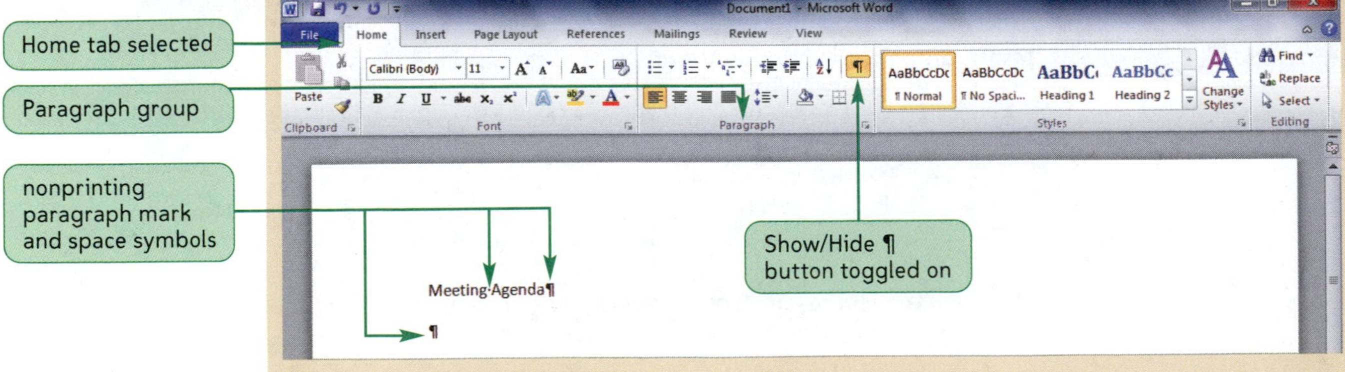

Trouble? If the nonprinting characters disappear from your screen, the Show/Hide ¶ button was already on. Repeat Step 2 to show nonprinting characters.

3. Position the insertion point to the left of the word "Meeting," press and hold the left mouse button, drag the pointer across the text of the first line but not the paragraph mark to highlight the text, and then release the mouse button. All the text in the first line of the document (but not the paragraph mark ¶) is selected.
4. In the Clipboard group on the Home tab, click the **Copy** button. The selected text is copied to the Clipboard.
5. Press the ↓ key. The text is deselected (no longer highlighted), and the insertion point moves to the second line in the document.
6. In the Clipboard group on the Home tab, point to the top part of the **Paste** button. Both parts of the Paste button are outlined in yellow, but the icon at the top is highlighted to indicate that it will be selected if you click the mouse button.
7. Point to the **Paste button arrow**. The button is outlined and the button arrow is highlighted.
8. Click the **Paste button arrow**. The paste commands and options are displayed. See Figure 9.

Figure 9 **Two-part Paste button**

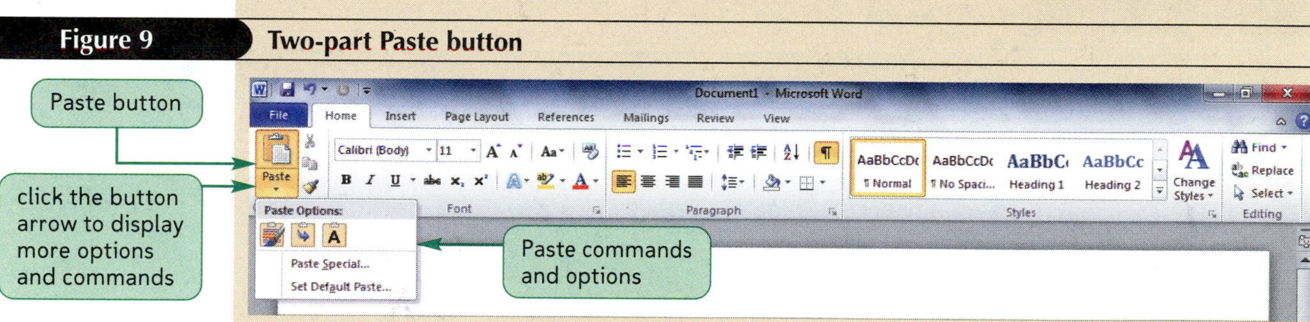

9. On the Paste Options menu, click the **Keep Text Only** button. The menu closes, and the text is duplicated in the second line of the document. The Paste Options button (Ctrl) appears below the duplicated text, providing access to the same paste commands and options.

INSIGHT

Using Keyboard Shortcuts and Key Tips

Keyboard shortcuts can help you work faster and more efficiently. A **keyboard shortcut** is a key or combination of keys you press to access a feature or perform a command. You can use these shortcuts to access options on the Ribbon, on the Quick Access Toolbar, and in Backstage view without removing your hands from the keyboard. To access the options on the Ribbon, press the Alt key. A label, called a Key Tip, appears over each tab. To select a tab, press the corresponding key. The tab is displayed on the Ribbon and Key Tips appear over each available button or option on that tab. Press the appropriate key or keys to select a button.

You can also press combinations of keys to perform specific commands. For example, Ctrl+S is the keyboard shortcut for the Save command (you press and hold the Ctrl key while you press the S key). This type of keyboard shortcut appears in ScreenTips next to the command's name. Not all commands have this type of keyboard shortcut. Identical commands in each Office program use the same keyboard shortcut.

Using Galleries and Live Preview

Galleries and Live Preview let you quickly see how your file will be affected by a selection. A **gallery** is a menu or grid that shows a visual representation of the options available for a button. For example, the Bullet Library gallery in Word shows an icon of each bullet style you can select. Some galleries include a More button that you click to expand the gallery to see all the options it contains. When you point to an option in a gallery, **Live Preview** shows the results that would occur in your file if you clicked that option. To continue the bullets example, when you point to a bullet style in the Bullet Library gallery, the selected text or the paragraph in which the insertion point is located appears with that bullet style. By moving the pointer from option to option, you can quickly see the text set with different bullet styles; you can then click the style you want.

To use the Bullet Library gallery and Live Preview:

1. In the Paragraph group on the Home tab, click the **Bullets button arrow**. The Bullet Library gallery opens.
2. Point to the **check mark bullet** style ✓. Live Preview shows the selected bullet style in your document. See Figure 10.

Figure 10 Live Preview of bullet icon

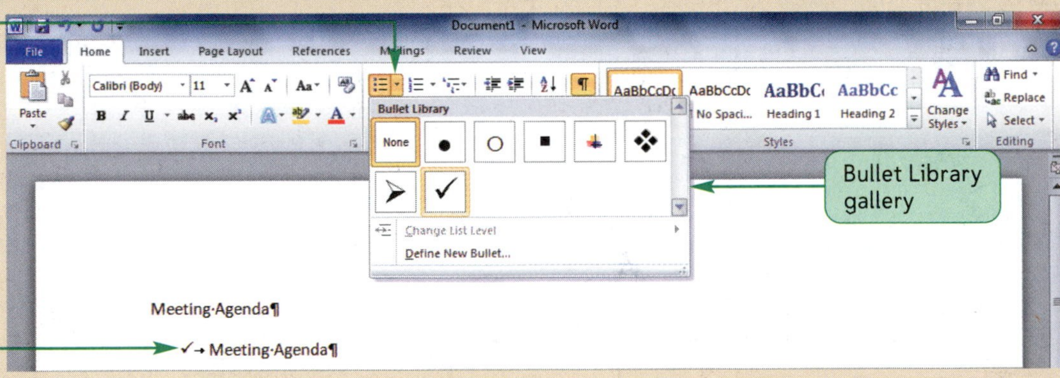

3. Place the pointer over each of the remaining bullet styles and preview them in your document.
4. Click the **check mark bullet** style ✓. The Bullet Library gallery closes, and the check mark bullet is added to the line, which is indented. The Bullets button remains toggled on when the insertion point is in the line with the bullet.
5. On the second line, next to the check mark bullet, select **Meeting Agenda**. The two words are highlighted to indicate they are selected.
6. Type **Brainstorm names for the new paint colors.** to replace the selected text with an agenda item.
7. Press the **Enter** key twice to end the bulleted list.

TIP

You can press the Esc key to close a gallery without making a selection.

Opening Dialog Boxes and Task Panes

The button to the right of some group names is the Dialog Box Launcher, which opens a task pane or dialog box related to that group of tasks. A **task pane** is a window that helps you navigate through a complex task or feature. For example, you can use the Clipboard task pane to paste some or all of the items that were cut or copied from any Office program during the current work session. A **dialog box** is a window from which you enter or choose settings for how you want to perform a task. For example, the Page Setup dialog box in Word contains options to change how the document looks. Some dialog boxes organize related information into tabs, and related options and settings are organized into groups, just as they are on the Ribbon. You select settings in a dialog box using option buttons, check boxes, text boxes, and lists to specify how you want to perform a task. In Excel, you'll use the Dialog Box Launcher to open the Page Setup dialog box.

To open the Page Setup dialog box using the Dialog Box Launcher:

1. On the taskbar, click the **Microsoft Excel** program button to switch from Word to Excel.
2. On the Ribbon, click the **Page Layout** tab. The page layout options appear on the Ribbon.
3. In the Page Setup group, click the **Dialog Box Launcher**. The Page Setup dialog box opens with the Page tab displayed. See Figure 11.

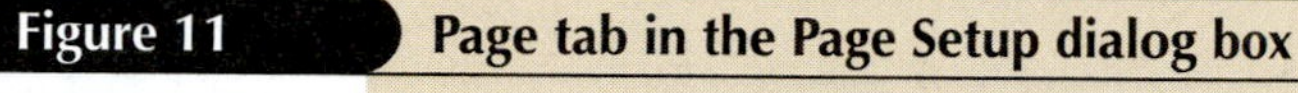

Figure 11 Page tab in the Page Setup dialog box

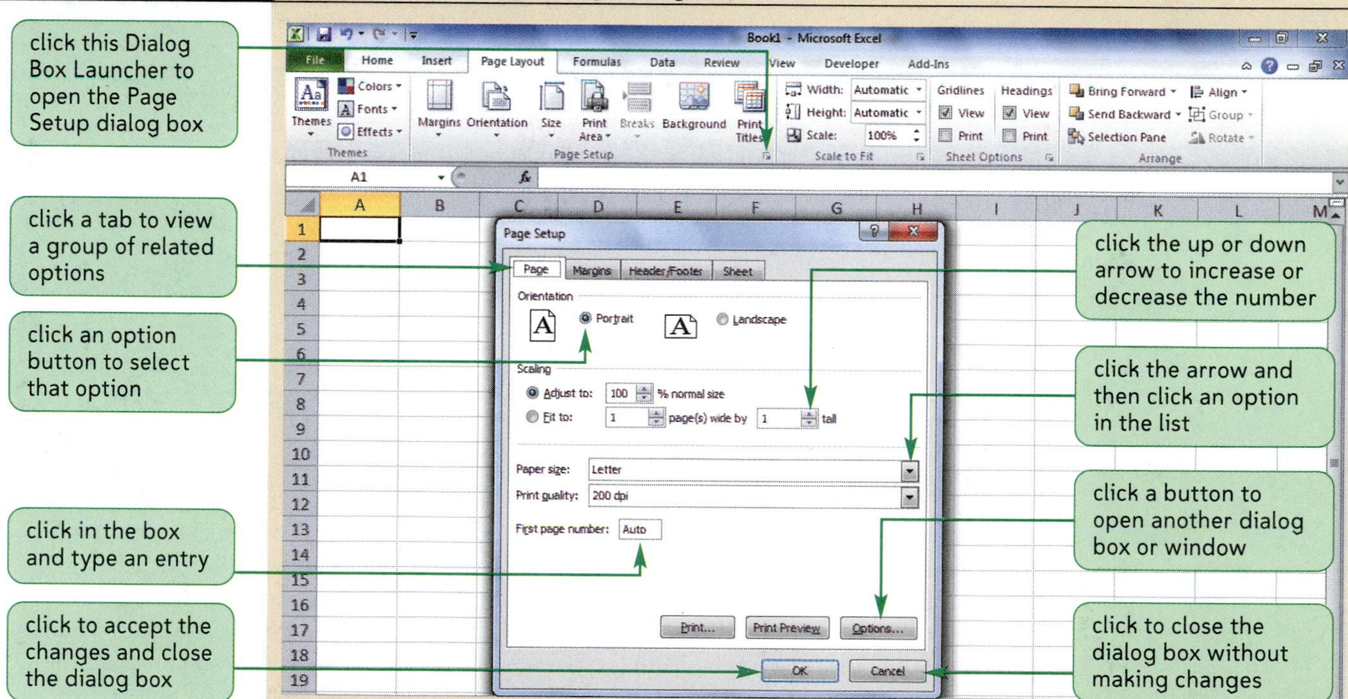

4. Click the **Landscape** option button. The workbook's page orientation changes to a page wider than it is long.
5. Click the **Sheet** tab. The dialog box displays options related to the worksheet. You can click a check box to turn an option on (checked) or off (unchecked).
6. In the Print section of the dialog box, click the **Gridlines** check box and the **Row and column headings** check box. Check marks appear in both check boxes, indicating that these options are selected.
7. Click the **Cancel** button. The dialog box closes without making any changes to the page setup.

TIP

You can check more than one check box in a group, but you can select only one option button in a group.

Using Contextual Tools

Some tabs, toolbars, and menus come into view as you work. Because these tools become available only as you might need them, the workspace remains less cluttered. However, tools that appear and disappear as you work can take some getting used to.

Displaying Contextual Tabs

Any object that you can select in a file has a related contextual tab. An **object** is anything that appears on your screen that can be selected and manipulated, such as a table, a picture, a shape, a chart, or an equation. A **contextual tab** is a Ribbon tab that contains commands related to the selected object so you can manipulate, edit, and format that object. Contextual tabs appear to the right of the standard Ribbon tabs just below a title label. For example, Figure 12 shows the Table Tools contextual tabs that appear when you select a table in a Word document. Although contextual tabs appear only when you select an object, they function in the same way as standard tabs on the Ribbon. Contextual tabs disappear when you click elsewhere on the screen, deselecting the object. Contextual tabs can also appear as you switch views. You'll use contextual tabs in later tutorials.

Figure 12 Table Tools contextual tabs

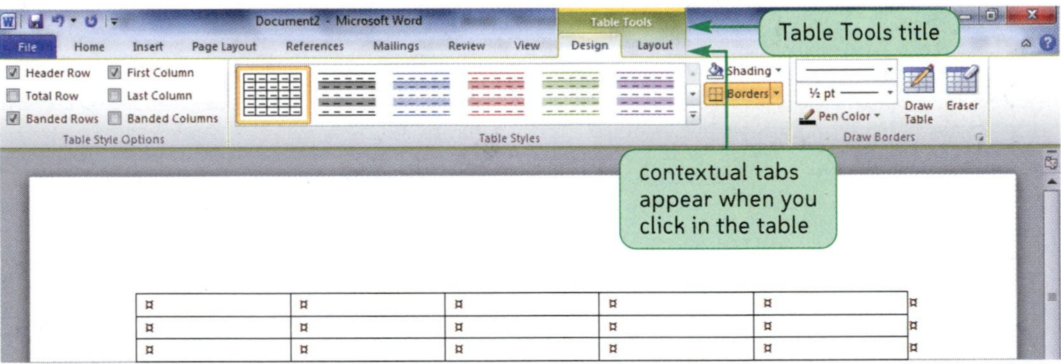

Accessing the Mini Toolbar

TIP

To turn off the Mini toolbar and Live Preview in Word, Excel, and PowerPoint, click the File tab, click the Options command, uncheck their check boxes in the Options dialog box, and then click the OK button.

The **Mini toolbar**, which appears next to the pointer whenever you select text, contains buttons for the most commonly used formatting commands, such as font, font size, styles, color, alignment, and indents. The Mini toolbar buttons differ in each program. A transparent version of the Mini toolbar appears immediately after you select text. When you move the pointer over the Mini toolbar, it comes into full view so you can click the appropriate formatting button or buttons. The Mini toolbar disappears if you move the pointer away from the toolbar, press a key, or click in the workspace. The Mini toolbar can help you format your text faster, but initially you might find that the toolbar disappears unexpectedly. All the commands on the Mini toolbar are also available on the Ribbon. Note that Live Preview does not work with the Mini toolbar.

You'll use the Mini toolbar to format text you enter in the workbook.

To use the Mini toolbar to format text:

1. If necessary, click cell **A1** (the rectangle in the upper-left corner of the worksheet).
2. Type **Budget**. The text appears in the cell.

3. Press the **Enter** key. The text is entered in cell A1 and cell A2 is selected.
4. Type **2013** and then press the **Enter** key. The year is entered in cell A2 and cell A3 is selected.
5. Double-click cell **A1** to place the insertion point in the cell. Now you can select the text you typed.
6. Double-click **Budget** in cell A1. The selected text appears white with a black background, and the transparent Mini toolbar appears directly above the selected text. See Figure 13.

Figure 13 Transparent Mini toolbar

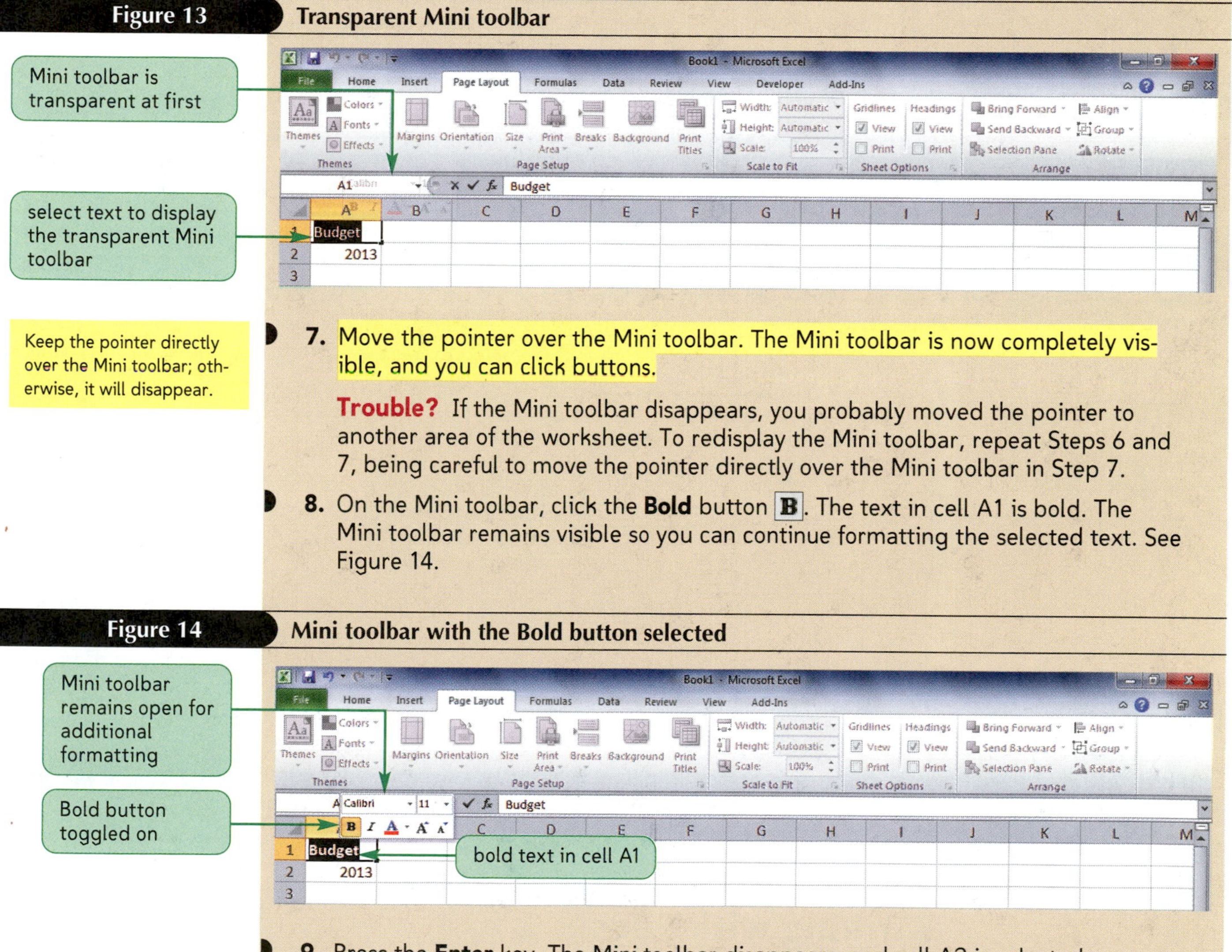

Keep the pointer directly over the Mini toolbar; otherwise, it will disappear.

7. Move the pointer over the Mini toolbar. The Mini toolbar is now completely visible, and you can click buttons.

   Trouble? If the Mini toolbar disappears, you probably moved the pointer to another area of the worksheet. To redisplay the Mini toolbar, repeat Steps 6 and 7, being careful to move the pointer directly over the Mini toolbar in Step 7.

8. On the Mini toolbar, click the **Bold** button **B**. The text in cell A1 is bold. The Mini toolbar remains visible so you can continue formatting the selected text. See Figure 14.

Figure 14 Mini toolbar with the Bold button selected

9. Press the **Enter** key. The Mini toolbar disappears, and cell A2 is selected.

Opening Shortcut Menus

A **shortcut menu** is a list of commands related to a selection that opens when you click the right mouse button. Shortcut menus enable you to quickly access commands that you're most likely to need in the context of the task you're performing without using the tabs on the Ribbon. The shortcut menu includes commands that perform actions, commands that open dialog boxes, and galleries of options that provide Live Preview. The Mini toolbar also opens when you right-click. If you click a button on the Mini toolbar, the rest of the shortcut menu closes while the Mini toolbar remains open so you can continue formatting the selection. For example, you can right-click selected text to open a shortcut menu with a Mini toolbar; the menu will contain text-related commands such as Cut, Copy, and Paste, as well as other program-specific commands.

You'll use a shortcut menu to delete the content you entered in cell A1.

To use a shortcut menu to delete content:

1. Right-click cell **A1**. A shortcut menu opens, listing commands related to common tasks you'd perform in a cell, along with the Mini toolbar. See Figure 15.

Figure 15 Shortcut menu with Mini toolbar

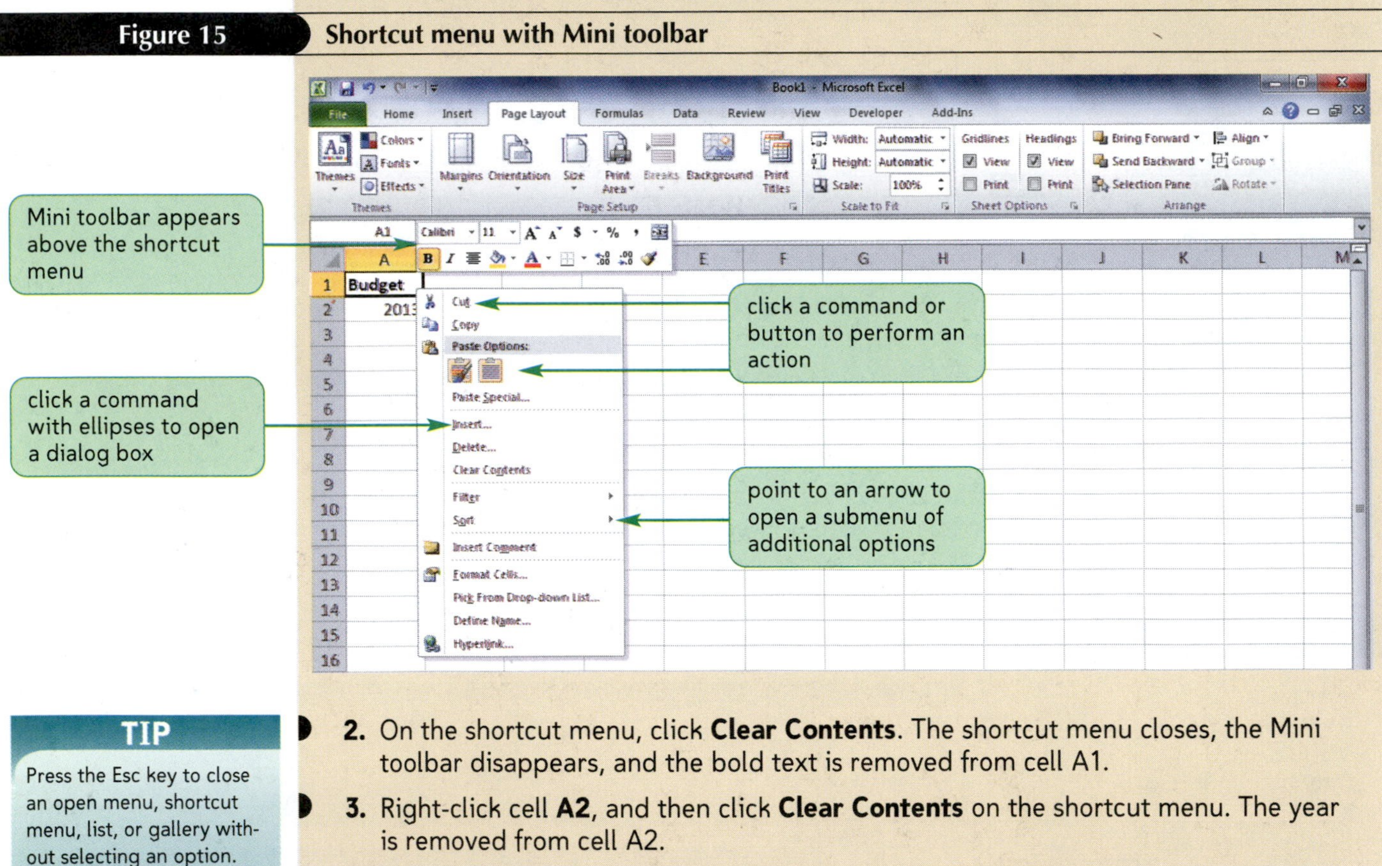

2. On the shortcut menu, click **Clear Contents**. The shortcut menu closes, the Mini toolbar disappears, and the bold text is removed from cell A1.
3. Right-click cell **A2**, and then click **Clear Contents** on the shortcut menu. The year is removed from cell A2.

TIP

Press the Esc key to close an open menu, shortcut menu, list, or gallery without selecting an option.

Working with Files

The most common tasks you perform in any Office program are to create, open, save, and close files. All of these tasks can be done from Backstage view, and the processes for these tasks are basically the same in all Office programs. To begin working in a program, you need to create a new file or open an existing file. When you start Word, Excel, or PowerPoint, the program opens along with a blank file—ready for you to begin working on a new document, workbook, or presentation. When you start Access, the New tab in Backstage view opens, displaying options for creating a new database or opening an existing one.

Saving a File

As you create and modify an Office file, your work is stored only in the computer's temporary memory, not on a hard drive. If you were to exit the program without saving, turn off your computer, or experience a power failure, your work would be lost. To prevent losing work, save your file frequently—at least every 10 minutes. You can save files to the hard drive located inside your computer, an external hard drive, a network storage drive, or a portable storage drive such as a USB flash drive.

To save a file, you can click either the Save button on the Quick Access Toolbar or the Save command in Backstage view. If it is the first time you are saving a file, the Save As dialog box will open so that you can specify save options. You can also click the Save As command in Backstage view to open the Save As dialog box, in which you can name the file you are saving and specify a location to save it.

TIP

Office 2003 and earlier files use the extensions .doc (Word), .xls (Excel), .mdb (Access), and .ppt (PowerPoint). To save in an earlier format, click the Save as type button in the Save As dialog box and click the 97-2003 format. When you open an earlier version file in Office 2010, you can save it in the same format or the Office 2010 format.

The first time you save a file, you need to name it. This **filename** includes a title you specify and a file extension assigned by Office to indicate the file type. You should specify a descriptive title that accurately reflects the content of the document, workbook, presentation, or database, such as "Shipping Options Letter" or "Fourth Quarter Financial Analysis." Your descriptive title can include uppercase and lowercase letters, numbers, hyphens, and spaces in any combination, but not the special characters ? " / \ < > * | and :. Each filename ends with a **file extension**, which is a period followed by several characters that Office adds to your descriptive title to identify the program in which that file was created. The default file extensions for Office 2010 are .docx for Word, .xlsx for Excel, .pptx for PowerPoint, and .accdb for Access. Filenames (the descriptive title and extension) can include a maximum of 255 characters. You might see file extensions depending on how Windows is set up on your computer. The figures in these tutorials do not show file extensions.

You also need to decide where to save the file—on which drive and in what folder. A **folder** is a container for your files. Just as you organize paper documents within folders stored in a filing cabinet, you can organize your files within folders stored on your computer's hard drive or on a removable drive such as a USB flash drive. Store each file in a logical location that you will remember whenever you want to use the file again. The default storage location for Office files is the Documents folder; you can create additional storage folders within that folder or navigate to a new location.

REFERENCE

Saving a File

To save a file the first time or with a new name or location:
- Click the File tab to open Backstage view, and then click the Save As command in the navigation bar (for an unnamed file, click the Save command or click the Save button on the Quick Access Toolbar).
- In the Save As dialog box, navigate to the location where you want to save the file.
- Type a descriptive title in the File name box, and then click the Save button.

To resave a named file to the same location with the same name:
- On the Quick Access Toolbar, click the Save button.

The text you typed in the Word window needs to be saved.

To save a file for the first time:

1. On the taskbar, click the **Microsoft Word** program button. Word becomes the active program.
2. On the Ribbon, click the **File** tab. Backstage view opens with commands and tabs for creating new files, opening existing files, and saving, printing, and closing files. See Figure 16.

Figure 16 **Backstage view**

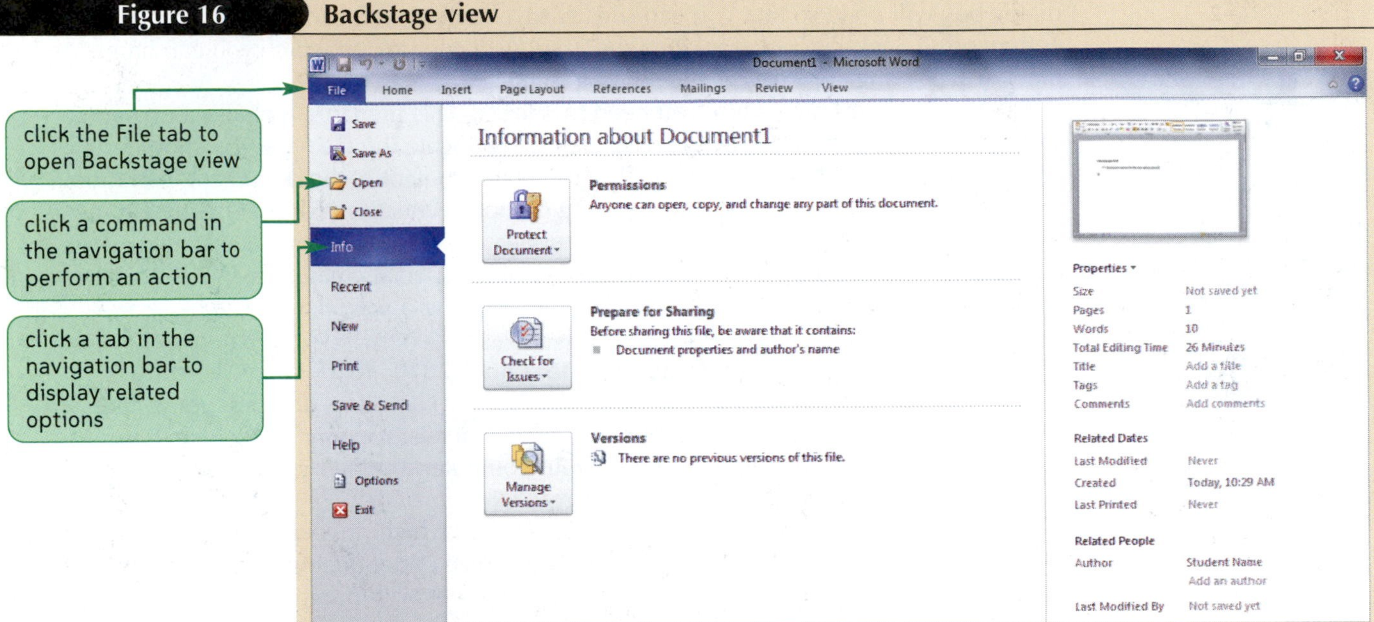

3. In the navigation bar, click the **Save As** command. The Save As dialog box opens because you have not yet saved the file and need to specify a storage location and filename. The default location is set to the Documents folder, and the first few words of the first line appear in the File name box as a suggested title.
4. In the Navigation pane along the left side of the dialog box, click the link for the location that contains your Data Files, if necessary.

   Trouble? If you don't have the starting Data Files, you need to get them before you can proceed. Your instructor will either give you the Data Files or ask you to obtain them from a specified location (such as a network drive). In either case, make a backup copy of the Data Files before you start so that you will have the original files available in case you need to start over. If you have any questions about the Data Files, see your instructor or technical support person for assistance.

5. In the file list, double-click the **Office** folder, and then double-click the **Tutorial** folder. This is the location where you want to save the document.
6. Type **Agenda** in the File name box. This descriptive filename will help you more easily identify the file. See Figure 17 (your file path may differ).

Figure 17 Completed Save As dialog box

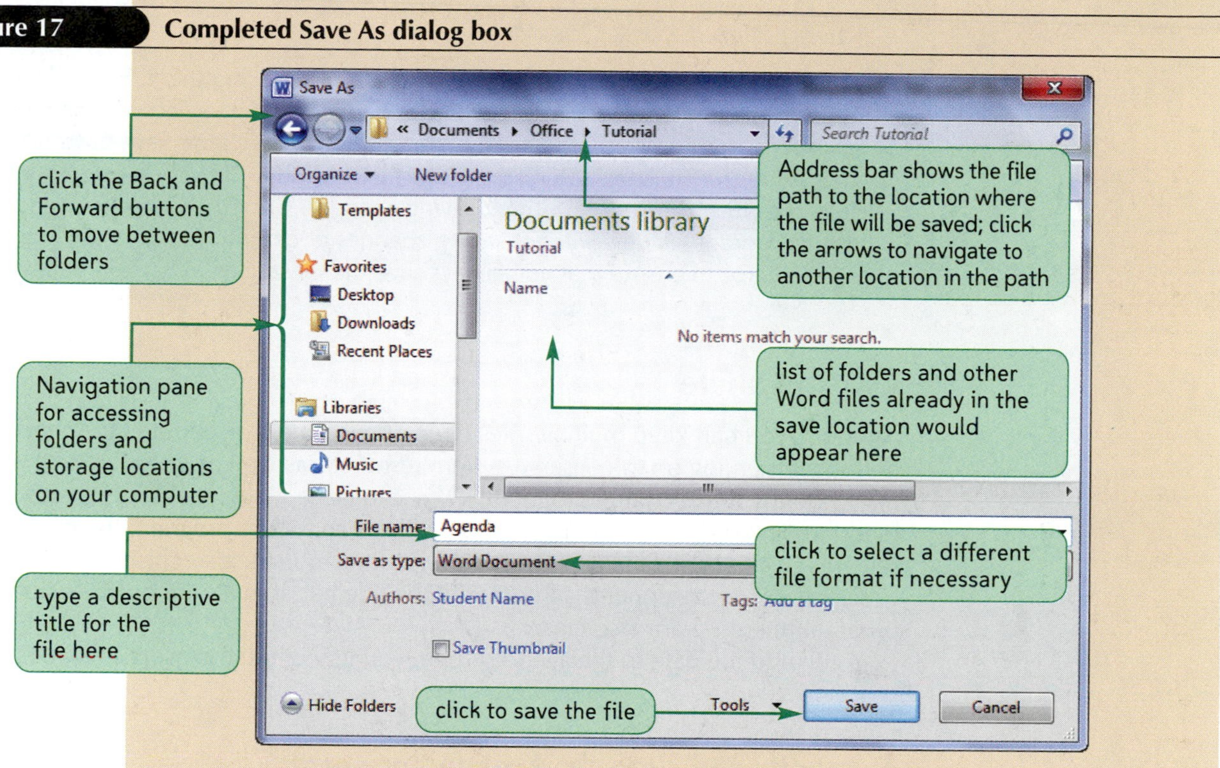

Trouble? If the .docx extension appears after the filename, your computer is configured to show file extensions. Continue with Step 7.

7. Click the **Save** button. The Save As dialog box closes, and the name of your file appears in the Word window title bar.

The saved file includes everything in the document at the time you last saved it. Any new edits or additions you make to the document exist only in the computer's memory and are not saved in the file on the drive. As you work, remember to save frequently so that the file is updated to reflect the latest content.

Because you already named the document and selected a storage location, you don't need to use the Save As dialog box unless you want to save a copy of the file with a different filename or to a different location. If you do, the previous version of the file remains on your drive as well.

You need to add your name to the agenda. Then, you'll save your changes.

To modify and save the Agenda document:

1. Type your name, and then press the **Enter** key. The text you typed appears on the next line.

2. On the Quick Access Toolbar, click the **Save** button. The changes you made to the document are saved in the file stored on the drive.

INSIGHT

Saving Files Before Closing

As a standard practice, you should save files before closing them. However, Office has an added safeguard: if you attempt to close a file without saving your changes, a dialog box opens, asking whether you want to save the file. Click the Save button to save the changes to the file before closing the file and program. Click the Don't Save button to close the file and program without saving changes. Click the Cancel button to return to the program window without saving changes or closing the file and program. This feature helps to ensure that you always save the most current version of any file.

Closing a File

Although you can keep multiple files open at one time, you should close any file you are no longer working on to conserve system resources as well as to ensure that you don't inadvertently make changes to the file. You can close a file by clicking the Close command in Backstage view. If that's the only file open for the program, the program window remains open and no file appears in the window. You can also close a file by clicking the Close button in the upper-right corner of the title bar. If that's the only file open for the program, the program also closes.

You'll add the date to the agenda. Then, you'll attempt to close it without saving.

To modify and close the Agenda document:

1. Type today's date, and then press the **Enter** key. The text you typed appears below your name in the document.
2. On the Ribbon, click the **File** tab to open Backstage view, and then click the **Close** command in the navigation bar. A dialog box opens, asking whether you want to save the changes you made to the document.
3. Click the **Save** button. The current version of the document is saved to the file, and then the document closes. Word is still open, so you can create additional new files in the open program or you can open previously created and saved files.

Opening a File

When you want to open a blank document, workbook, presentation, or database, you create a new file. When you want to work on a previously created file, you must first open it. Opening a file transfers a copy of the file from the storage location (either a hard drive or a portable drive) to the computer's memory and displays it on your screen. The file is then in your computer's memory and on the drive.

REFERENCE

Opening an Existing File

- Click the File tab to open Backstage view, and then click the Open command in the navigation bar.
- In the Open dialog box, navigate to the storage location of the file you want to open.
- Click the filename of the file you want to open.
- Click the Open button.
- If necessary, click the Enable Editing button in the Information Bar.

or

- Click the File tab, and then click the Recent tab in the navigation bar.
- Click a filename in the Recent list.

Any file you open that was downloaded from the Internet, accessed from a shared network, or received as an email attachment might open in a read-only format, called **Protected View**. In Protected View, you can see the file contents, but you cannot edit, save, or print them until you enable editing. To do so, click the Enable Editing button on the Information Bar, as shown in Figure 18.

Figure 18 **Protected View warning**

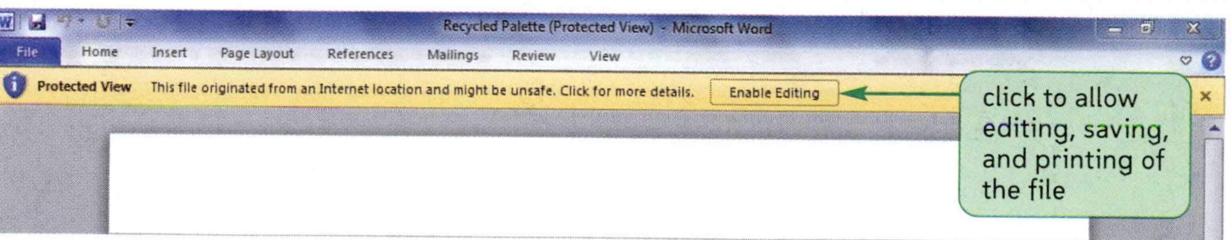

You need to print the meeting agenda you typed for Ean. To do that, you'll reopen the Agenda document.

To open the Agenda document:

1. On the Ribbon, click the **File** tab to display Backstage view.
2. In the navigation bar, click the **Open** command. The Open dialog box, which works similarly to the Save As dialog box, opens.
3. In the Open dialog box, use the Navigation pane or the Address bar to navigate to the **Office\Tutorial** folder included with your Data Files. This is the location where you saved the Agenda document.
4. In the file list, click **Agenda**. See Figure 19.

Figure 19 Open dialog box

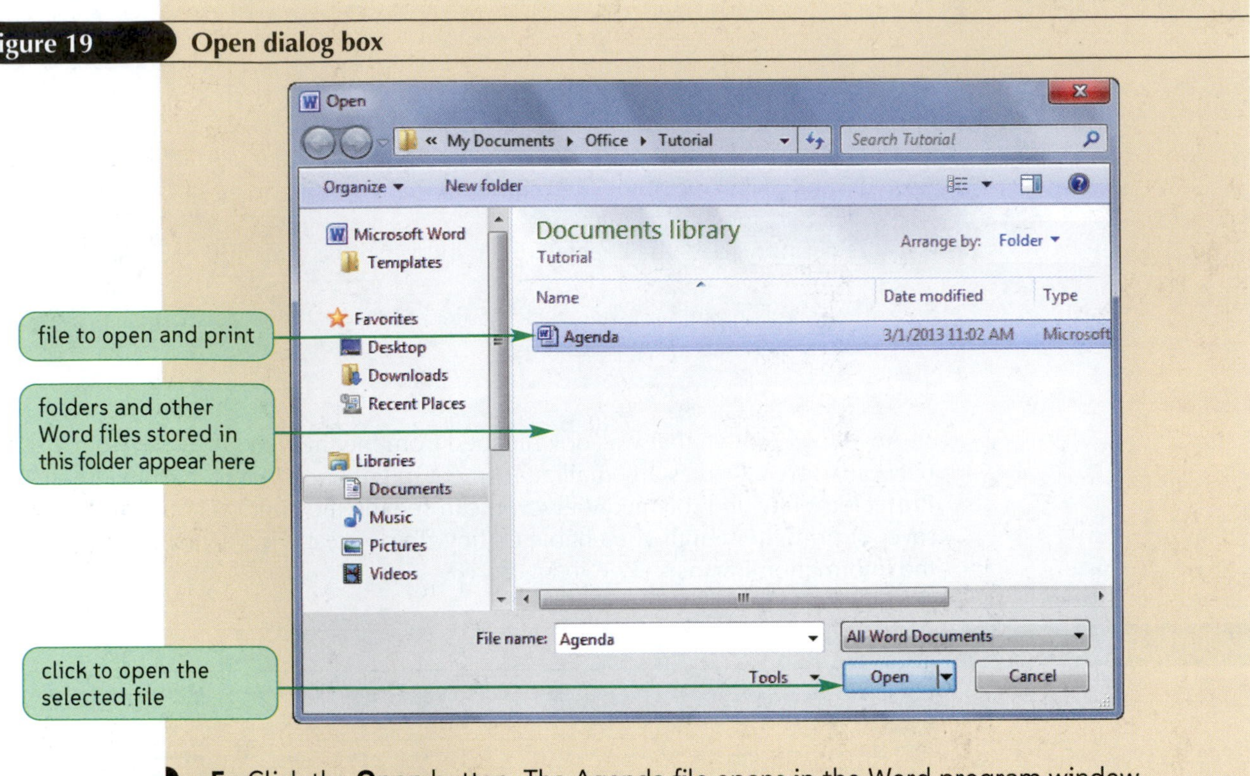

5. Click the **Open** button. The Agenda file opens in the Word program window.

Sharing Files Using Windows Live SkyDrive

Often the purpose of creating a file is to share it with other people—sending it attached to an email message for someone else to read or use, collaborating with others on the same document, or posting it as a blog for others to review. You can do all of these things in Backstage view from the Save & Send tab.

When you send a file using email, you can attach a copy of the file, send a link to the file, or attach a copy of the file in a PDF or another file format. You can also save to online workspaces where you can make the file available to others for review and collaboration. The Save to Web option on the Save & Send tab in Backstage view gives you access to **Windows Live SkyDrive**, which is an online workspace provided by Microsoft; your personal workspace comes with a Public folder for saving files to share as well as a My Documents folder for saving files you want to keep private. (SkyDrive is not available for Access.) Figure 20 shows the Save to Web options on the Save & Send tab in Backstage view of Word. SharePoint is an online workspace set up by an organization, such as a school, business, or nonprofit group.

TIP

To use SkyDrive, you need a Windows Live ID, which you can sign up for at no cost. After you sign in, you can create new folders and save files into the folders.

Files saved to an online workspace can be worked on by more than one person at the same time. The changes are recorded in the files with each author's name and the date of the change. A Web browser is used to access and edit the files. You choose who can have access to the files.

Figure 20 Save to Web options on the Save & Send tab

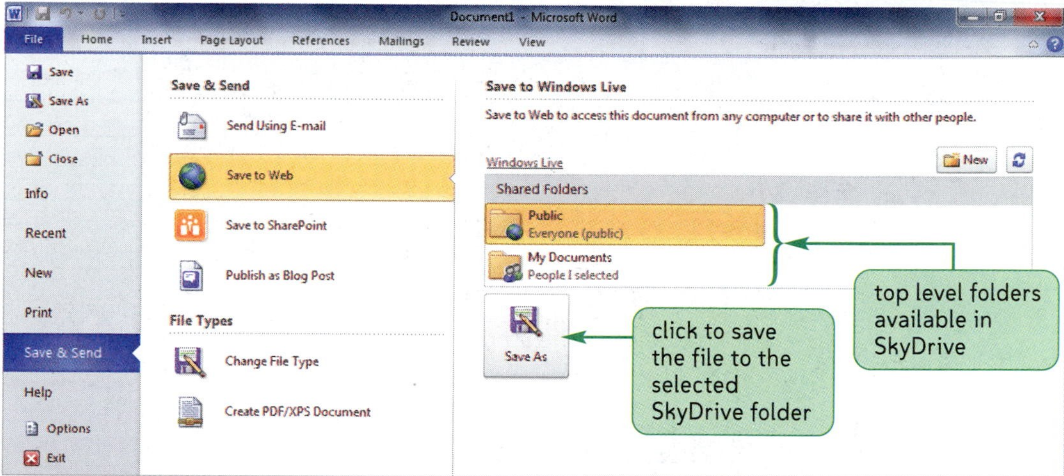

REFERENCE

Saving a File to SkyDrive

- Click the File tab to open Backstage view, and then click the Save & Send tab in the navigation bar.
- In the center pane, click Save to Web.
- In the right pane, click the Sign In button, and then use your Windows Live ID to log on to your Windows Live SkyDrive account.

Getting Help

If you don't know how to perform a task or want more information about a feature, you can turn to Office itself for information on how to use it. This information is referred to simply as **Help**. You can get Help in ScreenTips and from the Help window.

Viewing ScreenTips

ScreenTips are a fast and simple method you can use to get information about objects you see on the screen. A **ScreenTip** is a box with descriptive text about an object or button. Just point to a button or object to display its ScreenTip. In addition to the button's name, a ScreenTip might include the button's keyboard shortcut if it has one, a description of the command's function, and, in some cases, a link to more information so that you can press the F1 key while the ScreenTip is displayed to open the Help window with the relevant topic displayed.

To view ScreenTips:

1. Point to the **Microsoft Office Word Help** button. The ScreenTip shows the button's name, its keyboard shortcut, and a brief description. See Figure 21.

Figure 21 ScreenTip for the Help button

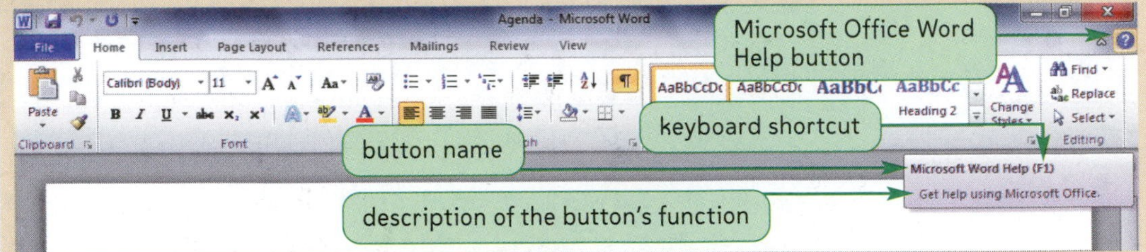

2. Point to other buttons on the Ribbon to display their ScreenTips.

Using the Help Window

For more detailed information, you can use the **Help window** to access all the Help topics, templates, and training installed on your computer with Office and available on Office.com. **Office.com** is a Web site maintained by Microsoft that provides access to the latest information and additional Help resources. For example, you can access current Help topics and training for Office. To connect to Office.com, you need to be able to access the Internet from your computer. Otherwise, you see only topics that are stored on your computer.

Each program has its own Help window from which you can find information about all of the Office commands and features as well as step-by-step instructions for using them. There are two ways to find Help topics—the search function and a topic list.

The Type words to search for box enables you to search the Help system for a task or a topic you need help with. You can click a link to open a Help topic with explanations and step-by-step instructions for a specific procedure. The Table of Contents pane displays the Help system content organized by subjects and topics, similar to a book's table of contents. You click main subject links to display related topic links. You click a topic link to display that Help topic in the Help window.

REFERENCE

Getting Help

- Click the Microsoft Office Help button (the button name depends on the Office program).
- Type a keyword or phrase in the Type words to search for box, click the Search button, and then click a Help topic in the search results list.

  or

  In the Table of Contents pane, click a "book," and then click a Help topic.
- Read the information in the Help window and then click other topics or links.
- On the Help window title bar, click the Close button.

You'll use Help to get information about printing a document in Word.

To search Help for information about printing:

1. Click the **Microsoft Office Word Help** button . The Word Help window opens.

2. If the Table of Contents pane is not open on the left side of the Help window, click the **Show Table of Contents** button on the toolbar to display the pane.
3. Click the **Type words to search for** box, if necessary, and then type **print document**. You can specify where you want to search.
4. Click the **Search button arrow**. The Search menu shows the online and local content available.
5. If your computer is connected to the Internet, click **All Word** in the Content from Office.com list. If your computer is not connected to the Internet, click **Word Help** in the Content from this computer list.
6. Click the **Search** button. The Help window displays a list of topics related to the keywords "print document" in the left pane. See Figure 22.

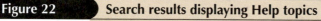

Figure 22 **Search results displaying Help topics**

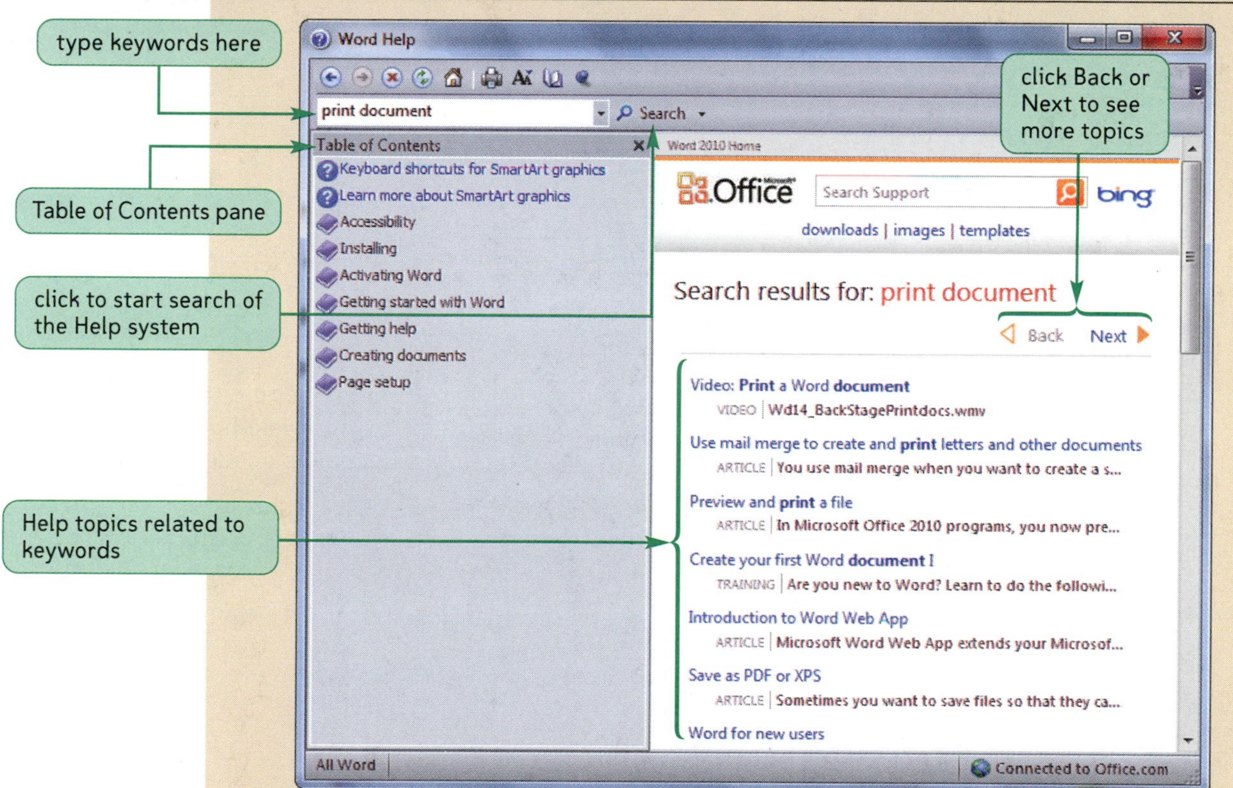

Trouble? If your search results list differs from the one shown in Figure 22, your computer is not connected to the Internet or Microsoft has updated the list of available Help topics since this book was published. Continue with Step 7.

7. Scroll through the list to review the Help topics.
8. Click **Preview and print a file**. The topic content is displayed in the Help window so you can learn more about how to print a document. See Figure 23.

Figure 23 Preview and print a file Help topic

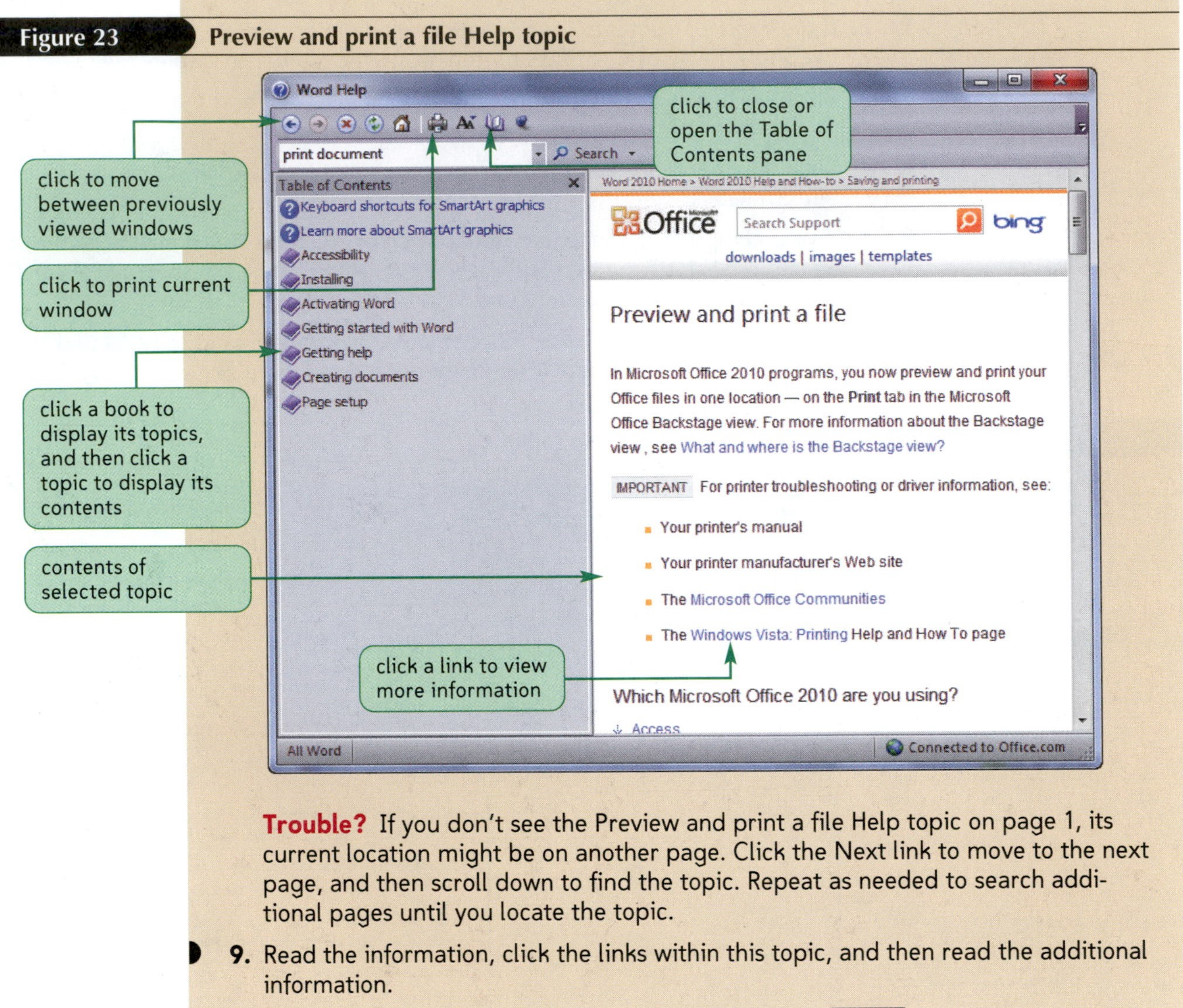

Trouble? If you don't see the Preview and print a file Help topic on page 1, its current location might be on another page. Click the Next link to move to the next page, and then scroll down to find the topic. Repeat as needed to search additional pages until you locate the topic.

9. Read the information, click the links within this topic, and then read the additional information.
10. On the Help window title bar, click the **Close** button to close the window.

Printing a File

At times, you'll want a paper copy of Office files. Whenever you print, you should review and adjust the printing settings as needed. You can select the number of copies to print, the printer, the portion of the file to print, and so forth; the printing settings vary slightly from program to program. You should also check the file's print preview to ensure that the file will print as you intended. This simple review will help you to avoid reprinting, which requires additional paper, ink, and energy resources.

REFERENCE

Printing a File

- On the Ribbon, click the File tab to open Backstage view.
- In the navigation bar, click the Print tab.
- Verify the print settings and review the print preview.
- Click the Print button.

You will print the agenda for Ean.

To print the Agenda document:

1. Make sure your printer is turned on and contains paper.
2. On the Ribbon, click the **File** tab to open Backstage view.
3. In the navigation bar, click the **Print** tab. The print settings and preview appear. See Figure 24.

Figure 24 **Print tab in Backstage view**

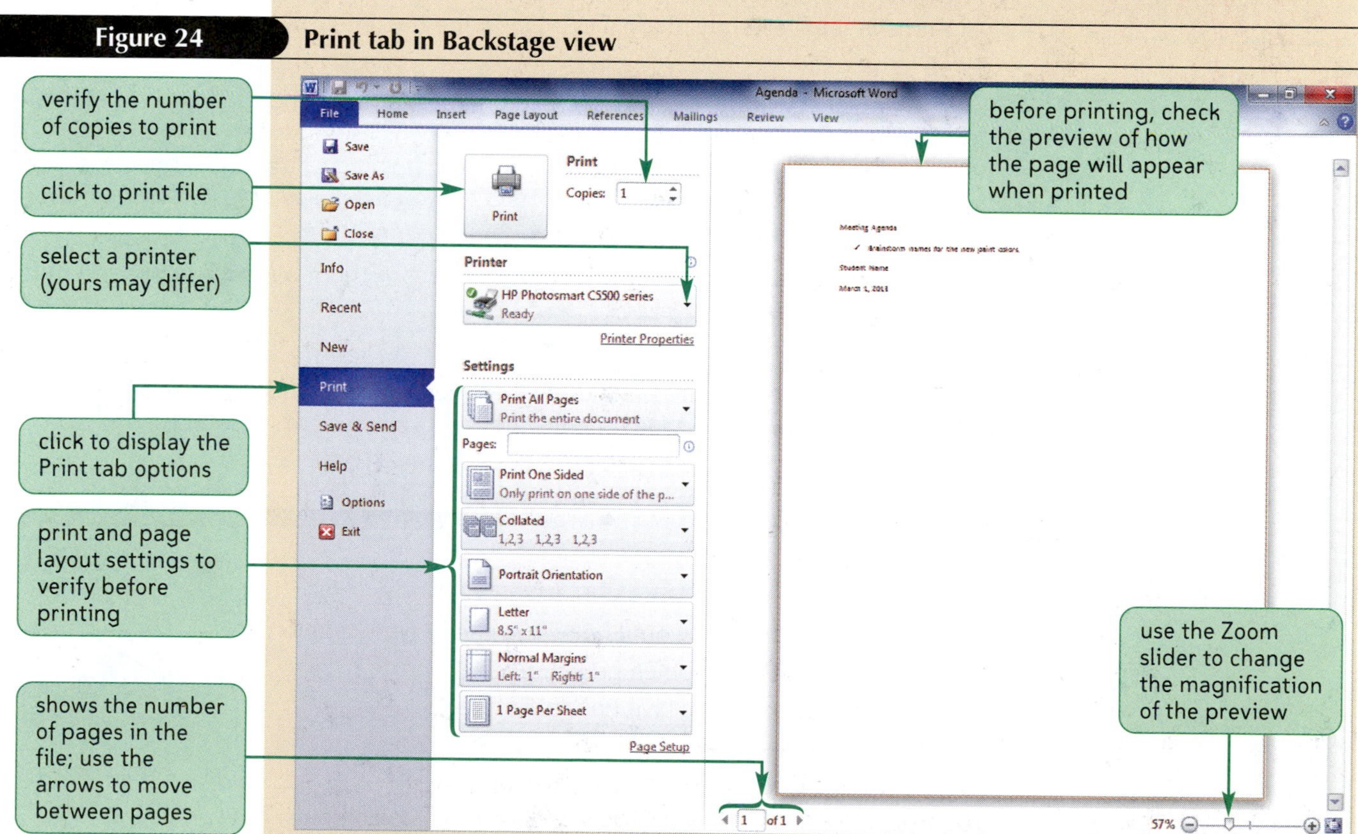

4. Verify that **1** appears in the Copies box.
5. Verify that the correct printer appears on the Printer button. If it doesn't, click the **Printer** button, and then click the correct printer from the list of available printers.
6. Click the **Print** button to print the document.

Trouble? If the document does not print, see your instructor or technical support person for help.

Exiting Programs

When you finish working with a program, you should exit it. As with many other aspects of Office, you can exit programs with a button or a command. You'll use both methods to exit Word and Excel. You can use the Exit command to exit a program and close an open file in one step. If you haven't saved the final version of the open file, a dialog box opens, asking whether you want to save your changes. Clicking the Save button in this dialog box saves the open file, closes the file, and then exits the program.

To exit the Word and Excel programs:

1. On the Word title bar, click the **Close** button. Both the Word document and the Word program close. The Excel window is visible again.

   Trouble? If a dialog box opens asking if you want to save the document, you might have inadvertently made a change to the document. Click the Don't Save button.

2. On the Ribbon, click the **File** tab to open Backstage view, and then click the **Exit** command in the navigation bar. A dialog box opens asking whether you want to save the changes you made to the workbook. If you click the Save button, the Save As dialog box opens and Excel exits after you finish saving the workbook. This time, you don't want to save the workbook.

3. Click the **Don't Save** button. The workbook closes without saving a copy, and the Excel program closes.

Exiting programs after you are done using them keeps your Windows desktop uncluttered for the next person using the computer, frees up your system's resources, and prevents data from being lost accidentally.

REVIEW

Quick Check

1. What Office program would be best to use to write a letter?
2. How do you start an Office program?
3. What is the purpose of Live Preview?
4. What is Backstage view?
5. Explain the difference between Save and Save As.
6. True or False. In Protected View, you can see file contents, but you cannot edit, save, or print them until you enable editing.
7. What happens if you open a file, make edits, and then attempt to close the file or exit the program without saving the current version of the file?
8. What are the two ways to get Help in Office?

Practice the skills you learned in the tutorial.

PRACTICE

Review Assignments

Data Files needed for the Review Assignments: Finances.xlsx, Letter.docx

You need to prepare for an upcoming meeting at Recycled Palette. You'll open and print documents for the meeting. Complete the following:

1. Start PowerPoint, and then start Excel.
2. Switch to the PowerPoint window, and then close the presentation but leave the PowerPoint program open. (*Hint*: Use the Close command in Backstage view.)
3. Open a blank PowerPoint presentation from the New tab in Backstage view. (*Hint*: Make sure Blank presentation is selected in the Available Templates and Themes section, and then click the Create button.)
4. Close the PowerPoint presentation and program using the Close button on the PowerPoint title bar; do not save changes if asked.
5. Open the **Finances** workbook located in the Office\Review folder. If the workbook opens in Protected View, click the Enable Editing button.
6. Use the Save As command to save the workbook as **Recycled Palette Finances** in the Office\Review folder.
7. In cell A1, type your name, press the Enter key to insert your name at the top of the worksheet, and then save the workbook.
8. Preview and print one copy of the worksheet using the Print tab in Backstage view.
9. Exit Excel using the Exit command in Backstage view.
10. Start Word, and then open the **Letter** document located in the Office\Review folder. If the document opens in Protected View, click the Enable Editing button.
11. Use the Save As command to save the document with the filename **Recycled Palette Letter** in the Office\Review folder.
12. Press and hold the Ctrl key, press the End key, and then release both keys to move the insertion point to the end of the letter, and then type your name.
13. Use the Save button to save the change to the Recycled Palette Letter document.
14. Preview and print one copy of the document using the Print tab in Backstage view.
15. Close the document, and then exit the Word program.
16. Submit the finished files to your instructor.

SAM

ASSESS

SAM: Skills Assessment Manager

For current SAM information, including versions and content details, visit SAM Central (http://samcentral.course.com). If you have a SAM user profile, you may have access to hands-on instruction, practice, and assessment of the skills covered in this tutorial. Since various versions of SAM are supported throughout the life of this text, check with your instructor for the correct instructions and URL/Web site for accessing assignments.

ENDING DATA FILES

Agenda.docx

Recycled Palette Finances.xlsx
Recycled Palette Letter.docx

ProSkills

Teamwork

Working on a Team

Teams consist of individuals who have skills, talents, and abilities that complement each other and, when joined, produce synergy—results greater than those a single individual could achieve. It is this sense of shared mission and responsibility for results that makes a team successful in its efforts to reach its goals. Teams are everywhere. In the workplace, a team might develop a presentation to introduce products. In the classroom, a team might complete a research project.

Teams meet face to face or virtually. A virtual team rarely, if ever, meets in person. Instead, technology makes it possible for members to work as if everyone was in the same room. Some common technologies used in virtual teamwork are corporate networks, email, teleconferencing, and collaboration and integration tools, such as those found in Office 2010.

Even for teams in the same location, technology is a valuable tool. For example, teams commonly collaborate on a copy of a file posted to an online shared storage space, such as SkyDrive. In addition, team members can compile data in the program that best suits the information related to their part of the project. Later, that information can be integrated into a finished report, presentation, email message, and so on.

PROSKILLS

Collaborate with Others

At home, school, or work, you probably collaborate with others to complete many types of tasks—such as planning an event, creating a report, or developing a presentation. You can use Microsoft Office to streamline many of these tasks. Consider a project that you might need to work on with a team. Complete the following steps:

1. Start Word, and open a new document, if necessary.
2. In the document, type a list of all the tasks the team needs to accomplish. If you are working with a team, identify which team member would complete each task.
3. For each task, identify the type of Office file you would create to complete that task. For example, you would create a Word document to write a letter.
4. For each file, identify the Office program you would use to create that file, and explain why you would use that program.
5. Save the document with an appropriate filename in an appropriate folder location.
6. Use a Web browser to visit the Microsoft site at *www.microsoft.com* and research the different Office 2010 suites available. Determine which suite includes all the programs needed for the team to complete the tasks on the list.
7. In the document, type which Office suite you selected and a brief explanation of why.
8. Determine how the team can integrate the different programs in the Office suite you selected to create the files that complete the team's goal or task. Include this information at the end of the Word document. Save the document.
9. Develop an efficient way to organize the files that the team will create to complete the goal or task. Add this information at the end of the Word document.
10. If possible, sign in to SkyDrive, and then save a copy of the file in an appropriate subfolder within your Public folder. If you are working with a team, have your teammates access your file, review your notes, and add a paragraph with their comments and name.
11. Preview and print the finished document, and then submit it to your instructor.

TUTORIAL 1

WORD

Creating a Document

Writing a Business Letter and Formatting a Flyer

OBJECTIVES

Session 1.1

- Enter a date with AutoComplete
- Enter text
- Select text and move the insertion point
- Correct errors and proofread a document
- Adjust paragraph spacing, line spacing, and margins
- Preview and print a document
- Create a new document
- Create an envelope

Session 1.2

- Open an existing document
- Change page orientation
- Change the font and font size
- Apply text effects and other formatting
- Align text
- Insert a paragraph border and shading

Case | *Carlyle University Press*

Carlyle University Press is a nonprofit book publisher associated with Carlyle State University in Albany, New York. The Press, as it is referred to by both editors and authors, publishes a variety of scholarly books. When a new author signs a contract for a book, he or she receives the *Author's Guide*, a handbook describing the process of creating a manuscript. In this tutorial, you will help the Managing Editor, Andrew Siordia, create a cover letter to accompany a copy of the *Author's Guide*. Then you will create a flyer announcing an appearance by an author at a local bookstore.

You will create the letter and flyer using **Microsoft Office Word 2010** (or simply **Word**), a word-processing program. You will type the text of the cover letter, save the letter, and then print the letter. In the process of entering the text, you'll learn several ways to correct typing errors and how to adjust paragraph and line spacing. You will also create an envelope for the letter. As you work on the flyer, you will learn how to open an existing document, change the way text is laid out on the page, format text, and insert and resize a photo.

STARTING DATA FILES

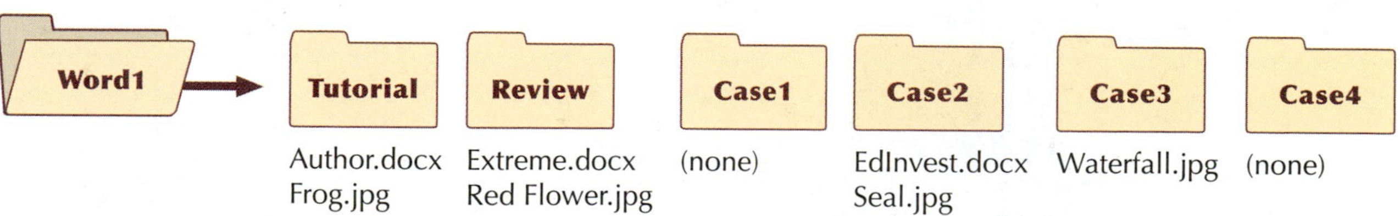

Tutorial	Review	Case1	Case2	Case3	Case4
Author.docx Frog.jpg	Extreme.docx Red Flower.jpg	(none)	EdInvest.docx Seal.jpg	Waterfall.jpg	(none)

SESSION 1.1 VISUAL OVERVIEW

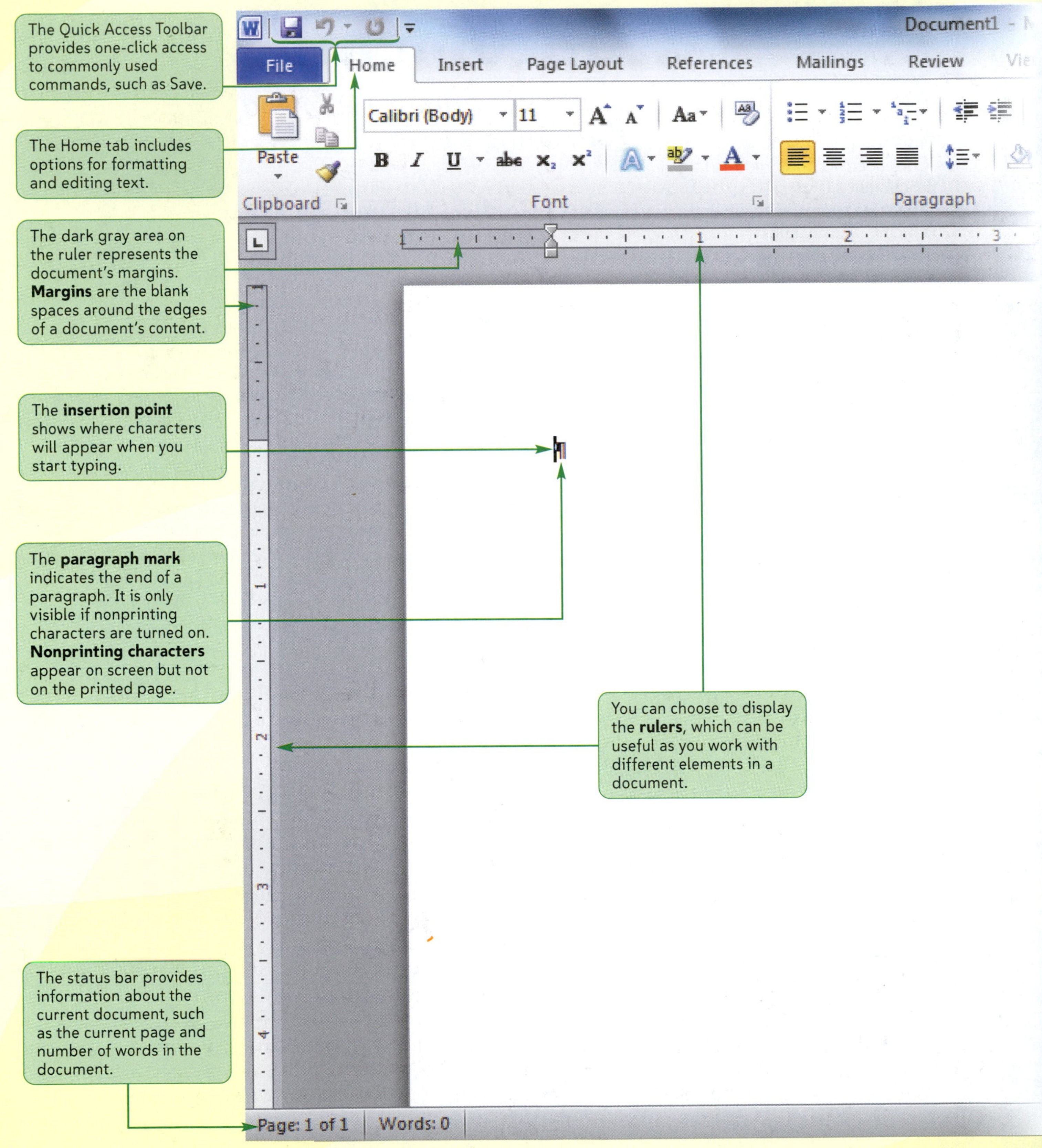

The Quick Access Toolbar provides one-click access to commonly used commands, such as Save.
The Home tab includes options for formatting and editing text.
The dark gray area on the ruler represents the document's margins. **Margins** are the blank spaces around the edges of a document's content.
The **insertion point** shows where characters will appear when you start typing.
The **paragraph mark** indicates the end of a paragraph. It is only visible if nonprinting characters are turned on. **Nonprinting characters** appear on screen but not on the printed page.
You can choose to display the **rulers**, which can be useful as you work with different elements in a document.
The status bar provides information about the current document, such as the current page and number of words in the document.
Document1
File
Home
Insert
Page Layout
References
Mailings
Review
Paste
Calibri (Body)
11
Clipboard
Font
Paragraph
Page: 1 of 1
Words: 0

THE WORD WINDOW

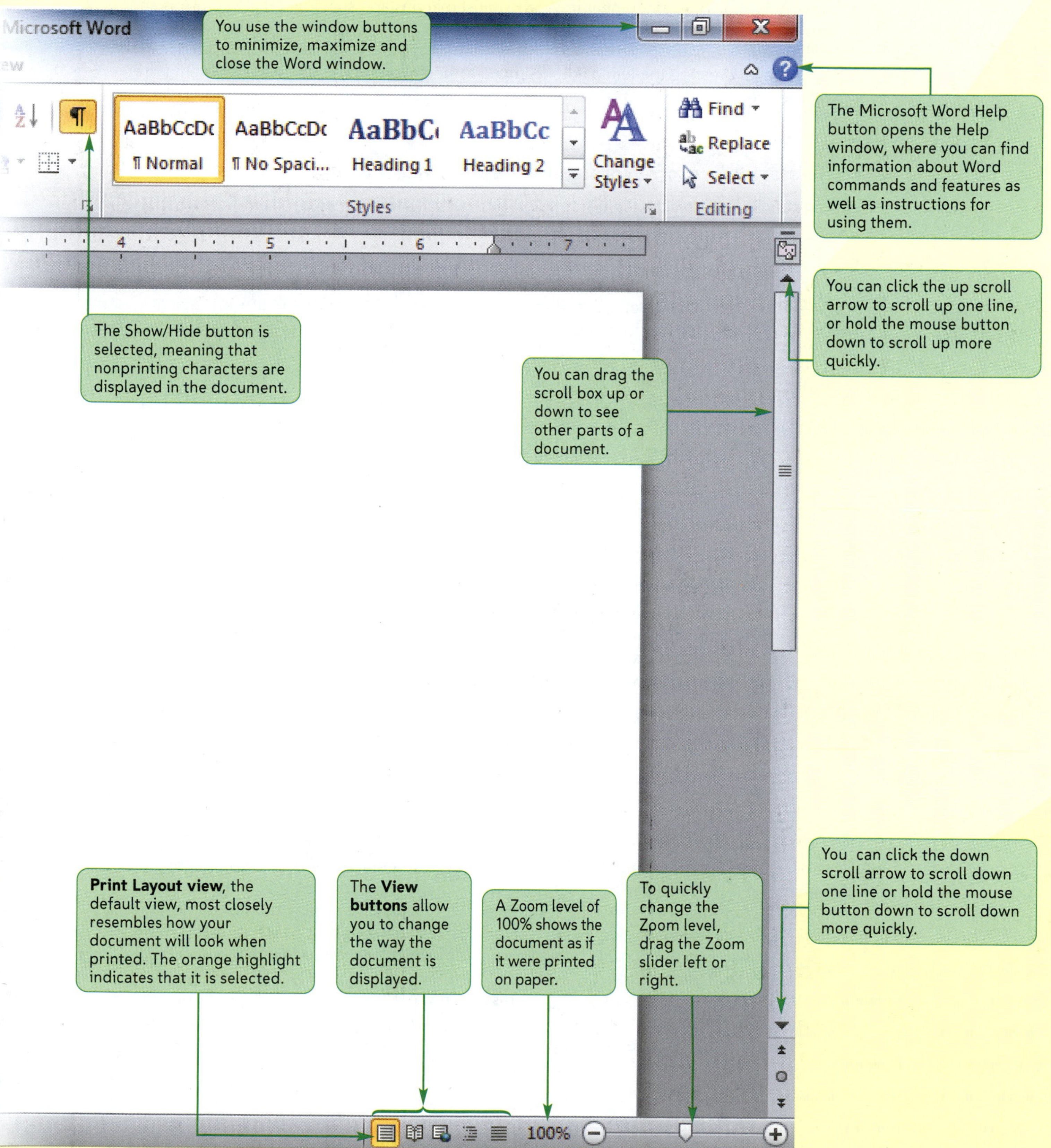

Microsoft Word
You use the window buttons to minimize, maximize and close the Word window.
The Microsoft Word Help button opens the Help window, where you can find information about Word commands and features as well as instructions for using them.
AaBbCcDc
¶ Normal
AaBbCcDc
¶ No Spaci...
AaBbCc
Heading 1
AaBbCc
Heading 2
Change Styles
Find
Replace
Select
Styles
Editing
The Show/Hide button is selected, meaning that nonprinting characters are displayed in the document.
You can click the up scroll arrow to scroll up one line, or hold the mouse button down to scroll up more quickly.
You can drag the scroll box up or down to see other parts of a document.
You can click the down scroll arrow to scroll down one line or hold the mouse button down to scroll down more quickly.
Print Layout view, the default view, most closely resembles how your document will look when printed. The orange highlight indicates that it is selected.
The **View buttons** allow you to change the way the document is displayed.
A Zoom level of 100% shows the document as if it were printed on paper.
To quickly change the Zoom level, drag the Zoom slider left or right.
100%

Starting Word

With Word, you can create polished, professional documents in a minimal amount of time. You can type a document in Word, adjust margins and spacing, create columns and tables, add graphics, and then easily make revisions and corrections. In this tutorial, you will create one of the most common types of documents, a block style business letter.

To begin creating the letter, you first need to start Word and then take a moment to set up the Word window.

To start Microsoft Word and set up the Word window:

1. Click the **Start** button on the taskbar, click **All Programs**, click **Microsoft Office**, and then click **Microsoft Word 2010**. The Word window opens, as shown in the Session 1.1 Visual Overview. You can refer to the Session 1.1 Visual Overview to locate and identify the different elements of the Word window.

   Trouble? If you don't see Microsoft Office Word 2010 on the Microsoft Office submenu, look for it on a different submenu or on the All Programs menu. If you still can't find Microsoft Office Word 2010, ask your instructor or technical support person for help.

2. If the Word window does not fill the entire screen, click the **Maximize** button in the upper-right corner of the Word window. It is useful to have the rulers displayed in the Word window while you work, so you will make sure they are displayed.
3. Click the **View** tab on the Ribbon. The View tab provides options for changing the appearance of the Word window.
4. In the Show group, click the **Ruler** check box to insert a check, if necessary. If the rulers were not displayed, they should be displayed now.

   Next, you'll change the Zoom level to a setting that ensures that your document will match the figures in this book. Instead of dragging the Zoom slider you will use a setting that automatically zooms the document so that the width of the page matches the width of the Word window.

5. In the Zoom group, click the **Page Width** button.
6. If necessary, click the **Print Layout** button on the status bar to select it. As shown in the Session 1.1 Visual Overview, the Print Layout button is the first of the View buttons located on the right side of the status bar.

TIP

Changing the Zoom affects only the way the document is displayed on the screen; it does not affect the document itself.

Before typing a document, you should make sure nonprinting characters are displayed. Nonprinting characters provide a visual representation of details you might otherwise miss. For example, the (¶) character marks the end of a paragraph, and the (•) character marks the space between words. It is helpful to display nonprinting characters so you can see whether you've typed an extra space, ended a paragraph, and so on. You will also find them useful when you work on the advanced formatting topics discussed in later tutorials.

Whether nonprinting characters are displayed when you start Word depends on the setting selected the last time Word was used on your computer. You will now make sure the nonprinting characters are displayed in the document window.

To verify that nonprinting characters are displayed:

1. In the blank Word document, look for the paragraph mark (¶) in the first line of the document, just to the right of the blinking insertion point.
2. If you don't see the paragraph mark, click the **Home** tab on the Ribbon, and then in the Paragraph group, click the **Show/Hide** ¶ button ¶. The Show/Hide ¶ button should now be highlighted in orange, indicating that it is selected, and the paragraph mark (¶) appears in the first line of the document, just to the right of the insertion point.

Creating a Block Style Business Letter

Andrew has asked you to type a block style letter to accompany an author guide that will be sent to new authors. Figure 1-1 shows an example of a block style letter.

Figure 1-1 Completed block style letter

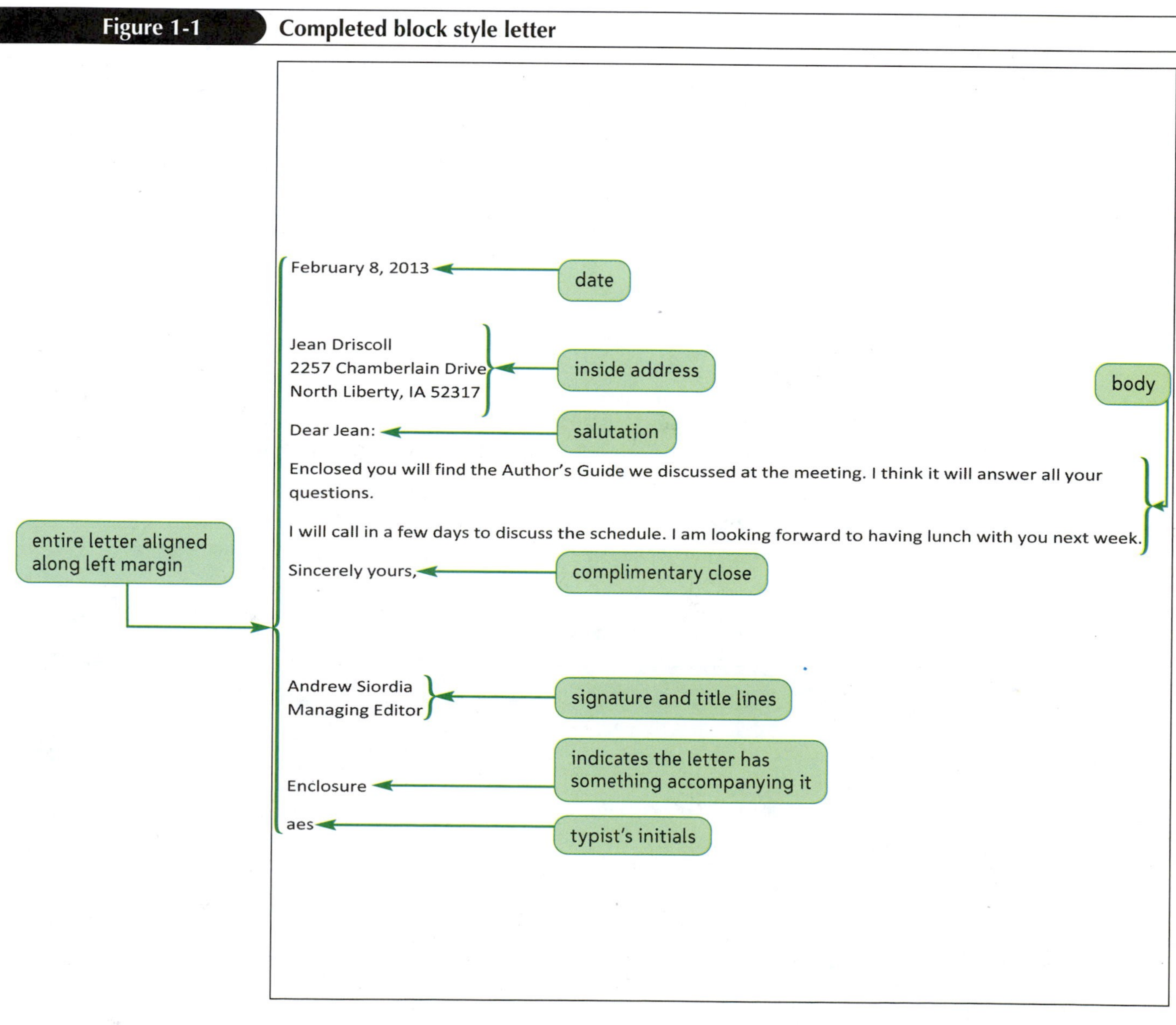

February 8, 2013

Jean Driscoll
2257 Chamberlain Drive
North Liberty, IA 52317

Dear Jean:

Enclosed you will find the Author's Guide we discussed at the meeting. I think it will answer all your questions.

I will call in a few days to discuss the schedule. I am looking forward to having lunch with you next week.

Sincerely yours,

Andrew Siordia
Managing Editor

Enclosure

aes

PROSKILLS

Written Communication: Creating a Business Letter

Several styles are considered acceptable for business letters. The main differences among them have to do with how parts of the letter are indented from the left margin. In the block style, which you will use to create the letter in this tutorial, each line of text starts at the left margin. In other words, nothing is indented. Another style is to indent the first line of each paragraph. The choice of style is largely a matter of personal preference, or it can be determined by the standards used in a particular business or organization. To further enhance your skills in writing business correspondence, you can consult an authoritative book for business writing that provides guidelines for creating a variety of business documents, such as *Business Communication: Process & Product*, by Mary Ellen Guffey.

Entering Text

The letters you type appear at the current location of the insertion point. You are ready to begin typing the letter for Andrew. The first item in a block style business letter is the date.

Inserting a Date with AutoComplete

Andrew wants to send the *Author's Guide* to Jean Driscoll on February 8, so you need to insert that date into the letter. To do so, you can take advantage of **AutoComplete**, a Word feature that automatically inserts dates and other regularly used items for you. In this case, you can type the first few characters of the month, and let Word insert the rest.

To insert the date:

1. Type **Febr** (the first four letters of February). A ScreenTip appears above the letters, as shown in Figure 1-2, suggesting "February" as the complete word. If you wanted to type something other than February, you could continue typing to complete the word. You want to accept the AutoComplete suggestion.

Figure 1-2 AutoComplete suggestion

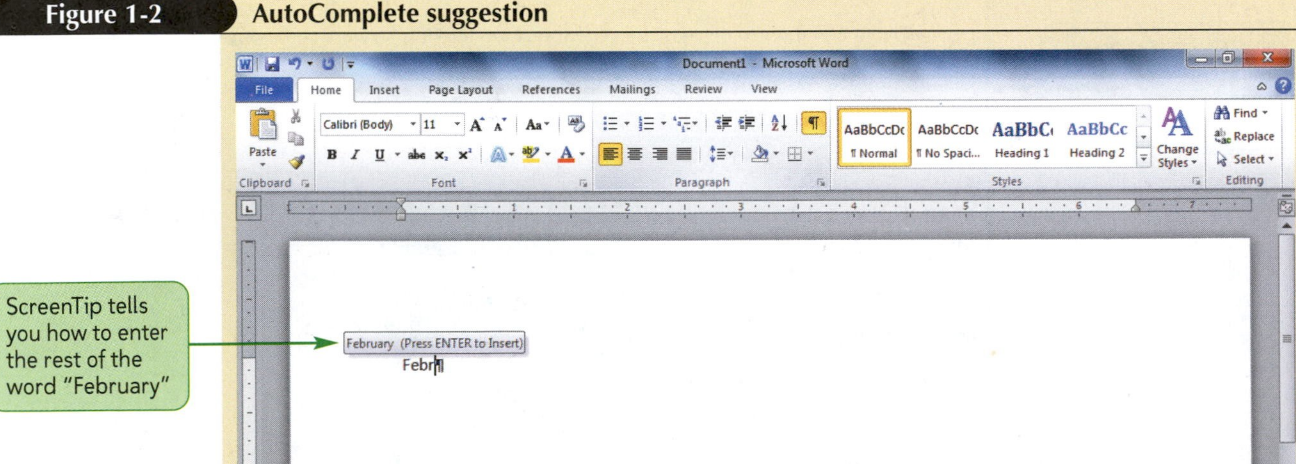

TIP

AutoComplete works for long month names like February, but not shorter ones like May, because "Ma" could be the beginning of many words, not just "May."

2. Press the **Enter** key. The rest of the word "February" is inserted in the document.
3. Press the **spacebar**, type **8, 2013** and then press the **Enter** key twice, leaving a blank paragraph between the date and the line where you will begin typing the inside address. Notice the nonprinting character (•) after the word "February" and before the number "2," which indicates a space. Word inserts this nonprinting character every time you press the spacebar.

   Trouble? If February happens to be the current month, you will see a second AutoComplete suggestion displaying the current date after you press the spacebar. To ignore that AutoComplete suggestion, continue typing the rest of the date as instructed in Step 3.

Next you will type the inside address.

Entering the Inside Address

In a block style business letter, the inside address appears below the date, with one blank paragraph in between. Note that some style guides recommend including even more space between the date and the inside address, but in the short letter you are typing more space would make the document look out of balance. The inside address is the address of the recipient of the letter, Jean Driscoll.

To insert the inside address:

1. Type the following information, pressing the **Enter** key after each item:

   Jean Driscoll

   2257 Chamberlain Drive

   North Liberty, IA 52317

   When you are finished typing the inside address, your screen should look like Figure 1-3. Don't be concerned if the lines of the inside address look like they are too far apart. You will adjust the spacing between lines of text after you finish typing the letter.

   Trouble? If you make a mistake while typing, press the Backspace key to delete the incorrect character and then type the correct character.

Figure 1-3 Letter with inside address

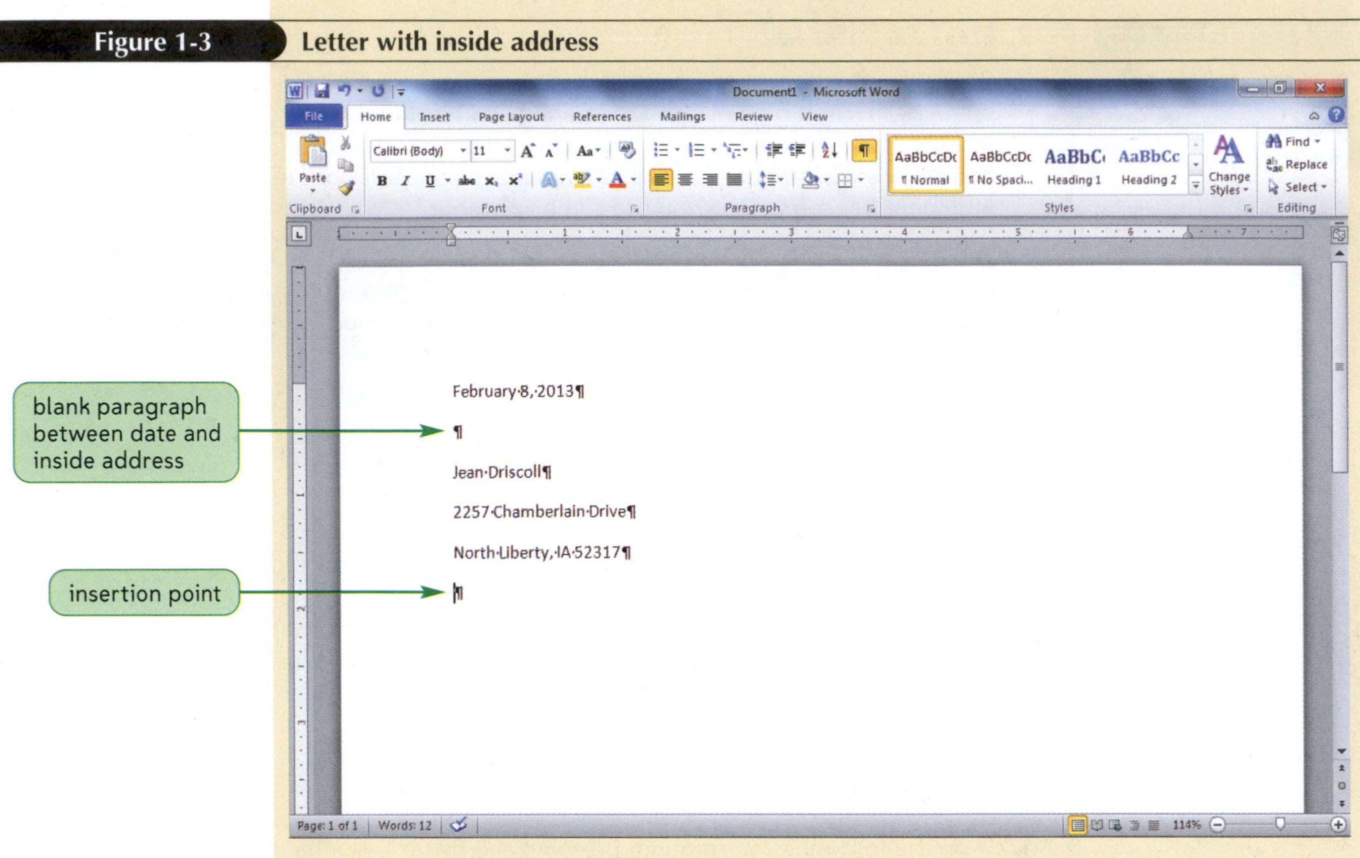

Now you can move on to the salutation and the body of the letter. As you type the body of the letter, notice that Word automatically moves the insertion point to a new line when it reaches the right margin.

To type the salutation and the body of the letter:

1. Type **Dear Jean:** and then press the **Enter** key to start a new paragraph for the body of the letter.
2. Type the following sentence, including the period: **Enclosed you will find the Author's Guide we discussed at the meeting.**
3. Press the **spacebar**.
4. Type the following sentence, including the period: **I think it will answer all your concerns.**
5. Press the **Enter** key.

   Notice how Word moves the insertion point to a new line when the current line is full. See Figure 1-4.

Figure 1-4 Partially completed letter

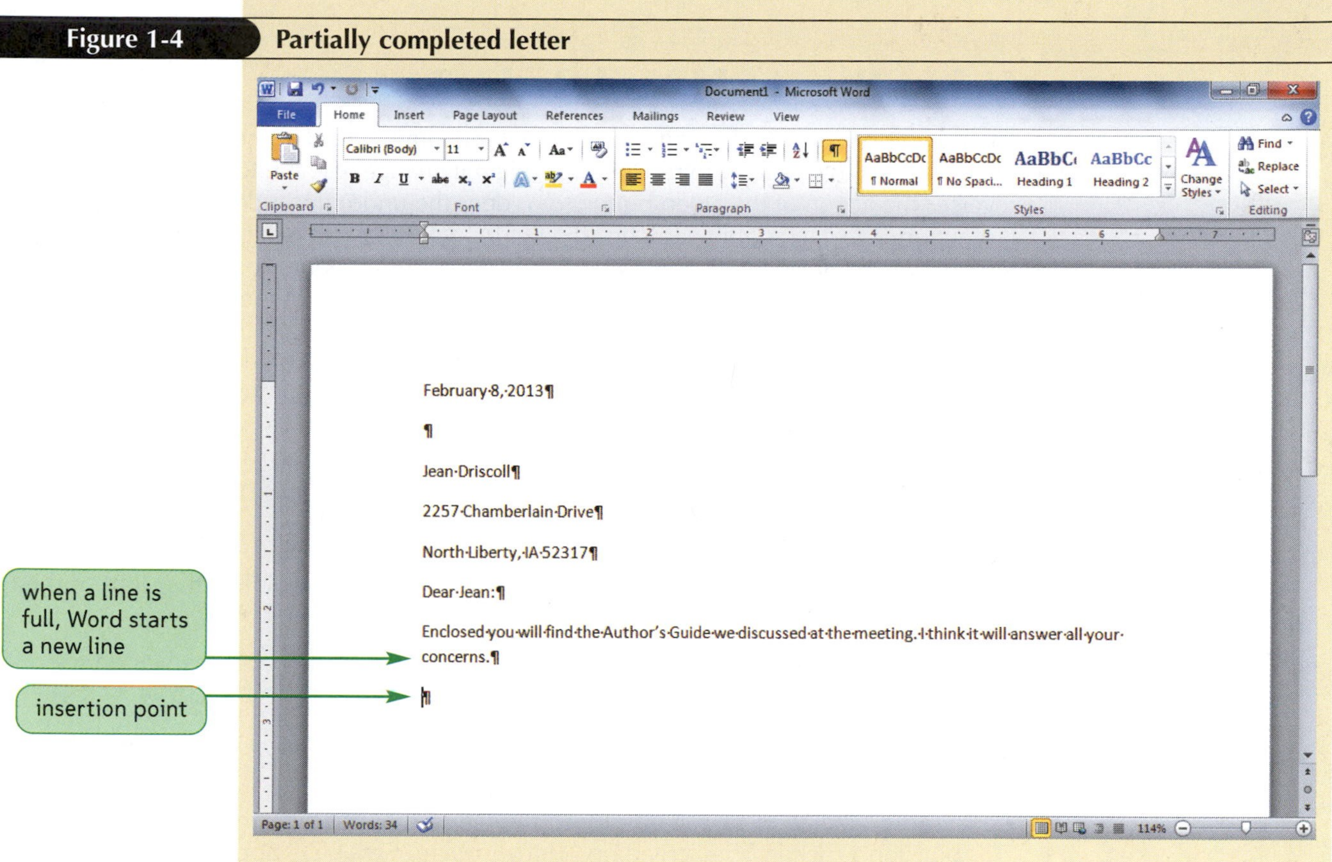

Before you continue with the rest of the letter, you should save what you have typed so far.

To save the document:

1. On the Quick Access Toolbar, click the **Save** button. The Save As dialog box opens. Note that Word suggests using the first line you typed ("February 8") as the filename.
2. Type **Driscoll Letter** in the File name box, replacing the suggested filename. Next, you need to specify a location in which to store the file.
3. Navigate to the Word1\Tutorial folder included with your Data Files.

   Trouble? If Word adds the .docx extension to your filename, your computer is configured to show file extensions. That's fine.

   Trouble? The Word1 folder is included with the Data Files for this text. If you don't have the Word Data Files, you need to get them before you can proceed. Your instructor will either give you the Data Files or ask you to obtain them from a specified location (such as a network drive). In either case, be sure that you make a backup copy of your Data Files before you start using them, so that the original files will be available on your copied disk in case you need to start over because of an error or problem. If you have any questions about the Data Files, see your instructor or technical support person for assistance.
4. Click the **Save** button in the Save As dialog box. The dialog box closes, and you return to the document window. The new document name (Driscoll Letter) appears in the title bar.

Now that the letter has been saved, you can continue working on it.

Using the Undo and Redo Buttons

To undo (or reverse) the last thing you did in a document, click the **Undo button** on the Quick Access Toolbar. To restore your original change, use the **Redo button**, which reverses the action of the Undo button (or redoes the undo). To undo more than your last action, you can continue to click the Undo button, or you can click the Undo button arrow on the Quick Access Toolbar. This opens a list of your most recent actions, in which you can click the action you want to undo; Word then undoes every action in the list, up to and including the action you clicked in the list.

Andrew asks you to change the word "concerns" to "questions" in the sentence "I think it will answer all your concerns." You'll make the change now. If Andrew decides he doesn't like it after all, you can always undo it.

To change the word "concerns":

1. Press the **left arrow** key ← twice to move the insertion point to the right of the "s" in the word "concerns."
2. Press the **Backspace** key eight times to delete the word "concerns," and then type **questions** as a replacement.

   After reviewing the sentence, Andrew decides he prefers the original wording, so you will undo the change.
3. On the Quick Access Toolbar, place the mouse pointer over the **Undo** button but don't click it. The ScreenTip "Undo Typing (Ctrl + Z)" appears, indicating that your most recent action involved typing. The item in parentheses is the keyboard shortcut for the Undo command. See Figure 1-5.

Figure 1-5 Using the Undo button

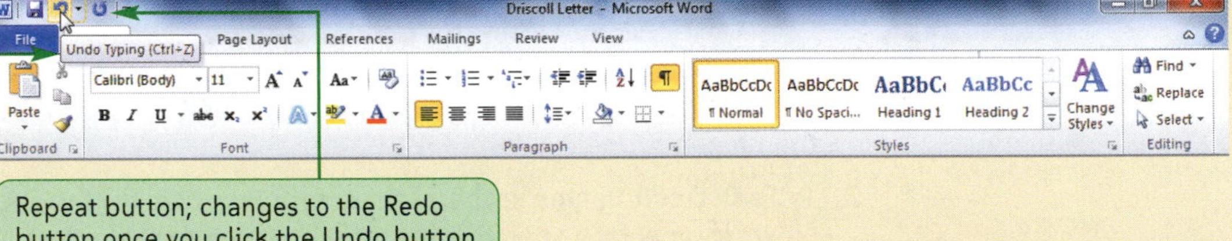

4. Click the **Undo** button on the Quick Access Toolbar. The Repeat button changes to the Redo button. The word "questions" is replaced with the original word, "concerns."

   Andrew decides that he does want to use "questions" after all. Instead of retyping it, you'll redo the undo.
5. On the Quick Access Toolbar, place the mouse pointer over the **Redo** button to display the "Redo Typing (Ctrl + Y)" ScreenTip.
6. Click the **Redo** button on the Quick Access Toolbar. The word "questions" replaces "concerns" in the document, so that the phrase reads "...answer all your questions."
7. On the Quick Access Toolbar, click the **Save** button. Word saves your letter with the same name and to the same location you specified earlier.

In the previous steps, you used the left arrow key ← to move the insertion point to a specific location in the document. You could also have clicked at that location instead of using an arrow key. As you become more experienced with Word, you'll see that you can use a number of different techniques for moving the insertion point around a document. The correct choice depends on your personal preference. For your reference, Figure 1-6 summarizes the most common keystrokes for moving the insertion point in a document.

Figure 1-6 **Keystrokes for moving the insertion point**

To move the insertion point	Press
Left or right one character at a time	← or →
Up or down one line at a time	↑ or ↓
Left or right one word at a time	Ctrl+← or Ctrl+→
Up or down one paragraph at a time	Ctrl+↑ or Ctrl+↓
To the beginning or to the end of the current line	Home or End
To the beginning or to the end of the document	Ctrl+Home or Ctrl+End
To the previous screen or to the next screen	Page Up or Page Down
To the top or to the bottom of the document window	Alt+Ctrl+Page Up or Alt+Ctrl+Page Down

Correcting Errors as You Type

As you have already learned, if you notice a typing error as soon as you make it, you can press the Backspace key, which deletes the characters and spaces to the left of the insertion point one at a time. You can also press the Delete key, which deletes characters to the right of the insertion point one at a time.

In many cases, however, Word's AutoCorrect feature will do the work for you. Among other things, **AutoCorrect** automatically corrects common typing errors, such as typing "adn" for "and." For example, you might have noticed AutoCorrect at work if you forgot to capitalize the first letter in a sentence as you typed the letter. After you type this kind of error, AutoCorrect automatically corrects it when you press the spacebar, the Tab key, or the Enter key.

Another useful tool for correcting errors is Word's **spelling checker**, which continually checks your document against Word's built-in dictionary. If you type a word that doesn't match the correct spelling in Word's dictionary, or if a word, such as a last name, is not in the dictionary at all, a wavy red line appears beneath it. A wavy red line also appears if you mistakenly type the same word twice in a row. Words that are spelled correctly but used incorrectly (for example, "you're" instead of "your") are underlined with a wavy blue line, although Word doesn't always catch every instance of this type of error, which is known as a **contextual spelling error**. Finally, the **grammar checker** marks grammatical errors with a wavy green line.

You'll see how this works as you continue typing the letter and make some intentional typing errors.

To learn more about correcting errors as you type:

1. Press the **down arrow** key ↓ to move the insertion point to the blank paragraph below the paragraph where you inserted the word "questions."
2. Type the following sentence, including the errors shown here: **i will call in a few few days to disuss teh shedule.**

As you type, AutoCorrect changes the lowercase "i" at the beginning of the sentence to uppercase. It also changes "teh" to "the" and "shedule" to "schedule." The spelling checker marks the spelling error "disuss" and the second "few" with wavy red lines. You will correct these errors after you finish typing the rest of the paragraph.

3. Press the **spacebar**, and then type the following sentence, including the errors: **I are looking forward too having lunch with you next week.** The word "too" is underlined in a wavy blue line, indicating a word that is spelled correctly but used incorrectly. The sentence also contains a grammatical error, but Word won't identify it until you press the Enter key to begin a new paragraph.
4. Press the **Enter** key to begin a new paragraph. As shown in Figure 1-7, a wavy green underline appears below "are," indicating a grammatical error.

Figure 1-7 **Spelling and grammatical errors marked in the document**

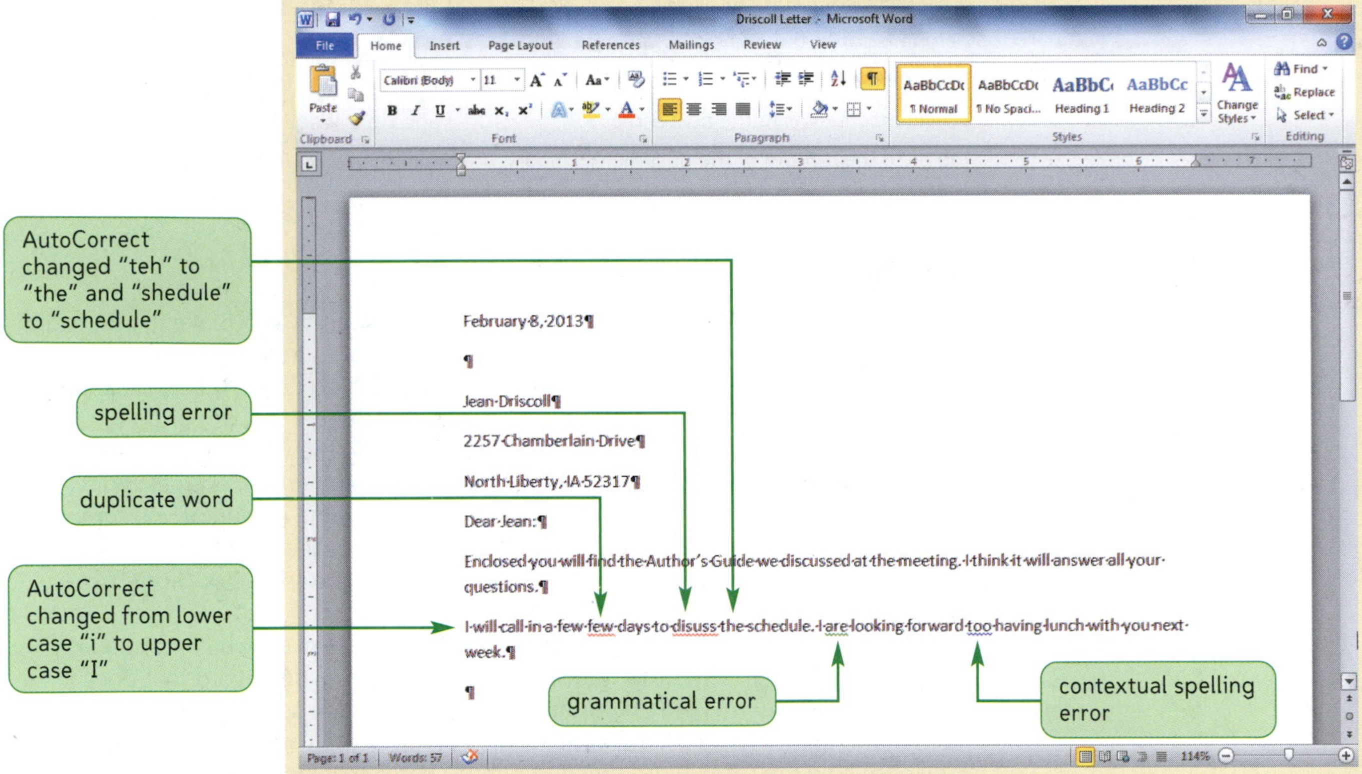

AutoCorrect changed "teh" to "the" and "shedule" to "schedule"
spelling error
duplicate word
AutoCorrect changed from lower case "i" to upper case "I"
grammatical error
contextual spelling error

To correct an error marked by either the spelling or grammar checker, you can right-click the error, and then select the correct replacement on the shortcut menu. If you don't see the correct word on the shortcut menu, you can click anywhere in the document to close the menu, and then type the correction yourself. If you know the correct spelling of a word marked as an error, you can bypass the shortcut menu, and simply delete the error and type a correction. You'll try both methods next.

To correct the spelling and grammar errors:

1. Right-click **disuss** to display the shortcut menu shown in Figure 1-8. The Mini toolbar also appears, providing easy access to some of the most commonly used options on the Home tab for the object you've right-clicked.

Figure 1-8 **Shortcut menu with suggested spellings**

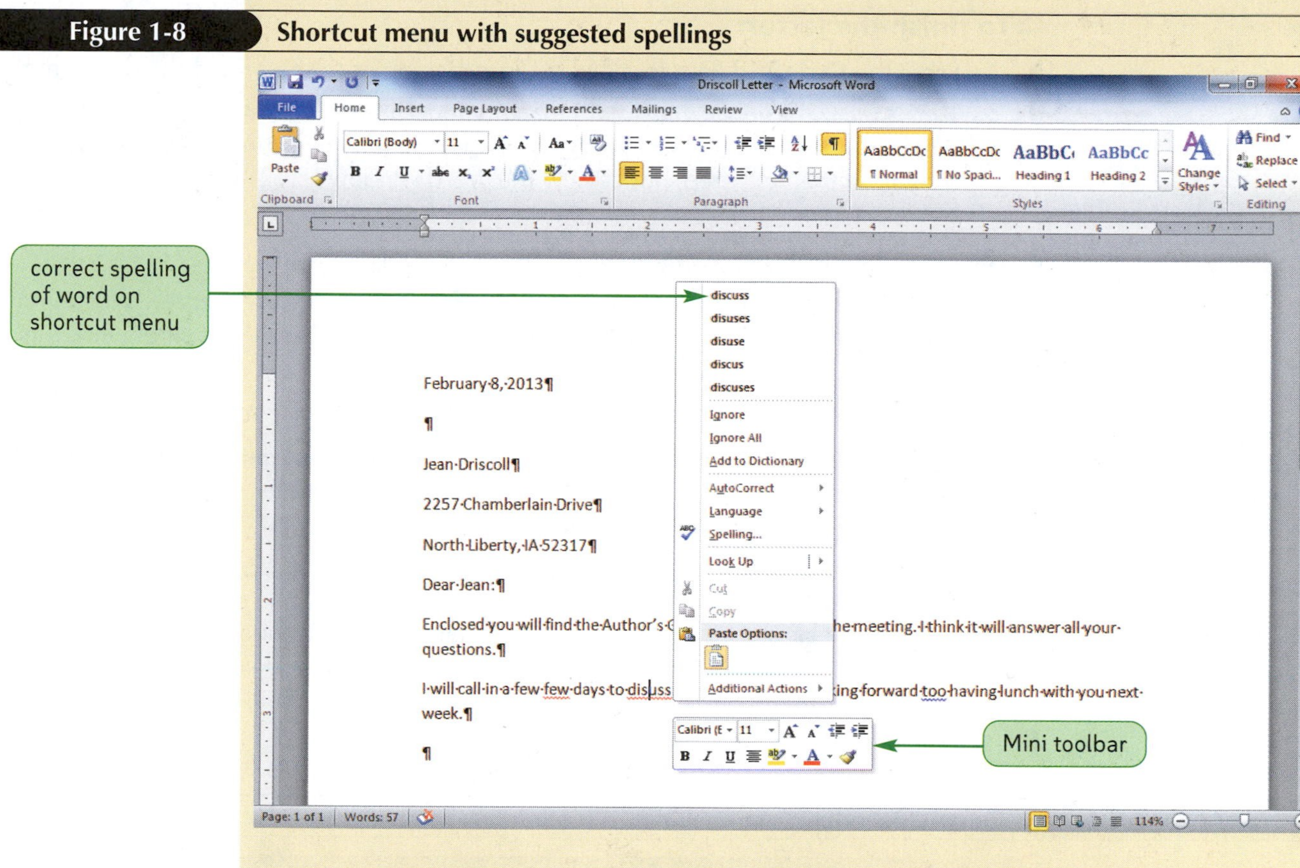

Trouble? If you see a menu other than the one shown in Figure 1-8, you didn't right-click exactly on the word "disuss." Press the Esc key to close the menu, and then repeat Step 1.

2. Click **discuss** on the shortcut menu. The correct word is inserted into the sentence, and the shortcut menu closes. You could use the shortcut menu to remove the second instance of "few" but in the next step you'll try a different method—selecting the word and deleting it.
3. Double-click the underlined word **few**. The word and the space following it are highlighted in blue, indicating that they are selected.

   Trouble? If the entire paragraph is selected, you triple-clicked the word by mistake. Click anywhere in the document to deselect it, and then repeat Step 3.
4. Press the **Delete** key. The second instance of "few" and the space following it are deleted from the sentence.
5. Using shortcut menus, replace the underlined word "are" with "am" and then replace the word "too" with "to."
6. On the Quick Access Toolbar, click the **Save** button.

TIP

To deselect highlighted text, click anywhere in the document.

You can see how quick and easy it is to correct common typing errors with AutoCorrect and the underlines displayed by the spelling and grammar checker. But you can't count on them to catch every possible error. After you finish the letter, you will still need to proofread it.

To finish the letter:

1. Press the **Ctrl+End** keys to move the insertion point to the end of the document.
2. Type **Sincerely yours,** (including the comma). Unless you are using a very large monitor, at this point your insertion point is probably near the bottom of the screen. In the next step, notice how the Word window scrolls down as you continue to type.
3. Press the **Enter** key three times to leave space for the signature.
4. Type **Andrew Siordia** and then press the **Enter** key. Because Andrew's last name is not in Word's dictionary, a wavy red line appears below it. You can ignore this for now.
5. Type **Managing Editor** and then press the **Enter** key twice and type **Enclosure**.
6. Press the **Enter** key once, type your first, middle, and last initials in lowercase, and then press the **Enter** key. AutoCorrect wrongly assumes your first initial is the first letter of a new sentence, and changes it to uppercase.
7. Click the **Undo** button on the Quick Access toolbar. Word reverses the change, replacing the uppercase initial with a lowercase one. At this point, your screen should look similar to Figure 1-9. Notice that, as you continue to add lines to the letter, the top part of the letter scrolls off the screen. For example, in Figure 1-9, you can no longer see the date.
8. Save the document.

Figure 1-9 Completed letter

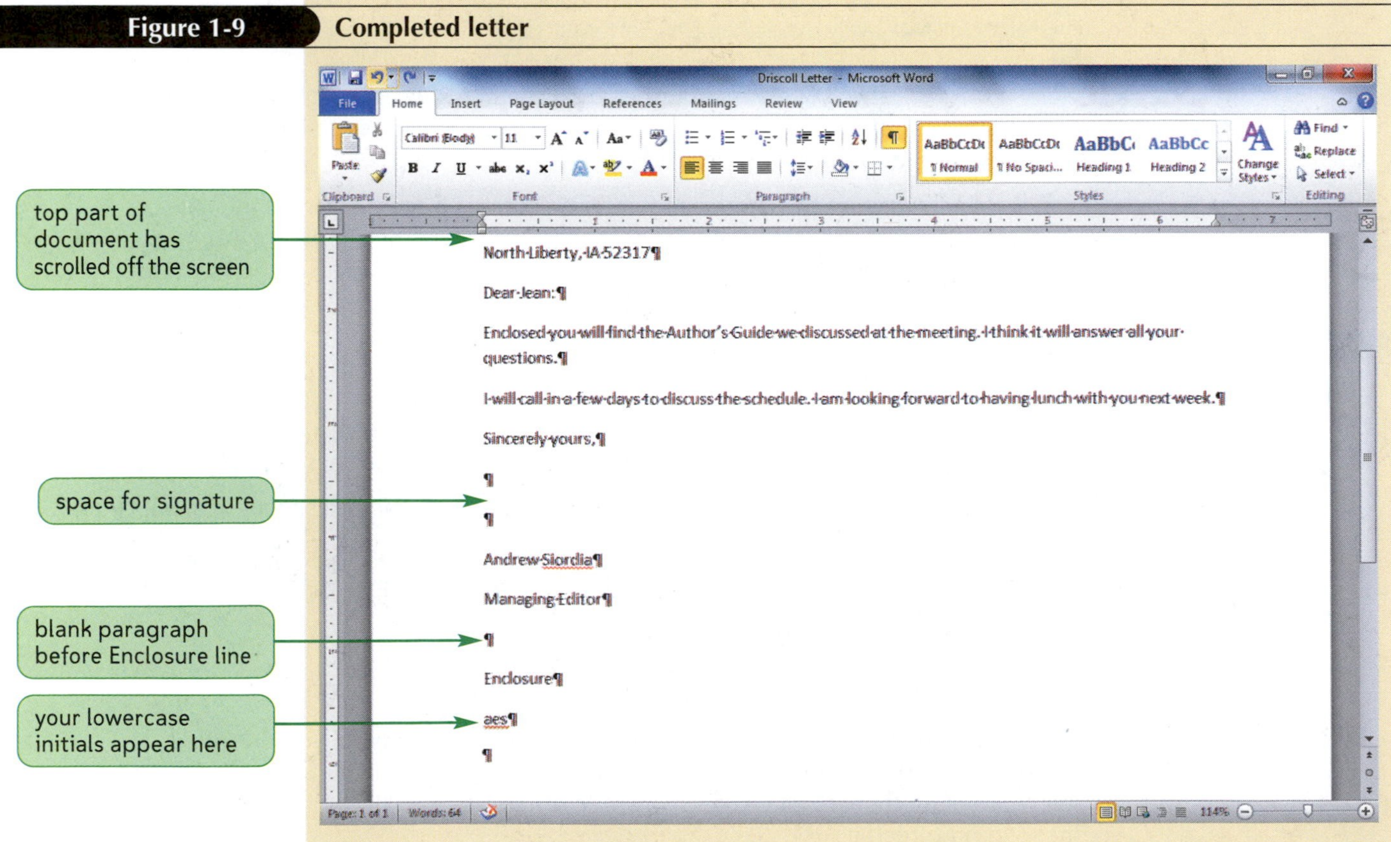

Now that you have finished typing the letter, you need to proofread it.

Proofreading a Finished Document

After you finish typing a document, you need to proofread it carefully from start to finish. Part of proofing a document in Word is removing all wavy underlines, either by correcting the text or by telling Word to ignore the underlined text because it isn't really an error. For example, Andrew's last name is marked as an error, when in fact it is correct. You need to tell Word to ignore "Siordia" wherever it occurs in the letter. You need to do the same for your initials.

To proofread and correct the remaining marked errors in the letter:

1. Right-click **Siordia**. A shortcut menu and the Mini toolbar open.
2. Click **Ignore All** on the shortcut menu to indicate Word should ignore the word "Siordia" each time it occurs in this document. The wavy red underline disappears from below Andrew's last name. Below your initials, you see a red wavy underline (if your initials do not form a word) or a green wavy underline.
3. If you see a wavy red underline below your initials, right-click your initials, and then click **Ignore All** on the shortcut menu to remove the red wavy underline. If you didn't see a wavy green underline below your initials before, you see one now.
4. Right-click your initials, and then on the shortcut menu click **Ignore Once** to remove the green wavy underline.
5. Scroll up to the beginning of the letter and read through the letter to proofread it for typing errors. Correct any errors using the techniques you have just learned.
6. Save your changes to the document.

The text of the letter is finished. Now you need to think about how it looks—that is, you need to think about the document's **formatting**. First, you need to adjust the spacing in the inside address and between the signature and title lines.

Adjusting Paragraph and Line Spacing

When typing a letter, you might need to adjust two types of spacing—paragraph spacing and line spacing. **Paragraph spacing** refers to the space that appears directly above and below a paragraph. In Word, any text that ends with a paragraph mark symbol (¶) is a paragraph. So, a **paragraph** can be a group of words that is many lines long, a single word, or even a blank line, in which case you see a paragraph mark alone on a single line. Paragraph spacing is measured in points; a **point** is 1/72 of an inch. The default setting for paragraph spacing in Word is 0 points before each paragraph and 10 points after each paragraph.

Line spacing is the amount of space that appears between lines of text within a paragraph. Word offers a number of preset line spacing options. The 1.0 setting, which is often called **single spacing**, allows the least amount of space between lines. All other line spacing options are measured as multiples of 1.0 spacing. For example, 2.0 spacing (sometimes called **double spacing)** allows for twice the space of single spacing. The default line spacing setting is 1.15, which allows a little more space between lines than 1.0 spacing.

Now consider the line and paragraph spacing in the Driscoll letter. The three lines of the inside address are too far apart. That's because each line of the inside address is actually a separate paragraph. As you can see in Figure 1-10, Word inserted the default 10 points of space after each of these separate paragraphs. To match the conventions of a block style business letter, the inside address should have the same spacing as the lines of text within a single paragraph. The same is true of the signature and title lines; they need to be closer together. You can accomplish this by removing the 10 points of space after each of these paragraphs.

Figure 1-10 **Line and paragraph spacing in the letter to Jean Driscoll**

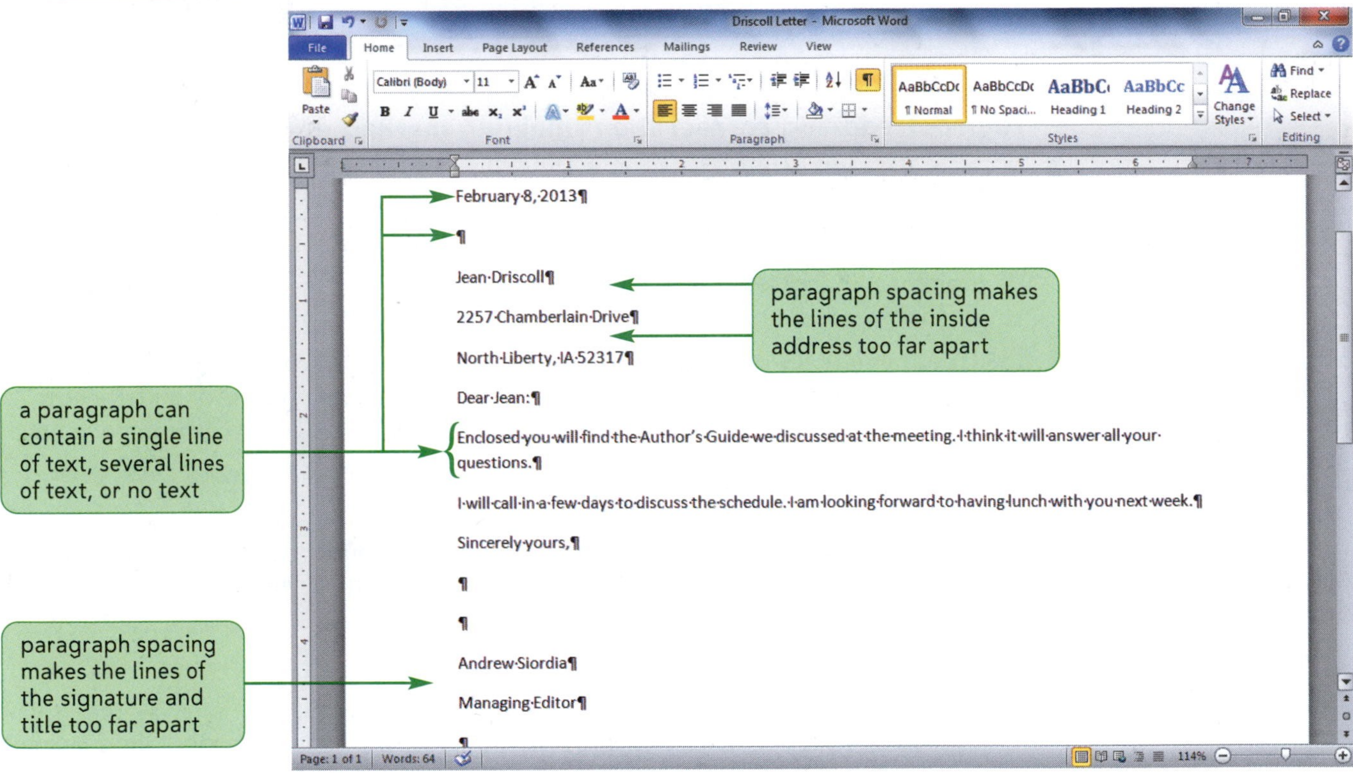

INSIGHT

Understanding Spacing Between Paragraphs

When discussing the correct format for letters, many business style guides talk about single spacing and double spacing between paragraphs. In these style guides, "to single space between paragraphs" means pressing the Enter key once after each paragraph. Likewise, "to double space between paragraphs" means pressing the Enter key twice after each paragraph. With the default paragraph spacing in Word 2010, however, you only need to press the Enter key once to insert a double space after a paragraph. Keep this in mind if you're accustomed to pressing the Enter key twice; otherwise, you could end up with more space than you want between paragraphs.

TIP

You can also adjust paragraph spacing using the Spacing options in the Paragraph group of the Page Layout tab.

To adjust paragraph and line spacing in Word, you use the Line and Paragraph Spacing button in the Paragraph group on the Home tab. Clicking this button displays a menu of the preset line spacing options (1.0, 1.15, 2.0, and so on). The paragraph spacing options that appear at the bottom of the menu are more streamlined: you can choose to add or remove the default 10 points of space before or after each paragraph.

Next you'll adjust the paragraph spacing in the inside address, and then turn your attention to the signature and title lines. In the process, you'll also learn some techniques for selecting text in a document.

To adjust the paragraph spacing in the inside address:

TIP

The white space in the left margin is sometimes referred to as the selection bar, because you click it to select text.

1. If necessary, scroll up to display the inside address.
2. Move the pointer to the white space just to the left of "Jean Driscoll" until the pointer changes to a right-facing arrow.
3. Click the mouse button. The entire name, including the paragraph symbol after it, is selected.
4. Press and hold the mouse button, drag the pointer down to select the next paragraph of the inside address as well, and then release the mouse button.

   The name and street address are selected as well as the paragraph marks at the end of each paragraph. You did not select the paragraph containing the city, state and zip code, because you do want to include paragraph spacing after that paragraph in order to separate the inside address from the salutation. See Figure 1-11.

Figure 1-11 Inside address selected

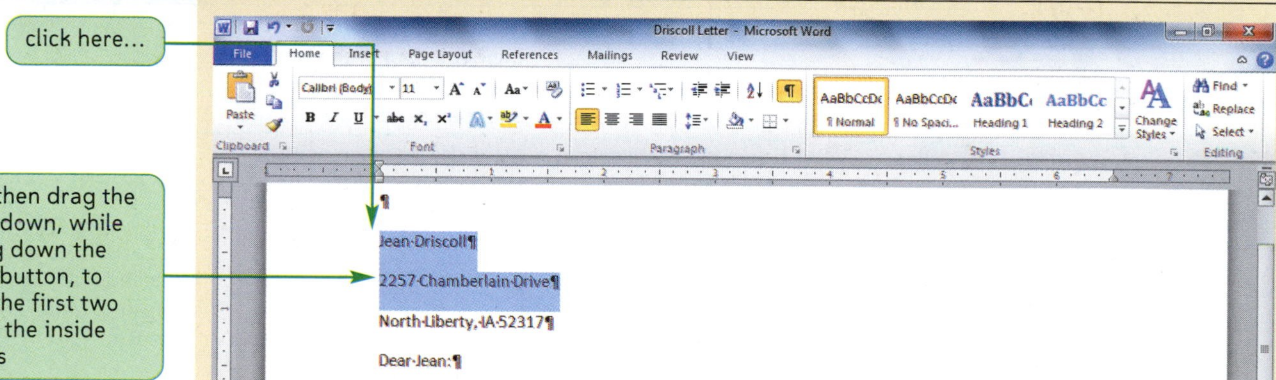

5. In the Paragraph group on the Home tab, click the **Line and Paragraph Spacing** button. A menu of line spacing options appears, with two paragraph spacing options at the bottom. See Figure 1-12. The default line spacing setting for the selected text (1.15) is indicated by a check mark. At the moment, you are only interested in the paragraph spacing options. Your goal is to remove the default 10 points of space after each paragraph in the inside address, so you need to use the last option on the menu, Remove Space After Paragraph.

Figure 1-12 Line and paragraph spacing options

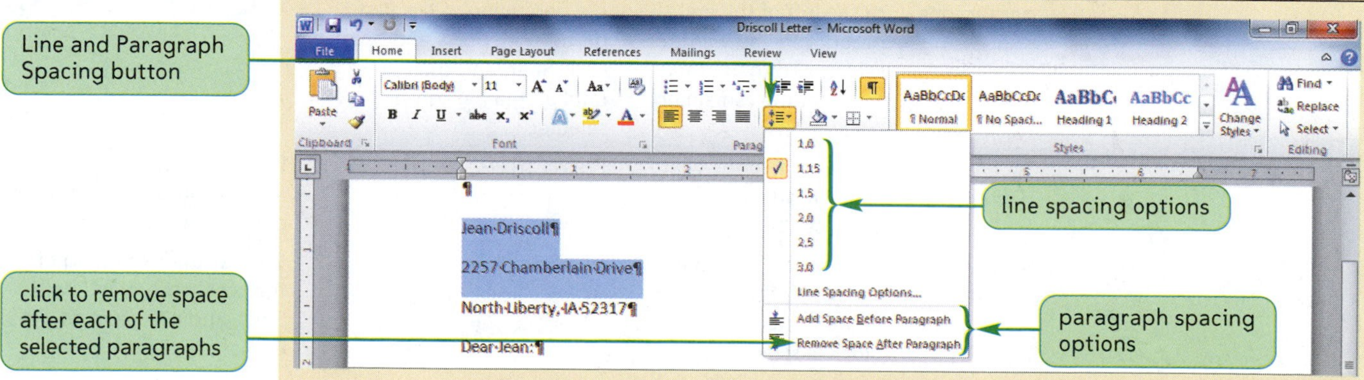

6. Click **Remove Space After Paragraph**. The menu closes, and the paragraphs are now closer together.

TIP

You can press the Shift+Enter key combination to move the insertion point to a new line without starting a new paragraph. This would allow you to type an inside address without inserting paragraph spacing.

7. Click anywhere in the document to deselect the inside address.
8. Select Andrew's name, click the **Line and Paragraph Spacing** button, and then click **Remove Space After Paragraph** to remove the extra paragraph spacing after the selected paragraph.
9. Click anywhere in the document to deselect Andrew's name, and then save your changes to the document.

As you corrected line and paragraph spacing in the previous set of steps, you used the mouse to select text. Word provides multiple ways to select, or highlight, text as you work. Figure 1-13 summarizes these methods and when to use them most effectively.

Figure 1-13 **Methods for selecting text**

To select	Mouse	Keyboard	Mouse and keyboard
A word	Double-click the word	Move the insertion point to the beginning of the word, press and hold Ctrl+Shift, and then press →	
A line	Click in the white space to the left of the line	Move the insertion point to the beginning of the line, press and hold Shift, and then press ↓	
A sentence	Click at the beginning of the sentence, then drag the pointer until the sentence is selected		Press and hold Ctrl, then click any location within the sentence
Multiple lines	Click and drag in the white space to the left of the lines	Move the insertion point to the beginning of the first line, press and hold Shift, and then press ↓ until all the lines are selected	
A paragraph	Double-click in the white space to the left of the paragraph, or triple-click at any location within the paragraph	Move the insertion point to the beginning of the paragraph, press and hold Ctrl+Shift, and then press ↓	
Multiple paragraphs	Click in the white space to the left of the first paragraph you want to select, and then drag to select the remaining paragraphs	Move the insertion point to the beginning of the first paragraph, press and hold Ctrl+Shift, and then press ↓ until all the paragraphs are selected	
An entire document	Triple-click in the white space to the left of the document text	Press Ctrl+A	Press and hold Ctrl, and click in the white space to the left of the document text
A block of text	Click at the beginning of the block, then drag the pointer until the entire block is selected		Click at the beginning of the block, press and hold Shift, and then click at the end of the block
Nonadjacent blocks of text	Press and hold Ctrl, then drag the mouse pointer to select multiple blocks of nonadjacent text		

Adjusting the Margins

Another aspect of document formatting is how the document fits on the printed page. You can check the document's margins by changing the zoom to display the entire page.

To change the zoom to display the entire page:

1. Click the **View** tab on the Ribbon. The View tab provides options for various ways to view the document and the elements of the Word window.
2. In the Zoom group, click the **One Page** button. The entire document is now visible in the Word window. See Figure 1-14.

Figure 1-14 Document zoomed to show entire page

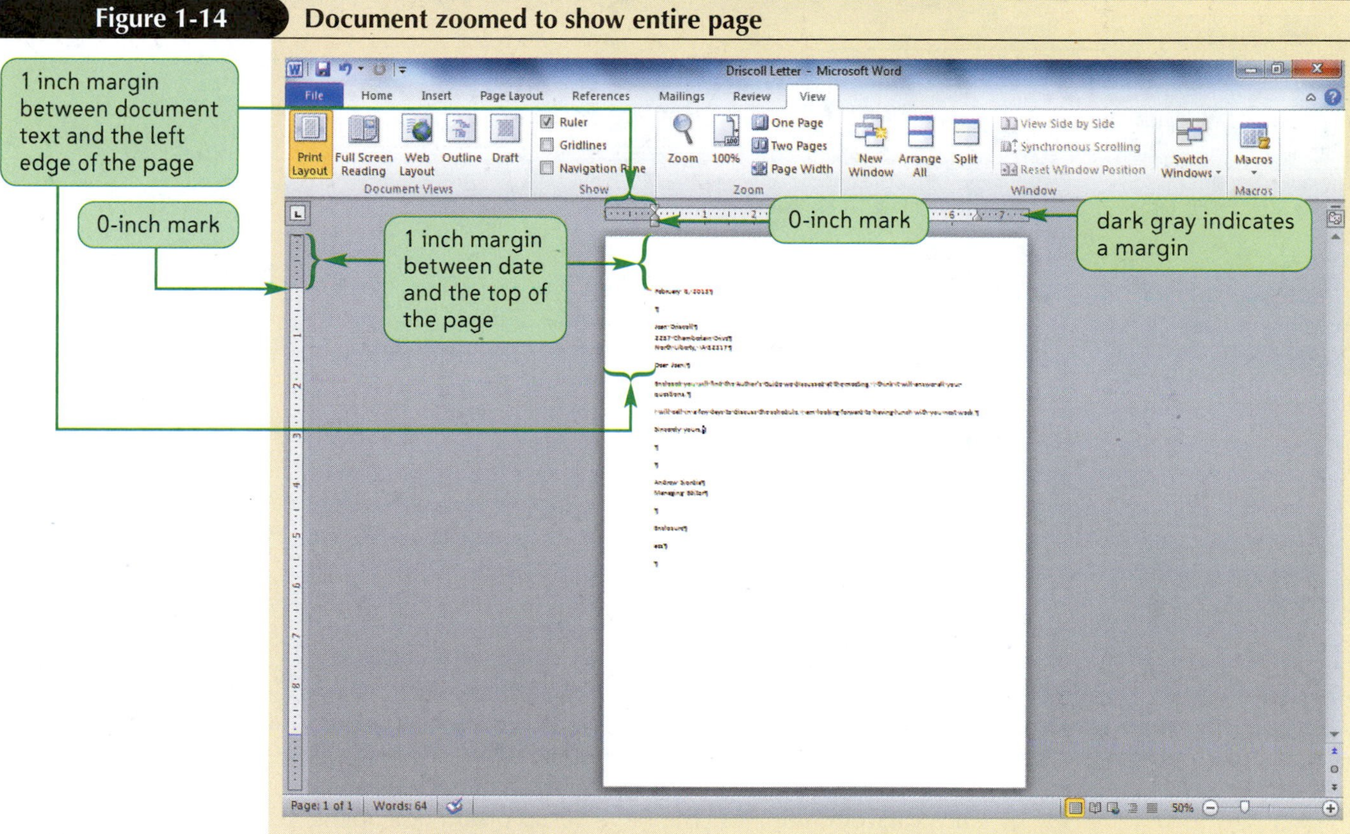

On the rulers, the margins appear dark gray. By default, Word documents include 1-inch margins on all sides of the document. By looking at the vertical ruler, you can see that the date in the letter, the first line in the document, is located 1 inch from the top of the page. Likewise, the horizontal ruler indicates the document text begins 1 inch from the left edge of the page.

Reading the measurements on the rulers can be tricky at first. On the horizontal ruler, the 0-inch mark is the right edge of the left margin. It's like the origin on a number line. You measure from the 0-inch mark to the left or to the right. On the vertical ruler, the 0-inch mark is the bottom edge of the top margin.

Andrew plans to print the letter on Carlyle University Press letterhead, which includes a graphic and the company's address. To allow more blank space for the letterhead, and to move the text down so it doesn't look so crowded at the top of the page, you need to increase the top margin. The settings for changing the page margins are located on the Page Layout tab on the Ribbon.

To change the page margins:

1. Click the **Page Layout** tab on the Ribbon. The Page Layout tab displays options for adjusting the layout of your document.
2. In the Page Setup group, click the **Margins** button. The Margins menu opens, as shown in Figure 1-15. Here you can choose from a number of predefined margin options, or you can click the Custom Margins command to select your own settings. After you create custom margin settings, the most recent set appears as an option at the top of the menu. In this case, you will create custom margins.

Figure 1-15 Margins menu

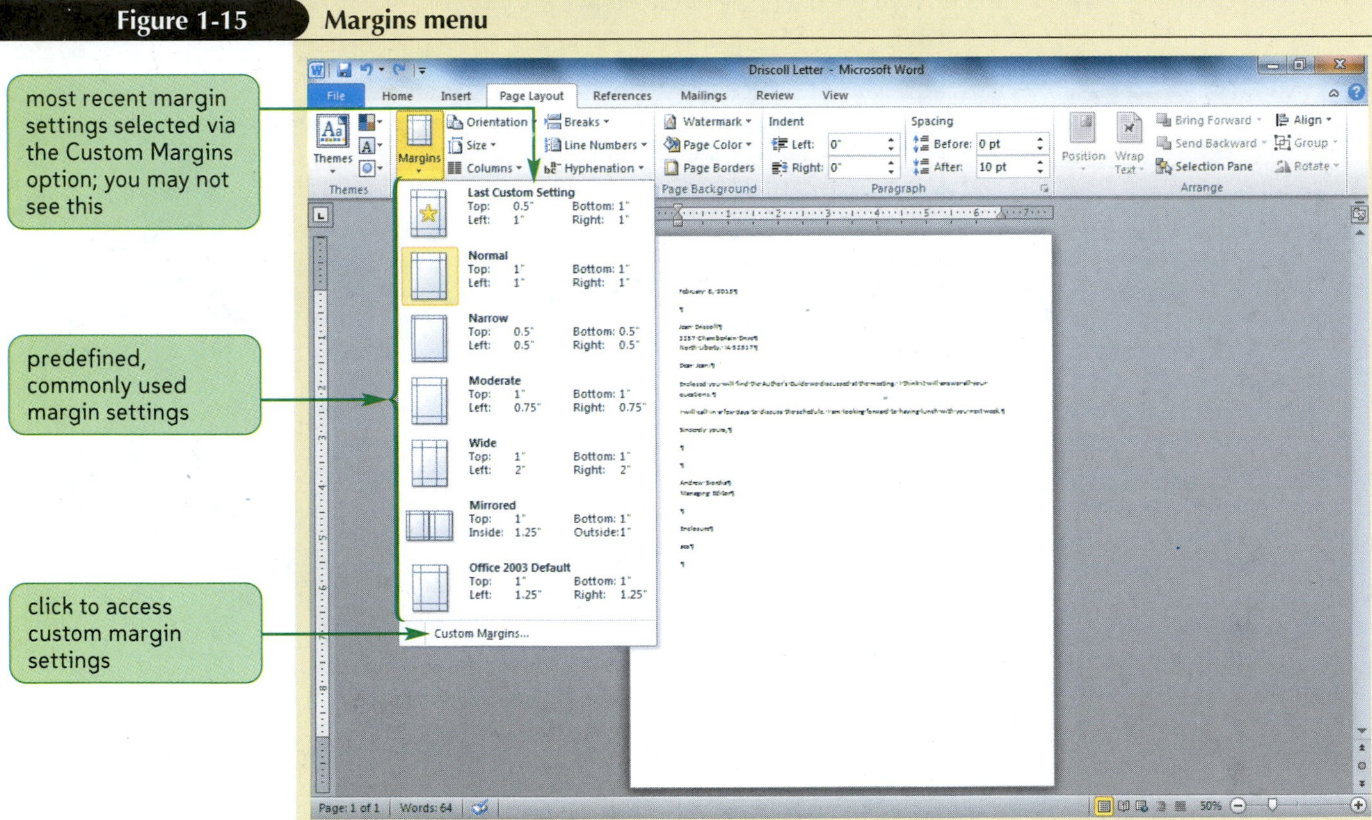

3. Click **Custom Margins**. The Page Setup dialog box opens, with the Margins tab displayed. The default margin settings are displayed in the boxes at the top of the Margins tab. The top margin of 1 is already selected, ready for you to type a new margin setting.
4. Type **2.5** in the Top box in the Margins section. See Figure 1-16.

Figure 1-16 Creating custom margins in the Page Setup dialog box

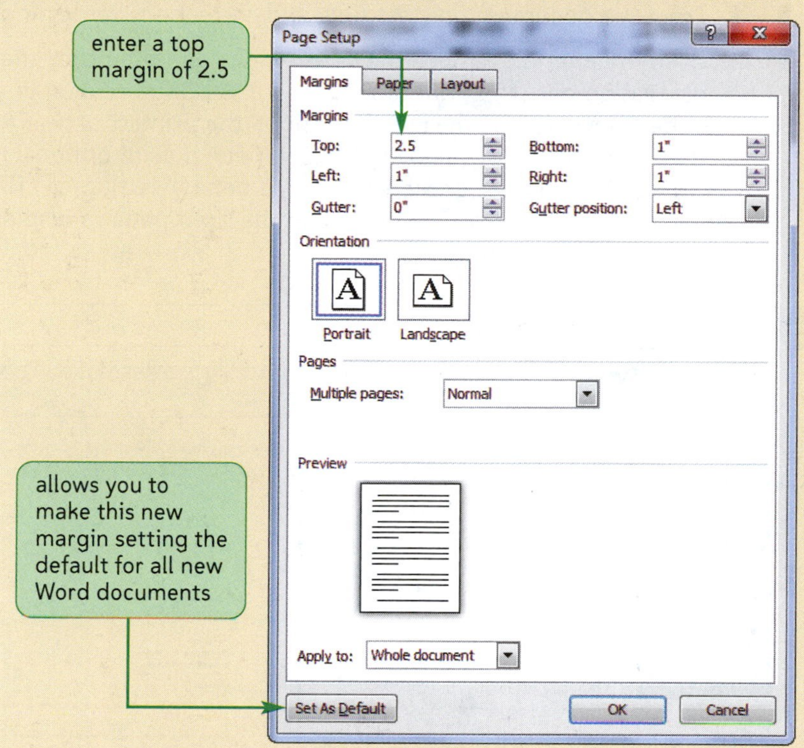

5. Click the **OK** button. The text of the letter is now lower on the page. The page looks less crowded, with room for the company's letterhead.
6. Change the zoom level back to Page Width, and then save your changes to the document.

INSIGHT

Working with Custom Margins

For most documents, the Word default of 1-inch margins is fine. In some professional settings, however, you might need to use a particular custom margin setting for all your documents. In that case, define the custom margins using the Margins tab of the Page Setup dialog box, and then click the Set As Default button to make your settings the default for all new documents. Keep in mind that most printers can't print to the edge of the page; if you select custom margins that are too narrow for your printer's specifications, Word alerts you to change your margin settings.

Previewing and Printing a Document

To be sure the document is ready to print, and to avoid wasting paper and time, you should first review it on the Print tab in Backstage view to make sure it will appear as you want it to when printed. Like the One Page zoom setting you used earlier, the Print tab displays a full-page view of the document, allowing you to see how it will fit on the printed page. However, you cannot actually edit the document on the Print tab. It simply provides one last quick look at the document before printing.

To preview the document:

1. Proof the document one last time and correct any remaining errors.
2. Click the **File** tab to open Backstage view, and then click the **Print** tab in the navigation bar. The Print tab displays a full-page version of your letter in the right pane, showing how the letter will fit on the printed page. The Print settings in the left pane allow you to control a variety of print options. For example, you can change the number of copies from the default setting of "1." You can also use the navigation controls at the bottom of the right pane to display other pages in a document. See Figure 1-17.

Figure 1-17 Print tab in Backstage view

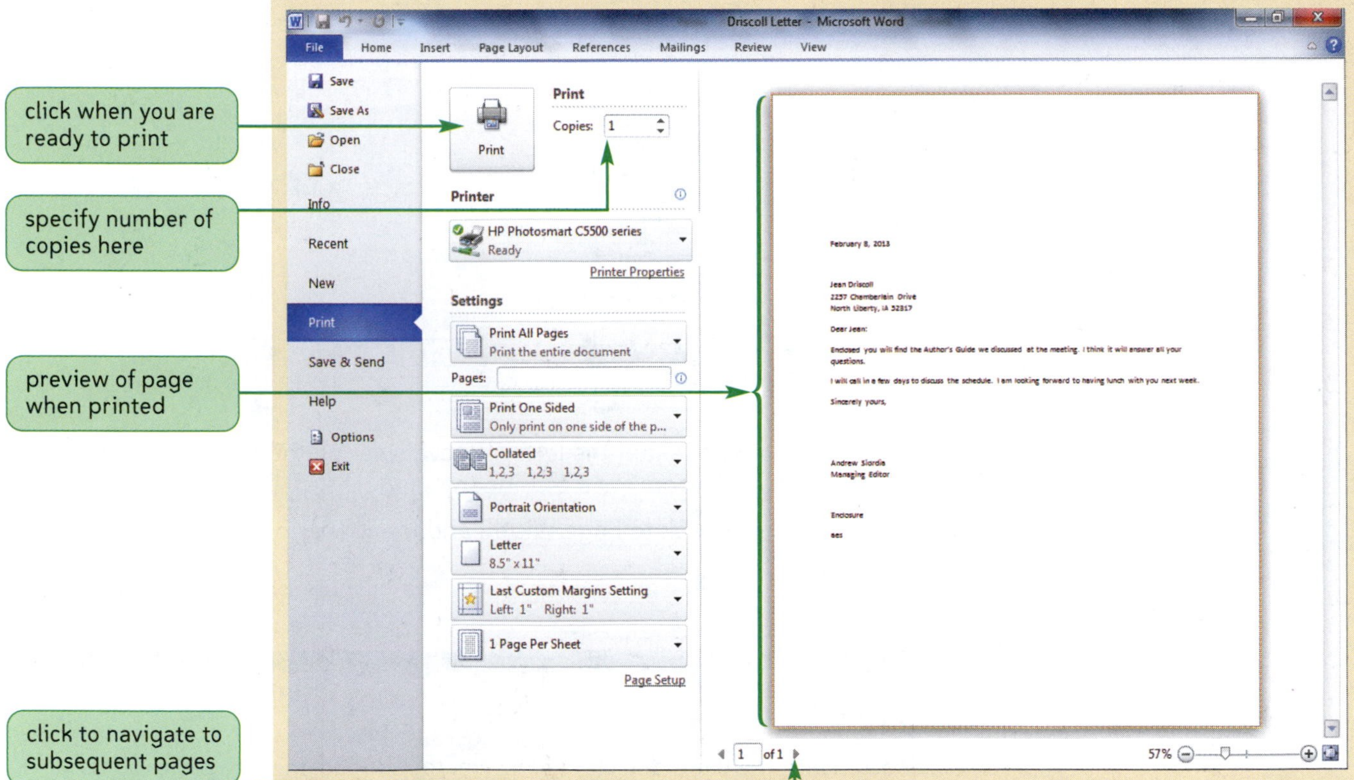

3. Review your document and make sure its overall layout matches the document in Figure 1-17. If you notice a problem with paragraph breaks or spacing, click the **Home** tab on the Ribbon, edit the document, and then repeat step 2.
4. Make sure your printer is turned on and contains paper.
5. Click the **Print** button in the left pane of the Print tab. Backstage view closes and the letter prints.
6. Click the **File** tab, and then click the **Close** command in the navigation bar to close the document without closing Word.

Now that the letter is completed, you need to create an envelope Andrew can use to mail the letter. You could add the envelope to the Driscoll Letter document, but Andrew would prefer to save the envelope as a separate document, so he can more easily find and reuse it for subsequent correspondence with Jean Driscoll. So before you can create the envelope, you need to open a new, blank document.

Opening a Blank Document and Creating an Envelope

When you create a new document, you can start with a new blank document, or you can start with one that already contains formatting and generic text commonly used in a variety of professional documents such as a fax cover sheet or a report. These preformatted files are called **templates**. You could use a template to create a formatted envelope, but first you'll learn how to create one on your own. You'll work with templates in the Case Problems at the end of this tutorial. To create an envelope on your own, you need to start with a new, blank document.

To create a new document for the envelope:

1. Click the **File** tab to open Backstage view, and then click the **New** tab in the navigation bar. The New tab displays a variety of template options. By default, the Blank document is selected. A sample of the selected option (in this case, an empty document) is displayed in the right pane of the New tab. The template options in the Home section are stored on your computer. The options in the Office.com Templates section are stored on the Office.com Web site, but are available to download for free. As you can see in Figure 1-18, Microsoft offers predesigned templates for all kinds of documents, including agendas, calendars, invoices, and letters.

Figure 1-18 The New tab in Backstage view

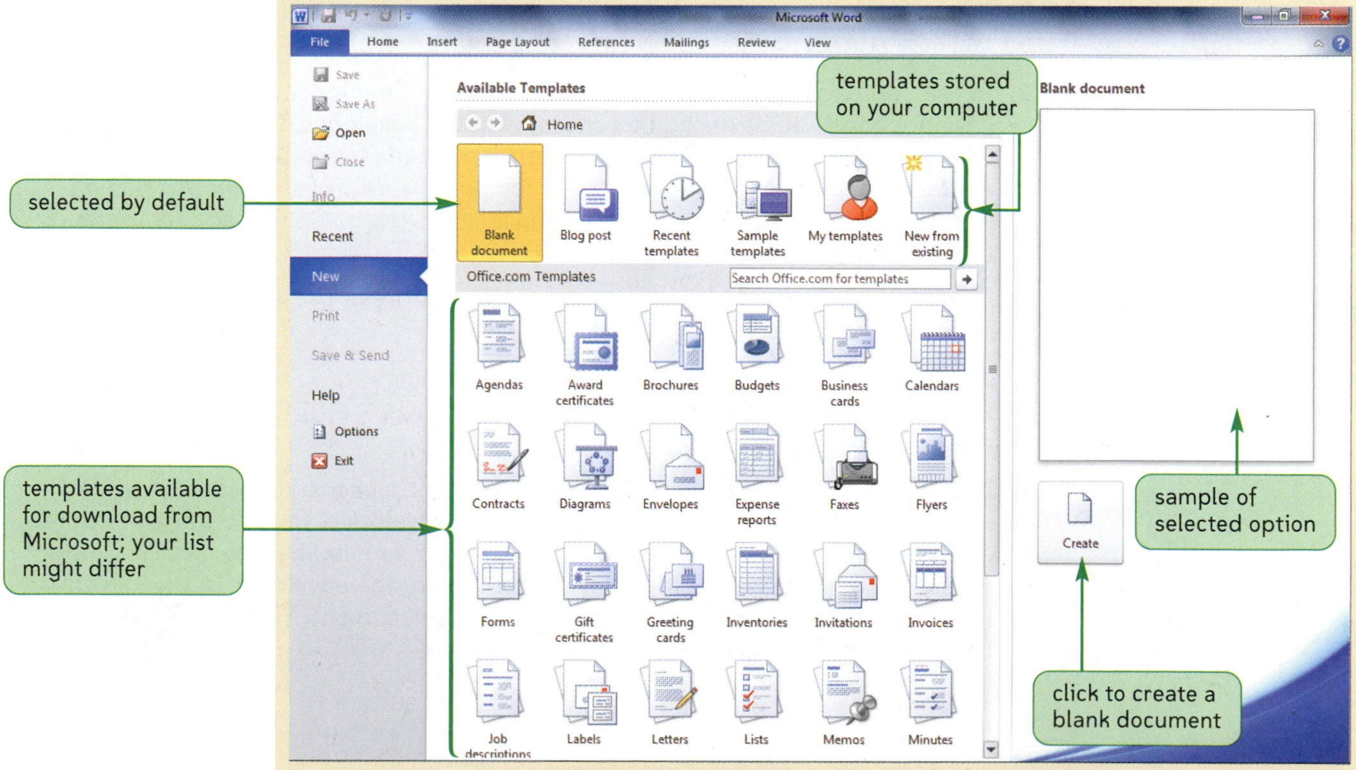

2. Verify that the **Blank document** option is selected, and then click the **Create** button. A new document named Document2 opens in the document window, with the Home tab selected on the Ribbon.
3. Save the new document as **Driscoll Envelope** in the Word1\Tutorial folder included with your Data Files.

REFERENCE

Creating an Envelope

- Click the Mailings tab on the Ribbon.
- In the Create group, click the Envelopes button to open the Envelopes and Labels dialog box.
- On the Envelopes tab, verify that the Delivery address box contains the correct address. If necessary, type a new address or edit the existing one.
- If necessary, type a return address. If you are using preprinted stationery that already includes a return address, click the Omit check box to insert a check mark.
- To print the envelope immediately, insert an envelope in your printer, and then click the Print button. Or, to store the envelope along with the rest of the document, click the Add to Document button and print the envelope later.

Now you can create an envelope in this new document. You start by clicking the Envelope button in the Create group on the Mailings tab. This opens the Envelopes and Labels dialog box, where you can type the address of the person you are sending the letter to (the recipient address) and adjust other settings. You can choose whether or not to include a return address; if you are using envelopes with a preprinted return address, you will not want to include a return address.

To create the envelope:

1. Click the **Mailings** tab on the Ribbon. The Ribbon changes to display the various Mailings options.
2. In the Create group on the Mailings tab, click the **Envelopes** button. The Envelopes and Labels dialog box opens, with the Envelopes tab on top. The insertion point appears in the Delivery address box, ready for you to type the recipient's address. Depending on how your computer is set up, and whether you are working on your own computer or a school computer, you might see an address in the Return address box.
3. In the Delivery address box, type the following address, pressing the Enter key to start each new line:

   Jean Driscoll
   2257 Chamberlain Drive
   North Liberty, IA 52317

4. If necessary, click the **Omit** check box to insert a check mark. Because Andrew will be using Carlyle University Press's printed envelopes, you don't need to print a return address on this envelope. At this point, if you had a printer stocked with envelopes, you could click the Print button to print the envelope. To save an envelope for printing later, you need to add it to the document. Your Envelopes and Labels dialog box should match the one in Figure 1-19.

TIP

You can add envelopes to existing documents. When you add an envelope to a letter, Word automatically uses the inside address from the letter as the delivery address.

Figure 1-19 Envelopes and Labels dialog box

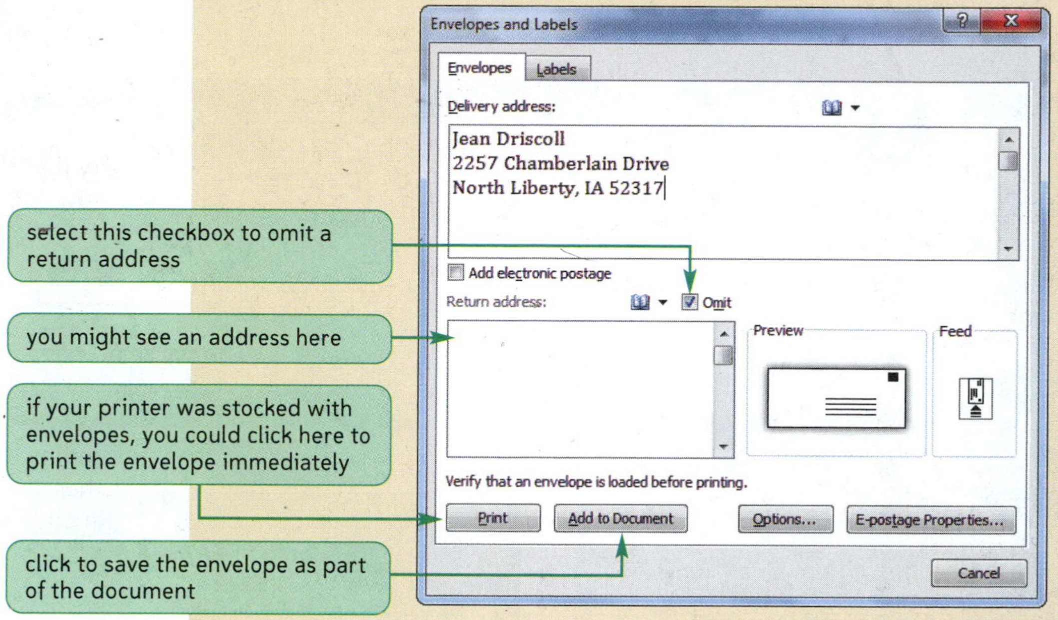

5. Click the **Add to Document** button. The dialog box closes, and you return to the document window. The envelope is inserted at the top of the document, with 1.0 line spacing. The double line with the words "Section Break (Next Page)" indicates how the envelope is formatted, and will not be visible when you print the envelope. The envelope will print in the standard business envelope format. Andrew will print the envelope later, so you can close the document now.
6. Save and close the document.

You have created and formatted the letter to the new author and created an envelope for it. In the next session, you will modify a flyer Andrew created, announcing an author appearance at a local bookstore, by formatting the text and adding a photo.

REVIEW

Session 1.1 Quick Check

1. True or False. In the block style letter, each line of text starts at the left margin, except for the date.
2. Explain how to display nonprinting characters.
3. True or False. Word adds the .docx extension to document filenames to identify them as Microsoft Word 2010 documents, whether your computer is set up to display them or not.
4. Explain how to open the Margins menu.
5. What is the default setting for paragraph spacing in a Word document?
6. True or False. A wavy red underline below a word indicates a grammatical error.

SESSION 1.2 VISUAL OVERVIEW

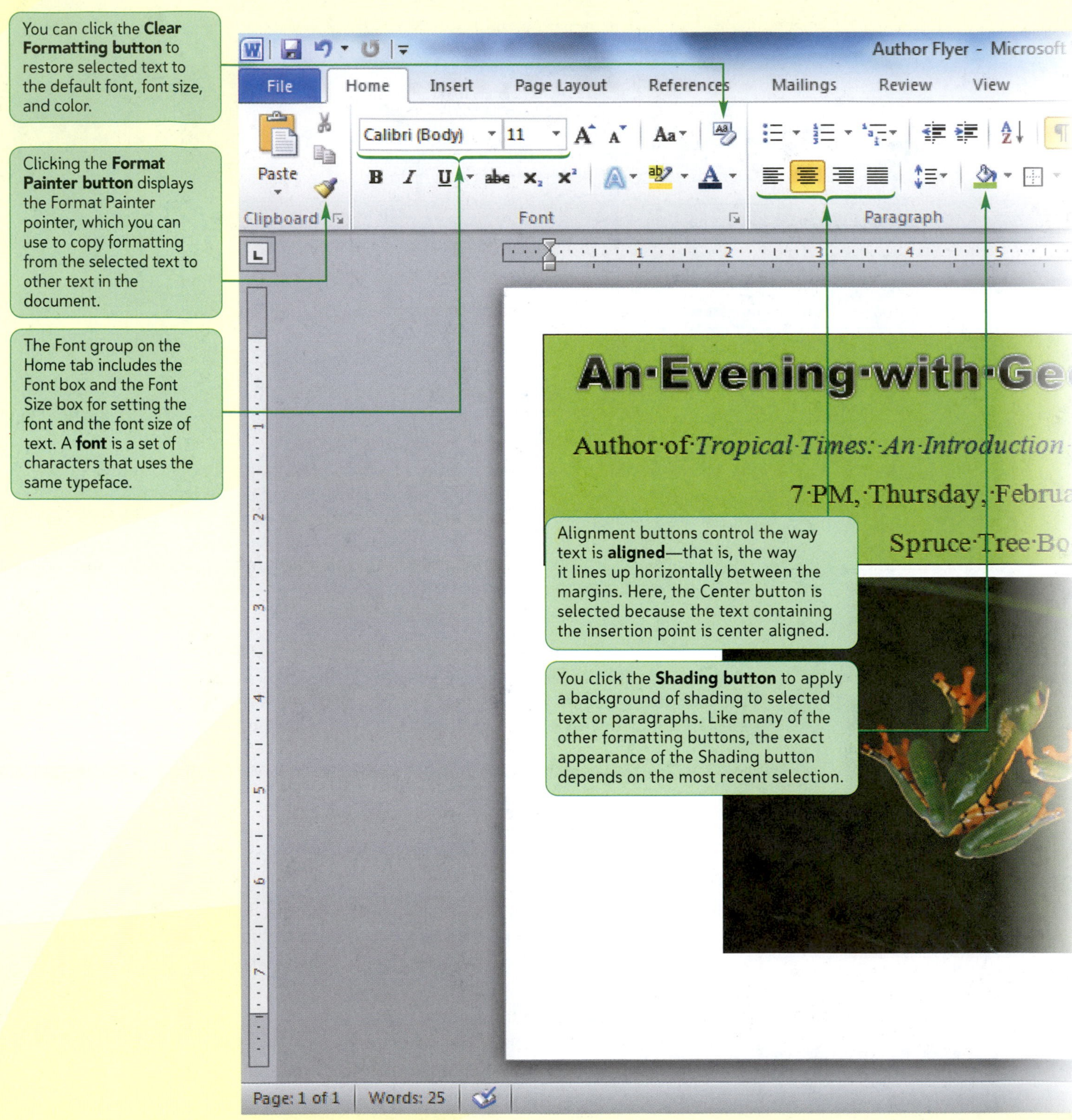

You can click the **Clear Formatting button** to restore selected text to the default font, font size, and color.
Clicking the **Format Painter button** displays the Format Painter pointer, which you can use to copy formatting from the selected text to other text in the document.
The Font group on the Home tab includes the Font box and the Font Size box for setting the font and the font size of text. A **font** is a set of characters that uses the same typeface.
Alignment buttons control the way text is **aligned**—that is, the way it lines up horizontally between the margins. Here, the Center button is selected because the text containing the insertion point is center aligned.
You click the **Shading button** to apply a background of shading to selected text or paragraphs. Like many of the other formatting buttons, the exact appearance of the Shading button depends on the most recent selection.
Author Flyer - Microsoft
File
Home
Insert
Page Layout
References
Mailings
Review
View
Calibri (Body)
11
Paste
Clipboard
Font
Paragraph
An·Evening·with·Ge
Author·of·Tropical·Times:·An·Introduction
7·PM,·Thursday,·Februa
Spruce·Tree·Bo
Page: 1 of 1
Words: 25

FORMATTING A DOCUMENT

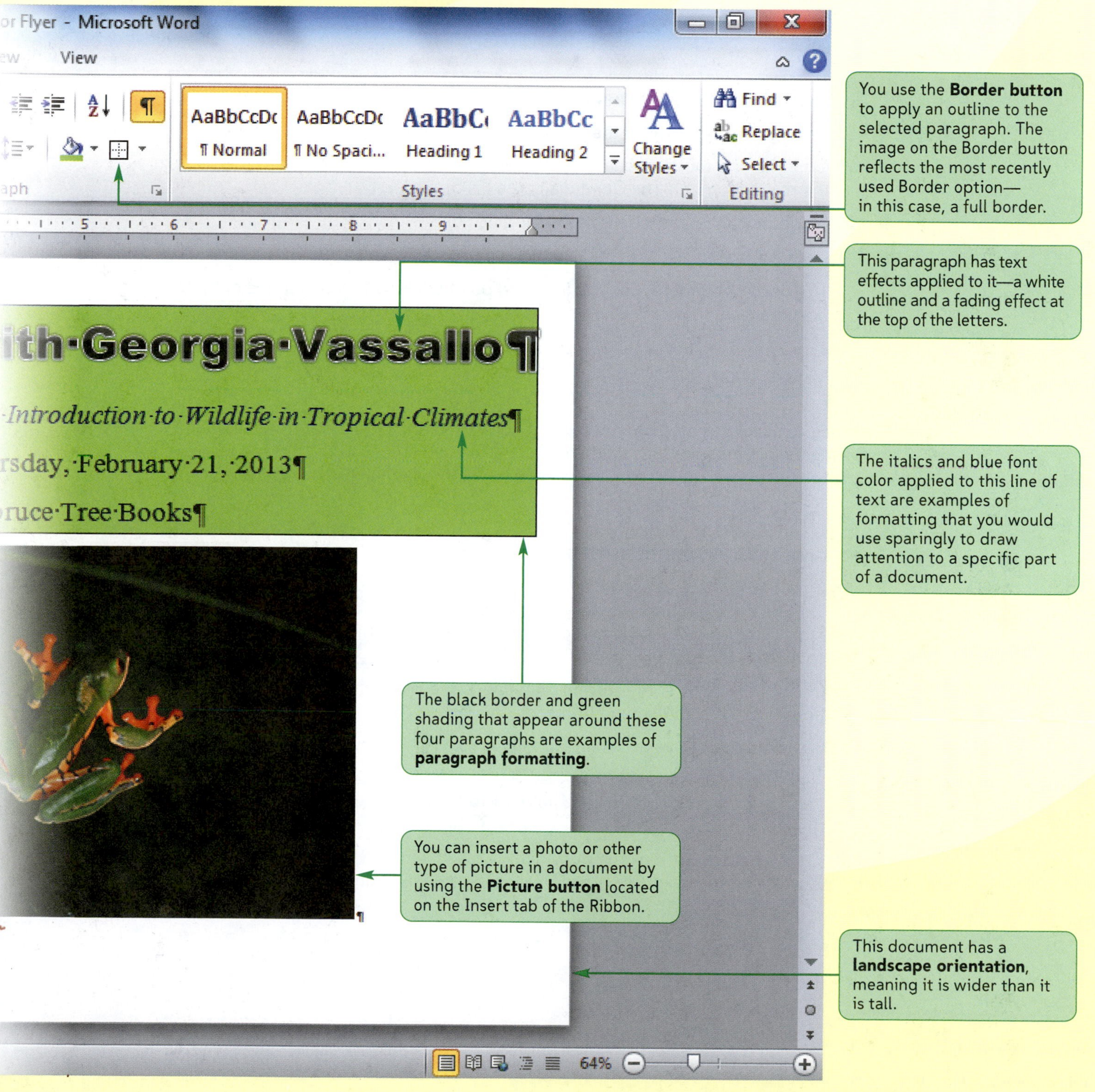
or Flyer - Microsoft Word
View
AaBbCcDc
¶ Normal
AaBbCcDc
¶ No Spaci...
AaBbC
Heading 1
AaBbCc
Heading 2
Change Styles
Find
Replace
Select
Styles
Editing
You use the **Border button** to apply an outline to the selected paragraph. The image on the Border button reflects the most recently used Border option—in this case, a full border.
This paragraph has text effects applied to it—a white outline and a fading effect at the top of the letters.
ith·Georgia·Vassallo¶
Introduction·to·Wildlife·in·Tropical·Climates¶
rsday,·February·21,·2013¶
ruce·Tree·Books¶
The italics and blue font color applied to this line of text are examples of formatting that you would use sparingly to draw attention to a specific part of a document.
The black border and green shading that appear around these four paragraphs are examples of **paragraph formatting**.
You can insert a photo or other type of picture in a document by using the **Picture button** located on the Insert tab of the Ribbon.
This document has a **landscape orientation**, meaning it is wider than it is tall.
64%

Opening an Existing Document

In this session, you need to complete a flyer announcing a bookstore appearance by Georgia Vassalo, a Carlyle University Press author. Andrew has already typed the text of the flyer, inserted a photo into it, and saved it as a Word document. He would like you to format the flyer in a way that makes it eye-catching and easy to read. You'll start by opening the document.

To open the flyer document:

1. If you took a break after the previous session, make sure Word is running.
2. Click the **File** tab to open Backstage view, and then click the **Open** command in the navigation bar. The Open dialog box is displayed.
3. Navigate to the Word1\Tutorial folder included with your Data Files.
4. Click **Author** to select the file, and then click the **Open** button.

   The document opens with the insertion point blinking in the first line of the document.

   Trouble? If the orange Protected View bar appears at the top of the document window, click the Enable Editing button.

Before making changes to Andrew's document, you will save it with a new name. Saving the document with a different filename creates a copy of the file and leaves the original file unchanged in case you want to work through the tutorial again.

To save the document with a new name:

1. Click the **File** tab to open Backstage view, and then click the **Save As** command in the navigation bar. The Save As dialog box opens with the current filename highlighted in the File name box. You could type an entirely new filename, or you could edit the current one.
2. Click to the right of the current filename in the File name box to place the insertion point after the "r" in "Author."
3. Press the **spacebar**, and then type **Flyer** so that the new filename is "Author Flyer."
4. Verify that the **Word1\Tutorial** folder is selected as the location for saving the file.
5. Click the **Save** button. The document is saved with the new filename, "Author Flyer," and the original Author file closes, remaining unchanged.

Decision Making: Creating Effective Documents

Before you create a new document or revise an existing document, take a moment to think about your audience. Ask yourself these questions:

- Who is your audience?
- What do they know?
- What do they need to know?
- How can the document you are creating change your audience's behavior or opinions?

Every decision you make about your document should be based on your answers to these questions. To take a simple example, if you are creating a flyer to announce an upcoming seminar on college financial aid, your audience would be students and their parents. They probably all know what the term "financial aid" means, so you don't need to explain that in your flyer. Instead, you can focus on telling them what they need to know—the date, time, and location of the seminar. The behavior you want to affect, in this case, is whether or not your audience will show up for the seminar. By making the flyer professional looking and easy-to-read, you increase the chance that they will.

You might find it more challenging to answer these questions about your audience when creating more complicated documents, like corporate reports. But the focus remains the same—connecting with the audience. As you are deciding what information to include in your document, remember that the goal of a professional document is to convey the information as effectively as possible to your target audience.

Before revising a document for someone else, it's a good idea to familiarize yourself with its overall structure.

To review the document:

1. Verify that the document is displayed in Print Layout view and that nonprinting characters are displayed.
2. Click the **View** tab, and then click the **One Page** button in the Zoom group. The Zoom changes to display the entire document on the screen.
3. Take a moment to review the document. At this point, the document is very simple. By the time you finish formatting it, it will look like the document shown in the Session 1.2 Visual Overview, formatted so it is wider than it is tall, with a green background, colored text, and a photo of a frog instead of a parrot. Figure 1-20 summarizes the tasks you will perform.

Figure 1-20 Formatting changes requested by Andrew

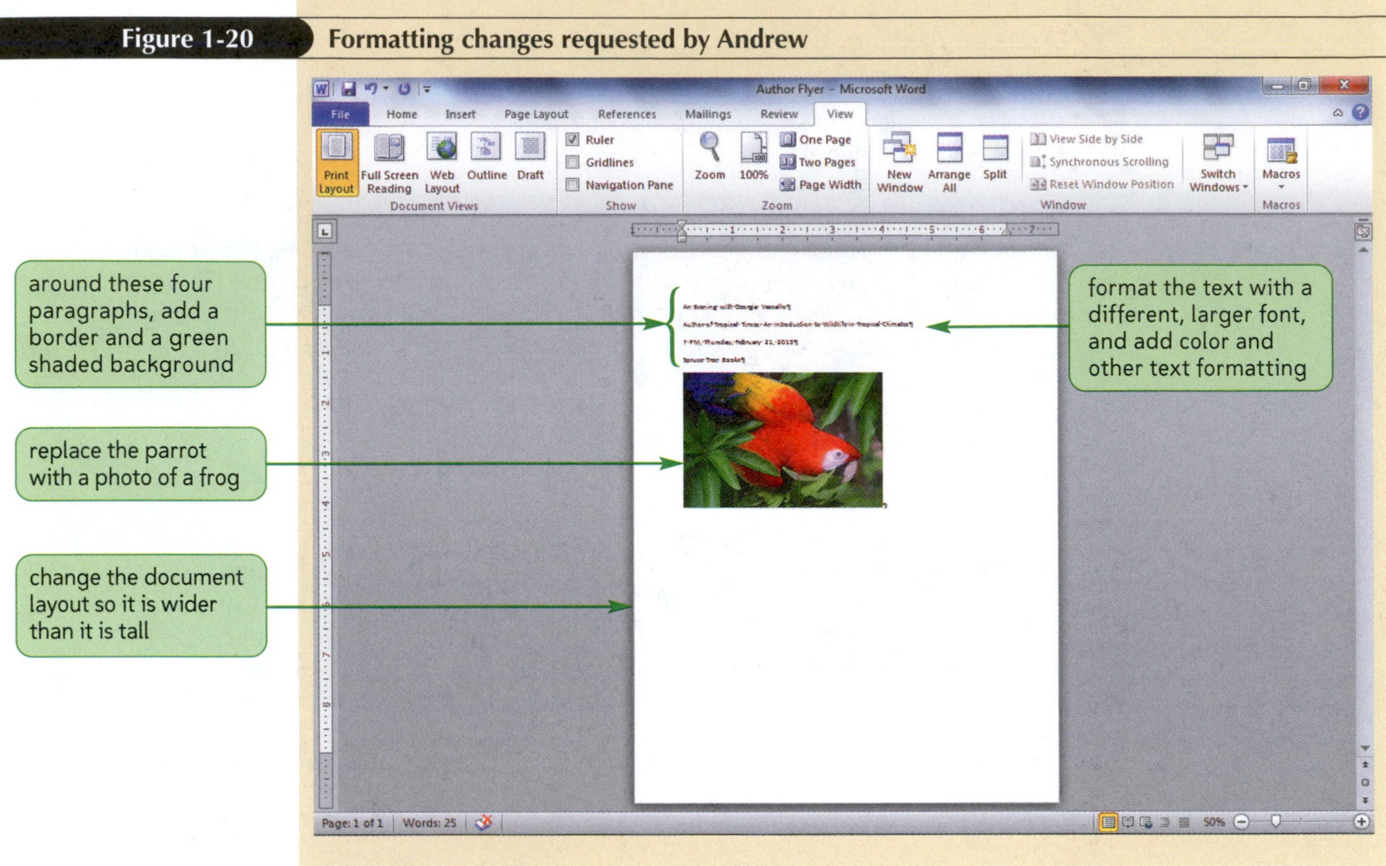

You will start by turning the page so it is wider than it is tall. In other words, you will change the document's **orientation**.

Changing Page Orientation

Portrait orientation, with the page taller than it is wide, is the default page orientation for Word documents because it is the orientation most commonly used for letters, reports, and other formal documents. However, Andrew wants to format the author flyer in **landscape orientation**—that is, with the page turned so it is wider than it is tall to better accommodate the photo. You can accomplish this task by using the Orientation button located on the Page Layout tab on the Ribbon. After you change the page orientation, you will select narrower margins so you can maximize the amount of color on the page.

To change the page orientation:

1. Click the **Page Layout** tab. The Ribbon changes to display options for formatting the overall layout of text and images in the document.
2. In the Page Setup group, click the **Orientation** button, and then click **Landscape** on the menu. The document changes to landscape orientation, with the page wider than it is tall.
3. In the Page Setup group, click the **Margins** button, and then click the **Narrow** option on the menu. The margins shrink from 1 inch to .5 inch on all four sides. See Figure 1-21.

Figure 1-21 Document in landscape orientation with narrow margins

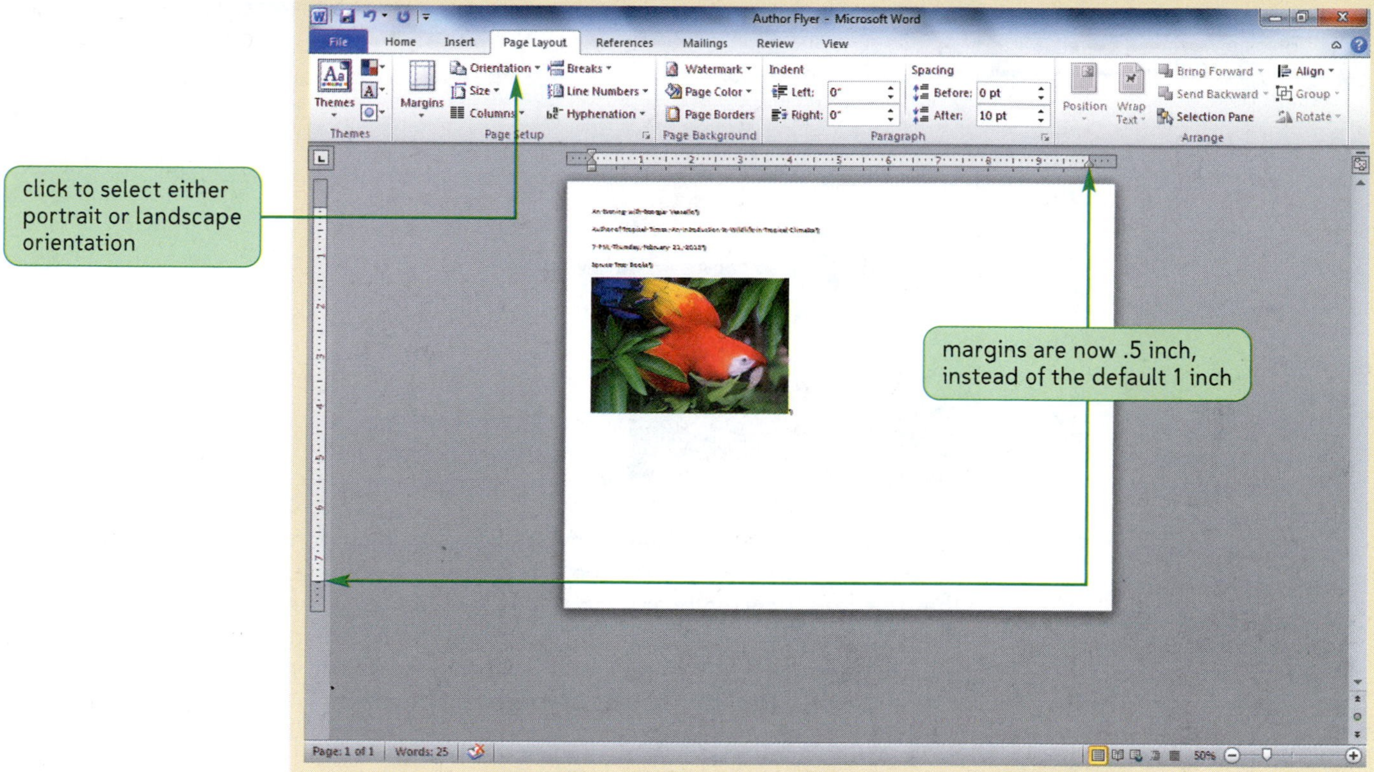

click to select either portrait or landscape orientation

margins are now .5 inch, instead of the default 1 inch

Changing the Font and Font Size

Andrew typed the document in the default font size, 11 point, and the default font, Calibri, but he would like to switch to the Times New Roman font instead. Also, he wants to increase the size of all four lines of the document text, with the first line appearing in the largest font. To apply these changes, you start by selecting the text you want to format. Then you select the options you want in the Font group on the Home tab.

To change the font and font size:

1. Click the **View** tab on the Ribbon, click the **Page Width** button to make it easier to see the document text, and then click the **Home** tab on the Ribbon.
2. To verify that the pointer is located at the beginning of the document, press the **Ctrl+Home** keys. If the insertion point was located anywhere else in the document, it moves to the beginning now, so that it is located to the left of the "A" in "An."
3. Press and hold the **Shift** key, and then click to the right of the fourth paragraph marker, at the end of the fourth line of text. The entire four lines of text are selected, as shown in Figure 1-22. The Font box in the Font group indicates the selected text is formatted in Calibri. The word "Body" next to the font name indicates that the Calibri font is intended for formatting body text. **Body text** is ordinary text, as opposed to titles or headings.

TIP

You could also have clicked and dragged the mouse to select the text, but then you might have accidentally selected the photo as well. In this case, a keyboard shortcut was more efficient.

Figure 1-22 Selected text, with default font displayed in Font box

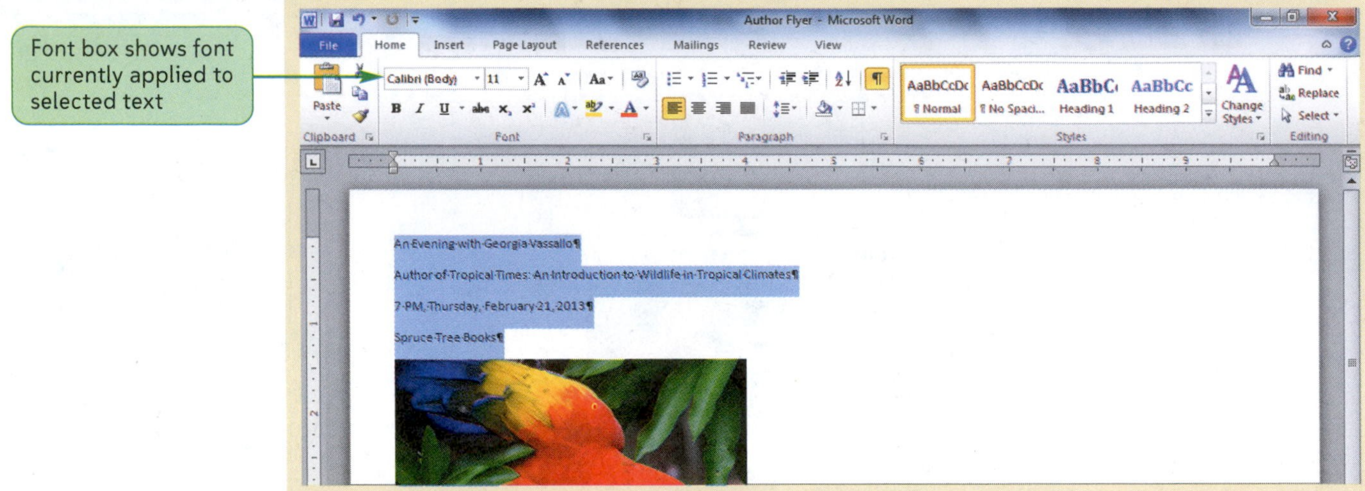

Font box shows font currently applied to selected text

4. In the Font group, click the **Font** arrow. A list of available fonts appears, with Cambria and Calibri at the top of the list. Calibri is highlighted in orange, indicating that this font is currently applied to the selected text. The word "Headings" next to the font name "Cambria" indicates that Cambria is intended for formatting headings. You'll learn more about Cambria, and its companion font, Calibri, in Tutorial 2, when you use Themes to format a document.

   Below Cambria and Calibri you might see a list of fonts that have been used recently on your computer, followed by a complete alphabetical list of all available fonts. (You need to scroll the list to see all the fonts.) Each name in the list is formatted with the relevant font. For example, "Arial" appears in the Arial font, and "Times New Roman" appears in the Times New Roman font. See Figure 1-23.

Figure 1-23 Font list

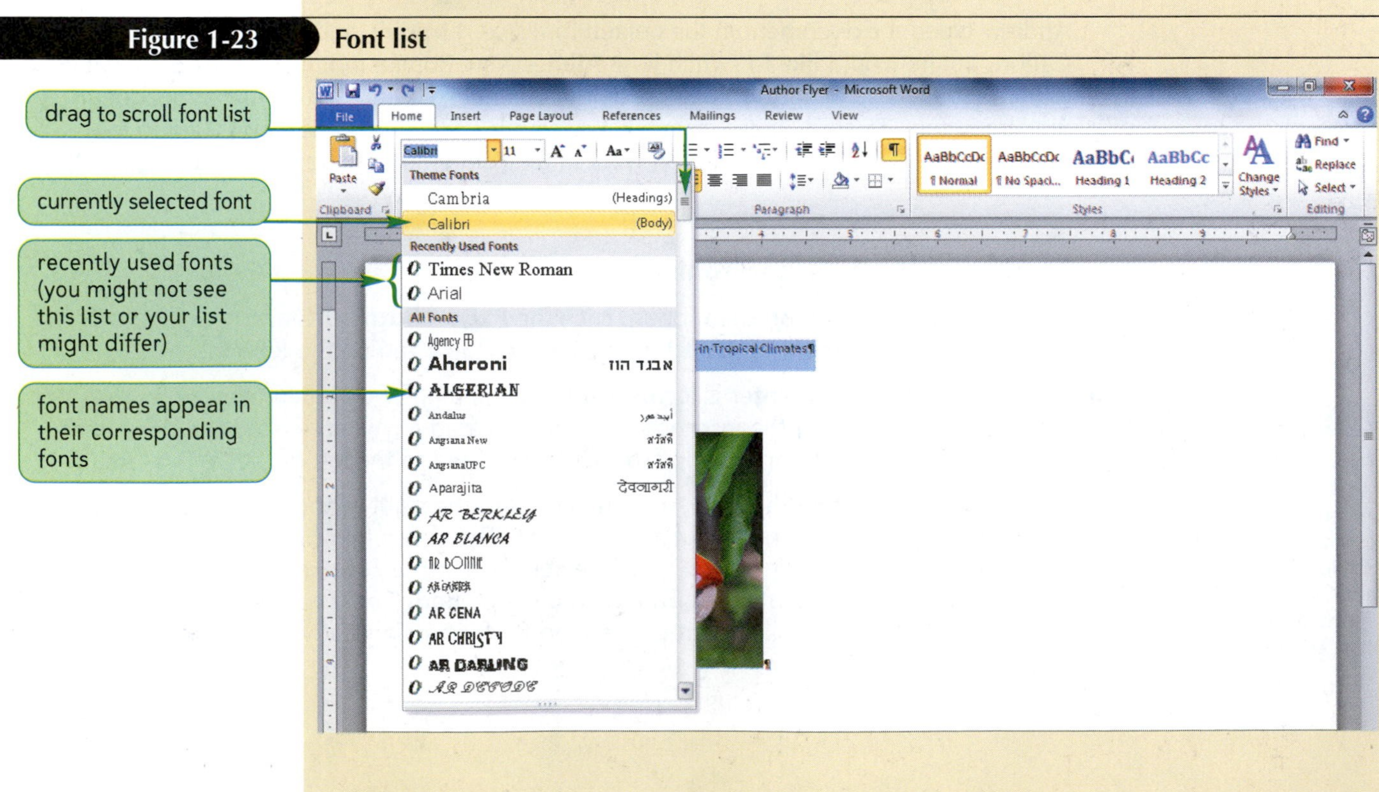

5. Without clicking, move the pointer over a dramatic-looking font in the font list, such as Algerian or Arial Black, and then move the pointer over another font. The selected text in the document changes to show a Live Preview of the font the pointer is resting on.
6. Scroll down the list and click **Times New Roman**. The Font menu closes, and the selected text is formatted in Times New Roman. You will make it more eye-catching as you increase the font size. The Font Size box currently displays the number "11" indicating that the selected text is formatted in 11-point font.
7. Verify that the four paragraphs of text are still selected, and then click the **Font Size** arrow to display a menu of font sizes. As with the Font menu, you can move the pointer over options in the Font Size menu to see a Live Preview of that option.
8. Click **22**. The selected text increases significantly in size and the Font Size menu closes.
9. Click a blank area of the document to deselect the text, and then save your changes to the document.

TIP

To quickly increase the font size of selected text, click the Grow Font button in the Font group on the Home tab. To decrease the font size, click the Shrink Font button.

Andrew looks over the flyer and decides he would like the first line of text to stand out from the rest. You will do this next by applying more text formatting.

Applying Text Effects, Font Colors, and Font Styles

To really make text stand out, you can use **text effects**, which are special visual enhancements such as outlines, shading, shadows, and reflections that you add to the text's font. You access these options by clicking the Text Effects button in the Font group on the Home tab. At other times, all it takes is different font color, or font style, such as **bold** or *italics*, to make a word, line, or paragraph of text stand out.

Andrew suggests increasing the font size of the flyer's first paragraph, and then applying text effects to it, so it really stands out from the rest of the text.

To apply text effects to the first paragraph:

1. Select the first paragraph in the flyer.
2. In the Font group, click the **Font** arrow, and then click **Arial Black**.
3. In the Font group, click the **Font Size** arrow, and then click **36**.
4. In the Font group, click the **Text Effects** button. A gallery of text effects appears, as shown in Figure 1-24. Some options that allow you to fine tune a particular text effect, perhaps by changing the color or adding an even more pronounced shadow, are listed below the predefined text effects in the gallery.

TIP

To restore selected text to the default font, size, and color, click the Clear Formatting button in the Font group on the Home tab.

Figure 1-24 Text Effects gallery

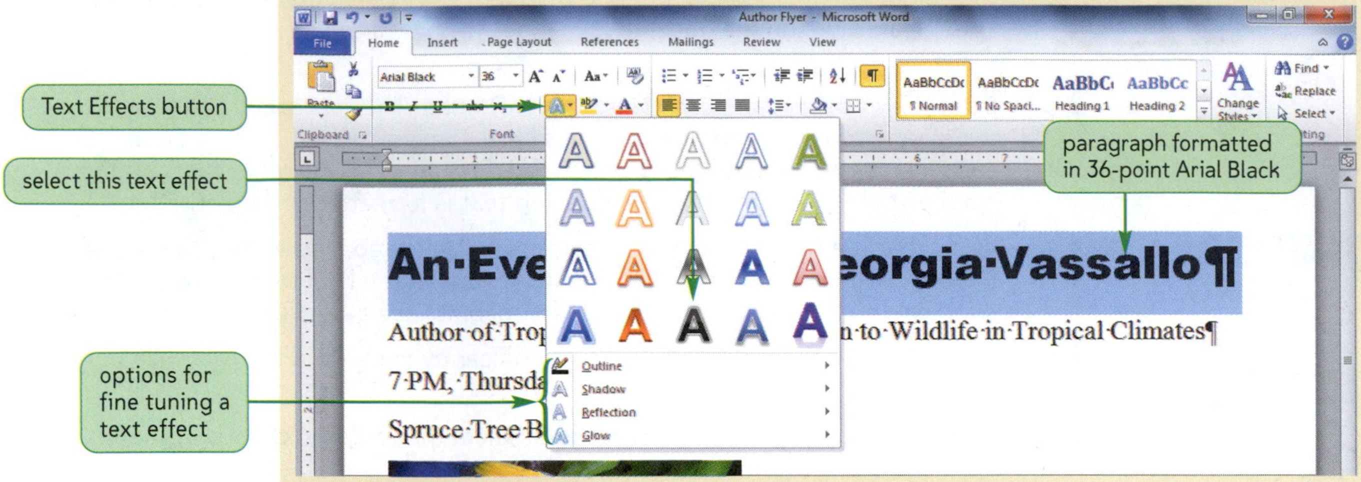

5. In the bottom row of the predefined text effects, place the pointer over the black letter "A" with the white outline to display a ScreenTip with a detailed description of the text effect, which reads "Gradient Fill – Black, Outline – White, Outer Shadow."
6. Click the black letter "A." The text effect is applied to the selected paragraph and the Text Effects gallery closes. The first paragraph is now formatted in Arial Black font, but with the additional text effects of a white outline and a fading effect at the top of each letter, as shown in the Session 1.2 Visual Overview.

Andrew wants to draw attention to the book title and the name of the bookstore where the event will take place. Book titles are typically italicized, so you'll add italics now as well as a font color for extra emphasis. Then you will use the Format Painter to copy the title's formatting to the name of the bookstore.

REFERENCE

Using the Format Painter

- Select the text whose formatting you want to copy.
- Click the Format Painter button in the Clipboard group on the Home tab. The mouse pointer changes to the Format Painter pointer, the I-beam pointer with a paintbrush.
- Drag the Format Painter pointer over the text you want to format.
- To copy formatting to nonadjacent paragraphs, double-click the Format Painter button, click the paragraphs you want to format, and then click the Format Painter button again to turn off the Format Painter.

To apply a font color and italics and use the Format Painter:

1. In the second paragraph, select the book title, "Tropical Times: An Introduction to Wildlife in Tropical Climates." It doesn't matter whether you select the paragraph symbol at the end of the title.

2. In the Font group, click the **Font Color button arrow** . A gallery of font colors appears. Black is the default font color and appears at the top of the Font Color list, with the word "Automatic" next to it. The options in the Theme Colors section of the menu are complementary colors that work well when used together in a document. The options in the Standard Colors section are the primary colors and simple variations of them. For more advanced color options, you could use the More Colors or Gradient options. Andrew prefers a simple dark blue.
3. In the Standard Colors section, place the mouse pointer over the second square from the right to display a ScreenTip with the color's name, "Dark Blue." See Figure 1-25. A Live Preview of the color appears in the document, where the text you selected in step 1 now appears formatted in dark blue.

Figure 1-25 **Selecting a font color**

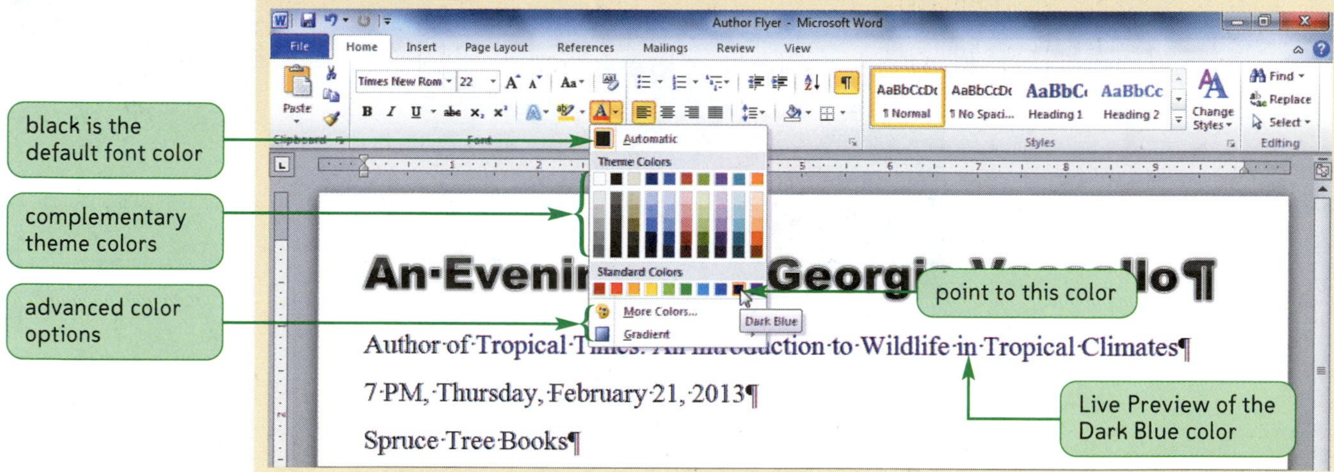

4. Click the **Dark Blue** square. The Font color gallery closes and the selected text is formatted in dark blue. On the Font Color button, the bar below the letter "A" is now dark blue indicating that, if you select text and click the Font Color button, it will automatically apply the dark blue color.
5. In the Font group, click the **Italic** button . The selected text is now italicized. Now you will copy the book title's formatting to the bookstore name using the Format Painter.
6. In the Clipboard group, click the **Format Painter** button to activate, or turn on, the Format Painter.
7. Move the pointer over the document. A small paint brush appears next to the I-beam pointer . See Figure 1-26. The text you select with the Format Painter pointer will automatically change to match the formatting of the selected text.

TIP

The Bold button (located in the Font group on the Home tab) can also be useful for emphasizing text.

Figure 1-26 Format Painter

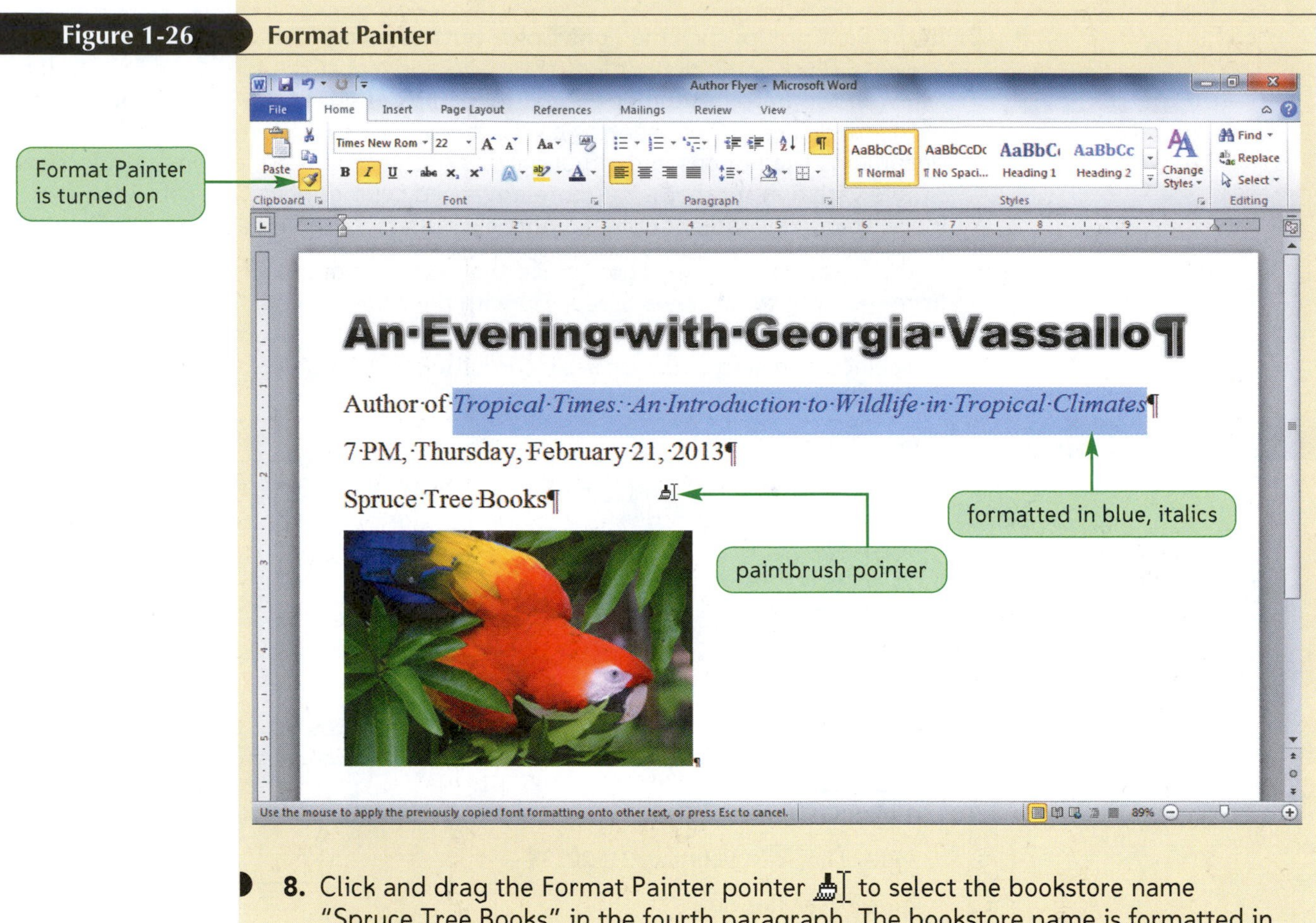

8. Click and drag the Format Painter pointer to select the bookstore name "Spruce Tree Books" in the fourth paragraph. The bookstore name is formatted in blue with italics. The mouse pointer returns to its original I-beam shape.
9. Save your changes to the document.

You have finished the text formatting Andrew requested. Next, you will complete some paragraph formatting, starting with paragraph alignment.

Aligning Text

Alignment refers to how the text lines up according to the margins on a page. By default, Word aligns text along the left margin, with the text along the right margin **ragged**, or uneven. This is called **left alignment**. With **right alignment**, the text is aligned along the right margin and is ragged along the left margin. With **center alignment**, text is centered between the left and right margins and is ragged along both the left and right margins. With **justified alignment**, full lines of text are spaced between both the left and the right margins, and the text is not ragged. Text in newspaper columns is often justified. See Figure 1-27.

Figure 1-27 Varieties of text alignment

left alignment
The term "alignment" refers to the way a paragraph lines up between the margins. The term "alignment" refers to the way a paragraph lines up between the margins.

right alignment
The term "alignment" refers to the way a paragraph lines up between the margins. The term "alignment" refers to the way a paragraph lines up between the margins.

center alignment
The term "alignment" refers to the way a paragraph lines up between the margins.

justified alignment
The term "alignment" refers to the way a paragraph lines up between the margins. The term "alignment" refers to the way a paragraph lines up between the margins.

The Paragraph group on the Home tab includes a button for each of the four major types of alignment described in Figure 1-27: the Align Text Left button, the Center button, the Align Text Right button, and the Justify button. To align a single paragraph, click anywhere in that paragraph and then click the appropriate alignment button. To align multiple paragraphs, select the paragraphs first, and then click an alignment button.

You need to center all the text in the flyer. The photograph is actually contained in its own paragraph, so you can also center it as well using an alignment button.

To center-align the text and photo:

1. Press the **Ctrl+A** keys. The entire document is selected, including the text and the paragraph containing the photo. In the Paragraph group, the Align Text Left button is highlighted, indicating that the selected text and photograph are left aligned.
2. In the Paragraph group, click the **Center** button, and then click a blank area of the document to deselect the selected paragraphs. The text and photo are now centered on the page. See Figure 1-28.

Figure 1-28 Centered text and photo

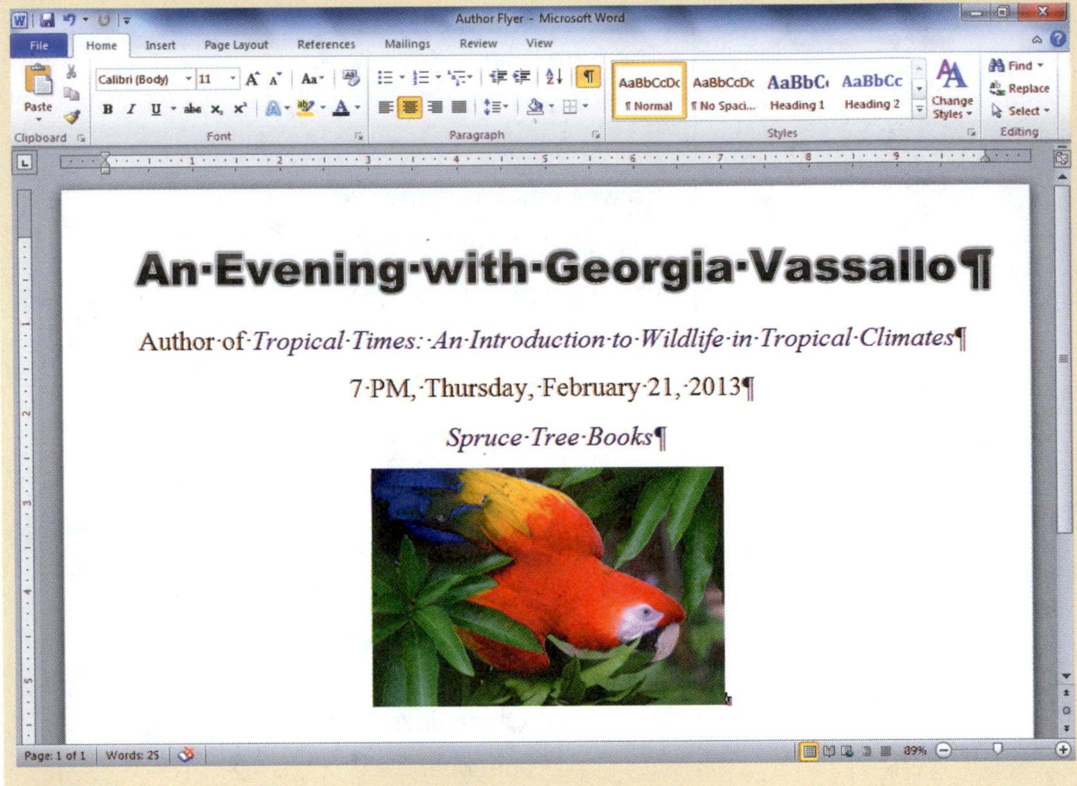

3. Save your changes to the document.

Adding a Paragraph Border and Shading

A **paragraph border** is an outline that appears around one or more paragraphs in a document. You can choose to apply only part of a border—for example, a bottom border that appears as an underline under the last line of text in the paragraph—or an entire box around a paragraph. You can select different colors and line weights for the border as well, making it more prominent or less prominent as needed. You apply paragraph borders using the Border button in the Paragraph group on the Home tab. **Shading** is background color that you can apply to one or more paragraphs and can be used in conjunction with a border for a more defined effect. You apply shading using the Shading button in the Paragraph group on the Home tab.

Now you will experiment with various border and shading options before applying the border and shading shown earlier in the Session 1.2 Visual Overview.

To add shading and a paragraph border:

1. Select the first paragraph in the document, which contains the text "An Evening with Georgia Vassallo."

2. In the Paragraph group, click the **Border button arrow**. A menu of border options appears, as shown in Figure 1-29. To apply a complete outline around the selected text, you use the Outside Borders option.

Figure 1-29 **Border menu**

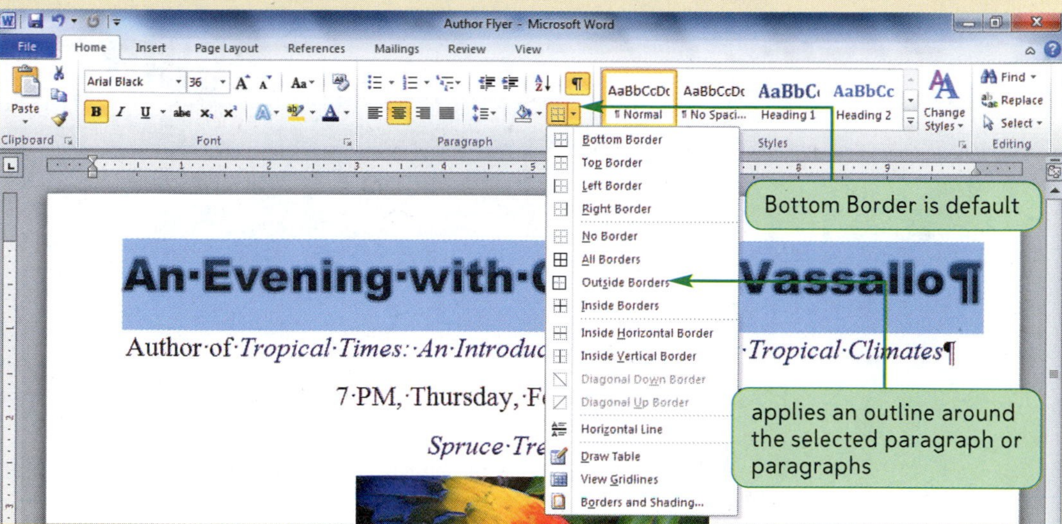

TIP

The exact name that appears in the ScreenTip for the Border button changes, depending on which border option is currently selected. In this case, the ScreenTip reads "Bottom Border" because the bottom border style is selected by default.

3. On the Border menu, click **Outside Borders**. The menu closes and a black border appears around the selected paragraph, and the Border button in the Paragraph group changes to show the Outside Borders option.
4. On the Quick Access Toolbar, click the **Undo** button to remove the border, click outside the first paragraph to deselect it, and then select all four paragraphs of text.
5. In the Paragraph group, click the **Border button arrow** and then click **All Borders**. Each paragraph appears with its own complete border around it.
6. On the Quick Access Toolbar, click the **Undo** button to remove the borders, click the **Border button arrow** in the Paragraph group, and then click **Outside Borders**. An outside border is applied to the selected paragraphs.

As you can see, the type of border Word applies depends on the number of paragraphs selected in the document and the option you choose on the Border menu. Andrew wants to keep the single outline around all four paragraphs, so you can now add shading. You don't have to use a border with shading, but the border helps add definition to the shading color.

To add paragraph shading to the paragraphs:

1. Verify that all four paragraphs of text are still selected.
2. In the Paragraph group, click the **Shading button arrow**. A gallery of shading options opens, divided into Theme Colors and Standard Colors. As with other formatting menus and galleries, you can move the pointer over an option to see a Live Preview of the option applied to the selected text in the document. Andrew asks you to use the light green shading option. See Figure 1-30.

Figure 1-30 Shading gallery

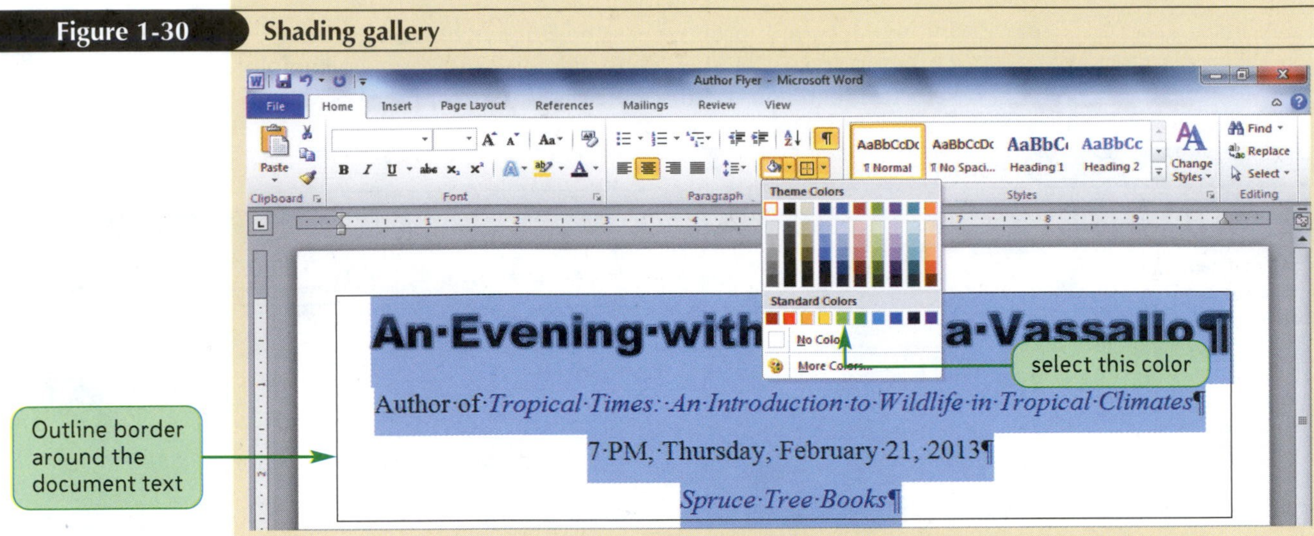

3. In the Standard Colors group, click the **Light Green** square, which is the fifth square from the left.
4. Click a blank area of the document to deselect the text. The green shading is applied to the paragraphs.
5. Save your changes to the document.

INSIGHT

Formatting Professional Documents

In professional documents, use color and special fonts sparingly. The goal of letters, reports, and other documents is to convey important information, not to dazzle the reader with fancy fonts and colors. Such elements only serve to distract the reader from your main point.

Andrew has found a great photo of a tree frog that he would prefer to use instead of the photo of the parrot. You can easily replace the parrot photo with this new photo.

Inserting, Deleting and Resizing a Photo

To work with a photo or other type of picture in a document, you first need to select it. Once a photo is selected, the Picture Tools Format tab appears on the Ribbon, with options for moving, resizing, editing, and formatting the photo with enhancements such as adding a frame or changing its shape. To insert a new photo or other type of picture, you use the Picture button in the Illustrations group on the Insert tab.

To delete the current photo and insert a new one:

1. Click the **View** tab, and then click the **One Page** button in the Zoom group so you can see the entire document on the screen at once.
2. Click the parrot photo to select it. The squares and circles, called **handles**, that appear around the edge of the photo indicate the photo is selected. See Figure 1-31. The Picture Tools Format tab also appears on the Ribbon.

Figure 1-31 Selected photo

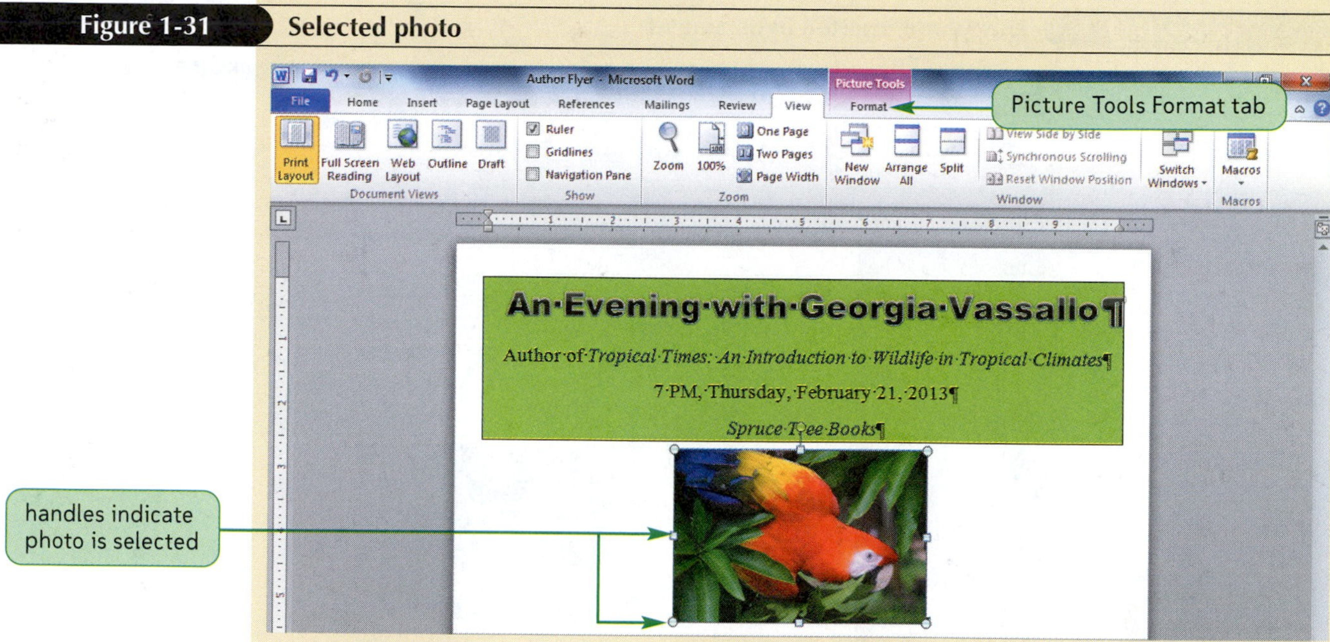

3. Press the **Delete** key. The photo is deleted from the document. The insertion point blinks next to a paragraph symbol that is centered below the green shaded text. You will insert the new photo in that paragraph.
4. Click the **Insert** tab on the Ribbon. The Ribbon changes to display the Insert options.
5. In the Illustrations group, click the **Picture** button. The Insert Picture dialog box opens.
6. Navigate to the Word1\Tutorial folder included with your Data Files.
7. Click **Frog** to select the file. The name of the selected file appears in the File name box.
8. Click the **Insert** button to close the dialog box and insert the photo. An image of a frog appears in the document, centered below the text, as shown in Figure 1-32. The photo is selected, as indicated by the border with handles that appears around it. You can drag one of the circular handles to make the photo a little bigger.

Figure 1-32 Frog photo inserted in document

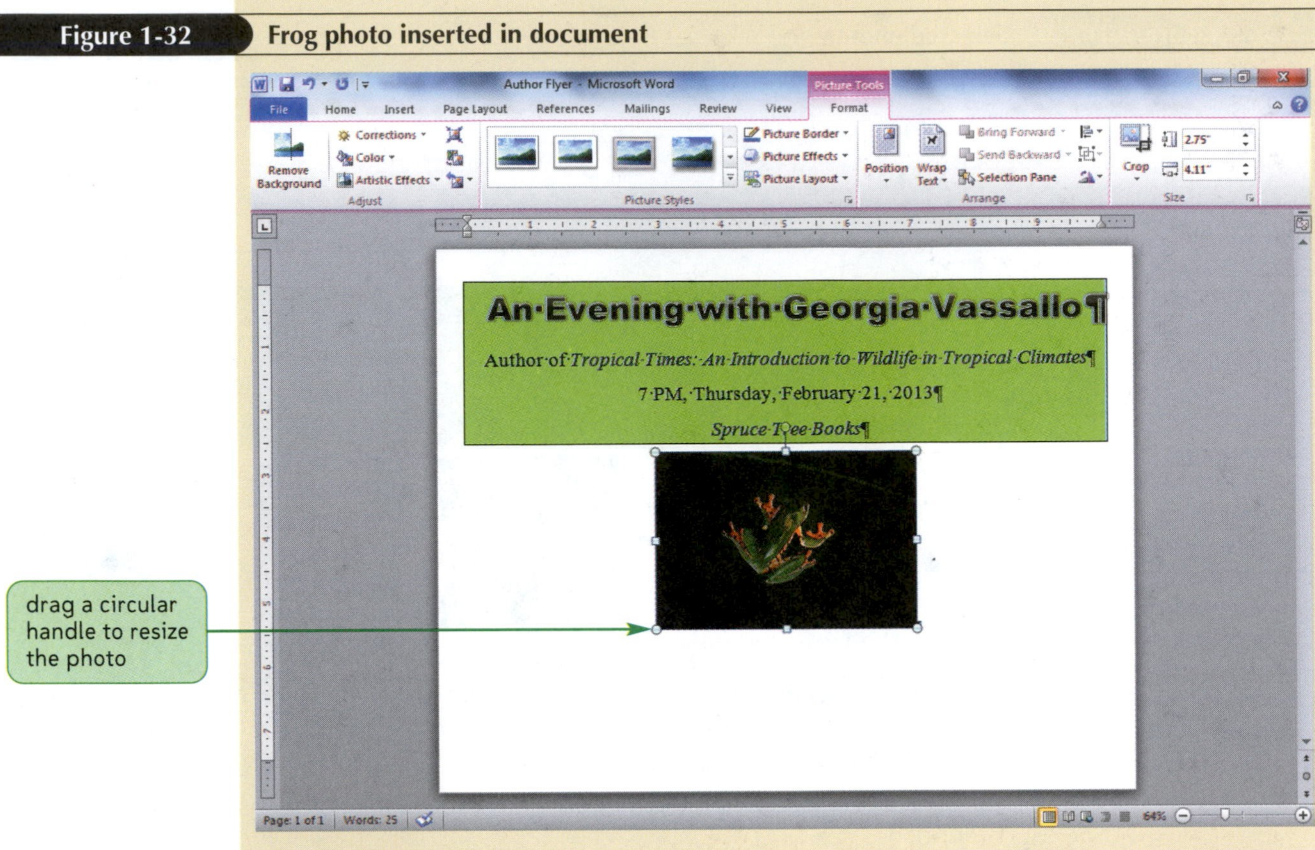

9. Place the pointer over the circular handle in the lower-right corner. The pointer changes to a double-white arrow.

Don't drag the pointer too far or the photo might become too large and move to a second page.

10. Press and hold the left mouse button, drag the handle down and to the right until the bottom of the photo outline reaches the edge of the bottom margin, as shown in Figure 1-33.

    As you drag the handle, the pointer changes shape to the black cross shown in Figure 1-33, and an outline of the photo showing the increase in its size appears.

Figure 1-33 Resizing the photo

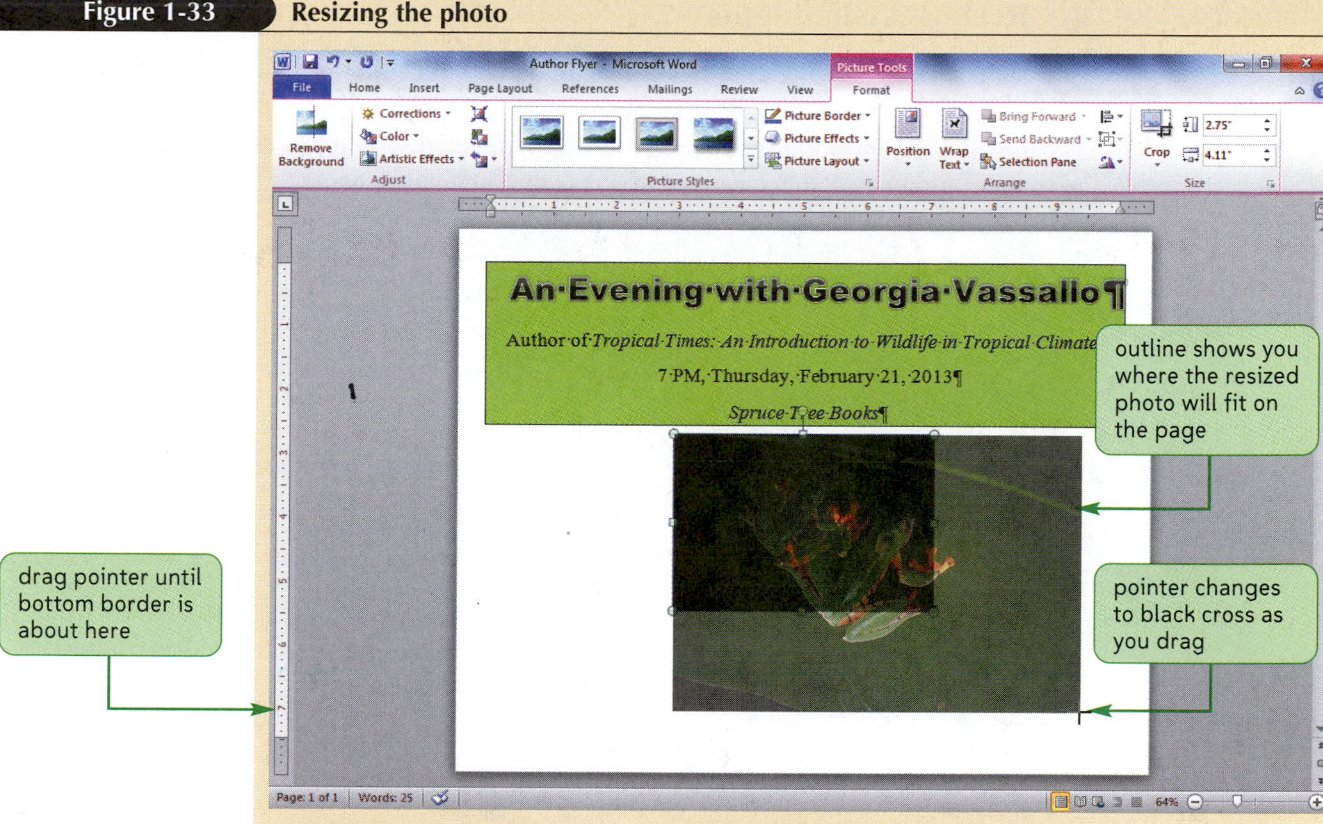

11. Release the mouse button, and then review the document and make additional adjustments to the photo, as necessary, until it is about the size of the photo shown in Figure 1-33, and then click a blank area of the document to deselect the photo.
12. Save the document, click the **File** tab, and then click the **Close** command in the navigation bar of Backstage view to close the document without closing Word.

The flyer is complete, and Andrew will print copies of it later. The flyer is visually striking, thanks to the text formatting you added and the new photo you inserted and sized.

REVIEW

Session 1.2 Quick Check

1. Describe the default page orientation for Word documents.
2. What is the default font?
3. What is the default font size?
4. Explain how to center-align text.
5. True or False. The type of border Word applies depends on the number of paragraphs selected in the document and the option you choose on the Border menu.
6. What button do you use to insert a photo in a document?

Practice the skills you learned in the tutorial using the same case scenario.

PRACTICE

Review Assignments

Data Files needed for the Review Assignments: Extreme.docx, Red Flower.jpg

Andrew asks you to write a letter to a local author, Charles Plaut, inviting him to an upcoming convention. He also asks you to format a flyer announcing an author appearance, and to create an envelope for the flyer. You'll create the letter, flyer, and envelope by completing the following steps.

1. Open a new blank document and then save the document as **Plaut Letter** in the Word1\Review folder provided with your Data Files.
2. Type the date **February 11, 2013** using AutoComplete for "February."
3. Press the Enter key twice, then type the following inside address, using the default paragraph spacing for now:
   Charles Plaut
   787 First Street
   Albany, NY 12205
4. Press the Enter key twice, then type the letter's salutation, body, complimentary closing, and signature line, as shown in Figure 1-34. Accept any relevant AutoCorrect suggestions. Use the default paragraph spacing; do not insert any extra blank paragraphs. Type your initials below the Enclosure line, instead of the initials you see in Figure 1-34.

Figure 1-34 **Plaut Letter**

February 11, 2013

Charles Plaut
787 First Street
Albany, NY 12205

Dear Charles:

The Albany Visitors Bureau will be hosting the 2013 convention for the National Editorial Association. The convention is scheduled for the last week in June. We'd like to invite you to attend the opening banquet as our guest. Our own editor-in-chief, Sally Ann Hamilton, will be the keynote speaker.

The complete convention schedule will be posted on the National Editorial Association's Web site on March 1. I'll e-mail you shortly afterward to confirm your reservation for the opening banquet. At that time, you can tell me if you will be available to attend any of the afternoon seminars.

Sincerely,

Andrew Siordia
Managing Editor

Enclosure

aes

type your initials here

5. Scroll to the beginning of the document and proofread your work.
6. Correct any misspelled words marked by wavy red underlines. If the correct spelling of a word does not appear on the shortcut menu, close the menu, and then make the correction yourself. Remove any red wavy underlines below words that are spelled correctly.
7. Remove the paragraph spacing from the first two lines of the inside address. Do the same for the signature line.
8. Change the top margin to 2 inches. Leave the other margins at their default settings.
9. Save your changes to the letter, preview and print it, and then close it.

10. Create a new, blank document, and then add an envelope to the document. Use Charles Plaut's address (from Step 3) as the delivery address. Use your address as the return address. If you are asked if you want to save the return address as the new return address, click No.
11. Save the document as **Plaut Envelope** in the Word1\Review folder provided with your Data Files.
12. Save your changes and close the document.
13. Open the file **Extreme** located in the Word1\Review folder included with your Data Files, and then check your screen to make sure your settings match those in the tutorial.
14. Save the document as **Extreme Flyer** in the same folder.
15. Correct any misspelled words marked by wavy red lines. Also, remove any red wavy underlines below words that are spelled correctly. (You can assume the author's name and "Thaler Hall" are spelled correctly.)
16. Change the Zoom level to One Page, and then change the page orientation to Landscape and the margins to Narrow.
17. Change the Zoom level to Page Width, and then format the document text in 22-point Times New Roman font.
18. Select the second paragraph, which contains the book title, and format it in 28-point Arial Black.
19. Format the book title with the text effect Gradient Fill – Black, Outline – White, Outer Shadow.
20. Italicize the author's name (Joseph Rudin) and then format it in the Blue font color, located in the Standard Colors section of the Font Color gallery.
21. Use the Format Painter to copy the blue font and italics to the third paragraph, which contains the time and date.
22. Select the entire document, and then center align the text and photo.
23. Add a single outside border surrounding the four paragraphs of text, and then add pale green shading to the four paragraphs, using the Olive Green, Accent 3, Lighter 40% color located in the Theme Colors section of the Shading gallery.
24. Delete the photo of the pink flower with green leaves and replace it with the **Red Flower.jpg** photo, located in the Word1\Review folder included with your Data Files.
25. Resize the photo so that it fills as much of the page as possible, without adding a second page to the document.
26. Save your changes to the flyer, preview and print it, and then close it.

APPLY

Case Problem 1

If you have a SAM 2010 user profile, your instructor may have assigned an autogradable version of this assignment. If so, log into the SAM 2010 Web site at www.cengage.com/sam2010 to download the instructions and start files.

There are no Data Files needed for this Case Problem.

Wingra Family Practice Clinic You are a nurse at Wingra Family Practice Clinic. You have organized a lunchtime lecture series for the clinic staff in which regional medical professionals will discuss topics related to pediatric health care. You have hired your first speaker and need to write a letter confirming your agreement and asking a few questions. Create the letter by completing the following steps. As you type the document, accept the default paragraph spacing until you are asked to change them. Because the clinic is currently out of letterhead, you will start the letter by typing a return address.

1. Open a new blank document and then save the document as **Wingra Letter** in the Word1\Case1 folder provided with your Data Files.
2. Type your name, press the Enter key, and then type the following return address:
   Wingra Family Practice Clinic
   2278 Norwood Place
   Middleton, WI 52247
3. Press the Enter key twice, and then type **September 5, 2013** as the date.
4. Press the Enter key twice, and then type this inside address:
   Dr. Maria Sundquist
   Prairie Land Medical Center
   4643 Frank Lloyd Wright Drive
   Madison, WI 53788
5. Press the Enter key twice, type the salutation **Dear Dr. Sundquist:** (don't forget the colon), and then press the Enter key once.
6. Type the following paragraph: T**hank you so much for agreeing to lecture about early childhood vaccinations on Friday, October 4. Before I can publicize your talk, I need some information. Please call by Tuesday with your answers to these questions:**
7. Press the Enter key, and then type the following questions as separate paragraphs, using the default paragraph spacing:
   Which vaccines will you cover in detail?
   Will you discuss common immune responses to vaccine antigens?
   Will you provide handouts with suggested vaccination schedules?
8. Move the insertion point to the beginning of the third question (which begins "Will you provide..."). Insert a new paragraph, and add the following as the new third question in the list: **Would you be willing to take questions from the audience?**
9. Insert a new paragraph after the last question, and then type the complimentary closing **Sincerely,** (including the comma).
10. Press the Enter key twice to leave room for your signature, and then type your full name. Press the Enter key and type **Wingra Family Practice Clinic**.
11. Correct any spelling errors indicated by red wavy lines. Because "Wingra" is spelled correctly, use the shortcut menu to remove the wavy red underline under the word "Wingra" and prevent Word from marking the word as a misspelling. Do the same for "Sundquist."
12. Select the four paragraphs containing the questions and italicize them.
13. Select the first three lines of the return address and remove the paragraph spacing. Do the same for the first three paragraphs of the inside address and the signature line.
14. Select the four paragraphs containing the return address, and then center them, format them in 16-point Times New Roman, and apply the Dark Blue font color.
15. Save the document, preview and print it, and then close it.

Apply your skills to create a flyer announcing a new investment program.

APPLY

Case Problem 2

Data Files needed for this Case Problem: EdInvest.docx, Seal.jpg

Pear Tree Investment Services You work as a financial planner at Pear Tree Investment Services. You are developing a new program, EdInvest, which encourages parents to save for their children's college educations. In order to get the word out, you asked a program assistant at the Department of Education to give a presentation at a local high school for parents of college-bound students. You will create a flyer announcing the presentation, and then create an envelope to use when you send the flyer to the school principal. Complete the following steps:

1. Open the file **EdInvest** located in the Word1\Case2 folder provided with your Data Files, and then save the document as **EdInvest Flyer** in the same folder.
2. Change the page orientation to Portrait and the margins to Moderate.
3. Replace YOUR NAME with your first and last name.
4. Select the first paragraph and format it with the text effect located in the lower-left corner of the Text Effect gallery (Gradient Fill – Blue, Accent 1, Outline – White, Glow – Accent 2), and then change the font size to 48 points. Finally, center the paragraph.
5. Use the Format Painter to copy the formatting of the first paragraph (with the new, blue text effect and the center alignment) to the last paragraph of text, which reads "Start saving today!"
6. Select the middle five paragraphs of text, format them in 16-point Arial Black, and change the font color to Dark Blue.
7. Right-align the five selected paragraphs, so the right edge of each paragraph aligns at the right margin. Depending on how long your name is, the paragraph containing your name might wrap to a second line.
8. **EXPLORE** Change the line spacing for the five selected paragraphs to 1.0 and then remove extra space between paragraphs.
9. Add a single outline border to surround the five right-aligned paragraphs, and then shade the paragraphs inside the border with blue shading, using the Blue, Accent 1, Lighter 40% color in the fourth row of the Theme Colors section of the Shading gallery.
10. Create a new paragraph at the end of the document, switch to One Page view, and insert the picture **Seal.jpg** from the Word1\Case2 folder provided with your Data Files.
11. Resize the picture until its bottom border is positioned just above the bottom page margin.
12. Save the document, preview and print it, and then close it.
13. Open a new, blank document, and save it as **Flyer Envelope** in the Word1\Case2 folder provided with your Data Files.
14. **EXPLORE** Create an envelope for the flyer, using the following address:
    Principal James Handke
    Monona Valley High School
    465 Ash Street
    Monona, ID 83756
    Click the Omit check box to deselect it (if necessary), and then, for the return address, type your own address. Add the envelope to the document. If you are asked if you want to save the return address as the new default return address, answer No. If your computer is connected to a printer that is stocked with envelopes, click the File tab to open Backstage view, click the Print tab, click the Pages option button, type 1 in the Pages box, and then click the OK button.
15. Save and close the document.

Use your skills to create the letter of recommendation shown in Figure 1-35.

CREATE

Case Problem 3

Data File needed for this Case Problem: Waterfall.jpg

Monterrey Mountain Bike Tours You are the owner of Monterrey Mountain Bike Tours, located in Portland, Oregon. One of your tour guides, Alyssa Greene, has decided to move to the Midwest to be closer to her family. She has applied for a job as a tour guide at Horicon Marsh in Wisconsin, and has asked you to write a letter of recommendation. Complete the following steps:

1. Open a new blank document and then save the document as **Alyssa Letter** in the Word1\Case3 folder provided with your Data Files.
2. Type the letter shown in Figure 1-35. Assume that you will print the letter on the company's letterhead, with the date positioned 2 inches from the top of the page. Replace "Student Name" with your first and last name. Remember to remove the paragraph spacing from the first three paragraphs of the inside address and from the signature line. For the photo, use the file **Waterfall** from the Word1\Case3 folder provided with your Data Files. Insert the photo in a blank paragraph just before the complimentary close, and size it so it takes up the same amount of space as the photo in Figure 1-35.

Figure 1-35 Letter of recommendation for Alyssa Greene

June 27, 2013

Carl Mellencamp
Horicon Marsh Administrative Office
675 Scales Bend Road
Horicon, Wisconsin 57338

Dear Mr. Mellencamp:

I am writing on behalf of Alyssa Greene, who has applied for a job as a tour guide at Horicon Marsh. I highly recommend that you hire Alyssa. She is enthusiastic, energetic, and extremely well organized.

I would be glad to tell you more over the phone. You can reach me during business hours at (555) 555-5555. In the meantime, I thought you might enjoy seeing this photo of Alyssa with a recent tour group, which gave her very high marks in their trip review.

Sincerely,

Student Name
Owner

3. Correct any typing errors.
4. Preview and print the letter.

EXPLORE

5. Create an envelope for the letter. Use the delivery address taken from the letter. Click the Omit check box to deselect it (if necessary), and then, for the return address, type your own address. Add the envelope to the document. If you are asked if you want to save the return address as the new default return address, answer No. If your computer is connected to a printer that is stocked with envelopes, click the Office Button, click Print, click the Pages option button, type **1** in the Pages box, and then click the OK button.
6. Save the document and close it.

Go beyond what you've learned to write a fax coversheet for a small engineering company.

CHALLENGE

Case Problem 4

There are no Data Files needed for this Case Problem.

Gladstone Engineering As the office manager for Gladstone Engineering, you are responsible for faxing technical drawings to clients. Along with each set of drawings, you need to include a coversheet that explains what you are faxing, lists the total number of pages, and provides the name and cell phone number of the engineer who created the drawings. The fastest way to create a professional-looking coversheet is to use a template. When you open a template, you actually open a new document containing the formatting and text stored in the template, leaving the original template untouched. To create the fax coversheet, complete the following steps.

1. Display the New tab in the Backstage view. Under "Home," click Sample templates.
2. (EXPLORE) In the Available Templates pane, scroll down, click Equity Fax, and then click the Create button. A fax template opens, containing generic text called placeholders that you replace with your own information. (You should always take care to remove any placeholders you don't replace with other text.)
3. (EXPLORE) Click the text "[Type the recipient name]." The placeholder text appears in a blue box with blue highlighting. The box containing the highlighted text (with the small rectangle attached) is called a document control. You can enter text in this document control just as you enter text in a dialog box.
4. Type **Pao Yang**, and then press the Tab key twice. A document control is now visible to the right of the word "From." If you see a name other than your own selected here, press the Delete key to delete the name.
5. If necessary, type your first and last name in the document control, and then press the Tab key to highlight the placeholder text "[Type the recipient fax number]."
6. Type **(555) 555-5555**, and then continue using the Tab key as necessary to enter **6** as the number of pages and **(333) 333-3333** as the phone number. If you press the Tab key too many times and skip past a document control, you can click the document control to select it.
7. (EXPLORE) Use the Tab key to select the placeholder text "[Pick the date]," click the list arrow on the document control, click the right-facing arrow above the calendar as necessary until you see the calendar for January 2013, and then click 10 in the calendar. The date 1.10.2013 appears in the Date document control.
8. Use the Tab key to select the placeholder text in the "Re:" section, and then press the Delete key to delete the placeholder text. Delete the "CC:" placeholder text as well.
9. Click the box to the left of "Please Reply," and then type an uppercase **X**.
10. Click the placeholder text "[Type comments]," and then type the following message: **Here are the latest drawings by Krista Richardson. Please review them and then call Krista on her cell phone to discuss the next phase of the project. Thank you very much**.
11. Save the coversheet as **Yang Fax** in the Word1\Case4 folder provided with your Data Files.
12. Zoom the document out until you can see the entire page on the screen. When you are finished reviewing the document, zoom the document until it returns to its original zoom setting.
13. Review the coversheet and correct any errors. Save the coversheet again, preview it, and then print it.
14. Close the document.

ASSESS

SAM: Skills Assessment Manager

For current SAM information, including versions and content details, visit SAM Central (http://samcentral.course.com). If you have a SAM user profile, you may have access to hands-on instruction, practice, and assessment of the skills covered in this tutorial. Since various versions of SAM are supported throughout the life of this text, check with your instructor for the correct instructions and URL/Web site for accessing assignments.

ENDING DATA FILES

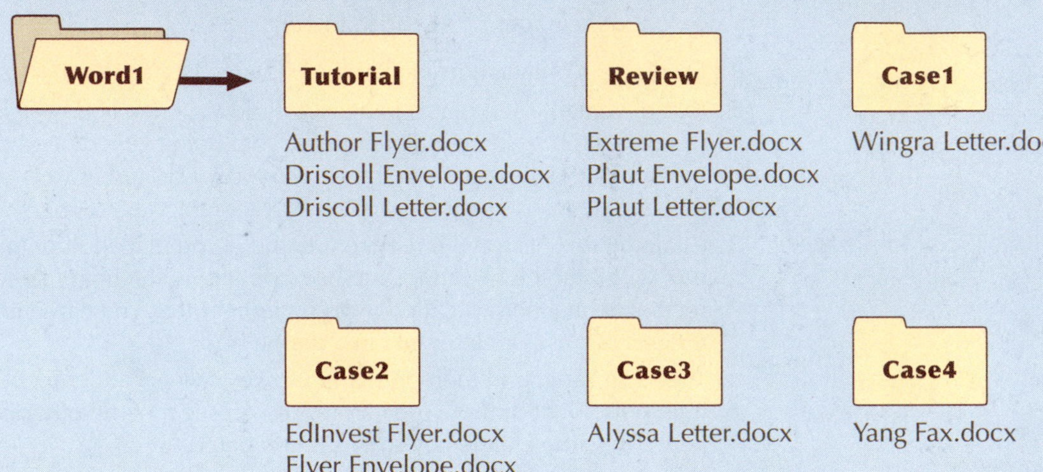

TUTORIAL 2

Editing and Formatting a Document

Editing an Academic Document According to MLA Style

OBJECTIVES

Session 2.1
- Create bulleted and numbered lists
- Move text within a document
- Find and replace text
- Check spelling and grammar
- Format documents with themes and styles

Session 2.2
- Review the MLA style for research papers
- Indent paragraphs
- Insert and modify page numbers
- Create citations and a bibliography

Case | *Pembrooke Community College*

Natalie Lanci is a student at Pembrooke Community College. As an assignment for her interior design class, she has drafted a one-page handout called "Getting the Look You Want," that a designer might give to customers. The handout still needs some revision; Natalie wants to reorganize some of the text. She also wants the finished document to look elegant and professional, while being easy to read. She has several ideas on how to format it to achieve these effects.

For her film history class, Natalie is writing a research paper on the history of disaster films. She needs to follow a set of very specific formatting and style guidelines for academic documents.

Natalie has asked you to help her edit these two very different documents. In Session 2.1 you will revise and format the interior design handout. In Session 2.2, you will review the MLA style for research papers, and then format Natalie's research paper on disaster films to match the MLA specifications.

STARTING DATA FILES

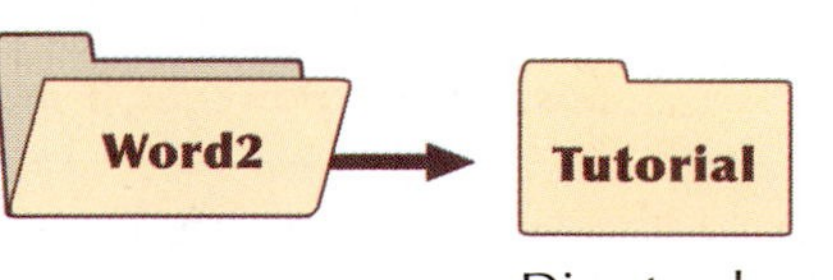

Tutorial	Review	Case1	Case2	Case3	Case4
Disaster.docx Interior.docx	Comedy.docx Services.docx Staff.docx	Classes.docx	Armstrong.docx	Management.docx	Elena.docx Goals.docx

SESSION 2.1 VISUAL OVERVIEW

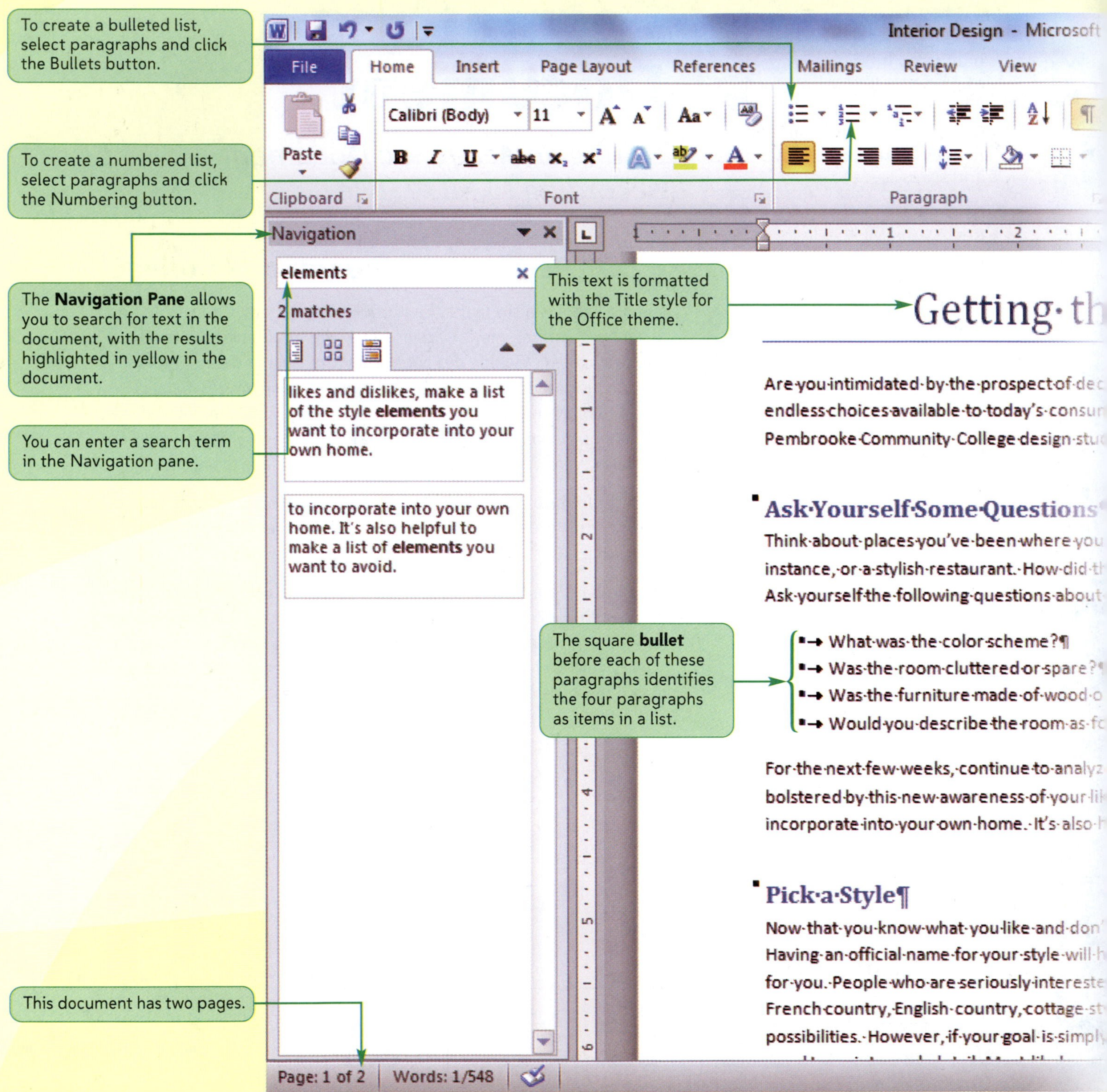

To create a bulleted list, select paragraphs and click the Bullets button.
To create a numbered list, select paragraphs and click the Numbering button.
The **Navigation Pane** allows you to search for text in the document, with the results highlighted in yellow in the document.
You can enter a search term in the Navigation pane.
This document has two pages.
This text is formatted with the Title style for the Office theme.
The square **bullet** before each of these paragraphs identifies the four paragraphs as items in a list.
Interior Design - Microsoft
File
Home
Insert
Page Layout
References
Mailings
Review
View
Calibri (Body)
11
Paste
Clipboard
Font
Paragraph
Navigation
elements
2 matches
likes and dislikes, make a list of the style elements you want to incorporate into your own home.
to incorporate into your own home. It's also helpful to make a list of elements you want to avoid.
Page: 1 of 2
Words: 1/548
Getting·th
Ask·Yourself·Some·Questions
What·was·the·color·scheme?¶
Was·the·room·cluttered·or·spare?
Was·the·furniture·made·of·wood·o
Would·you·describe·the·room·as·f
Pick·a·Style¶

FORMATTING A DOCUMENT

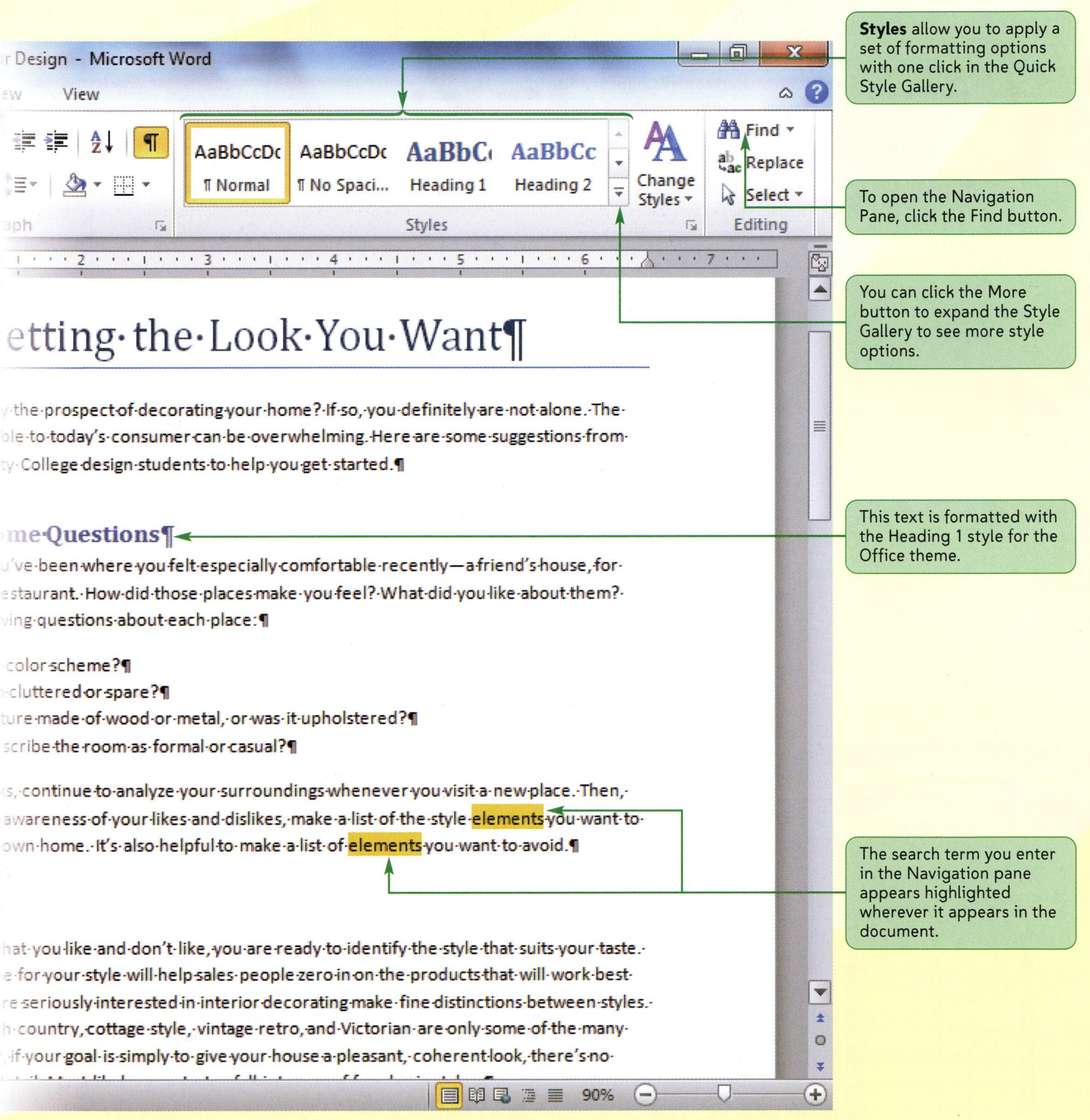

Styles allow you to apply a set of formatting options with one click in the Quick Style Gallery.
To open the Navigation Pane, click the Find button.
You can click the More button to expand the Style Gallery to see more style options.
This text is formatted with the Heading 1 style for the Office theme.
The search term you enter in the Navigation pane appears highlighted wherever it appears in the document.

Revising a Document

Before revising a document for someone else, it's a good idea to familiarize yourself with its overall structure, and the revisions that need to be made. Natalie's editing marks and notes on the first draft are shown in Figure 2-1.

Figure 2-1 Draft of handout with Natalie's edits (page 1)

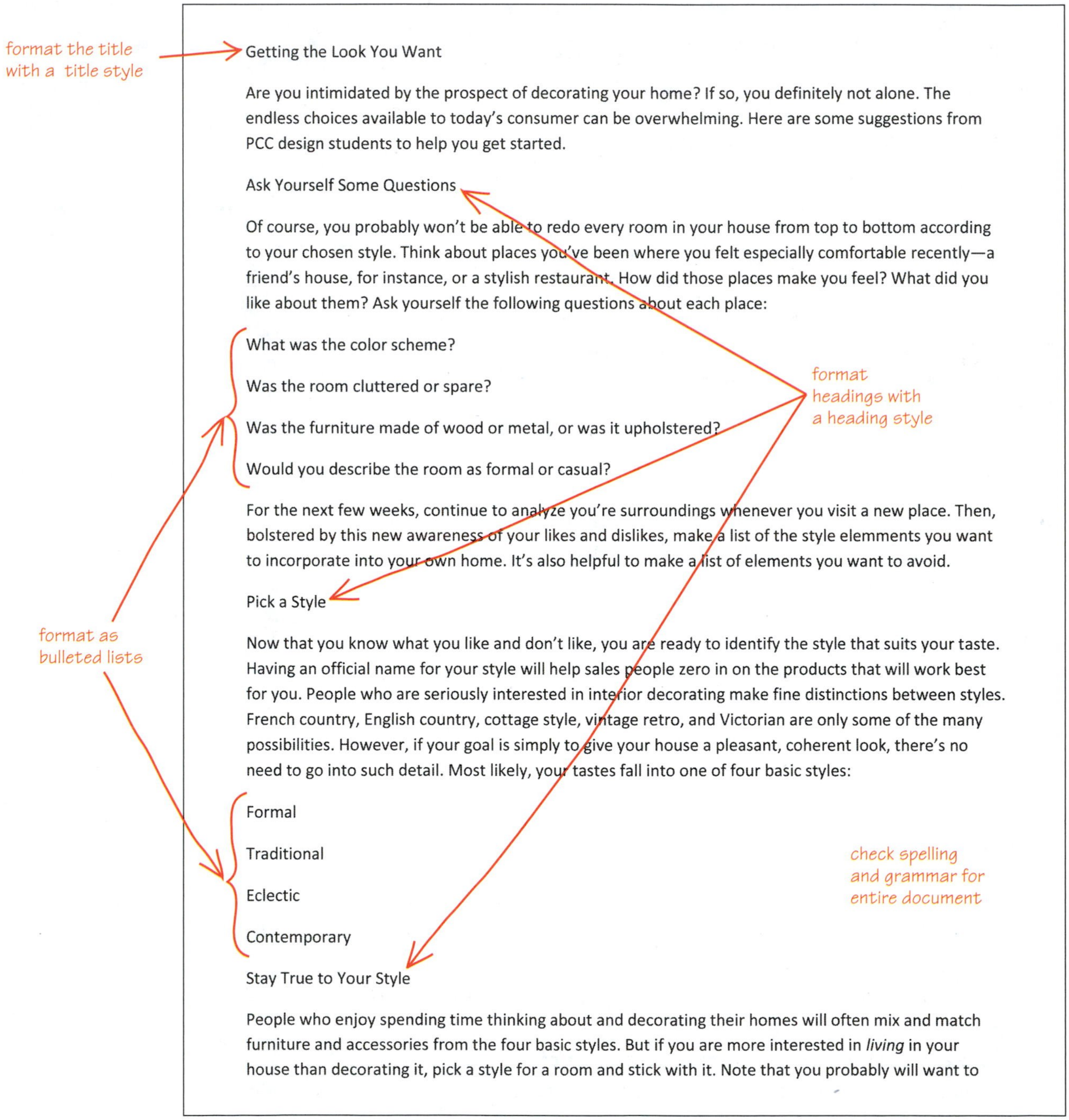

Getting the Look You Want

Are you intimidated by the prospect of decorating your home? If so, you definitely not alone. The endless choices available to today's consumer can be overwhelming. Here are some suggestions from PCC design students to help you get started.

Ask Yourself Some Questions

Of course, you probably won't be able to redo every room in your house from top to bottom according to your chosen style. Think about places you've been where you felt especially comfortable recently—a friend's house, for instance, or a stylish restaurant. How did those places make you feel? What did you like about them? Ask yourself the following questions about each place:

What was the color scheme?

Was the room cluttered or spare?

Was the furniture made of wood or metal, or was it upholstered?

Would you describe the room as formal or casual?

For the next few weeks, continue to analyze you're surroundings whenever you visit a new place. Then, bolstered by this new awareness of your likes and dislikes, make a list of the style elemments you want to incorporate into your own home. It's also helpful to make a list of elements you want to avoid.

Pick a Style

Now that you know what you like and don't like, you are ready to identify the style that suits your taste. Having an official name for your style will help sales people zero in on the products that will work best for you. People who are seriously interested in interior decorating make fine distinctions between styles. French country, English country, cottage style, vintage retro, and Victorian are only some of the many possibilities. However, if your goal is simply to give your house a pleasant, coherent look, there's no need to go into such detail. Most likely, your tastes fall into one of four basic styles:

Formal

Traditional

Eclectic

Contemporary

Stay True to Your Style

People who enjoy spending time thinking about and decorating their homes will often mix and match furniture and accessories from the four basic styles. But if you are more interested in *living* in your house than decorating it, pick a style for a room and stick with it. Note that you probably will want to

Figure 2-1 Draft of handout with Natalie's edits (page 2)

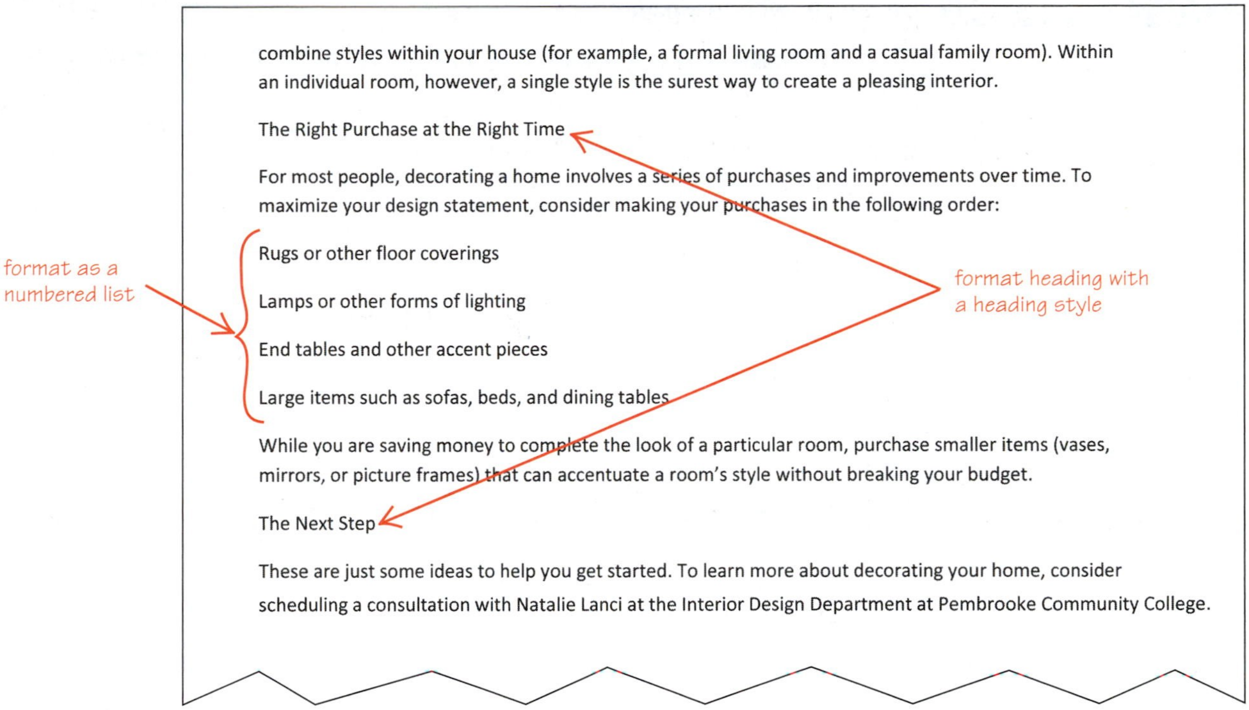

combine styles within your house (for example, a formal living room and a casual family room). Within an individual room, however, a single style is the surest way to create a pleasing interior.

The Right Purchase at the Right Time

For most people, decorating a home involves a series of purchases and improvements over time. To maximize your design statement, consider making your purchases in the following order:

Rugs or other floor coverings

Lamps or other forms of lighting

End tables and other accent pieces

Large items such as sofas, beds, and dining tables

While you are saving money to complete the look of a particular room, purchase smaller items (vases, mirrors, or picture frames) that can accentuate a room's style without breaking your budget.

The Next Step

These are just some ideas to help you get started. To learn more about decorating your home, consider scheduling a consultation with Natalie Lanci at the Interior Design Department at Pembrooke Community College.

You'll start revising Natalie's document by opening and saving it with a new name.

To open, rename, and review the document:

1. Open the document named **Interior** located in the Word2\Tutorial folder provided with your Data Files.
2. Save the document as **Interior Design** in the same location.
3. Verify that the document is displayed in Print Layout view and that the rulers and nonprinting characters are displayed. Make sure the Zoom level is set to **Page Width**.
4. Read the document. It includes a title, at the top, and headings (such as "Ask Yourself Some Questions" and "Pick a Style") that divide the document into parts. Right now the headings are hard to spot because they don't look any different from the surrounding text; Natalie used the default font size, 11-point, and the default font, Calibri (Body), for all the text in the document. Note, too, that the document includes some short paragraphs that would work better as bulleted or numbered lists. Word has also identified potential spelling and grammar errors that you will correct after you have made Natalie's revisions.
5. Scroll down until you can see the first line on page 2, "combine styles within your house…" as shown in Figure 2-2. The gray space below the first page's bottom margin indicates a page break. Word starts a new page automatically whenever your text fills up a page.

TIP

To reduce the gray space between pages to a gray line, double-click the gray space. To redisplay the gray space, double-click the gray line.

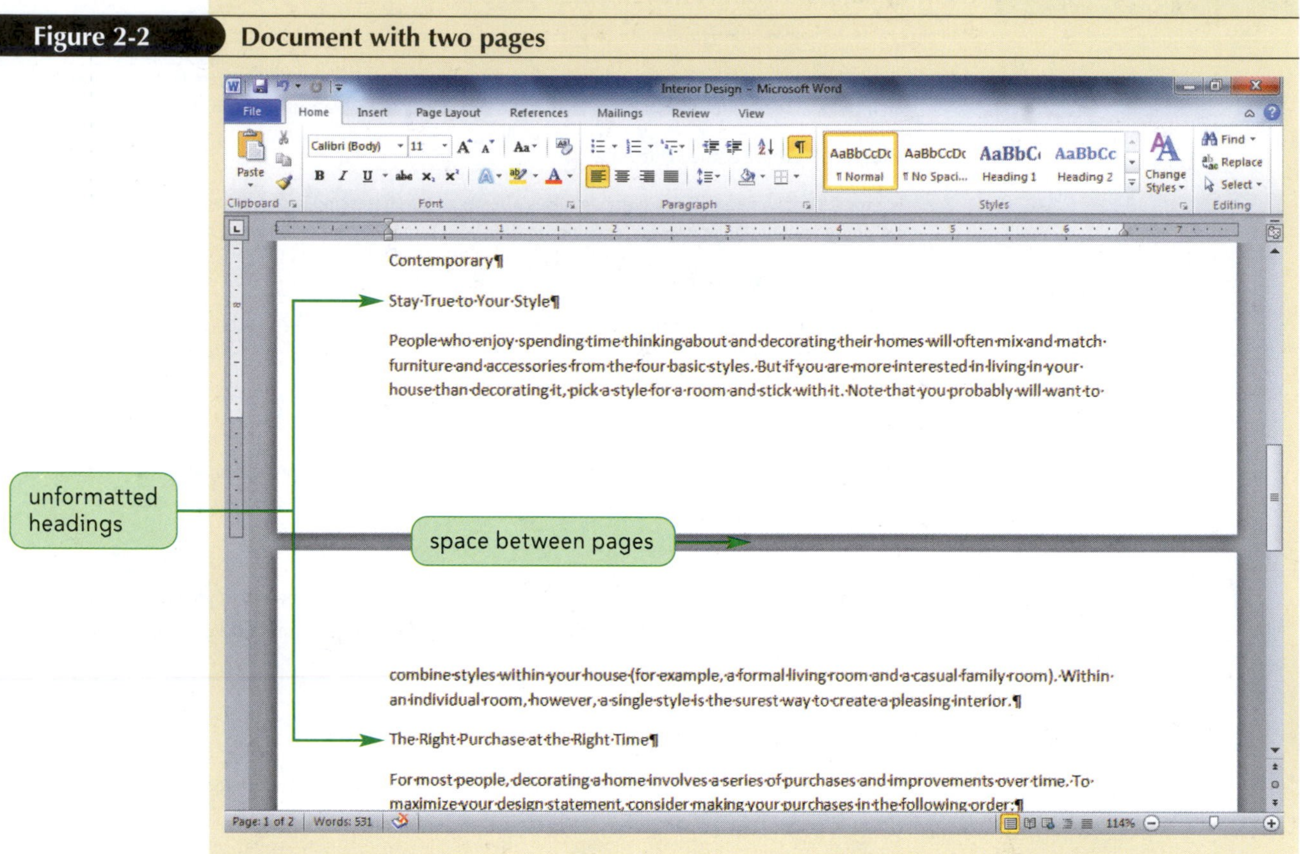

Figure 2-2 Document with two pages

Creating Bulleted and Numbered Lists

A **bulleted list** is a group of related paragraphs with a special symbol, such as a dot, dash, or other character, that appears to the left of each paragraph. For a group of related paragraphs that have a particular order (such as steps in a procedure), you can use numbers instead of bullets to create a **numbered list**. If you insert a new paragraph, delete a paragraph, or reorder the paragraphs in a numbered list, Word adjusts the numbers to make sure they remain consecutive.

To add bullets to a series of paragraphs, you use the Bullets button in the Paragraph group on the Home tab. To create a numbered list, you use the Numbering button in the Paragraph group instead. Both the Bullets button and the Numbering button have arrows that you can click to open a gallery of bullet or numbering styles.

Natalie asks you to format the paragraphs of questions on page 1 as a bulleted list. She also asks you to format the paragraphs on page 1 summarizing the four basic styles as a bulleted list. Finally you will need to format some of the paragraphs on page 2 as a numbered list.

To apply bullets to paragraphs:

1. Scroll up until you see the paragraphs containing questions on page 1, the first of which begins "What was the color scheme?," then select this paragraph and the three that follow it.
2. In the Paragraph group, click the **Bullets** button. Black circles appear as bullets before each item in the list. Also, the bulleted list is indented and the paragraph spacing between the items is reduced. After reviewing the default, circular bullet style in the document, Natalie decides she would prefer square bullets.
3. In the Paragraph group, click the **Bullets button arrow**. A gallery of bullet styles opens. The Recently Used Bullets section is shown at the top of the gallery of bullet styles; it displays the bullet styles that have been used since you started Word. You'll probably see just the round black bullet style, which was applied by default when you clicked the Bullets button. However, if you had used several different bullet styles, you would see them here. The **Bullet Library**, which offers a variety of bullet styles, is shown below the Recently Used Bullets. Natalie prefers the black square style. See Figure 2-3.

TIP

The Bullets button is a toggle button. To remove bullets from selected text, click the Bullets button.

Figure 2-3 Bullets gallery

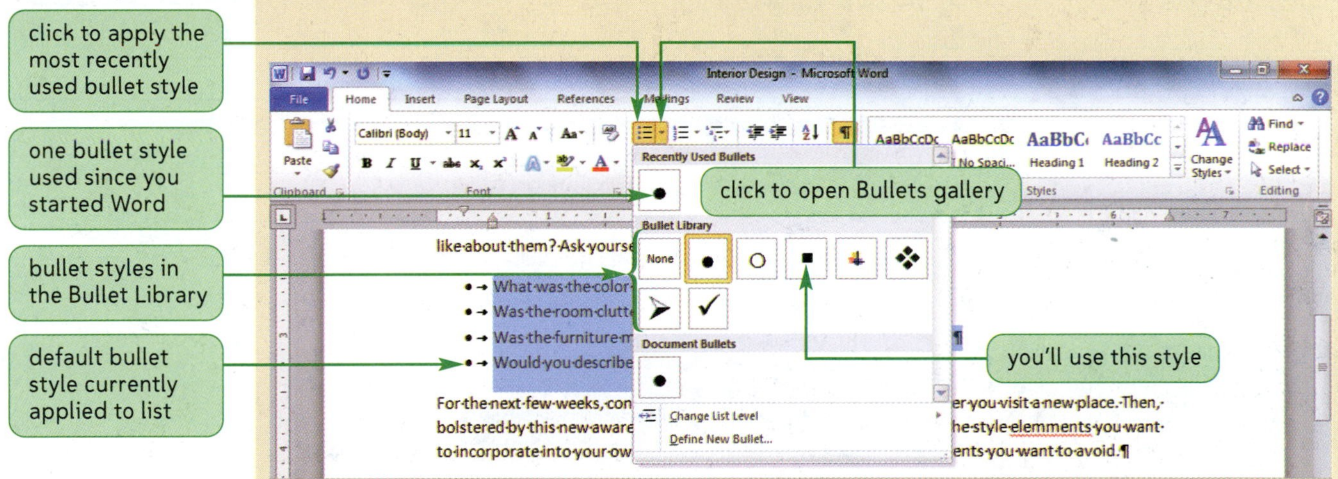

4. Move the mouse pointer over the bullet styles in the Bullet Library to see a Live Preview of the bullet styles in the document.
5. Click the **black square** in the Bullet Library. The round bullets are replaced with square bullets.

Next, you need to format the list of decorating styles on page 1 with square bullets. When you first start Word, the Bullets button applies the round bullets you saw earlier. But after you select a new bullet style, the Bullets button applies the last bullet style you used. So, to add square bullets to the decorating styles list, you just have to select the list and click the Bullets button.

To add bullets to the list of decorating styles:

1. Scroll down and select the paragraphs listing the four basic decorating styles (**Formal**, **Traditional**, **Eclectic**, **Contemporary**) near the bottom of page 1.
2. In the Paragraph group, click the **Bullets** button. The list is now formatted with square black bullets.

Next you will format the paragraphs listing suggested purchases on page 2. Natalie wants you to format this information as a numbered list because it specifies purchases in a sequential order.

TIP

The Numbering button is a toggle button, which means you can click it to turn numbering on or off. To remove numbers from selected text, click the Numbering button.

To apply numbers to the list of suggested purchases:

1. Scroll down to page 2 until you see the paragraph "Rugs or other floor coverings" and then select that paragraph and the three that follow it, the last one being "Large items such as sofas, beds, and dining tables."
2. In the Paragraph group, click the **Numbering** button. Consecutive numbers appear in front of each item in the list, with a period after each number. See Figure 2-4.

Figure 2-4 Numbered List

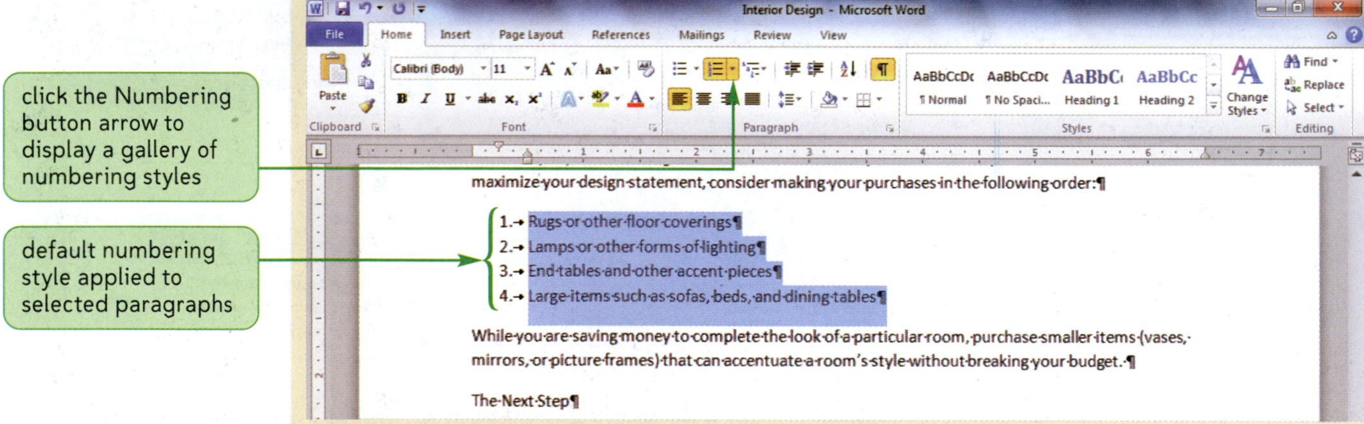

3. Click anywhere in the document to deselect the numbered list and save the document.

Just as with the Bullets button arrow, you can click the Numbering button arrow and then select from a gallery of numbering styles. For example, you could choose a style with Roman numerals or letters instead of the Arabic letters applied to the list in Figure 2-4.

Moving Text in a Document

One of the most useful features of a word-processing program is the ability to move text easily. For example, Natalie wants to reorder the information in four paragraphs on page 2. You could reorder the paragraphs by deleting a paragraph item and then retyping it at a new location, but it's easier to select and then move the text. Word provides several ways to move text: drag and drop, cut and paste, and copy and paste.

Dragging and Dropping Text

To move text with **drag and drop**, you select the text you want to move, press and hold the mouse button while you drag the selected text to a new location, and then release the mouse button.

In the numbered list you just created, Natalie wants you to move the paragraph that reads "Rugs and other floor coverings" down, so it is the third item in the list. You'll use the drag-and-drop method to drag this paragraph to the beginning of the fourth paragraph in the list. The fourth paragraph will then move down, making room for the new third paragraph. In the process, you'll see the advantage of using a numbered list, which automatically adjusts the numbering.

To move text using drag and drop:

1. Select the first paragraph in the numbered list, **Rugs and other floor coverings**, being sure to include the paragraph marker at the end. The number "1" remains unselected, because it's not actually part of the paragraph text.
2. Position the pointer over the selected text. The pointer changes to a left-facing arrow.
3. Press and hold the mouse button until the drag-and-drop pointer appears. Note that a dotted insertion point appears within the selected text. (You may have to move the mouse pointer slightly left or right to see the drag-and-drop pointer or the dotted insertion point.)
4. Without releasing the mouse button, drag the selected text down until the dotted insertion point is positioned to the left of the "L" in "Large items such as..." in the fourth item of the list. Make sure you use the dotted insertion point, rather than the mouse pointer, to guide the text to its new location. The dotted insertion point indicates exactly where the text will appear when you release the mouse button. See Figure 2-5.

   Trouble? If the numbers in the numbered list appear highlighted in gray, you moved the mouse pointer too close to the numbers. Ignore the highlighting, and position the dotted insertion point just to the left of the "L" in Large items such as...."

Figure 2-5 Moving text with drag-and-drop pointer

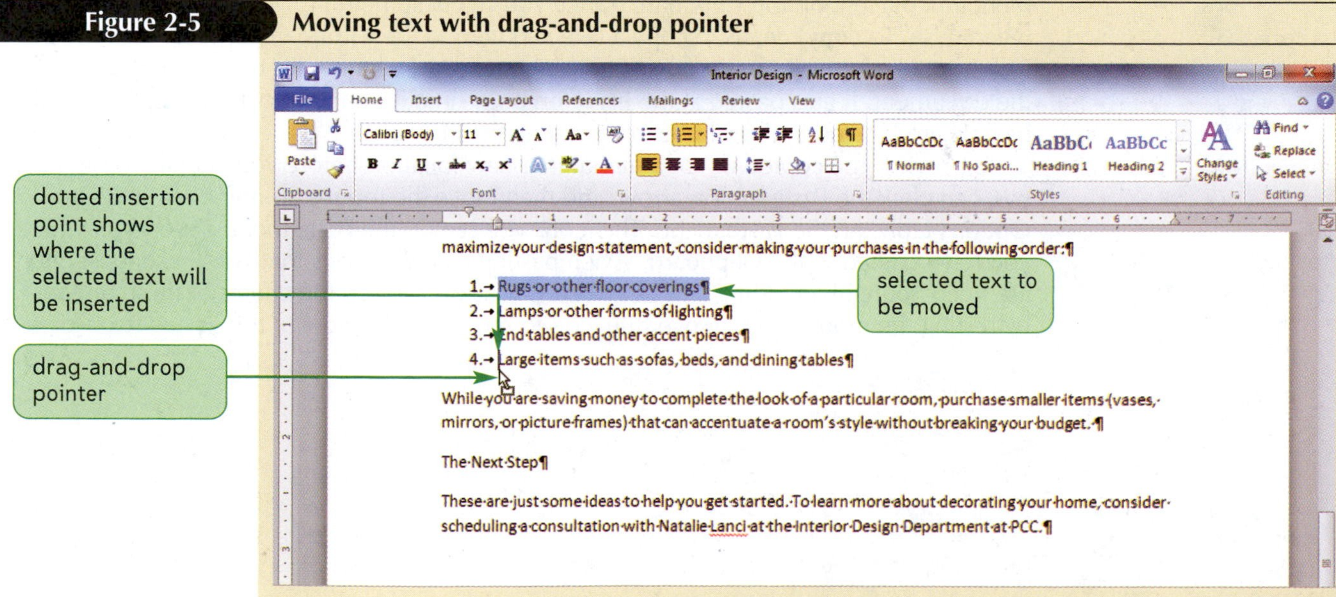

5. Release the mouse button, and then click a blank area of the document to deselect the text. As shown in Figure 2-6, the text is moved to its new location, numbered as paragraph 3, and the preceding paragraphs have been renumbered as paragraphs 1 and 2. The Paste Options button appears near the newly inserted text, providing access to more advanced options related to pasting text. You don't need to use the Paste Options button right now; it will disappear when you start performing another task.

Figure 2-6 Text in new location

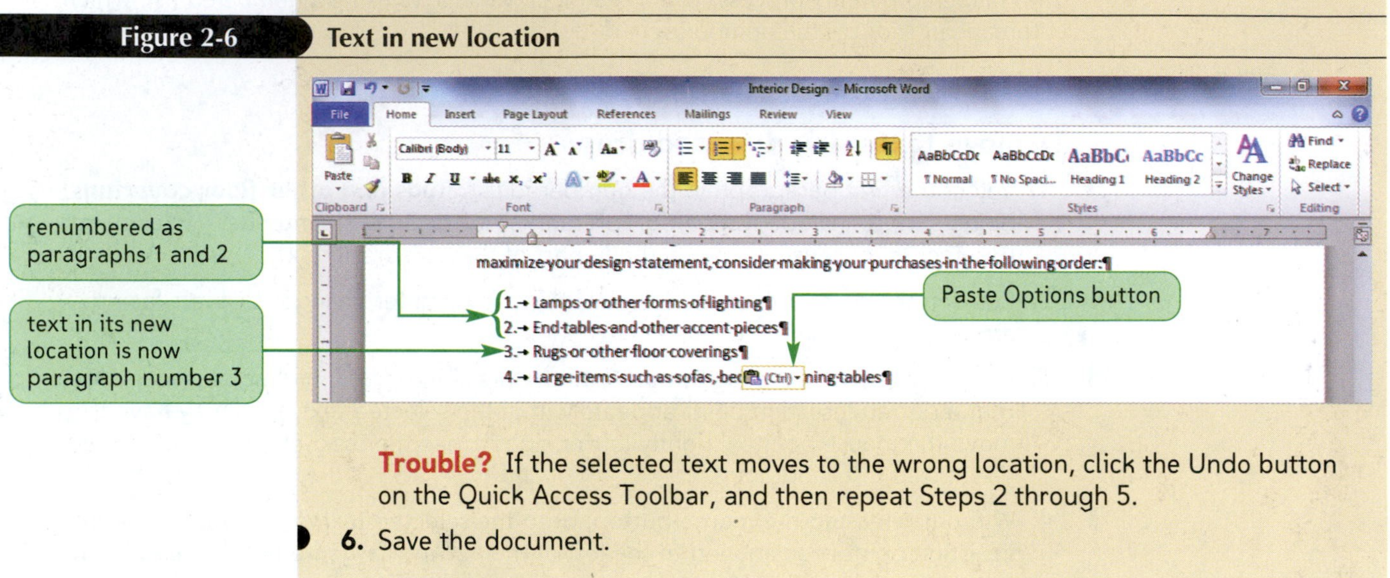

Trouble? If the selected text moves to the wrong location, click the Undo button on the Quick Access Toolbar, and then repeat Steps 2 through 5.

6. Save the document.

Dragging and dropping works well when you are moving text a short distance. When you are moving text from one page to another, it's easier to cut, copy, and paste text using the Clipboard.

Cutting or Copying and Pasting Text using the Clipboard

The **Clipboard** is a temporary storage area on your computer that holds objects such as text or graphics until you need them. To **cut** means to remove something from a document and place it on the Clipboard. Once you've cut something, you can paste it somewhere else. To **copy** means to copy a selected item to the Clipboard, leaving the item in its original location. To **paste** means to insert a copy of whatever is on the Clipboard into the document; it gets pasted at the insertion point. The buttons for cutting, copying, and pasting are located in the Clipboard group on the Home tab.

To preview the copied or cut material in a new location before you actually paste it, you can click the Paste button arrow, and then move the mouse pointer over the Paste Options icons on the Paste menu. The icons you see on the Paste menu depend on what you have copied to the Clipboard. When pasting text, the icons that you'll use most often are Keep Source Formatting and Keep Text Only. You can see the effects of these buttons by resting the mouse pointer over the icon to see a Live Preview of the pasted text. To actually paste the item, click the appropriate Paste Option icon on the menu. The Keep Source Formatting option allows you to retain the formatting that the copied or cut item had in its original location. The Keep Text Only option inserts the text using the formatting of the surrounding text in the new location. Note that when you paste an item from the Clipboard into a document, the item also remains on the Clipboard so you can paste it again somewhere else if you want.

REFERENCE

Cutting (or Copying) and Pasting Text

- Select the text or graphic you want to cut or copy.
- To remove the text or graphic, click the Cut button in the Clipboard group on the Home tab, or to copy, click the Copy button in the Clipboard group on the Home tab.
- Move the insertion point to the target location in the document.
- To insert the copied item at the insertion point, click the Paste button in the Clipboard group on the Home tab.
- To select options for how the copied or cut item will paste, click the Paste Options button arrow, and then click the appropriate Paste Option icon on the menu.

When you need to keep track of multiple pieces of cut or copied text, it's helpful to open the **Clipboard task pane**, which displays the contents of the Clipboard. You open the Clipboard task pane by clicking the Dialog Box Launcher in the Clipboard group on the Home tab. When the Clipboard task pane is not displayed, the Clipboard can hold only one item at a time. (Each newly copied item replaces the current contents of the Clipboard.) However, when the Clipboard task pane is displayed, the Clipboard can store up to 24 text items. The last item cut or copied to the Clipboard is the first item listed in the Clipboard task pane.

Natalie would like to move the first sentence in the paragraph under the heading "Ask Yourself Some Questions." You'll use cut and paste to move this sentence to a new location.

To move text using cut and paste:

1. Scroll up until you can see the paragraph below the heading "Ask Yourself Some Questions" on page 1.
2. Just below the heading, select the sentence **Of course, you probably won't be able to redo every room in your house from top to bottom according to your chosen style**. Make sure that you also select the space at the end of the sentence.
3. In the Clipboard group on the Home tab, click the **Cut** button. The selected text is removed from the document.
4. Scroll down to page 2, and click at the beginning of the first line on the page, just to the left of "F" in "For most people...."

TIP

You can also press Ctrl+X to cut selected text, and press Ctrl+V to paste the most recent copied item.

5. In the Clipboard group, click the **Paste** button. The sentence appears in its new location. The Paste Options button appears near the newly inserted sentence, as shown in Figure 2-7.

   Trouble? If a menu opens below the Paste button, you clicked the Paste button arrow instead of the Paste button. Press the Esc key to close the menu, and then repeat Step 5, taking care not to click the arrow below the Paste button.

   Trouble? If a wavy red underline appears below the text "style.For," you did not select the space after the sentence in Step 4. Press the spacebar to insert a space after the newly inserted sentence.

Figure 2-7 Sentence pasted in new location

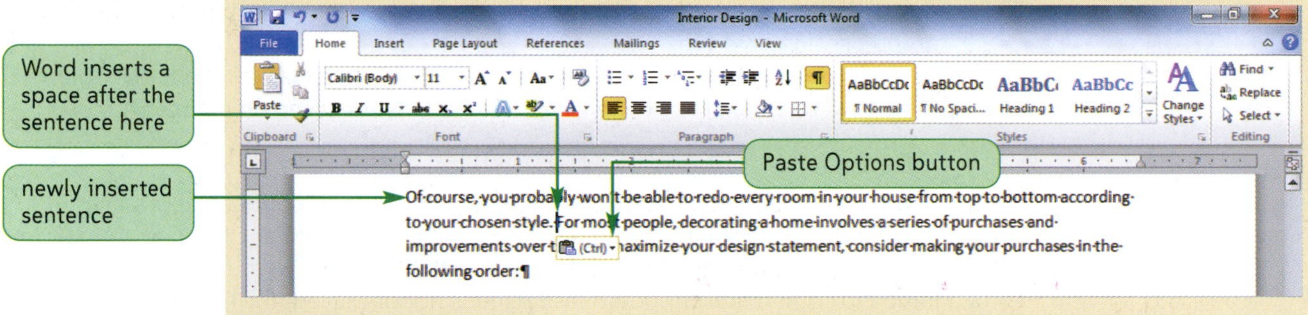

Natalie mentions that she'll be using two sentences from the Interior Design document as the basis for another assignment in her Interior Design class. She asks you to copy that information and paste it into a new document. You can do this using the Clipboard task pane.

To copy and paste text into a new document:

1. In the Clipboard group, click the **Dialog Box Launcher**. The Clipboard task pane opens on the left side of the document window, as shown in Figure 2-8. The document zooms out so that you can still see the full width of the page, even though the Clipboard task pane is open. Notice the Clipboard contains the sentence you copied to the Clipboard in the last set of steps, although you can only see the first part of the sentence. You can delete this because you do not need to paste it again elsewhere in the document.

Figure 2-8 Clipboard task pane

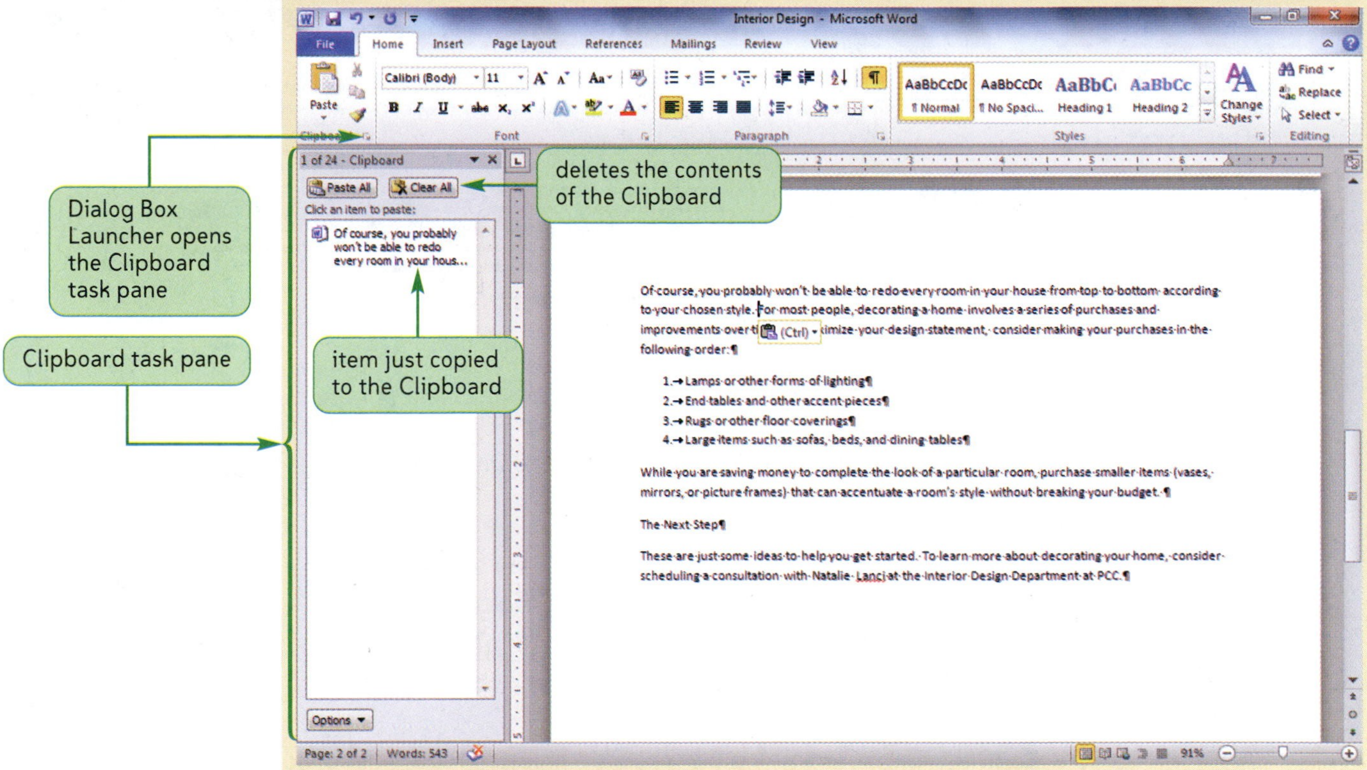

Dialog Box Launcher opens the Clipboard task pane

Clipboard task pane

deletes the contents of the Clipboard

item just copied to the Clipboard

- **2.** Click the **Clear All** button in the task pane. The current contents of the Clipboard are deleted, and you see the following message on the Clipboard task pane: "Clipboard empty. Copy or cut to collect items."
- **3.** In the paragraph above the numbered list, press and hold the **Ctrl** key and then click anywhere in the sentence **For most people, decorating a home involves a series of purchases and improvements over time.** The sentence and the space following it are selected.
- **4.** In the Clipboard group, click the **Copy** button. Only the first part of the sentence appears in the Clipboard task pane, but in fact the whole sentence is now stored on the Clipboard.
- **5.** Below the heading "Stay True to Your Style" (near the bottom of page 1) select the sentence **But if you are more interested in *living* in your house than decorating it, pick a style for a room and stick with it**.
- **6.** Click the **Copy** button. The sentence appears in the Clipboard task pane, as shown in Figure 2-9.

TIP

You can also copy selected text by pressing Ctrl+C.

Figure 2-9 Items in the Clipboard task pane

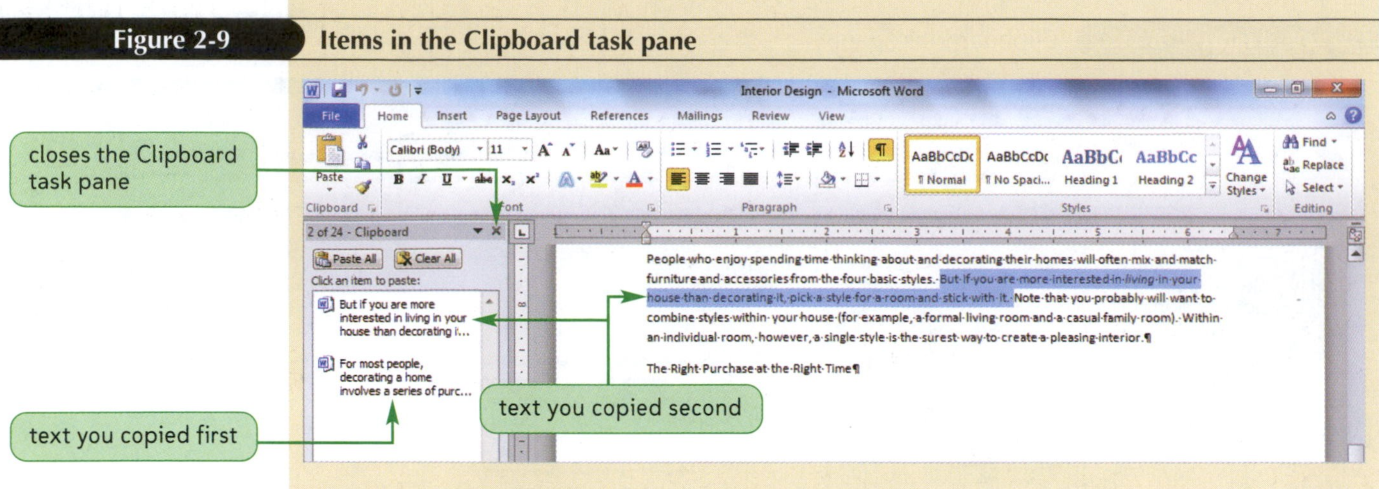

Now you can use the Clipboard task pane to insert the copied text into a new document.

To insert the copied text into a new document:

1. Click the **File** tab to open Backstage view, click the **New** tab, verify that **Blank document** is selected, and then click the **Create** button. A new, blank document opens.
2. In the Clipboard task pane, click the first item in the list of copied items, which begins "**But if you are more interested...**" The text is inserted in the document and the word "living" retains its italic formatting. However, Natalie decides she doesn't want to keep the italics in the newly pasted text. You can remove it by using the Paste Options button, which is visible just below the newly pasted text.
3. Click the **Paste Options** button (Ctrl) in the document. The Paste Options menu opens, as shown in Figure 2-10. The Keep Source Formatting button is selected by default; it tells Word to retain the text's original formatting when you paste it in a new location. That's exactly what happened in this case, when Word pasted the text with the word "living" italicized. To paste only the text, without the italics, you can click the Keep Text Only button.

TIP

To select a paste option before pasting an item, click the Paste button arrow in the Clipboard group on the Home tab, and then click the paste option you want.

Figure 2-10 Paste Options menu

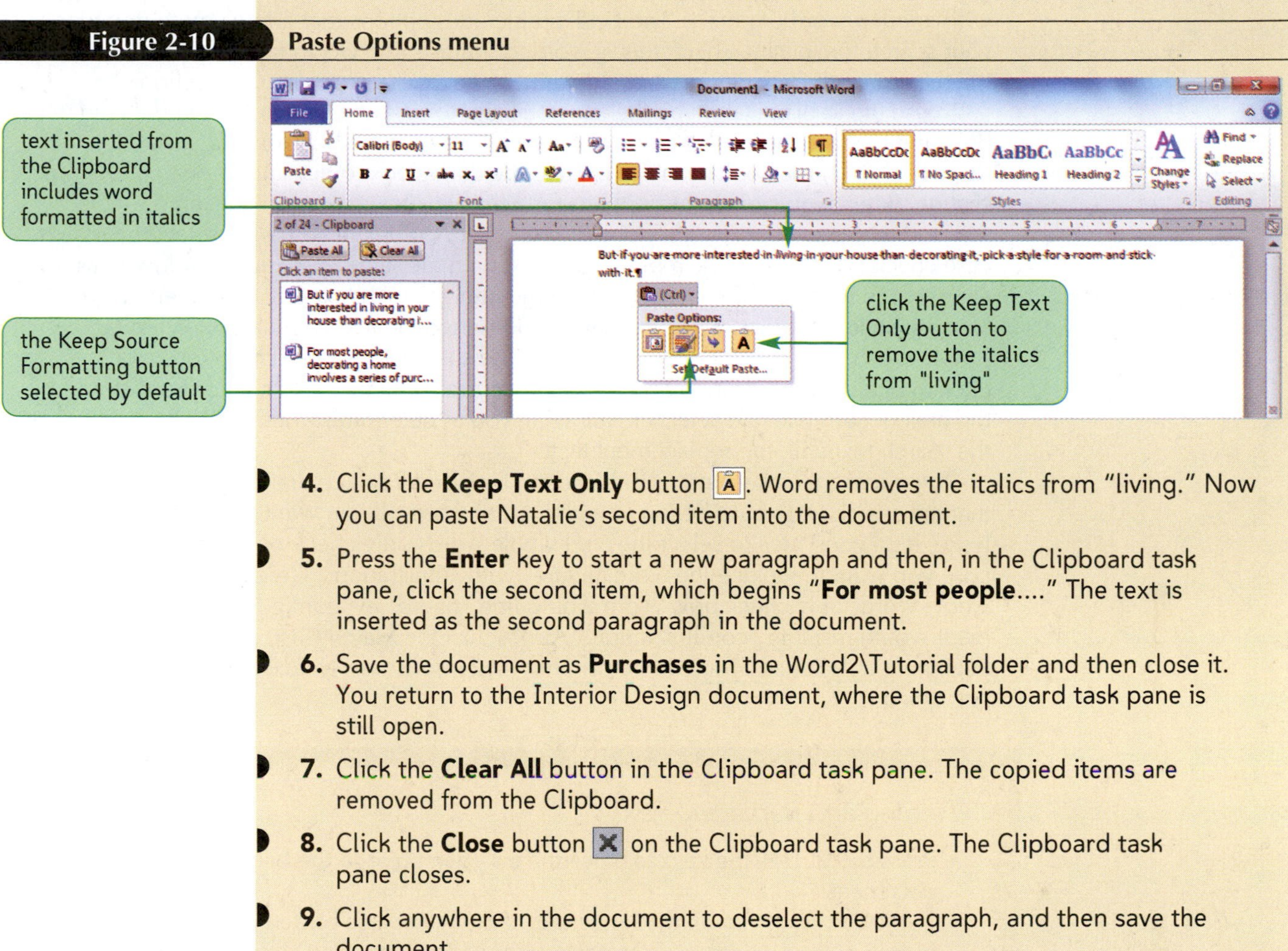
text inserted from the Clipboard includes word formatted in italics
the Keep Source Formatting button selected by default
click the Keep Text Only button to remove the italics from "living"

4. Click the **Keep Text Only** button [A]. Word removes the italics from "living." Now you can paste Natalie's second item into the document.
5. Press the **Enter** key to start a new paragraph and then, in the Clipboard task pane, click the second item, which begins "**For most people**...." The text is inserted as the second paragraph in the document.
6. Save the document as **Purchases** in the Word2\Tutorial folder and then close it. You return to the Interior Design document, where the Clipboard task pane is still open.
7. Click the **Clear All** button in the Clipboard task pane. The copied items are removed from the Clipboard.
8. Click the **Close** button [X] on the Clipboard task pane. The Clipboard task pane closes.
9. Click anywhere in the document to deselect the paragraph, and then save the document.

Finding and Replacing Text

When working with a longer document, you can waste a lot of time reading through the text to locate a particular word or phrase. It's more efficient to type the item you're searching for in the **Navigation Pane**. Word then highlights every instance of the search item in the document. At the same time, a list containing each instance of the search items (known as the **search results**) appears in the Navigation Pane. You can click a search result to go immediately to that location in the document. To open the Navigation Pane, click the Find button in the Editing group on the Home tab.

You can also find specific text using the **Find and Replace dialog box**, which you can open by clicking the Replace button in the Editing group on the Home tab. This dialog box contains three tabs, with the Replace tab displayed by default. The Replace tab provides options for finding a specific word or phrase in the document and replacing it with another word or phrase. The Find tab includes options that allow you to fine tune your search for specific characters, a word, or phrase. The Go To tab has options for moving the cursor to a specific part of a document, such as a page, line, or section.

To use the Replace tab, type the text you want to find (the **search text**) in the Find what box, and the text you want to substitute in the Replace with box. You can also click the More button on the Replace tab to expand the dialog box to display the Search Options section, where you can choose options for narrowing your search. For example, select the Find whole words only check box to search for complete words, or select the Match case check box to insert the replacement text with the same case (upper or lower) as in the Replace with text box. In that case, if the Replace with text box contained the words "English style," this would ensure that Word inserted the text with an uppercase "E".

Once you have specified the search text and specified any search options, you can click the Find Next button to find the next occurrence of the search text; Word stops at the next occurrence and selects it, allowing you to determine whether or not to substitute the search text with the replacement text.

When using the Navigation Pane and the Find and Replace dialog box, keep in mind that the search text might be found within other words. If you want to find a specific word, it's a good idea to select the Find whole words only check box. For example, suppose you want to replace the word "figure" with "illustration." Unless you select the Find whole words only check box, Word would find "figure" in "configure" and the replacement would result in "conillustration." Also, select the Match Case check box before beginning a search, so you can be certain Word inserts the replacement text exactly as you typed it.

REFERENCE

Finding and Replacing Text

- Press the Ctrl+Home keys to move the insertion point to the beginning of the document.
- In the Editing group on the Home tab, click the Replace button, or click the Find button in the Editing group on the Home tab, click the Find Options button in the Navigation pane, then click Replace.
- In the Find and Replace dialog box, on the Replace tab, click the More button if necessary to expand the dialog box and display the Search Options section.
- Type the characters you want to find in the Find what box.
- Type the replacement text in the Replace with box.
- Select the appropriate check boxes in the Search Options section of the dialog box to narrow your search.
- Click the Find Next button.
- Click the Replace button to substitute the found text with the replacement text and find the next occurrence.
- Click the Replace All button to substitute all occurrences of the found text with the replacement text, without reviewing each occurrence.

Throughout the document, Natalie wants to replace the initials "PCC" with the full school name, "Pembrooke Community College." You'll use the Find and Replace dialog box to make this change.

To replace "PCC" with "Pembrooke Community College":

1. Press the **Ctrl+Home** keys to move the insertion point to the beginning of the document.
2. In the Editing group on the Home tab, click the **Replace** button. The Find and Replace dialog box opens, with the Replace tab on top.
3. Click the **More** button in the lower-left corner of the dialog box to display additional search options.

   Trouble? If you see a Less button instead of the More button, the additional options are already displayed.
4. Click the **Find what** box, type **PCC**, press the **Tab** key, and then, in the Replace with box, type **Pembrooke Community College**.
5. Click the **Match case** check box to insert a check. This ensures that Word will insert the replacement text exactly as you have typed it in the Replace with box.
6. Click the **Find whole words only** check box to insert a check. Your Find and Replace dialog box should look like Figure 2-11.

Figure 2-11 Find and Replace dialog box

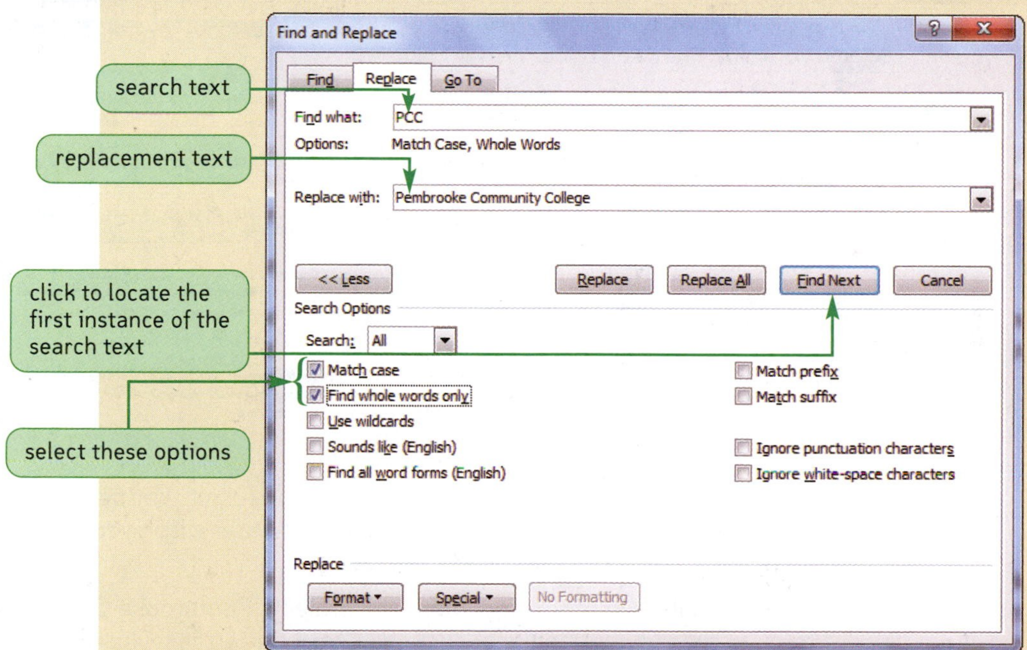

7. Click the **Find Next** button. Word highlights the first instance of "PCC" in the document.
8. Click the **Replace** button. Word replaces the first instance of "PCC" and then immediately jumps to the last line of the document, where the second instance of "PCC" is highlighted.
9. Click the **Replace** button. Word replaces "PCC" with "Pembrooke Community College" and then displays a message box telling you that Word has finished searching the document.
10. Click the **OK** button to close the message box, and then click the **Close** button to close the Find and Replace dialog box.

To quickly review the new instances of the full college name in the document, you can use the Navigation Pane.

To search for "Pembrooke Community College" in the document:

1. In the Editing group on the Home tab, click the **Find** button. The Navigation Pane opens on the left side of the Word window. The search text you entered when you used the Find and Replace dialog box is selected in the box at the top of the Navigation Pane. Instead of "PCC," you want to search for "Pembrooke Community College."
2. Type **Pembrooke Community College**. In the Navigation Pane, "PCC" is replaced by this new item. A list of search results containing two items appears in the Navigation Pane. In the document, the first instance of "Pembrooke Community College" is highlighted in yellow, as shown in Figure 2-12. To see the second instance, you can click the second search result in the Navigation Pane.

   Trouble? If the search results don't appear in the Navigation pane as shown in Figure 2-12, delete the search text you typed in Step 2, retype the search text, and then press the Enter key.

Figure 2-12 Navigation Pane with search results for "Pembrooke Community College"

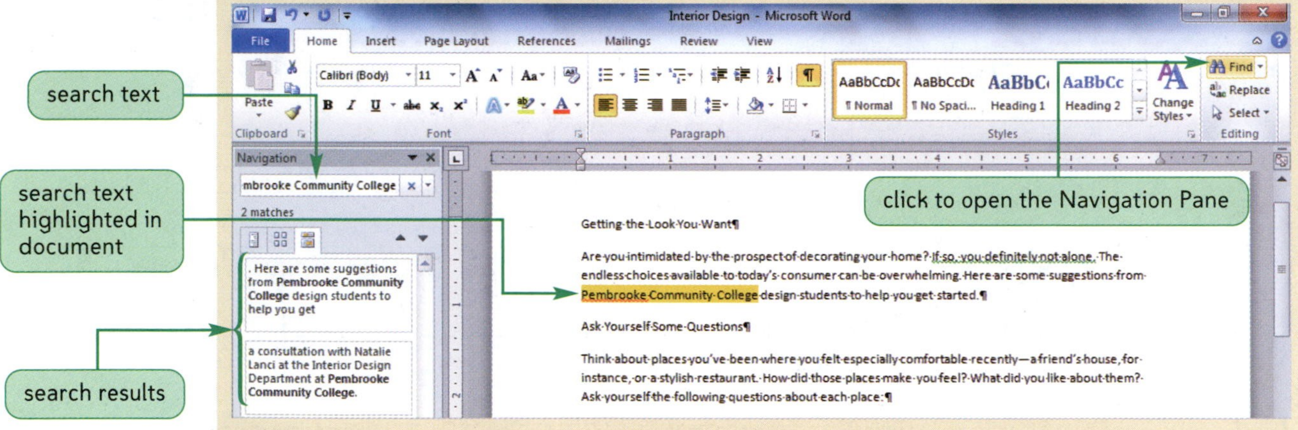

3. In the Navigation Pane, click the second search result that begins "a consultation with Natalie Lanci." The last line of the document is displayed, with the school name selected and highlighted in yellow.
4. Click a blank area of the document to deselect "Pembrooke Community College," then, in the Navigation Pane, click the **Close** button [X]. Closing the Navigation Pane removes the yellow highlighting from "Pembrooke Community College" in the document.
5. Save the document.

INSIGHT

Searching for Formatting

You can search for formatting using the Find and Replace dialog box in the same way that you can search for text. For example, you might want to check a document to see where you used bold formatting. To search for formatting, click the Format button located near the bottom of the Find tab of the Find and Replace dialog box, click the category of formatting that you want to look for (such as Font, Paragraph, Style, and so on), and then select the formatting you want to find.

You can also use the Replace tab to replace formatting in the same way you use it to replace text. To replace formatting, click the Replace tab in the Find and Replace dialog box, click the Format button, and click the category of formatting that you want to replace. You can look for formatting that occurs only on specific text, or you can look for formatting that occurs anywhere in a document. If you're looking for formatting on certain text (such as all instances of "Contemporary Furniture" that are bold), enter the text in the Find what box and then specify the formatting you're looking for. To find formatting on any text in a document, leave the Find what box empty and then specify the formatting.

The text of the document is finished. Now you need to proofread it and make sure it doesn't contain any spelling or grammar errors.

Using the Spelling and Grammar Checker

As you learned in Tutorial 1, the AutoCorrect feature in Word marks possible spelling and grammatical errors with wavy underlines as you type, so that you can quickly go back and correct those errors. Another, more thorough way of checking the spelling in a document is to use the **Spelling and Grammar Checker**, which checks a document word by word for a variety of errors. You start the Spelling and Grammar Checker by clicking the Spelling & Grammar button, located on the Review tab, in the Proofing group.

REFERENCE

Checking a Document for Spelling and Grammar Errors

- Move the insertion point to the beginning of the document, click the Review tab on the Ribbon, and then, in the Proofing group, click the Spelling & Grammar button.
- In the Spelling and Grammar dialog box, review any items highlighted in color. Possible grammatical errors appear in green, possible spelling errors appear in red, and words that are spelled correctly but possibly used incorrectly appear in blue. Review the suggested corrections in the Suggestions box.
- To accept a suggested correction, click it in the Suggestions box, and then click the Change button to make the correction and continue searching the document for errors.
- To skip the current instance of the potential error highlighted by the Spelling and Grammar Checker and continue searching the document for errors, click the Ignore Once button.
- Click the Ignore All button to skip all instances of the potential error and continue searching the document for errors. Click the Ignore Rule button to skip all instances of a highlighted error.
- To type your correction directly in the document, click outside the Spelling and Grammar dialog box, make the correction in the document, and then click the Resume button in the Spelling and Grammar dialog box.
- To add an unrecognized word to the dictionary, click the Add to Dictionary button.
- When a dialog box opens informing you that the spelling and grammar check is complete, click the OK button.

Use the Spelling and Grammar Checker to check the Interior Design document for mistakes.

To check the Interior Design document for spelling and grammatical errors:

Make sure the Spell Check begins at the start of the document.

1. Press the **Ctrl+Home** keys to move the insertion point to the beginning of the document, to the left of the "G" in "Getting the Look You Want."
2. Click the **Review** tab on the Ribbon. The Ribbon changes to display Reviewing options.
3. In the Proofing group, click the **Spelling & Grammar** button. The Spelling and Grammar: English (U.S.) dialog box opens, with a phrase displayed in green in the dialog box and that same phrase highlighted in blue in the document. The Suggestions box indicates that the highlighted text is a sentence fragment. The last part of the sentence should read "you definitely are not alone," but the verb "are" is missing. You can fix this error by clicking outside the Spelling and Grammar dialog box and typing the change directly in the document. See Figure 2-13.

Figure 2-13 Spelling and Grammar dialog box

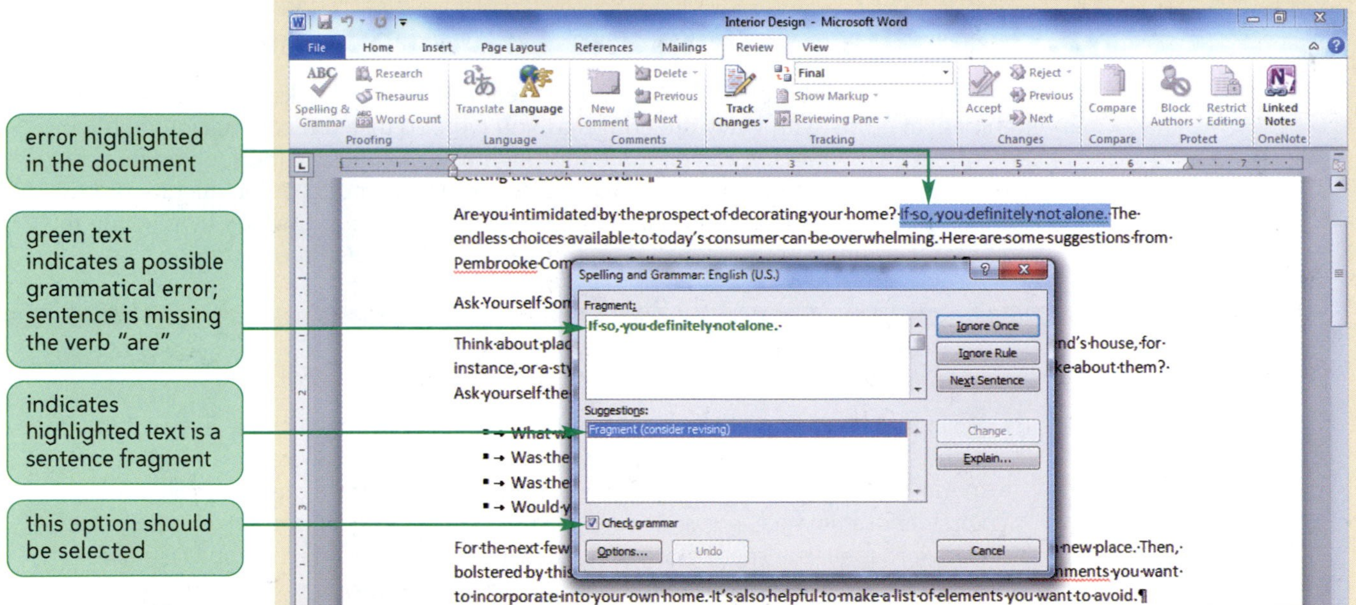
error highlighted in the document
green text indicates a possible grammatical error; sentence is missing the verb "are"
indicates highlighted text is a sentence fragment
this option should be selected

4. In the document, click the blue highlighted sentence **If so, you definitely not alone**. The blue highlight disappears, and the insertion point appears at the end of the sentence.

   Trouble? If you can't see the entire highlighted sentence, drag the dialog box to another location on the screen.

5. Click to the left of the "n" in "not," type **are**, and then press the **spacebar**. Verify that the last part of the sentence now correctly reads "you definitely are not alone." Now you can continue checking the document.
6. Click the **Resume** button in the Spelling and Grammar dialog box to continue checking the rest of the document. The word "Pembrooke" is displayed in red, indicating a possible spelling error. In the document, "Pembrooke" is highlighted in blue, with a wavy red underline. This isn't really an error.

TIP

If you want to check only for spelling errors, you can deselect the Check grammar check box.

7. Click the **Ignore All** button. Word ignores all instances of "Pembrooke" and continues checking the document. Next the word "you're" appears in blue in the Spelling and Grammar dialog box. In the document, the word is highlighted and has a wavy blue underline, indicating that it is spelled correctly, but used incorrectly. The correct choice, "your," appears in the Suggestions box.
8. Verify that "your" is selected in the Suggestions box, and then click the **Change** button. The Spelling and Grammar dialog box highlights the next error in the document, the misspelled word "elemments." The correct spelling, "elements," appears in the Suggestions box.
9. Verify that "elements" is selected in the Suggestions box, and then click the **Change** button. The Spelling and Grammar dialog box highlights "Lanci," Natalie's last name. You can ignore this, and then replace Natalie's name with your own after you are finished using the Spelling and Grammar checker.
10. Click the **Ignore Once** button. A message box opens indicating that the spelling and grammar check is complete.
11. Click the **OK** button to close the message box. You return to the Interior Design document.
12. In the last line of the document, replace "Natalie Lanci" with your first and last name, and then save the document.

PROSKILLS

Written Communication: Proofreading Your Document

Although the Spelling and Grammar Checker is a useful tool, there is no substitute for careful proofreading. Always take the time to read through your document to check for errors the Spelling and Grammar Checker might have missed. Keep in mind that the Spelling and Grammar Checker cannot pinpoint inaccurate phrases or poorly chosen words. You'll have to find those yourself. To produce a professional document, you must read it carefully several times. It's a good idea to ask one or two other people to read your documents as well; they might catch something you missed.

Now that the text is final, you will turn your attention to styles and themes, which affect the look of the entire document,

Working with Styles

A **style**, also known as a **Quick Style**, is a set of formatting options that you can apply by clicking its icon in the Quick Style gallery on the Home tab. Each style is designed for a particular use, with a name that reflects that use. For example, the Title style is intended for formatting the title at the beginning of a document.

All the text you type into a document has a style applied to it. By default, text is formatted in the Normal style, which applies 11-point Calibri font, left alignment, line spacing set to 1.15, and a small amount of extra space between paragraphs. In other words, the Normal style applies the default formatting you learned about when you first began typing a Word document.

Note that some styles apply **paragraph-level formatting**—that is, they are set up to format an entire paragraph, including changing the paragraph and line spacing. Other styles apply **character-level formatting**—that is, they are set up to format only a few characters or words (for example, formatting a book title in italics).

One row of the Quick Styles gallery is always visible on the Home tab. When you first open a document, the visible row contains the Normal, No Spacing, Heading 1, and Heading 2 styles. These all apply paragraph-level formatting, so to use one, you place the insertion point anywhere in the paragraph you want to format, and then click one of the visible styles. To access more styles, click the More button in the Styles group to display the entire Quick Styles gallery.

You will use a style to format the Interior Design document's title, at the top of page 1.

To format a title with a style:

1. Press the **Ctrl+Home** keys to position the cursor in the first line of the document, which contains the title "Getting the Look You Want."
2. In the Styles group on the Home tab, locate the More button in the Styles group, as shown in Figure 2-14.

Figure 2-14 **Locating the More button**

3. Click the **More** button. The Quick Styles gallery opens, displaying a total of 16 styles.
4. Point to (but don't click) the **Title style**, the first style in the second row of the gallery. The ScreenTip "Title" displays, and a Live Preview of the style appears in the paragraph containing the insertion point, as shown in Figure 2-15. The Title style inserts a blue line below the text, changes the font color to blue, and changes the font to 26-point Cambria.

Figure 2-15 **Title style in the Quick Styles gallery**

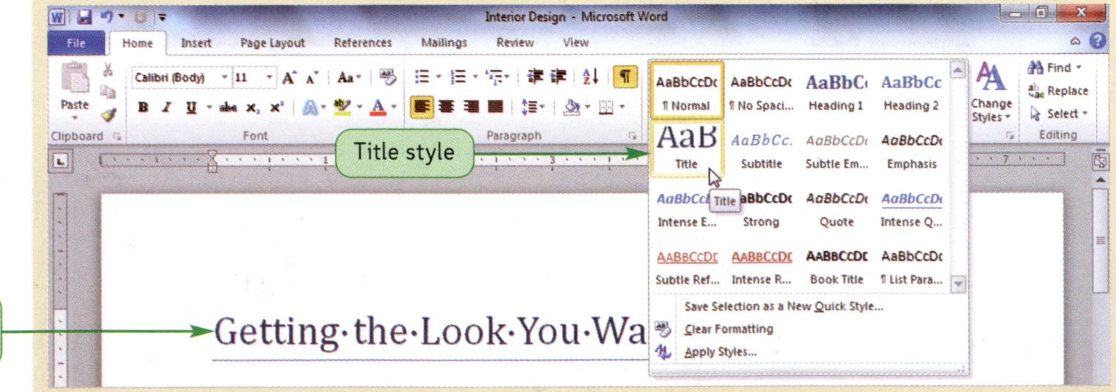

5. Click the **Title** style. The style is applied to the paragraph containing the heading "Getting the Look You Want." The row of styles visible in the Styles group on the Home tab now includes the Title style. Next, you need to center the document title.
6. Click the **Center** button in the Paragraph group on the Home tab. The title is centered in the document.

Next, you will format the document headings.

Working with Heading Levels

You can choose from different levels of heading styles. The highest level, Heading 1, is used for the major headings in a document and applies the most noticeable formatting, with a larger font than all the other heading styles. (In heading styles, the highest level has the lowest number.) The Heading 2 style is used for headings that are subordinate to the highest level headings; it applies slightly less dramatic formatting than the Heading 1 style.

The Interior Design handout only has one level of headings, so you will apply the Heading 1 style.

TIP

On most computers, you can press the F4 key to repeat your most recent action.

To format text with the Heading 1 style:

1. Click anywhere in the paragraph **Ask Yourself Some Questions**.
2. In the Styles group, click the **More** button to open the Quick Styles gallery, and then click the **Heading 1** style. The paragraph is now formatted in blue, 14-point Cambria, with bold. The Heading 1 style also inserts some paragraph space above the heading. The gallery row containing the Heading 1 style is now visible in the Styles group.
3. Scroll down, click in the paragraph containing the text **Pick a Style**, and then click the **Heading 1** style in the Styles group. The "Pick a Style" heading is formatted to match the other heading in the document.
4. Scroll down, click in the paragraph **Stay True to Your Style** at the bottom of page 1, and then apply the Heading 1 style.
5. Format the paragraphs "The Right Purchase at the Right Time," and "The Next Step" with the Heading 1 style, save the document, and then scroll up to review the document. See Figure 2-16.

Figure 2-16 Document with heading styles

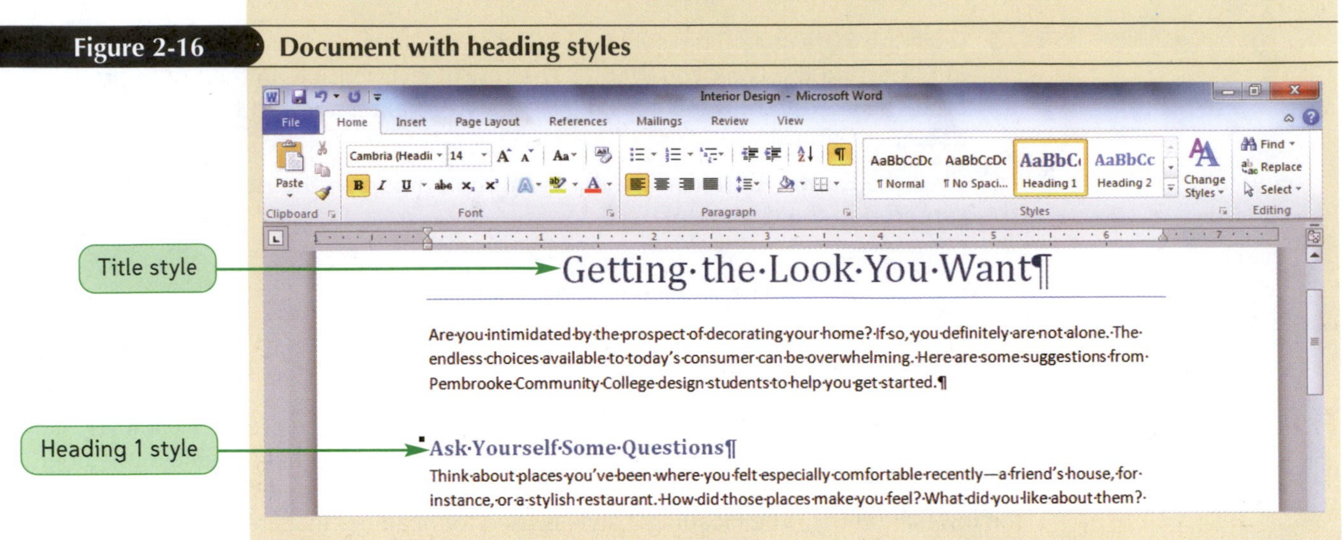

INSIGHT

Understanding the Benefits of Styles

By default, the Quick Style gallery offers 16 styles, each designed for a specific purpose. As you gain more experience with Word, you will learn how to use a wider array of styles. You'll also learn how to create your own styles. Styles allow you to change a document's formatting in an instant. But the benefits of heading styles go far beyond attractive formatting. Heading styles allow you to reorganize a document or generate a table of contents with a click of the mouse. Also, the heading styles are set up to keep a heading and the body text that follows it together, so a heading is never separated from its body text by a page break. Each Word document includes nine levels of heading styles, although only the Heading 1 and Heading 2 styles are available by default in the Quick Styles gallery. Whenever you use the lowest heading style on the Quick Styles gallery, the next lowest level is added to the Quick Styles gallery. For example, after you use the Heading 2 style, the Heading 3 style appears in the Styles group in the Quick Styles gallery.

After you format a document with a variety of styles, you can alter the look of the document by changing the document's theme.

Working with Themes

The document **theme** controls the variety of fonts, colors, and other visual effects available as you format a document. Forty-four different themes are included in Word, with each offering a coordinated assortment of fonts, colors, and text effects. Created by professional designers, themes ensure that a document has a polished, coherent look. When making formatting decisions, you often have the option of choosing a design element created for the current theme. For instance, when selecting a font color in Tutorial 1, you noticed that the colors on the Font Color palette are divided into Theme Colors and

Standard Colors. The Theme Colors are coordinated to look good together, so if you are going to use multiple colors in a document (perhaps for paragraph shading and font color), it's a good idea to stick with the Theme Colors.

When you open a new blank document in Word, the Office theme is applied by default. The Office theme is currently applied to the Interior Design document you are working on now, because Natalie has not changed the document's theme. To change the document's theme, click the Themes button, located in the Themes group on the Page Layout tab, and select the theme you want. The new theme is applied to the entire document and all the elements within it, with the colors and fonts changing to match the colors and fonts of the new theme.

When working with themes, you need to be aware of the difference between headings and body text. Natalie's document includes the headings "Ask Yourself Some Questions," "Pick a Style," "Stay True to Your Style," "The Right Purchase at the Right Time," and "The Next Step"—which you have now formatted with the Heading1 style. The title of the document, "Getting the Look You Want," is now formatted with the title style. Everything else in the Interior Design document is body text.

In order to ensure that your documents have a harmonious look, each theme assigns one font or font style for headings and one for body text. In some themes, the same font is assigned to each use. In the Office theme, the heading font is Cambria, and the body font is Calibri. These two fonts appear at the top of the Font list, as "Cambria (Headings)" and "Calibri (Body)" when you click the Font box arrow in the Font group on the Home tab. When you begin typing text in a new document with the Office theme, the text is by default formatted as body text with the Calibri font. If you change the document theme, the theme fonts in the Font list change to match the fonts for the new theme.

Figure 2-17 shows the heading and body fonts for two different themes.

Figure 2-17 **Office theme fonts and Newsprint theme fonts**

This is the Office theme's heading font, Cambria. This is the Office theme's body font, Calibri Office Theme	**This is the Newsprint theme's heading font, Impact.** This is the Newsprint theme's body font, Times New Roman. Newprint Theme

Each document theme is designed to convey a specific look and feel. The Office theme is designed to be appropriate for standard business documents. Other themes are designed to give documents a flashier look. Natalie thinks one of these more colorful themes might be appropriate for the Interior Design document. She asks you to apply the Opulent theme to it.

To change the document's theme:

1. Press the **Ctrl+Home** keys to move the insertion point to the beginning of the document. With the title and first heading visible, you will more easily be able to see what happens when you change the document's theme.
2. Click the **Page Layout** tab, and then in the Themes group, click the **Themes** button. The Themes gallery opens. See Figure 2-18.

Figure 2-18 **Themes gallery**

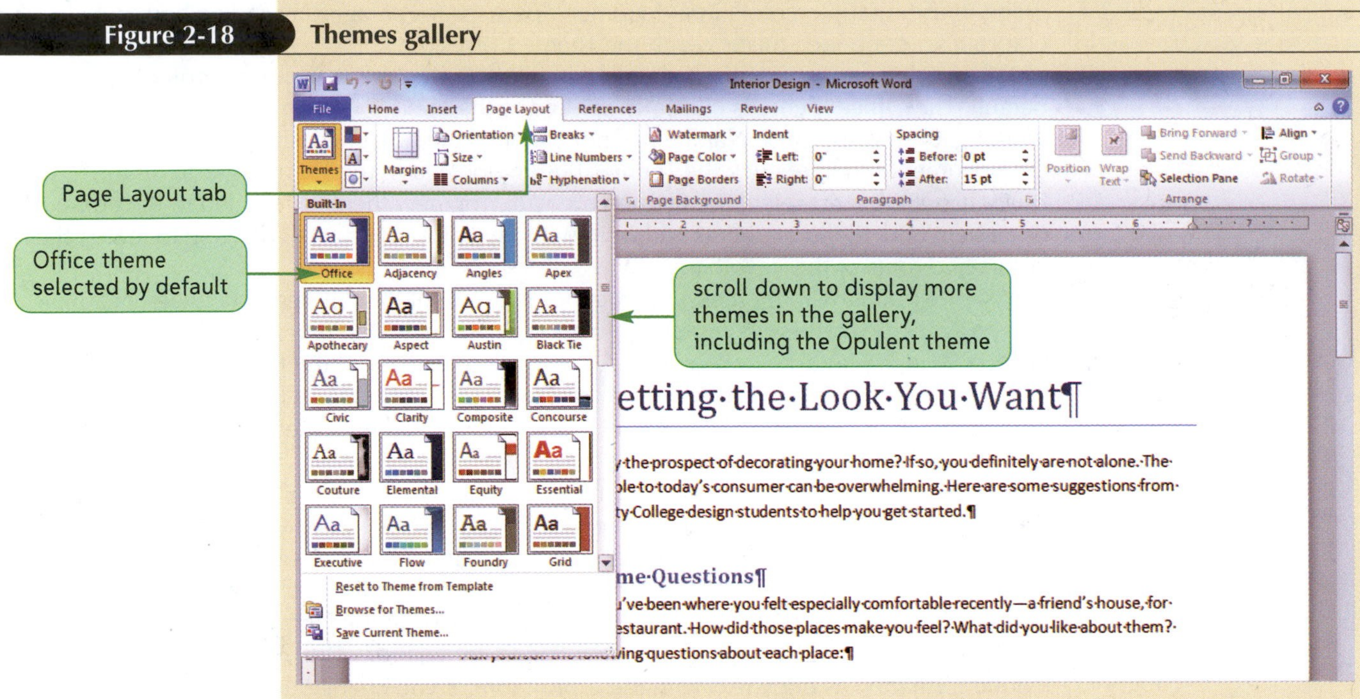

3. Move the mouse pointer (without clicking it) over the various themes in the gallery to see a Live Preview of each theme in the document. The heading and body fonts, and the heading colors, change to reflect the fonts associated with the various themes.
4. Scroll down the Themes gallery to see more themes, and then click the **Opulent** theme. The text in the Interior Design document changes to the body and heading fonts of the Opulent theme, with the headings formatted in purple. To see exactly what the Opulent theme fonts are, you can point to the Theme Fonts button in the Themes group.
5. Point to the **Theme Fonts** button [A] in the Themes group. A ScreenTip appears, listing the currently selected theme (Opulent), the heading font (Trebuchet MS), and the body font (also Trebuchet MS). These are the same two fonts listed at the top of the Fonts list on the Home tab. See Figure 2-19.

Figure 2-19 Fonts for the Opulent theme

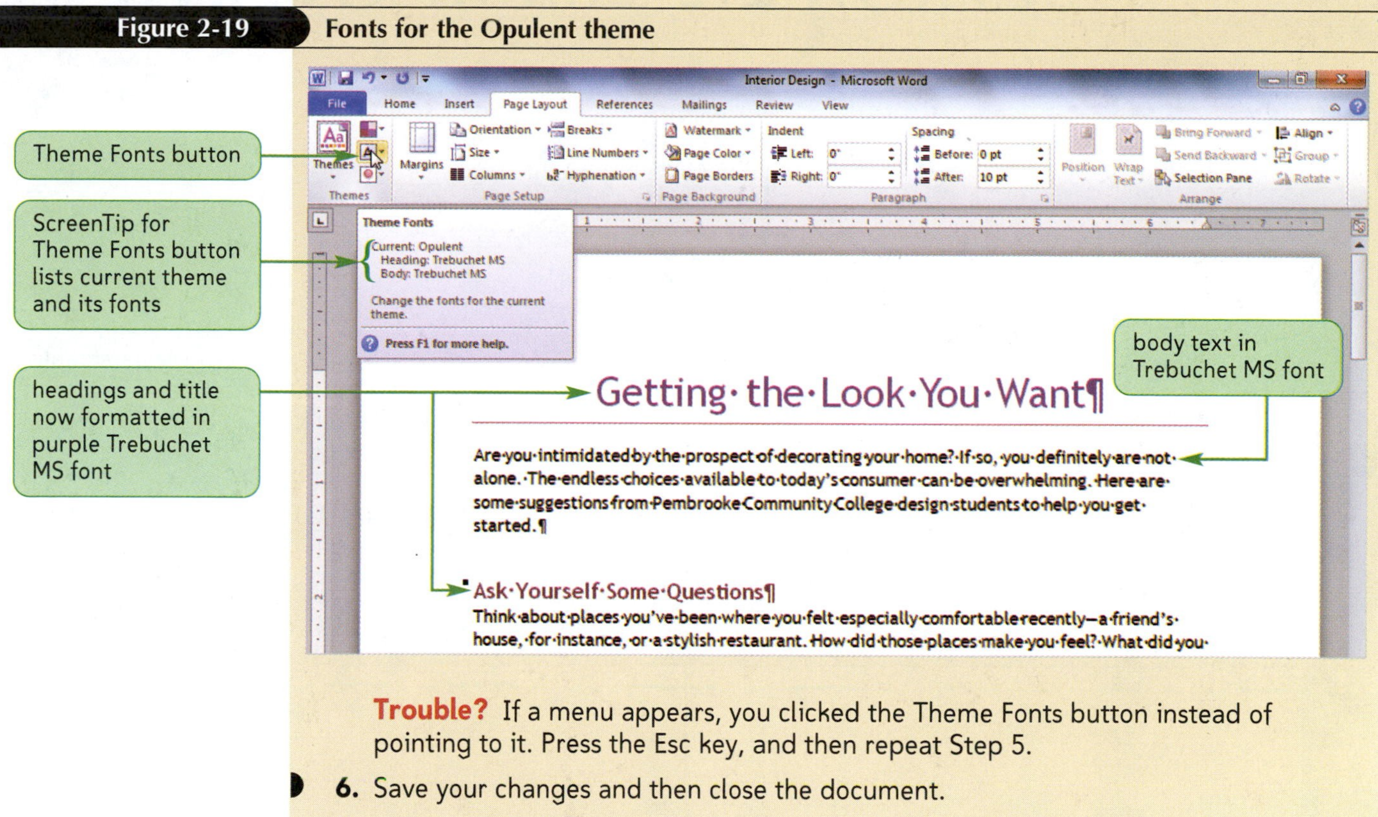

Trouble? If a menu appears, you clicked the Theme Fonts button instead of pointing to it. Press the Esc key, and then repeat Step 5.

6. Save your changes and then close the document.

Natalie's Interior Design paper is ready to be handed in to her instructor. The use of styles, bulleted and numbered lists, and a new theme give the document a professional look appropriate for use in an interior design studio handout.

REVIEW

Session 2.1 Quick Check

1. True or False. You should move the insertion point to the beginning of the document before starting the Spelling and Grammar checker.
2. Explain how to cut and paste text.
3. How can you ensure that Word will insert "ZIP code" instead of "zip code" when you use the Find and Replace dialog box?
4. What is a style?
5. True or False. All text in a document has a style applied to it.
6. Explain the relationship between a document's theme and styles.

SESSION 2.2 VISUAL OVERVIEW

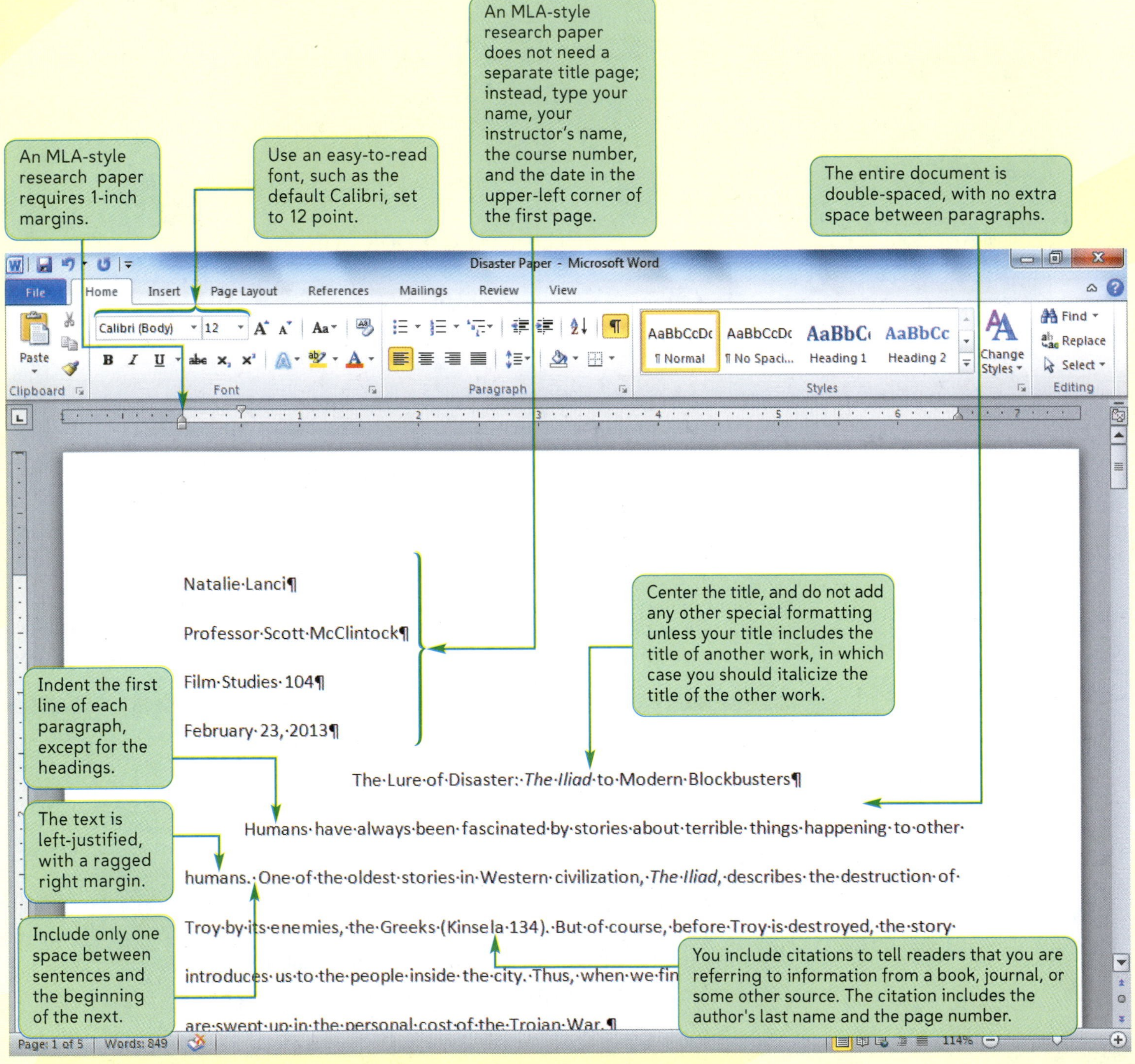

An MLA-style research paper requires 1-inch margins.
Use an easy-to-read font, such as the default Calibri, set to 12 point.
An MLA-style research paper does not need a separate title page; instead, type your name, your instructor's name, the course number, and the date in the upper-left corner of the first page.
The entire document is double-spaced, with no extra space between paragraphs.
Disaster Paper - Microsoft Word
File
Home
Insert
Page Layout
References
Mailings
Review
View
Paste
Clipboard
Calibri (Body)
12
Font
Paragraph
AaBbCcDc
¶ Normal
AaBbCcDc
¶ No Spaci...
AaBbC
Heading 1
AaBbCc
Heading 2
Styles
Change Styles
Find
Replace
Select
Editing
Natalie·Lanci¶
Professor·Scott·McClintock¶
Film·Studies·104¶
February·23,·2013¶
Center the title, and do not add any other special formatting unless your title includes the title of another work, in which case you should italicize the title of the other work.
Indent the first line of each paragraph, except for the headings.
The·Lure·of·Disaster:·*The·Iliad*·to·Modern·Blockbusters¶
The text is left-justified, with a ragged right margin.
Humans·have·always·been·fascinated·by·stories·about·terrible·things·happening·to·other·
humans.·One·of·the·oldest·stories·in·Western·civilization,·*The·Iliad*,·describes·the·destruction·of·
Troy·by·its·enemies,·the·Greeks·(Kinsela·134).·But·of·course,·before·Troy·is·destroyed,·the·story·
introduces·us·to·the·people·inside·the·city.·Thus,·when·we·fin
are·swept·up·in·the·personal·cost·of·the·Trojan·War.¶
Include only one space between sentences and the beginning of the next.
You include citations to tell readers that you are referring to information from a book, journal, or some other source. The citation includes the author's last name and the page number.
Page: 1 of 5
Words: 849
114%

MLA FORMATTING GUIDELINES

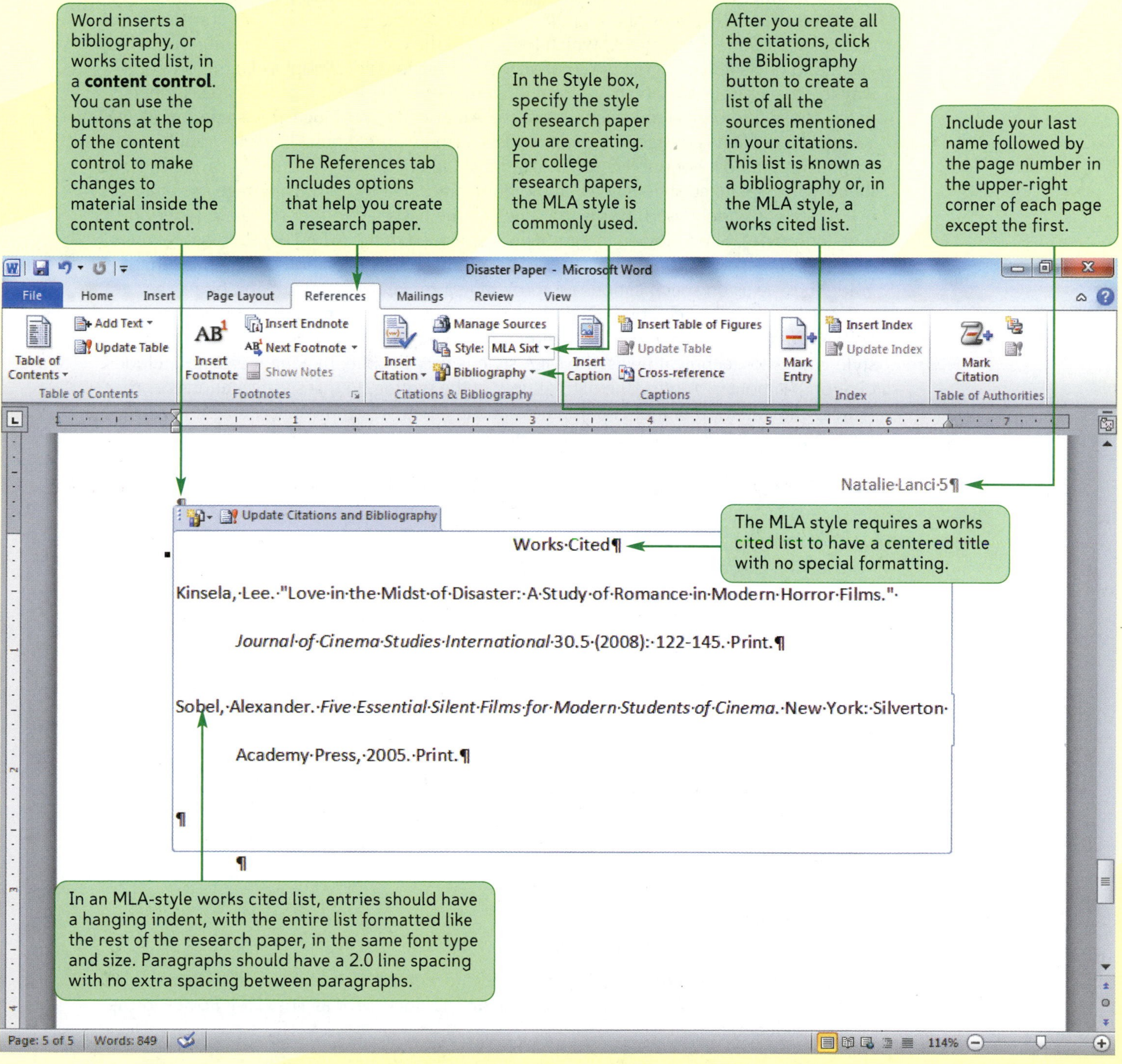
Word inserts a bibliography, or works cited list, in a **content control**. You can use the buttons at the top of the content control to make changes to material inside the content control.
The References tab includes options that help you create a research paper.
In the Style box, specify the style of research paper you are creating. For college research papers, the MLA style is commonly used.
After you create all the citations, click the Bibliography button to create a list of all the sources mentioned in your citations. This list is known as a bibliography or, in the MLA style, a works cited list.
Include your last name followed by the page number in the upper-right corner of each page except the first.
Disaster Paper - Microsoft Word
File Home Insert Page Layout References Mailings Review View
Add Text
Update Table
Table of Contents
Insert Endnote
Next Footnote
Show Notes
Insert Footnote
Footnotes
Manage Sources
Style: MLA Sixt
Bibliography
Insert Citation
Citations & Bibliography
Insert Table of Figures
Update Table
Cross-reference
Insert Caption
Captions
Mark Entry
Insert Index
Update Index
Index
Mark Citation
Table of Authorities
Natalie·Lanci·5¶
Update Citations and Bibliography
Works·Cited¶
The MLA style requires a works cited list to have a centered title with no special formatting.
Kinsela,·Lee.·"Love·in·the·Midst·of·Disaster:·A·Study·of·Romance·in·Modern·Horror·Films."·
Journal·of·Cinema·Studies·International·30.5·(2008):·122-145.·Print.¶
Sobel,·Alexander.·Five·Essential·Silent·Films·for·Modern·Students·of·Cinema.·New·York:·Silverton·
Academy·Press,·2005.·Print.¶
In an MLA-style works cited list, entries should have a hanging indent, with the entire list formatted like the rest of the research paper, in the same font type and size. Paragraphs should have a 2.0 line spacing with no extra spacing between paragraphs.
Page: 5 of 5 Words: 849 114%

Reviewing the MLA Style

A **style guide** is a set of rules that describe the preferred format and style for a certain type of writing. People in different fields use different style guides, with each style guide designed to suit the needs of a specific discipline. For example, journalists commonly use the *Associated Press Stylebook*, which focuses on the concise writing common in magazines and newspapers. In the world of academics, style guides emphasize the proper way to create **citations**, which are formal references to the work of others. Researchers in the social and behavioral sciences use the **American Psychological Association (APA)** style guide, which is designed to help readers scan an article quickly for key points and emphasizes the date of publication in citations. Other scientific and technical fields have their own specialized style guides. In the humanities, the **Modern Language Association (MLA)** style is widely used. This is the style Natalie has used for her research paper on disaster movies. She followed the guidelines specified in the *MLA Handbook for Writers of Research Papers*, published by The Modern Language Association of America. These guidelines focus on specifications for formatting a research document and citing the sources used in research conducted for a paper. The major formatting features of an MLA-style research paper are illustrated in the Session 2.2 Visual Overview. Compared to style guides for technical fields, the MLA style is very flexible, making it easy to include citations without disrupting the natural flow of the writing. In this style, citations of other writers take the form of a brief parenthetical entry, with a complete reference to each item included in the alphabetized bibliography at the end of the research paper.

INSIGHT

Formatting an MLA-Style Research Paper

The MLA guidelines were developed, in part, to simplify the process of transforming a manuscript into a journal article or a chapter of a book. The style calls for minimal formatting; the simpler formatting in a manuscript, the easier it is to turn the text into a published document. The MLA guidelines were also designed to ensure consistency in documents, so that all research papers look alike. Therefore, there should be no special formatting applied to the text in an MLA style research paper. Headings should be formatted like the other text in the document, with no bold or heading styles.

Natalie has started writing a research paper on disaster movies for her film history class. Next, you'll open the draft of her research paper, which is saved as a document named "Disaster," and determine what needs to be done to make it meet the MLA style guidelines for a research paper.

To open the document and review it for MLA style:

1. Open the document named **Disaster** located in the Word2\Tutorial folder provided with your Data Files, and then save the document as **Disaster Paper** in the same location.
2. Verify that the document is displayed in Print Layout view and that the rulers and nonprinting characters are displayed. Make sure the Zoom level is set to **Page Width**.
3. Review the document to familiarize yourself with its structure.

First, notice the parts of the document that already match the MLA style. Natalie included a block of information in the upper-left corner of the first page, giving her name, instructor, course name, and the date. The title at the top of the first page also meets the

MLA guidelines in that it is centered, and does not have any special formatting except for "The Illiad," which is italicized because it is the title of another work. Likewise, the headings ("Disasters in Silent Films," "World War II Cinema," "The First Modern Disaster Movies," and "The Seventies and Beyond") have no special formatting; but unlike the title, they are left-aligned. Finally, the body text is left-aligned with a ragged right margin, and the entire document is formatted in the same font, Calibri, which is easy to read.

Now what needs to be changed in order to make Natalie's paper consistent with the MLA style? Currently, the entire document is formatted using the default settings, in the Normal style for the Office theme. To transform it into an MLA-style research paper, you need to complete the checklist shown in Figure 2-20.

Figure 2-20 **Checklist for formatting a default Word document to match the MLA style**

- ✓ Double-space the entire document.
- ✓ Remove paragraph spacing from the entire document.
- ✓ Increase the font size for the entire document to 12 points.
- ✓ Indent the first line of each body paragraph .5 inch from the left margin.
- ✓ Add the page number (preceded by your last name) in the upper-right corner of each page. If you prefer, you can omit this from the first page.

You'll take care of the first three items in the checklist now.

To begin applying MLA formatting to the document:

1. Press the **Ctrl+A** keys to select the entire document.
2. In the Paragraph group on the Home tab, click the **Line and Spacing** button, and then click **2.0**.
3. Click the button again, and then click **Remove Space After Paragraph**. The entire document is now double-spaced, with no paragraph spacing, and the entire document is still selected.
4. In the Font group, click the **Font Size** arrow, and then click **12**. The entire document is formatted in 12-point font.
5. Click anywhere in the document to deselect the text.
6. In the first paragraph of the document, replace Natalie's name with your first and last name, and then save the document.

Now you need to indent the first line of each body paragraph.

Indenting a Paragraph

Word offers a number of options for indenting a paragraph. You can move an entire paragraph to the right, or you can create specialized indents, such as a **hanging indent**, where all lines except the first line of the paragraph are indented from the left margin. As you saw in the Session 2.2 Visual Overview, in MLA research papers all the body paragraphs (that is all the paragraphs except the information in the upper-left corner of the first page, the title, and the headings), have a first-line indent. Figure 2-21 shows some examples of other common paragraph indents.

Figure 2-21 **Common paragraph indents**

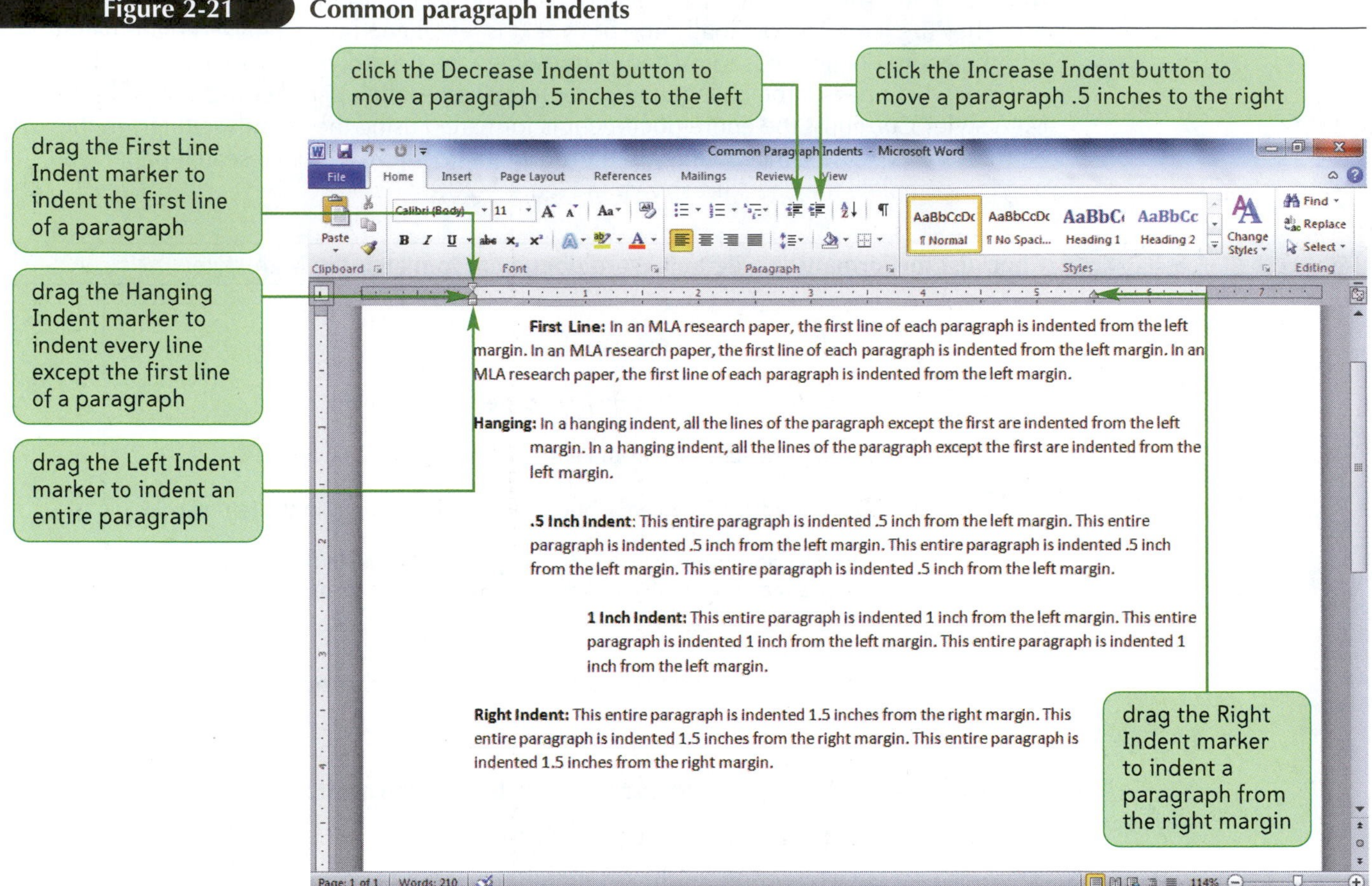

To quickly indent an entire paragraph .5 inch from the left, position the insertion point in the paragraph you want to indent and then click the Increase Indent button in the Paragraph group on the Home tab. You can continue to indent the paragraph in increments of .5 inches by repeatedly clicking the Increase Indent button. To move an indented paragraph back to the left .5 inch, click the Decrease Indent button.

To create first line, hanging, or right indents, you can use the indent markers on the ruler. First, click in the paragraph you want to indent, or select multiple paragraphs. Then drag the appropriate indent marker to the left or right on the horizontal ruler. The indent markers are small and can be hard to see. As shown in Figure 2-21, the **First Line Indent marker** looks like the top half of an hour glass; the **Hanging Indent marker** looks like the bottom half. The square below the Hanging Indent marker is the **Left Indent marker**. The **Right Indent Marker** looks just like the Hanging Indent marker, except that it is located on the far right side of the horizontal ruler.

TIP

You can also click in the paragraph you want to indent, or select multiple paragraphs, click the Dialog Box Launcher in the Paragraph group, and then adjust the Indentation settings.

Note that when you indent an entire paragraph using the Increase Indent button, the three indent markers, shown stacked on top of one another in Figure 2-21, move as a unit along with the paragraphs you are indenting.

In Natalie's Disaster paper, you will indent the first lines of the body paragraphs .5 inch from the left margin, as specified by the MLA style.

To indent the first line of each paragraph:

1. On the first page of the document, just below the title, click anywhere in the first main paragraph, which begins "Humans have always been fascinated...."
2. On the horizontal ruler, position the mouse pointer over the First Line Indent marker. When you see the ScreenTip that reads "First Line Indent" you know the mouse is positioned correctly.
3. Press and hold the mouse button as you drag the **First Line Indent** marker right to the .5 inch mark on the horizontal ruler. As you drag, a dotted vertical line appears over the document. You can use this line as a guide to align indents in a document. A dimmed version of the Left Indent marker remains in its original position until you release the mouse button. See Figure 2-22.

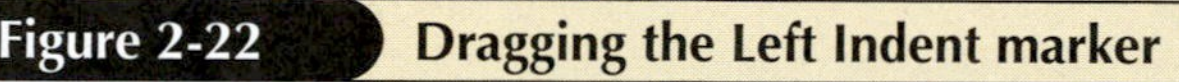

Figure 2-22 Dragging the Left Indent marker

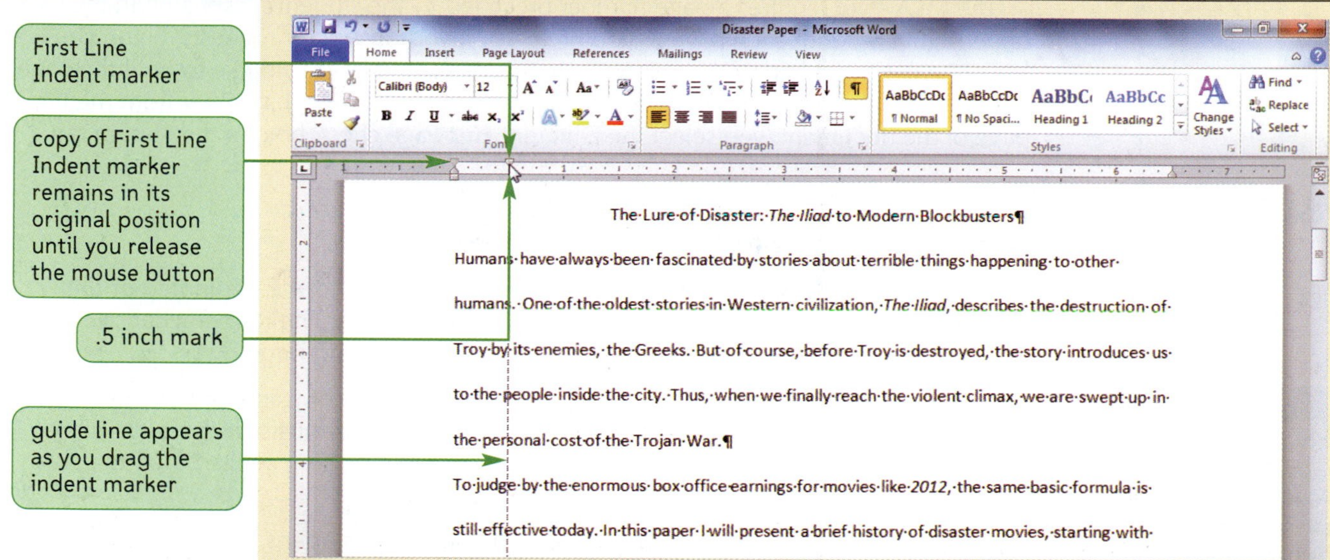
First Line Indent marker
copy of First Line Indent marker remains in its original position until you release the mouse button
.5 inch mark
guide line appears as you drag the indent marker
Disaster Paper - Microsoft Word
The·Lure·of·Disaster:·The·Iliad·to·Modern·Blockbusters¶
Humans·have·always·been·fascinated·by·stories·about·terrible·things·happening·to·other·
humans.·One·of·the·oldest·stories·in·Western·civilization,·The·Iliad,·describes·the·destruction·of·
Troy·by·its·enemies,·the·Greeks.·But·of·course,·before·Troy·is·destroyed,·the·story·introduces·us·
to·the·people·inside·the·city.·Thus,·when·we·finally·reach·the·violent·climax,·we·are·swept·up·in·
the·personal·cost·of·the·Trojan·War.¶
To·judge·by·the·enormous·box·office·earnings·for·movies·like·2012,·the·same·basic·formula·is·
still·effective·today.·In·this·paper·I·will·present·a·brief·history·of·disaster·movies,·starting·with·

4. When the Left Indent marker is positioned at the .5 inch mark on the ruler, release the mouse button. The marker remains in its new position and the vertical guide line disappears. The first line of the paragraph containing the insertion point indents .5 inch.
5. Click anywhere in the next paragraph in the document, which begins "To judge by the enormous box office earnings...", and then drag the First Line indent right to the .5 inch mark on the horizontal ruler. As you move the indent marker, you can use the vertical guide line as an extra check to make sure you match the first line indent of both paragraphs. You could continue to drag the indent marker to indent the first line of the remaining body paragraphs, but it's faster to use the Repeat button on the Quick Access toolbar.
6. Click in the paragraph below the heading "Disasters in Silent Films," and then click the **Repeat** button on the Quick Access toolbar.
7. Click in the next paragraph that begins "Personal dramas focus on," and then click the button.
8. Continue using the button to indent the first line of all the remaining body paragraphs.
9. Scroll to the top of the document, verify that you have correctly indented the first line of each body paragraph, and then save the document.

Next you need to insert page numbers.

Inserting and Modifying Page Numbers

When you insert page numbers in a document, you don't have to type a page number on each page. Instead, you insert a **page number field**, which is an instruction that tells Word to insert a page number on each page, no matter how many pages you eventually add to the document. Word inserts page number fields above the top margin, in the blank area known as the **header**, or below the bottom margin, in the area known as the **footer**. You can also insert page numbers in the side margins, although for business or academic documents, it's customary to place them in the header or footer.

After you insert a page number field, Word switches to Header and Footer view. In this view, you can add your name or other text next to the page number field, or use the Header & Footer Tools Design tab to change various settings related to headers and footers.

The MLA style requires a page number preceded by the student's last name in the upper-right corner of each page. If you prefer (or if your instructor requests it) you can leave the page number off the first page. In this case, Natalie would like to omit the page number from the first page of her research paper. To omit the page number from the first page of the document, you select the Different First Page check box on the Design tab.

TIP

To remove page numbers from a document, click the Remove Page Numbers command on the Page Number menu.

To add page numbers to the research paper:

1. Press the **Ctrl+Home** keys to move the insertion point to the beginning of the document, and then click the **Insert** tab on the Ribbon. The Ribbon changes to display the Insert options, including options for inserting page numbers.
2. In the Header & Footer group, click the **Page Number** button to open the Page Number menu. Here you can choose where you want to position the page numbers in your document—at the top of the page, the bottom of the page, the side margins, or at the current location of the insertion point.
3. Point to **Top of Page**. A gallery of page number styles opens. You can scroll the list to review the many styles of page numbers. Because the MLA style calls for a simple page number in the upper-right corner, you will use the Plain Number 3 style. See Figure 2-23.

Figure 2-23 Gallery of page number styles

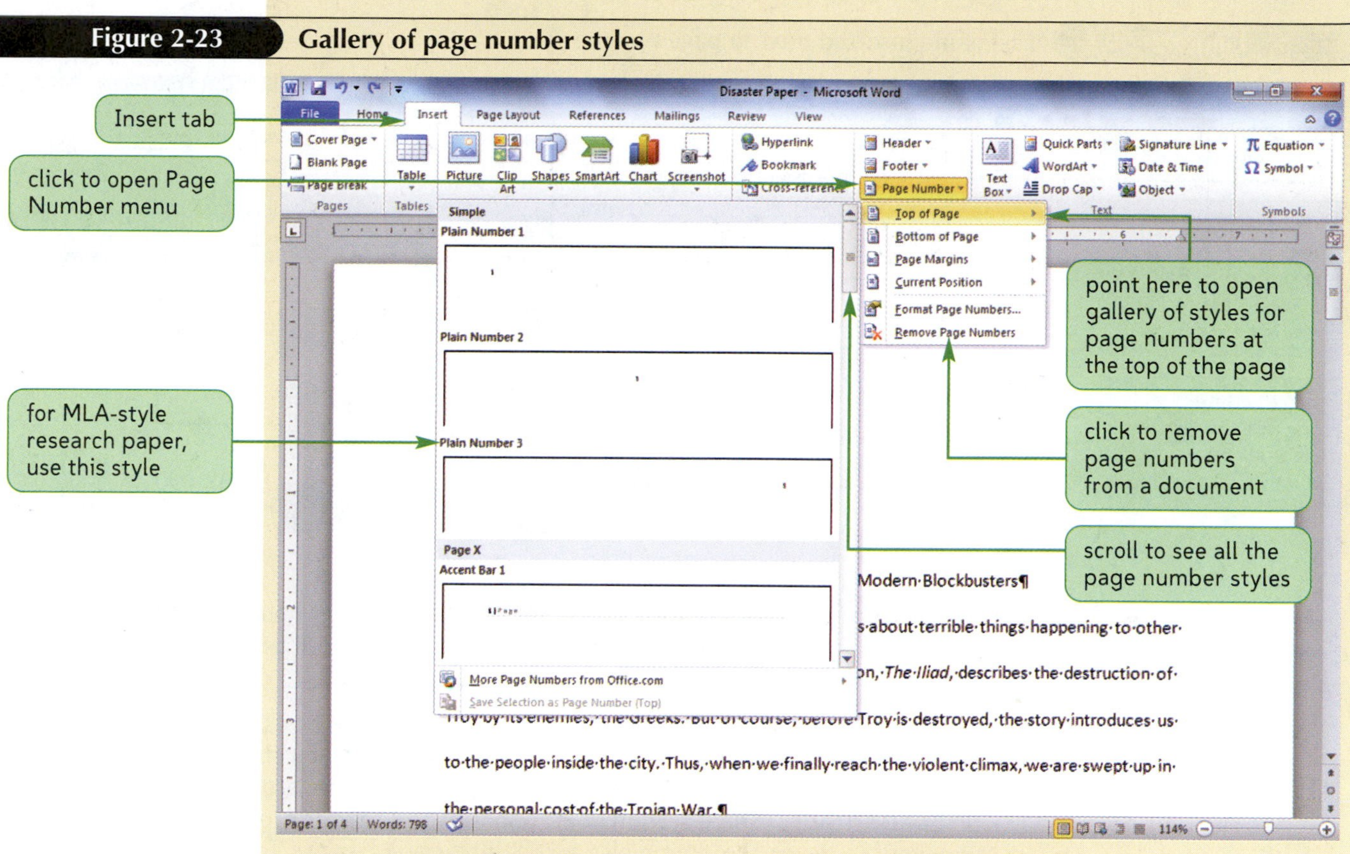

4. Click the **Plain Number 3** style. The Word window switches to Header and Footer view, with the page number for the first page in the upper-right corner. The page number has a gray background, indicating that it is actually a page number field and not simply a number that you typed. The Header & Footer Tools Design tab is displayed on the Ribbon, giving you access to a variety of formatting options. The insertion point blinks next to the page number field, ready for you to add text to the header if you wish. Note that in Header and Footer view, you can only type in the header or footer areas. The text in the main document area is a lighter shade of gray, indicating that it currently can't be edited.

5. Type your last name, press the **spacebar**, and then, if you see a wavy red line below your last name, right-click your name and then click **Ignore** on the Shortcut menu. See Figure 2-24.

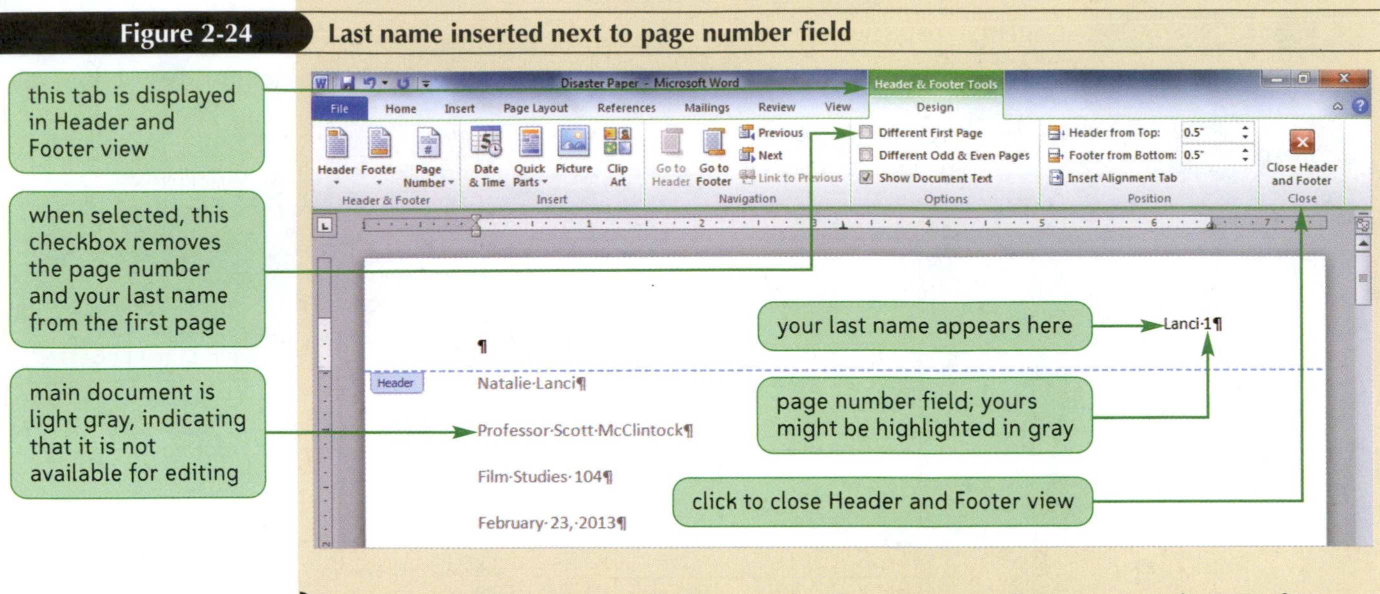

this tab is displayed in Header and Footer view
when selected, this checkbox removes the page number and your last name from the first page
main document is light gray, indicating that it is not available for editing
your last name appears here
page number field; yours might be highlighted in gray
click to close Header and Footer view
Header & Footer Tools
Design
Different First Page
Close Header and Footer
Header
Lanci·1¶
Natalie·Lanci¶
Professor·Scott·McClintock¶
Film·Studies·104¶
February·23,·2013¶

Figure 2-24 Last name inserted next to page number field

6. Scroll down and observe the page number (with your last name) at the top of pages 2, 3, and 4. As you can see, whatever you insert in the header on one page appears on every page of the document by default.
7. Scroll up, if necessary, so you can see the header on the first page, and then, on the Design tab in the Options group, click the **Different First Page** check box to insert a check. The page number field and your last name are removed from the first page header. The insertion point blinks at the header's left margin, in case you want to insert something else for the first page header. In this case, you don't.
8. On the Design tab, in the Close group, click the **Close Header and Footer** button. You return to Print Layout view, and the Header and Footer Tools Design tab no longer appears on the Ribbon.
9. Scroll down to review your last name and the page number in the headers for pages 2, 3, and 4. In Print Layout view, the text in the header is light gray, indicating that it is not currently available for editing.

TIP

After you insert a page number in a document, you can always reopen Header and Footer view by double-clicking the page number in Print Layout view.

You have finished all the tasks related to formatting the MLA-style research paper. Now Natalie wants your help in creating the essential parts of any research paper, the citations and bibliography.

Creating Citations and a Bibliography

A **bibliography** (or, as it is called in the MLA style, the **list of works cited**) is an alphabetical list of all the books, magazines, Web sites, movies, and other works that you refer to in your research paper. The items listed in a bibliography are known as **sources**. The entry for each source includes information such as the author, the title of the work, the publication date, and the publisher.

Within the research paper itself, you include a parenthetical reference, or **citation**, every time you quote or refer to a source. Every source included in your citations then has a corresponding entry in the works-cited list. A citation should include enough information to identify the quote or referenced material, so that the reader can easily locate the source in the accompanying works-cited list. The exact form for a citation varies, depending on the style guide you are using and the type of material you are referencing.

Some style guides are very rigid about the form and location of citations, but the MLA style offers quite a bit of flexibility. Typically, though, you insert an MLA citation at the end of a sentence in which you quote or refer to material from a source. For books or journals, the citation itself usually includes the author's last name and a page number. However, if the sentence containing the citation already includes the author's name, you only need to include the page number in the citation. Figure 2-25 provides some sample MLA citations for books and journals. For detailed guidelines, you can consult the *MLA Handbook for Writers of Research Papers, Seventh Edition*, which includes many examples.

Figure 2-25 **MLA Guidelines for citing a book or journal**

Citation Rule	Example
If the sentence includes the author's name, the citation should only include the page number.	Peterson compares the opening scene of the movie to a scene from Shakespeare (188).
If the sentence does not include the author's name, the citation should include the author's name and the page number.	The opening scene of the movie has been compared to a scene from Shakespeare (Peterson 188).

Word greatly simplifies the process of creating citations and a bibliography. You specify the style you want to use, and then Word takes care of setting up the citation and the list of works cited appropriately. Every time you create a citation for a new source, Word prompts you to enter the information needed to create the corresponding entry in the list of works cited. When you are ready, Word generates the bibliography automatically.

PROSKILLS

Written Communication: Acknowledging Your Sources

A research paper is a means for you to explore the available information about a subject and then present this information, along with your own understanding of the subject, in an organized and interesting way. Acknowledging all the sources of the information presented in your research paper is essential. If you fail to do this, you might be subject to charges of plagiarism, or trying to pass off someone else's thoughts as your own. Plagiarism is an extremely serious accusation, for which you could suffer academic consequences ranging from failing an assignment or even being expelled from school.

To ensure that you don't forget to cite a source, you should be careful about creating citations in your document as you type it. It's very easy to forget to go back and cite all your sources correctly after you've finished typing a research paper. If you do forget to cite a source, this could lead to accusations of plagiarism, and all the consequences that entails.

Creating Citations

Before you create citations, you need to select the style you want to use, which in the case of Natalie's paper is the MLA style. Then, to insert a citation, you click the Insert Citation button in the Citations & Bibliography group on the References tab. If you are citing a source for the first time, Word prompts you to enter all the information required for the source's entry in the bibliography or list of works cited. If you are citing an existing source, you simply select the source from the Insert Citation menu.

By default, an MLA citation includes only the author's name in parentheses. However, you can use the Edit Citation dialog box to add a page number. You can also use the Edit

Citation dialog box to remove, or suppress, the author's name, so only the page number appears in the citation. However, because Word will replace the suppressed author name with the title of the source, you need to suppress the title as well, by selecting the Title check box in the Edit Citation dialog box.

REFERENCE

Creating Citations

- Click the References tab, click the Bibliography Style button arrow in the Citations & Bibliography group, and then select the style you want.
- Click where you want to insert the citation. Typically, a citation goes at the end of a sentence, before the end punctuation.
- To add a citation for a new source, in the Citations & Bibliography group on the References tab, click the Insert Citation button, click Add New Source, enter information in the Create Source dialog box, and then click the OK button.
- To add a citation for an existing source, in the Citations & Bibliography group click the Insert Citation button, and then click the source.
- To add a page number to a citation, click the citation, click the Citation Options list arrow, click Edit Citation, type the page number, and then click the OK button.
- To display only the page number in a citation, click the citation, click the Citation Options list arrow, and then click Edit Citation. In the Edit Citation dialog box, select the Author and Title check boxes to suppress this information, and then click the OK button.

Natalie referenced information from two different sources when writing her research paper. You'll select a style and then begin adding the appropriate citations.

To select a style for the citation and bibliography:

1. Click the **References** tab on the Ribbon. The Ribbon changes to display references options.
2. In the Citations & Bibliography group, click the **Bibliography Style button arrow,** and then click **MLA Sixth Edition** in the list of styles if it is not already selected.
3. Click the **Home** tab, and then click the **Find** button in the Editing group to open the Navigation pane.
4. Use the Navigation pane to find the phrase "As at least one critic has observed," that appears on page 2 of the document, and then click in the document at the end of that sentence (between the end of the word "volcano" and the closing period).
5. Close the Navigation pane and then click the **References** tab. You need to add a citation that informs the reader which critic has made the observation described in the sentence. See Figure 2-26.

Figure 2-26 MLA style selected and insertion point positioned for new citation

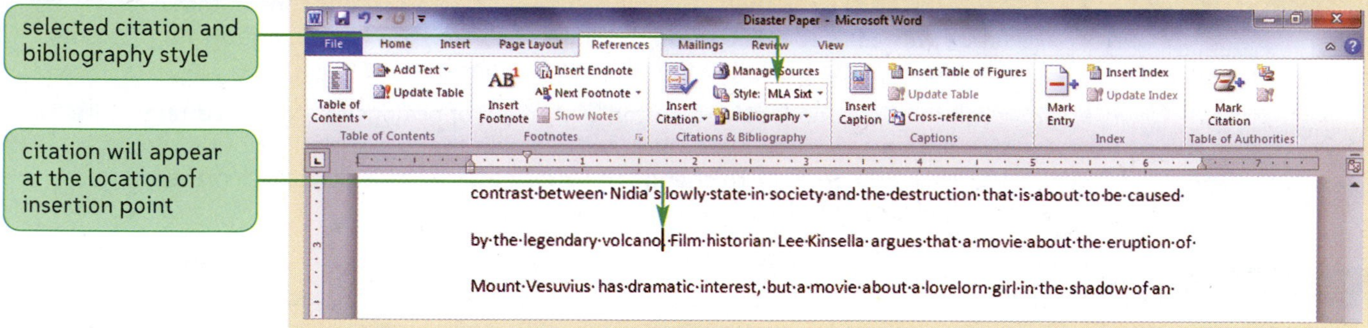

selected citation and bibliography style

citation will appear at the location of insertion point

contrast·between·Nidia's·lowly·state·in·society·and·the·destruction·that·is·about·to·be·caused·by·the·legendary·volcano.·Film·historian·Lee·Kinsella·argues·that·a·movie·about·the·eruption·of·Mount·Vesuvius·has·dramatic·interest,·but·a·movie·about·a·lovelorn·girl·in·the·shadow·of·an·

6. In the Citations & Bibliography group, click the **Insert Citation** button and then click **Add New Source**. The Create Source dialog box opens, ready for you to add the information required to create a bibliography entry for Alexander Sobel's book.
7. If necessary, click the **Type of Source** arrow and then click **Book**.
8. In the Author box, type **Alexander Sobel**.
9. Click in the **Title** box, and then type **Five Essential Silent Films for Modern Students of Cinema**.
10. Click in the **Year** box, and then type **2005**. This is the year the book was published. Next, you need to enter the name and location of the publisher.
11. Click in **City** box, type **New York**, click in the **Publisher** box, and then type **Silverton Academy Press**. See Figure 2-27.

Figure 2-27 Create Source dialog box with information for first source

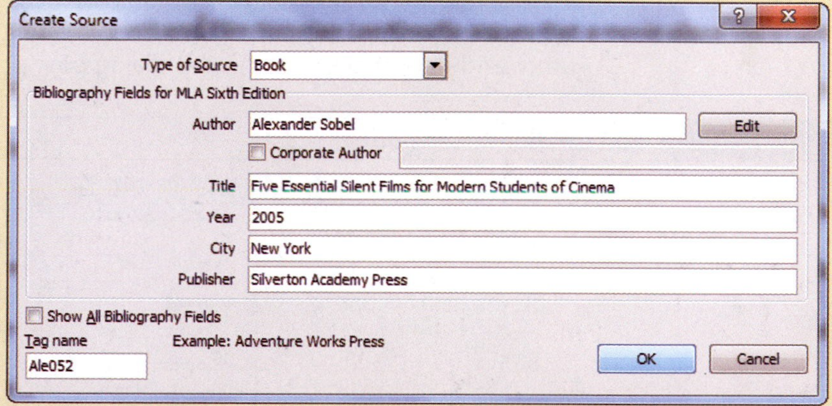

12. Click the **OK** button. Word inserts the parenthetical "(Sobel)" at the end of the sentence in the document.

Although the citation looks like ordinary text, it is actually contained inside a **content control**, a special feature used to display information that is inserted automatically and that may need to be updated later. You can only see the content control itself when it is selected. When it is unselected, you simply see the citation. In the next set of steps, you will select the content control, and then edit the citation to add a page number.

To edit the citation:

TIP

To delete a citation, click the citation to display the content control, click the tab on the left side of the content control, and then press the Delete key.

1. Click the citation **(Sobel)**. The citation appears in a content control that consists of a box with an arrow button on the right side, and, on the left, a tab with four dots. The arrow button is called the Citation Options button.
2. Click the **Citation Options** button. A menu of options related to editing a citation appears, as shown in Figure 2-28. To edit the information about the source, you click Edit Source. To change the information that is displayed in the citation itself, you use the Edit Citation option.

Figure 2-28 Citation Options menu

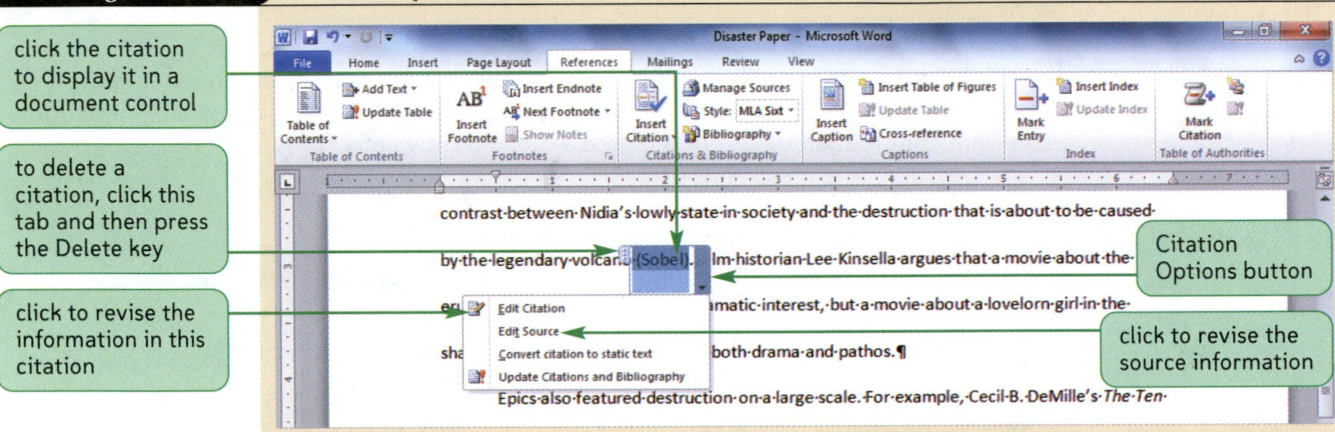

3. On the Citation Options menu, click **Edit Citation**. The Edit Citation dialog box opens, as shown in Figure 2-29. The insertion point appears in the Pages box, where you can add a page number for the citation. If you want to display only the page number in the citation (which would be necessary if you already mentioned the author's name in the same sentence in the text) then you would also select the Author and Title check boxes in this dialog box.

Figure 2-29 Edit Citations dialog box

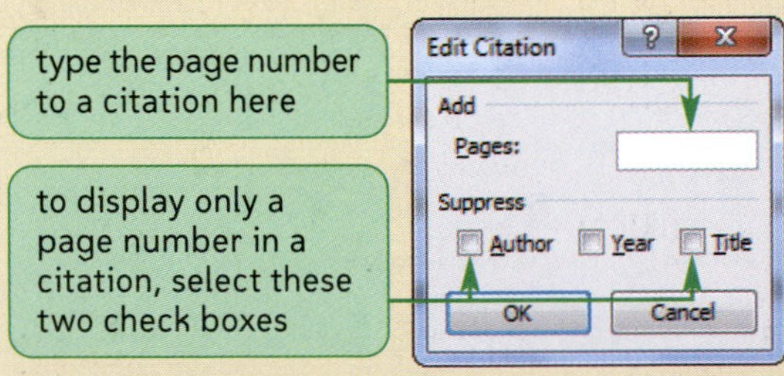

4. Type **45**, click the **OK** button, and then click anywhere in the document outside the citation content control. The revised citation now reads (Sobel 45).

Next, you will add two more citations, both for the same journal article.

To insert two more citations:

1. Move the insertion point to the end of the paragraph containing the Sobel citation, between the word "pathos" and the period ending the sentence. This sentence mentions film historian Lee Kinsella; you need to add a citation to one of her journal articles.
2. In the Citations & Bibliography group, click the **Insert Citation** button to open the Insert Citation menu. Notice that Alexander Sobel's book is now listed as a source on this menu. You could click Sobel's book in the menu to add a citation to it, but right now you need to add a new source.
3. Click **Add New Source** to open the Create Source dialog box, click the **Type of Source** arrow, and then click **Journal Article**. The Create Source dialog box displays the boxes, or fields, in which you need to enter information about a journal article. By default, Word displays text boxes for the information most commonly included in a bibliography. In this case, you also want to include the volume and issue numbers for Lee Kinsella's article, so you need to display more fields.

   Notice the information for citing a journal article differs from the information you entered earlier for the citation to the Sobel book. For journal articles, you are prompted to enter the page numbers for the entire article. If you want to display a particular page number in the citation, you can add it later.
4. Click the **Show All Bibliography Fields** check box to select this option. The Create Source dialog box expands to allow you to enter more detailed information. Red asterisks highlight the fields that are recommended, but they don't necessarily apply to every source.
5. Enter the following information, scrolling down to display the necessary text boxes:

   Author: **Lee Kinsella**

   Title: **Love in the Midst of Disaster: A Study of Romance in Modern Horror Films**

   Journal Name: **Journal of Cinema Studies International**

   Year: **2008**

   Pages: **122–145**

   Volume: **30**

   Issue: **5**

   When you are finished, your Create Source dialog box should look like the one shown in Figure 2-30.

Figure 2-30 Create Source dialog box with information for journal article

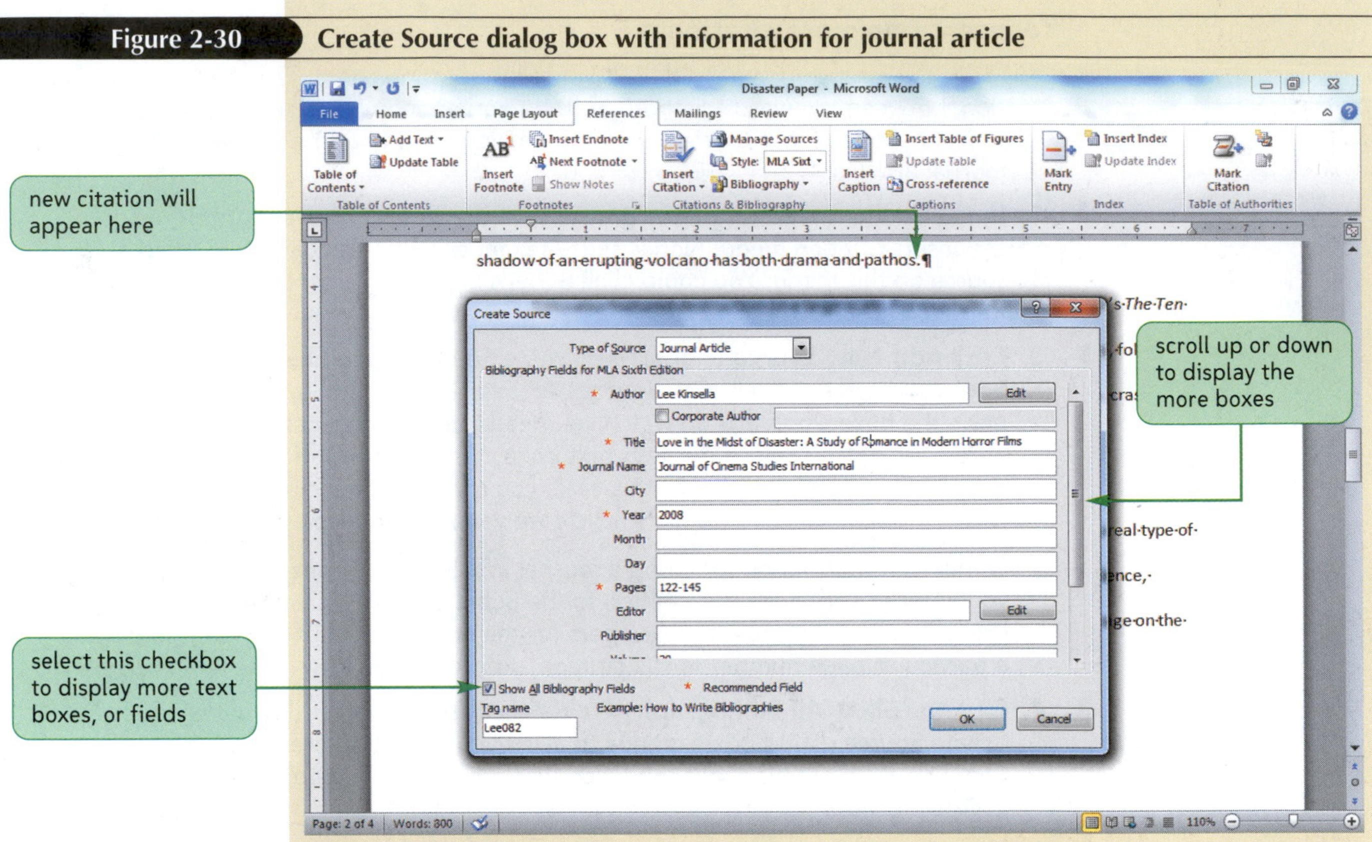

6. Click the **OK** button. The Create Source dialog box closes and the citation "(Kinsella)" is inserted in the text. Because the sentence containing the citation already includes the author's name, you will edit the citation to include the page number and suppress the author's name.
7. Click the **(Kinsella)** citation to display the content control, click the **Citations Options** button, and then click **Edit Citation** to open the Edit Citation dialog box.
8. Type **142** in the Pages box, and then click the **Author** and **Title** check boxes to select them. You need to suppress both the author's name and title, because otherwise Word will replace the suppressed author name with the title.
9. Click the **OK** button to close the Edit Citation dialog box, and then click anywhere outside the content control to deselect it. The end of the sentence now reads "...drama and pathos (142)."
10. Use the Navigation Pane to find the sentence that begins "This represents a completely new..." on the third page, click at the end of the sentence, to the left of the period after "film," and then close the Navigation Pane.

11. Click the **References** tab, click the **Insert Citation** button in the Citations & Bibliography group, and then click the **Kinsella, Lee** source at the top of the menu. You want the citation to refer to the entire article instead of just one page, so you will not edit the citation to add a specific page number.
12. Save the document.

You have entered the source information for two sources.

Generating a Bibliography

Once you have created a citation for a source in a document, you can generate a bibliography. When you do, Word scans all the citations in the document, collecting the source information for each citation, and then creates a list of information for each unique source. The format of the entries in the bibliography will reflect the style you specified when you created your first citation, which in this case is the MLA style. The bibliography itself is a **field**, similar to the page number field you inserted in Session 2.1. In other words, it is really an instruction that tells Word to display the source information for all the citations in the document. Because it is a field, and not actual text, you can update the bibliography later to reflect any new citations you might add.

You can choose to insert a bibliography with no style, which means without a title or heading, or you can choose a bibliography style option that includes the preformatted heading "Bibliography" or "Works Cited." Using a bibliography style is best because then Word inserts the bibliography field in a content control, which in turn includes some useful buttons that you can use to make additional changes to your bibliography. One of these buttons allows you to transform the bibliography field into static text—that is, into ordinary text that you can edit but that cannot be updated later. As you will see, you need to be able to change your final bibliography into static text so that you can then make some additional edits required to make your bibliography match the MLA style. The bibliography Word creates is close to the MLA style, but it's not perfect.

In the MLA style, the bibliography (or list of works cited) starts on a new page. So your first step is to insert a manual page break. A **manual page break** is one you insert at a specific location; it doesn't matter if the previous page is full or not. To insert a manual page break, use the Page Break button in the Pages group on the Insert tab.

To insert a manual page break:

1. Press the **Ctrl+End** keys to move the insertion point to the end of the document.
2. Click the **Insert** tab, and then in the Pages group, click the **Page Break** button. Word inserts a new, blank page 5, with the insertion point blinking at the top.
3. Scroll up to see the dotted line with the words "Page Break" at the bottom of the text on page 4. See Figure 2-31.

TIP

To insert a new, blank page in the middle of a document, position the insertion point where you want to insert the blank page, and then click the Blank Page button in the Pages group on the Insert tab.

Figure 2-31 Manual page break inserted into document

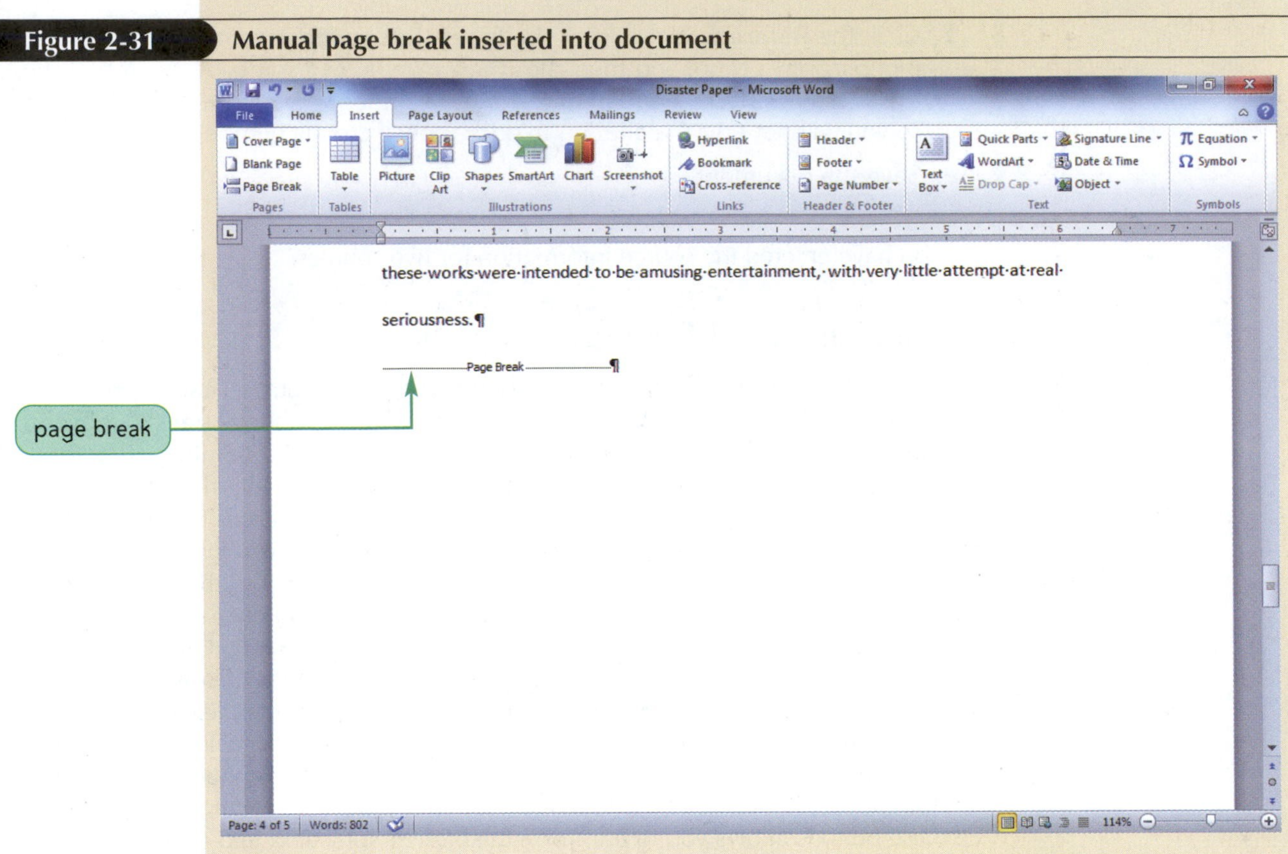

Now you can insert the bibliography on the new page 5.

To insert the bibliography:

1. Scroll down so you can see the insertion point at the top of page 5.
2. Click the **References** tab, and then in the Citations & Bibliography group, click the **Bibliography** button. The Bibliography menu opens, displaying two styles with preformatted headings, "Bibliography" and "Works Cited." The command at the bottom inserts a bibliography without a preformatted heading. See Figure 2-32.

Figure 2-32 Bibliography menu

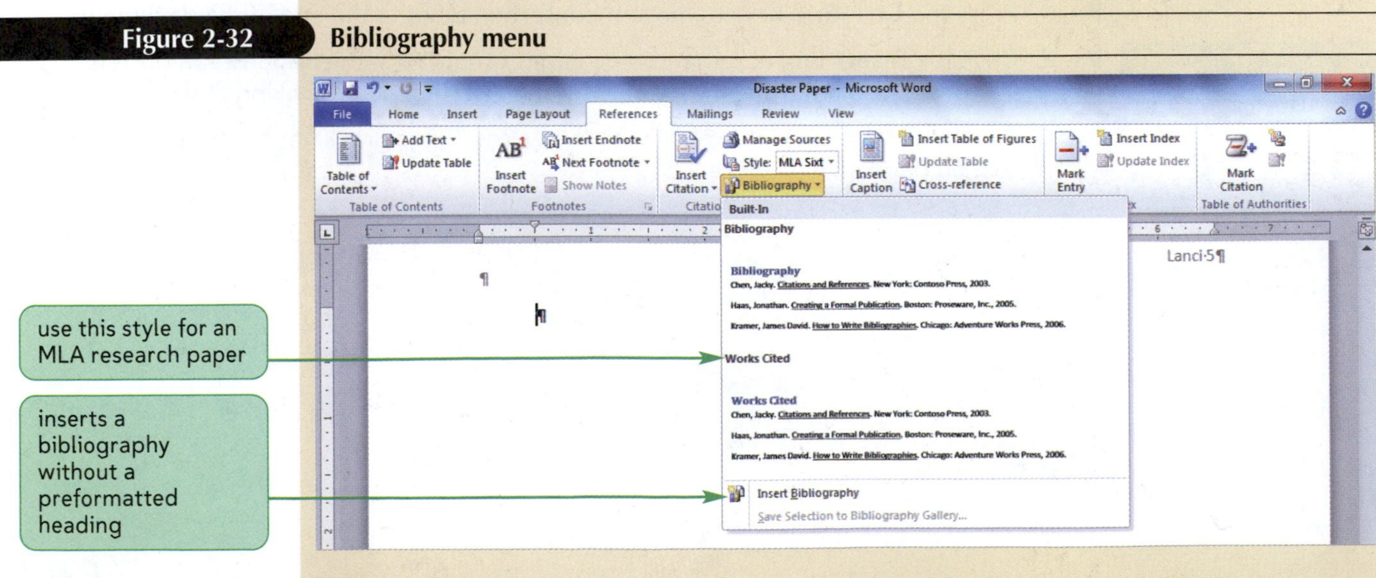

3. Click **Works Cited**. Word inserts the bibliography, with two entries, below the "Works Cited" heading. The bibliography text is formatted in Calibri, the default font for the Office theme. The "Works Cited" heading is formatted with the Heading 1 style. To see the content control that contains the bibliography, you need to select it.
4. Click the **bibliography**. The bibliography is highlighted in gray, indicating that it is a field and not regular text. The content control containing the bibliography is also visible, in the form of a blue border and a blue tab with two buttons. See Figure 2-33.

Figure 2-33 Bibliography displayed in a content control

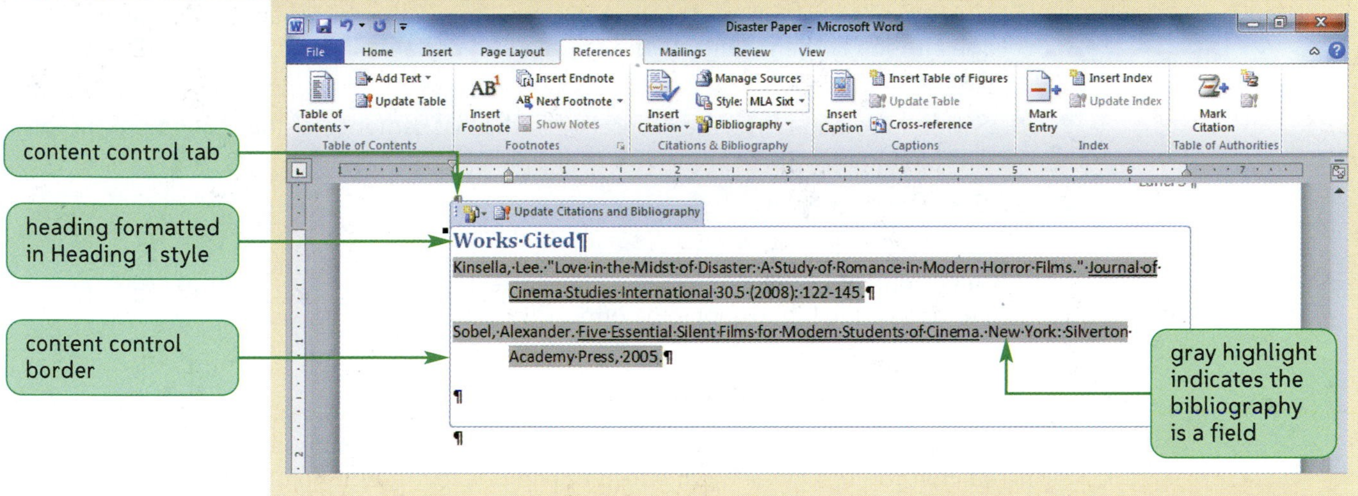

As Natalie looks over the works cited list, she realizes that she mispelled the last name of one of the authors. You'll correct the error now, and then update the works cited list.

Modifying an Existing Source

To modify information about a source, you click a citation to that source in the document, click the Citations Options button on the content control, and then click Edit Source. After you are finished editing the source, Word prompts you to update the master list and the source information in the current document. In almost all cases, you should click Yes to ensure that the source information is correct in all places it is stored on your computer.

INSIGHT

Managing Sources

When you create a source, Word adds it to a Master List of sources, which is available for use with any document created using the same user account on that computer. It also adds each new source to the Current List of sources for that document. Both the Master List and the Current List are accessible via the Source Manager dialog box, which you open by clicking the Manage Sources button in the Citations & Bibliography group on the References tab. Using this dialog box, you can copy sources from the Master List into the Current List. As you begin to focus on a particular academic field, and turn repeatedly to important works in your chosen field, you'll find this ability to reuse sources very helpful.

To edit a source in the research paper:

1. Scroll up to display the third paragraph on page 3, click the **(Kinsella)** citation you entered earlier. The content control appears around the citation.
2. Click the **Citations Options** button and then click **Edit Source**. The Edit Source dialog box opens. Note that Word displays the author's last name first in the Author box, just as it would appear in a bibliography.
3. Click the **Author** box, and edit the last name "Kinsella" by deleting the first "l" to change the last name to "Kinsela."
4. Click the **OK** button. A message dialog box opens asking if you want to update the master source list and the current document.
5. Click the **Yes** button, and then click anywhere on the third page to deselect the citation content control. The revised author name in the citation now reads "Kinsela."
6. Scroll up to page 2, locate "Kinsella" in the last sentence of the second paragraph on the page, and edit "Kinsella" so it reads "Kinsela."
7. Save the document.

You've edited the citation to include the correct spelling of "Kinsela," but now you need to update the bibliography to correct the spelling.

Updating a Bibliography

The bibliography does not automatically change to reflect changes you make to existing citations or to show new citations. To incorporate the latest information stored in the citations, you need to update it. To update a bibliography created with a bibliography style, click the bibliography, and then, in the content control tab, click Update Citations and Bibliography. To update a bibliography that was created without a style, right-click the bibliography, and then click Update Field on the Shortcut menu.

To update the bibliography:

1. Scroll down to page 5 and click anywhere in the works cited list to display the content control.
2. In the content control tab, click **Update Citations and Bibliography**. The works cited list is updated, with "Kinsella" changed to "Kinsela" in the first entry.

Natalie still has a fair amount of work to do on her research paper. After she finishes writing it and adding all the citations, she will update the bibliography again to include all her cited sources. At that point you might think the bibliography would be finished, but in fact a few steps remain to ensure that the works cited list matches the MLA style.

Finalizing an MLA Works Cited List

Figure 2-34 summarizes the steps for adapting a bibliography generated in Word to meet the MLA style guidelines for a works cited list.

Figure 2-34 **Steps for adapting a Word bibliography to match MLA guidelines for Works Cited list**

1. Format the "Works Cited" heading to match the formatting of the rest of the text in the document.
2. Center the title of the Works Cited list.
3. Change the formatting of the titles in the entries from underlined to italics.
4. For each item in the list that is a print publication, type "Print." at the end of the entry. Other types of media require similar notations. To learn more, review the examples in the *MLA Handbook for Writers of Research Papers.*
5. Double-space the entire works cited list, including the heading, with no extra space after the paragraphs.
6. Change the font size for the entire works cited list to 12 point.

TIP

After you convert a bibliography to static text, you can no longer update it to reflect changes to the document citations. So don't convert it until the bibliography contains all the necessary source information.

Before you finalize Natalie's works cited list to match the MLA style, you need to convert it from a field that can be updated automatically to **static text**—that is, text that can't be updated automatically. After that, you can make the changes shown in Figure 2-34.

To convert a bibliography to static text and format it as a MLA style works cited list:

1. In the tab at the top of the bibliography content control, click the **Bibliographies** button, and then click **Convert bibliography to static text**. The bibliography appears without the gray highlight, indicating that it is now regular text. The content control remains, but its buttons no longer have any effect on the static text bibliography.
2. Click in the **Works Cited** heading, click the **Home** tab, and then click the **Normal** style in the Styles group. The Works Cited heading is formatted in Calibri body font like the rest of the document. The MLA style for a works cited list requires this heading to be centered.
3. In the Paragraph group, click the **Center** button. Now you will change the formatting of the publication titles in the entries from underlined to italics, per the MLA style.
4. In the first entry in the list, select the title **Journal of Cinema Studies International**, click the **Underline** button **U** in the Font group to remove the underline, and then click the **Italic** button *I* to add italics.
5. In the second entry, format the title **Five Essential Silent Films for Modern Students of Cinema** to remove the underline, and apply italics. Next, you need to add a notation indicating the form of publication for each source. In both cases, they are print publications.
6. Click at the end of the Lee Kinsela source, press the **spacebar**, and then type **Print**. (including the period). Do the same for the Alexander Sobel source.
7. Select the entire works cited list, including the "Works Cited" heading, change the font size to **12** points, change the line spacing to **2.0**, and then remove paragraph spacing after each of the paragraphs.
8. Click anywhere outside the content control to deselect it, and then review your work. See Figure 2-35.

Figure 2-35 MLA-style works cited list

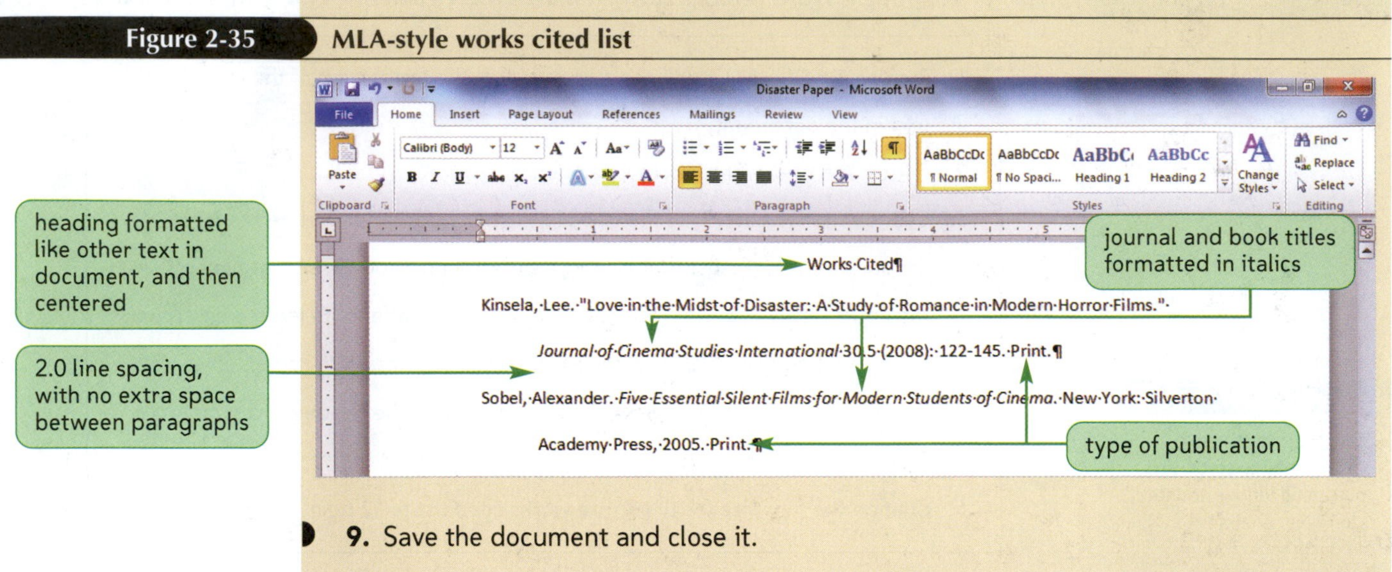

heading formatted like other text in document, and then centered
2.0 line spacing, with no extra space between paragraphs
journal and book titles formatted in italics
type of publication
Works·Cited¶
Kinsela,·Lee.·"Love·in·the·Midst·of·Disaster:·A·Study·of·Romance·in·Modern·Horror·Films."·
Journal·of·Cinema·Studies·International·30.5·(2008):·122-145.·Print.¶
Sobel,·Alexander.·Five·Essential·Silent·Films·for·Modern·Students·of·Cinema.·New·York:·Silverton·
Academy·Press,·2005.·Print.¶

9. Save the document and close it.

Natalie's research paper now meets MLA style guidelines.

REVIEW

Session 2.2 Quick Check

1. List the five tasks you need to perform to make a default Word document match the MLA style.
2. How do you indent a paragraph .5 inches from the left margin using an option on the Ribbon?
3. Explain how to remove a page number from the first page of a document.
4. What's the first step in creating citations and a bibliography?
5. Explain how to create a citation for a new source.
6. Explain how to edit a citation to display only the page number.
7. Explain how to insert a bibliography with a style that includes a preformatted heading.

Practice the skills you learned in the tutorial using the same case scenario.

PRACTICE

Review Assignments

Data Files needed for the Review Assignments: Services.docx, Staff.docx, Comedy.docx

Natalie is working part-time as a publicist for the Department of Design at Pembrooke Community College. She has created a document describing the professional design services offered by the instructors and their students. She asks you to help her spell check, proof, and format the document. Natalie also asks you to create a document listing the names of the department's interior designers and decorators. Finally, as part of her film class, she is working on a research paper on comedy throughout cinema history. She asks you to help her format the paper according to the MLA style, and to create some citations and a bibliography. She has inserted the uppercase word "CITATION" wherever she needs to insert a citation. Complete the following steps:

1. Open the file **Services** located in the Word2\Review folder included with your Data Files, and save the document as **Design Services** in the same folder.
2. Replace all instances of "PCC" with "Pembrooke Community College" being sure to match case.
3. Format the list of three interior designers (Peter Hernandez, Lynn O'Reilly, and Casey Rikli) as a bulleted list with square bullets. Do the same for the list of three interior decorators (Ernesto Livorni, Kaila Peterson, and Mai Yang Xiong).
4. Format the list of nine steps in the consultation process as a numbered list, using the "1), 2), 3)" numbering style. Note that the first paragraph in the list of steps begins "Schedule a free, forty-five minute consultation" and ends with the second to last paragraph in the document, which begins "Enjoy your beautiful..."
5. Move paragraph 3 ("Interview potential construction firms...") down to make it paragraph 4.
6. Use the Spelling and Grammar checker to correct any errors in the document. Assume that all names in the document are spelled correctly.
7. Proofread the document carefully to check for any additional errors. Look for and correct two errors in the last two paragraphs of the document that were not reported when you used the Spelling and Grammar checker.
8. In the last paragraph of the document, replace "Natalie Lanci" with your first and last name.
9. Format the title "Getting Started With Our Design Staff" using the Title style. Format the following headings with the Heading 1 style: Interior Designers, Interior Decorators, and Getting Started Step by Step.
10. Change the theme to the Pushpin theme.
11. Display the Clipboard task pane. Copy the bulleted list of interior designers and their specialties (starting with Peter Hernandez and ending with Casey Rikli) to the Clipboard. Also copy the list of interior decorators and their specialties (beginning with Ernesto Livorni and ending with Mai Yang Xiong) to the Clipboard.
12. Open the file **Staff** located in the Word2\Review folder included with your Data Files, and save the document as **Design Staff** in the same folder. In the subtitle, insert your first and last name after the word "by."
13. Below the heading "Interior Designers," paste the list of interior designers, which begins "Peter Hernandez." Below the heading "Interior Decorators," paste the list of interior decorators, which begins "Ernesto Liviorni." In each case, start by moving the insertion point to the blank paragraph below the heading.
14. Clear the contents of the Clipboard task pane, and then close it.
15. Save the **Design Staff** document and close it.

16. In the **Design Services** document, close the Clipboard task pane, save the document, and close it.
17. Open the file **Comedy** located in the Word2\Review folder included with your Data Files.
18. Save the document as **Comedy Paper** in the same folder.
19. In the upper-left corner, replace Natalie's name with your own.
20. Adjust the font size, line spacing, paragraph spacing, and paragraph indents to match the MLA style.
21. Insert your last name and a page number in the upper-right corner of every page except the first.
22. If necessary, select MLA Sixth Edition as the citations and bibliography style.
23. Use the Navigation Pane to highlight all instances of the upper-case word CITATION. Keep the Navigation Pane open so you can continue to use it to find the locations where you need to insert citations in the steps 24–28.
24. Delete the first instance of "CITATION" and the space before it, and then create a new source with the following information:

    Type of Source: **Book**

    Author: **Darcy Fitzwilliam-Browne**

    Title: **Comedy in a Tragic Age: A Study of Five Works**

    Year: **2002**

    City: **Atlanta**

    Publisher: **Georgia Valley Press**
25. Edit the citation to add "203" as the page number.
26. Delete the second instance of "CITATION" and the space before it, and then create a new source with the following information:

    Type of Source: **Journal Article**

    Author: **Douglas Chen**

    Title: **The Economy of Comedy in the Modern World**

    Journal Name: **North American Film Critique**

    Year: **2010**

    Pages: **88–103**

    Volume: **12**

    Issue: **3**
27. Edit the citation to add "95" as the page number.
28. Delete the third instance of "CITATION" and the space before it, and insert a citation for the book by Darcy Fitzwilliam-Browne. Edit the citation so that it only displays the page number "20" without the author's name.
29. At the end of the document, start a new page and insert a bibliography with the formatted heading "Works Cited."
30. In the first source you created, change the last name "Fitzwilliam-Browne" to "Fitzwilliam-Brown" and then update the bibliography. Make the same change wherever the name appears in the text.
31. Convert the bibliography to static text, and then finalize the bibliography to create an MLA-style Works Cited list. Assume that both sources are print publications.
32. Save the **Comedy Paper** document and close it.
33. Close any other open documents. Submit the finished documents to your instructor, either in printed or electronic form, as requested.

APPLY

Case Problem 1

If you have a SAM 2010 user profile, your instructor may have assigned an autogradable version of this assignment. If so, log into the SAM 2010 Web site at www.cengage.com/sam2010 to download the instructions and start files.

Data File needed for this Case Problem: Classes.docx

Peach Tree School of the Arts Students at Peach Tree School of the Arts, in Savannah, Georgia, can choose from a wide range of after-school classes in fine arts, music, and theater. Amanda Reinhardt, the school director, has created a flyer informing parents of some additional offerings. It's your job to format the flyer to make it professional looking and easy to read.

1. Open the file **Classes** located in the Word2\Case1 folder included with your Data Files, and save the file as **Summer Classes** in the same folder.
2. Format the document as shown in Figure 2-36.

Figure 2-36 **Edits for Summer Classes handout**

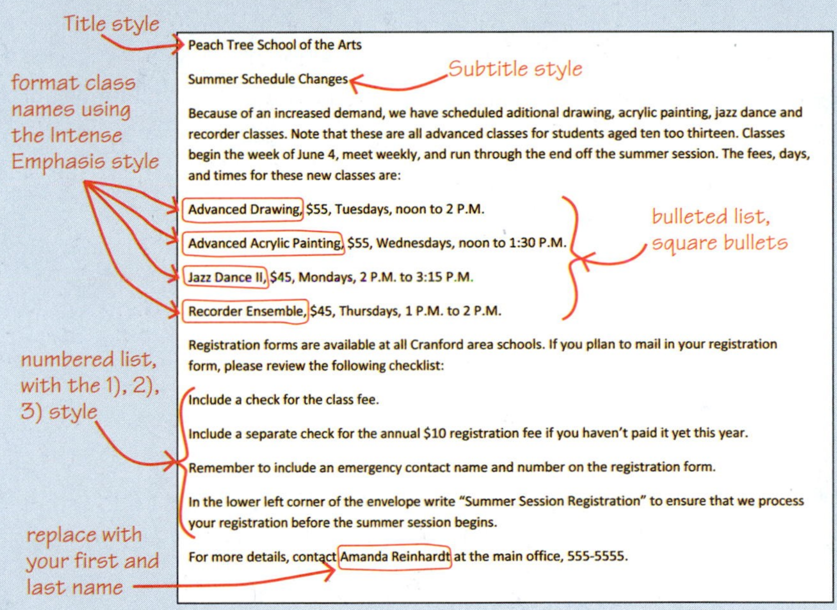

Peach Tree School of the Arts

Summer Schedule Changes

Because of an increased demand, we have scheduled aditional drawing, acrylic painting, jazz dance and recorder classes. Note that these are all advanced classes for students aged ten too thirteen. Classes begin the week of June 4, meet weekly, and run through the end off the summer session. The fees, days, and times for these new classes are:

Advanced Drawing, $55, Tuesdays, noon to 2 P.M.

Advanced Acrylic Painting, $55, Wednesdays, noon to 1:30 P.M.

Jazz Dance II, $45, Mondays, 2 P.M. to 3:15 P.M.

Recorder Ensemble, $45, Thursdays, 1 P.M. to 2 P.M.

Registration forms are available at all Cranford area schools. If you pllan to mail in your registration form, please review the following checklist:

Include a check for the class fee.

Include a separate check for the annual $10 registration fee if you haven't paid it yet this year.

Remember to include an emergency contact name and number on the registration form.

In the lower left corner of the envelope write "Summer Session Registration" to ensure that we process your registration before the summer session begins.

For more details, contact Amanda Reinhardt at the main office, 555-5555.

3. Replace all instances of uppercase "P.M." with lowercase "p.m." throughout the document.
4. Move the third bulleted item (which begins "Jazz Dance...") up to make it the first bulleted item in the list.
5. Correct any spelling or grammar errors. Ignore any potential grammar errors highlighted by the Spelling and Grammar checker that are in fact correct. In particular, ignore the sentence fragments, which are part of the bulleted list.
6. Proofread for other errors, such as words that are spelled correctly but used incorrectly.
7. Change the theme to the Civic theme, and then review the fonts applied by this theme.
8. Save the document and then close it. Submit the finished document to your instructor, either in printed or electronic form, as requested.

Apply the skills you learned to create an MLA-style research paper.

APPLY

Case Problem 2

Data File needed for this Case Problem: Armstrong.docx

Franklin College of the Arts Gabe Saydoff is a student at Franklin College of the Arts. He's working on a research paper about Louis Armstrong, the great jazz trumpet player. The research paper is only partly finished, with notes in brackets indicating the material Gabe still plans to write. He also inserted the uppercase word "CITATION" wherever he needs to insert a citation. Gabe asks you to help him format this early draft to match the MLA style. He also asks you to help him create some citations and a first attempt at a bibliography. He will update the bibliography later, after he finishes writing the research paper.

1. Open the file **Armstrong** located in the Word2\Case2 folder included with your Data Files, and then save the document as **Armstrong Paper** in the same folder.
2. In the first paragraph, replace "Gabe Saydoff" with your name, adjust the font size, line spacing, paragraph spacing, and paragraph indents to match the MLA style.
3. Insert your last name and a page number in the upper-right corner of every page except the first page in the document.
4. If necessary, select MLA Sixth Edition as the citations and bibliography style.
5. Use the Navigation Pane to find three instances of the uppercase word "CITATION."
6. Delete the first instance of "CITATION" and the space before it, and then create a new source with the following information:
   Type of Source: **Book**
   Author: **Phillip James Robins**
   Title: **Louis Armstrong, Man of Music: His Early Years in New Orleans and Chicago**
   Year: **2000**
   City: **New York**
   Publisher: **Blue Note Press**
7. Edit the citation to add "23" as the page number.
8. Delete the second instance of "CITATION" and the space before it, and then create a new source with the following information:
   Type of Source: **Sound Recording**
   Performer: **Louis Armstrong**
   Album Title: **The Complete Hot Five and Hot Seven Recordings, Remastered**
   Production Company: **Columbia**
   Year: **2000**
   Medium: **CD**
9. Edit the citation to suppress only the Author and the Year, so that it displays only the title.
10. Delete the third instance of "CITATION" and the space before it, and then insert a second reference to the book by Phillip Robins.
11. Edit the citation to add "35" as the page number.
12. At the end of the document, start a new page, and insert a bibliography with the preformatted heading "Works Cited."
13. Edit the source you created, changing the last name from "Robins" to "Robbins."
14. Update the bibliography so that it shows the new spelling of "Robbins."
15. Finalize the bibliography so that it matches the MLA style. The Robbins book is a print publication, and the recording is on CD. (Note that, although you entered the medium for the recording, you still need to add it to the bibliography.)

16. Use the Spelling and Grammar Checker to correct any errors in the document.
17. Save the **Armstrong Paper** document and close it. Submit the finished document to your instructor, either in printed or electronic form, as requested.

Apply the skills you learned to create a flyer about an entomology program.

CHALLENGE

Case Problem 3

Data File needed for this Case Problem: Management.docx

Hamilton Polytechnic Institute Finn Hansen is an associate researcher in the Department of Entomology at Hamilton Polytechnic Institute. He is working on a nationwide program that aims to slow the spread of a devastating forest pest, the gypsy moth. He has created a one-page flyer that will be used as part of a campaign to inform the public about current efforts to manage gypsy moths in North America. Format the document by completing the following steps.

1. Open the file **Management** located in the Word2\Case3 folder included with your Data Files, and then check your screen to make sure your settings match those in the tutorial.
2. Save the file as **Moth Management** in the same folder.
3. Format the document as shown in 2-37.

Figure 2-37 Edits for Gypsy Moth Management handout

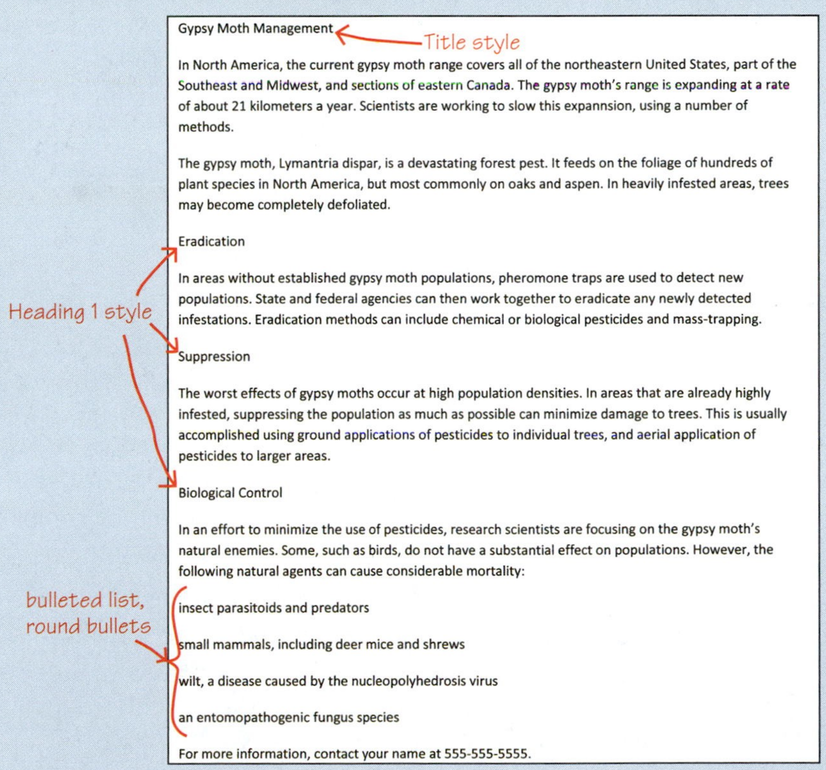

Gypsy Moth Management ← Title style

In North America, the current gypsy moth range covers all of the northeastern United States, part of the Southeast and Midwest, and sections of eastern Canada. The gypsy moth's range is expanding at a rate of about 21 kilometers a year. Scientists are working to slow this expannsion, using a number of methods.

The gypsy moth, Lymantria dispar, is a devastating forest pest. It feeds on the foliage of hundreds of plant species in North America, but most commonly on oaks and aspen. In heavily infested areas, trees may become completely defoliated.

Eradication

In areas without established gypsy moth populations, pheromone traps are used to detect new populations. State and federal agencies can then work together to eradicate any newly detected infestations. Eradication methods can include chemical or biological pesticides and mass-trapping.

Suppression

The worst effects of gypsy moths occur at high population densities. In areas that are already highly infested, suppressing the population as much as possible can minimize damage to trees. This is usually accomplished using ground applications of pesticides to individual trees, and aerial application of pesticides to larger areas.

Biological Control

In an effort to minimize the use of pesticides, research scientists are focusing on the gypsy moth's natural enemies. Some, such as birds, do not have a substantial effect on populations. However, the following natural agents can cause considerable mortality:

insect parasitoids and predators

small mammals, including deer mice and shrews

wilt, a disease caused by the nucleopolyhedrosis virus

an entomopathogenic fungus species

For more information, contact your name at 555-555-5555.

Heading 1 style

bulleted list, round bullets

EXPLORE

4. Open the Quick Styles gallery, and then use the Apply Styles command to open the Apply Styles window. In the second paragraph below the document title, select the Latin name for the gypsy moth, type **Quote** in the Style name box in the Apply Styles window, and then click the Apply button to apply the style to the selected text. Close the Apply Styles window.

5. Indent the paragraph below the "Eradication" heading .5 inches. Do the same for the paragraph below the "Suppression" heading, the paragraph below the "Biological Control" heading, and the last paragraph in the document. (*Hint*: To indent the paragraph above and below the bulleted list, you have to click the Indent Paragraph button twice.) Select the entire bulleted list and indent it so that the bullets align with the other indented paragraphs.
6. Use the Navigation Pane to find the text "your name" and replace it with your first and last name.

EXPLORE

7. In the last line of the document, delete the phone number, but not the space before it, type the email address **MothProgram@course.com**, and then press the spacebar. (Note that after you type an email address or a Web address and then press the spacebar or the Enter key, Word formats the address as a link.) Press and hold the Ctrl key and then click the email link. Your default email program opens, displaying a window where you could type an email message to MothProgram@course.com, if it were in fact an active email address. (If your computer is not set up for email, close any error messages or wizard dialog boxes that open.) Close the email window without saving any changes. The email link is now formatted in a color other than blue, indicating that the link has been clicked.
8. Delete the space after the email address, and then use the Spelling and Grammar checker to make corrections as needed, and proofread for additional errors. Assume the Latin name for the gypsy moth, the virus name, and the fungus name are correct.
9. Change the document theme to the Austin theme. Review the new fonts and colors applied to the various parts of the document, including the email address.

EXPLORE

10. Right-click the email address and then click Remove Hyperlink on the Shortcut menu to format the email address as regular text.
11. Save the document, and then close it. Submit the finished document to your instructor, either in printed or electronic form, as requested.

Apply the skills you learned to format a resume and a fund-raising document.

CHALLENGE

Case Problem 4

Data Files needed for this Case Problem: Elena.docx, Goals.docx

Educational Publishing Elena Pelliterri has over a decade of experience in education. She worked as a writing teacher and then as a college supervisor of student teachers. Now she would like to pursue a career as a sales representative for a company that publishes textbooks and other educational materials. She has asked you to edit and format her resume. She also needs help formatting a document she created for a literacy organization for which she volunteers. Complete the documents by completing the following steps.

1. Open the file **Elena** located in the Word2\Case4 folder included with your Data Files, and then save the file as **Elena Resume** in the same folder.
2. Search for the text "your name", and replace it with your first and last name.
3. Replace all occurrences of "Aroyo" with "Arroyo."
4. Format the resume as described in Figure 2-38. Use the Format Painter to copy formatting as necessary.

Figure 2-38 Formatting for Pelliteri Resume

Resume Element	Format
Name "Elena Pelliterri"	Title style
Address, phone number, and email address	Subtitle style
OBJECTIVE EXPERIENCE EDUCATIONAL HISTORY COMPUTER SKILLS VOLUNTEER EXPERIENCE REFERENCES	Heading 1 style
Rio Mesa College, Phonix Arizona, College Supervisor, 2006-2010 Middleton Public Schools writing teacher, Middleton, Arizona, 2000-2006	Heading 2 style
Lists of teaching experience, educational history, computer skills, and volunteer experience.	Bulleted lists with square bullets

5. Change the document theme to Executive.
6. Reorder the two items under the "COMPUTER SKILLS" heading so that the item about Microsoft Office becomes the first in the list.

EXPLORE

7. Use the Spelling and Grammar checker to check for spelling errors, but not grammar errors in the document. Note that this document contains lines that the Spelling and Grammar checker might consider sentence fragments but that are acceptable in a resume.

EXPLORE

8. Open a new, blank document, type some text, and experiment with the Change Case button in the Font group on the Home tab. Close the document without saving it, and then change the name "Elena Pelliterri" at the top of the resume to all uppercase.
9. Save the document.

EXPLORE

10. Use Word Help to learn how to save a Word document as a PDF file, and then save Elena's resume as a PDF file in the Word2\Case4 folder as **Elena Resume PDF**. If the new PDF file opens automatically in Adobe Acrobat, review it in Adobe Acrobat and then close it. If it does not open automatically, open the Word2\Case3 folder in Windows Explorer, and then double-click the **Elena Resume PDF** file to open it in Adobe Acrobat. Review the file, close Adobe Acrobat, and then close the Elena Resume document.
11. Open the file **Goals** located in the Word2\Case4 folder included with your Data Files, and then save the file as **Goals List** in the same folder. Search for the text "your name", and replace it with your first and last name.
12. Select the three paragraphs below your name, and then decrease the indent for the selected paragraphs so that they align at the left margin. Create a .5 inch hanging indent for the selected paragraphs instead.
13. Save and close the document. Submit the finished documents to your instructor, either in printed or electronic form, as requested.

SAM

ASSESS

SAM: Skills Assessment Manager

For current SAM information, including versions and content details, visit SAM Central (http://samcentral.course.com). If you have a SAM user profile, you may have access to hands-on instruction, practice, and assessment of the skills covered in this tutorial. Since various versions of SAM are supported throughout the life of this text, check with your instructor for the correct instructions and URL/Web site for accessing assignments.

ENDING DATA FILES

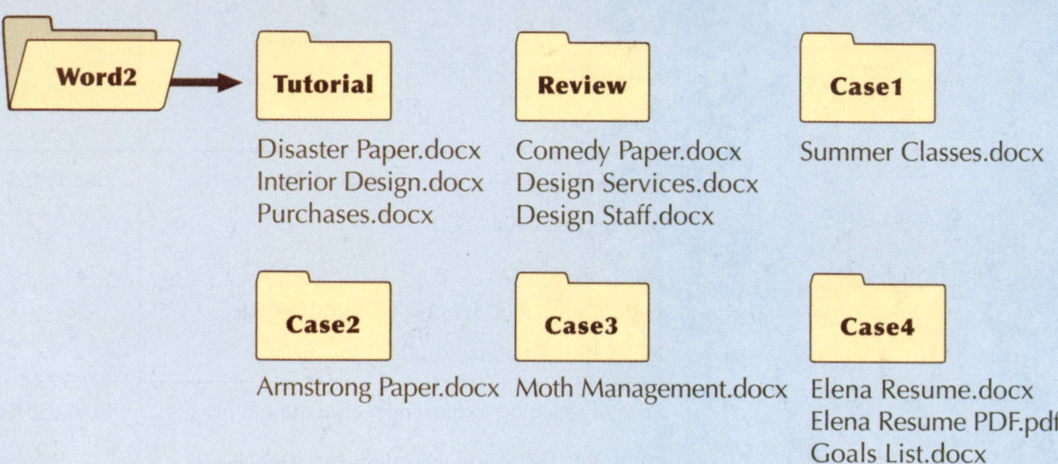

TUTORIAL 3

Creating a Multiple-Page Report

Writing a Recommendation

WORD

OBJECTIVES

Session 3.1

- Work with a document's headings in the Navigation pane
- Create and edit a table
- Sort rows in a table
- Modify a table's structure
- Format a table

Session 3.2

- Set tab stops
- Create footnotes and endnotes
- Divide a document into sections
- Create a SmartArt graphic
- Create headers and footers
- Insert a cover page

Case | *Parkside Housing Coalition*

Robin Hunter is the director of Parkside Housing Coalition, a nonprofit organization that provides low-cost rental housing in Evanston, Illinois, at more than 50 properties it owns and manages. Robin has been investigating a plan to reduce utility bills for Parkside residents through a process known as an energy audit. Robin has written a multiple-page report for the board of directors at Parkside Housing Coalition summarizing basic information about energy audits. She has asked you to finish formatting the report. She also needs your help in adding a table to the end of the report.

In this tutorial, you will use the Navigation pane to review the document headings and reorganize the document, insert a table, and modify it by changing the structure and formatting. You will also set tab stops, create footnotes and endnotes, and insert a section break. Finally, you will create a SmartArt graphic, add headers and footers, and insert a cover page.

STARTING DATA FILES

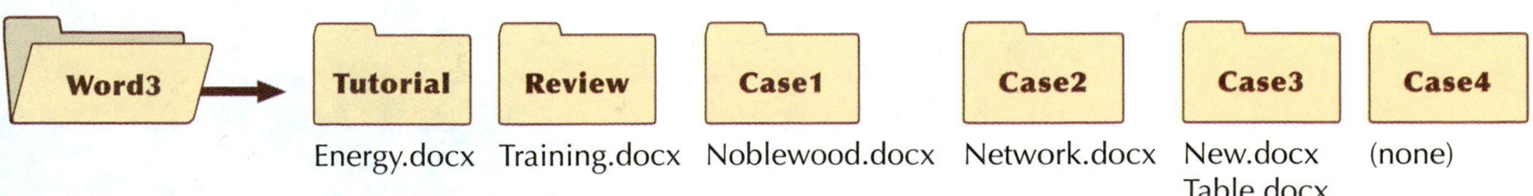

Energy.docx Training.docx Noblewood.docx Network.docx New.docx Table.docx (none)

SESSION 3.1 VISUAL OVERVIEW

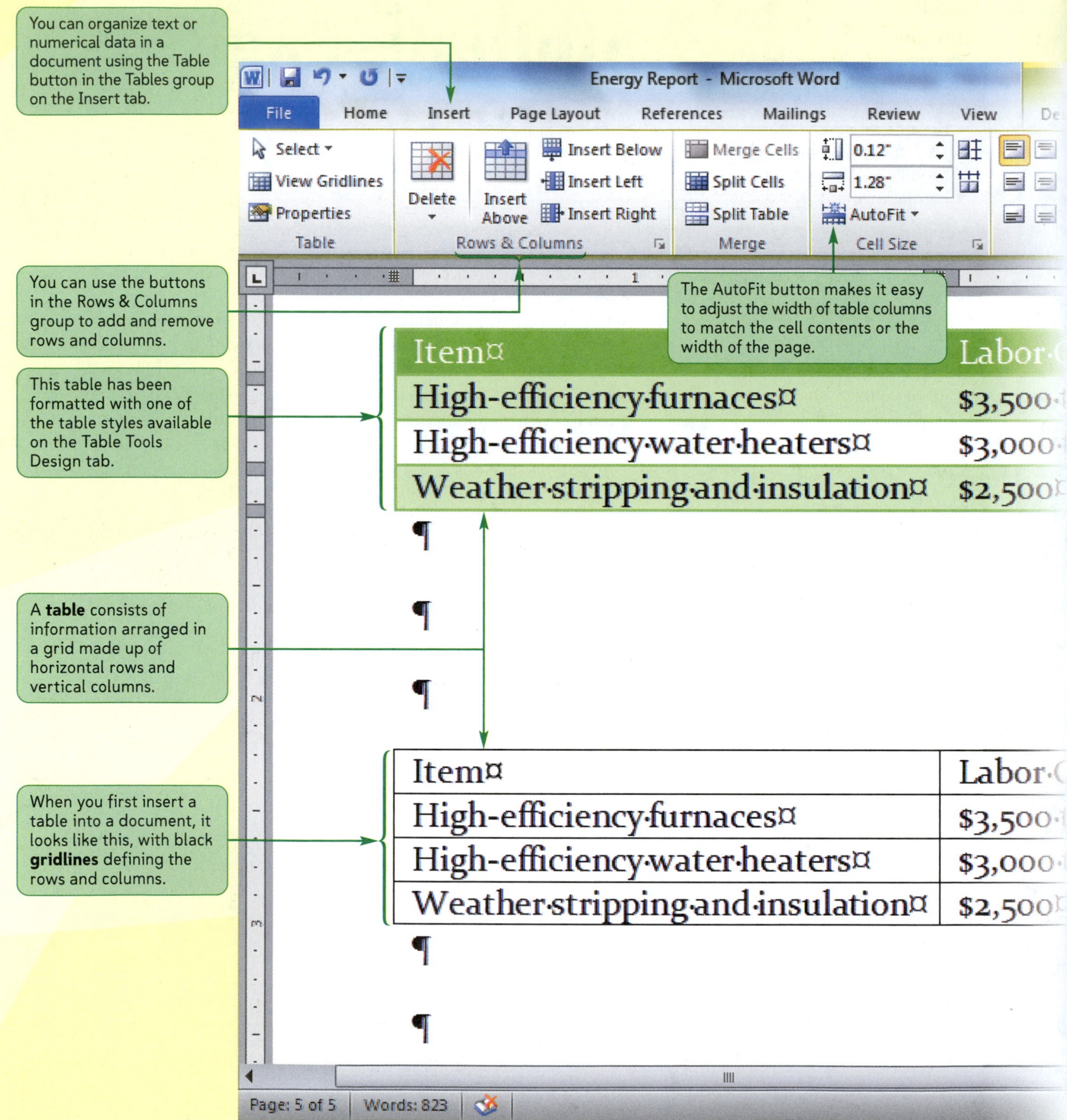
You can organize text or numerical data in a document using the Table button in the Tables group on the Insert tab.
You can use the buttons in the Rows & Columns group to add and remove rows and columns.
This table has been formatted with one of the table styles available on the Table Tools Design tab.
A **table** consists of information arranged in a grid made up of horizontal rows and vertical columns.
When you first insert a table into a document, it looks like this, with black **gridlines** defining the rows and columns.
The AutoFit button makes it easy to adjust the width of table columns to match the cell contents or the width of the page.
Energy Report - Microsoft Word
File
Home
Insert
Page Layout
References
Mailings
Review
View
Select
View Gridlines
Properties
Table
Delete
Insert Above
Insert Below
Insert Left
Insert Right
Rows & Columns
Merge Cells
Split Cells
Split Table
Merge
0.12"
1.28"
AutoFit
Cell Size
Item
Labor
High-efficiency furnaces
$3,500
High-efficiency water heaters
$3,000
Weather stripping and insulation
$2,500
Page: 5 of 5
Words: 823

ORGANIZING INFORMATION IN TABLES

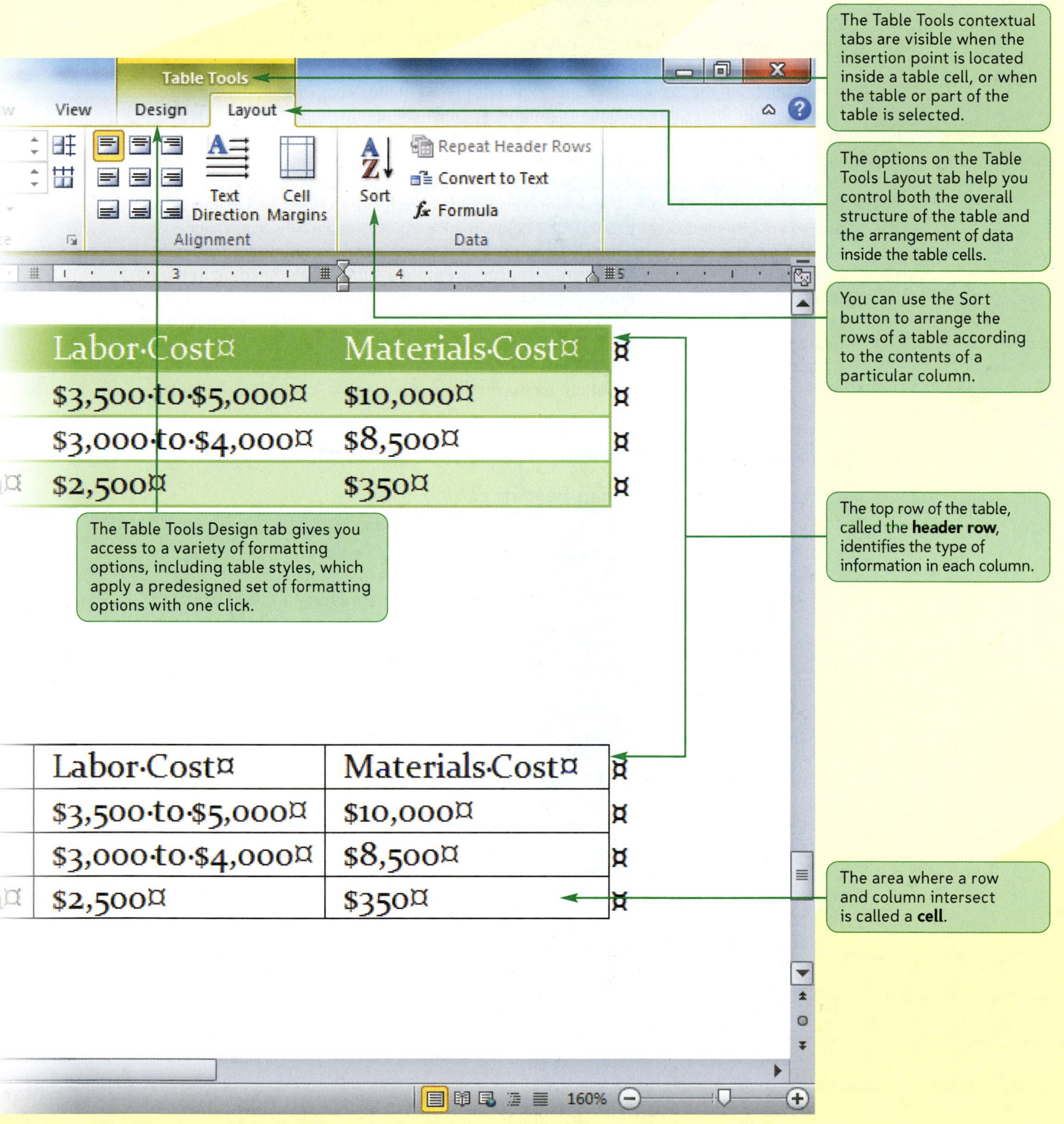

The Table Tools contextual tabs are visible when the insertion point is located inside a table cell, or when the table or part of the table is selected.

The options on the Table Tools Layout tab help you control both the overall structure of the table and the arrangement of data inside the table cells.

You can use the Sort button to arrange the rows of a table according to the contents of a particular column.

The Table Tools Design tab gives you access to a variety of formatting options, including table styles, which apply a predesigned set of formatting options with one click.

The top row of the table, called the **header row**, identifies the type of information in each column.

The area where a row and column intersect is called a **cell**.

Working with Headings in the Navigation Pane

The Navigation pane offers two different ways to view a document's structure and then navigate within it. You can view and navigate the document's outline by displaying its headings in the document, or you can view and navigate the document's pages by displaying thumbnail images of the pages.

To view the headings in the document, you click the Browse the headings in your documents button in the Navigation pane. When displayed in the Navigation pane, this list of headings constitutes the document's **outline**. Reviewing the outline can help you keep track of your document's overall organization. It also lets you see, at a glance, the hierarchy of the document headings. Paragraphs formatted with the Heading 1 style are considered the highest level headings, and appear aligned at the left margin of the Navigation pane. Paragraphs formatted with the Heading 2 style are considered subordinate to Heading 1 paragraphs, and so are indented slightly to the right below the Heading 1 paragraphs. Each successive level of heading styles (Heading 3, Heading 4, and so on) is indented further to the right.

From within the Navigation pane, you can **promote** a subordinate heading to the next level up in the heading hierarchy. For example, you can promote a Heading 2 paragraph to a Heading 1 paragraph. You can also do the opposite—that is, you can **demote** a heading to a subordinate level. For example, you can demote a Heading 1 paragraph to a Heading 2 paragraph. To promote a heading, right-click it in the Navigation pane, and then click Promote on the Shortcut menu. To demote a heading, click Demote on the Shortcut menu.

INSIGHT

Promoting and Demoting Headings Using Styles

When you promote or demote a heading, Word applies the next higher or lower level of heading style to the heading paragraph. You could accomplish the same thing by formatting the heading paragraph with a style within the document, but it's easy to lose track of the overall organization of the document that way. Promoting and demoting headings from within the Navigation pane ensures that you can see how these changes affect the overall document outline.

You can display a heading in the document by clicking it in the Navigation pane. You can also click and drag a heading in the Navigation pane to a new location in the document's outline. When you do so, the heading and the body text that follows it move to the new location in the document. To simplify your view of the outline in the Navigation pane, you can choose to hide lower level headings from view, leaving only the major headings visible.

If you just want to move quickly among the pages in your document, you can click the Browse the pages in your document button in the Navigation pane. This displays the pages of your document as thumbnails; you can click a thumbnail to instantly move to that page in the document.

Robin saved the draft of her report as a Word document named "Energy." In its current form, the report is two pages long. Robin organized the information in her report using headings formatted with the Heading 1, Heading 2, and Heading 3 styles. You will use the Navigation pane to review the outline of Robin's report and make some changes to its organization.

To review the document and its headings in the Navigation pane:

1. Open the file **Energy** located in the Word3\Tutorial folder included with your Data Files, and save the file with the name **Energy Report** in the same folder.

2. Verify that the document is displayed in Print Layout view and that the rulers and nonprinting characters are displayed. Make sure the Zoom level is set to **Page Width**.

3. On the Home tab, in the Editing group, click the **Find** button. The Navigation pane opens to the left of the document. You want to view the pages in the document first.

4. Click the **Browse the pages in your document** button, which appears below the Search Document box in the Navigation pane. The two pages of the document appear as thumbnails in the Navigation pane, with the first page thumbnail selected and the page itself displayed in the document window. See Figure 3-1.

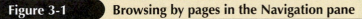

Figure 3-1 Browsing by pages in the Navigation pane

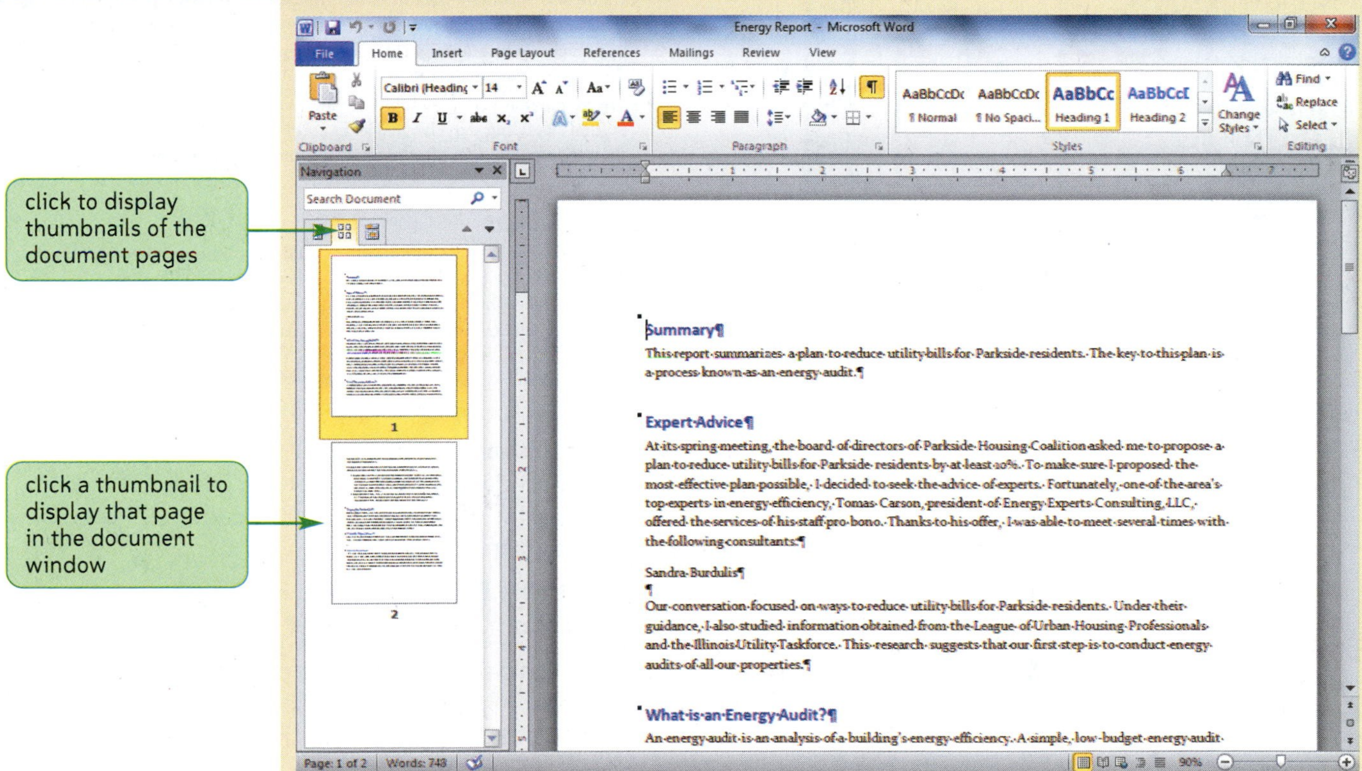

5. Click the **page 2** thumbnail to move to the second page in the document. Now you want to view the headings in the document.

6. Click the **Browse the headings in your document** button. An outline of the document headings is displayed in the Navigation pane, as shown in Figure 3-2. The orange highlighted heading ("Final Recommendation") indicates which part of the document currently contains the insertion point. The Navigation pane treats a heading and the body text that follows it as a single unit, so in this case, the insertion point is located somewhere within the heading Final Recommendation or within the body text that follows it.

Figure 3-2 **Headings displayed in the Navigation pane**

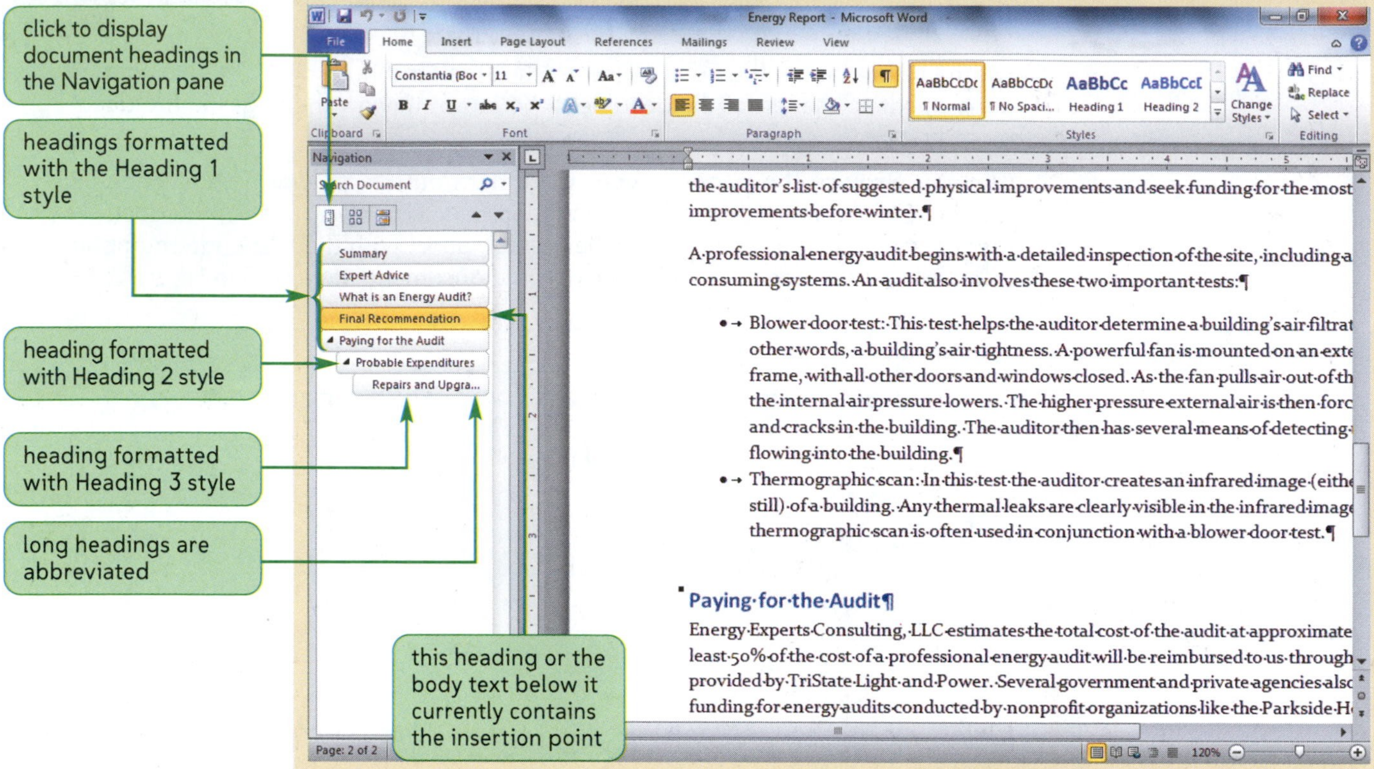

click to display document headings in the Navigation pane

headings formatted with the Heading 1 style

heading formatted with Heading 2 style

heading formatted with Heading 3 style

long headings are abbreviated

this heading or the body text below it currently contains the insertion point

7. In the Navigation pane, click the **What is an Energy Audit?** heading. Word displays the heading in the document window, with the insertion point at the beginning of the heading, and the "What is an Energy Audit?" heading is now highlighted in orange in the Navigation pane.
8. In the Navigation pane, click the **Probable Expenditures...** heading. Word displays the heading in the document window, at the bottom of page 2.
9. In the Navigation pane, click the **Collapse** arrow ◢ next to the "Paying for the Audit" heading. The Heading 2 and Heading 3 text is no longer visible in the Navigation pane. Note that this has no effect on the text in the actual document. See Figure 3-3.

Figure 3-3 **Heading 2 and Heading 3 text hidden in Navigation pane**

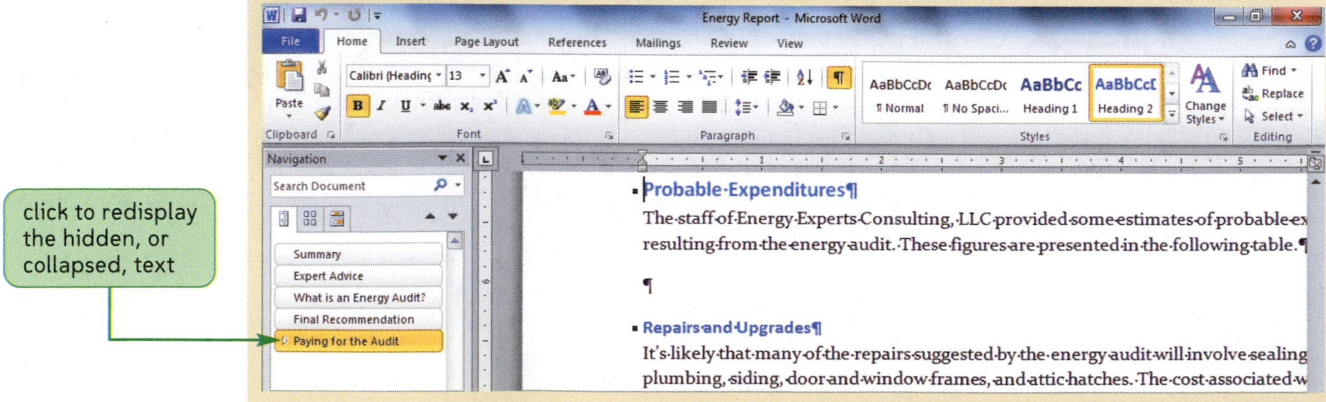

10. In the Navigation pane, click the **Expand** arrow next to the "Paying for the Audit" heading. The Heading 2 and Heading 3 text are again visible in the Navigation pane.

Now that you are familiar with the report, you need to make a few organizational changes. Robin wants to promote the Heading 3 text "Repairs and Upgrades" to Heading 2 text. Then she wants to move the "Repairs and Upgrades" heading and its body text so it precedes the "Probable Expenditures" section.

To use the Navigation pane to reorganize text in the document:

TIP

You can also use Outline view to display, promote, and demote headings, and reorganize a document. Click the Outline button on the right side of the status bar, and then use the buttons on the Outlining tab.

1. In the Navigation pane, right-click the heading **Repairs and Upgr...** to display the shortcut menu.
2. Click **Promote**. The heading, which is no longer abbreviated, moves to the left in the Navigation pane, so it aligns below the "Probable Expenditures" heading. In the document window, the text is now formatted with the Heading 2 style, with its larger, more prominent font.
3. In the Navigation pane, click and drag the **Repairs and Upgrades** heading up. As you drag the heading, a black guideline appears, which you can use to position the heading in its new location, and the pointer changes to .
4. Position the black guideline below the "Paying for the Audit" heading, as in Figure 3-4.

Figure 3-4 Moving a heading in the Navigation pane

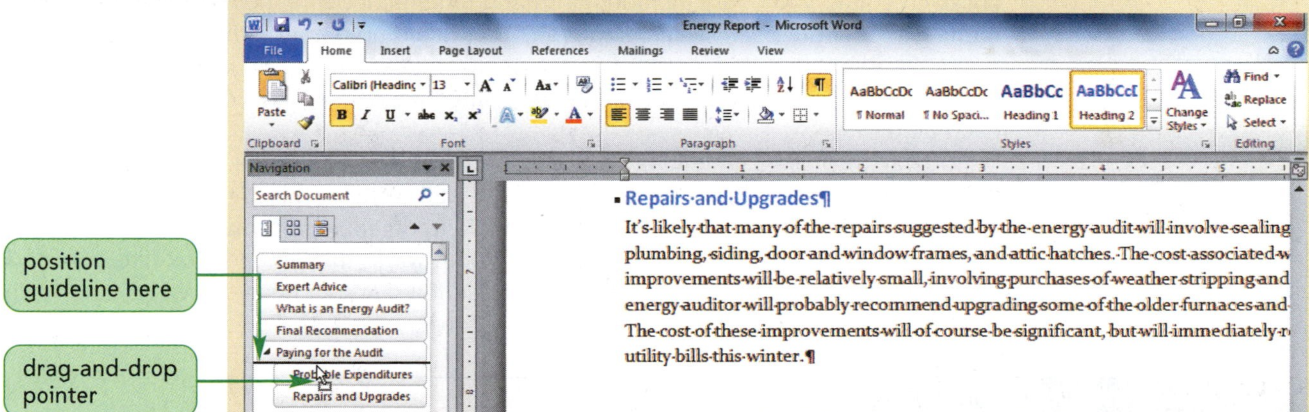

5. Release the mouse button. The "Repairs and Upgrades" heading appears in its new position in the Navigation pane, as the second to last heading in the outline. The heading and its body text appear in their new location in the document, before the "Probable Expenditures" heading. See Figure 3-5.

Figure 3-5 **Heading and body text in new location**

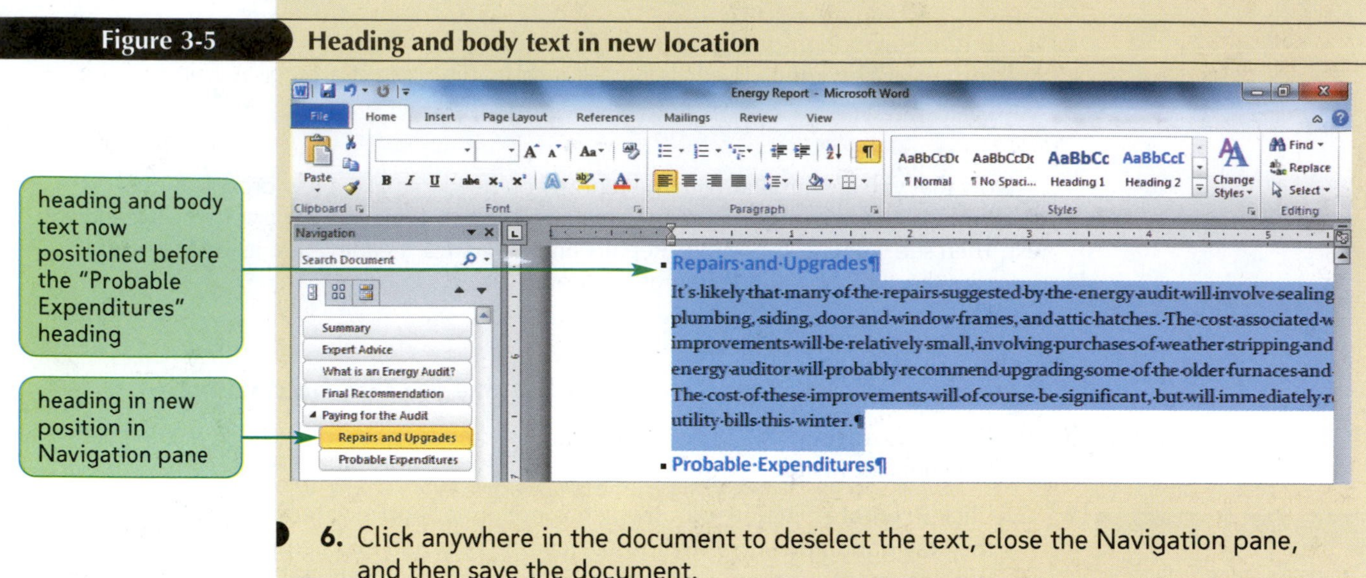

6. Click anywhere in the document to deselect the text, close the Navigation pane, and then save the document.

The document is now structured the way Robin wants it. Next you need to create a table summarizing her data on probable expenditures.

Inserting a Blank Table

A table is a useful way to present information that is organized into categories, or **fields**. For example, you could use a table to organize contact information for a list of clients. For each client, you could include information in the following fields: first name, last name, street address, city, state, and zip code. The complete set of information about a particular client is called a **record**. In a typical table, each column is a separate field, and each row is a record. A row at the top, called the **header row**, contains the names of each field.

You can also use a table to lay out text and graphics on the page. You'll have a chance to use a table in this way in the Case Problems at the end of this tutorial.

For Robin's report, you need to create a table to organize information in rows and columns. The sketch in Figure 3-6 shows what Robin wants the table to look like. It includes two columns, or fields: Item and Materials Cost. It includes a header row, containing the names of the two fields, and three rows, or records.

Figure 3-6 **Table sketch**

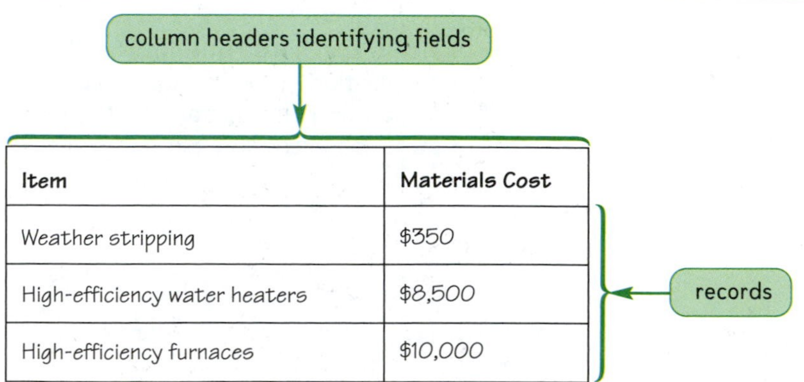

Item	Materials Cost
Weather stripping	$350
High-efficiency water heaters	$8,500
High-efficiency furnaces	$10,000

Creating a table in Word is a three-step process. First, you use the Table button on the Insert tab to insert a blank table structure. Then you enter information into the table. Finally, you format the table to make it easy to read.

The Table button allows you to drag the mouse pointer across a blank grid to select the numbers of rows and columns you want to include in your table. A Live Preview of the table structure appears in the document as you drag the mouse pointer. The table is inserted in the document when you release the mouse button.

You need to move the "Probable Expenditures" section to a new page, so you will have plenty of room for the new table. You will insert a manual page break to move this section to its own page.

To insert a page break and insert a blank table:

1. Click at the beginning of the heading "Probable Expenditures" and then press the **Ctrl+Enter** keys. The heading and the body text following it move to a new, third page.
2. Press the **Ctrl+End** keys to move the insertion point to the blank paragraph at the end of the document.
3. Click the **Insert** tab, and then click the **Table** button in the Tables group. A table grid opens, with a menu at the bottom.
4. Click in the upper-left cell of the grid, and then hold the left mouse button down as you drag the pointer down and across the grid to highlight **two columns** and **four rows**. (The outline of a cell turns orange when it is highlighted.) As you drag the pointer across the grid, Word indicates the size of the table (columns by rows) at the top of the grid. A Live Preview of the table structure appears in the document. See Figure 3-7.

Figure 3-7 Inserting a blank table

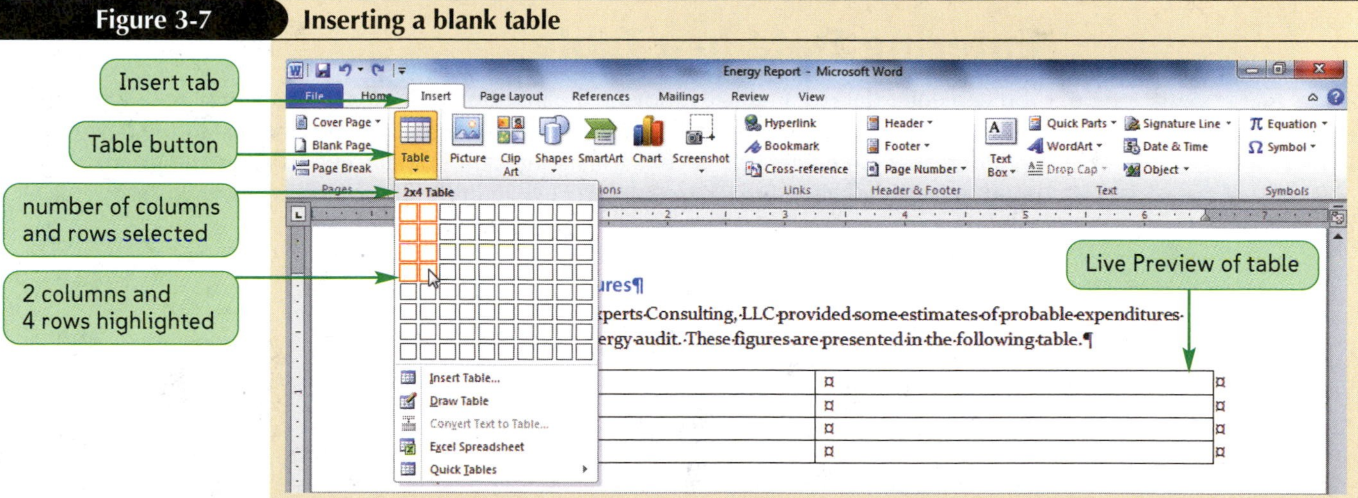

5. When the table size is 2 × 4, release the mouse button. An empty table consisting of two columns and four rows is inserted in the document, with the insertion point in the upper-left cell. The two columns are of equal width. Because nonprinting characters are displayed in the document, each cell contains an end-of-cell mark, and each row contains an end-of-row mark, which are important for selecting parts of a table. The Table Tools Design and Layout contextual tabs appear on the Ribbon.

TIP

To delete a table, select it, right-click it, and then click Cut. If you press the Delete key instead, you'll delete the contents of the table, but not the table itself.

Trouble? If you inserted a table with the wrong number of rows or columns, click the Undo button to remove the table, and then repeat Steps 3 through 5.

6. Move the mouse pointer over the empty table to display handles for moving and sizing the table. The Table Select handle appears in the table's upper-left corner. You can click to select the entire table, or you can drag it to move the table. You can drag the Table Resize handle, the small rectangular handle in the lower-right corner, to change the size of the table. See Figure 3-8.

Figure 3-8 Blank table inserted in document

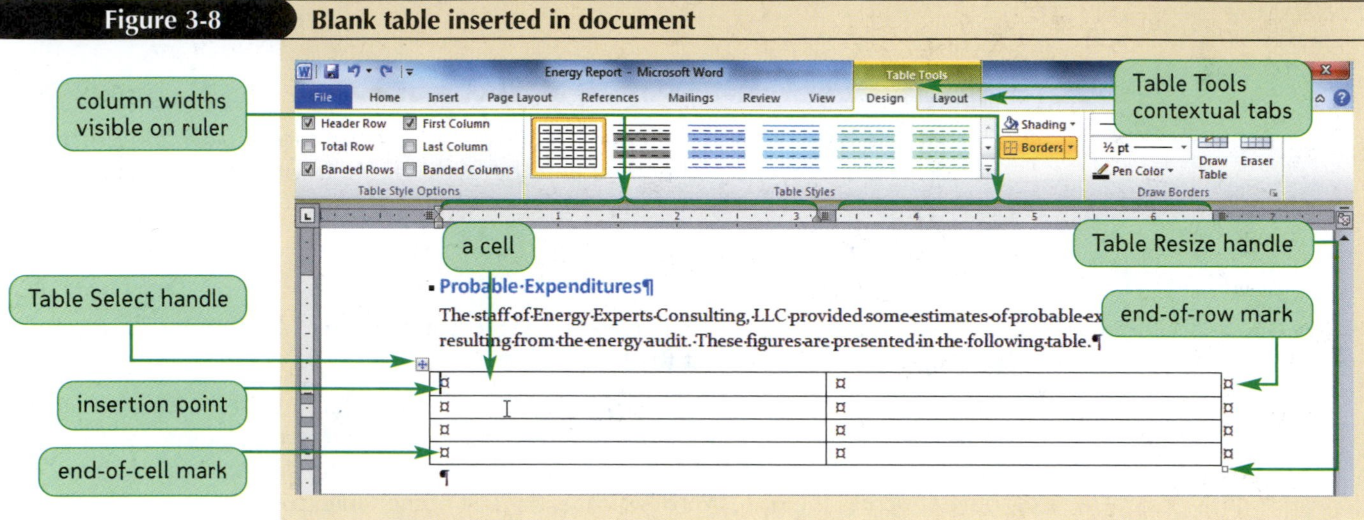

The blank table is ready for you to begin entering information.

Entering Data in a Table

You can enter data in a table by moving the insertion point to a cell and typing. If the data takes up more than one line in the cell, Word automatically wraps the text to the next line and increases the height of that cell (and all the cells in that row). To move the insertion point to another cell in the table, you can click in that cell, use the arrow keys, or use the Tab key.

To enter data into the table:

1. Verify that the insertion point is located in the upper-left cell.
2. Type **Item**. As you type, the end-of-cell mark moves right to accommodate the text.
3. Press the **Tab** key to move the insertion point to the next cell to the right.

   Trouble? If Word created a new paragraph in the first cell rather than moving the insertion point to the second cell, you pressed the Enter key instead of the Tab key. Press the Backspace key to remove the paragraph mark, and then press the Tab key to move to the second cell in the first row.

4. Type **Materials Cost**, and then press the **Tab** key to move to the first cell in the second row. Notice that when you press the Tab key in the right column, the insertion point moves to the first cell in the next row.

You have finished entering the header row—the row that identifies the information in each column. Now you can enter the information about the various expenditures.

To continue entering information in the table:

1. Type **weather stripping**, and then press the **Tab** key to move to the second cell in the second row. Notice that the "w" in "weather stripping" is capitalized, even though you typed it in lowercase. By default, AutoCorrect capitalizes the first letter in a cell entry.
2. Type **$350**, and then press the **Tab** key to move the insertion point to the first cell in the third row.
3. Type the following information, pressing the Tab key to move from cell to cell.

   High-efficiency water heaters **$8,500**

   High-efficiency furnaces **$10,000**

At this point, the table consists of a header row and three records. Robin realizes that she needs to add one more row to the table. To add a new row to the bottom of a table, make sure the insertion point is located in the right-most cell in the bottom row, and then press the Tab key.

To add a row to the table:

1. Verify that the insertion point is in the bottom-right cell (which contains the value "$10,000") and then press the **Tab** key. A new, blank row is added to the bottom of the table.
2. Type **Insulation**, press the **Tab** key, and then type **$700**. When you are finished, your table should look like the one shown in Figure 3-9.

Figure 3-9 Table with all data entered

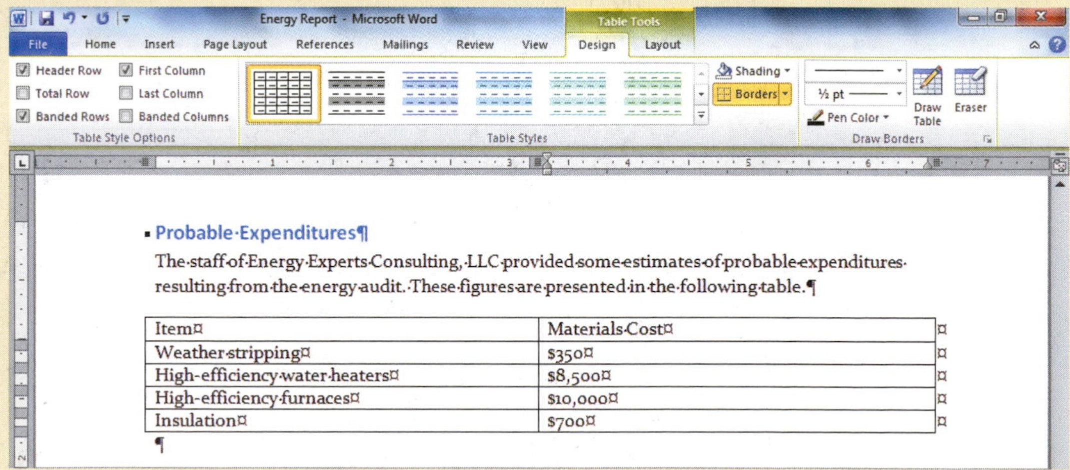

Trouble? If a new row appears at the bottom of your table, you pressed the Tab key when the insertion point was in the last cell in the table. Click the Undo button on the Quick Access Toolbar to remove the extra row from the table.

The table you've just created presents information about expenditures in an easy-to-read format. You want to format the header row in bold so it stands out from the rest of the table. To do that, you need to first select the header row in the table.

Selecting Part of a Table

When selecting a part of a table, you need to make sure you select the end-of-cell mark in a cell or the end-of-row mark at the end of a row. The foolproof way to select part of a table is to click the Select button on the Table Tools Layout tab and then click the appropriate command—Select Cell, Select Column, or Select Row. Alternatively, to select an entire row, you can click in the left margin next to the row. Similarly, you can click just above a column to select it. After you've selected an entire row, column, or cell, you can drag the mouse to select adjacent rows, columns, or cells.

To select and format the header row:

1. Move the mouse pointer to the left of the top row (which contains the word "Item"). The pointer changes to a right-facing arrow.
2. Click the mouse button. The entire header row, including the end-of-cell mark in each cell and the end-of-row mark, is selected. See Figure 3-10.

Figure 3-10 Header row selected

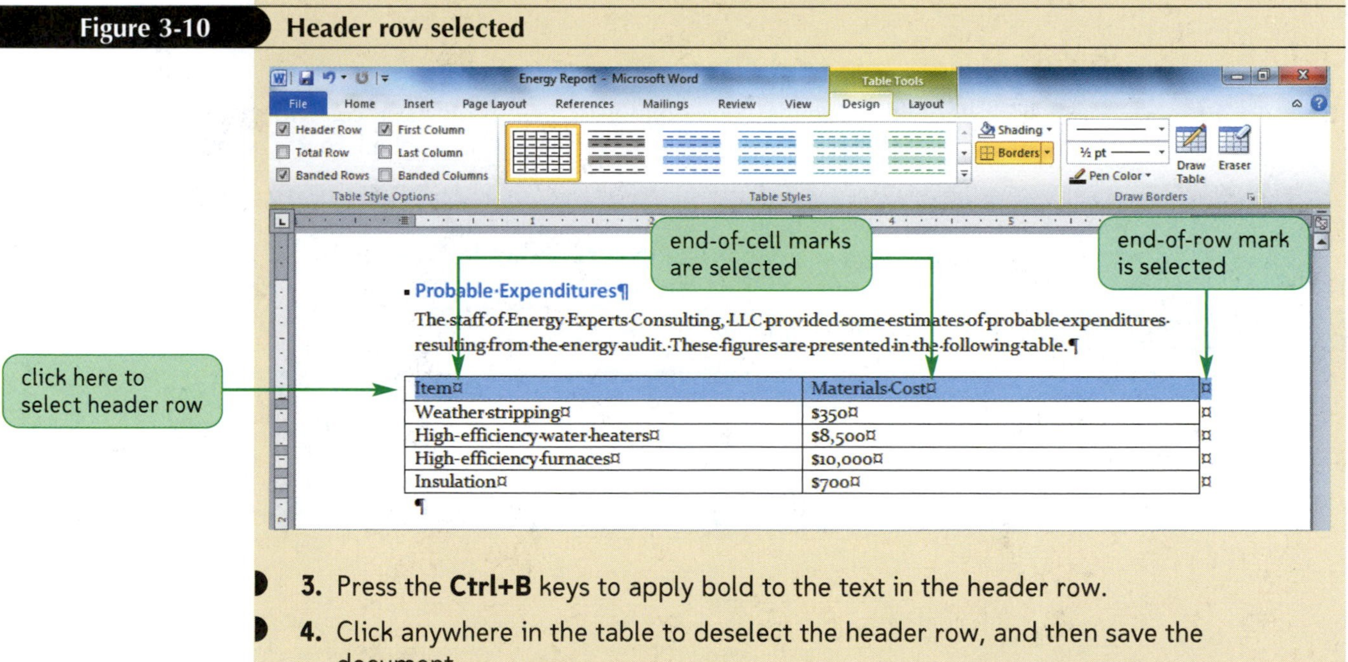

3. Press the **Ctrl+B** keys to apply bold to the text in the header row.
4. Click anywhere in the table to deselect the header row, and then save the document.

Now that you have created a very basic table, you can sort the information in it and improve its appearance.

Sorting Rows in a Table

The term **sort** refers to the process of rearranging information in alphabetical, numerical, or chronological order. You can sort a series of paragraphs, including the contents of a bulleted list, or you can sort the rows of a table.

When you sort a table, you arrange the rows based on the contents of one of the columns. For example, you could sort the table you just created based on the contents of the Item column—either in ascending alphabetical order (from *A* to *Z*) or in descending alphabetical order (from *Z* to *A*). Alternately, you could sort the table based on the contents of the Materials Cost column—either in ascending numerical order (lowest to highest) or in descending numerical order (highest to lowest).

To sort a table, select the table, then, on the Table Tools Layout tab, click the Sort button to open the Sort dialog box. This dialog box provides a number of options for fine-tuning the sort, including options for sorting a table by the contents of more than one column. This is useful if, for example, you want to organize the table rows by last name, and then, within each last name, by first name. You'll have to change fewer settings in the Sort dialog box if you first take the time to format the headers in bold, as you just did. That way Word recognizes the bold text as headers and excludes them from the sorting process, leaving them at the top of the table.

REFERENCE

Sorting the Rows of a Table

- Format the column headers in bold, and then click anywhere within the table.
- In the Data group on the Table Tools Layout tab, click the Sort button.
- In the Sort dialog box, click the Sort by arrow, and then select the header for the column you want to sort by.
- In the Type box located to the right of the Sort by box, select the type of information stored in the column you want to sort by; you can choose text, numbers, or dates.
- To sort in alphabetical, chronological, or numeric order, verify that the Ascending option button is selected. To sort in reverse order, click the Descending option button.
- To sort by a second column, click the Then by arrow and click a column header. If necessary, specify the type of information in the Then by column, and the sort order of ascending or descending.
- Make sure the Header row option button is selected. This indicates that the table includes a header row that should not be included in the sort.
- Click the OK button.

Robin would like you to sort the contents of the table in ascending alphabetical order, based on the contents of the Item column.

To sort the information in the table:

1. Make sure the insertion point is somewhere in the table, and then click the **Table Tools Layout** tab.
2. In the Data group, click the **Sort** button. The Sort dialog box opens, as shown in Figure 3-11. By default, the Item column is already selected in the Sort by box, indicating the sort will be based on the contents in this column. The contents of the Item column is text, so "Text" is selected in the Type box. The Ascending option button is selected by default, indicating that Word will sort the contents of the Item column from *A* to *Z*. The Header row option button is selected in the lower-left corner of the dialog box, ensuring this row will not be included in the sort.

TIP

If the Sort by column contained dates or numbers, the Type box would display Date or Number.

Figure 3-11 Sort dialog box

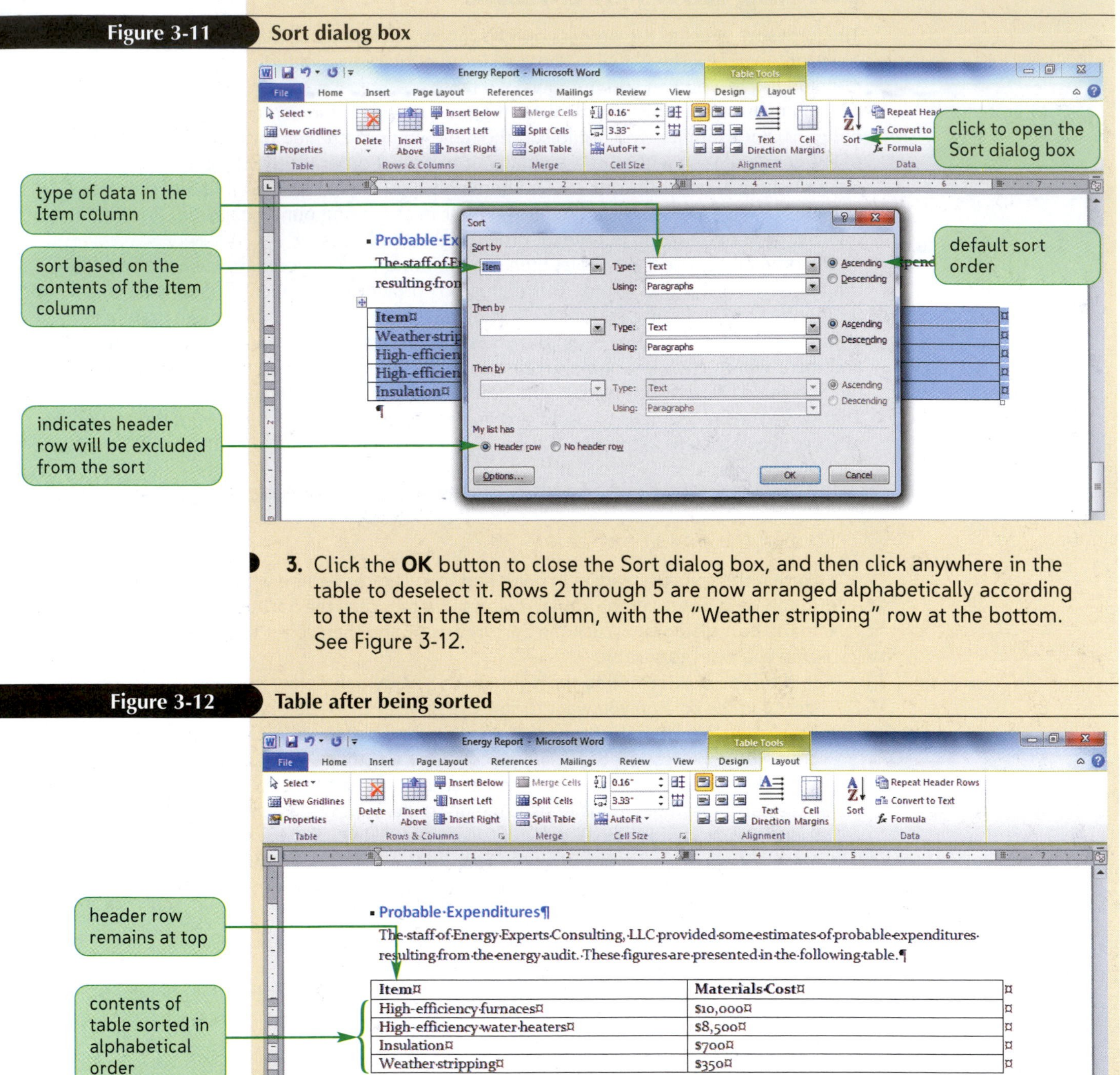

3. Click the **OK** button to close the Sort dialog box, and then click anywhere in the table to deselect it. Rows 2 through 5 are now arranged alphabetically according to the text in the Item column, with the "Weather stripping" row at the bottom. See Figure 3-12.

Figure 3-12 Table after being sorted

4. Save the document.

Robin decides that the table should include an estimate of the labor cost for each item. She asks you to insert a "Labor Cost" column.

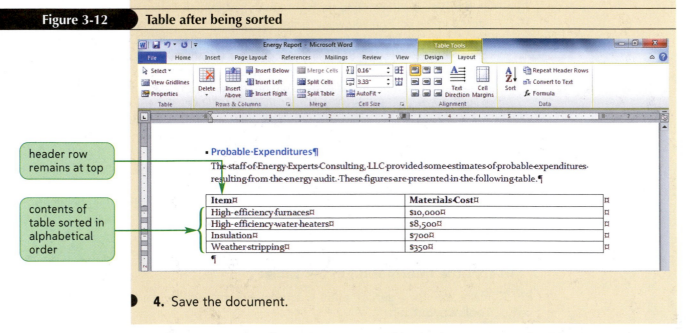

Inserting Rows and Columns in a Table

You will often need to modify a table structure by adding or deleting rows and columns. To insert a column, first click anywhere in the column to the left or right of the location where you want to insert a new column, and then click either the Insert Left or Insert Right button in the Rows & Columns group on the Table Tools Layout tab. Inserting a row is similar to inserting a column. First, click anywhere in a row above or below where you want to insert the new row, and then, in the Rows & Columns group, click either the Insert Above button or the Insert Below button.

To insert a column in the table:

1. Click any cell in the Item column.
2. In the Rows & Columns group, click the **Insert Right** button. A new, blank column is inserted to the right of the Item column. The three columns in the table are narrower than the original two columns; the overall width of the table does not change.
3. Click in the top cell of the new column, and enter the following header and data. Use the ↓ key to move the insertion point down through the column.

   Labor Cost

   $3,500 to $5,000

   $3,000 to $4,000

   $1,000

   $2,500

   When you are finished, your table should look like the one in Figure 3-13. Because you selected the entire header row when you formatted the original headers in bold, the newly inserted header, "Labor Cost," is also formatted in bold.

Figure 3-13 New Labor Cost column

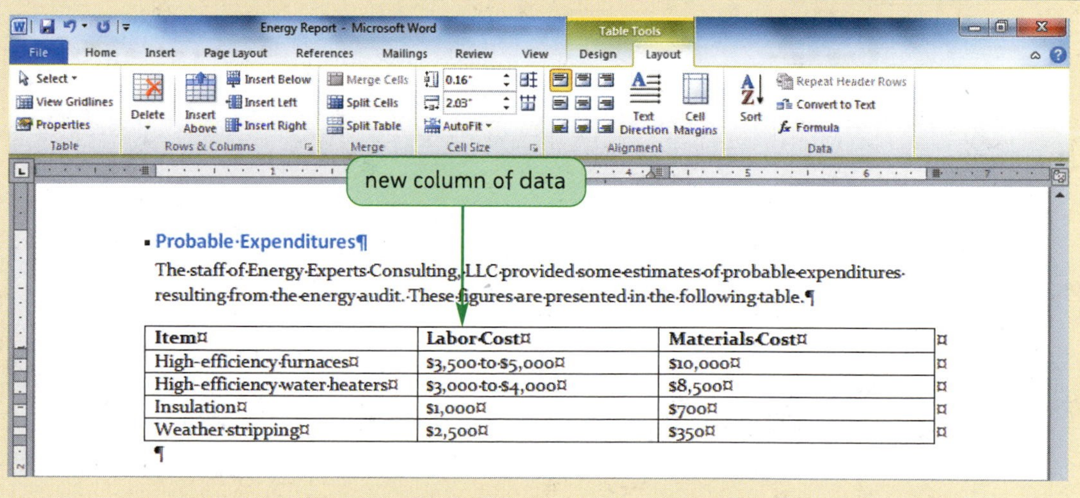

Robin just learned that the costs listed for weather stripping actually cover both weather stripping and insulation. Therefore, she would like you to delete the Insulation row from the table.

Deleting Rows and Columns

When you consider deleting a row, you need to be clear about whether you want to delete the *contents* of the row, or the contents and the *structure* of the row. You can delete the *contents* of a row by selecting the row and pressing the Delete key. This removes the information from the row, but leaves the row structure intact. The same is true for deleting the contents of an individual cell, a column, or the entire table. To delete the *structure* of a row, column, or the entire table—including its contents—you select the row (or column or the entire table) and then use the Delete button in the Rows & Columns group. To delete multiple rows or columns, start by selecting all the rows or columns you want to delete.

Before you delete the Insulation row, you need to edit the contents in the last cell in the first column to indicate that the items in that row are for weather stripping and insulation.

To delete the Insulation row:

1. In the cell containing the text "Weather stripping," click to the right of the "g," press the **spacebar**, and then type **and insulation**. The cell now reads "Weather stripping and insulation." Part of the text wraps to a second line within the cell. Next, you can delete the Insulation row, which is no longer necessary.
2. Select the **Insulation** row by clicking to the left of the row in the left margin.
3. In the Rows & Columns group on the Layout tab, click the **Delete** button. The Delete menu opens, displaying options for deleting cells, columns, rows, or the entire table. See Figure 3-14.

Figure 3-14 Deleting a row

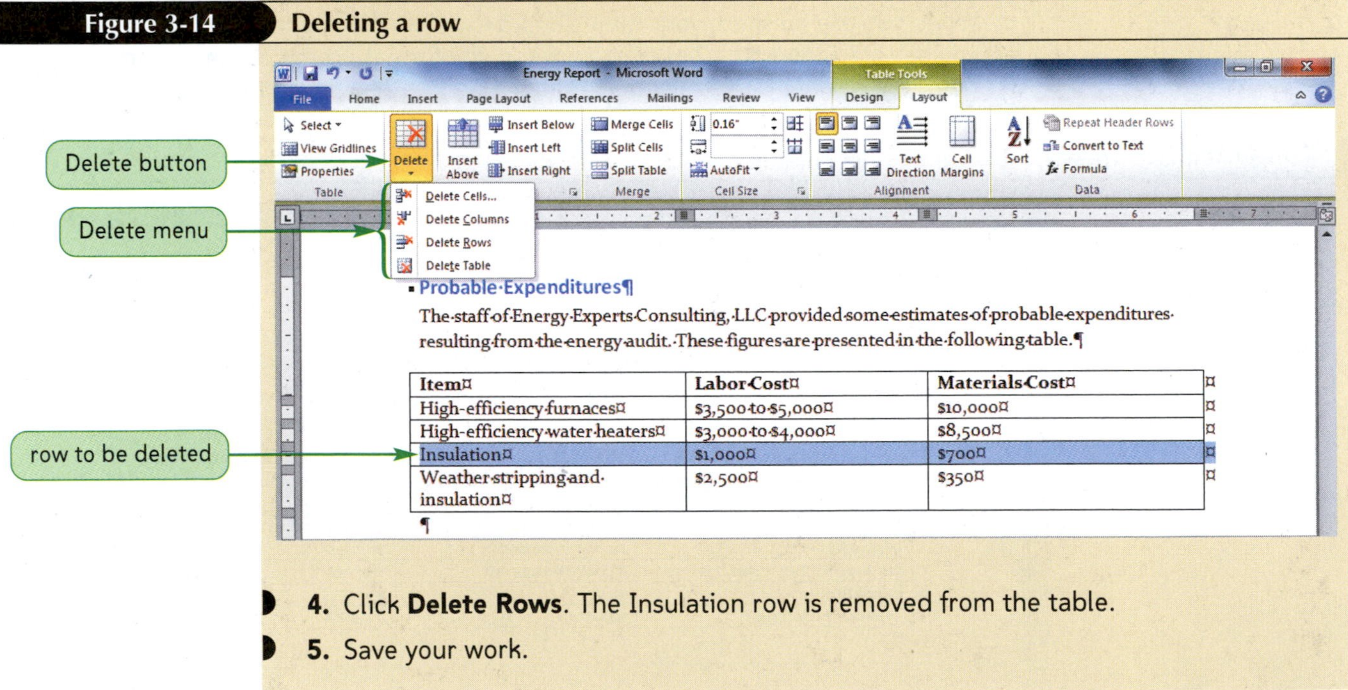

4. Click **Delete Rows**. The Insulation row is removed from the table.
5. Save your work.

The table now contains all the information Robin wants to include. Now you need to adjust the widths of the three columns.

Changing Column Widths

Columns that are too wide for the material they contain can make a table hard to read. You can change a column's width by dragging the column's right border to a new position. Or, if you prefer, you can double-click a column border to make the column width adjust automatically to accommodate the widest entry in the column. To adjust the width of all the columns to match their widest entries, click anywhere in the table, click the AutoFit button in the Cell Size group on the Table Tools Layout tab, and then click AutoFit Contents. To adjust the width of the entire table to span the width of the page, click the AutoFit Contents button and then click AutoFit Window.

You will adjust the columns in Robin's table by double-clicking the right column border. You need to start by making sure that no part of the table is selected. Otherwise, when you double-click the border, only the width of the selected part of the table will change.

To change the width of the columns in the table:

1. Verify that no part of the table is selected, and then position the mouse pointer over the right border of the Labor Cost column until the pointer changes to ↔. See Figure 3-15.

Figure 3-15 Adjusting the column width

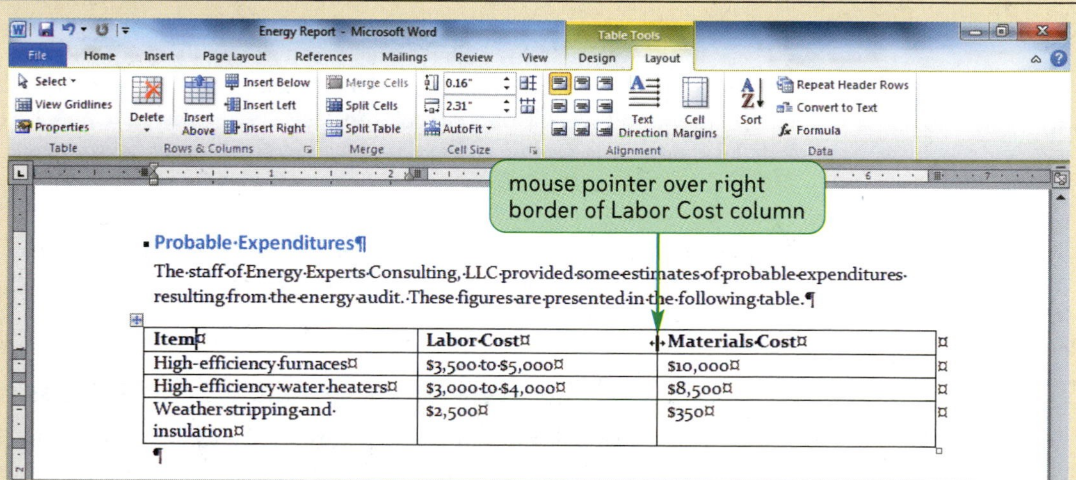

TIP

To change the height of a row, position the mouse pointer over the bottom row border and drag the border up or down.

2. Double-click the mouse button. The right column border moves left so that the Labor Costs column is just wide enough to accommodate the widest entry in the column.
3. Click any cell in the table, click the **AutoFit** button in the Cell Size group, and then click **AutoFit Contents**. The table columns adjust so that each is just wide enough to accommodate its widest entry. The text "Weather stripping and insulation" in the bottom left cell no longer wraps to a second line.

To finish the table, you will add some formatting to improve the table's appearance.

Formatting Tables with Styles

Word includes a variety of built-in table styles that you can use to add shading, color, borders, and other design elements with a single click. You can choose a style that includes different formatting for the header row than for the rest of the table. Or you can choose a style that instead applies different formatting to the **first column**, or header column (that is, the far-left column, which sometimes contains headers that identify the type of information in each row). Some styles format the rows in alternating colors, called **banded rows**, while others format the columns in alternating colors, called **banded columns**.

You select a table style from the Table Styles group on the Table Tools Design tab, which displays a selection of table styles. To see the complete collection, click the More button in the Table Styles group to open the Table Styles gallery. When you move your mouse pointer over a table style, a Live Preview of it appears in the table in the document. After you apply a table style, you can modify elements of it by selecting or deselecting the check boxes in the Table Style Options group on the Table Tools Design tab.

REFERENCE

Formatting a Table with a Table Style

- Click in the table you want to format, and then click the Table Tools Design tab.
- In the Table Styles group, click the More button to display the Table Styles gallery.
- Position the mouse pointer over a style in the Table Styles gallery to see a Live Preview of the table style in the document.
- In the Table Styles gallery, click the style you want.
- To apply or remove style elements (such as special formatting for the header row, banded rows, or banded columns), select or deselect check boxes as necessary in the Table Style Options group.

Robin wants to use a table style that emphasizes the header row with special formatting, does not include column borders, and uses color to separate the rows.

To apply a table style to the Probable Expenditures table:

1. Click anywhere in the table, and then click the **Table Tools Design** tab. In the Table Styles group, the plain black-and-white grid style is highlighted, indicating that it is the table's current style. See Figure 3-16.

Figure 3-16 Table styles visible on the Design tab

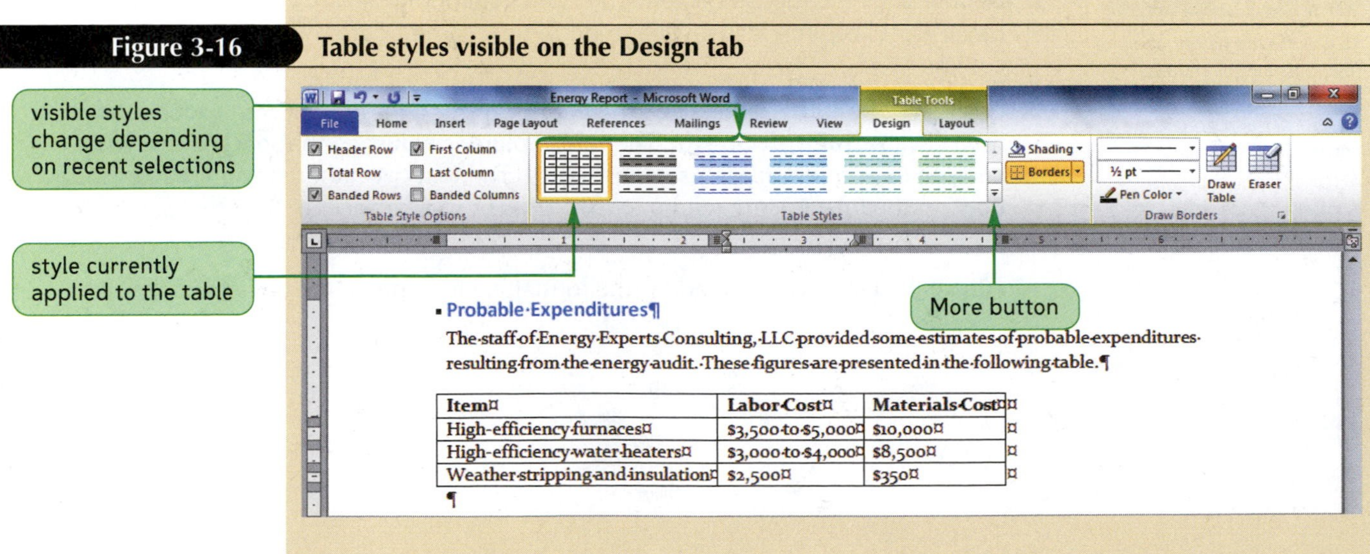

Item	Labor Cost	Materials Cost
High-efficiency furnaces	$3,500 to $5,000	$10,000
High-efficiency water heaters	$3,000 to $4,000	$8,500
Weather stripping and insulation	$2,500	$350

2. In the Table Styles group, click the **More** button. The Table Styles gallery opens. Now the plain black-and-white grid style appears at the top of the gallery, under the heading "Plain Tables." The more elaborate Table Styles appear below, in the "Built-In" section of the gallery.
3. Use the gallery's vertical scroll bar to view the complete collection of table styles. When you are finished looking, scroll up until you can see the Built-In section again.
4. Move the mouse pointer over the style located in the fourth row of the Built-In section, second column from the right. See Figure 3-17. A ScreenTip displays the style's name, "Medium Shading 1 – Accent 5." The style consists of a dark green heading row, with alternating rows of light green and white below and no borders between the columns. A Live Preview of the style is visible in the document.

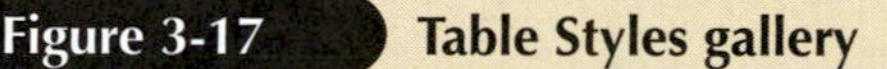

Figure 3-17 Table Styles gallery

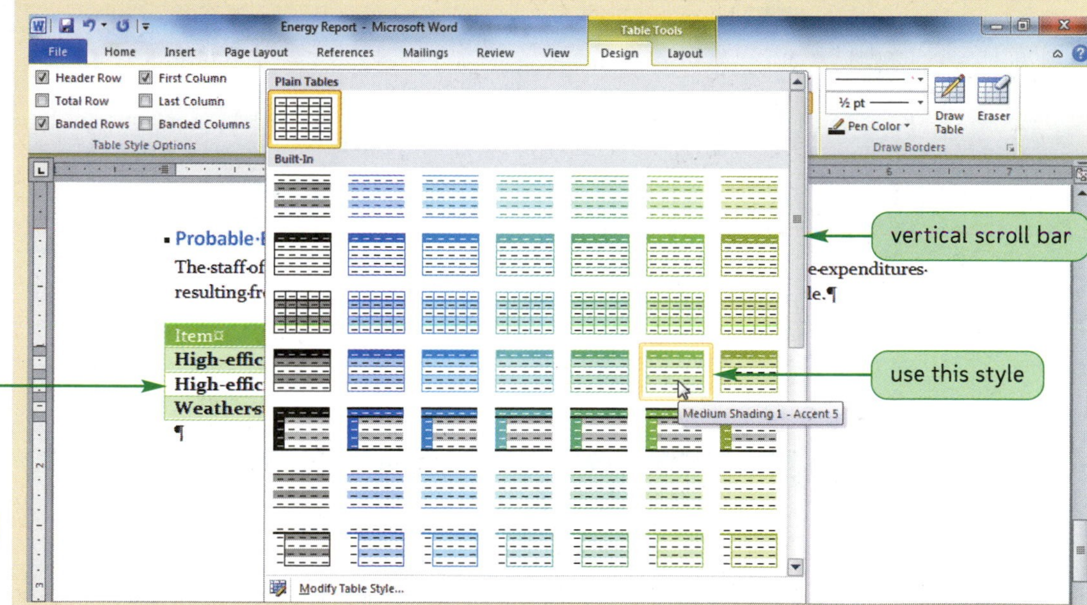

TIP

If you change the theme after applying a table style, the table's formatting will change to match the colors of the newly applied theme.

5. Click the **Medium Shading 1 – Accent 5** style. The Table Styles gallery closes. The table's header row is formatted with dark green shading and white text. The rows below appear in alternating colors of light green and white.

The only problem with the newly formatted table is that the text in the first column is formatted in bold. In tables where the first column contains headers, bold would be appropriate, but this isn't the case with Robin's table. You'll fix this by deselecting the First Column check box in the Table Style Options group.

To remove the bold formatting from the first column:

1. In the Table Style Options group, click the **First Column** check box to deselect this option. The bold formatting is removed from the entries in the Item column. Note that the Header Row check box is selected. This indicates that the table's header row is emphasized with special formatting (dark green shading with white text). The Banded Rows check box is also selected because the table is formatted with banded rows of green and white. Figure 3-18 shows the finished table.

Figure 3-18 Completed table

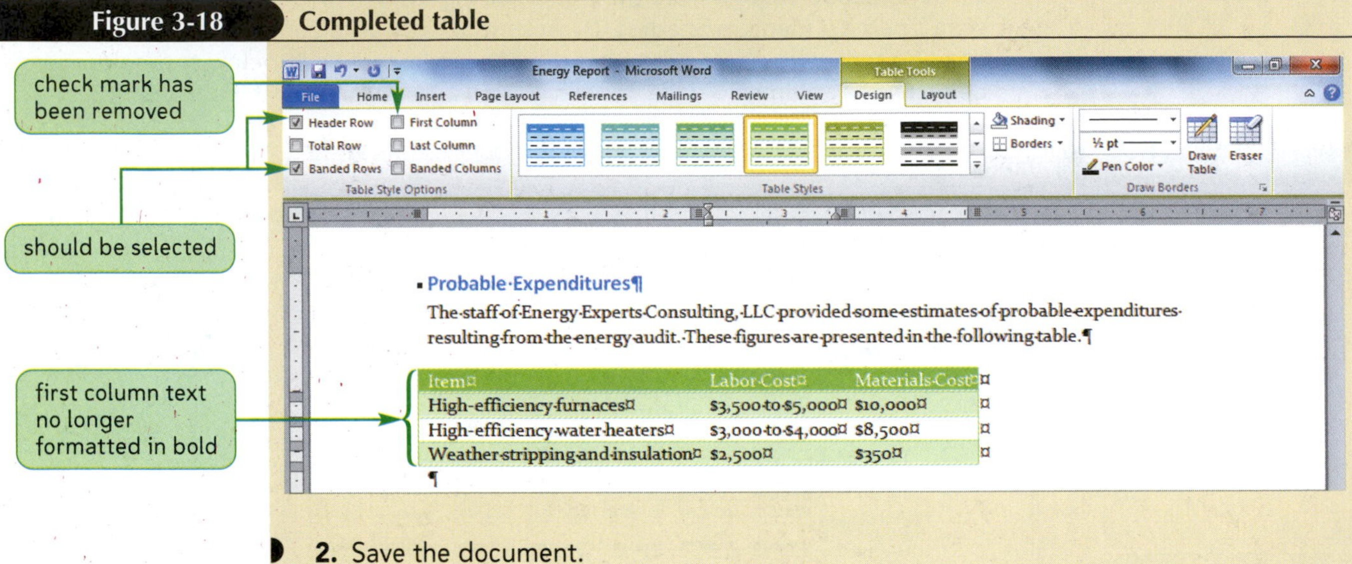

2. Save the document.

PROSKILLS

Problem Solving: Fine-tuning Table Styles

After you apply a table style to a table, you might like the look of the table, but find that it no longer effectively conveys your information or is not quite as easy to read. To solve this problem, you might be inclined to go back to the Table Styles gallery to find another style that might work better. Another method to correct problems with a table style is to identify the table elements with problematic formatting, and then manually make formatting adjustments to just those elements using the options on the Table Tools Design tab. For example, you can change the thickness and color of the table borders using the options in the Draw Borders group, and you can add shading using the Shading button in the Table Styles group. Also, if you don't like the appearance of table styles in your document, consider changing the document's theme and preview the table styles again. The table styles have a different appearance in each theme. When applying table styles, remember there are many options for attractively formatting the table without compromising the information being conveyed.

The completed table looks crisp and professional. In the next session, you will complete the rest of the report by organizing information using tab stops, creating footnotes and endnotes, dividing the document into sections, inserting headers and footers, and finally inserting a cover page.

REVIEW

Session 3.1 Quick Check

1. List three tasks you can perform using the Navigation pane.
2. Explain how to insert a table in a document.
3. Explain how to add a row to the bottom of a table.
4. List two ways to select a row in a table.
5. Explain how to sort a table.
6. True or False. To insert a column, you begin by selecting a column to the left or right of the location where you want to insert a column.
7. How can you adjust a table style so that the first column in the table is formatted like all the others?

SESSION 3.2 VISUAL OVERVIEW

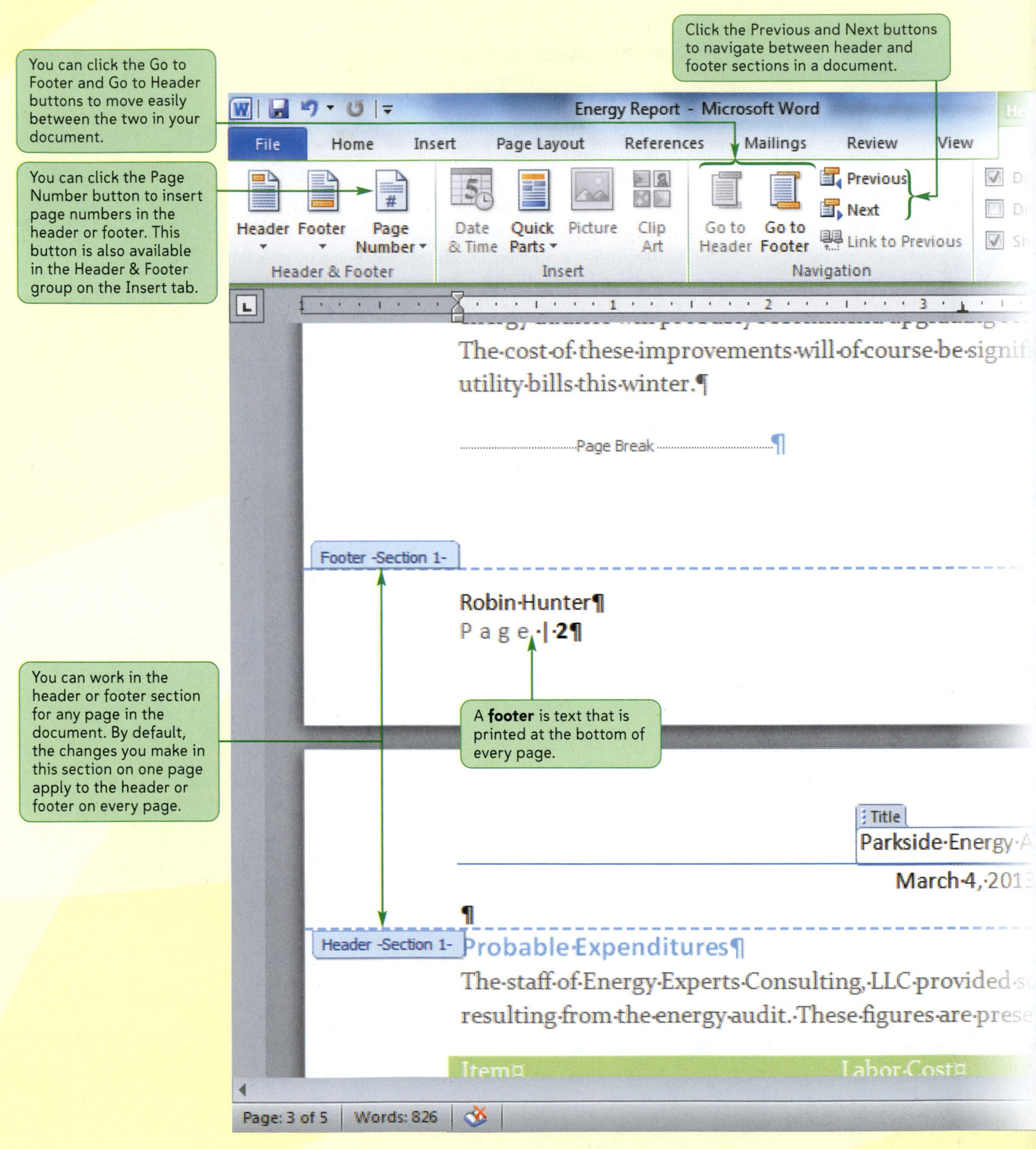

Click the Previous and Next buttons to navigate between header and footer sections in a document.
You can click the Go to Footer and Go to Header buttons to move easily between the two in your document.
You can click the Page Number button to insert page numbers in the header or footer. This button is also available in the Header & Footer group on the Insert tab.
Energy Report - Microsoft Word
File
Home
Insert
Page Layout
References
Mailings
Review
View
Header
Footer
Page Number
Date & Time
Quick Parts
Picture
Clip Art
Go to Header
Go to Footer
Previous
Next
Link to Previous
Header & Footer
Insert
Navigation
The·cost·of·these·improvements·will·of·course·be·signi
utility·bills·this·winter.¶
Page Break
Footer -Section 1-
Robin·Hunter¶
Page·|·2¶
You can work in the header or footer section for any page in the document. By default, the changes you make in this section on one page apply to the header or footer on every page.
A **footer** is text that is printed at the bottom of every page.
Title
Parkside·Energy·A
March·4,·201
Header -Section 1-
Probable·Expenditures¶
The·staff·of·Energy·Experts·Consulting,·LLC·provided·s
resulting·from·the·energy·audit.·These·figures·are·pres
Item
Labor·Cost
Page: 3 of 5
Words: 826

WORKING WITH HEADERS AND FOOTERS

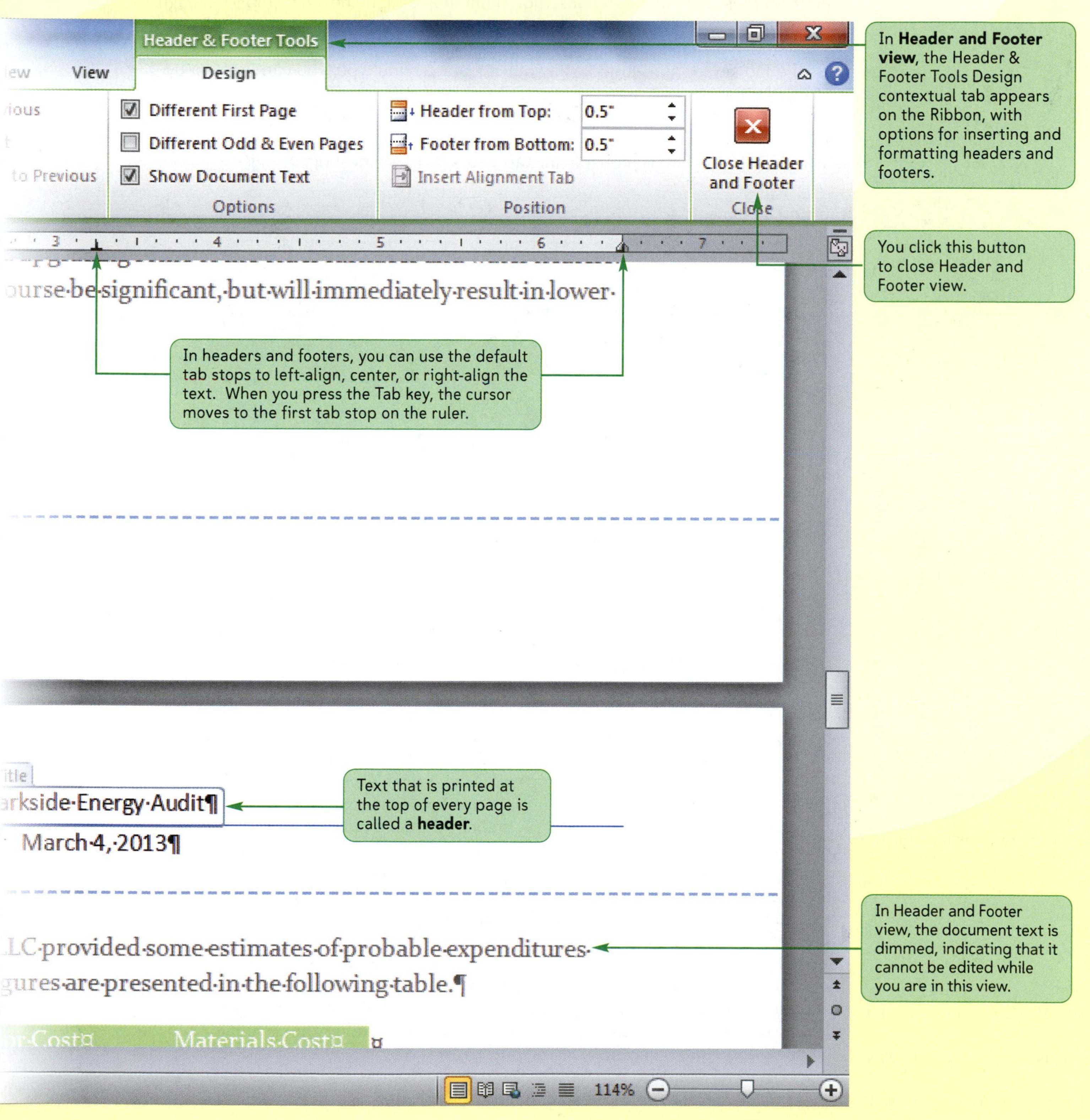

Header & Footer Tools
View
Design
Different First Page
Different Odd & Even Pages
Show Document Text
Options
Header from Top: 0.5"
Footer from Bottom: 0.5"
Insert Alignment Tab
Position
Close Header and Footer
Close
In **Header and Footer view**, the Header & Footer Tools Design contextual tab appears on the Ribbon, with options for inserting and formatting headers and footers.
You click this button to close Header and Footer view.
In headers and footers, you can use the default tab stops to left-align, center, or right-align the text. When you press the Tab key, the cursor moves to the first tab stop on the ruler.
Text that is printed at the top of every page is called a **header**.
March·4,·2013¶
In Header and Footer view, the document text is dimmed, indicating that it cannot be edited while you are in this view.
114%

Setting Tab Stops

A **tab stop** (often called a **tab**) is a location on the horizontal ruler where the insertion point moves when you press the Tab key. Tab stops are useful for aligning small amounts of data in columns. There are default tab stops every one-half inch on the horizontal ruler, indicated by the small tick marks that appear along the ruler's bottom edge. When you press the Tab key, the insertion point moves to the next tab stop to the right. It's important to have the Show/Hide ¶ button selected when you work with tab stops, because then you can see the nonprinting tab character (→) that is inserted when you press the Tab key. A tab is just like any other character you type; you can delete it by pressing the Backspace key or the Delete key.

You can use tab stops to align text in a variety of ways. The five major types of tab stops are Left, Center, Right, Decimal, and Bar, as shown in Figure 3-19. The Left style is selected by default and is probably the tab style you'll use most often.

Figure 3-19 **Tab stop alignment styles**

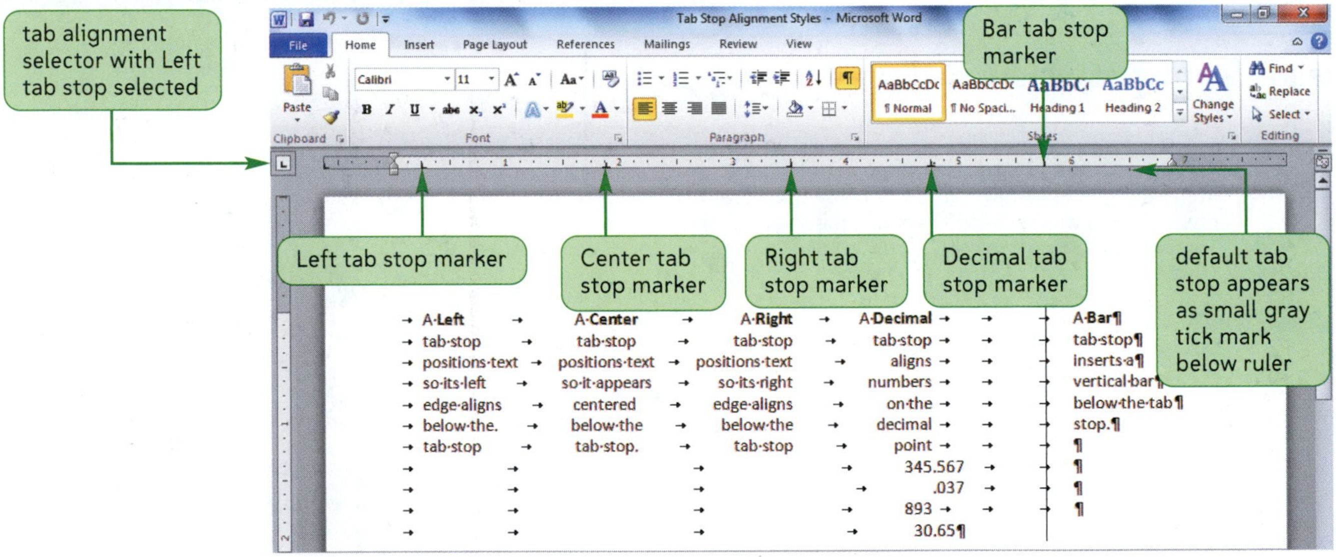

You can set tab stops a few different ways. The simplest is to first select an alignment style from the tab alignment selector, located at the left end of the horizontal ruler, and then click the horizontal ruler where you want to insert the tab stop. When you insert a tab stop, all of the default tab stops to its left are removed. This means you have to press the Tab key only once to move the insertion point to the newly created tab stop.

To create more complicated tab stops, you can use the Tabs dialog box. Among other things, the Tabs dialog box allows you to insert a **dot leader**, which is a row of dots (or other characters) between tabbed text. A dot leader makes it easier to read a long list of tabbed material because the eye can follow the dots from one item to the next. You've probably seen dot leaders used in the table of contents in a book, where the dots separate the chapter titles from the page numbers. To create a left tab stop with a dot leader, click the Dialog Box Launcher in the Paragraph group on the Home tab, click the Indents and Spacing tab if necessary, and then click the Tabs button at the bottom of the dialog box. In the Tab stop position text box, type the location on the ruler where you want to insert the tab. For example, to insert a tab stop at the 4-inch mark, type 4. Verify that the Left option button is selected in the Alignment section, and then, in the Leader section, click the option button for the type of dot leader you want. Click the Set button and then click the OK button.

REFERENCE

Setting and Clearing Tab Stops

- Click the tab alignment selector on the far left of the horizontal ruler until the appropriate tab stop alignment style appears.
- Click the horizontal ruler where you want to position the tab stop.
- Press the Tab key to move the insertion point to the new tab stop.
- To remove a tab stop, drag it off the ruler.

In the Energy Report document you have been working on, you need to type the list of consultants and their titles. You can use tab stops to quickly format this small amount of information in two columns. As you type, you'll discover whether Word's default tab stops are appropriate for this document or whether you need to add a new tab stop.

To enter the list of consultants using tabs:

1. If you took a break after the previous session, make sure Word is running and that the Energy Report document is open. Check that the ruler and nonprinting characters are displayed and that the document is displayed in Print Layout view.
2. Scroll as necessary to display the Expert Advice section that appears near the top of the first page, and then click to the right of the last "s" in "Sandra Burdulis."
3. Press the **Tab** key. A tab character appears, and the insertion point moves to the first tab stop after the "s" in "Burdulis." This tab stop is the default tab located at the 1.5-inch mark on the horizontal ruler. See Figure 3-20.

Figure 3-20 Tab character

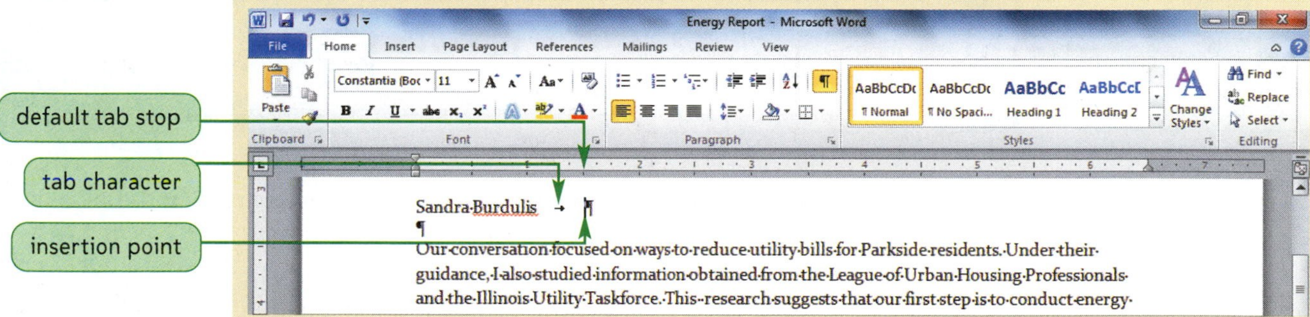

4. Type **Associate Engineer**. You could press the Enter key now to end the paragraph and start a new paragraph in which you can type the name and title for another expert. However, remember that Word inserts paragraph space after every paragraph; this will result in a list in which the items are spaced too far apart. Instead, you can use the Shift+Enter key combination to insert a manual line break. A **manual line break** moves the insertion point to the next line without actually starting a new paragraph, and no extra space is inserted.
5. Press the **Shift+Enter** keys. The insertion point moves to the next line, and Word inserts a manual line break nonprinting character. See Figure 3-21.

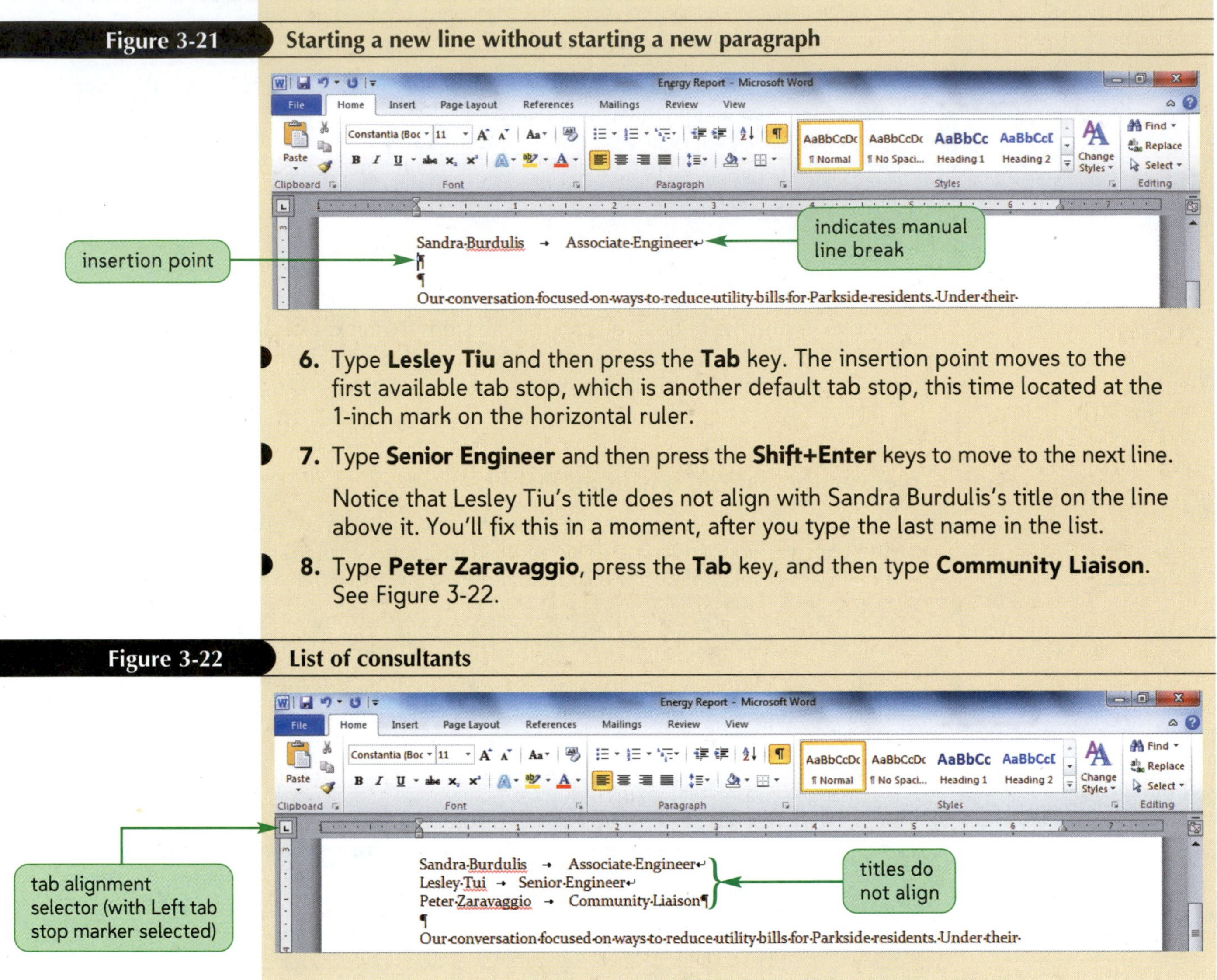

Figure 3-21 Starting a new line without starting a new paragraph

6. Type **Lesley Tiu** and then press the **Tab** key. The insertion point moves to the first available tab stop, which is another default tab stop, this time located at the 1-inch mark on the horizontal ruler.
7. Type **Senior Engineer** and then press the **Shift+Enter** keys to move to the next line.

   Notice that Lesley Tiu's title does not align with Sandra Burdulis's title on the line above it. You'll fix this in a moment, after you type the last name in the list.
8. Type **Peter Zaravaggio**, press the **Tab** key, and then type **Community Liaison**. See Figure 3-22.

Figure 3-22 List of consultants

The list of names and titles is not aligned properly. You can fix this by inserting a new tab stop.

To add a new tab stop to the horizontal ruler:

1. Click anywhere in the paragraph containing the list of consultants and their titles. Note that the current tab stop alignment style is Left tab.
2. Click the tick mark at the 2.5-inch location on the ruler. Word inserts a Left tab stop at that location and removes the default tab stops to its left. The column of titles shifts to the new tab stop. See Figure 3-23.

Figure 3-23 Titles aligned at new tab stop

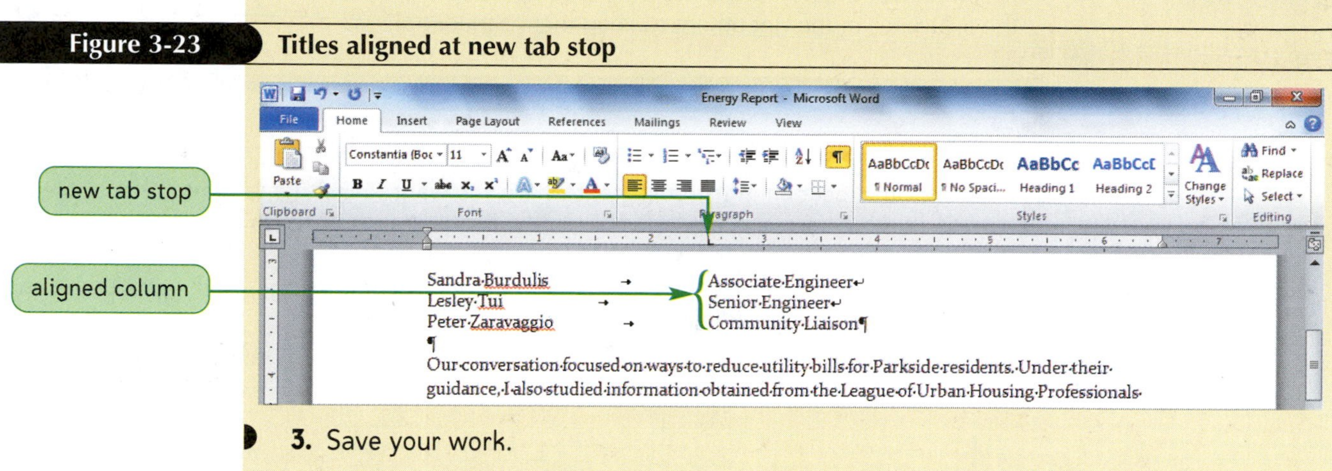

3. Save your work.

PROSKILLS

Decision Making: Choosing Between Tabs and Tables

When you have information that you want to align in columns in your document, you need to decide the best way to accomplish this. Whatever you do, don't try to align columns of data by adding extra spaces with the spacebar. Although the text might seem precisely aligned on the screen, it might not be aligned when you print the document. Furthermore, if you edit the text, the spaces you inserted to align your columns will be affected by your edits; they get moved just like regular text, ruining your alignment.

So what is the most efficient way to align text in columns? It depends. Inserting tabs works well for aligning small amounts of information in just a few columns and rows, such as two columns with three rows, but they become cumbersome when you need to organize a lot of data over multiple columns and rows. In this case, using a table to organize columns of information is better. Unlike with tabbed columns of data, it's easy to add data to tables by inserting columns. You might also choose tables over tab stops when you want to take advantage of the formatting options available with table styles. No matter which method you decide to use, tab stops and tables will ensure that when you edit the information in the columns, the alignment of the information will remain intact.

Robin would like to add two footnotes that provide further information about topics discussed in Robin's report. You will do that next.

Creating Footnotes and Endnotes

A **footnote** is an explanatory comment or reference that appears at the bottom of a page. When you create a footnote, Word inserts a small, superscript number (called a **reference marker**) in the text. The term **superscript** means that the number is raised slightly above the line of text. Word then inserts the same number in the page's bottom margin and positions the insertion point next to it so you can type the text of the footnote. **Endnotes** are similar, except that the text of an endnote appears at the end of a section, or in the case of a document without sections, at the end of the document. (You'll learn about dividing a document into sections later in this tutorial.) Also, by default, the reference marker for an endnote is a lowercase Roman numeral.

Word automatically manages the reference markers for you, keeping them sequential from the beginning of the document to the end, no matter how many times you add, delete, or move footnotes or endnotes. For example, if you move a paragraph containing footnote 4 so that it falls before the paragraph containing footnote 1, Word renumbers all the footnotes in the document to keep them sequential.

REFERENCE

Inserting a Footnote or an Endnote

- Click the location in the document where you want to insert a footnote or endnote.
- Click the References tab, and then in the Footnotes group, click the Insert Footnote button or the Insert Endnote button.
- Type the text of the footnote in the bottom margin of the page, or the text of the endnote at the end of the document.
- When you are finished typing the text of a footnote, click in the body of the document to continue working on the document.

Robin asks you to insert a footnote at the end of the paragraph just above the heading "Final Recommendation." The last sentence of this paragraph refers to studies on the effectiveness of residential energy audits. Robin wants a footnote that explains where more information about those studies can be found.

To add a footnote to the report:

1. Near the bottom of page 1, click at the end of the paragraph located just before the heading "Final Recommendation" to position the insertion point to the right of the period after "household."
2. Click the **References** tab, and then click the **Insert Footnote** button in the Footnotes group. A superscript "1" is inserted to the right of the period after "household." Word also inserts the number "1" in the bottom margin below a separator line. The insertion point is now located next to the number in the bottom margin, ready for you to type the text of the footnote. See Figure 3-24.

Figure 3-24 **Inserting a footnote**

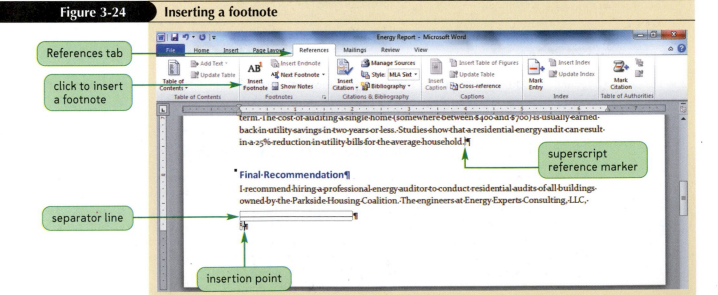

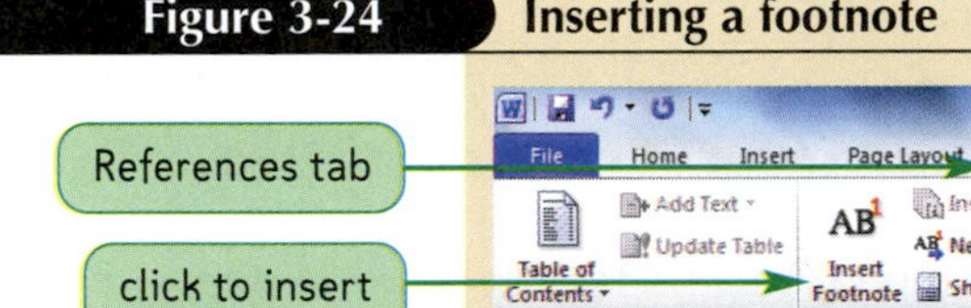

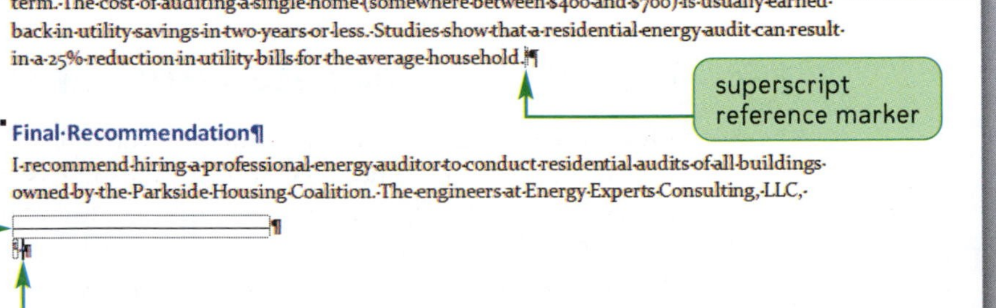

3. Type **For more information, see "A Consumer's Guide to Energy," available at www.course.com/consumer/energy. This helpful Web site is maintained by Course Energy Consultants.**

   When you press the spacebar after the Web address, Word underlines the address and formats it in a different font color, indicating that it is a live hyperlink, as shown in Figure 3-25. This means people reading the document can open the Web site by pressing the Ctrl key and clicking the link. Because Robin plans to distribute only a hard copy of the report, she asks you to disable the hyperlink.

TIP

Different themes format hyperlinks in different colors. In the default Office theme, hyperlinks are formatted in blue.

Figure 3-25 Footnote containing live hyperlink

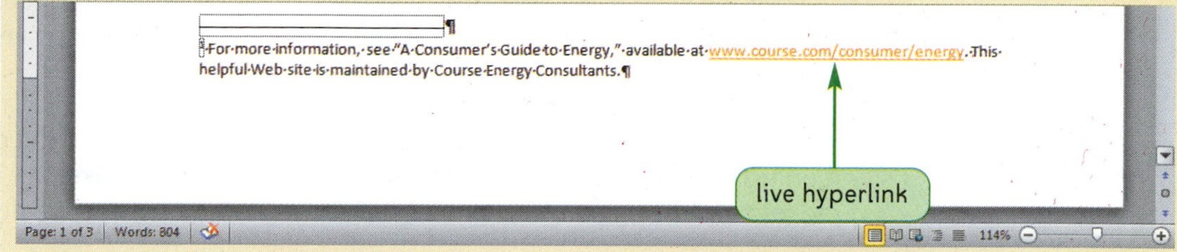

4. Right-click the **hyperlink** and then on the shortcut menu, click **Remove Hyperlink**. The disabled hyperlink is formatted to match the footnote text.

Robin would like you to insert a second footnote.

To insert a second footnote:

1. In the same paragraph, click at the end of the sentence which begins "The cost of auditing..." to position the insertion point to the right of the period after "less."
2. In the Footnotes group, click the **Insert Footnote** button, and then type **The cost of an audit is usually based on a home's square footage.** Because this footnote is placed earlier in the document than the one you just created, Word inserts a superscript "1" for this footnote, the other footnote is now numbered "2," and the "Final Recommendation" heading and its body text move to the next page. See Figure 3-26.

Figure 3-26 Inserting a second footnote

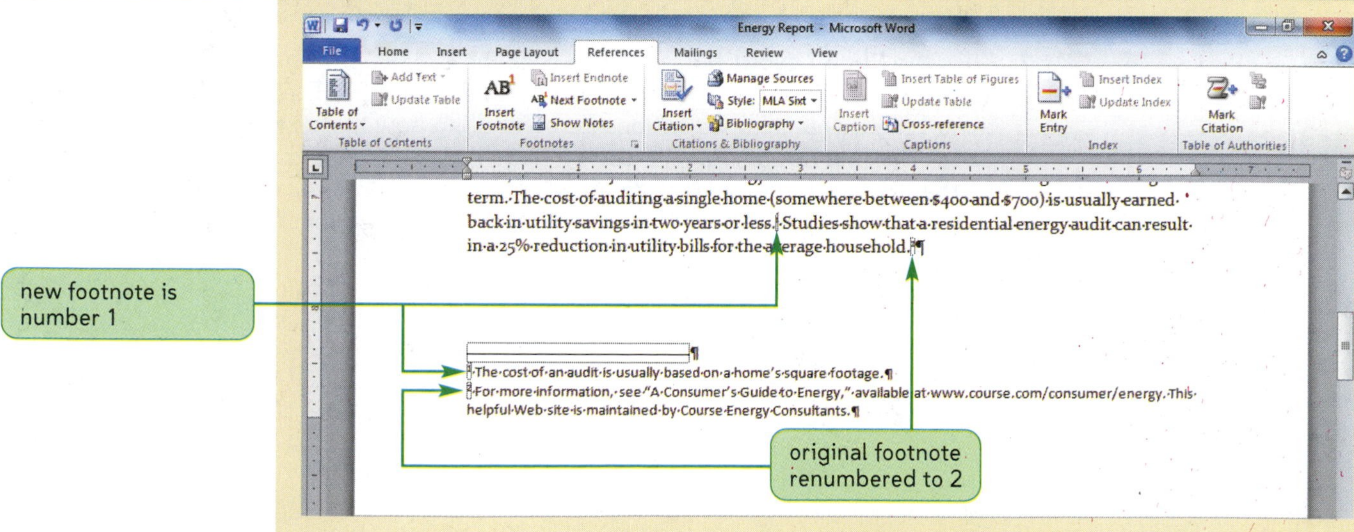

INSIGHT

Understanding Endnotes, Footnotes, and Citations

It's easy to confuse footnotes with endnotes and endnotes with citations. Remember, a footnote appears at the bottom, or foot, of a page, and always on the same page as its reference marker. You might have one footnote at the bottom of page 3, three footnotes at the bottom of page 5, and one at the bottom of page 6. By contrast, an endnote appears at the end of the document or section, with all the endnotes compiled into a single list. Both endnotes and footnotes can contain any kind of information you think might be useful to your readers. Citations, however, are only used to list specific information about a book or other source you refer to or quote from in the document. A citation typically appears in parentheses at the end of the sentence containing information from the source you are citing, and the sources for all the document's citations are listed in a bibliography, or list of works cited, at the end of the document.

Next, Robin wants to include a sample of the type of handout she plans to post on community bulletin boards at Parkside, encouraging residents to take part in the energy audit process. Before you can create the handout, you need to divide the document into sections.

Formatting a Document in Sections

Robin wants to format the handout in landscape orientation, but the rest of the report is currently formatted in portrait orientation. To format part of a document in an orientation different from the rest of the document, you need to divide the document into sections.

A **section** is a part of a document that can have its own page orientation, margins, headers, footers, and so on. Each section, in other words, is like a document within a document. To divide a document into sections, you insert a **section break**, which appears as a dotted line with the words "Section Break." You can select from a few different kinds of section breaks. For example, a Next page section break inserts a page break and starts the new section on the next page. A Continuous section break starts the section at the location of the insertion point, without changing the page flow. To insert a section break, you use the Breaks button in the Page Setup group on the Page Layout tab to select the type of section break you want to insert.

To insert a section break below the table:

1. Press the **Ctrl+End** keys to move the insertion point to the end of the document. The insertion point appears in the blank paragraph below the table.
2. Click the **Page Layout** tab, and then click the **Breaks** button in the Page Setup group. The Breaks menu opens, as shown in Figure 3-27. The Page Breaks section of the menu includes options for controlling how the text flows from page to page. The first option, Page, inserts a page break (just like the Page Break button on the Insert tab that you used earlier). The Section Breaks section of the menu includes four types of section breaks. The two you'll use most often are Next Page and Continuous.

Figure 3-27 Breaks menu

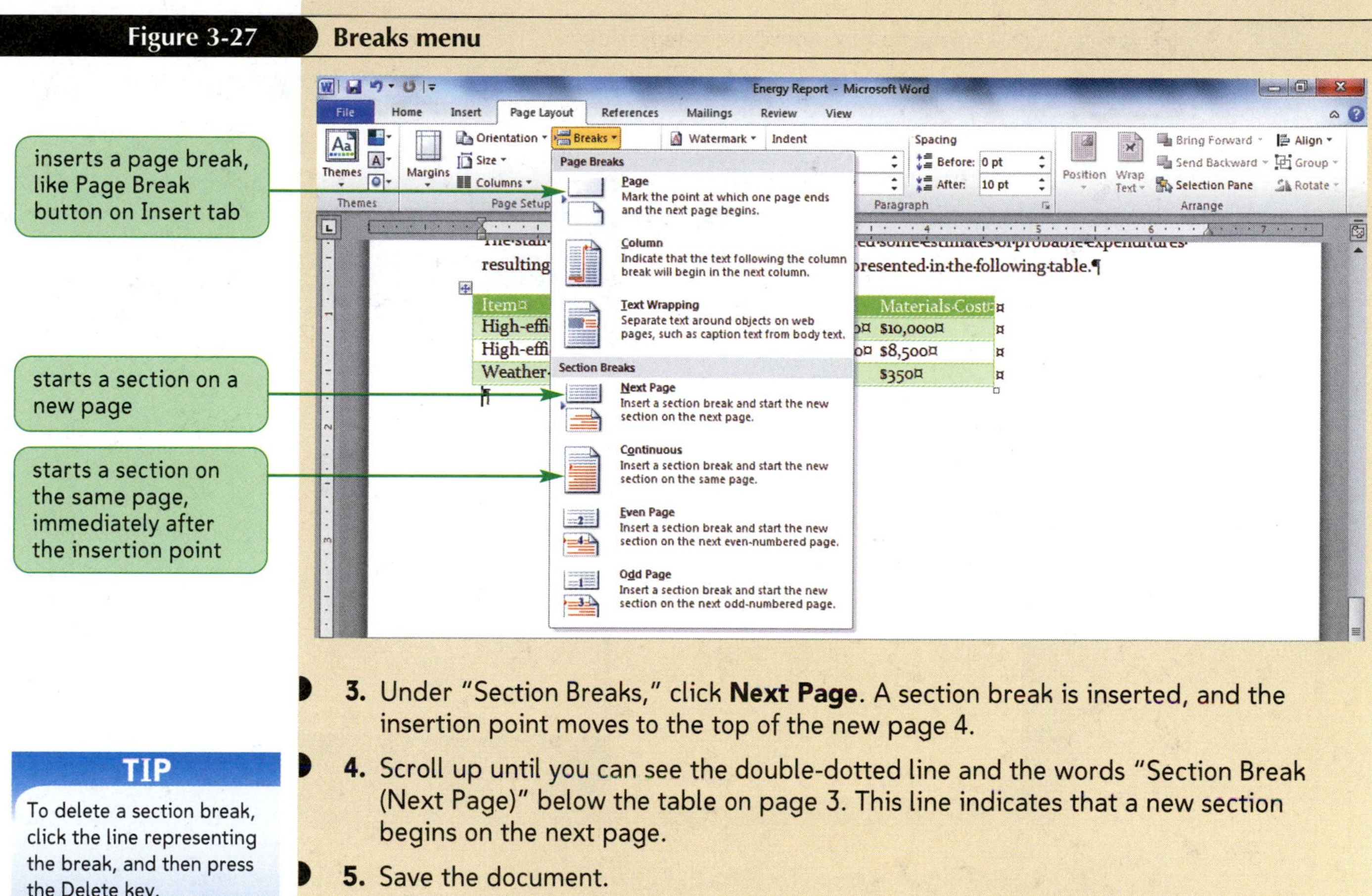

3. Under "Section Breaks," click **Next Page**. A section break is inserted, and the insertion point moves to the top of the new page 4.
4. Scroll up until you can see the double-dotted line and the words "Section Break (Next Page)" below the table on page 3. This line indicates that a new section begins on the next page.
5. Save the document.

TIP

To delete a section break, click the line representing the break, and then press the Delete key.

You've created a new page that is a separate section from the rest of the report. The sections are numbered consecutively, so that the first part of the document is section 1 and the new page is section 2. Now you can format section 2 in landscape orientation without affecting the rest of the document.

To format section 2 in landscape orientation:

1. Scroll down if necessary and verify that the insertion point is positioned at the top of the new page 4, and then click the **View** tab.
2. In the Zoom group, click the **Two Pages** button. The last two pages of the document appear side-by-side.
3. Click the **Page Layout** tab, click the **Orientation** button in the Page Setup group, and then click **Landscape**. Section 2, which consists solely of page 4, changes to landscape orientation, as shown in Figure 3-28. Section 1, which consists of pages 1–3, remains in portrait orientation.

Figure 3-28 Page 4 formatted in landscape orientation

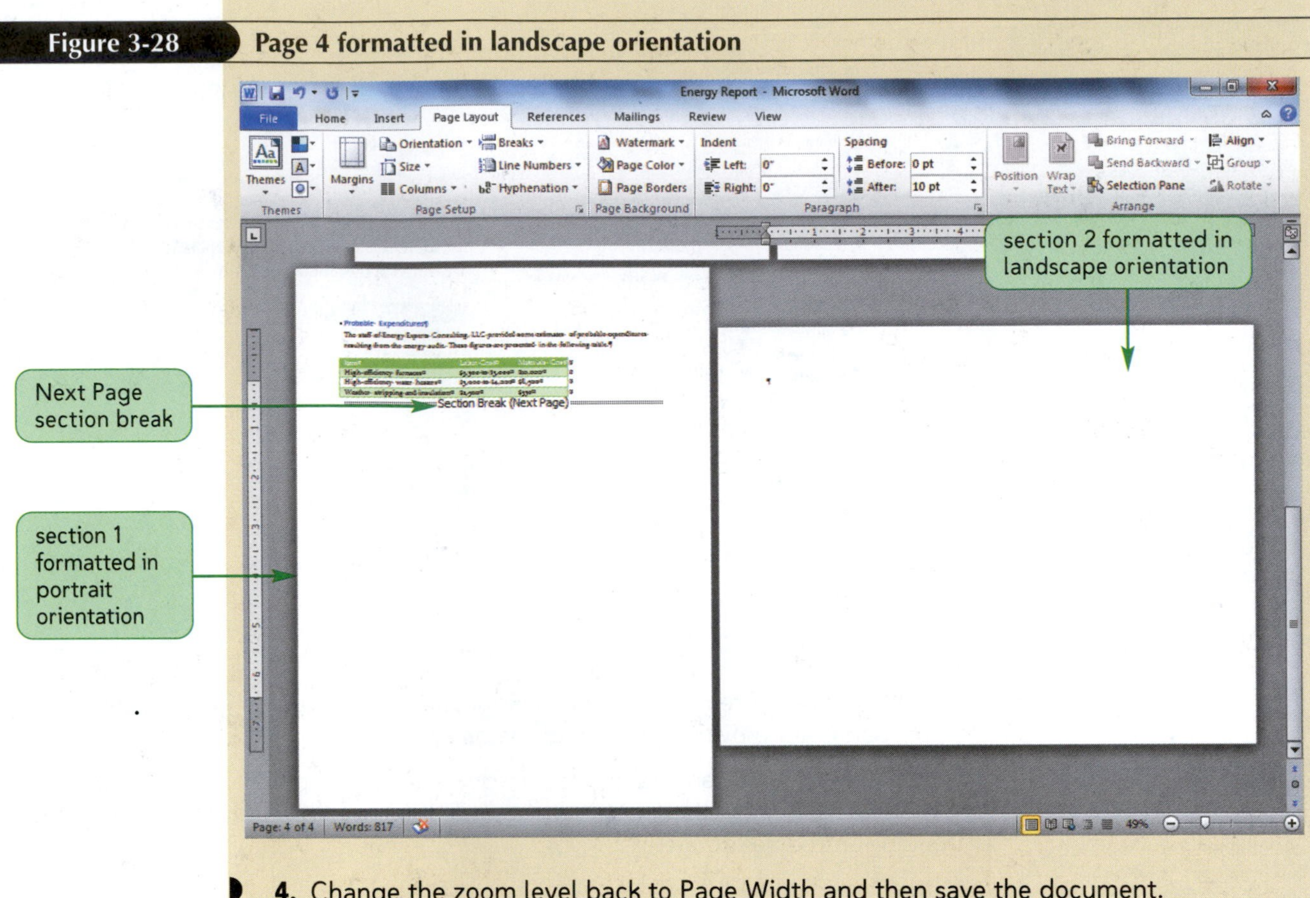

4. Change the zoom level back to Page Width and then save the document.

Page 4 is now formatted in landscape orientation, ready for you to create Robin's handout, which will consist of an illustration, or graphic, that explains the stages and ultimate goal of the energy audit process. You will use Word's SmartArt feature to create the graphic.

Creating SmartArt

A **SmartArt** graphic is a diagram or chart that illustrates concepts that would otherwise require several paragraphs of explanation. To create a SmartArt graphic, you switch to the Insert tab and then, in the Illustrations group, click the SmartArt button. This opens the Choose a SmartArt Graphic dialog box, where you can select from seven categories of graphics, including graphics designed to illustrate relationships, processes, and hierarchies. Within each category, you can then choose from numerous designs. Once inserted into your document, a SmartArt graphic contains placeholder text that you replace with your own text. When a SmartArt graphic is selected, the SmartArt Tools Design and Format tabs appear on the Ribbon.

On page 4 of Robin's report, you need to create a SmartArt graphic that summarizes the energy audit process.

To create a SmartArt graphic:

1. Verify that the insertion point is located at the top of page 4, which is blank, and then click the **Insert** tab.
2. In the Illustrations group, click the **SmartArt** button. The Choose a SmartArt Graphic dialog box opens, listing categories of SmartArt graphics in the left panel. The middle panel displays the graphics associated with the category selected in the left panel. The right panel displays a larger image of the graphic that is currently selected in the middle panel, along with an explanation of the graphic's purpose. Currently, All is selected in the left panel.
3. Explore the Choose a SmartArt Graphic dialog box by selecting categories in the left panel and viewing the graphics displayed in the middle panel.
4. In the left panel, click **Relationship**, and then scroll the middle panel and click the **Equation** graphic (in the third column from the left, sixth row from the top), which shows three circles in an equation. In the right panel, you see an explanation of the Equation graphic, as shown in Figure 3-29.

Figure 3-29 **Selecting a SmartArt graphic**

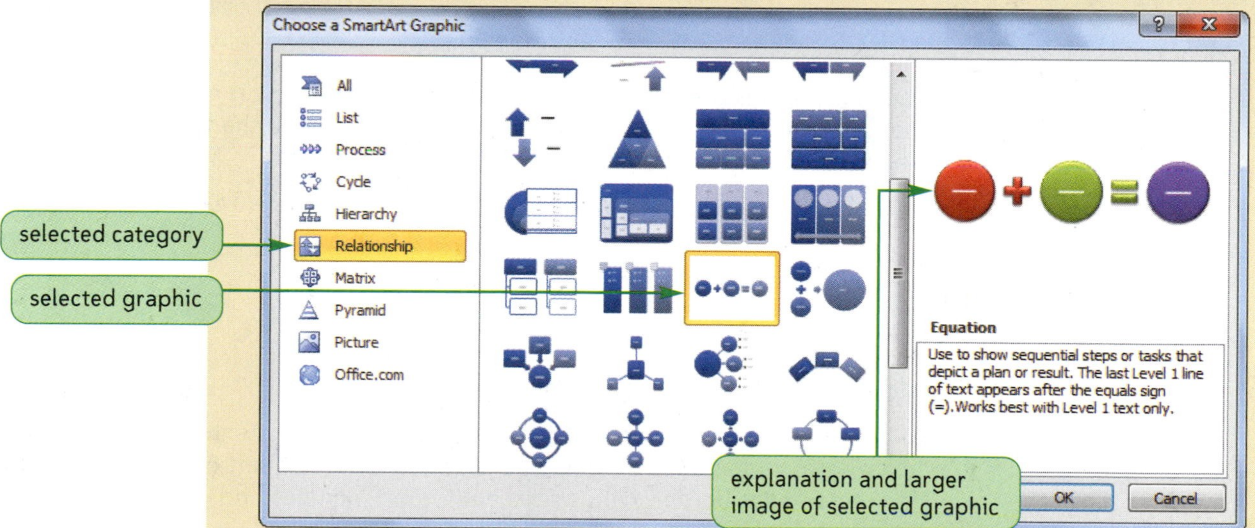

5. Click the **OK** button. The Choose a SmartArt Graphic dialog box closes, and the Equation graphic, with placeholder text, is inserted at the top of page 4. The graphic is surrounded by a rectangular border, indicating that it is selected. The SmartArt Tools tabs appear on the Ribbon. To the left or right of the graphic, you might also see the Text Pane, a small window with a title bar that reads "Type your text here."
6. If you do *not* see the Text Pane, click the **left-facing arrow** on the left side of the SmartArt Border, as shown in Figure 3-30.

Figure 3-30 SmartArt graphic with Text Pane displayed

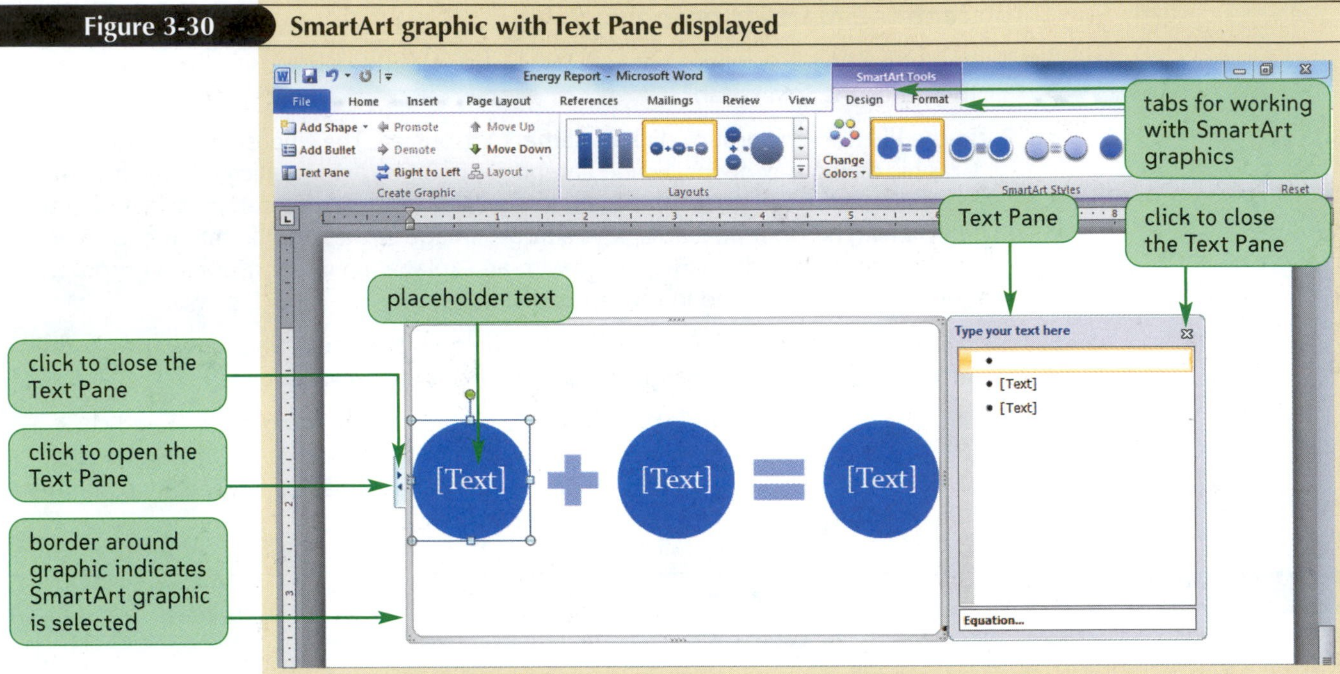

The Text Pane is useful for complicated graphics containing many parts. However, the Equation graphic is simple enough that you can type the text directly in the circles, so you will close the Text Pane.

7. Click the **Close** button in the upper-right corner of the Text Pane.

Now you are ready to add text to the graphic.

To add text to the SmartArt graphic:

1. In the blue circle on the left, click the **[Text]** placeholder text. The placeholder text disappears and the insertion point blinks inside the left circle. The dotted-line rectangular border, with circles and square handles, indicates the shape is selected. See Figure 3-31.

   Trouble? If the circle is selected, but the placeholder text is still visible, you clicked the circle, but not the placeholder text within the circle. Repeat Step 1, being sure to click the placeholder text.

Figure 3-31 Entering text in the SmartArt graphic

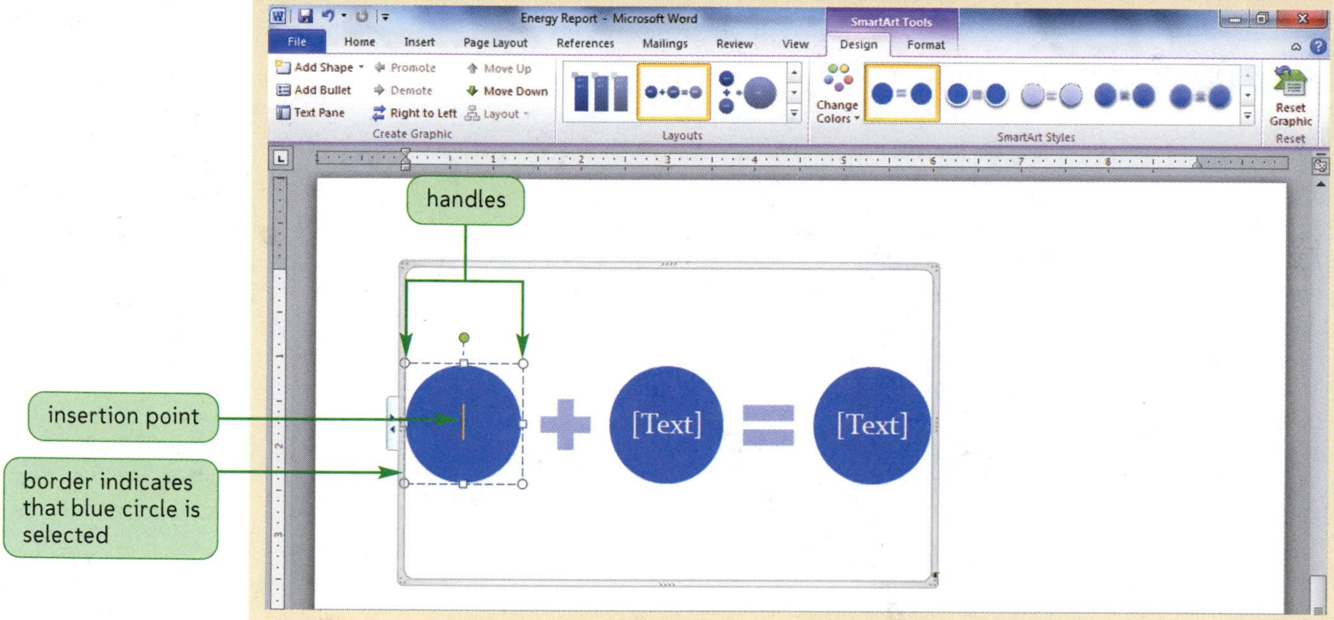

2. Type **Energy Audit**. The font size gets smaller as you type to accommodate each new letter without increasing the size of the circle.
3. Click the **[Text]** placeholder text in the middle circle, type **Repairs and Upgrades**, click the **[Text]** placeholder text in the right circle, and type **Lower Utility Bills**. The right circle remains selected.

   Trouble? If you make a typing mistake, click the circle containing the error and edit the text as you would ordinary text, using the Backspace or Delete keys as necessary.
4. Click in the white area inside the SmartArt border to deselect the right circle. The equation now reads "Energy Audit + Repairs and Upgrades = Lower Utility Bills."

You want the graphic to fill the page. To resize the entire SmartArt graphic, you drag its border.

To adjust the size of the SmartArt graphic:

1. Zoom out so you can see the entire page. As you can see on the ruler, the SmartArt is currently about six inches wide.
2. Position the mouse pointer over the lower-right corner of the SmartArt border. The pointer changes to ⤡.

   Trouble? If the pointer changes to ✥, you haven't positioned the pointer correctly over the lower-right corner. Reposition the pointer until it changes to ⤡.
3. Drag the pointer down and to the right. As you drag, the pointer changes to a crosshair +. A rectangular outline moves with the pointer, showing how the dimensions of the SmartArt border will appear when you release the mouse button. The size of the graphic won't actually change until you release the mouse button.

4. Using the ruler as a guide, drag the border until the outline is approximately 9 inches wide and 6.5 inches high, as shown in Figure 3-32.

Figure 3-32 **Resizing SmartArt**

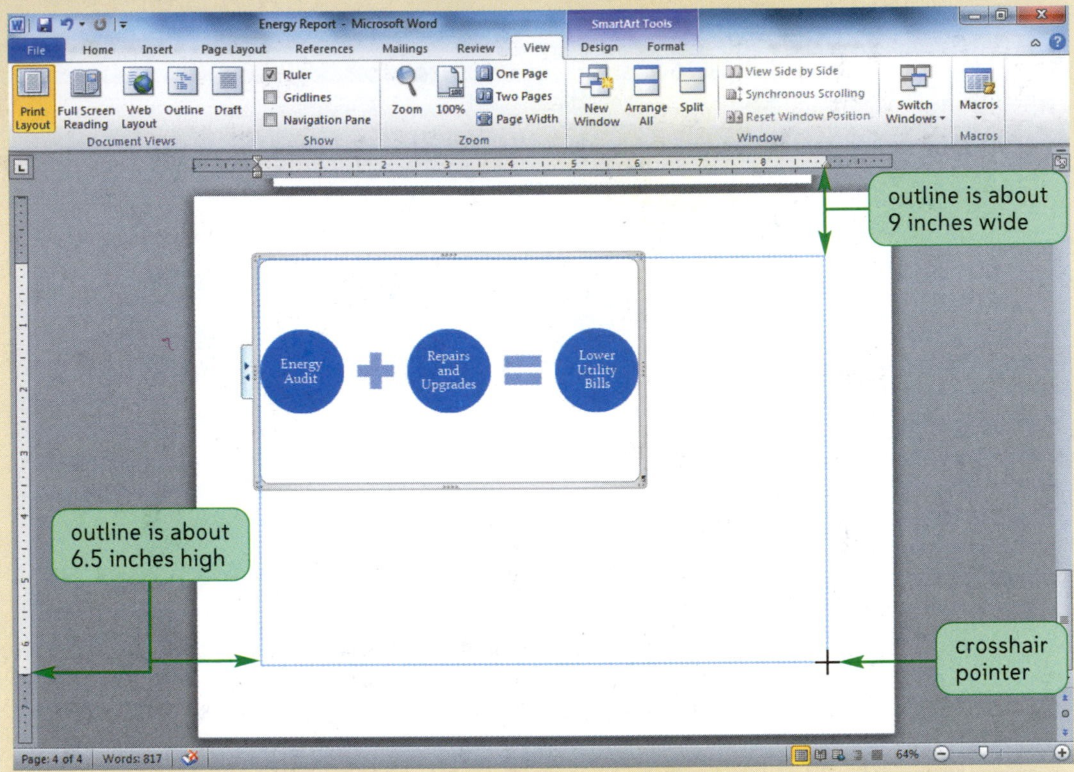

5. Release the mouse button. The SmartArt graphic resizes, so that it is now 9 inches wide and 6.5 inches high, taking up most of the page.

6. Click outside the SmartArt border to deselect it, and view the graphic centered on the page.

Next, you need to insert headers at the top of each page in the report and footers at the bottom of each page in the report. Because the document is divided into sections, you will create separate headers and footers for these sections.

Adding Headers and Footers

As you learned when you inserted page numbers in a document in Tutorial 2, you can only edit the header and footer area of a document in Header and Footer view. There are three ways to open Header and Footer view: (1) insert a page number using the Page Number button in the Header & Footer group on the Insert tab; (2) double-click in the header area (in a page's top margin) or in the footer area (in a page's bottom margin); or (3) click the Header button or the Footer button on the Insert tab.

By default, Word assumes that when you add something to the header or footer on any page of the document, you want the same text to appear on every page of the document. To create a different header or footer for the first page (as you did when you created an MLA-style research paper) you select the Different First Page check box in the Options group on the Header & Footer Tools Design tab. When a document is divided into sections like the Energy Report document, you can choose to create a different header or footer for each section.

For a simple header or footer, switch to Header and Footer view, and then type the text you want directly in the header or footer area, formatting the text as you would any other text in a document. To choose from a selection of predesigned header or footer styles, use the Header and Footer buttons on the Header & Footer Tools Design tab (or on the Insert tab). These buttons open galleries that you can use to select from a number of header and footer styles, some of which include page numbers and graphic elements such as horizontal lines or shaded boxes. Some also include document controls that are similar to the kinds of controls (text boxes, list boxes, etc.) that you might encounter in a dialog box. Most of the document controls you'll see in headers and footers are text boxes, where you can enter pertinent information such as the document title or the name of the document's author. Any information that you enter in a document control is displayed in the header or footer as ordinary text, but it is also stored in the Word file so that Word can easily reuse it in other parts of the document. For example, later in this tutorial you will create a cover page for the report. Word's predefined cover pages include document controls similar to those found in headers and footers. So if you use a document control to enter the document title in the header, that same document title will show up in the cover page; there's no need to retype it.

You will next create a footer for the whole document (sections 1 and 2) that includes the page number and your name. As shown in Figure 3-33, you'll also create a header for section 1 (pages 1 through 3) that includes the document title and the date.

Figure 3-33 Plans for headers and footers in the report

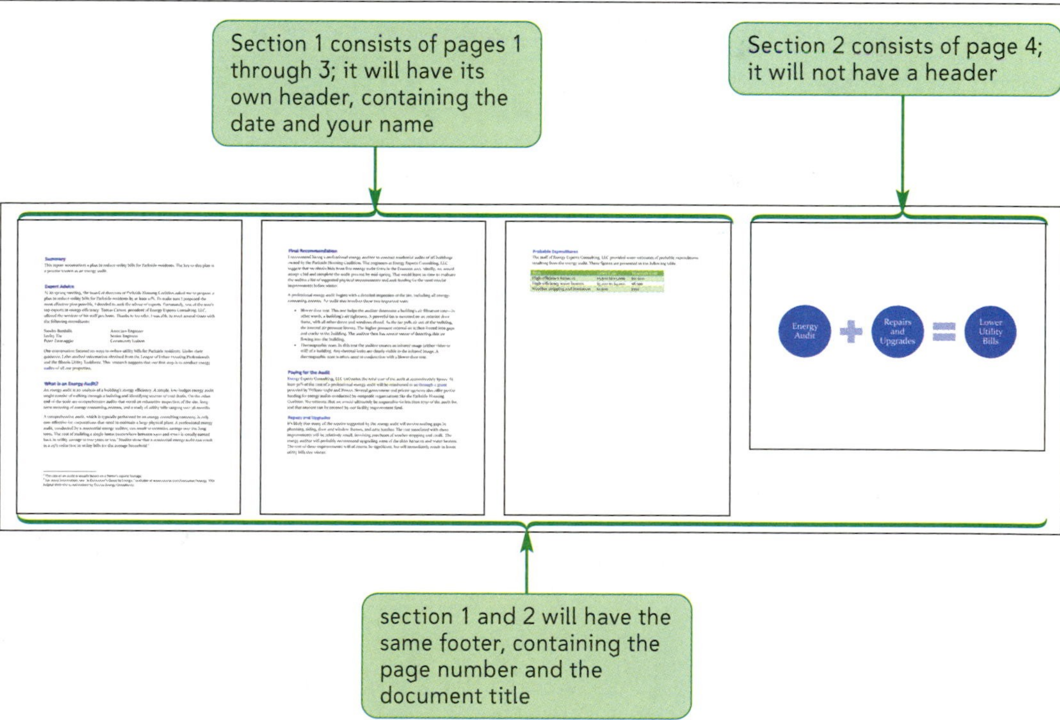
Section 1 consists of pages 1 through 3; it will have its own header, containing the date and your name
Section 2 consists of page 4; it will not have a header
Energy Audit
Repairs and Upgrades
Lower Utility Bills
section 1 and 2 will have the same footer, containing the page number and the document title

First you will create the footer on page 1, so you can see how the footer fits below the footnotes at the bottom of the page.

To create a footer for the entire document:

1. Change the zoom level to Page Width, and then scroll up until you can see the bottom of page 1.
2. Double-click in the white space below the footnotes. The document switches to Header and Footer view. On the Ribbon, the Header & Footer Tools Design tab appears. The insertion point is positioned on the left side of the footer area, ready for you to begin typing. The label "Footer -Section 1-" tells you that the insertion point is located in the footer for section 1. The document text (including the footnotes) is gray, indicating that you cannot edit it in Header and Footer view. The header area for section 1 is also visible on top of page 2. The default footer tab stops are visible on the ruler. See Figure 3-34.

Figure 3-34 Creating a footer

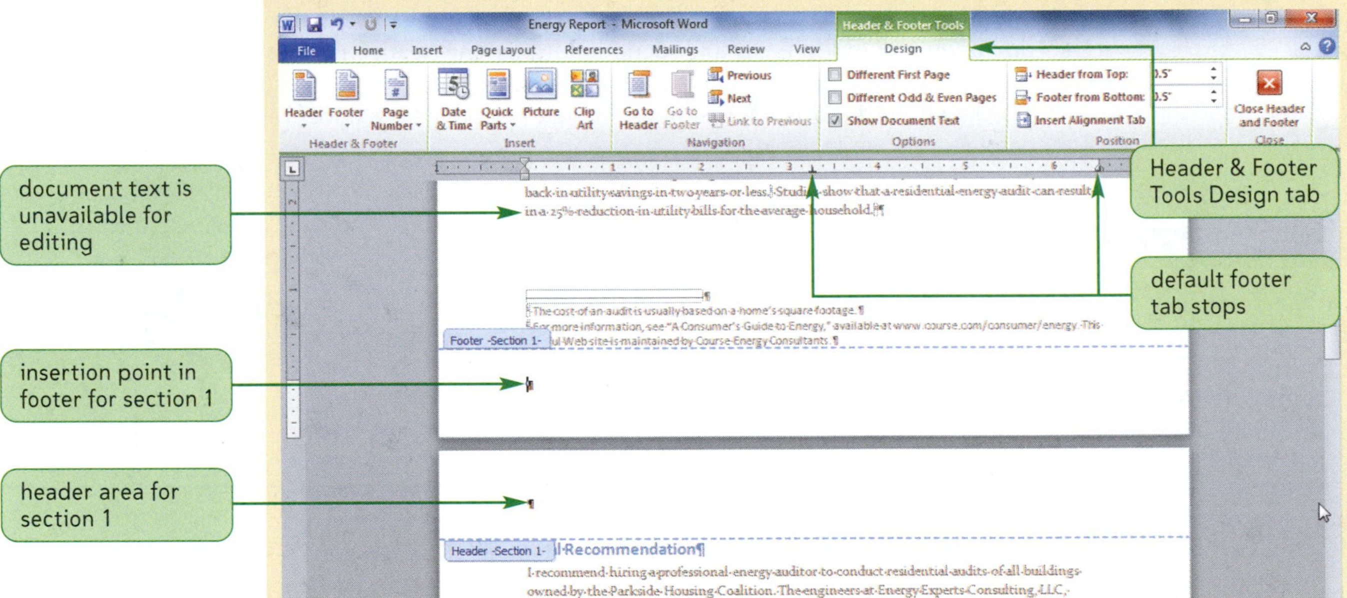

3. Type your first and last name, and then press the **Enter** key. The insertion point moves to the second line in the footer, aligned along the left margin. This is where you will insert the page number.
4. In the Header & Footer group, click the **Page Number** button. The Page Number menu opens. Because the insertion point is already located where you want to insert the page number, you will use the Current Position option.
5. Point to **Current Position**. A gallery of page number styles opens. Robin wants to use the Accent Bar 2 style.
6. Click the **Accent Bar 2** style (the third from the top). The word "Page," a vertical bar, and the page number are inserted in the footer.

Next, you'll check to make sure that the footer you just created for section 1 also appears in section 2. To move between headers or footers in separate sections, you can use the buttons in the Navigation group on the Design tab.

TIP

To change the numbering style for a page number or to specify a number to use as the first page number, click the Page Number button in the Header & Footer group, and then click Format Page Numbers.

7. In the Navigation group, click the **Next** button. Word displays the footer for the next section in the document—that is, the footer for section 2, which appears at the bottom of page 4. The label at the top of the footer area reads "Footer -Section 2-" and it contains the same text (your name and the page number) in this footer as in section 1, because Word assumes, by default, that when you type text in one footer, you want it to appear in all the footers in the document.

Now you need to create a header for section 1. Robin does not want to include a header in section 2 because it would distract attention from the SmartArt graphic. So you will first separate the header for section 1 from the header for section 2.

To separate the headers for section 1 and section 2:

1. If necessary, click anywhere in the section 2 footer area at the bottom of page 4. To switch from the footer to the header in the current section, you can use the Go to Header button in the Navigation group.
2. In the Navigation group, click the **Go to Header** button. The insertion point moves to the section 2 header at the top of page 4. Notice that in the Navigation group, the Link to Previous button is selected and the blue tag on the right side of the header border contains the message "Same as Previous," indicating that the section 2 header is linked to the header in the previous section, which is section 1. Anything you add to the section 1 header will also be added to the section 2 header. To make the section 2 header a separate entity, you need to break that link.
3. In the Navigation group, click the **Link to Previous** button to deselect it. Deselecting this button ensures that the header you create in section 1 will not appear in section 2. The Same as Previous tab disappears from the right side of the header border. See Figure 3-35.

Figure 3-35 Breaking the link between the section 1 and section 2 headers

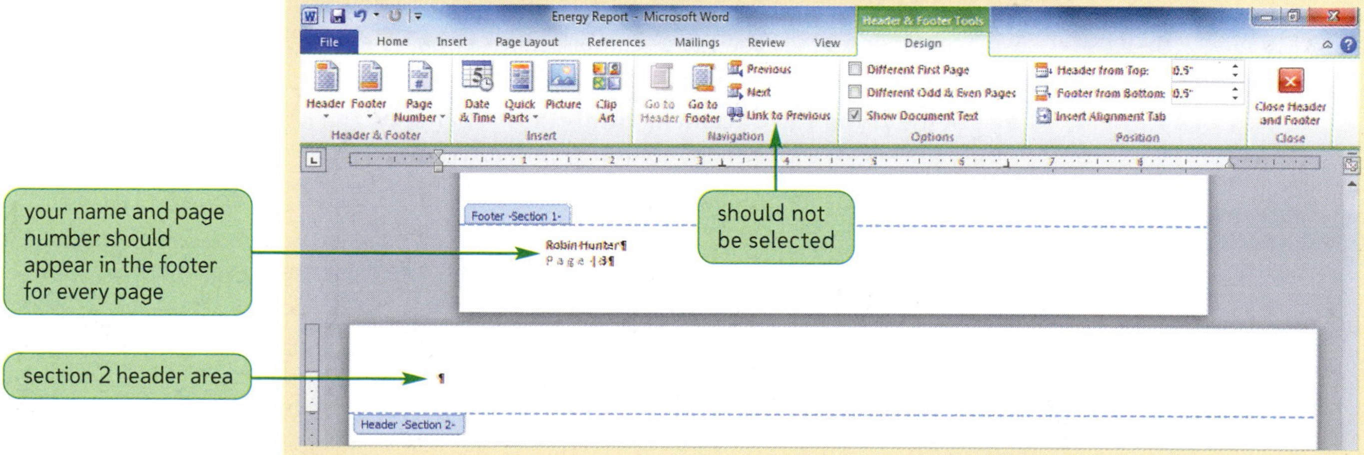

your name and page number should appear in the footer for every page

should not be selected

section 2 header area

TIP

When you create a header for a section, it doesn't matter what page you're working on, as long as the insertion point is located in a header in that section.

4. In the Navigation group, click the **Previous** button. The insertion point moves up to the nearest section 1 header, which is at the top of page 3. The label "Header -Section 1-" identifies this as a section 1 header.
5. In the Header & Footer group, click the **Header** button. A gallery of header styles opens. See Figure 3-36.

Figure 3-36 Header gallery

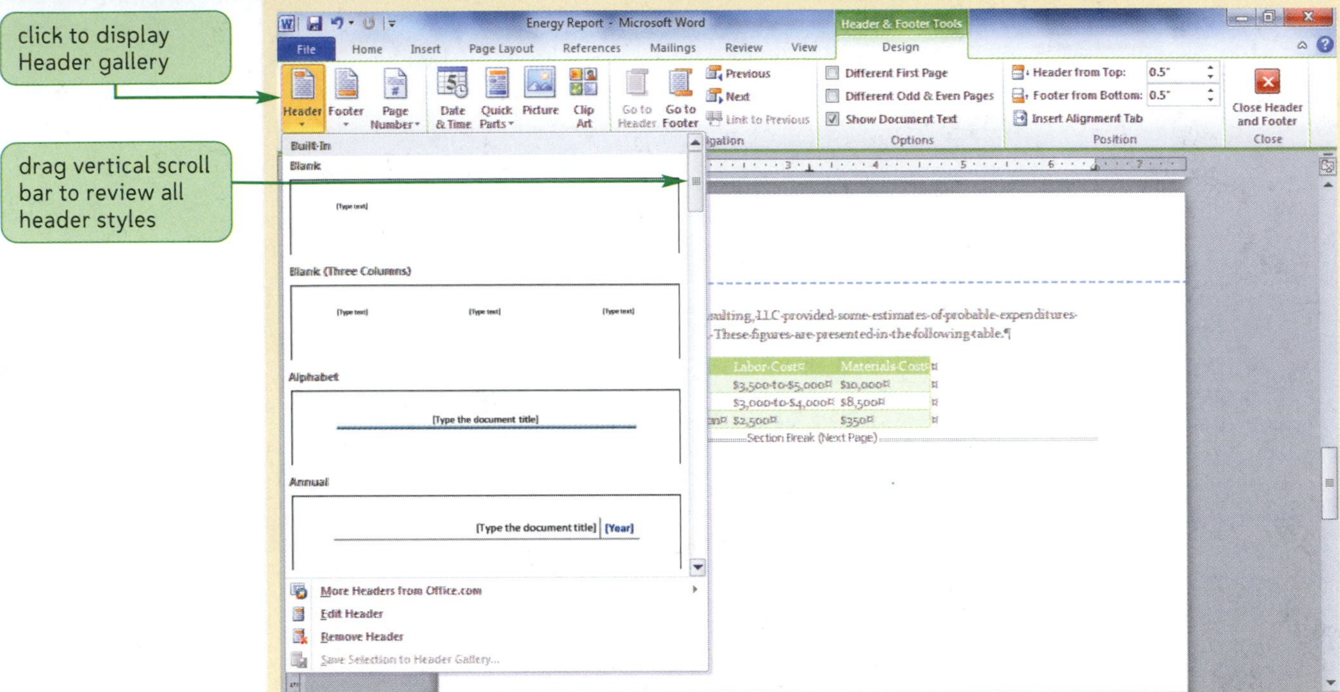

6. Scroll down and review the various header styles, and then click the **Conservative** style (eighth from the top). A horizontal line is inserted in the document. The placeholder text "[Type the document title]" appears above the line. The placeholder text "[Pick the date]" appears below the line.
7. Click the **[Type the document title]** placeholder text. The placeholder text appears within a document control. See Figure 3-37.

Figure 3-37 Adding a header to section 1

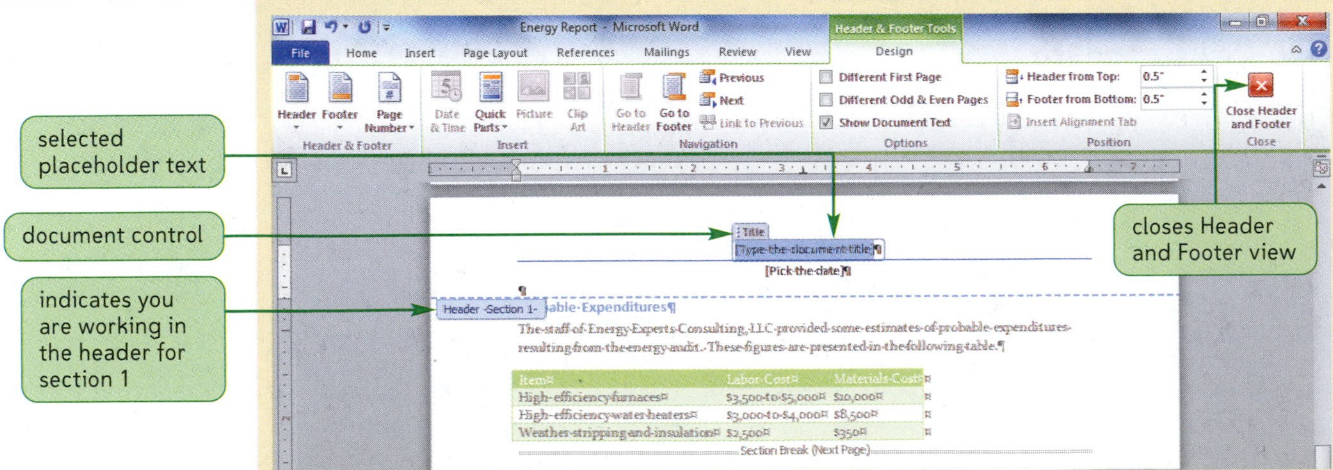

8. Type **Parkside Energy Audit**. As soon as you begin typing, the placeholder text and the blue highlight disappear. The text, "Parkside Energy Audit," is displayed in the document control. Next, you need to add the date. The header style you selected includes a date picker document control, which allows you to select the date from a calendar.
9. Click the **[Pick the date]** placeholder text to display an arrow in the document control, and then click the arrow. A calendar appears, as shown in Figure 3-38. In the calendar, the current date is outlined in orange.

Figure 3-38 Adding a date to the section 1 header

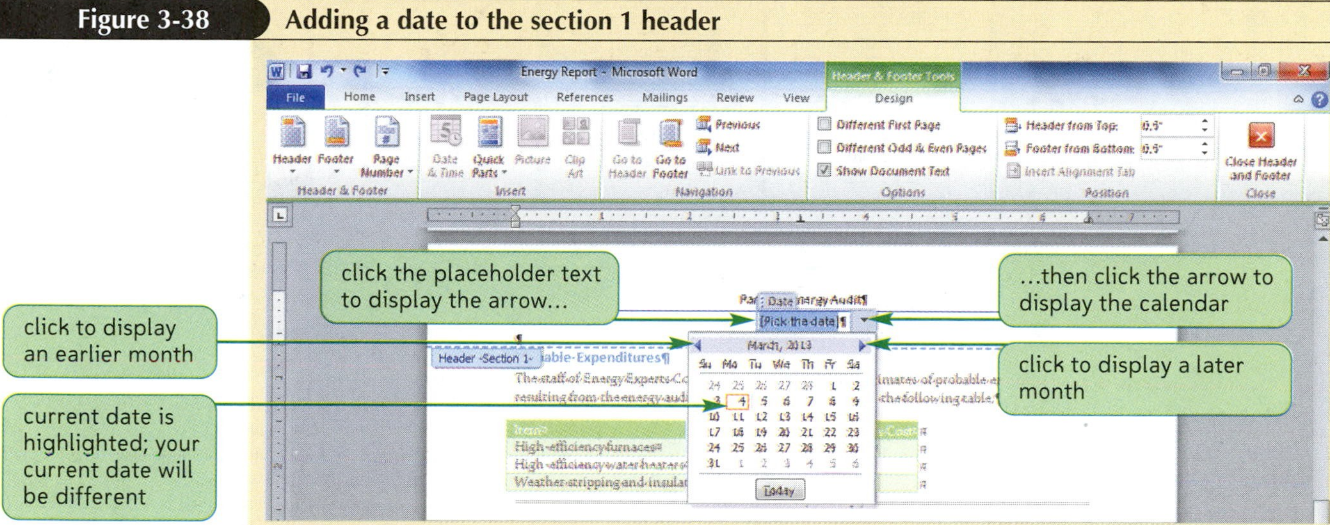
click the placeholder text to display the arrow...
...then click the arrow to display the calendar
click to display an earlier month
click to display a later month
current date is highlighted; your current date will be different

10. Click the current date.
11. Click anywhere in the Section 1 footer (on the preceding page) to deselect the date document control. You are finished creating the header and footer for Robin's report, so you can close Header and Footer view and return to Print Layout view.
12. In the Close group, click the **Close Header and Footer** button, save your work, and then drag the Zoom slider left until you can see all four pages of the document, including the header at the top of pages 1–3 and the footer at the bottom of pages 1–4. See Figure 3-39.

Figure 3-39 Document with new header and footer

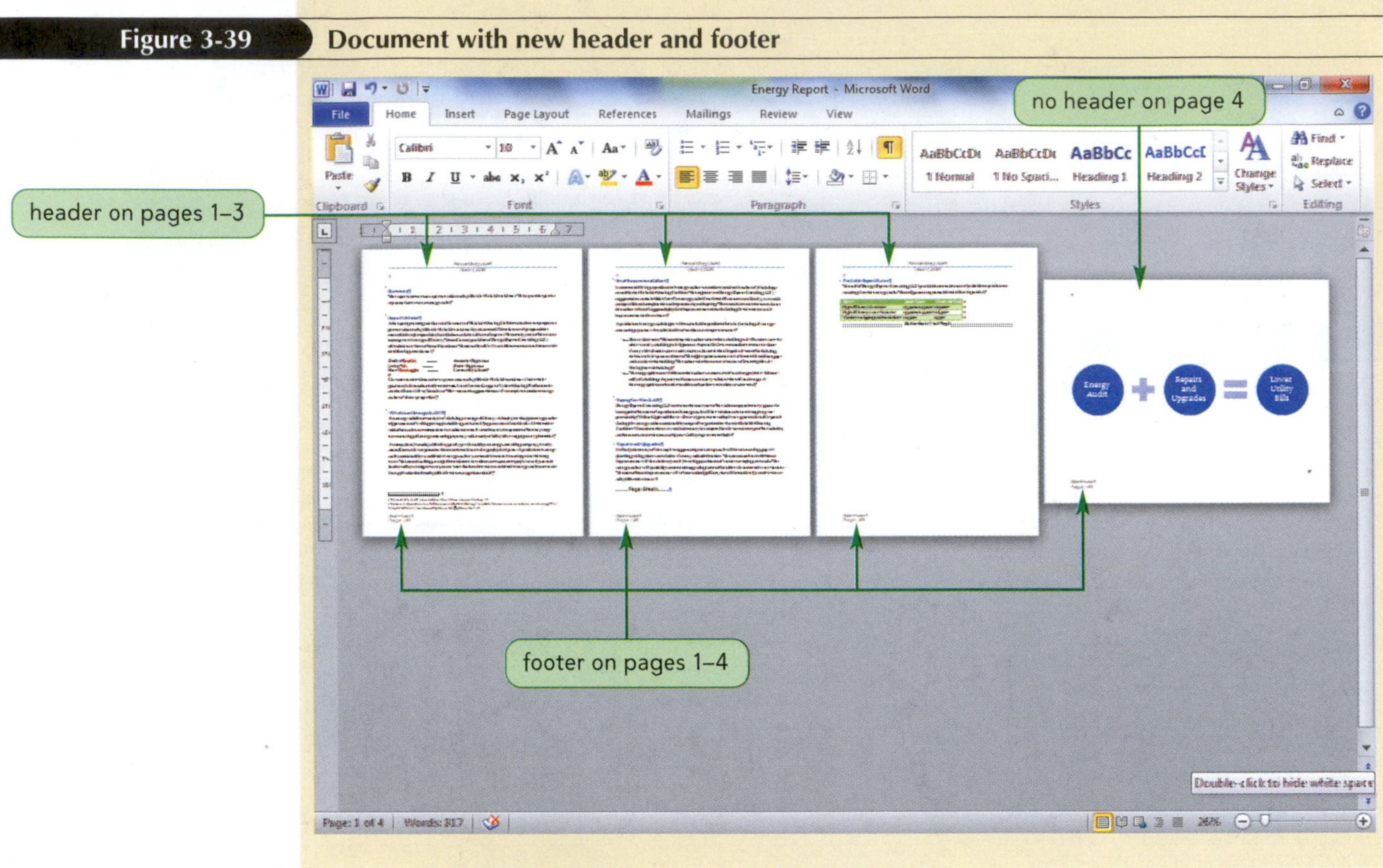

Finally, you need to insert a cover page for the report.

Inserting a Cover Page

A document's cover page typically includes the title and the name of the author. Some people also include a summary of the report on the cover page; this is commonly referred to as an abstract. In addition, you might include the date, the name and possibly the logo of your company or organization, and a subtitle. A cover page should not include the document header or footer.

To create a cover page, you can use the Cover Page button on the Insert tab. The Cover Page button inserts a cover page with a predefined style at the beginning of the document. The cover page includes document controls in which you can enter the document title, the document's author, the date, and so on. These document controls are linked to any other document controls in the document. For example, you already entered "Parkside Energy Audit" into a document control in the header of Robin's report, so if you use a cover page that contains a similar document control, "Parkside Energy Audit" will appear on the cover page automatically. Note that document controls sometimes display, by default, information entered when either Word or Windows was originally installed on your computer. If your computer has multiple user accounts, the information displayed in some document controls might reflect the information for the current user. In any case, you can easily edit the contents of a document control.

To insert a cover page at the beginning of the report:

1. Verify that the document is still zoomed so that you can see all four pages, and then press the **Ctrl+Home** keys. The insertion point moves to the beginning of the document.
2. Click the **Insert** tab, and then click the **Cover Page** button in the Pages group. A gallery of cover page styles opens. Notice that the names of the cover page styles match the names of the preformatted header styles you saw earlier. For example, the list includes a Conservative cover page, which is similar in design to the Conservative header used in this document. To give a document a coherent look, it's helpful to use elements (such as cover pages and headers) with the same style throughout.
3. Scroll down the gallery to see the cover page styles, and then locate the Conservative cover page style (second style in the second row.)
4. Click the **Conservative** cover page style. The new cover page is inserted at the beginning of the document.
5. Change the Zoom level to **One Page**. The Company document control, at the top of the page, is selected. In the middle of the cover page, the report title "Parkside Energy Audit" appears, which you previously entered into a document control in the document header. The cover page also contains the current date from the header. It also includes an Author document control which displays "Robin Hunter," the Author for the document. The cover page also includes a document control for a subtitle and a document control for an abstract giving a brief document summary. See Figure 3-40.

TIP

A document's Author is listed on the Info tab in Backstage view. By default this will be the user name for the account that was used to create the document.

Figure 3-40 Newly inserted cover page

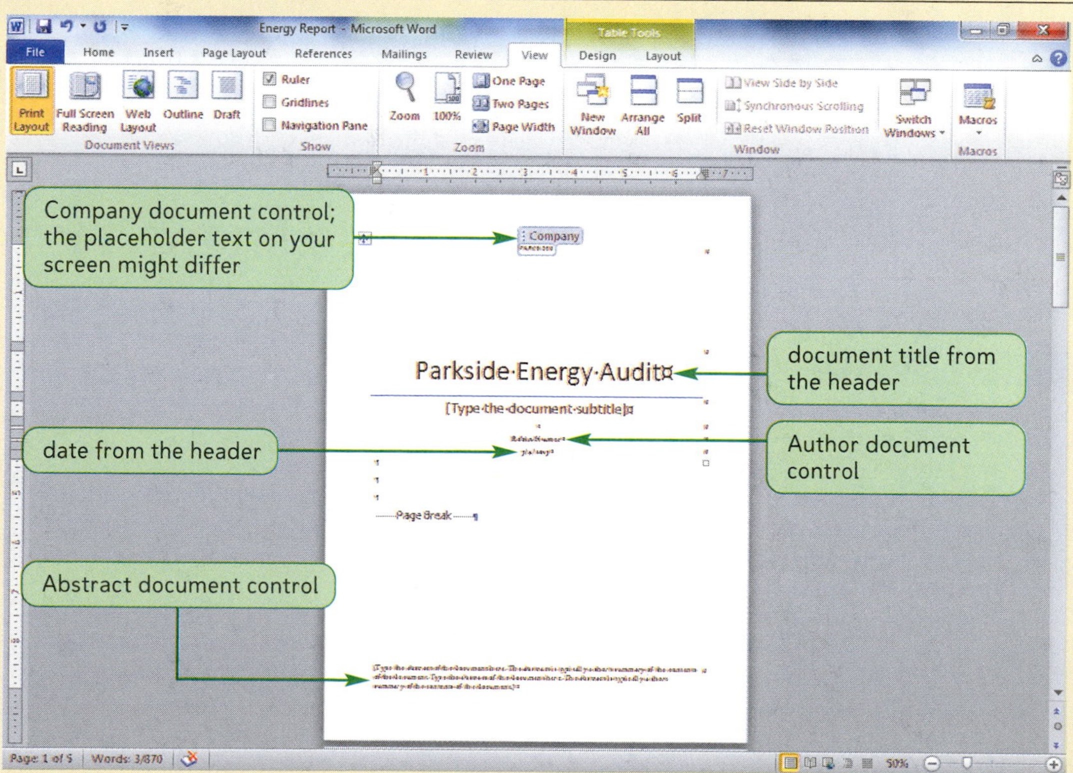

You need to edit the information in the Company document control at the top of the page.

6. Change the Zoom level to **Page Width**, click to the right of "PARKSIDE" in the Company document control, press the **spacebar**, and then type **Housing Coalition**. The organization name appears in all upper case letters, because that is the formatting for this document control. Next you will remove the document subtitle placeholder because you do not need it for this cover page.

7. Click the **[Type the document subtitle]** placeholder text to select the Subtitle document control, and then click the blue **Subtitle** label on the control to select the entire document control. The Table Tools contextual tabs appear on the Ribbon because, although you can't tell by looking at them, the document controls are actually organized on the page in a table structure. When you clicked the Subtitle document control, you clicked within the table. See Figure 3-41.

Figure 3-41 **Selected document control**

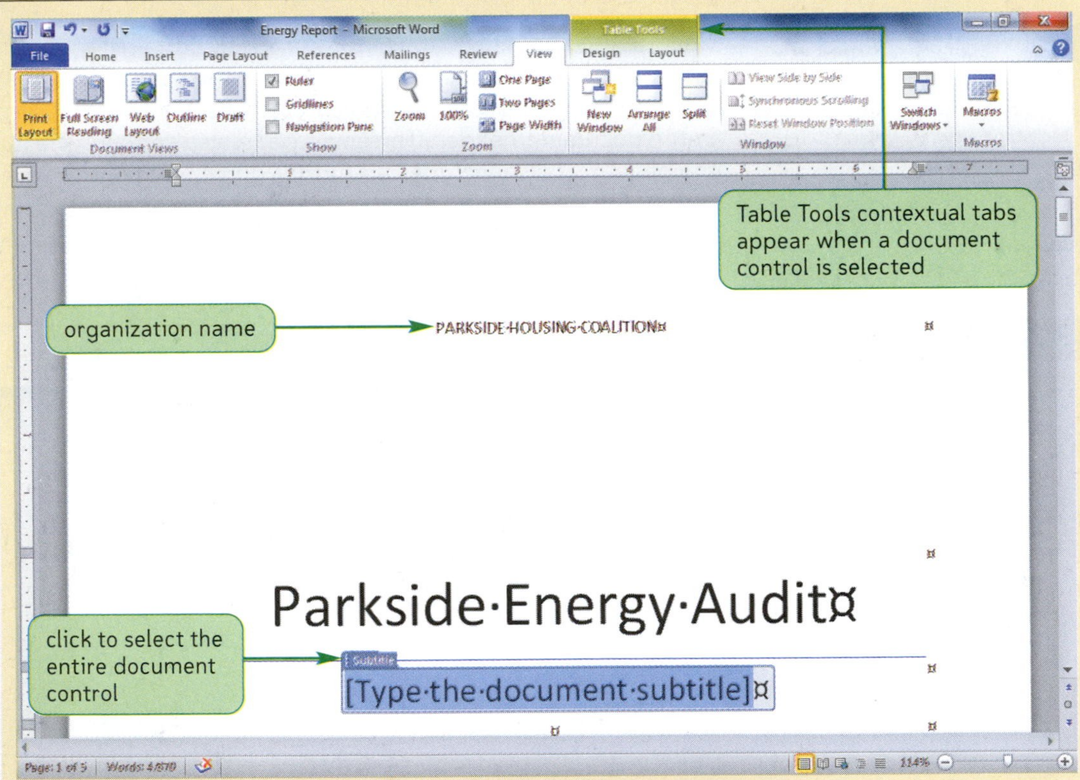

> **TIP**
>
> To delete a cover page that you inserted from the Cover Page gallery, click the Cover Page button in the Pages group, and then click Remove Current Cover Page.

8. Press the **Delete** key. The document control is removed from the cover page.

9. Scroll down, click the **Author** document control, and if necessary, replace the contents of the control with your first and last name.

10. Scroll down, delete the **Abstract** document control, and then save the document.

INSIGHT

Creating a Simple Cover Page Manually

To create a simple cover page for a report, insert a Next Page section break at the beginning of the document, being sure to adjust the header and footer settings so the header and footer do not appear on the cover page. Type the title and other information you want to include on the cover page, and format it appropriately. If you want the cover page text to appear centered on the page, click the Dialog Box Launcher in the Page Setup group on the Page Layout tab, click the Layout tab of the Page Setup dialog box, click the Vertical alignment arrow, and then click Center.

Your work on the report is finished. You should preview the report before closing it.

To preview the report:

1. Click the **File** tab to open Backstage view, and then click the **Print** tab. The cover page of the report appears in the document preview in the right pane.
2. Examine the document preview, using the arrow buttons at the bottom of the pane to display each page. Make sure that the header is only visible on pages 2–4, and that the footer is visible on pages 2–5. Also, notice that Word renumbered the pages to account for the addition of the cover page, which is the new page 1.
3. If you need to make any changes to the report, return to Print Layout view, edit the document, preview the document again, and then save and close the document.

You now have a draft of Energy Report document, including a cover page, the report text, a nicely formatted table, and the SmartArt graphic (in landscape orientation).

REVIEW

Session 3.2 Quick Check

1. True or False. There are default tab stops every one-half inch on the horizontal ruler.
2. Explain how to create a footnote.
3. What button do you use to insert a section break, and where is it located?
4. True or False. By default, Word assumes that the text you type in a header should be used only for the header on that page.
5. Explain how to create separate headers for section 1 and section 2.
6. Explain how to delete a document control.

Apply the skills you learned in the tutorial using the same case scenario.

PRACTICE

Review Assignments

Data File needed for the Review Assignments: Training.docx

In conjunction with a local community college, Robin Hunter has organized a series of computer training classes for Parkside residents to be held in the Parkside community center. She has begun work on a report for the board that outlines basic information about the classes and introduces the instructors. You need to format the report, add a table at the end containing a preliminary schedule, and create a sample graphic that Robin could use in a handout advertising the classes.

Complete the following:

1. Open the file **Training** located in the Word3\Review folder included with your Data Files, and then save it as **Training Report** in the same folder.
2. Use the Navigation pane to promote the headings "Equipment Needs" and "Schedule" to Heading 1 text, and then move the "Schedule" heading and its body text to the end of the document.
3. Insert a page break before the Schedule heading, and then at the bottom of the new page 2 create a table using the following information. Format the header row in bold.

Start Date	Topic
April 20	The Internet
March 30	Spreadsheets and tables
January 20	Computer literacy
May 15	Databases
June 8	Simple Web programming

4. Sort the table by the contents of the Start Date column in ascending order, keeping in mind that you are sorting dates and not text.
5. In the appropriate location, insert a new row for a class on word processing that starts on February 15.
6. Delete the "Simple Web Programming" row at the bottom of the table.
7. Modify the widths of both columns to accommodate the widest entry in each.
8. Apply the Medium Shading 1 – Accent 1 built-in table style to the table, and then change the document theme to Equity.
9. On page 1, replace the text "[instructor names]" with the following list of instructors and their specialties. Insert a tab after each name, remembering that the list of specialties won't align properly until you complete Step 10. Remember to press the Shift+Enter keys to insert a new line for each name without adding extra space:
   Kristina K. Connelly-Brown **Word processing**
   Carl Morales **Multimedia software**
   Heinrich Burser **Web design**
   Amelia Carolina Guntz **Database design and SQL programming**
10. Select the list of instructors and their specialties, and then insert a left tab stop 2.5 inches from the left margin.
11. Below the heading "Equipment Needs," locate the first sentence of the second paragraph, which begins "We need four more computers...." At the end of that sentence, insert a footnote that reads **The computers should run either Windows Vista or Windows 7.**

12. Insert a Next Page section break after the table on page 2, format the new page 3 in landscape orientation, and then insert a SmartArt graphic that illustrates the advantages of computer classes. Use the Continuous Block Process graphic from the Process category, and, from left to right, include the following text in the SmartArt diagram: **Computer Education**,**Technological Advantage**, and **New Career Prospects**. Size the SmartArt graphic to fill the page.
13. Create a footer for sections 1 and 2 that aligns your first and last name at the left margin. Insert the page number, without any design elements and without the word "Page," below your name.
14. Separate the section 1 header from the section 2 header, create a header for section 1 using the Conservative header style, enter **Parkside Computer Training** as the document title, pick the current date, and then close Header and Footer view.
15. Insert a cover page using the Conservative style, delete the Company document control, verify that the document title is automatically inserted in the cover page, enter **An Informational Report** for the subtitle, enter your name for the author, verify that the current date appears below your name, and then delete the Abstract document control.
16. Save and preview the report, and then submit the finished document to your instructor, either in printed or electronic form, as requested.

APPLY

Case Problem 1

If you have a SAM 2010 user profile, your instructor may have assigned an autogradable version of this assignment. If so, log into the SAM 2010 Web site at www.cengage.com/sam2010 to download the instructions and start files.

Data File needed for this Case Problem: Noblewood.docx

Noblewood Textiles, Inc. As an assistant manager of Noblewood Textiles in San Diego, California, you must help prepare an annual report for the board of directors.

Complete the following:

1. Open the file **Noblewood** located in the Word3\Case1 folder included with your Data Files, and then save it as **Noblewood Report** in the same folder.
2. Use the Navigation pane to promote the headings "Children's Knitting Hour" to Heading 2 text, and then move the "Company Philosophy" heading and its body text up before the "Goal" heading.
3. Select the list of members under the heading "Board of Directors," and then insert a left tab stop with a dot leader at the 4-inch mark. (*Hint*: Click the Page Layout tab, and then, in the Paragraph group, click the Dialog Box Launcher, click the Indents and Spacing tab if necessary, and then click the Tabs button at the bottom of the dialog box to open the Tabs dialog box.)
4. Near the middle of page 2, at the end of the paragraph below the heading "Summer Fiber Art Festival," insert the following endnote: **NetMind Solutions currently hosts our Web site.**
5. On page 1, at the end of the paragraph below the heading "Company Philosophy," insert the following footnote: **Boardman Fabrics is our statewide competitor.**
6. Move the insertion point to the blank paragraph at the end of the document, and then insert a table consisting of three columns and four rows.

7. In the table, enter the following column headers and data. Format the header row in bold.

Department	July-December	Projected January-June
Yarn	$175,000	$165,000
Quilting	$185,000	$150,000
Garment	$120,000	$85,000

8. Sort the table in ascending order by department.
9. Insert a row above the Garment row and enter the following information:

Embroidery	$130,000	$110,000

10. Adjust the column widths so each column accommodates the widest entry.
11. Format the table using the Light Shading- Accent 2 table style.
12. Create a footer for the document that aligns your name at the left margin and the page number (in the Accent Bar 3 style) at the right margin. (*Hint*: Press the Tab key twice to move the insertion point to the right margin before inserting the page number.)
13. Insert a cover page using the Sideline style. Enter the company name, **Noblewood Textiles**, and the title, **Annual Report** in the appropriate document controls. In the subtitle document control, enter **Prepared by Your Name** (but replace "Your Name" with your first and last name). Delete the Author document control, and then insert the current date in the Date document control.
14. Change the document theme to Austin and then review the changes that occur throughout the document as a result, including the cover page and the table.
15. Save and preview the document, and then submit the finished document to your instructor, either in printed or electronic form, as requested.

Apply your skills to create a report on a municipal wireless network.

APPLY

Case Problem 2

Data File needed for this Case Problem: Network.docx

Report on a Municipal Wireless Network Like many communities, the town of Grand Island, Nebraska, is considering a city-wide wireless (or WiFi) network to provide low-cost Internet access for all residents. A task force appointed by the mayor has investigated the issue and summarized its findings in a report. As you format the report in the following steps, you will create a cover page from scratch, without relying on predefined elements provided by Word. You will also create and edit a SmartArt graphic to illustrate the process of creating the network. Complete the following:

1. Open the file named **Network** located in the Word3\Case2 folder included with your Data Files, and then save it as **Network Report** in the same folder.
2. Replace "Student Name" in the first page with your first and last name.
3. Use the Navigation pane to Promote the heading "Low Cost" to Heading 2 text, and to move the heading "Summary" and the body text that follows it before the "Task Force Members" heading.
4. Insert a Next Page section break just before the "Summary" heading.
5. Position the insertion point somewhere in the page 1 text.
6. Change the vertical alignment in section 1 to center. (*Hint*: Click the Page Layout tab, and then click the Dialog Box Launcher in the Page Setup group.)

7. Insert a tab stop at the 2-inch mark in the list of task force members that appear on page 2.
8. Change the section 2 header so it is no longer linked to section 1, move the insertion point to the center tab stop in the section 2 header, and then type the header **Grand Island WiFi Report, Prepared by Student Name** (replacing "Student Name" with your first and last name). Format the header text using the Intense Emphasis style.

EXPLORE

9. Create a footer for just section 2 with a plain page number in the center. Use the Format Page numbers command on the Page Number menu to format the page number with a hyphen before and after it.
10. Insert a Next Page section break at the end of the document, and then format the new page in landscape orientation.
11. Change the section 3 header and footer so they are no longer connected to section 2, delete the page number field from the section 3 footer, and then review the footers in all three sections, verifying that section 2 still contains a page number field. In the section 3 header, drag the Center Align tab stop right to the 4.5-inch mark on the ruler, so that the header text is centered over the page.
12. Insert a SmartArt graphic on the new page 4. In the Process category, select the Upward Arrow graphic. Starting at the bottom of the arrow and moving up, enter the text **Hire Networking Firm**, **Construct Network**, and **Sell Broadband Rights**. When you are finished, keep the "Sell Broadband Rights" text box selected.

EXPLORE

13. On the SmartArt Tools Design tab, in the Create Graphic group, click the Add Shape button arrow, click Add Shape After, and then type **Sell Network Subscriptions**.
14. Click anywhere in the white area of the SmartArt Graphic, inside the border, to deselect the text, and then resize the graphic to fill the page.
15. Change the document theme to Essential, and then review the document's new look.
16. Save the document, preview it, and then submit the finished document to your instructor, either in printed or electronic form, as requested.

Go beyond what you've learned to convert text into a table and use other advanced table options.

CHALLENGE

Case Problem 3

Data Files needed for this Case Problem: New.docx and Table.docx

Contact List for Parson's Graphic Design Amanda Parson recently launched a new graphic design firm that specializes in creating Web ads for small businesses in the Seattle area. A colleague has just emailed her a list of potential clients. The list consists of names, email addresses, and phone numbers. Because it was exported from another program, the information is formatted as simple text, with the pieces of information separated by commas. Amanda asks you to convert this text into a table and then format the table to make it easy to read. When you're finished, she needs you to sum a column of numbers in her Office Expense table. Complete the following:

1. Open the file named **New** located in the Word3\Case3 folder included with your Data Files, and then save it as **New Clients** in the same folder.

EXPLORE

2. Use Word Help to learn how to convert text to a table. (*Hint*: Search on "Add or delete a table" and then read the "Convert text to a table" topic.) Use what you learn to convert the document to a table with 4 columns and 6 rows. Adjust the column widths to accommodate the widest entry in each column.

3. Insert a header row using the bold headers **Company**, **Contact**, **Phone**, and **Email**.
4. Sort the list alphabetically by Company, and then replace the name "Katherine Shropshire" with your first and last name.
5. Change the page orientation to landscape, and then drag the Table Resize handle (located just outside the lower-right corner of the table) until the table is 7 inches wide and 3 inches high.
6. Format the table using the Light List – Accent 6 style, and change the document theme to Angles.
7. Save and preview the document, and then submit the finished document to your instructor, either in printed or electronic form, as requested. Close the document.
8. Open the file named **Table** located in the Word3\Case3 folder included with your Data Files, and then save it as **Expense Table** in the same folder.

EXPLORE

9. Select the cell containing the word TOTAL, and the blank cell to its right, then click the Merge Cells button in the Merge group on the Tables Tools Layout tab.

EXPLORE

10. Experiment with the Alignment buttons on the Table Tools Layout tab, and then align the word "TOTAL" on the right of the new, larger cell using the Align Top Right button. Do the same for the four cells below the Expense header (including the blank cell at the bottom of the Expense column).

EXPLORE

11. Click the blank cell at the bottom of the Expense column and then, in the Data group, click the Formula button. The Formula dialog box opens. Make sure the formula "=SUM(ABOVE)" appears in the Formula text box, make sure the other two text boxes are blank, and then click the OK button to display the total in the selected cell.
12. Adjust the width of each column so it is just wide enough for its widest entry, change the document theme to Angles, and then format the table with the Colorful List table style.
13. Save and preview the document, and then submit the finished document to your instructor, either in printed or electronic form, as requested.

Use your table skills to create the instruction sheet shown in Figure 3-42.

CREATE

Case Problem 4

There are no Data Files needed for this Case Problem.

Herschel Astronomical Society Sarah Vernon coordinates star-gazing tours for the Herschel Astronomical Society. To ensure that participants can see as well as possible in the night sky, they are asked to follow a set of rules that astronomers refer to as a dark sky protocol. You can use Word table features to create an instruction sheet describing the club's dark sky protocol. Figure 3-42 shows Sarah's sketch.

Figure 3-42 **Sketch for dark sky protocol sheet**

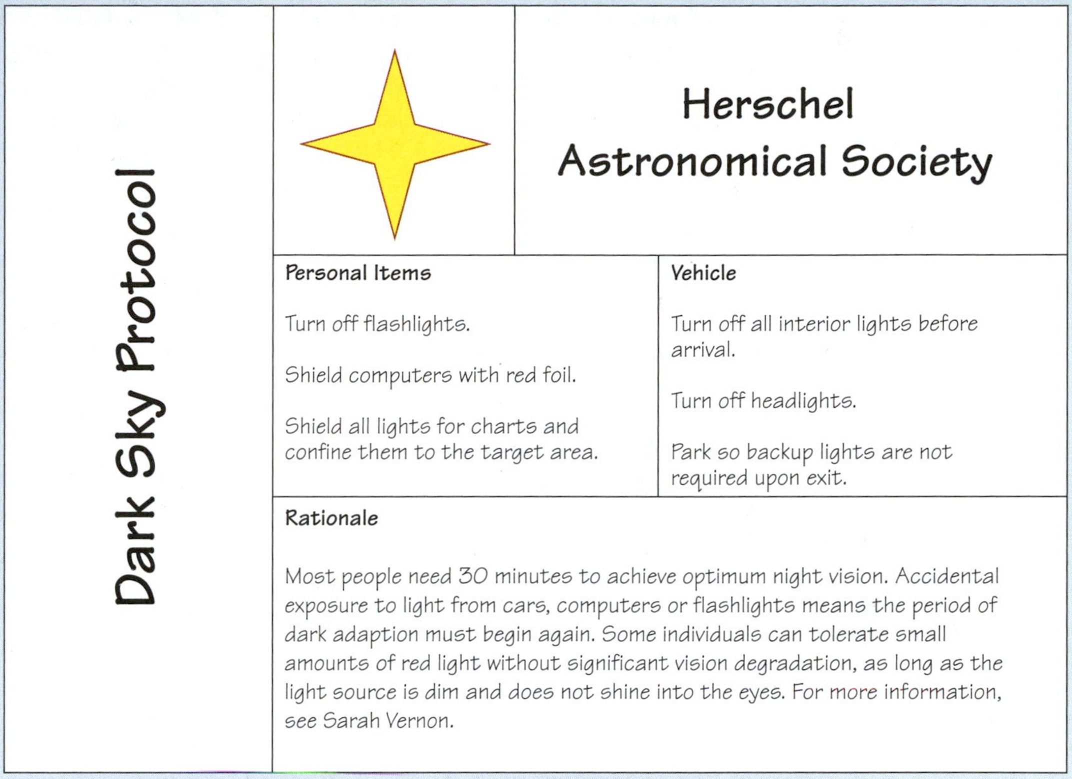

Dark Sky Protocol

Herschel Astronomical Society

Personal Items

Turn off flashlights.

Shield computers with red foil.

Shield all lights for charts and confine them to the target area.

Vehicle

Turn off all interior lights before arrival.

Turn off headlights.

Park so backup lights are not required upon exit.

Rationale

Most people need 30 minutes to achieve optimum night vision. Accidental exposure to light from cars, computers or flashlights means the period of dark adaption must begin again. Some individuals can tolerate small amounts of red light without significant vision degradation, as long as the light source is dim and does not shine into the eyes. For more information, see Sarah Vernon.

Complete the following steps:

1. Open a new, blank document, and save it as **Herschel Society** in the Word3\Case4 folder included with your Data Files.
2. Change the document's orientation to landscape.

EXPLORE

3. On the Insert tab, click the Table button, and then click Draw Table at the bottom of the Insert Table menu. The Draw Table pointer (which looks like a pencil) appears. You drag this pointer horizontally or vertically to create a straight line, and diagonally to create a rectangle.

EXPLORE

4. Click in the upper-left corner of the document (near the paragraph mark), and then drag down and to the right to draw a rectangle that stretches to the right and bottom margins. The rectangle should be a little less than nine inches wide and six inches high.

EXPLORE

5. Use the Draw Table pointer to draw the columns and rows shown in Figure 3-42. For example, to draw the column border for the "Dark Sky Protocol" column, click the top of the rectangle where you want the column to begin, and drag down to the bottom of the rectangle. Use the same technique to draw rows. (If you make a mistake, use the Undo button. To delete a border, click the Eraser button on the Table Tools Design tab, click the border you want to erase, and then click the Eraser button again to turn it off. Click the Draw Table button to turn on the Draw Table pointer again.)
6. Press the Escape key to turn off the Draw Table pointer.

EXPLORE

7. In the left column, type the text **Dark Sky Protocol**. With the pointer still in that cell, click the Table Tools Layout tab, then in the Alignment group, click the Text Direction button twice to position the text vertically so that it reads from bottom to top. Using the formatting options on the Home tab, format the text in 36-point font. Click the

Table Tools Layout tab, and then, in the Alignment group, click the Align Center button. (*Hint*: You will probably have to adjust and readjust the row and column borders throughout these steps, until all the elements of the table are positioned properly.)

8. Type the remaining text, as shown in Figure 3-42. Replace "Sarah Vernon" with your own name. Use bold as shown in Figure 3-42 to draw attention to key elements. Use the default font, but change the font sizes as necessary to make your table look like the one in Figure 3-42. Likewise, use the Center Align button on the Table Tools Layout tab as necessary. (*Hint:* For the bottom three cells, use 16-point or 18-point font for the bold items and 14-point or 16-point font for the other text.)

EXPLORE

9. Switch to the Insert tab. In the Illustrations group, click the Shapes button and then, under "Stars and Banners," click the 4-Point Star shape. In the blank cell in the top row, position the mouse pointer over the upper-left corner, and then click and drag the mouse pointer down and to the right to draw a four-pointed star. If the star isn't centered neatly in the cell, click the Undo button and try again until you draw a star that looks similar to the one in Figure 3-42. On the Drawing Tools Format tab, in the Shape Styles group, click the Shape Fill button arrow and, under "Standard Colors," click the yellow square. Click anywhere outside the star to deselect it.
10. Change the document theme to Civic.

EXPLORE

11. Remove the borders by selecting the entire table, clicking the Table Tools Design tab, clicking the Borders button arrow (in the Table Styles group), and then selecting No Border.
12. Save your work, preview the document, make any necessary adjustments, and then submit the finished document to your instructor, either in printed or electronic form, as requested.

ASSESS

SAM: Skills Assessment Manager

For current SAM information, including versions and content details, visit SAM Central (http://samcentral.course.com). If you have a SAM user profile, you may have access to hands-on instruction, practice, and assessment of the skills covered in this tutorial. Since various versions of SAM are supported throughout the life of this text, check with your instructor for the correct instructions and URL/Web site for accessing assignments.

ENDING DATA FILES

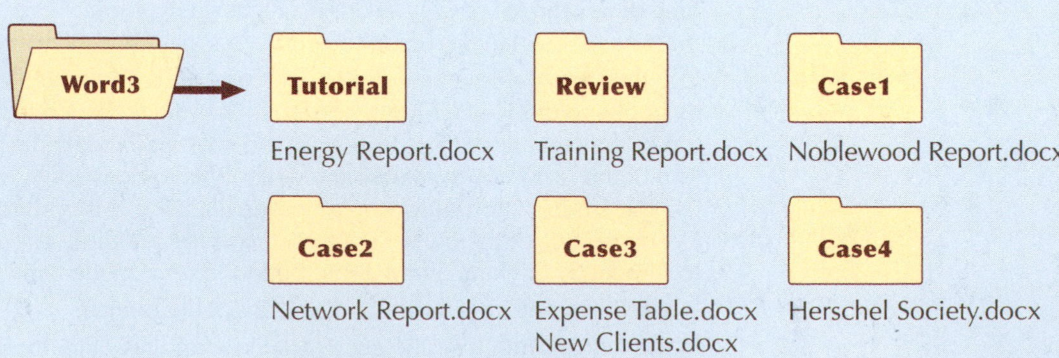

TUTORIAL 4

Desktop Publishing and Mail Merge

Creating a Newsletter and Cover Letter

OBJECTIVES

Session 4.1

- Identify desktop publishing features
- Format text in columns
- Insert drop caps
- Insert symbols and special characters
- Create WordArt
- Edit, resize, and move WordArt
- Align and wrap text around graphics
- Add clip art to a document
- Edit clip art

Session 4.2

- Edit a photograph
- Add a page border
- Balance columns
- Perform a mail merge

Case | *Shepherd Bay Medical Center*

Joel Conchola, a public outreach specialist at Shepherd Bay Medical Center, needs to create a one-page newsletter that explains the importance of exercise and diet in preventing type II diabetes. He has asked you to help him create the newsletter and a cover letter to accompany it.

Joel has already written the newsletter text. He wants you to transform the text into a publication that is organized and professional looking. He wants the newsletter to contain a headline and newspaper-style columns.

In this tutorial, you'll get acquainted with some desktop publishing features available in Word that you will use to create the newsletter. You will create a headline using WordArt, and format the text in columns to make it easier to read. To add interest, you'll include clip art and edit a photograph. You'll fine-tune the newsletter layout and add a border around the page to give the newsletter a finished look. Lastly, you will use Word's mail merge feature to insert personalized information into the cover letter that will accompany the newsletter.

STARTING DATA FILES

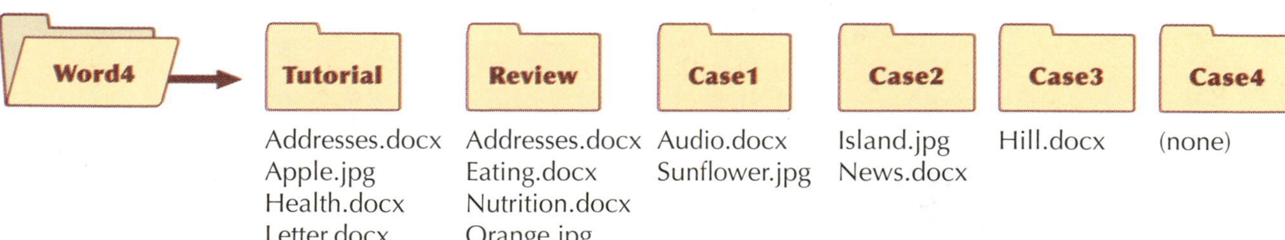

SESSION 4.1 VISUAL OVERVIEW

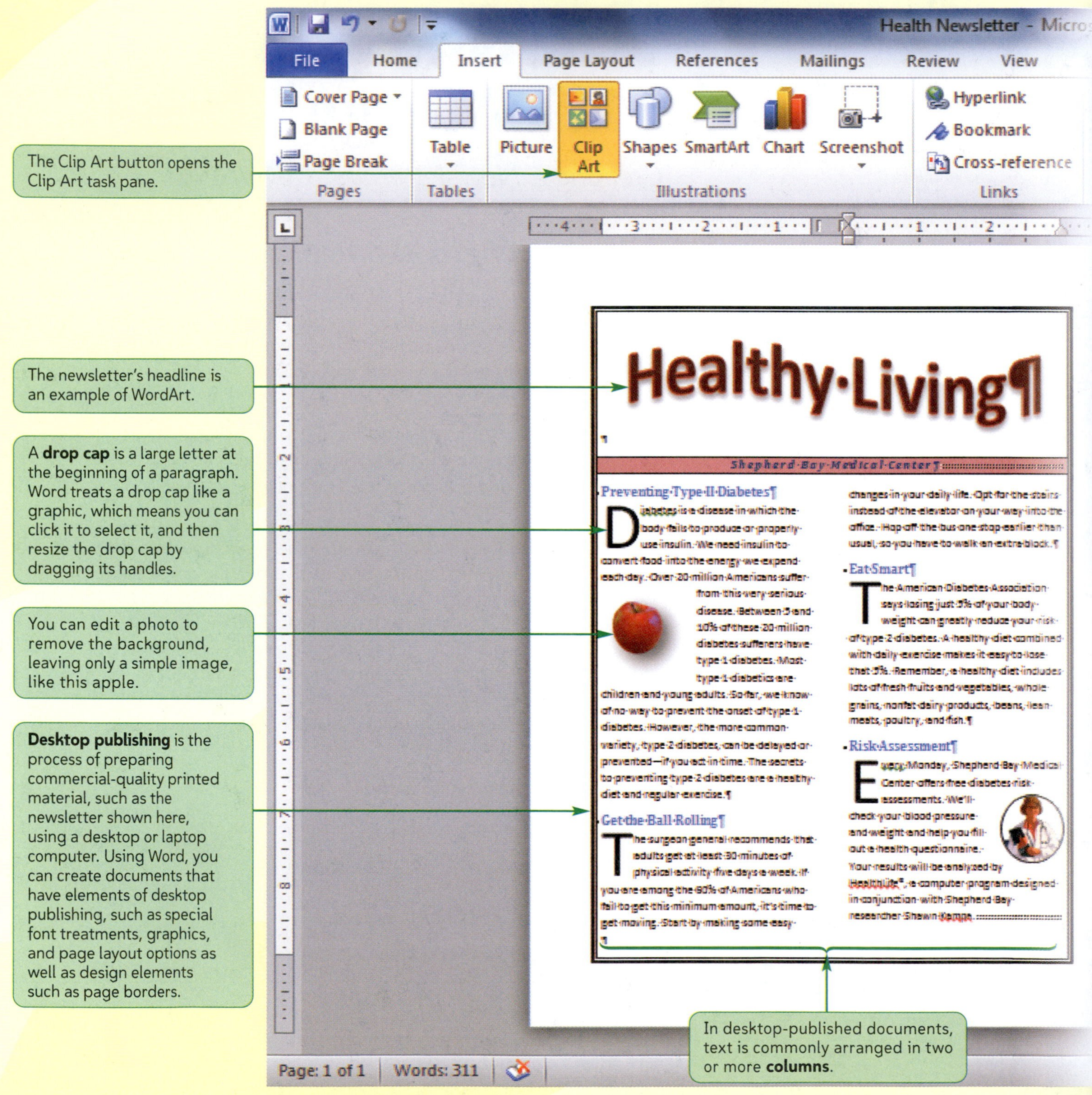
The Clip Art button opens the Clip Art task pane.
The newsletter's headline is an example of WordArt.
A **drop cap** is a large letter at the beginning of a paragraph. Word treats a drop cap like a graphic, which means you can click it to select it, and then resize the drop cap by dragging its handles.
You can edit a photo to remove the background, leaving only a simple image, like this apple.
Desktop publishing is the process of preparing commercial-quality printed material, such as the newsletter shown here, using a desktop or laptop computer. Using Word, you can create documents that have elements of desktop publishing, such as special font treatments, graphics, and page layout options as well as design elements such as page borders.
In desktop-published documents, text is commonly arranged in two or more **columns**.
Health Newsletter
File
Home
Insert
Page Layout
References
Mailings
Review
View
Cover Page
Blank Page
Page Break
Pages
Table
Tables
Picture
Clip Art
Shapes
SmartArt
Chart
Screenshot
Illustrations
Hyperlink
Bookmark
Cross-reference
Links
Healthy·Living¶
Shepherd·Bay·Medical·Center¶
Preventing·Type·II·Diabetes¶
Eat·Smart¶
Risk·Assessment¶
Get·the·Ball·Rolling¶
Page: 1 of 1
Words: 311

ELEMENTS OF DESKTOP PUBLISHING

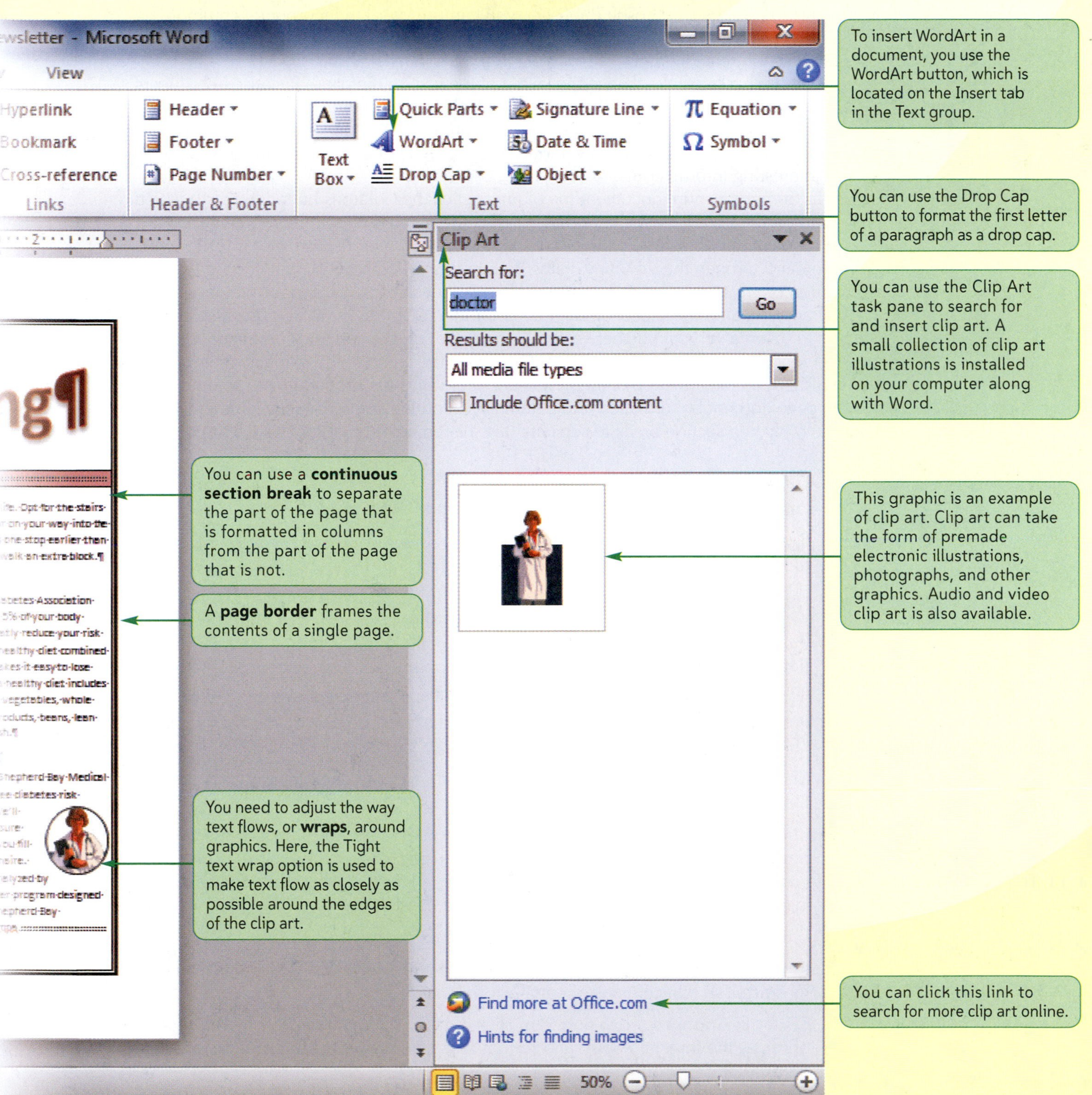

ewsletter - Microsoft Word
View
Hyperlink
Bookmark
Cross-reference
Links
Header
Footer
Page Number
Header & Footer
Text Box
Quick Parts
WordArt
Drop Cap
Signature Line
Date & Time
Object
Text
Equation
Symbol
Symbols
Clip Art
Search for:
doctor
Go
Results should be:
All media file types
Include Office.com content
Find more at Office.com
Hints for finding images
50%
To insert WordArt in a document, you use the WordArt button, which is located on the Insert tab in the Text group.
You can use the Drop Cap button to format the first letter of a paragraph as a drop cap.
You can use the Clip Art task pane to search for and insert clip art. A small collection of clip art illustrations is installed on your computer along with Word.
You can use a **continuous section break** to separate the part of the page that is formatted in columns from the part of the page that is not.
This graphic is an example of clip art. Clip art can take the form of premade electronic illustrations, photographs, and other graphics. Audio and video clip art is also available.
A **page border** frames the contents of a single page.
You need to adjust the way text flows, or **wraps**, around graphics. Here, the Tight text wrap option is used to make text flow as closely as possible around the edges of the clip art.
You can click this link to search for more clip art online.

Formatting Text in Columns

Although professional desktop publishers use software specially designed for desktop publishing, such as Microsoft Publisher, you can use Word to incorporate common desktop publishing elements. In this tutorial, you will use a variety of desktop publishing elements to create the newsletter shown in the Session 4.1 Visual Overview.

First, Joel asks you to change the layout of the text on the page. Because newsletters are meant for quick reading, they are usually laid out in columns. Text flows down one column, continues at the top of the next column, flows down that column, and so forth. Columns are useful because they allow the eye to take in a lot of text and to scan quickly for interesting information.

To format an entire document in columns, click the Columns button in the Page Setup group on the Page Layout tab, and then select the number of columns you want on the Columns menu. To format only part of a document in columns, use the More Columns command to open the Columns dialog box. In this dialog box you can choose to insert a section break at the current location of the insertion point, and then format only the text that appears after the section break into columns. The Columns dialog box also allows you to insert a vertical line between columns, and select a specific column width.

As shown in the Session 4.1 Visual Overview, the name of the medical center appears in a shaded box at the top of the newsletter. Joel wants the shaded box to span the top of the page and not be formatted into columns, so you'll need to use the Columns dialog box to insert a section break to separate this shaded box from the newsletter text .

To format the newsletter text in columns:

1. Open the file **Health** from the Word4\Tutorial folder included with your Data Files, then save the document as **Health Newsletter** in the same folder.
2. Display nonprinting characters, switch to Print Layout view, display the rulers, and set the zoom to Page Width. Notice the newsletter is formatted with the Office theme, and the Heading 2 style is applied to all headings in the document. The first paragraph is formatted with a paragraph border, red shading, dark blue font, and italics.
3. Press the **Ctrl+End** keys to move to the end of the document, and then replace "Shawn Kampa" with your first and last name in the last sentence.
4. Click at the beginning of the second paragraph in the document, just to the left of the "P" in "Preventing Type II Diabetes."
5. Click the **Page Layout** tab, and then, in the Page Setup group, click the **Columns** button. The Columns menu opens. To format all the document text in columns, you could click the Two, Three, Left, or Right options on this menu. However, to insert a section break at the same time, you need to use the More Columns option.
6. Click **More Columns**. The Columns dialog box opens.
7. In the Presets section, click the **Two** icon. The Preview section shows a document formatted in two columns of equal width.
8. Click the **Apply to** arrow and then click **This point forward**. This inserts a section break at the insertion point and formats the columns immediately after the section break. See Figure 4-1.

Figure 4-1 **Columns dialog box**

formats text in two columns

places a line between columns

creates columns of the same width

adds a section break at the insertion point

shows how columns will look with current settings

Columns

Presets

One Two Three Left Right

Number of columns: 2

Line between

Width and spacing

Col #: Width: Spacing:

1: 3" 0.5"

2: 3"

Preview

Equal column width

Apply to: This point forward

Start new column

OK Cancel

9. Click the **OK** button. The Columns dialog box closes. A section break appears at the end of the first paragraph, and the rest of the document text is formatted in two columns. The shaded box at the top of the page remains in its original position.

10. Zoom out so you can see the entire page. The text fills the left column but not the right column. You'll make sure the columns are equal length later, after you make some other changes to the newsletter. See Figure 4-2.

Figure 4-2 **Document formatted in two columns**

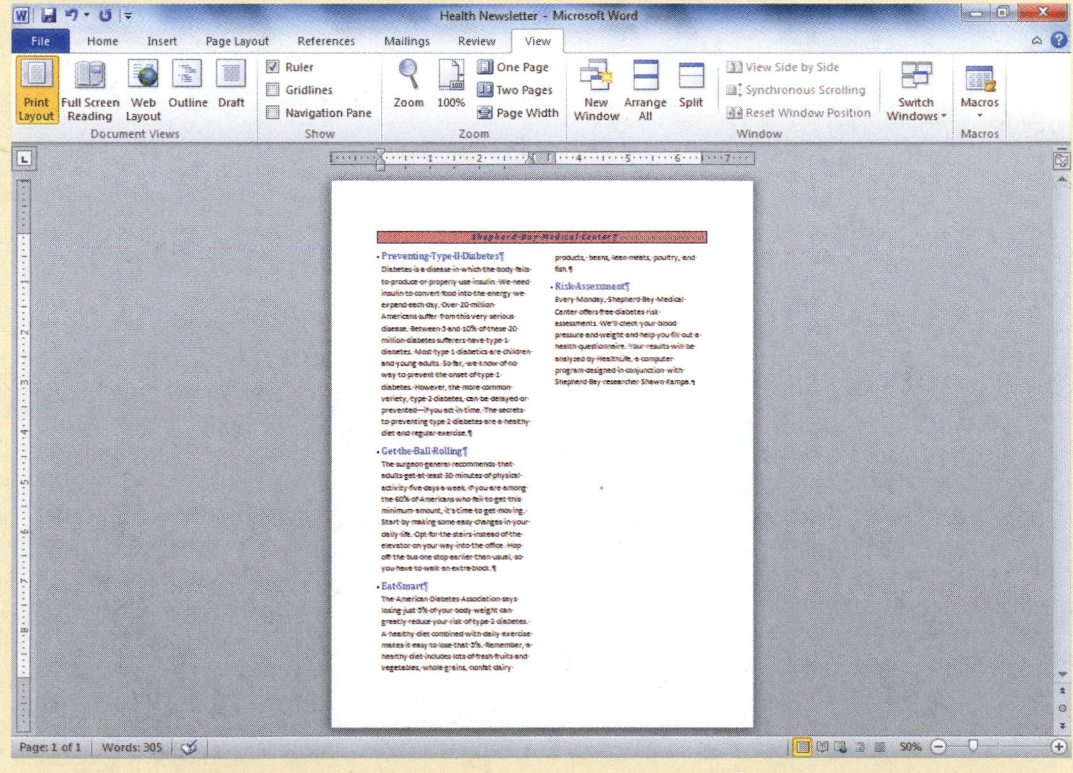

11. Save the document.

Keep in mind that you can modify columns as you work on a document by changing the number of columns. You can also return the document to its original format by formatting it as one column.

Inserting Drop Caps

Like newspapers and magazines, newsletters often include special design elements, called drop caps, which draw the reader's attention to the beginning of an article or paragraph. As you saw earlier in the Session 4.1 Visual Overview, a drop cap is a large, graphical version of a letter that replaces the first letter of a paragraph.

You can place a drop cap in the margin, next to the paragraph, or you can have the text of the paragraph wrap around the drop cap. Joel asks you to create a drop cap for each of the four body paragraphs that follow the level 2 headings. The drop cap will extend three lines into the paragraph, with the text wrapping around it.

To insert drop caps in the newsletter:

1. Change the Zoom level to Page Width, and then move the insertion point to the paragraph below the heading "Preventing Type II Diabetes."
2. Click the **Insert** tab, and then click the **Drop Cap** button in the Text group. The Drop Cap menu opens.
3. Move the mouse pointer over the **In margin** option and then the **Dropped** option, and observe the Live Preview of the two types of drop caps in the document. The default settings applied by these two options are fine for most documents. Clicking Drop Cap Options, at the bottom of the menu, opens the Drop Cap dialog box, where you can select more detailed settings. See Figure 4-3.

Figure 4-3 Drop Cap menu

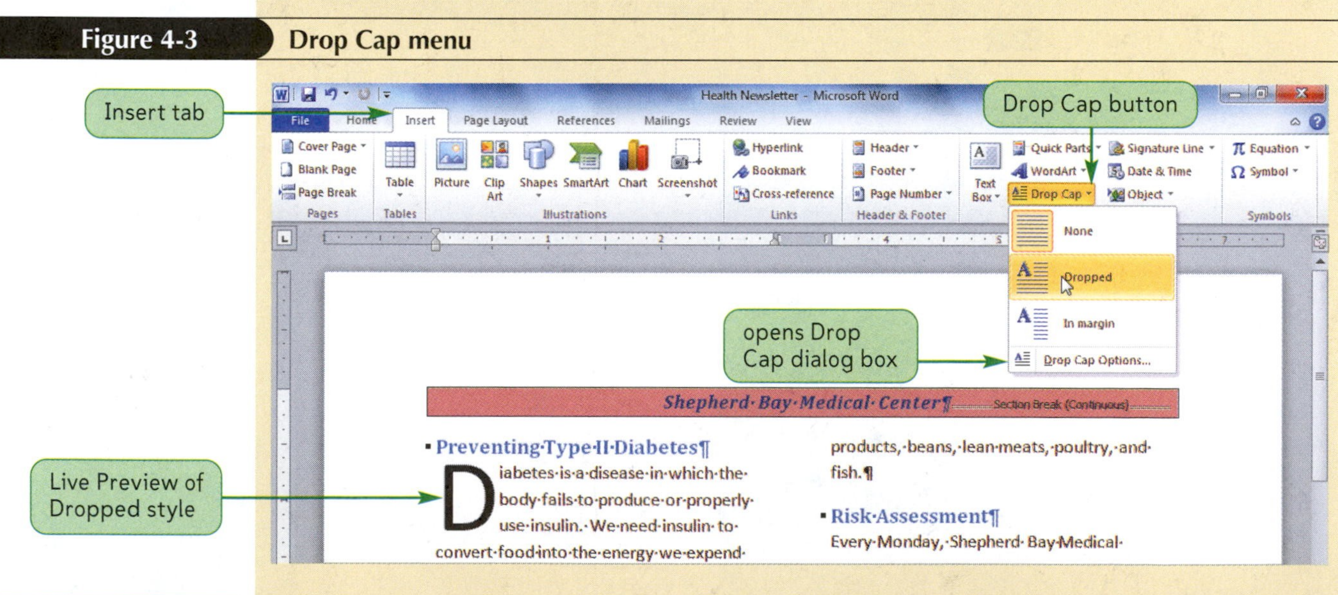

TIP

To change the size of the drop cap, drag the sizing handle in its lower-right corner.

4. Click **Dropped** on the Drop Cap menu. The Drop Cap menu closes, and Word formats the first character of the paragraph as a drop cap. The blue box with square selection handles around the drop cap indicates it is selected.
5. Click in the paragraph following the heading "Get the Ball Rolling," and then repeat Steps 2 and 4 to insert a drop cap in that paragraph.

6. Insert a drop cap in the paragraph following the heading "Eat Smart."
7. Insert a drop cap in the paragraph following the last heading, "Risk Assessment," click anywhere in the text to deselect the drop cap, and then save your work.

As Joel looks over the newsletter, he notices that in the last paragraph he uses the name Healthlife, which is a registered trademark and needs to appear with the registered trademark symbol (®) next to it.

Inserting Symbols and Special Characters

In printed publications, it is customary to change some of the characters available on the standard keyboard into specialized characters or symbols called **typographic characters**. Word's AutoCorrect feature automatically converts some standard characters into typographic characters as you type. For instance, as Joel typed the paragraph under the heading "Preventing Type II Diabetes," he typed two hyphens after the phrase "be delayed or prevented." As he began to type the rest of the sentence, "if you act in time," Word automatically converted the two hyphens into a single, longer character called an em dash.

Figure 4-4 lists some of the character combinations that AutoCorrect automatically converts to typographic characters. In most cases you need to press the spacebar and type more characters before Word inserts the appropriate typographic character. If you don't need the typographic character inserted by Word, click the Undo button to revert to the characters you originally typed.

Figure 4-4 Common typographic characters

To insert this symbol or character	Type	After you press the spacebar, Word converts to
em dash	word--word	word—word
Smiley	:)	☺
Copyright symbol	(c)	©
Trademark symbol	(tm)	TM
Registered trademark symbol	(r)	®
Ordinal numbers	1st, 2nd, 3rd, etc.	1st, 2nd, 3rd, etc.
Fractions	1/2, 1/4	½, ¼
Arrows	<-- or -->	← or →

Most of the typographic characters in Figure 4-4 can also be inserted using the Symbol button on the Insert tab, which opens a gallery of commonly used symbols, and the More Symbols command, which opens the Symbol dialog box. The Symbol dialog box provides access to all the symbols and special characters you can insert into a Word document.

REFERENCE

Inserting Symbols and Special Characters

- Move the insertion point to the location where you want to insert a particular symbol or special character.
- Click the Insert tab, and then, in the Symbols group, click the Symbol button.
- If you see the symbol or character you want in the Symbol gallery, click it. For a more extensive set of choices, click More Symbols to open the Symbol dialog box.
- In the Symbol dialog box, locate the symbol or character you want on either the Symbols tab or the Special Characters tab.
- Click the symbol or special character you want, click the Insert button, and then click the Close button.

Joel forgot to include a registered trademark symbol (®) after "HealthLife" in the last paragraph of the newsletter. He asks you to add one now, using the Symbol dialog box.

To insert the registered trademark symbol:

1. In the paragraph below the heading "Risk Assessment" at the bottom of the right column, click to the right of the word "HealthLife" to position the insertion point between the final "e" and the comma.
2. Click the **Insert** tab, if necessary, click the **Symbol** button in the Symbols group, and then click **More Symbols**. The Symbol dialog box opens.
3. If necessary, click the **Special Characters** tab. See Figure 4-5.

Figure 4-5 Symbol dialog box

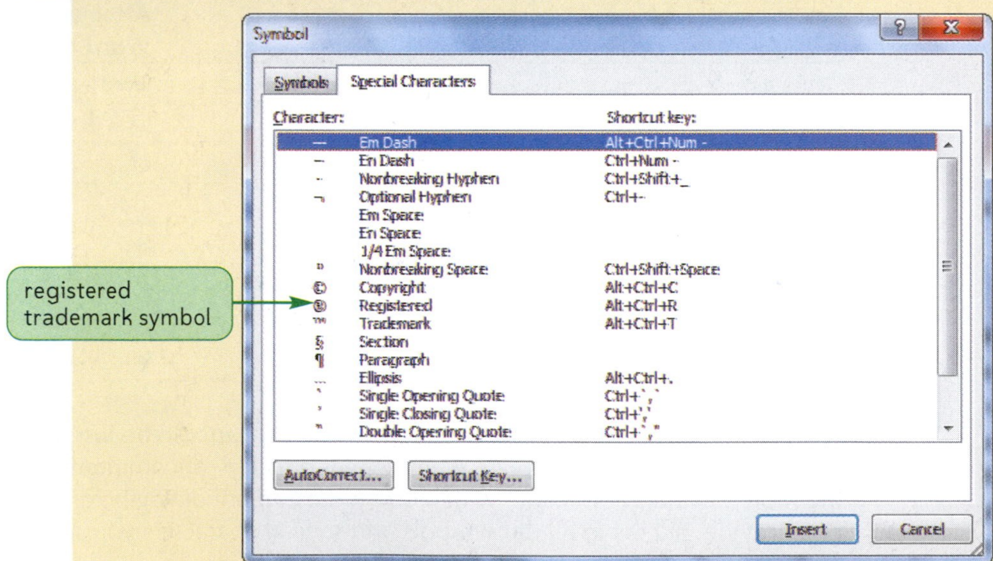

4. Click **Registered** to select it, and then click the **Insert** button.
5. Click the **Close** button to close the Symbol dialog box. Word inserts an ® symbol as a superscript character immediately after the word "HealthLife."

Next, you need to add the graphics to the newsletter. You will begin by creating a headline for the newsletter, using WordArt.

Using WordArt to Create a Headline

Joel asks you to create a title for the newsletter that looks like a newspaper headline. You will use WordArt to achieve this effect. **WordArt** is specially formatted, decorative text. In addition to the formatting you apply to regular text, you can apply to WordArt special effects such as shadows, outlines, and fill colors similar to those you would use to enhance other graphical objects. You can create WordArt out of existing text in a document by first selecting the text, and then, in the Text group on the Insert tab, clicking the WordArt button, and then selecting a WordArt style from the gallery that opens. You can also click the WordArt button in the Text group on the Insert tab, and then click the style you want in the WordArt gallery to open a WordArt text box containing placeholder text, which you can then replace with the text you want to format as WordArt. After you type your new WordArt text, you can format it just as you would ordinary text, by changing its font and font size, adding bold and italics, and so on.

WordArt is considered an **object**—that is, something that you can manipulate independently of the text. You can drag the WordArt to a new location, wrap text around it, and choose from a greater variety of text effects than are available with ordinary text. In addition to the glow, shadow, and reflection text effects that you can use with ordinary text, you can add rounded, or **beveled**, edges to the individual letters, format the text in 3-D, and transform the text into waves, circles, and other shapes. You can also rotate WordArt text so it stretches vertically on the page. Another advantage of WordArt over regular text is that you can edit the colors of WordArt text in two ways: by changing the **fill** (the interior color) or the **outline** (exterior color). You can also change the style of the outline, by, for example, making it thicker, or breaking it into dashes.

By default, a new WordArt text box is attached to, or anchored to, the paragraph containing the insertion point. This means that, in some cases, formatting applied to the paragraph will also affect the WordArt text. For example, the first paragraph of the Health Newsletter document is formatted with shading. If you insert the WordArt in that paragraph, the WordArt will also have pale red background shading. To avoid unexpected formatting results like this, it's a good idea to anchor a WordArt text box to a paragraph that has no special formatting.

Before using WordArt to create a title for the newsletter, you will insert a new, blank paragraph at the beginning of the newsletter document that has the Normal style applied.

To create the title of the newsletter using WordArt:

1. Move the insertion point to the beginning of the document, and then press the **Enter** key to insert a new paragraph. A new paragraph is inserted inside the red shaded box.

To avoid unexpected results, clear formatting from the paragraph before inserting WordArt.

2. Press the ↑ key to move the insertion point to the new paragraph, click the **Home** tab, and then click the **Clear Formatting** button in the Font Group. The blank paragraph reverts to the Normal style, without the shading, the paragraph border, or any other special formatting elements.
3. Click the **Insert** tab, and then click the **WordArt** button in the Text group. The WordArt gallery opens. Joel wants to use the WordArt style in the bottom row.
4. Position the mouse pointer over the second WordArt style from the left in the bottom row. A ScreenTip describes some elements of this WordArt style: "Fill – Orange, Accent 6, Warm Matte Bevel." See Figure 4-6.

Figure 4-6 WordArt gallery

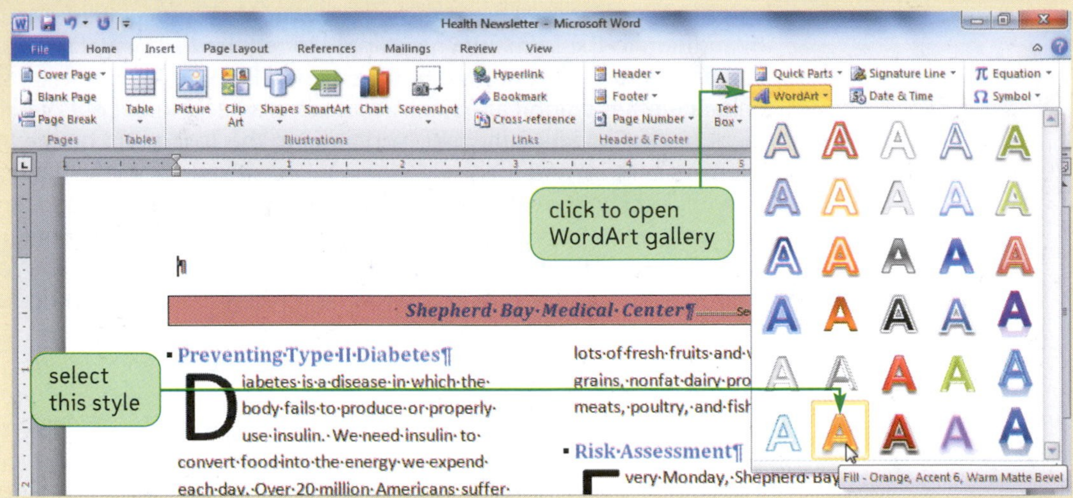

5. Click the WordArt style **Fill – Orange, Accent 6, Warm Matte Bevel**. The gallery closes, and a text box containing WordArt placeholder text appears over the document text. The placeholder text is selected, ready for you to replace it with something new. The Drawing Tools Format tab appears as the active tab on the Ribbon, displaying a variety of tools that you can use to edit the WordArt. The anchor icon to the left of the first paragraph of the document tells you that the WordArt text box is currently anchored to, or attached to, that paragraph. See Figure 4-7.

Figure 4-7 WordArt text box inserted in document

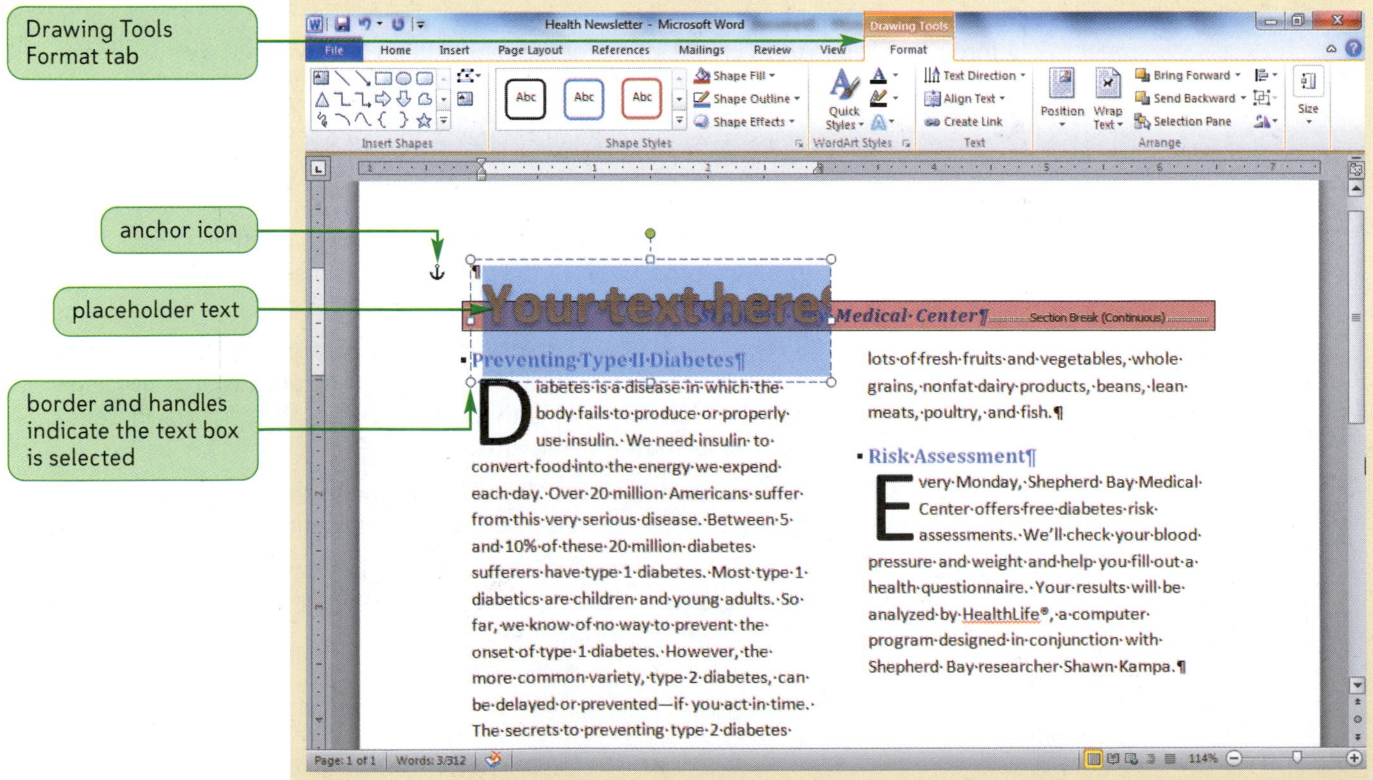

6. Type **Healthy Living** to replace the placeholder text, and then click anywhere outside the text box to deselect it. The anchor icon and the text box border are no longer visible, and the Ribbon displays the Home tab. See Figure 4-8.

Figure 4-8 **WordArt inserted into document**

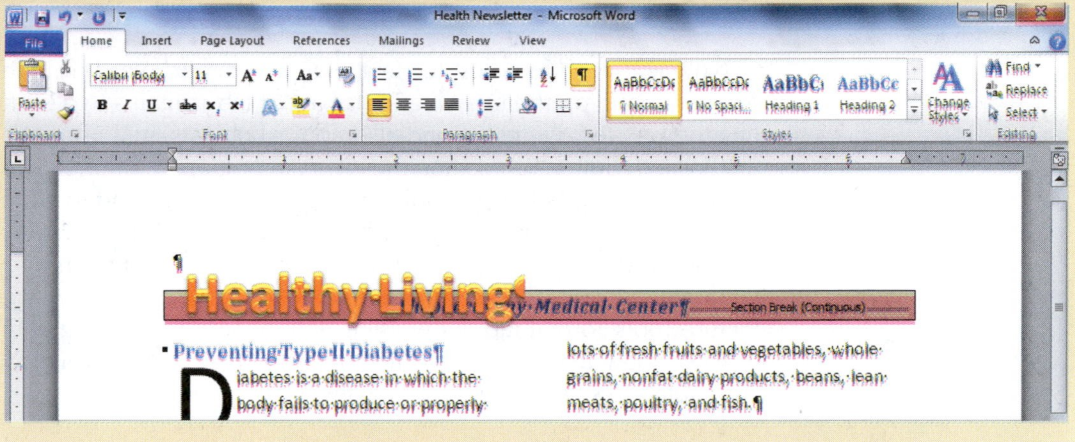

Before you make any more edits to the WordArt, you will adjust its text wrap setting so the WordArt does not overlap the document text.

Wrapping Text Around a Graphic

TIP

You can think of a "floating graphic" as similar to a boat which, though anchored, is free to float above the spot to which it is anchored.

Graphic objects in a document can be either floating or inline. WordArt is considered a **floating graphic**, meaning it is attached, or anchored, to a specific paragraph. In the case of the WordArt in the newsletter, it is currently anchored to the first paragraph of the newsletter. It can still be moved, however, to a new location in the document, as you have just seen. When you move a floating graphic, its **text wrap setting** dictates how text will wrap around it in its new location. If you add text to a document, the floating graphic does not move to accommodate the new text. Instead, the floating graphic remains in position, with the new text flowing around it. The default text wrap setting for WordArt is In Front of Text. The other wrap settings for graphics are:

- **Square**—Text flows around the straight edges of an object's border.
- **Tight**—Text flows around the curved edges of the object itself—for example, following the contours of the WordArt letters, or the lines of a drawing.
- **Through**—Similar to Tight text wrapping, except that text also fills any open spaces in the graphic.
- **Top and Bottom**—Text stops at the top border of an object and resumes below the bottom border. If the object is anchored to the first paragraph in the document, the first line of text begins below the bottom border of an object.
- **Behind Text**—Text flows over the graphic.

Other graphic objects you have inserted into Word documents, such as photos in Tutorial 1 and the Smart Art diagram in Tutorial 3, were examples of **inline graphics**. An inline graphic differs from a floating graphic in that it is located in a specific position in a specific line of text in the document. Text does not wrap around an inline graphic; instead, the graphic moves along with the text. For example, if you type text to the left of an inline graphic, the graphic moves right to accommodate the new text.

INSIGHT

Working with Inline Graphics

A document containing inline graphics is hard to work with because every time you edit the text, the graphics move to a new position. You can change an inline graphic to a floating graphic by applying one of the text wrap settings to it. You will learn more about this later in the session when you insert and work with clip art.

Now you need to adjust the text wrapping for the WordArt in the newsletter. The Arrange group on the Drawing Tools Format tab contains two useful tools for controlling the way text wraps around all graphical objects, including WordArt. You can use the Position button to position the WordArt or graphic in one of several preset locations on the page (top left, top middle, top right, and so on) and to wrap the document text around it. You can also use the Wrap Text button, which allows you to move the WordArt or graphic after you wrap text around it, and allows you to choose from a number of wrapping options. (The Wrap Text button also appears in the Arrange Group of the Picture Tools Format tab, for working with photos and other graphics.)

Now you will use the Wrap Text button in the Arrange group of the Drawing Tools Format tab to select an appropriate text wrap option.

To wrap the newsletter text below the WordArt object:

1. Click the WordArt to select it. The WordArt border and the anchor icon appear, and the insertion point is positioned in the WordArt. Also, the Drawing Tools Format tab is now visible.
2. Click the **Drawing Tools Format** tab, and then click the **Wrap Text** button in the Arrange group. A menu of text wrapping options opens, with the default option In Front of Text selected. See Figure 4-9.

Figure 4-9 Wrap Text menu

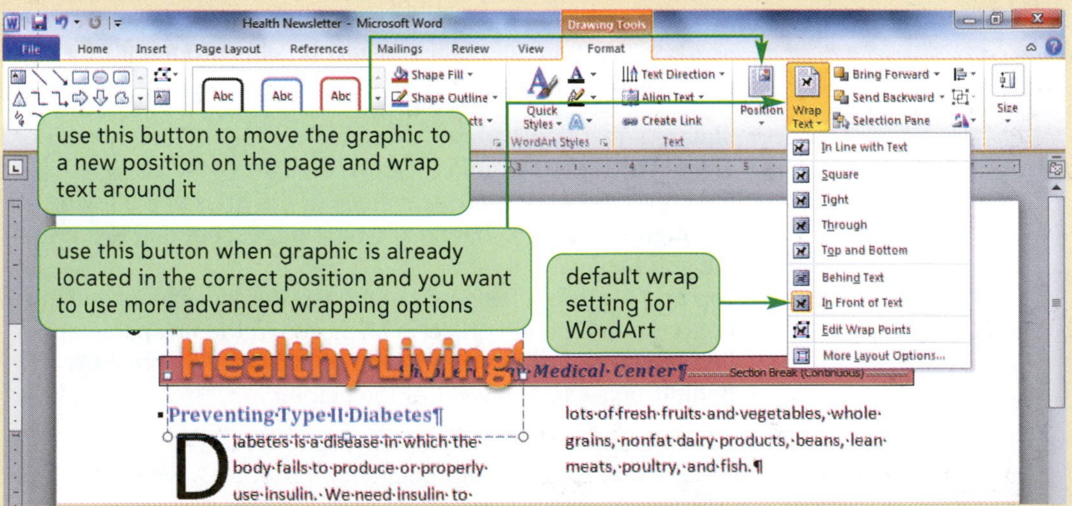

3. Click **Top and Bottom**. The document text moves down, so that the first paragraph, "Shepherd Bay Medical Center," begins immediately below the bottom border of the WordArt text box. See Figure 4-10.

Figure 4-10 WordArt with Top and Bottom text wrap setting

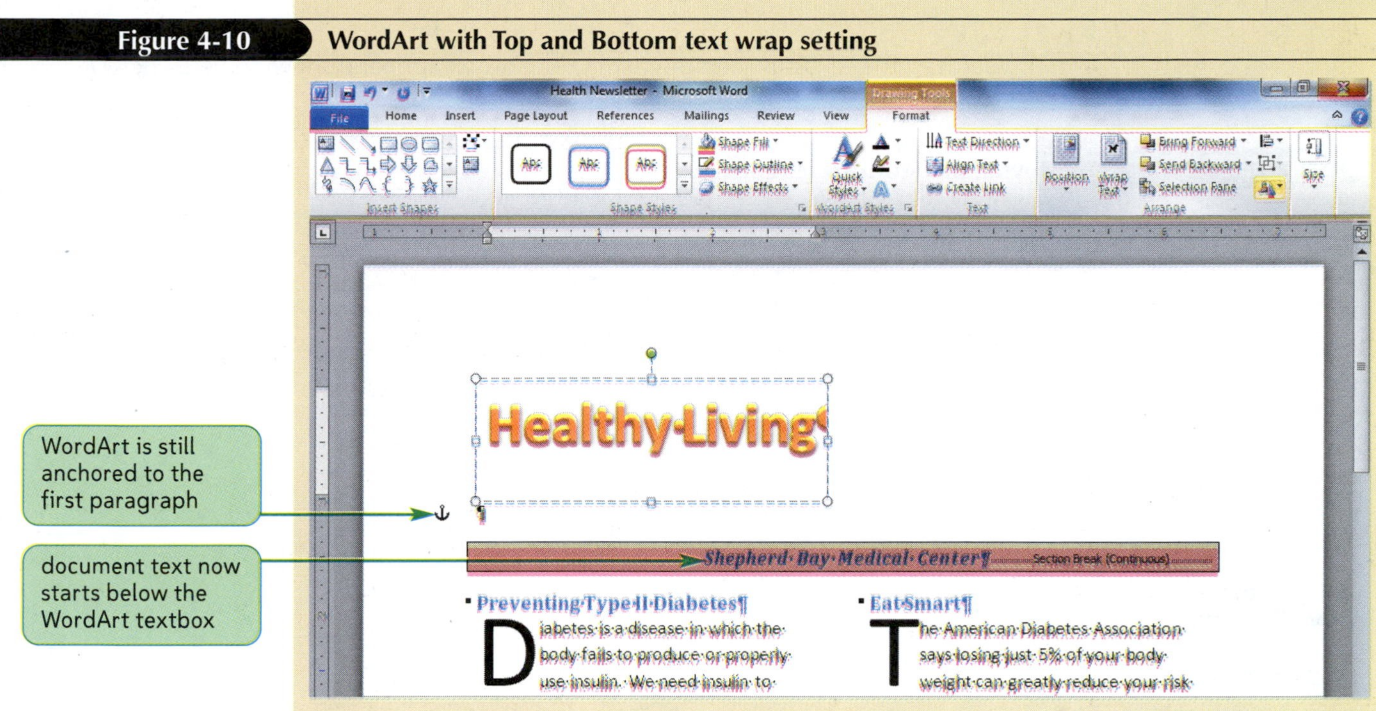

Now that the document text is wrapped below the headline, you can continue to modify it in several ways. First, you will increase its font size, and then center it at the top of the page.

Resizing WordArt

When resizing WordArt, you need to consider both the font size of the text and the size of the text box that contains the WordArt. You change the font size for WordArt text just as you would for ordinary text, by selecting it and then choosing a new font size using the Font size box in the Font group on the Home tab. If you choose an especially large font for a headline, you might also need to resize the text box to ensure that the resized text appears on a single line. To resize a text box, you drag the text box's handles.

To change the font size of the WordArt text:

1. Verify that the WordArt is selected, and then click the **Home** tab.
2. Drag the mouse to select the WordArt text **Healthy Living**, click the **Font Size** arrow in the Font group, and then click **48**. The WordArt text increases in size.

> **TIP**
>
> To delete WordArt, click the WordArt text to display the dashed line text box border, click the text box border again so it appears as a solid line, and then press the Delete key.

Moving WordArt

Joel wants you to position the WordArt so it is centered above the shaded box at the top of the newsletter. You can move a WordArt text box to a new location by dragging it.

To move the WordArt text box down and center it:

1. Move the mouse pointer over the bottom border of the WordArt text box. The pointer changes to ✥.

2. Click and drag the WordArt text box right to center it, as shown in Figure 4-11. As you drag the text box, an outline of the text box appears, showing you where it will be positioned once you release the mouse button.

Figure 4-11 Moving the WordArt text box

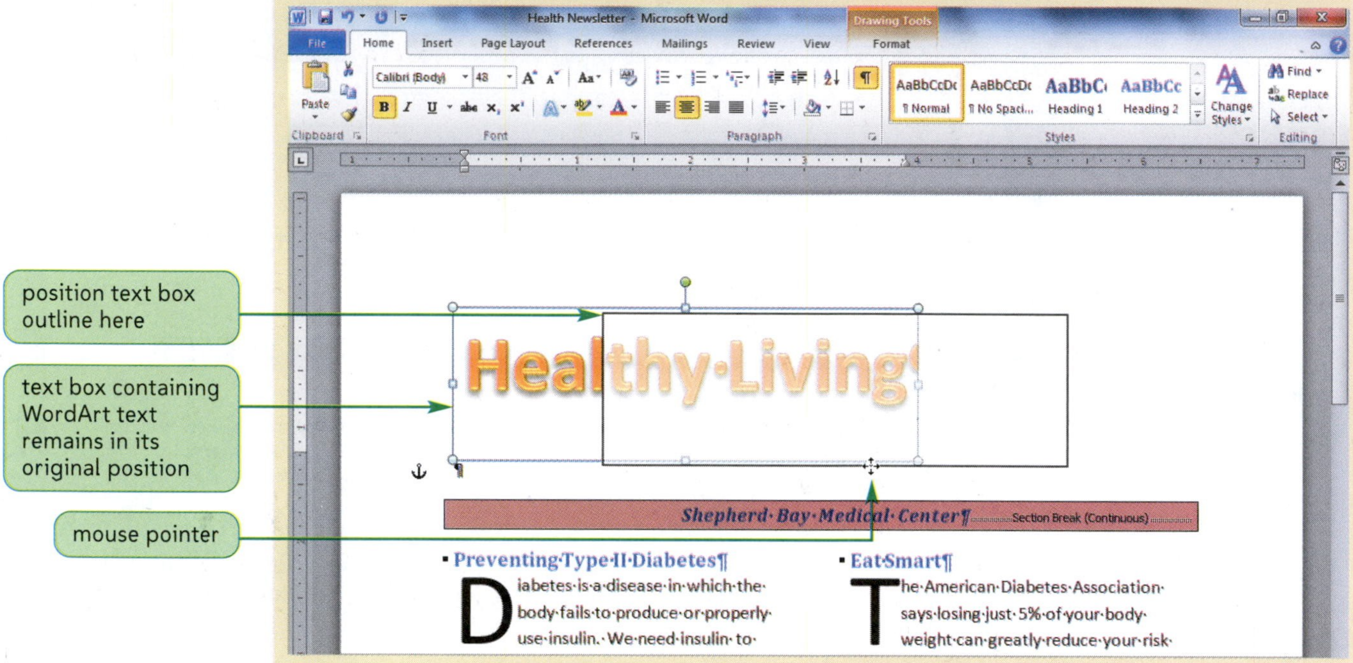

position text box outline here

text box containing WordArt text remains in its original position

mouse pointer

3. Release the mouse button. The WordArt text box moves to the new location, centered at the top of the page. See Figure 4-12.

Figure 4-12 WordArt text box in new location

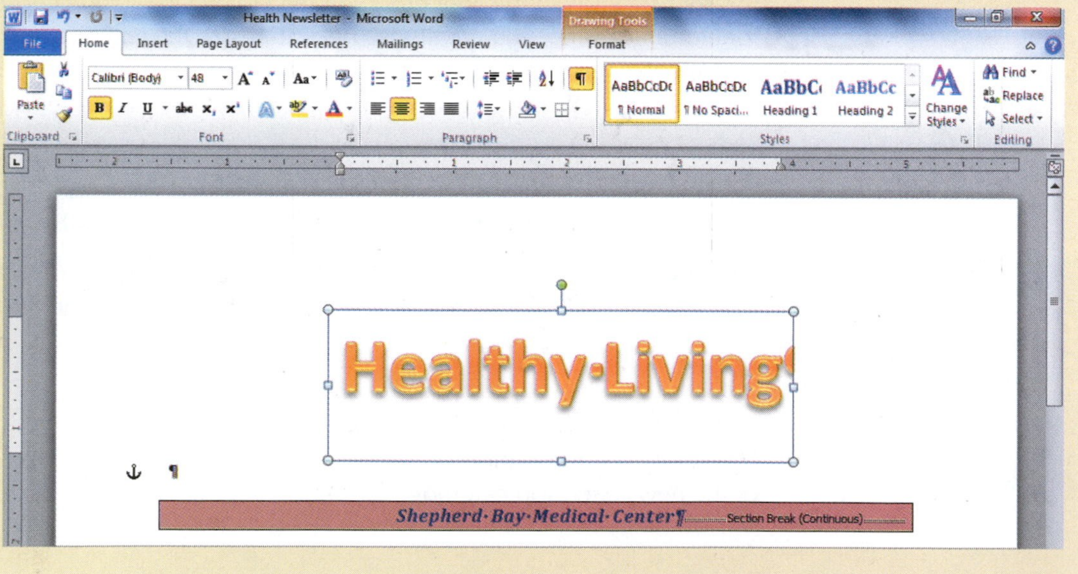

Applying WordArt Styles

The WordArt Styles group on the Drawing Tools Format tab includes four tools that allow you to alter the color, shape, and overall look of WordArt. If you don't like the style you selected when you originally created your WordArt, you can select a new style using the Quick Styles button. To change the fill color, use the Text Fill button, or, to change the outline color, use the Text Outline button. Finally, the Text Effects button gives you access to a variety of special effects, including shadows, beveling, and 3-D rotation, and transforming the shape of the WordArt. If your WordArt already includes some of these features, you can use the Text Effects button to fine tune the effects, perhaps by making a shadow or bevel more noticeable, or by removing an effect entirely.

Joel wants you to change the fill color for the WordArt text to red, and then transform the shape of the text.

To change the color and shape of WordArt:

1. Verify that the WordArt text box is still selected, click the **Drawing Tools Format** tab, and then, in the WordArt Styles group, click the **Text Fill button arrow**. A color palette opens.
2. In the bottom row of the Theme Colors section, position the mouse pointer over the red color in the fifth column from the right, to display the ScreenTip "Red, Accent 2, Darker 50%."
3. Click the **Red, Accent 2, Darker 50%** color. The headline is now red.
4. Click the **Text Effects** button in the WordArt Styles group, and then point to **Transform**. A gallery of transform effects appears, as shown in Figure 4-13. As with any palette in Word, you can move the mouse pointer over the options in the palette to preview the changing effects in the document before clicking to select one. In this case, Joel asks you to use the Wave 1 effect.

Figure 4-13 Transform effects

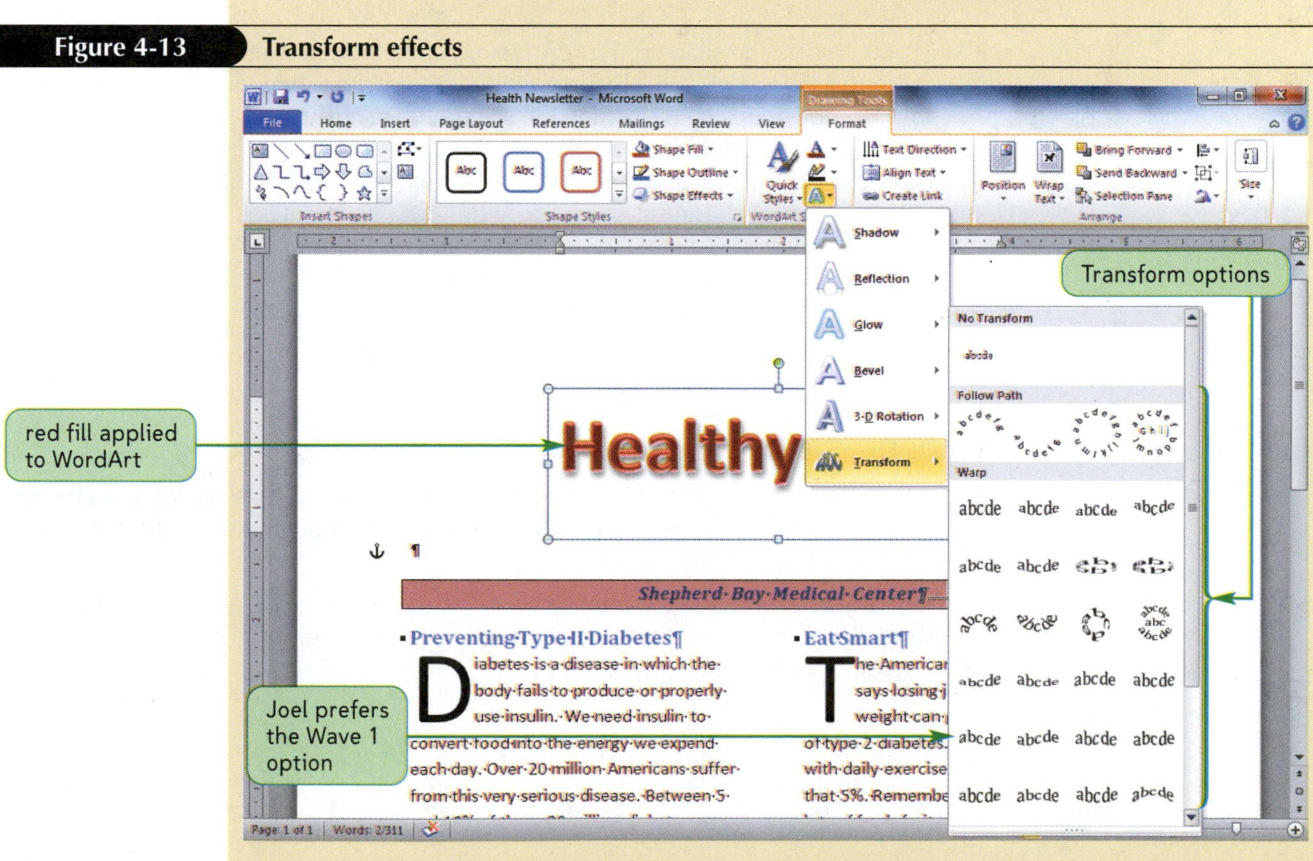

5. Preview several transform effects, and then, under the "Warp" heading, in the first column, fifth row, click the **Wave 1** effect. The text is formatted in a wave shape. Pink diamond-shaped handles appear in the middle of the bottom border and towards the top of the left border of the text box. You can drag a pink diamond handle to make a transform effect more or less noticeable. See Figure 4-14.

Figure 4-14 **WordArt text formatted with the Wave 1 transform effect**

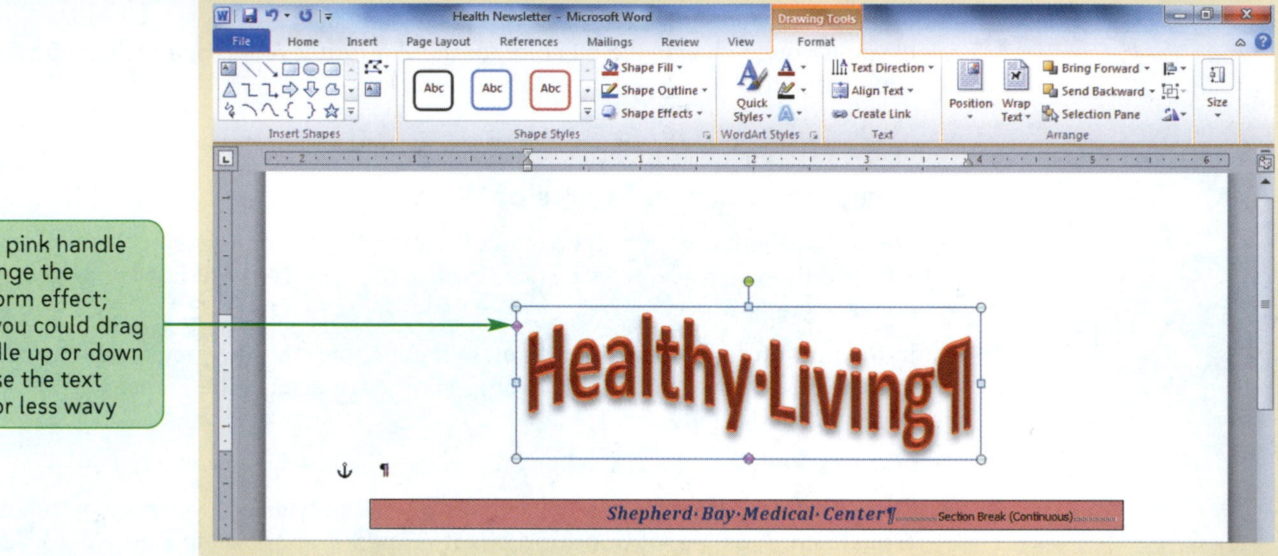
drag a pink handle to change the transform effect; here, you could drag a handle up or down to make the text more or less wavy
Healthy·Living¶
Shepherd·Bay·Medical·Center¶
Section Break (Continuous)

6. Click anywhere outside the WordArt text box to deselect it, and then save the document.

After you change the shape of WordArt text, you will often want to adjust its size and position. In this case, Joel wants the headline to be nearly as wide as the document text. You can accomplish this by increasing the size of the WordArt text box. The WordArt text inside will expand to fill the larger text box.

You can use two methods to resize a WordArt text box. First, you can drag its sizing handles, just as you would resize a photo by dragging its handles. Or, if you prefer, you can use the Size button to enter specific height and width settings.

To resize the WordArt text box, you need to select it. When you do, the transform effect will no longer be visible. However, when you deselect the text box, the transform effect will reappear.

To use the Size button to resize the WordArt text box:

1. Click the WordArt text to select the WordArt text box and to display the Drawing Tools Format tab. The WordArt text temporarily appears in a straight line, without the Wave1 transform effect.

2. Click the **Drawing Tools Format** tab, and then click the **Size** button in the Size group. The Size menu opens, displaying the current height and width of the WordArt text box. See Figure 4-15.

Figure 4-15 **Size menu**

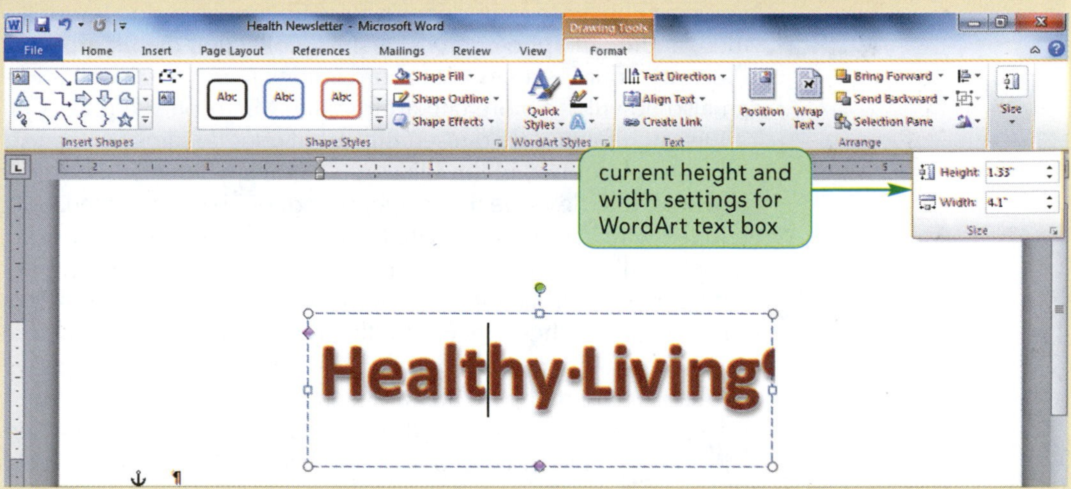

3. Click in the **Width** box, type **6**, press the **Enter** key, and then click outside the WordArt text box to deselect it so you can see the transform effect again. The WordArt is resized, but now needs to be repositioned so it is centered.
4. Select the WordArt again, and then drag the WordArt text box slightly left to center it over the document text. The pink handle at the bottom of the text box should be positioned just above the "M" in "Medical Center." See Figure 4-16.

Figure 4-16 **Resized and centered WordArt text box**

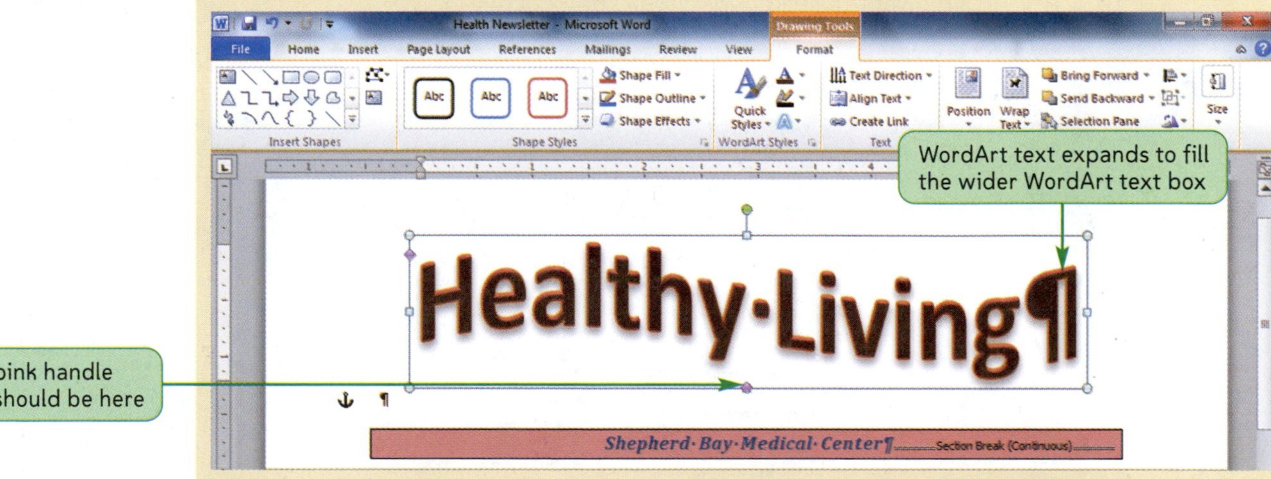

5. Click a blank area of the document to deselect the WordArt, and then save your work.

The WordArt headline is complete. Now you will add clip art to the newsletter.

Inserting Clip Art

As you saw in the Session 4.1 Visual Overview, you can add premade illustrations known as clip art to your documents. Clip art comes in all forms of media, including video, audio, and photographs. A small collection of clip art is included on your computer with your installation of Word, and you are free to use it in your documents. You can also download more clip art from the Microsoft Web site, Office.com.

To search for and then insert clip art in your document, you use the Clip Art task pane. In the Search for box in the Clip Art task pane, you enter words or phrases, known as **keywords**, that describe the image, sound, or video you need. Each of the clip art files included with Word is associated with a set of keywords. For example, clip art of a car might have the keywords "car" and "racing" associated with it, and if the clip art is a car going down a road, additional keywords might be "road" and "driving." If you search using any one of these keywords, that image will appear in your results, along with images of cars not on a road and images of cars without drivers.

After you insert clip art into a document, you can resize it, drag it to a new location, and wrap text around it using the same techniques you used when editing WordArt.

Joel asks you to insert clip art of a doctor in the last paragraph, below the heading "Risk Assessment."

To insert clip art into the newsletter:

1. Click at the beginning of the fourth to last line of the document, which begins "health questionnaire…".
2. Click the **Insert** tab, and then click the **Clip Art** button in the Illustrations group. The Clip Art task pane opens, as shown in Figure 4-17. The Search for box on your computer might be empty, or it might contain text from a previous search. You want to search for clip art of a doctor.

Figure 4-17 Clip Art task pane

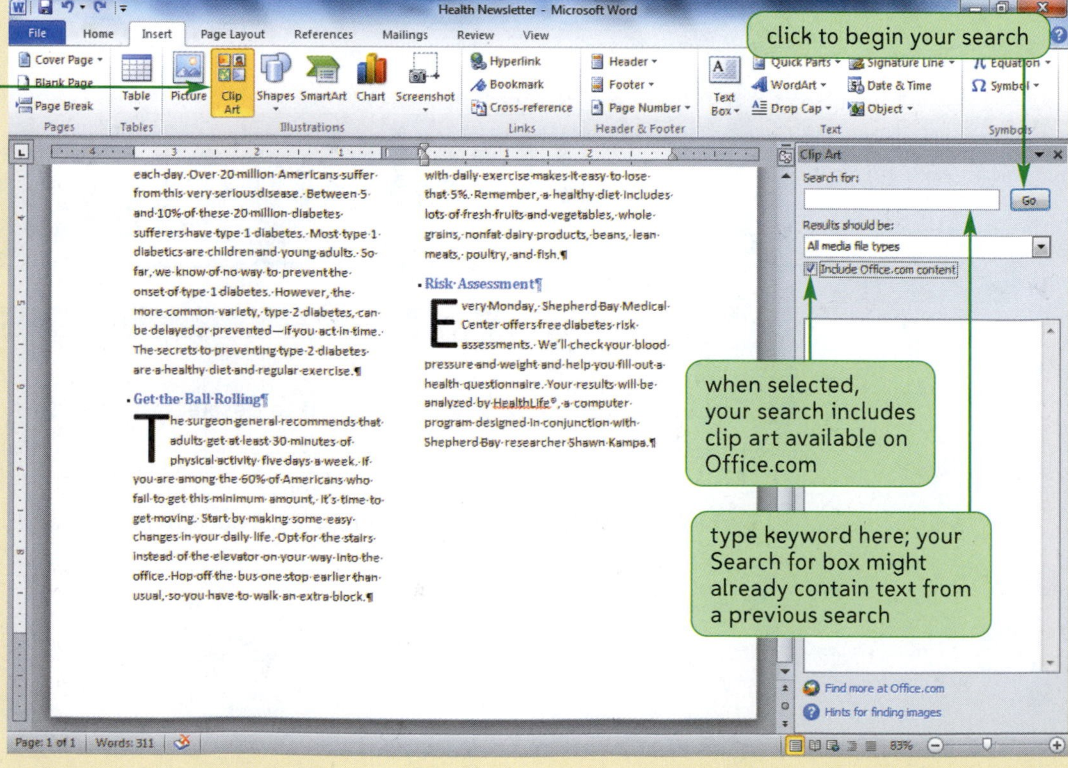

3. Click in the **Search for** box, delete its contents if necessary, and then type **doctor**.
4. Make sure **All media file types** appears in the Results should be box. This ensures that your search will include results for all media types.

   Trouble? If All media file types does not appear in the Results should be box, click the arrow and click the All media file types check box to select it, then click a blank area of the Clip Art task pane to close the menu.
5. Deselect the Include Office.com content check box, if necessary. This ensures that only clip art stored on your computer will be searched.
6. Click the **Go** button. A clip art graphic of a doctor appears in the Clip Art task pane.
7. Click the **doctor clip art**. The clip art is inserted as an inline graphic, at the current location of the insertion point, in the middle of the last paragraph, as shown in Figure 4-18. The text moves to make room for the clipart, but does not wrap around it, because the clip art is an inline graphic. The clip art is selected, as indicated by its border with handles, and the Picture Tools Format tab is available and active on the Ribbon.

Figure 4-18 **Clip art inserted in document**

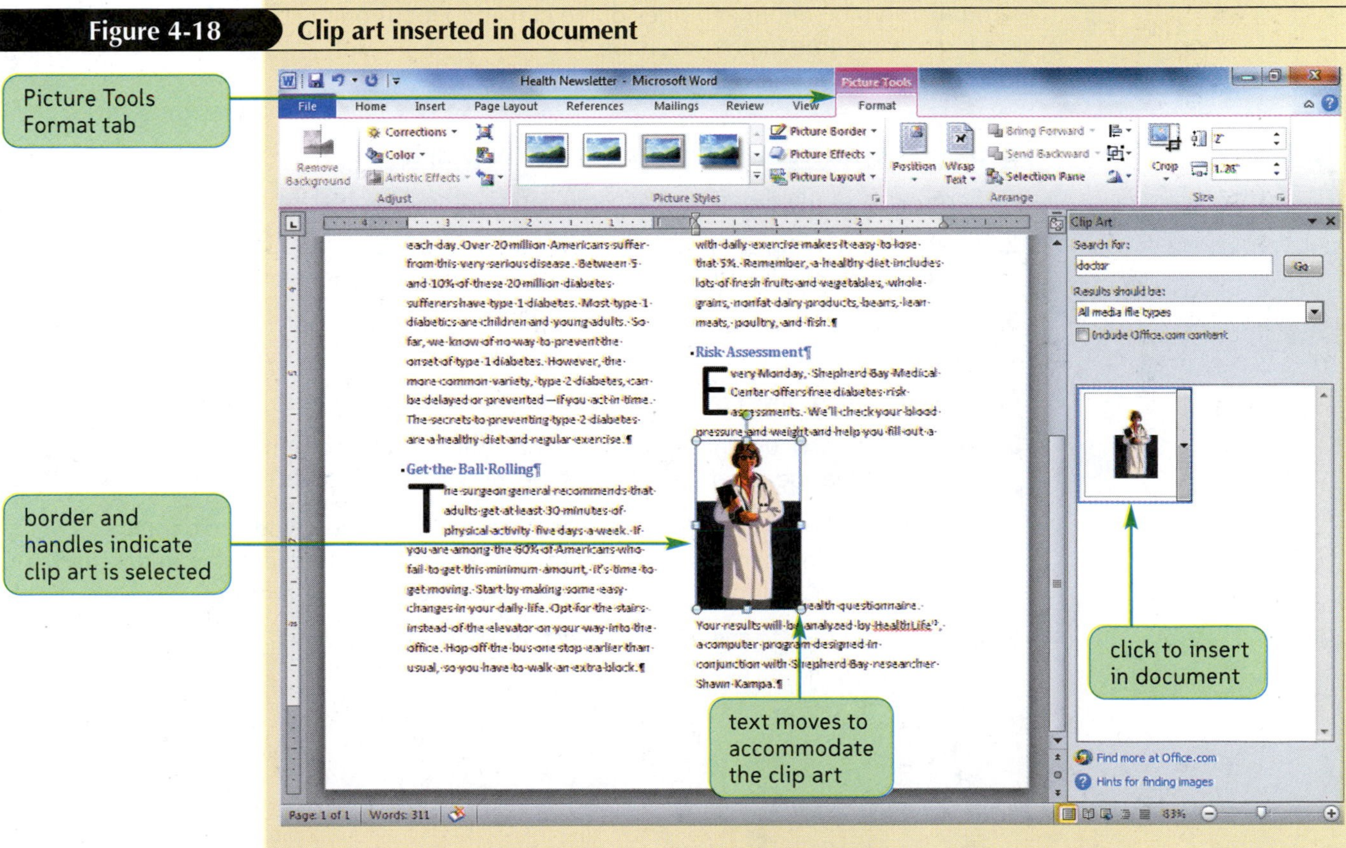

8. Close the Clip Art task pane.

Occasionally you will encounter clip art that comes with preset text wrap settings, so it appears in your document as a floating graphic. However, most clip art images appear as inline graphics, like the doctor graphic you just inserted in the newsletter. In this case, then, you need to change the clip art's text wrap setting to make it a floating graphic. Before you do that for the doctor clip art, you need to modify the graphic by cropping it to adjust its size and shape.

Cropping a Graphic

Word offers two ways to adjust the size of a graphic such as WordArt, clip art, or a photo—you can resize it, using the techniques you learned earlier with resizing WordArt, or you can crop it. **Cropping a graphic** means cutting off part of the graphic. For example, you could crop an illustration of an ice cream cone by cropping off the cone, leaving only the ice cream itself. Word also offers several more advanced cropping options; of these, the one you'll probably use most often is cropping to a shape, which means trimming the edges of a graphic so it fits into a star, oval, arrow, or other shape.

Once you crop a graphic, the part you cropped is hidden from view. However, it remains a part of the graphic, in case you change your mind and want to restore the cropped graphic to its original form. To begin cropping a graphic, you click the Crop button in the Size group on the Picture Tools Format tab.

You'll crop the bottom and sides of the clip art to focus on the doctor's face, and then crop it a second time to an oval shape.

To crop the bottom and sides of the clip art:

1. Scroll up slightly if necessary so you can see the top border of the clip art.
2. Verify that the clip art is selected, and then, in the Size group, click the **Crop** button. Dark black sizing handles appear on the clip art's border.
3. Position the pointer directly over the middle sizing handle on the bottom border. The pointer changes to ┳.
4. Press and hold down the mouse button. The pointer changes to +.
5. Drag the pointer up and down to see how the bottom portion of the clip art disappears and reappears, depending on the location of the pointer.

   Trouble? If the picture shrinks instead of being cropped, you accidentally dragged a sizing handle instead of the black cropping handle in the middle of the bottom border. Undo the change, and repeat Steps 3 through 5.
6. Drag the pointer to the doctor's waist, as shown in Figure 4-19.

Figure 4-19 Cropping the clip art

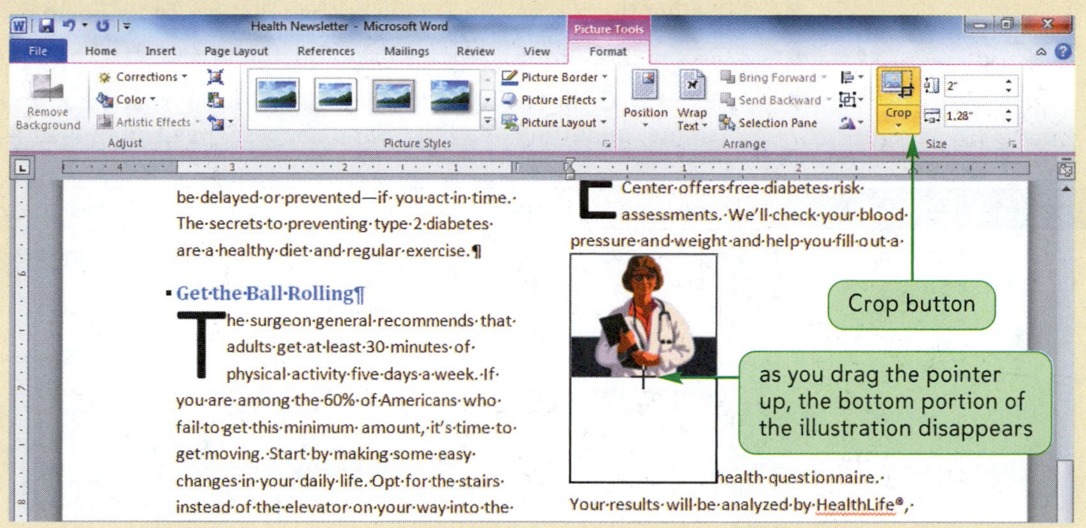

7. When the clip art looks like the one shown in Figure 4-19, release the mouse button. The bottom portion of the clip art is no longer visible. The original border remains, indicating that the cropped portion is still saved as part of the clip art, in case you want to undo the cropping.
8. Drag the middle handle on the right border to crop the right side of the clip art to just before the doctor's elbow, leaving a small amount of the dark green background visible.
9. Crop the left side of the clip art so that it matches the crop you made on the right side.
10. Click a blank area of the document to deselect the clip art, and then save the document. See Figure 4-20.

Figure 4-20 Cropped clip art

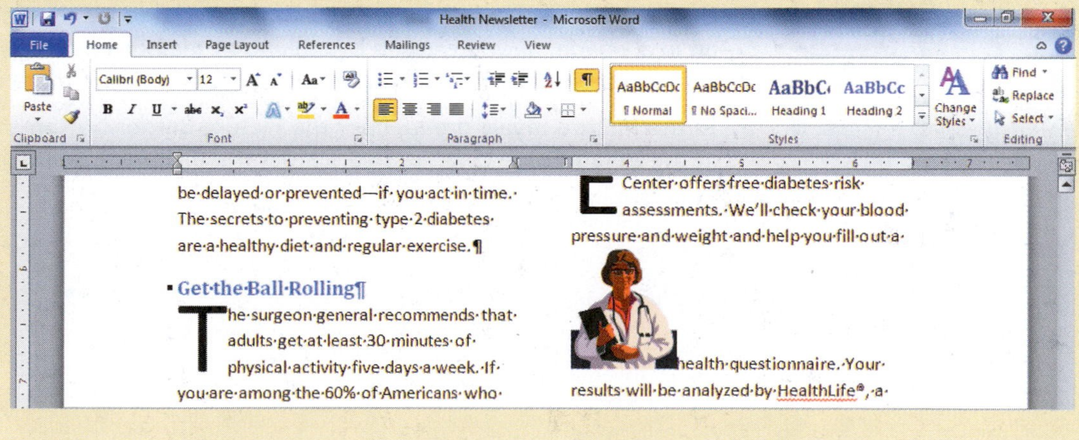

You can also crop a graphic to a specific shape.

To crop the clip art to an oval shape:

1. Select the clip art, and then click the **Picture Tools Format** tab.
2. In the Size group, click the **Crop button arrow**. The Crop menu opens.
3. Point to **Crop to Shape** to display a gallery of shapes. Joel wants to use the oval shape, under the heading "Basic Shapes." See Figure 4-21.

Figure 4-21 Selecting a crop shape

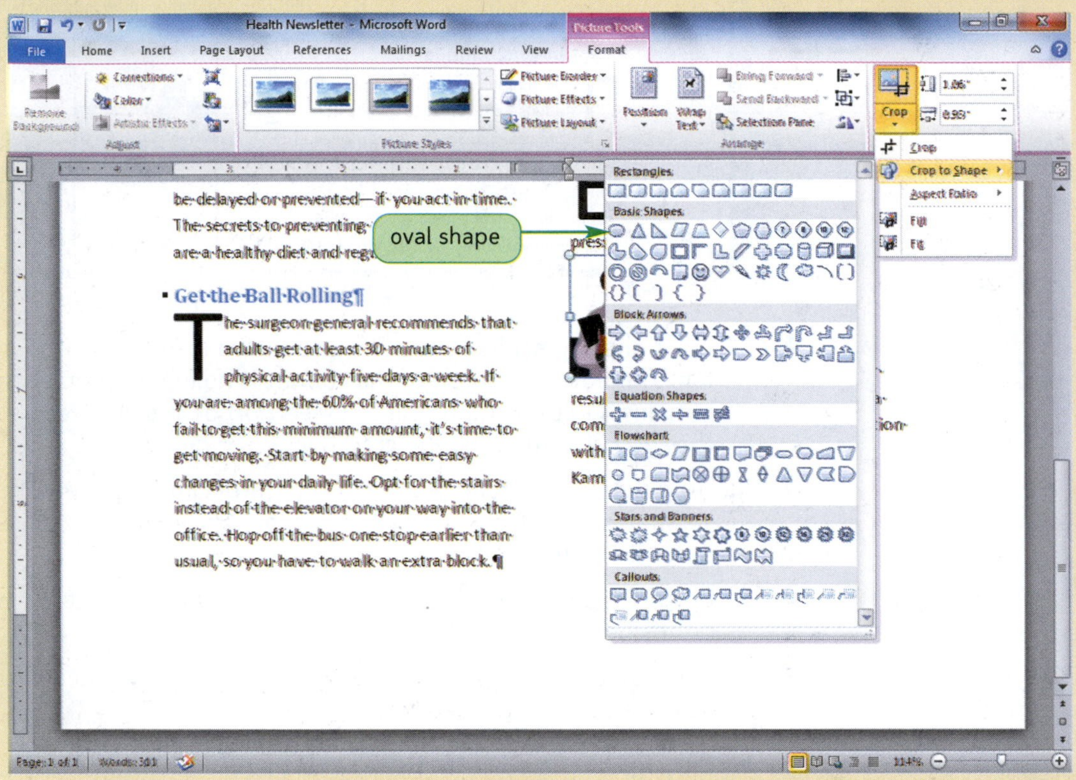

> **TIP**
>
> To change the clip art's colors, click the Color button in the Adjust group on the Picture Tools Format tab.

4. Under Basic Shapes, click the **Oval** shape. Word crops the edges of the clip art to an oval shape, as you can see by looking at the bottom border of the clip art. You can add a border to the clip art to make its new shape more evident.
5. In the Picture Styles group, click the Picture Border button. A simple border, in the default blue color, appears around the clip art. See Figure 4-22.

Figure 4-22 Clip art cropped to an oval shape

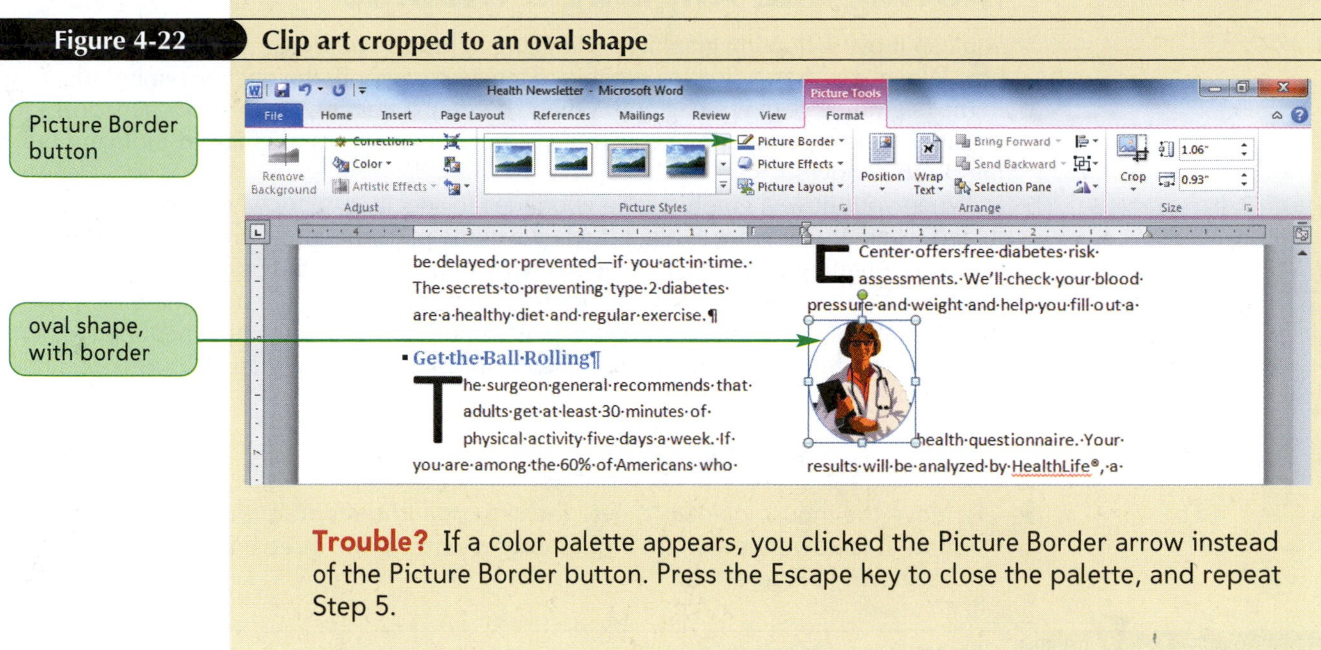

Trouble? If a color palette appears, you clicked the Picture Border arrow instead of the Picture Border button. Press the Escape key to close the palette, and repeat Step 5.

Now that the clip art has been modified, you need to position it properly on the page by changing its text wrap setting.

To change the text wrap setting for the clip art:

> **TIP**
>
> Make sure you separate drop caps from clipart and photos by at least one full line of text to avoid text wrapping issues.

1. Verify that clip art is selected, and then, in the Arrange group, click the **Wrap Text** button. A menu of text wrapping options appears.
2. Click **Tight**. The paragraph text wraps to the right of the clip art, roughly following its oval shape. An anchor symbol appears near the beginning of the paragraph, indicating the clip art is now a floating graphic anchored to this paragraph. See Figure 4-23.

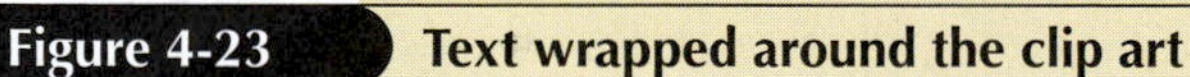

Figure 4-23 Text wrapped around the clip art

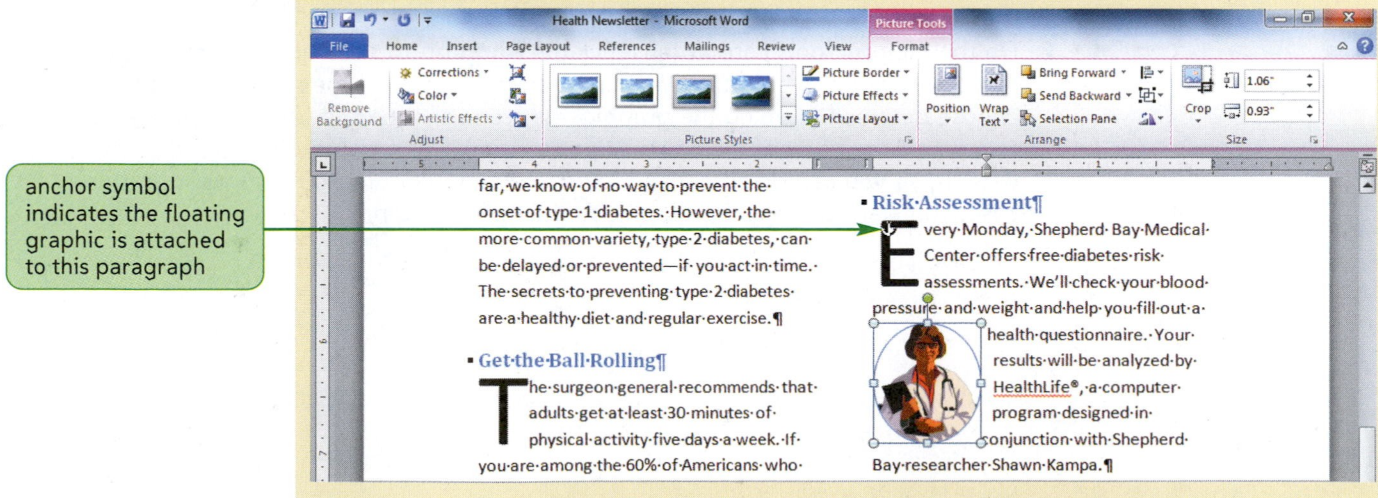

Finally you need to move the clip art to the right side of the paragraph.

Moving and Aligning a Graphic

You can move a floating graphic by dragging it, just as you dragged the WordArt text box. When you drag a floating graphic to a new paragraph, the anchor symbol moves to the beginning of that paragraph. When you drag a floating graphic to a new position within the same paragraph, the anchor symbol remains in its original position and only the graphic moves.

When you move a graphic, it's a good idea to specify exactly where you want to align it, and whether you want to align it relative to the page margins or relative to the edge of the page. Aligning a graphic relative to the margin is usually the best choice, because it ensures that you don't accidentally position a graphic outside the page margins, causing the graphic to get cut off when the page is printed. To specify alignment options for graphics, you use the Align button in the Arrange group on the Picture Tools Format tab.

To move and align the clip art:

1. Move the mouse pointer over the clip art and then drag it right, and up slightly, until it is positioned on the right margin, with two or three lines of text above it, as shown in Figure 4-24.

Figure 4-24 Clip art in new location

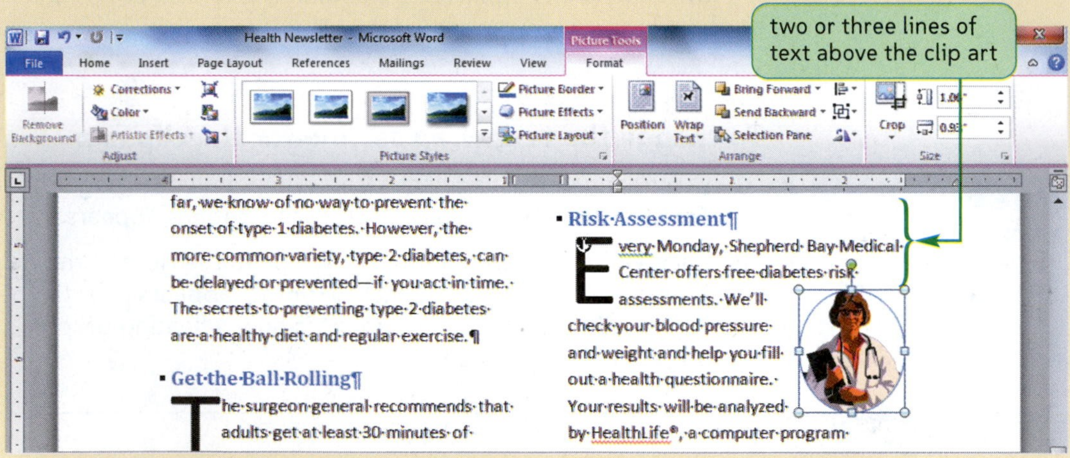

2. On the Picture Tools Format tab, click the **Align** button in the Arrange group. A menu of alignment options opens. Near the bottom of the menu, you can choose between aligning the graphic relative to the margin (Align to Margin) or relative to the edge of the page (Align to Page). Align to Margin is selected by default, so you can go ahead and select the alignment margin you want. In this case, you want to align the graphic to the right margin.

3. On the Align menu, click **Align Right**. Depending on exactly where you positioned the clip art when you dragged it in Step 1, it moves slightly left or right to align to the right margin.
4. Click anywhere outside the clip art to deselect it, and then save your work.

PROSKILLS

Written Communication: Writing for a Newsletter

Photos, clip art, WordArt, and other design elements can make a newsletter very appealing to readers. They can also be a lot of fun to create and edit. But don't let the design elements in your desktop-published documents distract you from the most important aspect of any document: clear, effective writing. Because the newsletter format feels less formal than a report or letter, some writers are tempted to use a casual, familiar tone. If you are creating a newsletter for friends or family, that's fine. But in most other settings—especially in a business or academic setting—you should strive for a professional tone, similar to what you find in a typical newspaper. Avoid jokes; you can never be certain that what amuses you will also amuse all your readers. Worse, you run the risk of unintentionally offending your readers. Also, space is typically at a premium in any printed document, so you don't want to waste space on anything unessential. Finally, keep in mind that the best writing in the world will be wasted in a newsletter that is overburdened with too many design elements. You don't have to use every element covered in this tutorial in a single document. Instead, use just enough to attract the reader's attention to the page, and then let the text speak for itself.

Joel asks you to add another graphic to the newsletter—this time, a photograph. In the next session you will add the photograph and modify it to improve its appearance. Then you'll finalize the newsletter and create the cover letter with mail merge.

REVIEW

Session 4.1 Quick Check

1. How would you format only part of a document in columns?
2. Explain how to open the menu that allows you to create a drop cap.
3. Explain how to create a WordArt headline.
4. True or False. The default text wrapping style for a WordArt text box is Tight.
5. True or False. By default, clip art is inserted as a floating graphic.
6. Explain how to crop a graphic.
7. Why should you align a graphic to the margin after moving it?

SESSION 4.2 VISUAL OVERVIEW

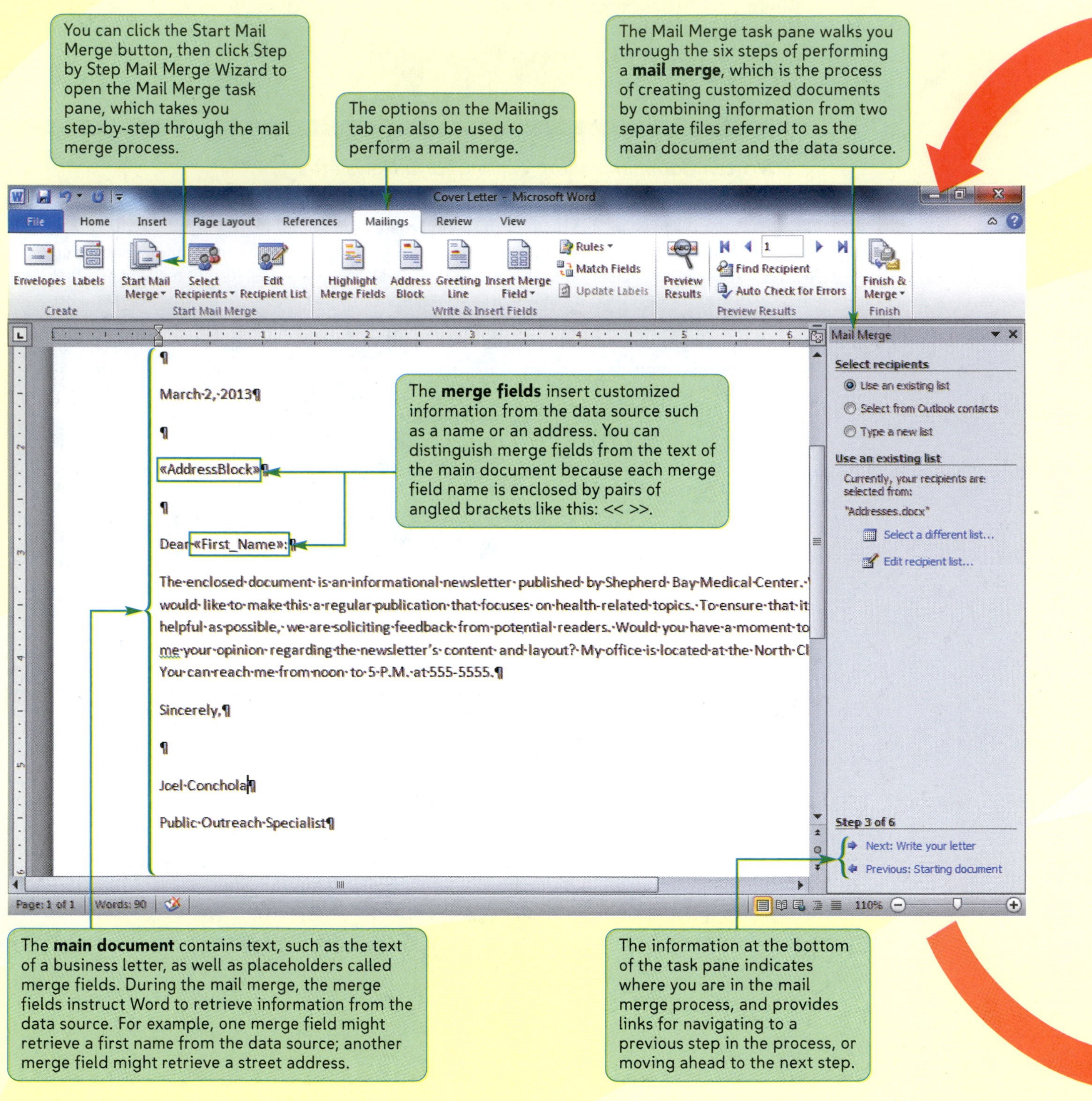
You can click the Start Mail Merge button, then click Step by Step Mail Merge Wizard to open the Mail Merge task pane, which takes you step-by-step through the mail merge process.
The options on the Mailings tab can also be used to perform a mail merge.
The Mail Merge task pane walks you through the six steps of performing a **mail merge**, which is the process of creating customized documents by combining information from two separate files referred to as the main document and the data source.
Cover Letter - Microsoft Word
File Home Insert Page Layout References Mailings Review View
Envelopes Labels
Create
Start Mail Merge Select Recipients Edit Recipient List
Start Mail Merge
Highlight Merge Fields Address Block Greeting Line Insert Merge Field
Rules
Match Fields
Update Labels
Write & Insert Fields
Preview Results
Find Recipient
Auto Check for Errors
Preview Results
Finish & Merge
Finish
March·2,·2013¶
«AddressBlock»¶
Dear·«First_Name»:¶
The·enclosed·document·is·an·informational·newsletter·published·by·Shepherd·Bay·Medical·Center.
would·like·to·make·this·a·regular·publication·that·focuses·on·health-related·topics.·To·ensure·that·it
helpful·as·possible,·we·are·soliciting·feedback·from·potential·readers.·Would·you·have·a·moment·to
me·your·opinion·regarding·the·newsletter's·content·and·layout?·My·office·is·located·at·the·North·Cl
You·can·reach·me·from·noon·to·5·P.M.·at·555-5555.¶
Sincerely,¶
Joel·Conchola¶
Public·Outreach·Specialist¶
The **merge fields** insert customized information from the data source such as a name or an address. You can distinguish merge fields from the text of the main document because each merge field name is enclosed by pairs of angled brackets like this: << >>.
Mail Merge
Select recipients
Use an existing list
Select from Outlook contacts
Type a new list
Use an existing list
Currently, your recipients are selected from:
"Addresses.docx"
Select a different list...
Edit recipient list...
Step 3 of 6
Next: Write your letter
Previous: Starting document
Page: 1 of 1 Words: 90
110%
The **main document** contains text, such as the text of a business letter, as well as placeholders called merge fields. During the mail merge, the merge fields instruct Word to retrieve information from the data source. For example, one merge field might retrieve a first name from the data source; another merge field might retrieve a street address.
The information at the bottom of the task pane indicates where you are in the mail merge process, and provides links for navigating to a previous step in the process, or moving ahead to the next step.

PERFORMING A SIMPLE MAIL MERGE

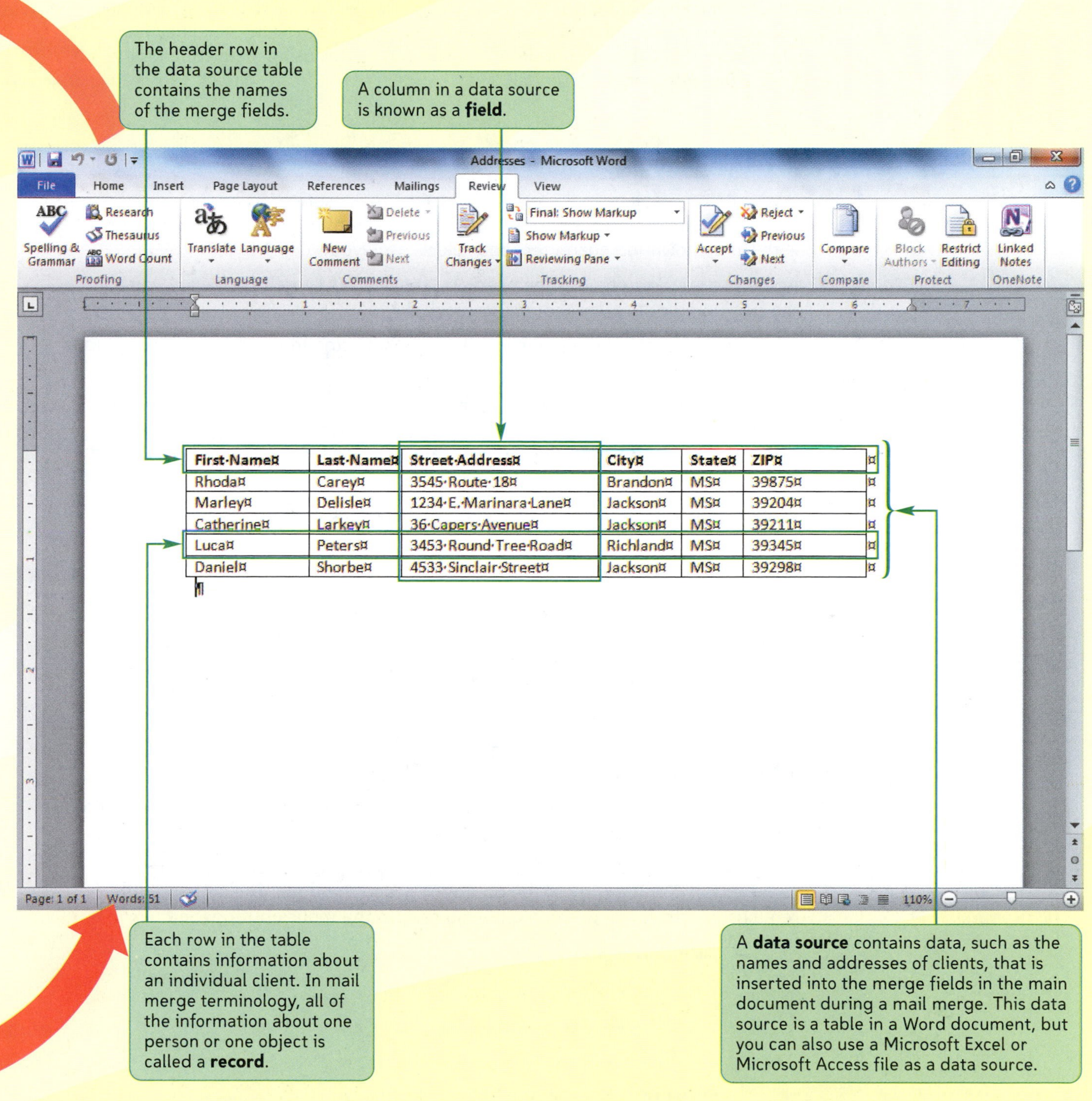
The header row in the data source table contains the names of the merge fields.
A column in a data source is known as a **field**.
Addresses - Microsoft Word
First Name | Last Name | Street Address | City | State | ZIP
Rhoda | Carey | 3545 Route 18 | Brandon | MS | 39875
Marley | Delisle | 1234 E. Marinara Lane | Jackson | MS | 39204
Catherine | Larkey | 36 Capers Avenue | Jackson | MS | 39211
Luca | Peters | 3453 Round Tree Road | Richland | MS | 39345
Daniel | Shorbe | 4533 Sinclair Street | Jackson | MS | 39298
Each row in the table contains information about an individual client. In mail merge terminology, all of the information about one person or one object is called a **record**.
A **data source** contains data, such as the names and addresses of clients, that is inserted into the merge fields in the main document during a mail merge. This data source is a table in a Word document, but you can also use a Microsoft Excel or Microsoft Access file as a data source.

Editing Photographs

Before you work on the mail merge topics presented in the Session 4.2 Visual Overview, Joel asks you to insert a photograph into the newsletter.

Because a photograph is also a graphic object, all of the techniques you have learned for manipulating and editing graphics such as clip art also can be applied to photographs. Joel asks you to insert a photo of an apple in the paragraph below the heading "Preventing Type II Diabetes." Recall from Tutorial 1 that you can do this using the Picture button, in the Illustrations group on the Insert tab.

To insert a photograph:

1. If you took a break after the previous session, make sure Word is running and that the Health Newsletter file is open with the document in Print Layout view and with the nonprinting characters and rulers displayed.
2. In the first paragraph after the heading "Preventing Type II Diabetes," click at the beginning of the line that starts "each day...".
3. Click the **Insert** tab, and then click the **Picture** button in the Illustrations group to open the Insert Picture dialog box.
4. Insert the photo file named **Apple.jpg** from the Word4\Tutorial folder included with your Data Files. The photo of a red apple is inserted in the paragraph as an inline graphic, and the Picture Tools Format tab appears on the Ribbon.

The apple photograph needs to be rotated so that the apple appears right side up.

Rotating a Photo

Digital photographs are sometimes saved with the image turned on its side, so when you insert the photo into a document it appears sideways. You can rotate a photo by dragging the Rotation handle that appears on the photo's border when the photo is selected, or you can use the Rotate button in the Arrange group on the Picture Tools Format tab.

To rotate a photograph:

1. Position the mouse pointer over the green Rotation handle at the top of the photo. The mouse pointer changes to .
2. Drag the mouse pointer down and to the right, around the photo. The pointer changes to and a copy of the photo rotates to the right. The actual photo remains in its original position until you release the mouse button. See Figure 4-25.

Figure 4-25 Dragging the Rotation handle

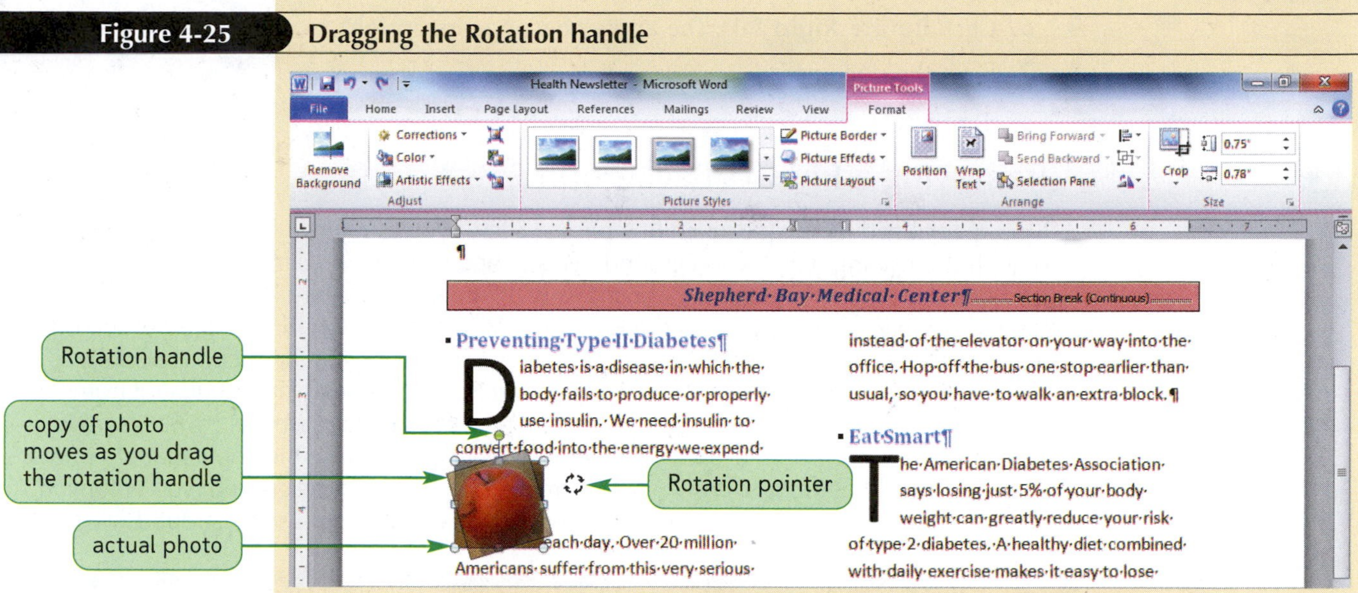

3. Release the mouse button. The photo appears in the new, rotated position. Dragging the Rotation handle is helpful if you want to position a photo on a diagonal, or if its exact position doesn't really matter. For more precise rotation options, you can use the Rotate button.

4. Click the Undo button on the Quick Access toobar to return the apple to its original position, with the stem pointing to the left.

5. On the Picture Tools Format tab, click the **Rotate** button in the Arrange group to open the Rotate menu. As you can see in Figure 4-26, you can use the first two options, Rotate Right 90° and Rotate Left 90°, to turn a graphic 90 degrees either right or left. The Flip Vertical and Flip Horizontal options are useful when you want to completely flip a photo, as if it were a transparency with an image visible on both sides, and you were flipping the transparency over. In this case, you just want to turn the photo 90 degrees to the right.

Figure 4-26 Rotate menu

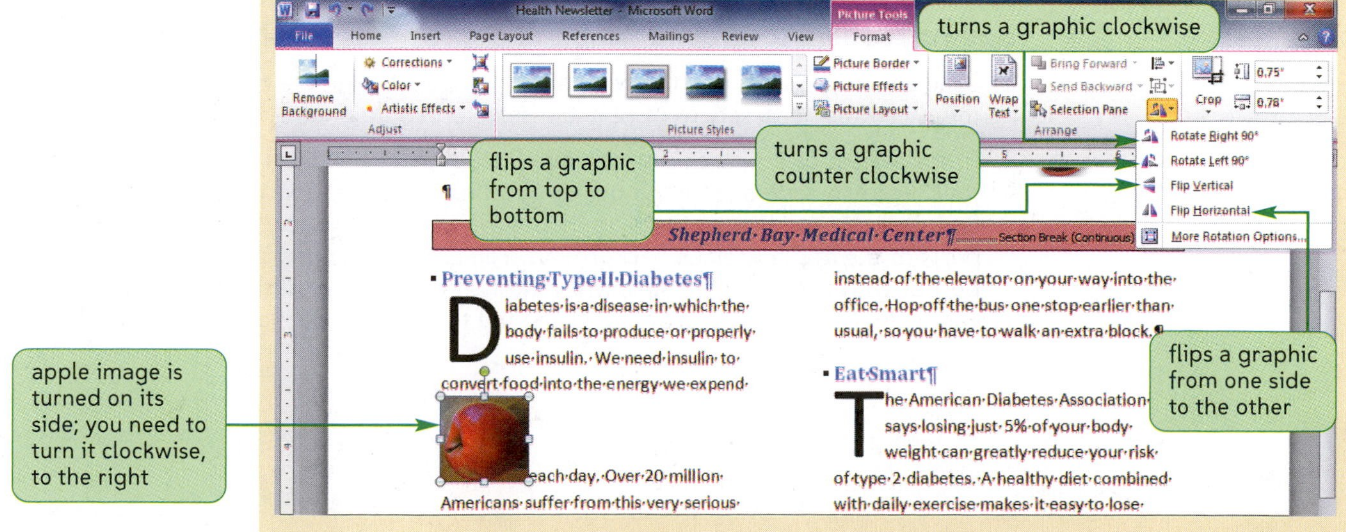

6. Click **Rotate Right 90°**. The apple now appears upright.
7. Save the document.

Removing a Photo's Background

One specialized technique for editing photos allows you to remove the background of a photo, leaving only the foreground image. For example, you can edit a photo of a bird in the sky to remove the sky, leaving only the image of the bird. To edit a photo to remove the background, you use the Remove Background button in the Adjust group on the Picture Tools Format tab. Removing a photo's background can be tricky, especially if you are working on a photo with a background that is not clearly differentiated from the foreground image. For example, you might find it difficult to remove a white, snowy background from a photo of an equally white snowman. Because the apple in Joel's photo contains a small amount of brown that is similar to the brown background, you will need to make some adjustments to completely separate the apple from its background.

REFERENCE

Removing a Photo's Background

- Select the photo, and then click the Remove Background button in the Adjust group on the Picture Tools Format tab.
- Drag the handles on the blue border as necessary to include parts of the photo that have been incorrectly marked for removal.
- For marking specific areas to keep, click the Mark Areas to Keep button in the Refine group of the Background Removal tab, and then use the drawing pointer to select areas of the photo to keep.
- For marking specific areas to remove, click the Mark Areas to Remove button in the Refine group of the Background Removal tab, and then use the drawing pointer to select areas of the photo to remove.
- Click the Keep Changes button in the Close group.

You'll start by zooming in, so you can clearly see the photo as you edit it.

To remove the background from the apple photograph:

1. Drag the **Zoom slider** all the way to the right to change the zoom to 500%, and then scroll as necessary to display the selected apple photo.
2. In the Adjust group, click the **Remove Background** button. The part of the photo that Word considers to be the background turns purple, and the Background Removal tab appears on the Ribbon. See Figure 4-27. Notice that Word marks parts of the apple itself as background. You can change this by expanding the border with the white handles, which now surrounds part of the apple. Then you can make additional adjustments using the tools on the Background Removal tab.

Figure 4-27 **Removing a photo's background**

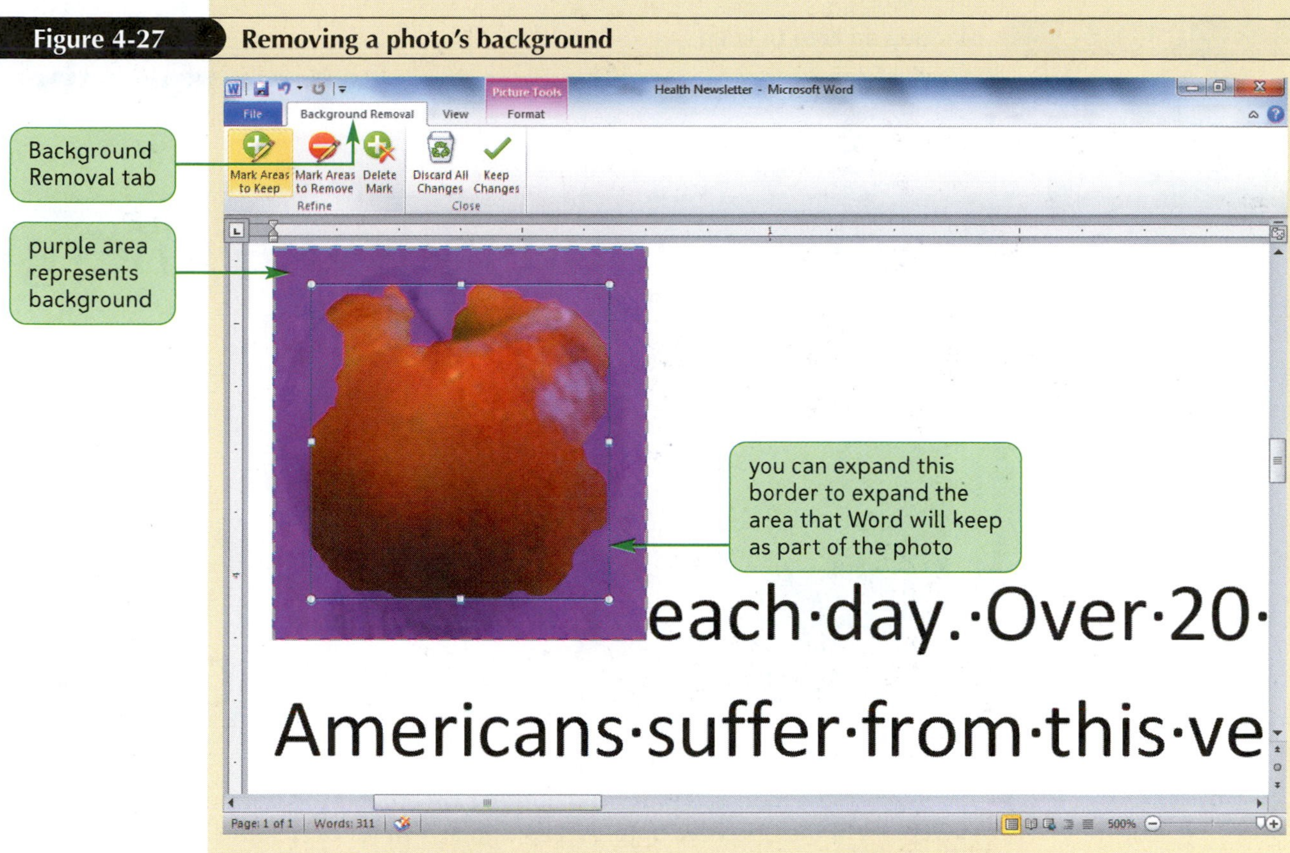

3. Drag the circular handle in the lower-right corner of the blue border down to the bottom-right corner of the photo. The entire right-side of the apple turns red, indicating Word no longer considers it to be part of the background.

   Trouble? If part of the brown background also reverts to its original color, undo the change, and then repeat Step 3. If a small part of the right side of the apple is still purple, ignore the purple part for now and continue with Step 4.

4. Drag the circular handle in the lower-left corner of the blue border down to the bottom-left corner of the photo. The entire left-side of the apple turns red.

5. Drag the top, middle handle of the blue border up to just below photograph's top border.

   At this point, the entire apple has reverted to its original color, except for a small purple area near the stem. Now you need to identify this specific area to be kept as part of the photo.

6. On the Background Removal tab, click the **Mark Areas to Keep** button in the Refine group, and then move the drawing pointer over the apple. You can use the drawing pointer to draw lines through the purple areas you want to keep as part of the photo.

7. Click in a red part of the apple below the stem, and drag the mouse pointer up to a red area above the stem. The pointer changes to a white arrow and a dotted line appears as you drag the pointer. See Figure 4-28.

Figure 4-28 Marking an area to keep

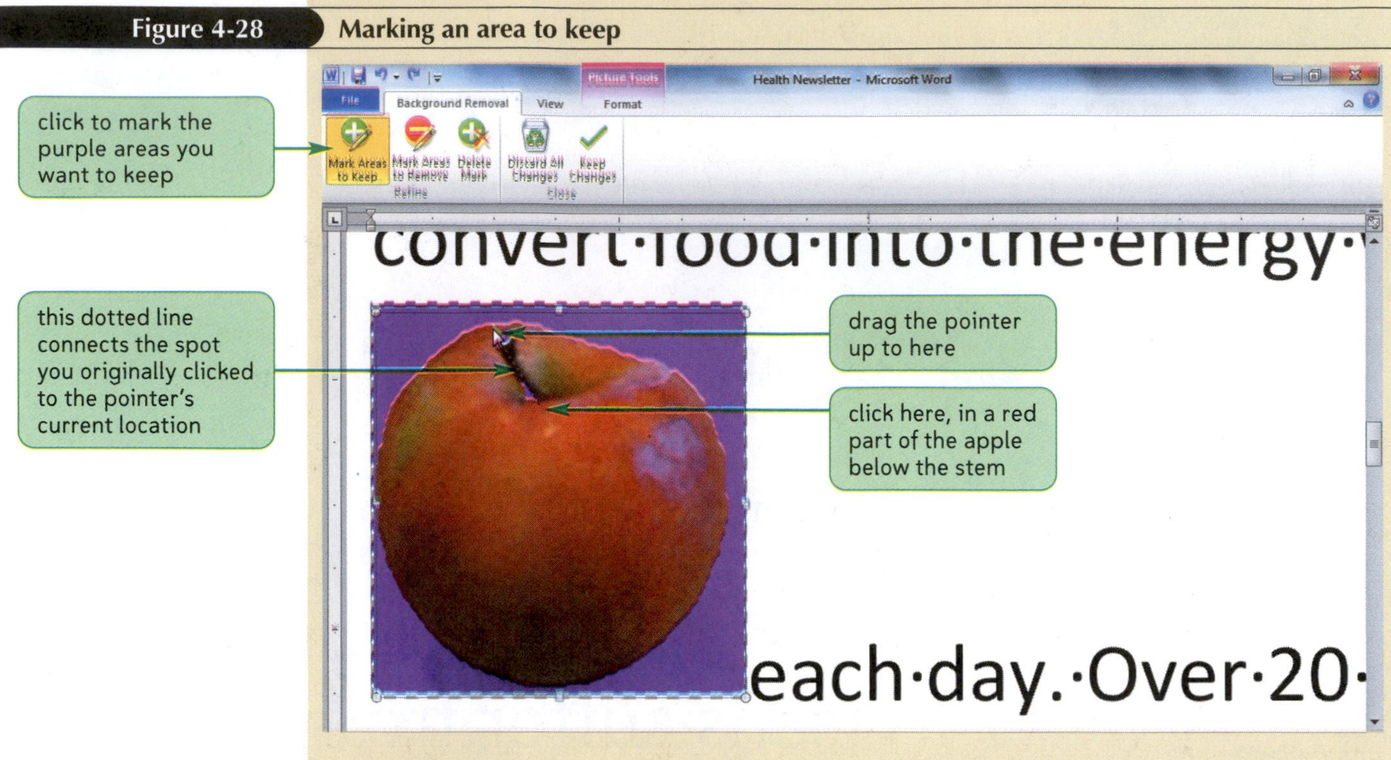
click to mark the purple areas you want to keep
this dotted line connects the spot you originally clicked to the pointer's current location
drag the pointer up to here
click here, in a red part of the apple below the stem
Health Newsletter - Microsoft Word
Background Removal
View
Format
convert·food·into·the·energy·
each·day.·Over·20·

8. Release the mouse button. The purple area around the dotted line reverts to the colors of the original photo. A plus sign in a white circle appears on the dotted line, indicating that you have marked that part of the photo as an area to keep.
9. If parts of the apple are still purple, draw additional lines as necessary to mark them as areas to keep, until all of the apple appears in its original color, with the background marked in purple. Now you will make the changes to the photo permanent, and remove the background from it.
10. In the Close group, click the **Keep Changes** button. The background is removed from the photo, leaving only the image of the apple, as shown in Figure 4-29.

Figure 4-29 Apple with background removed

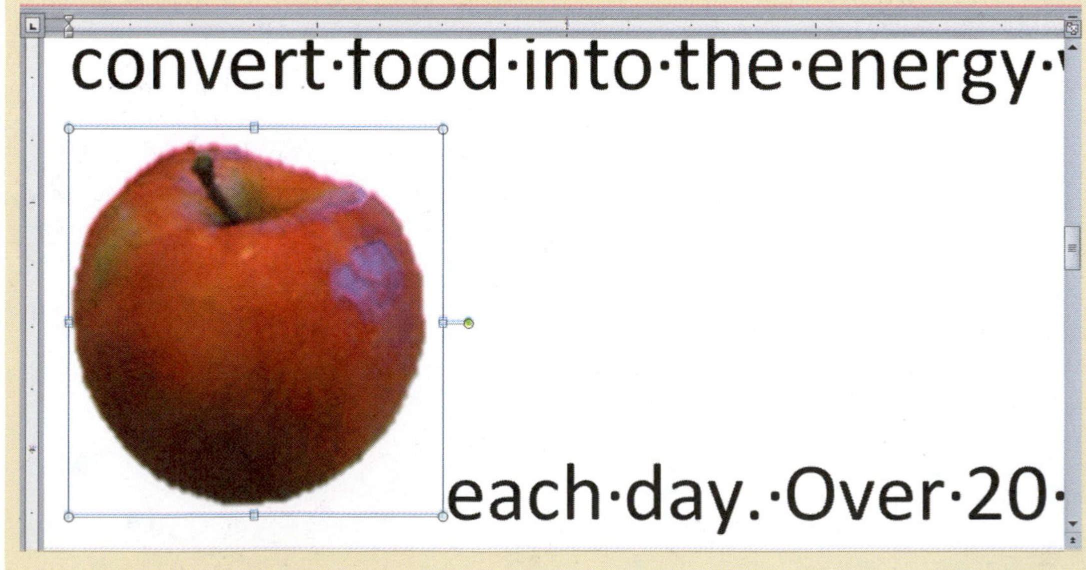
convert·food·into·the·energy·
each·day.·Over·20·

Now that the apple is cropped the way Joel wants it, you need to move it to a new location, align it, and apply a text wrap setting. You can perform all three tasks at once by using the Position button.

To move, align, and wrap text around the photo:

1. Change the Zoom level to **One Page**, so you can see the position of the photo relative to the rest of the document. The photo is currently an inline graphic.
2. Click the **Picture Tools Format** tab, and then click the **Position** button in the Arrange group to display a gallery of position options. You want to place the apple photo in the middle of the left side of the page, so you will use the option Position in Middle Left with Square Text Wrapping, as shown in Figure 4-30.

Figure 4-30 Position gallery

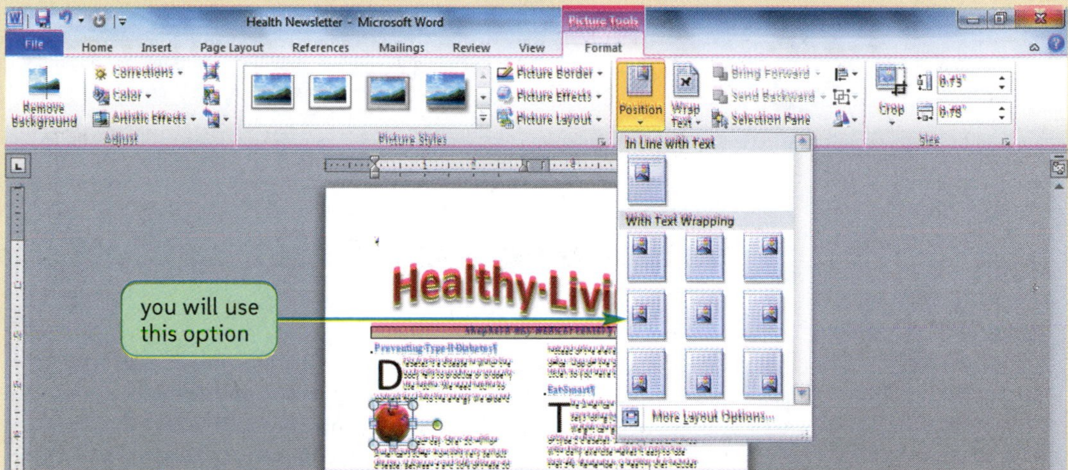

3. Click the **Position in Middle Left with Square Text Wrapping** option. The photo moves down slightly, to the middle of the left side of the page. Text wraps around the photo in a square shape.

Applying a Picture Style

You can change a graphic's overall look by selecting a **picture style** from the Picture Styles gallery on the Picture Tools Format tab. For example, you can use a picture style that adds a shadow, a fading effect around the edges, or a border that looks like a picture frame. Joel asks you to apply a picture style that adds a shadow to the apple photo.

To add a picture style to the apple photo:

1. Change the Zoom level to **Page Width**, scroll as necessary so you can see the apple photo, and then verify that the photo is selected.
2. Click the **Picture Tools Format** tab and then click the **More** button in the Picture Styles group to display the gallery of picture styles.
3. Move the mouse pointer over the various styles and observe the Live Preview of the picture styles on the apple photo.

4. Click the **Drop Shadow Rectangle** style, in the top row, second from the right. The gallery closes and a shadow appears below and to the right of the apple. See Figure 4-31.

Figure 4-31 Photo formatted with a picture style

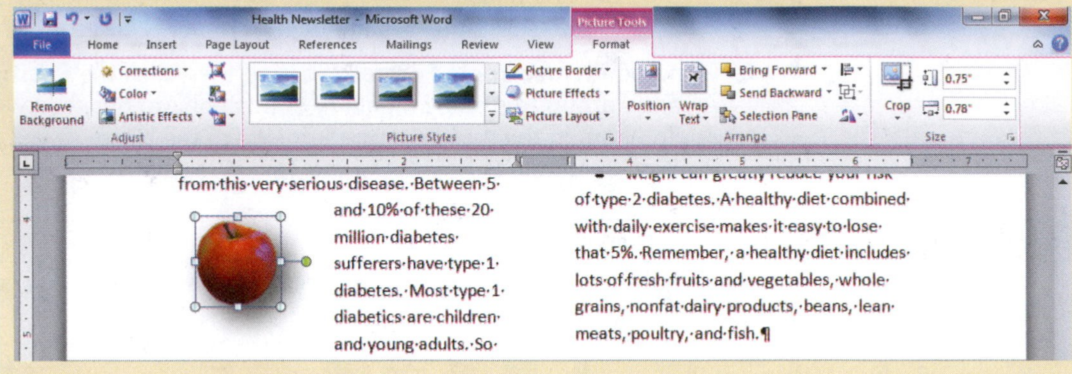

5. Save the document.

INSIGHT

Working with Graphics Files

Graphics come in two main types—vector graphics and raster graphics. A vector graphic file stores an image as a mathematical formula, which means you can increase or decrease the size of the image as much as you want without affecting its overall quality. They are often used for line drawings and, because they tend to be small, are widely used on the Web. File types for vector graphics are often proprietary, which means they only work in specific graphics programs. In Word, you will sometimes encounter files with the .wmf file extension, which is short for Windows Metafiles. A .wmf file is a type of vector graphic file created specifically for Windows.

In most cases, though, you will work with raster graphics, also known as bitmap graphics. A **bitmap** is a grid of square colored dots, called **pixels**, that form a picture. A bitmap graphic, then, is essentially a collection of specific pixels. The most common types of bitmap files are:

- BMP—These files, which have the .bmp file extension, tend to be very large, so it's best to resave them in a different format before using them in a Word document.
- TIFF—Commonly used for photographs or scanned images. TIFF files are usually much larger than GIF or JPEG files, but smaller than BMP files. A TIFF file has the file extension .tif.
- GIF—Suitable for most types of simple art, without complicated colors. A GIF file is compressed, so it doesn't take up much room on your computer. A GIF file has the file extension .gif.
- PNG—Similar to GIF, but suitable for art containing a wider array of colors. PNG files are slowly replacing GIF files as the preferred type for uncomplicated art consisting of a few simple lines.
- JPEG—Suitable for photographs and drawings. Files stored using the JPEG format are even more compressed than GIF files. A JPEG file has the file extension .jpg. To save file space, use JPEG graphics as much as possible.

Now that all the graphics are finished in the newsletter, you need to work on the layout of the newsletter text. For example, notice that left-hand column is longer than the column on the right. Joel wants you to fix this so that the two columns in the newsletter are balanced on the page.

Balancing Columns

If you want the columns in a document to appear **balanced** on a page, meaning of equal length, you can insert a continuous section break at the end of the document. When you insert a continuous section break, Word adjusts the flow of content between the columns so they are of equal or near equal length. The columns remain balanced no matter how much material you remove from either column later. The columns also remain balanced if you add material that causes the columns to flow to a new page; the overflow will also be formatted in balanced columns.

You need to add a continuous section break to balance the newsletter columns.

To balance the columns:

1. Press the **Ctrl+End** keys to move the insertion point to the end of the document, just after the period following your name.
2. Change the Zoom level to One Page, and then click the **Page Layout** tab.
3. In the Page Setup group, click the **Breaks** button. The Breaks menu opens.
4. Below "Section Breaks," click **Continuous**. Word inserts a continuous section break at the end of the text. Word balances the text between the two columns, moving some text from the bottom of the left column to the right column, so the two columns are approximately the same length. The longer column of text on the right moved down slightly around the doctor clip art, with the clip art itself remaining in its original position on the page. See Figure 4-32.

Figure 4-32 Newsletter with balanced columns

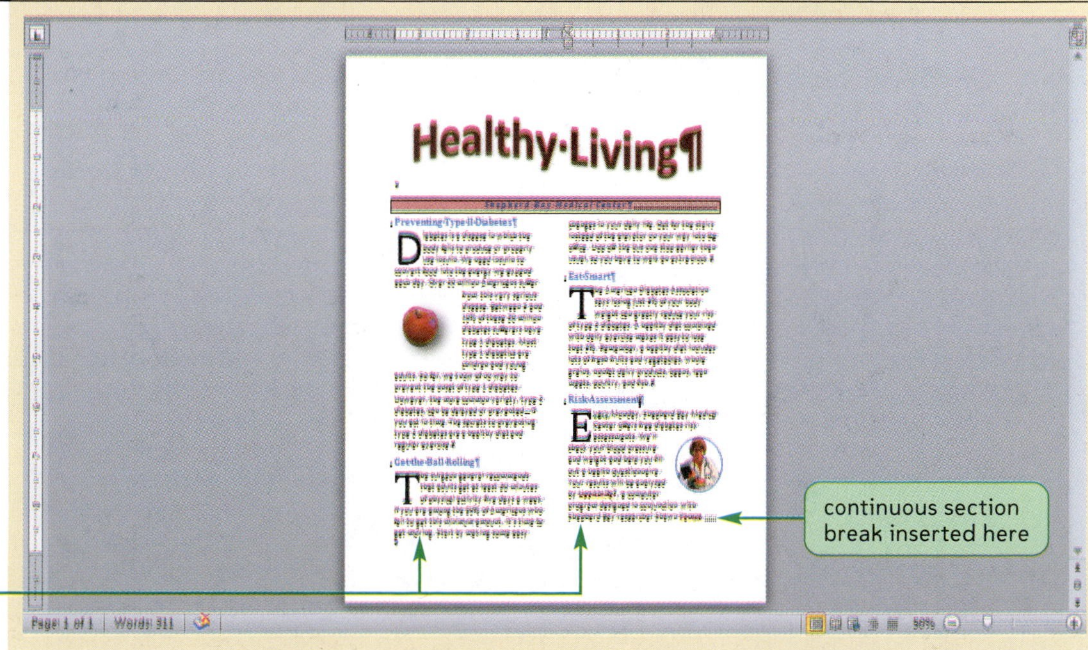

Note that you can also adjust the length of a column by inserting a column break using the Breaks button in the Page Setup group on the Page Layout tab. A column break moves all the text and graphics following it to the next column. Column breaks are useful when you have a multi-page document formatted in three or more columns, with only enough text on the last page to fill some of the columns. In that case, balancing columns on the last page won't work. Instead, you can use a section break to distribute an equal amount of text over all the columns on the page.

Inserting a Border Around a Page

You already know how to add definition to a paragraph by adding a border. You can do the same thing to a page by adding a page border. Joel asks you to add a border around the entire page of the newsletter.

To insert a border around the newsletter:

1. In the Page Background group, click the **Page Borders** button. The Borders and Shading dialog box opens, with the Page Border tab displayed. You can use the Setting options on the left side of this tab to specify the type of border you want. In this case, you want a simple box.
2. In the Setting section, click the **Box** option. Now you can choose the style of line that will be used to create the border.
3. In the Style box, scroll down and select the ninth style down from the top (the thick line with the thin line underneath), and then verify that the Apply to option is set to **Whole document**. See Figure 4-33.

TIP

Use the Art box on the Page Border tab to select a border consisting of graphical elements like apples and stars, or to select specially designed borders.

Figure 4-33 Adding a border to the newsletter

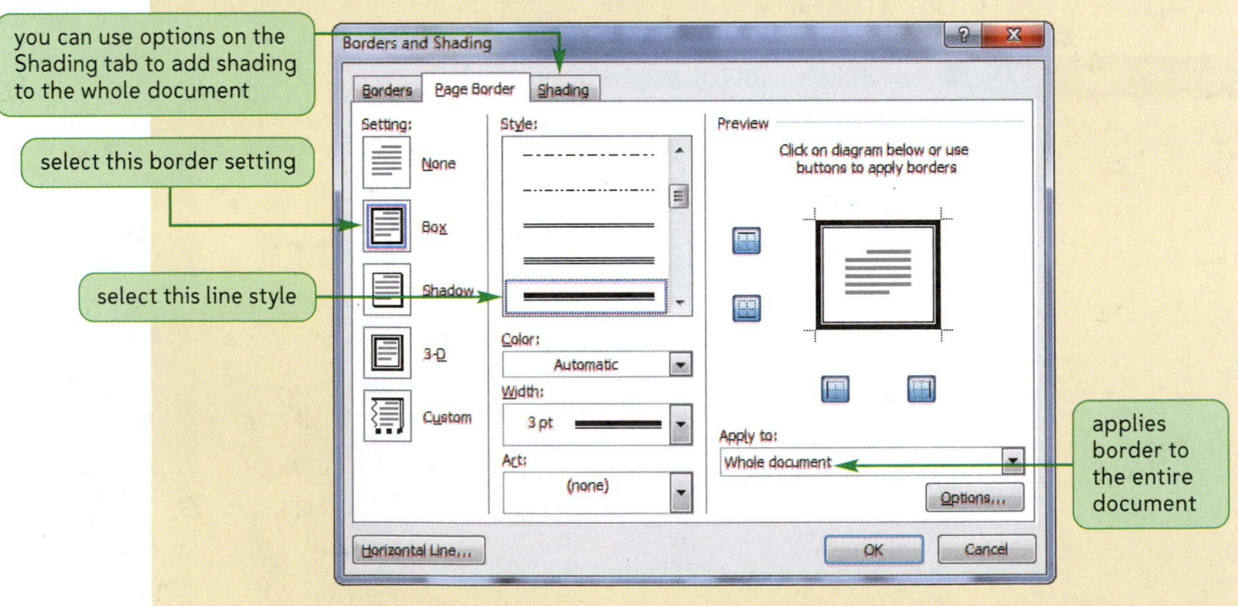

4. Click the **Options** button in the lower-right corner of the Borders and Shading dialog box. The Border and Shading Options dialog box opens. By default, the border is positioned 24 points from the edges of the page. To ensure that your printer will print the entire border, you need to change the Measure from setting so that it is positioned relative to the outside edge of the text rather than the edge of the page.
5. Click the **Measure from** arrow and then click **Text**. The settings in the Top and Bottom boxes change to 1 pt, and the settings in the Left and Right boxes change to 4 pt, indicating the border's position relative to the edge of the text.
6. Click the **OK** button in the Border and Shading Options dialog box, and then click the **OK** button in the Borders and Shading dialog box. The newsletter now has an attractive border. See Figure 4-34.

Figure 4-34 Newsletter with border

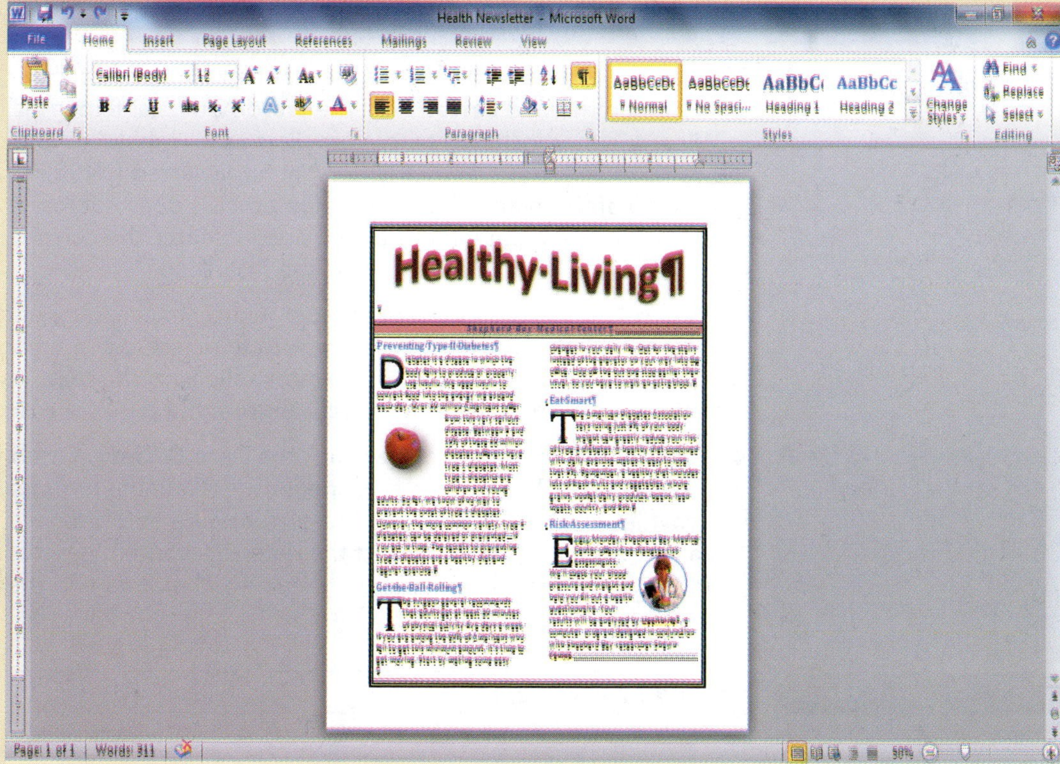

Trouble? If the WordArt and clip art move out of position after inserting the page border, drag the WordArt text box, as necessary, to center it above the columns, and then drag the clip art to position it as shown in Figure 4-34.

7. Save and close the document

Now Joel asks you to use Word's mail merge feature to insert customer names and addresses into the cover letter he will send with the newsletter.

Performing a Simple Mail Merge

As described in the Session 4.2 Visual Overview, mail merge is a process in Word that combines information from two separate documents—a main document and a data source—to create many final documents, each containing customized information that you specify using merge fields.

In this case, Joel's main document is the letter shown in the Session 4.2 Visual Overview. He plans to send the newsletter to a small test group of clients. His data source is a table in a Word document (also shown in the Session 4.2 Visual Overview) that contains the names and addresses of five Shepherd Bay Medical Center clients.

Before beginning a mail merge, it is a good idea to open your data source and your main document, to ensure they are properly set up.

To review the data source and the main document:

1. Open the document named **Addresses** from the Word4\Tutorial folder included with your Data Files. Review the table, which contains addresses for five clients of Shepherd Bay Medical Center.
2. Close the Addresses document without making any changes, and then open the document named **Letter** from the Word4\Tutorial folder included with your Data Files. Joel has included text in brackets as placeholders to indicate where he wants to insert the merge fields. Joel has inserted **[INSERT CURRENT DATE]** at the top of the letter. The mail merge process does not insert the current date in the merged document; rather you need to enter the current date using the Date & Time button in the Text group on the Insert tab.
3. Change the document zoom to Page Width, if necessary, and then delete the text **[INSERT CURRENT DATE]**, being sure to delete the opening and closing brackets. Do not delete the paragraph mark following the text. Verify that the insertion point is located in the fifth paragraph from the top of the document.
4. Click the **Insert** tab, and then click the **Date & Time** button in the Text group. The Date and Time dialog box opens. The Available formats list in this dialog box provides options for inserting the current date and time in a variety of formats. In this case, you want to insert the date as a content control in a format that includes the complete name of the month, the date, and the year (for example, February 26, 2013). See Figure 4-35.

Figure 4-35 Date and Time dialog box

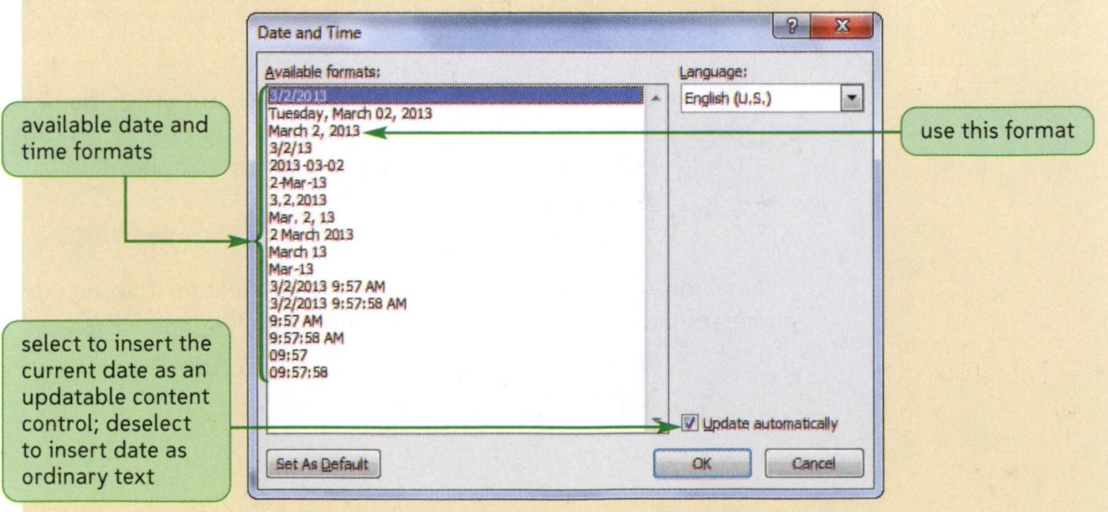

5. In the Available formats list, click the third format from the top, which is the month, day, year format. Next, you need to make sure the date is inserted as a content control that updates automatically every time you open the document.
6. Make sure the **Update automatically** check box is selected, and then click the **OK** button. The current date is inserted in the document. At this point it looks like ordinary text. To see the content control, you have to click the date.
7. Click the **date** to display the content control. See Figure 4-36. If you closed the document, and then opened it a day later, the content control would automatically display the new date.

TIP

If you use a Date format that includes the time, click the Update tab at the top of the content control, or press the F9 key to update the time while the document is open.

Figure 4-36 **Date content control**

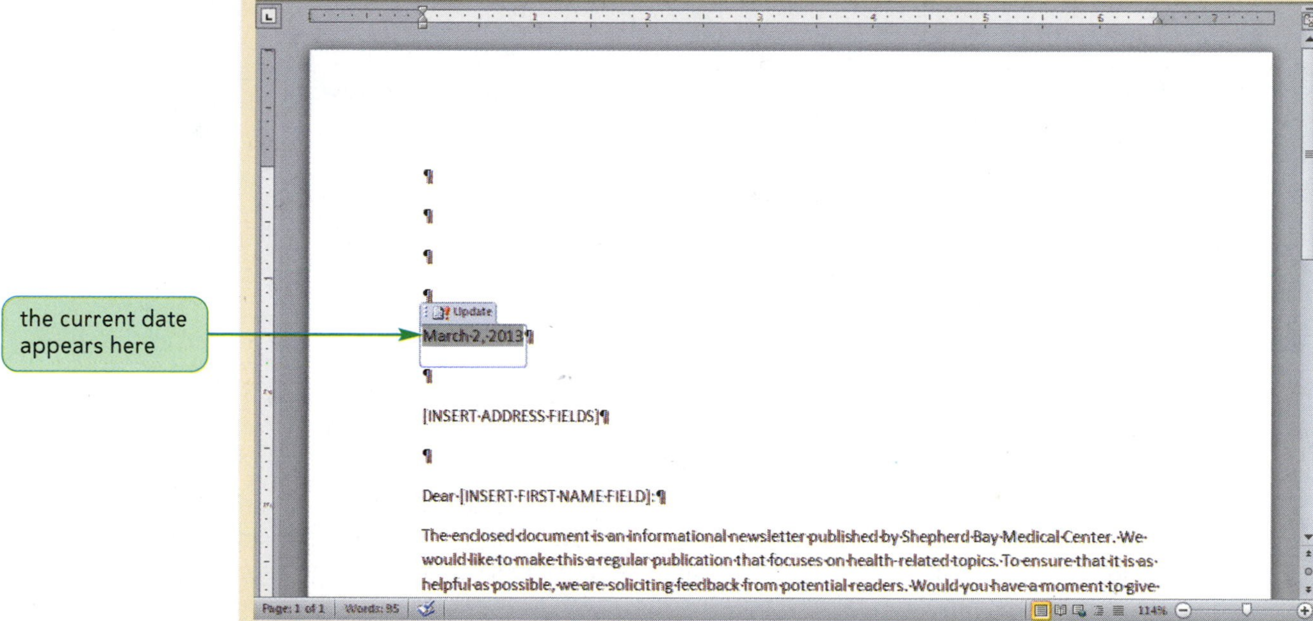

8. Click anywhere outside the date content control to deselect it.
9. Scroll to the bottom of the letter, replace "Joel Conchola" with your first and last name, and then save the document as **Cover Letter** in the Word4\Tutorial folder included with your Data Files.

Now that you are familiar with the data source, and you have inserted the current date in the main document, you are ready to begin the mail merge. The Mailings tab contains all the options you need for performing a mail merge. However, when you're just getting started with mail merge, it's helpful to use the Mail Merge task pane, which walks you through the process.

To start the mail merge process:

1. Click the **Mailings** tab, and then click the **Start Mail Merge** button in the Start Mail Merge group. The Start Mail Merge menu opens.
2. On the Start Mail Merge menu, click **Step by Step Mail Merge Wizard**. The Mail Merge task pane opens, displaying the first of six steps related to completing a mail merge. See Figure 4-37. Your first task is to specify the type of main document you want to use for the merge.

Figure 4-37 Mail Merge task pane

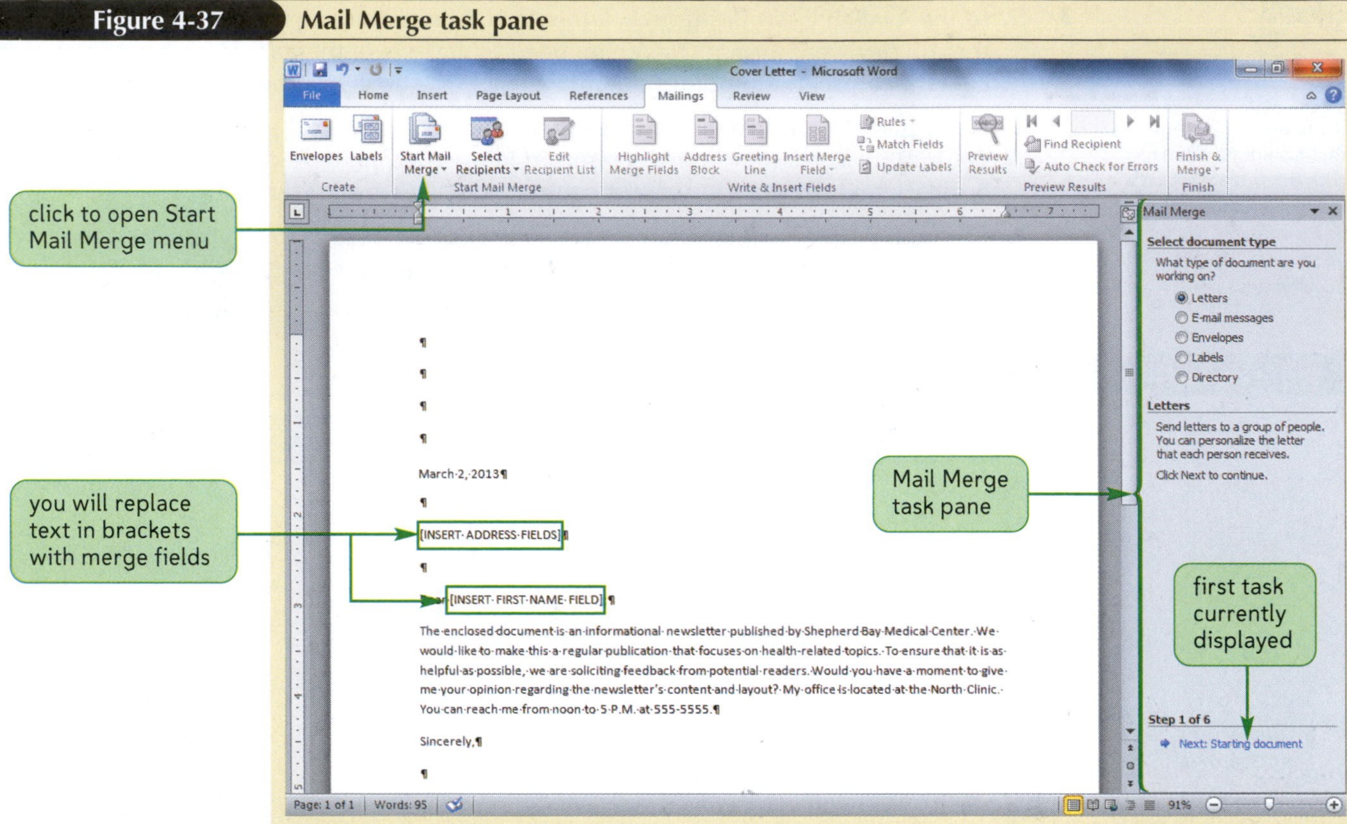

3. Verify that the **Letters** option button is selected in the Mail Merge task pane.
4. At the bottom of the Mail Merge task pane, click **Next: Starting document**. The Mail Merge task pane now displays information and options that you can use to select a starting document—that is, to select a main document. In this case, you want to use the current document, Cover Letter.
5. Verify that the **Use the current document** option button is selected.
6. At the bottom of the Mail Merge task pane, click **Next: Select recipients**.

At this point in the mail merge process, you need to select the data source for the mail merge, which would be the list of recipients that Joel has saved in the Addresses document.

Selecting a Data Source

TIP

It's a good idea to store the main document and the data source in the same folder. If you move the data source after you set up a merge, you might have to reselect the data source before the merge will work.

You can use many kinds of files as data sources for a mail merge, including Word tables, Excel worksheets, Access databases, or Contacts lists from Microsoft Outlook. You can select a preexisting file or you can create a new data source. In this case, you will use the table in the Addresses document, which you examined earlier.

To select the data source:

1. In the Mail Merge task pane, verify that the **Use an existing list** option button is selected.
2. Click **Browse** in the Mail Merge task pane. The Select Data Source dialog box opens. This dialog box works similarly to the Open dialog box.

3. Navigate to the Word4\Tutorial folder, select the **Addresses** document, and then click the **Open** button. The table from the Addresses document is displayed in the Mail Merge Recipients dialog box. See Figure 4-38.

Figure 4-38 **Mail Merge Recipients dialog box**

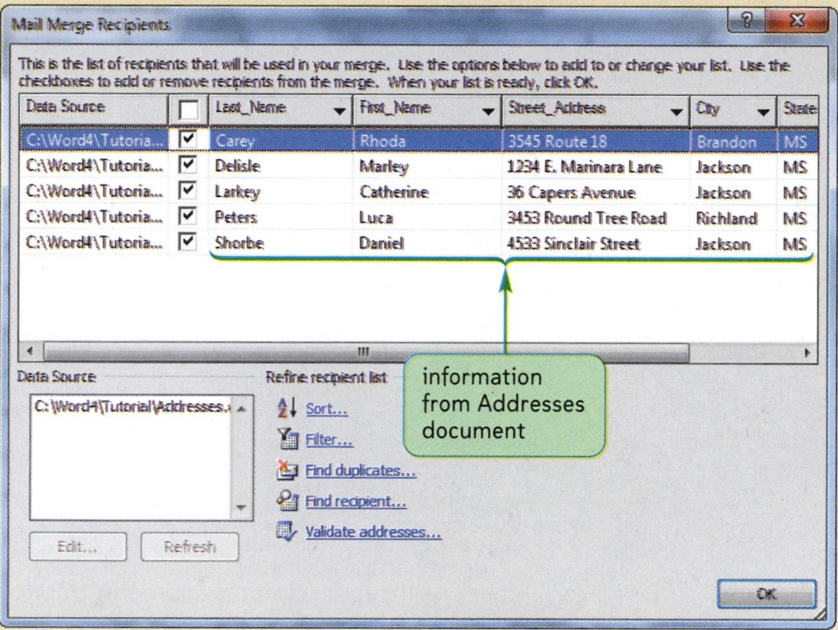

4. Click the **OK** button. The Mail Merge Recipients dialog box closes, and you return to the Cover Letter document with the Mail Merge task pane open. Under "Use an existing list," you see the name of the file selected as the data source—or, depending on where you store your Data Files, you might see only the beginning of a directory path, which identifies the location where the data source file is stored.
5. Click **Next: Write your letter** at the bottom of the Mail Merge task pane. The task pane displays options related to inserting merge fields in the main document.

Inserting Merge Fields

Joel's letter is a standard business letter, so the recipient's name and address belong below the date. You could insert individual merge fields for the client's first name, last name, address, city, and zip code. But it's easier to use the **Address block** link in the Mail Merge task pane, which inserts a merge field for the entire address with one click.

To insert an Address Block merge field:

1. Select the text **[INSERT ADDRESS FIELDS]**, and then delete it. Remember to delete the opening and closing brackets. Do not delete the paragraph mark following the text.
2. Verify that there are three blank paragraphs between the date and the salutation and that the insertion point is positioned in the second blank paragraph below the date.

3. Click **Address block** in the Mail Merge task pane. The Insert Address Block dialog box opens. See Figure 4-39. The options in this dialog box allow you to fine-tune the way the address will be inserted in the letter. The Preview box shows you how the address will look in the document after the merge is complete.

Figure 4-39 **Insert Address Block dialog box**

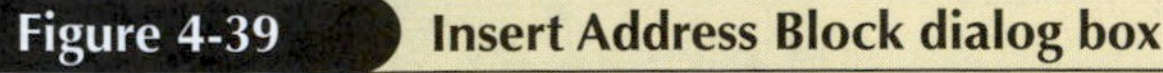

4. Verify that the **Insert recipient's name in this format** check box is selected, and also verify that **Joshua Randall Jr.** is selected in the Specify address elements box. This ensures that Word will insert each recipient's first and last name.

5. Verify that the **Insert postal address** check box is selected. It doesn't matter whether the other check box and option buttons are selected; you only need to be concerned with them when working with more complicated data sources.

TIP

A selected merge field is highlighted with a gray background to distinguish it from regular text.

6. Click the **OK** button. An Address Block merge field is inserted in the letter. See Figure 4-40. Notice the angled brackets that surround the merge field. The brackets are automatically inserted when you insert a merge field. It is important to note that you cannot type the angled brackets and merge field information—you must enter it by making a dialog box selection.

Figure 4-40 **Address Block merge field in letter**

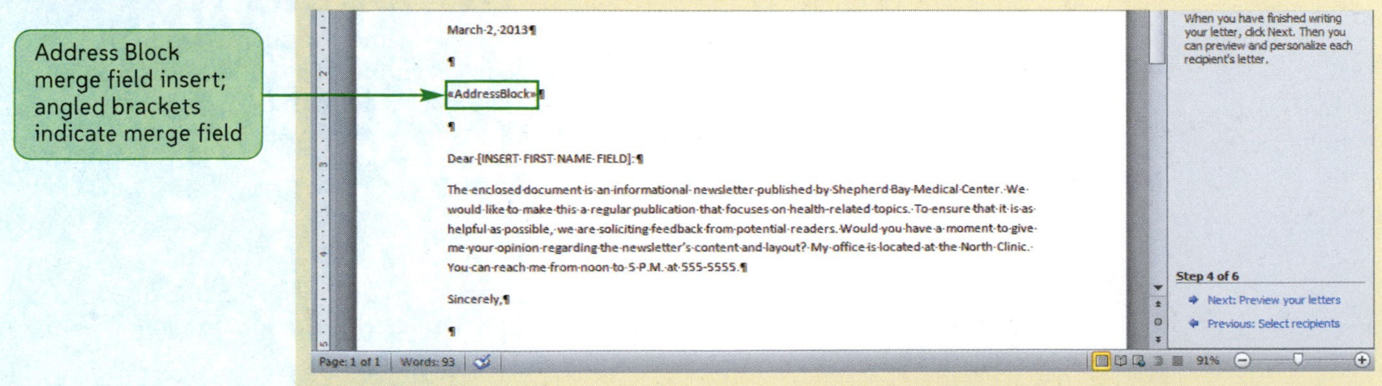

Later, when you merge the main document with the data source, Word will replace the Address Block merge field with the address information for each record in the data source. Note that you can also build an inside address out of separate merge fields for the recipient's first name, last name, address, and so on, using the More items option in the Mail Merge task pane. In most cases, though, the Address Block merge file is the simplest option.

Next, you need to insert a merge field that will include each client's first name in the salutation.

To insert the merge field for the salutation:

1. Select and delete **[INSERT FIRST NAME FIELD]** in the salutation. Remember to delete the opening and closing brackets. Do not delete the colon.
2. If necessary, insert a space to the left of the colon. The insertion point should be positioned between the space and the colon.
3. In the Mail Merge task pane, click **More items**. The Insert Merge Field dialog box opens. The Fields list shows all the merge fields in the data source. See Figure 4-41. Note that merge fields cannot contain spaces, so Word replaces any spaces in the merge field names with underlines. You want to insert the client's first name into the main document, so you need to make sure the First_Name merge field is selected.

Figure 4-41 Insert Merge Field dialog box

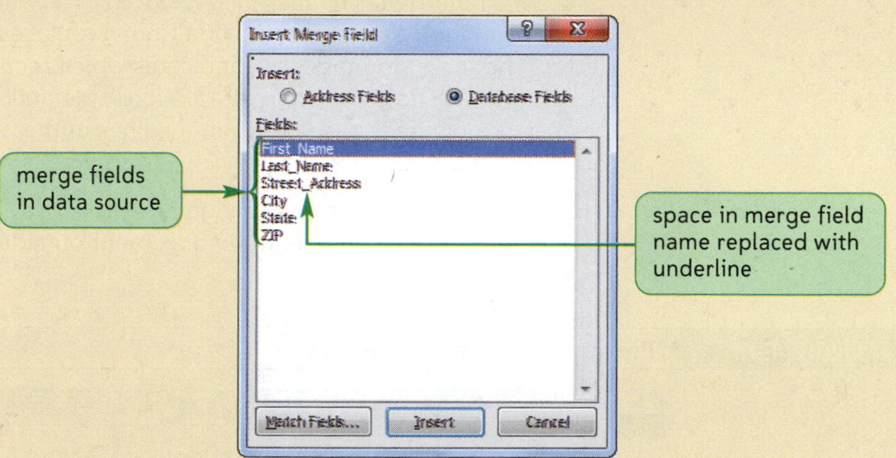

4. Verify that **First_Name** is selected, click the **Insert** button, and then click the **Close** button to close the Insert Merge Field dialog box. The First_Name merge field is inserted in the document at the location of the insertion point. See Figure 4-42.

Figure 4-42 First_Name merge field inserted in document

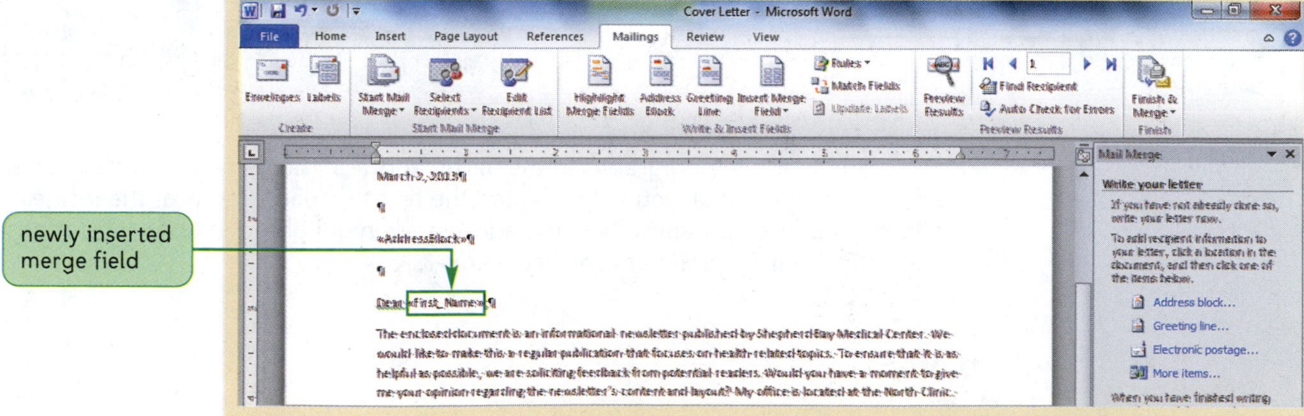

Trouble? If you make a mistake and insert the wrong merge field or insert the correct field in the wrong location, undo the insertion and then repeat Steps 1 through 4.

5. Save your changes to the main document.

The main document now contains all the necessary merge fields, so you're ready to merge the main document with the data source. First, however, you should preview the merged document.

Previewing the Merged Document

When you preview the merged document, you see the main document with the customized information inserted in place of the merge fields. Previewing a merged document allows you to check for errors or formatting problems before you perform the merge.

To preview the merged document:

1. In the Mail Merge task pane, click **Next: Preview your letters**. The data for the first client in the data source (Rhoda Carey) replaces the merge fields in the cover letter. The top of the task pane indicates which record is currently displayed in the document. As shown in Figure 4-43, Word's default paragraph and line spacing results in too much space between the lines of the address. You can fix this by adjusting the spacing in the preview letter, just as you would for an ordinary letter.

   Trouble? If the address is highlighted with a gray background, the merge field is selected. Click anywhere in the document outside the address to deselect the merge field.

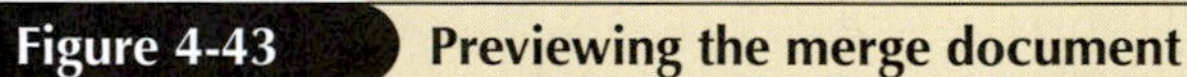

Figure 4-43 Previewing the merge document

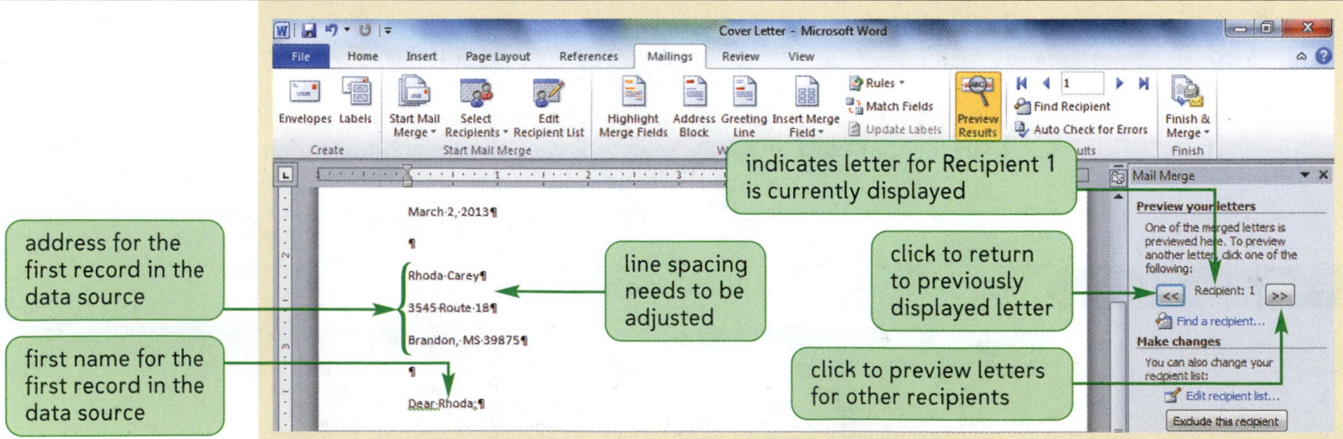

2. Select the first two paragraphs of the inside address (the name and the street address). Even though you only selected the first two paragraphs of the inside address, all three paragraphs of the address are highlighted in gray, indicating that they are fields and not ordinary text.

3. Click the **Home** tab, click the **Line and Paragraph Spacing** button in the Paragraph group, and then click **Remove Space After Paragraph**. The spacing now looks appropriate for an inside address. This formatting change affects all the letters in the merged document.
4. Preview the rest of the letter to make sure the text and formatting are correct. In particular, check to make sure that the spacing before and after the first name in the salutation is correct.

You are ready for the final step—completing the merge.

Merging the Main Document and Data Source

Because your data source consists of five records, merging the main document with the data source will result in five copies of the letter to five different clients of Shepherd Bay Medical Center. Each letter will appear on its own page. Keep in mind that mail merges more often involve hundreds or even thousands of records. As a result, the resulting document can be extremely long, with one page for every record in the data source.

To complete the mail merge:

1. In the Mail Merge task pane, click **Next: Complete the merge**. The task pane displays options related to merging the main document and the data source. You can use the Print option to have Word print the customized letters immediately, without displaying them on the screen. This is useful when you are using a data source with many records. In this case, though, you'll use the Edit individual letters option to merge to a new document.
2. Click **Edit individual letters** in the Mail Merge task pane. The Merge to New Document dialog box opens. Here, you need to specify which records you want to include in the merge. You want to include all the records in the data source.
3. Verify that the **All** option button is selected, click the **OK** button, and then scroll as needed to display the entire first letter. Word creates a new document (the merged document) called Letters1, which contains five pages, one for each record in the data source. Each letter is separated from the one that follows it by a Next Page section break. See Figure 4-44. The main document with the merge fields (Cover Letter) remains open.

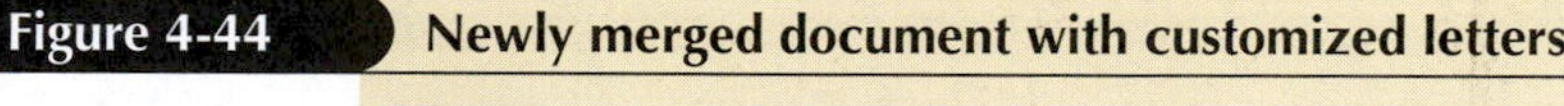
Figure 4-44 Newly merged document with customized letters

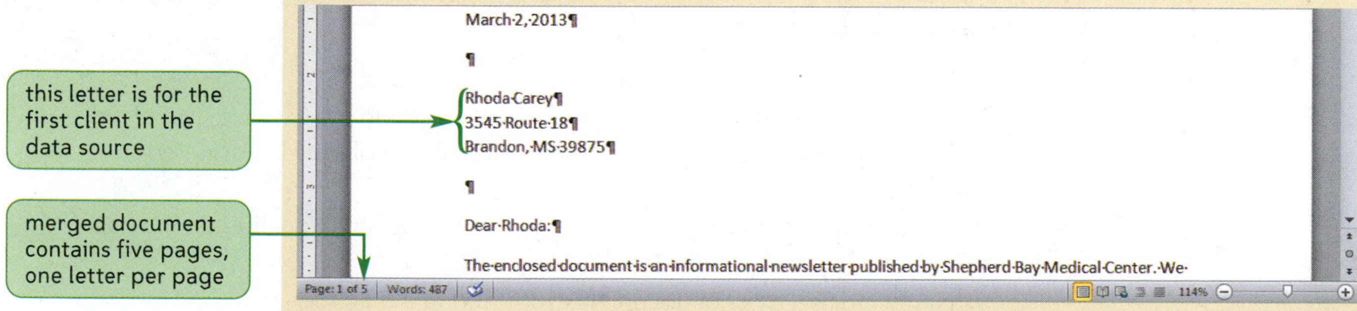

TIP

To avoid wasting disk space, you do not need to save large merged documents after printing them.

4. Save the merged document in the Word4\Tutorial folder, using the filename **Merged Cover Letters**.
5. Scroll down and review the five letters. Note the different address and salutation in each.
6. Close the Merged Cover Letters document. You return to the Cover Letter document.
7. Save the document and then close it.

PROSKILLS

Teamwork: Incorporating Work from Team Members

Newsletters often contain articles and graphics from several people, with one person, the editor, responsible for combining all this material into a single, coherent newsletter. Likewise, in a mail merge, the data file and the main document often come from two different sources. For example, a sales representative might supply a data file with names of potential clients, while a marketing associate might write a letter announcing a new product. Meanwhile, a sales assistant might be the one charged with merging the data file and the main document to create the letters that will ultimately be sent out to potential clients.

Dividing up work like this often makes it possible to finish a project far more quickly than if you had to supply everything yourself. But that's only true if every member of the team understands exactly what he or she needs to supply. If you're the one in charge of the finished product, it is important to communicate with the team ahead of time to ensure that you get what you need. Remember to do this by email or in writing, so your team has something to refer to when they are putting together their contributions. In particular, specify the following:

- Deadline—State the date you need each person's contribution.
- Description—Describe the content each person should provide (for example, "a short article on projected sales for the third quarter" or "a list of new employees").
- Length—Specify the required word and page count.
- File types—List the acceptable file types for graphics, text, or data.

Clear directions such as these will ensure the document is finished on time, and contains all the necessary elements.

You have completed a mail merge and generated a merged document. Joel will send the cover letters out with sample copies of his newsletter.

REVIEW

Session 4.2 Quick Check

1. Name five types of bitmap files.
2. Explain how to rotate a graphic using a menu command.
3. How does Word indicate that a particular part of a photo is considered background?
4. What button allows you to move a graphic to a specific location on the page, wrap text around it, and align it all at once?
5. Name the two types of documents you need in a mail merge.
6. List the steps in the Step By Step Mail Merge wizard.

Practice the skills you learned in the tutorial using the same case scenario.

PRACTICE

Review Assignments

Data Files needed for the Review Assignments: Addresses.docx, Orange.jpg, Eating.docx, and Nutrition.docx

The Nutrition Department of the Shepherd Bay Medical Center has asked Joel to create another newsletter. This one will provide information and encouragement for Shepherd Bay clients to eat well. Joel has already written the text and asks you to transform it into a professional-looking newsletter. He also asks you to create an accompanying cover letter using Word's mail merge feature. Complete the following steps:

1. Open the file **Eating** from the Word4\Review folder included with your Data Files, then save the document as **Eating Well** in the same folder.
2. In the last paragraph, replace "STUDENT NAME" with your first and last name.
3. Format everything in the newsletter except the paragraph containing the text "Shepherd Bay Medical Center" in two columns.
4. Create a drop cap in the first paragraph under each Heading 2 heading.
5. In the paragraph below the heading "Eating Well in a Busy World," insert a registered trademark symbol after "20 Fast Food Friends."
6. At the top of the document, create the headline **Healthy Food** using WordArt. In the WordArt Gallery, choose the middle style in the bottom row (Fill – Red, Accent 2, Matte Bevel).
7. Change the font size of the WordArt text to 48 points.
8. Apply the Top and Bottom text wrap style to the WordArt text box and then center the WordArt over the document text.
9. Change the text fill color to Orange, Accent 6, Darker 25%.
10. Apply the Wave 1 transform effect to the WordArt text, enlarge it by changing the width setting to 6 inches, and then drag the WordArt text box to center it again over the document text.
11. In the paragraph below the heading "Eating Well in a Busy World," click at the beginning of the line that starts "in a busy world…."
12. On your computer, find a blue and black clip art illustration of a business woman (the woman is running with a cell phone in her hand), and then insert the clip art at the insertion point.
13. Resize the clip art so it is approximately 1.5 inches square.
14. Crop the clip art on the left to remove the satellite dish, then crop the clip art to an oval shape and add a simple blue border.
15. Use the Position button to wrap text around the graphic, and position it in the middle of the left margin.
16. In the paragraph under the heading "Fresh is Better," click at the beginning of the line that begins "conditions. Experts suggest…" and insert the photo named **Orange** from the Word4\Review folder included with your Data Files.
17. Rotate the photo so the orange is upright, with the stem end on top, and then size it so it is 1-inch wide.
18. Remove the brown background, retaining only the image of the orange.
19. Add a shadow to the orange using the Drop Shadow Rectangle picture style, and then position and align it along the right margin, below the "Fresh is Better" heading, with Tight text wrapping.
20. Balance the columns.
21. Add a border around the page using the border style with three thin lines, and specify the border placement should be measured from the edge of text. Adjust the position of the graphics as necessary.

22. Preview, save, and close the newsletter. Submit the finished documents to your instructor, either in printed or electronic form, as requested.
23. Open the file **Nutrition** located in the Word4\Review folder, replace "Joel Conchola" at the end of the letter with your name, and then save the document as **Nutrition Letter** in the same folder.
24. Insert the current date as a content control, using the format February 26, 2013.
25. Merge the Nutrition Cover Letter document with the Addresses file found in the Word4\Review folder. Use the Address Block merge field for the inside address. Also, include a merge field that will insert the customer's first name in the salutation. Preview the merged letters and make any necessary changes before completing the merge. Remember to adjust the spacing for the inside address.
26. Save the merged document as **Merged Nutrition Letters** and close it. Save your changes to the main document and close it. Close the task pane if necessary.
27. Submit the finished documents to your instructor, either in printed or electronic form, as requested.

APPLY

Case Problem 1

If you have a SAM 2010 user profile, your instructor may have assigned an autogradable version of this assignment. If so, log into the SAM 2010 Web site at www.cengage.com/sam2010 to download the instructions and start files.

Data Files needed for this Case Problem: Audio.docx, Sunflower.jpg

Florentina, Arizona, Public Library Michaela Novoa is the director of the Florentina, Arizona, Public Library. She and her staff have developed a new program that makes it possible for library patrons to download audio books over the Web via a service called Sunflower Audio. Michaela has written the text of a newsletter explaining the Sunflower Audio system. She asks you to finalize the newsletter. Complete the following steps:

1. Open the file **Audio** located in the Word4\Case1 folder included with your Data Files.
2. At the end of the document, replace "STUDENT NAME" with your first and last name. Save the document as **Sunflower Audio** in the same folder.
3. At the top of the document, create the WordArt headline **Downloading Sunflower Books** attached to a new, blank paragraph. In the WordArt Gallery, choose the third style from the left, in the second row from the bottom (Fill – Orange, Accent 2, Warm Matte Bevel).
4. Set the text wrapping style to Top and Bottom.
5. Resize the WordArt text box so it is just wide enough and tall enough to allow the WordArt text to fit on a single line. Center the WordArt text at the top of the page, a suitable distance from the top margin.
6. Apply the Chevron Up transform effect, and change the width of the WordArt text box to 6.7 inches.
7. Format all the text below "Florentina, Arizona, Public Library" in two columns, with a line between them.
8. On your computer, find clip art related to computers, and then locate the image of the man in a brown suit typing on a keyboard.
9. Insert the clip art of the man in the paragraph under the heading "HOW DO I LISTEN TO A DOWNLOADED BOOK?"
10. Resize the clip art so that it is 1.5 inches wide.
11. Apply Square text wrapping. Position and align the clip art on the right border, near the middle of the paragraph.
12. In the first paragraph in the left column, insert the photo named **Sunflower** from the Word4\Case1 folder included with your Data Files.
13. Rotate the photo 90° to the right.

EXPLORE 14. Flip the photo horizontally.
15. Resize the photo so it is 1.5 inches tall, and then remove the green background, retaining only the image of the sunflower.
16. Apply Tight text wrapping, then position and align the photo in the middle of the paragraph, on the left margin.
EXPLORE 17. Use the Picture Effects button in the Picture Styles group on the Picture Tools Format tab to add an olive green glow to the sunflower.
18. Balance the columns.
19. Save your work, submit the finished documents to your instructor, either in printed or electronic form, as requested, and then close the files.

Expand your skills to create an employee newsletter.

CHALLENGE

Case Problem 2

Data Files needed for this Case Problem: Island.jpg, News.docx

Flannery Investments You work in the Personnel Department for Flannery Investments, a national investment company with headquarters in Minneapolis, Minnesota. You've been assigned the task of preparing the monthly newsletter *Flannery News*, which provides news about employees of Flannery Investments. You will use text written by other employees for the body of the newsletter. Complete the following steps:

1. Open the file **News** located in the Word4\Case2 folder included with your Data Files, and then save it as **Flannery Newsletter** in the same folder.
2. Replace all instances of the name "Daniela" in the document with your first name. Then replace all instances of "Alford" with your last name.
3. At the top of the newsletter, create a **Flannery News** WordArt headline attached to a new, blank paragraph. Use the WordArt style in the bottom row, in the far right column.
4. Apply Top and Bottom text wrapping, change the font size to 45 points, and then center the WordArt at the top of the page 1 inch from the top margin.
5. Format the body of the newsletter into three newspaper-style columns. Don't be concerned that the newsletter spans more than one page.
6. Insert a drop cap in the first paragraph after each Heading 2 heading.
7. In the paragraph below the heading "Win a Vacation Get-Away," insert the photo named **Island** from the Word4\Case2 folder included with your Data Files.
8. Crop about a third of the photo from the left and right sides, so that you only see the pier stretching out into the water, and the photo is about .5 inches wide.
9. Use the Position button to position and align the photo in the middle of the page, along the left margin.
10. Balance the columns on the first page of the newsletter.
11. In the left column on page 2, insert clip art of a golfer from the collection on your computer, resize it so it is 1 inch wide, apply Tight text wrapping, and then position and align it on the left margin, two lines below the drop cap.

EXPLORE 12. Flip the clip art horizontally, so the golfer is facing the middle of the page.
EXPLORE 13. Use the Color button in the Adjust group on the Picture Tools Format tab to change the color of the clip art to Green, Accent color 1 Light.
EXPLORE 14. Insert two column breaks on page 2 to create a total of three columns of approximately equal length.
EXPLORE 15. Add a page border of yellow stars to the entire document, and have the border measured from the text margins.
16. Save your work, submit the finished documents to your instructor, either in printed or electronic form, as requested, and then close any open files.

Explore new techniques as you create the two-sided brochure shown in Figure 4-45.

CHALLENGE

Case Problem 3

Data File needed for this Case Problem: Hill.docx

Hill Star Dairy Cooperative Haley Meskin is the publicity director for Hill Star Dairy Cooperative in Lawrence, Kansas. Local residents pay a membership fee to join the co-op and then receive a 10 percent discount on purchases of organic dairy products. Many members don't realize that they can take advantage of other benefits, such as monthly mailings with recipe cards and coupons. To spread the word, Haley would like to create a brochure describing the benefits of joining the co-op. She has already written the text of the brochure. She would like the brochure to consist of one piece of paper folded in three parts, with text on both sides of the paper, as shown in Figure 4-45.

Figure 4-45 Hill Star two-sided brochure

side one

Welcome to Hill Star
Hill Star Dairy Cooperative is owned by its more than 3000 members. Under the oversight of its board of directors, the co-op is run by a staff of 24, including 12 full-time and 12 part-time employees.

Everyone is invited to shop at the co-op, but members are always needed. Your membership payments are invested in the co-op. Among other things, they help pay the light bills and the mortgage. A portion of each year's membership fees goes to our Capital Improvement account—our special "rainy day" fund.

Become a Member!
Joining makes you, essentially, a part owner in Hill Star Organic Dairy Cooperative. To join, fill out a membership form at the store or visit our Web site at www.hill-star-organic.net.

The current membership fee is $55.

Advantages of Membership
You might be wondering—"If anyone can shop at the co-op, why should I pay the $55 membership fee?" In addition to supporting a vital part of our community, members:

- Save 10% on everyday prices
- Cash personal checks for less than $50.
- Order specialty items at a 15% discount.
- Receive our monthly mailings, with recipes and discounts.
- Attend one free class per month, on topics such as making homemade ice cream.

side two

JOIN NOW

Hill Star
An Organic Dairy Cooperative
5790 Creamery Way
Lawrence, KS 66054
555-555-5555
www.hill-star.course.com
Student Name, Manager

HILL STAR

cover after brochure is folded

HILL STAR

1. Open the file **Hill** located in the Word4\Case3 folder included with your Data Files, and then save it as **Hill Star Brochure** in the same folder. This document contains a graphic of a cow. Because no text wrapping has been applied, it is an inline graphic. You want it to remain an inline graphic, because you want it to move with text.
2. On the second page, replace "STUDENT NAME" with your first and last name.
3. Format the entire document in three columns of equal width. Do not include a vertical line between columns. Ignore the page break at the bottom of page 1.

EXPLORE

4. Insert a column break at the beginning of the heading "Become a Member!" Insert another column break before the heading "Advantages of Membership." On the second page, insert a column break in the first paragraph. When you are finished, the document should consist of two pages, with the cow graphic and the co-op address in the middle of the second page.
5. Copy the cow graphic to the Clipboard, and then paste it on page 1, just before the heading "Become a Member!" Insert two blank paragraphs before the "Become a Member!" heading to separate the heading from the cow graphic. The middle column of the first page now contains the cow graphic, with the heading "Become a Member!" below, followed by two paragraphs of text.
6. On page 2, create a WordArt headline that reads "JOIN NOW" (all upper case) using the WordArt style in the fourth row from the top, second column from the right (Gradient Fill – Indigo, Accent 1, Outline – White).

EXPLORE

7. In the Text group of the Drawing Tools Format tab, use the Text Direction button to arrange the WordArt so you have to start reading at the bottom of the WordArt text box.
8. Position the WordArt text box in the middle of the first column on page 2, change the text box height to 5.5 inches, change its width to 2 inches, and then change the font for the WordArt text to 72 points. Adjust the position of the WordArt text box as necessary to center it horizontally and vertically in the left column of page 2.
9. Copy the WordArt text box to the Clipboard, click anywhere on page 2, paste the WordArt text box at the insertion point, and then drag the text box to position it in the right column on page 2.
10. Select the newly pasted WordArt text, change the text to **HILL STAR**, then adjust the size and position of the WordArt text box so the WordArt text is centered in the right column. When you are finished, page 2 should consist of the JOIN NOW WordArt in the left column, the cow graphic and address information in the middle column, and the HILL STAR WordArt in the right column.

EXPLORE

11. Click the Page Layout tab, and then, in the Page Setup group, click the Dialog Box Launcher. In the Page Setup dialog box, click the Layout tab, click the Vertical alignment arrow, click Center, and then click the OK button. This centers the text vertically on the page (between the top and bottom margins) and ensures that the brochure will look right when folded. Save your work.
12. To print the brochure, you need to print the first page and then print the second page on the reverse side. "JOIN NOW" should print on the reverse side of the list of member benefits; likewise, "HILL STAR" should print on the reverse side of the "Welcome to Hill Star" text. Whether you should place the printed page upside down or right-side up depends on your printer. You may have to print a few test pages until you get it right. When you finish, you should be able to turn page 1 (the page with the heading "Welcome to Hill Star") face up, and then fold it inward in thirds, along the two column borders. Fold the brochure, so that the "HILL STAR" column lies on top.
13. Save your work, submit the finished documents to your instructor, either in printed or electronic form, as requested, and then close any open files.

Create and use the table shown in Figure 4-46, to complete a mail merge.

CREATE

Case Problem 4

There are no Data Files needed for this Case Problem.

Internship Search Cover Letters You're ready to start looking for an internship, and you plan to use Word to create customized cover letters to accompany your resume. You've decided to use mail merge to customize the letters. You'll start by creating the table shown in Figure 4-46 and filling it with address information for potential internship sponsors. Then you'll create a cover letter to use as a main document, and customize it by inserting the appropriate mail merge fields. Complete the following:

1. Open a new, blank document, and then save it as **Intern Data** in the Word4\Case4 folder included with your Data Files.
2. Create the table shown in Figure 4-46, and then enter information for three potential internship sponsors. The information can be real or fictitious. For the First Name and Last Name columns, use a fictitious name for an appropriate contact at each company. Use Ms. or Mr. for the Title field. Note that the Title field has to be the column on the far right, or the Address Block merge field won't work correctly. (The Address Block merge field assumes the first seven columns on the left are the fields you want to include in the address.) Save your work and close the document.

Figure 4-46 **Table structure for data source**

First Name	Last Name	Company Name	Street Address	City	State	ZIP	Title

3. Open a new, blank document and save it as **Intern Letter** in the Word4\Case4 folder.
4. Create a cover letter that introduces yourself and describes your experience and education. Instead of an inside address, include the placeholder text **[INSIDE ADDRESS]**. For the salutation, use **Dear [TITLE] [LAST NAME]**. Refer the reader to your resume (even if you don't have one) for more information. Use a proper business letter style for your cover letter. Include a sentence in the cover letter that mentions the company name. Use the placeholder **[COMPANY NAME]** to remind you to insert the appropriate merge field later.
5. Save the letter, and then open the Mail Merge task pane and follow the steps outlined in it. Use the Intern Letter document as the main document, and select the Intern Data file as the data source.
6. Use the Address block merge field for the inside address (in the "Joshua Randall Jr." format), and verify that the Insert company name check box is selected in the Insert Address Block dialog box. Adjust the paragraph and line spacing for the paragraph containing the Address Block merge field to remove paragraph spacing from the first three paragraphs of the inside address.

EXPLORE

7. Add a merge field for the title and the last name in the salutation of the letter, and add a merge field to replace the company name placeholder text in the body of the letter. Save your changes to the main document before completing the merge.
8. Preview your letters and then complete the merge (choosing the Edit individual letters option). Save the merged document as **Merged Intern Letters** in the Word4\Case4 folder, close all open documents, and close the Mail Merge task pane.
9. Open a new, blank document, and then save it as **Intern Envelopes** in the Word4\Case4 folder.

EXPLORE

10. Open the Mail Merge task pane, click the Envelopes option button under Select document type, and then click Next: Starting document. Click Envelope options, and then click the OK button in the Envelope Options dialog box to select the default settings. The document layout changes to resemble a business size envelope.
11. Continue with the steps in the Mail Merge task pane, selecting the Intern Data file as the data source.
12. Click Next: Arrange your envelope, and notice that the insertion point is positioned in the return address, ready for you to begin typing. Type your name and address as the return address. Click the paragraph mark in the center of the document and insert an Address block merge field in the "Joshua Randall Jr." format. You do not have to adjust the paragraph or line spacing for the Address block field for an envelope. Save your work.
13. Preview the envelopes, and complete the merge (choosing the Edit individual envelopes option). Don't worry about the section break that appears after the return address; the envelopes will print correctly. Save the merged document as **Merged Intern Envelopes** in the Word4\Case4 folder. Close the Mail Merge task pane and save your changes to the main document.
14. Submit the finished documents to your instructor, either in printed or electronic form, as requested, and then close any open files.

SAM

ASSESS

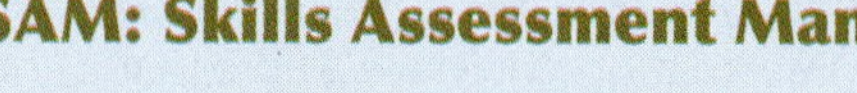

SAM: Skills Assessment Manager

For current SAM information, including versions and content details, visit SAM Central (http://samcentral.course.com). If you have a SAM user profile, you may have access to hands-on instruction, practice, and assessment of the skills covered in this tutorial. Since various versions of SAM are supported throughtout the life of this text, check with your instructor for the correct instructions and URL/Web site for accessing assignments.

ENDING DATA FILES

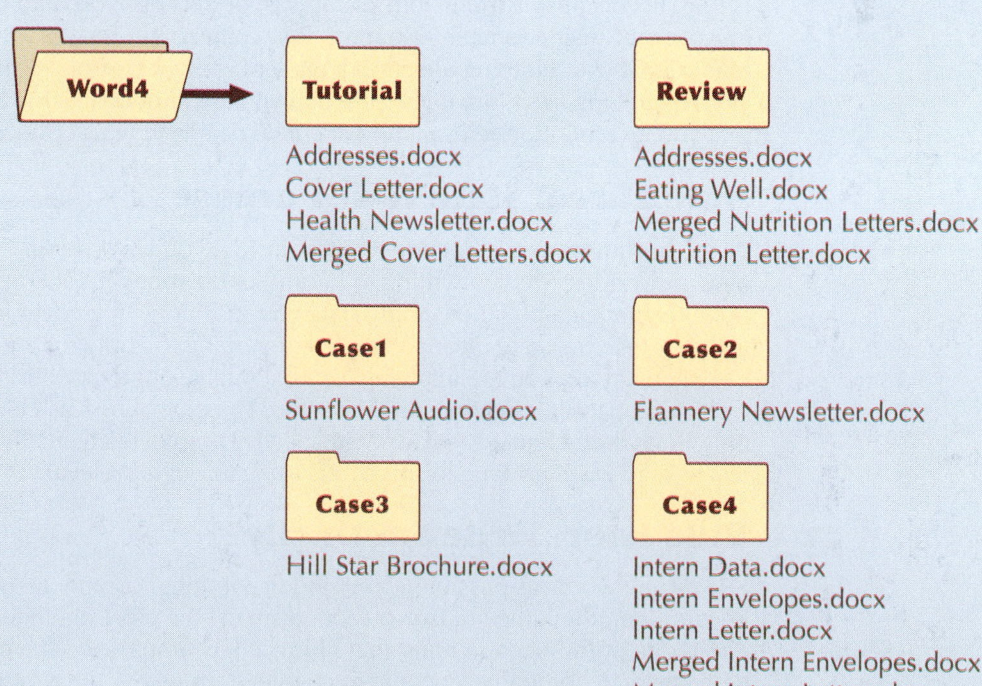

ProSkills

Written Communication

Writing Clear and Effective Business Documents

Whether it's a simple email message sent to a group, a memo to provide information on an upcoming event, or a press release introducing a new product to the market, the quality of your written communications tells the world how prepared, informed, and detail-oriented you are. When searching for a job, an ability to write clearly and effectively is essential. After all, your first contact with a company is often a cover letter and resume. For a prospective employer, these documents provide the first indicators of the kind of employee you might be. To make the best possible impression, follow these important rules in all types of business communication.

Rule One: Identify Your Audience

Who will read your document? What do they already know about your subject? For starters, you can assume your audience is made up of busy people who will only take the time to read what is important and relevant to them. They don't want to be entertained. They just want to read the information you have to present as quickly as possible. In the case of a resume and cover letter, your audience is typically one or more professional people who don't know you. The goal of your resume and cover letter, then, should be to introduce yourself quickly and efficiently.

Rule Two: Do Your Research

Provide all the information the reader will need to make a decision or take action. Be absolutely certain that the facts you present are correct. Don't assume that something is true just because a friend told you it was, or because you read it on the Web. Verify all your facts using reputable sources. Remember, your goal as a writer is to make the reader trust you. Nothing alienates a reader faster than errors or misleading statements. When applying for a job, make sure that you are knowledgeable about the company, so that you can mention relevant and accurate details in your cover letter.

Rule Three: State Your Purpose

At the beginning of the document, explain why you are writing. The reader shouldn't have to wonder. Are you writing to inform, or do you want action to be taken? Do you hope to change a belief or simply state your position? In a cover letter accompanying your resume, state clearly that you are writing to apply for a job, and then explain exactly what job you are applying for. That might sound obvious, but many job applicants forget about directness in their efforts to come across as clever or interesting. This only hurts their chances, because prospective employers typically have many cover letters to read, with no time to spare for sorting through irrelevant information.

Rule Four: Write Succinctly

Use as few words as possible. Don't indulge in long, complicated words and sentences because you think they make you sound smart. The most intelligent writing is often short and to the point. Keep in mind that hiring a new employee is a very time-consuming process. In small companies, people in charge of hiring often have to do it while performing their regular duties. Thus, the more succinct your resume and cover letter, the greater the chances that a potential employer will actually read both documents.

ProSkills

Rule Five: Use the Right Tone

Be professional and courteous. In the case of writing to a prospective employer, don't make the mistake of being overly friendly, as it might indicate to the reader that you are not taking the job application process seriously.

Rule Six: Revise, Revise, Revise

After you finish a document, set it aside for a while, and then proof it when it's no longer fresh in your mind. Even a small grammar or punctuation error can cause a potential employer to set aside your resume in favor of a more polished one with no errors. Remember, the best writers in the world seek out readers who can provide constructive suggestions, so consider having a friend or colleague read it and provide feedback. If someone points out an unclear passage, make every attempt to improve it.

Following these basic rules will help to ensure that you develop strong, professional written communication skills.

PROSKILLS

Create a Resume and Cover Letter

You've seen how Microsoft Word 2010 allows you to create polished, professional-looking documents in a variety of business settings. The word-processing skills you've learned will be useful to you in many areas of your life. For example, you could create a Word table to keep track of a guest list for a wedding, or you could use Word's desktop publishing features to create a flyer promoting a garage sale or a concert for a friend's band. In the following exercise, you'll create a table summarizing information about prospective employers, and then use that information to create a resume and a cover letter.

Note: Please be sure *not* to include any personal information of a sensitive nature in the documents you create to be submitted to your instructor for this exercise. Later on, you can update the documents with such information for your own personal use.

1. Pick a field that you would look to work in, and then use the Web to look up information about four companies or organizations in that field that you would like to work for.
2. Create a table that summarizes your research. Your table should include all the fields necessary for a mail merge, as well as three fields with general information that would be useful for you in a job interview. For example, you might include a "Most Important Product" field and a "Facts About Company Founder" field. Create a complete record for each company, and then sort the table alphabetically by company name.
3. Create a resume that you could use to apply for jobs at the four companies you researched. Take care to create a resume that is suitable for your chosen field. You can create the resume from scratch, or you can use one of the templates that are available on the New tab in Backstage view. In the Office.com Templates section of the New tab, click Resumes and CVs, click any one of the three folders, and then double-click any template to open it as a Word document. To use a template after you've opened it, save it like an ordinary document, and then

ProSkills

replace the placeholder text with your own information. If a template includes a sample picture, you can replace the picture with your own photo file.

4. After creating your resume, be sure to proof it for any errors, and revise it for proper tone and clear and succinct content. If possible, ask a classmate or a family member to read it over and provide constructive feedback.
5. Create a cover letter to accompany your resume. Where appropriate, insert placeholders for merge fields. Make sure that your letter clearly states your purpose, and that the letter is written succinctly. When reviewing your cover letter and revising it, make sure your writing is professional, and uses an appropriate tone.
6. Perform a mail merge, using your cover letter as the main document and the table you created in Step 2 as the data source. Save the merged document.
7. Perform a second mail merge to create the envelopes for your cover letter and resume. In the first step of the Mail Merge task pane, click the Envelopes option button. In the second step, click Envelope options, and then click the OK button to accept the default envelope settings. Continue following the steps in the Mail Merge task pane. Save the merged document.
8. Review all your documents carefully in Print Preview, then submit the finished documents to your instructor, either in printed or electronic form, as requested.

TUTORIAL 5

Working with Templates, Themes, and Styles

Creating a Site Selection Report

WORD

OBJECTIVES

Session 5.1
- Create a new document from a template
- Insert a Word file into a document
- Customize the document theme
- Select a style set
- Change character and paragraph spacing
- Modify a style

Session 5.2
- Create a new style
- Inspect and compare styles
- Create a table of contents
- Use the Research task pane
- Translate text
- Create and use a new template

Case | *Department of City Planning*

Clarenbach, Tennessee is a rapidly growing suburb of Nashville. Clarenbach's Department of City Planning prepares reports on many public projects that contribute to this growing community. Sam Hooper, a senior member of the department, has asked you to help prepare a report on possible sites for a new public swimming pool. He'd like you to use a Word template as the basis for the new report. He also wants you to create a template that can be used for all reports produced by the department. You will create a custom theme for the reports, and you will work with creating and modifying style sets.

STARTING DATA FILES

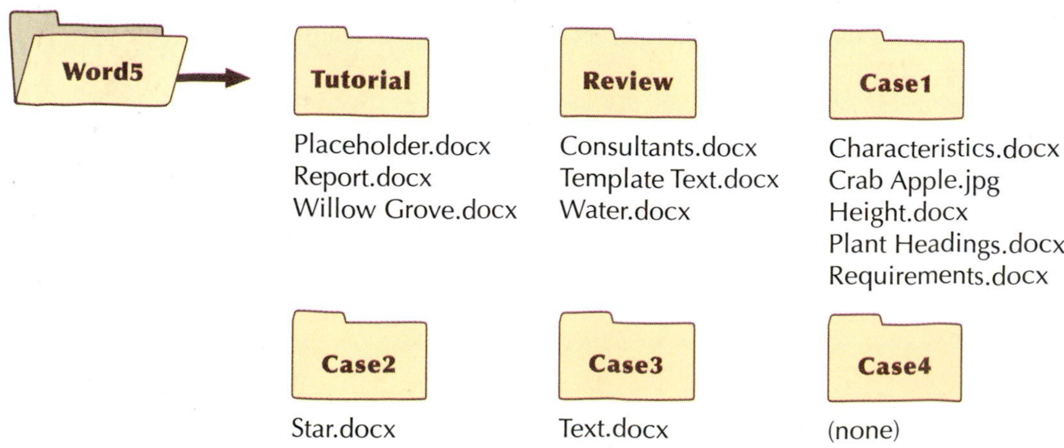

SESSION 5.1 VISUAL OVERVIEW

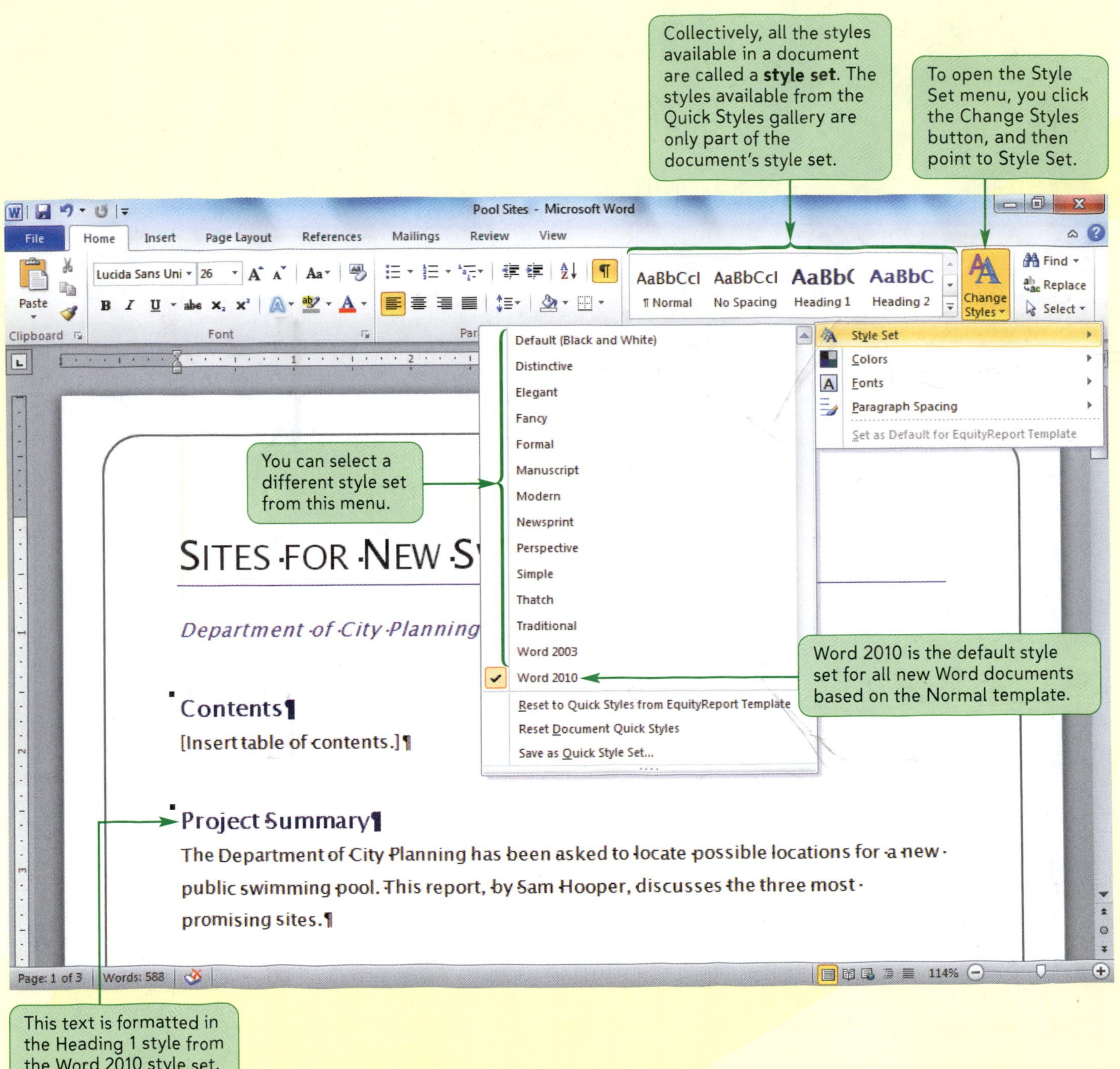

CUSTOM THEMES AND STYLE SETS

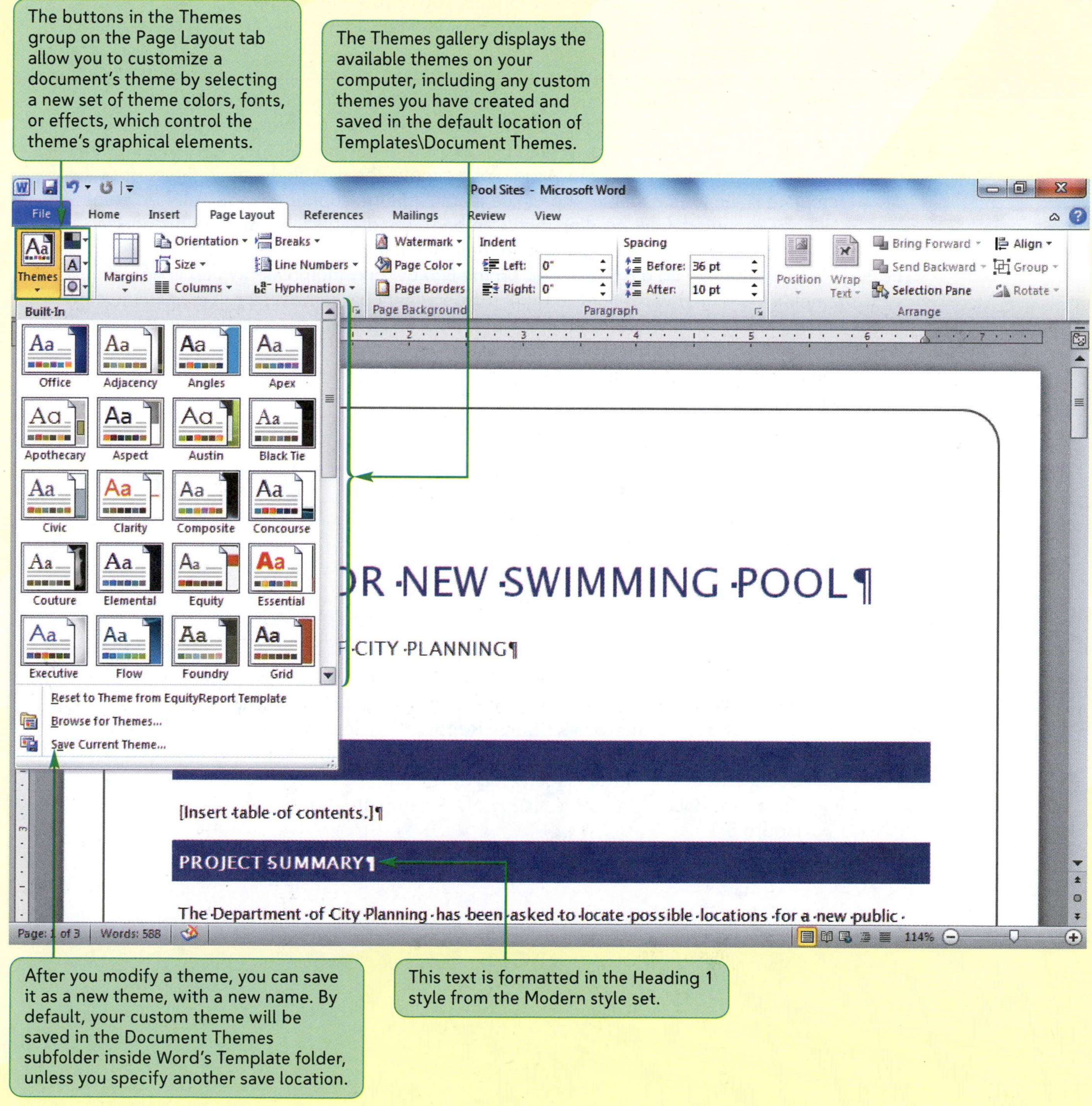
The buttons in the Themes group on the Page Layout tab allow you to customize a document's theme by selecting a new set of theme colors, fonts, or effects, which control the theme's graphical elements.
The Themes gallery displays the available themes on your computer, including any custom themes you have created and saved in the default location of Templates\Document Themes.
Pool Sites - Microsoft Word
File
Home
Insert
Page Layout
References
Mailings
Review
View
Themes
Margins
Orientation
Size
Columns
Breaks
Line Numbers
Hyphenation
Watermark
Page Color
Page Borders
Page Background
Indent
Left: 0"
Right: 0"
Spacing
Before: 36 pt
After: 10 pt
Paragraph
Position
Wrap Text
Bring Forward
Send Backward
Selection Pane
Align
Group
Rotate
Arrange
Built-In
Office
Adjacency
Angles
Apex
Apothecary
Aspect
Austin
Black Tie
Civic
Clarity
Composite
Concourse
Couture
Elemental
Equity
Essential
Executive
Flow
Foundry
Grid
Reset to Theme from EquityReport Template
Browse for Themes...
Save Current Theme...
R NEW SWIMMING POOL¶
F CITY PLANNING¶
[Insert table of contents.]¶
PROJECT SUMMARY¶
The Department of City Planning has been asked to locate possible locations for a new public
Page: 1 of 3
Words: 588
114%
After you modify a theme, you can save it as a new theme, with a new name. By default, your custom theme will be saved in the Document Themes subfolder inside Word's Template folder, unless you specify another save location.
This text is formatted in the Heading 1 style from the Modern style set.

Creating a New Document from a Template

A **template** is a file that you use as a starting point for a series of similar documents so that you don't have to re-create formatting and text for each new document. A template can contain customized styles, text, graphics, or any other element that you want to repeat from one document to another. Word includes templates that you can use to create reports, fax cover sheets, letters, and other types of documents. For an even wider selection of templates, you can look online, where you'll find templates for certificates, contracts, brochures, and greeting cards, just to name a few. You can also create your own templates to suit your specific needs.

TIP

Templates have the file extension .dotx to differentiate them from regular Word documents, which have the extension .docx.

Although you might not realize it, you already have experience working with templates. Every new, blank document that you open in Word is a copy of the Normal template. Unlike the other templates included with Word, the **Normal template** does not have any text, formatting, or graphics, but it does include all the default settings that you are accustomed to using in Word. For example, the default theme in the Normal template is the Office theme. The Office theme, in turn, supplies the default body font (Calibri) and the default heading font (Cambria). The default 1.15 line spacing and the paragraph spacing are also specified in the Normal template.

Sam would like to base his report on the Equity Report template, which is one of the templates installed with Word. You open a document based on a template from the New tab in Backstage view, the same tab you use to open a new, blank document. When you open a template, Word actually creates a document that is an exact copy of the template. The template itself remains unaltered, so that you can continue to use it as the basis for other documents.

To open a new document based on the Equity Report template:

1. In Word, click the **File** tab to open Backstage view, and then click the **New** tab in the navigation bar. The left pane of the New tab gives you access to templates that are stored on your computer and templates available online at Office.com. The default selection, Blank document, opens a new, blank document based on the Normal template. In this case, you want to open a document based on a different template.
2. In the Home section, click **Sample templates.** The left pane of the New tab displays thumbnails of the templates that were installed with Word. Scroll down, if necessary, and then click **Equity Report**. The right pane of the New tab displays a preview of the first page of the selected template. Below the preview, the Document option button is selected by default, indicating that Word will create a new document that is a copy of the template, *not the template itself*. See Figure 5-1.

Figure 5-1 **Selecting the Equity Report template**

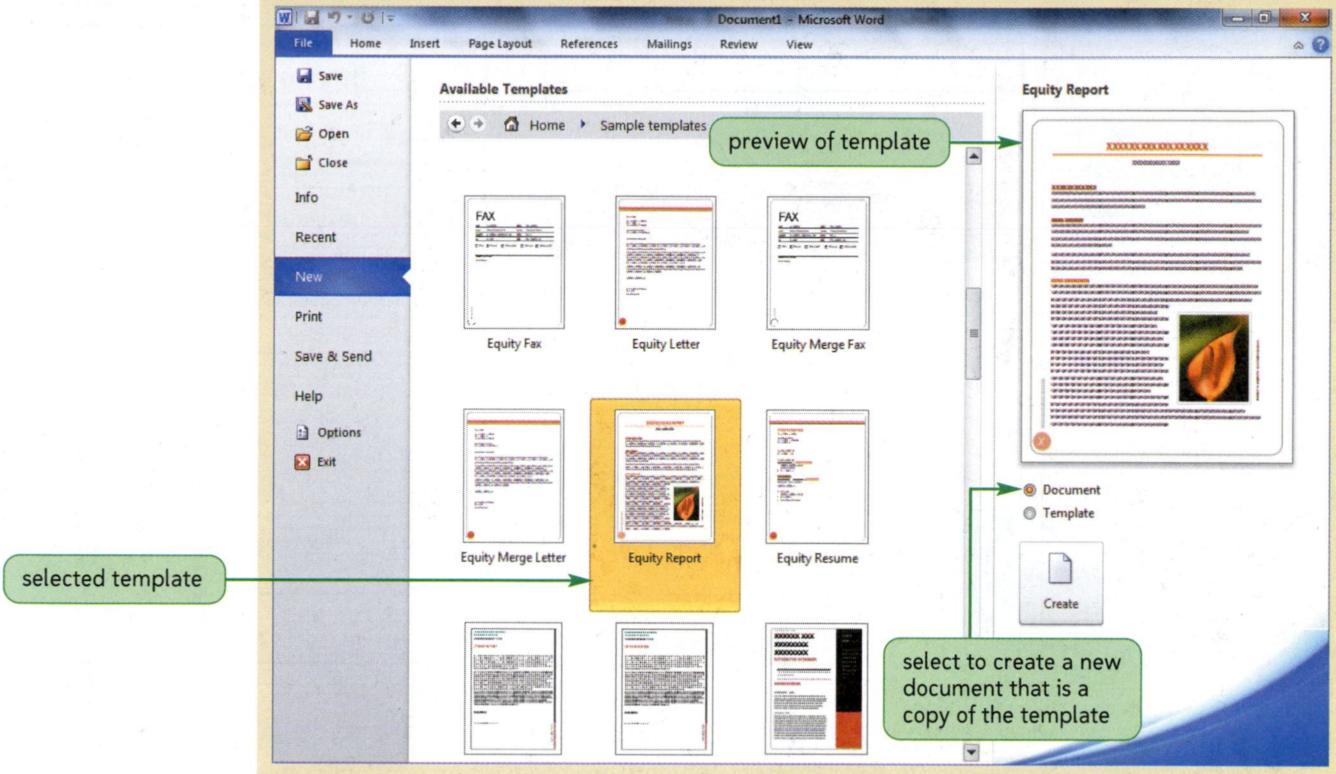

3. Click the **Create** button. A new document, named Document2, opens. It contains a number of content controls designed specifically for the Equity Report template.

4. Switch to **Print Layout** if necessary, change the Zoom setting to **Page Width**, display nonprinting characters if necessary, and then scroll down and review the parts of the document. Figure 5-2 shows all the elements of the Equity Report template.

TIP

The sample text in the Equity Report is actually a helpful summary of techniques for working with templates, rather than text one might use in a report.

Figure 5-2 Equity Report template

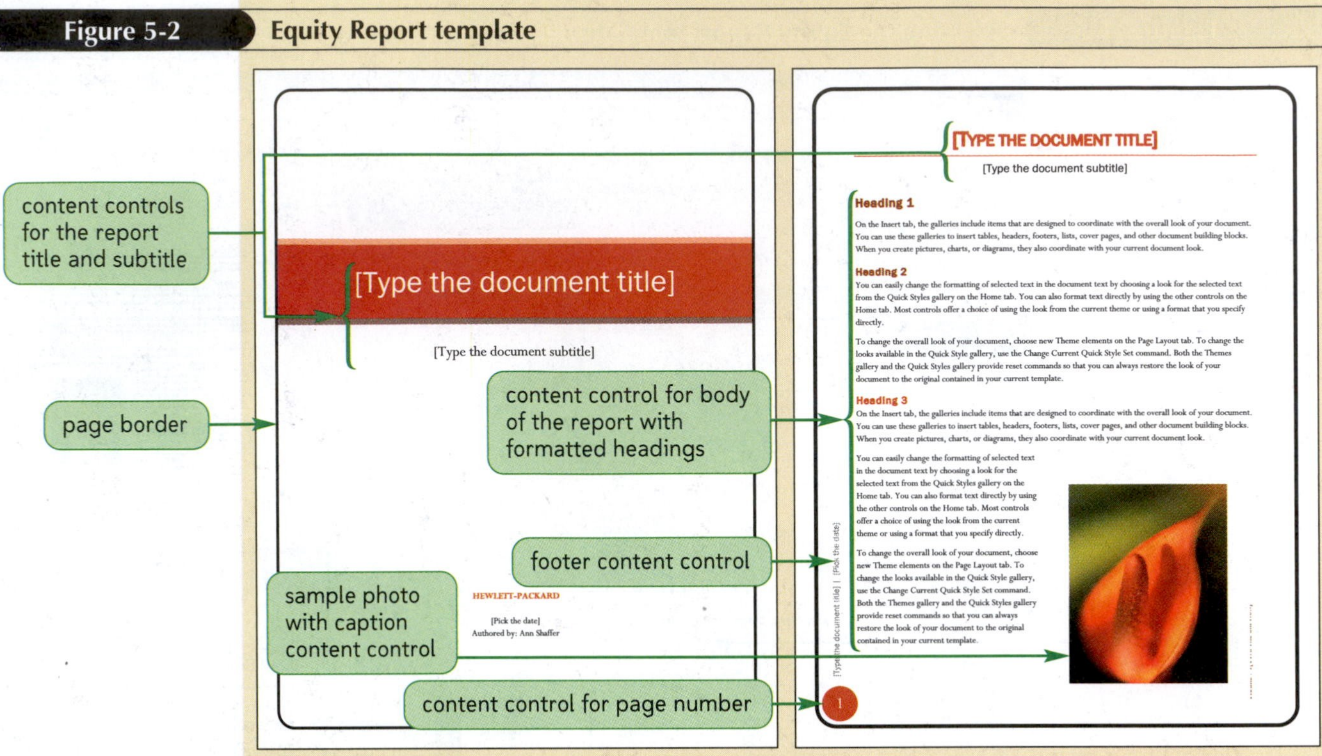

The first page is a cover page with several content controls for the document title, subtitle, and other elements. The second page contains similar content controls as well as a sample photograph with a content control for a caption. Each page is surrounded by a border with rounded corners. The colors, fonts, and other elements you see in the document are specified by the Equity theme, which is the default theme for the Equity Report template.

5. Save the document as **Pool Sites** in the Word5\Tutorial folder included with your Data Files.

After you use a template to create a new document, you can delete the elements you don't want to use, type appropriate text in the content controls that you want to keep, and then replace the sample body text with text that is specific to your document. In this case, you do not need the cover page, so you can begin by deleting that from the Pool Sites document, and then enter the appropriate text for this report into the content controls.

To modify the document created from the Equity template:

1. Click the **Insert** tab, click the **Cover Page** button in the Pages group, and then click **Remove Current Cover Page**. The cover page is removed from the document, leaving only the page with the sample photograph, which is now page 1.
2. Press the **Delete** key to delete the blank paragraph at the top of the remaining page.
3. Replace the **[Type the document title]** placeholder text with **Sites for New Swimming Pool**. The new title replaces the placeholder text. Next, you need to enter the subtitle.

4. Replace the **[Type the document subtitle]** placeholder text with **Department of City Planning**. The new subtitle appears in the control. Next, you need to add the date to the vertical footer. To do this, you need to switch to Header and Footer view.
5. In the Header & Footer group, click the **Footer** button, and then, under the Footer gallery, click **Edit Footer**. The document switches to Header and Footer view and scrolls down to display the vertical footer in the lower-left corner of the page. The Document Title content control in the footer displays the document title, "Sites for New Swimming Pool," which you entered earlier. The Date content control contains the [Pick the date] placeholder.
6. Click the **[Pick the date]** placeholder text to display the content control, click the **Date button arrow** to display the calendar, and then click the current date. The calendar closes and the current date is displayed in the Date content control.
7. On the Header & Footer Tools Design tab, click the **Close Header and Footer** button in the Close group. You return to Page Layout view. The Subtitle content control is still active, because it was active when you switched to Header and Footer view.

TIP

To remove the preformatted footer from the document, you click Remove Footer on the Footer menu.

Sam wants the report to begin with the heading "Contents" followed by a table of contents. You'll insert the heading now, and then insert the table of contents information later in this tutorial.

To enter the Contents heading:

1. Move the mouse pointer over the text in the body of the report, which begins with "Heading 1." The text area is highlighted in light blue.
2. Click anywhere in the body of the report. The blue highlight darkens and now covers only the text itself. A blue tag above the highlighted text indicates that the body of the report is actually a content control. See Figure 5-3. Unlike with other content controls, you can delete this one simply by typing something new.

Figure 5-3 **Document with sample text highlighted**

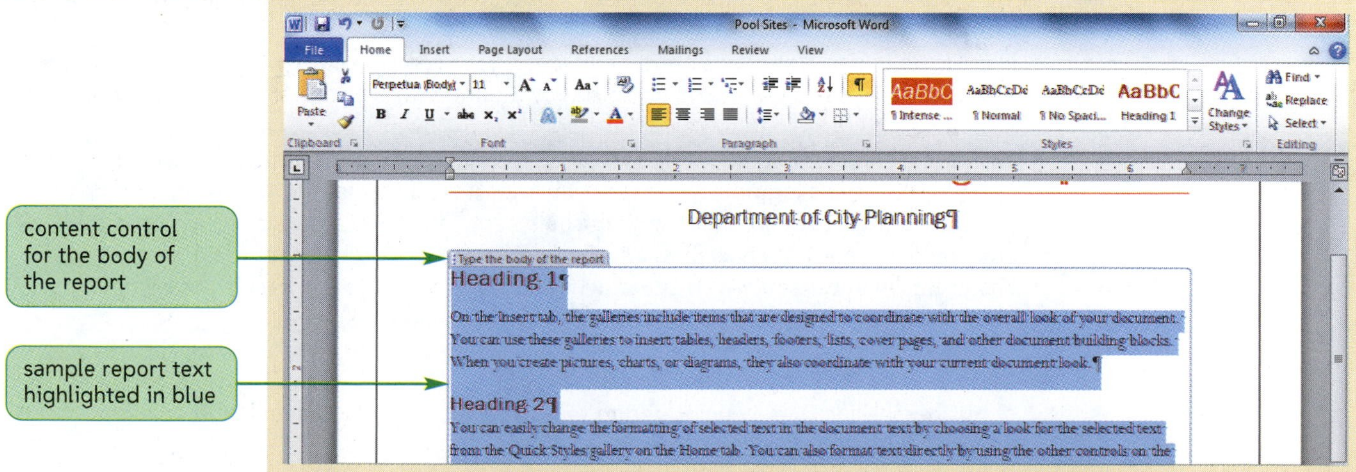

3. Type **Contents**. The content control is removed, along with the sample text and the sample photograph. The new text is formatted in the Perpetua font, which is the default body font for the Equity Report template.
4. In the Styles group, click the **Heading 1** style. The Contents heading is formatted in 14-point Franklin Gothic Book font with a dark orange color.
5. Press the **Enter** key to start a new paragraph, type **[Insert table of contents.]**, and then press the **Enter** key again. This placeholder text will remind Sam to insert a table of contents later, after his report is created. The new text is formatted in the Normal style, not in the Heading 1 style. A new paragraph after a heading is formatted in the Normal style by default. See Figure 5-4.

Figure 5-4 Report with new heading

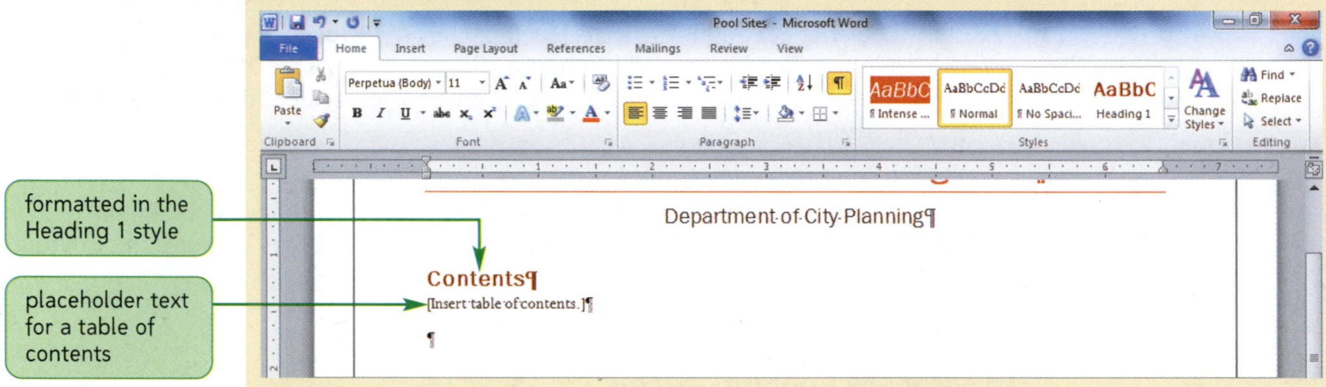

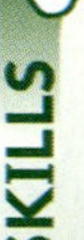

PROSKILLS

Decision Making: Using Templates from Other Sources

The templates installed with Word are only a small sample of the templates available to you. The Microsoft Office Online Web site offers a huge variety of templates that are free to registered Microsoft Office users. Countless other sites offer templates for free, for individual sale, as part of a subscription service, or a combination of all three. However, you need to be wary when searching for templates online. Keep in mind the following when deciding what sites to use:

- Files downloaded from the Internet can infect your computer with viruses and spyware, so make sure your computer is up-to-date with antivirus and antispyware software before attempting to download any templates.
- Evaluate a site carefully to verify that it is a reputable source of virus-free templates. Verifying the site's legitimacy is especially important if you intend to pay for a template with a credit card. Search for the Web site's name and Web address on several different search engines (such as Bing and Google) to see what other people say about it. The Better Business Bureau's Web site at *www.bbb.org* allows you to search for complaints against an online business by entering its URL (Web address).
- Some Web sites claim to offer templates for free, when in fact the offer is primarily a lure to draw visitors to sites that are really just online billboards, with ads for any number of businesses completely unrelated to templates or Word documents. You should avoid downloading templates from these Web sites.
- Many templates available online were created for earlier versions of Word that did not include themes or many other design features that you are accustomed to in Word 2010. Make sure you know what you're getting before you pay for an out-of-date template.

Sam has typed a draft of his report and saved it in a separate Word document. You can insert this Word file into the Pool Sites document.

Inserting a File into a Word Document

To insert a file into a document, you start by clicking the Object button in the Text group on the Insert tab. When you insert a Word file into an open Word document, the text is inserted at the location of the insertion point, so you need to make sure the insertion point is at the correct location. Word always inserts a blank paragraph at the end of text inserted from another file. If you don't want to include this extra paragraph, you can delete it. Before inserting the file, you will open it and review the formatting.

To insert a file into the Pool Sites document:

1. Open the file **Report** from the Word5\Tutorial folder included with your Data Files. As you can see, the document is formatted in the Office theme. It contains text formatted with the familiar blue color of the Office theme Heading 1 and Heading 2 styles.
2. Close the Report document and return to the Pool Sites document, verify that the insertion point is located in the blank paragraph below the [Insert table of contents.] text.
3. Click the **Insert** tab, and then in the Text group, click the **Object button arrow**. A menu appears with two options.

   Trouble? If the Object dialog box opens, you clicked the Object button instead of the Object button arrow. Close the dialog box, and then click the Object button arrow instead.
4. On the Object menu, click **Text from File**. The Insert File dialog box opens, which is very similar to the Open dialog box.
5. If necessary, navigate to the Word5\Tutorial folder included with your Data Files, click the **Report** document, and then click the **Insert** button. The text of the Report document is inserted in the Pool Sites document. It takes on the theme of the current document (the Equity theme), with the headings now formatted in a dark orange color.
6. Scroll up to review the beginning of the document, as shown in Figure 5-5.

Figure 5-5 Report document inserted into the Pool Sites document

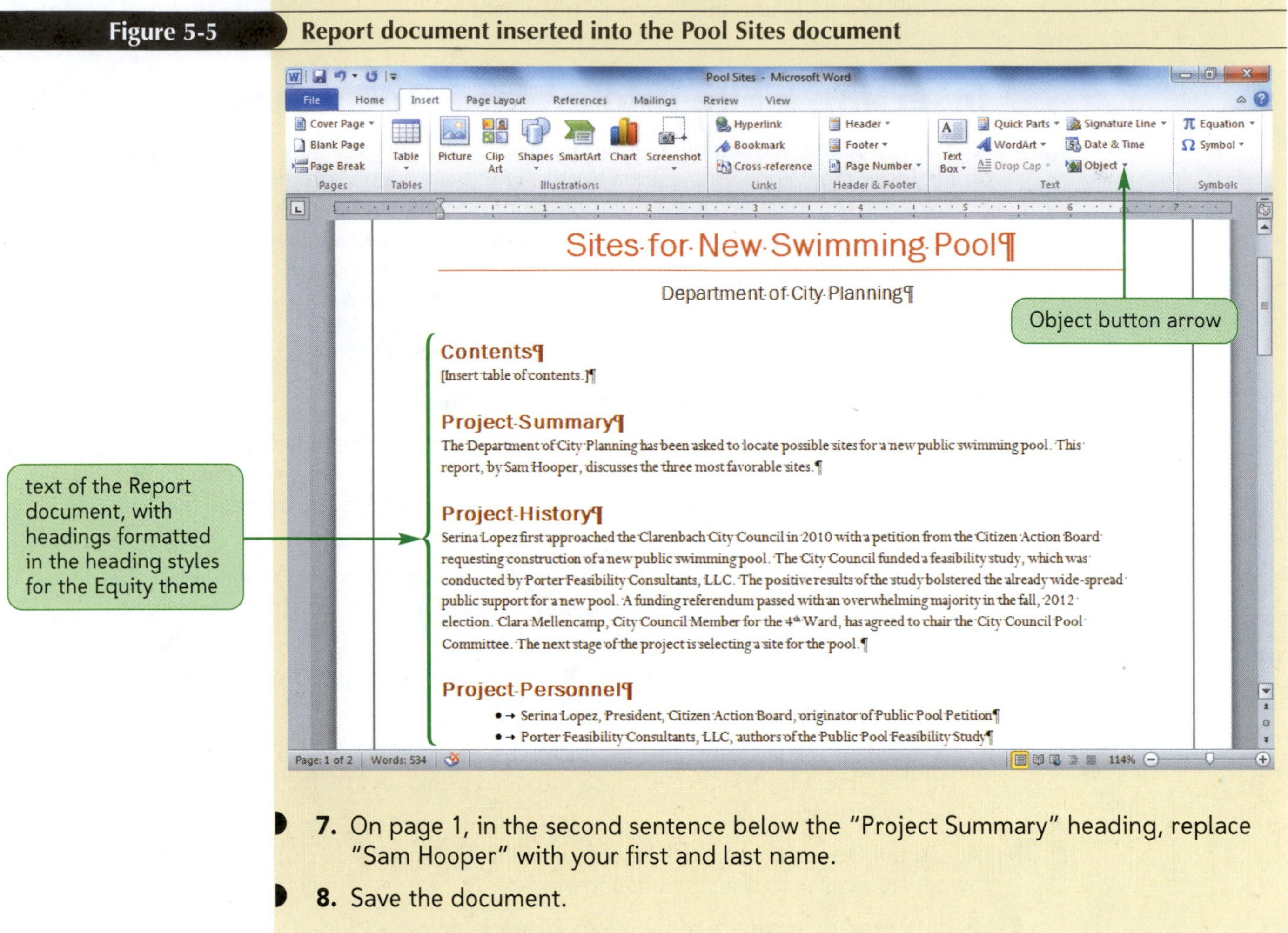

7. On page 1, in the second sentence below the "Project Summary" heading, replace "Sam Hooper" with your first and last name.
8. Save the document.

Now that the document contains the report text, Sam asks you to customize the formatting. You'll start with the document theme.

Customizing the Document Theme

A document theme consists of three main components—theme colors, theme fonts, and theme effects. A specific set of colors, fonts, and effects is associated with each theme, but you can mix and match them to create a customized theme for your document.

As you saw in the Session 5.1 Visual Overview, you change the theme colors, fonts, and effects for a document using the options in the Themes group on the Page Layout tab. When you change the theme colors, fonts, and effects for a document, the changes affect only that document.

The Pool Sites document, which was based on the Equity Report template, is formatted with the Equity theme. Although Sam likes the overall layout of the document, he wants to select different theme colors and theme fonts. He doesn't plan to include any graphics, so there's no need to customize the theme effects. You'll start with the theme colors.

Changing the Theme Colors

Theme colors are the coordinated colors used by a theme to format headings, body text, and other elements. For example, the Equity theme, which is currently applied to Sam's report, uses orange for the headings and the circle graphic in the footer, and a coordinating gray for the page border and footer text. Sam prefers something more neutral than the orange color used in the Equity theme. He asks you to apply a different set of theme colors.

To change the theme colors in the Pool Sites document:

1. Click the **Page Layout** tab, and then click the **Theme Colors** button. A gallery of theme colors opens, with one coordinated set of colors for each theme. A pale orange outline indicates that the Equity theme color set is currently applied to the document. The gallery displays eight colors in each set of colors. The third color from the left is the color used for headings. For example, the third color from the left in the Equity theme color set is dark orange, which is currently applied to the headings in the document. The remaining colors are used for other types of elements, such as hyperlinks, page borders, shading, and so on. See Figure 5-6.

Figure 5-6 Theme Colors gallery

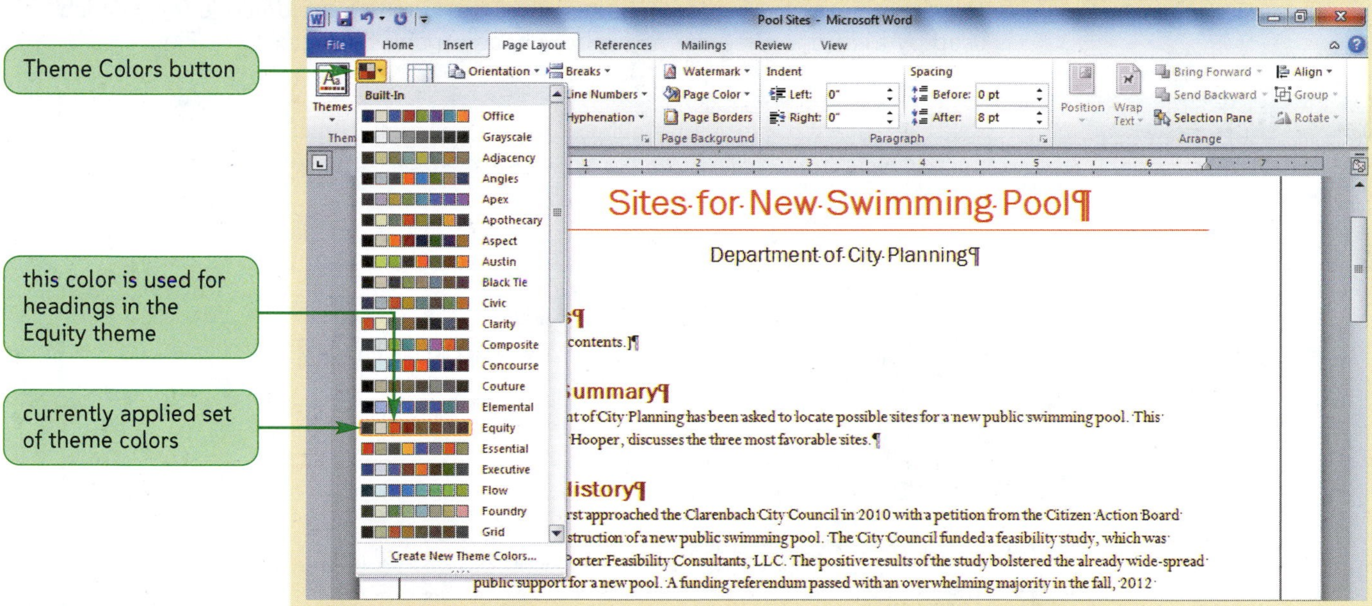

Trouble? If you see additional theme colors at the top of the menu under the heading "Custom," then custom theme colors have been created and stored on your computer.

2. Move the mouse pointer over the options in the gallery to observe the Live Preview of the colors in the document.
3. Scroll down, and then click the **Urban** color set, which is the third from the bottom. The document headings are now formatted in dark blue.
4. Save your work.

The new colors you just selected affect only the Pool Sites document. Your changes do not affect the Equity theme that was installed with Word and that is available to all new documents. Next, Sam asks you to customize the document theme further by changing the theme fonts.

Changing the Theme Fonts

As with theme colors, you can change the **theme fonts** in a document to suit your needs. You know from Tutorial 2 that each theme uses two coordinating fonts or font styles—one for the headings and one for the body text. For example, the Equity theme in the Pool Sites document includes the Franklin Gothic Book font for headings, and Perpetua for body text. When changing the theme fonts, you can select from all the font combinations available in any of the themes installed with Word.

To select a different set of theme fonts for the Pool Sites document:

1. In the Themes group, move the mouse pointer over the **Theme Fonts** button [A]. A ScreenTip appears, indicating that the current fonts are Franklin Gothic Book for headings and Perpetua for body text.
2. Click the **Theme Fonts** button [A]. The Theme Fonts gallery opens, displaying the heading and body font combinations for each theme.
3. Scroll down to review the fonts. Sam prefers the Lucida Sans Unicode font, which is used by the Concourse theme for both heading and body text. See Figure 5-7.

Figure 5-7 Theme Fonts gallery

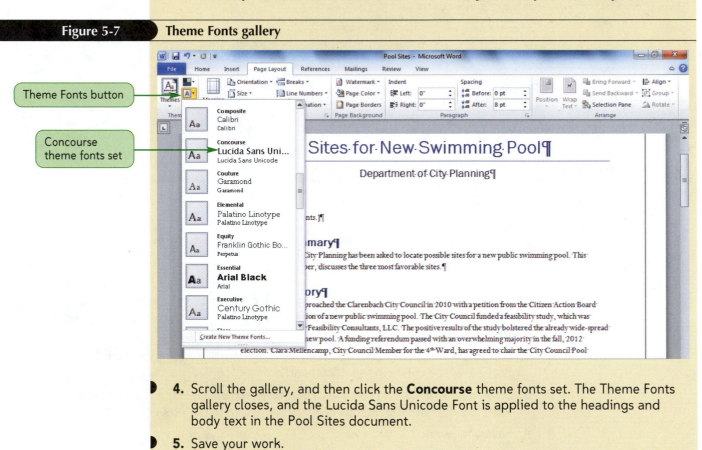

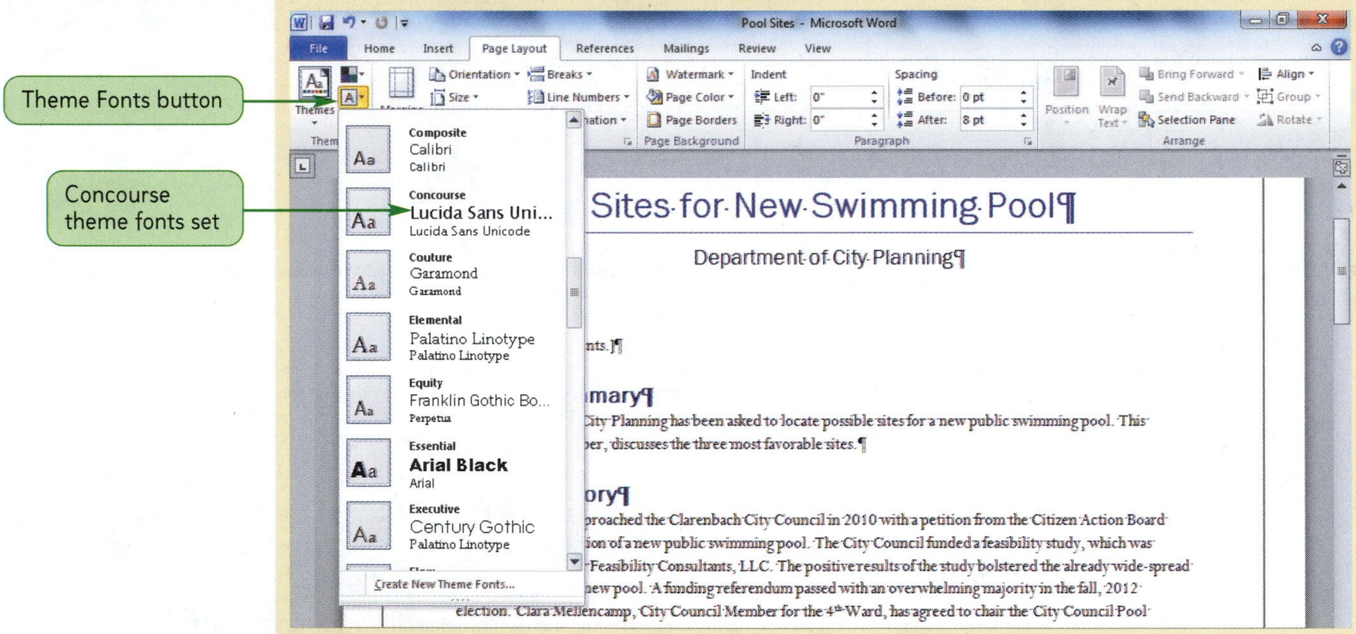

4. Scroll the gallery, and then click the **Concourse** theme fonts set. The Theme Fonts gallery closes, and the Lucida Sans Unicode Font is applied to the headings and body text in the Pool Sites document.
5. Save your work.

The changes you have made to the theme fonts for the Pool Site do not affect the original Equity theme that was installed with Word and that is available to all new documents. To make your new combination of theme fonts and theme colors available to other documents, you can save them as a new, custom theme.

INSIGHT

Creating Custom Theme Colors and Theme Fonts

The theme colors and theme fonts installed with Word were created by Microsoft designers who are experts in creating harmonious-looking documents. It's always best to stick with these predesigned options, rather than trying to create your own set. However, in some specialized situations you might need to create customized sets of theme fonts and colors. When you create a customized set, the theme fonts and colors are saved as part of Word so that you can use them in other documents. To create a custom set of theme colors, you click the Theme Colors button in the Themes group on the Page Layout tab, click Create New Theme Colors to open the Create New Theme Colors dialog box, in which you can select colors for different theme elements, and enter a descriptive name for the new theme colors. The custom set of theme colors appears as an option in the Themes Color gallery.

To create a custom set of heading and body fonts, you click the Theme Fonts button in the Themes group on the Page Layout tab, click Create New Theme Fonts, select your custom heading and body, and then enter a descriptive name for the new set of fonts in the Name box. The custom set of theme fonts appears as an option in the Theme Fonts menu.

Saving a Custom Theme

You can save a new custom theme to any folder, but when you save a custom theme to the default location—the Document Themes subfolder inside the Word Templates folder—it appears as an option in the Themes gallery. To save a custom theme, you click the Themes button in the Themes group on the Home tab, and then click Save Current Theme.

Sam asks you to save his combination of theme fonts and theme colors as a new theme.

To save a new theme:

1. In the Themes group, click the **Themes** button, and then, in the menu below the Themes gallery, click **Save Current Theme**. The Save Current Theme dialog box opens. The Document Themes folder is the default location. The default theme name is "Theme1." You can select a different save location and enter a more meaningful theme name. See Figure 5-8.

Figure 5-8 Save Current Theme dialog box

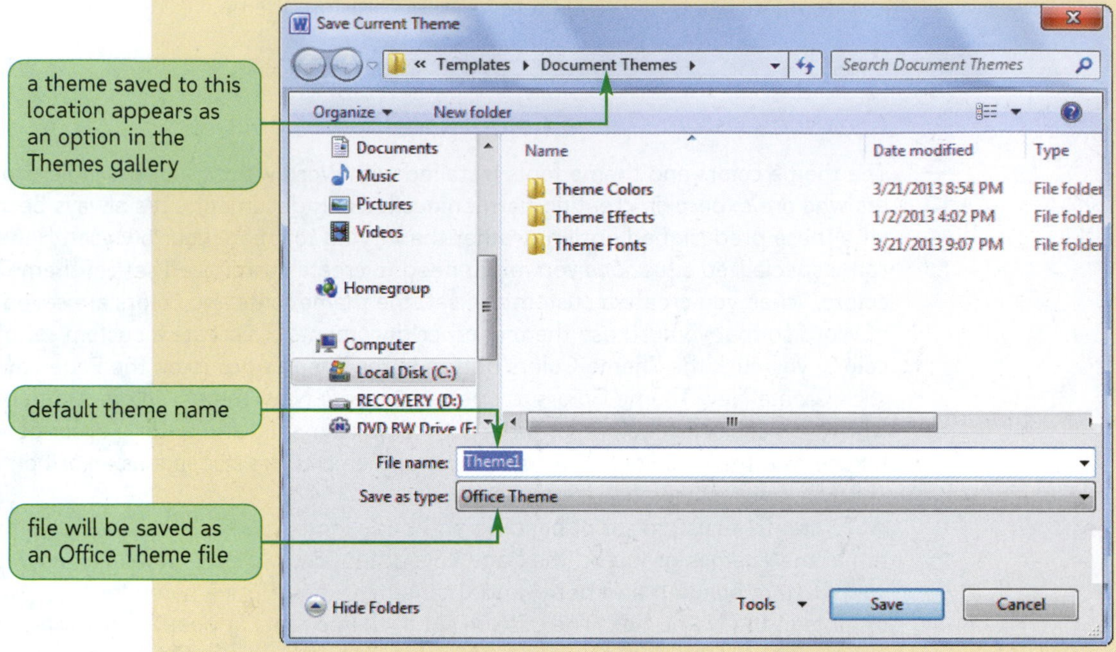

TIP

To delete a theme from the Document Themes folder and remove it from the Themes gallery, click the Themes button in the Themes group on the Page Layout tab, right-click the theme you want to delete, click Delete, and then click Yes.

2. Navigate to the Word5\Tutorial folder included with your Data Files. Next you'll type the new filename, using "DCP," the acronym for "Department of City Planning," as part of the filename.
3. Click in the File name box, type **DCP Theme**, and then click the **Save** button. The Save Current Theme dialog box closes.

Sam plans to use the new DCP theme later to help standardize the look of all documents created in his department. When he is ready to apply it to a document, he can click the Themes button in the Themes group on the Page Layout tab, click Browse for Themes, navigate to the folder containing the custom theme, and then select and open the theme.

Selecting a Style Set

TIP

Once you have applied a style set, you can still change the theme. Changing the theme only affects the theme colors and theme fonts.

Recall that a style is a set of formatting options that you can apply to a specific text element in a document, such as a document's title, heading, or body text. A **style set** is a coordinated set of styles in a document. By default, the Quick Styles gallery displays styles from the Word 2010 style set, and this is the style set you see in the Quick Styles gallery when you open a new, blank document. You can choose from 12 additional style sets using the Change Styles button in the Styles group on the Home tab, as shown in the Session 5.1 Visual Overview.

Each style set has a Normal style, a Heading 1 style, a Heading 2 style, and so on. The styles in a style set are designed to convey a specific look. For example, the Thatch style set shown in Figure 5-9 has a bold, modern look. The Heading 1 style includes a thick band of color with an outline and a contrasting font color. The Heading 2 style in the Thatch style set has white letters that are outlined in the same color used as the background color in the Heading 1 style.

Figure 5-9 Styles from two different style sets

Word 2010 style set	Title style Heading 1 style Heading 2 style Normal style
Thatch style set	Title style Heading 1 style Heading 2 style Normal style

Sam asks you to select a different style set for the Pool Sites document.

To select a new style set for the Pool Sites document:

1. Click the **Home** tab, and then click the **Change Styles** button in the Styles group. The Change Styles menu opens. To select a new style set, you use the Style Set option.
2. Point to **Style Set**. The Style Set menu opens, displaying a list of style sets.
3. Drag the mouse pointer down the menu, and then point to **Modern**. As you drag the mouse pointer, a Live Preview shows some of the styles that make up the different style sets in the menu. In the Modern style set, the Heading 1 style applies a blue box that spans the left and right margins, with the heading text in white. Notice that the theme fonts you specified earlier—Lucida Sans Unicode for both headings and the body text—are still applied, as are the Concourse theme colors. See Figure 5-10.

Figure 5-10 Live Preview of the Modern style set

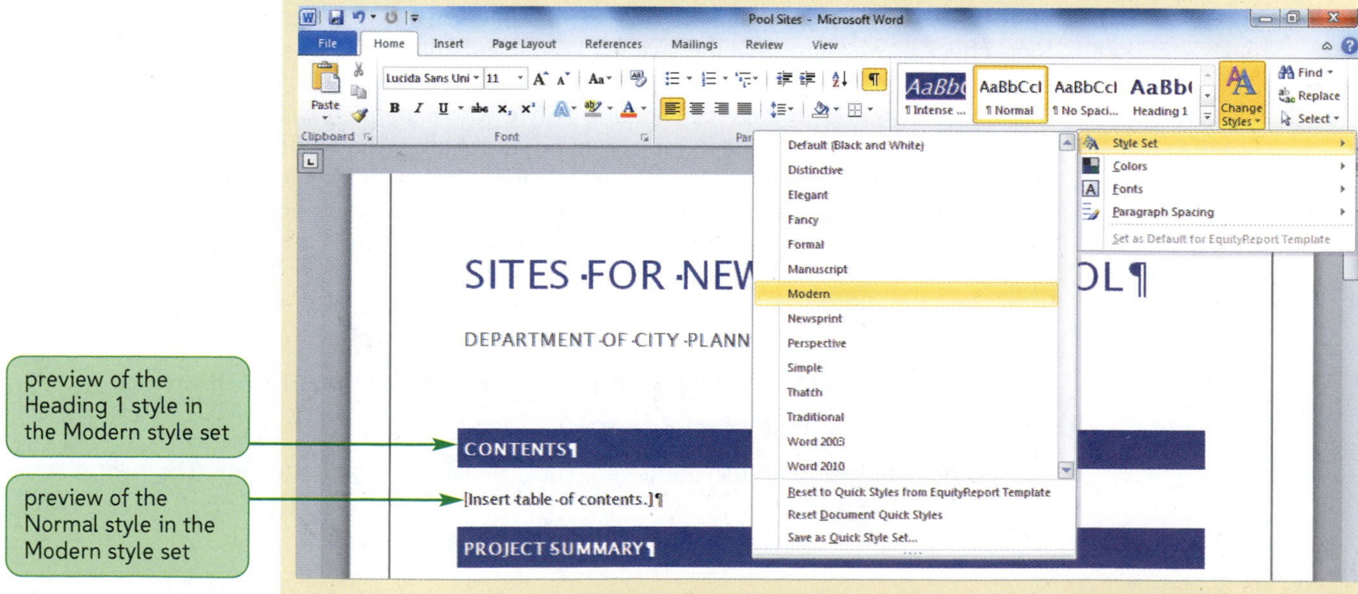

4. Click **Modern** on the Style Set menu. The styles in the document change to reflect the styles in the Modern style set, and the Quick Styles gallery in the Styles group displays the first four styles in the Modern Style set.
5. In the Styles group, click the **More** button to review the set of styles available in the Quick Styles gallery, and then click anywhere in the document to close the Quick Styles gallery.

The ability to select a new style set gives you a lot of flexibility when formatting a document. However, sometimes you will want to modify a style to better suit your particular needs.

Modifying Styles

To modify a style, you select text formatted with the style you want to modify, apply new formatting, and then update the style by saving your changes. Sam asks you to modify the Heading 1 style for the report by increasing the character spacing and paragraph spacing and applying italics. You'll start by adjusting the character spacing.

Changing Character Spacing

The term **character spacing** refers to the space between individual characters. To add emphasis to text, you can expand or contract the spacing between characters. As with line and paragraph spacing, space between characters is measured in points, with one point equal to 1/72 of an inch.

To adjust character spacing for selected text, click the Dialog Box Launcher in the Font group on the Home tab, and then click the Advanced tab in the Font dialog box. Of the numerous settings available on this tab, you'll find two especially useful.

First, the Spacing box allows you to choose Normal spacing (which is the default character spacing you normally see in documents), Expanded spacing (with the characters farther apart than with the Normal setting) and Condensed spacing (with the characters closer together than with the Normal setting). With both Expanded and Condensed spacing, you can specify the number of points between characters.

Secondly, the Kerning for fonts check box allows you to adjust the spacing between characters to make them look like they are spaced evenly. Kerning is helpful when you are working with large font sizes, which can sometimes cause characters to appear unevenly spaced even though they are in fact spaced evenly. Selecting the Kerning for fonts check box ensures that the spacing is adjusted automatically so that letters appear evenly spaced.

Sam wants you to update the Heading 1 style with expanded character spacing, and he wants the Heading 1 style to include italics formatting. You will begin by making these changes to a paragraph that is currently formatted with the Heading 1 style. Later, you will update the Heading 1 style to match the new formatting of the paragraph you modified and, as a result, all the paragraphs formatted with the Heading 1 style will be updated as well.

To modify the character spacing of the Project Summary heading:

1. Select the heading **Project Summary**.
2. In the Font group on the Home tab, click the **Dialog Box Launcher**. The Font dialog box opens.

TIP

The more advanced options, under "OpenType Features," allow you to fine tune the appearance of characters.

3. Click the **Advanced** tab. This tab includes several options for changing the space between characters. The Character Spacing settings at the top of this tab reflect the style settings for the currently selected text. The Spacing box is set to Expanded.
4. Click the **Spacing** arrow to see the available spacing options. If you wanted to move the selected characters closer together, you would click Condensed. In this case, you will keep the Expanded setting but increase the space between the characters by changing the setting in the By box next to the Spacing box.
5. Click the **Spacing** arrow again to close the menu without making any changes, and then next to the Spacing box, delete the contents in the By box, type **2** (you don't have to type "pt"), and then press the **Tab** key. The Preview section shows a sample of the expanded character spacing. See Figure 5-11.

Figure 5-11 **Changing character spacing in the Font dialog box**

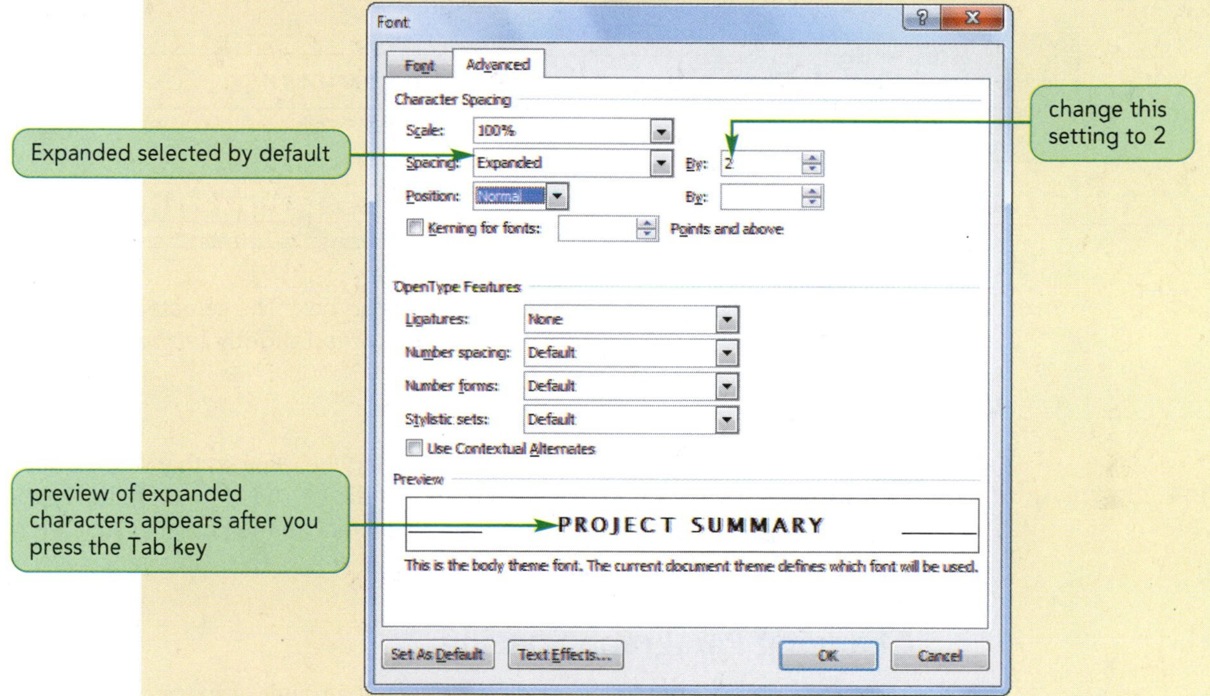

Next, you need to apply italics, which you can do from the Font tab.

6. In the Font dialog box, click the **Font** tab. Here you can make numerous changes affecting the appearance of the selected text, including adding special effects such as shadows or outlines.
7. In the Font style box, click **Bold Italic**. The Preview section of the Font tab shows a preview of the italics formatting applied to the Project Summary heading, which also has the Heading 1 style applied to it. See Figure 5-12.

Figure 5-12 **Applying italics to text formatted with the Heading 1 style**

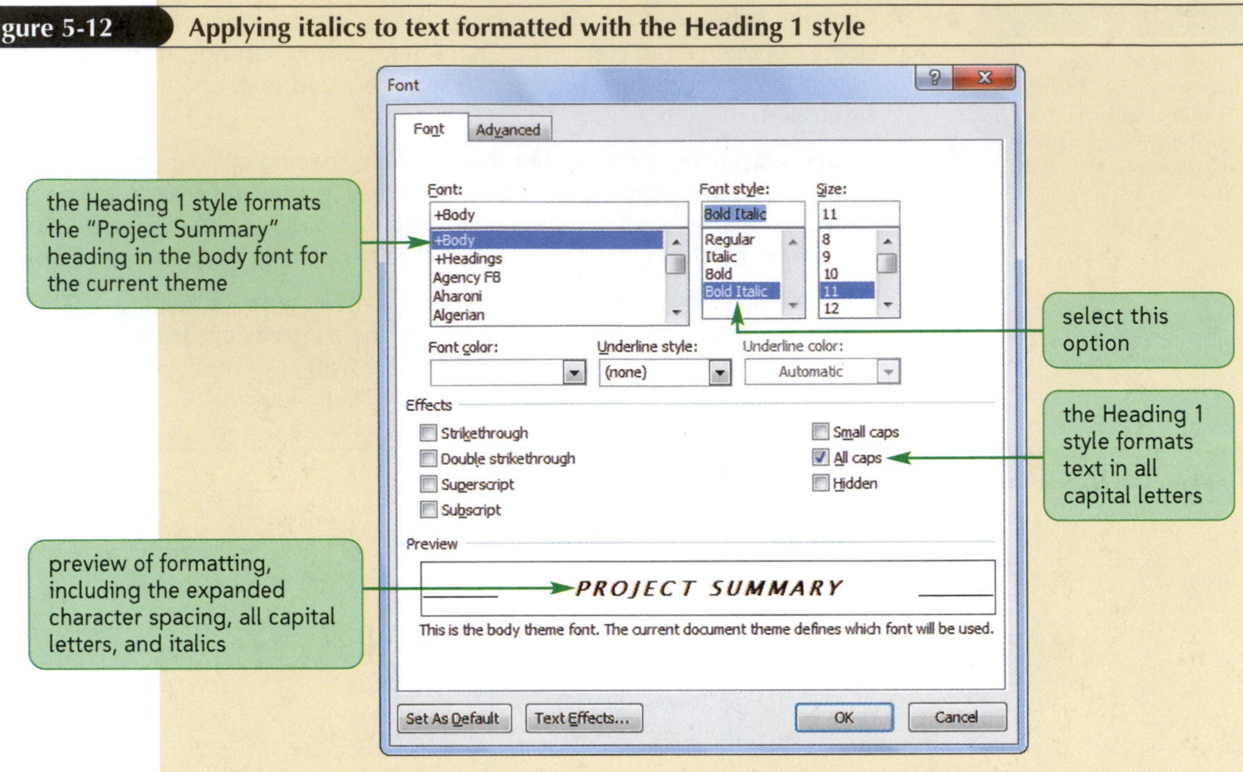

8. Click the **OK** button to close the Font dialog box. The selected heading is now italicized, with the individual characters spread slightly farther apart.
9. Save your work.

Next, you need to change the Project Summary heading so that some extra spacing appears below it. Then you will update the Heading 1 style to match the new formatting of the Project Summary heading. This will affect all the headings that are currently formatted with the Heading 1 style.

Changing Paragraph Spacing

You already know how to add or delete a default amount of space before or after a paragraph using the Line and Paragraph Spacing button in the Paragraph group on the Home tab. To specify an exact amount of space, you use the options in the Paragraph group on the Page Layout tab. Sam wants 15 points of space after the Contents heading. The extra space will help further distinguish the heading from the body text that follows it.

To increase the space after the Project Summary heading:

1. Verify that the Project Summary heading is still selected.
2. Click the **Page Layout** tab. Note that the Paragraph group on this tab includes settings for paragraph indents and paragraph spacing. You use the Spacing Before and After boxes to add space before or after the selected paragraph. Currently, the selected paragraph has 10 points of space before it and 0 points after it. Sam wants to change the After setting to 15.

3. In the Spacing section of the Paragraph group, click the **After** box, type **15,** and then press the **Enter** key to apply the change to the selected paragraph. See Figure 5-13.

Figure 5-13 Changing paragraph spacing

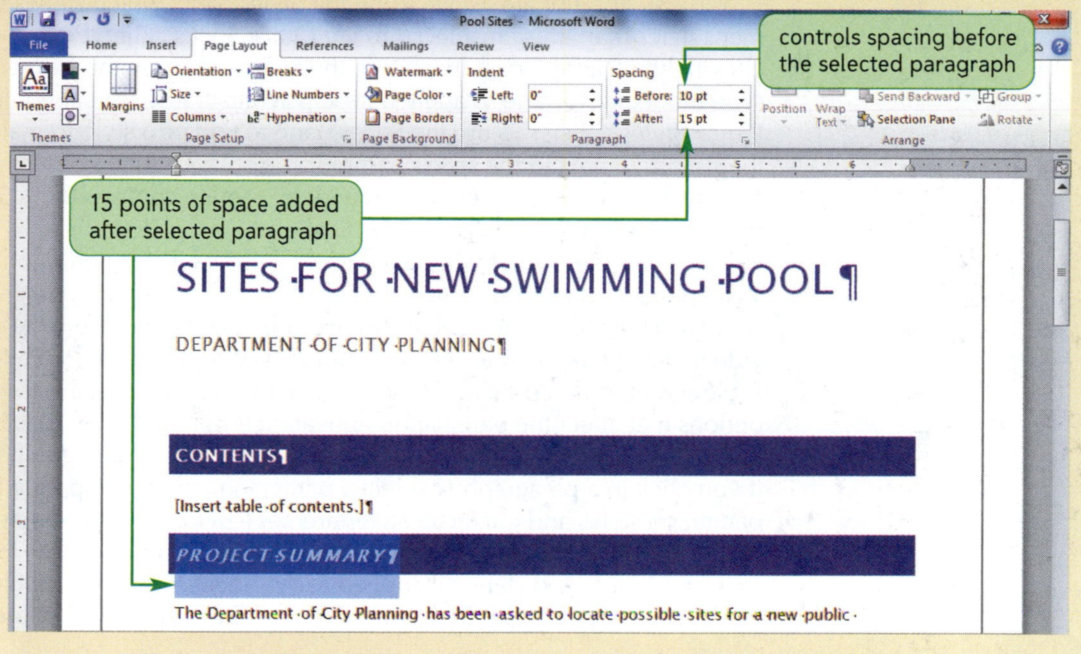

Updating a Style

Now that the selected heading is formatted the way you want, you can update the Heading 1 style to match it. When updating a style, you need to decide whether you want to save the style to the current document or to the current template—that is, the template from which your document draws its default formatting settings. As you know, when you open a new blank document, it is based on the Normal template. In the case of Sam's Pool Site document, the current template is the Equity Report template. When you save a modified style to the current template, the modified version of the style appears in all new documents based on that template. Unless you have a very good reason for saving a modified style to the current template, you should save it to the current document instead.

INSIGHT

Modifying and Saving Styles to a Template

Making changes to a template, especially to the Normal template, is not something you should do casually, because your changes will affect all future documents created from that template. Also, continually modifying or creating styles in the Normal template can result in a Quick Styles gallery that is disorganized, making it hard to find the styles you want. To avoid this problem, consider saving modified styles to the current document (rather than to the current template), and then saving the current document as a template. All future documents based on that template will contain your new styles. Meanwhile, the Normal template will remain unaffected by the new styles.

To update a style to match the currently selected text, you can right-click the style in the Quick Styles gallery and then click Update *Style* to Match Selection, where *Style* is the name of the style you want to update. For example, to update the Heading 1 style, you could right-click it and then click Update Heading 1 to Match Selection. This saves the updated style to the current document. To save a modified style to the current template, right-click the style, click Modify, and then, in the Modify Style dialog box, select the New documents based on this template option button.

You can also update a style using the Styles pane, which shows you more of the document styles than those displayed in the Quick Styles gallery. You open the Styles pane by clicking the Dialog Box Launcher in the Styles group on the Home tab. You can click a style in the Styles pane to apply it to selected text, just as you would click a style in the Quick Styles gallery. To use the Styles pane to update a style to match selected text, click the list arrow next to the style's name. This displays a menu containing the same Update *Style* to Match Selection command and the Modify command that you see when you right-click a style in the Quick Styles gallery.

The Styles pane can be useful because it provides detailed information about each style. In particular, it differentiates between character styles, paragraph styles, and linked styles. A **character style** contains formatting options that affect the appearance of individual characters, such as font style, font color, font size, bold, italics, and underline. A **paragraph style** contains all the character formatting options as well as formatting options that affect the paragraph's appearance—line spacing, text alignment, tab stops, and borders. A **linked style** contains both character and paragraph formatting options. If you click in a paragraph or select a paragraph, and then apply a linked style, both the paragraph styles and character styles are applied to the entire paragraph. If you apply a linked style to a selected word or group of words in a paragraph, then only the character styles for that linked style are applied to the selected text; the paragraph styles are not applied to the paragraph itself. All of the heading styles in Word are linked styles.

REFERENCE

Modifying Styles Using the Style pane

- In the document, select text formatted with the style you want to modify, and make the formatting changes you want to add to the style.
- In the Styles group on the Home tab, click the Dialog Box Launcher to open the Styles pane.
- With the text still selected in the document, move the mouse pointer over the style you want to modify in the Styles pane to display an arrow next to the style's name, and then click the arrow.
- To save the modified style to the current document, click Update *Style Name* to Match Selection (where *Style Name* is the name of the style you want to modify).
- To save the modified style to the current template, click Modify to open the Modify Style dialog box, click the New documents based on this template option button, and then click the OK button.

To open the Styles pane and modify the Heading 1 style:

1. Click the **Home** tab, and then, in the Styles group, click the **Dialog Box Launcher**. The Styles pane opens. It might be docked on the right side of the document window, or it might be floating over the document.

TIP

To change how the styles are displayed in the Styles pane, click the Options link in the bottom-right corner of the Styles pane to open the Style Pane Options dialog box.

2. If the Styles pane is not docked on the right side of the document window, double-click the title bar of the pane. The Styles pane attaches itself to the right side of the document window, and the document zoom adjusts so you can see the full width of the page next to the Styles pane. See Figure 5-14. The blue outline around the Heading 1 style in the Styles pane indicates that the currently selected text, the "Project Summary" heading, is formatted with the Heading 1 style. A paragraph symbol to the right of a style name indicates a paragraph style, a lowercase letter "a" indicates a character style, and a combination of both a paragraph symbol and a lowercase letter "a" indicates a linked style. You can display even more information about a style by moving the mouse pointer over the style name in the Styles pane.

Figure 5-14 **Styles pane**

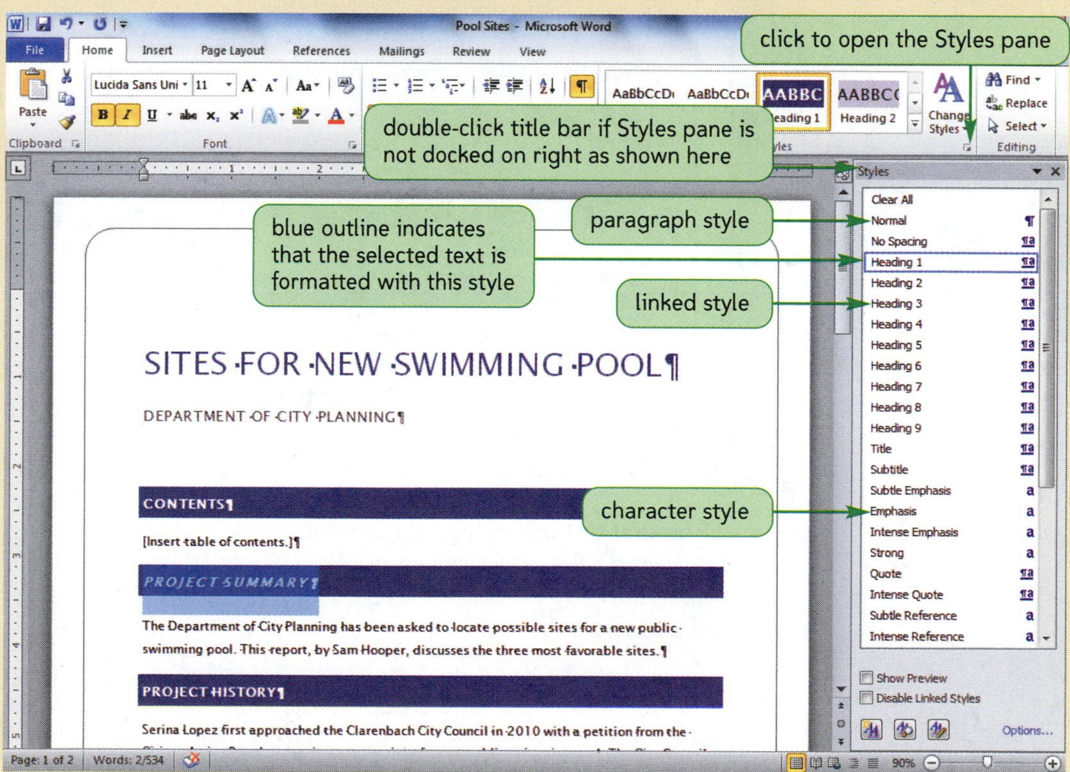

3. In the Styles pane, move the mouse pointer over **Heading 1**. An arrow next to the Heading 1 style name appears, and a ScreenTip with detailed information about the Heading 1 style opens below the style name. The information in the ScreenTip relates only to the formatting applied by default with the Heading 1 style; it makes no mention of italics, expanded character spacing, or the 15 points of space after the paragraph. Although you applied these formatting changes to the Project Summary heading, they are not yet part of the Heading 1 style.

4. Click the **Heading 1** arrow. A menu opens with options related to working with the Heading 1 style. See Figure 5-15.

Figure 5-15 Heading 1 style menu

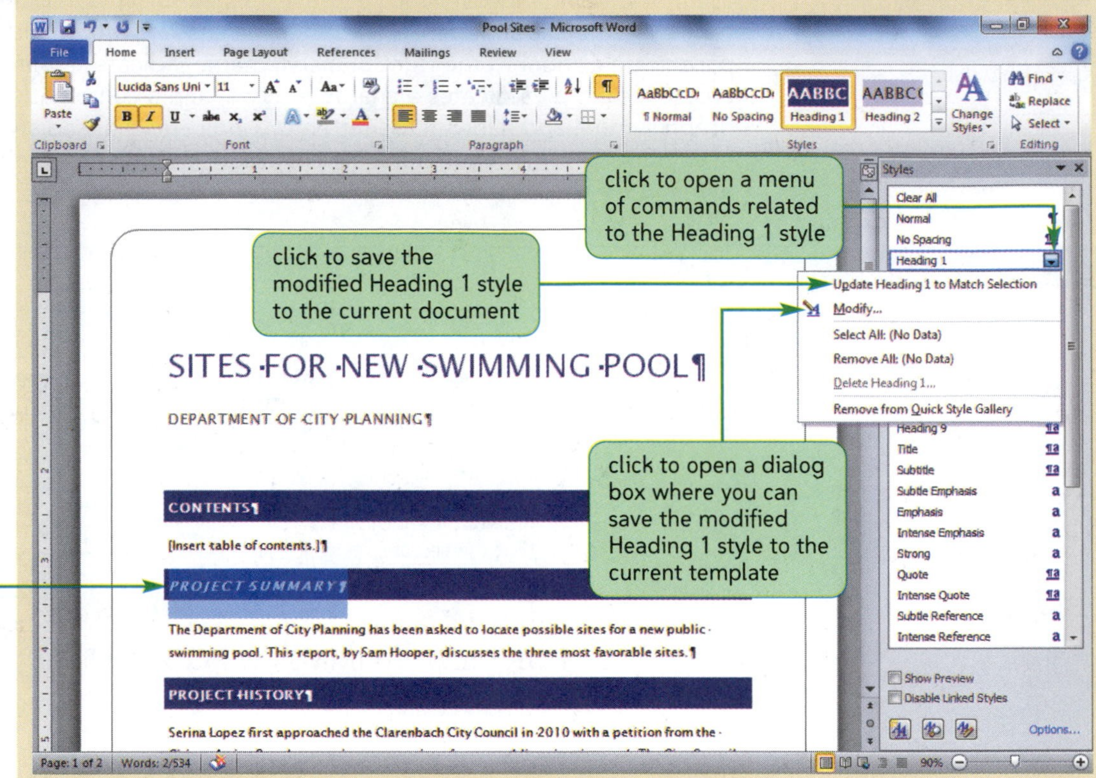

The first option on the menu modifies the Heading 1 style to match the selected text and saves the newly modified style to the current document. Sam wants to save the newly modified Heading 1 style to the current document, so you'll use the first option.

5. Click **Update Heading 1 to Match Selection**. The Heading 1 style changes to include all the changes Sam asked you to make to the Project Summary heading. As a result, all the headings in the document formatted in the Heading 1 style are now formatted with italics, expanded character spacing, and additional paragraph spacing.

6. In the Styles pane, click the **Close** button, and then save your work. The modified version of the Heading 1 style is saved along with the document. No other documents are affected by this change to the Heading 1 style.

You can also create a new style for a document, also from the Styles pane. You will do that in the next session.

REVIEW

Session 5.1 Quick Check

1. What template is used when you create a new blank document?
2. Explain how to insert a Word file into a document.
3. What are the three main components of a document theme?
4. Explain how to save a new theme.
5. Explain how to select a new style set.
6. Explain how to display the dialog box tab where you can adjust the character spacing for selected text.
7. True or False. The Quick Styles gallery shows the same styles as the Styles pane.
8. Explain how to save a modified style to the current document using the Styles pane.

SESSION 5.2 VISUAL OVERVIEW

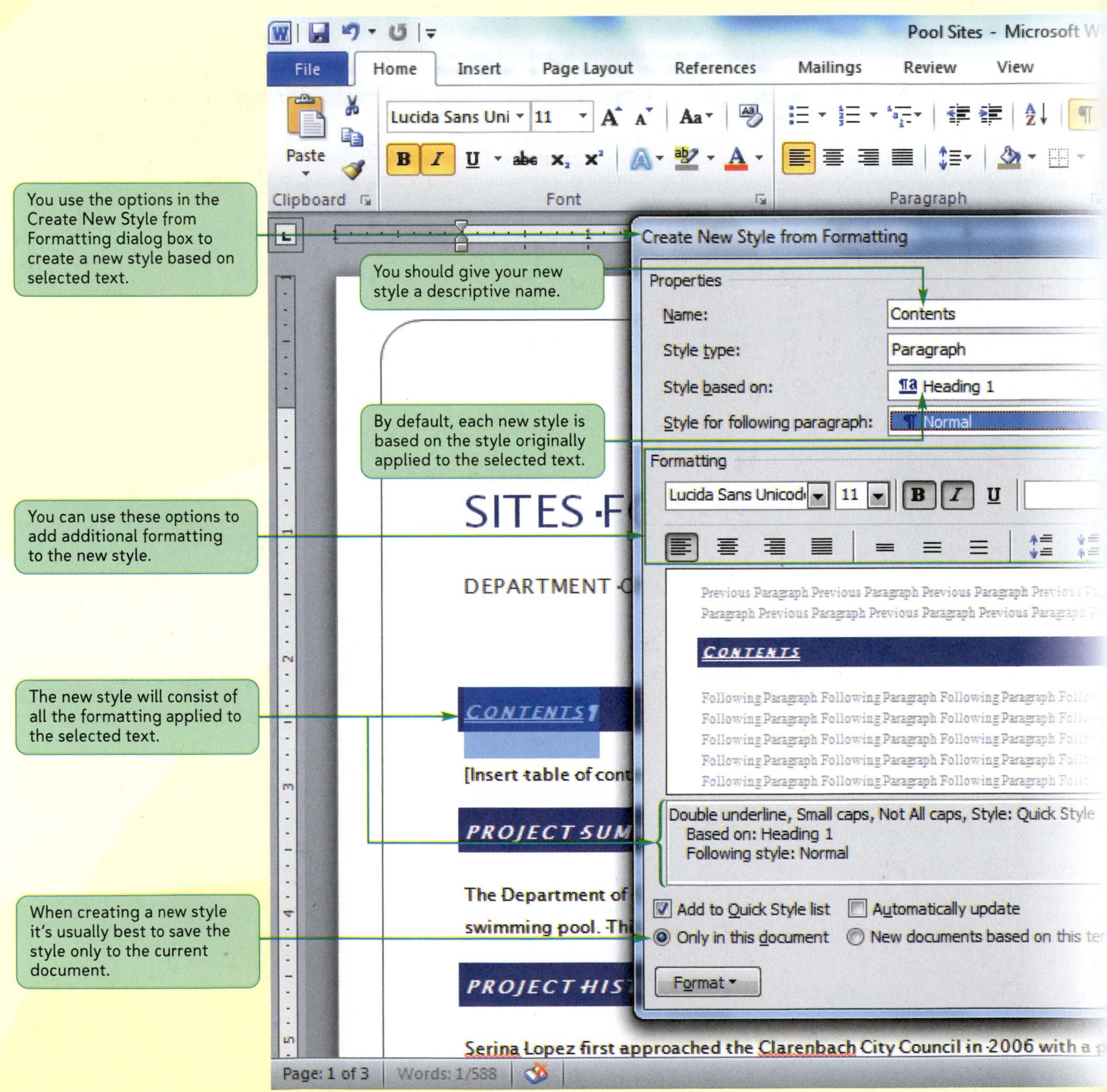
You use the options in the Create New Style from Formatting dialog box to create a new style based on selected text.
You should give your new style a descriptive name.
By default, each new style is based on the style originally applied to the selected text.
You can use these options to add additional formatting to the new style.
The new style will consist of all the formatting applied to the selected text.
When creating a new style it's usually best to save the style only to the current document.
Pool Sites - Microsoft W
File
Home
Insert
Page Layout
References
Mailings
Review
View
Lucida Sans Uni
11
Paste
Clipboard
Font
Paragraph
Create New Style from Formatting
Properties
Name:
Contents
Style type:
Paragraph
Style based on:
Heading 1
Style for following paragraph:
Normal
Formatting
Lucida Sans Unicod
SITES ·F
DEPARTMENT ·C
CONTENTS
[Insert table of cont
PROJECT SUM
The Department of
swimming pool. Thi
PROJECT HIST
Serina Lopez first approached the Clarenbach City Council in 2006 with a
Double underline, Small caps, Not All caps, Style: Quick Style
Based on: Heading 1
Following style: Normal
Add to Quick Style list
Automatically update
Only in this document
New documents based on this te
Format
Page: 1 of 3
Words: 1/588

CREATING A NEW STYLE

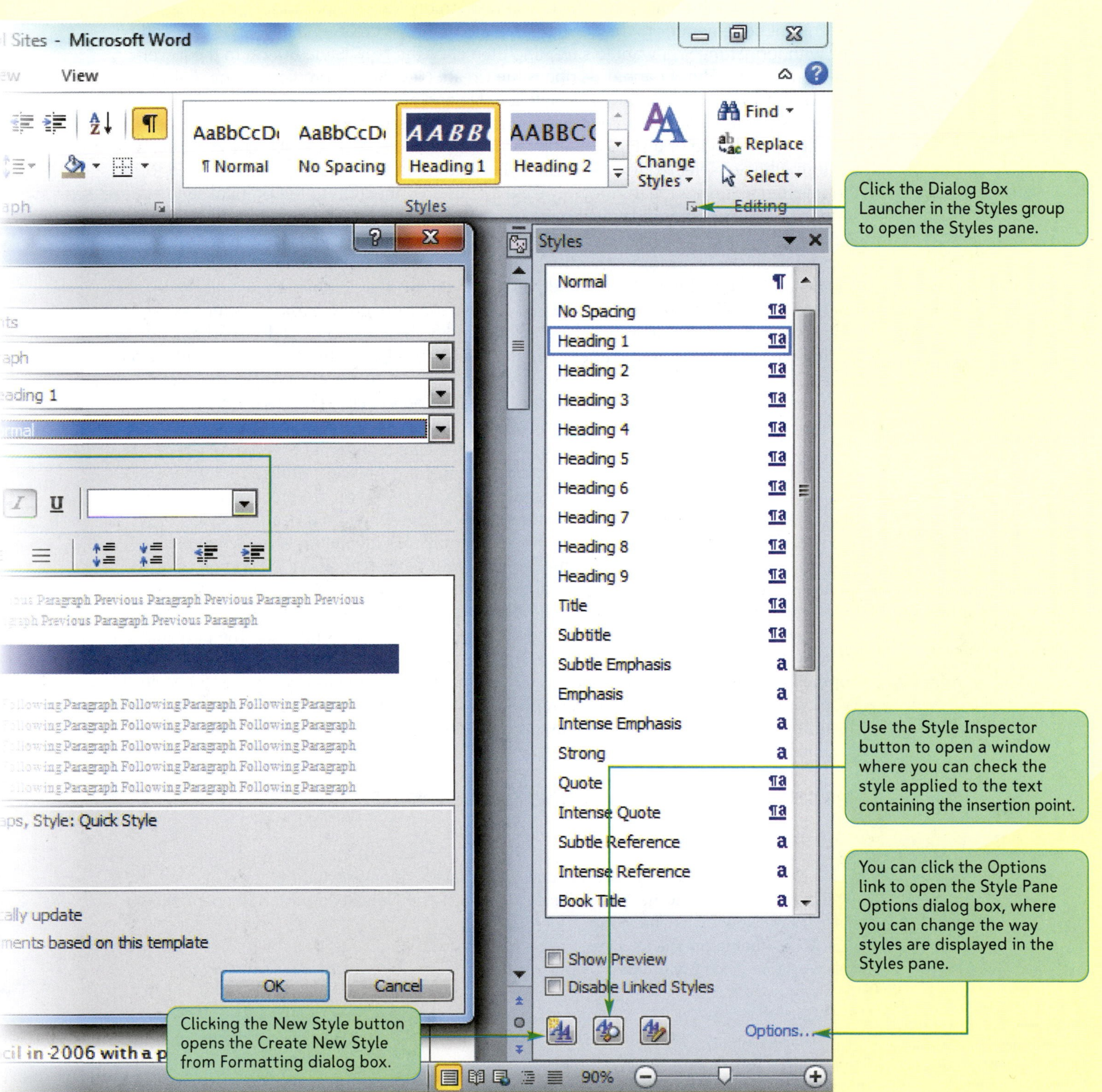

Creating a New Style

Creating a new style is similar to the steps you followed in the previous session to modify a style, except that, instead of updating an existing style to match the formatting of selected text, you save the formatting of the selected text as a new style. As when modifying styles, when creating a new style you need to decide whether to save the style to the current document or to the current template. To begin creating a new style, select the text with formatting you want to save, and then click the New Style button in the lower-left corner of the Styles pane. This opens the Create New Style from Formatting dialog box, where you can assign the new style a name and adjust other settings.

Remember that all text in your document has a style applied to it, whether it is the default Normal style or a style you applied. When you create a new style based upon the formatting of selected text, the new style is based on the style originally applied to the selected text. That means the new style retains a connection to the original style, so that if you make modifications to the original style, these modifications will also be applied to the new style. For example, suppose you need to create a new style that will be used exclusively for formatting the heading "Budget" in all upcoming reports. You could start by selecting text formatted with the Heading 1 style, then change the font color of the selected text to purple, and then save the formatting of the selected text as a new style named "Budget." Later on, if you modify the Heading 1 style—perhaps by adding italics—the text in the document that is formatted with the Budget style will also have italics, because it is based on the Heading 1 style. Note that the opposite is not true: changes to the new style do *not* affect the style on which it is based.

This connection between a new style and the style on which it is based enforces a consistent look among styles, encouraging you to create a document with a coherent design. To take full advantage of this feature, you need to think carefully about what style you want to use as the basis for a new style. For example, if you are creating a new style that will be used as a heading, you should base that new style on a heading style.

TIP

To delete a new style, point to the style's name in the Styles pane, click the down arrow next to the style name, click Revert to *Style Name*, and then click Yes.

When creating a new style, you also need to think about what happens when the insertion point is in a paragraph formatted with your new style, and then you press the Enter key to start a new paragraph. With the default heading styles in Word, a new paragraph created in this way is formatted in the Normal style. That makes sense, because you typically only want to format a single paragraph with a heading style. The paragraph after a heading style is usually body text formatted in the Normal style. Unless you have compelling reason to do otherwise, you should also select the Normal style as the style Word will use to format a new paragraph following your new heading style. You make this selection using the Style for following paragraph box in the Create New Style from Formatting dialog box.

REFERENCE

Creating a New Style

- Select text with the formatting you want to save as a new style.
- In the lower-left corner of the Styles pane, click the New Style button to open the Create New Style from Formatting dialog box.
- Type a name for the new style in the Name box.
- Verify that the Style based on box displays the style on which you want to base your new style.
- Click the Style for following paragraph arrow, and click Normal.
- To save the new style to the current document, verify that the Only in this document option button is selected.
- To save the style to the current template, click the New documents based on this template option button.
- Click the OK button.

Sam is ready for you to create a new style for the "Contents" heading. The new style will be based on the Heading 1 style. It will look just like the Heading 1 style, except that instead of formatting text in all capital letters, it will format text in smaller versions of capital letters known as **small caps**. Also, the new style will apply an underline.

To format the Contents heading with the options for the new style:

1. If you took a break after the last session, make sure the Pool Sites document is open in Print Layout view with the nonprinting characters and the ruler displayed.
2. Select the **Contents** heading. You use the Font dialog box to format text in small caps.
3. In the Font group on the Home tab, click the **Dialog Box Launcher** and then, in the Font dialog box, click the **Font** tab if necessary. In the Effects section, the All caps check box is currently selected. Instead of All caps (which formats text in regularly sized capital letters), you need to select Small caps.
4. In the Effects section, click the **Small caps** check box to add a check. The check is removed from the All caps check box.
5. Click the **Underline style** arrow, and click the **double underline** style. The Preview section of the Font dialog box displays a preview of the new formatting. See Figure 5-16.

TIP

To change the case of selected text, use the Change Case button in the Font group on the Home tab.

Figure 5-16 Formatting the Contents heading

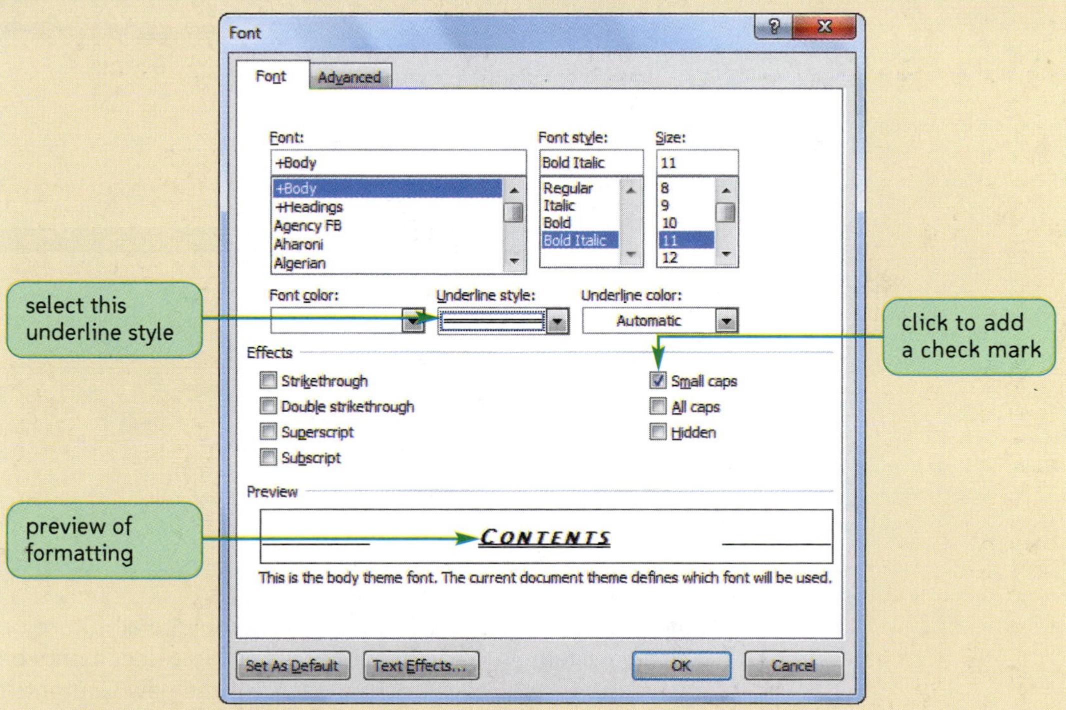

6. Click the **OK** button. The Font dialog box closes, and the "Contents" heading is formatted in small caps with a double underline.

Now that the text is formatted the way you want, you can save its formatting as a new style.

To save the formatting of the Contents heading as a new style:

1. In the Styles group, click the **Dialog Box Launcher** to open the Styles pane.
2. With the **Contents** heading still selected, click the **New Style** button in the lower-left corner of the Styles pane. The Create New Style from Formatting dialog box opens. A default name for the new style, "Style1," appears selected in the Name box. The name "Style1" also appears in the Style for following paragraph box.
3. Type **Contents**. The default style name is replaced with the new one. The Style based on box tells you that the new Contents style is based on the Heading 1 style, which is what you want. The Style for following paragraph box is now blank. You need to select the Normal style.
4. Click the **Style for following paragraph** arrow and then click **Normal**. See Figure 5-17.

Figure 5-17 Creating a new style

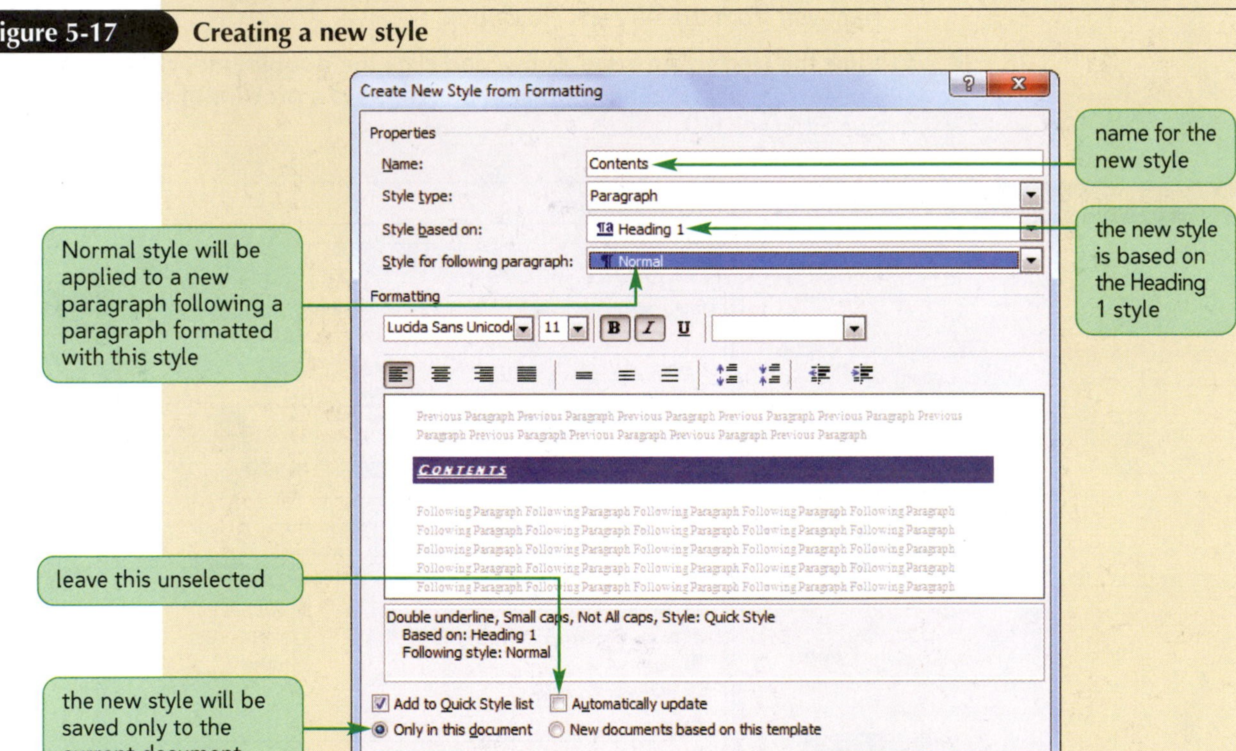

If you wanted to make the new style available to all future documents based on the current template, you would click the New documents based on this template option button. However, you want to save the new Contents style only to the current document, so you will accept that default setting, with the Only in this document option button selected. Note that, by default, the Automatically update check box is *not* selected. As a general rule, you should never select this check box, because it can produce unpredictable results in future documents based on the same template.

5. Click the **OK** button. The Create New Style from Formatting dialog box closes. The new Contents style is added to the Quick Styles gallery and to the Styles pane. If Sam needs to format additional headings with this new style, he can access it in either location. See Figure 5-18.

Figure 5-18 **Contents style added to Quick Styles gallery and Styles pane**

TIP

To remove a style from the Quick Styles gallery, right-click it in the Quick Styles gallery and then click Remove from Quick Style Gallery.

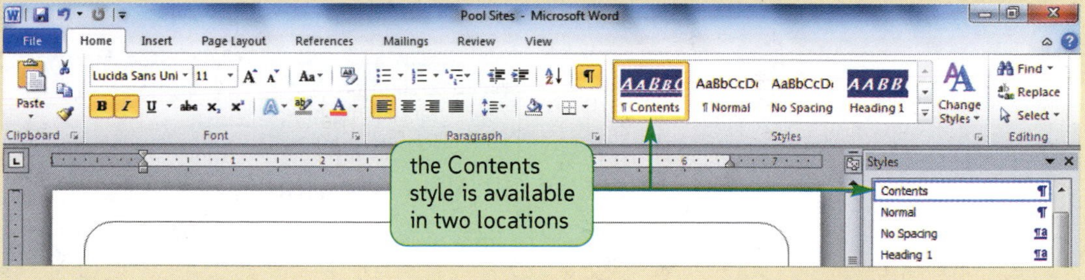
the Contents style is available in two locations

6. Save the document.

Inspecting and Comparing Styles

If you create a document with many styles, it's easy to lose track of the style applied to each paragraph and the formatting associated with each style. To see a comparison of two styles, you can use the **Reveal Formatting pane**. To quickly determine which style is applied to a paragraph, you can click a paragraph, and then look to see which style is selected in the Styles Pane. However, if you need to check numerous paragraphs in a long document, it's easier to use the **Style Inspector pane**, which remains open while you scroll through the document and displays only the style for the paragraph that currently contains the insertion point.

Sam asks you to show him how to use the Style Inspector and the Reveal Formatting panes in order to learn more about the Normal and the Heading 2 styles.

To use the Style Inspector and Reveal Formatting panes:

1. Click anywhere in the **[Insert table of contents.]** paragraph.
2. At the bottom of the Styles pane, click the **Style Inspector** button. The Style Inspector opens. The top pane displays the name of the style applied to the paragraph that currently contains the insertion point. See Figure 5-19.

Figure 5-19 Style Inspector window

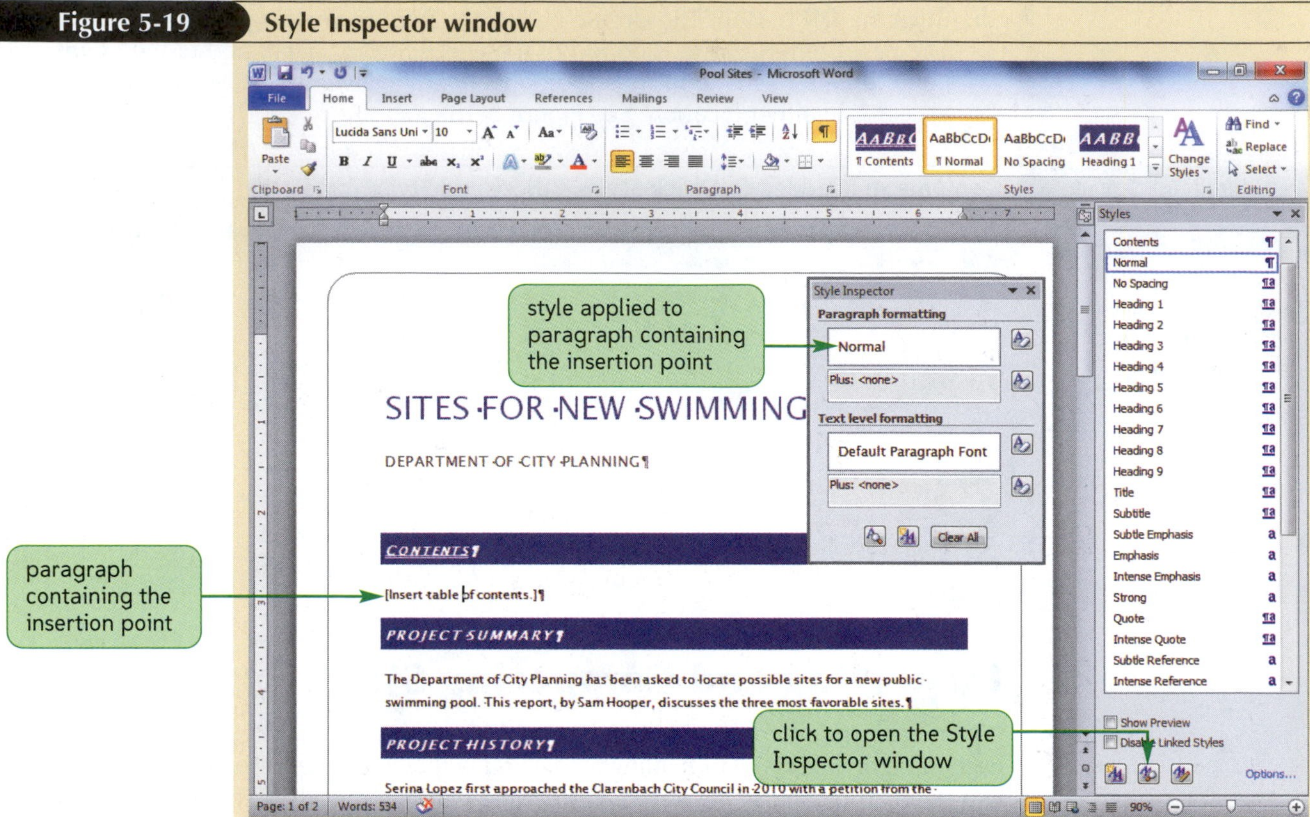

3. Press the **Ctrl+↓** keys. In the document, the insertion point moves down to the next paragraph. The Style Inspector tells you that this paragraph is formatted with the Heading 1 style.

4. Continue to use the **Ctrl+↓** key combination to move the insertion point down through the paragraphs of the document, observing the style names displayed in the Style Inspector.

5. Scroll up and select the paragraph **[Insert table of contents.]**, click the **Reveal Formatting** button at the bottom of the Style Inspector window to open the Reveal Formatting pane, and then close the Style Inspector. The Reveal Formatting pane displays detailed information about the Normal style, the style applied to the selected paragraph.

6. In the Reveal Formatting pane, click the **Compare to another selection** check box to select it. The options in the Reveal Formatting pane change to allow you to compare one style to another. Under Selected text, both text boxes display copies of the selected text, "[Insert a table of contents.]" This tells you that, currently, the style applied to the selected text (that is, the Normal style) is being compared to itself. Now you'll compare the Normal style to the Heading 2 style.

7. In the document, scroll down to page 2 and select the text **Villas Park**, which is formatted with the Heading 2 style. The text "Villas Park" appears in the Reveal Formatting pane, in the text box below "[Insert a table of contents.]" The Formatting differences section displays information about the styles applied to the two different text samples. The information in the Reveal Formatting pane contains a lot of detail. But, generally, if you see two settings separated by a hyphen and a greater than symbol, the item on the right relates to the text in the bottom box. For example, in the Font section, you see "10pt -> 11 pt." This tells you

TIP

Text formatted in a white font, such as the Contents heading, is not visible in the text boxes at the top of the Reveal Formatting pane. To use the Reveal Formatting pane with white text, temporarily format it in black.

that the item in the top text box, "[Insert a table of contents.]," is formatted in a 10-point font, whereas the item in the bottom text box, "Villas Park," is formatted in an 11-point font. See Figure 5-20.

Figure 5-20 Comparing two styles

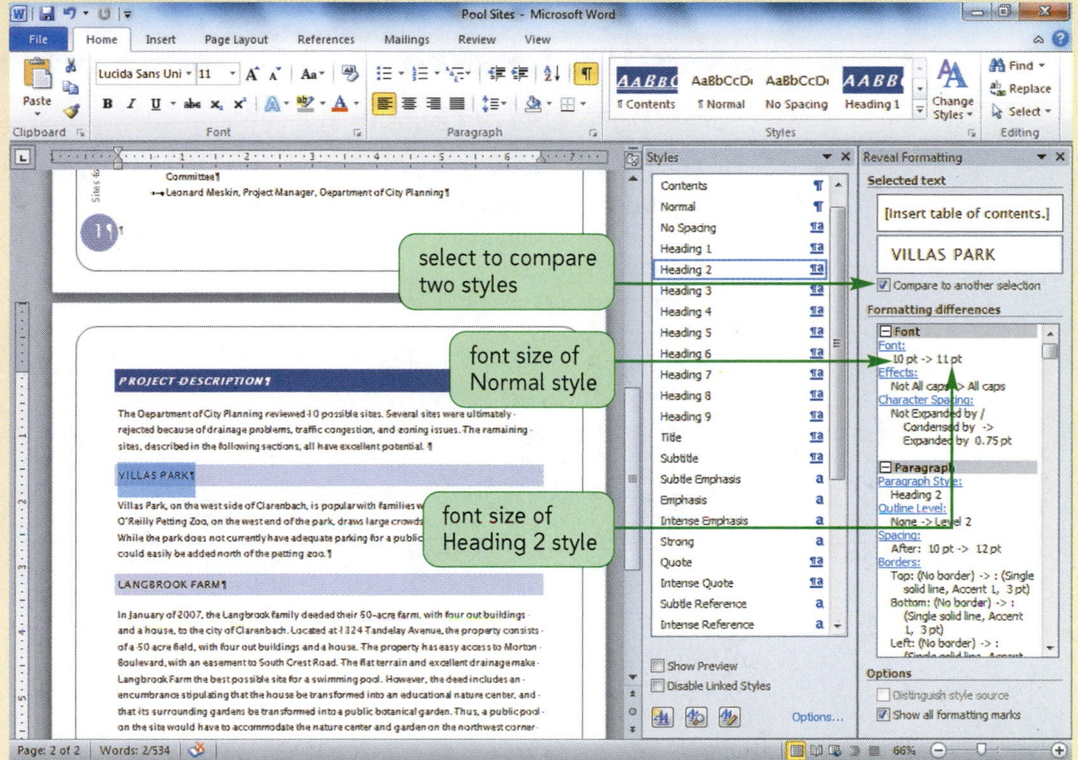

8. In the Reveal Formatting pane, click the **Close** button ✖, and then click the **Close** button ✖ in the Styles pane.

You are finished formatting the Pool Sites report with themes and styles. Now Sam asks you to create a table of contents for the report.

Creating a Table of Contents

You can use the Table of Contents button in the Table of Contents group on the References tab to generate a table of contents that includes any text to which you have applied heading styles. A table of contents is essentially an outline of the document. By default, Heading 1 text is aligned on the left, Heading 2 text is indented slightly to the right below the Heading 1 paragraphs, Heading 3 text is indented slightly to the right below the Heading 2 paragraphs, and so on.

The page numbers and headings in a table of contents in Word are hyperlinks that you can click to jump to a particular part of the document. If you add or delete a heading in the document, or add body text that causes one or more headings to move to a new page, you can quickly update the table of contents by clicking the Update Table button in the Table of Contents group on the References tab. To add text that is not formatted as a heading to the table of contents, you can select the text, format it as a heading, and then update the table of contents. However, if you already have the References tab displayed, it's more efficient to select the text in the document, use the Add Text button in the Table of Contents group to add a Heading style, and then update the table of contents.

When inserting a table of contents, you can insert one of the predesigned formats available from the Table of Contents button in the Table of Contents group on the References tab. If you prefer to select from more options, you can open the Table of Contents dialog box. From within the Table of Contents dialog box, you can adjust the level assigned to each style within the table of contents.

REFERENCE

Creating a Table of Contents

- Apply the built-in heading styles, such as Heading 1, Heading 2, and Heading 3, to the appropriate text in the document.
- Move the insertion point to the location in the document where you want to insert the table of contents.
- Click the References tab, and then click the Table of Contents button in the Table of Contents group.
- To insert a predesigned table of contents, click one of the Automatic table of contents styles in the Table of Contents menu.
- To open a dialog box where you can choose from a variety of table of contents settings, click Insert Table of Contents to open the Table of Contents dialog box. Click the Formats arrow and select a style, change the Show levels setting to the number of heading levels you want to include in the table of contents, verify that the Show page numbers check box is selected, and then click the OK button.

The current draft of Sam's report is fairly short, but the final document will be much longer. He asks you to create a table of contents for the report now, just after the "Contents" heading. Then, as Sam adds sections to the report, he can update the table of contents.

To insert the table of contents into the Pool Sites document:

1. On page 1, below the heading "Contents," delete the placeholder text **[Insert a table of contents.]**. Do not delete the paragraph mark after the placeholder text. Your insertion point should now be located in the blank paragraph between the "Contents" heading and the "Project Summary" heading.

TIP

To delete a table of contents, click the Table of Contents button, and then click Remove Table of Contents.

2. Click the **References** tab, and then click the **Table of Contents** button in the Table of Contents group. The Table of Contents menu opens, displaying a gallery of table of contents formats. See Figure 5-21. The Automatic options insert a table of contents made up of the first three levels of document headings, in a predefined format. Each of the Automatic options also includes a heading for the Table of Contents. Because Sam's document already contains the heading "Contents," you do not want to use either of the Automatic options. The Manual option is useful only in specialized situations, when you need to type the table of contents yourself—for example, when creating a book manuscript for an academic publisher. Instead of using one of the Automatic options, you will use the Insert Table of Contents command to open the Table of Contents dialog box.

Figure 5-21 Table of Contents gallery

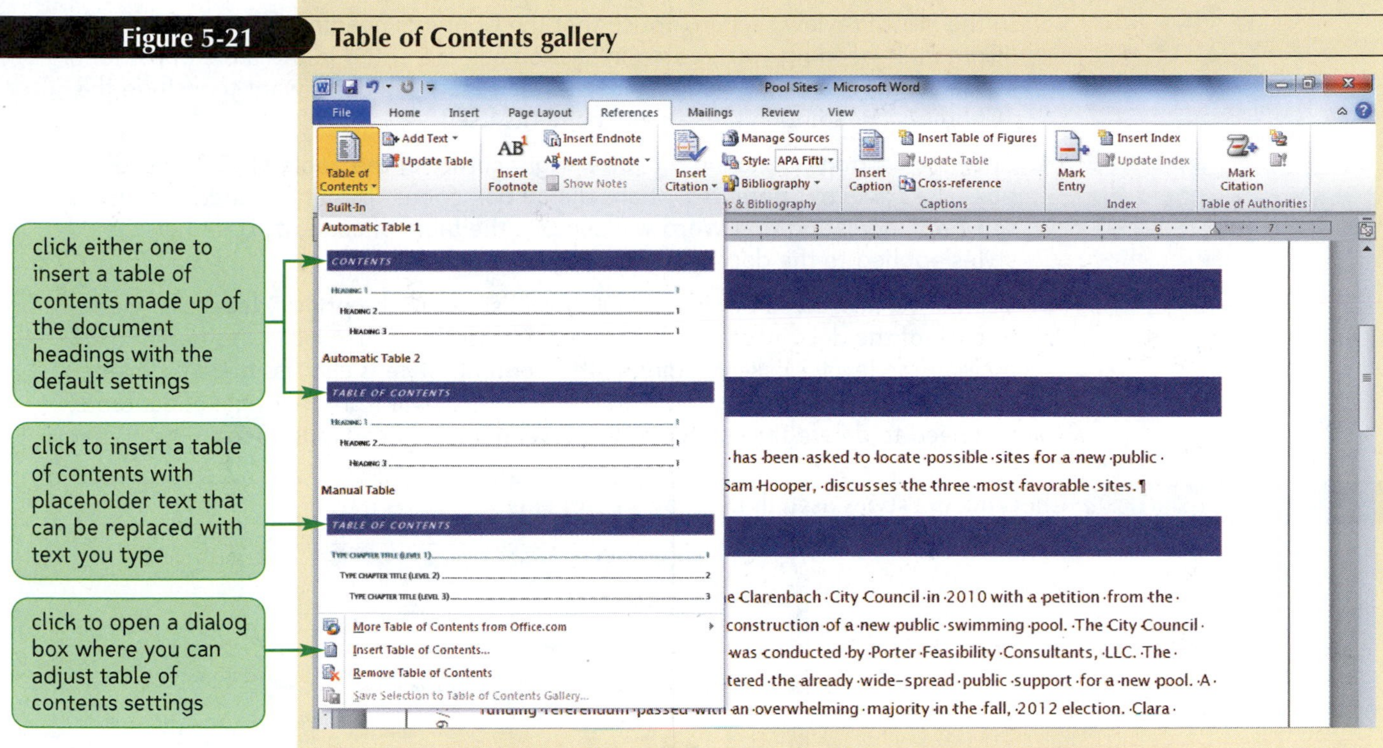

3. Below the Table of Contents gallery, click **Insert Table of Contents**. The Table of Contents dialog box opens, with the Table of Contents tab displayed. See Figure 5-22. The Print Preview on the left shows the appearance of the table of contents in a Print Layout view, while the Web Preview on the right shows what the table of contents would look like if you displayed it in Web Layout view. The Formats box shows the default option, From template, which applies the table of contents styles provided by the document's template.

Figure 5-22 Table of Contents dialog box

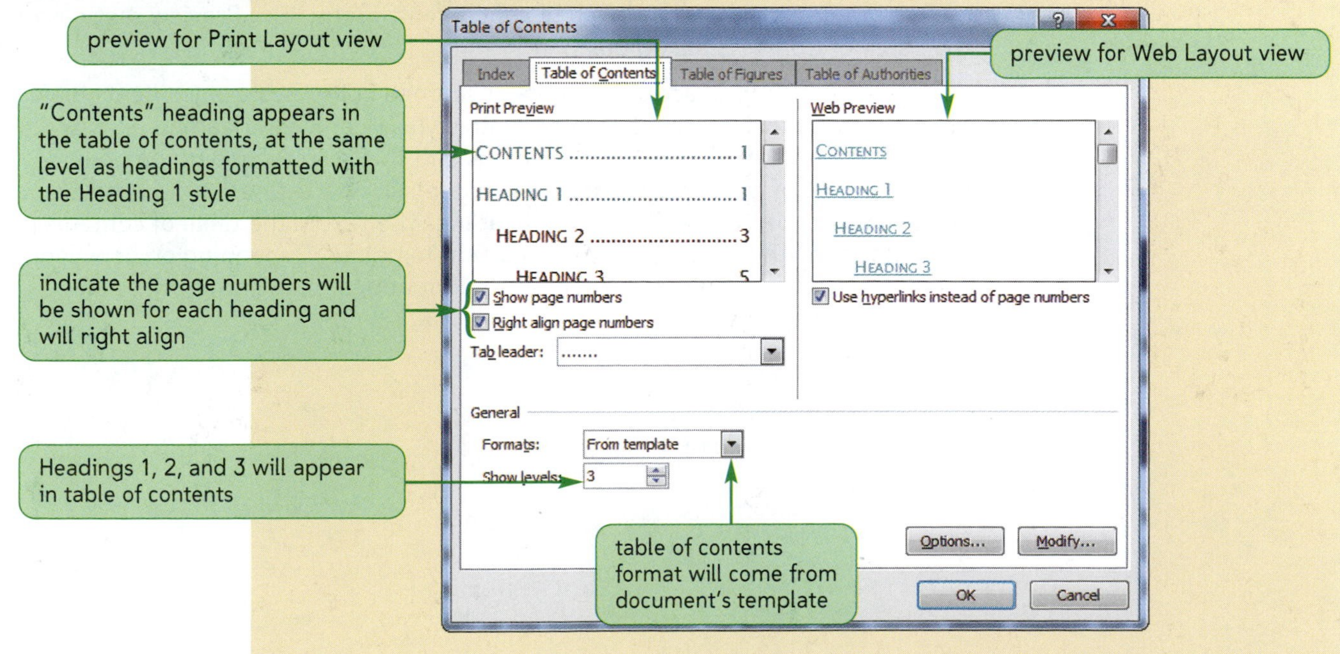

In the Print Preview section, notice that the Contents heading style, applied to the "Contents" heading you created in Session 5.1, is treated in the table of contents at the same level as the Heading 1 style. However, you don't want to include the "Contents" heading in the table of contents itself.

4. Click the **Options** button in the lower-right corner of the Table of Contents dialog box. The Table of Contents Options dialog box opens. The Styles check box is selected, indicating that Word will compile the table of contents based on the styles applied to the document headings.

5. Use the vertical scroll bar in the TOC level list to see the priority level assigned to each of the document styles. Heading 1 is assigned to level 1, and Heading 2 is assigned to level 2. Like Heading 1, the Contents style is also assigned to level 1. To remove any text formatted with the Contents style from the table of contents, you need to delete the Contents style level number. See Figure 5-23.

Figure 5-23 **Checking the styles used in the table of contents**

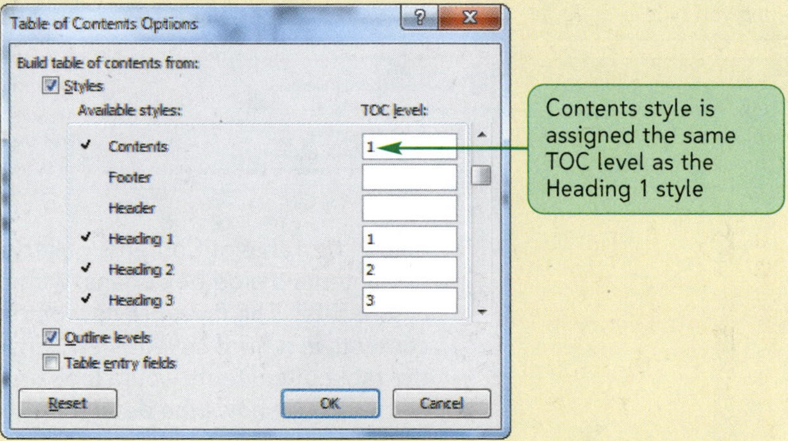

6. Delete the **1** from the TOC level box for the Contents style, and then click the **OK** button to close the Table of Contents Options dialog box. The "Contents" heading no longer appears in the sample table of contents in the Print Preview sections of the Table of Contents dialog box.

7. Click the **OK** button to accept the default settings in the Table of Contents dialog box. Word searches for text formatted with styles Heading 1, Heading 2, and Heading 3, and then places those headings and their corresponding page numbers in a table of contents. The table of contents is inserted at the insertion point, which appears below the "Contents" heading. The text in the table of contents is formatted with the TOC styles for the current template. Depending on how your computer is set up, the table of contents might appear on a light gray background. See Figure 5-24.

Figure 5-24 Table of contents inserted into document

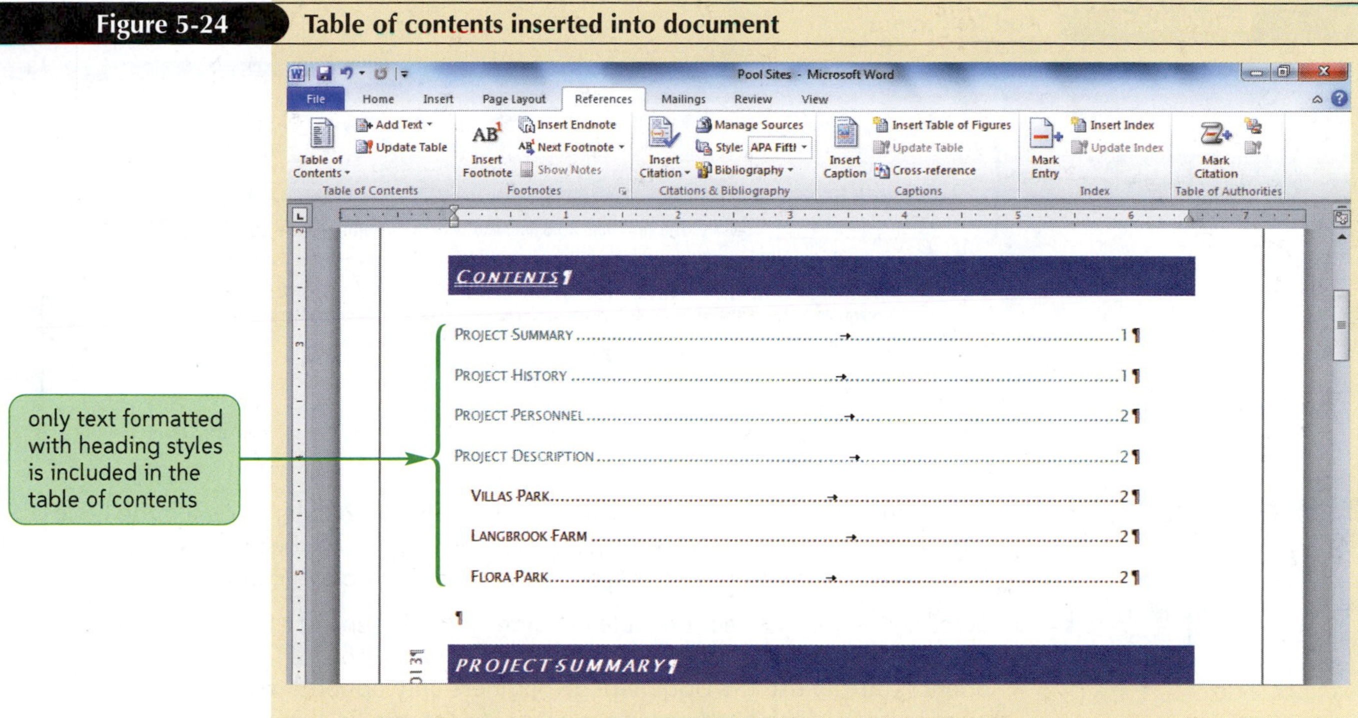

You can check the hyperlink formatting to make sure the headings really do function as links.

8. Press and hold the **Ctrl** key while you click **LANGBROOK FARM** in the table of contents. The insertion point moves to the beginning of the "Langbrook Farm" heading near the bottom of page 2.
9. Save the document.

Sam just finished compiling information on another potential pool site. He has the information saved as a Word file, which he asks you to insert at the end of the Pool Sites document. You will do this next, and then add the new heading to the table of contents.

To add a section to the Pool Sites document and then update the table of contents:

1. Press the **Ctrl+End** keys to move the insertion point to the end of the document, and then insert the file **Willow Grove** from the Word5\Tutorial folder included with your Data Files.
2. Select the paragraph **Willow Grove**.
3. Click the **References** tab, and then click the **Add Text** button in the Table of Contents group. The Add Text menu opens. See Figure 5-25.

Figure 5-25 Add Text menu

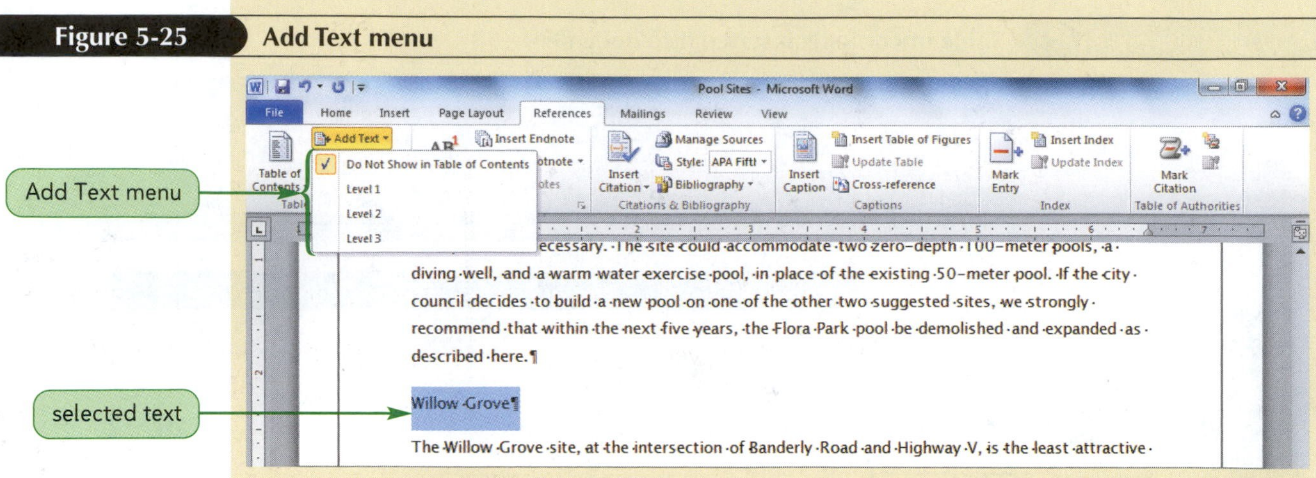

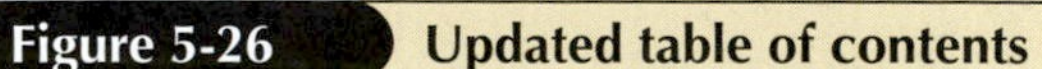

TIP

You can also format new text with a heading style in the Quick Styles gallery, and then update the table of contents.

4. Click **Level 2**. The text is formatted with the Heading 2 style, to match the headings for the sections about the other possible pool sites. Now that the text is formatted with a heading style, you can update the table of contents.
5. Scroll up so you can see the table of contents, and then click the **Update Table** button in the Table of Contents group. The Update Table of Contents dialog box opens. You can use the Update page numbers only option button if you don't want to update the headings in the table of contents. In this case, you have added a new section, so you want to update the entire table of contents.
6. Click the **Update entire table** option button to select it, and then click the **OK** button. The table of contents is updated to include the Willow Grove heading. See Figure 5-26.

Figure 5-26 Updated table of contents

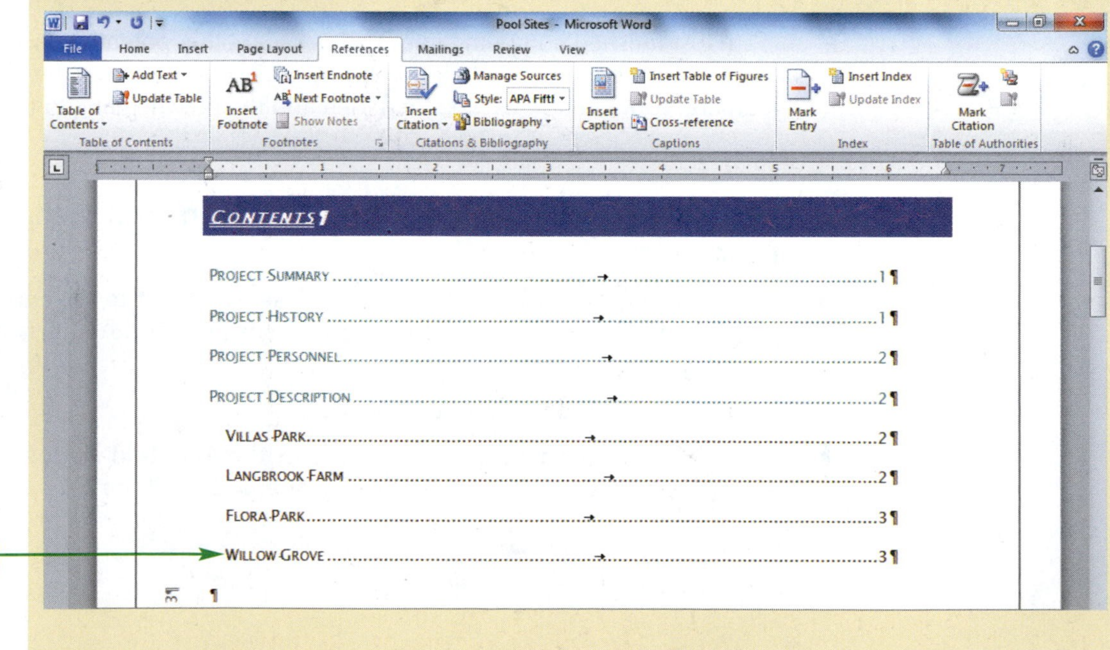

7. Save your work.

Now Sam needs you to perform a few research tasks, starting with looking up a definition and a synonym.

Using the Research Task Pane

You can use the **Research task pane** to look up dictionary definitions in the Encarta Dictionary, which is installed with Word, and to search for synonyms in Word's thesaurus. In addition, you can search for information in online general interest encyclopedias and in sources devoted to particular topics, such as business and finance. If you prefer, you can use Microsoft's Bing search engine to search the entire Web from the Research task pane. The Research and Thesaurus buttons in the Proofing group both open the Research task pane. However, it's easiest to right-click the word or the selected phrase you want to look up, and then select an option on the shortcut menu.

First, Sam wants to make sure he understands the term *encumbrance,* in the paragraph at the bottom of page 2.

To look up a definition in the Research task pane:

1. Find the word **encumbrance** in the last paragraph on Page 2, right-click **encumbrance**, and then point to **Look Up** on the shortcut menu. A submenu of research sources opens, as shown in Figure 5-27. Sam would like to look up the term "encumbrance" in Word's Encarta Dictionary.

Figure 5-27 **Look Up command in shortcut menu**

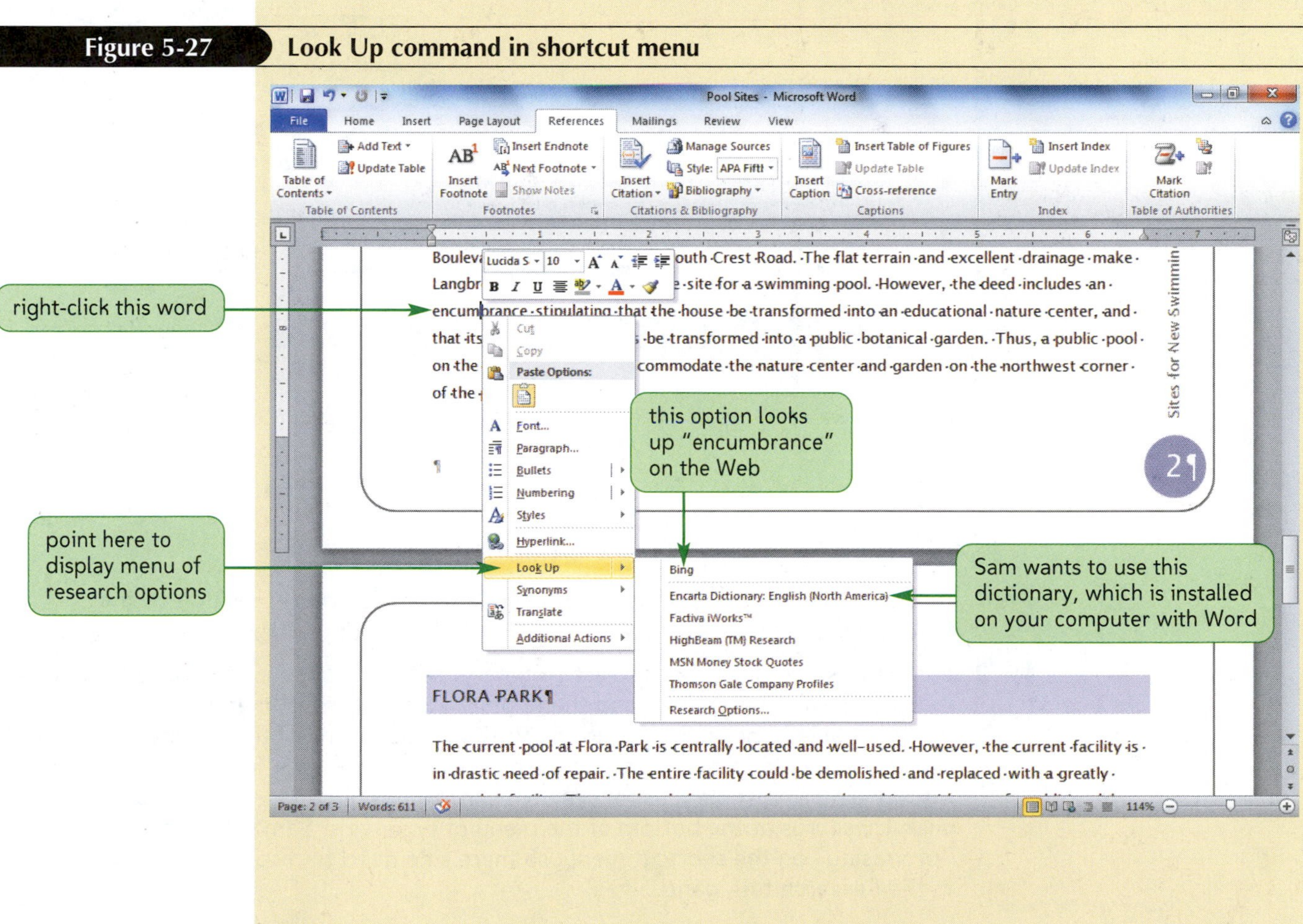

2. Click **Encarta Dictionary: English (North America)**. The Research task pane opens on the right side of the document window, displaying two definitions for the noun *encumbrance*. Definition 2, a "burden or claim on property" is the relevant definition in this case. See Figure 5-28. If you wanted to copy this definition to the Clipboard so you could use it in a document, you could right-click it in the Research task pane and then click Copy. Sam doesn't need you to do that in this case, however.

Figure 5-28 Definitions displayed in the Research task pane

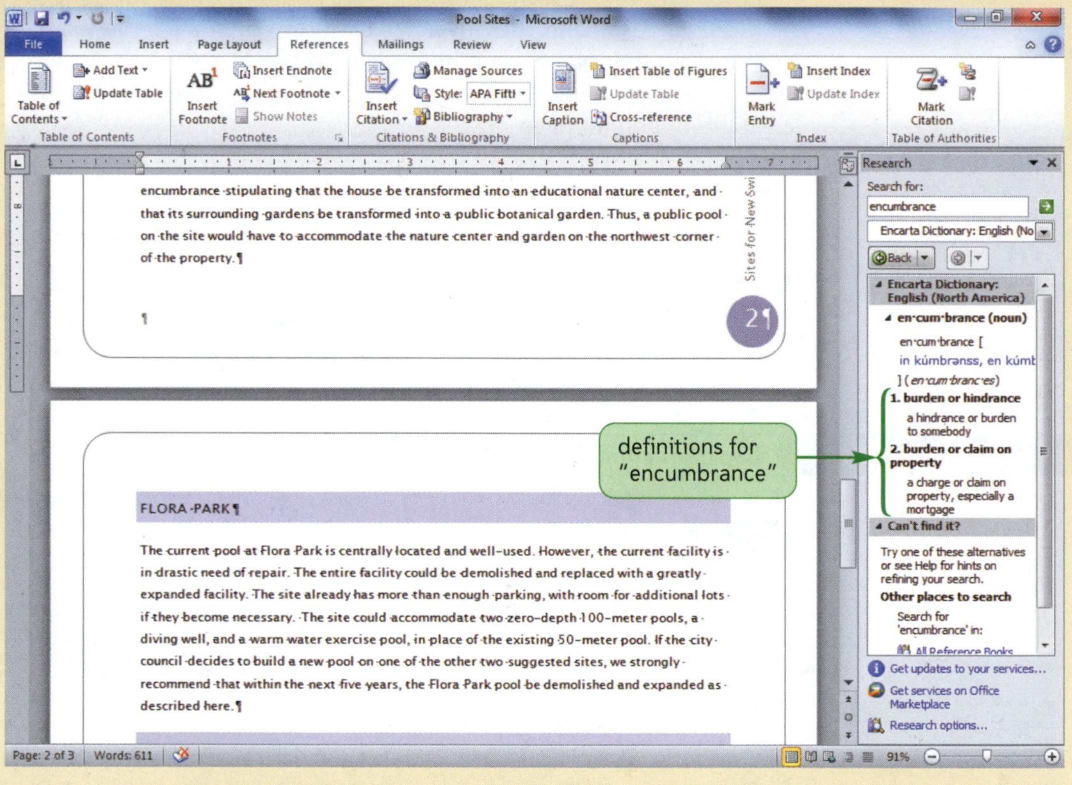

Next, Sam wants to replace the word "favorable" in the Project Summary section with a synonym.

To look up a synonym in the thesaurus:

1. In the document, scroll up to display the "Project Summary" section on the first page.
2. In the last sentence of the "Project Summary" section, right-click the word **favorable** to open the shortcut menu, and then point to **Synonyms**. A menu of synonyms for "favorable" opens. See Figure 5-29. You can click any of the synonyms on the shortcut menu to insert it in the document as a replacement for "favorable." To display a more complete list of synonyms in the Research task pane, you could click Thesaurus at the bottom of the menu of synonyms. Sam likes the synonym "promising" on the shortcut menu, so there's no need to display more synonyms in the Research task pane.

Figure 5-29 Synonyms for "favorable"

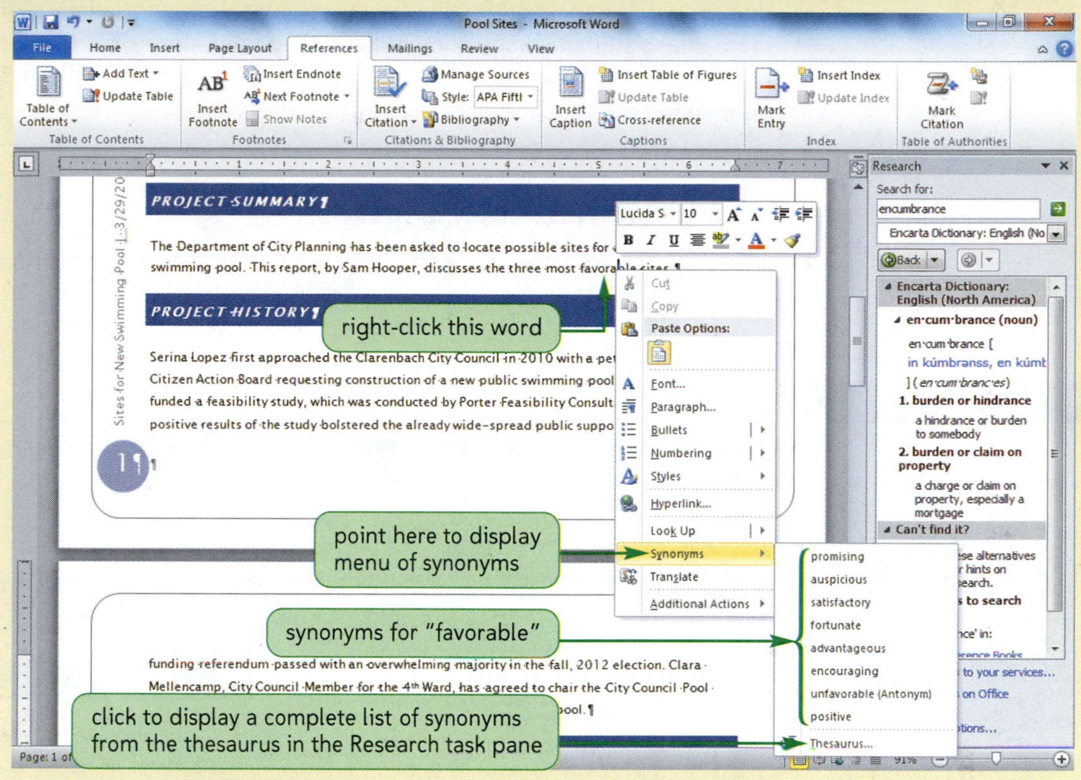

3. Click **promising**. The shortcut menus close and the word "promising" is inserted in the document, as a replacement for "favorable."
4. Close the Research task pane, and then save the document.

Next, Sam needs to view a Spanish translation of part of the document.

Translating Text

The Translate button in the Language group on the Review tab offers three options for translating text into other languages. The Translate Document option sends your entire document to the Microsoft Translator Web site, which then displays your original document in a browser, side-by-side with the translated version. The Translate Selected Text option opens the Research task pane (if it is not already open), where you can select the language you want to translate your text into, and then read the translation in the Research task pane. The Mini Translator option opens a small window that displays a translation when you point to selected text in your document.

Before you can use the Translate Document option or the Mini Translator, you need to select the original language and the translation language. To do that, you click the Choose Translation Language command on the Translate menu to open the Translation Language Options dialog box. This dialog box includes two sections, one for the Translate Document option, and one for the Mini Translator, where you can select the language into which you want to translate the current text.

As you use Word's translation tools, keep in mind that the translations are generated by computer, so they are not necessarily perfect. That is, they might not sound exactly right to a native speaker. After you translate all or part of a document, make sure to have an expert in the language review the translation and make any necessary corrections.

Sam plans to distribute Spanish versions of his Pool Site report to the organization that provided a major donation for the new pool, the Association of Latino Businesses. He will ask a Spanish-speaking colleague to help him prepare a complete translation. For now, he wants to try out the translation tools. First you will select the translation languages.

To select a translation language:

1. Click the **Review** tab, and then click the **Translate** button in the Language group. The Translate menu opens. You might see translation languages specified in brackets next to some of these options or you might not. See Figure 5-30.

Figure 5-30 Translate menu

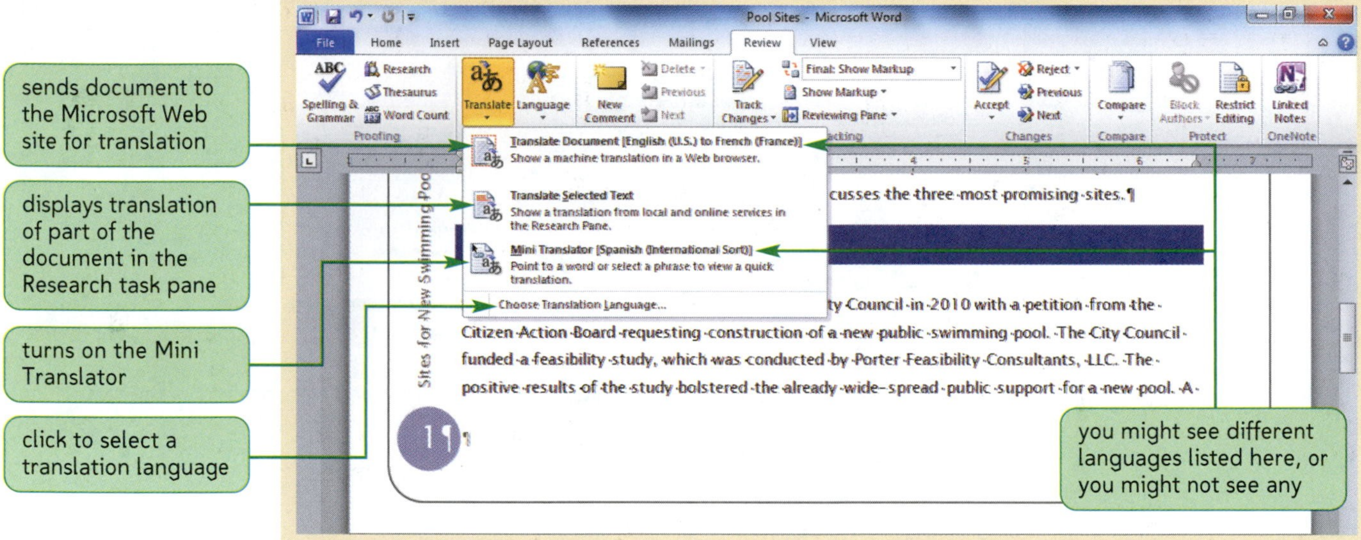

sends document to the Microsoft Web site for translation

displays translation of part of the document in the Research task pane

turns on the Mini Translator

click to select a translation language

you might see different languages listed here, or you might not see any

2. Click **Choose Translation Language**. The Translation Language Options dialog box opens. You can use the top box to select the language that the Mini Translator will translate the current document into. You can use the bottom two boxes to select the languages you want to translate to and from when using the Translate Document option on the Translate menu.
3. In the Choose Mini Translator language section, click the **Translate to** arrow to display a list of languages, scroll down the list if necessary, and then, if necessary, click **Spanish (International Sort)**.
4. In the Choose document translation languages section, click the **Translate from** arrow, select **English (U.S.)**, if necessary, click the **Translate to** arrow, and then click **Spanish (International Sort)**, if necessary. See Figure 5-31.

Figure 5-31 Selecting the translation language for the Mini Translator

5. Click the **OK** button to close the dialog box and return to the document.

Once you have selected a translation language, you can begin translating text in your document. Next you will start the Mini Translator and translate some text.

Note: The following steps require an Internet connection. If your computer is not connected to the Internet, read the following steps but do not perform them.

To use the translator to translate portions of the Pool Sites document:

1. In the Language group, click the **Translate** button, and then click **Mini Translator [Spanish (International Sort)]**. The Translate menu closes. To display the Mini Translator, you need to point to a word or a selected phrase.
2. In the "Project Summary" section, select the sentence that begins **The Department of City Planning...**
3. Position the mouse pointer  over the selected text. A faint image of the Mini Translator appears.
4. Move the mouse pointer down or up over the Mini Translator window to display it fully. See Figure 5-32. If your computer has speakers installed, you can click the Mini Translator's Play button to hear the selected text read aloud.

TIP

To display a translation of a single word, click in the word and then use the mouse pointer to display the Mini Translator.

Figure 5-32 Mini Translator window

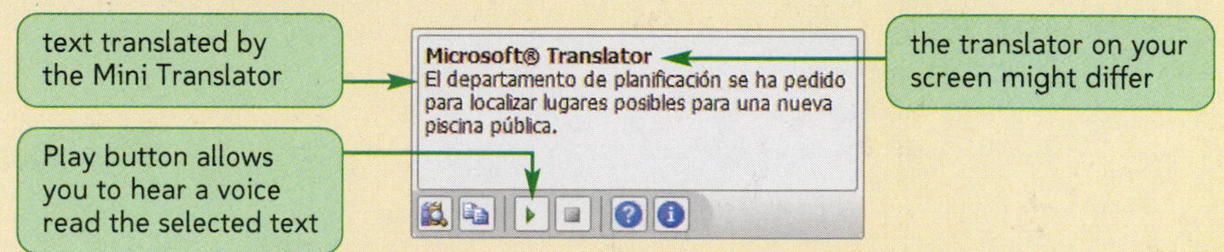

5. Click the **Play** button. If your computer has speakers installed, you hear a computer-generated voice reading the English sentence. The ability to hear a sentence read aloud can be useful if you are translating text from a language you don't understand very well, and you want to listen to the text in the original language.
6. If necessary, redisplay the Mini Translator window, and then click the **Expand** button. The Research task pane opens, displaying the translation. To replace the selected text with a copy of the translation, you could click the Insert button. However, Sam has no need for a copy of the translation now. Next, he wants to review a complete translation of the document.
7. Click the **Translate** button, and then click **Translate Document [English (U.S.) to Spanish (International Sort)]**. The Translate Whole Document dialog box opens. It displays a message explaining that the entire document will be sent over the Web to a translation service.

   Trouble? If the Translate Document option is not available on the Translate menu, you may not have the necessary translation options installed on your computer. In that case, read but do not attempt to complete Steps 7 through 9.
8. Click the **Send** button. Your computer's Web browser opens, displaying the original English document side-by-side with a Spanish translation. See Figure 5-33.

Figure 5-33 Spanish translation side-by-side with original English text

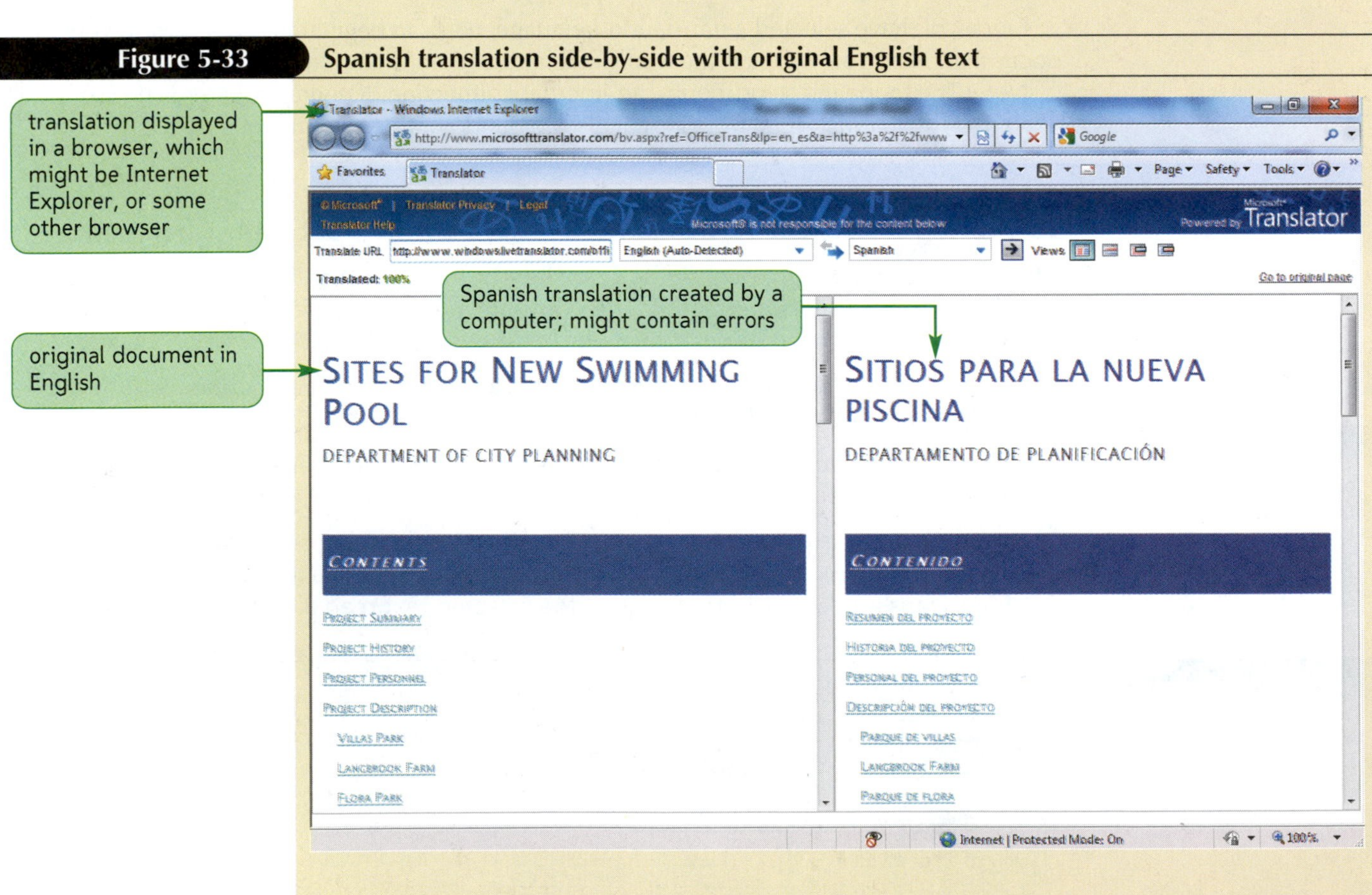

9. Close the browser window. You no longer need the Mini Translator, so you should turn it off.
10. In the Language group, click the **Translate** button, and then click **Mini Translator [Spanish (International Sort)]** to turn off the Mini Translator.
11. Close the Research task pane, deselect the text, and then save your work.

The Mini Translator will continue to appear and translate text until you turn it off.

You are finished working on the Pool Sites document. Sam thinks the document looks great, and would like to save it as a template to use for future department reports.

Saving a Document as a Template

If you will frequently need to create a particular type of document, it's a good idea to create your own template for that type of document. In this case, Sam wants to create a template that will be used for all reports issued by the Department of City Planning. When creating a template, you can save it to any folder on your computer. However, if you save it to the Templates folder that is installed with Word, you can easily open the template later by clicking the My templates option on the New tab in Backstage view.

REFERENCE

Saving a Document as a Template

- Click the File tab, and then click Save As to open the Save As dialog box.
- Click the Save as type arrow, and then click Word Template.
- Navigate to the folder in which you want to save the template. To save the template to the Templates folder that is installed with Word, click the Templates folder in the Navigation pane of the Save As dialog box.
- In the File name box, type a name for the template.
- Click the Save button.

You will save the new template in the Word5\Tutorial folder, so that you can easily submit the completed tutorial files to your instructor.

To save the Pool Sites document as a new template:

1. Save the Pool Sites document to ensure that you have saved your most recent work.
2. Click the **File** tab, and then click **Save As**. The Save As dialog box opens.
3. Click the **Save as type** arrow, and then click **Word Template**.
4. If necessary, navigate to the Word5\Tutorial folder included with your Data Files. Next you'll type the new filename using "DCP," the acronym for "Department of City Planning."
5. Delete the default filename in the File name box, and then type **DCP Report**. See Figure 5-34.

Figure 5-34 Saving a document as a template

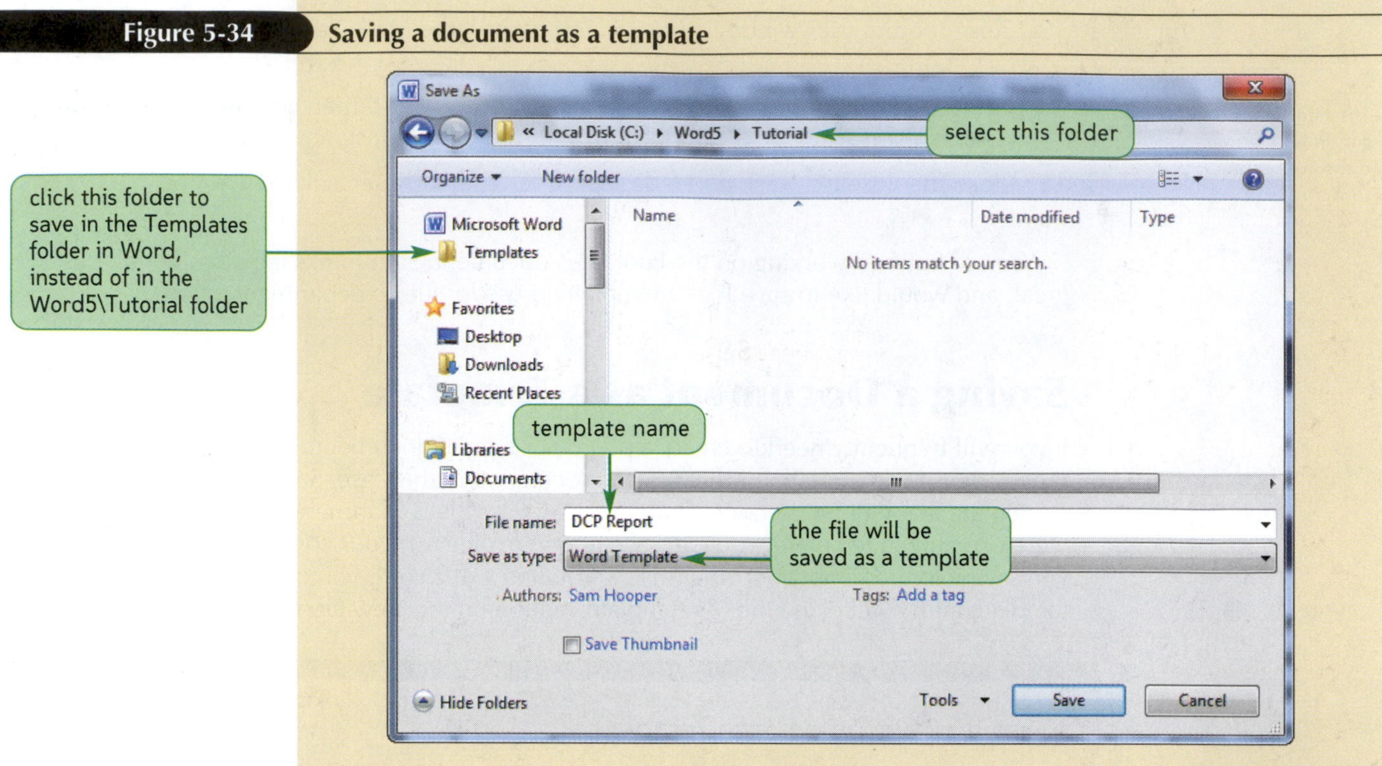

6. Click the **Save** button. The Save As dialog box closes, and the document, which is now a template with the .dotx file extension, remains open.

PROSKILLS

Written Communication: Standardizing the Look of Your Documents

Large companies often ask their employees to use a predesigned template for all corporate documents. If you work for an organization that does not require you to use a specific template, consider using one anyway in order to create a standard look for all of your documents. A consistent appearance is especially important if you are responsible for written communication for an entire department, because it ensures that colleagues and clients will immediately recognize documents from your department.

Take care to use a professional-looking template. If you decide to create your own, make sure to use document styles that make text easy to read, with colors that are considered appropriate in your workplace. Don't try to dazzle your readers with design elements. In nearly all professional settings, a simple, elegant look is ideal.

To make the new DCP Report template really useful to Sam's colleagues, you need to delete the specific information related to the Pool Sites report and replace it with placeholder text explaining the type of information required in each section. You'll start by editing the content controls. Then you will delete the body of the report and replace it with some placeholder text that Sam has already typed and saved as a separate Word document. Sam wants to use the current subtitle, "Department of City Planning," as the subtitle in all department reports, so there's no need to change it. However, the title will vary from one report to the next, so you need to replace it with a suitable placeholder. You'll retain the table of contents. When Sam's colleagues use the template to create future reports, they can update the table of contents to include the headings they add to their new documents.

To replace the Pool Sites report information with placeholder text:

1. Replace the report title "Sites for New Swimming Pool" with the text **[INSERT TITLE HERE.]**. Be sure to include the brackets, so it will be readily recognizable as placeholder text.
2. Switch to Header and Footer view, and then in the footer, replace the current date with the text **[Select current date.]**, making sure that you do not delete the Date Picker content control in the process.
3. Return to Print Layout view, and then delete everything in the document between the "Project Summary" heading and the final, blank paragraph, so all that remains is the Project Summary heading and a blank paragraph below it. Now you can insert a file containing placeholder text for the body of the report template.
4. In the blank paragraph under the Project Summary heading, insert the **Placeholder** file from the Word5\Tutorial folder included with your Data Files. See Figure 5-35. Scroll down to review the document and notice that the headings are all correctly formatted with the Heading 1 style. When Sam created the Placeholder document, he formatted the text in the default Heading 1 style provided by the Office theme. But when you inserted the file into the Pool Sites document, Word automatically reformatted the headings with your modified Heading 1 style. Now you can update the table of contents.

Figure 5-35 Template with placeholder text

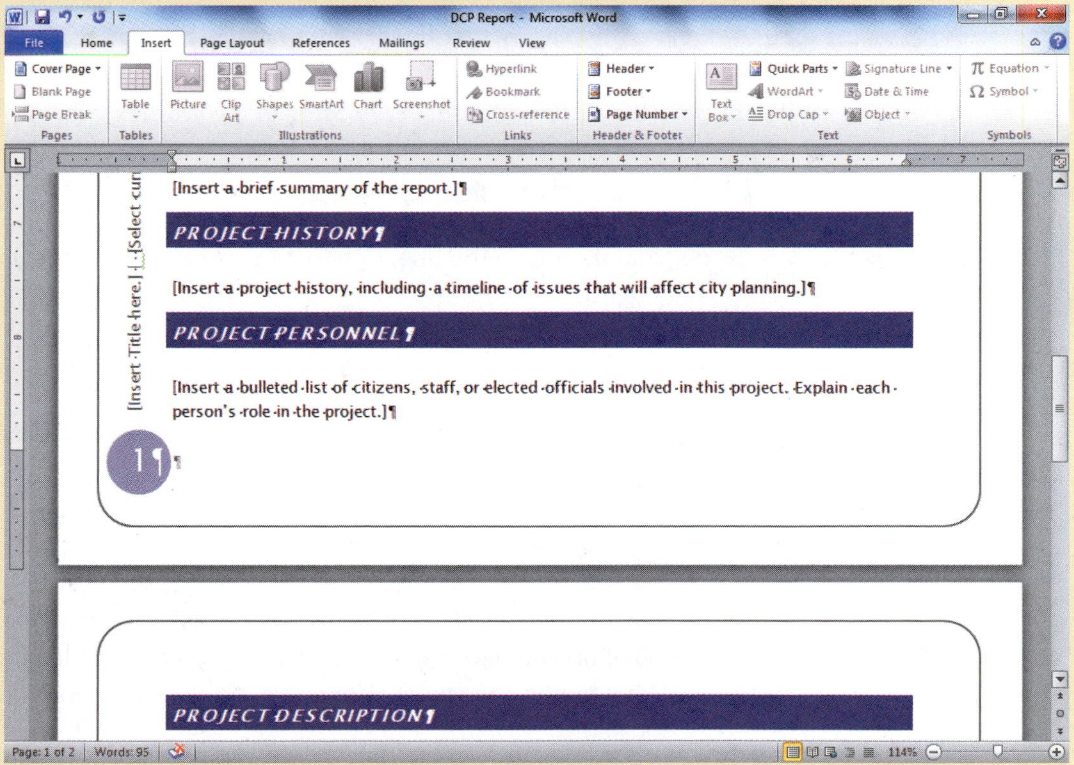

5. Click the **References** tab, and then click the **Update Table** button in the Table of Contents group. The table of contents is updated to include the headings currently in the template.
6. Save your work and close the template file.

The template you just created will simplify the process of creating new reports in Sam's department. Next you will use the template as the basis for a new document.

Opening a New Document Based on Your Template

The new template is ready to be used by the Department of City Planning for all new reports. In fact, Sam would like to use it now to begin a report on possible sites for a new public library.

To begin a new document based on the DCP Report template:

1. Click the **File** tab, and then click the **New** tab. The New tab in Backstage view displays a variety of template options.
2. Under "Home," click **New from existing**. The New from Existing Document dialog box opens. You can use this dialog box to open a copy of a template as a new document, or to open a copy of a regular document as a new document.
3. If necessary, navigate to the Word5\Tutorial folder included with your Data Files, click **DCP Report**, and then click the **Create New** button. A new document opens containing the text and formatting from the DCP Report template. Changes you make to this new document will not affect the DCP Report template file, which remains unchanged in the Word5\Tutorial folder.
4. Delete the placeholder **[Insert title here.]** and type **POSSIBLE SITES FOR NEW LIBRARY**, and then click anywhere outside the Title control to deselect it.
5. Save the document as **Library Sites** in the Word5\Tutorial folder included with your Data Files.

   Trouble? If the Title control displays the placeholder text "[Insert Title here.]" after you save the document, you didn't deselect the control before saving the document. Retype the title, deselect the control, and save your changes to the document.
6. Close the document.

REVIEW

Session 5.2 Quick Check

1. Explain how to create a new style.
2. What tool do you use to see a quick comparison of two styles?
3. What is the advantage of saving a template to the Templates folder?
4. What do you have to do before you can create a table of contents?
5. What button can you click to revise a table of contents, and where is the button located?
6. How do you begin looking up a word in the dictionary or thesaurus?
7. What do you need to do before you can use the Mini Translator?

Apply the skills you learned in the tutorial using the same case scenario.

PRACTICE

Review Assignments

Data Files needed for the Review Assignments: Consultants.docx, Template Text.docx, Water.docx

Sam's DCP Report template is now used for all reports created by employees of the Clarenbach Department of City Planning. Inspired by Sam's success with the template, the director of the Department of Water Utility (DWU), Heather Sheehan, wants you to help with a report on improving the city's water testing system. After you format the report, she'd like you to save the document as a new template. Finally, she'd like you to look up some terms using the Research task pane.

Complete the following steps:

1. Open a new Word document based on the **Oriel Report** template, and then save the document as **Water Testing** in the Word5\Review folder included with your Data Files.
2. Remove the cover page, and then delete the blank paragraph at the top of the new page 1.
3. Replace the title placeholder text with **Improving City Water Testing**. Replace the subtitle placeholder text with **Department of Water Utility**. Use the date control in the header to add the current date.
4. Delete the content control for the body of the report, and then select and delete the text box in the lower-right corner of the page.
5. In the blank paragraph below the subtitle, insert the file named **Water** from the Word5\Review folder included with your Data Files. This is just a skeletal draft of the report, but it includes the necessary headings.
6. At the end of the report, replace "Student Name" with your first and last name.
7. Change the theme colors to Newsprint, and then change the theme's fonts to the Apex fonts.
8. Save the new colors and fonts as a theme named **DWU Theme** in the Word5\Review folder included with your Data Files.
9. Select the Traditional style set.
10. Modify the Project Background heading by changing the character spacing to condensed, changing the paragraph spacing after the heading to 12 points, and adding italics.
11. Update the Heading 1 style to match the newly formatted Project Background heading.
12. Create a new style for the Contents heading that is based on the Heading 1 style. The style should be identical to the Heading 1 style, except that it should format text in 18-point font, with paragraph shading that uses the color Brown, Accent 3, Lighter 40%. Name the new style **Contents** and save it to the current document.
13. Open the Style Inspector and check the style applied to each paragraph in the document. Then use the Reveal Formatting pane to compare the Contents style with the Heading 1 style.
14. Insert a table of contents below the Table of Contents heading that does not include the "Contents" heading. Use the default settings in the Table of Contents dialog box.
15. At the end of the document, insert the Word file **Consultants** from the Word5\Review folder included with your Data Files, and then add the text "Outside Contributors" to the table of contents as a Level 1 heading.
16. Use the Mini Translator to display a Spanish translation of the paragraph below the "Project Background" heading.
17. Display the translation in the Research task pane, copy it to the Clipboard, and then paste it into a new document.

18. Save the new document as **Translation** in the Word5\Review folder included with your Data Files, close it, and then turn off the Mini Translator.
19. Find the word *aquifer* in the document, look up the term's meaning in the Encarta dictionary, copy the definition that begins "a layer of permeable rock…" to the Clipboard, click to the right of the word *aquifer* in the document, create a footnote that begins **According to the Encarta Dictionary, an aquifer is** and then insert the definition into the footnote, followed by a period.
20. In the "Project Background" section, find the first instance of the word *new*, and then replace it with an appropriate synonym.
21. Save your changes to the Water Testing document.
22. Save the Water Testing document as a template named **DWU Report** in the Word5\Review folder included with your Data Files.
23. On page 1, replace the title with the placeholder **[Insert title here.]**. Replace the current date with the placeholder **[Insert current date here.]**.
24. Delete everything in the report after the table of contents.
25. In the blank paragraph below the table of contents, insert the Word file **Template Text** from the Word5\Review folder included with your Data Files.
26. At the end of the template, replace "Student Name" with your first and last name, and then update the table of contents.
27. Save the template, and close it.
28. Open a new document based on the DWU Report template, enter **Estimate for New Wells** as the document title, save the new document as **New Wells** in the Word5\Review folder included with your Data Files, and close it.
29. Submit the finished documents to your instructor, either in printed or electronic form, as requested.

Apply your skills to create a template for a handout.

APPLY

Case Problem 1

Data Files needed for this Case Problem: Characteristics.docx, Crab Apple.jpg, Height.docx, Plant Headings.docx, Requirements.docx.

Bluestem Landscape Design Carla Niedenthal is the manager of the retail garden store owned by Bluestem Landscape Design. Customers often ask her for information about particular plants. Over the years, she has created fact sheets for some of the most popular plants, but now Carla would like to create a set of one-page plant descriptions. Her first step is to create a template that will serve as the basis of the handouts. As you'll see in the following steps, you can use templates intended for one purpose, such as a letter, for a different purpose, such as a handout.

Complete the following steps:

1. Open a new document based on the **Median Letter** template, and then save the document as **Plant** in the Word5\Case1 folder included with your Data Files. This document is set up as a table.
2. Use the View Gridlines button in the Table group on the Table Tools Layout tab to make sure the blue gridlines are visible.
3. Replace the placeholder text in the Company Name control with **Bluestem Landscape Design**. Replace the sender company address placeholder text with **Plant-at-a-Glance**.
4. Delete the date control, and then type **[Insert common plant name]** in the brown cell that used to contain the date control. Click the blue cell next to the brown cell and type **[Insert Latin plant name.]**.

5. Delete the contents of the bottom-right cell, including all the content controls and any blank paragraphs, and then delete the bottom row of the table, so that the table consists of only two rows with two cells each.
6. In the blank paragraph below the table, insert the file **Plant Headings** from the Word5\Case1 folder included with your Data Files.
7. Format the three headings, Characteristics, Mature Height, and Requirements, with the Heading 1 style. Remember that if you can't find a style in the Quick Styles gallery, you can look in the Styles pane.
8. Change the theme colors to Foundry.
9. Change the theme fonts to Verve.
10. Modify the Heading 1 style for the current document by changing the character spacing to Expanded, changing the paragraph spacing after the heading to 12 points, and adding italics.
11. At the bottom of the document, replace "STUDENT NAME" with your first and last name, and then save the document.
12. Save the Plant document as a template named **Plant Template** in the Word5\Case1 folder included with your Data Files, and then close the template.
13. Open a document based on your template. Save the new document as **Crab Apple** in the Word5\Case1 folder included with your Data Files.
14. For the common plant name, enter **Crab Apple**. For the Latin plant name, enter **Malus**.
15. Under the Characteristics heading, replace the placeholder text with the Word file **Characteristics** from the Word5\Case1 folder included with your Data Files. Delete the extra paragraph mark at the end of the new text.
16. Replace the placeholder text below the Mature Height heading and the Requirements heading with the files **Height** and **Requirements** from the Word5\Case1 folder included with your Data Files. Delete any extra new paragraphs.
17. At the bottom of the document, read the placeholder text about inserting a photograph. Delete the placeholder text (but not the paragraph mark at the end of it), and insert the photo named **Crab Apple.jpg** from the Word5\Case1 folder included with your Data Files. Format the photograph with the Drop Shadow Rectangle style.
18. Save and close the Crab Apple document.
19. Submit the finished documents to your instructor, either in printed or electronic form, as requested.

Apply your skills to create a template for a consultant's report.

APPLY

Case Problem 2

Data File needed for this Case Problem: Star.docx

Star Avenue Consulting Steven Yang is a consultant for Star Avenue Consulting, a firm that helps retail chains evaluate and improve the organization of their retail floor space. Steven and his colleagues often have to produce reports that summarize their recommendations. Your job is to create a template they can use to generate these reports.

Complete the following steps:

1. Open the document **Star** from the Word5\Case2 folder included with your Data Files. In the third paragraph, replace "CONSULTANT NAME" with your first and last name, and then save it as **Star Report** in the same folder.
2. Change the document's theme to the Opulent theme, and change the theme colors to Flow. Change the style set to Traditional.

3. Format the "Assessment of Current Layout" heading by changing the character spacing to Expanded, changing the font size to 16 points, and changing the paragraph spacing after the paragraph to 18 points. Update the Heading 1 style for the current document to match the newly formatted heading.
4. Create a new style for the company name at the top of the document that is based on the Title style. The new style should be identical to the Title style, except that the text should be 20-point font, with bold and italic formatting and 6 points of space after the paragraph. Name the new style **Company**, select the Normal style as the style for following paragraphs, and save the new style to the current document.
5. In the blank paragraph above the heading "Assessment of Current Store Layout," insert a table of contents using the Automatic Table 2 format. Delete the blank paragraph after the content control that contains the table of contents.
6. In the placeholder text after the heading "Assessment of Current Store Layout," replace "current" with an appropriate synonym.
7. Save your changes to the Star Report document, and then save the Star Report document as a template named **Star Template** in the Word5\Case2 folder included with your Data Files. Close the template.
8. Open a document based on your new template. You will use this document as the basis of a new report for Gametron, a chain of video game stores. You will not complete the entire report; instead you'll leave the placeholder text in the body of the report for another consultant to replace.
9. Save the new document as **Gametron** in the Word5\Case2 folder included with your Data Files.
10. For the client name, insert **Gametron Inc. and Subsidiaries**.
11. Save and close the Gametron document.
12. Submit the finished documents to your instructor, either in printed or electronic form, as requested.

Go beyond what you've learned to edit a business plan for a new Internet company.

CHALLENGE

Case Problem 3

Data File needed for this Case Problem: Text.docx

AllSecure, Inc. Camden Lui has written a business plan for his new Internet business, AllSecure, Incorporated. On its Web site, the company will publish security information on data storage and transmission services. Camden has written part of the report and needs help formatting it.

Complete the following steps:

1. Open a new document based on the Origin Report template and save it as **AllSecure Plan** in the Word5\Case3 folder included with your Data Files.
2. Remove the cover page, and then delete the blank paragraph at the top of the remaining page.
3. Use **AllSecure, Inc.** for the document title and **Business Plan** for the subtitle.
4. Delete the body control, and insert the file named **Text** from the Word5\Case3 folder included with your Data Files. At the end of the document, replace "Student Name" with your first and last name.
5. Create a new character style for the company name where it is used in the body of the report. (*Hint*: In the Create New Style from Formatting dialog box, click the Style type arrow and then click Character.) Base the style on the Intense Reference style. The new style should be identical to the Intense Reference style, except that it should format text in small caps. Name the style **Company Name** and save it to the current document.

EXPLORE

6. In the bottom-right corner of the Styles pane, click the Options link, and then review the Style Pane Options dialog box. Using Word Help as a reference, set up the Style pane to list the styles in the current document in alphabetical order.

EXPLORE

7. Replace all instances of "AllSecure" formatted in the Normal style with "AllSecure" formatted in the Company Name style. To do this, open the Find and Replace dialog box, type AllSecure in the Find what box, click the Format button, click Style, select the Normal style, and then click OK. Type AllSecure in the Replace with box, and then use the Format button to select the Company Name style. Continue the find and replace process as usual.
8. Insert a new paragraph before the Executive Summary heading, and then format the new paragraph with the Normal style.

EXPLORE

9. Use the Table of Contents dialog box to insert a table of contents without page numbers in the new, blank paragraph. Use the Distinctive format.
10. At the end of the document, change the heading Audience Needs to **Audience Requirements**, and then update the table of contents.
11. In the last paragraph on the first page, replace "crucial" with an appropriate synonym.

EXPLORE

12. Select the "Requirements for Success" heading, open the Paragraph dialog box, click the Line and Page Breaks tab, select the Keep with next check box, and then click the OK button. Update the Heading 1 style to match the newly formatted "Requirements for Success" heading, so that all text formatted with the Heading 1 style stays with the body text that follows it. This will prevent headings from being stranded at the bottom of a column, with the body text at the top of the next column.
13. Save and close the document.
14. Submit the finished documents to your instructor, either in printed or electronic form, as requested.

Look up information about Web sites that offer Word 2010 templates.

RESEARCH

Case Problem 4

There are no Data Files needed for this Case Problem.

Deca Publishing Associates You work as an editorial assistant at Deca Publishing Associates, a small firm that performs a variety of editorial tasks for larger publishing companies. Your supervisor would like to take advantage of the many Word templates available online from companies other than Microsoft. She asks you to do some research and write a short report summarizing your findings. She also asks you to include screenshots of sites that provide templates online. *Note:* To complete this case problem, you will need a connection to the Internet.

Complete the following steps:

1. Open a new document based on the Urban Report template, and then save the document as **Word Templates** in the Word5\Case4 folder included with your Data Files.
2. Remove the cover page.
3. Enter **Word Templates** as the document title and **A Sample of Online Sources** as the subtitle document control, and then delete the document control for the body of the report.
4. Enter your first and last name in the content control in the document header.
5. Open the Research task pane and use the Bing search engine to look up information about sites that offer Word 2010 templates. You can click View all results on Live Search to display the information in your browser, and then continue searching from there. Learn as much as you can about the various sites. Review the Microsoft site, as well as several other sites. Look for sites that offer templates for sale and for free.

6. Write a brief report describing the options available on the Microsoft site and on one other site. For each site, include the site's name formatted with the Heading 1 style, followed by a bulleted list that includes the site's Web address, a brief description of the types of templates available, and information about template prices. After you type a site's Web address, remember to press the spacebar or the Enter key to transform the Web address into a live hyperlink.
7. Add a blank paragraph formatted in the Normal style at the end of each bulleted list.
8. EXPLORE Look up the term **screenshot** in Word Help and learn how to insert a screenshot of an open Window into a Word document. In the blank paragraph at the end of each bulleted list, insert a screenshot of the relevant Web site.
9. Save and close the document.
10. Submit the finished documents to your instructor, either in printed or electronic form, as requested

ASSESS

SAM: Skills Assessment Manager

For current SAM information, including versions and content details, visit SAM Central (http://samcentral.course.com). If you have a SAM user profile, you may have access to hands-on instruction, practice, and assessment of the skills covered in this tutorial. Since various versions of SAM are supported throughout the life of this text, check with your instructor for the correct instructions and URL/Web site for accessing assignments.

ENDING DATA FILES

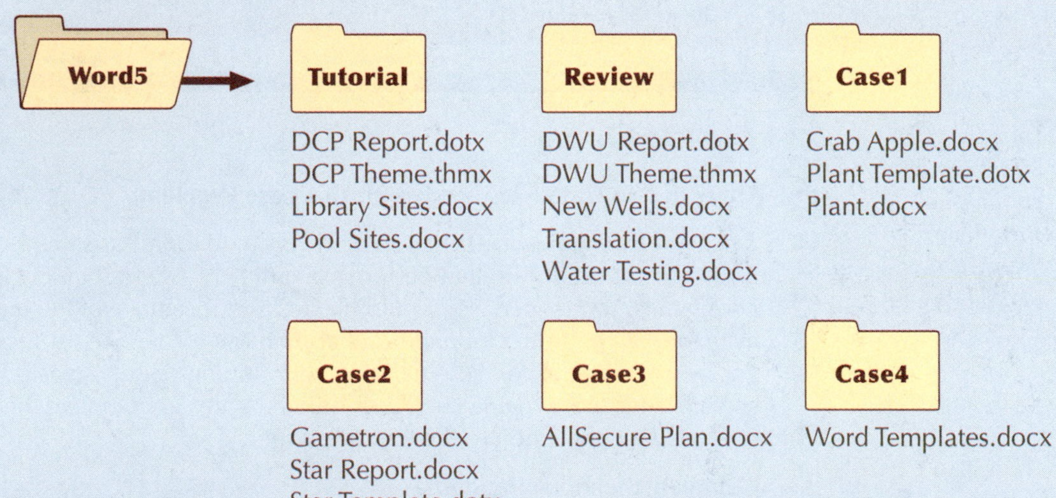

TUTORIAL 6

Using Mail Merge

Creating a Form Letter, Mailing Labels, and a Telephone Directory

WORD

OBJECTIVES

Session 6.1
- Learn about the mail merge process
- Select a main document
- Create a data source
- Insert mail merge fields into a main document
- Edit a main document
- Preview a merged document
- Complete a mail merge

Session 6.2
- Edit an existing data source
- Sort and filter records
- Create mailing labels and a phone directory
- Convert tables to text and text to tables
- Create multilevel lists

Case | *Lily Road Yoga Studio*

Nina Ranabhat is the owner and chief instructor at Lily Road Yoga Studio in Boise, Idaho. The studio has just moved to a new, expanded location. Nina wants to invite clients to try out the new facility during free, open-studio days in the month of June. She plans to send a form letter to each client announcing the location and the open-studio days. The form letter will also contain specific details for individual clients, such as name, address, and each client's favorite class and instructor. Nina has already written the text of the form letter. She plans to use the mail merge process to add the personal information for each client. She asks you to complete the form letter using the Mail Merge feature in Word. She also needs a set of letters that will go just to the clients who like a particular teacher. After you create the merged letters, she'd like you to create the mailing labels for the envelopes and a telephone directory that lists a phone number for each teacher. Next, you will create an additional document with name and address information by converting text to a table, and converting a table to text. Finally, you will create and format an outline with information about the studio's teachers.

STARTING DATA FILES

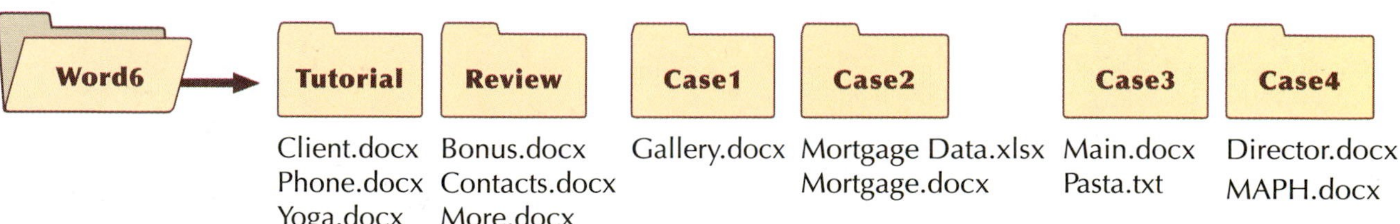

Tutorial	Review	Case1	Case2	Case3	Case4
Client.docx	Bonus.docx	Gallery.docx	Mortgage Data.xlsx	Main.docx	Director.docx
Phone.docx	Contacts.docx		Mortgage.docx	Pasta.txt	MAPH.docx
Yoga.docx	More.docx				

SESSION 6.1 VISUAL OVERVIEW

To complete the merge, you click the Finish & Merge button. This creates a new document, the **merged document**, which contains a separate copy of the main document for each record in the data source.

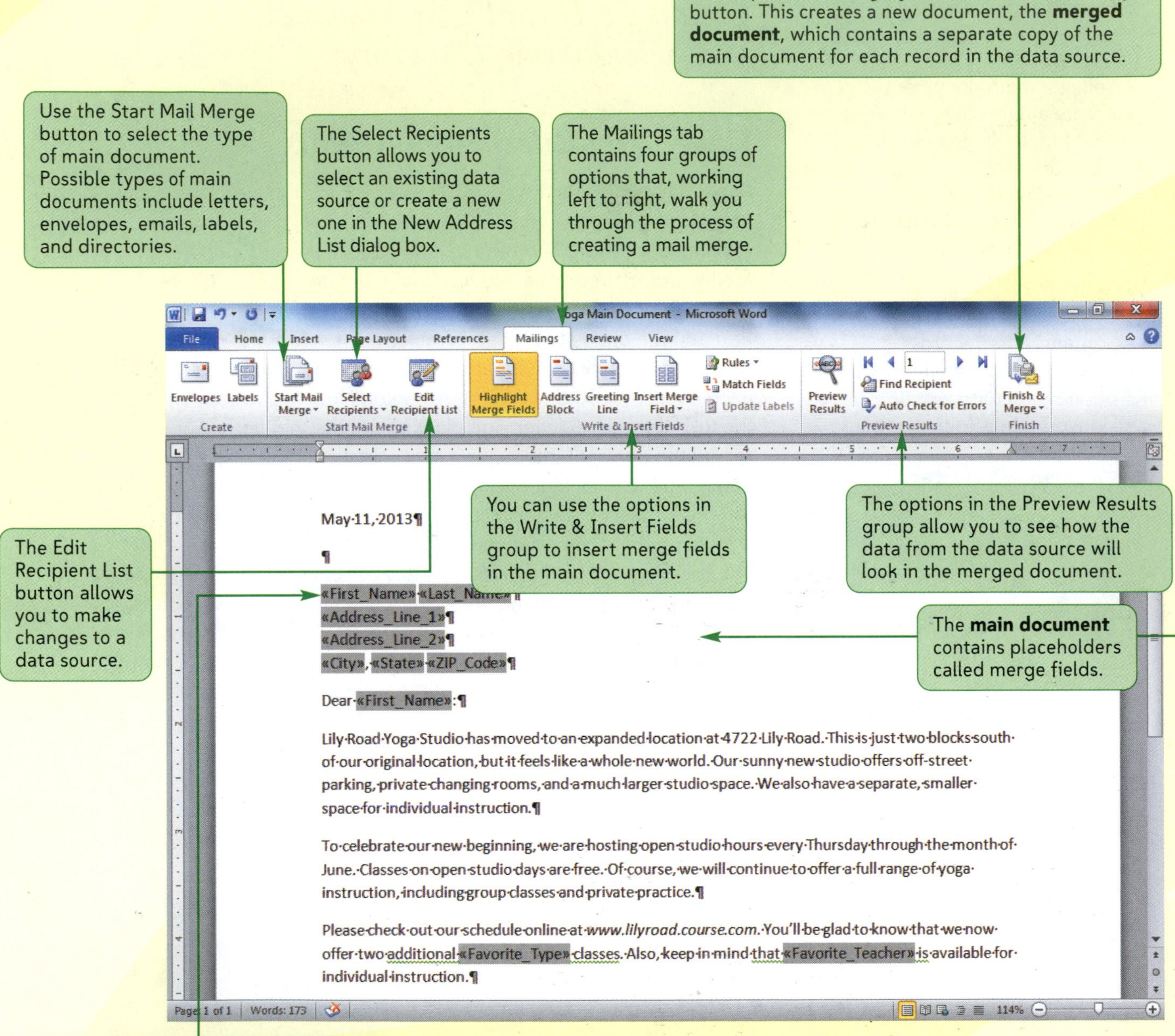
Use the Start Mail Merge button to select the type of main document. Possible types of main documents include letters, envelopes, emails, labels, and directories.
The Select Recipients button allows you to select an existing data source or create a new one in the New Address List dialog box.
The Mailings tab contains four groups of options that, working left to right, walk you through the process of creating a mail merge.
The Edit Recipient List button allows you to make changes to a data source.
You can use the options in the Write & Insert Fields group to insert merge fields in the main document.
The options in the Preview Results group allow you to see how the data from the data source will look in the merged document.
The **main document** contains placeholders called merge fields.
May 11, 2013
«First_Name» «Last_Name»
«Address_Line_1»
«Address_Line_2»
«City», «State» «ZIP_Code»
Dear «First_Name»:
Lily Road Yoga Studio has moved to an expanded location at 4722 Lily Road. This is just two blocks south of our original location, but it feels like a whole new world. Our sunny new studio offers off-street parking, private changing rooms, and a much larger studio space. We also have a separate, smaller space for individual instruction.
To celebrate our new beginning, we are hosting open studio hours every Thursday through the month of June. Classes on open studio days are free. Of course, we will continue to offer a full range of yoga instruction, including group classes and private practice.
Please check out our schedule online at www.lilyroad.course.com. You'll be glad to know that we now offer two additional «Favorite_Type» classes. Also, keep in mind that «Favorite_Teacher» is available for individual instruction.

A **merge field** indicates what information you want to retrieve from the data source and display in the main document. For example, a merge field might retrieve a name or a zip code. A merge field is enclosed by angled brackets, or **chevrons**, like this: << >>.

MAIL MERGE

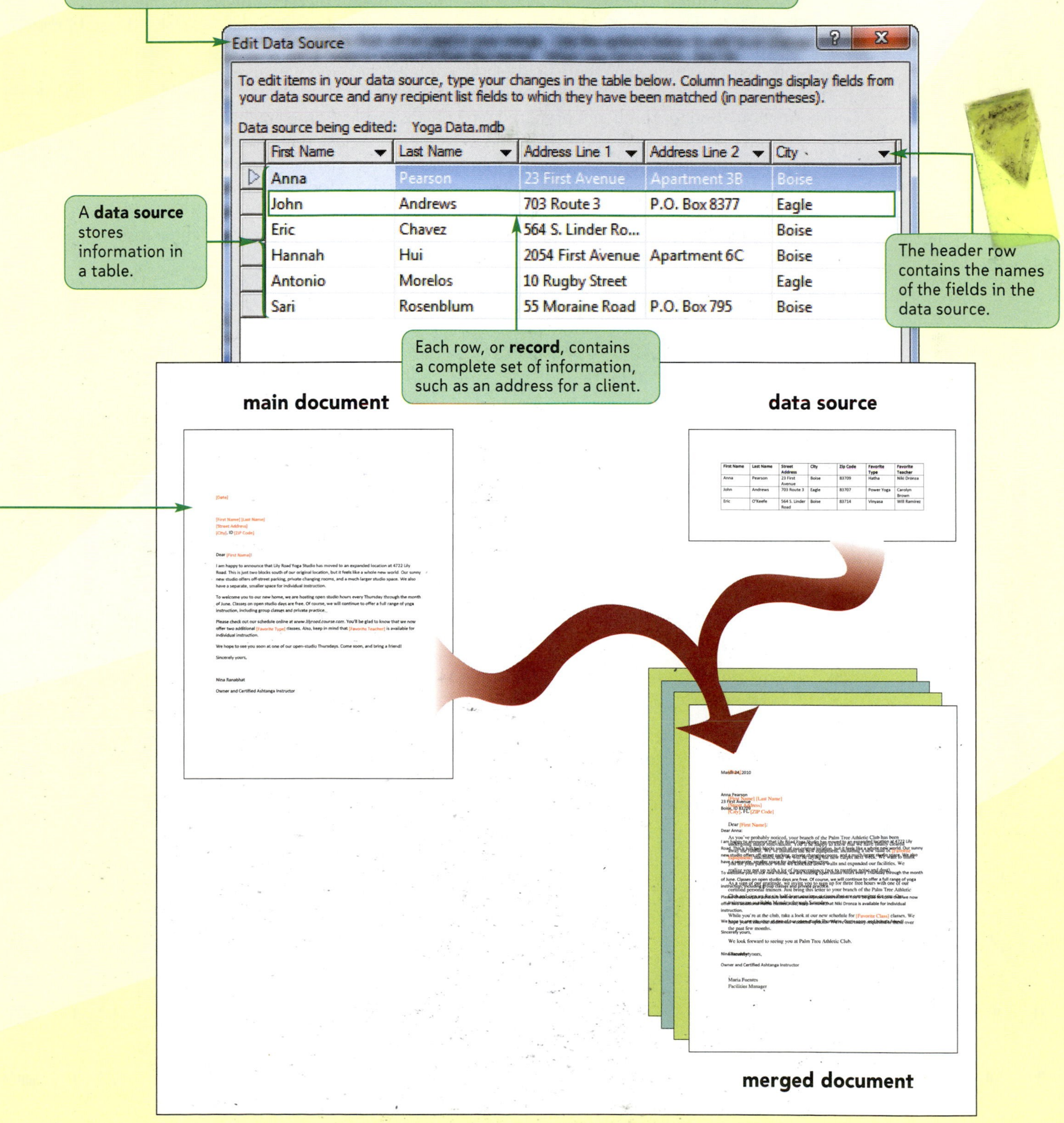
A **data source** contains information, such as names and addresses, that is displayed in the main document by the merge fields. You can use a Word table, an Excel spreadsheet, or other types of files as data sources, or you can create a new one using the New Address List dialog box.
Edit Data Source
To edit items in your data source, type your changes in the table below. Column headings display fields from your data source and any recipient list fields to which they have been matched (in parentheses).
Data source being edited: Yoga Data.mdb
First Name | Last Name | Address Line 1 | Address Line 2 | City
Anna | Pearson | 23 First Avenue | Apartment 3B | Boise
John | Andrews | 703 Route 3 | P.O. Box 8377 | Eagle
Eric | Chavez | 564 S. Linder Ro... | | Boise
Hannah | Hui | 2054 First Avenue | Apartment 6C | Boise
Antonio | Morelos | 10 Rugby Street | | Eagle
Sari | Rosenblum | 55 Moraine Road | P.O. Box 795 | Boise
A **data source** stores information in a table.
The header row contains the names of the fields in the data source.
Each row, or **record**, contains a complete set of information, such as an address for a client.
main document
data source
merged document

Performing a Mail Merge

When you perform a mail merge, you insert individualized information from a data source into a main document. A main document can be a letter or any other kind of document containing merge fields that tell Word where to insert names, addresses, and other variable information from the data source. When you **merge** the main document with the data source, you produce a new document called a **merged document**. The Session 6.1 Visual Overview summarizes mail merge concepts.

Nina's main document is the letter shown in the Session 6.1 Visual Overview. In this session, you will insert the merge fields shown in this letter. You will also create Nina's data source, which will include the name and address of each client. It will also include information about each client's preferred type of class and favorite teacher.

You can perform a mail merge by using the Mail Merge task pane, which walks you through the steps of performing a mail merge. You can also use the options on the Mailings tab, which streamlines the process and offers more tools. In this tutorial you will work with the Mailings tab to complete the mail merge for Nina. The Mailings tab organizes the steps in the mail merge process so that you can move from left to right across the Ribbon using the buttons to complete the merge.

The first step is to open the document you want to use as the main document, and then use the Start Mail merge button in the Start Mail Merge group to select the type of document. Selecting the type of main document affects the commands that are available to you later as you continue through the mail merge process, so it's important to make the correct selection at the beginning. In this case, you will use a letter as the main document.

To open the main document and begin the mail merge process:

1. Open the file **Yoga** from the Word6\Tutorial folder included with your Data Files, then save the document as **Yoga Main Document** in the same folder.
2. Display nonprinting characters, switch to Print Layout view, display the rulers, and set the zoom to Page Width.
3. Review the contents of the letter. Notice that the first paragraph includes a date field, which automatically updated to display the current date when you opened the document.
4. Scroll down to display the letter's closing, change "Nina Ranabhat" to your name, and then scroll back up to the beginning of the letter.
5. Click the **Mailings** tab on the Ribbon. Notice that most of the buttons in the groups on the Mailings tab are grayed out, indicating the options are unavailable. These options only become available after you begin the mail merge process by specifying a main document and a data source.
6. In the Start Mail Merge group, click the **Start Mail Merge** button. The Start Mail Merge menu opens. See Figure 6-1. The first five options on the menu allow you to specify the type of main document you will be creating. Most of the options involve print items, such as labels and letters, but you can also select an email as the type of main document. In this case, you will be creating a letter.

TIP

After you have completed a mail merge, you can break the connection between a main document and its data source by clicking Normal Word Document on the Start Mail Merge menu.

Figure 6-1 Start Mail Merge menu

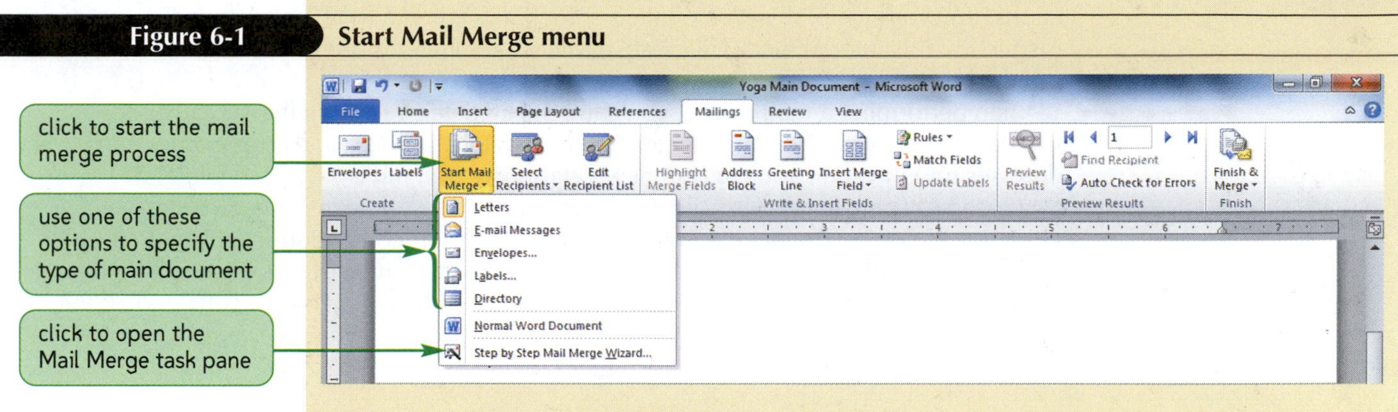

7. Click **Letters**. The Start Mail Merge menu closes.

   Next, you need to select the list of recipients for Nina's letter—the data source.

8. In the Start Mail Merge group, click the **Select Recipients** button. The Select Recipients menu allows you to use an existing list, select from Outlook Contacts (the address book in Outlook), or create a new recipient list. Because Nina hasn't had a chance to create a data source yet, she asks you to create one.

9. Click **Type New List**. The New Address List dialog box opens, as shown in Figure 6-2. The default fields for a data source appear in this dialog box. However, before you begin creating the data source, you need to identify the fields and records Nina wants you to include.

Figure 6-2 New Address List dialog box

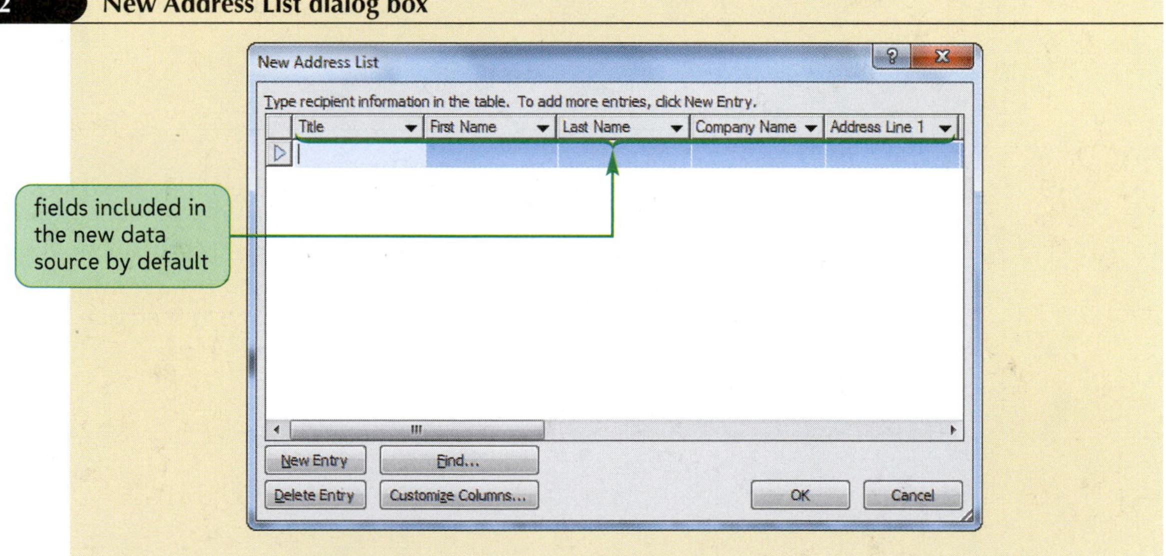

Creating a Data Source

As described in the Session 6.1 Visual Overview, a data source is a file with information organized into fields and records. Typically, the data source for a mail merge contains a list of names and addresses, but it can also contain email addresses, telephone numbers, and other data. Various kinds of files can be used as the data source, including a simple text file, Word table, Excel worksheet, Access database, or a Microsoft Office Address

Lists file, which stores addresses for Microsoft Outlook and other Microsoft Office applications. (In Word Help, this type of file is sometimes called a Microsoft Office Contacts Lists file.) In this tutorial, you will create a Microsoft Office Address Lists file to use as your data source.

When performing a mail merge, you can select a data source file that already contains names and addresses, or you can create a new data source and enter names and addresses into it. When you create a new data source, the file is saved by default as a Microsoft Office Address Lists file. Creating a new data source involves two steps—deciding which fields to include in the data source and entering address information.

You need to create a data source that contains information on Nina's clients, including the name, address, preferred type of class, and favorite teacher. Nina collected all the necessary information by asking clients to fill out a form when they registered for their first yoga class. Figure 6-3 shows one of these forms.

Figure 6-3 Client information form

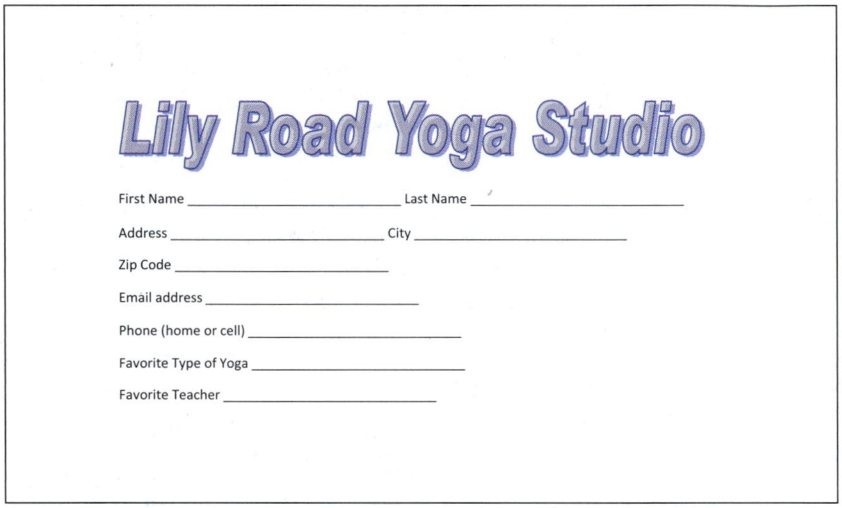

Lily Road Yoga Studio

First Name __________ Last Name __________

Address __________ City __________

Zip Code __________

Email address __________

Phone (home or cell) __________

Favorite Type of Yoga __________

Favorite Teacher __________

The information on each form will make up one record in the data source. Each blank on the form translates into one field in the data source as shown in Figure 6-4. Even though you won't need the clients' email addresses or phone numbers to complete the mail merge, you can still include them in the data source. That way Nina can reuse the same data source in the future when using mail merge to send out emails to her clients, or when creating a directory of client phone numbers.

Figure 6-4 **Fields to include in data source**

Field Names	Description
First Name	Client's first name
Last Name	Client's last name
Address Line 1	Client's street address
Address Line 2	Additional address information, such as an apartment number
City	City
State	State
ZIP Code	Zip code
E-mail Address	Client's email address
Phone	Client's home or cell phone number
Favorite Type	Client's preferred type of yoga
Favorite Teacher	Client's preferred yoga teacher

When you create a new data source, Word provides a number of default fields, such as First Name, Last Name, and Company. You can customize the data source by adding new fields and removing the default fields that you don't plan to use. As you create a data source, keep in mind that each field name must be unique; you can't have two fields with the same name.

REFERENCE

Creating a Data Source for a Mail Merge

- On the Mailings tab, click the Select Recipients button in the Start Mail Merge group, and then click Type New List to open the New Address List dialog box.
- To create the fields for your data source, click the Customize Columns button to open the Customize Address List dialog box.
- To delete an unnecessary field, select it, click the Delete button, and then click the Yes button.
- To add a new field, click the Add button, type the name of the field in the Add Field dialog box, and then click the OK button.
- To rearrange the order of the field names, click a field name, and then click the Move Up or Move Down button.
- To rename a field, click a field name, click the Rename button to open the Rename Field dialog box, type a new field name, and then click the OK button to close the Rename Field dialog box.
- Click the OK button to close the Customize Address List dialog box.
- In the New Address List dialog box, enter information for the first record, click the New Entry button, and type another record. Continue until you are finished entering information into the data source, and then click the OK button to open the Save Address List dialog box.
- Type a name for the data source in the File name box, and then click the Save button. The file is saved with the .mdb file extension.

You're ready to create the data source for Nina's form letter using information Nina has given you for three of her clients. You will use the New Address List dialog box to enter one record per client. However, before you begin entering information, you need to customize the list of fields to include only the fields Nina requires.

To customize the list of fields before creating the data source:

1. In the New Address List dialog box, click the **Customize Columns** button. The Customize Address List dialog box opens. Here you can delete the fields you don't need, add new ones, and arrange the fields in the order you want. You'll start by deleting fields.
2. In the Field Names box, verify that **Title** is selected, and then click the **Delete** button. A message appears asking you to confirm the deletion.
3. Click the **Yes** button. The Title field is deleted from the list of field names.
4. Continue using the Delete button to delete the following fields: **Company Name**, **Country or Region**, and **Work Phone**. Next, you need to add some new fields. When you add a new field, it is inserted below the selected field, so you will start by selecting the last field in the list.
5. In the Field Names box, click **E-mail Address**, and then click the **Add** button. The Add Field dialog box opens, asking you to type a name for your field.
6. Type **Favorite Type**, and then click the **OK** button. The field "Favorite Type" is added to the Field Names list.
7. Use the Add button to add a **Favorite Teacher** field below the Favorite Type field. Next, you need to move the E-mail Address field up above the Home Phone field, so that the fields are in the same order as they appear on the form shown previously in Figure 6-3.
8. Click **E-mail Address**, and then click the **Move Up** button. The E-mail Address field moves up, so it now appears just before the Home Phone field. Finally, because Nina's form asks clients to fill in a home or cell phone number, you need to change "Home Phone" to simply "Phone."
9. Click **Home Phone**, and then click the **Rename** button to open the Rename Field dialog box.
10. In the To box, replace "Home Phone" with **Phone**, and then click the **OK** button to close the Rename Field dialog box and return to the Customize Address List dialog box. See Figure 6-5.

Figure 6-5 Customized list of field names

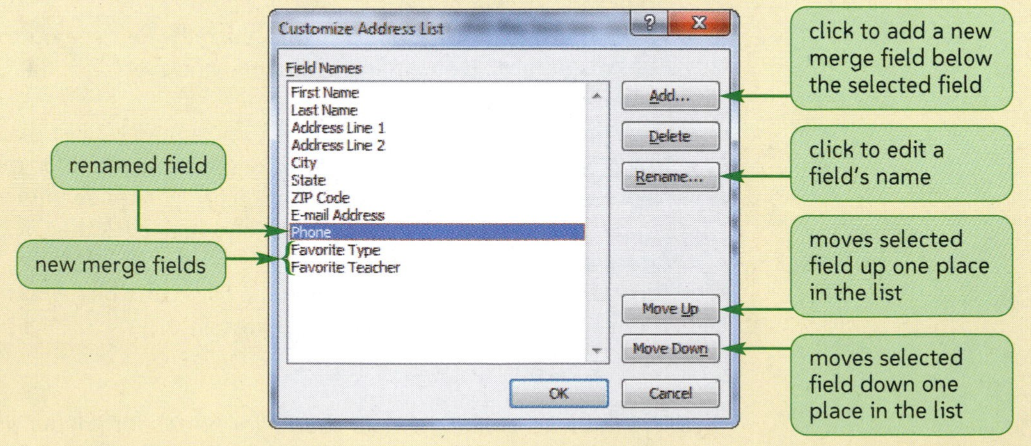

11. Click the **OK** button in the Customize Address List dialog box to close it and return to the New Address List dialog box. This dialog box reflects the changes you just made. For instance, it no longer includes the Title field. The fields are listed in the same order they appeared in the Customize Address List dialog box.

12. Use the horizontal scroll bar near the bottom of the New Address List dialog box to display the Favorite Type and Favorite Teacher fields. Although part of "Favorite Teacher" is cut off in the dialog box, the entire field name is stored as part of the data source. See Figure 6-6.

Figure 6-6 Changes made to New Address List dialog box

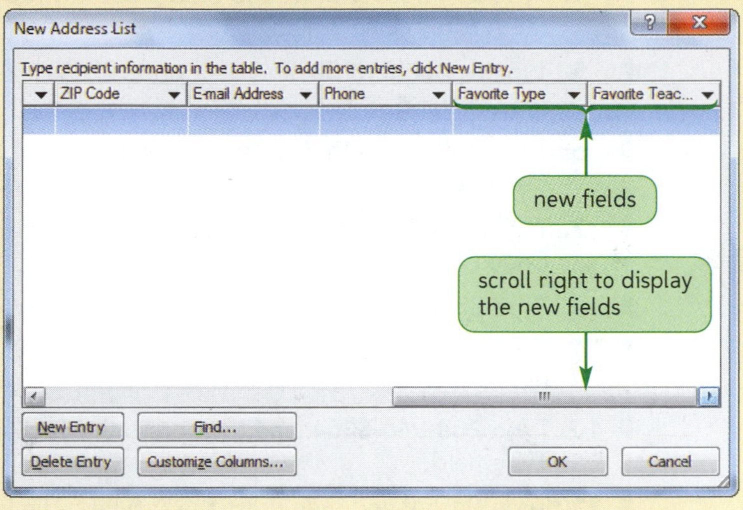

INSIGHT

Organizing Field Names

Although the order of field names in the data source doesn't affect their placement in the main document, it's helpful to arrange field names logically in the data source so you can enter information quickly and efficiently. For example, you'll probably want the First Name field next to the Last Name field. To make it easier to transfer information from a paper form to a data source, it's a good idea to arrange the fields in the same order as on the form, just like you did in the preceding steps. Also, note that if you include spaces in your field names, Word will replace the spaces with underscores when you insert the fields into the main document. For example, Word transforms the field name First Name into First_Name.

Now that you have specified the fields you want to use, you are ready to enter the client information into the data source.

Entering Data into a Data Source

Nina gives you three completed client information forms and asks you to enter the information from the forms into the data source. You'll use the New Address List dialog box to enter the information. As you press the Tab key to move right from one field to the next, the dialog box will scroll to display fields that are not currently visible.

TIP

You can press the Shift+Tab keys to move the insertion point to the previous field.

To enter data into a record using the New Address List dialog box:

1. Scroll left to display the First Name field, click in the **First Name** field, if necessary, and then type **Anna** to enter the first name of the first client. Make sure you do not press the spacebar after you finish typing an entry in the New Address List dialog box. You should add spaces only in the text of the main document, not in the data source, to prevent too many or too few spaces between words.
2. Press the **Tab** key to move the insertion point to the Last Name field.
3. Type **Pearson**, and then press the **Tab** key to move the insertion point to the Address Line 1 field.
4. Type **23 First Avenue**, and then press the **Tab** key to move the insertion point to the Address Line 2 field.
5. Type **Apartment 3B**, and then press the **Tab** key to move the insertion point to the City field.
6. Type **Boise**, and then press the **Tab** key to move the insertion point to the State field.
7. Type **ID**, and then press the **Tab** key to move the insertion point to the ZIP Code field.
8. Type **83709**, and then press the **Tab** key to move to the E-mail Address field.
9. Type **pearson22@mount-tech.net**, and then press the **Tab** key to move to the Phone field.
10. Type **208-946-5264**, and then press the **Tab** key to move to the Favorite Type field.
11. Type **Hatha**, and then press the **Tab** key. The insertion point is now in the Favorite Teacher field, which is the last field in the data source.
12. Type **Niki Dronza**, but do *not* press the Tab key. See Figure 6-7.

Figure 6-7 **Completed record**

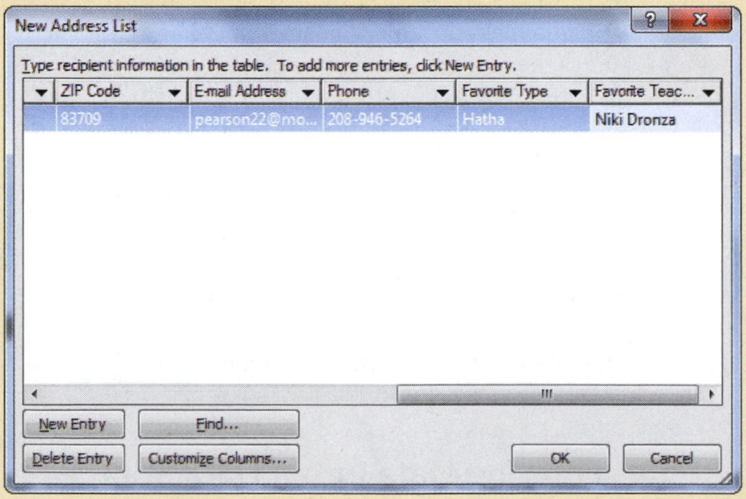

New Address List

Type recipient information in the table. To add more entries, click New Entry.

ZIP Code	E-mail Address	Phone	Favorite Type	Favorite Teac...
83709	pearson22@mo...	208-946-5264	Hatha	Niki Dronza

New Entry | Find... | Delete Entry | Customize Columns... | OK | Cancel

You have completed the information for the first record of the data source. Now you're ready to enter information for the next two records. You can create a new record by clicking the New Entry button, or by pressing the Tab key after you have finished entering information into the last field for a record. As you enter the next two records, you will use both methods. Note that, within a record, you can leave some fields blank. For example, only two of Nina's three clients included information for the Address Line 2 field.

To add additional records to the data source:

1. In the New Address List dialog box, click the **New Entry** button. A new, blank record is created.
2. Enter the information shown in Figure 6-8 for the next two records in the data source. To create an Eric Chavez record, press the Tab key after entering the Favorite Teacher field for the John Andrews record. Also, leave the Address Line 2 field blank for the Eric Chavez record.

Figure 6-8 **Information for records 2 and 3**

First Name	Last Name	Address Line 1	Address Line 2	City	State	ZIP Code	E-mail Address	Phone	Favorite Type	Favorite Teacher
John	Andrews	703 Route 3	P.O. Box 8377	Eagle	ID	83707	john23@world-org.org	208-477-3843	Power Yoga	Carolyn Ramirez
Eric	Chavez	564 S. Linder Road		Boise	ID	83714	chavez55@boise4quest.edu	208-773-0990	Vinyasa	Will Brown

Trouble? If you create a fourth record by mistake, click the Delete Entry button to remove the blank fourth record.

You have entered the records for three clients. Nina's data source eventually will contain hundreds of records for Lily Road Yoga Studio clients. The current data source, however, contains only the records Nina wants to work with now. Next, you need to save the data source.

Saving a Data Source

You have finished entering data, so you can close the New Address List dialog box. When you close this dialog box, the Save Address List dialog box opens, where you can save the data source as a Microsoft Office Address Lists file.

To save the data source:

1. In the New Address List dialog box, click the **OK** button. The New Address List dialog box closes, and the Save Address List dialog box opens, as shown in Figure 6-9. The Save as type box indicates that the data source will be saved as a Microsoft Office Address Lists file. The File name box is empty; you need to name the file before saving it.

Figure 6-9 Saving the data source

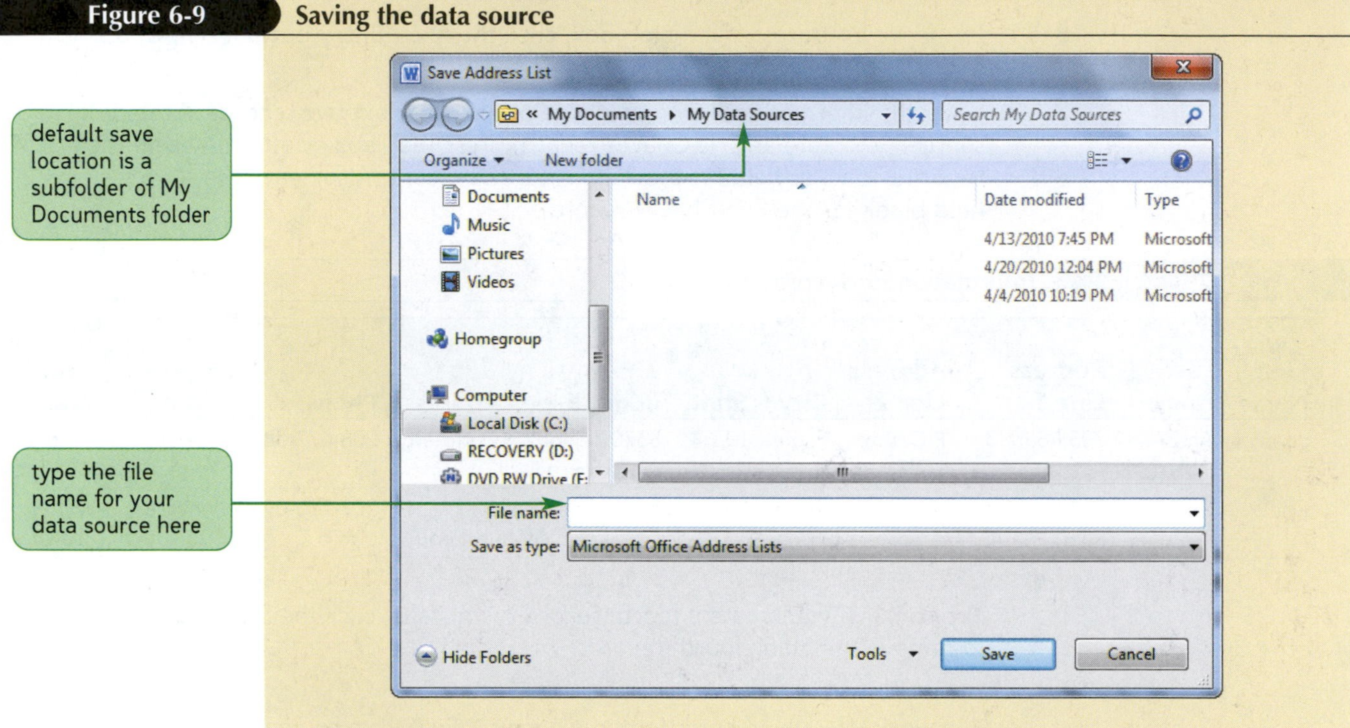

2. Click the **File name** box, and then type **Yoga Data**. By default, Word will save the file to the My Data Sources folder, which is a subfolder of the Documents folder, unless you specify another save location. In this case, you will save the data source in the Word6\Tutorial folder.
3. Navigate to the Word6\Tutorial folder included with your Data Files, and then click the **Save** button. The Save Address List dialog box closes, and you return to the main document.

Decision Making: Planning Your Data Source

When creating a data source, think beyond the current mail merge task to possible future uses for your data source. For example, Nina's data source includes both an E-Mail Address field and a Phone field, not because she wants to use that information in the current mail merge project, but because she can foresee needing these pieces of information at a later date as a means for communicating with her clients. Having all relevant client information in one data source will make it easier to retrieve and use the information effectively.

In some cases, you'll also want to include information that might seem obvious. For example, Nina's data source includes a State field even though all of her current clients live in or around Boise, Idaho. However, she included a state field because she knows that her pool of addresses might expand sometime in the future to include residents of other states.

Finally, think about the structure of your data source before you create it. Try to break information down into as many fields as seems reasonable. For example, it's always better to include a First Name field and a Last Name field, rather than simply a Name field, because including two separate fields makes it possible, later, to alphabetize the information in the data source by last name. If you entered first and last names in a single Name field, you could only alphabetize by first name, because the first name would appear first in the Name field.

If you're working with a very small data source, breaking information down into as many fields as possible is less important. However, it's very common to start with a small data source, and then, as time goes on, find that you need to continually add information to the data source, until you have a large file. If you failed to plan the data source adequately at the beginning, the expanded data source could become difficult to manage.

Next, you need to add the merge fields to the main document.

Inserting Merge Fields

You will build an inside address for the letter by inserting individual merge fields for the address elements. Nina's letter is a standard business letter, so you'll place merge fields for the client's name and address below the date. You must include proper spacing around the fields so that the information in the merged document will be formatted correctly. To insert a merge field, you move the insertion point to the location where you want to insert the merge field, and then click the Insert Merge Field button arrow in the Write & Insert Merge Fields group.

To insert a merge field:

1. Click in the second blank paragraph below the date.
2. In the Write & Insert Fields group, click the **Insert Merge Field button arrow**. A menu containing all the merge fields in the data source opens. Note that the spaces in the merge field names have been replaced with underlines. See Figure 6-10.

Figure 6-10 Insert Merge Field menu

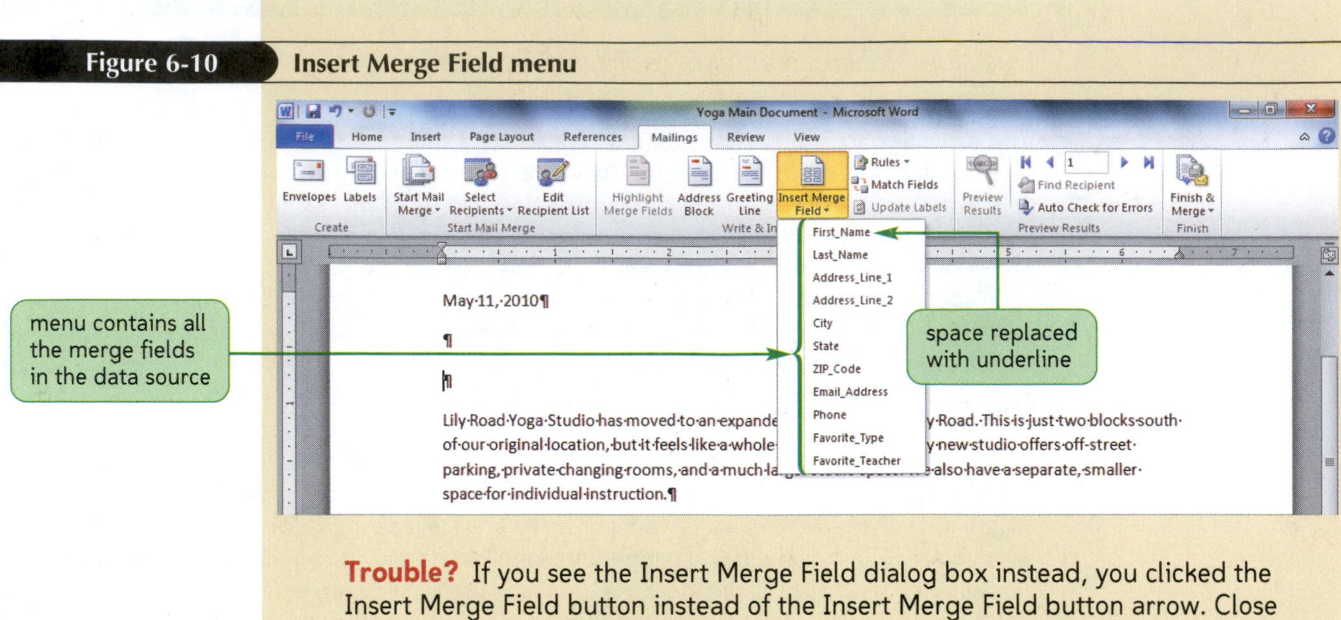

Trouble? If you see the Insert Merge Field dialog box instead, you clicked the Insert Merge Field button instead of the Insert Merge Field button arrow. Close the dialog box and repeat Step 2.

TIP

You can only insert merge fields into a main document by using the tools on the Mailings tab or in the Mail Merge task pane. You cannot simply type merge fields into the main document—even if you type the angled brackets.

3. Click **First_Name**. The Insert Merge Field menu closes, and the merge field is inserted into the document. The merge field consists of the field name surrounded by double angled brackets << >>, also called chevrons. In the Write & Insert Fields group, the Highlight Merge Fields button is now available, which means you can use it to display the merge field on a gray background.

   Trouble? If you make a mistake and insert the wrong merge field, click to the left of the merge field, press the Delete key to select the field, and then press the Delete key again to delete it.

4. In the Write & Insert Fields group, click the **Highlight Merge Fields** button. The First Name merge field is displayed on a gray background, making it easier to see in the document. See Figure 6-11.

Figure 6-11 First_Name merge field highlighted in main document

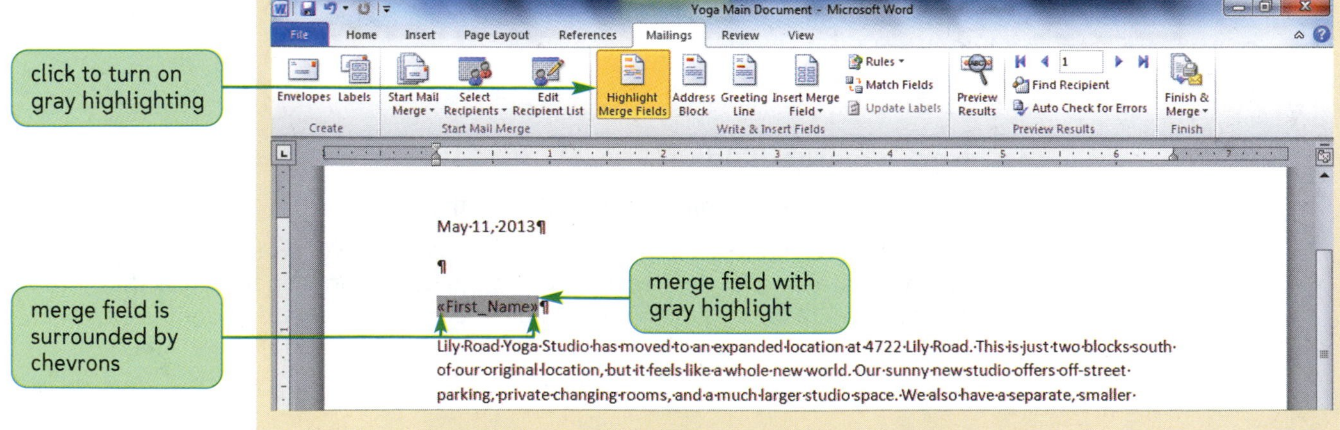

Later, when you merge the main document with the data source, Word will replace this merge field with information from the First Name field in the data source. Now, you're ready to insert the merge fields for the rest of the inside address. You'll add the

necessary spacing and punctuation between the merge fields as well. You might be accustomed to pressing the Shift+Enter key combination to start a new line in an inside address without inserting paragraph spacing. However, because your data source includes a record in which one of the fields (the Address Line 2 field) is blank, you need to press the Enter key to start each new line. As you will see later in this tutorial, this ensures that, in the final merged document, Word hides the Address Line 2 field whenever it is blank. To maintain the proper spacing in the main document, you will adjust the paragraph spacing after you insert all the fields.

To insert the remaining merge fields for the inside address:

1. Press the **spacebar** to insert a space after the First Name field, click the **Insert Merge Field button arrow**, and then click **Last_Name**.
2. Press the **Enter** key to start a new paragraph, click the **Insert Merge Field button arrow**, and then click **Address_Line_1**. Word inserts the Address Line 1 merge field into the form letter. Some of the records in the data source include an entry in the Address Line 2 field, so you will insert the Address Line 2 merge field next.
3. Press the **Enter** key, click the **Insert Merge Field button arrow**, and then click **Address_Line_2**. Word inserts the Address Line 2 merge field into the form letter.
4. Press the **Enter** key, insert the **City** merge field, type **,** (a comma), press the **spacebar** to insert a space after the comma, insert the **State** merge field, press the **spacebar**, and then insert the **ZIP_Code** merge field. The inside address now contains all the necessary merge fields. See Figure 6-12. Next you will adjust the paragraph spacing for the inside address.

Figure 6-12 Main document with merge fields for inside address

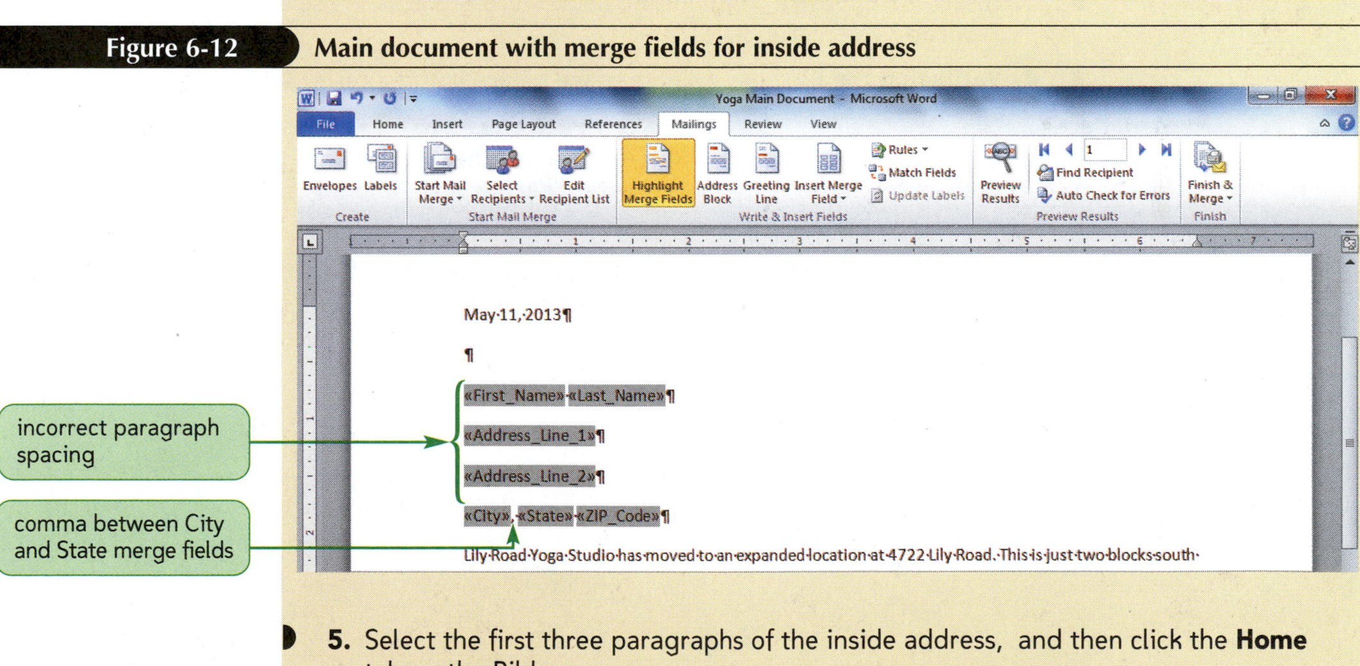

5. Select the first three paragraphs of the inside address, and then click the **Home** tab on the Ribbon.
6. In the Paragraph group, click the **Line and Paragraph Spacing** button, and then click **Remove Space After Paragraph.** The paragraph spacing is removed, so that the paragraphs of the inside address are now correctly spaced.

You can now add the salutation of the letter, which will contain each client's first name.

To insert the merge field for the salutation:

1. Insert a new paragraph after the ZIP_Code field, type **Dear**, and then press the **spacebar**.
2. Click the **Mailings** tab on the Ribbon.
3. In the Write & Insert Fields group, click the **Insert Merge Field** button, click **First_Name** to insert this field into the document, and then type **:** (a colon).
4. Save your work.

You'll further personalize the letter by including merge fields that will allow you to reference each client's favorite type of class and teacher.

To add merge fields for each client's favorite type of class and teacher:

1. Scroll down to display the third paragraph in the body of the letter, which begins "Please check out our schedule...."
2. In the third paragraph in the body of the letter, select the placeholder **[Favorite Type]**, including the brackets. You'll replace this phrase with a merge field. Don't be concerned if you also select the space following the closing bracket.
3. Insert the **Favorite_Type** merge field. Word replaces the selected text with the Favorite Type merge field.
4. Verify that the field has a single space before it and after it. Add a space on either side if necessary.
5. Replace the placeholder text **[Favorite Teacher]** in the third paragraph in the body of the letter with the **Favorite_Teacher** field, and adjust the spacing as necessary. See Figure 6-13.

   Trouble? The text before and after the inserted merge fields might appear with a wavy green underline. This is not a problem.

Figure 6-13 **Main document after inserting merge fields**

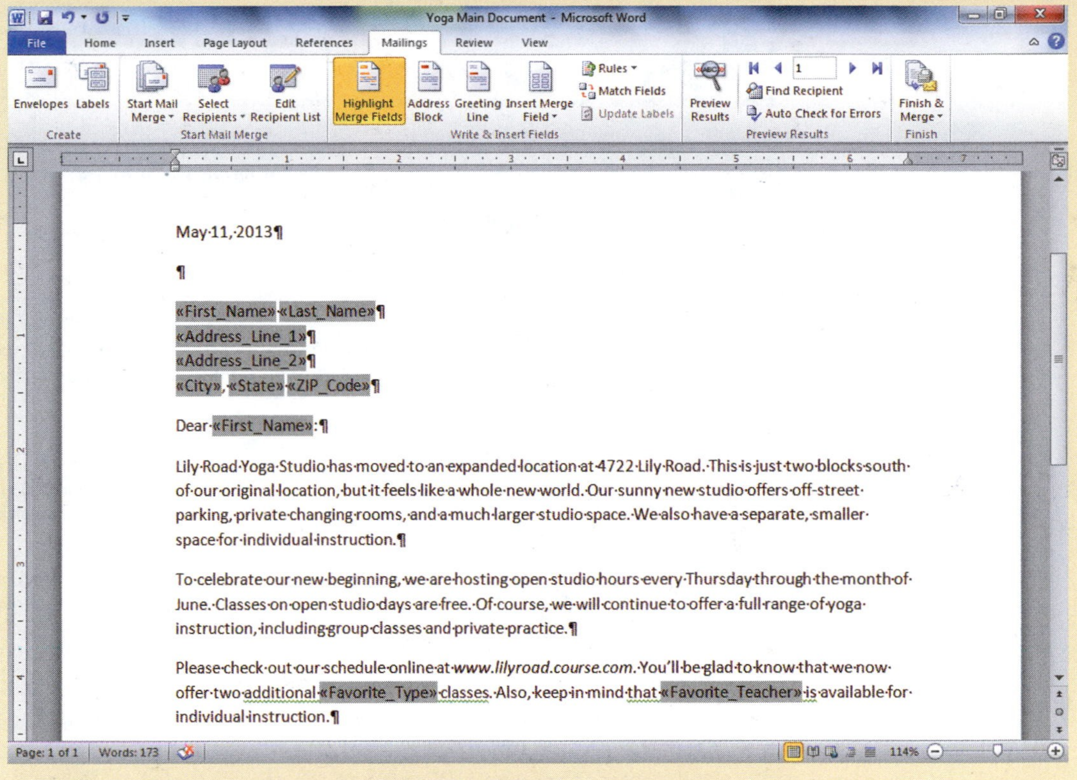

6. Save the document.

The main document now contains all the necessary merge fields. The next step is to merge the main document and the data source. Word allows you to preview the merged document before you complete the merge.

Previewing the Merged Document

Your next step is to preview the merged document to see how the letter will look after Word inserts the information for each client. When you preview the merged document, you can check one last time for any missing spaces between the merge fields and the surrounding text. You can also look for any other formatting problems, and, if necessary, make final changes to the data source.

To preview the merged document:

1. In the Preview Results group, click the **Preview Results** button. The data for the first record (Anna Pearson) replaces the merge fields in the form letter. The inside address for Anna Pearson includes information from the Address Line 2 field, for a total of four lines. The Go to Record box in the Preview Results group shows which record is currently displayed in the document. See Figure 6-14.

Figure 6-14 First letter with merged data

Last Record button

First Record button

Previous Record button

Next Record button

data from the first record

data from the Address_Line_2 field

Go to Record box indicates the record currently displayed

May·11,·2013¶

¶

Anna·Pearson¶
23·First·Avenue¶
Apartment·3B¶
Boise,·ID·83709¶

Dear·Anna:¶

Lily·Road·Yoga·Studio·has·moved·to·an·expanded·location·at·4722·Lily·Road.·This·is·just·two·blocks·south·of·our·original·location,·but·it·feels·like·a·whole·new·world.·Our·sunny·new·studio·offers·off-street·parking,·private·changing·rooms,·and·a·much·larger·studio·space.·We·also·have·a·separate,·smaller·space·for·individual·instruction.¶

To·celebrate·our·new·beginning,·we·are·hosting·open·studio·hours·every·Thursday·through·the·month·of·June.·Classes·on·open·studio·days·are·free.·Of·course,·we·will·continue·to·offer·a·full·range·of·yoga·

2. Carefully check the Anna Pearson letter to make sure the text and formatting are correct, and make any necessary corrections. In particular, check to make sure that the spaces before and after the merged data are correct; it is easy to accidentally omit spaces or add extra spaces around merge fields.
3. In the Preview Results group, click the **Next Record** button ▶. The data for John Andrews is displayed in the letter. As with the preceding record, the inside address for this record includes four lines of information.
4. Click the **Next Record** button ▶ to display the data for Eric Chavez in the letter. In this case, the inside address includes only three lines of information. See Figure 6-15.

Figure 6-15 Address for third record

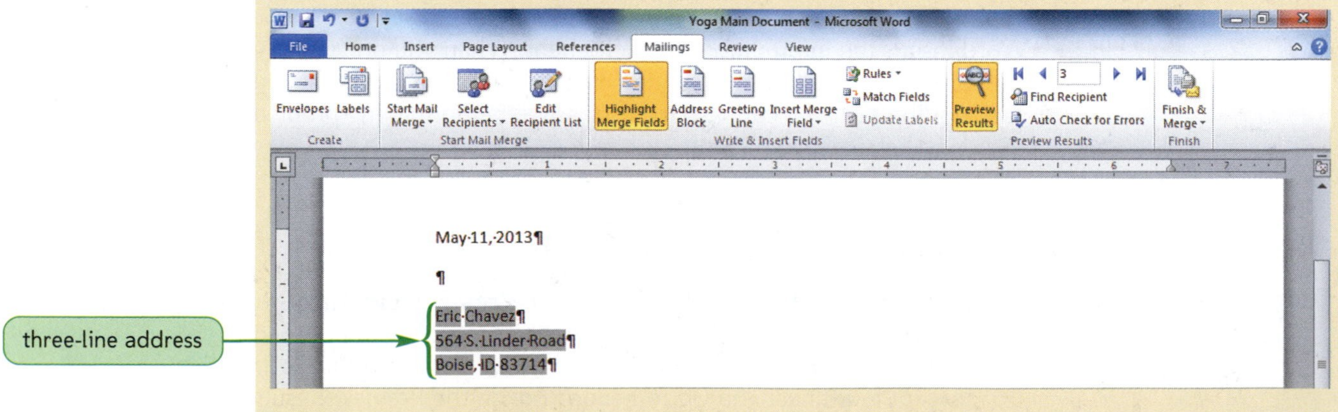

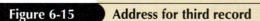

5. In the Preview Results group, click the **First Record** button ⏮ to redisplay the first record in the letter (with data for Anna Pearson).

The main document of the mail merge is complete. Now that you have previewed the merged documents, you can finish the merge.

Merging the Main Document and the Data Source

TIP

If your data source includes an E-mail Address field, you can merge to email, generating one email for every email address in the data source.

When you finish a merge, you can choose to merge directly to the printer. In other words, you can choose to have Word print the merged document immediately without saving it as a separate file. However, Nina wants to save an electronic copy of the merged document for her records. So you'll merge the data source and main document to a new document.

To complete the mail merge:

1. In the Finish group, click the **Finish & Merge** button. As shown in Figure 6-16, the Finish & Merge menu displays the three merge options.

Figure 6-16 Finishing the merge

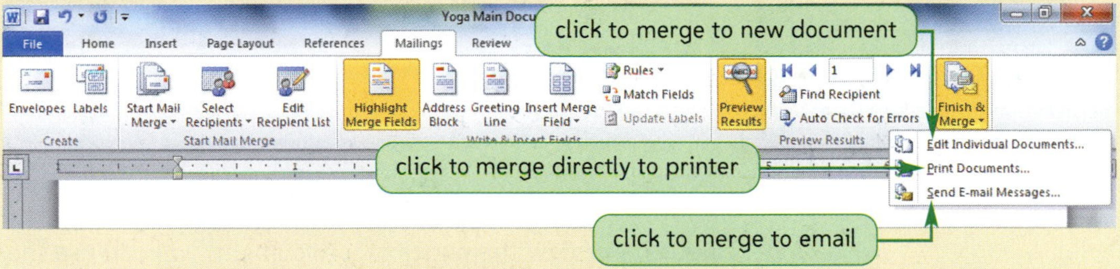

2. In the Finish & Merge menu, click **Edit Individual Documents**. The Merge to New Document dialog box opens. Here, you need to specify which records to include in the merge. You want to include all three records from the data source.
3. Verify that the **All** option button is selected, and then click the **OK** button. Word creates a new document named Letters1, which contains three pages, one for each record in the data source. In this new document, the merge fields have been replaced by the specific names, addresses, and so on, from the data source. See Figure 6-17. The date field appears at the top of every page, highlighted in gray. The gray highlighting will not print.

Figure 6-17 Merged document

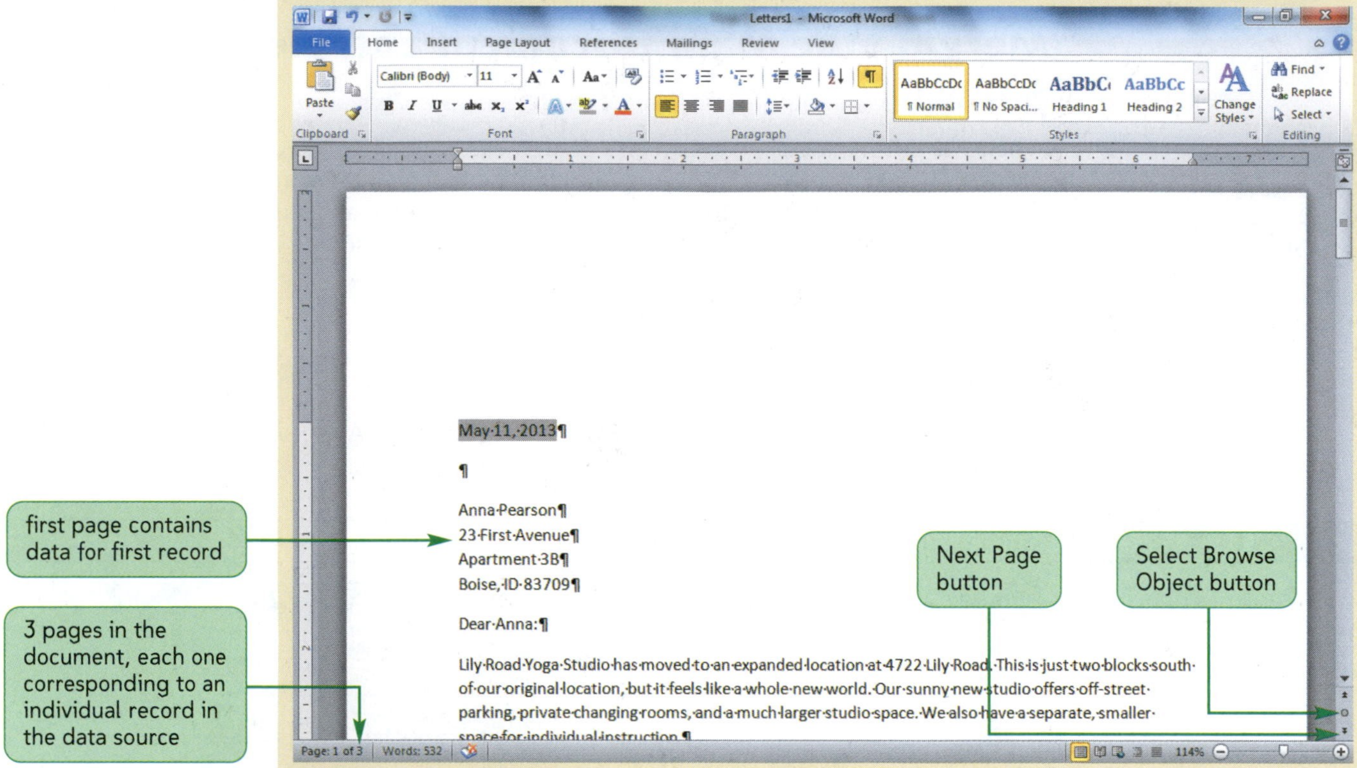

first page contains data for first record

3 pages in the document, each one corresponding to an individual record in the data source

Next Page button

Select Browse Object button

To quickly review the pages of a document, you can use the Select Browse Object button at the bottom of the vertical scroll bar.

4. Click the **Select Browse Object** button near the bottom of the vertical scroll bar, click the **Browse by Page** button on the palette to move to page 2, the letter for John Andrews, and then, below the Select Browse Object button, click the **Next Page** button to move to the letter addressed to Eric Chavez. Note that each letter is addressed to a different client and that the favorite type and teacher vary from one letter to the next.

5. Scroll back to the first page of the document, and as you scroll, notice that the letters are separated by page breaks.

6. Save the merged document in the Word6\Tutorial folder, using the filename **Yoga Merged Letters 1**.

7. Close the **Yoga Merged Letters 1** document. The document named "Yoga Main Document" is now the active document. After completing a merge, you need to save the main document. That ensures that any changes you might have made to the data source in the course of the mail merge are saved along with the main document.

8. Save and close the **Yoga Main Document** document.

Note that if you need to take a break while working on a mail merge, you can save the main document and close it. The data source and field information are saved along with the document. When you're ready to work on the merge again, you can open the main document and update the connection to the data source. You'll see how this works at the beginning of the next session, in which you will learn how to use additional Mail Merge features.

REVIEW

Session 6.1 Quick Check

1. Define the following:
   a. date field
   b. main document
   c. merge field
   d. record
2. A ______________ is a file with information organized into fields and records.
3. True or False. You cannot use an Excel worksheet as a data source.
4. Explain how to use the options in the Mailings tab to insert a merge field into a main document.
5. List the three different ways to complete a merge.

SESSION 6.2 VISUAL OVERVIEW

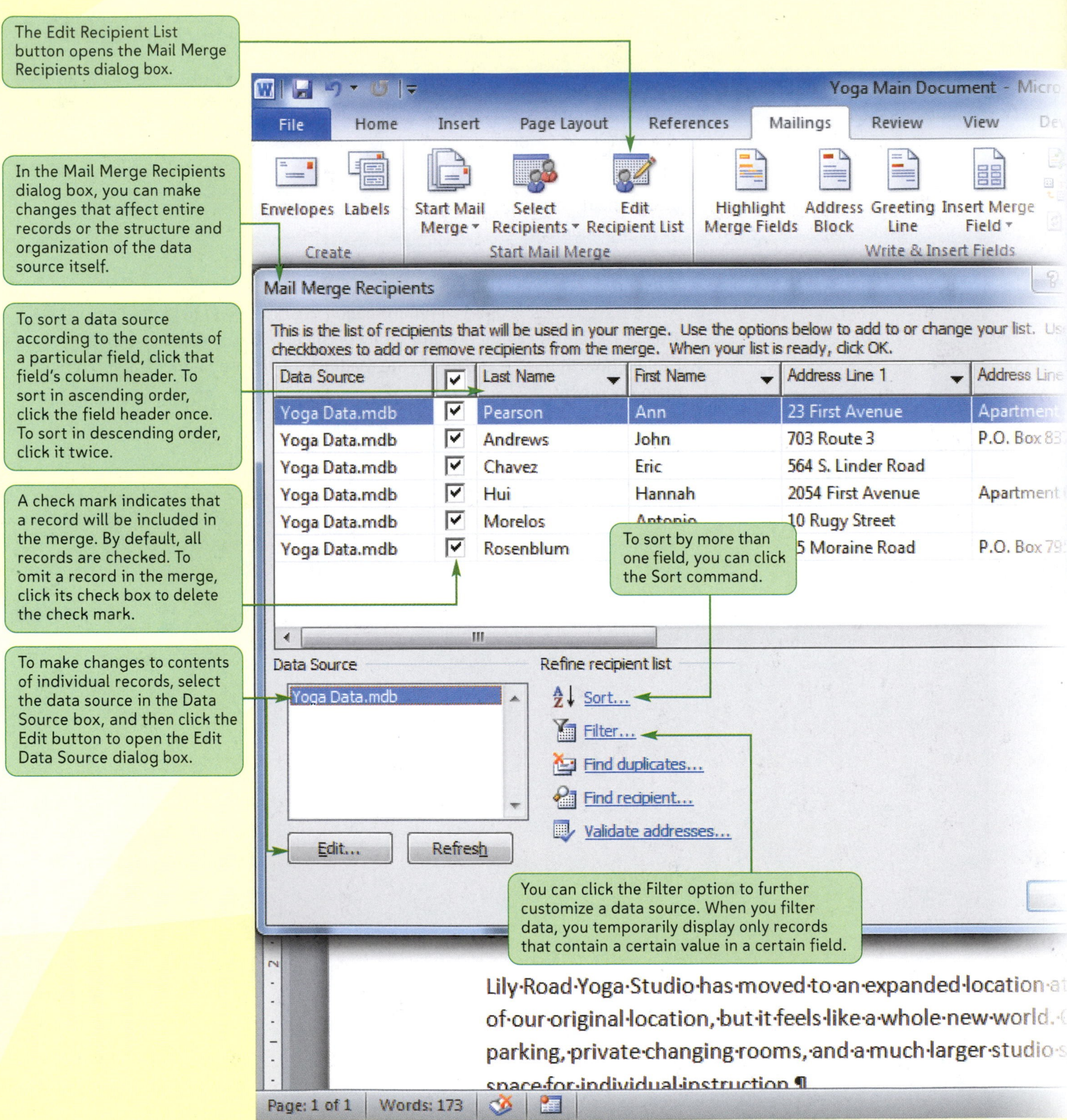
The Edit Recipient List button opens the Mail Merge Recipients dialog box.
In the Mail Merge Recipients dialog box, you can make changes that affect entire records or the structure and organization of the data source itself.
To sort a data source according to the contents of a particular field, click that field's column header. To sort in ascending order, click the field header once. To sort in descending order, click it twice.
A check mark indicates that a record will be included in the merge. By default, all records are checked. To omit a record in the merge, click its check box to delete the check mark.
To make changes to contents of individual records, select the data source in the Data Source box, and then click the Edit button to open the Edit Data Source dialog box.
To sort by more than one field, you can click the Sort command.
You can click the Filter option to further customize a data source. When you filter data, you temporarily display only records that contain a certain value in a certain field.
Yoga Main Document
File
Home
Insert
Page Layout
References
Mailings
Review
View
Envelopes
Labels
Create
Start Mail Merge
Select Recipients
Edit Recipient List
Start Mail Merge
Highlight Merge Fields
Address Block
Greeting Line
Insert Merge Field
Write & Insert Fields
Mail Merge Recipients
This is the list of recipients that will be used in your merge. Use the options below to add to or change your list.
checkboxes to add or remove recipients from the merge. When your list is ready, click OK.
Data Source
Last Name
First Name
Address Line 1
Yoga Data.mdb
Pearson
Ann
23 First Avenue
Andrews
John
703 Route 3
P.O. Box
Chavez
Eric
564 S. Linder Road
Hui
Hannah
2054 First Avenue
Morelos
10 Rugy Street
Rosenblum
5 Moraine Road
Data Source
Refine recipient list
Yoga Data.mdb
Sort...
Filter...
Find duplicates...
Find recipient...
Validate addresses...
Edit...
Refresh
Lily·Road·Yoga·Studio·has·moved·to·an·expanded·location
of·our·original·location,·but·it·feels·like·a·whole·new·world.
parking,·private·changing·rooms,·and·a·much·larger·studio
Page: 1 of 1
Words: 173

EDITING A DATA SOURCE

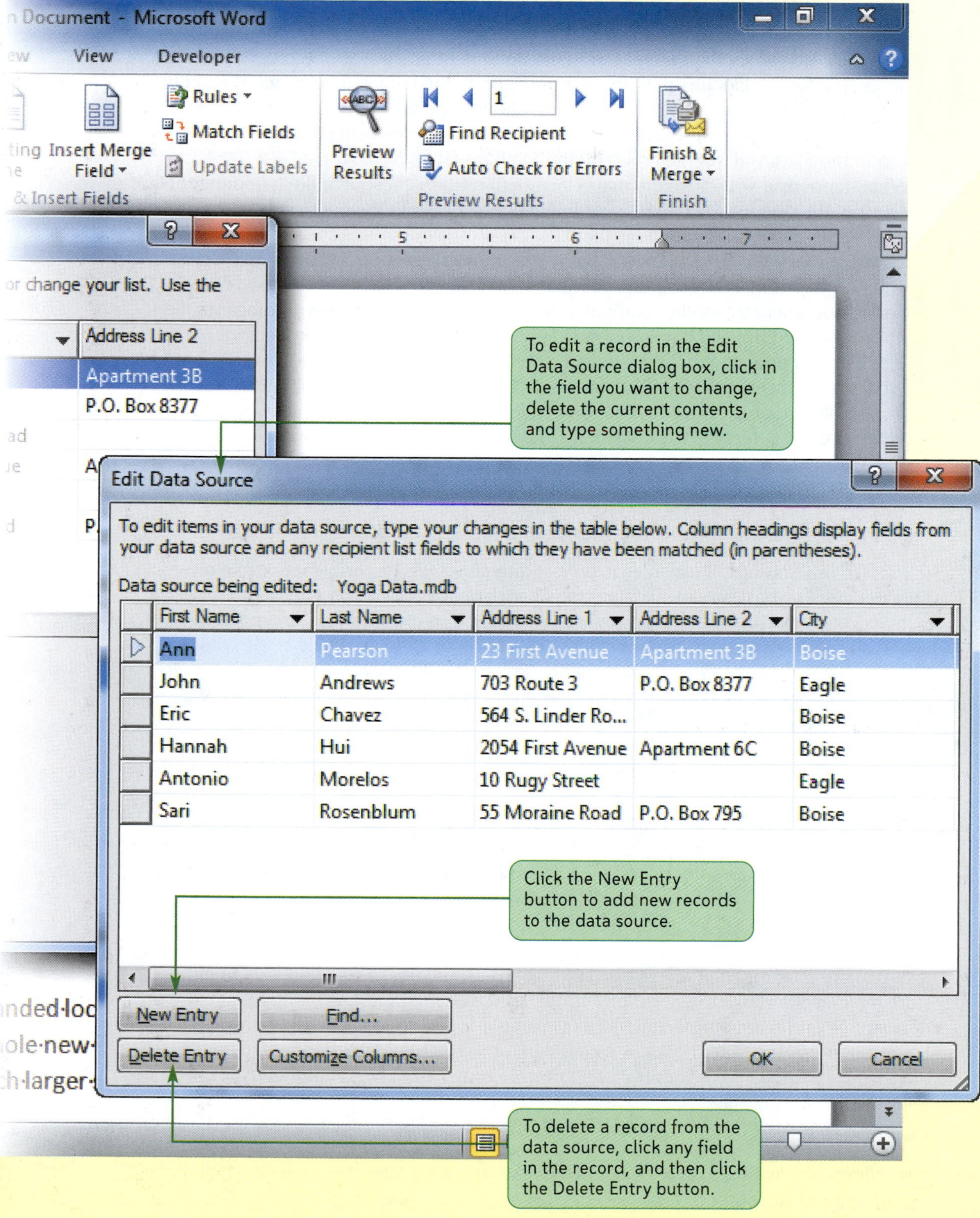
Document - Microsoft Word
View
Developer
Rules
Match Fields
Update Labels
Insert Merge Field
& Insert Fields
Preview Results
1
Find Recipient
Auto Check for Errors
Preview Results
Finish & Merge
Finish
To edit a record in the Edit Data Source dialog box, click in the field you want to change, delete the current contents, and type something new.
Edit Data Source
To edit items in your data source, type your changes in the table below. Column headings display fields from your data source and any recipient list fields to which they have been matched (in parentheses).
Data source being edited: Yoga Data.mdb
First Name
Last Name
Address Line 1
Address Line 2
City
Ann Pearson 23 First Avenue Apartment 3B Boise
John Andrews 703 Route 3 P.O. Box 8377 Eagle
Eric Chavez 564 S. Linder Ro... Boise
Hannah Hui 2054 First Avenue Apartment 6C Boise
Antonio Morelos 10 Rugy Street Eagle
Sari Rosenblum 55 Moraine Road P.O. Box 795 Boise
Click the New Entry button to add new records to the data source.
New Entry
Find...
Delete Entry
Customize Columns...
OK
Cancel
To delete a record from the data source, click any field in the record, and then click the Delete Entry button.

Reopening a Main Document

After you complete a mail merge, a connection exists between the main document file and the data source file, even after you close the main document and exit Word. The connection is maintained as long as you keep both files in their original locations. The two files don't have to be in the same folder; each file just has to remain in the folder it was in when you first created the connection between the two files. When you reopen a main document, you see a warning dialog box explaining that data from a database (that is, the data source) will be placed in the document you are about to open. You can click Yes to open the document with its connection to the data source intact. If you click No, the main document opens with no connection to the data source. In that case, to perform a mail merge, you would have to select a data source using the Select Recipients button in the Start Mail Merge group on the Mailings tab.

What happens if you move the main document or the data source file to a different folder from the one in which they were originally saved? That depends on how your computer is set up and where you move the files. On most Windows 7 computers, you can't move the *data source* file on its own, but if you move the *main document* file to another location on the same computer, the connection is usually maintained. However, if you move the document to another computer on a network, or to a different storage media (say from the hard drive to a memory stick), the connection might be broken. In that case, when you open the main document, you'll see a series of message boxes informing you that the connection to the data source has been broken. Eventually, you will see a Microsoft Word dialog box with a button labeled Find Data Source, which you can click, and then use the Select Data Source dialog box to locate and select your data source.

PROSKILLS

Teamwork: Sharing Main Documents and Data Sources

In professional settings, a mail merge project often involves files originating from multiple people. The best way to manage these files depends on your particular situation. For instance, at a small office supply company, the marketing manager might supply the text of a main document introducing monthly sales on printer supplies, while a sales representative might supply an updated list of names and addresses of potential customers every month. Suppose that you are the person responsible for performing the mail merge on the first of every month. You will be able to perform your work more efficiently if you, the marketing manager, and the sales representative know ahead of time where to store your contributions to the project. For example, you might have a special folder on the company network set up for storing these files.

In large companies, which maintain massive databases of customer information, a data source is typically stored at a fixed network location. In such cases, maintaining the security of the data is extremely important. You usually can't access such a data source without a password and the appropriate encryption software.

If you are creating mail merges for your own personal use, it's a good idea to either store the data source in the default My Data Sources folder and keep it there, or store the data source and the main document in the same folder (a folder other than the My Data Sources folder). The latter option is best if you think you might need to move the files to a different computer. That way, if you do need to move them, you can move the entire folder.

Nina has new client information she wants you to add to the data source used in the last mail merge, and she wants to perform another merge with the new data. To add the new client information, you will start by opening the Yoga Main Document, which is linked to the data source.

To reopen the main document:

1. Open the document named **Yoga Main Document** from the Word6\Tutorial folder included with your Data Files. A warning message appears, indicating that opening the document will run an SQL command. SQL is the database programming language that controls the connection between the main document and the data source.
2. Click the **Yes** button to open the main document with its link to the data source intact, and then click the **Mailings** tab on the Ribbon. The main document displays the data for the last record you examined when you previewed the merged document (Anna Pearson). You can alternate between displaying the merge fields and the client data by toggling the Preview Results button on the Mailings tab.

   Trouble? If you see the merge fields instead of the data for one of the yoga clients, skip to Step 4.
3. In the Preview Results group, click the **Preview Results** button to deselect it. The merge fields are displayed in the main document. The date field, at the beginning of the letter, displays the current date.
4. If necessary, highlight the merge fields by clicking the **Highlight Merge Fields** button in the Write & Insert Fields group.

Editing a Data Source

After you complete a mail merge, you might find that you need to make some changes to the data source and redo the merge. You can edit a data source in two ways—from within the program used to create the data source, or via the Mail Merge Recipients dialog box in Word. If you are familiar with the program used to create the data source, the simplest approach is to edit the file from within that program. For example, if you were using an Excel worksheet as your data source, you could open the file in Excel, edit it (perhaps by adding new records), save it, and then reselect the file as your data source. To edit a Microsoft Office Address Lists file from within Word, you can use the Mail Merge Recipients dialog box.

REFERENCE

Editing a Data Source in Word

- Open the main document for the data source you want to edit.
- In the Start Mail Merge group on the Mailings tab, click the Edit Recipient List button.
- In the Data Source box in the Mail Merge Recipients dialog box, select the data source you want to edit, and then click the Edit button.
- To add a record, click the New Entry button, and then type a new record.
- To delete a record, click any field in the record, and then click the Delete Entry button.
- To add or remove fields from the data source, click the Customize Columns button, make any changes, and then click the OK button. Remember that if you remove a field, you will delete any data entered into that field.
- Click the OK button in the Edit Data Source dialog box, click the Yes button in the Microsoft Office Word dialog box, and then click the OK button in the Mail Merge Recipients dialog box.

Nina would like you to add information for three new clients to the data source.

To edit the data source by adding records:

1. In the Start Mail Merge group on the Mail Merge tab, click the **Edit Recipient List** button. The Mail Merge Recipients dialog box opens, displaying the three records you added when you first created the data source. The Data Source box in the lower-left corner allows you to select a data source to edit. If you had multiple data sources stored in the Word6\Tutorial folder, you would see them all in this list box.
2. In the Data Source box, click **Yoga Data.mdb**. The filename is selected.
3. Click the **Edit** button. The Edit Data Source dialog box opens.
4. Use the New Entry button to enter the information for the three new records shown in Figure 6-18. When you are finished, you will have a total of six records in the data source. Notice that the record for Antonio Morelos contains no Address Line 2 data.

Figure 6-18 New client data

First Name	Last Name	Address Line 1	Address Line 2	City	State	Zip Code	E-Mail Address	Phone	Favorite Type	Favorite Teacher
Hannah	Hiu	2054 First Avenue	Apartment 6C	Boise	ID	83709	hiu@surgery.hospital.net	208-775-3093	Hatha	Niki Dronza
Antonio	Morelos	10 Rugby Street		Eagle	ID	83707	morelos-a@bfjorgen.com	208-787-1000	Hatha	Niki Dronza
Sari	Rosenblum	55 Moraine Road	P.O. Box 795	Boise	ID	83710	sari@rosenblum78.course.com	208-987-0098	Power Yoga	Carolyn Ramirez

5. Click the **OK** button, and then click the **Yes** button in the message box that appears, asking if you want to update the Yoga Data.mdb file. You return to the Mail Merge Recipients dialog box, as shown in Figure 6-19.

   Trouble? If your records look different from those in Figure 6-19, select the data source, click the Edit button, edit the data source, and then click the OK button.

Figure 6-19 New records added to data source

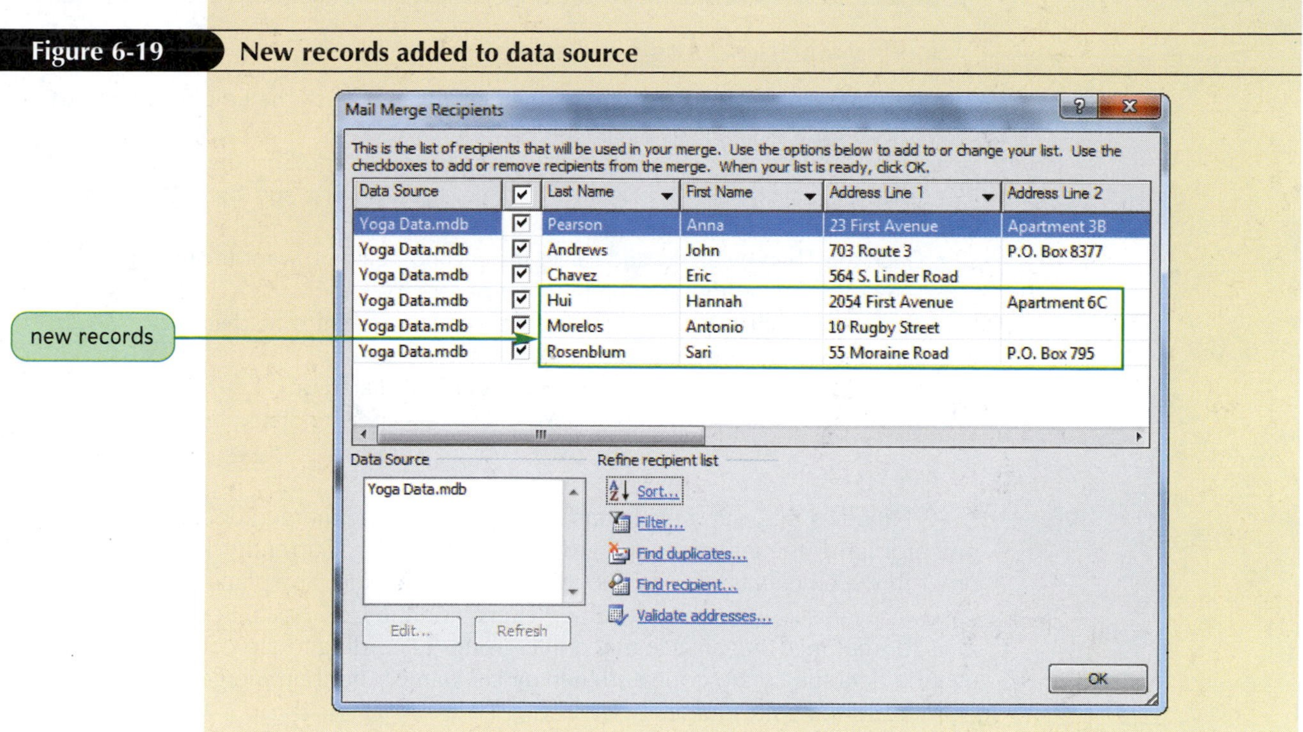

You'll leave the Mail Merge Recipients dialog box open so you can use it to make other changes to the data source.

Sorting Records

You can sort information in a data source table just as you sort information in any other table. Recall that to sort means to rearrange a list or a document in alphabetical, numerical, or chronological order. To quickly sort information in ascending order (*A* to *Z*, lowest to highest, or earliest to latest) or in descending order (*Z* to *A*, highest to lowest, or latest to earliest), click a field's heading in the Mail Merge Recipients dialog box. The first time you click the heading, the records are sorted in ascending order. If you click it a second time, the records are sorted in descending order.

To perform a more complicated sort, you can click the Sort command in the Mail Merge Recipients dialog box. This opens the Filter and Sort dialog box, where you can choose to sort by more than one field. For example, you could sort records in ascending order by last name, and then in ascending order by first name, in which case the records would be organized alphabetically by last name, and then, in cases where multiple records contained the same last name, those records would be sorted by first name.

REFERENCE

Sorting a Data Source by Multiple Fields

- In the Start Mail Merge group on the Mailings tab, click the Edit Recipient List button to open the Mail Merge Recipients dialog box.
- Click Sort to open the Sort Records tab of the Filter and Sort dialog box.
- Click the Sort by arrow, select the first field you want to sort by, and then select the Descending option button if necessary.
- Click the Then by arrow and select the second field you want to sort by, and then select the Descending option button if necessary.
- If necessary, click the Then by arrow and select the third field you want to sort by, and then select the Descending option button if necessary.
- Click the OK button to close the Filter and Sort dialog box.
- Click the OK button to close the Mail Merge Recipients dialog box.

As Nina looks through the letters to her clients in the merged document, she notices one problem—the letters are not grouped by zip codes. Currently, the letters are in the order in which clients were added to the data source file. She plans to use business mail (also known as bulk mail) to send her letters, and the U.S. Postal Service offers lower rates for mailings that are separated into groups according to zip code. She asks you to sort the data file by zip code and then by last name, and then merge the main document with the sorted data source.

To sort the data source by zip code:

1. In the Mail Merge Recipients dialog box, click **Sort**. The Filter and Sort dialog box opens, with the Sort Records tab displayed.
2. Click the **Sort by** arrow, and then click **ZIP Code**.
3. Click the first **Then by** arrow, and then click **Last Name**. See Figure 6-20.

Figure 6-20 **Sorting by zip code and by last name**

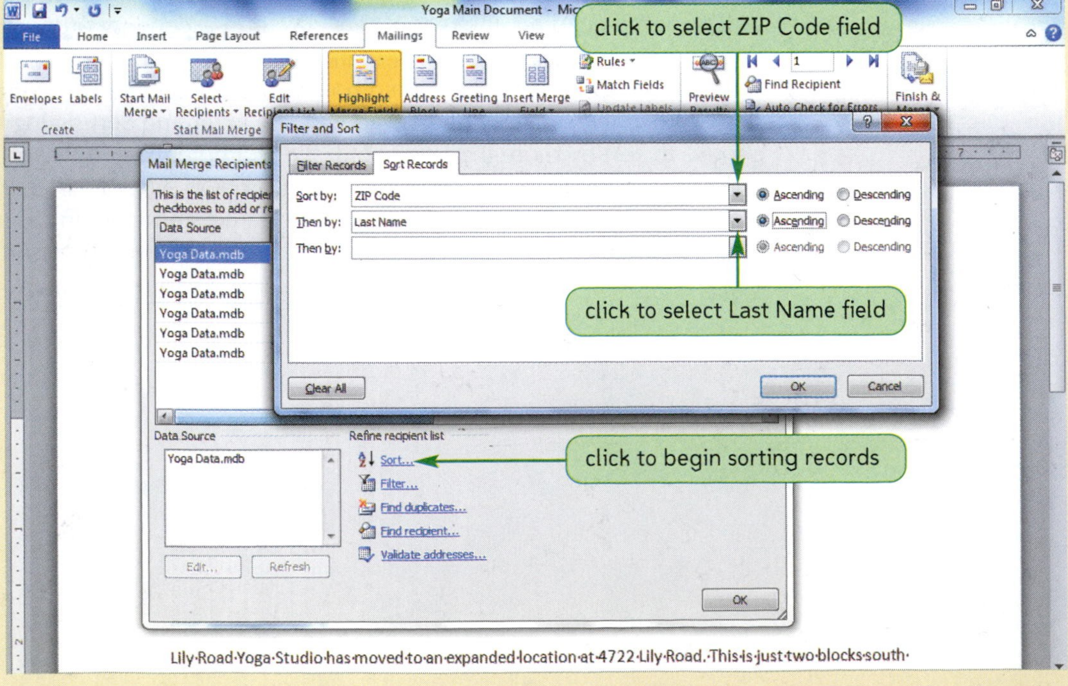

4. Click the **OK** button. Word sorts the records from lowest zip code number to highest, and then, within each zip code, it sorts the records by last name. In the Mail Merge Recipients dialog box, the record for John Andrews, with zip code 83707, is now at the top of the data source list. The record for Antonio Morelos, which also has a zip code of 83707, comes second. The remaining records are sorted similarly, with the record for Eric Chavez the last in the list. When you merge the data source with the form letter, the letters will appear in the merged document in this order.
5. Click the **OK** button. The Mail Merge Recipients dialog box closes.
6. In the Preview Results group, click the **Preview Results** button. The data for John Andrews is displayed in the main document.
7. In the Finish group, click the **Finish & Merge** button, click **Edit Individual Documents**, verify that the **All** option button is selected in the Merge to New Document dialog box, and then click the **OK** button. Word generates the new merged document with six letters, one letter per page as before—but this time the first letter is to John Andrews, who has the lowest zip code (83707) and a last name that comes before "Morelos" in the alphabet.
8. Use the Select Browse Object button to browse by page and verify that the letters in the newly merged document are arranged in ascending order by zip code.
9. Save the new merged document in the Word6\Tutorial folder, using the filename **Yoga Merged Letters 2**, and then close it. You return to the Yoga Main Document.
10. Save the Yoga Main Document file.

Next, Nina would like you to create a set of letters to just those clients who listed Carolyn Ramirez as their favorite teacher.

Filtering Records

Nina wants to inform clients that the teacher Carolyn Ramirez is available for individual instruction only on Tuesdays and Thursdays. She asks you to modify the form letter and then merge it with the records of clients who have indicated that Carolyn is their favorite teacher. To select specific records in a data source, you **filter** the data source to temporarily display only the records containing a particular value in a particular field. To filter a data source, open the Mail Merge Recipients dialog box, click the arrow button in the column header for the field for which you want to specify a value to filter by, and then click the value you want to filter by.

To filter the data source to select specific records for the merge:

1. In the Preview Results group, click the **Preview Results** button to deselect it and display the merge fields in the Yoga Main Document file instead of the data from the data source.
2. Scroll the document, and then in the body of the letter, click at the end of the third paragraph, which begins "Please check out our schedule online...."
3. Press the ← key to move the insertion point to the left of the period, insert a space, type **on Tuesdays and Thursdays**, and then verify that the sentence reads "...<<Favorite_Teacher>> is available for individual instruction on Tuesdays and Thursdays."

4. Save the Yoga Main Document with the new name, **Carolyn Main Document**, in the Word6\Tutorial folder included with your Data Files.

TIP

To remove an individual record from a merge, deselect the corresponding check box in the Mail Merge Recipients dialog box.

5. In the Start Mail Merge group, click the **Edit Recipient List** button to open the Mail Merge Recipients dialog box, and then scroll right so you can see the Favorite Teacher field.

6. Click the arrow button in the Favorite Teacher column header. A menu opens, listing all the entries in the Favorite Teacher field as well as a few other options. You can use the (All) option to redisplay all records after previously filtering a data source. See Figure 6-21.

Figure 6-21 Filtering records in a data source

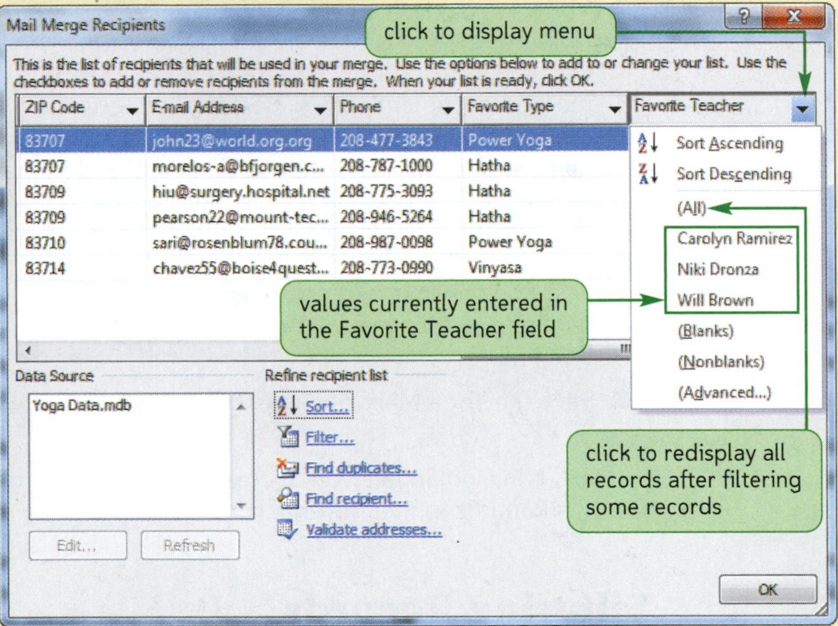

You can use the Advanced option in the Filter menu to open the Filter Records tab in the Filter and Sort dialog box, where you can perform complex filter operations that involve comparing the contents of one or more fields to a particular value to determine if a record should be displayed or not.

7. Click **Carolyn Ramirez**. Word temporarily hides all the records in the data source except those that contain "Carolyn Ramirez" in the Favorite Teacher field. See Figure 6-22. Now you can complete the merge.

Figure 6-22 Filtered data source

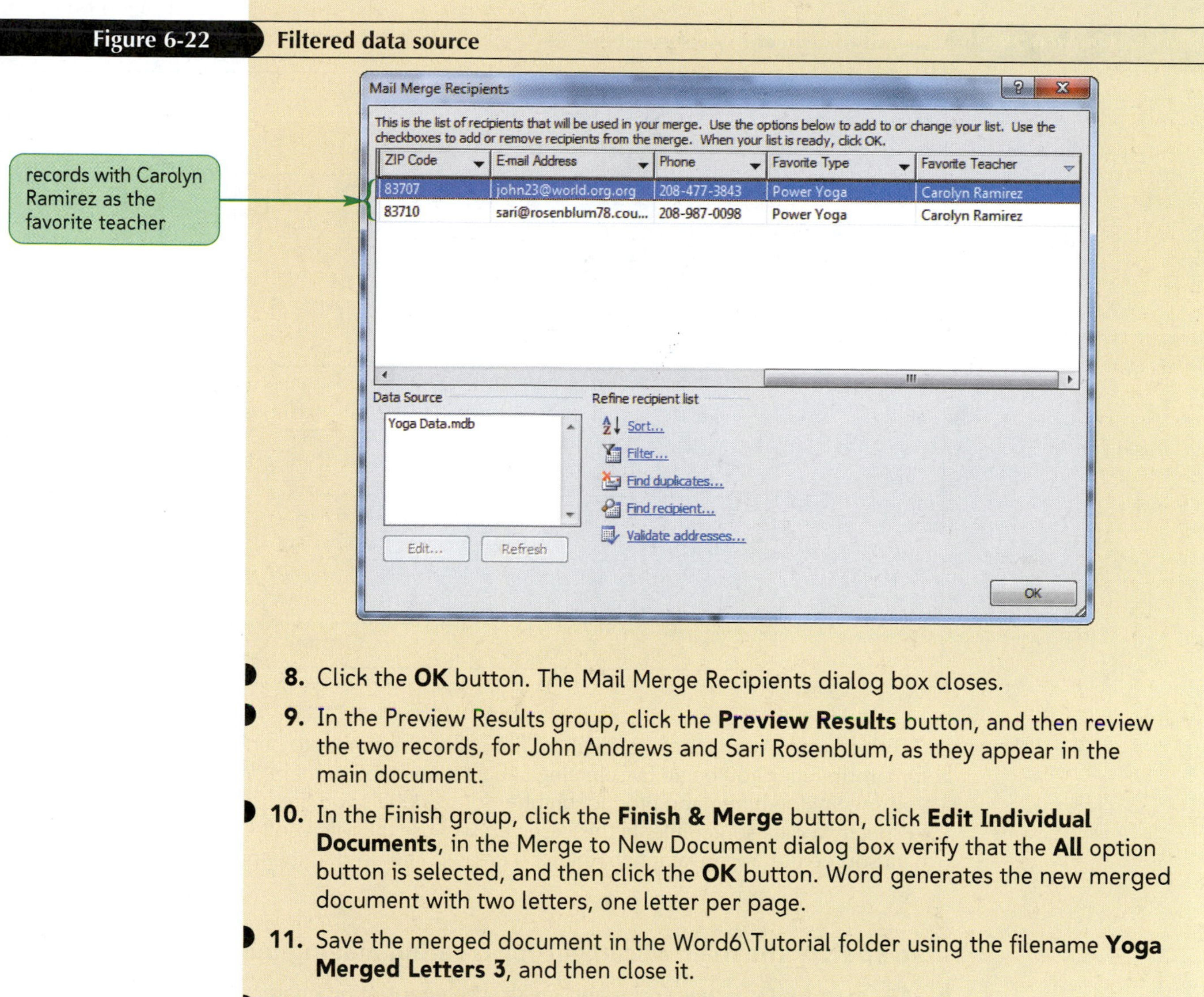

8. Click the **OK** button. The Mail Merge Recipients dialog box closes.
9. In the Preview Results group, click the **Preview Results** button, and then review the two records, for John Andrews and Sari Rosenblum, as they appear in the main document.
10. In the Finish group, click the **Finish & Merge** button, click **Edit Individual Documents**, in the Merge to New Document dialog box verify that the **All** option button is selected, and then click the **OK** button. Word generates the new merged document with two letters, one letter per page.
11. Save the merged document in the Word6\Tutorial folder using the filename **Yoga Merged Letters 3**, and then close it.
12. Save the **Carolyn Main Document** file, and then close it.

Next, you'll create and print mailing labels for the form letters.

Creating Mailing Labels

Nina could print the names and addresses for the letters directly on envelopes, or she could perform a mail merge to create mailing labels. The latter method is easier because she can print 14 labels at once, rather than printing one envelope at a time.

Nina has purchased Avery® Laser Printer labels, which are available in most office-supply stores. Word supports most of the Avery label formats, allowing you to choose the layout that works best for you. Nina purchased labels in 8 1/2 × 11-inch sheets that are designed to feed through a printer. Each label measures 4 × 1.33 inches. Each sheet contains seven rows of labels, with two labels in each row, for a total of 14 labels. See Figure 6-23.

Figure 6-23 Layout of a sheet of Avery® labels

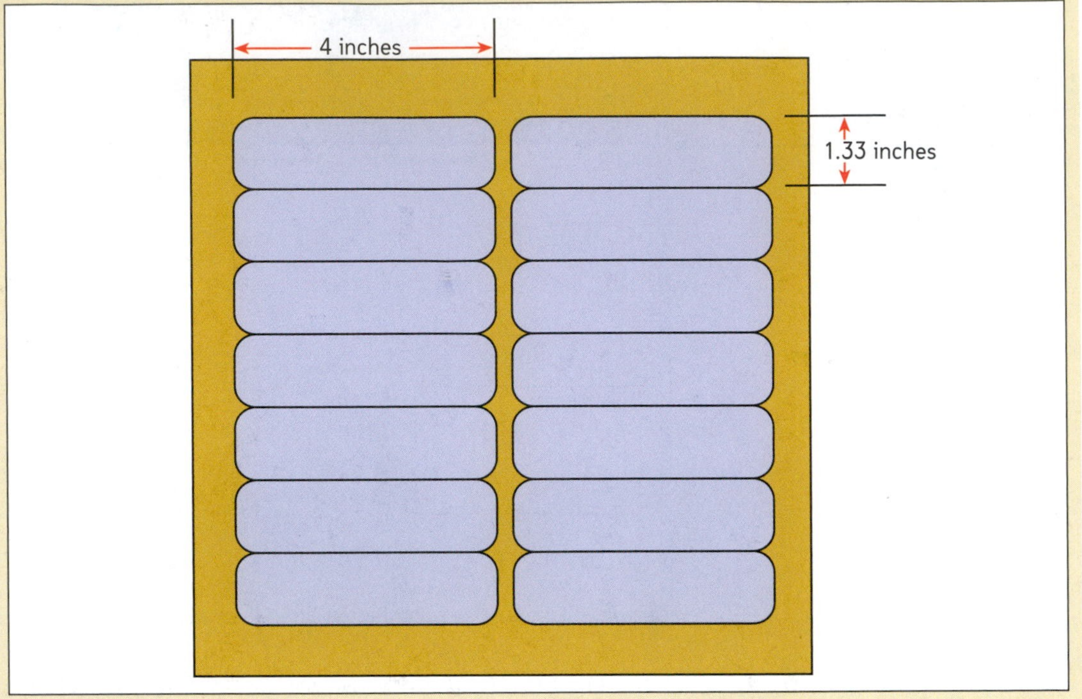

Performing a mail merge to create mailing labels is similar to performing a mail merge for a form letter. You begin by selecting Labels as the type of main document, and then you specify the brand and product number for the labels you are using. You will also need to specify a data source file. In this case you will use the Microsoft Office Address Lists data source file, Yoga Data.mdb, that you created and used in the form letter mail merges.

To specify the main document for creating mailing labels:

1. Open a new, blank document, make sure nonprinting characters are displayed, and zoom out so you can see the whole page.
2. Save the document to the Word6\Tutorial folder using the filename **Yoga Labels Main Document**.
3. Click the **Mailings** tab on the Ribbon.
4. In the Start Mail Merge group, click the **Start Mail Merge** button, and then click **Labels**. The Label Options dialog box opens.
5. Click the **Label vendors** arrow, and then click **Avery US Letter**.
6. Scroll down the Product number box, and then click **5162 Easy Peel Address Labels**. See Figure 6-24.

Figure 6-24 Label Options dialog box

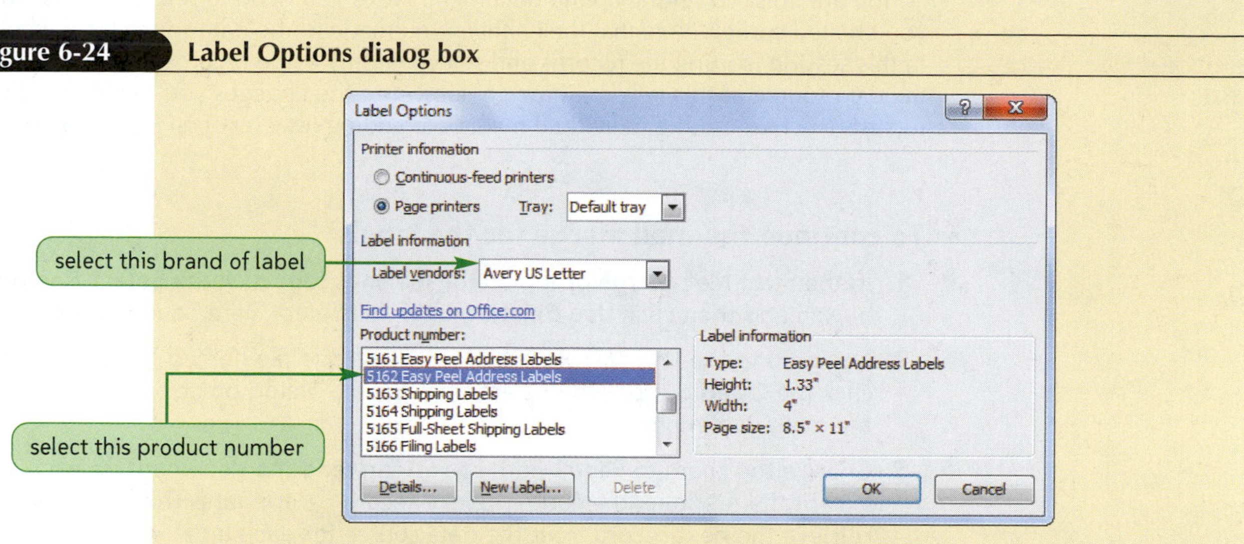

7. Click the **OK** button. The Label Options dialog box closes and Word inserts a table structure into the document, with one cell for each of the 14 labels on the page, as shown in Figure 6-25. The gridlines are visible only on the screen; they will not be visible on the printed labels.

Figure 6-25 Document ready for labels

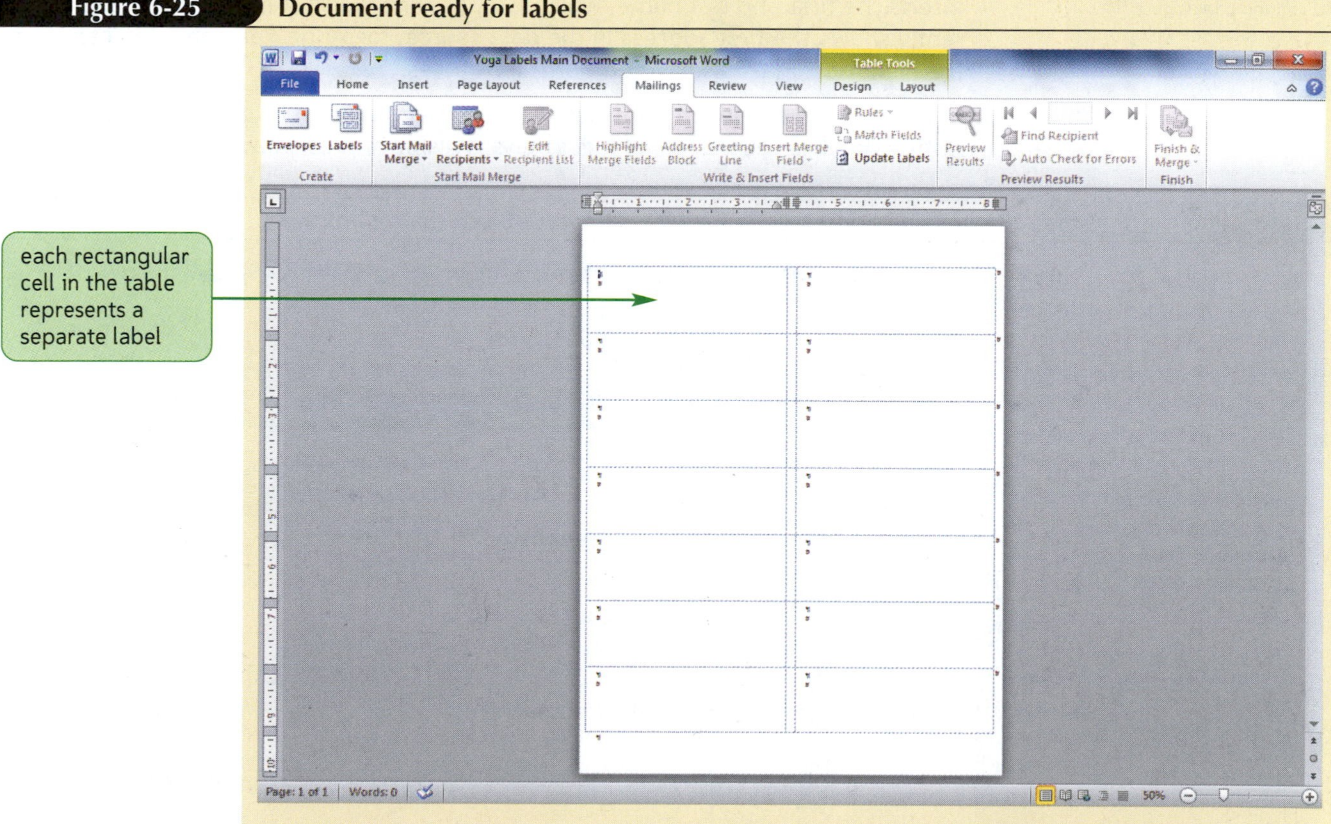

Trouble? If you don't see the table gridlines, click the Table Tools Layout tab, and then, in the Table group, click the View Gridlines button to select it.

You are finished setting up the document. Next, you need to select the data source you created earlier. Note that the changes you made to the data source as a whole earlier in this session (sorting the records and selecting only some records) have no effect on the data source in this new mail merge. However, the changes you made to individual records (such as editing individual records or adding new records) are retained.

To continue the mail merge for the labels:

1. In the Start Mail Merge group on the Mailings tab, click the **Select Recipients** button and then click **Use Existing List**. The Select Data Source dialog box opens.
2. Navigate to the Word6\Tutorial folder, select the file named **Yoga Data**, and then click the **Open** button. The Select Data Source dialog box closes and you return to the main document.
3. Change the zoom to Page Width so you can read the document. In each label except the first one, the code <<Next Record>> appears. This code tells Word to retrieve the next record from the data source for each label.
4. Verify that the insertion point is located in the upper-left label, and then click the **Mailings tab** on the Ribbon.
5. In the Write & Insert Fields group, click the **Address Block** button. The Insert Address Block dialog box opens. The left pane displays possible formats for the name in the address block. The default format, "Joshua Randall Jr.," simply inserts the first and last name, which is what Nina wants. The Preview pane currently shows the first address in the data source, for Anna Pearson. You can click the Next button to display additional addresses.
6. In the Preview section of the Insert Address Field dialog box, click the **Next** button ▷. The record for John Andrews is displayed, as shown in Figure 6-26.

> **TIP**
>
> You can only use the Address Block merge field if you include a State field in your data source.

Figure 6-26 Previewing addresses in the Insert Address Block dialog box

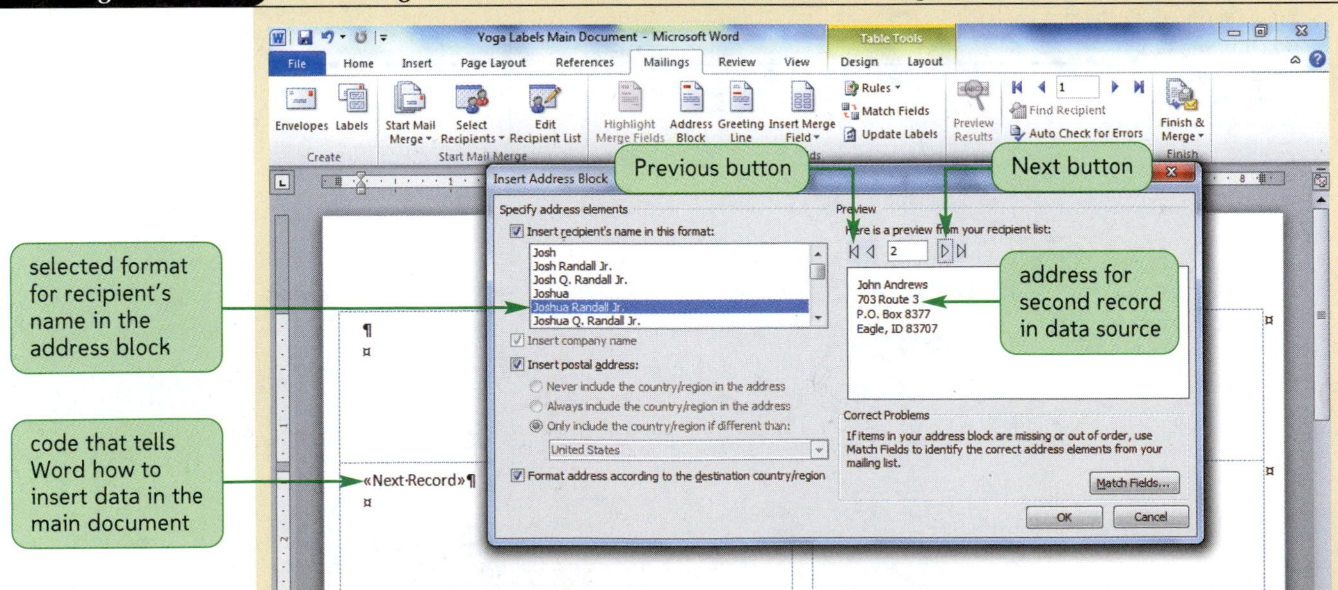

7. Click the **OK** button. The Insert Address Block dialog box closes, and an Address Block merge field appears in the upper-left label on the page. Next, you need to update the remaining labels to match the one containing the Address Block merge field.

8. In the Write & Insert Fields group, click the **Update Labels** button. The Address Block merge field is inserted into all the labels in the document, as shown in Figure 6-27. In all except the upper-left label, the Next Record code appears to the left of the Address Block merge field.

Figure 6-27 Field codes inserted into document

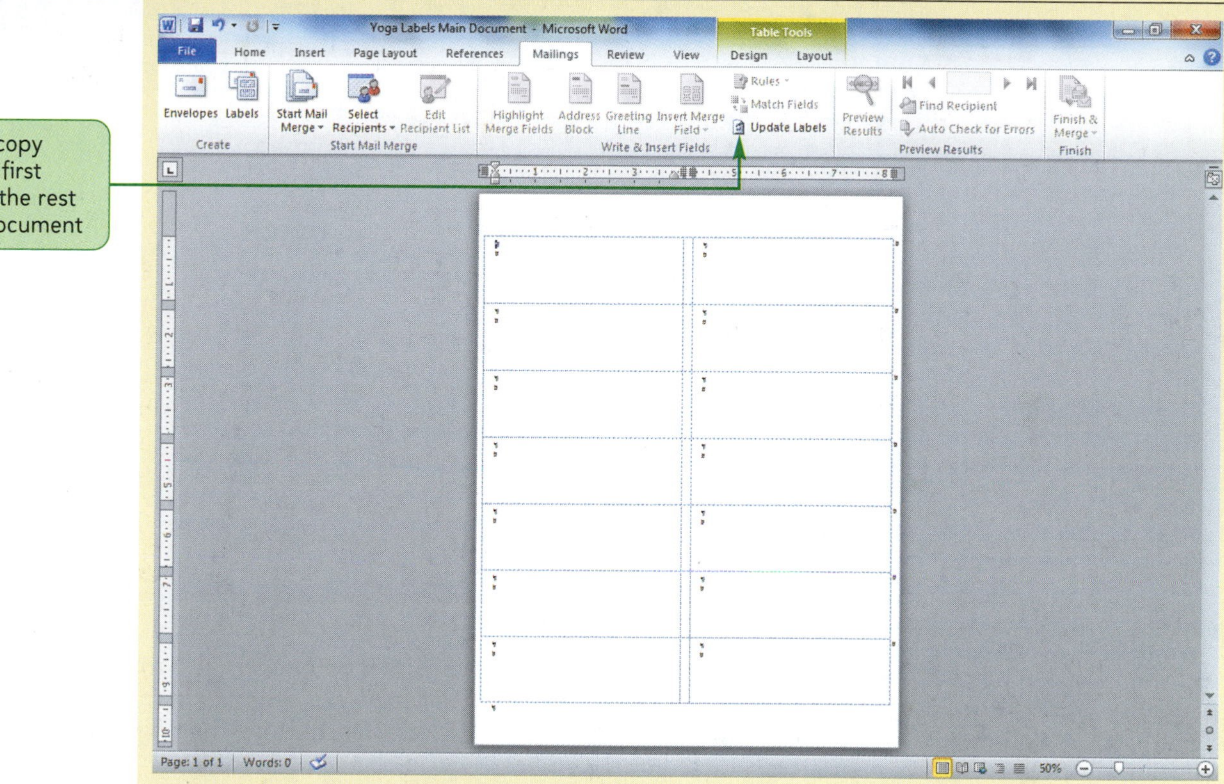

You are ready to preview the labels and complete the merge. To ensure that you see all the labels in the preview, make sure the Go to Records box in the Preview Results group displays the number "1".

To preview the labels and complete the merge:

1. If necessary, click the **First Record** button in the Preview Results group to display "1" in the Go to Record box.
2. In the Preview Results group, click the **Preview Results** button. The data for Nina's six clients is displayed in the main document. See Figure 6-28.

Figure 6-28 **Previewing addresses in labels**

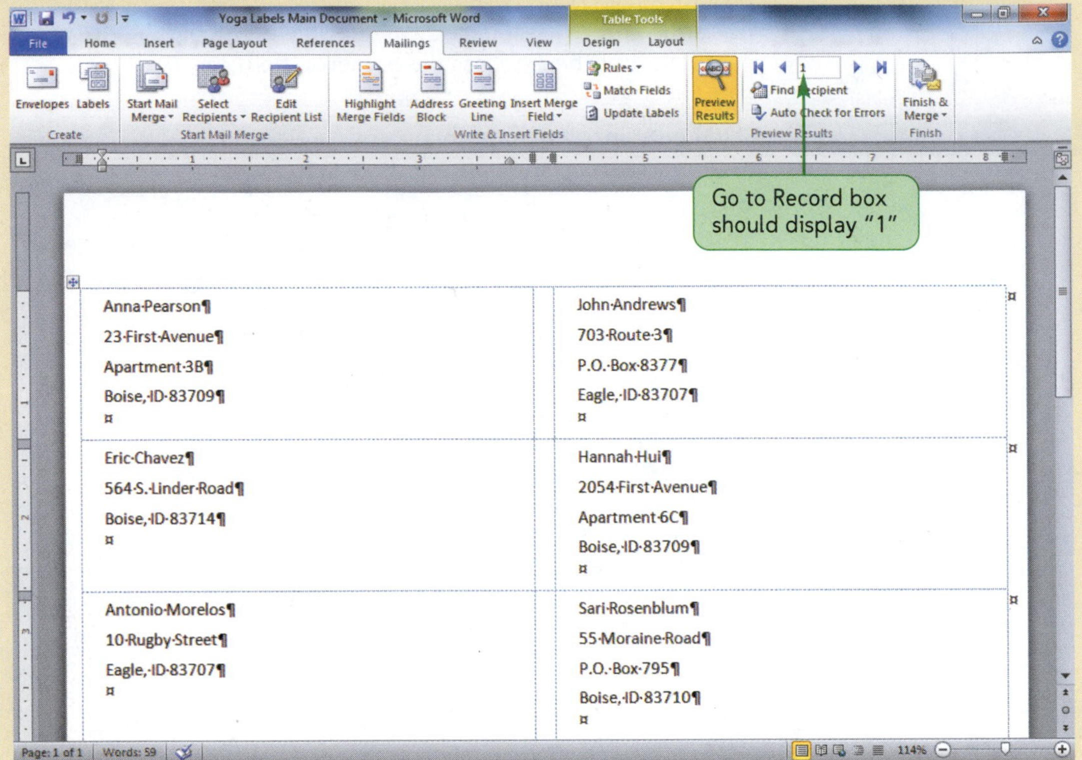

3. In the Finish group, click the **Finish & Merge** button, click **Edit Individual Documents**, verify that the **All** option button is selected in the Merge to New Document dialog box, and then click the **OK** button. The finished labels are inserted into a new document.

4. Scroll through the document. The document contains space for 14 labels, but because the data source contains only six records, the new document contains addresses for six labels.

5. In the upper-left label, change "Anna Pearson" to your name, and then save the merged document in the Word6\Tutorial folder using the filename **Yoga Merged Labels**.

6. Close the **Yoga Merged Labels** document, then save and close the Yoga Labels Main Document file.

TIP

It is a good idea to print one page of a label document on regular paper so you can check your work before printing on the more expensive sheets of adhesive labels.

Creating a Telephone Directory

Next, Nina wants you to create a list of telephone numbers for all the teachers at Lily Road Yoga Studio. Nina has already created a Word document containing the phone numbers; you will use that document as the data source for the merge. You'll set up a mail merge as before, except this time you'll select Directory as the main document type. You'll start by examining the Word document that Nina wants you to use as the data source and then create the main document.

To review the data source and create the main document for the merge:

1. Open the document named **Phone** from the Word6\Tutorial folder, and then save it as **Phone Data** in the same folder. The information in this document is arranged in a table with three column headings: "First Name," "Last Name," and "Phone." The information in the table has already been sorted in alphabetical order by last name.
2. In the bottom row, replace "Nina Ranabhat" with your first and last name, and then save and close the Phone Data document.
3. Open a new, blank document, display nonprinting characters and the rulers, if necessary, and change the Zoom to Page Width.
4. Save the main document in the Word6\Tutorial folder using the filename **Phone Directory with Merge Fields**.
5. Click the **Mailings** tab on the Ribbon.
6. In the Start Mail Merge group, click the **Start Mail Merge** button, and then click **Directory**.
7. In the Start Mail Merge group, click the **Select Recipients** button, and then click **Use Existing List** to open the Select Data Source dialog box.
8. Navigate to and select the file named **Phone Data** in the Word6\Tutorial folder, and click the **Open** button. The main document is still blank; you'll insert the merge fields next.

You're ready to insert the fields in the main document. Nina wants the telephone list to include the names at the left margin of the page and the phone numbers at the right margin. You'll set up the main document so that the phone number is preceded by a dot leader. A **dot leader** is a dotted line that extends from the last letter of text on the left margin to the beginning of the nearest text aligned at a tab stop.

To set up the directory main document with dot leaders:

1. With the insertion point in the first line of the document, insert the **First_Name** merge field, insert a space, insert the **Last_Name** merge field, and then in the Write & Insert Fields group, click the **Highlight Merge Fields** button. The First Name and Last Name merge fields are displayed on a gray background. Now you'll set a tab stop at the right margin (at the 6-inch mark on the ruler) with a dot leader.
2. Click the **Home** tab on the Ribbon.
3. In the Paragraph group, click the **Dialog Box Launcher** to open the Paragraph dialog box, and then in the lower-left corner of the Indents and Spacing tab, click the **Tabs** button. The Tabs dialog box opens.
4. Type **6** in the Tab stop position box, click the **Right** option button in the Alignment section, and then click the **2 ....** option button in the Leader section. See Figure 6-29.

TIP

You can click the Clear All button in the Tabs dialog box to delete all the tab stops in the document.

Figure 6-29 Creating a tab with a dot leader

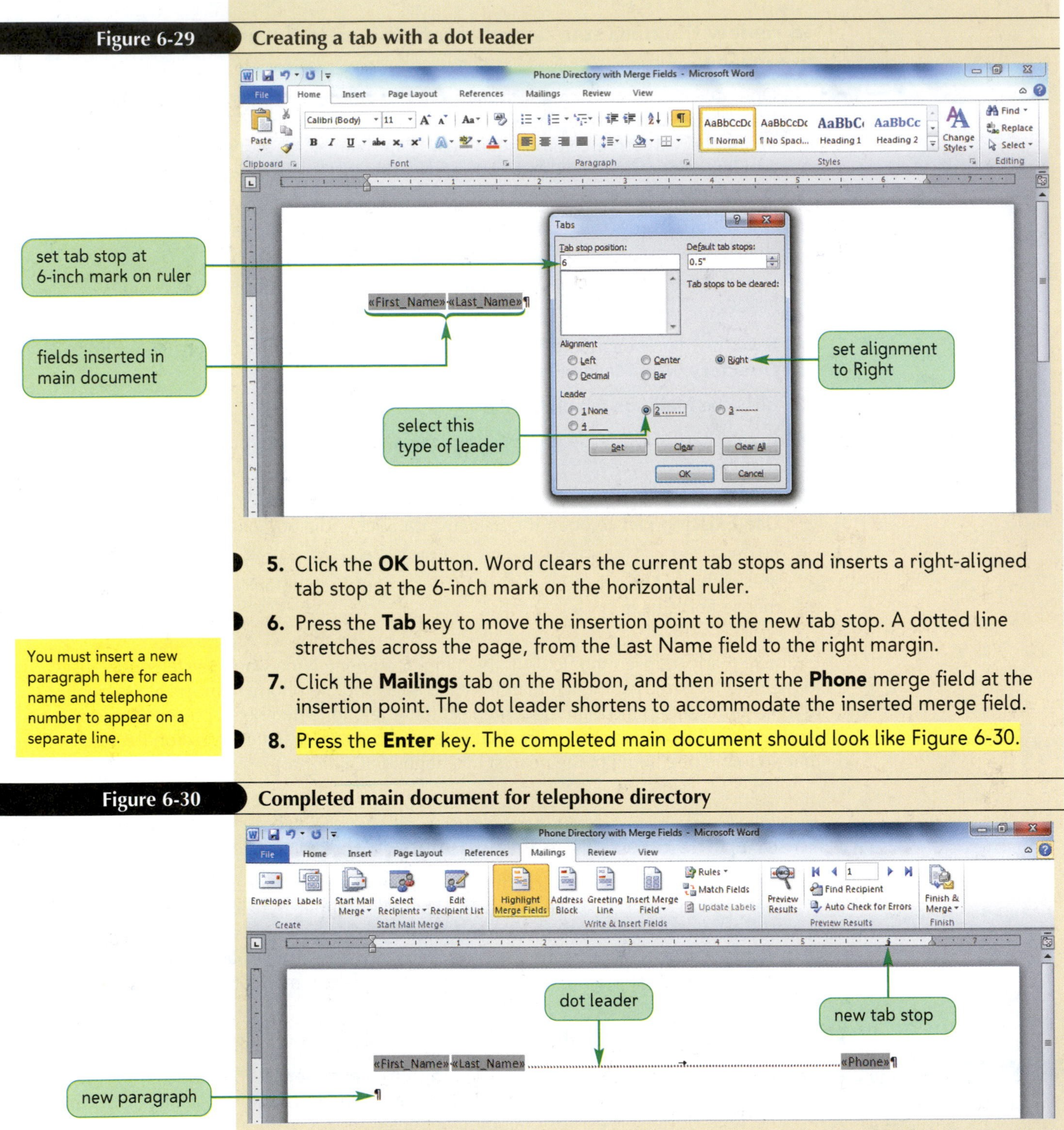

5. Click the **OK** button. Word clears the current tab stops and inserts a right-aligned tab stop at the 6-inch mark on the horizontal ruler.
6. Press the **Tab** key to move the insertion point to the new tab stop. A dotted line stretches across the page, from the Last Name field to the right margin.
7. Click the **Mailings** tab on the Ribbon, and then insert the **Phone** merge field at the insertion point. The dot leader shortens to accommodate the inserted merge field.
8. Press the **Enter** key. The completed main document should look like Figure 6-30.

You must insert a new paragraph here for each name and telephone number to appear on a separate line.

Figure 6-30 Completed main document for telephone directory

You are now ready to merge this file with the data source.

To finish the merge for the phone list:

1. In the Preview Results group, click the **Preview Results** button, and then review the data for the first record in the document.
2. In the Finish group, click the **Finish & Merge** button, click **Edit Individual Documents**, verify that the **All** option button is selected in the Merge to New Document dialog box, and then click the **OK** button. Word creates a new document named Directory1 that contains the completed telephone list. See Figure 6-31.

Figure 6-31 Completed telephone directory

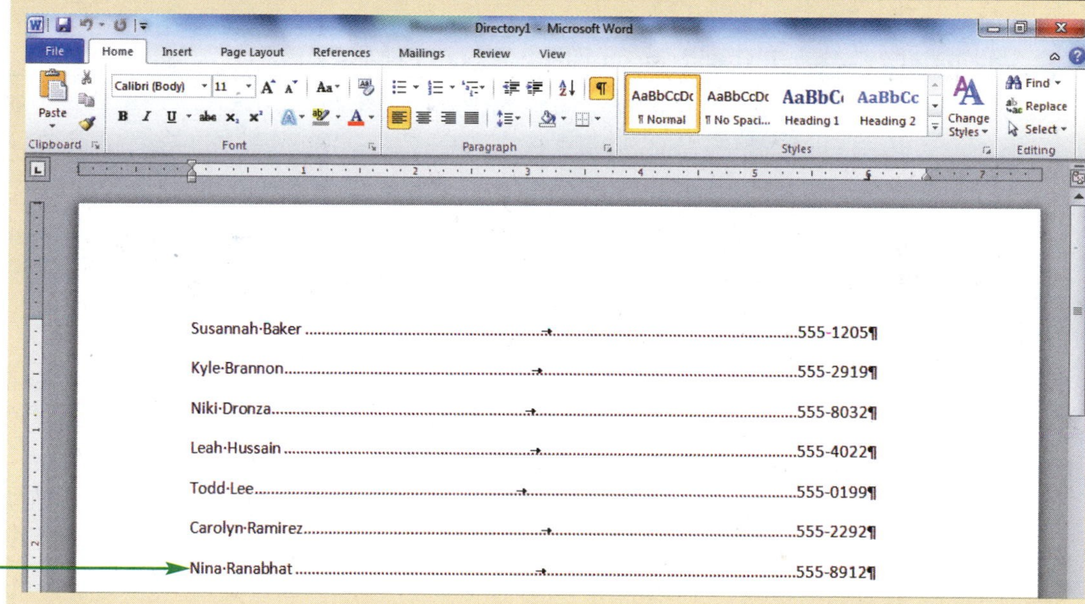

your name should appear here

3. Save the document as **Phone Directory** in the Word6\Tutorial folder, and then close it.
4. Save and close the **Phone Directory with Merge Fields** document.

Converting Text to a Table

Nina needs your help with a few other tasks related to managing information about the teachers and clients at Lily Road Yoga Studio. First, she needs to prepare some information about new clients, which her assistant typed, to make it suitable for use as a data source. Because her assistant is not familiar with mail merge, she typed it as simple text in a Word document, instead of adding it to Nina's data source. Also, she forgot to include an email address and phone number for each client.

Nina can resolve these issues by converting the text to a Word table, and then adding columns for phone numbers and email addresses. Then, the next time she sees the clients she can get the missing information from them and add it to the table.

Before you can convert text into a table, you need to make sure it is set up correctly. That is, you need to make sure that **separator characters**—typically commas or tabs—are used consistently to divide the text into individual pieces of data to represent fields. Also, you need to make sure each paragraph in the document contains the same number of fields. Upon conversion, each field is formatted as a separate cell in a column, and each paragraph mark starts a new row, or record.

TIP

Address information exported from email and contact management programs often takes the form of a text file, with the fields separated by commas.

To convert text into a table:

1. Open the document named **Client** from the Word6\Tutorial folder, and then save it as **Client Table** in the same folder. Display nonprinting characters, if necessary, and change the Zoom level to **Page Width**. See Figure 6-32. The document consists of three paragraphs, each of which contains a name, address, city, state, zip code, favorite type of yoga, and favorite teacher. Some of the fields are separated by commas (for example, the address and the city) but some are only separated by spaces (for example, the first and last name). Also, the favorite type of yoga and favorite teacher are enclosed in parentheses. You need to edit this information so that fields are separated by commas, with no parentheses enclosing the last two items.

Figure 6-32 Text with inconsistent separator characters

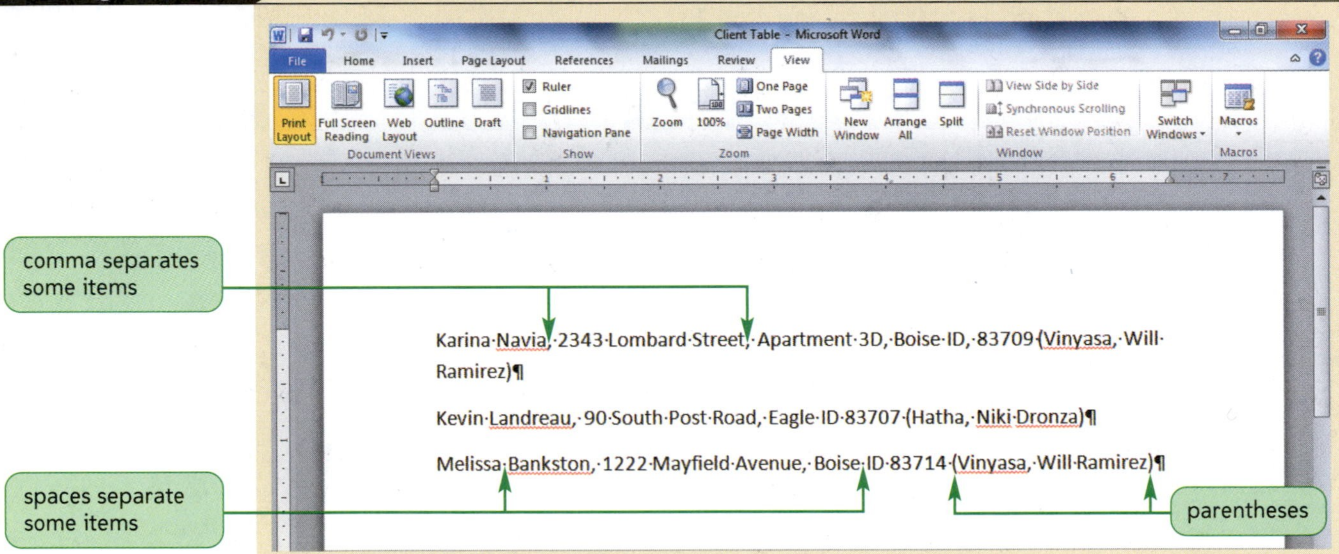

comma separates some items
spaces separate some items
parentheses
Karina·Navia,·2343·Lombard·Street,·Apartment·3D,·Boise·ID,·83709·(Vinyasa,·Will·Ramirez)¶
Kevin·Landreau,·90·South·Post·Road,·Eagle·ID·83707·(Hatha,·Niki·Dronza)¶
Melissa·Bankston,·1222·Mayfield·Avenue,·Boise·ID·83714·(Vinyasa,·Will·Ramirez)¶

2. Edit the document to insert a comma after each first name, city, and zip code, and then delete the parentheses in each paragraph.

   In order to convert the text to a table, the paragraphs in the document must contain the same number of items that will become fields. The first paragraph includes two pieces of address information—a street address and an apartment number, which is equivalent to an Address Line 1 field and an Address Line 2 field. However, the other paragraphs only include an Address Line 1 field. Before you can convert the text into a table, you need to make sure each paragraph includes the same fields.

3. In the second paragraph, click to the right of the comma after "Road," press the **spacebar**, and then type **,** (a comma).

4. In the third paragraph, click to the right of the paragraph after "Avenue," press the **spacebar**, and then type **,** (a comma). Now the second two paragraphs each contain a blank field. See Figure 6-33.

Figure 6-33 Text set up for conversion to a table

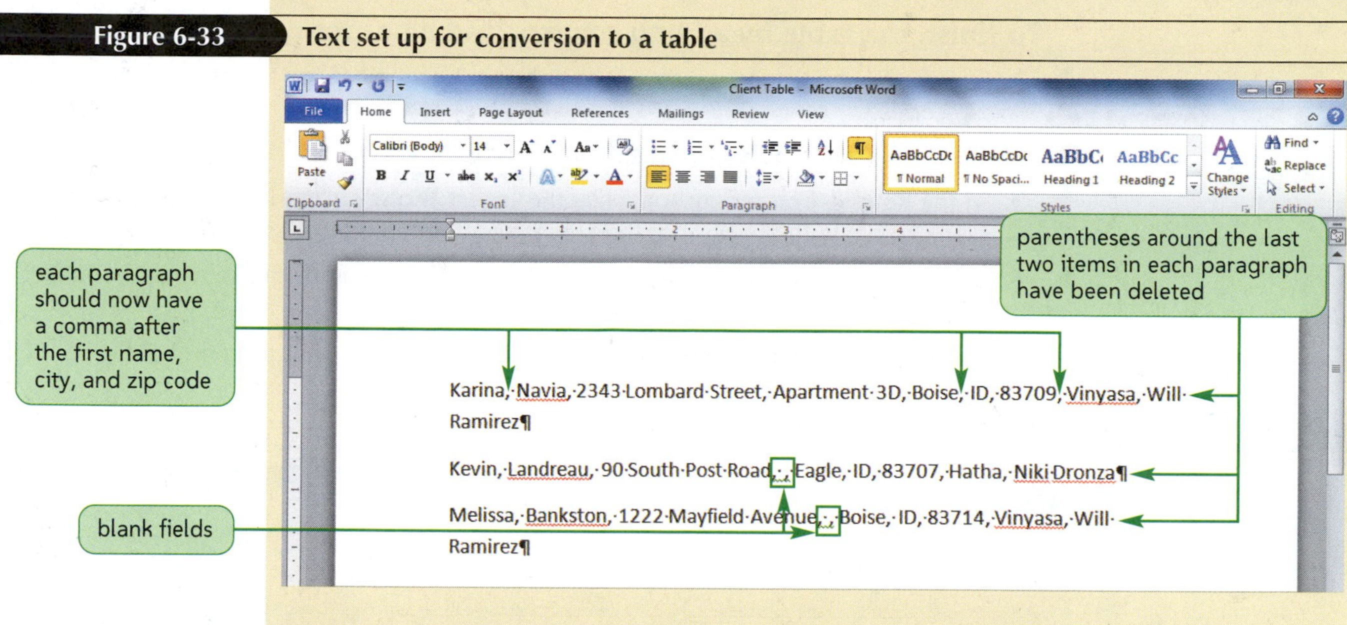

TIP

If a conversion does not turn out the way you expect, undo it and then review the text to make sure each paragraph contains the same number of data items, with the items divided by the same separator character.

5. Press the **Ctrl+A** keys to select the entire document, and then click the **Insert** tab on the Ribbon.
6. In the Tables group, click the **Table** button, and then click **Convert Text to Table**. The Convert Text to Table dialog box opens. Because the information in each paragraph is separated by commas, you need to select the Commas option button in the Separate text at section of the dialog box.
7. Click the **Commas** option button. See Figure 6-34. Note that the Number of columns setting is 9, and the Number of rows setting is 3. This corresponds to the nine fields in each of the three paragraphs.

Figure 6-34 Converting text to a table

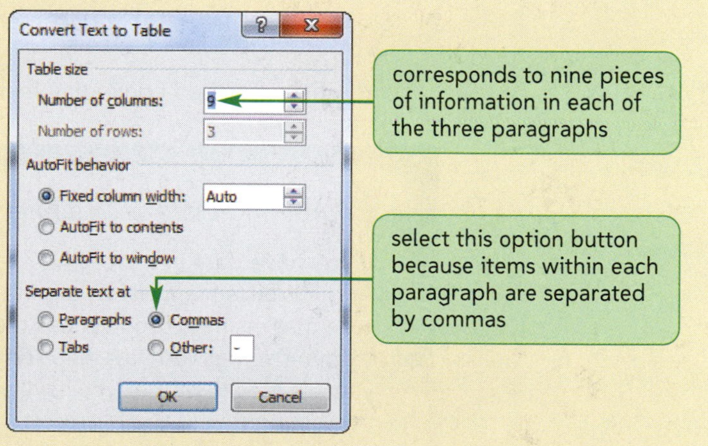

8. Click the **OK** button. The Convert Text to Table dialog box closes, and the text in the document is converted into a table consisting of nine columns and three rows.

Now that you have converted the text to a table, you need to finish the table by adding the columns for the phone number and email address, and adding a header row to identify the field names.

To finish the table by adding columns and a header row:

1. Switch to Landscape orientation, and then select the column containing the zip codes.
2. Click the **Table Tools Layout** tab on the Ribbon.
3. In the Rows & Columns group, click the **Insert Right** button twice to add two blank columns to the right of the column containing zip codes.
4. Select the table's top row, and then in the Rows & Columns group, click the **Insert Above** button.
5. Enter the column headings shown in Figure 6-35 and format them in bold.

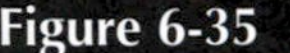
Figure 6-35 Table with new columns and column headings

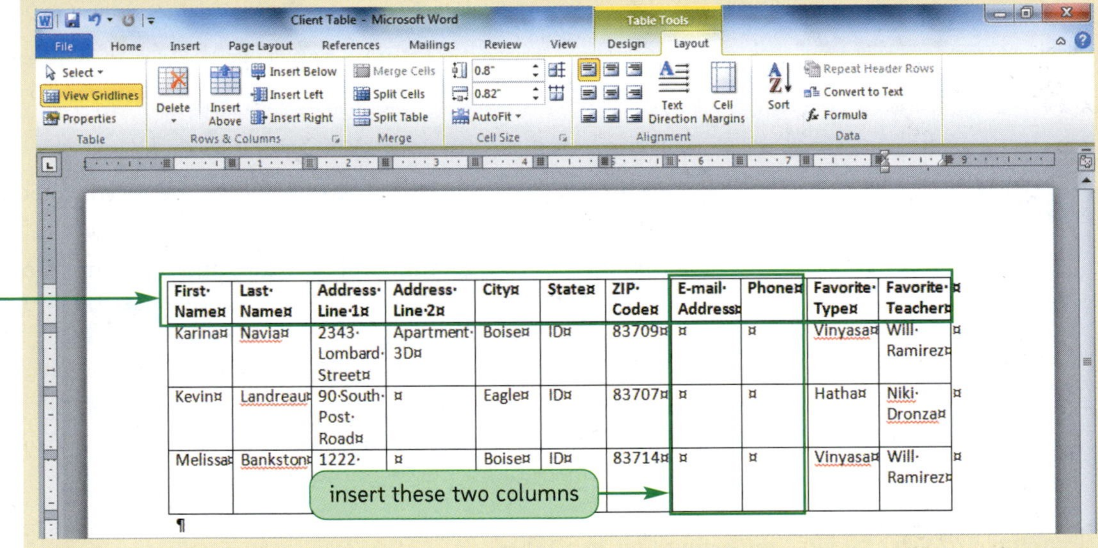

6. Save the Client Table document, and then close it.

You have finished converting text into a table.

INSIGHT

Combining Data with a Microsoft Address Lists File

If you have data in a Word file that you want to combine with data in a Microsoft Address Lists file, start by setting up the Word document as a table. That way you can be sure that each record includes the same fields. You can also check over the table quickly to confirm that you have entered data in the various fields in a consistent format. Once you are confident that you have set up the table correctly, you can begin the process of combining it with the Microsoft Address Lists file. First, delete the heading row, and then convert the table back to text, separating the fields with commas. Next, save the Word file as a text file, with the .txt file extension. Finally, open the Microsoft Office Address Lists file in Access, and then, on the Import & Link tab in the External Data group, click the Text File button to begin importing the text file into the Microsoft Address Lists file.

Converting a Table to Text

At an upcoming open house, Nina plans to give a brief talk in which she introduces all the teachers at the studio. She wants to create a list of the teachers detailing their areas of specialty that she can refer to while she talks.

To create this list, Nina suggests you start with the Phone Data document that contained the table of yoga teachers and their phone numbers that you worked with earlier. You will begin by converting this table of information into text. As when you converted text into a table, you will need to specify how the individual pieces of information in the table will be separated in the document once it is removed from the table structure.

To convert a table into text:

1. Open the document **Phone Data** from the Word6\Tutorial folder, and then save it as **Teacher List** in the same folder. Display nonprinting characters, if necessary, and change the Zoom to **Page Width**. You want to include only the names of Nina's teachers, so you will start by deleting the header row and the Phone column.
2. Delete the header row and the column of phone numbers from the table. The table now contains only the first and last name of each yoga teacher. You are ready to convert this table into text.
3. Select the entire table, click the **Table Tools Layout** tab, if necessary, to display this tab, and then in the Data group, click **Convert to Text**. The Convert to Text dialog box opens.
4. Click the **Other** option button. You want to separate the first and last names by a space.
5. In the Other box, delete the hyphen, verify that the insertion point is at the far-left edge of the text box, and then press the **spacebar** to insert a space. See Figure 6-36.

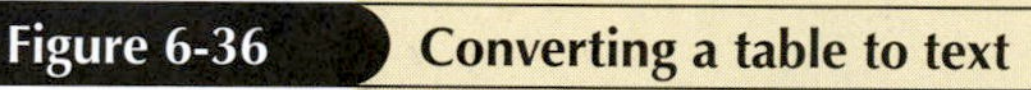

Figure 6-36 Converting a table to text

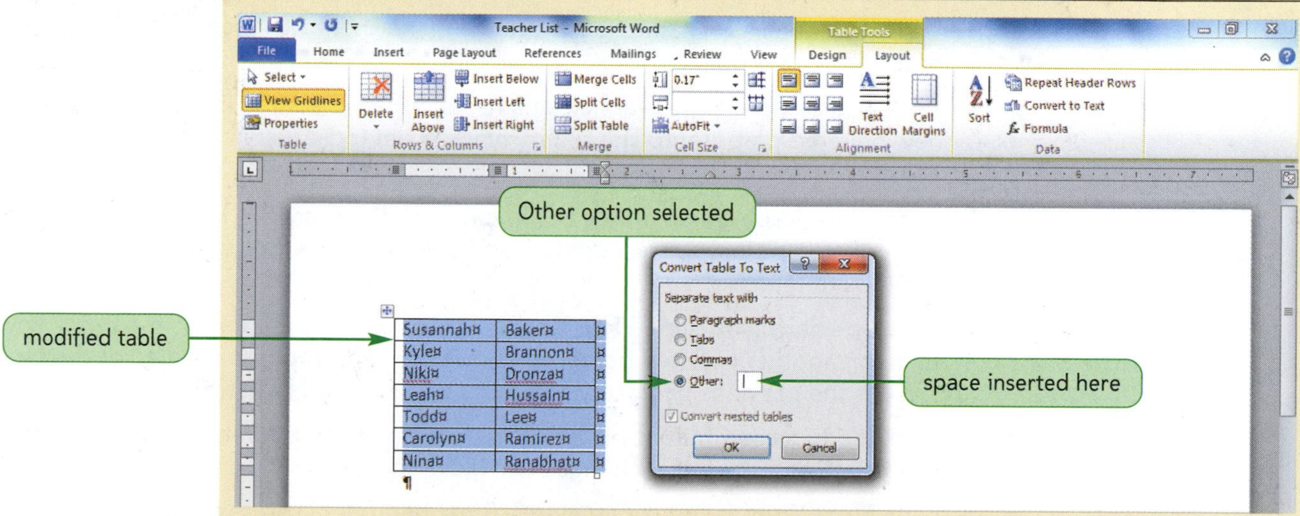

6. Click the **OK** button. The Convert Table to Text dialog box closes. The contents of the table are now formatted as seven separate paragraphs, one for each row in the table. Each first name is separated from its corresponding last name by a space.
7. Save the document.

Working with Lists

Now that you have converted the table of information into text, you can work with it as you would any other text. For example, Nina wants you to create a detailed list of teachers and their classes. Because most people at the studio refer to the teachers by their first names, she asks you to first sort the list of teachers by first name.

To sort the list:

1. If necessary, select the seven paragraphs containing the names of the yoga teachers, and then, in the Paragraph group, click the **Sort** button. The Sort Text dialog box opens. This is similar to the dialog box you've used before to sort tables. You want to sort the paragraphs in the list in ascending alphabetical order.
2. Verify that **Paragraphs** appears in the Sort by box and that the **Ascending** option button is selected, and then click the **OK** button. The Sort Text dialog box closes, and the paragraphs are arranged alphabetically. The list begins with Carolyn Ramirez, unless your first name comes alphabetically before "Carolyn," in which case your name appears at the top of the list.
3. Save the document.

Now that the list is sorted, you can use it to create an outline, or **multilevel list**. To create a multilevel list, first format text as a bulleted or numbered list, and then indent, or demote, some paragraphs within the list to create an outline structure. To demote a paragraph, click at the beginning of the paragraph and then press the Tab key or click the Increase Indent button in the Paragraph group on the Home tab. To promote, or unindent, a paragraph, click at the beginning of the paragraph and then press the Shift+Tab keys, or click the Decrease Indent button in the Paragraph group on the Home tab.

To create a multilevel list:

1. Verify that the list of names is still selected, and then click the **Bullets** button to format it as a bulleted list.
2. Click at the end of Kyle Brannon's name, and then press the **Enter** key to insert a new bulleted paragraph. The round, black bullet looks just like the other bullets in the list.
3. In the Paragraph group on the Home tab, click the **Increase Indent** button. The bulleted paragraph is indented, and the bullet changes to a white circle with a black outline.
4. Type **Specialties include Flow Yoga and Pilates**, and then press the **Enter** key to insert another bulleted paragraph. The new paragraph is indented at the same level as the previous paragraph, with the same style of bullet.
5. Click the **Increase Indent** button. The bulleted paragraph is indented to the next level, and the bullet changes to a black square.
6. Type **Flow Yoga is not recommended for beginners**, press the **Enter** key, and then type **Pilates requires four hours of individual instruction**.
7. Press the **Enter** key to insert a new bulleted paragraph, and then click the **Decrease Indent** button in the Paragraph group to promote the new bulleted paragraph.
8. Type **His classes are generally considered very challenging**.

If you don't like the bullets or numbering styles that Word applies by default to a multilevel list, you can apply new styles by using the Multilevel List button in the Paragraph group on the Home tab. You can also use a multilevel list style to change a bulleted outline into a numbered outline. After looking over the list, Nina decides she would like to use a more eye-catching set of bullets.

To apply a multilevel bullet style to the list:

1. Select the entire list, and then click the **Multilevel List** button to open a gallery of list styles. As shown in Figure 6-37, one of the list styles applies fancy bullets, two apply outline numbering, and three apply outline numbering and heading styles. The last is specially designed for creating a book outline. Finally, the None option retains any heading styles previously applied by one of the other multilevel list styles, but removes any outline numbering. Right now, Nina is interested in the bullets.

Figure 6-37 Multilevel List menu

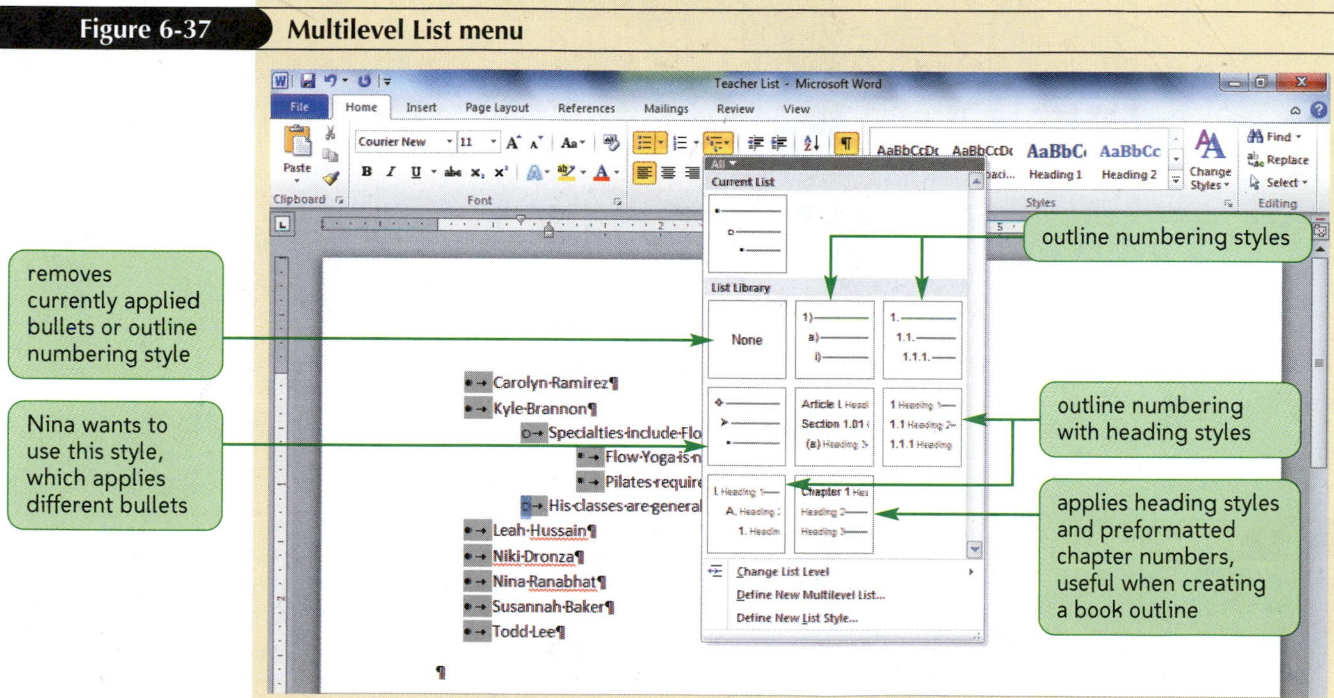

2. Click the bullet style in the second row of the List Library section, as shown in Figure 6-37. Your bulleted list should look like the list in Figure 6-38.

Figure 6-38 Bulleted list with multiple levels

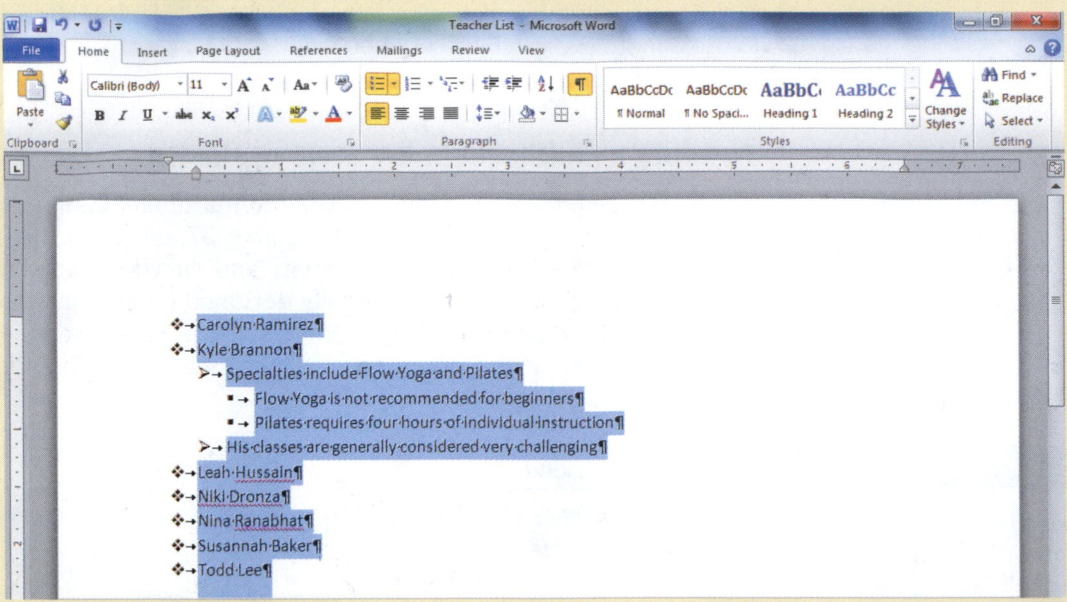

Nina decides the list would be more useful to her if it had outline numbering instead of bullets. You can make this change by applying a different multilevel list style.

3. With the list still selected, click the **Multilevel List** button to open the Multilevel List gallery, and then in the top row of the List Library section, click the middle style, which uses a combination of numbers and letters.
4. Deselect the list, and save the document. Your completed list should look like Figure 6-39.

Figure 6-39 Multilevel list with outline numbering

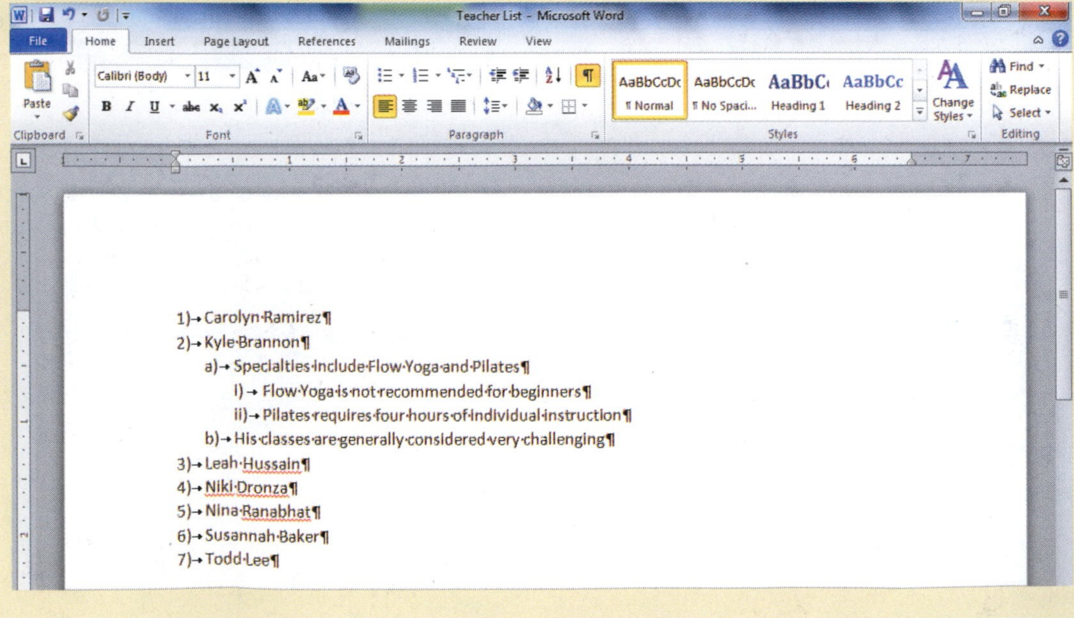

You have completed the mail merges Nina requested, and you have created an outline of yoga teachers she can use as she meets with potential new clients at the yoga studio open house.

REVIEW

Session 6.2 Quick Check

1. True or False. After you complete a mail merge and close the main document, the connection between the main document file and the data source file is broken.
2. Explain how to edit a data source for a main document that is already open.
3. What's the quickest way to sort a data source by one field?
4. Explain how to filter a data source.
5. When you create a directory with a dot leader, what do you have to do after you insert the merge field on the right side of the page?
6. True or False. You can convert data in a document to a table only if the individual pieces of data are separated by tabs.

Apply the skills you learned in the tutorial using the same case scenario.

PRACTICE

Review Assignments

Data Files needed for the Review Assignments: Bonus.docx, Contacts.docx, More.docx

Nina's clients are happy with the new facility, and the open-studio days she offered in June were a big success. Nina was pleased with how convenient it was to send out form letters with the Word Mail Merge feature. Now she wants to send a letter inviting clients who have purchased an annual membership to sign up for their membership bonus—either a massage or a meditation session, depending on which option they selected when they purchased their membership. Complete the following steps:

1. Open the file **Bonus** from the Word6\Review folder included with your Data Files, then save the document as **Bonus Main Document** in the same folder.
2. In the letter's closing, replace Nina's first and last name with your own.
3. Begin the mail merge by selecting Letters as the type of main document.
4. Create a new data source with the following fields in the following order: First Name, Last Name, Address Line 1, Address Line 2, City, State, ZIP Code, E-mail Address, Phone, and Bonus. Remove any extra fields. Rename fields as necessary.
5. Create four records using the information shown in Figure 6-40.

Figure 6-40 **Information for new data source**

First Name	Last Name	Address Line 1	Address Line 2	City	State	ZIP Code	E-mail Address	Phone	Bonus
Jane	Cussler	299 Hollister Street	Apartment 8D	Boise	ID	83722	cussler@curlygraphics.boise.net.	208-399-1948	massage
Carl	Hesse	933 Wildway Avenue		Beatty	ID	83776	yogaguy@world-net-global.com	208-322-8294	massage
William	Greely	52 Eton Road	P.O. Box 9080	Boise	ID	83776	william.greely@greely-productions.boise.org	208-234-7766	meditation session
Katya	Pushkin	821 Ruby Road		Boise	ID	83722		208-909-2893	meditation session

6. Save the data source as **Bonus Data** in the Word6\Review folder.
7. Edit the data source to replace "Carl Hesse" with your first and last name.
8. Sort the data source in ascending order by zip code and then by last name.
9. Create an inside address consisting of the necessary merge fields. Adjust the paragraph spacing in the inside address as necessary. Add a salutation that includes the First Name merge field. Insert the Bonus field into the body of the letter where indicated.
10. Save your changes to the main document, and then preview the merged document. Correct any formatting or spacing problems.
11. Merge to a new document, save the merged document as **Merged Bonus Letters**, and then close the file.
12. Filter the data source to display only records for clients interested in a massage, and then complete a second merge. Save the new merged document as **Merged Massage Letters**. Close all documents, saving all changes.
13. Open a new, blank document, and create a set of mailing labels using the vendor Avery US Letters and product number 5162. Save the main document as **Labels Main Document** in the Word6\Review folder.

14. Select the **Bonus Data** file you created earlier in this assignment as the data source.
15. Insert an Address Block merge field in the "Joshua Randall Jr." format and then update the labels.
16. Preview the merged labels, merge to a new document, and then save the new document as **Merged Labels** in the Word6\Review folder and close it. Save and close all open documents.
17. Create a telephone directory with a dot leader. Use the file named **Contacts** from the Word6\Review folder as the data source. Set a right tab at six inches and use a dot leader. Save the main document as **Directory Main Document** in the Word6\Review folder and the merged document as **Merged Directory** in the same folder. Save and close all open documents.
18. Open the document named **More** from the Word6\Review folder and save it as **More Bonus Data**. Convert the data in the document to a table with eight columns. Insert a header row with the following column headers formatted in bold: First Name, Last Name, Address Line 1, Address Line 2, City, State, ZIP Code, and Bonus. Replace "Daniel Einstein" with your name. Save and close the document.
19. Open the **Contacts** document from the Word6\Review folder and save it as **Contacts Info** in the same folder. Delete the header row and the phone number column, and then convert the table to four paragraphs of text.
20. In "Regent Property Management," change "Regent" to your last name.
21. Format the four paragraphs as a bulleted list, and then add the additional bullets and sub bullets of information shown in Figure 6-41.

Figure 6-41 **List of company information**

- Clear Pane Window Cleaning
    - Scheduled for the first Monday of every month
        - In summer, may have to switch to the first Tuesday of every month
        - Move the table away from the front window before cleaners arrive
    - Paid by direct deposit
- Sampson Security
- Boise Federal Savings
    - Deposits must be in by 5 PM
    - Include a yellow deposit slip with every deposit
- Regent Property Management

22. Apply the bulleted multilevel list style.
23. Save the document as **Contacts Info Outline** in the Word6\Review folder, apply the multilevel list style that inserts outline numbering in the form 1), a), and i), then save the document again and close it.
24. Submit the documents to your instructor, either in printed or electronic form, as requested.

Apply the skills you learned to create a letter to customers of an art gallery.

APPLY

Case Problem 1

Data File needed for this Case Problem: Gallery.docx

Nightingale Gallery Nell Williams owns Nightingale Gallery, a purveyor of fine art photography in Saginaw, Michigan. She wants to send out a letter to past customers informing them of an upcoming show by a local photographer. Complete the following steps:

1. Open the document named **Gallery** from the Word6\Case1 folder, and then save it in the same folder as **Gallery Main Document**. In the closing, replace "Student Name" with your name.
2. Select Letters as the type of main document, and then create a data source with the following field names, in the following order: Title, First Name, Last Name, Street Address, City, State, ZIP Code, and E-mail Address.
3. Enter the following four records shown in Figure 6-42.

Figure 6-42 **Four records for new data source**

Title	First Name	Last Name	Street Address	City	State	ZIP Code	E-mail Address
Mr.	David	Joliet	1577 Cooperville Drive	Saginaw	MI	48601	joliet@world-country5.net
Mr.	Paul	Robertson	633 Wentworth	Bay City	MI	48707	d_roberts@p-m-c-57.org
Mrs.	Delia	Suyemoto	4424 Bedford Avenue	Saginaw	MI	48602	d_suyemoto@filkins-incorporated.com
Ms.	Kira	Gascoyne	844 Winter Way	Midland	MI	33075	gascoyne@saginaw.school65.edu

4. Save the data source as **Gallery Data** in the Word6\Case1 folder, and then sort the records alphabetically by last name.
5. Edit the data source to replace "Kira Gascoyne" with your name. Change the title to "Mr." if necessary.
6. Build an inside address from separate merge fields, and then add a salutation using the Title and Last Name merge fields. Adjust paragraph spacing as necessary.
7. Save your changes to the Gallery Main Document file. Preview the merged document, and then merge to a new document.
8. Save the merged letters document as **Merged Gallery Letters** in the Word6\Case1 folder and then close it.
9. Save the **Gallery Main Document** document and close it.

EXPLORE

10. Open a new, blank document, save it as **Gallery Envelopes** in the Word6\Case1 folder. Assume Nell will be using envelopes with a preprinted return address, so you don't have to type a return address. Select Envelopes as the type of main document, select the 10 (4 1/8 × 9 1/2 in) size of envelopes in the Envelope Options dialog box, and use the **Gallery Data** file you created earlier as the data source. In the recipient address area of the envelope, insert the appropriate merge fields, and then merge to a new document.
11. Save the merged document as **Merged Gallery Envelopes** in the Word6\Case1 folder, and then close it. Save the main document and close it.

12. Create a customer email directory that includes first and last names but not titles. Use the file named **Gallery Data** (which you created earlier) as the data source. Do not include the record for David Joliet in the merge. Use a dot leader, with the right tab stop set at the 6-inch mark, to separate the name on the left from the email address on the right.
13. Save the main document for the email directory as **Directory Main Document** in the Word6\Case1 folder. Complete the merge to create the directory, and then save the merged document as **Merged Gallery Directory** in the Word6\Case1 folder.
14. Save and close all open documents. Submit the documents to your instructor, in either printed or electronic form, as requested.

Apply your skills to create a form letter for a mortgage company.

APPLY

Case Problem 2

Data Files needed for this Case Problem: Mortgage.docx, Mortgage Data.xlsx

Lensville Mortgage Corporation As an account manager at Lensville Mortgage Corporation, you need to send out letters to past customers asking them to consider refinancing. Your data for the mail merge is saved as an Excel file. Complete the following steps:

1. Open the document **Mortgage** from the Word6\Case2 folder, in the letter's closing, replace "Student Name" with your name, and then save it in the same folder as **Mortgage Main Document**.
2. Select Letters as the type of main document. In the closing, replace "Student Name" with your name.
3. EXPLORE For the data source, select the Excel file **Mortgage Data** from the Word6\Case2 folder. Click the OK button in the Select Table dialog box.
4. Edit the data source to replace "Barb Russ" with your name.
5. EXPLORE Insert an Address Block merge field for the inside address in the format "Joshua Randall Jr.," and format the Address block merge field using the No Spacing style. Insert a salutation using the First Name merge field. Add paragraph spacing before the salutation paragraph to account for the fact that the No Spacing style removed paragraph spacing after the preceding paragraph.
6. In the body of the letter, replace the placeholders [NUMBER OF YEARS], [CURRENT LOAN TERM], and [NEW LOAN TERM] with the appropriate merge fields.
7. Sort the records in the data source in ascending order by Current Loan Term.
8. Preview the merged document, and then merge to a new document. Save the merged document as **Merged Mortgage Letters** in the Word6\Case2 folder.
9. Close all open documents, saving all changes.
10. Create a main document for generating mailing labels on sheets of Avery US Letter Address labels, product number 5162, using the **Mortgage Data** file as your data source. Use the Address Block merge field in the format "Joshua Randall Jr.". Save the main document as **Labels Main Document** in the Word6\Case2 folder.
11. Preview the merged document, merge to a new document, and then save the merged document as **Merged Mortgage Labels** in the Word6\Case2 folder. Close all open documents, saving any changes.
12. Open the **Mortgage Main Document** file from the Word6\Case2 folder, maintaining the connection to its data source, and save it as **Mortgage Filtered**. Filter out all records in the data source except records for customers in Fort Myers.
13. Preview the merged document, and then complete the merge to a new document. Save the merged document as **Merged Fort Myers** in the Word6\Case2 folder.
14. Close all open documents, saving any changes. Submit the documents to your instructor, in either printed or electronic form, as requested.

Convert a text file into a table, and then use the table as a data source for a mail merge.

CHALLENGE

Case Problem 3

Data Files needed for this Case Problem: Letter.docx, Pasta.txt

Fierenze Pasta Kayla Souza is manager of Fierenze, a manufacturer of fresh pasta in Racine, Wisconsin. Fierenze has just bought out a competitor, JD Pasta. Now Kayla wants to send a letter to JD Pasta's longtime customers, who she hopes will become Fierenze customers. She wants to use the mail merge feature in Word to create a letter that informs each customer of the price of his or her favorite type of pasta. The customer data has been saved in the form of a text file, with the data fields separated by commas. Kayla needs your help to convert the text file to a Word table, which she can then use as the data source for a mail merge. Complete the following steps:

1. In Word, open the text file named **Pasta.txt** from the Word6\Case3 folder included with your Data Files. (*Hint*: If the file is not listed in the Open dialog box, make sure All Files is specified in the box to the right of the File name box.) Save the Pasta.txt file as a Word document in the same folder using the filename **Pasta Data**.
2. Format the text in the document using the Normal style, and switch to Landscape orientation.
3. Convert the text to a table with the following nine columns: First Name, Last Name, Address Line 1, Address Line 2, City, State, Zip Code, Type, and Price. Insert your first and last name where indicated. Insert a header row with the appropriate column headers formatted in bold. Save the document and close it.
4. Open the file **Main** from the Word6\Case3 folder, and then save it as **Pasta Main Document** in the same folder. In the closing, replace "Student Name" with your first and last name.
5. Select Letter as the type of main document, select the **Pasta Data** document as the data source, and then sort the records in ascending alphabetical order by the Type field.
6. Insert an Address Block merge field for the inside address in the format "Joshua Randall Jr.," and format the Address block merge field using the No Spacing style.
7. **EXPLORE** For the salutation, experiment with the Greeting Line button on the Mailings tab. Use the Greeting Line dialog box to insert a salutation that includes "Dear" and the customer's first name, followed by a colon. Add paragraph spacing before the salutation paragraph.
8. Edit the body of the form letter to replace the placeholder text with the corresponding merge field names.
9. **EXPLORE** Use the Rules button in the Write & Insert Fields group on the Home tab to replace [PLACEHOLDER] with a merge field that displays "We hope to see you soon at our new Chicago location, opening early next year!" if the value in the State field is equal to IL; otherwise, the field should display "We hope to see you soon!" (*Hint*: Click If...Then...Else... in the Rules menu, select State as the Field name, select Equal to as the Comparison, and enter IL in the Compare to box. Insert the appropriate word in the Insert this text box and in the Otherwise insert this text box.)
10. **EXPLORE** Use the Filter command in the Mail Merge Recipients dialog box to display only the records that include either linguini or ravioli in the Type field. (*Hint:* In the Filter Records tab of the Query Options dialog box, you need to fill in two rows. Select Type in the Field box in both rows, select Equal to in the Comparison box for both rows, type the correct types of pasta in the Compare to boxes, and in the list box on the far left, select Or instead of And.)
11. Save the document and then finish the merge to a new document. Save the merged document as **Merged Pasta Letters** in the Word6\Case3 folder.
12. Save the main document and close it. Submit the documents to your instructor, in either printed or electronic form, as requested.

Create the outline shown in Figure 6-43, to use as a basis for a report.

CREATE

Case Problem 4

Data Files needed for this Case Problem: Director.docx, MAPH.docx

Public Health Report Outline Shakira Ankor is a communications specialist at the Municipal Association for Public Health (MAPH). Each year she begins her work on the association's annual report by creating an outline using the multilevel list feature in Word. She has asked you to help her create the outline. She also asks you to begin the report itself by inserting a Word file. Complete the following steps:

1. Open the document **MAPH** from the Word6\Case4 folder included with your Data Files, and then save it as **MAPH Outline** in the same folder.
2. Switch to Print Layout view, if necessary, and make sure nonprinting characters are displayed.
3. Replace "Student Name" with your first and last name, and then, in the paragraph below your name, create the outline shown in Figure 6-43. Format the list with the multilevel list style that numbers paragraphs 1, 1.1, 1.1.1, with heading styles.

Figure 6-43 Outline for annual report

1. A Message from the Director
2. Report Highlights
3. Summaries from Regional Committees
   3.1. Northeast Region
   3.2. Southeast Region
   3.3. Midwest Region
   3.4. West Region
4. National Health Information Campaigns
   4.1. Vaccinations for Adolescents and Young Adults
      4.1.1. Special Needs of High School Students
      4.1.2. Considerations for the College-Bound
   4.2. Childhood Obesity
   4.3. Geriatric Nutrition Needs
      4.3.1. Calcium Intake
      4.3.2. Protein Requirements

4. Save the MAPH Outline document, and then save it again as **MAPH Report** in the Word6\Case4 folder.
5. Select the list and apply the None Multilevel list style. Insert a new paragraph after the paragraph "A Message from the Director," and then insert the Word file **Director** from the Word6\Case4 folder. Delete the blank paragraph at the end of the newly inserted text.
6. Save and close the document.
7. Submit the finished documents to your instructor, either in printed or electronic form, as requested.

ASSESS

SAM: Skills Assessment Manager

For current SAM information, including versions and content details, visit SAM Central (http://samcentral.course.com). If you have a SAM user profile, you may have access to hands-on instruction, practice, and assessment of the skills covered in this tutorial. Since various versions of SAM are supported throughout the life of this text, check with your instructor for the correct instructions and URL/Web site for accessing assignments.

ENDING DATA FILES

Tutorial

Carolyn Main Document.docx
Client Table.docx
Phone Data.docx
Phone Directory with Merge Fields.docx
Phone Directory.docx
Teacher List.docx
Yoga Data.mdb
Yoga Labels Main Document.docx
Yoga Main Document.docx
Yoga Merged Labels.docx
Yoga Merged Letters 1.docx
Yoga Merged Letters 2.docx
Yoga Merged Letters 3.docx

Review

Bonus Data.mdb
Bonus Main Document.docx
Contacts Info.docx
Contacts Info Outline.docx
Directory Main Document.docx
Labels Main Document.docx
Merged Bonus Letters.docx
Merged Directory.docx
Merged Labels.docx
Merged Massage Letters.docx
More Bonus Data.docx

Case1

Directory Main Document.docx
Gallery Data.mdb
Gallery Envelopes.docx
Gallery Letter.docx
Gallery Main Document.docx
Merged Gallery Directory.docx
Merged Gallery Envelopes.docx
Merged Gallery Letters.docx

Case2

Labels Main Document.docx
Merged Fort Myers.docx
Merged Mortgage Labels.docx
Merged Mortgage Letters.docx
Mortgage Data.xlsx
Mortgage Filtered.docx
Mortgage Main Document.docx

Case3

Merged Pasta Letters.docx
Pasta Data.docx
Pasta Main Document.docx

Case4

MAPH Outline.docx
MAPH Report.docx

TUTORIAL 7

Collaborating with Others and Creating Web Pages

Writing a Program Description

OBJECTIVES

Session 7.1
- Track changes in a document
- Insert and delete comments
- Accept and reject changes
- Compare and combine documents
- Embed and modify an Excel worksheet
- Link an Excel chart
- Modify and update a linked chart

Session 7.2
- Share files on SkyDrive
- Create bookmarks
- Insert and edit hyperlinks
- Save a Word document as a Web page
- Format a Web document
- View a Web document in a Web browser

Case | *Green Fields Fresh Lunch Program*

Zoe Rios is the owner and president of Rios Communications in Dubuque, Iowa, a public relations company that specializes in developing publicity documents and Web sites in the field of public health. She is currently working on a program description for Green Fields, an organization that is devoted to improving the quality of meals served in area schools. She asked Henry Davis, a writer at Rios Communications, to review a draft of the program description. While Henry is revising the program description, Zoe has asked you to work on it, making additional changes. When you are finished, Zoe wants you to merge Henry's edited version of the document with your most recent draft.

After you create a new version of the document for Zoe, she wants you to add some budget figures from an Excel workbook. She also needs you to add a pie chart created by Henry. Finally, to make the program description available to the organization's members, she asks for your help to distribute it in electronic form and publish it on her company's Web site.

STARTING DATA FILES

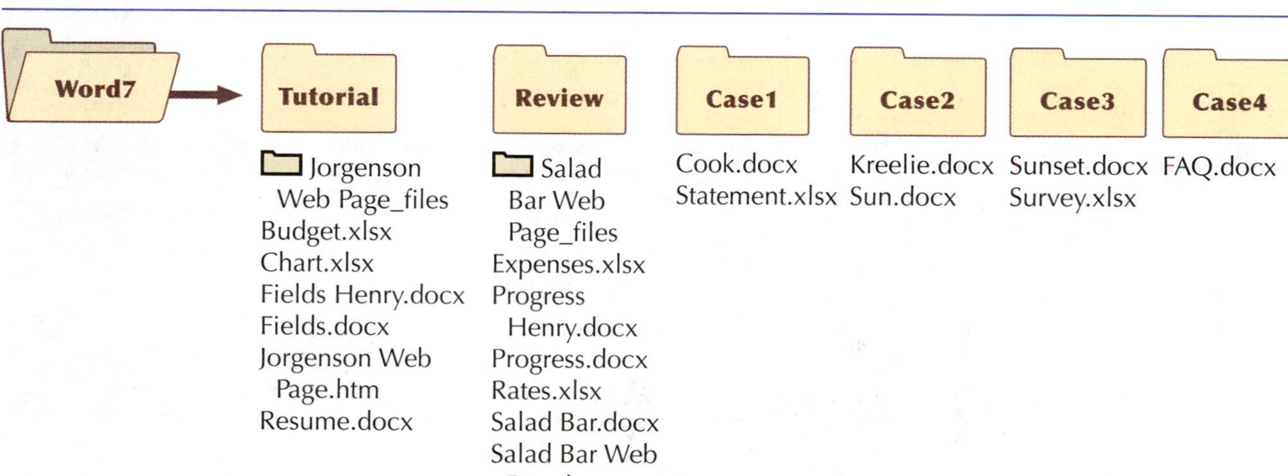

SESSION 7.1 VISUAL OVERVIEW

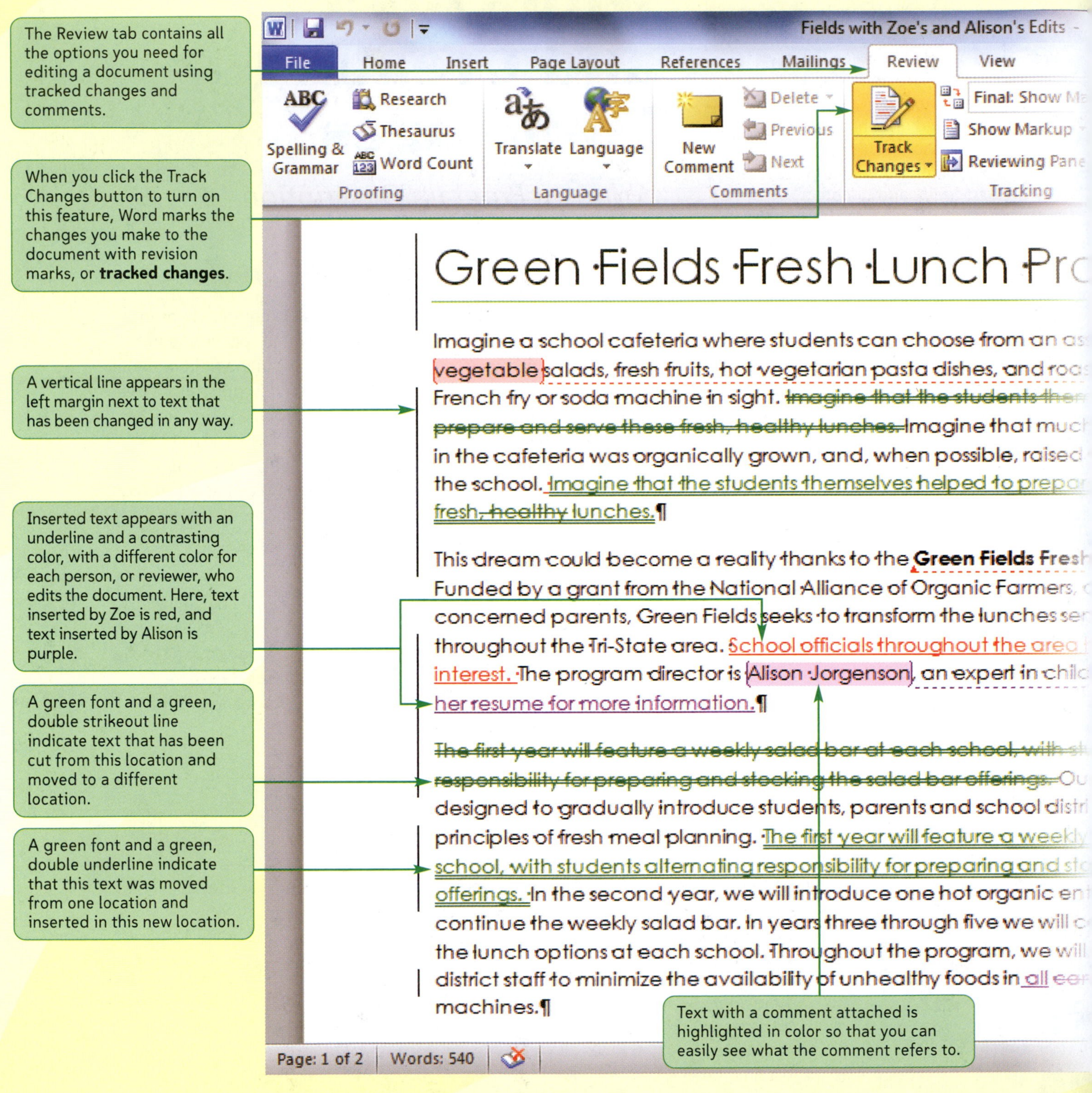

The Review tab contains all the options you need for editing a document using tracked changes and comments.
When you click the Track Changes button to turn on this feature, Word marks the changes you make to the document with revision marks, or **tracked changes**.
A vertical line appears in the left margin next to text that has been changed in any way.
Inserted text appears with an underline and a contrasting color, with a different color for each person, or reviewer, who edits the document. Here, text inserted by Zoe is red, and text inserted by Alison is purple.
A green font and a green, double strikeout line indicate text that has been cut from this location and moved to a different location.
A green font and a green, double underline indicate that this text was moved from one location and inserted in this new location.
Text with a comment attached is highlighted in color so that you can easily see what the comment refers to.
Fields with Zoe's and Alison's Edits
File
Home
Insert
Page Layout
References
Mailings
Review
View
Spelling & Grammar
Research
Thesaurus
Word Count
Proofing
Translate
Language
Language
New Comment
Delete
Previous
Next
Comments
Track Changes
Show Markup
Tracking
Page: 1 of 2
Words: 540

TRACKING CHANGES

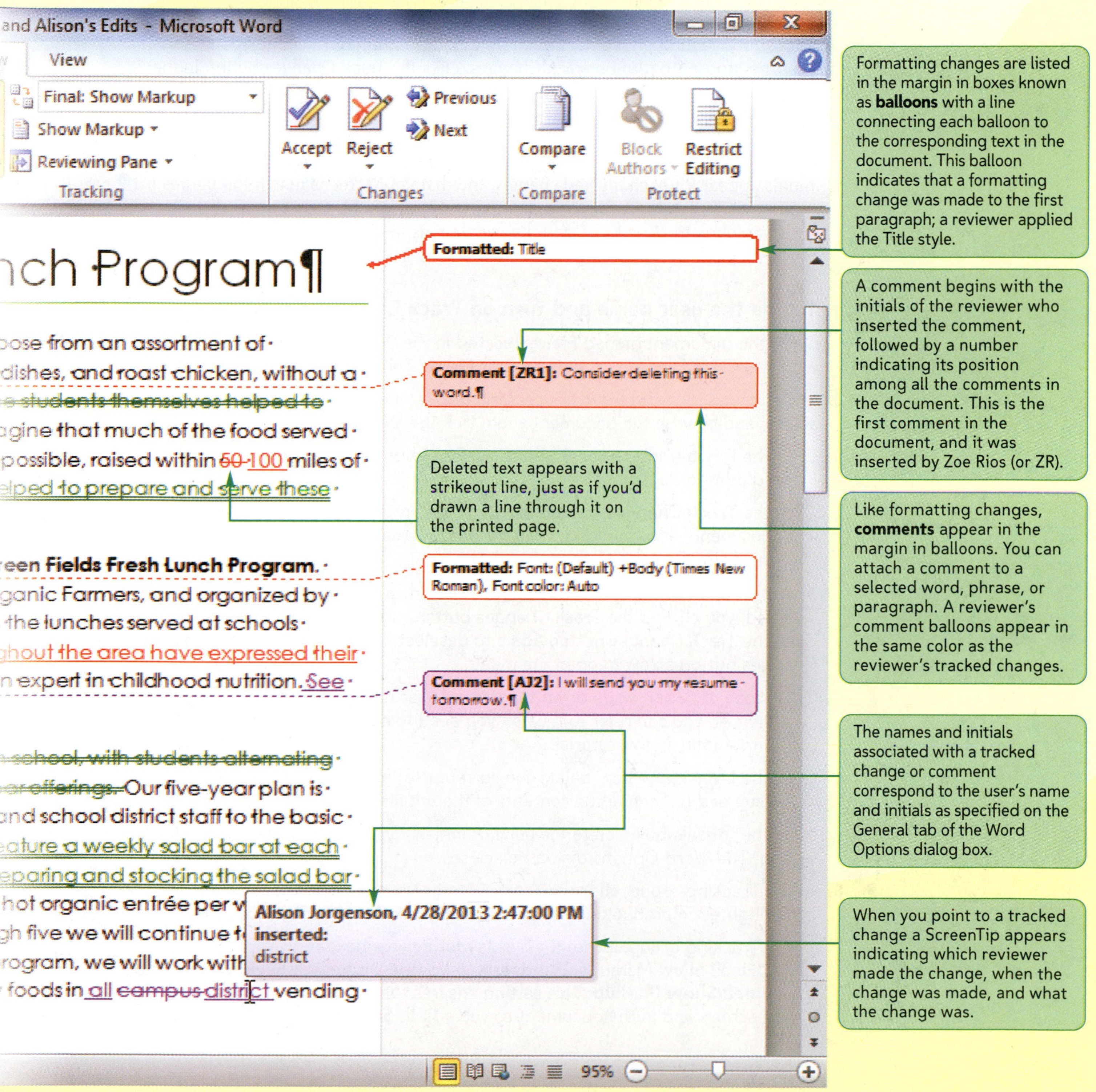

and Alison's Edits - Microsoft Word
View
Final: Show Markup
Show Markup
Reviewing Pane
Tracking
Accept
Reject
Previous
Next
Changes
Compare
Compare
Block Authors
Restrict Editing
Protect
Formatted: Title
Comment [ZR1]: Consider deleting this word.¶
Formatted: Font: (Default) +Body (Times New Roman), Font color: Auto
Comment [AJ2]: I will send you my resume tomorrow.¶
Alison Jorgenson, 4/28/2013 2:47:00 PM
inserted:
district
95%
Formatting changes are listed in the margin in boxes known as **balloons** with a line connecting each balloon to the corresponding text in the document. This balloon indicates that a formatting change was made to the first paragraph; a reviewer applied the Title style.
A comment begins with the initials of the reviewer who inserted the comment, followed by a number indicating its position among all the comments in the document. This is the first comment in the document, and it was inserted by Zoe Rios (or ZR).
Deleted text appears with a strikeout line, just as if you'd drawn a line through it on the printed page.
Like formatting changes, **comments** appear in the margin in balloons. You can attach a comment to a selected word, phrase, or paragraph. A reviewer's comment balloons appear in the same color as the reviewer's tracked changes.
The names and initials associated with a tracked change or comment correspond to the user's name and initials as specified on the General tab of the Word Options dialog box.
When you point to a tracked change a ScreenTip appears indicating which reviewer made the change, when the change was made, and what the change was.

Editing a Document with Tracked Changes

The Track Changes feature in Word simulates the process of marking up a hard copy of a document with a colored pen, but with many more advantages. Word keeps track of who makes each change, assigning a different color to each reviewer, and providing ScreenTips indicating details of the change, such as the reviewer's name and the date and time the change was made. Using the buttons in the Tracking group on the Review tab, you can move through the document quickly, accepting or rejecting changes with a click of the mouse. To turn on Track Changes, click the Track Changes button in the Tracking group on the Review tab.

Zoe is ready to revise her first draft of the lunch program description. In particular, she wants to make some changes to the first paragraph of the document. She asks you to turn on Track Changes before you begin making the edits for her. To ensure that her name and initials appear for each tracked change, and that your screens match the figures in this tutorial, you will temporarily change the user name on the General tab of the Word Options dialog box to "Zoe Rios" and the user initials to "ZR."

To change the user name and turn on Track Changes:

1. Open the document named **Fields** located in the Word7\Tutorial folder included with your Data Files, and then save it as **Fields Zoe** in the same folder.
2. Switch to Print Layout view if necessary, display the rulers and nonprinting characters, and change the document zoom to **Page Width**.
3. Click the **Review** tab on the Ribbon. The Review tab provides options for reviewing and editing documents.
4. Click the **Track Changes button arrow** in the Tracking group to open the Track Changes menu, and then click **Change User Name**. The General tab of the Word Options dialog box opens.

   Trouble? If you don't see a menu and if the Track Changes button is now selected, you clicked the Track Changes button rather than the arrow below it. Click the Track Changes button again to deselect it, and then click the Track Changes button arrow to open the menu.

5. On a piece of paper, write down the current user name and initials, if they are not your own, so you can refer to it when you need to restore the original user name and initials later in this tutorial.
6. Click the **User name** box, delete the current user name, and then type **Zoe Rios**. You also need to change the contents of the Initials box.
7. Click the **Initials** box, delete the current initials, type **ZR**, and then click the **OK** button. The Word Options dialog box closes.
8. In the Tracking group, click the **Track Changes** button. The Track Changes button is highlighted in orange, indicating that the Track Changes feature is turned on.
9. In the Tracking group, locate the Display for Review box, and verify that it displays "Final: Show Markup." If it doesn't, click the Display for Review arrow and click **Final: Show Markup**. This setting ensures that tracked changes will appear on the screen and in the document as you edit it. See Figure 7-1.

TIP

You can also open the General tab of the Word Options dialog box by clicking the File tab and then clicking Options.

Figure 7-1 Track Changes turned on

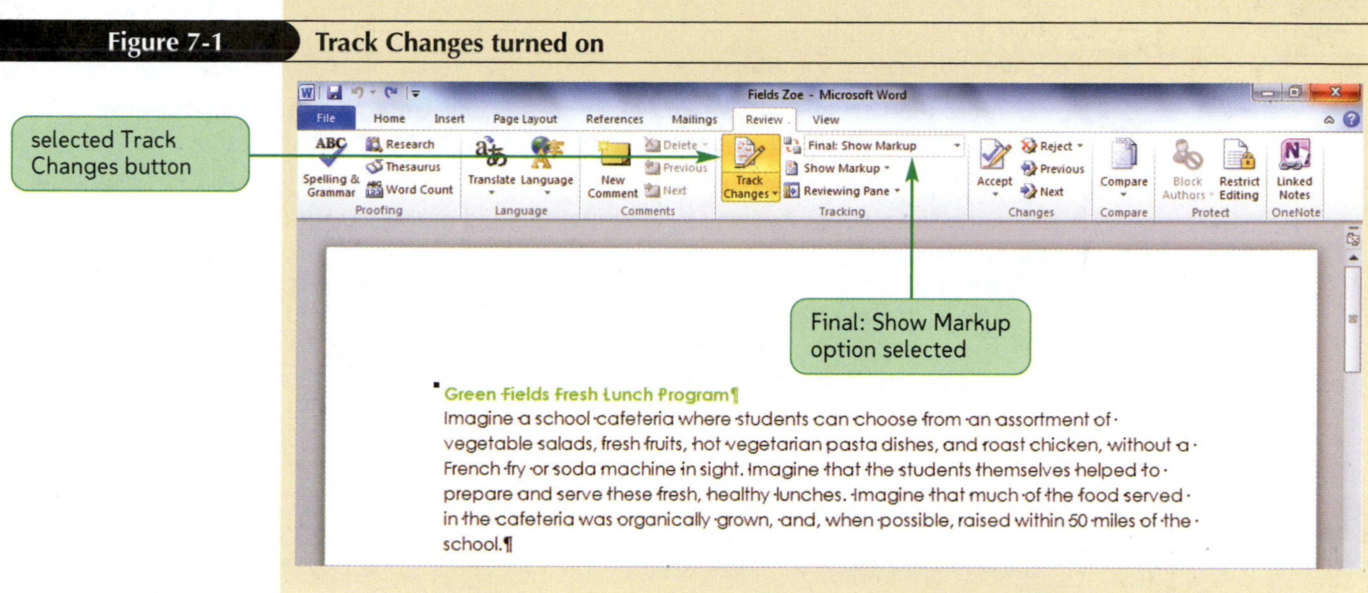

Now that Track Changes is turned on, you can begin editing Zoe's document. First, Zoe needs to change "50" in the last sentence of the second paragraph to "100."

TIP

Use the Word Count button in the Proofing group to display a document's total word count and other information about its contents.

To edit Zoe's document:

1. In the paragraph below the first heading, select the number **50** in the last sentence, and then type **100**. A strikeout line appears through the number 50, and the new number, 100, appears in red. The new number is also underlined, and a vertical line appears in the left margin, drawing attention to the change.

   Trouble? If you see the number 100 in a color other than red, your computer is set up to display tracked changes in a different color.

2. Move the mouse pointer over the newly inserted number 100. A ScreenTip appears displaying the type of edit (an insertion), the user name associated with the edit, in this case "Zoe Rios," and the date and time the edit was made. See Figure 7-2.

Figure 7-2 ScreenTip with user name and date

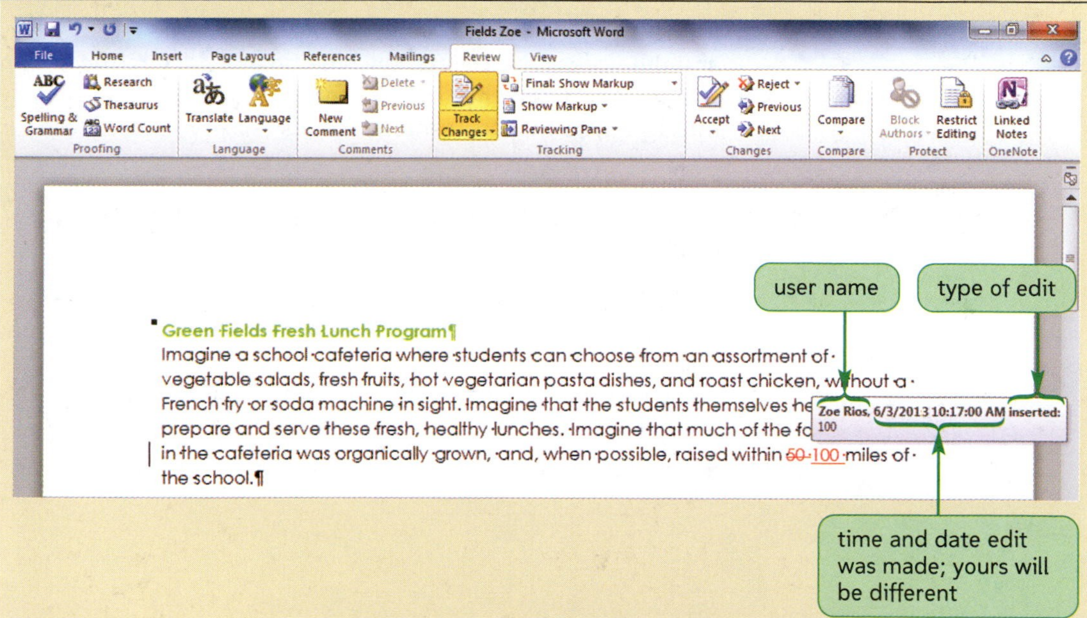

Next, Zoe wants you to move the second to last sentence in this paragraph to the end of the paragraph.

3. Press the **Ctrl** key, and then click in the sentence **Imagine that the students themselves helped to prepare and serve these fresh, healthy lunches.** The entire sentence is selected.

4. Drag the sentence down to insert it at the end of the paragraph, and then click anywhere in the document to deselect it. The sentence is inserted with a double underline, in green. The color is different from the one used for the number "100" earlier, because Word uses a separate color to denote moved text. See Figure 7-3. The sentence is still visible in its original location, but now it is displayed in green, with a double strikeout line through it. A vertical line appears in the left margin, next to the sentence in its original location, and also next to the sentence in its new location.

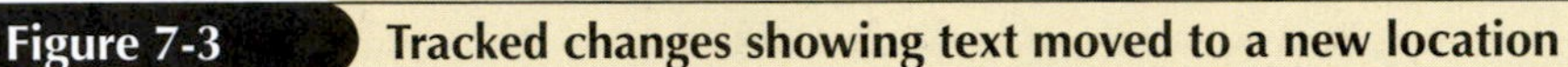

Figure 7-3 Tracked changes showing text moved to a new location

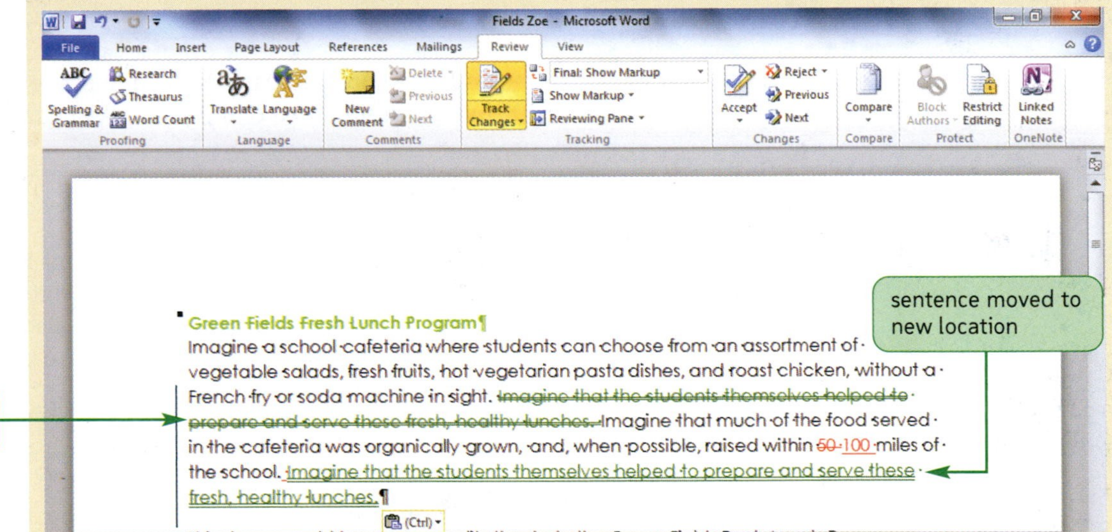

After reviewing the sentence in its new location at the end of the paragraph, Zoe decides she wants to delete the word "healthy" from the sentence.

5. In the sentence you moved in Step 4, click to the left of the comma after "fresh," and then press the **Delete** key nine times to delete the comma, the space after it, and the word **healthy**. The deleted text ", healthy" appears with a strikeout line through it, so that the sentence reads "...serve these fresh lunches."

Finally, you need to format the first heading in the document with the Title style.

6. Click in the heading **Green Fields Fresh Lunch Program**, and then click the **Home** tab.

7. In the Styles group, click the **More** button, and then click the **Title** style in the gallery. A vertical line appears in the left margin next to the heading, and a balloon appears in the right margin containing the text "Formatted: Title" indicating that you changed the formatting of the paragraph to the Title style. See Figure 7-4.

Figure 7-4 Tracked changes showing formatted text

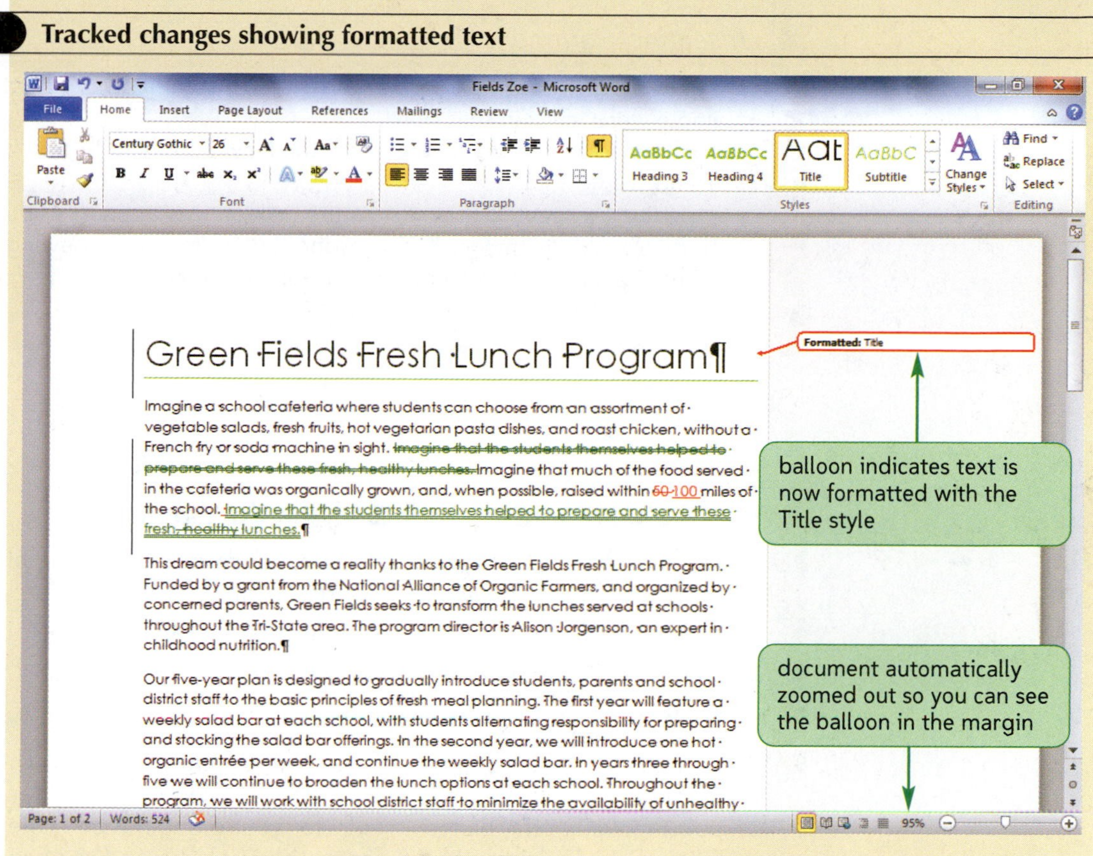

In addition to tracking changes, you can also add comments to the document you are editing.

Inserting Comments

Comments are another useful revision tool. For example, you can use comments to insert notes to yourself as you create a document, or as a means of communicating ideas and feedback to coworkers who are also contributing to the same document. As shown earlier in the Session 7.1 Visual Overview, the text of your comment appears in a balloon in the right margin, along with the name of the person who made the comment and the date and time it was made.

Although comments are often used in conjunction with tracked changes, you don't have to turn on Track Changes to insert comments in a document. The buttons in the Comments group on the Review tab contain options for inserting, deleting, and navigating through comments in a document.

REFERENCE

Inserting Comments

- Select the text to which you want to attach a comment, or, to attach a comment to a single word, click in that word.
- Click the Review tab, and then click the New Comment button in the Comments group.
- Type the text of your comment in the balloon that appears in the margin.
- To display comments in the Reviewing Pane, click the Reviewing Pane button arrow in the Tracking group on the Review tab, and then click Reviewing Pane Vertical or Reviewing Pane Horizontal.

Zoe would like you to add a comment in the Budget section on page 2.

To add a comment to page 2 of the document:

1. Scroll down until you can see the Budget section at the top of page 2. The second sentence says that a complete budget will be available soon. Zoe wants to include a reminder to be more precise about exactly when the full budget will be ready.
2. At the end of the Budget section, click anywhere in the word **soon**.
3. Click the **Review** tab on the Ribbon.
4. In the Comments group, click the **New Comment** button. The word "soon" is highlighted in red, a balloon is inserted in the right margin, and the insertion point moves to the balloon, ready for you to begin typing the comment. See Figure 7-5. The default color for the highlighting and the balloon is red, but it might be a different color on your computer. In Figure 7-5, you see "Comment [ZR1]." The letters "ZR" are Zoe's initials; the number 1 after the initials tells you that this is the first comment in the document.

Figure 7-5 **Inserting a comment**

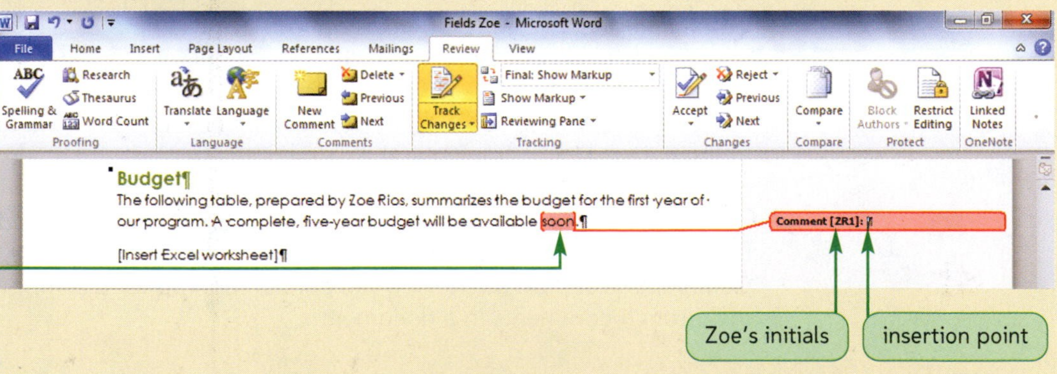

5. With the insertion point in the comment balloon, type **Insert precise date for new budget.** The comment is displayed in the balloon in the right margin. The insertion point remains in the comment balloon until you click in the document.
6. Click anywhere in the document. The comment balloon dims, but remains visible in the margin.
7. Save your work.

Adjusting Track Changes Options

The default settings for Track Changes worked well as you edited Zoe's document. Note, however, that you can change these settings if you prefer. For instance, you could select a larger balloon for comments or a different color for inserted text. You could also change the user name that appears in the ScreenTip for each edit.

To view the settings for the Track Changes options:

1. In the Tracking group on the Review tab, click the **Track Changes button arrow**. A menu appears below the Track Changes button.
2. Click **Change Tracking Options**. The Track Changes Options dialog box opens. As shown in Figure 7-6, you can use the options in the Balloons section to control the size and location of the balloons in the margins. Other options in this dialog box allow you to select the colors you want to use for various types of edits. For example, you can use the Color box next to the Insertions box to select a color to use for inserted text. Note that the default setting for Insertions, Deletions, Comments, and Formatting is By author. This means that Word assigns one color to each person who edits the document. You'll see the significance of that later in this tutorial, when you merge your copy of the document with Henry's. Right now there's no need to change any of the settings in the Track Changes Options dialog box, so you can close it.

Figure 7-6 **Examining the Track Changes Options dialog box**

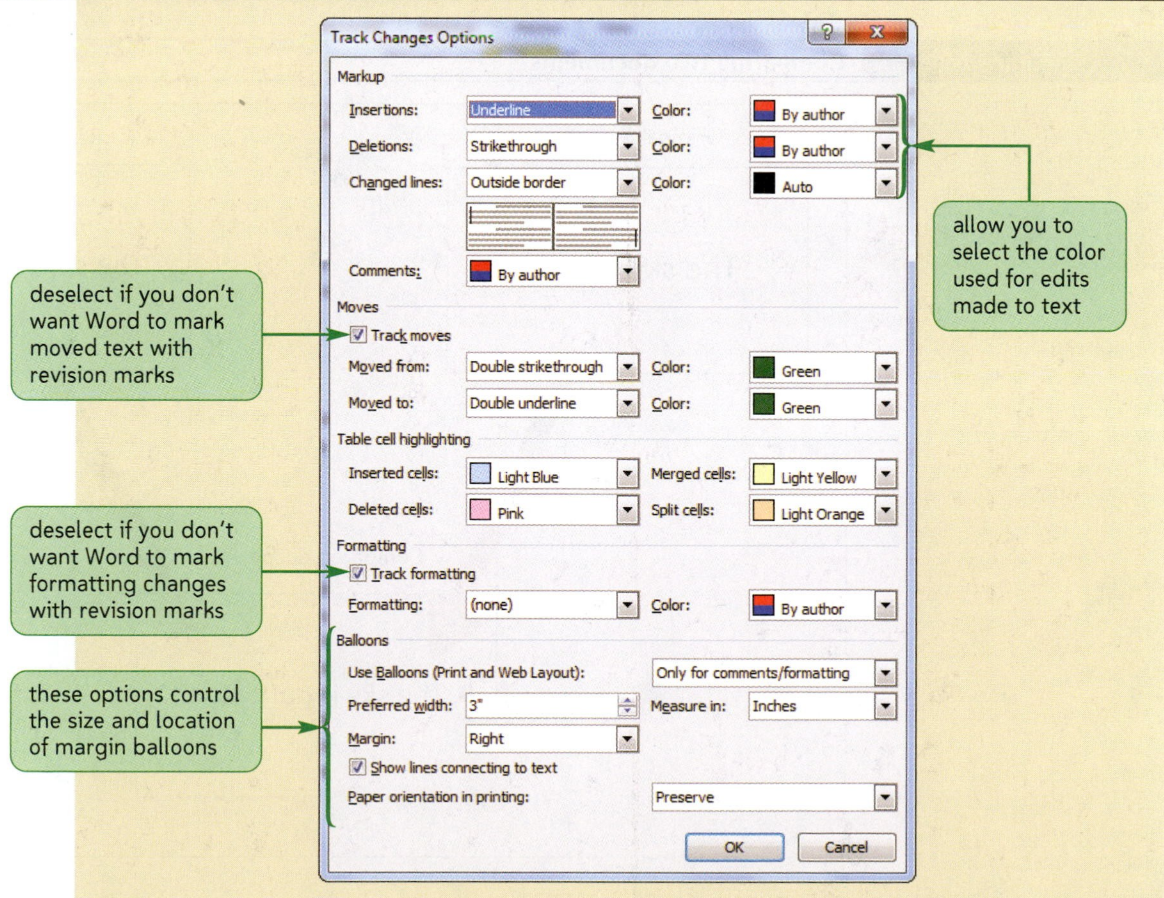

3. Click the **Cancel** button to close the Track Changes Options dialog box.

Zoe has received Henry's edited copy of the first draft via email, and now she'd like your help in combining her edited copy of the Fields Zoe document with Henry's.

Comparing and Combining Documents

When you work in a collaborative environment with multiple people contributing to the same document, Word's Compare and Combine features are essential tools. They allow you to compare documents, with tracked changes highlighting the differences. The Compare and Combine features are similar, but they have different purposes.

Use the **Compare** feature when you have two different versions of a document and you want to see the differences between the two. Use the **Combine** feature when you have two or more versions of a document that you want to combine into a single document. Note that it's also common to use the term **merge** rather than "combine" when talking about combining documents. However, keep in mind that merging, when used in this context, is different from the mail merge process you learned about earlier.

When you compare two documents, you select one document as the original and one as the revised document. Word then creates a new, third document, which consists of the original document with tracked changes added to show how the revised document differs from the original. The original document and the revised document are left unchanged.

For example, suppose the original document contains the sentence "The sky is blue." Also, suppose that in the revised document, the sentence reads "The sky is dark blue." When you compare these two documents, you create a third document where the sentence looks as if you took the original document, turned on tracked changes, and inserted the word "dark." Figure 7-7 illustrates how this works.

Figure 7-7 Comparing two documents

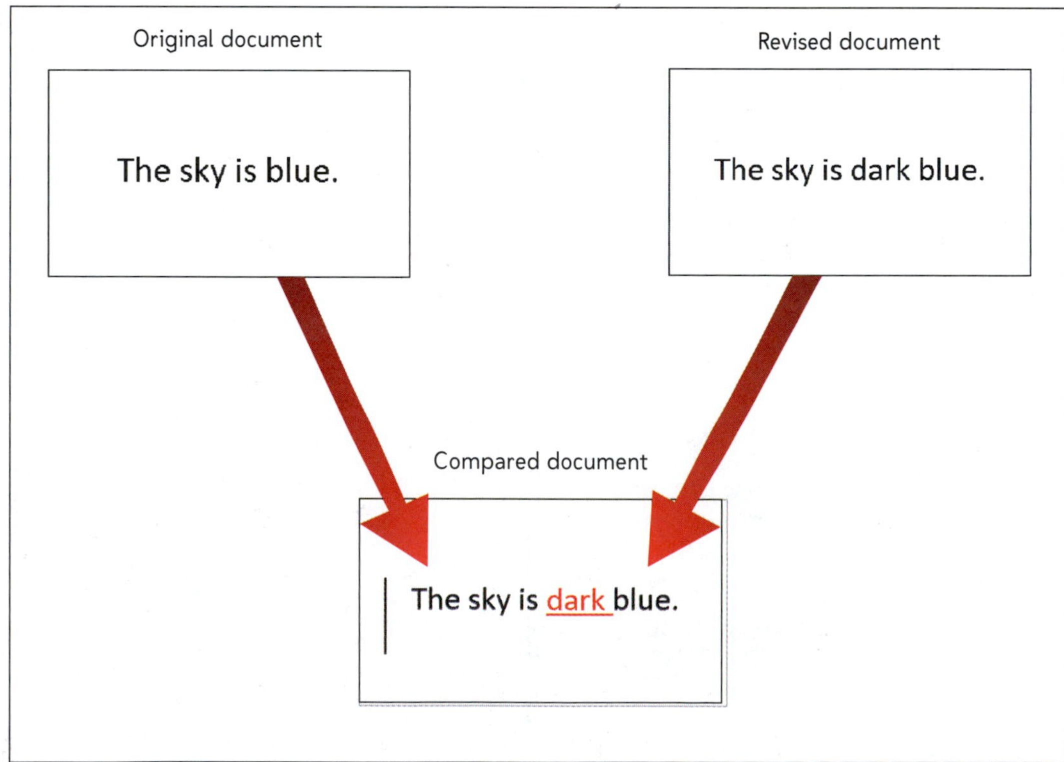

When combining documents, you also start by selecting one document as the original and the other document as the revised document. Word then creates a new document that contains the tracked changes from both the original document and the revised document. If you want, you can then take this new document and combine it with a third. You can continue using this process to incorporate changes from as many authors as you want.

When comparing or combining documents, it doesn't matter if they were originally edited with Tracked Changes turned on. Word marks all differences between the two documents using Tracked Changes, whether or not the original documents themselves contain tracked changes.

REFERENCE

Comparing and Combining Documents

- Click the Compare button in the Compare group on the Review tab.
- Click either Compare (to open the Compare Documents dialog box) or Combine (to open the Combine Documents dialog box).
- Next to the Original document box, click the Browse button, navigate to the location of the document, select the document, and then click the Open button.
- Next to the Revised document box, click the Browse button, navigate to the location of the document, select the document, and then click the Open button.
- Click the More button, if necessary, to display options that allow you to select which items you want marked with tracked changes, and then make any necessary changes.
- Click the OK button.

When you start combining or comparing documents, it's not necessary to have either the original document or the revised document open. In this case, the Fields Zoe document, which you will use as the original document, is currently open. You will combine this document with Henry's edited version of it.

To combine Zoe's document with Henry's document:

1. Make sure you have saved your changes to the **Fields Zoe** document.
2. In the Compare group on the Review tab, click the **Compare** button. A menu opens with options for comparing or combining two versions of a document. You want to combine two documents.
3. Click **Combine**. The Combine Documents dialog box opens.
4. If necessary, click the **More** button. The dialog box expands to display check boxes, which you can use to specify the items you want marked with tracked changes.

   Trouble? If the dialog box has a Less button instead of a More button, the dialog box is already expanded to show the check boxes for selecting additional options. In this case, skip Step 4.

   In the Show changes section at the bottom of the dialog box, the New document option button is selected by default, indicating that Word will create a new, combined document rather than importing the tracked changes from the original document into the revised document, or vice versa. Now you need to specify the Fields Zoe document as the original document. Even though this document is currently open, you still need to select it.

5. Next to the Original document box, click the **Browse** button to open the Open dialog box.
6. If necessary, navigate to the Word7\Tutorial folder included with your Data Files, click **Fields Zoe** in the file list, and then click the **Open** button. You return to the Combine Documents dialog box, where the filename "Fields Zoe" now appears in the Original document box. The "Label unmarked changes with" box displays Zoe's name, indicating that any changes that have been made without tracked changes turned on will be labeled with Zoe's name in the combined document. Next, you need to select the document you want to use as the revised document.
7. Next to the Revised document box, click the **Browse** button, navigate to and select the file **Fields Henry** in the Word7\Tutorial folder included with your Data Files, and then click the **Open** button. The filename "Fields Henry" appears in the Revised document box, and Henry's first and last name appear in the Label unmarked changes with box. See Figure 7-8.

Figure 7-8 Selecting the original and revised documents

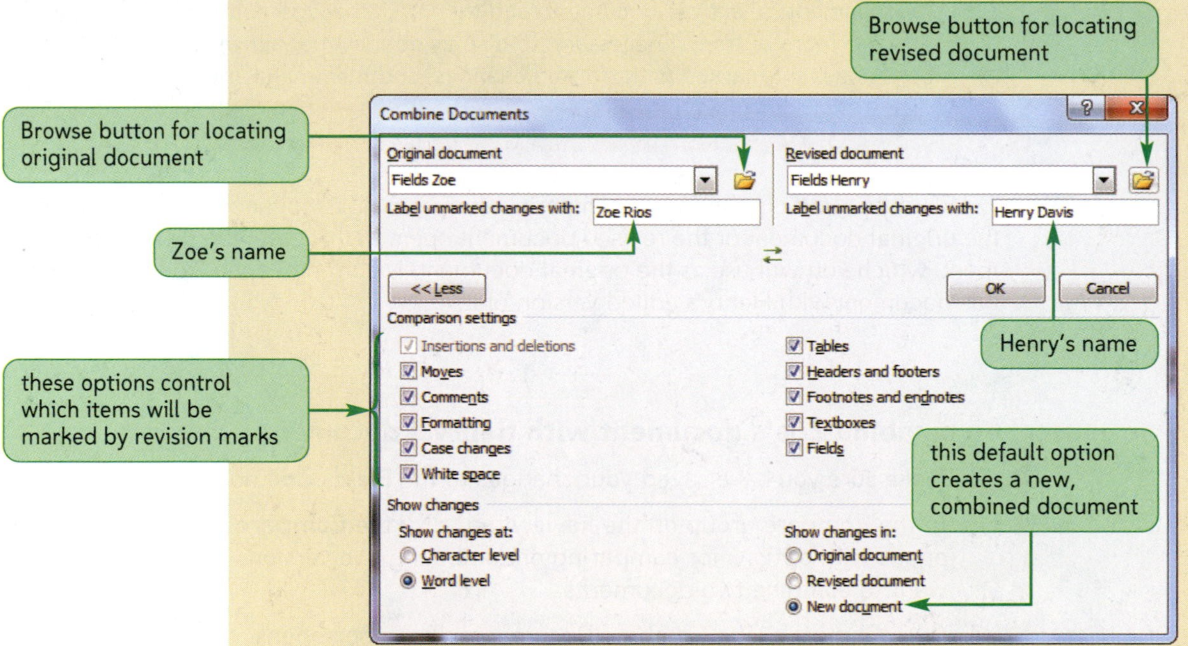

8. Click the **OK** button. The Combine dialog box closes, and a new document named either "Combine Result 1" or "Document1" opens. It contains the tracked changes from both the original document and the revised document. At this point, you might see only the new, combined document, or you might also see the original and revised documents open in separate windows, as shown in Figure 7-9. You might also see the Reviewing Pane, which lists each change in the new, combined document, also shown in Figure 7-9.

Figure 7-9 Two documents combined

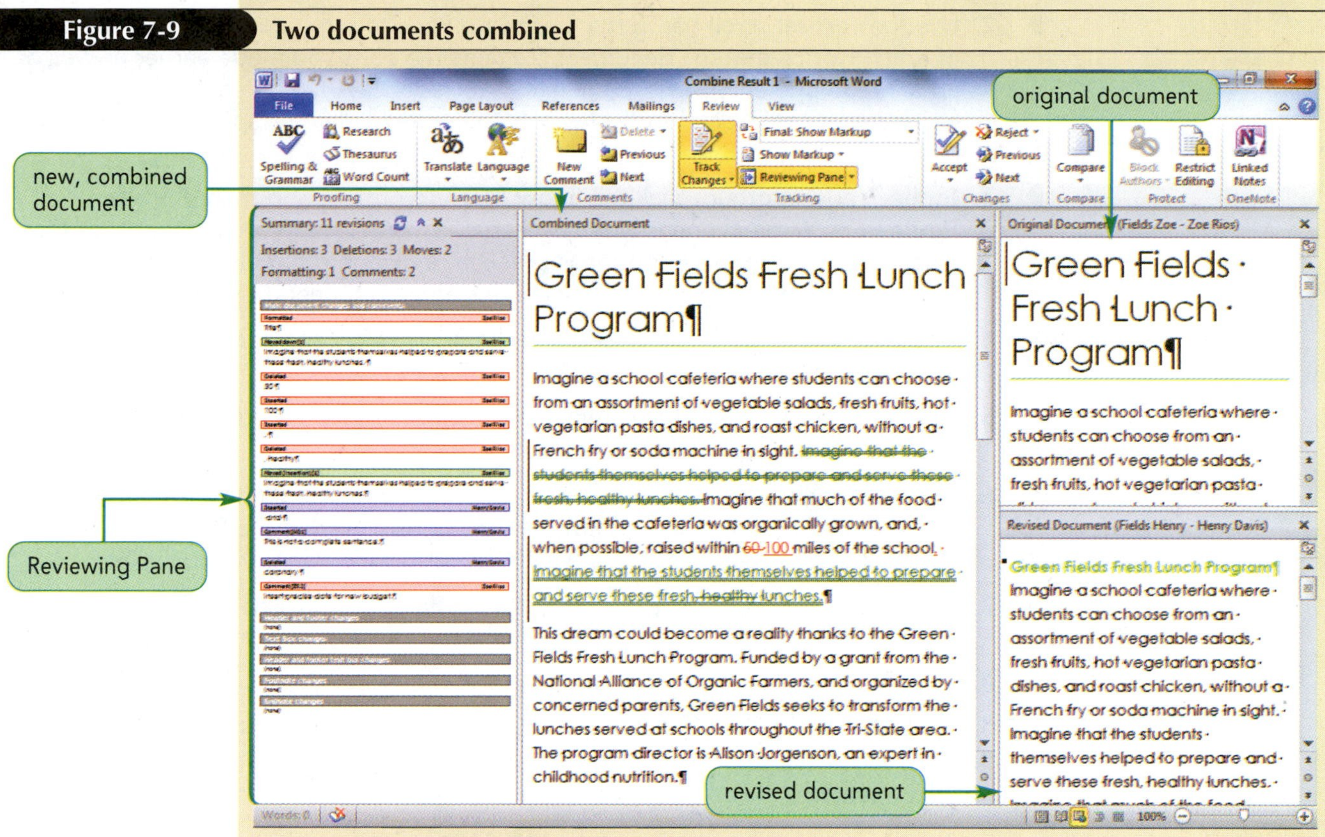

You will make sure your screen is set up to show the original and revised documents and the Reviewing Pane.

9. In the Compare group, click the **Compare** button, point to **Show Source Documents**, and, if you do not see a check mark next to Show Both, click **Show Both**. If you do see a check mark next to Show Both, press the **Escape** key to close the menu.

10. If the Reviewing Pane shown in Figure 7-9 is not displayed, click the **Reviewing Pane** button in the Tracking group to display the Reviewing Pane. The Reviewing Pane will be displayed either in a horizontal window at the bottom of the screen or vertically on the left side of the screen.

11. If your Reviewing Pane is displayed horizontally, click the **Reviewing Pane button arrow** in the Tracking group, and then click **Reviewing Pane Vertical**. Your screen should now match Figure 7-9.

On a small screen, displaying the original and revised documents makes it harder to review the edits in the new, combined document. In that case, you can hide them.

To hide the source documents and review the edits in the Reviewing Pane:

1. In the Compare group, click the **Compare** button, point to **Show Source Documents** button, and then click **Hide Source Documents**. The panes displaying the original and revised documents close.

2. Use the vertical scroll bar in the Reviewing Pane to scroll down and review the list of edits. Notice that the document contains the edits you made earlier as well as edits made by Henry Davis. By default, Word displays all the edits by all reviewers, but you can choose to display only the edits made by a specific reviewer or reviewers.
3. In the Tracking group, click the **Show Markup** button, and then point to **Reviewers**. A menu opens with check marks next to Henry's name and Zoe Rios. Also, the "All Reviewers" option is checked, indicating that all the edits from all the reviewers are displayed. To hide Zoe's edits, you need to deselect her name.
4. Click **Zoe Rios**. The menu closes, and the Reviewing Pane and document show only Henry's edits.
5. Scroll down through the document so you can see that the edits for Zoe Rios are no longer displayed in the document.
6. Click the **Show Markup** button again, point to **Reviewers**, and then click **All Reviewers**. Zoe's and Henry's edits are again displayed in the Reviewing Pane and in the document. You are finished with the Reviewing Pane, so you can close it.
7. In the Tracking group, click the **Reviewing Pane** button. The Reviewing Pane closes.
8. Save the document as **Fields Combined** in the Word7\Tutorial folder included with your Data Files.
9. Click the **Track Changes** button to turn off Track Changes. This ensures that you won't accidentally add any additional edit marks as you review the document.

Next you will review the edits to accept and reject the changes as appropriate.

Accepting and Rejecting Changes

The document you just created contains all the edits from two different reviewers—Zoe's changes made in the original document, and Henry's changes as they appeared in the revised document. Each reviewer's edits appear in a different color, with ScreenTips, making it easy to see which reviewer has made each change.

When you review tracked changes in a document, the best approach is to move the insertion point to the beginning of the document, and then navigate through the document one change at a time using the Next and Previous buttons. In this way, you'll be sure not to miss any edits. As you review a tracked change, you can either accept the change or reject the change.

As you accept and reject changes, you often need to delete comments as well. To delete a comment, click in the comment balloon, and then click the Delete button in the Comment group. To delete all the comments in a document, click the Delete button arrow in the Comment group, and then click Delete All Comments in Document.

REFERENCE

Accepting and Rejecting Changes

- Move the insertion point to the beginning of the document.
- In the Changes group on the Review tab, click the Next button to select the first edit or comment in the document.
- To accept a selected change, click the Accept button in the Changes group.
- To reject a selected change, click the Reject button in the Changes group.
- To accept all the changes in the document, click the Accept button arrow, and then click Accept All Changes in Document.
- To reject all the changes in the document, click the Reject button arrow, and then click Reject All Changes in Document.

Now you will review the document of combined changes.

To accept and reject changes in the Fields Combined document:

1. Press the **Ctrl+Home** keys to move the insertion point to the beginning of the document.
2. In the Changes group on the Review tab, click the **Next** button. The heading "Green Fields Fresh Lunch Program" is selected, as shown in Figure 7-10. Recall that in the Fields Zoe document that you edited earlier, you formatted this heading with the Title style.

   Trouble? If the insertion point moves to Henry's comment at the bottom of page 1, you clicked the Next button in the Comments group instead of the Next button in the Changes group. Repeat Steps 1 and 2.

Figure 7-10 **First change in the document selected**

3. In the Changes group, click the **Accept** button. The margin balloon disappears, indicating that the change has been accepted. The next change in the document is now selected. This is the sentence that you moved to a new location at the end of the paragraph. Both the deleted sentence and the inserted copy of the sentence at the end of the paragraph appear in green. You need to accept the change of moving this sentence.

Trouble? If you see a menu below the Accept button, you clicked the Accept button arrow by mistake. Press the Escape key to close the menu, and then click the Accept button.

4. Click the **Accept** button. The sentence with the strikeout line through it is removed from the document, and the moved sentence in its new location at the end of the paragraph reverts to regular, black font. The next change in the document, the deleted number 50, is now selected.
5. Accept the deletion of the number 50 and the rest of the changes on page 1. At the top of page 2, the word "and" is selected as the next change. This is one of Henry's changes.
6. Scroll down to display the changes Henry made to page 2. See Figure 7-11.

Figure 7-11 **Reviewing Henry's changes**

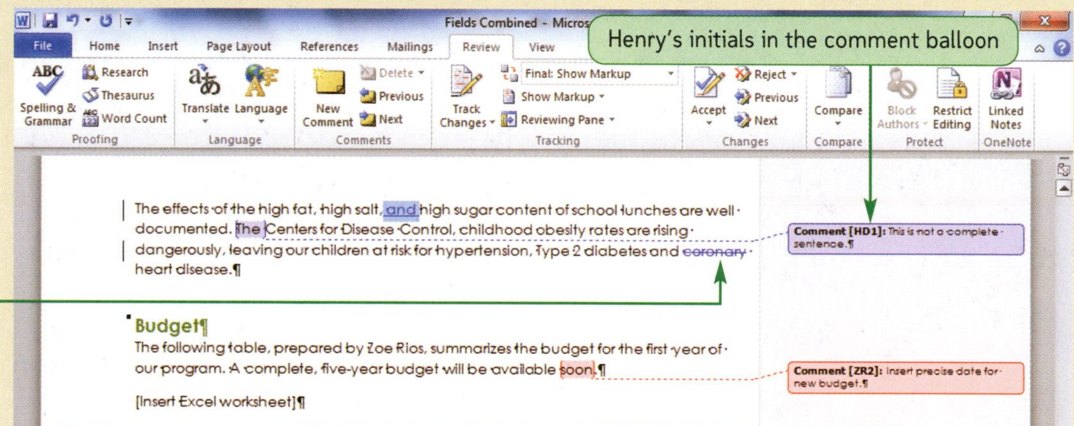

7. Click the **Accept** button to accept the insertion of the word "and." The insertion point moves to Henry's comment, which reads "This is not a complete sentence."
8. In the Comments group, click the **Delete** button. The comment is deleted and the insertion point moves back to the document.

You need to edit the sentence that Henry was concerned about, and then continue reviewing changes in the document.

To edit the incomplete sentence, and then continue accepting and rejecting changes:

1. Edit the sentence that begins "The Centers for Disease Control, childhood…" so that it reads **According to the Centers for Disease Control, childhood….**
2. In the Changes group, click the **Next** button to select the next change in the document. The deleted word "coronary," which appears with a strikeout line through it, is highlighted. Zoe prefers to keep "coronary," so you will reject this change.
3. In the Changes group, click the **Reject** button. The word "coronary" is no longer marked for deletion, and the insertion point moves to the comment balloon in the margin containing Zoe's comment. See Figure 7-12.

Figure 7-12 Rejected change

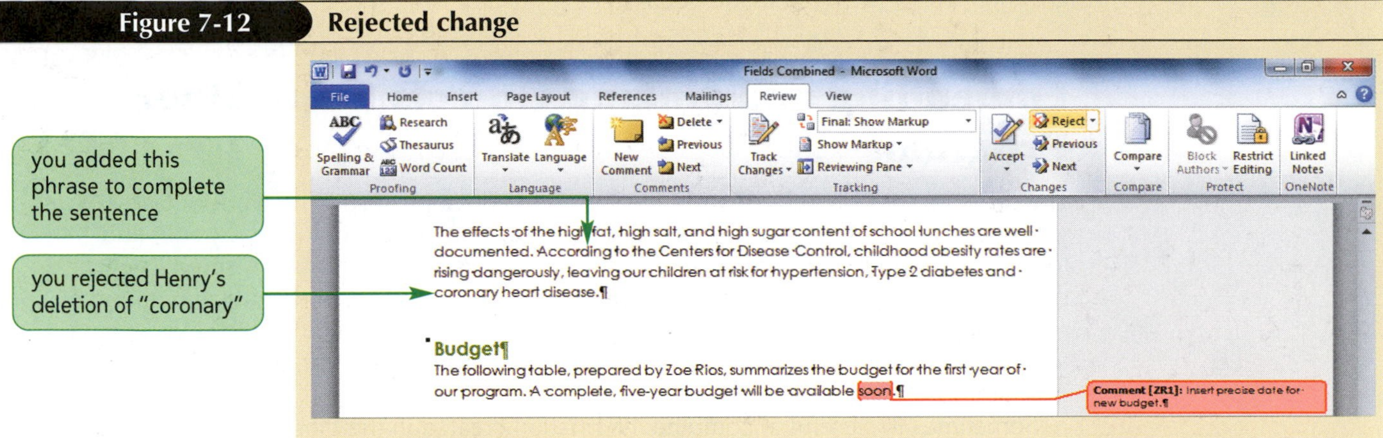

4. Click anywhere in the comment balloon, and then click the **Delete** button in the Comments group. The comment is deleted, and the document zoom adjusts because the document no longer contains any tracked changes or comments in the margins.

5. Change the document view to Page Width, and then, in the first sentence under the "Budget" heading, replace "Zoe Rios" with your first and last name. Now that you are finished editing and reviewing the document with tracked changes, you need to restore your original user name and initials settings.

6. Click the **Review** tab, click the **Track Changes button arrow** in the Tracking group, click **Change User Name,** change the user name and initials back to their original settings on the General tab of the Word Options dialog box, and then click the **OK** button.

7. Click the **Word** button in the taskbar, click the **Fields Zoe – Microsoft Word** thumbnail to display the document, close the **Fields Zoe** document, and then save the **Fields Combined** document.

TIP

To delete all the comments in a document, click in any comment balloon, click the Delete button arrow in the Comments group, and then click Delete All Comments in Document.

INSIGHT

Understanding Tracked Changes

Once a document is finished, you want to make sure it does not contain any tracked changes or comments. You can't always tell if a document contains comments or tracked changes just by looking at it, because the comments or changes for some or all of the reviewers might be hidden. Also, the Display for Review box in the Tracking group on the Review tab might be set to Final instead of Final: Show Markup. In that case, the tracked changes would not be visible, but could easily be redisplayed by changing the Display for Review setting to Final: Show Markup. To determine whether or not a document contains any tracked changes or comments:

- In the Tracking group on the Review tab, verify that the Display for Review box is set to Final: Show Markup.
- In the Tracking group on the Review tab, click the Show Markup button, point to Reviewers, and confirm a check mark appears next to All Reviewers.
- Press the Ctrl+Home keys to move the insertion point to the beginning of the document, and then in the Changes group on the Review tab, click the Next button. This will either display a dialog box indicating the document contains no comments or tracked changes, or the insertion point will move to the next comment or tracked change.

Now that you have combined Henry's edits with Zoe's, you are ready to add the budget and Henry's pie chart to the document.

Embedding and Linking Objects from Other Programs

The programs in Office 2010 are all designed to accomplish specific types of tasks. As you've seen with Word, you can use a word-processing program to create, edit, and format documents such as letters, reports, newsletters, and proposals. A **spreadsheet program**, on the other hand, allows you to organize, calculate, and analyze numerical data in a grid of rows and columns. A spreadsheet created in Microsoft Excel is known as a **worksheet**. Excel also has tools for analyzing and representing data graphically in charts.

Sometimes it is useful to combine information created in the different Office programs into one file. For example, in the Green Fields Fresh Lunch Program description, Zoe wants to include budget information that was created in an Excel worksheet. She also wants to include an Excel chart, created by Henry, that shows the percentage of fresh fruits and vegetables served in local schools. You can incorporate the Excel data and chart into Zoe's Word document by taking advantage of **object linking and embedding**, or **OLE**, a technology that allows you to share information between the Office programs. This process is commonly referred to as **integration**.

Recall that an object is anything that can be selected and modified as a whole, such as a table, picture, or block of text. When referring to OLE, the program used to create the original version of the object is called the **source program**. The program into which the object is integrated is called the **destination program.** Similarly, the original file that contains the object you are integrating is called the **source file**, and the file into which you integrate the object is called the **destination file**. You can integrate objects by either embedding or linking.

Embedding is a technique that allows you to insert a copy of an object into a destination document. In the destination document, you can double-click an embedded object to access the tools of the source program, allowing you to edit the object within the destination document using the tools of the source program. Because the embedded object is a copy, any changes you make to it are not reflected in the original source file, and vice versa. For instance, you could embed a worksheet named Itemized Expenses into a Word document named Travel Report. Later, if you change the Itemized Expenses file, those revisions would not appear in the Travel Report document. The opposite is also true; if you edit the embedded object from within the Travel Report file, those changes will not be reflected in the source file Itemized Expenses. The embedded object retains a connection to the source program, Excel, but not to the source file.

Figure 7-13 illustrates the relationship between an embedded Excel object in Zoe's Word document and the source file.

Figure 7-13 **Embedding an Excel worksheet in a Word document**

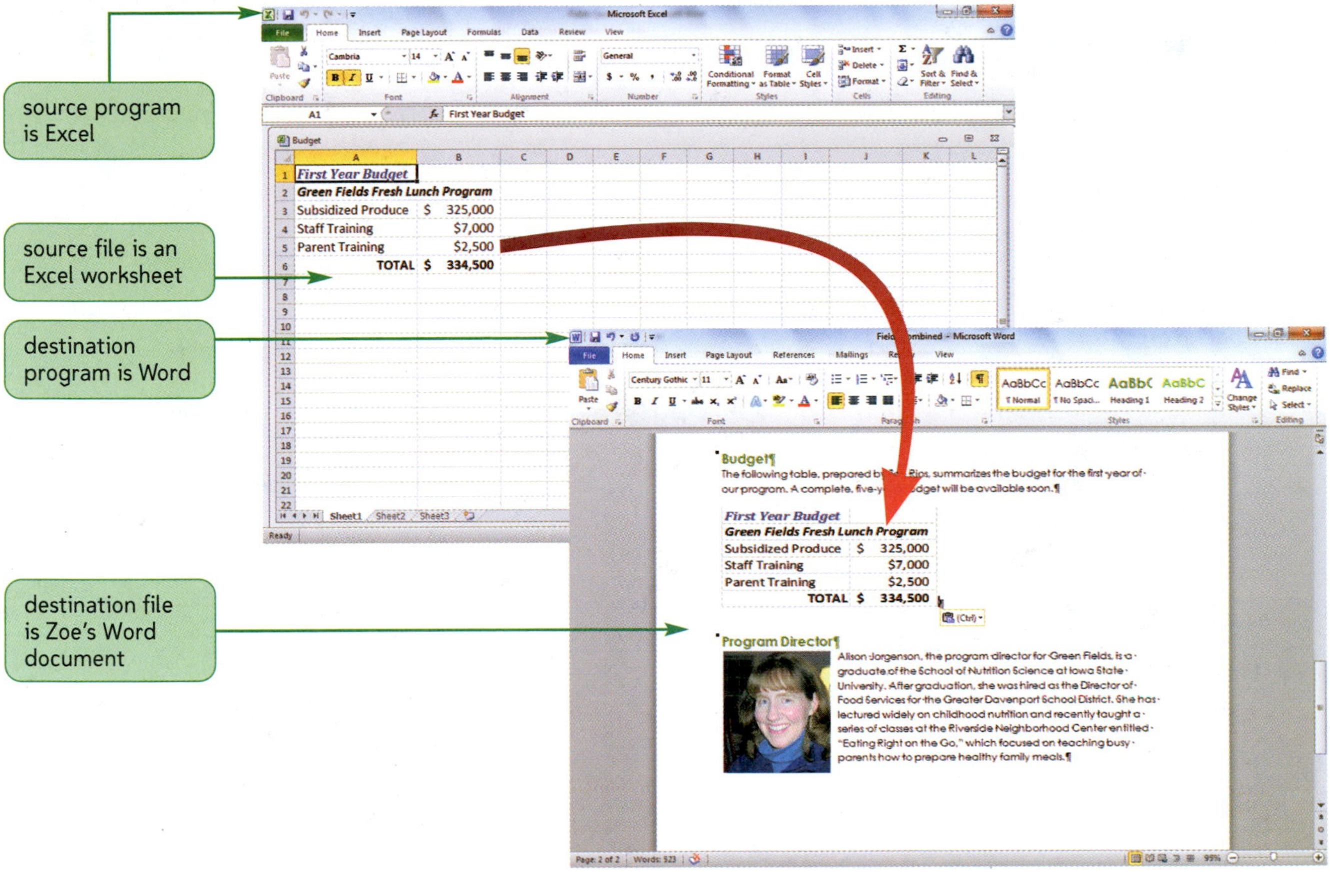

source program is Excel

source file is an Excel worksheet

destination program is Word

destination file is Zoe's Word document

First Year Budget	
Green Fields Fresh Lunch Program	
Subsidized Produce	$ 325,000
Staff Training	$7,000
Parent Training	$2,500
TOTAL	$ 334,500

TIP

A document that contains a linked object takes up less space on a disk than does a document containing an embedded version of the same object.

Linking is similar to embedding, except that the object inserted into the destination file maintains a connection to the source file—not just the source program. Just as with an embedded object, you can double-click a linked object to access the tools of the source program. However, unlike with an embedded object, if you edit the source file in the source program, those changes appear in the linked object; likewise, if you change the object from the destination program, the changes will also appear in the file in the source program. The linked object in the destination document is not a copy; it is a shortcut to the original object in the source file.

INSIGHT

Storing Linked Files

When linking objects, it is important to keep the source and destination files in their original storage locations. If you move the files or the folders in which they are stored, you will disrupt the connection between the source file and the document containing the linked object, because the shortcut in the destination file will no longer have a valid path to the source file. For example, if you insert a linked Excel file into a Word document, close the Word document and the Excel file, and then later a colleague moves the source file (the Excel file) to a different folder or even deletes it, the next time you open the Word document containing the linked object, you will get an error message or you won't be able to update the linked object. To update the path for linked objects, click the File tab, click the Info tab in Backstage view, and then click Edit Links to Files in the right pane of the Info tab. In the Links dialog box that opens, click the link whose location has changed, click the Change Source button, and then navigate to the new location of the source file.

Figure 7-14 illustrates the relationship between the data in Henry's Excel chart and the linked object in Zoe's Word document.

Figure 7-14 **Linking an Excel chart to a Word document**

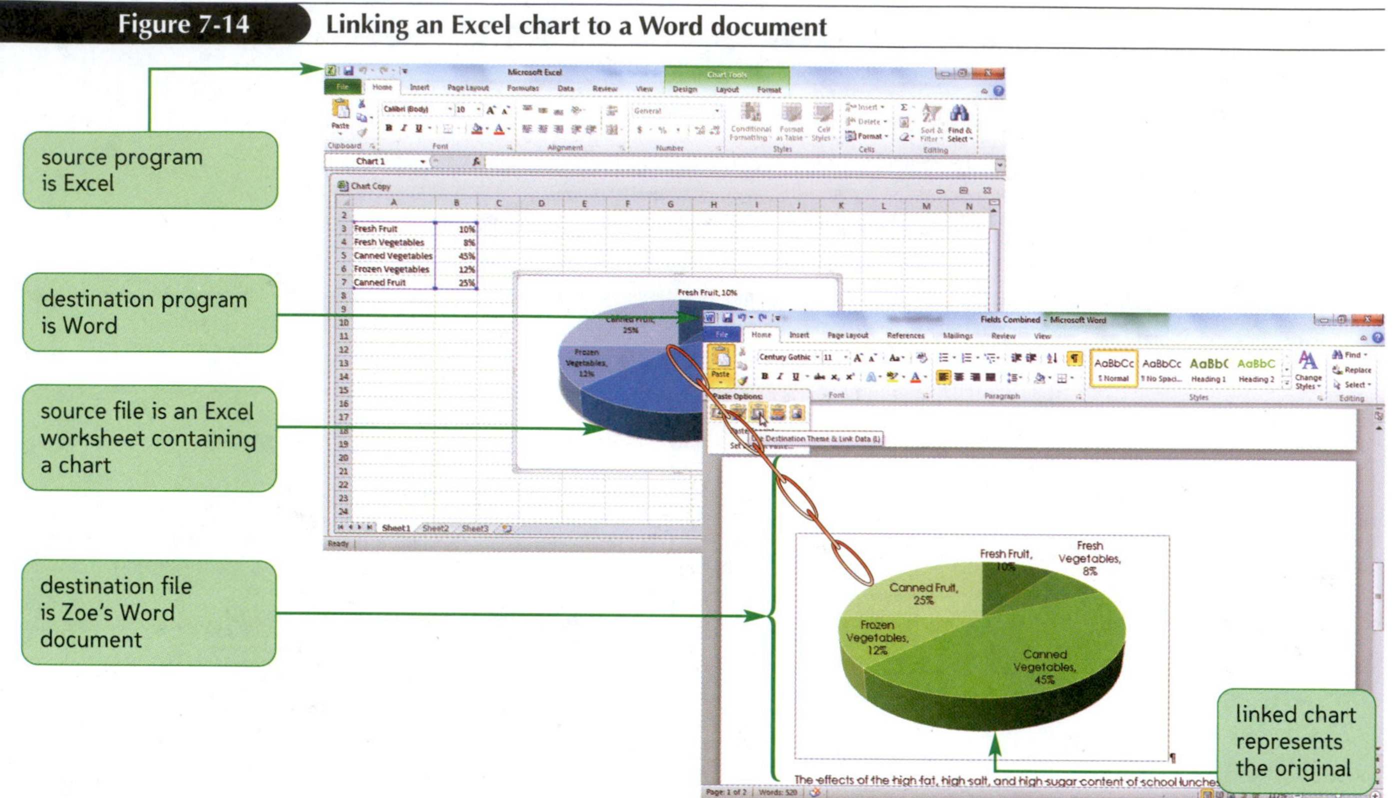

PROSKILLS

Decision Making: Choosing Between Embedding and Linking

Embedding and linking are both useful when you know you'll want to edit an object after inserting it into Word. But how do you decide whether to embed or link the object? Create an embedded object if you won't have access to the original source file in the future, or if you don't need to maintain the connection between the source file and the document containing the linked object. An advantage of embedding is that the source file is unaffected by any editing in the destination document, and the two files can be stored separately. You could even delete the source file from your disk without affecting the copy embedded in your Word document. A disadvantage is that the file size of the Word document containing the embedded object will be larger.

Create a linked object whenever you have data that is likely to change over time and when you want to keep the object in your document up to date. The advantage to linking is that the data in both the source file and destination file can reflect recent revisions. A disadvantage to linking is that you have to keep track of two files (the Excel file and the Word file) rather than just one.

Embedding an Excel Worksheet

To embed an object from an Excel worksheet into a Word document, you start by opening the Excel worksheet (the source file) and copying the Excel object that you want to embed to the Office Clipboard. You then open the Word document (the destination file), click the Paste button arrow in the Clipboard group on the Home tab, and then click Paste Special to open the Paste Special dialog box. In this dialog box, you can choose to paste the copied Excel object in a number of different forms. To embed it, you select Microsoft Office Excel Worksheet Object.

Zoe wants to include the budget for the lunch program in her program description document. If she needs to adjust numbers in the budget later, she will need access to the Excel tools for recalculating the data. Therefore, you will embed the Excel object in the Word document, replacing the "[Insert Excel worksheet]" placeholder on page 2. Then you can use Excel commands to modify the embedded object from within Word.

To embed the Excel data in the Word document:

1. On page 2, delete the placeholder **[Insert Excel worksheet]** that appears under the Budget heading, being careful not to delete the paragraph mark after it. The insertion point should now be located in a blank paragraph above the "Program Director" heading. Now you need to open Henry's Excel file and copy the budget.
2. Start Microsoft Excel 2010, open the file **Budget** located in the Word7\Tutorial folder included with your Data Files, and then maximize the Excel program window if necessary. See Figure 7-15.

Figure 7-15 **Budget file open in Excel**

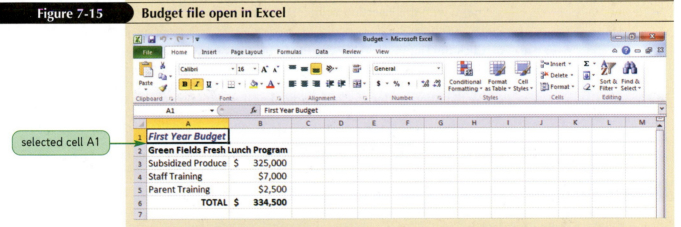

An Excel worksheet is arranged in rows and columns, just like a Word table. The intersection between a row and column is called a **cell**; an individual cell takes its name from its column letter and row number. For example, the intersection of column A and row 1 in the upper-left corner of the worksheet is referred to as cell A1, and it is currently selected, as indicated by its dark outline. To copy the budget data to the Office Clipboard, you need to select the entire block of cells containing the budget.

3. Click cell **A1** (the cell containing the text "First Year Budget"), press and hold the **Shift** key, and then click cell **B6** (the cell containing "$334,500"). See Figure 7-16.

Figure 7-16 **Budget data selected in the worksheet**

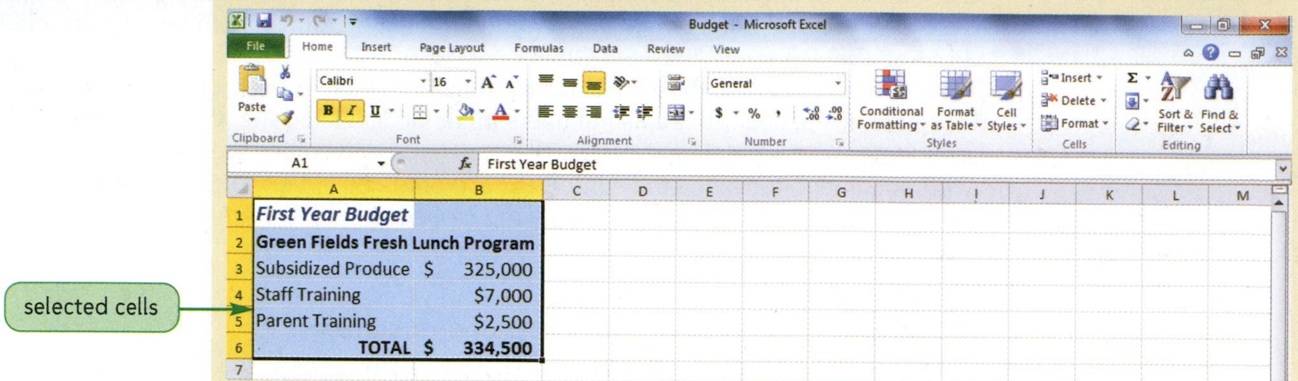

Now that the data is selected, you can copy it to the Office Clipboard, and return to Word. You need to keep Excel open, otherwise you will not have access to the commands for embedding the data in Word.

4. Press the **Ctrl+C** keys. The border around the selected cells is flashing, indicating that you have copied the data in these cells to the Office Clipboard.
5. Click the **Word** button in the taskbar. You return to the Fields Combined document, with the insertion point located in the blank paragraph above the heading "Program Director."
6. Click the **Home** tab, click the **Paste button arrow** in the Clipboard group, and then click **Paste Special** to open the Paste Special dialog box. Here you can choose to embed the Excel object or link it, depending on whether you select the Paste option button (for embedding) or the Paste link option button (for linking). The Paste option button is selected by default. To embed the data, you need to select Microsoft Office Excel Worksheet Object in the As list.
7. In the As list, click **Microsoft Office Excel Worksheet Object**. See Figure 7-17.

Figure 7-17 **Paste Special dialog box**

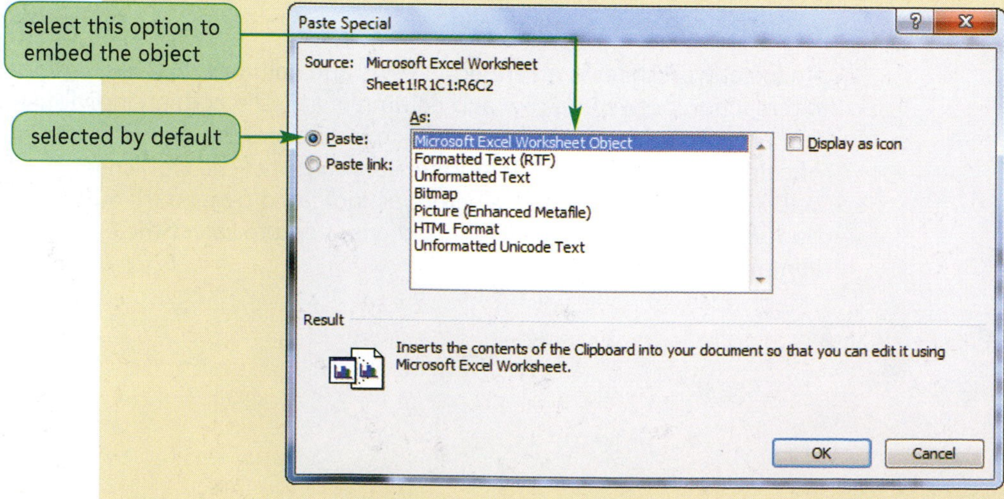

8. Click the **OK** button. The Excel object is inserted in the Word document, as shown in Figure 7-18.

Figure 7-18 Excel object embedded in the Word document

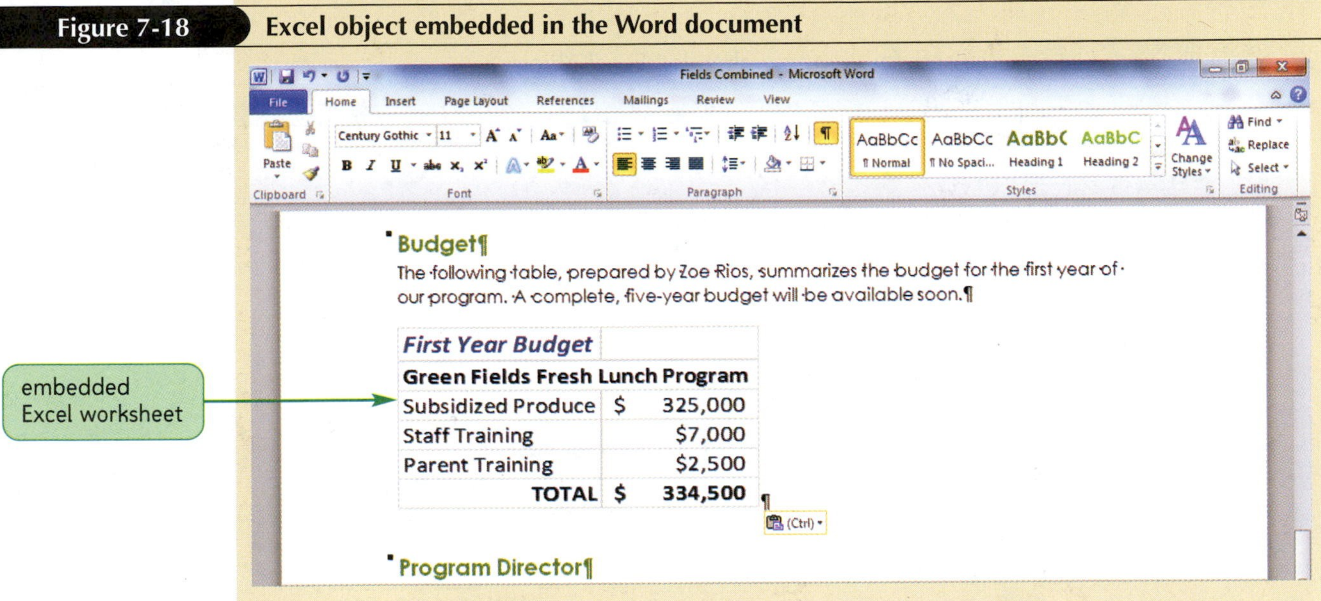

At this point, the Excel data looks like an ordinary table. But because you embedded it as an Excel worksheet object, you can modify it from within Word, using Excel tools and commands.

Modifying the Embedded Worksheet

After you embed an object in Word, you can modify it two different ways. First, you can click the object to select it, and then move or resize it, just as you would a graphic object. Second, you can double-click the object to display the tools of the source program on the Word Ribbon, and then edit the contents of the object. After you modify the embedded object using the source program tools, you can click anywhere else in the Word document to deselect the embedded object and redisplay the usual Word tools on the Ribbon.

Zoe would like to center the Excel object on the page. She also explains that the value for Staff Training is incorrect, so she asks you to update the budget with the new data.

To modify the Excel object:

1. Click anywhere in the embedded budget. Selection handles and a dotted blue outline appear around the Excel object, indicating that it is selected. With the object selected, you can center it as you would center any other selected item.
2. In the Paragraph group on the Home tab, click the **Center** button. The Excel object is aligned to the center of the page.
3. Double-click anywhere inside the Excel object. The object's border changes to resemble the borders of an Excel worksheet, with horizontal and vertical scroll bars, row numbers, and column letters. The Word tabs on the Ribbon are replaced with Excel tabs. You need to change the value for Staff Training from $7,000 to $6,000. This should also decrease the budget total by $1,000 because of the formula used in the worksheet to calculate this value.

4. Click cell **B4**, which contains the value $7,000, type **6000**, and then press the **Enter** key. The new value of "$6,000" replaces the old value of "$7,000." The budget total in cell B6 decreases from $334,500 to $333,500. See Figure 7-19.

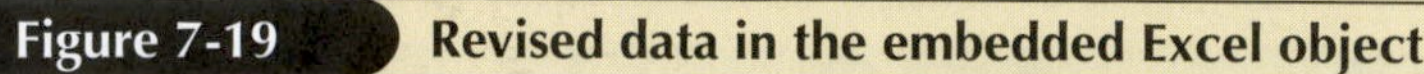

Figure 7-19 **Revised data in the embedded Excel object**

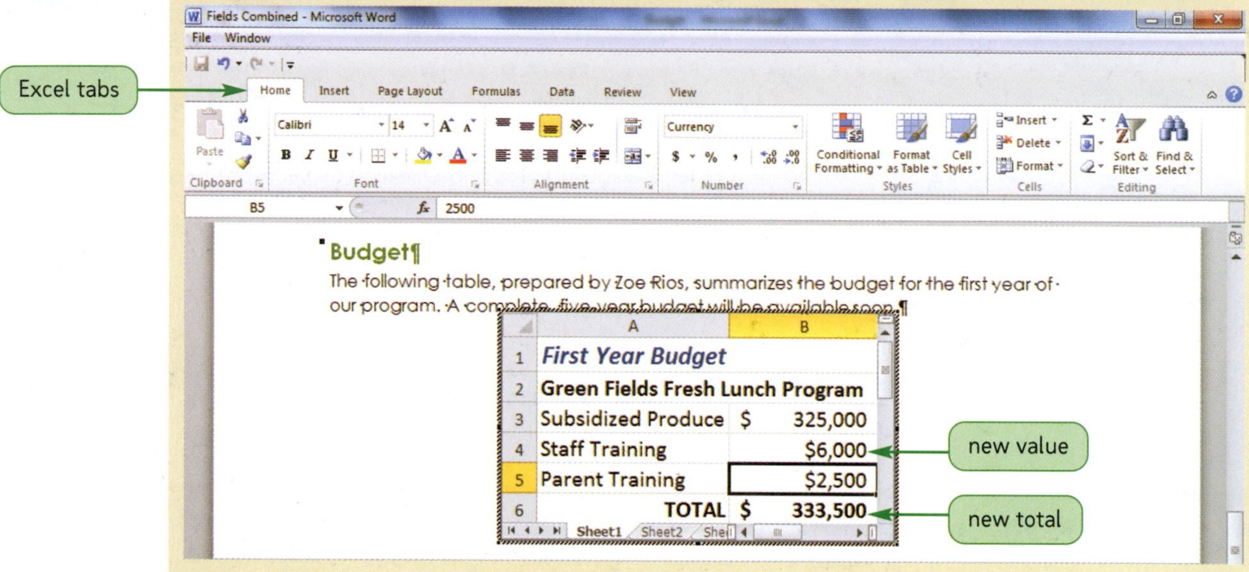

5. Click outside the borders of the Excel object to deselect it. The Word tabs are now visible on the Ribbon again.

6. Click the **Microsoft Excel** button in the taskbar to display the Excel window. Because you embedded the data from the Excel worksheet instead of linking it, the original Budget workbook, with the original Staff Training value of $7,000, remains unchanged.

7. Click the **File** tab, and then click **Close** in the navigation bar. The Budget workbook closes.

Next, Zoe wants you to insert Henry's Excel chart, which illustrates the percentage of fresh fruits and vegetables served in school lunches. Because Henry plans to revise the chart soon, Zoe decides to link the chart in the Excel file rather than embed it. That way, once Henry updates the chart in the source file, the new data will appear in Zoe's Word document as well.

Linking an Excel Chart

When you link an object, you start by selecting it in the source program and copying it to the Office Clipboard. Then you return to Word and select one of the linking options from the Paste Options menu. The Paste Options menu displays different options depending on what you have copied to the Office Clipboard. Figure 7-20 describes some of the commands you will see on the Paste Options menu for different objects. Note that the ScreenTip (button name) for some of these buttons changes depending on the object you have selected to copy and paste.

Figure 7-20 **Commands on the Paste Options menu**

Button	Button Name	Function	Available when...
	Keep Text Only	Pastes formatted text as unformatted text; also, pastes text from a table as tabbed, unformatted text	You copy text to the Clipboard
	Use Destination Theme	Pastes or embeds copied element from another document or file using theme colors and fonts of destination document	You copy formatted text or a graphic from another document or file and the insertion point is located in a Word document
	Keep Source Formatting	Pastes or embeds copied item from Clipboard with the same formatting it had in source file	You copy text or a graphic from another document or file and the insertion point is located in a Word document
	Use Destination Theme & Link Data	Pastes copied element from another document or file using theme colors and fonts of destination document; also, retains link to source document or file	You copy formatted text or a graphic from another document or file and the insertion point is located in a Word document
	Keep Source Formatting & Link Data	Pastes copied item from Clipboard with the same formatting it had in source file; also retains link to source document or file	You copy formatted text or a graphic from another document or file and the insertion point is located in a Word document
	Picture	Pastes copied Excel data or chart as a picture	You copy data or a chart from an Excel workbook and the insertion point is located in a Word document
	Nest Table	Pastes multiple cells inside a single cell	You copy cells in a table to the Clipboard and the insertion point is located in a table
	Merge Table	Pastes copied table or rows at the bottom of the current table	You copy a table or table rows to the Clipboard and the insertion point is located in a table
	Insert as New Rows	Pastes copied rows as new rows in the current table	You copy table rows to the Clipboard and the insertion point is located in a table
	Insert as New Columns	Pastes copied columns as new columns in the current table	You copy table rows to the Clipboard and the insertion point is located in a table

The chart Zoe wants to use is stored in a workbook named Chart, located in the Word7\Tutorial folder included with your Data Files. Because you'll make changes to the chart after you link it, you will make a copy of the Chart workbook before you link it. This leaves the original workbook file unchanged in case you want to repeat the tutorial steps later. Normally you don't need to copy a file before you link it to a Word document.

To link an Excel chart to the program description document:

1. Open the Excel file named **Chart** from the Word7\Tutorial folder included with your Data Files, and then save the Excel file with the name **Chart Copy** in the same folder. The worksheet includes some data and the pie chart created from the data.
2. Click the chart border. Do not click any part of the chart itself. A selection border appears around the chart. The worksheet data is also outlined in color to indicate this is the data used to create the chart. See Figure 7-21.

Figure 7-21 Pie chart selected in the worksheet

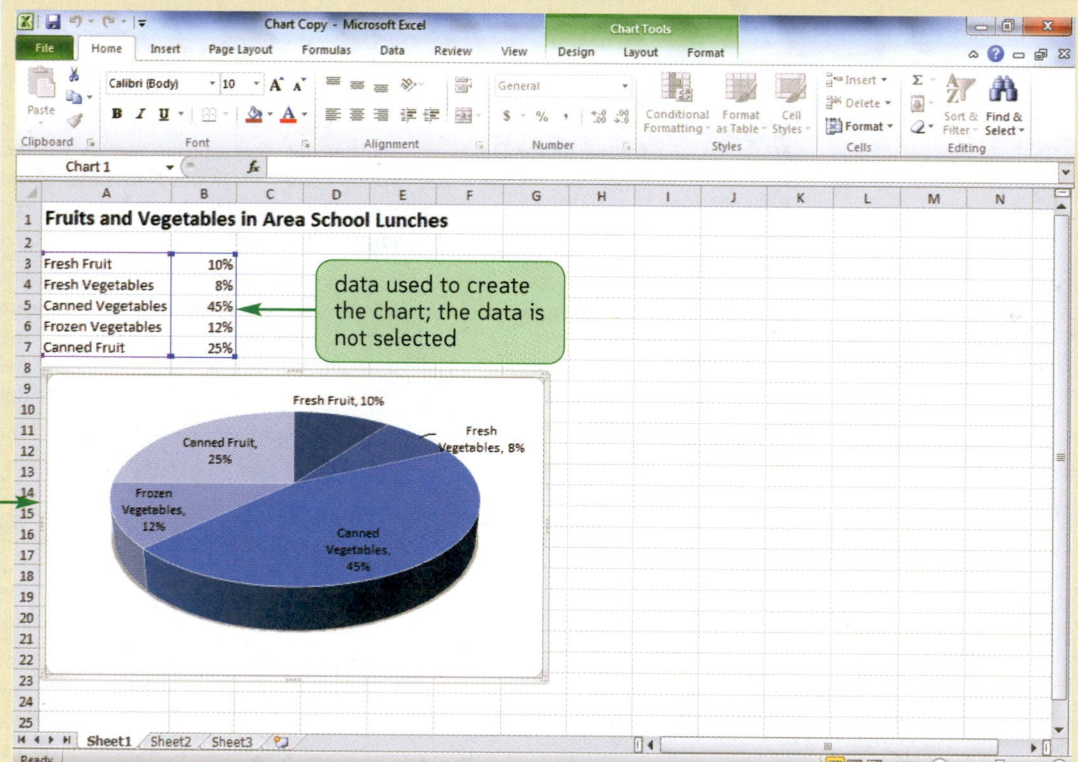

selection border around chart

Trouble? If you see borders or handles around individual elements of the pie chart, click in the worksheet outside the chart border, and then repeat Step 2.

3. Press the **Ctrl+C** keys to copy the pie chart to the Office Clipboard, and then click the **Microsoft Word** button in the taskbar. The Fields Combined document is displayed in the Word window.
4. Scroll up to the bottom of page 1, delete the text **[Insert Excel chart]**, and verify that the insertion point is located in the blank paragraph at the bottom of page 1.
5. In the Clipboard group on the Home tab, click the **Paste button arrow** to display the Paste Options menu.

6. Move the mouse pointer over the icons in the Paste Options menu and notice the changing appearance of the chart, depending on which Paste Option you are previewing. Note that, for linking, you can choose between the Keep Source Formatting & Link Data option, which retains the font and blue colors from the Excel workbook, or Use Destination Theme & Link Data, which formats the chart with the font and green colors of the document's current theme. See Figure 7-22.

Figure 7-22 Linking options in the Paste Options menu

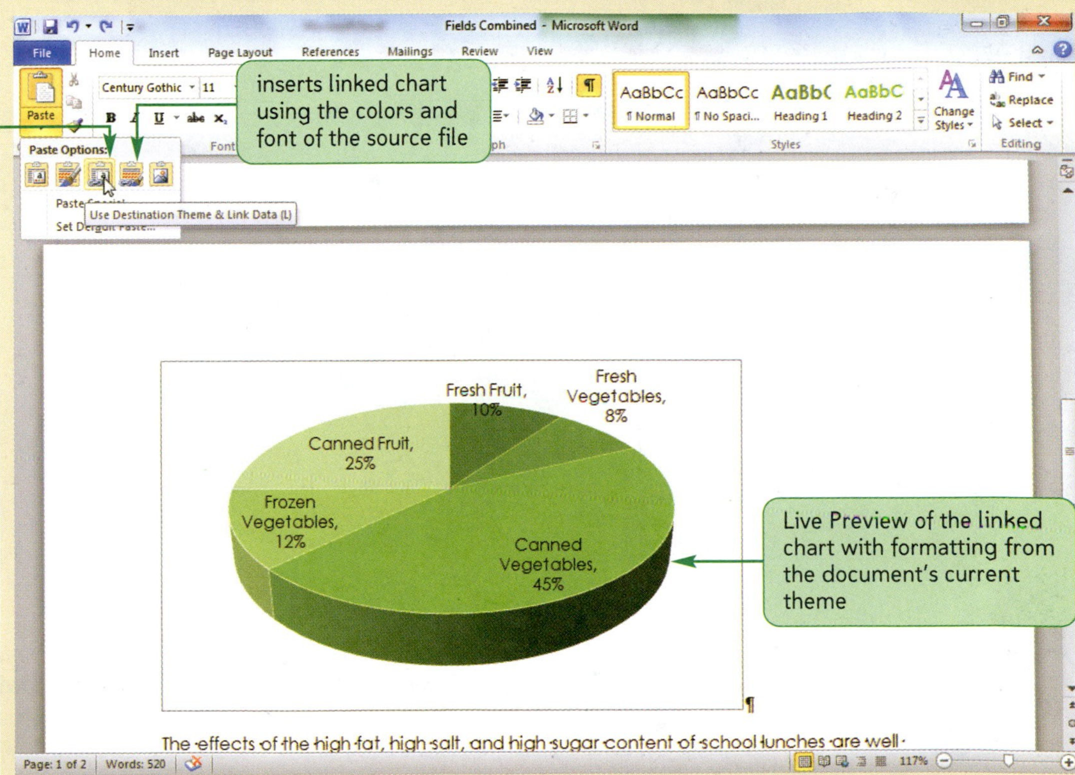

7. On the Paste Options menu, click the **Use Destination Theme & Link Data** button. The chart is inserted at the top of page 2. It is formatted with the green colors and font of the Austin theme used in the document.

Modifying the Linked Chart

The advantage of linking compared to embedding is that you can update the data in the source file, and those changes will automatically be reflected in the destination file as well.

Zoe has received Henry's updated percentages of fruit and vegetables served, and she wants the chart in her program description to reflect this new information. You will update the data in the Excel chart in the source file. You start by selecting the chart, and then clicking the Edit Data button in the Data group on the Chart Tools Design tab. This displays the source and destination files side by side, so you can edit the source file and see the results in the destination file.

To modify the chart in the source file:

1. Click anywhere in the white area inside the chart border. The gray chart border appears, and the three Chart Tools contextual tabs appear on the Ribbon, indicating that the chart is selected. See Figure 7-23.

Figure 7-23 **Chart selected in Word**

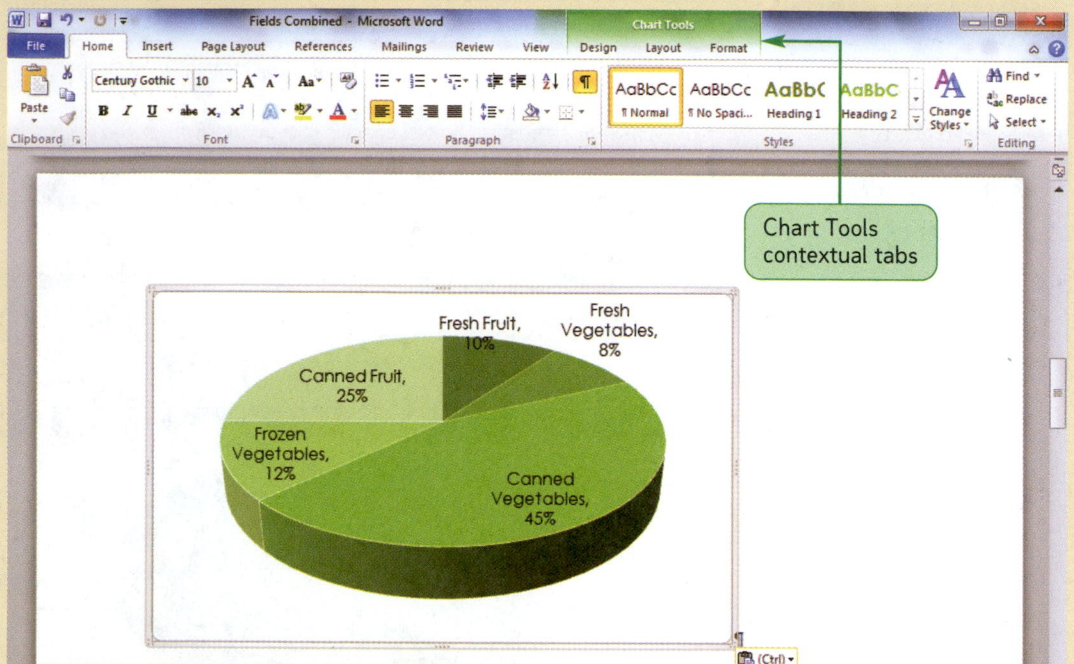

2. Click the **Chart Tools Design** tab, and then click the **Edit Data** button in the Data group. The Excel and Word windows are displayed side-by-side, with the Chart Copy workbook displayed in the Excel window on the right.
3. In the Excel window, click anywhere outside the chart to deselect it. To modify the chart, you need to edit the data in the worksheet.
4. In the Excel window, click cell **B5**, which contains the percentage for Canned Vegetables, type **40**, and then press the **Enter** key. The new percentage is entered in cell B5, and the label in the Canned Vegetables section of the pie chart changes from 45% to 40% in both the Excel workbook and the linked chart in the Word document.

   Trouble? If the chart in the Word document does not change to show the new value for Canned Vegetables, click the Refresh Data button in the Data group of the Chart Tools Design tab in the Word window.

5. In the Excel window, click cell **B7**, which contains the percentage for Canned Fruit, type **30**, and then press the **Enter** key. The new percentage is entered in cell B7, and the label in the Canned Fruit section of the pie charts in both the Excel and Word windows changes from 25% to 30%. See Figure 7-24.

Figure 7-24 Modifying the chart in Excel

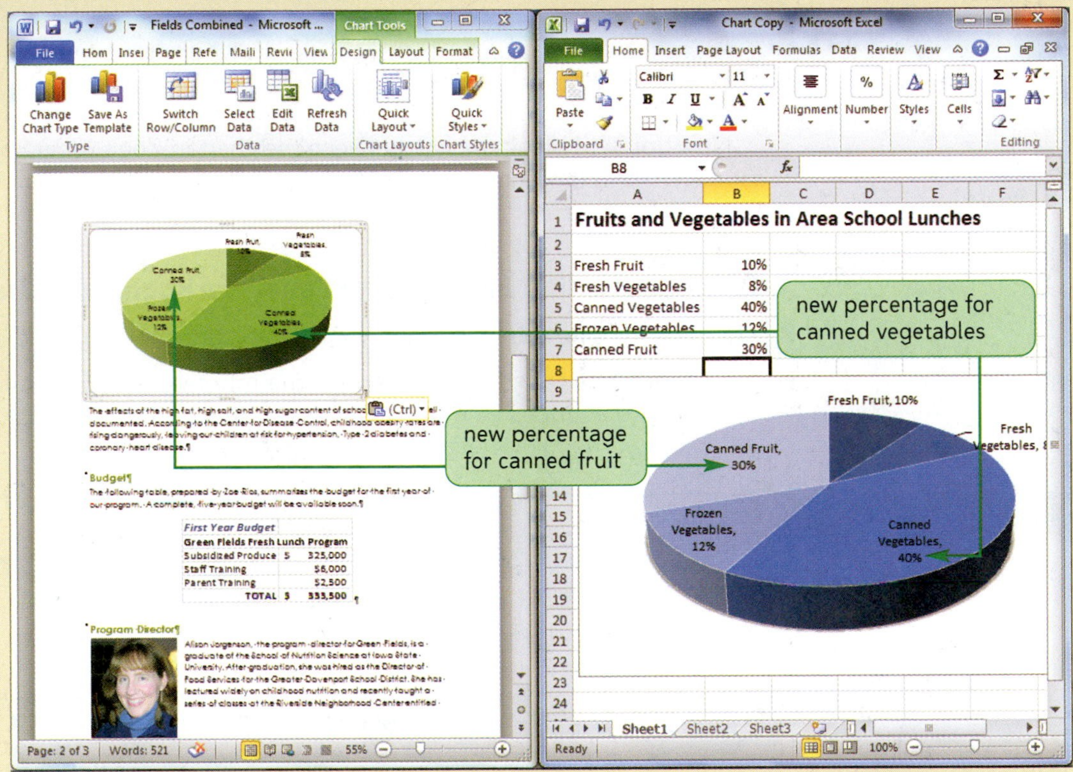

Trouble? If the chart in the Word document does not change to show the new value for Canned Vegetables, click the Refresh Data button in the Data group of the Chart Tools Design tab in the Word window.

6. On the Quick Access Toolbar in the Excel window, click the **Save** button, and then close the Chart Copy file and exit Excel. The Word window maximizes to fill the screen.

7. Click anywhere outside the chart to deselect it, and then save your work.

Zoe is finished with her work on the chart, and does not expect the data in it to change, so she decides to break the link between the Excel workbook and the Word document.

Breaking Links

If you no longer need a link between files, you can break it. When you break a link, the object in the source file and the object in the destination file no longer have any connection to each other, and changes made to one object do not affect the other object.

REFERENCE

Breaking a Link to a Source File

- Click the File tab to open Backstage view, and then click the Info tab, if necessary.
- Click Edit Links to Files in the right pane of the Info tab to open the Links dialog box.
- In the list of links in the document, click the link that you want to break.
- Click the Break Link button.
- Click the Yes button in the dialog box that opens asking you to confirm breaking the link.
- Click the OK button to close the Links dialog box.

Now you will break the link between the chart in Zoe's program description and the source chart in the Chart Copy workbook.

To break the link between the Excel workbook and the Word document:

1. Click the **File** tab. Backstage view opens with the Info tab displayed.
2. At the bottom of the right pane of the Info tab, click **Edit Links to Files**. The Links dialog box opens with the only link in the document (the link to the Chart Copy Excel workbook) selected. See Figure 7-25.

Figure 7-25 Links dialog box

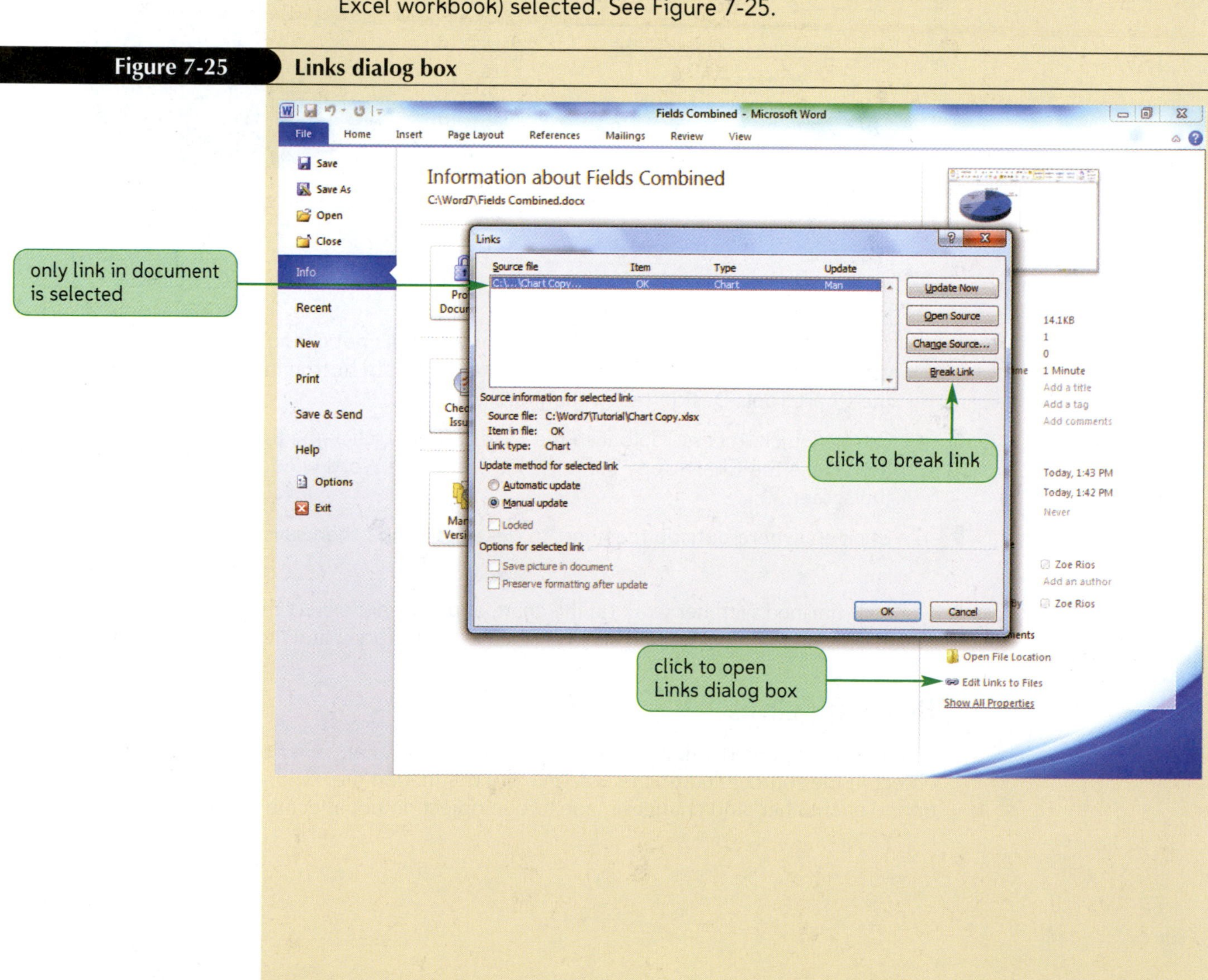

3. Click the **Break Link** button, and then click **Yes** in the dialog box that opens asking if you are sure you want to break the link. The list in the Links dialog box now indicates there is no source file for the chart in the document.
4. Click the **OK** button in the Links dialog box to close it. You return to the Info tab in Backstage view. With the link broken, you can no longer edit the Excel data from within Word. You can verify that by checking the Chart Tools Design tab.
5. Click the **Home** tab to display the document, click the white area inside the chart to select it, click the **Chart Tools Design** tab, and then notice that the Edit Data button in the Data group is grayed out, indicating this option is no longer available.
6. Click anywhere outside the chart to deselect it, and then save your work.

Zoe wants to focus on the task of distributing the document electronically, which you'll do in the next session.

REVIEW

Session 7.1 Quick Check

1. Explain how to use Track Changes to edit a document.
2. What button do you use to insert a comment and on what tab is it located?
3. Explain the difference between comparing and combining documents.
4. True or False. You need to turn on Tracked Changes to insert a comment in a document.
5. Explain the difference between a linked object and an embedded object.
6. What button do you use in Word to embed or link an object from another program that you've copied to the Clipboard?
7. Explain how to break a link between a Word file and another file.

SESSION 7.2 VISUAL OVERVIEW

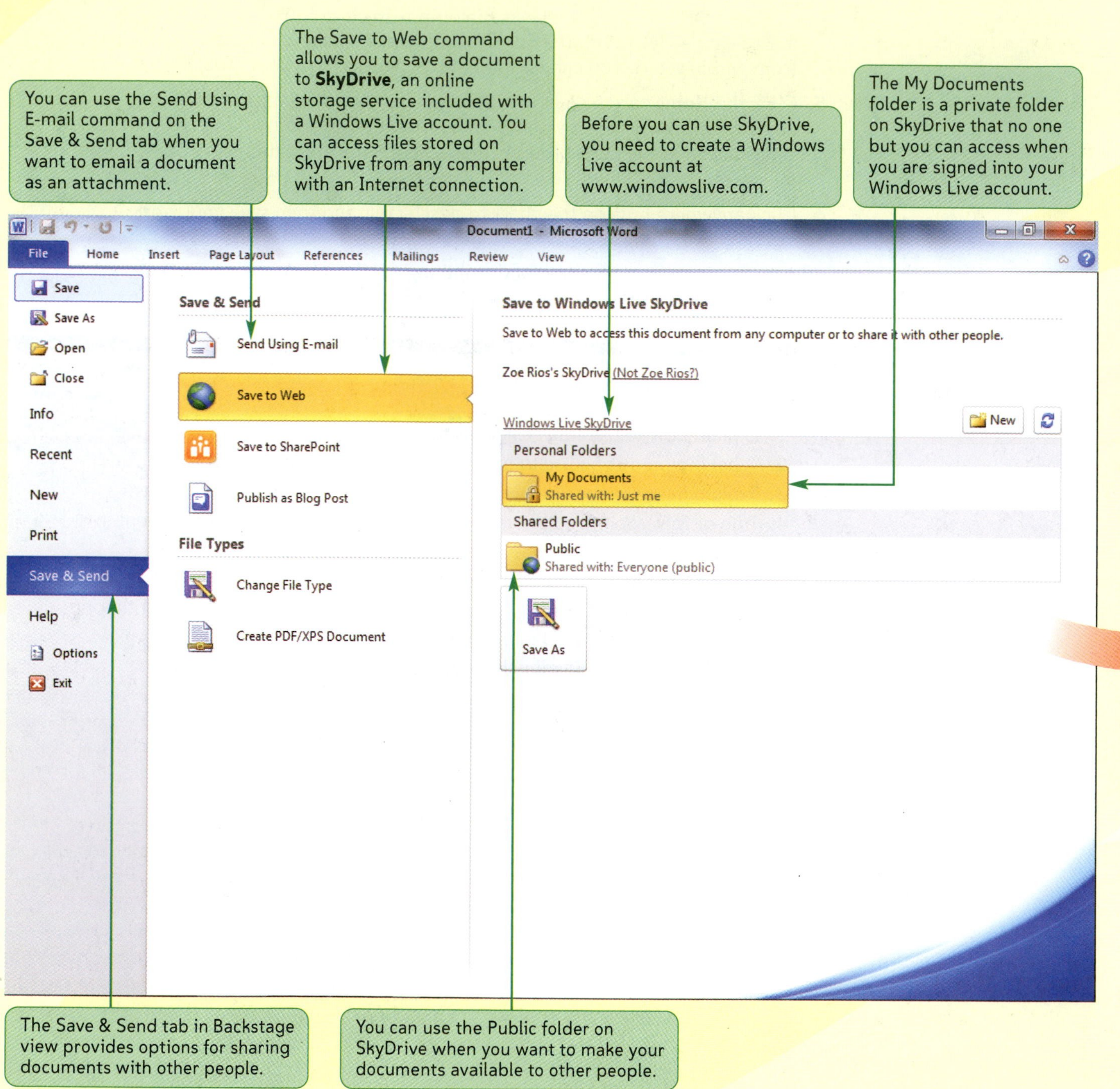

You can use the Send Using E-mail command on the Save & Send tab when you want to email a document as an attachment.
The Save to Web command allows you to save a document to **SkyDrive**, an online storage service included with a Windows Live account. You can access files stored on SkyDrive from any computer with an Internet connection.
Before you can use SkyDrive, you need to create a Windows Live account at www.windowslive.com.
The My Documents folder is a private folder on SkyDrive that no one but you can access when you are signed into your Windows Live account.
Document1 - Microsoft Word
File
Home
Insert
Page Layout
References
Mailings
Review
View
Save
Save As
Open
Close
Info
Recent
New
Print
Save & Send
Help
Options
Exit
Save & Send
Send Using E-mail
Save to Web
Save to SharePoint
Publish as Blog Post
File Types
Change File Type
Create PDF/XPS Document
Save to Windows Live SkyDrive
Save to Web to access this document from any computer or to share it with other people.
Zoe Rios's SkyDrive (Not Zoe Rios?)
Windows Live SkyDrive
New
Personal Folders
My Documents
Shared with: Just me
Shared Folders
Public
Shared with: Everyone (public)
Save As
The Save & Send tab in Backstage view provides options for sharing documents with other people.
You can use the Public folder on SkyDrive when you want to make your documents available to other people.

VIEWING A WORD DOCUMENT ON SKYDRIVE

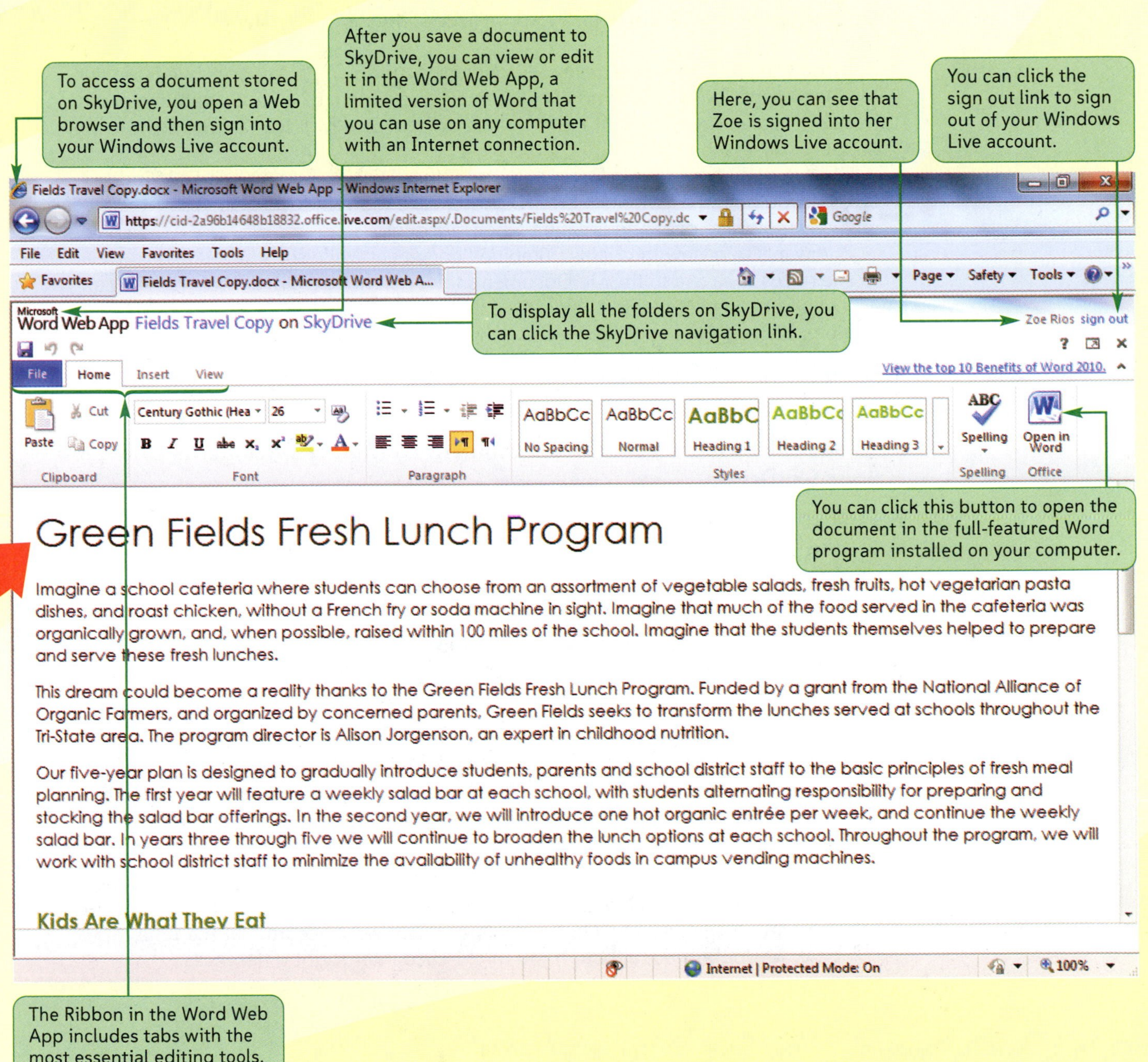

Saving and Sharing Files on SkyDrive

SkyDrive is Microsoft's online storage and file sharing service, which you can access with a free Windows Live account. You upload files to SkyDrive so you can access the documents from another computer, share the documents with other people, or use SkyDrive's additional storage. Each Windows Live account comes with its own SkyDrive. After you have saved a document on SkyDrive, you can edit it in the Word Web App, which is a limited version of Word 2010 that you can access from any computer connected to the Internet.

If you want to save a document to SkyDrive for your own private use, save it to your My Documents folder, which no one else can access. To make a file available to other people, you can save it to your Public folder, or create a new folder and invite individual people to access the file.

To save documents to SkyDrive or to use Office Web Apps, you need a Windows Live ID. You obtain a Windows Live ID by going to the Windows Live Web site at *www.windowslive.com* and creating a new account.

Zoe wants to review the Fields Combined document while she's traveling next week, so she needs to save it to the My Documents folder on her SkyDrive. That way she can access it from any computer connected to the Internet.

Note: The steps in this section assume that you already have a Windows Live ID and account.

To save the Fields Combined document to the My Documents folder on your SkyDrive:

1. If you took a break after the previous session, make sure the Fields Combined document is open in Print Layout view.
2. Click the **File** tab, and then click the **Save & Send** tab in the navigation bar. The Save & Send options available in Word appear in Backstage view.
3. In the Save & Send section, click **Save to Web**. The right pane changes to display a Sign In button that you can use to sign into your Windows Live account. See Figure 7-26.

   Trouble? If you do not already have a Windows Live account, your screen will look different from the one in the figure. Before you can complete the rest of these steps, you need to set up a Windows Live account, which is free, by going to the Windows Live Web site at *www.windowslive.com* and following the steps on the site to create a new account.

   Trouble? SkyDrive and the Office Web Apps are dynamic Web pages and might change over time, including the way they are organized and how commands are performed. The steps and figures in this section were accurate at the time this book was published, although you might encounter slight differences.

Figure 7-26 Save & Send tab in Backstage view

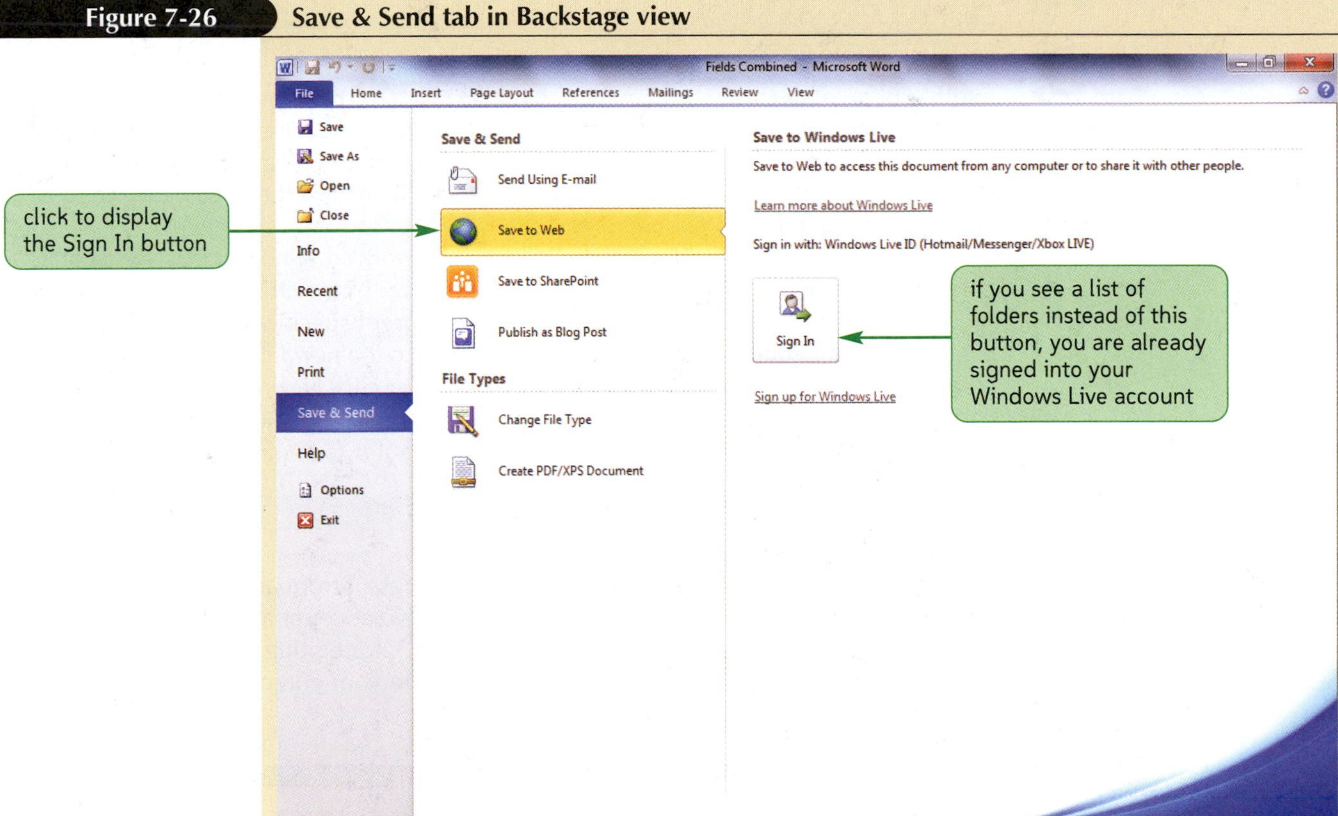

Trouble? If you are already signed into Windows Live, you see the folders in your SkyDrive account listed instead. Skip Steps 4–6 and continue with Step 7.

4. Click the **Sign In** button. The Connecting to docs.live.net dialog box opens.
5. In the E-mail address box, type the email address associated with your Windows Live account, press the **Tab** key, and then type the password associated with your Windows Live account in the Password box.
6. Click the **OK** button. The dialog box closes, and after a few moments, the right pane in Backstage view changes to list the folders on your SkyDrive, as shown earlier in the Session 7.2 Visual Overview.
7. In the right pane, click the **My Documents** folder to select it (if necessary), and then click the **Save As** button. Backstage view closes, and then after a few moments the Save As dialog box opens.
8. In the Save As dialog box, change the filename to **Fields Travel Copy**, and then click the **Save** button. The Save As dialog box closes. The Fields Travel Copy document is currently open on your computer, but it is stored on your SkyDrive.
9. Close the **Fields Travel Copy** document and exit Word.

INSIGHT

Sharing Files on SkyDrive

After you save a document to your Public folder on SkyDrive, you can make it available to other people by emailing them the URL for the file. To copy a document's URL, display the document on SkyDrive, right-click the URL in the Address bar, click Copy on the shortcut menu, then open your email program and paste the URL into a new email message. Anyone who receives the email can click the URL to view the document, whether or not they are signed into Windows Live.

Another option is to invite people to join your network on Windows Live. By default, anyone in your network has access to your Public folder from within their own SkyDrive.

Finally, you can create a new folder on SkyDrive, grant specific people access to the contents of the folder, and then upload a document to the new folder. To create a new folder, sign in to Windows Live, display your Sky Drive, click New, click Folder, type a name for the folder, click Change, select the sharing options you want, click Next, click Add files, and then select documents from your computer to begin uploading them to your SkyDrive.

TIP

If your computer is part of a network that runs Microsoft SharePoint, you can use Word's co-authoring feature, which allows you and one or more colleagues to edit a document on SkyDrive simultaneously.

After you save a document to SkyDrive, you can access it from any computer connected to the Internet by logging into your Windows Live account and displaying your SkyDrive. You can simply view the document, or open it for editing either from within the Word Web App or from the Word program stored on your computer. In both cases, any changes are saved to the document on your SkyDrive.

REFERENCE

Accessing Files Stored on SkyDrive

- Start Internet Explorer, go to *www.windowslive.com*, and sign into your Windows Live account.
- If you don't see the folders for your SkyDrive account, click Office.
- Click the folder in which you stored the document, and then click the document.
- To edit the document on your computer, click Open in Word.
- To edit the document online in the Word Web App, click Edit in Browser.

Zoe wants to view her document on SkyDrive.

To view the Fields Travel Copy document on SkyDrive:

1. Click the **Internet Explorer** button on the taskbar, click in the Address bar, type **www.windowslive.com**, and then sign into your Windows Live account.
2. If you do not see your SkyDrive folders on the left side of the Windows Live page, click the **Office** link at the top of the page to display them. (Ignore the menu that opens when you move the mouse pointer over the Office link.) Your SkyDrive folders are divided into Personal folders (which only you can access), Shared folders (which other people can access), and Shared with me folders (which other people have shared with you). In Figure 7-27, the My Documents folder is the only Personal folder, and the Public folder is the only Shared folder. There are no Shared with me folders shown in Figure 7-27. In the center of the page you see information about documents you've worked with recently on your SkyDrive. In particular, you see a link for the Fields Travel Copy document. You could click that link now to display the file. However, to get some experience opening folders on SkyDrive, you'll click the My Documents link instead.

Figure 7-27 SkyDrive folders

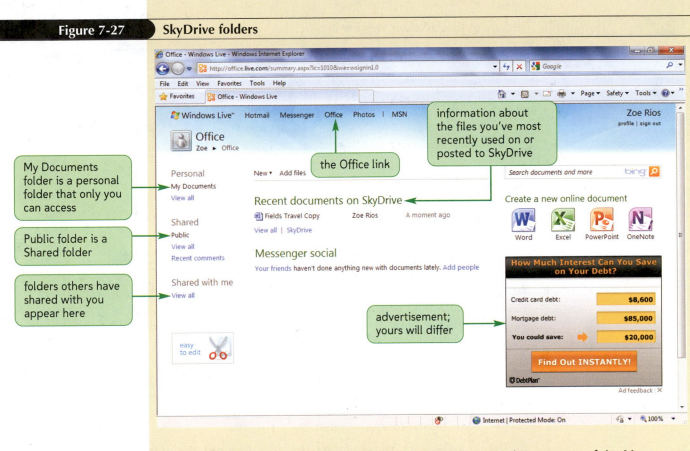

My Documents folder is a personal folder that only you can access

Public folder is a Shared folder

folders others have shared with you appear here

the Office link

information about the files you've most recently used on or posted to SkyDrive

advertisement; yours will differ

3. In the Personal section, click **My Documents**. You see the contents of the My Documents folder, which includes the Fields Travel Copy document.

4. Point to the **Fields Travel Copy** document to display the file management options shown in Figure 7-28. You could click the Delete button on the far right to delete the Fields Travel Copy document from your SkyDrive.

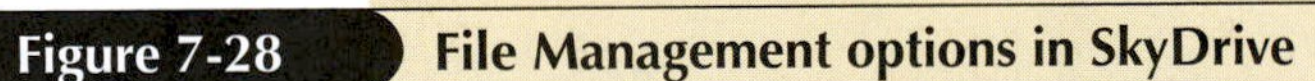

Figure 7-28 File Management options in SkyDrive

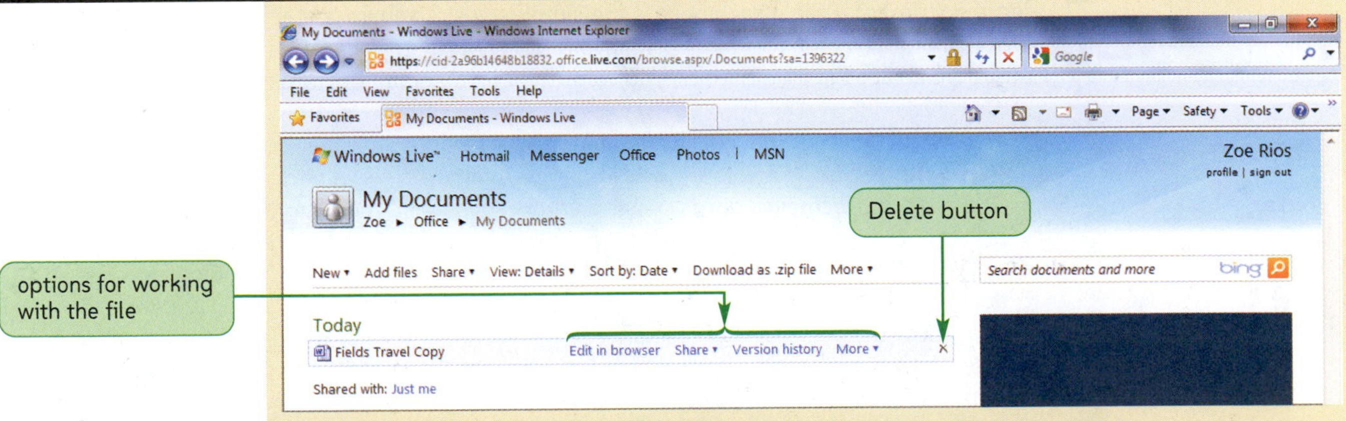

TIP

To open a new Word Web App file in your browser, point to Office and then click New Word document.

5. Click **Fields Travel Copy**. The document is displayed in the browser window for viewing only, with a menu bar above it, providing options for working with the document. If you want to open the document in Word on your computer, you can click Open in Word. If you want to open the document in your browser and edit it using the Web App version of Word, you can click Edit in Browser. See Figure 7-29.

Figure 7-29 Document displayed for viewing in SkyDrive

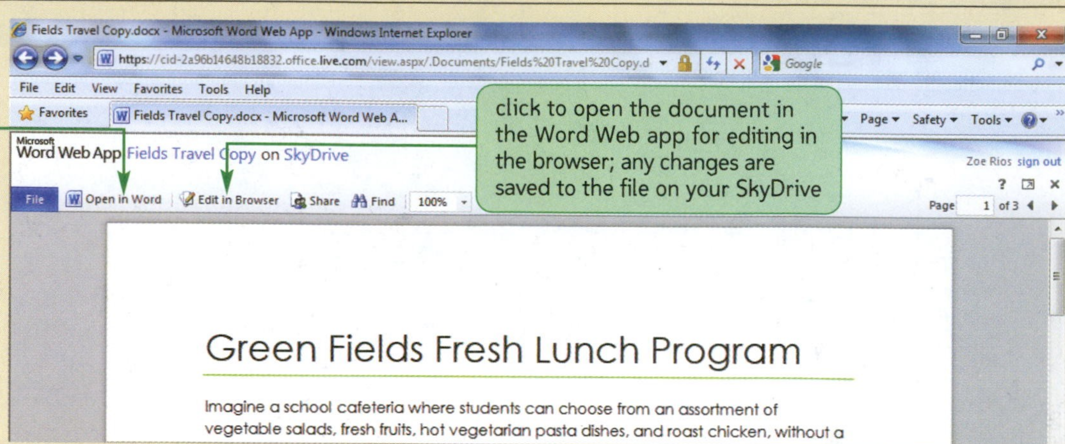

6. In the menu bar, click **Edit in Browser**. The document opens in the Word Web App. This limited version of Word is useful when you need to edit a Word document on a computer that does not have a copy of Word installed. Before you sign out of Windows Live, you can try out the navigation links.
7. In the navigation links at the top of the Windows Live page, click the **SkyDrive** link to return to the My Documents folder, and then, at the top of the page, click **Office** to display all your SkyDrive folders again. When you are finished using Windows Live, it's important to sign out, so another person using your computer can't gain access to your account.
8. In the upper-right corner of the page, click **sign out**, and then close Internet Explorer.

PROSKILLS

Teamwork: Emailing Word Documents

SkyDrive is a powerful tool for sharing documents among co-workers. But sometimes emailing a document as an attachment is the simplest way to share a file. To get started emailing a document, click the File tab, click Save & Send, verify that Send Using E-mail is selected, and then select the email option you want. When you email documents, keep in mind a few basic rules:

- Many email services have difficulty handling attachments larger than 4 MB. Consider storing large files in a compressed (or zipped) folder to reduce their size before emailing.
- Other word-processing programs and early versions of Word might not be able to open files created in Word 2010. To avoid problems with conflicting versions, you have two options. You can save the Word document as a rich text file (using the Rich Text File document type in the Save As dialog box) before emailing it. All versions of Word can open rich text files. Another option is to convert the document to PDF format, which is essentially a picture of a Word document that can be read on any computer system using Adobe Acrobat Reader. To save a Word Document as a PDF file, use the Create PDF/XPS Document command from the Save & Send tab in Backstage view.
- If you plan to email a document that contains links to other files, remember to email all the linked files.
- Attachments, including Word documents, are sometimes used maliciously to spread computer viruses. Remember to include an explanatory note with any email attachment so that the recipient can be certain the attachment is legitimate. Also, it's important to have a reliable virus checker program installed if you plan to receive and open email attachments.

Next, Zoe turns her attention back to the Fields Combined document, which is stored on her computer. First, she asks you to add some hyperlinks. While hyperlinks are widely used in Web pages, you can also use them in ordinary Word documents.

Using Hyperlinks in Word

TIP

Hyperlinks are commonly referred to as "links," but take care not to confuse them with the OLE links you worked with earlier in this tutorial.

A **hyperlink** is a word, phrase, or graphic that you can click to jump to another part of the same document, to a separate Word document, to a file created in another program, or to a Web page. You can also include email links, which you can click to create an email message from a document.

Zoe wants you to add two hyperlinks to the program description—one that jumps to a location within the program description and one that will open a different document.

Inserting a Hyperlink to a Bookmark in the Same Document

Creating a hyperlink within a document is actually a two-part process. First, you need to mark the text you want the link to jump to—either by formatting the text with a heading style or by inserting a bookmark. A **bookmark** is an electronic marker that refers to a specific point in a document. Second, you need to select the text that you want users to click, format it as a hyperlink, and specify the bookmark or heading as the target of the hyperlink. The **target** is the place in the document to which the link connects. In this case, Zoe wants to create a hyperlink that targets the name of the Program Director, Alison Jorgenson, near the end of the document. Figure 7-30 illustrates this process.

Figure 7-30 Hyperlink that targets a bookmark

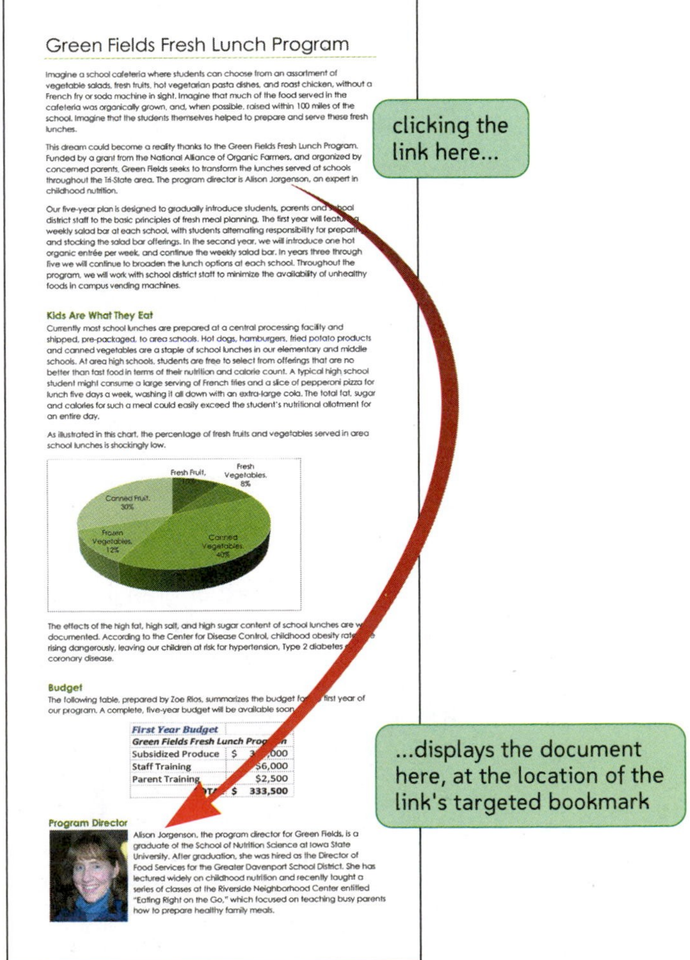

Green Fields Fresh Lunch Program

Imagine a school cafeteria where students can choose from an assortment of vegetable salads, fresh fruits, hot vegetarian pasta dishes, and roast chicken, without a French fry or soda machine in sight. Imagine that much of the food served in the cafeteria was organically grown, and, when possible, raised within 100 miles of the school. Imagine that the students themselves helped to prepare and serve these fresh lunches.

This dream could become a reality thanks to the Green Fields Fresh Lunch Program. Funded by a grant from the National Alliance of Organic Farmers, and organized by concerned parents, Green Fields seeks to transform the lunches served at schools throughout the Tri-State area. The program director is Alison Jorgenson, an expert in childhood nutrition.

Our five-year plan is designed to gradually introduce students, parents and [illegible] district staff to the basic principles of fresh meal planning. The first year will featu[illegible] weekly salad bar at each school, with students alternating responsibility for prepari[illegible] and stocking the salad bar offerings. In the second year, we will introduce one hot organic entrée per week, and continue the weekly salad bar. In years three through five we will continue to broaden the lunch options at each school. Throughout the program, we will work with school district staff to minimize the availability of unhealthy foods in campus vending machines.

Kids Are What They Eat

Currently most school lunches are prepared at a central processing facility and shipped, pre-packaged, to area schools. Hot dogs, hamburgers, fried potato products and canned vegetables are a staple of school lunches in our elementary and middle schools. At area high schools, students are free to select from offerings that are no better than fast food in terms of their nutrition and calorie count. A typical high school student might consume a large serving of French fries and a slice of pepperoni pizza for lunch five days a week, washing it all down with an extra-large cola. The total fat, sugar and calories for such a meal could easily exceed the student's nutritional allotment for an entire day.

As illustrated in this chart, the percentage of fresh fruits and vegetables served in area school lunches is shockingly low.

The effects of the high fat, high salt, and high sugar content of school lunches are w[illegible] documented. According to the Center for Disease Control, childhood obesity rat[illegible] rising dangerously, leaving our children at risk for hypertension, Type 2 diabetes [illegible] coronary disease.

Budget

The following table, prepared by Zoe Rios, summarizes the budget fo[illegible] first year of our program. A complete, five-year budget will be available soon.

First Year Budget	
Green Fields Fresh Lunch Prog[illegible]n	
Subsidized Produce	$ 3[illegible],000
Staff Training	$6,000
Parent Training	$2,500
[illegible]	$ 333,500

Program Director

Alison Jorgenson, the program director for Green Fields, is a graduate of the School of Nutrition Science at Iowa State University. After graduation, she was hired as the Director of Food Services for the Greater Davenport School District. She has lectured widely on childhood nutrition and recently taught a series of classes at the Riverside Neighborhood Center entitled "Eating Right on the Go," which focused on teaching busy parents how to prepare healthy family meals.

To create a hyperlink in Zoe's document, you'll need to insert a bookmark in the Program Director section.

To insert a bookmark:

1. Start Word and open the **Fields Combined** document from the Word7\Tutorial folder included with your Data Files. Switch to Print Layout view if necessary, display the rulers and nonprinting characters, and change the document zoom to Page Width.
2. Scroll down and select the name **Alison Jorgenson** at the beginning of the Program Director section, near the bottom of page 2.
3. Click the **Insert** tab, and then click the **Bookmark** button in the Links group. The Bookmark dialog box opens. You can now type the bookmark name, which cannot contain spaces.
4. Type **Director**. See Figure 7-31.

Figure 7-31 Creating a bookmark

TIP

The Bookmark dialog box lists all the document's bookmarks. To delete a bookmark, click it in the dialog box and then click the Delete button.

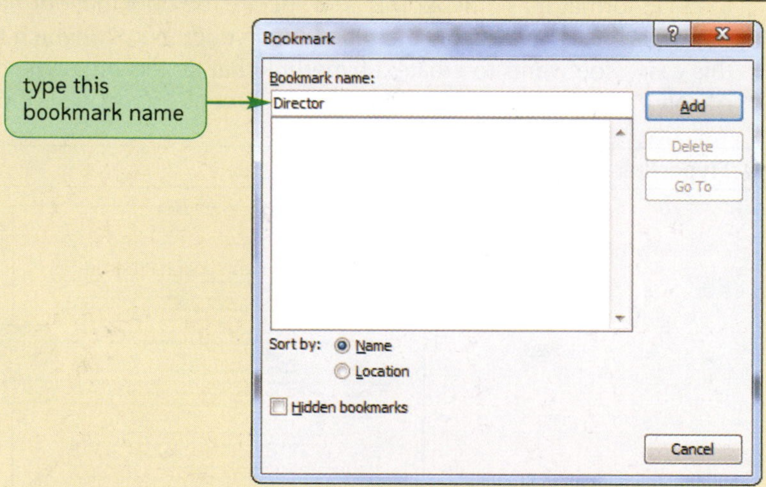

5. Click the **Add** button. The Bookmark dialog box closes. Although you can't see it, a bookmark has been inserted before Alison's name.

The bookmark you just created will be the target of the hyperlink you will create next.

REFERENCE

Creating a Hyperlink to a Location in the Same Document

- Select the text or graphic you want to format as the hyperlink.
- In the Links group on the Insert tab, click the Hyperlink button to open the Insert Hyperlink dialog box.
- In the Link to pane, click Place in This Document.
- In the list displayed, click the bookmark or heading you want to link to and then click the OK button.

Zoe wants you to create a hyperlink from the program director's name (Alison Jorgenson) on the first page of the document that will target the bookmark you created at the beginning of the program director's description on the second page.

To create a hyperlink to the bookmark:

1. Scroll up to page 1, and then, in the last sentence of the second paragraph under the heading "Green Fields Fresh Lunch Program," select the name **Alison Jorgenson**.
2. In the Links group on the Insert tab, click the **Hyperlink** button. The Insert Hyperlink dialog box opens.
3. In the Link to pane, click **Place in This Document**. The Select a place in this document list shows the headings and bookmarks in the document. Here you can click the bookmark or heading you want as the target for the hyperlink.
4. Under "Bookmarks," click **Director**. See Figure 7-32.

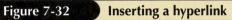

Figure 7-32 Inserting a hyperlink

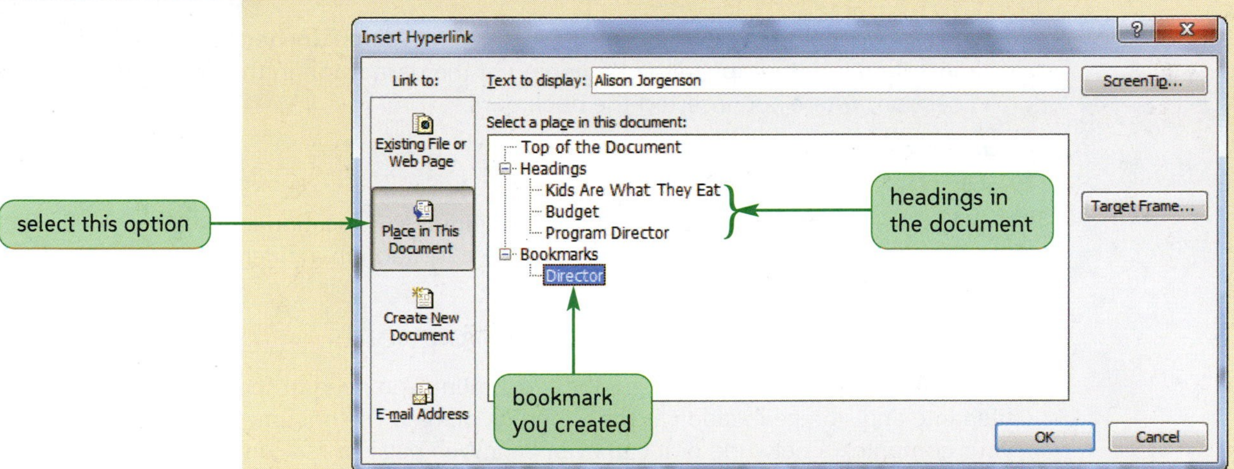

5. Click the **OK** button. The name "Alison Jorgenson" is formatted in the hyperlink style for the Austin theme, which applies an orange font color with an underline. The hyperlink now targets the Director bookmark that you created in the last set of steps.

After inserting a hyperlink into a document, you should test it.

To test the hyperlink in your document:

TIP

To edit the text that appears in a hyperlink's ScreenTip, click the ScreenTip button in the Insert Hyperlink dialog box, type the text you want for a ScreenTip, and then click the OK button.

1. Move the mouse pointer over the hyperlink, **Alison Jorgenson**. A ScreenTip appears with the name of the bookmark (Director) and instructions for following the link. See Figure 7-33.

Figure 7-33 Displaying the ScreenTip for a hyperlink

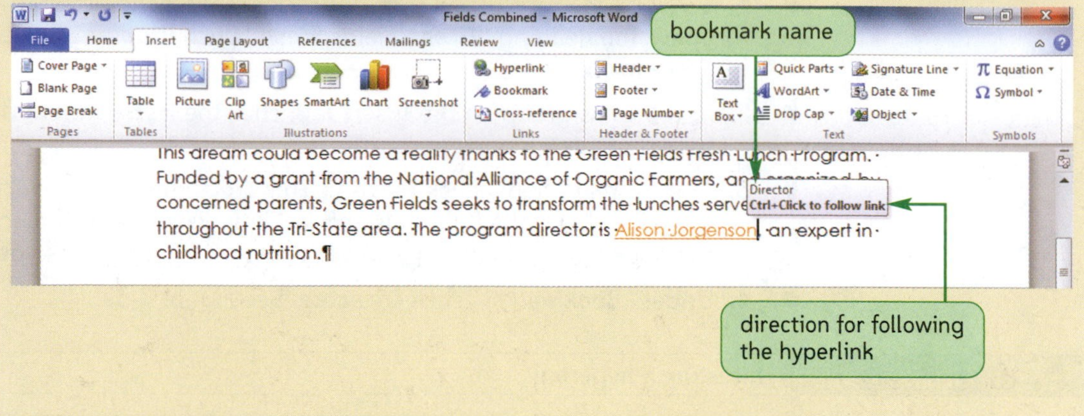

2. Press and hold the **Ctrl** key, and then click the **Alison Jorgenson** hyperlink. The insertion point jumps to the beginning of the paragraph in the Program Director section, where you inserted the bookmark.
3. Save your work.

You have finished creating a hyperlink that jumps to a location in the same document. Next, you will create a hyperlink that jumps to a location in a different document.

Creating Hyperlinks to Other Documents

When you create a hyperlink to another document, you need to specify the document's filename and storage location as the hyperlink's target. The document can be stored on your computer, a network, or it can even be a Web page stored somewhere on the Web. In that case, you need to specify the Web page's URL (Web address) as the target. When you click a hyperlink to another document, the document opens on your computer, with the beginning of the document displayed. Keep in mind that if you move the source or target documents after you create a hyperlink, the hyperlink will no longer work.

REFERENCE

Creating a Hyperlink to Another Document

- Select the text you want to format as a hyperlink.
- In the Links group on the Insert tab, click the Hyperlink button to open the Insert Hyperlink dialog box.
- In the Link to pane, click Existing File or Web Page.
- To target a specific file on your computer or network, use the Look in arrow to open the folder containing the file, and then click the file in the file list.
- To target a Web page, type its URL in the Address box.

Zoe wants to insert a hyperlink that, when clicked, will open a Word document containing Alison's resume. Because she wants the hyperlink to take users to the beginning of the resume, you don't need to insert a bookmark. Instead, you can specify just the name and location of the target document.

To create a hyperlink to the resume document:

1. Press the **Ctrl+End** keys to move the insertion point to the blank paragraph at the end of the document. This is where you'll insert text, some of which will become the hyperlink.
2. Type **See Alison's resume.**
3. Select the word **resume** in the text you just typed.
4. In the Links group on the Insert tab, click the **Hyperlink** button. The Insert Hyperlink dialog box opens.
5. In the Link to pane, click **Existing File or Web Page**. The dialog box displays options related to selecting a file or a Web page.
6. Navigate to the Word7\Tutorial folder included with your Data Files (if necessary), and then click **Resume** in the file list. See Figure 7-34.

Figure 7-34 **Inserting a hyperlink to a different document**

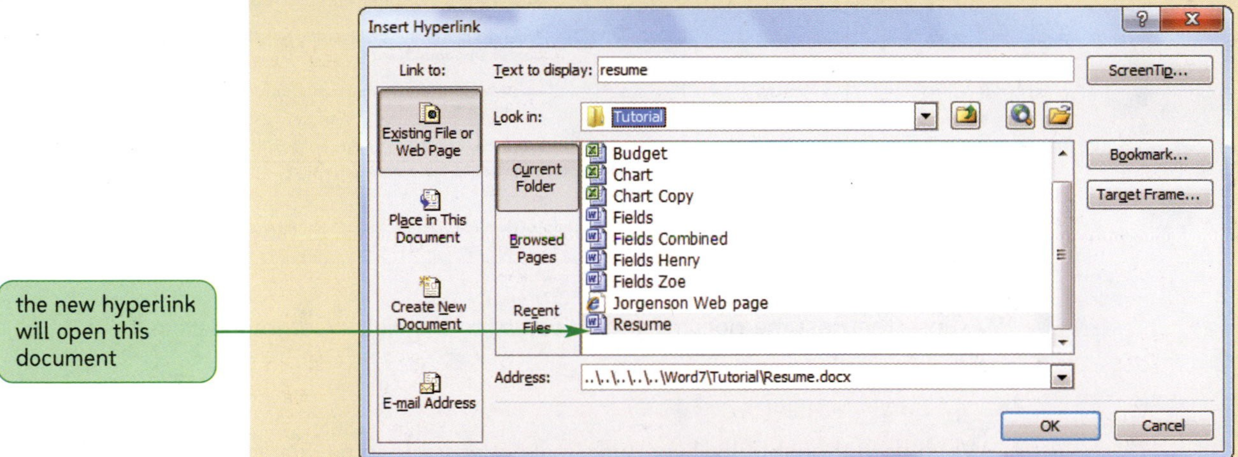

7. Click the **OK** button. The word "resume" is now formatted as a hyperlink. Now you will test the hyperlink.
8. Press and hold the **Ctrl** key, and then click the **resume** hyperlink. The Resume document opens. See Figure 7-35.

Figure 7-35 Resume document

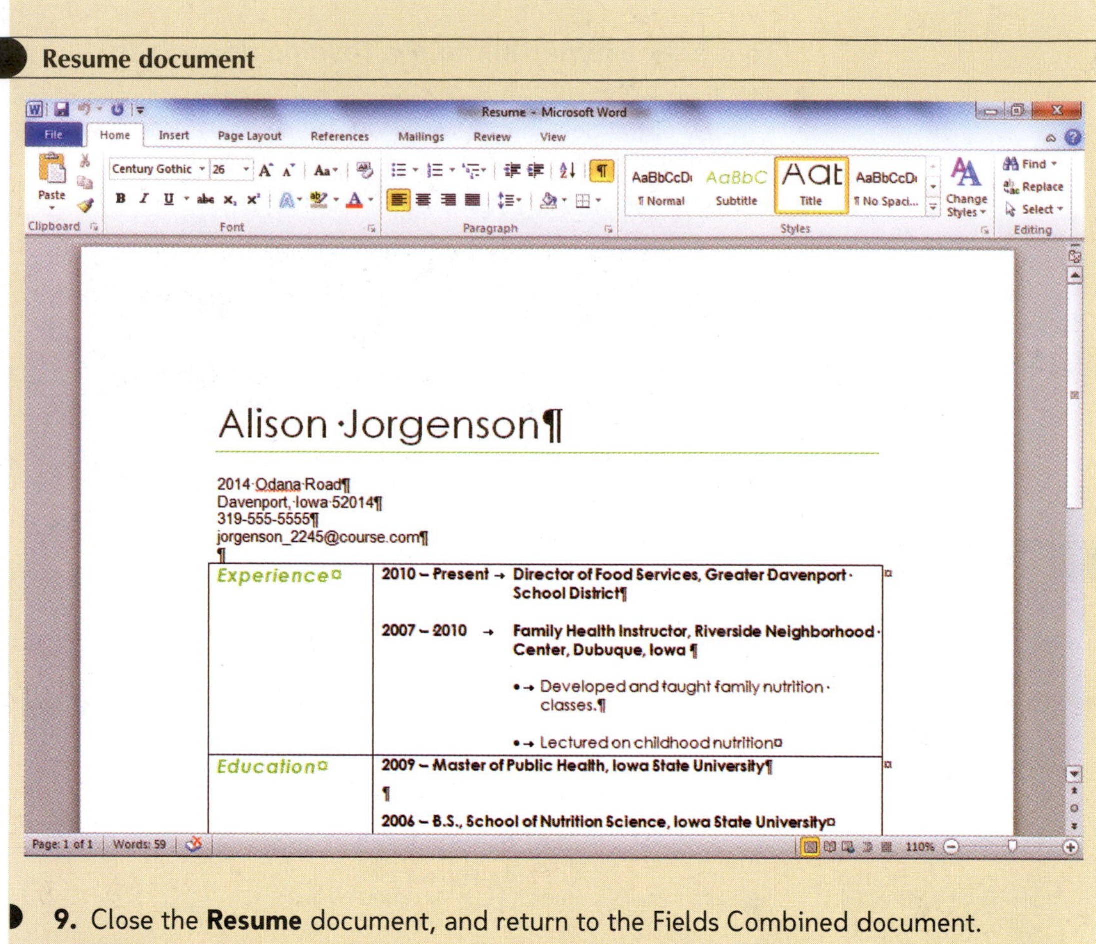

9. Close the **Resume** document, and return to the Fields Combined document.
10. Save your work.

When used thoughtfully, hyperlinks make it possible to navigate a complicated document or a set of files quickly and easily. Next, you need to save the document as a Web page.

Saving a Word Document as a Web Page

Web pages are special documents designed to be viewed in a program called a **browser**. One widely used browser is Internet Explorer 8. Because Web pages include code written in the **Hypertext Markup Language**, or **HTML**, they are often referred to as **HTML documents**.

To create sophisticated Web pages (or a complete Web site), you'll probably want to use a dedicated HTML editor, such as Adobe Dreamweaver. However, in Word you can create a simple Web page from an existing document by saving it as a Web page. When you do so, Word inserts HTML codes that tell the browser how to format and display the text and graphics. Fortunately, you don't have to learn the Hypertext Markup Language to create Web pages with Word. When you save the document as a Web page, Word creates all the necessary HTML codes (called tags). This process is transparent to you, so you won't actually see the HTML codes in your Web page.

When you save a document as a Web page, Word saves the document as an HTML file and places the graphics that appear in the document in a separate folder. A group of smaller files travels across the Web faster than one large file, so this division of files makes it easier to share your documents on the Web.

You can choose from three different Web page file types in Word. The main differences among these file types are file size and the way special elements, such as WordArt or embedded or linked objects, are treated when they are displayed in a browser:

- **Single File Web Page**—Saves the document as an MHTML file, which is similar to an HTML file, with all graphics stored in the file along with the text. A Single File Web Page can be more than three or four times the size of the original Word document.
- **Web Page**—Saves the document as an HTML file, with a separate folder containing graphics and other elements that control the page's formatting. The HTML file created using the Web Page file type is approximately the same size as the original Word document, but the total size of the accompanying files can be two or three times the size of the Word document.
- **Web Page, Filtered**—Saves the document as an HTML file, with graphics stored in a separate folder. This file type retains less information than the other two formats. Any formatting differences are apparent only when you open the filtered Web page in a browser, or the next time you open the file in Word. Before you save a Word document as a filtered Web page, Word displays a dialog box warning you that some Office features (typically formatting) may not be available when you reopen the page. The total file size of a filtered Web page and its accompanying graphics files is smaller than the Word document from which it is created.

The Single File Web Page file type is a good choice when you plan to share your Web page only over a small network and not over the Internet. Having to manage only one file is more convenient than having to keep track of a group of files. But when you want to share your files over the Internet, it's better to use the Web Page, Filtered option. This will keep your overall file size as small as possible. Note that the folder Word creates to store the accompanying files has the same name as your Web page, plus an underscore and the word "files." For instance, a Web page saved as "Finance Summary" would be accompanied by a folder named "Finance Summary_files."

REFERENCE

Saving a Word Document as a Web Page

- Click the File tab, and then click Save As to open the Save As dialog box.
- Click the Save as type arrow, and then click Single File Web Page; Web Page, Filtered; or Web Page.
- If desired, type a new filename in the File name box.
- Click the Change Title button to open the Enter Text dialog box, type a title for the Web page in the Page title box, and then click the OK button.
- Click the Save button in the Save As dialog box. If you saved the document using the Web Page, Filtered option, click Yes in the warning dialog box.

After you save a document as a Web page, Word displays it in **Web Layout view**, which displays the document similarly to the way it would appear in a Web browser. For example, in Web Layout View, the text spans the width of the screen (as it would in a browser), with no page breaks, and without any margins or headers and footers. Also, text wrapping around graphics often changes in Web Layout view, as the text expands to fill the wider area of the screen. For example, on the second page of the Fields Combined document, some text currently wraps below the Program Director's photograph, flowing onto a third page. When this document is saved as a Web page, the text wrapping will adjust to the wider page.

To save the Fields Combined document as a Web page:

1. Click the **File** tab, and then click **Save As**. The Save As dialog box opens.
2. Navigate to the Word7\Tutorial folder included with your Data Files (if necessary), click the **Save as type** arrow, and then click **Web Page, Filtered**.
3. In the File name box, change the filename to **Fields Web Page**.
4. Click the **Change Title** button to open the Enter Text dialog box, and then type **Green Fields Fresh Lunch Program** in the Page title box. This title will appear in the browser title bar. See Figure 7-36.

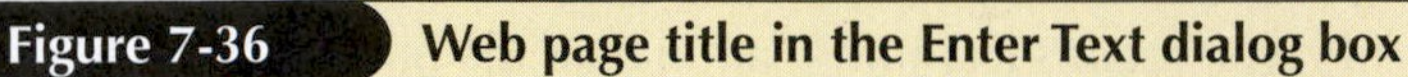

Figure 7-36 Web page title in the Enter Text dialog box

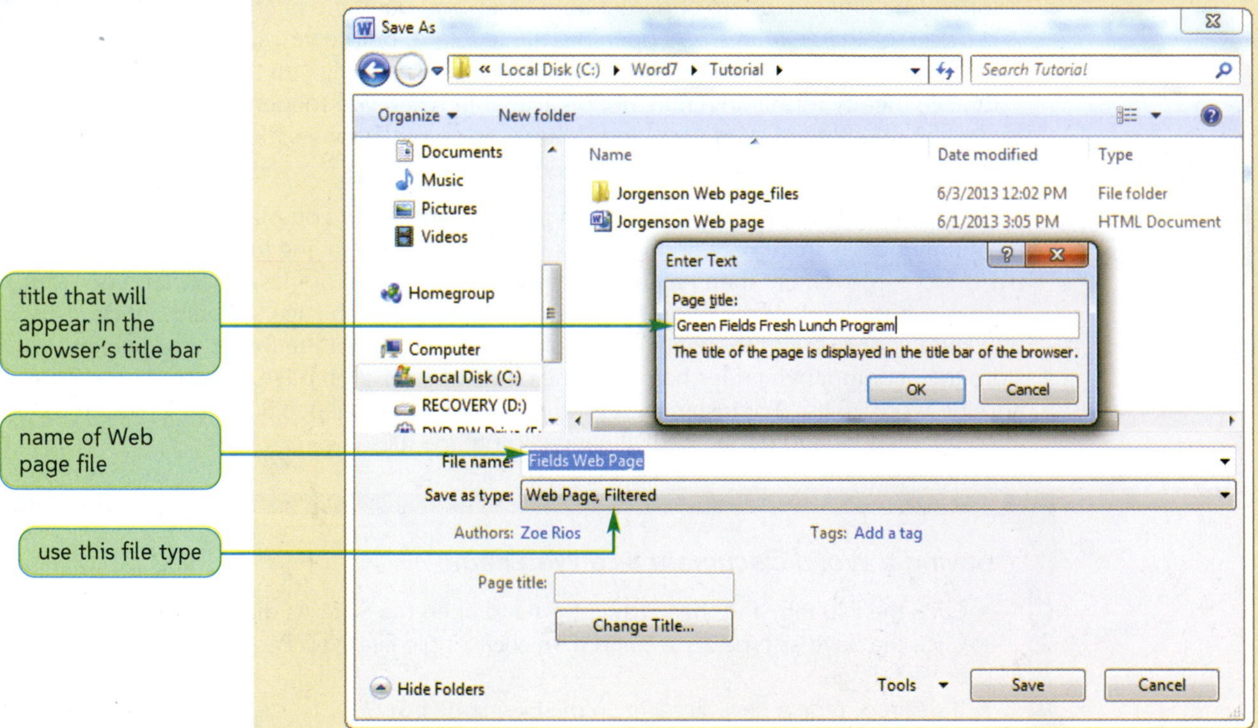

5. Click the **OK** button in the Enter Text dialog box.
6. Click the **Save** button in the Save As dialog box. A dialog box opens warning you that using the Web Page, Filtered file type will remove Office-specific tags that control how the document is displayed in Word.
7. Click the **Yes** button. The document is converted into a Web page and displayed in Web Layout view. The text spans the document window, no longer constrained by the page margins. The revised filename, "Fields Web Page," appears in the Word title bar, as usual. The title you specified in Step 4 won't be visible until you open the Web page in a browser, at which point it will be displayed in the browser's title bar. You need to zoom to make the text easier to read.
8. Drag the Zoom slider to change the document zoom to **100%**. The text wrapping adjusts to the new zoom setting.
9. Scroll down and review the Web page. Note the lack of page breaks and the way the text wraps next to the photo, near the end of the Web page. Because the text spans all the way to the edge of the Word window, it all fits to the right of the photograph, without wrapping below. See Figure 7-37.

Figure 7-37 New Web page displayed in Web Layout view

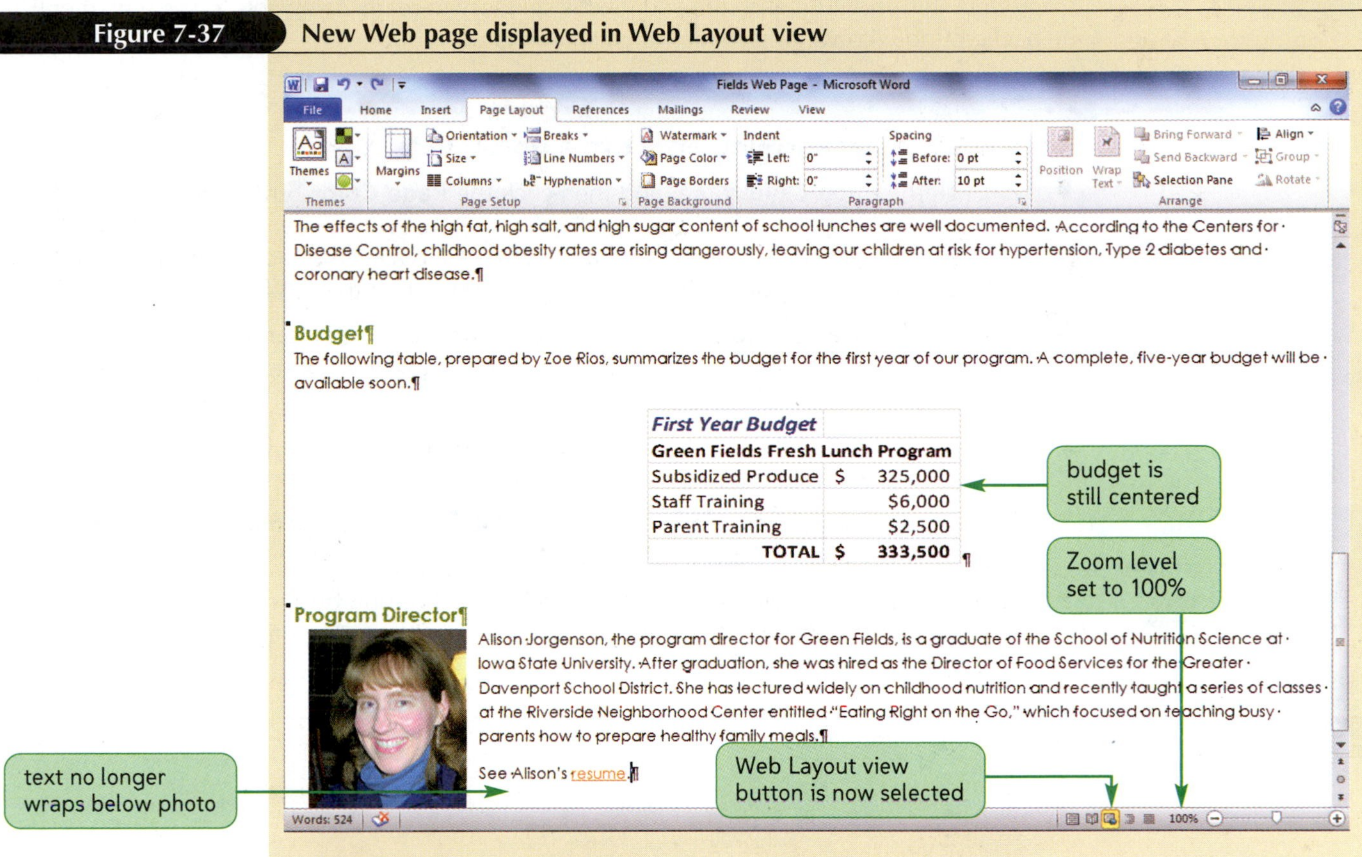

The total file size for the new Web page plus the accompanying files is 38 KB, compared to 50 KB for the Fields Combined document. This smaller size, plus the fact that the graphics files are stored separately from the text, means the Fields Web Page can travel more quickly over the Web than the Fields Combined document file.

Next, you'll make some changes to the Fields Combined document that will improve its online appearance.

Formatting a Web Page

You can edit and format text and graphics in a Web page the same way you edit and format a normal Word document.

Applying a Background Effect

To make the document more visually interesting for online viewers, Zoe would like to add a background effect. You can apply one of the following background effects:

- Solid color
- Gradient—a single color combined with gray, or a combination of colors that varies in intensity
- Texture—a design that mimics the look of various textured materials, including linen and marble
- Pattern—a repetitive design such as checks, polka dots, and stripes, in colors you specify
- Picture—a single image

Note that backgrounds do not appear in printed documents. After you apply a background, you should make sure your text is still easy to read. Zoe wants to use a gradient background with varying shades of green and gray.

To apply a background effect to a document:

1. Click the **Page Layout** tab, and then click the **Page Color** button in the Page Background group. The Page Color gallery opens, with a menu at the bottom. You could click a color in the gallery to select it as a background color for the page. To select any other type of background effect, you need to click Fill Effects.
2. Click **Fill Effects**, and then click the **Gradient** tab (if necessary). Note that you could use other tabs in this dialog box to add a textured, patterned, or picture background.
3. In the Colors section, click the **One color** option button. The Color 1 box and scroll bar appear. You can use them to select the color and specify its intensity.
4. Click the **Color 1** arrow and then click **Light Green, Background 2, Lighter 60%**, in the third row, third color from the left.
5. In the Shading Styles section, click the **Vertical** option button to change the gradient pattern so it stretches vertically up and down the page. Compare your dialog box to Figure 7-38.

TIP

You can use the scroll bar below the Color 1 box to increase or decrease the intensity of the gradient color.

Figure 7-38 Selecting a gradient

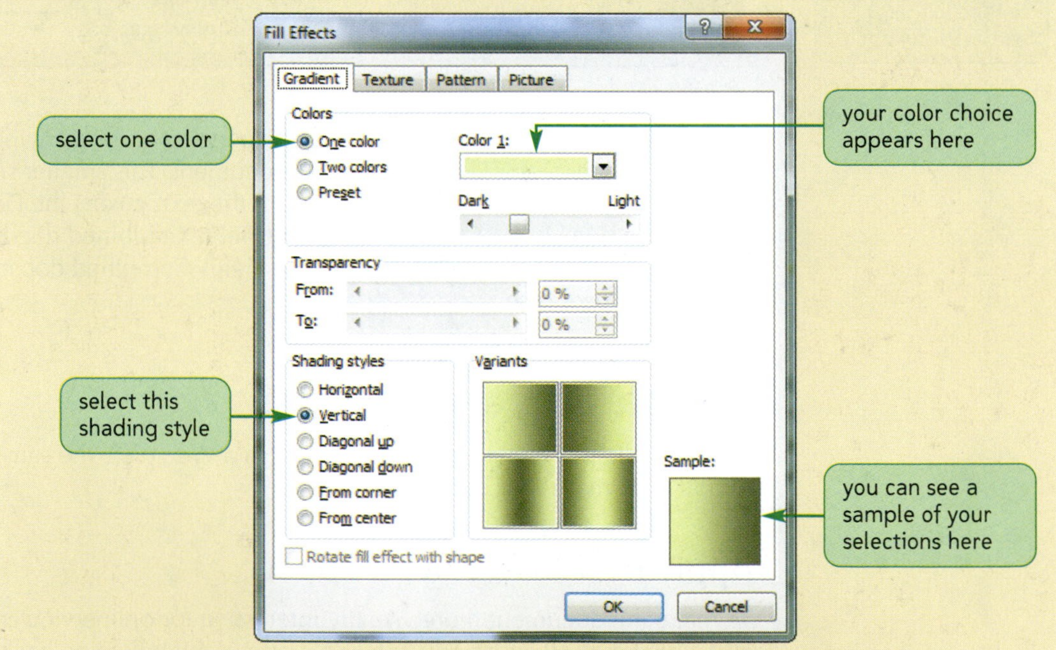

6. Click the **OK** button. The document's background is now a gradient that varies between shades of green. On the new background, the gridlines of the Excel worksheet data appear white.
7. Save the document, clicking **Yes** in the warning dialog box.

The background is attractive and light enough to make the document text easy to read. Next, you will add lines to separate the various sections of the Web page.

Inserting Horizontal Lines

Horizontal lines allow you to see at a glance where one section ends and another begins. You can also add horizontal lines to regular Word documents. If you don't like a horizontal line after you insert one into a document, you can delete it by clicking the line and then pressing the Delete key.

Zoe wants you to add a horizontal line at the end of each section except the last one. To add a horizontal line using a simple, default style, click the Border button in the Paragraph group on the Home tab, and select the Horizontal Line command. To add a more elaborate horizontal line, you need to use the Horizontal Line dialog box.

To insert horizontal lines into the Web page:

1. Click at the beginning of the heading "Kids Are What They Eat" on the first page of the document, and then click the **Home** tab on the Ribbon.
2. In the Paragraph group, click the **Border button arrow** to open the Borders menu. You could click the Horizontal Line command to insert a default gray line, but Zoe wants to select a line that will work better on the gradient background.
3. At the bottom of the Border menu, click **Borders and Shading**. The Borders and Shading dialog box opens, with the Borders tab displayed.
4. Click the **Horizontal Line** button. The Horizontal Line dialog box opens, displaying several styles of horizontal lines.
5. Scroll down and click the olive green line, ninth from the top in the right column, as shown in Figure 7-39.

Figure 7-39 Selecting a horizontal line style

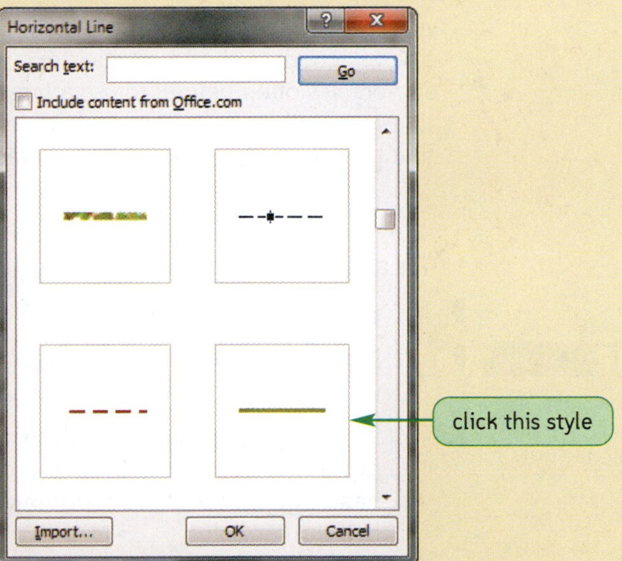

6. Click the **OK** button. An olive green line is inserted into the Web page above the "Kids Are What They Eat" heading. Your Web page should look similar to Figure 7-40.

Figure 7-40 Newly inserted horizontal line

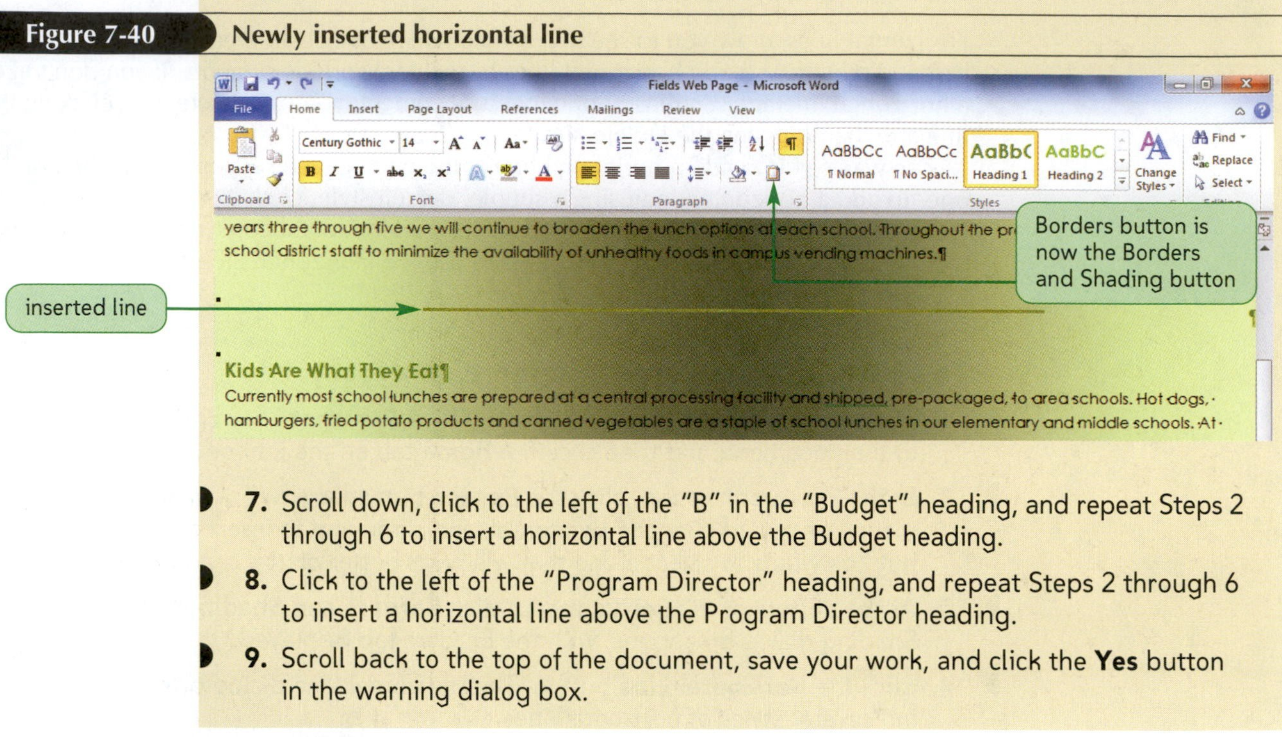

7. Scroll down, click to the left of the "B" in the "Budget" heading, and repeat Steps 2 through 6 to insert a horizontal line above the Budget heading.
8. Click to the left of the "Program Director" heading, and repeat Steps 2 through 6 to insert a horizontal line above the Program Director heading.
9. Scroll back to the top of the document, save your work, and click the **Yes** button in the warning dialog box.

Now that you've used horizontal lines to help organize the Web page, you decide to improve the appearance of the Web page's text.

Formatting Text and Hyperlinks in a Web Page

After you convert a Word document to a Web page, you often need to adjust the formatting to accommodate the wider text, which spans the width of the viewer's screen. For starters, it's often helpful to use a larger font size for headings. Zoe asks you to make the title larger. She also asks you to center it. Then she asks you to format the hyperlinks so that they are easier to read on the gradient background.

To adjust the formatting for the page title and hyperlinks:

1. Select the title **Green Fields Fresh Lunch Program** at the top of the Web page.
2. In the Font group on the Home tab, click the **Grow Font** button twice to increase the font size from 26-point to 36-point.
3. In the Paragraph group, click the **Center** button to center the heading at the top of the document, and then click anywhere in the document to deselect the heading. To make the hyperlinks easier to read, you can format them in bold and in a darker color.
4. In the second paragraph below the title, select the **Alison Jorgenson** hyperlink, format it in bold, then change the font color to Orange, Accent 6, Darker 50%. Do the same for the resume hyperlink at the bottom of the Web page.
5. Save your work, clicking the **Yes** button in the warning dialog box.

TIP

You can use the Shrink Font button to reduce the font size of selected text.

Next, you'll create a new hyperlink and edit the existing one.

Editing Hyperlinks

Zoe's Web page contains two hyperlinks—the Alison Jorgenson link, which jumps to the Program Director section at the end of the Web page, and the resume link, which jumps to a Word document containing Alison's resume. You originally created these hyperlinks in Zoe's Word document, but they remained functional after you saved the document as a Web page. Now that Zoe is ready to publish her program description on the Web, she has also saved the Resume document as a Web page. She asks you edit the Resume hyperlink to jump to this new Web page, rather than to the original Resume.docx file.

To edit a hyperlink:

1. Position the pointer over the **resume** hyperlink at the end of the Web page. A ScreenTip appears indicating that the link will jump to a document named Resume.docx.
2. Right-click the **resume** hyperlink, and then click **Edit Hyperlink** on the shortcut menu. The Edit Hyperlink dialog box opens. This looks just like the Insert Hyperlink dialog box, which you have already used. To edit the hyperlink, you simply select a different target file.
3. In the Link to pane, verify that the **Existing File or Web Page** option is selected.
4. If necessary, navigate to the Word7\Tutorial folder, click **Jorgenson Web Page** in the file list, and then click the **OK** button. You return to the Fields Web Page.
5. Place the mouse pointer over the **resume** hyperlink. A ScreenTip appears, indicating that the link will now jump to a Web page named Jorgenson Web Page.htm.

The edited hyperlink in the program description Web page now correctly targets the Web page with Alison's resume. After users read the resume, they most likely will want to return to the program description, so Zoe asks you to insert a hyperlink in the Jorgenson Web Page file containing Alison's resume, that jumps back to the Fields Web Page file. You insert hyperlinks into Web pages just as you do in Word documents. To open the Jorgenson Web Page file, you might be tempted to click the "resume" hyperlink in the Fields Web Page. However, if you do, the Web page would open in Internet Explorer. Instead, you need to open it using the Open command in Backstage view.

To insert a hyperlink in the Jorgenson Web page:

1. Click the **File** tab, click **Open**, navigate to the Word7\Tutorial folder included with your Data Files if necessary, click the **Jorgenson Web Page** file, and then click the **Open** button.
2. Press the **Ctrl+End** keys, and then at the bottom of the resume, select the text **Return to Green Fields Fresh Lunch Program page.**
3. Click the **Insert** tab, click the **Hyperlink** button, and then, in the Link to pane of the Insert Hyperlink dialog box, click **Existing File or Web Page** if it is not already selected.
4. If necessary, navigate to the Word7\Tutorial folder included with your Data Files, click **Fields Web Page**, and then click the **OK** button. Word formats the selected text as a hyperlink.
5. Save the Jorgenson Web page, and then close the Web page. You return to the Fields Web Page.
6. Save and close the Fields Web Page.

The resume now contains a hyperlink that takes users back to the Fields Web Page.

INSIGHT

Keeping Track of Documents Containing Hyperlinks

When your documents or Web pages include hyperlinks to other documents or Web pages, you must keep track of where you store the target files. If you move a target file to a different location, hyperlinks to it will not function properly. In this case, you created a hyperlink in the Fields Web Page file that links to the Jorgenson Web Page file, and vice versa. Both Web pages are stored in the Word7\Tutorial folder, which is most likely located on your computer's hard disk. To ensure that these hyperlinks continue to function, you must store the two Web pages in the same folder as when you created the link. If you have to move a target Web page, then be sure to edit the hyperlink to select the target Web page in its new location.

Now Zoe suggests you view both Web pages in a browser, and test the hyperlinks.

Viewing the Web Page in a Browser

You're now ready to view the finished Web pages in Internet Explorer, a Web browser. In the browser, you can test the hyperlinks and verify that the formatting looks the way you intended. In a browser, you don't have to press the Ctrl key to use a hyperlink. Instead, you simply click the link.

To view the Web pages in a Web browser:

1. Click the **Internet Explorer** button on the taskbar.
2. If the program window does not fill the screen entirely, click the **Maximize** button on the Internet Explorer title bar.
3. If you do not see a menu bar directly below the title bar, right-click a blank area of the Favorites bar to open the shortcut menu, and then click **Menu Bar** to place a check next to this option.
4. On the menu bar, click **File**, and then click **Open**. The Open dialog box opens.
5. Click the **Browse** button, navigate to the Word7\Tutorial folder, click **Fields Web Page**, and then click the **Open** button. You return to the Open dialog box.
6. Click the **OK** button. The Open dialog box closes, and Zoe's Web page is displayed in the browser window. The title "Green Fields Fresh Lunch Program," appears in the Internet Explorer title bar. See Figure 7-41.

Figure 7-41 **Web page displayed in Internet Explorer 8**

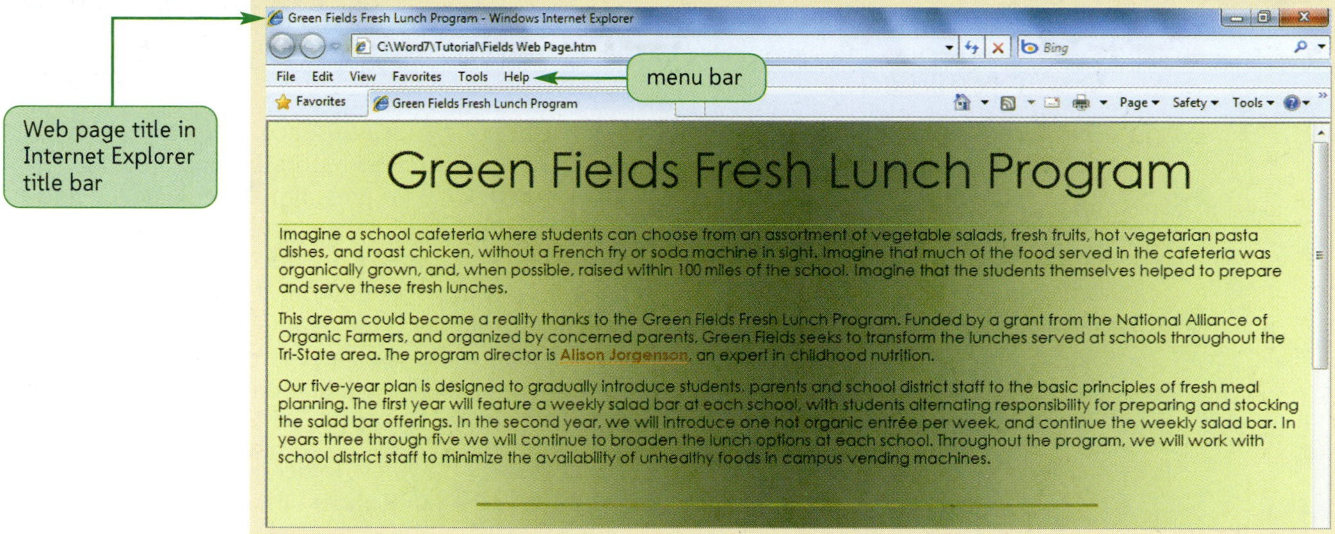

Web page title in Internet Explorer title bar

menu bar

7. Scroll down and review the Web page, then scroll back up and click the **Alison Jorgenson** hyperlink. The Program Director section is displayed in the browser window.
8. In the last paragraph of the document, click the **resume** hyperlink. The browser opens the Jorgenson Web page.
9. Scroll down to review the resume.
10. At the bottom of the resume, click the **Return to Green Fields Fresh Lunch Program page.** hyperlink. The browser displays the Fields Web Page.

    Trouble? If any of the hyperlinks don't work properly, close the browser, return to Word, edit the hyperlinks so they link to the proper files, and then test the links again in Internet Explorer.
11. Close Internet Explorer.

REVIEW

Session 7.2 Quick Check

1. If you want to save a file to SkyDrive for your own private use, what folder can you save it in?
2. True or False. A Web page is the same thing as an HTML document.
3. What is the first step in creating a hyperlink to a location in the same document?
4. What kind of page backgrounds can you apply using the Fill Effects dialog box?
5. True or False. When you save a document as a Web page, Word automatically displays it in Print Layout view.
6. Explain how to insert a horizontal line in a document or Web page in a simple, default style.
7. Explain how to edit a hyperlink.

Apply the skills you learned in the tutorial using the same case scenario.

PRACTICE

Review Assignments

Data Files needed for the Review Assignments: Expenses.xlsx, Progress.docx, Progress Henry.docx, Rates.xlsx, Salad Bar.docx, Salad Bar Web Page.htm, Salad Bar Web Page_Files (folder)

The first year of the Green Fields Fresh Lunch program was a success. Now Zoe and the staff of Rios Communications need to create a progress report to summarize the program's effectiveness. Zoe has written a draft of the progress report and emailed it to Henry. While he reviews it, Zoe plans to turn on Track Changes and continue work on the document. Then she can combine her edited version of the document with Henry's, accepting or rejecting changes as necessary. Next, she needs to insert some data from an Excel worksheet as an embedded object and insert an Excel chart as a linked object. She then wants to create a version of the document with hyperlinks, format the document for viewing as Web page, save it as a Web page, and view it in a browser. Complete the following steps:

1. Open the file named **Progress** from the Word7\Review folder included with your Data Files. Save the file as **Progress Zoe** in the same folder.
2. Change the user name to "Zoe Rios" and the user initials to "ZR," and then turn on Track Changes.
3. Format the first heading with the Title style.
4. Delete **concerned** in the first sentence below the title.
5. In the third line below the title, insert the word **generous** before the word "grant," so the sentence reads "...by a generous grant...."
6. In the third paragraph below the title, select the word "thirty" and insert a comment that reads **Remember to verify this number**.
7. In the Current Membership section at the end of the document, replace "Marti Sundra" with your name. Save your work.
8. Combine the **Progress Zoe** document with Henry's edited version, named **Progress Henry**, located in the Word7\Review folder included with your Data Files. Use the Progress Zoe document as the Original document.
9. Turn off Track Changes, accept the formatting change on the document title, then accept all the remaining changes in the document except Henry's deletion of "extremely." Review the comments, and then delete all comments in the document.
10. Change the user name and initials back to their original settings.
11. Save the new document as **Progress Combined** in the Word7\Review folder included with your Data Files, and then save it as **Progress Sky Drive** to the My Documents folder on your Sky Drive and close it.
12. Close the **Progress Zoe** document, and then reopen the **Progress Combined** document from the Word7\Review folder.
13. Replace the placeholder [Insert Excel worksheet] on the second page with the budget in the **Expenses.xlsx** file in the Word7\Review folder included with your Data Files. Insert the budget as an embedded object, and then close Excel.
14. Center the embedded object, and then edit it to change the Parent Training value from $2,500 to **$3,000**.
15. Open the workbook named **Rates.xlsx** file in the Word7\Review folder included with your Data Files, save it as **Rates Copy.xlsx,** and then copy the chart to the Office Clipboard.
16. Return to the Progress Combined document, and replace the placeholder [Insert Excel chart] at the bottom of the first page with a linked copy of the chart in the Rates Copy workbook using the destination theme. Save your work.

17. Edit the data in the Rates Copy workbook by changing the Last Month participation rate for middle schools from 35% to **80%**. Save and close the **Rates Copy.xlsx** file and close Excel.
18. Save your work, and then save the document with the new name **Progress No Links** in the same folder.
19. Break the link to the Excel workbook, and then save your work.
20. In the list of board members at the end of the document, select the word Chair and insert a bookmark named **Board**. In the second line of the document, format the word "parents" as a hyperlink that targets the Board bookmark. Test the hyperlink to make sure it works.
21. In the line below the heading "Year One: What Went Right?" format **salad bars** as a hyperlink that targets the Word document named **Salad Bar** in the Word7\Review folder included with your Data Files. Test the hyperlink to make sure it works, and then close the Salad Bar document. Save the Progress Combined document.
22. Save the document as a Web page in the Word7\Review folder using the Web Page, Filtered file type. Use **Progress Web Page** for the filename and **Green Fields First Year Progress** as the page title.
23. Add a gradient page color using Indigo, Accent 1, Lighter 80% as the color, with the Dark/Light scroll box at its default setting, and the shading style set to From center.
24. Before every heading except the title, insert a black horizontal line with circles on each end.
25. Increase the font size for the first heading, "Green Fields Progress Report," to 36-point, and then center the heading. Save the Web page.
26. Edit the "salad bar" hyperlink to open the **Salad Bar Web Page** file stored in the Word7\Tutorial folder included with your Data Files.
27. Open the **Salad Bar Web Page** file in Word, and format the last paragraph as a hyperlink that targets the **Progress Web Page** file.
28. Save all files, close Word, start Internet Explorer, and then open the **Progress Web Page**. Review the Web page in the browser, test the hyperlinks, and then close the browser.
29. Submit the documents to your instructor in printed or electronic form, as requested.

Apply the skills you learned to create an investment statement.

APPLY

Case Problem 1

Data Files needed for this Case Problem: Cook.docx, Statement.xlsx

KingFish Financial Planning You have just started work as a certified financial planner at KingFish Financial Planning. At the end of every quarter, you need to send a letter to each client containing a statement that summarizes the client's investment portfolio. The letter is a Word document, and the investment data for each client is stored in an Excel file. You need to insert the Excel data in the Word document as an embedded object. In the following steps, you will create a statement for a client named Isabella Cook.

1. Open the file named **Cook** from the Word7\Case1 folder included with your Data Files. Save the file as **Cook Letter** in the same folder.
2. In the signature line, replace "Student Name" with your name.
3. Delete the placeholder "[Insert Excel worksheet.]."
4. Start Excel and open the file named **Statement** from the Word7\Case1 folder included with your Data Files.
5. Copy the two columns of account names and current holdings to the Clipboard and insert it into the Word document in the blank paragraph that previously contained the placeholder text. Insert the data as an embedded Microsoft Excel Worksheet Object.

6. Return to the **Statement** worksheet and close Excel.
7. In the Cook Letter document, change the value for the Roth IRA to **$27,000.00**, and then save the document.
8. Save the document as **Cook Letter Sky Drive** to the My Documents folder on your SkyDrive and close it.
9. Submit the finished documents to your instructor, either in printed or electronic form, as requested.

Apply the skills you learned to create a Web page for a dog kennel.

APPLY

Case Problem 2

Data Files needed for this Case Problem: Kreelie.docx, Sun.docx

Kreelie Kennels Web Page Brianna Kreelie is the owner of Kreelie Kennels, an upscale dog boarding facility in Knoxville, Kentucky. She would like your help in creating a Web page for her business. She has created a first draft and saved it as a Word document. In the document, she included some comments explaining the edits she would like you to make. After you edit the document and remove the comments, she would like you to format it and save it as a Web page. Complete the following steps:

1. Open the file **Kreelie** from the Word7\Case2 folder included with your Data Files, and then save it as **Kreelie Edited** in the same folder.
2. Turn on Track Changes, review the comments, and make the changes requested in the comments. When you are finished, delete the comments. At the end of the document, attach a comment to the word "pool" that reads **I made all the changes you requested**.
3. Save the **Kreelie Edited** document.
4. Save the document as **Kreelie Final** in the Word7\Case2 folder.
5. Turn off Track Changes, and then accept all your changes in the document. Delete your comment at the end of the document, and then save your work.
6. Open the document named **Sun** from the Word7\Case2 folder, save it as **Sundeck** in the same folder, and then close it.
7. In the **Kreelie Final** document, at the end of the "Fun in the Sun" section, format the word "here" as a hyperlink that opens the **Sundeck** document.
8. Test the link, and then, in the Sundeck document, format the text **Back to main page.** as a hyperlink that jumps to the **Kreelie Final** document. Test the link.
9. Format the page background for the **Kreelie Final** document and the **Sundeck** document with the Parchment texture. (*Hint*: On the Texture tab of the Fill Effects dialog box, click a texture to see its name in the box.) Save the **Kreelie Final** and **Sundeck** documents.
10. Save the Kreelie Final document as **Kreelie Web Page** in the Word7\Case2 folder, using the Web Page, Filtered file type. Use **Kreelie Kennels** as the page title. Save the Sundeck document as **Sundeck Web Page** in the same folder, using the same file type. Use **Kreelie Kennels Sundeck** as the page title.
11. Edit the hyperlinks so they target the correct files, and then save the files.
12. In the Kreelie Web Page file, add a wavy orange horizontal line before each paragraph formatted with the Heading 1 style.
13. Save your work, close Word, open the **Kreelie Web Page** file in Internet Explorer, and note the formatting applied to the kennel name at the top of the page. Test the hyperlink. Close the browser.
14. Open the **Kreelie Edited** document and attach a comment to the Kreelie Kennels title at the top of the page, explaining how the title's formatting differs when the page is saved as a Web page and displayed in a browser.

15. Save and close the document. Submit the finished file to your instructor, either in printed or electronic form, as requested.

Use the Web to find a copyright-free, public domain photo to use in a Web page.

RESEARCH

Case Problem 3

Data Files needed for this Case Problem: Sunset.docx, Survey.xlsx

Sunset Optical Web Page You have been asked to create a Web page for Sunset Optical, a supplier of high-quality eyeglasses in Bellingham, Washington. Complete the following steps:

1. Open the file **Sunset** from the Word7\Case3 folder included with your Data Files, and then save it as **Sunset Optical** in the same folder.
2. In the second to last line, replace "Student Name" with your name.
3. Review the comments and delete them.
4. Use the Research task pane to look up information on the Web about public domain, copyright-free photos. Click the link to one of the sites listed in the Research task pane to open the Web site offering public domain, copyright-free photos, and then search the site to locate a public domain photo of a sunset. If the photo is displayed as a thumbnail image, click it to display it in a larger size.
5. Right-click the photo, and then, on the shortcut menu, click Save Picture As. Save the photo file to the Word7\Case3 folder included with your Data Files. Leave the browser open with the photo displayed.
6. Delete the [Insert Photo] placeholder text at the beginning of the Word document, and insert the photo. Crop or resize it as necessary so the photo is approximately 6 inches wide and between 3 and 4 inches tall.

EXPLORE

7. Return to the browser, select the URL for the photo in the browser's address bar, and then press Ctrl+C to copy the address to the Clipboard. Return to the Word document, right-click the photo, and then click Hyperlink on the shortcut menu to format the photo as a hyperlink. In the Address box at the bottom of the Insert Hyperlink dialog box, paste the URL from your browser. Close your browser, test the link in the Word document, and then close the browser again.
8. Open the Excel file named **Survey** from the Word7\Case3 folder included with your Data Files, and then save it as **Survey Copy**.
9. Delete the [Insert chart] placeholder text, and in its place insert a linked copy of the chart from the Survey Copy file in the Word document. Use the formatting of the destination file. Close Excel.
10. Revise the linked chart to change the value for "Surprised to find they needed glasses" to **200**. Change the value for "Have worn glasses most of their life" to **275**. Save your changes to the **Survey Copy** workbook and close Excel.
11. In Word, drag the border of the chart until it is small enough to fit on the same page as the document text and the document is only one page long.
12. Apply a theme with theme colors that complement your photo.

EXPLORE

13. Format the page background using a two-color gradient with a horizontal style. Choose colors that match your photo and make the text easy to read.
14. Save the **Sunset Optical** document, and then save it again as a Web page using the Single File Web Page file type. Use **Sunset Web Page** as the filename and **Sunset Optical** as the page title.
15. Close Word, open the Web page in a browser, test the photo hyperlink, and then close your browser.
16. Submit the finished files to your instructor, either in printed or electronic form, as requested.

Go beyond the skills you've learned to create a FAQ Web page.

CHALLENGE

Case Problem 4

Data File needed for this Case Problem: FAQ.docx

Great Falls Health Resource Sebastian Morey is publications director at Great Falls Health Resource, a county agency in Great Falls, Montana, that helps county residents manage health and health insurance-related issues. Sebastian asks you to help create a FAQ (Frequently Asked Questions) page that answers some basic questions related to health insurance. So far, he has created the basic structure of the FAQ and inserted a few questions. He wants you to add the necessary hyperlinks. Complete the following steps:

1. Open the file named **FAQ** from the Word7\Case4 folder included with your Data Files, and then save it as a Word document using the name **Insurance FAQ** in the same folder.
2. At the bottom of the document, replace "Student Name" with your name. Replace "Date" with the current date.
3. EXPLORE Create a system of hyperlinks that makes it possible for a user to click a topic in the Table of Contents and jump immediately to the relevant heading in the document. Use a heading as the target of each hyperlink rather than a bookmark. Add hyperlinks to the "Back to top" text that jump to the "Table of Contents" heading at the beginning of the document.
4. At the bottom of page 1, delete the placeholder "[Insert chart here.]," and then verify that the insertion point is located in a blank paragraph between two other blank paragraphs.
5. EXPLORE In the Illustrations group on the Insert tab, use the Chart button to insert the default type of column chart. In the Excel workbook, drag the lower-right corner of the blue selection box so that it only encloses rows 1 through 4 in columns A and B. Drag the border between column headers for columns A and B to the right to make Column A about four times wider than its default width.
6. EXPLORE Replace "Category 1" with the **No employee contribution**, replace "Category 2" with **Required for family coverage**, and then replace "Category 3" with **Required for employee coverage**. Enter the following data in Column B:
   - No employee contribution: 5%
   - Required for family coverage: 60%
   - Required for employee coverage: 80%

   Replace "Series1" with **Employee Contributions**. Close Excel. There's no need to save the data because it will be saved with the Word document.
7. EXPLORE Select the chart in the Word document, and then examine the various Chart Tools tabs. Use a button on the Chart Tools Layout tab to turn off the chart legend. Use the Edit Data button on the Design tab to edit the data, changing the percentage for "Required for family coverage" from 60% to 93%. Close Excel.
8. Near the end of page 2, in the section on finding health insurance statistics on the Web, format the word "here" as a hyperlink that targets the Web site for the U.S. Census Bureau. In the Address box of the Insert Hyperlink dialog box, enter the following URL: **www.census.gov**. (Do not include the period at the end.) If your computer is connected to the Internet, test the hyperlink, and then close the browser. Save the document.
9. Save the document as **Insurance FAQ Sky Drive** to the My Documents folder on your SkyDrive and close it.
10. Open the **Insurance FAQ** document from the Word7\Case4 folder, and then save the document as a Web page using the Single File Web Page file type. Use **FAQ Web Page** as the filename and **Frequently Asked Questions** as the page title.
11. Close Word and open the **FAQ Web Page** in a browser. Test all the table of contents and "Back to top" hyperlinks, and then test the U.S. Census Bureau hyperlink.
12. Submit the finished files to your instructor, either in printed or electronic form, as requested.

ENDING DATA FILES

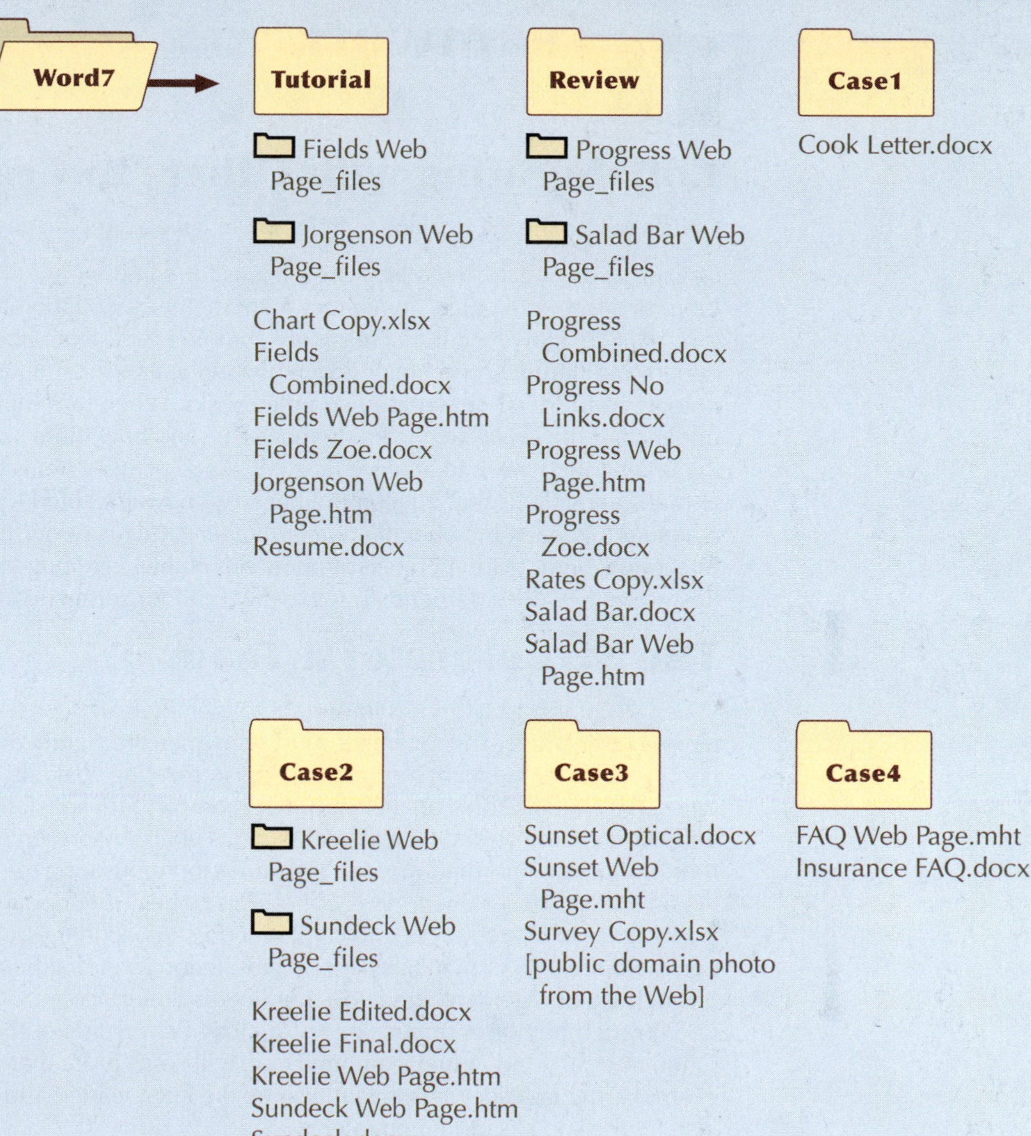
Word7
Tutorial
Fields Web Page_files
Jorgenson Web Page_files
Chart Copy.xlsx
Fields Combined.docx
Fields Web Page.htm
Fields Zoe.docx
Jorgenson Web Page.htm
Resume.docx
Review
Progress Web Page_files
Salad Bar Web Page_files
Progress Combined.docx
Progress No Links.docx
Progress Web Page.htm
Progress Zoe.docx
Rates Copy.xlsx
Salad Bar.docx
Salad Bar Web Page.htm
Case1
Cook Letter.docx
Case2
Kreelie Web Page_files
Sundeck Web Page_files
Kreelie Edited.docx
Kreelie Final.docx
Kreelie Web Page.htm
Sundeck Web Page.htm
Sundeck.docx
Case3
Sunset Optical.docx
Sunset Web Page.mht
Survey Copy.xlsx
[public domain photo from the Web]
Case4
FAQ Web Page.mht
Insurance FAQ.docx

ProSkills

Teamwork

Collaborating with Others to Create Documents

Collaboration means working together to achieve a specific goal through teamwork.

Organizations establish collaborative teams for completing a wide variety of tasks, with long- or short-term goals. Sometimes team members collaborate on projects by working side-by-side. However, it's increasingly common for the members of a team to collaborate from different corporate or geographical locations, using telecommunications technologies and social networks to complete tasks. When forming a team, it is important to understand the skills each team member has, and how these skills can best be used as the team collaborates to achieve its goals. An effective team is made up of people with abilities and talents that are complementary, and well-suited to the tasks at hand. It's also essential that each member of the team understand his or her responsibilities. On a truly integrated team, team members support each other, agreeing to share new responsibilities when they arise, rather than waiting around for someone else to pick up the slack.

The Structure of a Team

When structuring a team it is important to identify team leaders, work coordinators, idea people, and critics. Each member must recognize the significance of their individual contributions to the team's overall success in meeting its goals. Some team members will serve specific roles on the team. For example, task specialists spend a lot of time and effort ensuring that the team achieves its goals by presenting ideas, sharing opinions, collecting information, sorting details, and motivating the team to keep on track. When stresses occur due to time constraints or heavy workloads, positive team morale and a sense of shared focus and camaraderie can become essential. Some team members hold the role of managing social satisfaction by strengthen the team's social bonds through encouragement, empathy, conflict resolution, compromise, and tension reduction through humor or organizing social activities outside of the work environment. Oftentimes, the individual team members will serve more than one role on the team. For example, the task specialist might also be the team leader, and the idea person might also fill the social satisfaction role.

In this exercise you will work with a team to create documents. As you structure your team to complete these tasks, consider the roles you need the team members to fill. Before beginning, you might want to discuss the roles each member is comfortable assuming, and determine how complementary your collective abilities might be.

To ensure your team works effectively to complete tasks and achieve its goals:

- Recognize that everyone brings something of value to the team.
- Respect and support each other as you work toward the common goal.
- Try to see things from the other person's perspective when conflict or criticisms arise.
- Encourage or support team members that might need assistance.
- Address negative or unproductive attitudes immediately so they don't damage team energy and attitude.
- Seek outside help if the team gets stuck and can't move forward.
- Provide periodic positive encouragement or rewards for contributions.

ProSkills

Using Technology in Teamwork

Team members often work together from separate locations. Also, most of the time, teams need to produce work on accelerated schedules, and therefore need to do so efficiently. In these instances, teams depend on technology to accomplish work tasks. For example, corporate intranets and networks, email and voice mail, texting and instant messaging, teleconferencing and software collaboration tools, social networks, and cell phones can support teamwork. Before beginning a team project, identify the most appropriate technology tools the team will use to communicate and document work activities. Then you should determine how the team will organize, combine, and make available the documents and files the team produces.

PROSKILLS

Create a Report Template, Directory, and Web Page

At this point, you should feel confident that you have the word-processing skills required to create, revise, and distribute useful documents in your professional and personal life. But there's no need to wait to use these new skills. You can create some practical documents right now, starting with a template for a report that you need to create routinely. In the following exercise, work with your team members to create documents using the Word skills and features presented in Tutorials 5 through 7.

Note: Please be sure *not* to include any personal information of a sensitive nature in the documents you create to be submitted to your instructor for this exercise. Later on, you can update the documents with such information for your own personal use.

1. Meet with your team to plan a new report template to use for school reports or another type of report that you might have to create on a regular basis. Work with your group to select an appropriate template installed with Word, delete or edit document controls as necessary, insert placeholder text as necessary, and customize the theme. Select an appropriate style set, and create at least one new style that will be useful in your report. As a group, take the time to plan your template to ensure that it will be useful for a series of similar documents.
2. Use your template as the basis for a new report. Insert a file containing the text of a report you or a team member wrote for one of your classes, or insert appropriate text of your choosing, and then format the text using the template styles. Remember to include a table of contents in the report. At the end of the report, include a hyperlink that jumps to the beginning of the report.
3. If you or a team member are familiar with Excel, open a new workbook, enter some data that supports one of the points in the team's report, and then embed the worksheet data in the report. If you don't know how to enter data in Excel, you can embed the data from the Budget file in the Word7\Tutorial folder included with your Data Files, and then edit the data as necessary. Note that you can widen a column in Excel by dragging the right border of the column's header (the letter at the top of the column).
4. Email a copy of your report to a team member. Have him or her edit the document with Track Changes turned on and then send the report back to you.

ProSkills

5. Combine your edited copy of the document with the copy edited by your team member. Accept or reject changes as necessary. Save the new, combined document with a new name.
6. Meet with your team and choose a type of information, such as email addresses or birthdays, that the group would like to organize in a single document. Create a Word table, and then enter fictitious versions of the information into the table. You can replace this with real information later for your personal use, after you've handed in your assignments. Sort the information based on one of the columns.
7. Create a main document for a directory that includes a dot leader. Use the group's Word table from Step 6 as the data source. Insert the necessary merge codes into the main document and complete the merge.
8. Format the merged document with a gradient page color and add a title. Format the title appropriately. Save the document as a Web page that consists of only one file.
9. Submit your team's completed documents to your instructor in electronic or printed form, as requested. Also, save a copy of the documents to the My Documents folder on your SkyDrive.

TUTORIAL 8

Customizing Word and Automating Your Work

Automating Documents for a Function Hall

OBJECTIVES

Session 8.1
- Correct the color of photos
- Learn about picture compression
- Add a shape with text
- Add a custom paragraph border
- Create a watermark
- Create columns of different widths
- Insert a text box

Session 8.2
- Create and insert Quick Parts
- Manage building blocks
- Customize AutoCorrect
- Add document properties
- Insert fields

Session 8.3
- Learn about Trust Center settings
- Record and run macros
- Edit macros using Visual Basic
- Import and run Visual Basic macros
- Record an AutoMacro
- Customize the Quick Access Toolbar and the Ribbon

Case | *Forsythe Plaza*

Geoff McKay manages the Forsythe Plaza, a building with four large function halls in Quechee, Vermont. The function halls are rented out for weddings and other large parties, and are usually booked more than a year in advance. Geoff sends letters confirming bookings to customers who have sent in deposits. He wants to create letterhead for these letters. Also, prospective customers often visit or call to choose the rooms, caterer, and band they want for their event. Geoff wants to create a form he can use to collect this information. Finally, Geoff is working to market the Plaza more aggressively for corporate functions, and he wants to create a brochure for these events. He asks you to help him create these documents.

STARTING DATA FILES

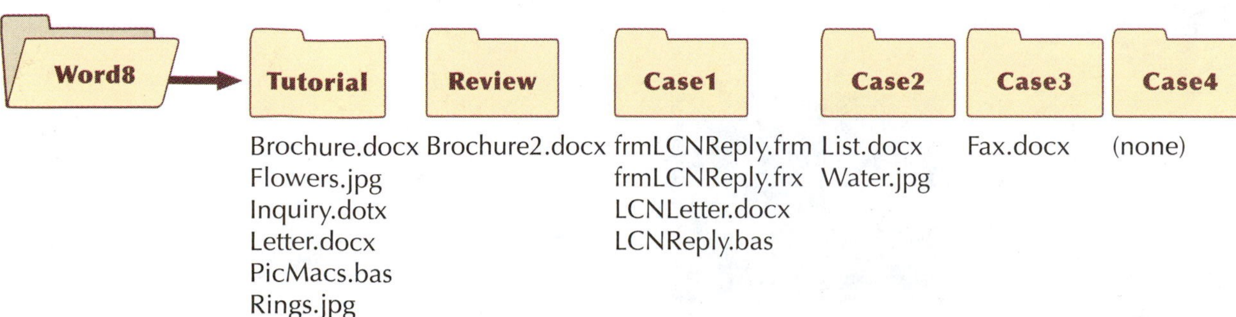

SESSION 8.1 VISUAL OVERVIEW

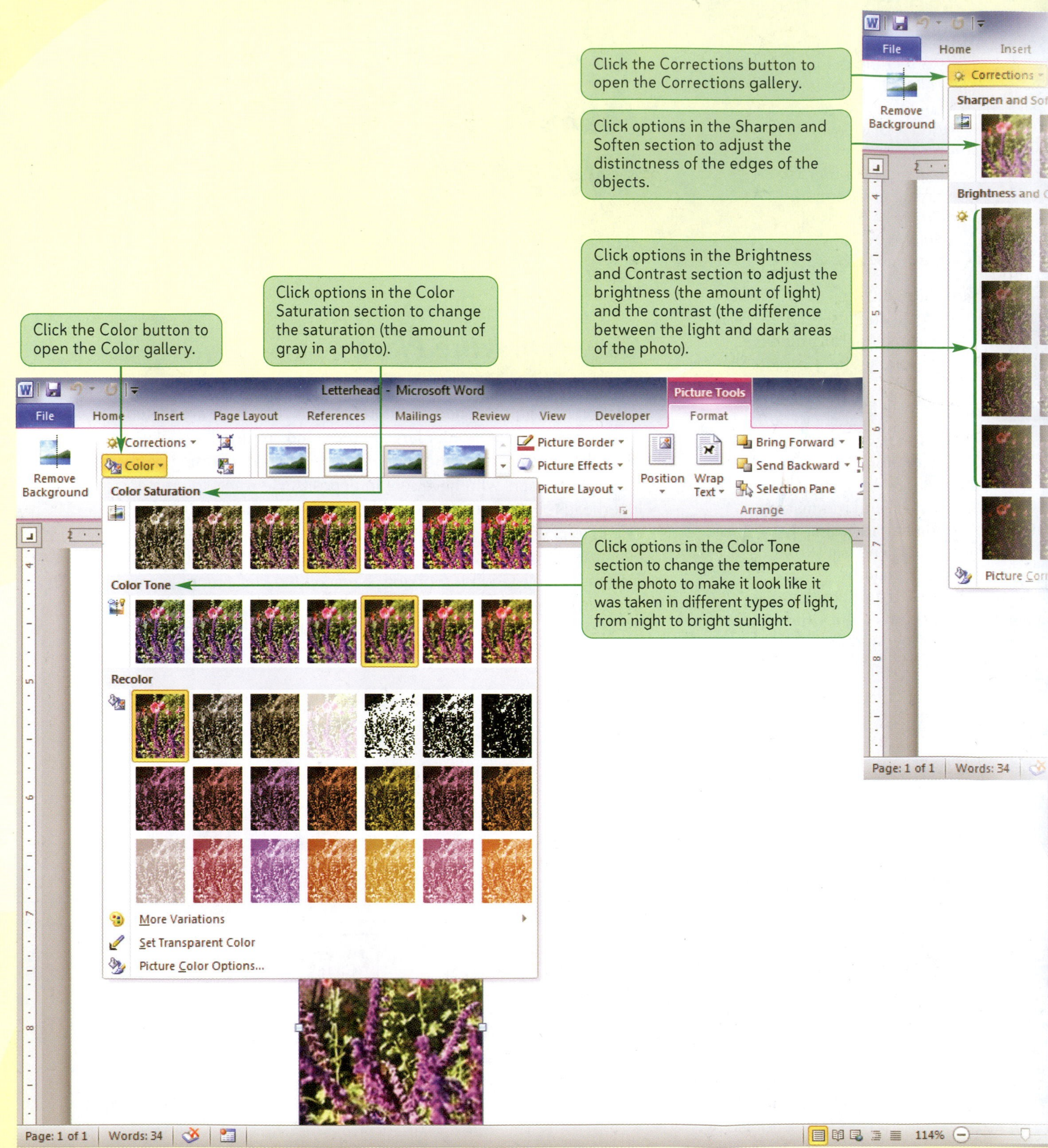
Click the Corrections button to open the Corrections gallery.
Click options in the Sharpen and Soften section to adjust the distinctness of the edges of the objects.
Click options in the Brightness and Contrast section to adjust the brightness (the amount of light) and the contrast (the difference between the light and dark areas of the photo).
Click the Color button to open the Color gallery.
Click options in the Color Saturation section to change the saturation (the amount of gray in a photo).
Click options in the Color Tone section to change the temperature of the photo to make it look like it was taken in different types of light, from night to bright sunlight.
Letterhead - Microsoft Word
Picture Tools
File
Home
Insert
Page Layout
References
Mailings
Review
View
Developer
Format
Remove Background
Corrections
Color
Picture Border
Picture Effects
Picture Layout
Position
Wrap Text
Bring Forward
Send Backward
Selection Pane
Arrange
Color Saturation
Color Tone
Recolor
More Variations
Set Transparent Color
Picture Color Options...
Sharpen and Sof
Brightness and C
Picture Corr
Page: 1 of 1
Words: 34
114%

CORRECTING PHOTOS

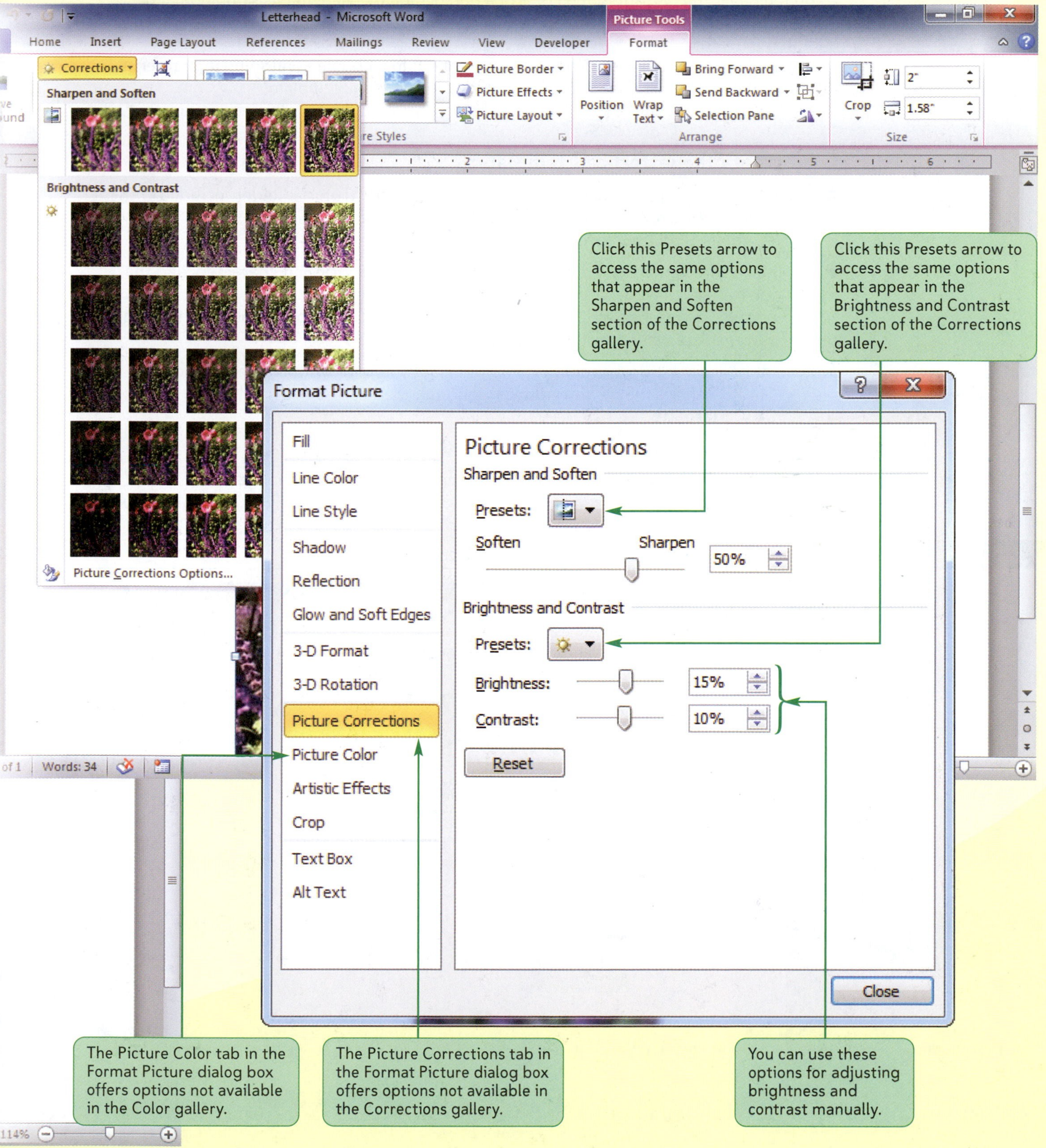
Letterhead - Microsoft Word
Picture Tools
Home Insert Page Layout References Mailings Review View Developer Format
Corrections
Sharpen and Soften
Brightness and Contrast
Picture Corrections Options...
Picture Border
Picture Effects
Picture Layout
Position
Wrap Text
Bring Forward
Send Backward
Selection Pane
Arrange
Crop
2"
1.58"
Size
Words: 34
114%
Format Picture
Fill
Line Color
Line Style
Shadow
Reflection
Glow and Soft Edges
3-D Format
3-D Rotation
Picture Corrections
Picture Color
Artistic Effects
Crop
Text Box
Alt Text
Picture Corrections
Sharpen and Soften
Presets:
Soften
Sharpen
50%
Brightness and Contrast
Presets:
Brightness:
15%
Contrast:
10%
Reset
Close
Click this Presets arrow to access the same options that appear in the Sharpen and Soften section of the Corrections gallery.
Click this Presets arrow to access the same options that appear in the Brightness and Contrast section of the Corrections gallery.
The Picture Color tab in the Format Picture dialog box offers options not available in the Color gallery.
The Picture Corrections tab in the Format Picture dialog box offers options not available in the Corrections gallery.
You can use these options for adjusting brightness and contrast manually.

Color Correcting Photos

When you add photos to a document, you might need to adjust them so they look better on the page. You can adjust the color of a photograph by changing its saturation and tone. You can also adjust the brightness and the contrast of a photo as well as sharpen or soften the photo.

Geoff wants you to use a letter that was sent out to a couple confirming their reservation of the hall as a starting point for creating the letterhead template.

To create the letterhead template:

1. Open the template file **Letter** located in the Word8\Tutorial folder included with your Data Files, open the Save As dialog box, change the Save as type to Word Template, and then save it as **Letterhead**.
2. Make sure you are in Print Layout view, and that nonprinting characters and the ruler are displayed. Notice that the date in the letter is the current date. This is because it was inserted as a date field that is updated automatically to show the current date whenever the document is opened.
3. In the inside address, replace "Ms. Pamela Lindeman" with **Name**, replace "145 South Main St." with **Address**, and then replace "Dover, NH 03820" with **City, State Zip**.
4. In the salutation, delete **Ms. Lindeman,** (including the comma).
5. Delete the rest of the text in the letter, and then save your changes. See Figure 8-1.

Figure 8-1 Letterhead template based on original Letter document

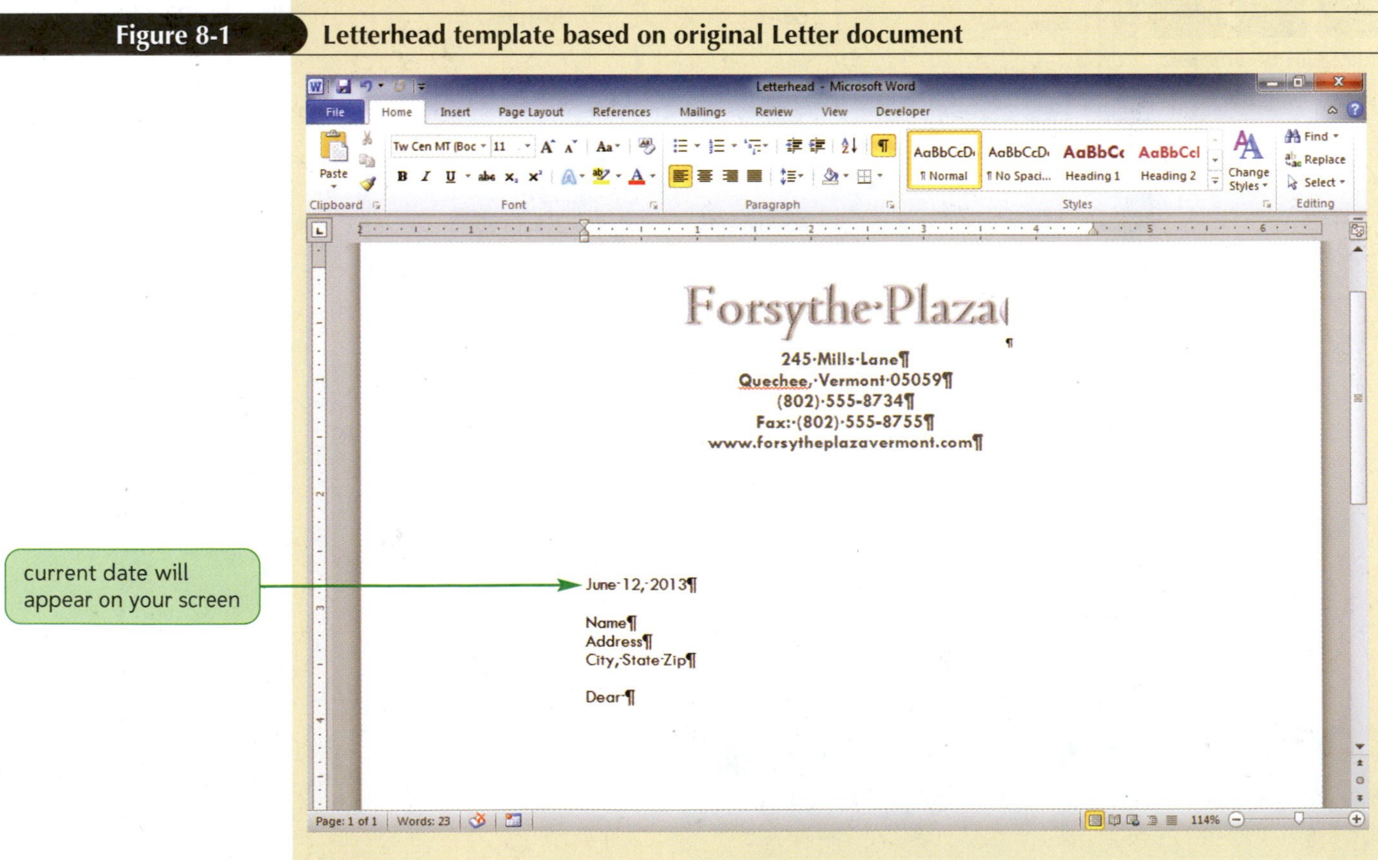

At the bottom of the letterhead template is a photo of flowers in one of the gardens at the Plaza. Geoff asks you to apply some color corrections to make the photo stand out on the page.

TIP

You can apply artistic effects to a photo, such as making it look like a watercolor painting or a pencil sketch, by clicking the Artistic Effects button in the Adjust group on the Picture Tools Format tab.

To sharpen the photo and adjust its brightness and contrast:

1. Scroll to the bottom of the document, click the photo of the flowers, and then click the **Picture Tools Format** tab. First, Geoff wants you to sharpen the edges of the objects in the photo.
2. In the Adjust group, click the **Corrections** button. A gallery of preset options for correcting the photo appears.
3. Under Sharpen and Soften, click the **Sharpen: 50%** option. The edges of the flowers in the photo are sharpened. Next, Geoff wants you to make the photo a little brighter and to adjust the contrast.
4. In the Adjust group, click the **Corrections** button, and then point to several of the options under Brightness and Contrast. None of the preset options provide the right amount of brightness and contrast.
5. At the bottom of the gallery, click **Picture Corrections Options**. The Format Picture dialog box opens with Picture Corrections selected in the list on the left.
6. Drag the **Brightness** slider to the right until the percentage is **15%**, and then drag the **Contrast** slider to the right until the percentage is **10%**.
7. Click the **Close** button. The brightness and the contrast in the picture are increased slightly.

Now Geoff wants you to adjust the tone of the photo to make the lighting look more like a sunny day.

To adjust the tone of the photo:

1. In the Adjust group on the Picture Tools Format tab, click the **Color** button. A gallery of options for adjusting the color of the photo appears.
2. In the Color Saturation section, point to several of the options. The options on the left remove color and add more gray to the photo, and the options on the right remove gray to make the colors more vivid. Geoff decides the color saturation of the photo is fine, so you won't adjust this now.
3. In the Color Tone section, click the **Temperature: 7200 K** option. The photo is modified to look as if it were taken in more direct sunlight. See Figure 8-2.

Figure 8-2 Color-corrected photo in the template

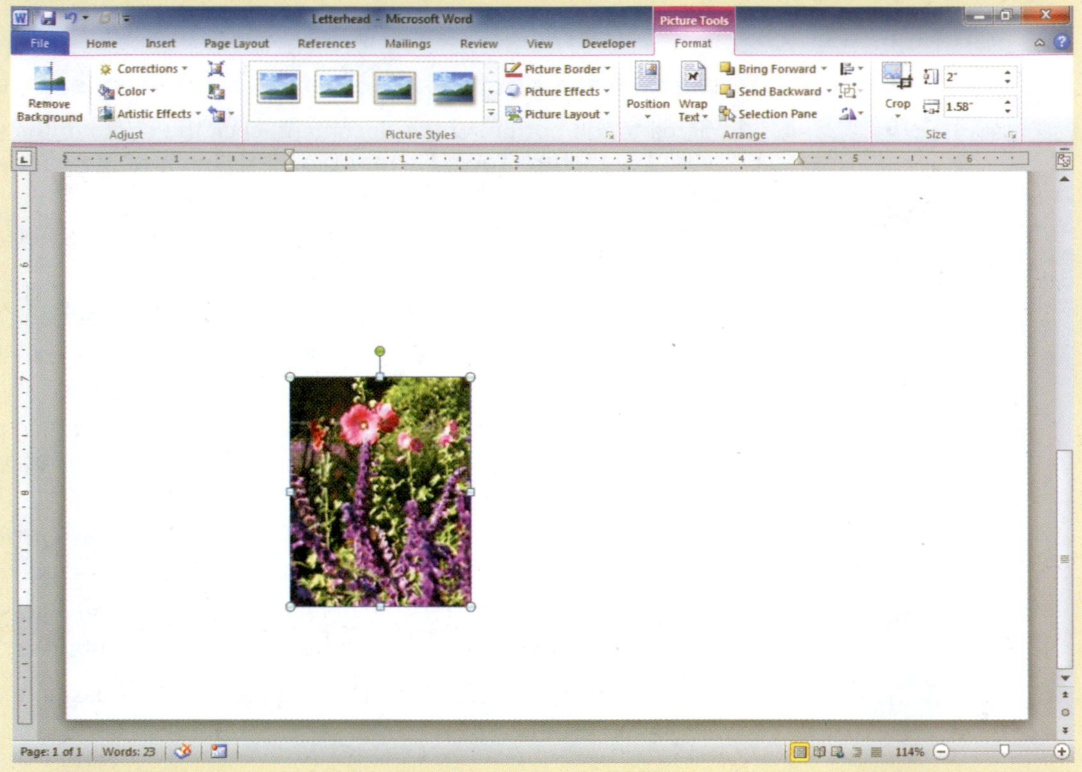

4. Deselect the photo, and then save your changes.

Understanding Picture Compression

Pictures added to documents are compressed by default to 220 pixels per inch (ppi). This setting is set in the Word Options dialog box and is applied automatically to all pictures in the document. You can change this default setting to 110 or 96 ppi, or turn off the automatic compression feature. For some pictures, you can choose to compress them further after you insert them. When you compress pictures, you remove pixels. If the picture is small, some compression won't matter, but if the picture is large or if you remove too many pixels, the difference in quality will be noticeable.

Geoff wants you to verify that the picture compression setting in the document is at least 220 ppi. You'll do this now.

TIP

To compress an individual picture using a different setting than the default, click the Compress Pictures button in the Adjust group on the Picture Tools Format tab.

To check the picture compression setting for the Letterhead template:

1. Click the **File** tab, and then click **Options** in the navigation bar. The Word Options dialog box opens.
2. In the list on the left, click **Advanced** to display the Advanced options, and then scroll down until you can see the Image Size and Quality section. See Figure 8-3.

Figure 8-3 Word Options dialog box displaying Advanced options

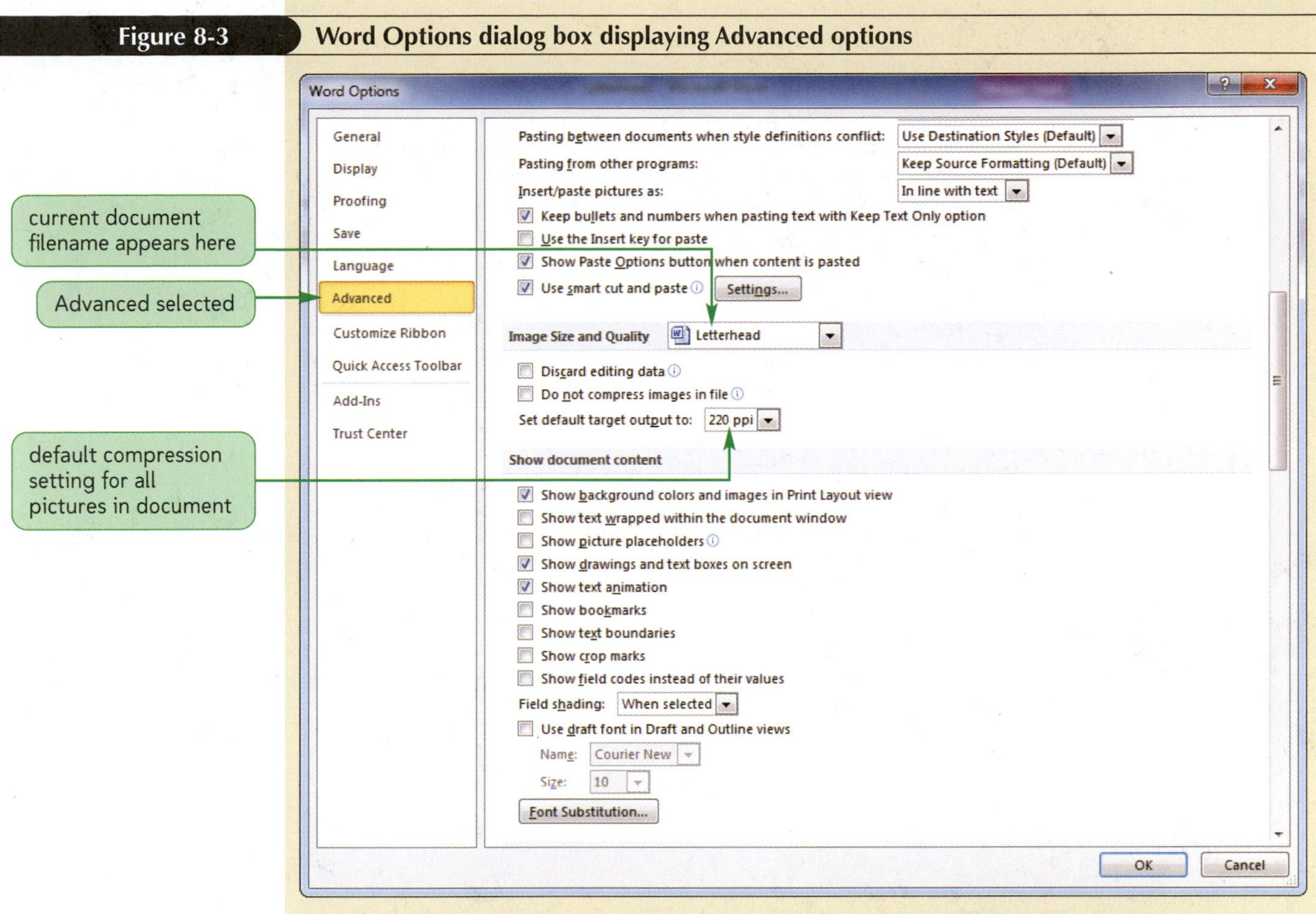

3. In the Image Size and Quality section, verify that the box next to "Set default target output to" contains 220 ppi.

4. Click the **Cancel** button to close the dialog box without making any changes.

In the letter Geoff will be sending to clients, he wants to let people know that they can take photographs at their events using the Plaza gardens as a backdrop. He asks you to add text to the letterhead template identifying the gardens in the picture and noting its availability for photographs.

Adding a Shape with Text

You can add shapes to your documents to draw attention to something or to add interest. You can leave the shapes empty or you can add text to them. On the Insert tab, click the Shapes button in the Illustrations group to open a menu of shapes organized in categories, such as lines, rectangles, circles, and many types of arrows. In addition, callouts are a special category of shapes. **Callouts** are shapes that contain text and have a line attached to them so that you can point to something in the document. To add text to a drawn shape, select the shape, and then just start typing.

REFERENCE

Adding a Shape with Text

- Click the Insert tab, and then in the Illustrations group, click the Shapes button.
- Click the desired shape.
- Drag the pointer to draw the shape in the document.
- Use the options on the Drawing Tools Format tab to format the size, placement, color, lines, and other characteristics of the shape.
- With the shape selected, type the text in the shape.
- Select the text and format it as necessary.

Geoff asks you to add a rounded rectangle shape below the picture of the gardens, and then add text to the shape to label the picture.

To add a shape with text:

1. Click the **Insert** tab, and then click the **Shapes** button in the Illustrations group. The Shapes gallery opens, as shown in Figure 8-4.

Figure 8-4 **Shapes gallery**

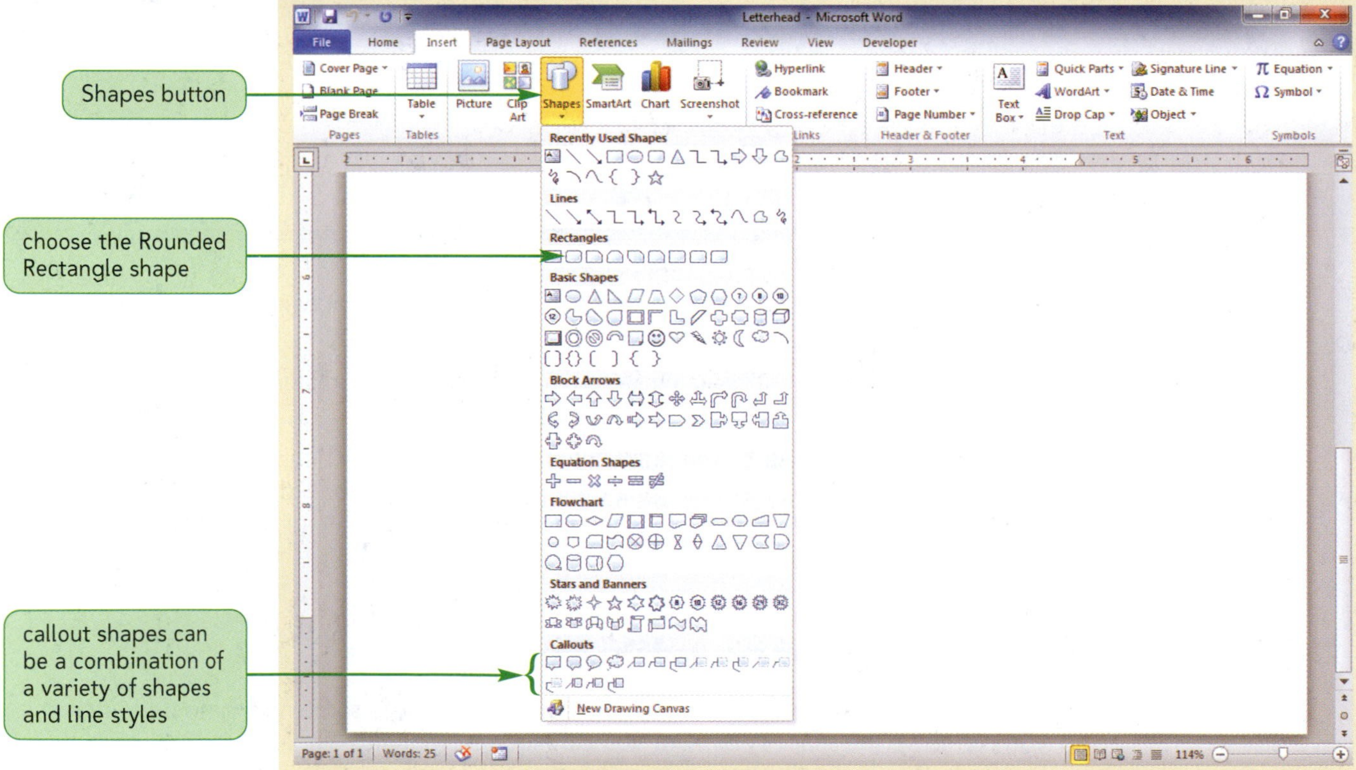

2. Under Rectangles, click the **Rounded Rectangle** shape (second shape in the row). The menu closes and the pointer changes to +.
3. Below the flowers picture, drag to draw a rectangle approximately three inches long and one-half inch high. The rectangle appears in the document.
4. Type **Take photographs in any of our three beautiful gardens!**

5. Click the edge of the rectangle to select it, click the **Drawing Tools Format** tab if necessary, click the **Shape Fill button arrow** in the Shape Styles group, and then click **No Fill**. The colored background is removed from the shape.
6. In the Shape Styles group, click the **Shape Outline button arrow**, point to **Weight**, and then click **½ pt**. The weight of the outline of the shape is decreased to one-half point.
7. Click the **Home** tab, change the font color to **Pink, Text 2**, change the font size to **8 points**, and then italicize the text.
8. If necessary, drag either of the side sizing handles to resize the width of the rectangle so that it's large enough to fit the text all on one line, drag the bottom sizing handle up to decrease the height of the rectangle to about one-third of an inch, and then use the arrow keys to position the rectangle so it is centered just under the image, as shown in Figure 8-5.

   Trouble? If pressing the arrow keys has no effect, you probably accidentally deselected the shape. Click the shape again to select it, and then use the arrow key to position the rectangle so it is centered under the image.

Figure 8-5 Shape with text below image

9. Deselect the shape, and then save your changes. You're finished creating the Letterhead template for Geoff.
10. Close the document, but do not exit Word.

Geoff is pleased with the completed Letterhead template. Next, you'll format the inquiry form that Geoff created.

Adding Custom Paragraph Borders

You already know how to add a basic border around a paragraph. You can also add a custom border. Borders not only draw attention to text, they can separate parts of a document so the user doesn't get confused.

The next document you'll work on for Geoff is a form that Forsythe Plaza employees can use when collecting information from prospective customers about reserving a function room for a wedding. Geoff already added the basic information to a template he created. He wants you to start formatting it by adding a border to separate the top part of the form, which contains the customer data, and the bottom of the form, which contains information about the event. First, you'll open Geoff's template.

To insert a custom border in the template:

1. Open the template file **Inquiry**, located in the Word8\Tutorial folder, and then save it as a template to the same folder as **Inquiry Form**. See Figure 8-6.

Figure 8-6 Inquiry Form template

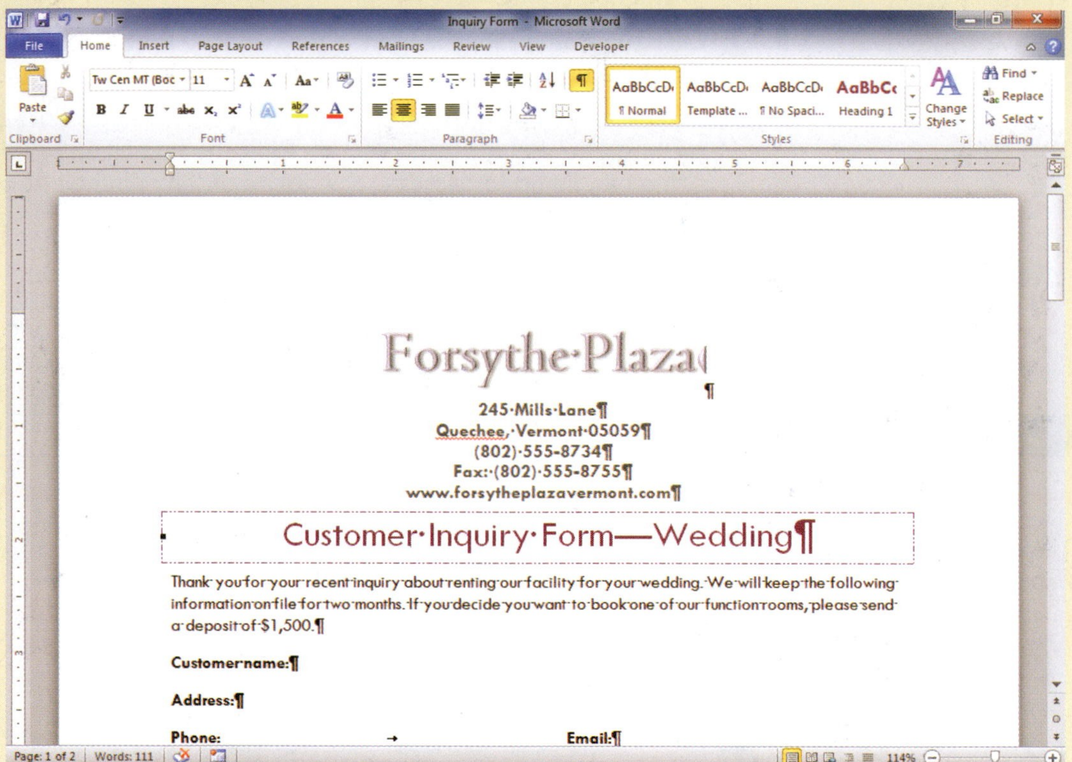

2. Scroll down until the colored text "Customer Inquiry Form—Wedding" is at the top of the document window, and then click anywhere in the line starting with "Phone:". This is the last line that contains customer information. The next line is the start of information about the event.
3. In the Paragraph group on the Home tab, click the **Bottom Border button arrow**, and then click **Borders and Shading**. The Borders and Shading dialog box opens with the Borders tab on top. You already know how to insert a Horizontal Line picture border. You want to use one of the border styles available in the Style list.
4. In the Setting list on the left, click the **Custom** button, in the Style list click the **down arrow** three times, and then click the three-lines style at the bottom of the list.
5. Click the **Color** arrow, and then click the **Pink, Text 2** color (fourth color in the top row).
6. In the Preview section, click at the bottom of the paragraph. A pink triple line appears at the bottom of the paragraph in the Preview section. Notice that the bottom button to the left of the preview box is selected. See Figure 8-7.

TIP

To adjust the distance between the border line and the text, click the Options button on the Borders tab in the Borders and Shading dialog box.

Figure 8-7 Borders tab in the Borders and Shading dialog box after applying a custom border

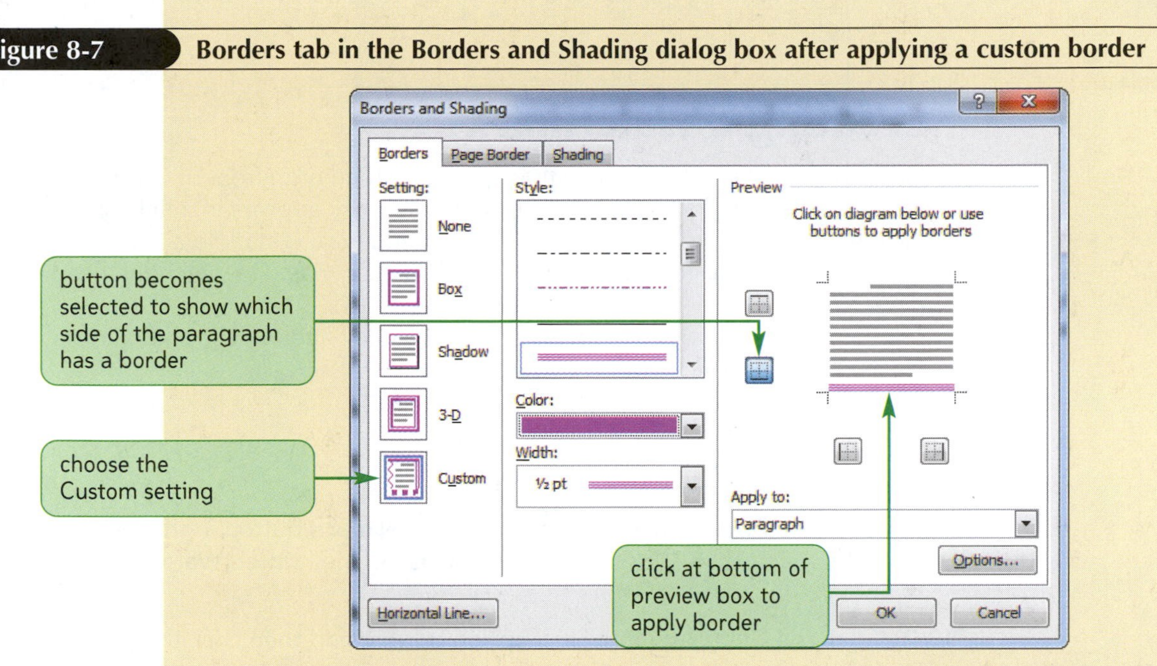

7. Click the **OK** button. A dark pink triple line appears below the Phone: line, as shown in Figure 8-8.

Figure 8-8 Template with custom border

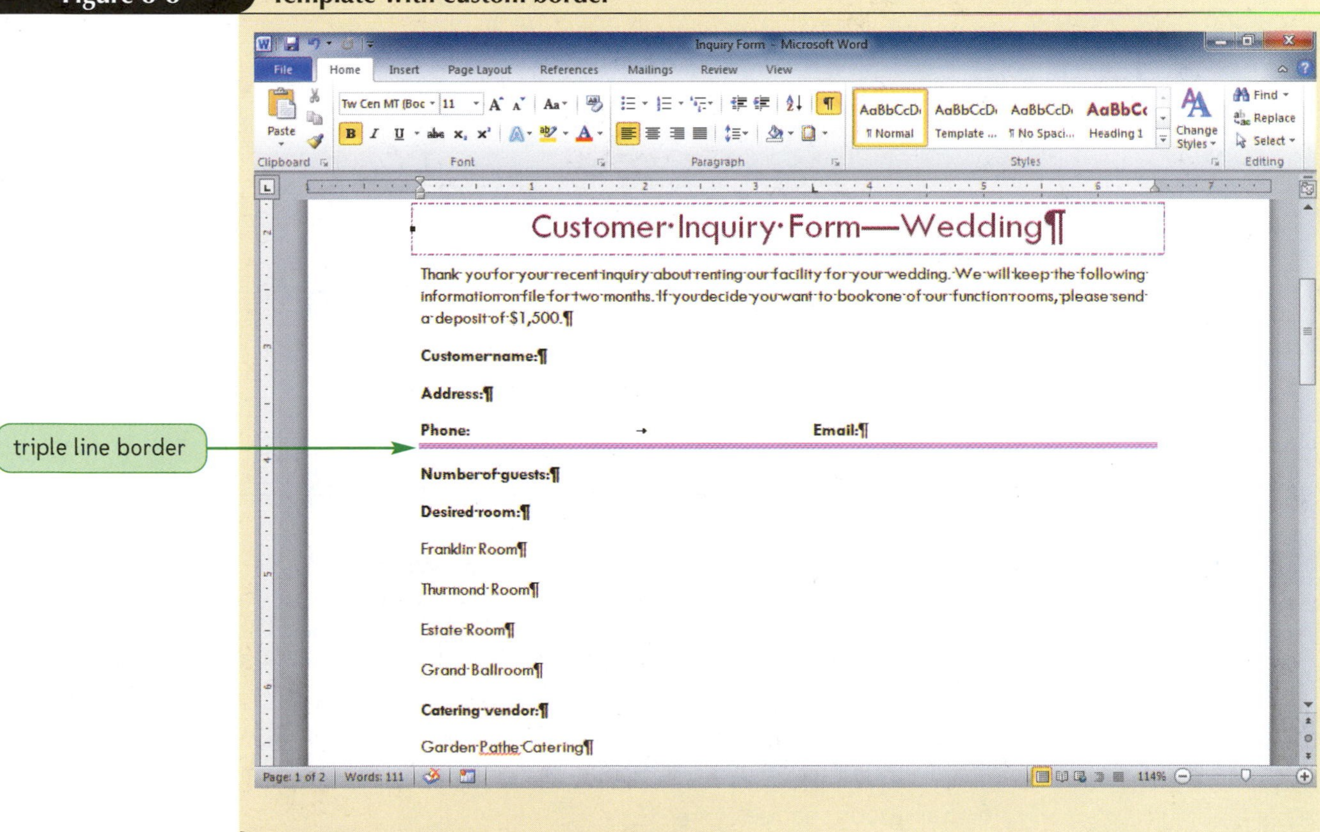

8. Save your changes to the template.

Next, Geoff wants you to add a picture of two hands with wedding rings as a watermark.

Creating a Watermark

A **watermark** is text or a graphic that appears behind or in front of existing text on the printed pages of a document. Usually, the watermark appears in a light shade in the background of each printed page. When you add a watermark to a header or footer, it appears on every page in the document (or on every page on which the header or footer appears).

Geoff gave you a file containing a picture of the hands with wedding rings. You'll use this as the watermark.

To insert the photo as a watermark:

1. Click the **Page Layout** tab, click the **Watermark** button in the Page Background group, and then click **Custom Watermark**. The Printed Watermark dialog box opens.
2. Click the **Picture watermark** option button, and then click the **Select Picture** button. The Insert Picture dialog box opens.
3. Navigate to the Word8\Tutorial folder included with your Data Files, click **Rings**, and then click the **Insert** button. The Printed Watermark dialog box should look like the one shown in Figure 8-9.

Figure 8-9 Printed Watermark dialog box with photo selected

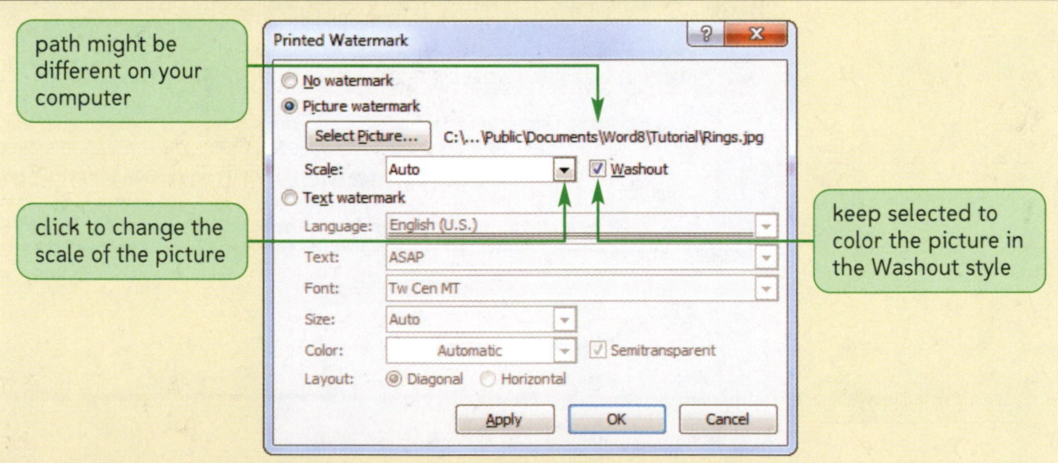

4. Click the **Scale** arrow, click **150%**, click the **Washout** check box to deselect it, if necessary, and then click the **Apply** button. The picture of hands with wedding rings appears as the background of the form behind the dialog box, however, it's too dark and makes the text difficult to read. You'll reapply the Washout effect.
5. In the Printed Watermark dialog box, click the **Washout** check box to select it, and then click the **OK** button. The dialog box closes and picture colors appear washed out, making the text much easier to read.
6. Save your changes.

TIP

Another way to add a picture as a watermark is to insert a picture using the Picture button on the Insert tab, change it to a floating graphic behind the text, and then on the Picture Tools Format tab, click the Recolor button and click the Washout style under Color Modes.

Creating Columns of Different Widths

You already know how to format text into columns of equal width. In Word, you also can format text into two or more columns with varying widths.

To make space for a customer quote, Geoff suggests you format the middle part of the form in two columns with the categories on the left and the choices in a list on the right. Instead of creating columns of equal width, you'll create a narrow left column and a wider right column.

TIP

To customize the width of the columns, click the Columns button in the Page Setup group on the Page Layout tab, and then click More Columns. In the Columns dialog box that opens, change the values in the Width and Spacing boxes as desired.

To create columns of different widths:

1. Select all the lines of text from **Desired room:** through **Other:** just above the sentence "If you have any questions, please call me."
2. In the Page Setup group on the Page Layout tab, click the **Columns** button. A menu of column options appears. The first three commands on this menu are used to format selected text into columns of equal width. The Left command formats selected text into two columns where the left column is narrower than the right, and the Right command does the opposite.
3. Click **Left**, and then scroll up so you can see that the selected text is formatted in two columns, and the left column is narrower than the right column. See Figure 8-10.

Figure 8-10 Document after formatting text in two columns

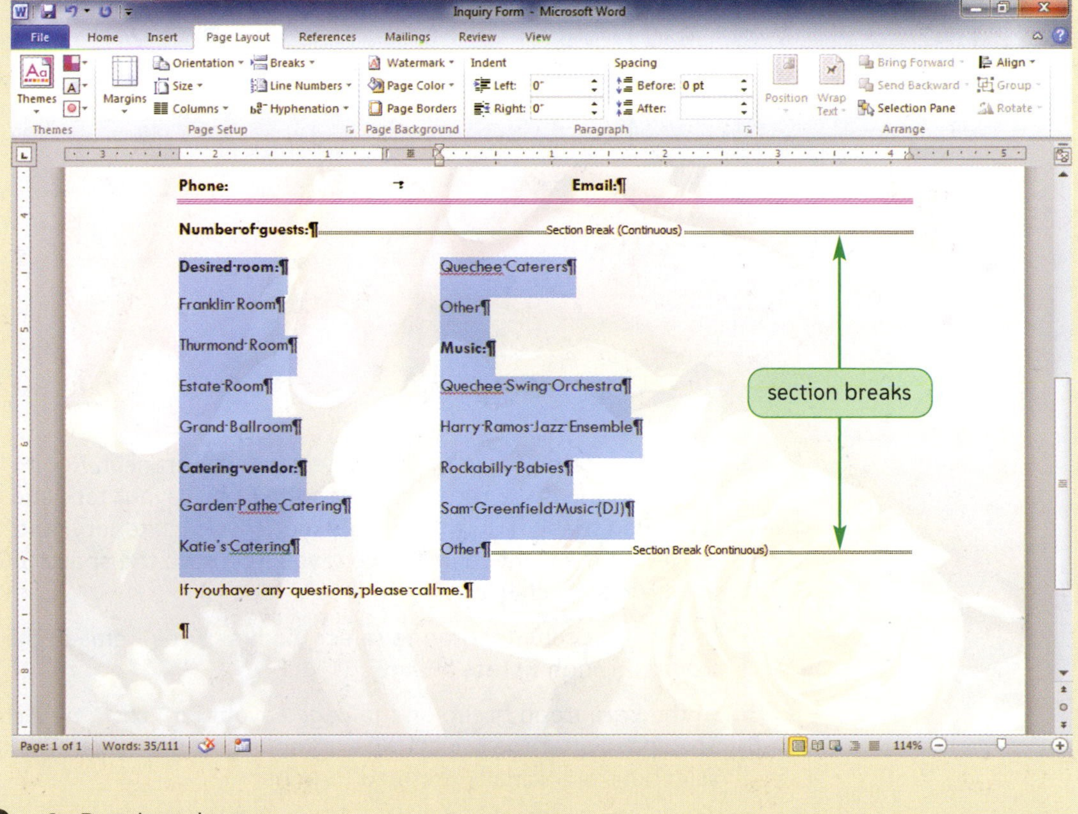

4. Deselect the text.

Now that you've formatted the text in columns, you need to adjust the order of the items so that the categories are on the left and the choices are on the right. Then you can adjust the spacing after the paragraphs to make the columns attractive and easy to read.

To restructure the text in the columns and format the columns:

1. In the left column, drag across **Catering vendor:** and the paragraph mark to select it, and then drag the selected text up to position it to the left of the text "Franklin Room." "Catering vendor:" becomes the second item in the left column.
2. In the right column, drag across **Music:** and the paragraph mark after it to select it, and then drag the selected text to position it to the left of the text "Franklin Room." "Music:" becomes the third item in the left column. See Figure 8-11. Now you need to force the choices to appear in the right column. To do this, you'll insert a column break.

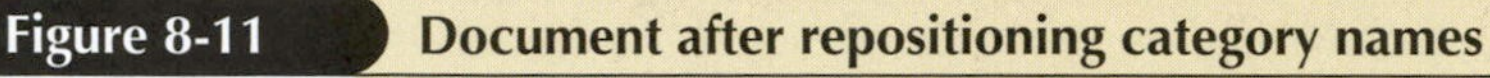

Figure 8-11 Document after repositioning category names

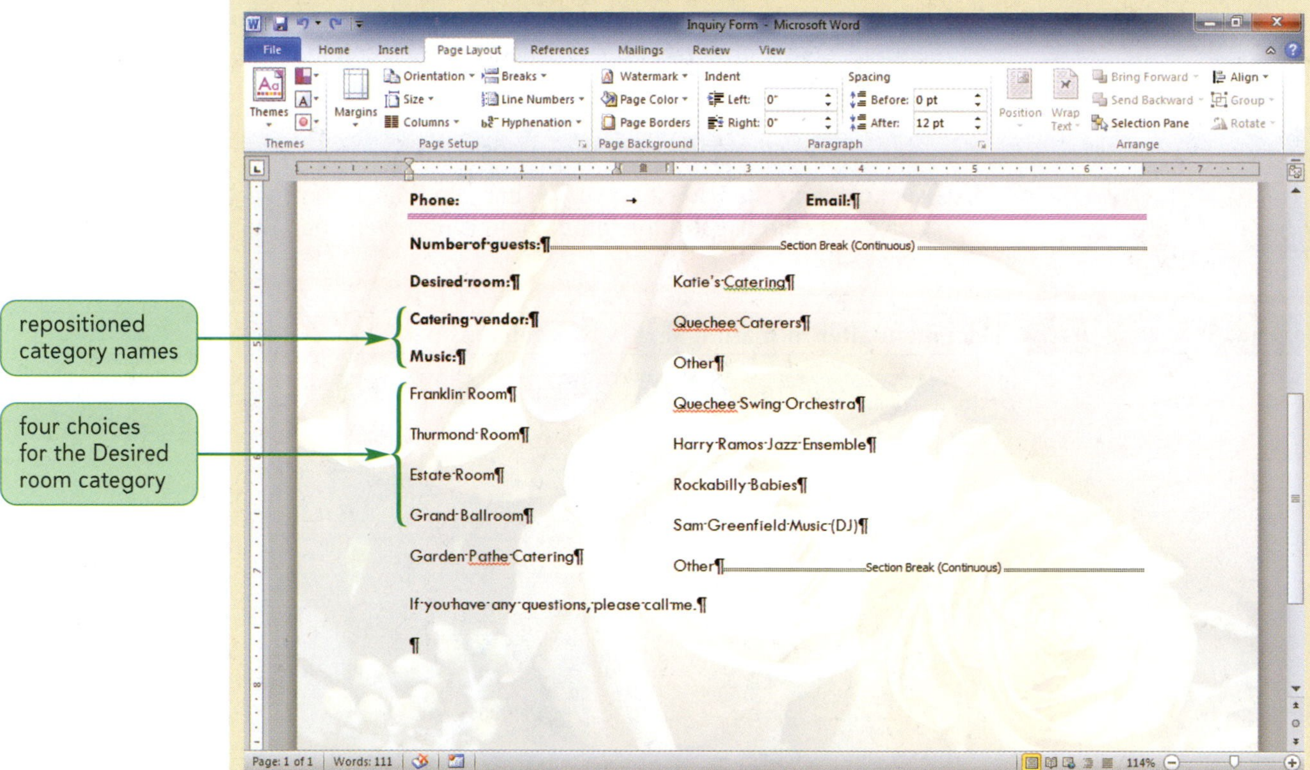

3. In the left column, click immediately before "Franklin Room," click the **Breaks** button in the Page Setup group on the Page Layout tab, and then click **Column**. A column break is inserted below the "Music" category, and the list of choices is moved to the right column. Next, you'll remove the space after the paragraphs in each group of choices.
4. In the right column, drag to select the first three items in the list, from **Franklin Room** through **Estate Room**.
5. In the Paragraph group on the Page Layout tab, click the **After** down arrow twice. The space after the selected paragraphs changes to zero points, and all the room selections are visually grouped together.
6. Select **Garden Pathe Catering** through **Quechee Caterers**, and then click the **After** down arrow in the Paragraph group on the Page Layout tab twice to visually group the caterer choices.

7. Select **Quechee Swing Orchestra** through **Sam Greenfield Music (DJ)**, and then remove the space after these paragraphs to visually group the music choices. Finally, you need to adjust the space after the paragraphs in the left column to align the categories with their choices.
8. Click anywhere in the category name **Desired room:**, and then change the value in the After box in the Paragraph group to **54 pt**.
9. Change the paragraph spacing after the paragraph containing **Catering vendor:** to **54** points as well. Now the choices are aligned with each category label. See Figure 8-12.

Figure 8-12 Text in columns repositioned and aligned

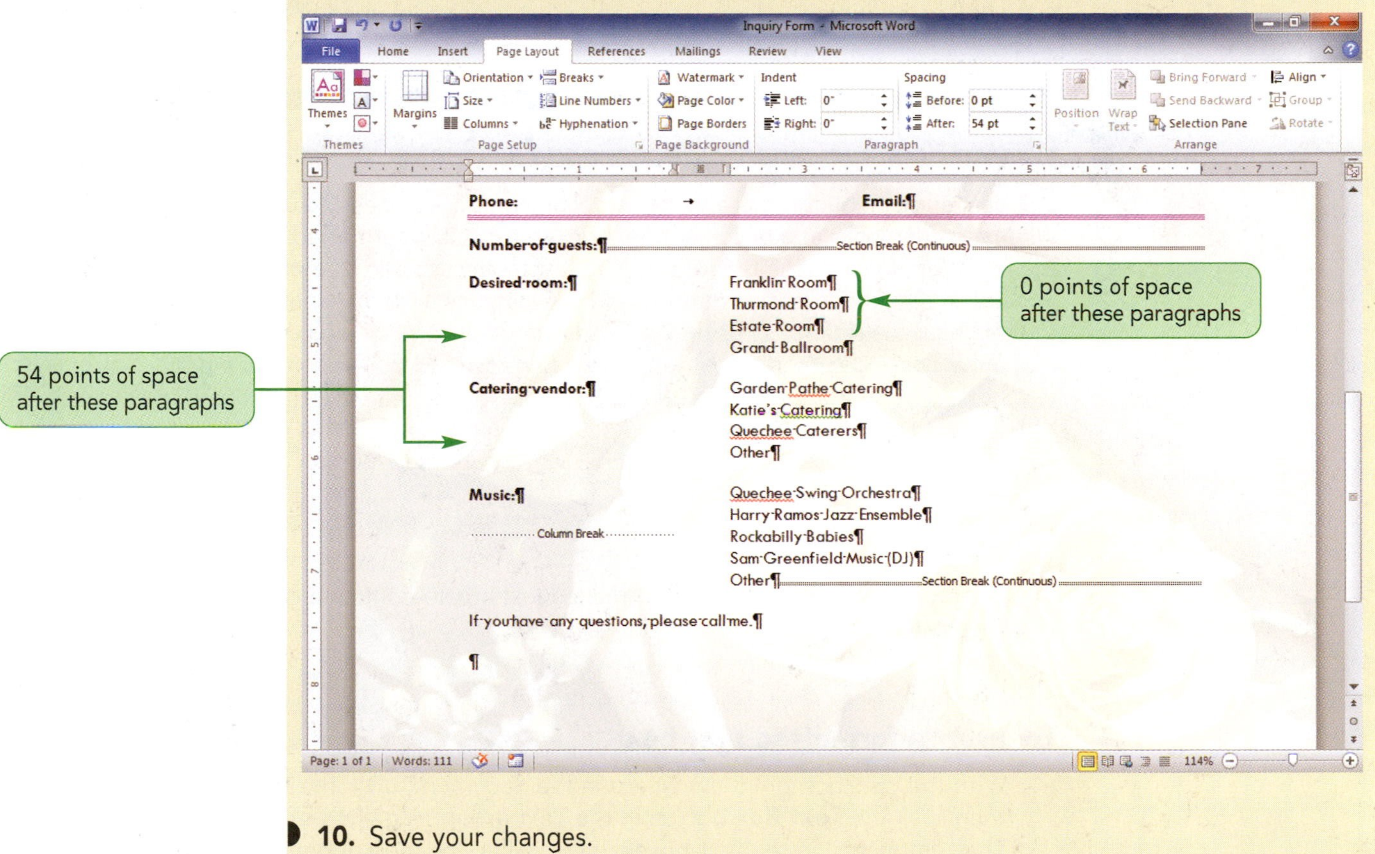

10. Save your changes.

Now space is available on the right where you can insert a text box with a quote from a satisfied customer.

Inserting Text Boxes

> **TIP**
> To create a text box from existing text, select the text, click the Insert tab, click the Text Box button in the Text group, and then click Draw Text Box.

Recall that a text box is an object that contains text and that you can treat it as an inline or a floating object in a document. Essentially, when you drew a shape and added text to it earlier in this session, you created a text box. You can also create a text box in a document by clicking the Text Box button in the Text group on the Insert tab, and then clicking Draw Text Box. You can create plain text boxes that you leave as is or format yourself, or you can insert preformatted text boxes from the Text Box gallery. If you start with a plain text box, you can format it with fill color and border color as well as change the font and font styles used in the text box. When you insert a preformatted text box, you can of course change the formatting if you choose.

Another aspect of text boxes you have to consider is whether they are inline with the text of the document or whether they float on top of the document text. You also have to decide how you want the document text to wrap around the text box. You've made similar formatting decisions for other elements you've worked with, including pictures, WordArt, clip art objects, and charts. When you insert a preformatted text box, it is formatted as an inline object with Square text wrapping by default.

You can use text boxes to create pull quotes and sidebars. Text boxes that contain text copied (not cut) from the document are called **pull quotes**, because they contain text "pulled" from the document. Pull quotes are eye-catching, offer an opportunity to reiterate an important point, and provide relief from unbroken text, which is especially important in long documents. A variation on pull quotes is **sidebars**, which are text boxes that contain additional, related information that is not contained in the main document.

PROSKILLS

Written Communication: Sidebars and Pull Quotes

Sidebars and pull quotes can enhance a document, but you need to use them judiciously. When a reader looks at a document, text boxes, especially formatted text boxes, will be the first thing to catch the reader's eye. Text you select to add as a pull quote should be important enough to bear repeating. Text you insert as a sidebar should be related to the text near the sidebar's position in the document, and it should contain information that enhances understanding without distracting the reader. If you select a preformatted text box, make sure it fits the style of the document, and make adjustments if it doesn't. Keeping your audience and the purpose of the document in mind as you choose the content and format of sidebars and pull quotes will ensure that your documents are always professional.

Geoff would like you to insert a formatted text box to contain a quote from one of his satisfied customers.

To insert a formatted text box:

1. With the insertion point anywhere in the document, click the **Insert** tab, and then click the **Text Box** button in the Text group. A gallery of text boxes opens. The colors used in the text boxes in the gallery change depending on the theme colors. See Figure 8-13.

Figure 8-13 Text Box gallery

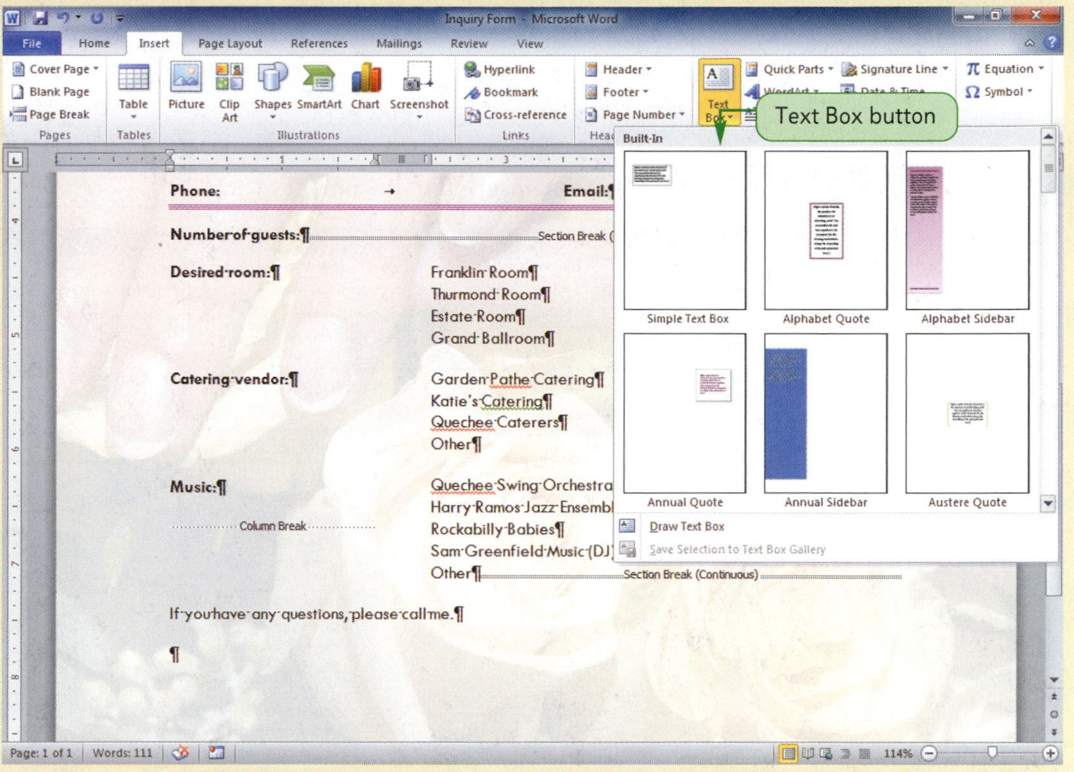

TIP

You can use the Quote or Intense Quote Quick Style to format text as a quote. Both styles italicize the text.

2. In the gallery, click the down scroll arrow twice, and then click the **Braces Quote 2** text box. A blue text box is inserted in the right middle of the page. The placeholder text is selected in the content control.
3. Type **Thanks to the fantastic staff at Forsythe Plaza, all of our guests had a wonderful time at our wedding.**
4. Press the **Enter** key, and then type **Jack and Camille Perreira**.
5. Select the text in the text box, and then change it to **12 points**.
6. Click the **Drawing Tools Format** tab, and then click the **Size** button. The Size group expands to show the Shape Height and Shape Width boxes.

7. Select the value in the Width box, type **2**, select the value in the Height box, type **2.1**, and then click a blank area of the document. The size of the text box is modified to fit the text.
8. Drag the text box to position it approximately centered in the area to the right of the list of choices. See Figure 8-14.

Figure 8-14 **Formatted text box inserted in document**

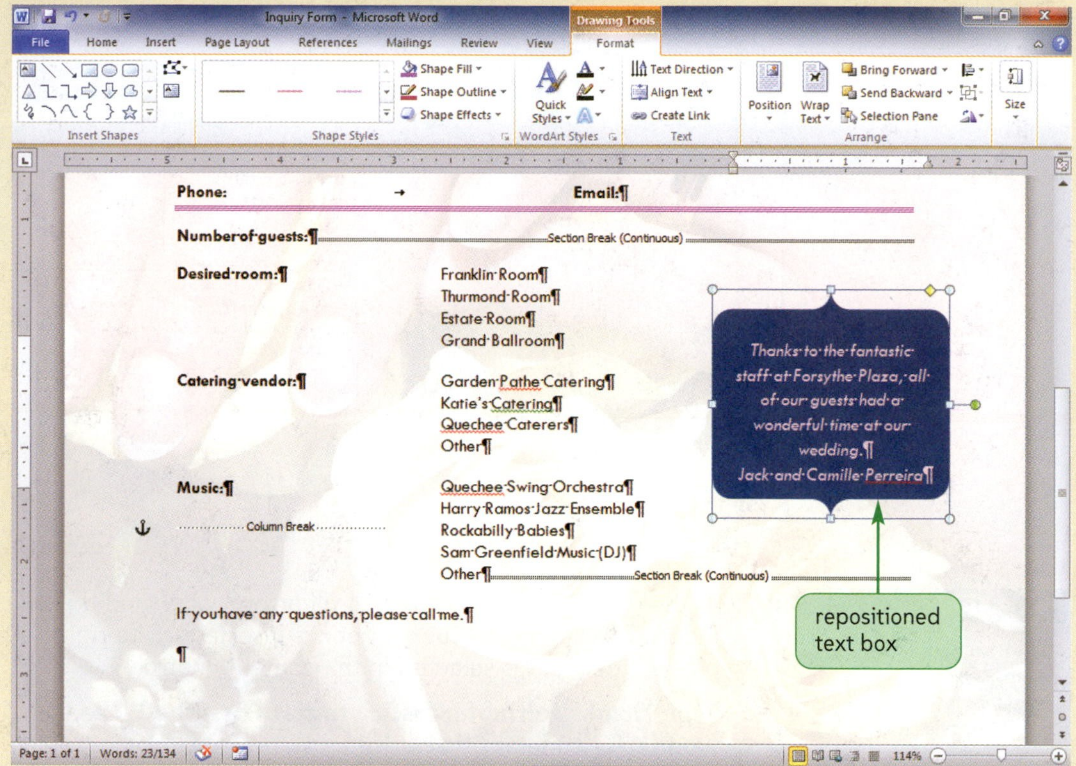

9. In the Shape Styles group, click the **Shape Effects** button, point to **Shadow**, and click the **Offset Bottom** style in the gallery (the second style in the first row in the Outer section).
10. Deselect the text box, and then save your changes.

INSIGHT

Linking Text Boxes

Linked text boxes are useful if you have a large amount of text that you need to place in different locations in a document, but you want the text to continue from one text box to another. For example, if you created a newsletter in Word, you might have a story that starts in a text box on page 1 of the newsletter and continues in a text box on page 3. To flow the text automatically from the first text box to the second, first select the text you want to link, click the Text Box button in the Text group on the Insert tab, and then click Draw Text Box. The selected text is placed in a text box. Next, click outside the text box, click the Text Box button again, click Draw Text Box, and then drag the pointer in the document window to draw a second, empty text box. Click in the first text box—the text box containing the content—click the Drawing Tools Format tab, click the Create Link button in the Text group, and then click the pointer in the empty text box. The text boxes are linked. You can now resize the first text box so it is the size you want, without worrying about how much text fits in the box. The text that no longer fits in the first text box is moved to the second text box.

You've finished formatting the template. In the next session, you'll add contact information and save it to be inserted into other documents. You'll also add document properties and fields to the documents.

REVIEW

Session 8.1 Quick Check

1. Name four ways you can correct a photograph.
2. What is the default compression for photos in a document?
3. How do you add text to a shape that you draw?
4. What is a watermark?
5. True or False. You can add a border on any side of a paragraph.
6. What is a pull quote?

SESSION 8.2 VISUAL OVERVIEW

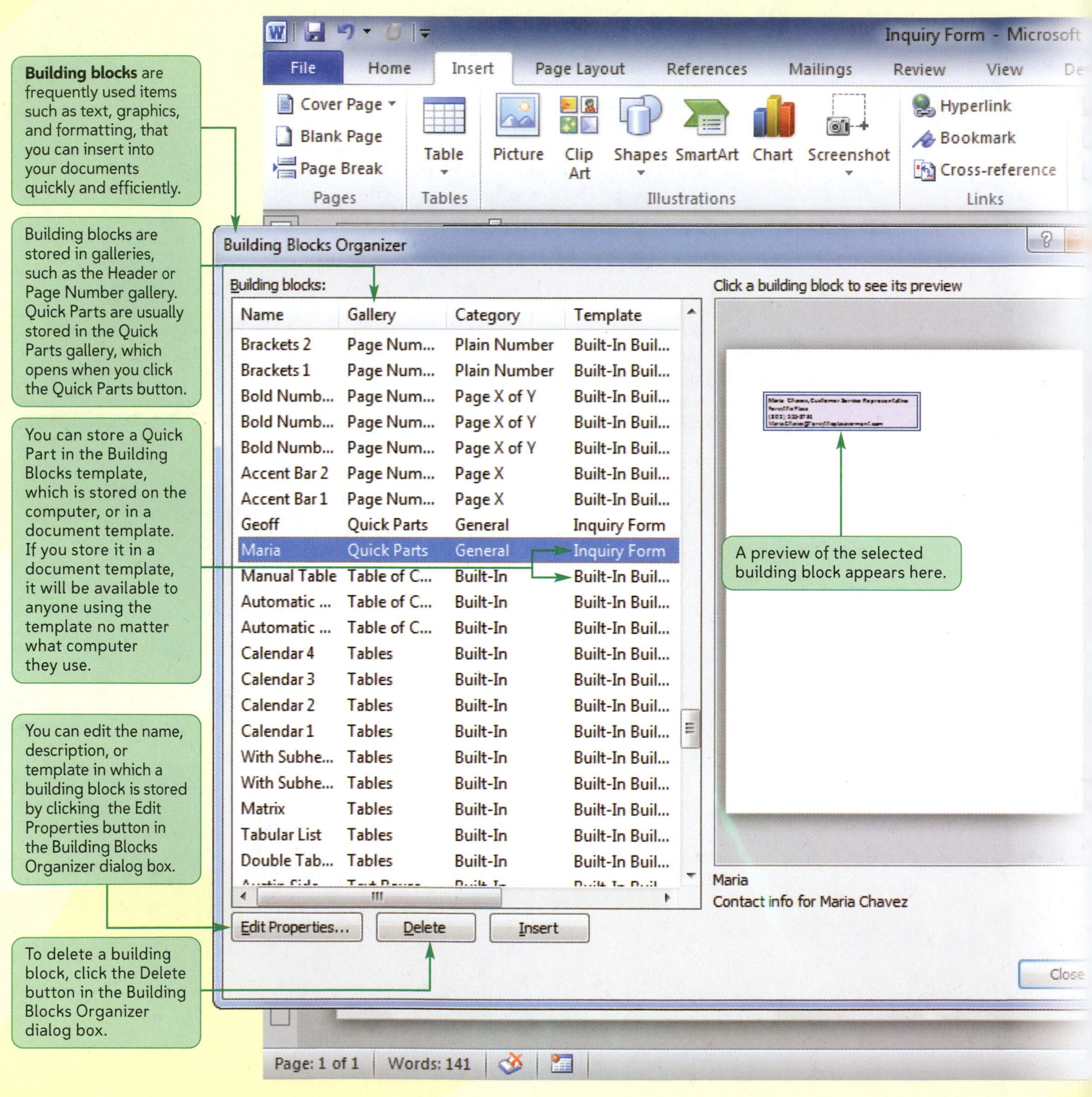

BUILDING BLOCKS

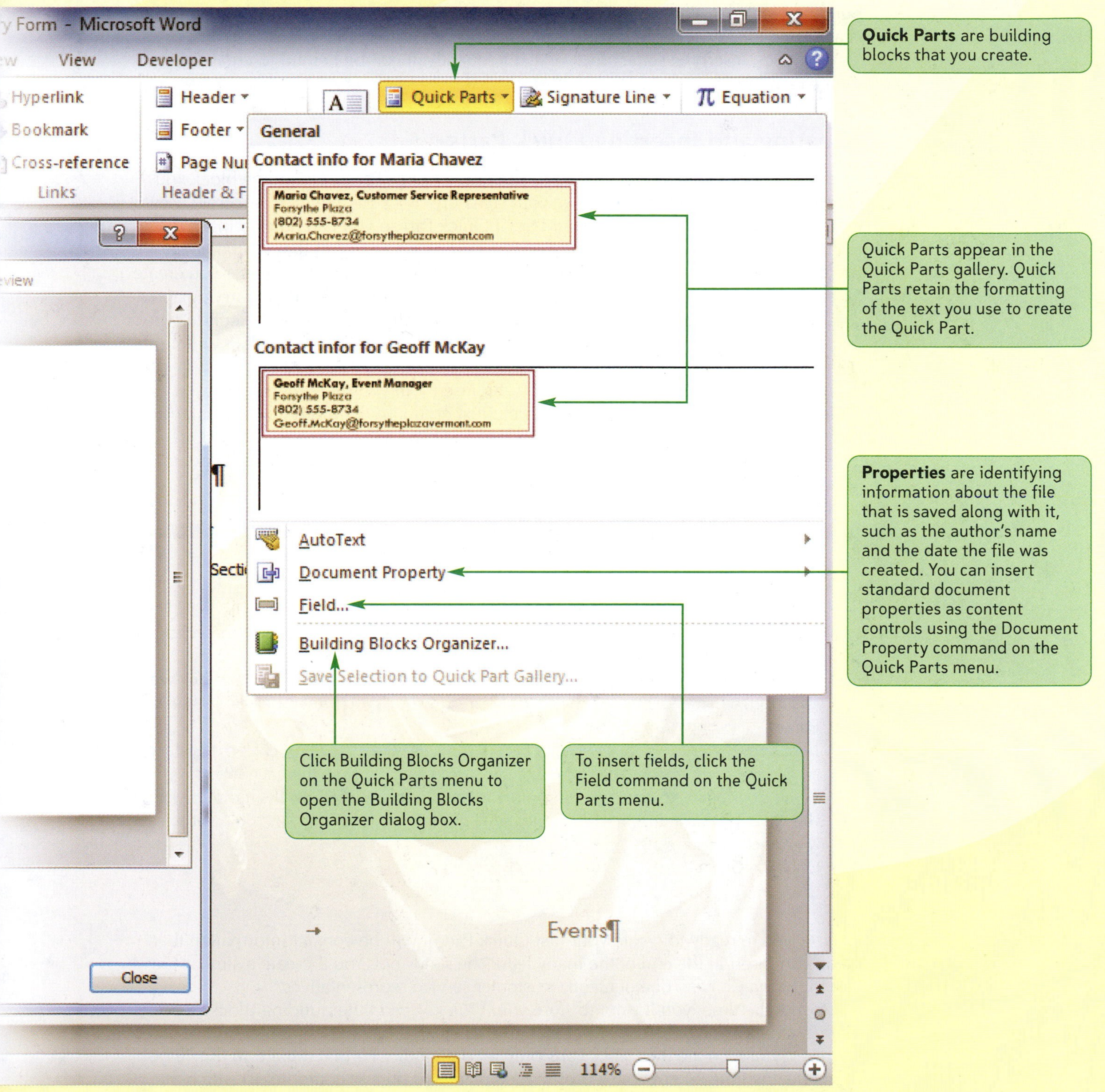
y Form - Microsoft Word
View
Developer
Hyperlink
Bookmark
Cross-reference
Links
Header
Footer
Page Nu
Header & F
Quick Parts
Signature Line
Equation
General
Contact info for Maria Chavez
Maria Chavez, Customer Service Representative
Forsythe Plaza
(802) 555-8734
Maria.Chavez@forsytheplazavermont.com
Contact infor for Geoff McKay
Geoff McKay, Event Manager
Forsythe Plaza
(802) 555-8734
Geoff.McKay@forsytheplazavermont.com
AutoText
Document Property
Field...
Building Blocks Organizer...
Save Selection to Quick Part Gallery...
Close
Events¶
114%
Quick Parts are building blocks that you create.
Quick Parts appear in the Quick Parts gallery. Quick Parts retain the formatting of the text you use to create the Quick Part.
Properties are identifying information about the file that is saved along with it, such as the author's name and the date the file was created. You can insert standard document properties as content controls using the Document Property command on the Quick Parts menu.
Click Building Blocks Organizer on the Quick Parts menu to open the Building Blocks Organizer dialog box.
To insert fields, click the Field command on the Quick Parts menu.

Automating Tasks with Building Blocks

Word has many predesigned building blocks for a wide variety of items, including cover pages, calendars, numbering, text boxes, and more. You've already used some of them, probably without realizing that they are building blocks. For example, on the Insert tab, when you click the Header or Footer button, the predesigned choices in the gallery are building blocks. Building blocks are stored in the global Building Blocks template, which is available to all Word documents.

When you insert the same block of text frequently, it can be helpful to create a Quick Part.

Creating and Inserting Quick Parts

As described in the Session 8.2 Visual Overview, a Quick Part is a building block you create. For example, you might make your signature block for a letter ("Sincerely," several blank lines, your name, and your title) a Quick Part so you can quickly insert that text without typing it every time; or, you might create a Quick Part that is a company name and logo. Two advantages of Quick Parts are speed and accuracy. After you create an error-free Quick Part, you can easily insert it into documents without worrying about creating spelling or typographical errors. This is especially valuable for difficult-to-type text such as phone numbers, serial numbers, email addresses, or other words and numbers not in the Word dictionary.

Once you've created a Quick Part, you can insert it in your documents. To insert a Quick Part, use the Quick Parts button in the Text group on the Insert tab. You can use the same button to access the various built-in building blocks that come with Word.

In Geoff's Inquiry Form template, you'll create Quick Parts to insert formatted contact information for Geoff and another employee.

REFERENCE

Creating a Quick Part

- Select the text or graphics you want to be a Quick Part.
- Click the Insert tab, click the Quick Parts button in the Text group, and then click Save Selection to Quick Part Gallery.
- In the Create New Building Block dialog box, replace the text in the Name box with a descriptive name for the Quick Part, if desired, to help you remember what the Quick Part is.
- If you don't want to save the Quick Part in the Quick Parts gallery, click the Gallery arrow, and then choose the gallery to which you want to save the Quick Part.
- If you don't want to save the Quick Part to the global Building Blocks template, click the Save in arrow, and then click the name of the template in which you want to save the Quick Parts.
- Click the OK button.

Now you're ready to create your first Quick Part; it will be contact information that Geoff can insert at the end of the many letters he sends out. You'll create a similar Quick Part for Maria Chavez, one of Geoff's customer service representatives.

Most of the time, you'll want to store your Quick Parts in the Building Blocks template, so that they can be used in all documents created on your computer. In this case, however, you'll create the Quick Parts only for the Inquiry Form template so they'll be available any time an employee uses the template and on any computer to which the template is copied. In addition, by saving the Quick Part to the template, you'll leave the Normal template unchanged, which is important if you are using a computer in a lab.

You must use the Open dialog box to open the template itself.

To create the text for Geoff's contact information:

1. If you took a break after the last session, click the **File** tab, click **Open** in the navigation pane, navigate to the Word8\Tutorial folder included with your Data Files, click **Inquiry Form**, and then click the **Open** button.
2. Make sure that the ruler and paragraph marks are displayed.
3. Move to the bottom of the document, and then in the blank paragraph below the last line type the following:

   Geoff McKay, Event Manager

   Forsythe Plaza

   (802) 555-8734

   Geoff.McKay@forsytheplazavermont.com
4. Select all four lines of text, apply the **No Spacing** style, select **Geoff McKay, Event Manager**, change the font size to **12** points, and then apply **bold** formatting.
5. Select the four lines again, click the **Border button arrow** in the Paragraph group, click **Borders and Shading**, and then in the Setting list on the left of the Borders tab, click the **Box** button.
6. In the Style group, click the **down arrow** 10 times, select the bottom style (a double line consisting of a thick line above a thin line), click the **Color** arrow, and then click the **Pink, Accent 1, Darker 25%** color (fifth row, fifth column).
7. Click the **Shading** tab, click the **Fill** arrow, and then click the **Gold, Accent 4, Lighter 80%** color (eighth color in the second row). The Preview box shows a pale yellow fill color.
8. Click the **OK** button. The dialog box closes, and the four lines of text have a border around them and are shaded with pale gold.
9. With the four lines of text selected, drag the **Right Indent** marker on the ruler to the 3.5-inch mark. The right border of the paragraph is indented to the 3.5-inch mark, as shown in Figure 8-15.

Figure 8-15 Formatted contact information

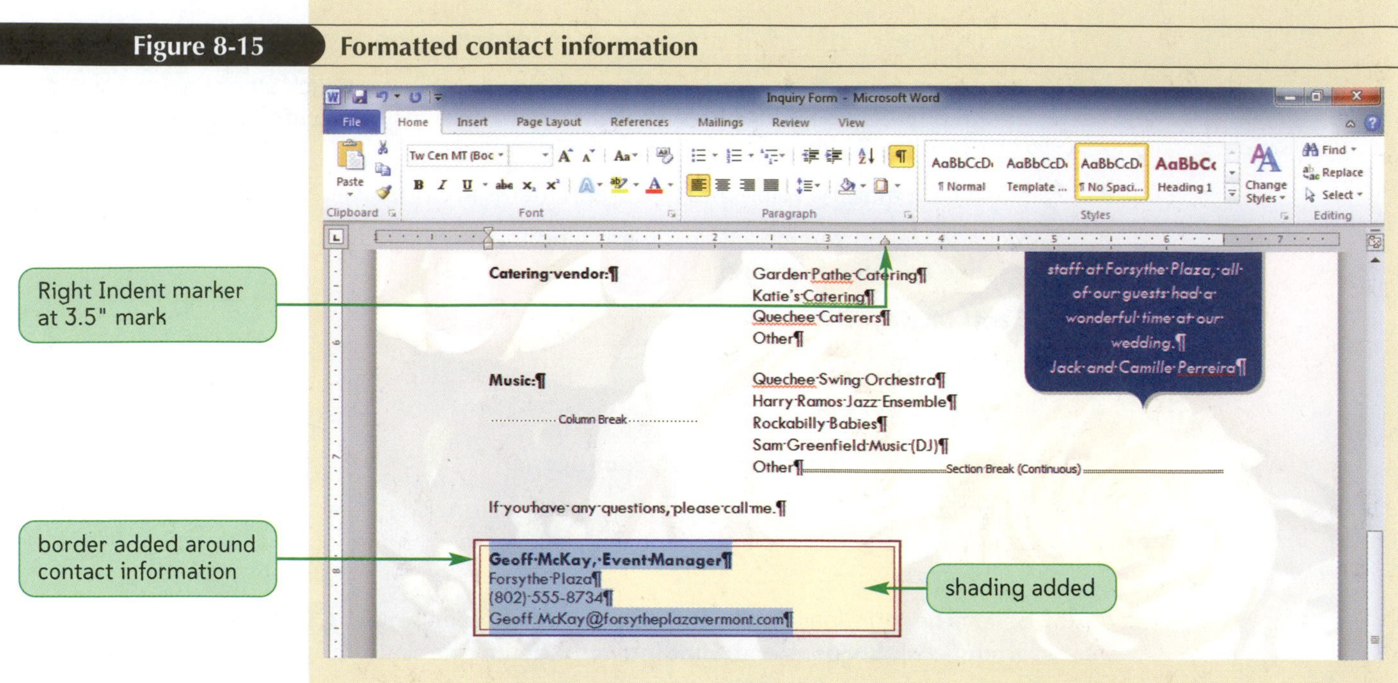

Now that you've inserted and formatted the text, you can save it as a Quick Part.

To create the Quick Part:

1. With the four lines of text selected, click the **Insert** tab, click the **Quick Parts** button in the Text group, and then click **Save Selection to Quick Part Gallery**. The Create New Building Block dialog box opens.
2. In the **Name** box, delete "McKay," so that the contents of the Name box is "Geoff." See Figure 8-16. Because this document is a template, the default location for this Quick Part is in the document template, as indicated by the name in the Save in box. The default gallery is the Quick Parts gallery.

Figure 8-16 Create New Building Block dialog box with new Quick Part name

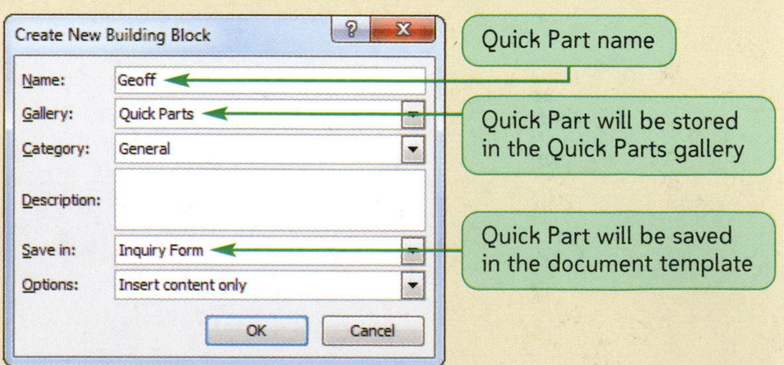

3. Click the **OK** button. You'll also create a Quick Part for another employee, Maria Chavez, who is a Customer Service Representative.
4. In the document, replace "Geoff McKay, Event Manager" with **Maria Chavez, Customer Service Representative**, and then replace "Geoff.McKay" in the email address with **Maria.Chavez**.

5. Select the four lines surrounded by the border, and then click the **Quick Parts** button in the Text group. The Quick Part named Geoff appears at the top of the Quick Parts gallery. See Figure 8-17.

Figure 8-17 Quick Part on Quick Parts menu

Quick Part added to Quick Parts gallery

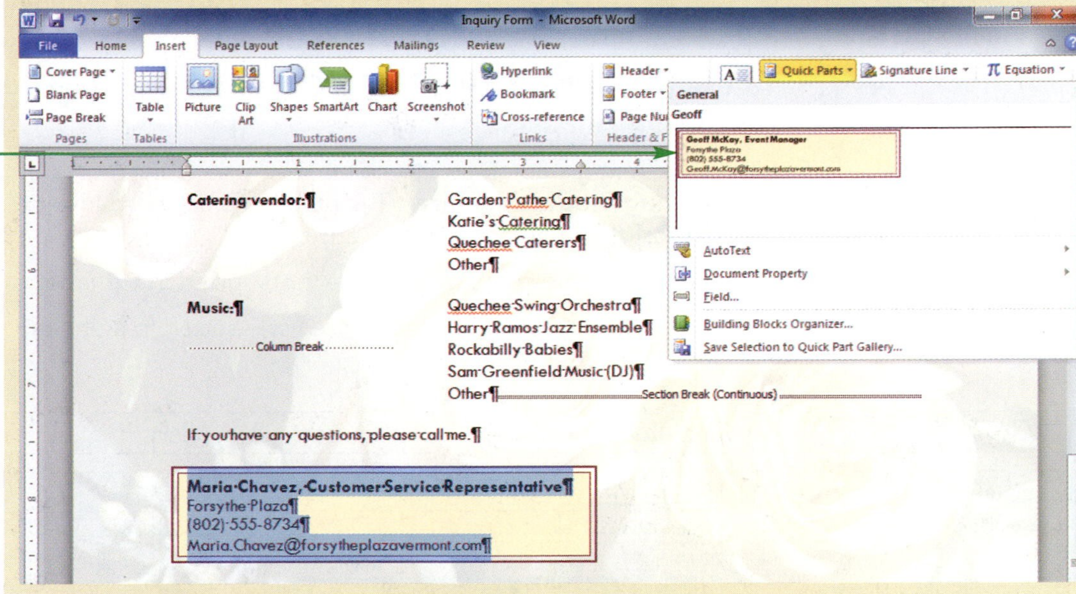

6. Click **Save Selection to Quick Part Gallery**, change the text in the Name box to **Maria**, and then click the **OK** button. Now two Quick Parts are saved in the template.

You should test one of the Quick Parts you created for this template to make sure it works properly.

TIP

To quickly insert a Quick Part that appears on the Quick Parts menu, place the insertion point where you want the Quick Part inserted, type the Quick Part name, and then press the F3 key.

To test Geoff's new signature Quick Part:

1. Delete the four lines of text surrounded by the border, and then create a blank paragraph below the last line of text in the document, if necessary.
2. In the Text group, click the **Quick Parts** button. The two Quick Parts you created appear at the top of the Quick Parts gallery in alphabetical order.
3. Click the **Geoff** Quick Part. Geoff's formatted information appears at the location of the insertion point.
4. Save your changes.

The Quick Part works as it should.

Managing Building Blocks

Geoff would like you to look at all the building blocks available in Word to see if there are some that he could be using to save time as he creates documents for Forsythe Plaza. You can see a list of all the building blocks in the global Building Blocks template by opening the Building Blocks Organizer dialog box. If you have a template open when you open the Building Blocks Organizer, any building blocks that are part of that template will also be listed. With the Building Blocks Organizer dialog box, you can sort the building blocks in various ways. You can also use the Building Blocks Organizer to insert a building block into the document, edit the properties of a building block, or delete a building block.

Geoff would like you to explore the Building Blocks Organizer and then modify the two Quick Parts you created for him earlier.

To examine the Building Blocks Organizer and then edit the properties for the Quick Parts:

1. In the Text group on the Insert tab, click the **Quick Parts** button, and then click **Building Blocks Organizer**. The Building Blocks Organizer dialog box opens. You can sort the building blocks by any column.
2. Click the **Name** column head. The list is sorted in alphabetical order by name.
3. Click the **Gallery** column head. The list is sorted in alphabetical order by gallery. See Figure 8-18.

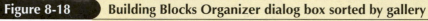

Figure 8-18 Building Blocks Organizer dialog box sorted by gallery

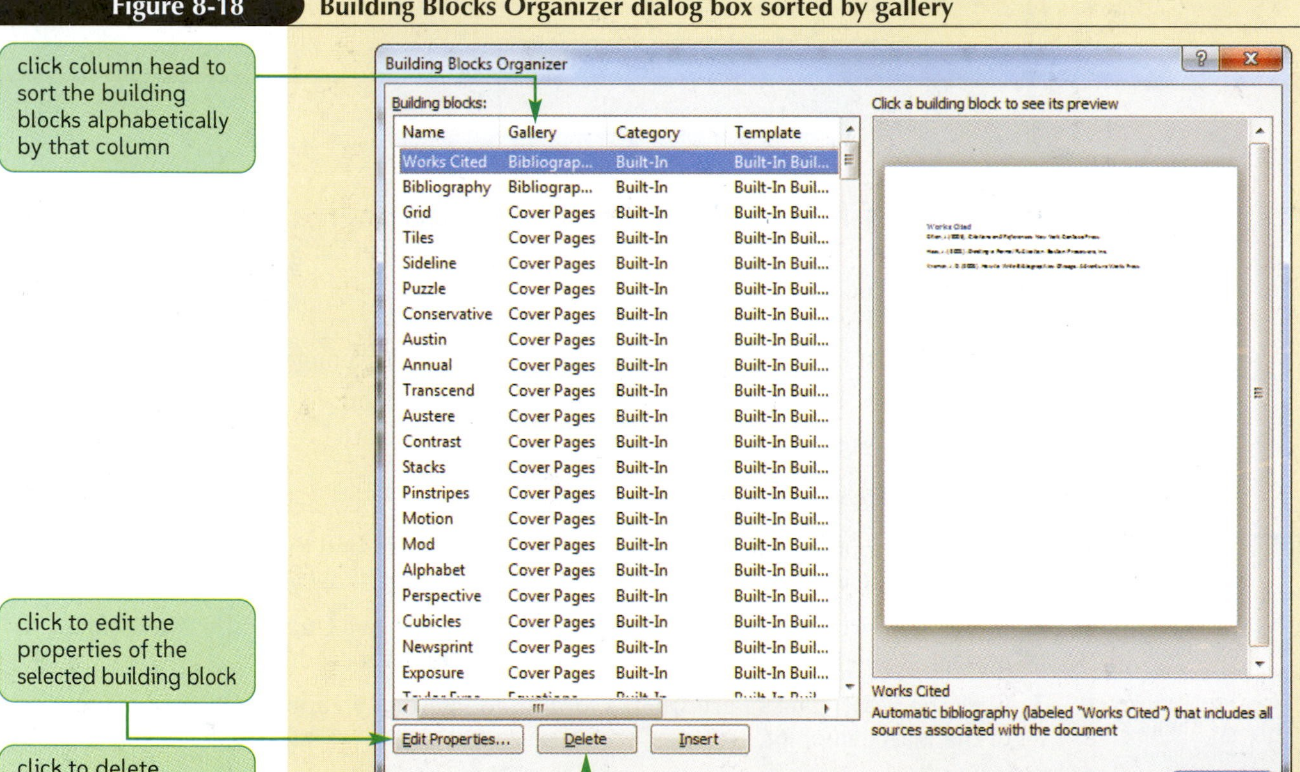

TIP

You can insert any building block from the Building Blocks Organizer dialog box by selecting it and then clicking the Insert button.

4. Scroll down until you see the two entries in the Quick Parts gallery, click the **Geoff** building block, and then click the **Edit Properties** button. The Modify Building Block dialog box opens. It is identical to the Create New Building Block dialog box.
5. Click in the **Description** box, type **Contact info for Geoff McKay**, and then click the **OK** button. A dialog box opens asking if you want to redefine the building block entry.
6. Click the **Yes** button.

7. In the list of building blocks, scroll down until you see the two entries in the Quick Parts gallery, click the **Maria** Quick Part, click the **Edit Properties** button, click in the Description box, type **Contact info for Maria Chavez**, click the **OK** button, and then click the **Yes** button. The properties for both Quick Parts that you created have been updated.
8. In the Building Blocks Organizer dialog box, click the **Close** button.
9. Save your changes.

INSIGHT

Organizing Building Blocks Using Categories

Another way to organize building blocks is to use categories. When you open the Create New Building Block dialog box, you can click the Category arrow, and then click Create New Category to open the Create New Category dialog box. Type a category name, and then click the OK button. You can sort the building blocks in the Building Blocks Organizer dialog box by category to help you keep track of Quick Parts you create.

Next, you'll learn how to customize the Word AutoCorrect feature.

Customizing AutoCorrect

Recall that Word's AutoCorrect feature corrects certain spelling and typographical errors as you type, such as correcting letter transposition errors ("adn" to "and"), capitalizing a sentence that begins with a lowercase letter, and correcting two initial capital letters ("PHotography" to "Photography"). You can customize AutoCorrect by adding words that you frequently misspell or mistype to the AutoCorrect list. For example, Geoff frequently mistypes the word "Forsythe" as "Frosythe," so he wants this misspelling added to the AutoCorrect list.

Sometimes AutoCorrect makes unwanted corrections. For example, the default setting "Capitalize first letter of sentences" capitalizes any word that follows a period, exclamation point, or question mark. This is usually a good thing. But because Forsythe Plaza is owned by a larger corporation called Diamond Luxury Properties, Ltd., the next word following "Ltd." should not always be capitalized. Geoff would like you to create an exception to the "Capitalize the first letter of sentences" rule so that he can type "Ltd." without the next word being capitalized automatically. To set this exception, you need to add "Ltd." to the Exceptions list in the AutoCorrect dialog box.

REFERENCE

Customizing AutoCorrect

- Click the File tab, and then click Options to open the Word Options dialog box.
- In the list on the left, click Proofing, click the AutoCorrect Options button, and then click the AutoCorrect tab in the AutoCorrect dialog box.
- Select or deselect the check boxes on the tab to set AutoCorrect options.
- To add an entry to the AutoCorrect list at the bottom of the dialog box, click in the Replace box, type the misspelling you want to add, click in the With box, type the correct spelling, and then click the Add button.
- To remove an entry from the AutoCorrect list, click the entry, and then click the Delete button.
- To add an exception to the AutoCorrect rules, click the Exceptions button to open the AutoCorrect Exceptions dialog box, click the appropriate tab, type the exception, click the Add button, and then click the OK button.
- To delete an exception, click the exception in the list in the AutoCorrect Exceptions dialog box, click the Delete button, and then click the OK button.
- Click the OK button in the AutoCorrect dialog box, and then click the OK button in the Word Options dialog box.

You'll customize the AutoCorrect options next.

To create an AutoCorrect entry and add an Exception:

1. Click the **File** tab, click **Options** in the navigation bar to open the Word Options dialog box, and then click **Proofing** in the list on the left. The Word Options dialog box shows proofing options.
2. Click the **AutoCorrect Options** button. The AutoCorrect: English (U.S.) dialog box opens with the AutoCorrect tab selected. See Figure 8-19. You use the check boxes on this tab to set the AutoCorrect options. Commonly misspelled or mistyped words are listed alphabetically in the box at the bottom of the tab. The correct spellings that AutoCorrect inserts in the document when you press the Enter key appear on the right side of the list. The first few items listed in the box are not misspellings but characters that represent a symbol. If you type the sequence of characters, AutoCorrect automatically inserts the symbol in place of the characters.

Figure 8-19 AutoCorrect tab in the AutoCorrect: English (U.S.) dialog box

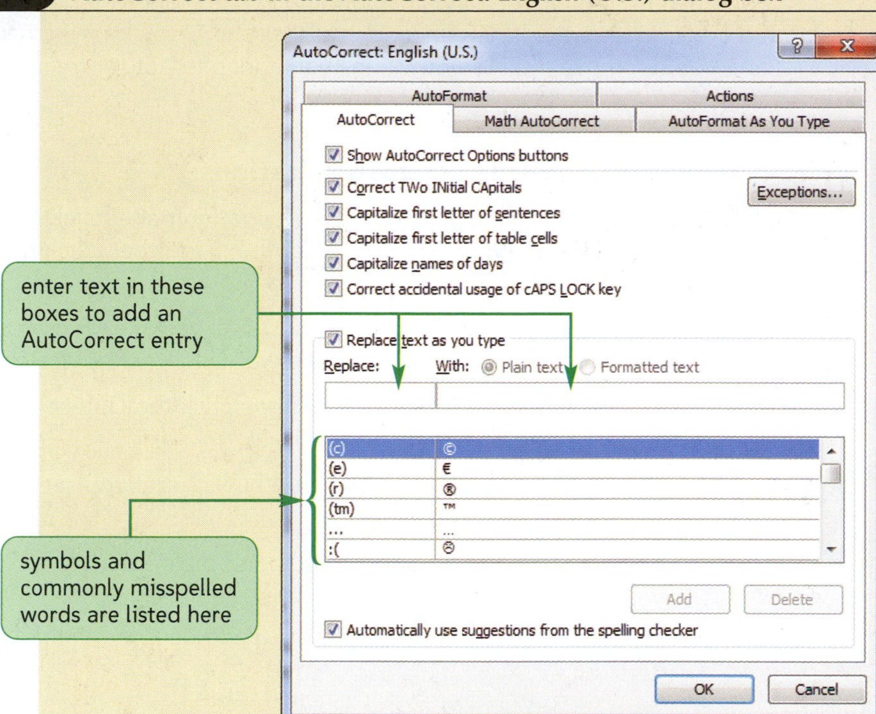

3. Click in the **Replace** box, and then type **Frosythe**.
4. Click in the **With** box, type **Forsythe**, and then click the **Add** button. The misspelling is added to the list. The check boxes at the top of the tab control the AutoCorrect options. The third option is the one that controls the automatic capitalization of words after end-of-sentence punctuation marks.
5. Click the **Exceptions** button in the AutoCorrect dialog box to open the AutoCorrect Exceptions dialog box with the First Letter tab selected. Here you'll type the text you want as an exception to the Capitalize first letter of sentences rule.
6. Type **Ltd.** in the Don't capitalize after box, and then click the **Add** button. The word "Ltd." is added to the list of exceptions in the AutoCorrect Exceptions dialog box so that when Geoff types "Ltd.", AutoCorrect won't capitalize the following word.
7. Click the **OK** button in the AutoCorrect Exceptions dialog box, and then click the **OK** button in the AutoCorrect dialog box. The dialog boxes close and AutoCorrect is customized with your changes.
8. Click the **OK** button in the Word Options dialog box. Now you'll insert text using the customized AutoCorrect entry and exception.
9. Scroll up until you can see the paragraph under the heading "Customer Inquiry Form—Wedding," select **our facility** in the first line, type **Frosythe**, and then press the **spacebar**. The word you typed autocorrects to "Forsythe."
10. Type **Plaza (a Diamond Luxury Properties, Ltd. company)**. The word "company" does not change to "Company" even though it is the first word after a period because "Ltd." was added to the exceptions list.
11. Save your changes to the template.

Generally, AutoCorrect entries are short and are not formatted. Also, keep in mind that AutoCorrect corrections happen automatically once you add them to the AutoCorrect list. You need to undo them as you're working if you decide you don't want the correction to occur in a particular instance.

Now you'll remove the customizations you added to AutoCorrect.

To remove the AutoCorrect customizations:

1. Click the **File** tab, click **Options** in the navigation pane, click **Proofing** in the list on the left of the Word Options dialog box, and then click the **AutoCorrect Options** button.
2. Scroll down the list of AutoCorrect entries until you see "Frosythe." (Note that the list is sorted in alphabetical order by the words in the Replace column.)
3. Click **Frosythe** to select that entry, and then click the **Delete** button. The entry you added is deleted.
4. Click the **Exceptions** button, scroll down the list until you see ltd., click **ltd.**, and then click the **Delete** button.
5. Click the **OK** button in each of the three open dialog boxes.

Next Geoff asks you to add properties to the file to describe the document.

Working with File Properties

When you save a file, the file properties are saved with it. You can use properties to organize documents based on specific properties or to search for files that have specific properties.

Some content controls are linked to document properties so that the controls "pick up" and display the property information. For example, if you insert a header that includes a Title content control in your document, that control is automatically tied to the Title document property, and if you have specified a Title document property for the document, it displays in the Title content control in the header. The connection works both ways, so that if you change the Title document property the change will appear in every Title content control in the document.

Adding Document Properties

To add properties, you need to display the Info tab in Backstage view. Geoff wants you to add yourself as a document author and Forsythe Plaza as the Company property. He also wants you to add a title property and tags, which are keywords that help identify the document on your computer. Finally, he wants you to add Draft as the Status property.

To add document properties on the Info tab:

1. Click the **File** tab, and then click the **Info** tab in the navigation pane, if necessary. The Info tab displays the document properties in the right pane. See Figure 8-20. When a document is created, the Author property is picked up from the User name box in the Word Options dialog box. Because Geoff created the original document, his name is listed as the Author. The name in the Last Modified By box below the Author box is also picked up from the User name box in the Word Options dialog box. First, you'll add yourself as an author.

Figure 8-20 Info tab for the Inquiry Form template

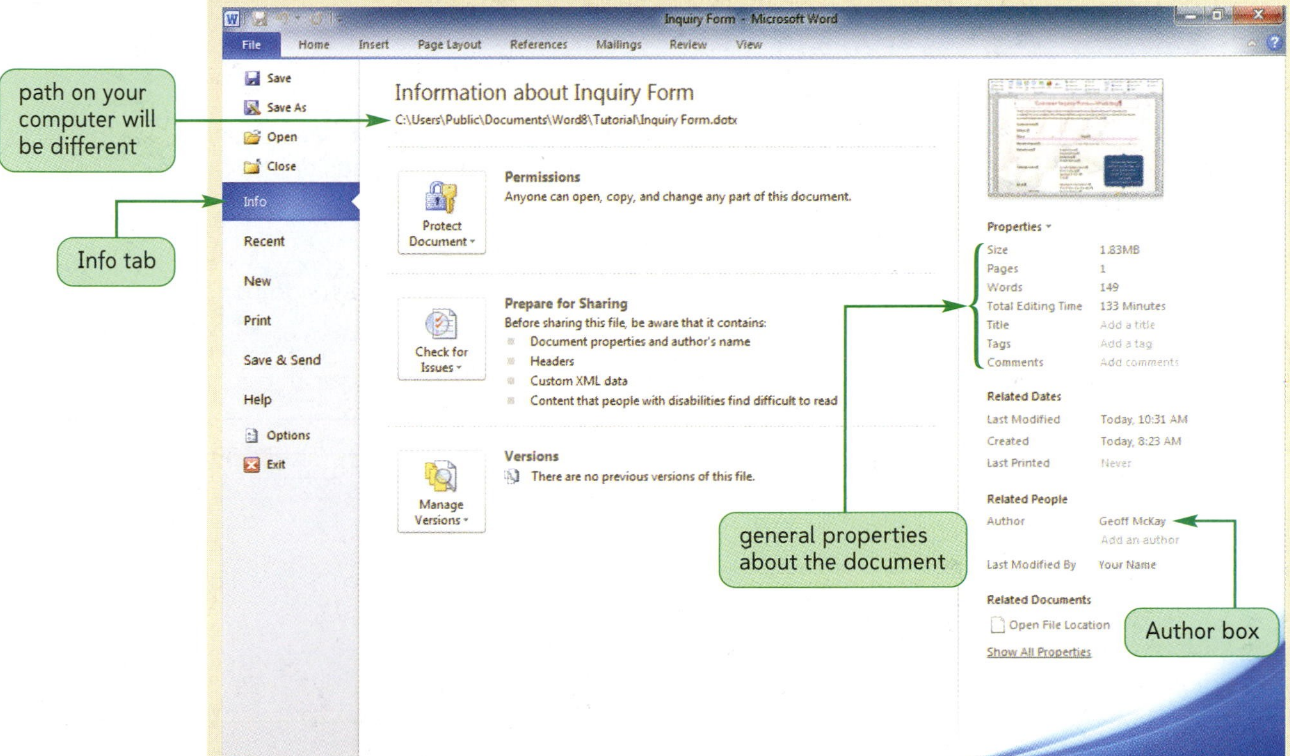

2. In the Related People section, click **Add an author**, type your name in the box that appears, and then click a blank area of the screen. You are added as an author.

   Trouble? If you pressed the Enter key after typing your name and the Check Names dialog box opened, click the Cancel button.

3. In the Properties section at the top of the right pane, click **Add a title**, and then type **Customer Inquiry Form** in the box that appears. The Title property is not the same as the filename. The title you insert here appears in any Title controls you insert in the template, and it would appear in the title bar of a browser if you saved the document as a Web page.
4. Click **Add a tag**, and then type **new customers, weddings, inquiry** in the box that appears. Now you need to add the Status and Company properties. These properties are not currently visible.
5. At the bottom of the right pane, click the **Show All Properties** link. The list in the right pane expands to include all of the document properties.

6. In the Properties section at the top of the right pane, click **Add text** next to Status, type **Draft**, click **Specify the company** next to Company, and then type **Forsythe Plaza**.

   Trouble? If a company name appears in the box next to Company, delete it, and then type Forsythe Plaza.

Geoff decides he would like you to indicate that this template was created by the Events department at Forsythe Plaza. The Department property is not listed on the Info tab. To add this property, you need to open the Properties dialog box for the template, and then add the property on the Custom tab.

To add a custom document property:

1. At the top of the right pane, click **Properties**, and then click **Advanced Properties**. The Inquiry Form Properties dialog box opens.
2. Click the **Summary** tab. The Title, Author, Company, and Keywords boxes reflect the changes you made on the Info tab.
3. Click the **Custom** tab. See Figure 8-21. This tab lists additional properties you can add.

Figure 8-21 Custom tab in the Inquiry Form Properties dialog box

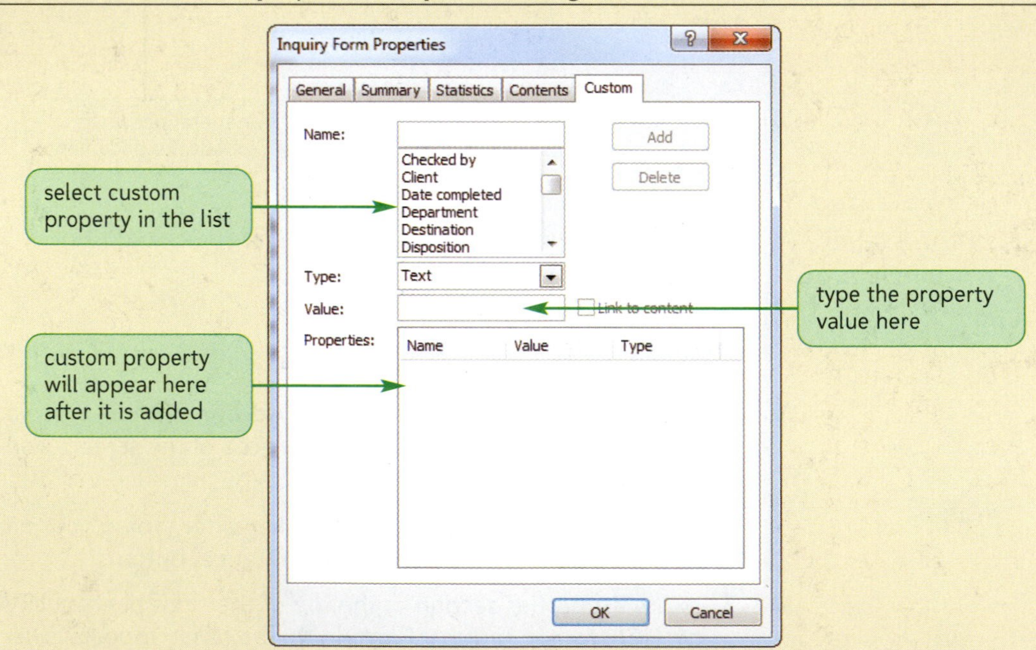

4. In the Name list near the top of the dialog box, click **Department**. "Department" appears in the Name box above the list.
5. Click in the **Value** box, type **Events**, and then click the **Add** button. "Department" and the value you gave it appear in the Properties list.
6. Click the **OK** button. The dialog box closes.
7. Click the **File** tab to close Backstage view, and then save your changes.

TIP

To create a new property, type its name in the Name box, and then click the Add button.

The properties you inserted will make it easy for Geoff to organize and locate files based on these properties, and now he won't have to insert text into content controls that are linked to these properties.

Inserting Document Properties into the Template

When you send the Inquiry Form template to Geoff's manager at Diamond Luxury Properties, Geoff wants you to indicate that the document is a draft. You could use the built-in Draft watermark, but that would remove the picture he inserted as a watermark. Instead you'll insert into the footer the document property that holds this information. The standard document properties are listed in a submenu on the Quick Parts menu, so you can insert it from there. When you insert a document property from the Quick Parts menu, you insert it as a content control.

To insert a document property as a Quick Part:

1. Click the **Insert** tab (if necessary), click the **Footer** button in the Header & Footer group, and then click **Edit Footer**. The footer area in the document becomes active, and the Header & Footer Tools Design tab is active on the Ribbon.
2. Click the **Insert** tab, click the **Quick Parts** button in the Text group, and then point to **Document Property**. A submenu of many of the document properties opens. See Figure 8-22.

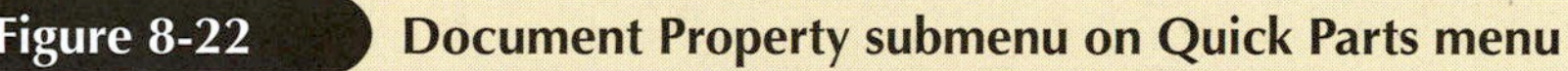

Figure 8-22 Document Property submenu on Quick Parts menu

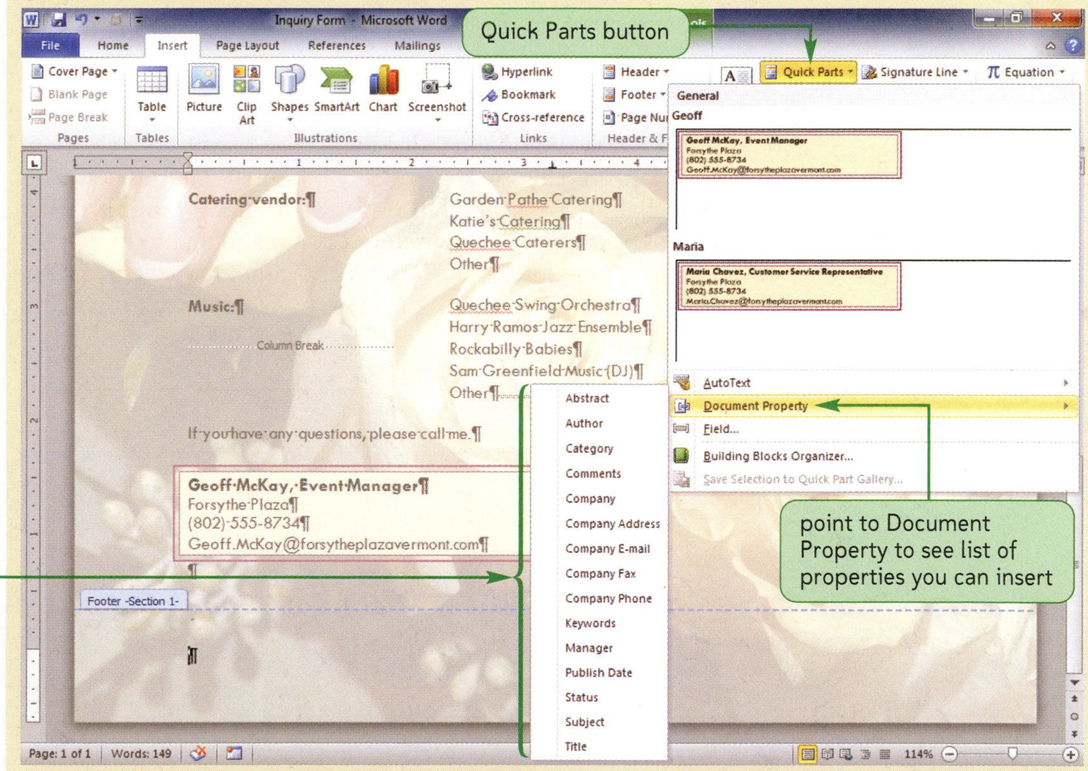

3. Click **Status**. A content control labeled Status appears in the footer with "Draft" in it.

Now, you want to insert the Department property, but that property does not appear on the Document Property submenu on the Quick Parts menu. To insert this custom property, you'll need to insert it as a field.

Automating Documents Using Fields

Using fields is a powerful method for automating a document. As you recall from completing the Mail Merge process, a field is a special code that instructs Word to insert information that might change into a document. Word provides many fields that you can insert. When you learned how to insert the current date and kept the Update automatically check box selected, you actually inserted a field. Figure 8-23 lists common fields that you can include in documents.

Figure 8-23 Common fields

Field	Code (Example)	Action
Date	{DATE \@ "MMMM d, yyyy"}	Inserts the current date/time according to a date-time picture
Fill-in	{FILLIN "Your name?" * MERGEFORMAT}	Inserts information filled in by the user
NumPages	{NUMPAGES}	Inserts the total number of pages in the document
Page	{PAGE}	Inserts the current page number
Ref	{REF BookmarkName}	Inserts the contents of the specified bookmark

When you insert a field into a document, the corresponding field code includes the name of the field and optional instructions and switches, which are enclosed in braces { } (also called French brackets or curly brackets). An **instruction** is a word or phrase that specifies what the field should do, such as display a **prompt**, which is a phrase that tells the user how to proceed. A **switch** is a command that follows *, \#, \@, or \! and turns on or off certain features of the field. For example, a switch can specify how the result of the field is formatted. Figure 8-24 shows a field code that contains a field name, instructions, and a switch.

Figure 8-24 Components of a field code

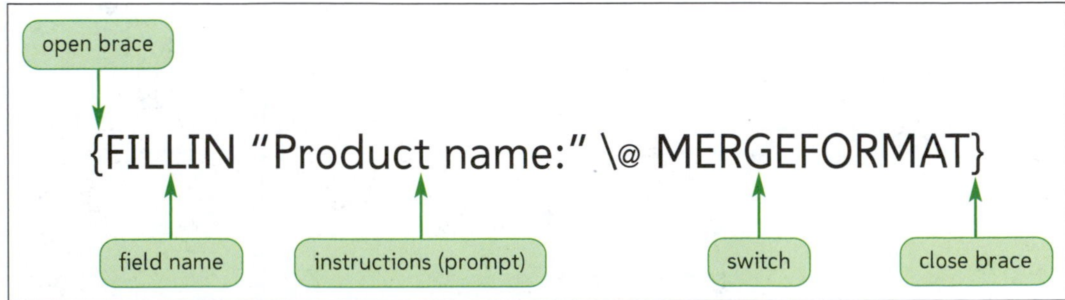

The field name, FILLIN, specifies that this field asks the user to supply (fill in) some information. The instruction is a prompt (Product name:) that tells the user what to type. The switch (\@ MERGEFORMAT) specifies that the field's result (the user fill-in information) should retain any formatting applied to the field even if the user fills in new information. All field codes must include braces and a field name, but not all field codes include instructions and switches.

Inserting a Custom Property Using the Field Dialog Box

One of the things you can insert as a field is a custom file property. When you inserted the Status property, you actually inserted a field—you just used a shortcut method provided by Word for inserting the common file properties. The Department property is a custom property, so to insert it in the footer, you need to insert it using the Fields dialog box. You'll do this now.

TIP

To see if a field has any switches available, click the Field Codes button in the Field dialog box to see the code, and then click the Options button that appears to see the available switches.

To insert a custom property as a field:

1. With the Status content control still selected, press the → key, and then press the **Tab** key twice to position the insertion point at the right margin in the footer.
2. In the Text group, click the **Quick Parts** button, and then click **Field**. The Field dialog box opens.
3. Click the **Categories** arrow, and then click **Document Information**. The Field names list is filtered to include only fields in the Document Information category.
4. In the Field names list, click **DocProperty**. The middle section of the dialog box changes to display options for the DocProperty field. See Figure 8-25.

Figure 8-25 Field dialog box

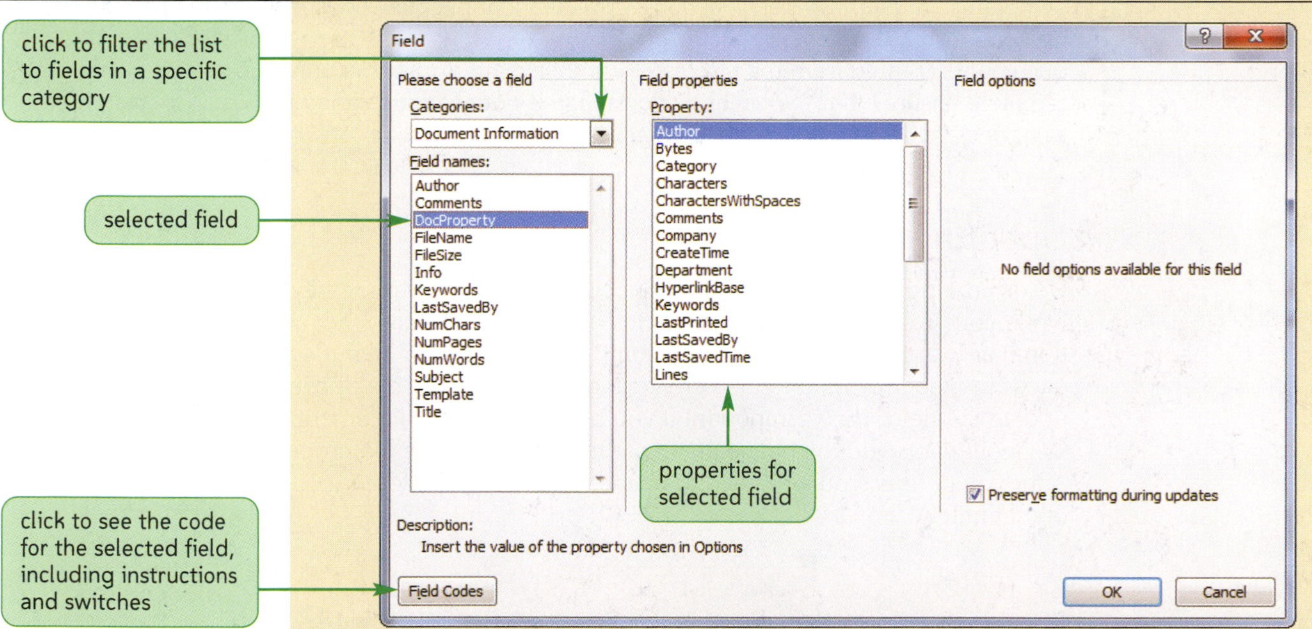

5. In the Property list, click **Department**, and then click the **OK** button. "Events," the Department property for the document, appears in the footer.

   Trouble? If you see the field code instead of the word "Events," click the File tab, click Options in the navigation bar, and then click Advanced in the list on the left. Scroll down to locate the Show document content section, click the Show field codes instead of their values check box to deselect it, and then click the OK button.

You'll examine the field code for the Department field now.

To examine field codes:

1. In the footer, right-click **Events**, and then click **Toggle Field Codes** on the shortcut menu. The field codes for the field you right-clicked appear instead of the content. The field code for the Department document property is { DOCPROPERTY Department * MERGEFORMAT }.
2. Right-click **Draft**. The Toggle Field Codes command is not on this shortcut menu because this is a content control, not a field, and although some content controls contain fields, this one does not. Notice that this shortcut menu does include the command Remove Content Control.
3. Right-click the field code for "Events" at the right margin in the footer, and then click **Toggle Field Codes**. The field codes are hidden, and you again see only the contents of the field.

Next, you'll insert the current date, examine the field code, and then revise its format.

PROSKILLS

Teamwork: Using Properties and Fields

Templates are helpful when you work with a team of people who all need to create similar documents. If you want specific document properties to be inserted by all users in the documents created from the template, using fields to display document properties in the template ensures that the needed information is not overlooked and is always inserted in each document. Keep this in mind if you need to create a template for use by a group.

Updating a Field

Fields are updated when you open a document, but sometimes they must be updated while you are working on a document to ensure they contain the most recent information. For example, if you insert the NumPages field, which identifies the total number of pages in a document, and then create additional pages in the document, you need to update the field. This is important if you plan to print the document before closing it.

Geoff wants you to change the department name in the file properties to Functions. After you do this, you will need to update the field in the footer to reflect the new value of that field.

To change the custom property and update the field:

1. Click the **File** tab. Backstage view appears with the Info tab selected.
2. At the top of the right pane, click **Properties**, and then click **Advanced Properties**. The Inquiry Form Properties dialog box opens with the Custom tab selected.
3. In the Properties box at the bottom of the dialog box, click **Departm...**, and then click the **Delete** button. The custom property is deleted from the list.
4. In the Name list, click **Department**, click in the Value box, type **Functions**, and then click the **Add** button. The new custom Department property appears in the Properties list.
5. Click the **OK** button, and then click the **File** tab. Now you need to update the property in the footer.
6. In the footer, right-click **Events**, and then click **Update Field** on the shortcut menu. The field is updated to reflect the change you made to the custom property.

TIP

To edit a field, right-click it, and then click Edit Field on the shortcut menu to open the Field dialog box.

Make sure you save your changes or you will lose all your work when you start the next set of steps.

7. Click the **Header & Footer Tools Design** tab, if necessary, and then click the **Close Header and Footer** button in the Close group. The footer area is no longer active.
8. Save your changes.

Next, you'll create a new template that uses the Fill-in field, making it easy for Geoff and his staff to modify the template for events other than weddings.

Inserting and Editing a Fill-In Field

The Fill-in field opens a dialog box that requests input from the user when the document is first opened. When you insert a Fill-in field, you type the text that will prompt the user for the required information.

Although Forsythe Plaza is very popular for weddings, it can also host other types of functions, such as company dinners, lectures, and retreats. Geoff has been working on an extensive advertising program to market the Plaza to corporations for business functions. He decided that he wants to print customized inquiry forms for various functions. To create a customizable form, he will start with the template you just created, and then remove the picture watermark and insert the Fill-in field to prompt the user to insert the new title.

Geoff would like you to insert a Fill-in field in place of the word "Wedding" in the boxed purple text at the top of the form. The field will prompt the user to insert the name for the type of event requested. First you need to save the file with a new name to create the new template.

To create a new template and insert a Fill-in field:

1. Click the **File** tab, click **Save As**, and then save the template as **General Inquiry** to the Word8\Tutorial folder included with your Data Files.
2. Click the **Page Layout** tab, click the **Watermark** button in the Page Background group, and then click **Remove Watermark**. The watermark is removed.
3. In the title "Customer Inquiry Form—Wedding", delete the word **Wedding**. You want the text in the title to be customized to reflect the type of event.
4. Click the **Insert** tab, click the **Quick Parts** button in the Text group, and then click **Field**. The Field dialog box opens.
5. Click the **Categories** arrow, and then click **(All)**. The Field names list now lists all available fields.
6. Scroll the list and then click Fill-in. You need to type the text that will appear as an instruction in the dialog box that opens when the document is opened.
7. Click in the **Prompt** box in the Field properties section of the dialog box, and then type **Enter type of function:** (with a colon at the end).
8. Click the **Preserve formatting during updates** check box to uncheck it. When this check box is checked, Word preserves any formatting that the user applies to the field; that is, if the user changes the format to, say, red italics, and the check box is checked, the red italics will appear when you update the field. If you clear this check box, Word will update the field information but retain the original formatting; that is, Word will clear the red italics.
9. Click the **OK** button. A Microsoft Office Word dialog box appears with the prompt you typed, "Enter type of function:". This is the dialog box that will appear when a document based on this template is first opened. Anything the user types in the box will appear at the location of the Fill-in field in the document. You want the

field to be empty in the template so that the user can enter the type of form each time a new document is created from the template, so you will close this dialog box without entering any text.

10. Click the **OK** button without entering any text. The dialog box closes. It looks as if there is no change in the document. The insertion point is blinking after the dash in the boxed purple text.
11. Right-click between the dash and the paragraph mark, and then click **Toggle Field Codes** on the shortcut menu. The Fill-in field code appears in the title. The Fill-in field code has no switch, but it does include the text you specified for the prompt. You can click anywhere in the field code to modify the prompt or to add a switch.
12. Right-click the Fill-in field code, and then click **Toggle Field Codes** to hide the field codes, and then save your changes.

When a Forsythe Plaza employee uses this template to create new queries, the template will provide a prompt to change the event title. You'll try this now to make sure it works.

To create a new document based on the template and add text to the Fill-in field:

1. Click the **File** tab, click **New** in the navigation bar, and then click **New from existing**.
2. In the New from Existing Document dialog box, click **General Inquiry**, and then click the **Create New** button. A new document is created based on the General Inquiry template, and the dialog box with the prompt "Enter type of function:" opens. See Figure 8-26.

Figure 8-26 New document created from the General Inquiry template

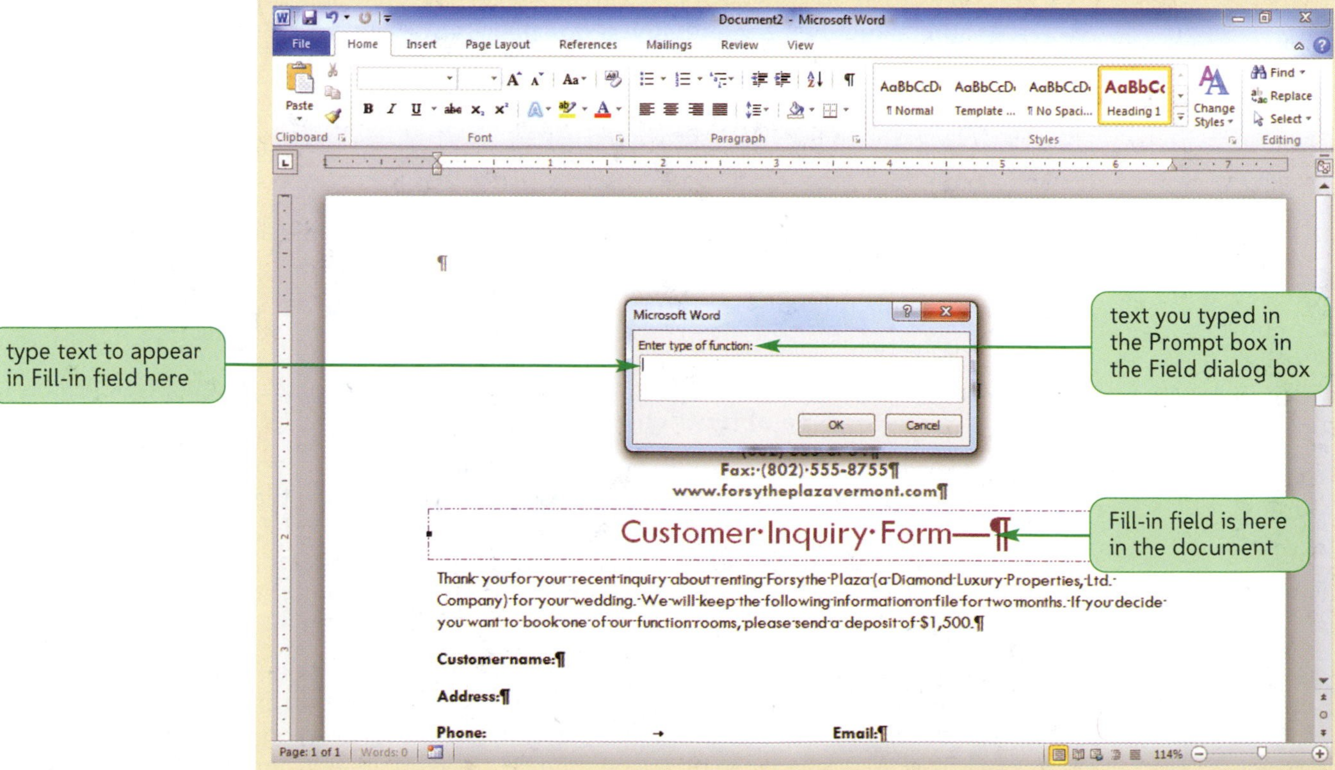

3. In the Enter type of function box, type **Graduation**, and then click the **OK** button. The dialog box closes and "Graduation" appears after the dash in the document's title.
4. Close the document without saving changes. The General Inquiry template is the active document again.

In addition to the fields you used, it is useful to be familiar with the fields described in Figure 8-27. These fields are all available in the Field dialog box.

Figure 8-27 **Useful fields**

Field	Description of inserted text
FileName	Name of the saved file
FileSize	Size of the file on disk
NumPages	Total number of pages
SaveDate	Date the document was last saved
UserInitials	User initials on the Popular page in the Word Options dialog box
UserName	User name on the Popular page in the Word Options dialog box

In the next session, you'll explore how to customize various Word Options settings, and you'll record a macro to help create a brochure for Geoff.

REVIEW

Session 8.2 Quick Check

1. What is a Quick Part?
2. How can you see all the available building blocks?
3. Define "exception" in the AutoCorrect feature.
4. How do you access document properties?
5. How do you update a field?
6. What symbol surrounds field codes?

SESSION 8.3 VISUAL OVERVIEW

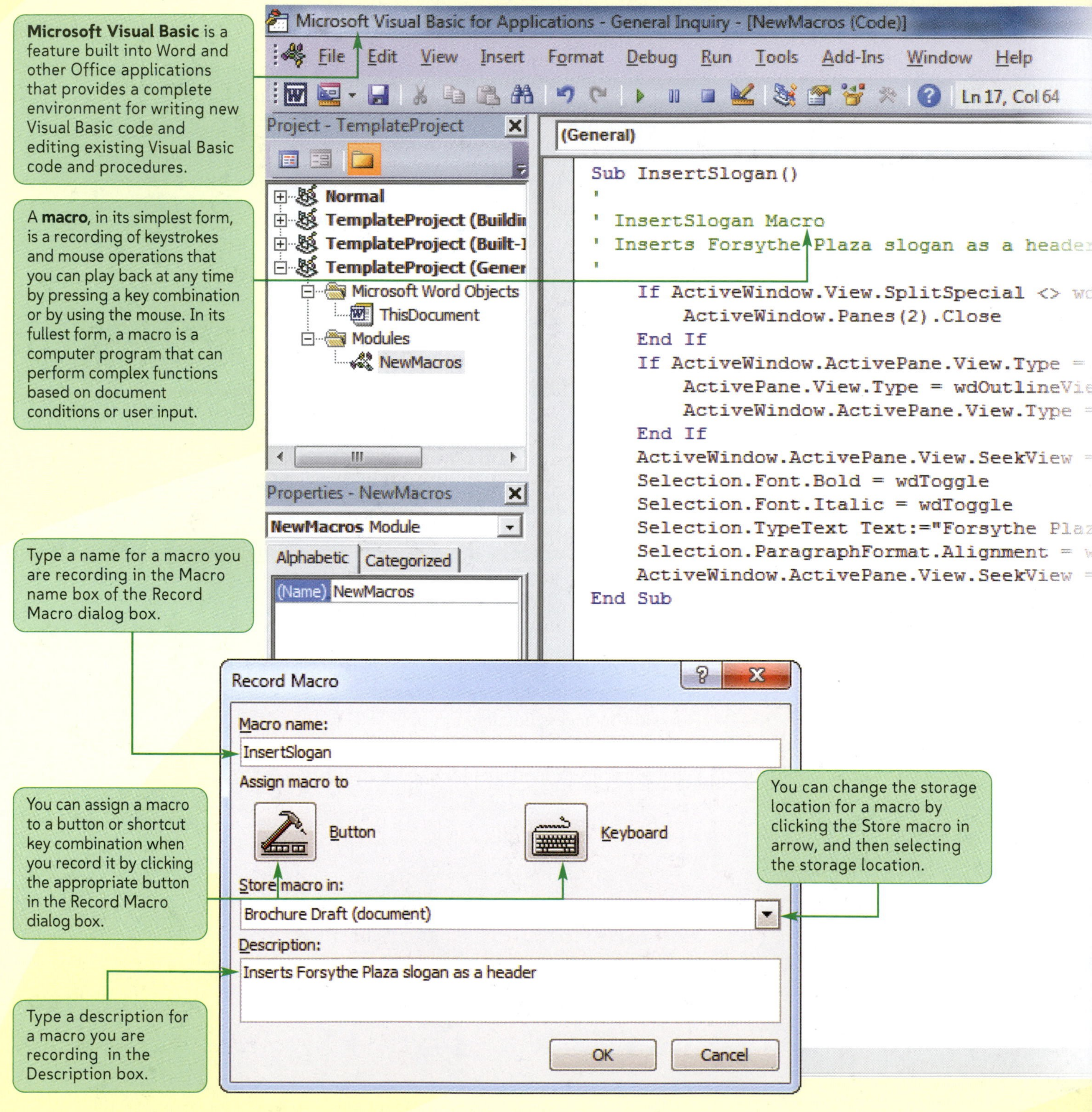

MACROS

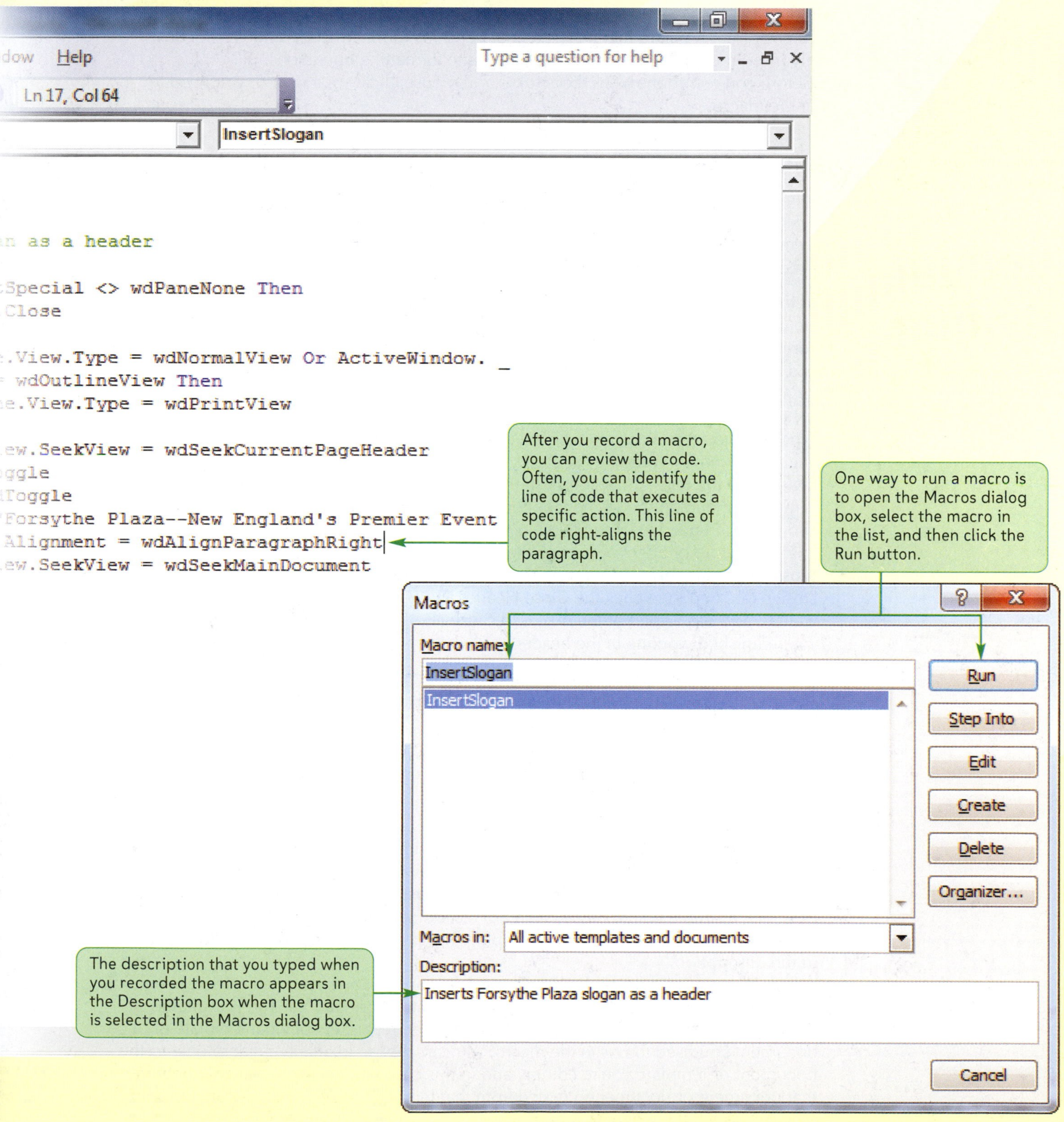
dow Help
Type a question for help
Ln 17, Col 64
InsertSlogan
n as a header
Special <> wdPaneNone Then
.Close
.View.Type = wdNormalView Or ActiveWindow. _
= wdOutlineView Then
e.View.Type = wdPrintView
ew.SeekView = wdSeekCurrentPageHeader
ggle
Toggle
'Forsythe Plaza--New England's Premier Event
.Alignment = wdAlignParagraphRight
ew.SeekView = wdSeekMainDocument
After you record a macro, you can review the code. Often, you can identify the line of code that executes a specific action. This line of code right-aligns the paragraph.
One way to run a macro is to open the Macros dialog box, select the macro in the list, and then click the Run button.
Macros
Macro name:
InsertSlogan
InsertSlogan
Run
Step Into
Edit
Create
Delete
Organizer...
Macros in:
All active templates and documents
Description:
Inserts Forsythe Plaza slogan as a header
Cancel
The description that you typed when you recorded the macro appears in the Description box when the macro is selected in the Macros dialog box.

Automating Word with Macros

Geoff has heard a great deal about macros and how they can help automate repetitive tasks. Using macros to run frequently executed commands has two main advantages. Combining a number of keystrokes and mouse operations into a macro saves time and helps you complete your work faster. Also, assuming you record a macro accurately—without typos or other mistakes—the keystrokes and mouse operations will always play back error-free. A macro that inserts text or performs formatting operations will consistently insert the same text and perform the same formatting operations.

Before you record the steps (keystrokes and mouse clicks) of a macro, you need to plan the macro.

Planning a Macro

Geoff wants you to create a macro that he can run to insert the company slogan into the header of a document. First, you'll plan the steps you'll be recording. Because you will be recording keystrokes and mouse clicks, you don't want to make an error when you are recording. To insert formatted text in the header, you need to:

- **Activate the header area**—To accomplish this, you'll click the Insert tab, click the Header button in the Header & Footer group, and then click Edit Header on the menu.
- **Turn on bold and italic formatting**—To accomplish this, you'll click the Home tab, and then click the Bold and Italic buttons in the Font group. By turning on the character formatting before you type the text, you save yourself the step of needing to select the text after you type it.
- **Type the text**—You'll simply type the slogan for the plaza, "Forsythe Plaza--New England's Premier Wedding Facility."
- **Right-align the text**—To accomplish this, you'll click the Align Text Right button in the Paragraph group on the Home tab. Because this is a paragraph formatting command and you don't need to do anything to select the current paragraph, you could perform this step before or after you type the text.
- **Close the header area**—To accomplish this, you'll click the Header & Footer Tools Design tab, and then click the Close Header and Footer button in the Close group. You want to add this as part of the macro because after you insert the text in the header, you're finished working in the header area.

Now that you have a plan, you can set up the recording in the Macros dialog box. In the Macros dialog box, you need to do the following:

- **Name the macro**—A macro name must begin with a letter and can contain a maximum of 80 letters and numbers; the name can't contain spaces, periods, or other punctuation (although you can use the underscore character). The macro name should summarize its function. For example, if you record a macro to resize a picture, you could name the macro "ResizePic."
- **Describe the macro (optional)**—You should provide a detailed description of a macro to help you recall its exact function. This is especially important if a macro performs a complex series of operations that can't be summarized in the macro name. For example, a simple macro name, such as PositionPicLeft, doesn't describe the picture features, such as borders and text wrapping. You could include that type of information in the description.
- **Attach the macro to a template or document**—Unless you specify otherwise, every macro you create is attached to the global template, Normal.dotx, and is available in every Word document created on that computer, regardless of what template or document you used to create the macro. You can choose to attach a macro only to the document or template you're editing, and in this case, the macro is available only in that document or documents created from that template, but is available on any computer on which the template is opened.

- **Assign the macro to a toolbar button, menu, or keyboard shortcut (optional)**—A macro is easier to run if you assign it to a button that you add to the Quick Access Toolbar or assign it a keyboard shortcut. Otherwise, it requires at least four mouse clicks to run.

Examining Trust Center Settings

A macro virus is a virus written into a macro code. Because you can't tell if a macro has a virus when you open a document, Word has built-in security settings to protect your computer. The default setting is to disable all macros, but when you try running a macro, to display a yellow Security Warning bar at the top of the document with a message stating that macros have been disabled. See Figure 8-28. In this case, you can click the Enable Content button if you are sure the macro is safe to run.

Figure 8-28 **Security Warning stating that macros have been disabled**

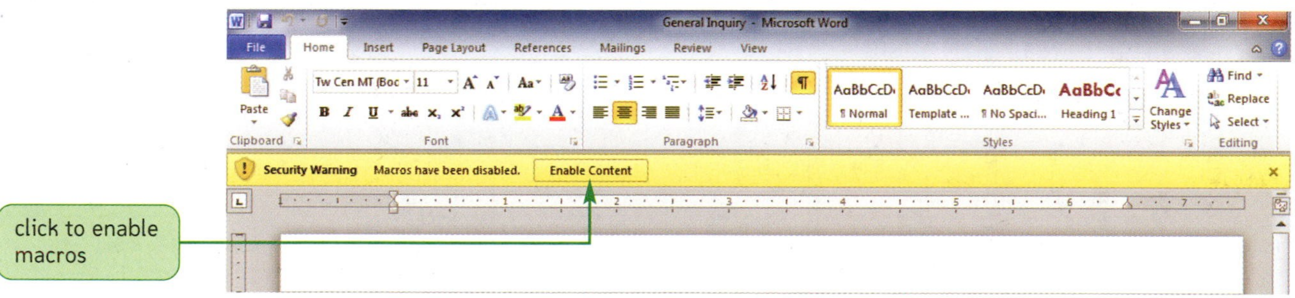

Another setting disables macros, but when you try to run one, displays a dialog box stating that macros are disabled, rather than the Security Warning bar.

You'll check your macro security settings now.

To check macro security settings:

1. Click the **File** tab, click **Options** in the navigation bar to display the Word Options dialog box, and then click **Trust Center** in the list on the left. The dialog box changes to display links to articles about security and privacy on the Internet and the Trust Center Settings button.
2. Click the **Trust Center Settings** button. The Trust Center dialog box opens.
3. If necessary, click **Macro Settings** in the list on the left. The Trust Center shows the current macro settings. See Figure 8-29.

Figure 8-29 Trust Center displaying Macro Settings

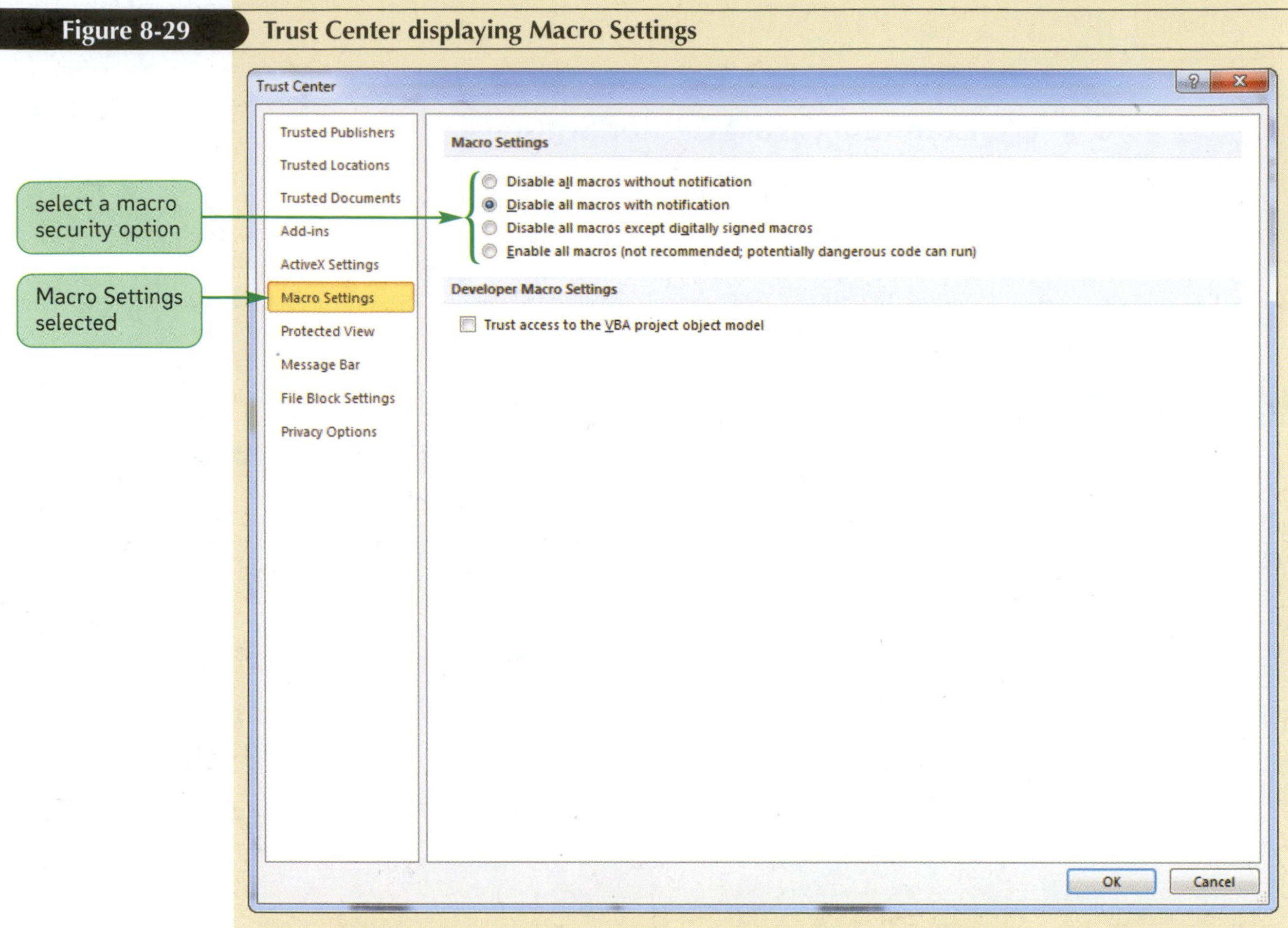

4. If the Disable all macros with notification option button is not selected, note which option is selected, and then click the **Disable all macros with notification** option button.

5. Click the **OK** button, and then click the **OK** button in the Word Options dialog box.

Recording a Macro

Recording a macro in Word is similar to recording and replaying your voice on a tape or digital recorder. To record a macro, you turn on the macro recorder, perform keystrokes and mouse operations, and then turn off the macro recorder. When you play back the macro, Word performs the same sequence of keystrokes and mouse clicks. Note that you can't record mouse operations within the document window while you record a macro—for example, you can't select text with the mouse or drag and drop text—but you can use the mouse to select buttons and options on the Ribbon.

You are ready to record the macro that inserts the slogan for Forsythe Plaza as a right-aligned header. Once you've recorded the macro in the template, Geoff can use it in other documents to save time.

REFERENCE

Recording a Macro

- Click the View tab, in the Macros group, click the Macros button arrow, and then click Record Macro; *or* click the Developer tab, and then in the Code group, click the Record Macro button; *or* on the status bar, click the Start Recording button.
- In the Record Macro dialog box, type a name for the macro in the Macro name box.
- To save the macro in the current document or template, click the Store macro in arrow, and then select the desired active document or template.
- Use the Button or Keyboard button to assign the macro to a button or assign a short-cut key combination.
- Click the OK button to start recording the macro.
- Perform the mouse actions and keystrokes you want to record the macro.
- On the View tab in the Macros group, click the Macros button arrow, and then click Stop Recording; *or* on the Developer tab in the Code group, click the Stop Recording button; *or* on the status bar, click the Stop Recording button.

Before you record the macro, you'll name the macro, attach it to the template, add a description of the macro, and assign it to a shortcut key combination.

TIP

You can also click the Start Recording button in the status bar at the bottom of the document window to start recording a macro, or you can click the Developer tab, and then click the Record Macro button in the Code group.

To prepare to record the InsertSlogan macro:

1. If you took a break after the last session, click the **File** tab, click **Open** in the navigation pane, navigate to the Word8\Tutorial folder included with your Data Files, click **General Inquiry**, and then click the **Open** button.
2. Make sure that the ruler and paragraph marks are displayed.
3. Click the **View** tab, click the **Macros button arrow** in the Macros group, and then click **Record Macro**. The Record Macro dialog box opens. The temporary name Macro1 appears in the Macro name box.
4. Type **InsertSlogan** in the Macro name box.
5. Click the **Store macro in** arrow, and then click **Documents Based On General Inquiry** to attach the macro only to the current document.
6. Click in the **Description** box, and then type **Inserts Forsythe Plaza slogan as a header**. Next, you'll assign the macro to a shortcut key combination so that you don't need to open the Macros dialog box to run it.
7. Click the **Keyboard** button. The Customize Keyboard dialog box opens. See Figure 8-30. The macro is selected in the Commands list, and the insertion point is blinking in the Press new shortcut key box.

Figure 8-30 Customize Keyboard dialog box

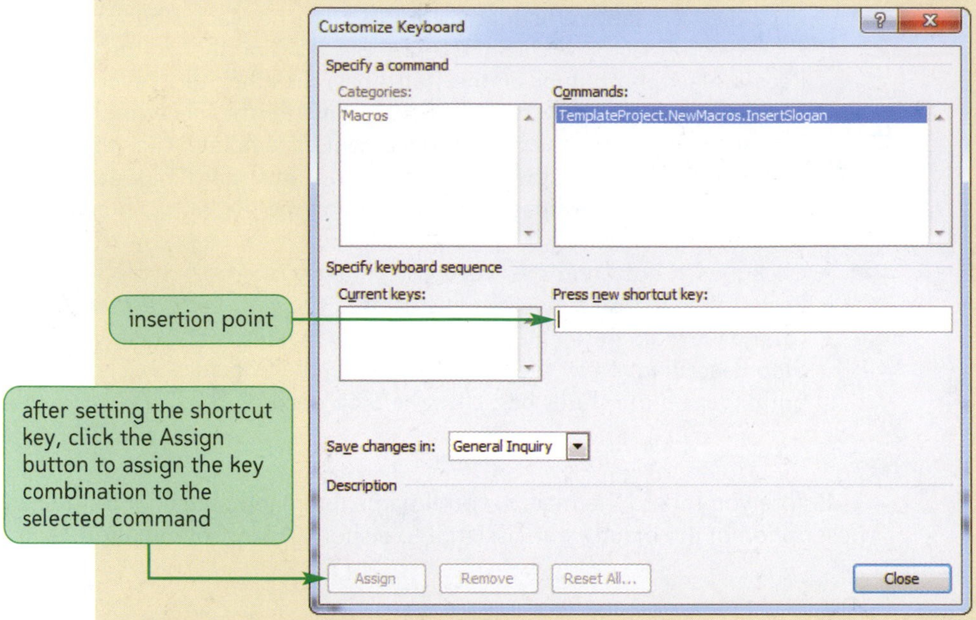

8. Press the **Alt+Ctrl+Shift+Z** keys. A message appears below the Current keys box stating that this key combination is unassigned.
9. Click the **Assign** button. The key combination you chose appears in the Current keys list. Now when you press the Alt+Ctrl+Shift+Z keys, the macro you are about to record will run.
10. Click the **Close** button in the Customize Keyboard dialog box. The dialog boxes close, and the pointer changes to , indicating that you are recording a macro. On the status bar, the Stop Recording button appears (in place of the Start Recording button).

From this point, Word records every keystroke and mouse operation until you stop the recording, so perform these steps carefully, and complete them exactly as shown. If you make a mistake, you can stop recording and start over. It does not matter how long you take to perform the steps. When the macro is run, the steps will execute very quickly.

To record the InsertSlogan macro:

1. Click the **Insert** tab, click the **Header** button in the Header & Footer group, and then click **Edit Header**. The header becomes active.
2. Click the **Home** tab, click the **Bold** button **B**, and then click the **Italics** button *I*. The text you type will be formatted in bold and italics.
3. Type **Forsythe Plaza--New England's Premier Event Facility**.
4. Click the **Align Text Right** button in the Paragraph group. The text is right-aligned.
5. Click the **Header & Footer Tools Design** tab, and then click the **Close Header and Footer** button in the Close group.

TIP

You can also stop the recording of a macro by clicking the Stop Recording button in the status bar.

6. Click the **View** tab, click the **Macros button arrow** in the Macros group, and then click **Stop Recording**. The pointer changes back to the normal pointer, and the button on the status bar changes back to the Start Recording button.

   Trouble? If you made a mistake while recording the macro, repeat the previous set of steps, clicking the Yes button when asked if you want to replace the existing macro, and then repeat this set of steps.

Now that you've recorded a macro, you're ready to run it.

Running Macros

To "run" a macro means to execute it—to perform the recorded or programmed steps. To run a macro, you can open the Macros dialog box, select the macro in the list, and then click the Run button. To open the Macros dialog box, you click the Macros button in the Macros group on the View tab. If you assigned the macro to a button when you recorded it, you can click the button to run the macro. Finally, if you assigned a keyboard shortcut to the macro when you recorded it, as you did when you recorded the InsertSlogan macro, you can press the shortcut keys you assigned.

Geoff wants you to test the macro now. First, you need to remove the header that was inserted when you recorded the macro.

To run the InsertSlogan macro:

1. Double-click in the header area, select the entire line and the paragraph mark, and then press the **Delete** key. The header is deleted.
2. Double-click anywhere in the document to make the header inactive.
3. Press the **Alt+Ctrl+Shift+Z** keys. The formatted header is entered in the header area, the document window becomes active, and the header area becomes inactive. The macro works as it should. You can use the Undo button to see the list of tasks the macro performed.
4. On the Quick Access Toolbar, click the **Undo button arrow**. See Figure 8-31. Notice that the top several actions all begin with "VBA-" (for the Visual Basic programming language). These are the recorded actions that the macro performed.

Figure 8-31 Undo list after running the macro

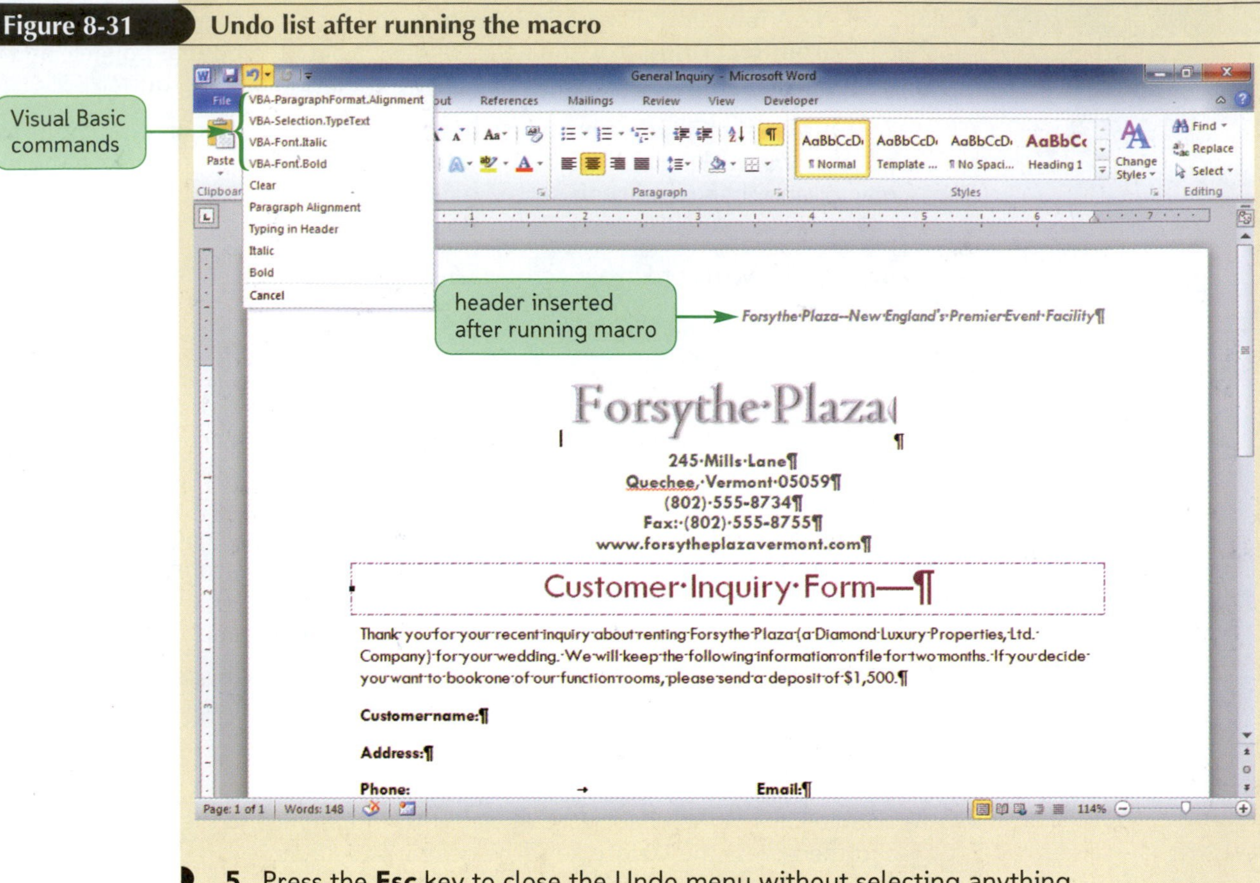

5. Press the **Esc** key to close the Undo menu without selecting anything.

Geoff decides he wants the slogan to be centered in the header. You could record a new macro, but it's easier to edit the one you already recorded.

Editing a Macro Using the Visual Basic Window

When you record a macro, you are actually creating a Visual Basic program. Microsoft Visual Basic is a feature built into Word and other Office applications that provides a complete environment for writing new Visual Basic code and editing existing Visual Basic code and procedures. Each action you performed while recording the macro created a line of code in Visual Basic. You can see the code by opening the Visual Basic window. You can usually examine the code and identify specific actions even if you don't have a thorough understanding of Visual Basic.

You'll edit the macro in the Visual Basic window now.

To edit the InsertSlogan macro:

1. Click the **View** tab, and then click the **Macros button** in the Macros group. The Macros dialog box opens listing the macro you recorded.

   Trouble? If you see other macros listed in the Macros dialog box, they are probably stored in the Normal template on your computer. Just continue with the next step.

2. In the list of macros, click **InsertSlogan**, if necessary, and then click the **Edit** button. The Microsoft Visual Basic for Applications window opens. See Figure 8-32. Instead of a Ribbon with tabs and buttons, the Visual Basic window contains a menu bar and toolbar. This window also contains various smaller windows (called panes) for creating and editing macros. The InsertSlogan macro commands appear in the right pane. Notice that most lines of the code begin with "Selection." This is a Visual Basic command that performs an action on the selected text. The third line from the bottom is the line that was recorded when you clicked the Align Text Right button.

Figure 8-32 **Visual Basic window displaying the code for the InsertSlogan macro**

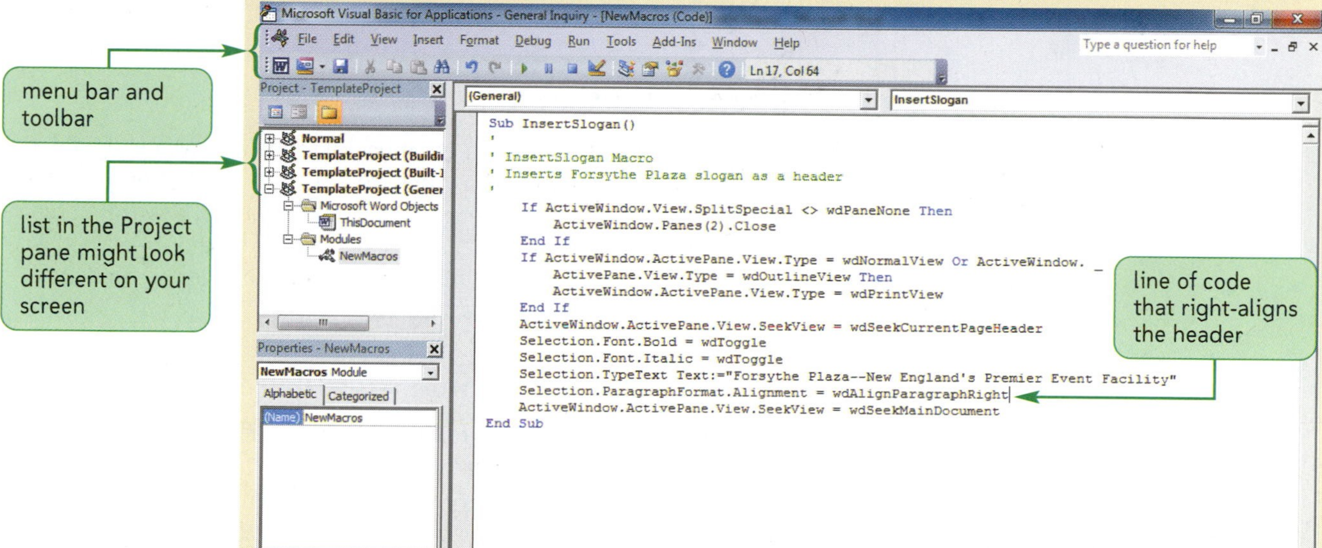

Trouble? If the Visual Basic window is not maximized, maximize it now.

Trouble? If the Project – TemplateProject pane isn't open, click View on the Visual Basic menu bar, and then click Project Explorer.

Trouble? If the Properties – NewMacros pane isn't open, click View on the Visual Basic menu bar, and then click Properties Window.

3. In the third line of code from the bottom, select **Right,** and then type **Center**.

Trouble? If the second to last line beginning with "ActiveWindow" moves up to the end of the line that you just modified, position the insertion point after the word "Center," and then press the Enter key.

4. Close the Visual Basic window. Changes you have made to the code are saved automatically with your Word document, and will be saved to the disk when you save the document. Now you'll test the revised macro.

5. Delete the header, and then close the header area. This time, you'll run the macro from the Macros dialog box.

6. Click the **View** tab, and then click the **Macros** button in the Macros group. The Macros dialog box opens with InsertSlogan listed.

7. If necessary, click **InsertSlogan** to select it, and then click the **Run** button. The header entered in the header area is now centered.

   Trouble? If you used the Remove Header command on the Header menu in Step 5 instead of deleting all of the text including the paragraph mark in the active header, the header won't be bold or italicized. This is because if you use the Remove Header command, the formatting is not removed, and then when the macro applies the bold and italic formatting to the inserted text, it actually toggles these commands off. Double-click in the header to make it active, delete the header, and then run the macro again.

Now that you've recorded and tested the macro, you want to save the document with the macro.

Saving a Document with Macros

In order to run macros in a document, the document must be saved as a Macro-Enabled Document or a Macro-Enabled Template. If you try to save a document or a template that contains macros in the ordinary Word Document or Template file format, a warning dialog appears asking if you want to save the document as a "macro-free" document—in other words, without the macros—and you are given the opportunity to change the file type.

To save a document with the macros into the Brochure Draft document:

1. On the Quick Access Toolbar, click the **Save** button. A dialog box opens warning you that the macro cannot be saved in a macro-free document and asking if you want to continue saving as a macro-free document. This is not what you want.
2. Click the **No** button. The dialog box closes, and the Save As dialog box appears.
3. Click the **Save as type** arrow. Notice that two file types are macro-enabled: a Word document and a Word template. You want to save this as a macro-enabled template.
4. Click **Word Macro-Enabled Template**, and then click the **Save** button. The document is saved along with the macro.

INSIGHT

Understanding Filename Extensions

Recall that all files have filename extensions, which are several letters after a period at the end of a filename. The default setting in Windows is to hide filename extensions. Filename extensions identify the file type, such as .docx for normal Word documents, .jpeg or .bmp for pictures, .exe for program files, and so on. When you save a document as a Word Template, the filename extension is .dotx, which distinguishes these documents from ordinary Word documents. When you save a file as a Macro-Enabled Document, the filename extension is .docm, and when you save a file as a Macro-Enabled Template, the extension is .dotm. You should also be aware of the .doc extension for Word documents created in versions of Word prior to Word 2007.

Importing Macros

Geoff wants to learn more about macros. A friend of his used Visual Basic code to write two macros for resizing and repositioning a picture. The macros are named ResizePictureLeft and ResizePictureRight. The two macros are similar: each opens a simple dialog box, asks the user to type a percentage, expands or reduces the picture size by the given percentage, and then positions the picture at the left or right margin.

Geoff's friend wrote the two macros in a Word document and then exported them from Word into the file PicMacs.bas. The .bas file extension indicates that the file contains one or more Visual Basic macros. You will import the PicMacs.bas file into a document and then test it to see how a macro works.

To access Visual Basic directly, you need to display the Developer tab, which contains commands for working with codes, controls, XML, and document protection in Word. Geoff is working on a new brochure that he plans to send out in a direct mail campaign. He asks you to import the two macros into the brochure, and then run them to see how they work.

To open the Brochure document and display the Developer tab:

1. Open the file **Brochure** from the Word8\Tutorial folder included with your Data Files, save the document as **Brochure Draft** to the same folder, and then display nonprinting characters and the rulers, if necessary.
2. Click the **File** tab, and then click **Options** in the navigation bar. The Word Options dialog box opens with General selected in the list on the left.
3. In the list on the left, click **Customize Ribbon**. The right pane of the dialog box changes to show two lists—one listing Word commands and the other listing Ribbon tabs. See Figure 8-33.

Figure 8-33 Word Options dialog box with Customize Ribbon selected

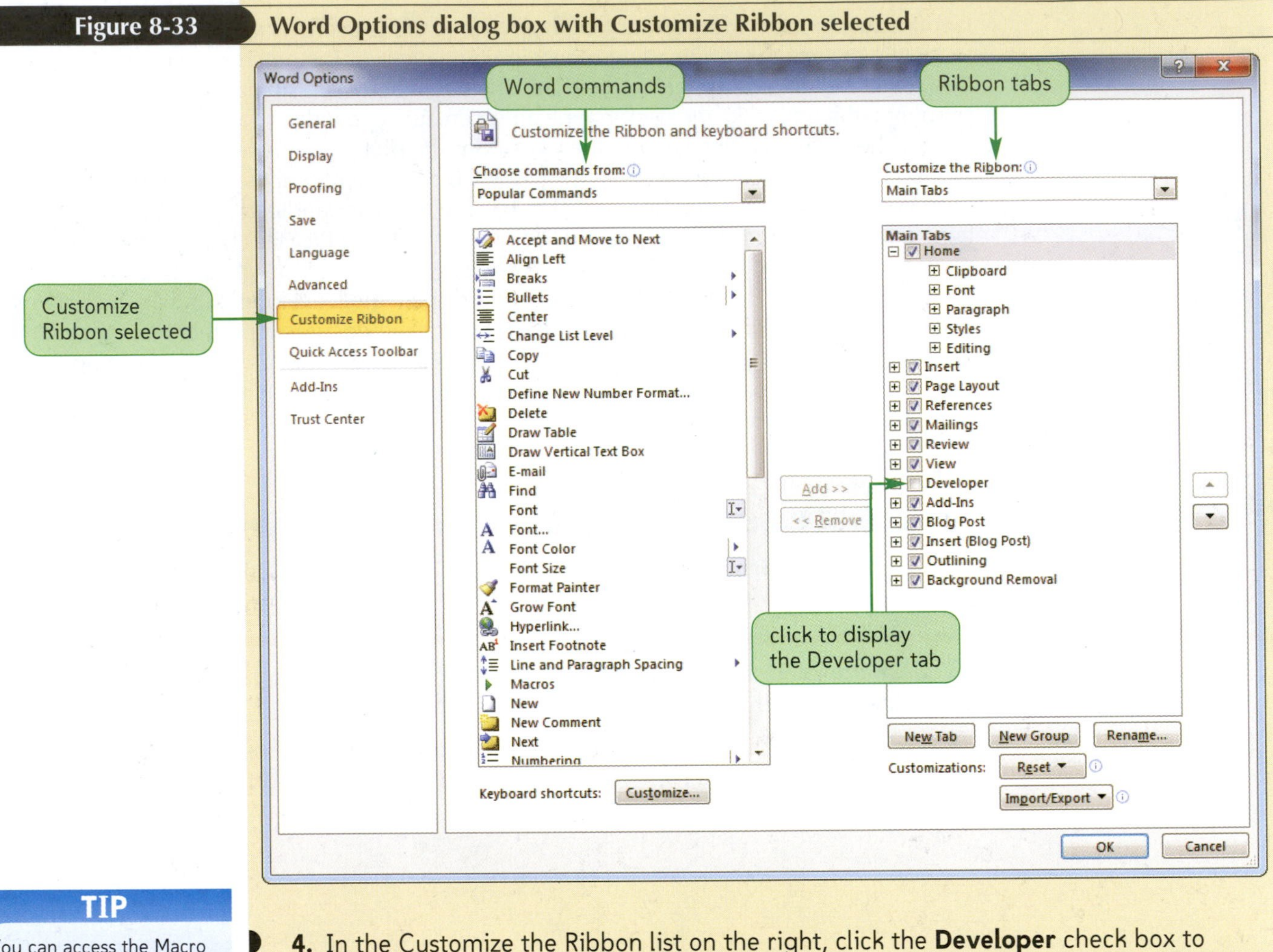

TIP

You can access the Macro Settings in the Trust Center by clicking the Macro Security button in the Code group on the Developer tab.

4. In the Customize the Ribbon list on the right, click the **Developer** check box to select it, if necessary, and then click the **OK** button. The dialog box closes and the Developer tab appears on the Ribbon to the right of the View tab.
5. Click the **Developer** tab.

The Code group on the Developer tab contains commands for working with macros, including the Macros button, which opens the Macros dialog box and the Record Macro button, which starts recording a macro. Geoff is ready for you to import his friend's macros into the Brochure Draft document so you can test them.

To import the macros into the Brochure Draft document:

1. In the Code group, click the **Visual Basic** button. The Microsoft Visual Basic for Applications window opens listing the code for the InsertSlogan macro you recorded earlier. You need to select the current document in the Project – TemplateProject pane on the left.
2. In the Project – TemplateProject pane, scroll up if necessary, and then click **Project (Brochure Draft)**. Project (Brochure Draft) is selected and the name of the pane changes to Project – Project. With the correct document selected, you're ready to import the macros.

3. On the menu bar in the Visual Basic window, click **File**, and then click **Import File**. The Import File dialog box opens.
4. Click the **Look in** arrow, select the drive or folder in which your Data Files are stored, and then double-click folders as needed to navigate to the Word8\Tutorial folder.
5. Click **PicMacs.bas**, and then click the **Open** button. A folder named "Modules" appears in the Project (Brochure Draft) section in the Project – Project pane. See Figure 8-34.

Figure 8-34 **New Modules folder listed under the Brochure document**

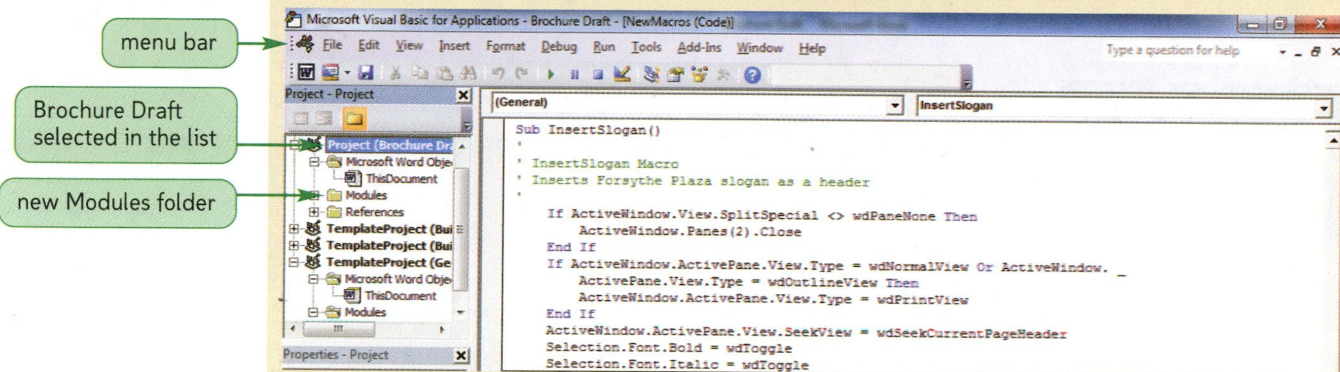

6. In the Project (Brochure Draft) section in the Project – Project pane, click the **plus sign** next to the Modules folder. The folder opens, and the macros in the folder are listed below it. You see PicMacs, which is the name of the set of macros that you imported.
7. In the Project – Project pane, double-click **PicMacs**. The macro code for PicMacs replaces the InsertSlogan code on the right. The first macro is ResizePictureLeft, which resizes a photograph and positions it at the left margin of your Word document. If you scroll down the macro window, you can see the second macro, ResizePictureRight, which has the same function as ResizePictureLeft, except that it positions the picture at the right margin.
8. On the Visual Basic window title bar, click the **Close** button [X] to close it and return to the document.

Because the imported macros are designed to format pictures, before you can run the macros you must have a picture inserted into your document, and the picture must be selected.

To insert and select a picture and then run the PictureResize macros:

1. Click the **Insert** tab, click the **Picture** button in the Illustrations group, navigate to the Word8\Tutorial folder, and then double-click **Flowers**. The Flowers photo is inserted in the document. The picture is selected, as indicated by the sizing handles, and the picture is inserted as an inline graphic. Now you're ready to run one of the macros.

TIP

You can also open the Macros dialog box by clicking the Developer tab, and then in the Code group, clicking the Macros button.

2. Click the **View** tab, and then click the **Macros button** in the Macros group. The Macros dialog box opens, listing the two imported macros.
3. If necessary, click **ResizePictureLeft** to select it, and then click the **Run** button. The macro displays a dialog box titled Select Picture Size and waits for you to type a percentage of the current picture size. For example, if you wanted the height and width of the picture to be half their current values, you would type 50; if you wanted the height and width to be double their current values, you would type 200.
4. Type **50**, and then click the **OK** button. The macro reduces the size of the picture by 50 percent, changes the picture to a floating graphic, sets the picture so that the document text wraps around it on the right side, and positions the picture at the left margin. See Figure 8-35. Next, you'll test the other macro, ResizePictureRight.

Figure 8-35 **Picture after running the ResizePictureLeft macro**

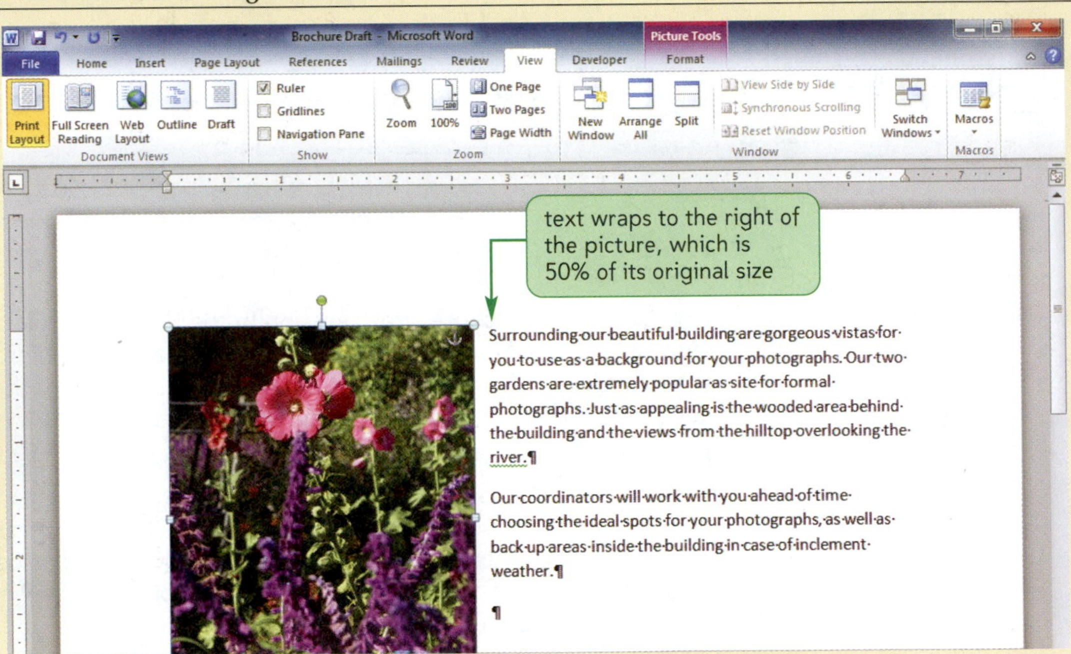

5. With the picture of the flowers still selected, run the **ResizePictureRight** macro, using **40** as the percentage. The macro reduces the picture width and height to 40 percent of its current values and positions it at the right margin. Note that the picture dimensions are 40 percent of the current picture size, not 40 percent of the original size. Now you can save the document with the macros in it.
6. On the Quick Access Toolbar, click the **Save** button, and then click the **No** button in the dialog box that asks if you want to continue saving as a macro-free document.
7. In the Save As dialog box, click the **Save as type** arrow, click **Word Macro-Enabled Document**, and then click the **Save** button.
8. Close the **Brochure Draft** document. The General Inquiry template is the current document again.

Now you'll return to the General Inquiry template, where you'll record a macro that finds the word "wedding" in the introductory paragraph so that the person filling in the form remembers to change it to suit the event being planned.

Recording an AutoMacro

To make the General Inquiry Template even more useful, you will add an AutoMacro. An **AutoMacro** is a macro that runs automatically when you perform certain basic operations, such as starting Word, creating a document, opening a document, closing a document, and exiting Word. AutoMacros have special reserved names so that when you create a macro using one of them, the macro runs at the point determined by the code built into that AutoMacro. For example, if you create a macro named AutoNew and save it in a template, when you create a new document based on that template, the macro will run at that point. Figure 8-36 lists the AutoMacros and their purposes.

Figure 8-36 Description of AutoMacros built into Word

AutoMacro Name	Purpose
AutoExec	Runs each time you start Word
AutoNew	Runs when you start a new document
AutoOpen	Runs each time you open an existing document
AutoClose	Runs each time you close a document
AutoExit	Runs each time you exit Word

Geoff asks you to record an AutoNew macro in the General Inquiry Template so that whenever a new document is created from the template, the macro will execute the Find command and select the word "wedding" in the introductory paragraph. This will remind the employee to change that word to match the event for which the customer is planning a party.

To create the AutoNew macro:

1. Make sure the General Inquiry template is the current document, and then press the **Ctrl+Home** keys to move the insertion point to the beginning of the document.
2. Click the **Developer** tab, and then click the **Record Macro** button in the Code group. The Record Macro dialog box opens.
3. Type **AutoNew** in the Macro name box. This macro name tells Word to run the macro when you begin a new document based on this template.
4. Click the **Store macro in** arrow, and then click **Documents Based On General Inquiry** so the macro runs only if a new document is opened from the General Inquiry Template.
5. In the Description box, type **Find instance of "wedding"**. You won't assign this macro to a toolbar or the keyboard because it will run automatically when the new document is opened.
6. Click the **OK** button. You're now ready to record the commands of the AutoNew macro.
7. Click the **Home** tab, click the **Find button arrow** in the Editing group, and then click **Advanced Find**. The Find and Replace dialog box opens with the Find tab selected.
8. Type **wedding** in the Find what box, and then click the **Find Next** button. The word "wedding" in the introductory paragraph is selected.
9. In the dialog box, click the **Cancel** button. This completes the operations for the AutoNew macro.

10. Click the **Developer** tab, and then click the **Stop Recording** button in the Code group.
11. Save your changes.

The AutoNew macro will run whenever an employee starts a new document from the General Inquiry with macros template. Now you need to test your template.

To test the AutoNew macro in a new document based on the General Inquiry with macros template:

TIP

You can drag the scroll bar over to see the Type list so that you can identify the file type of each document.

1. Click the **File** tab, click **New** in the navigation bar, and then click the **New from existing** button under Available Templates. The New from Existing Document dialog box opens listing the files in the Word8\Tutorial folder. There are two files named General Inquiry. A small yellow bar is at the top of the icons for both files, indicating they are template files. One of the icons has an exclamation point on it. This indicates that the template or document is macro-enabled.
2. Click the **General Inquiry** file with the icon that has the exclamation point, and then click the **Create New** button. The New from Existing Document dialog box closes, and another dialog box opens as a result of the Fill-in field, asking you to enter the type of function.
3. In the Enter the type of function box, type **Retirement Party**, and then click the **OK** button. The dialog box closes, and the document opens. "Retirement Party" appears in the title line to the right of "Customer Inquiry Form." This is where the Fill-in field is located in the document. The word "wedding" is highlighted in the introductory paragraph. This is a result of the AutoNew macro running.
4. Type **retirement party** to replace the selected word "wedding" in the introductory paragraph.
5. Save the document as a regular Word document named **Retirement Party Inquiry** in the Word8\Tutorial folder.

Customizing Word Options

Now that you have created macros for the Forsythe Plaza template, Geoff asks you to explore other customization features in Word. You know that you can customize many features of Word using the Word Options dialog box. The dialog box has a list of categories on the left, and when you click a category, the right side of the dialog box changes to display options and commands for that category. The categories in the Word Options dialog box are described in Figure 8-37.

Figure 8-37 Word Options dialog box categories

Category	Description
General	Options for selecting common customizations in Word, including changing the user name and initials
Display	Options for changing how a document looks on the screen and when it is printed
Proofing	Options and commands for changing the way text is corrected when using the spelling and grammar checker and the AutoCorrect feature
Save	Options and commands for changing the default format in which documents are saved and the default locations to where files are saved
Language	Options for changing the language used for editing, display, and Help
Advanced	Advanced options and commands for changing the display, proofing, and save defaults
Customize Ribbon	A list of the commands available in Word and commands for adding them to or removing them from the existing groups on Ribbon tabs or creating new Ribbon tabs
Quick Access Toolbar	A list of the commands available in Word and commands for adding them to or removing them from the Quick Access Toolbar
Add-Ins	Commands for working with add-ins, small programs that enhance Word's functionality
Trust Center	Links to Web sites that explain Microsoft privacy and security policies, and a command for opening the Trust Center, where you can set security settings

By now, you have opened the Word Options dialog box several times to change some of the options. For example, you accessed the Trust Center via the Word Options dialog box. Recall that to open the Word Options dialog box, you click the File tab, and then click Options in the navigation bar. The dialog box always opens with the General tab selected in the list on the left. Several common customization options are listed here, including the personalization section, where you can add your name and initials. As you learned when you used the Track Changes feature in Tutorial 7, you can change the user name and initials so that your name appears as the author of the tracked changes. The name in this box is also picked up as the Author property in new documents.

Another helpful customization is to change the default Save location. When you use the Open or the Save As command, the Open or Save As dialog box lists the Documents folder as the default location for documents. If you store your documents in another location, it can be time consuming to change the location every time you open or save a file. You can change the default location by clicking Save in the list on the left in the Word Options dialog box, and then changing the path and folder name in the Default file location box. See Figure 8-38. Note that you can also change the default file format here as well, by clicking the Save files in this format arrow, and then clicking the new default file format.

Figure 8-38 Save tab in Word Options dialog box

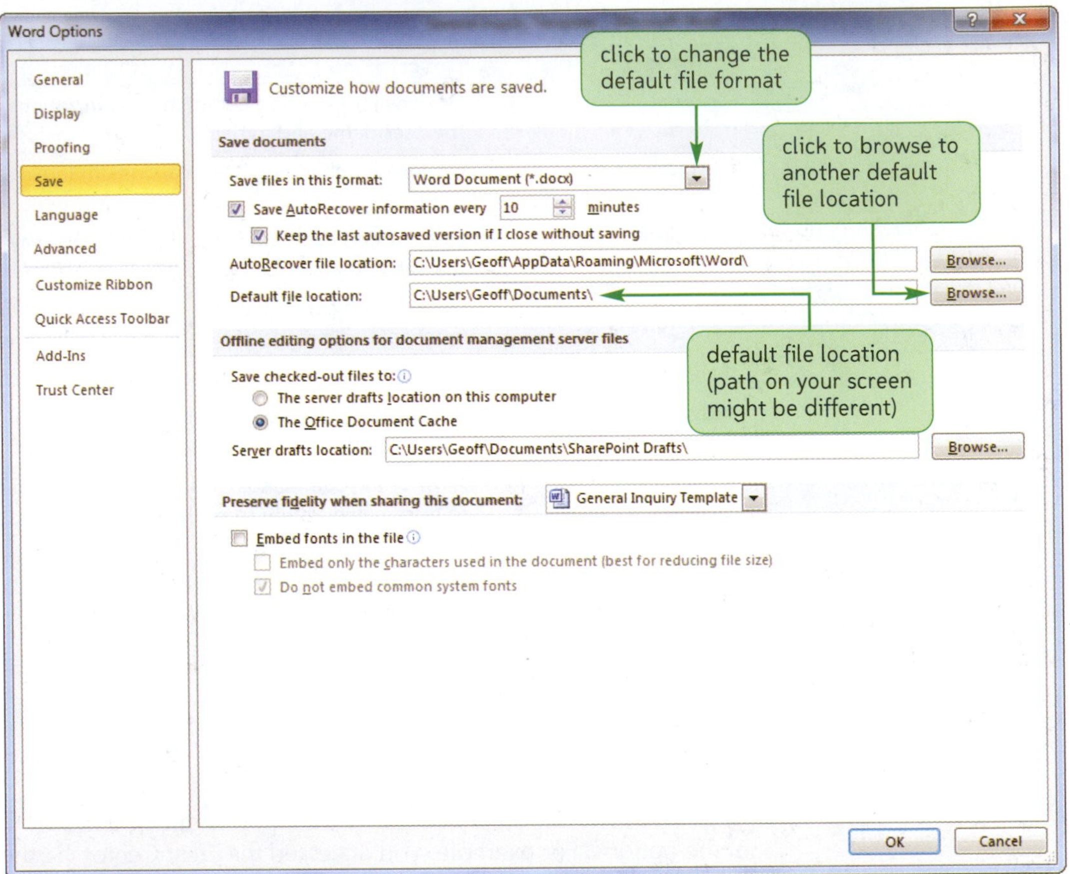

Two of the tabs in the Word Options dialog box provide options for modifying the Ribbon and the Quick Access Toolbar to suit your working style. For example, you can customize the Quick Access Toolbar by adding buttons to it or removing buttons from it. You'll do this next.

REFERENCE

Adding a Button to the Quick Access Toolbar

- On the Quick Access toolbar, click the Customize Quick Access Toolbar button, and then click a command in the list or click More Commands to open the Quick Access Toolbar tab in the Word Options dialog box; *or* click the File tab, click Options, and then in the list on the left, click Quick Access Toolbar.
- Click the Choose commands from arrow above the list of commands on the left, and then click a category of commands to filter the list of commands.
- In the Choose commands from list, click the command you want to add to the Quick Access Toolbar, and then click the Add button.
- Click the OK button to close the dialog box.

Geoff asks you to add the View Field Codes button to the Quick Access Toolbar so that he can easily see the field codes in the document you created.

To add a button to the Quick Access Toolbar:

1. On the Quick Access Toolbar, click the **Customize Quick Access Toolbar** button. A menu opens displaying common commands that you can add to the Quick Access Toolbar. Notice that the Save, Undo, and Redo commands have check marks next to them; these are the commands that already appear on the Quick Access Toolbar.
2. Click **More Commands**. The Word Options dialog box opens displaying the Quick Access Toolbar tab. The list on the left contains commands available in Word; the list on the right contains commands that appear on the Quick Access Toolbar. The list on the left is filtered to show popular commands.
3. Above the list on the left, click the **Choose commands from** arrow. A list of categories of commands opens.
4. Click **Commands Not in the Ribbon**. The list changes to show only commands that are not available on the Ribbon.
5. In the list on the left, drag the scroll box to the bottom of the scroll bar.
6. Near the top of the list, click **View Field Codes**, and then click the **Add** button. The View Field Codes command is added to the Customize Quick Access Toolbar list on the right, as shown in Figure 8-39.

Figure 8-39 View Field Codes command added to the Customize Quick Access Toolbar list

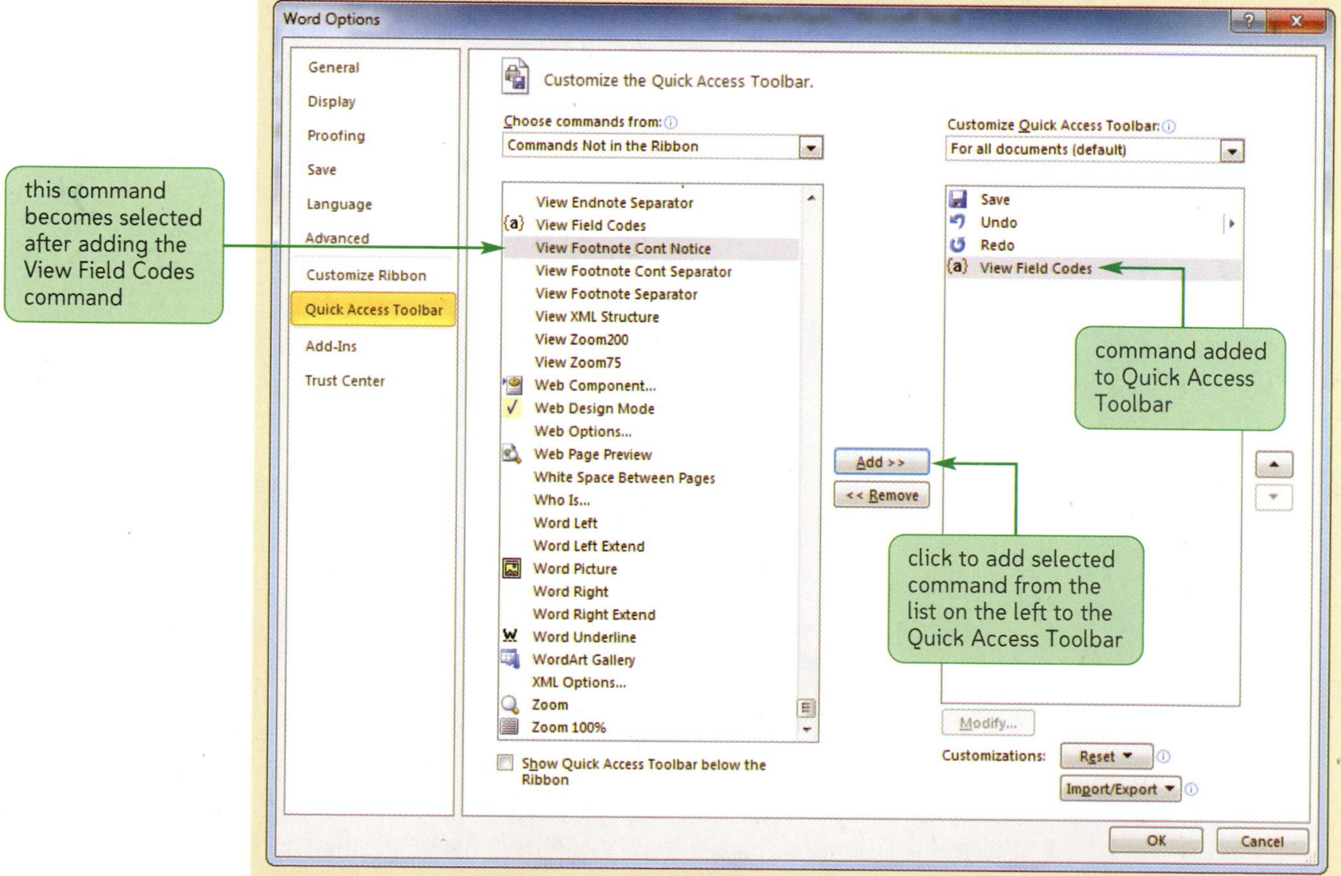

7. Click the **OK** button. The dialog box closes and the View Field Codes button appears on the Quick Access Toolbar.

Now Geoff can use the button to use the View Field Codes command.

You can customize the Ribbon as well. You can add buttons to existing groups on the current tabs, you can hide current tabs, and you can create new tabs.

Geoff finds that he uses some commands frequently as he works. He asks you to create a new tab on the Ribbon and put the buttons for his frequently-used commands on it.

To add new tab to the Ribbon:

1. Click the **File** tab, click **Options** in the navigation bar, and then click the **Customize Ribbon** tab. The right side of the Word Options dialog box changes to show two lists. On the left, you see the same lists of commands you saw when you were adding a button to the Quick Access Toolbar. On the right, the tabs on the Ribbon are listed. The tab that was selected before you opened this dialog box is expanded. See Figure 8-40.

Figure 8-40 Word Options dialog box with the Customize Ribbon options displayed

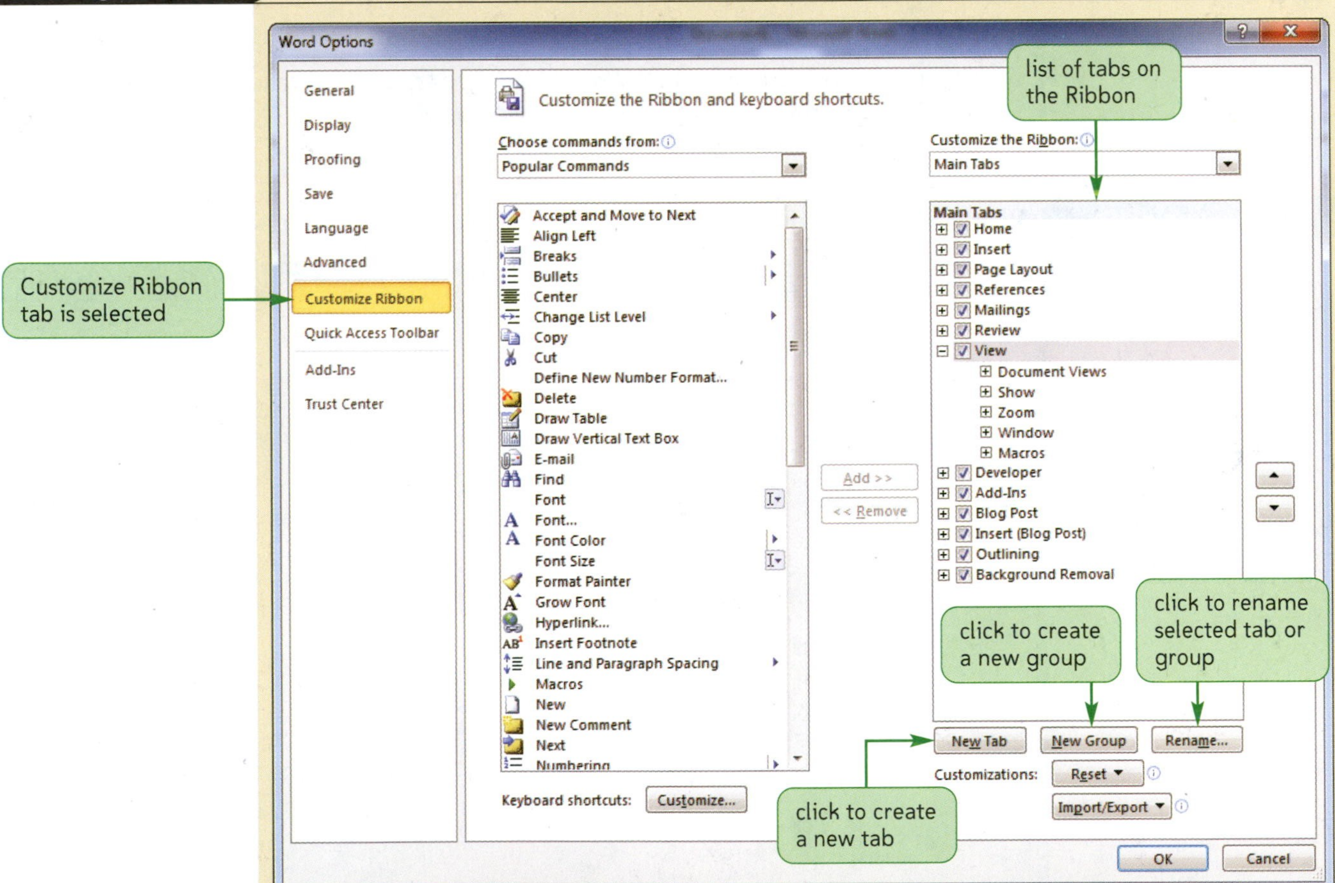

2. In the Customize the Ribbon list on the right, click the **New Tab** button. A new tab appears below the currently selected tab. One group is listed below the new tab.
3. Click **New Tab (Custom)** in the list, and then click the **Rename** button below the list. The Rename dialog box opens.
4. In the Display name box, type **Geoff**, and then click the **OK** button.
5. In the list, click **New Group (Custom)**, and then click **Rename**. A different Rename dialog box opens.

6. In the Display name box, type **Frequently Used**, and then click the **OK** button. Now you can add buttons to the group on the new tab.

TIP

You cannot add a button to a tab without first selecting a group on the tab.

7. In the list on the left, click **Macros**, and then click the **Add** button.
8. In the list on the left, scroll down, click **Page Width**, and then click the **Add** button. Geoff will add more commands later. He wants this custom tab to appear as the last tab on the Ribbon.
9. In the list on the right, click **Geoff (Custom)**, and then click the **Move Down** button as many times as necessary to move it below the Add-Ins tab. See Figure 8-41. Note that you cannot move a custom tab so it appears after the contextual tabs listed.

Figure 8-41 New tab repositioned in the Customize the Ribbon list

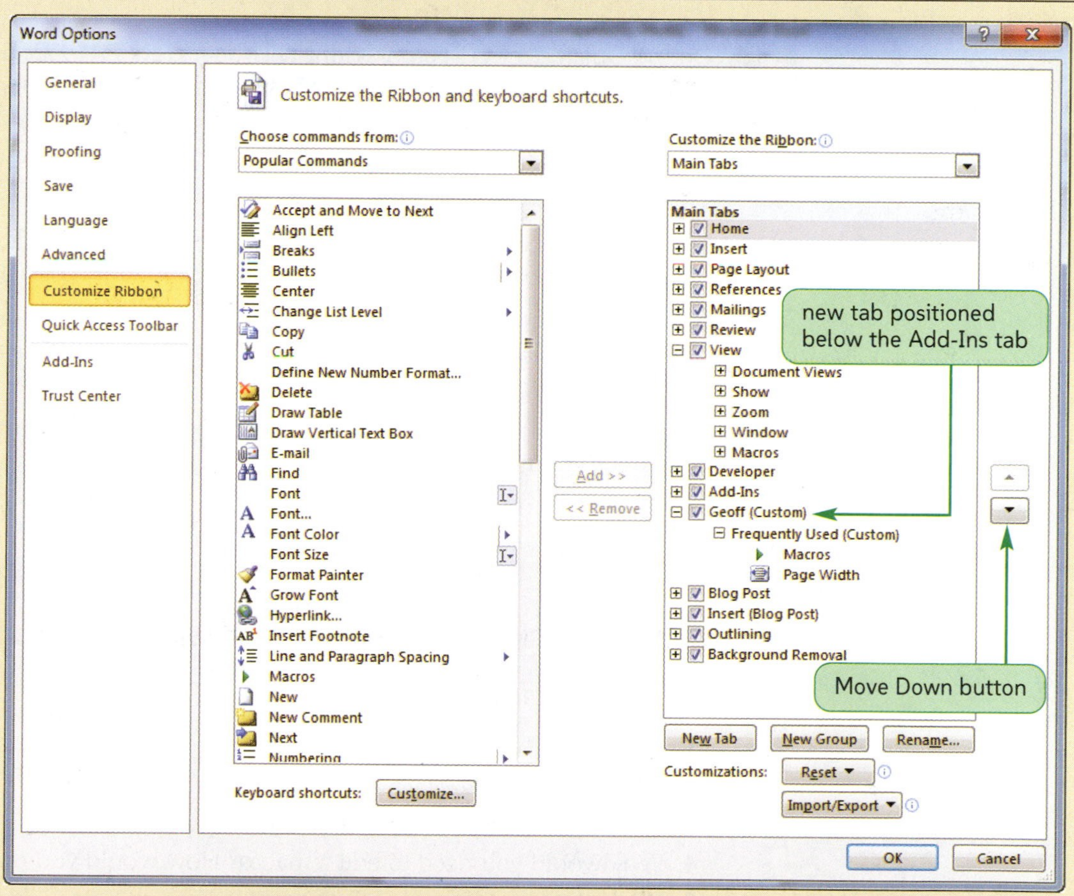

10. Click the **OK** button. The dialog box closes and you see the new tab on the Ribbon to the right of the Developer tab.

After adding buttons to the Quick Access Toolbar or creating a new Ribbon tab, you might decide that you don't want them there after all. If you're not working on your own computer, you should remove any customizations you make.

You'll test the button and the keyboard shortcut you created, and then you'll remove both of these customizations.

To test the customizations and then return Word to its default state:

1. On the Quick Access Toolbar, click the **View Field Codes** button. The button works as it should: the field codes appear in the document and the button on the Quick Access Toolbar is selected.
2. Click the **Geoff** tab, and then in the Frequently Used group, click the **Macros** button. The Macros dialog box opens.
3. Click the **Cancel** button to close the dialog box. Now you'll return Word to its original state.
4. If you changed the macro security settings, click the **Developer** tab, click the **Macro Security** button in the Code group to open the Trust Center dialog box with Macro Settings selected in the list on the left, click the option button that was selected before you changed this setting in the Macro Settings section, and then click the **OK** button.
5. On the Quick Access Toolbar, right-click the **View Field Codes** button, and then click **Remove from Quick Access Toolbar**. The shortcut menu closes, and the button is removed from the toolbar.
6. Click the **File** tab, click **Options** in the navigation bar, and then click the **Customize Ribbon** tab.
7. In the Customize the Ribbon list, click **Geoff (Custom)**, and then click the **Remove** button. The custom tab is deleted. Now you'll hide the Developer tab.
8. In the Customize the Ribbon list, click the **Developer** check box, and then click the **OK** button. The dialog box closes, and both the Geoff tab and the Developer tab no longer appear on the Ribbon.
9. Close the **Retirement Party Inquiry** and the **General Inquiry** template, saving changes if prompted.

Geoff is pleased with the final documents. He thinks they will help his staff work more efficiently.

REVIEW

Session 8.3 Quick Check

1. What is a macro?
2. What are two advantages to using a macro?
3. Briefly describe how to record a macro.
4. Why would you need to edit a macro? How would you do it?
5. What are AutoMacros?
6. Why might a template need an AutoNew macro?
7. How do you run a macro named MyMacro if it's not assigned to a button on the Quick Access Toolbar or to a shortcut key combination?
8. What is the name of the dialog box in which you can customize many of the options in Word?

Apply the skills you learned in the tutorial using the same case scenario.

PRACTICE

Review Assignments

Data File needed for the Review Assignments: Brochure2.docx

Geoff McKay, Event Manager at Forsythe Plaza, wants you to create a brochure. He first wants you to create a brochure for customers who want to hold their wedding reception at the Plaza. Then he wants you to make suggestions for customizing the brochure for other functions. Complete the following steps:

1. Open the file **Brochure2** from the Word8\Review folder included with your Data Files, and then save it as a template in the same folder with the filename **New Brochure**.
2. Format the entire document in two columns, with the left column narrower than the right column. On the Page Layout tab, click the Columns button in the Page Setup group, and then click More Columns. In the Col # 1 row, change the Width box to 2.8", and then click the OK button.
3. Insert a column break before the third paragraph, which starts with "Gorgeous," even if it is already at the top of the second column. (This way, it will always start the second column even if you move other text around.)
4. Soften the photo of the bride by 25 percent, and adjust its color saturation by reducing it to 66 percent.
5. Change the brightness of the photo of the flowers to +10% and the contrast to –20%, and adjust its tone by increasing its temperature to 8800 K.
6. Change the compression settings for all photos in this document so that images are not compressed by selecting the Do not compress images in file check box on the Advanced tab in the Word Options dialog box.
7. Using the Rounded Rectangle shape, draw a rectangle below the picture of the flowers that is the same width as the flower picture and approximately one-quarter inch high. Add the text **The rear garden** to the shape. Change the fill color of the shape to Pink, Text 2, Lighter 80%; change the outline to Lavender, Background 2, Darker 10%; and then change the text color to Black. Adjust the size of the shape as needed so that it is not touching the text underneath it.
8. Insert a watermark that identifies the document as a draft by opening the Watermark menu, and then clicking the Draft 1 style in the gallery.
9. Insert a next page section break after the URL at the bottom of the right column. Change the format of page 2 to a single column, and change the orientation to Portrait.
10. On page 1, select the last six lines of text in the right column (the address information), and then apply a custom border above and below the selected text. Use the third style from the bottom of the Style list on the Borders tab in the Borders and Shading dialog box. Change the color of the border to Purple, Accent 2, Lighter 40%. Add light purple shading using the Purple, Accent 2, Lighter 80% color.
11. Click immediately after the URL at the bottom of the right column, and then press the Enter key to insert a paragraph mark if one is not there already. Save the formatted address as a Quick Part named FP Address stored in the New Brochure template.
12. On page 2, insert the formatted text box called Sideline Sidebar. In the text box, type **Forsythe Plaza—New England's Premier Event Facility**. Drag the text box down to the bottom of page 2 and position it approximately two inches above the bottom of the page and approximately centered horizontally.
13. On page 2, insert the FP Address Quick Part at the top of the page.
14. Add your name as an Author document property, and add the custom property Checked by with a value of **Geoff McKay**.

15. Make the footer area on page 2 active, type **Prepared by:**, press the spacebar, and then insert the author name as a field using the Quick Parts menu.
16. Press the Right Arrow key, press the Tab key twice, type **Checked by:**, press the spacebar, and then insert the custom Checked by property as a field.
17. Change the value of the custom Checked by property to **Matt Sargent**, and then update the Checked by field in the footer to display the new value.
18. On page 1, in the first paragraph in the left column, delete the word "weddings," and then insert a second space. (If the Forsythe Plaza box is interfering with your ability to select the text, drag the bottom middle sizing handle of the WordArt logo up to just above the first line of text.) Position the insertion point between the spaces, and then insert the Fill-in field with the prompt **Enter type of event:**. Save the changes to the template.
19. Record a macro named **Slogan2** stored in documents based on the New Brochure template. Type **Inserts new slogan as a header** as the description. Use the Button button to add a button for the macro to the Quick Access Toolbar. When the macro starts recording, do the following:
    a. Click the Insert tab, click the Header button in the Header & Footer group, and then click Edit Header.
    b. Click the Home tab, and then change the font formatting to 16-point, Purple, Accent 2, Lighter 40%, italic.
    c. Type **Forsythe Plaza makes it an event to remember!**
    d. Center the text.
    e. Close the Header area.
    f. Stop recording.
20. Edit the macro so that the header is right-aligned instead of centered by changing the appropriate word in the code to **Right**.
21. Remove the header and then run the macro. (You might need to reformat the header area to 11-points Trebuchet MS (Body) font, not italicized, black text, and left-aligned.)
22. Create an AutoNew macro stored in the New Brochure template with the description **Changes the zoom to Two Pages**. The steps for this macro are:
    a. Click the View tab.
    b. In the Zoom group, click the Two Pages button.
    c. Stop recording.
23. Change the zoom to Page Width, save the template as a macro-enabled template, and then close the template without exiting Word.
24. If necessary, change your macro security settings so that you can run macros, and then create a new document based on the New Brochure template. Type **corporate event** in the Fill-in field dialog box that opens. Save the document as a macro-enabled document named **Corporate Brochure Draft** to the Word8\Review folder.
25. If you changed the security settings for macros, reset the security to its original level.
26. Delete the button you added to the Quick Access Toolbar.
27. Submit the documents to your instructor in electronic form, if requested, and then close all open documents.

Apply your skills to create and use a new template and import and use macros.

APPLY

Case Problem 1

Data Files needed for this Case Problem: LCNLetter.docx, LCNReply.bas, frmLCNReply.frm, frmLCNReply.frx

Linnea's Crafts and Needles Linnea Brown is the owner of Linnea's Crafts and Needles in Atlanta, Georgia. Linnea takes orders via telephone, mail, and the Internet from customers throughout Canada and the United States, and ships her crafts, sewing, and knitting products to customers. One of her best sellers is gift boxes of supplies for different types of crafts (for example, scrapbooking, knitting, stamping). One of her responsibilities is to respond to customer complaints. Linnea asks you to help her prepare a document template to increase the efficiency with which she responds to complaints. Complete the following steps:

1. Open the file **LCNLetter** from the Word8\Case1 folder included with your Data Files, and then save it as a template in the same folder with the filename **LCN Response**. Change your macro security settings, if necessary, so that all macros are enabled.
2. EXPLORE Use clip art to create a watermark. Search for appropriate clip art (try using "knitting" as the keyword). Insert the clip, recolor it using the Washout style (on the Color menu), and then change the text wrapping so it is behind the text. If it is still too dark, adjust the brightness to a higher percentage until it is light enough to look like a watermark.
3. Customize the Ribbon by creating a tab named Linnea and a group named Favorites, and then add the Quick Parts button and the Building Blocks Organizer button to the new group. (*Hint*: Don't forget to change the filtering options for the commands by clicking the Choose commands from arrow.)
4. EXPLORE Edit the date field at the top of the letter so the date appears in the format 12 June 2014.
5. Select and replace the first occurrence of NAME (in the inside address) with a Fill-in field code to fill in the customer's name. Type an appropriate prompt.
6. Display the Fill-in field code.
7. Copy the field code for the Fill-in field you just entered, and then paste it so that it replaces NAME after "Dear." Edit the prompt to request just the customer's first name.
8. Select and replace STREET and then CITY, STATE, ZIP with an appropriate Fill-in field for each. Hide all visible field codes.
9. Add a double-line border, colored Dark Purple, Text 2, below the URL.
10. Use the Quick Parts button you added to the new Linnea Ribbon tab to create a Quick Part from the company name and return address. (Be sure not to select the empty paragraph at the top of the document.) Name it **LCN Address** and save the Quick Part in this template. Delete the company name and address in the letter, and then insert the Quick Part you created to test it. Create a second Quick Part consisting of just the company name (do not include the paragraph mark after the company name), and name this **LCN**, saved in the template as well.
11. Use the Building Blocks Organizer button on the Linnea tab to open the Building Blocks Organizer. Edit the LCN Quick Part by adding the description **Formatted company name**.
12. Save your changes to the template.

13. Position the insertion point at the beginning of the letter, and then create an AutoNew macro that moves the insertion point to the blank paragraph after the first sentence in the body of the letter. (Use the keyboard to move the insertion point.) Make sure the macro is saved in the template. Include the description **Moves insertion point to body of letter**.
14. Open a Visual Basic window, and import the file **LCNReply.bas**, located in the Word8\Case1 folder, into TemplateProject LCN Response. (You might not see the .bas file extension when you open the Import File dialog box.) This contains part of the code for a macro that Linnea wrote to help automate writing the response letter.
15. Import the file **frmLCNReply.frm**, located in the Word8\Case1 folder, into the TemplateProject LCN Response. This file contains a macro User Form, which is a customized dialog box. When you import this file, the file frmLCNReply.frx is imported automatically as well.
16. Close the Visual Basic window.
17. Add a button for running the macro LCNReply to the Quick Access Toolbar. (*Hint*: Filter the commands list to include Macros only.)
18. Move the insertion point to the end of the document, and then test the LCNReply macro by clicking the button you added to the Quick Access Toolbar. The macro dialog box named "Response to Customer" appears and gives you the option of inserting one of four paragraphs, based on the type of customer complaint. The macro works as follows:
    - Click "Nothing (Didn't receive order)" if the customer didn't receive an order
    - Click "Wrong Order" if the customer received a product but not the correct order
    - Click "Damaged Box" if the customer received the correct order but the gift box was damaged.
    - Click "Poor Quality Product" if the customer complained about the quality of the crafts, sewing, or knitting products order
    - Click the OK button.

    Test each option of the macro, and when finished, delete the inserted paragraphs and blank lines.
19. Save your changes as a macro-enabled template, and then close the document.
20. Open a new document based on the LCN Response macro-enabled template.
21. When prompted by the Fill-in fields, use your own name and address as the person to whom the letter is being written (the customer).
22. With the insertion point located in the blank paragraph below the first paragraph of the body of the letter, run the LCNReply macro, selecting the Damaged Box option. Move the insertion point to the left of the final period in the paragraph that you just inserted with the macro, press the spacebar, type **from**, press the spacebar, and then use the LCN Quick Part to insert the company name.
23. Save the new letter as a macro-enabled document using the filename **Letter Final**, and then submit it to your instructor, either in electronic or printed form, as requested. If you changed the macro security settings, reset the security to its original level.
24. Remove the button you added from the Quick Access Toolbar, remove the custom tab from the Ribbon, and then change the macro security settings back to the original setting, if necessary. Close all open documents.

Apply your skills to create a shipping list template.

APPLY

Case Problem 2

Data Files needed for this Case Problem: List.docx, Water.jpg

Seely Tech Books Patric Melio is the manager of Seely Tech Books, a bookseller specializing in books about all forms of engineering. He has asked you to help him create a document template for a shipping list that he can include with each book shipment. Complete the following steps:

1. Open the file **List** in the Word8\Case2 folder included with your Data Files, and then save it as a macro-enabled template in the same folder with the filename **Shipping List**.
2. Insert a watermark using the file named **Water** from the Word8\Case2 folder included with your Data Files. Apply the Washout effect.
3. To the right of the tab after "Shipment Method," type **Federal Express**, select that phrase (do not select the paragraph mark), and then make it a Quick Part named **FedEx** in this template only. Delete the text "Federal Express" from the template. Repeat this action with **USPS**, saved as **USPS**, and **Fed Ex Ground**, saved as **Ground**. Delete the "Fed Ex Ground" text from the template.
4. To the right of the tab after "Payment Method," type **Credit Card**, and then save that phrase as a Quick Part named **CC** in this template only. Delete the text "Credit Card" from the template. Repeat this action with **Check**, saved as **Check**. Delete the text "Check" from the template.
5. Insert Fill-in fields to the right of the tab after Title, Author, Edition/Volume, and Copyright Year. You should choose an appropriate prompt for each of the four items. (*Hint*: Create one Fill-in field, create the prompt, display field codes, select the Fill-in field, copy it to all the other locations where you want a Fill-in field, and then directly edit the prompt within the field code.)
6. Toggle the Date field code to the right of "Date" below the section break. Edit the switch to M/d/yy so it appears in the style 4/8/14. Toggle the field codes off, and then update the field.
7. In the same section of the template, insert Fill-in fields to the right of the tab for Customer Number, Order Number, Date Ordered, Name, Company, and Street. You should choose an appropriate prompt for each of the items.

8. Insert Fill-in fields to the right of the tab for City, State, and ZIP. Set the Default response for City to "Augusta", for State to "GA", and for ZIP to "30903", because most of the orders are from local customers. (*Hint*: Select the appropriate check box in the Field Options section of the Field dialog box, and type the default there.)
9. Insert a Fill-in field for the Price in cell B1 of the table. (*Note*: Cells B2 and B4 contain special calculation fields. Inserting a calculation field in a table is covered in Tutorial 9.)
10. Press the Ctrl+Home keys, and then create an AutoNew macro for this template only that moves the insertion point to the right of the tab after "Shipment Method" when a new document is opened based on this template. (Use the keyboard to position the insertion point.) Type an appropriate description for the macro.
11. Save your changes, and then close the template.
12. Change the macro security settings to enable all macros, if necessary. Open a new document based on the Shipping List template.
13. When prompted by the Fill-in fields, type the information as follows (the dialog boxes for the fields in your document might appear in a different order):
    - Customer Number: **99743**
    - Order Number: **42-0987**

- Date Ordered: Use the current date.
- Name: Use your name.
- Company: Leave blank.
- Street: Use your school or another street address.
- City, State, Zip: Accept the default values.
- Title: **Ancient Bridges**
- Author: **Maria Fasuli**
- Edition/Volume: **4th**
- Copyright Year: **2012**
- Price: **82.75**

14. Verify that the insertion point is to the right of the tab after "Shipment Method," and then insert the FedEx Quick Part to insert "Federal Express." Move the insertion point to the right of the tab after "Payment Method," and then insert the CC Quick Part.

EXPLORE

15. In the table, update the Tax and Total fields (in the cells to the right of those labels), which are the calculation fields. (*Hint*: You update calculation fields the same way you update the results of other fields.)
16. Save the packing slip as a Word document in the Word8\Case2 folder included with your Data Files using the filename **Sample Shipping List**.
17. If you changed the security settings for macros, reset security to the original level, and then submit the files to your instructor, in either printed or electronic form, as requested. Close all open documents.

Create a template and a Word document for a blacksmith company.

CREATE

Case Problem 3

Data File needed for this Case Problem: Fax.docx

Sierra Top Blacksmiths Petra Mincberg is the general manager of Sierra Top Blacksmiths, a company that creates hand-forged iron products for solid-wood door manufacturers. Because shipping blacksmith products is so expensive, Petra wants to fax every customer an order acknowledgement that provides general information and lists the number of items in each style ordered. Petra wrote the text for the acknowledgement fax, and asks you to create a document template, as shown in Figure 8-42, to generate the faxes. Then she asks you to use the document template to prepare a fax for a customer, as shown in Figure 8-43. Complete the following steps:

1. Open the file named **Fax** from the Word8\Case3 folder included with your Data Files and save it as a macro-enabled template using the name **Fax Template**.
2. Insert a transparent hexagon shape that encloses the address at the top of the fax. Change the fill color of the shape to No Fill. Resize the shape as necessary so that the hexagon encloses the address without crowding it.
3. In the table below the company address, insert the fields shown in Figure 8-42.

Figure 8-42 Fax template for Sierra Top Blacksmiths

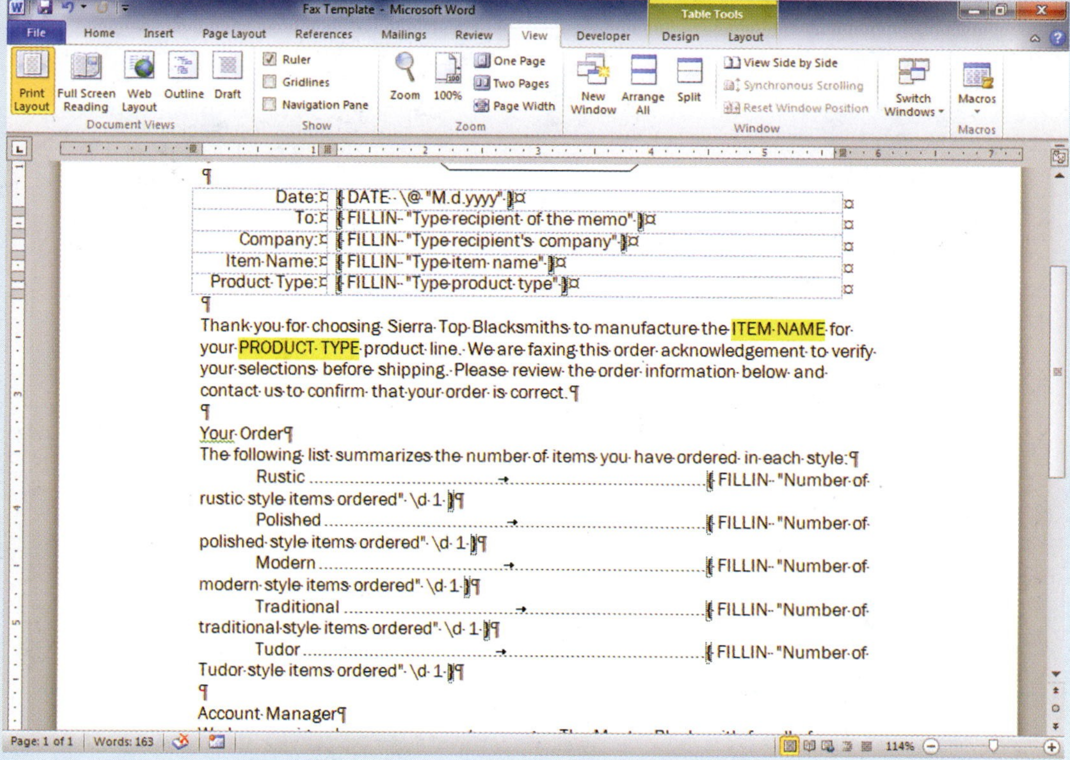

4. In the paragraph below the table, replace the highlighted placeholder text with the same fill-in fields that you used next to Item Name and Product Type in the table.

EXPLORE

5. To the right of the dot-leaders in the "Your Order" section, insert Fill-in fields as shown in Figure 8-42. In each case, set the default number to **1**. (*Hint*: Select the Default response to prompt check box in the Field dialog box, and type **1** in the box next to that check box.)
6. Use Quick Parts to facilitate entering the six names in the second to last paragraph (under the heading "Account Manager"). The completed template document should have six Quick Parts, three for the account managers and three for master blacksmiths. Use the person's initials as the Quick Part name. The completed template should have a space where a name should be located (rather than the highlighted list of names in brackets).
7. Include a macro in the template that moves the insertion point to the place where the first name should be inserted with a Quick Part in the paragraph below "Account Manager." The macro should run automatically when you start a new document using the template.
8. Toggle all field codes off, save the completed **Fax Template** file to the Word8\Case3 folder, and then close it.
9. Use the **Fax Template** file to create the document shown in Figure 8-43. Use the current date. When you see the To: prompt, type your name.

Figure 8-43 Fax template for Sierra Top Blacksmiths

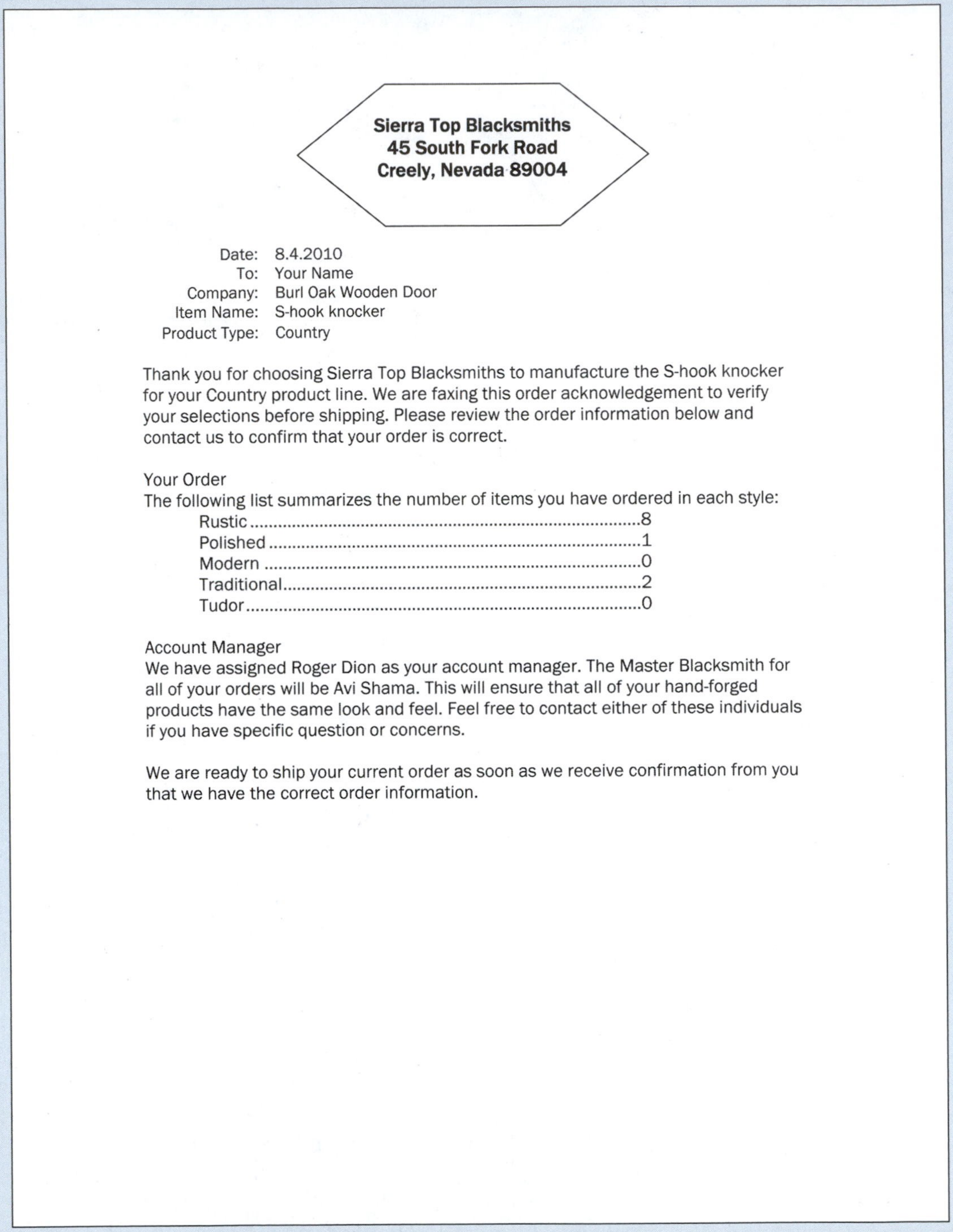

Sierra Top Blacksmiths
45 South Fork Road
Creely, Nevada 89004

Date: 8.4.2010
To: Your Name
Company: Burl Oak Wooden Door
Item Name: S-hook knocker
Product Type: Country

Thank you for choosing Sierra Top Blacksmiths to manufacture the S-hook knocker for your Country product line. We are faxing this order acknowledgement to verify your selections before shipping. Please review the order information below and contact us to confirm that your order is correct.

Your Order
The following list summarizes the number of items you have ordered in each style:

Rustic 8
Polished 1
Modern 0
Traditional 2
Tudor 0

Account Manager
We have assigned Roger Dion as your account manager. The Master Blacksmith for all of your orders will be Avi Shama. This will ensure that all of your hand-forged products have the same look and feel. Feel free to contact either of these individuals if you have specific question or concerns.

We are ready to ship your current order as soon as we receive confirmation from you that we have the correct order information.

10. In the second-to-last paragraph, insert **Roger Dion** as the account manager, and **Avi Shama** as the Master Blacksmith.
11. Save the new letter as a document using the filename **Sample Fax**.
12. Submit your documents to your instructor in electronic or printed form, as requested, and then close all open documents.

Create a newsletter introducing a theater company's production of that play.

RESEARCH

Case Problem 4

There are no Data Files needed for this Case Problem.

Riverland Communications You are a writer employed by Riverland Communications, a public relations firm located in Spring Green, Wisconsin. Riverland has been hired to create a series of newsletters for Red Barn Theater, a local community theater company, to publicize upcoming plays. Each newsletter should include the following three articles: a description of the play, information about the lead actor, and a biographical sketch of the playwright. It's your job to create a template that any writer at Riverland Communications can use to create these newsletters. Complete the following steps:

1. Create a sketch of the newsletter on paper. Plan to include a WordArt heading with the name of the theater company (Red Barn Theater). It should also include a subheading for the name of the current play. Plan to format the newsletter with multiple columns. Use varying widths if appropriate. Plan to include at least one shape with text. The Buildings folder in the Office Collections Clipart folder includes a clip art image of a barn and silo, which you could use as the logo for Red Barn Theater. Include any other newsletter features you want, such as drop caps, lines between columns, and a border.
2. Create a document and save it as a macro-enabled template named **Theater** in the Word8\Case4 folder.
3. Create the structure of the newsletter according to the plan you created in Step 1. Where appropriate, insert placeholder headings. Insert temporary text below the headings so you can see how the columns will look when filled with text. To insert temporary text (also known as random text), move the insertion point to a new paragraph, type **=rand()** and then press the Enter key.
4. Format the newsletter template and add any elements you planned in Step 1. Remember to include at least one shape with text as a decorative element and at least one piece of clip art.
5. Use fields to customize parts of the newsletter. For example, you might want to use Date and Fill-in fields. Keep in mind that the letter should have enough placeholder text and enough prompts so that you can use your document template to create a newsletter for any play staged by Red Barn Theater.
6. As part of the document template, create at least one macro. For example, create an AutoNew macro to move the insertion point to a certain location within the document when the document is first created, or record a macro that resizes a picture or clip art.
7. Create at least two Quick Parts that you save in the template. For example, one might be a Quick Part for the name of the company director, Milo Levetan, and for the name of the theater company, Red Barn Theater.
8. Close the **Theater** template, and then start a new document based on the **Theater** template. Save the document as a document named **Sample Newsletter** in the Word8\Case4 folder included with your Data Files.
9. Search the Internet for information on a play and then use the template to create a newsletter introducing Red Barn Theater's staging of the play. Based on your research, write the articles about the play and the playwright. Pick any famous actor as the lead actor, and then, doing more Internet research as necessary, write the article about the lead actor.
10. Save the completed newsletter, submit your documents to your instructor in electronic or printed form, as requested, and then close all open documents.

ASSESS

SAM: Skills Assessment Manager

For current SAM information, including versions and content details, visit SAM Central (http://samcentral.course.com). If you have a SAM user profile, you may have access to hands-on instruction, practice, and assessment of the skills covered in this tutorial. Since various versions of SAM are supported throughout the life of this text, check with your instructor for the correct instructions and URL/Web site for accessing assignments.

ENDING DATA FILES

Word8 →

Tutorial

Brochure Draft.docm
Brochure Draft.docx
General Inquiry.dotm
General Inquiry.dotx
Inquiry Form.dotx
Letterhead.dotx
Retirement Party Inquiry.docx

Review

Corporate Brochure Draft.docm
New Brochure.dotm
New Brochure.dotx

Case1

LCN Response.dotm
LCN Response.dotx
Letter Final.docm

Case2

Sample Shipping List.docx
Sample List.dotm

Case3

Fax Template.dotm
Sample Fax.docx

Case4

Sample Newsletter.docx
Theater.dotm

TUTORIAL 9

Creating Online Forms Using Advanced Table Techniques

Developing an Order Form

OBJECTIVES

Session 9.1
- Plan and design an online form
- Merge and split cells
- Move gridlines
- Draw and erase borders
- Align and rotate text
- Format text and shade cells

Session 9.2
- Learn about content controls
- Insert content controls
- Modify placeholder text in a content control
- Test content controls

Session 9.3
- Learn about cell referencing in formulas
- Use formulas in a table
- Protect a document
- Fill in an online form
- Learn how to fax and email a form

Case | *Scarborough Kung Fu Studios*

Peter Dietz is the owner of Scarborough Kung Fu Studios in Scarborough, Maine. He teaches Kung Fu classes to children and teens. He realized recently that his staff was spending quite a bit of time entering data for new students when they sign up for classes, so he decided to set up a computer on which new students or their parents could enter their own information in an online form.

In this tutorial, you'll create and then test an online registration form. You'll start with a partially completed form, which is a Word table that Pete created. First, you'll modify the structure and the format of the table. Next, you'll create different types of content controls and special fields to accept certain types of information, and you'll add placeholder text to help the user fill out the form. You'll add a formula to the table and use form fields to perform a calculation. When the form is complete, you'll add a password to protect the form from being changed accidentally, and then you'll test the form by completing a sample registration. Finally, you'll explore how Pete can fax or email the form rather than printing it.

STARTING DATA FILES

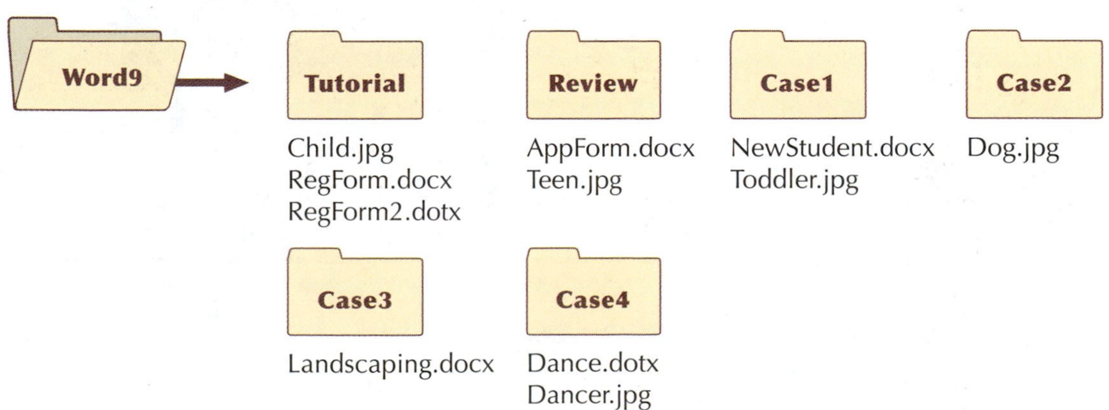

SESSION 9.1 VISUAL OVERVIEW

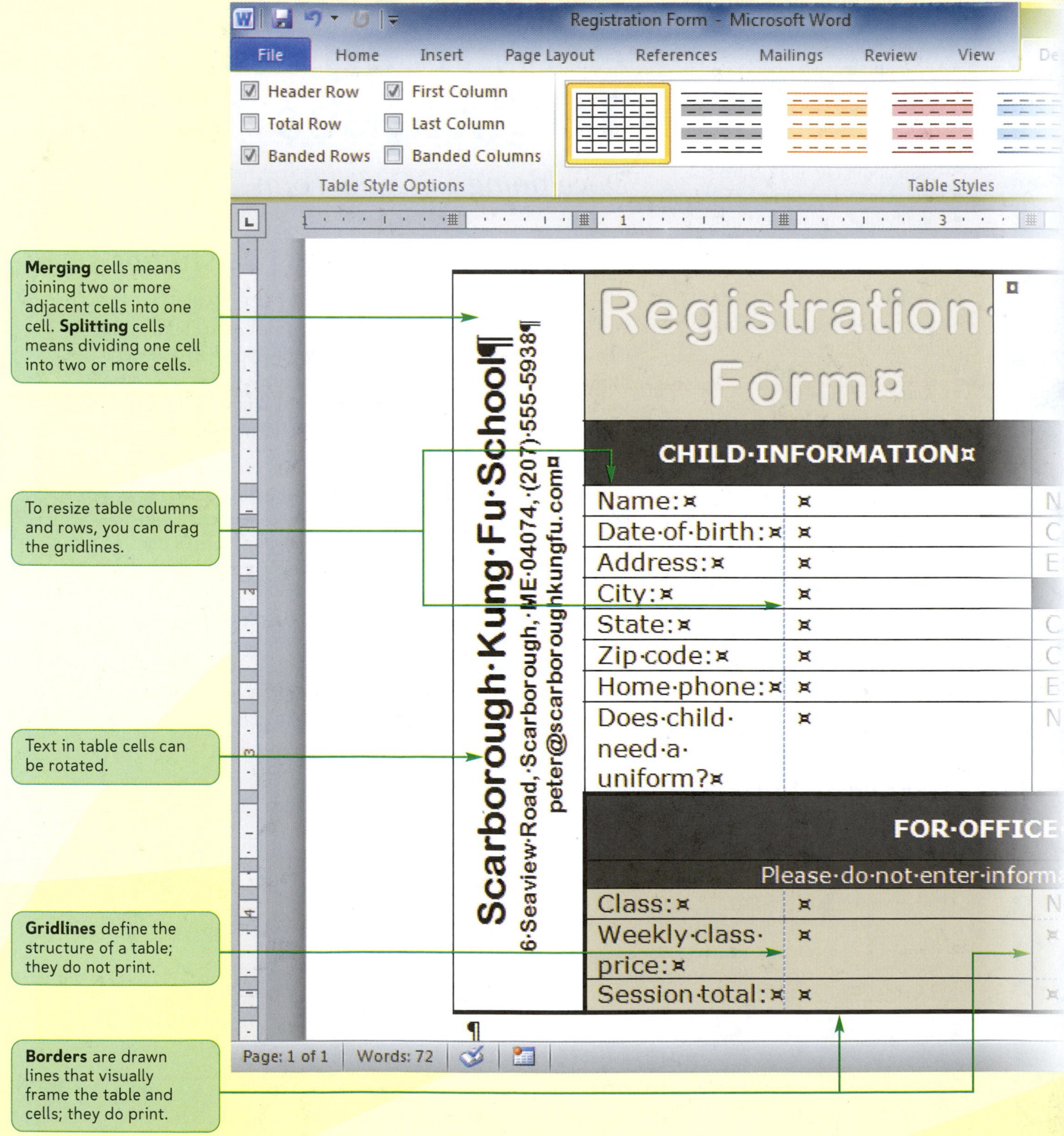

Registration Form - Microsoft Word
File
Home
Insert
Page Layout
References
Mailings
Review
View
Header Row
First Column
Total Row
Last Column
Banded Rows
Banded Columns
Table Style Options
Table Styles
Merging cells means joining two or more adjacent cells into one cell. **Splitting** cells means dividing one cell into two or more cells.
To resize table columns and rows, you can drag the gridlines.
Text in table cells can be rotated.
Gridlines define the structure of a table; they do not print.
Borders are drawn lines that visually frame the table and cells; they do print.
Scarborough·Kung·Fu·School
6·Seaview·Road,·Scarborough,·ME·04074,·(207)·555-5938
peter@scarboroughkungfu.com
Registration Form
CHILD·INFORMATION
Name:
Date·of·birth:
Address:
City:
State:
Zip·code:
Home·phone:
Does·child·need·a·uniform?
FOR·OFFICE
Please·do·not·enter·inform
Class:
Weekly·class·price:
Session·total:
Page: 1 of 1
Words: 72

CUSTOM TABLE

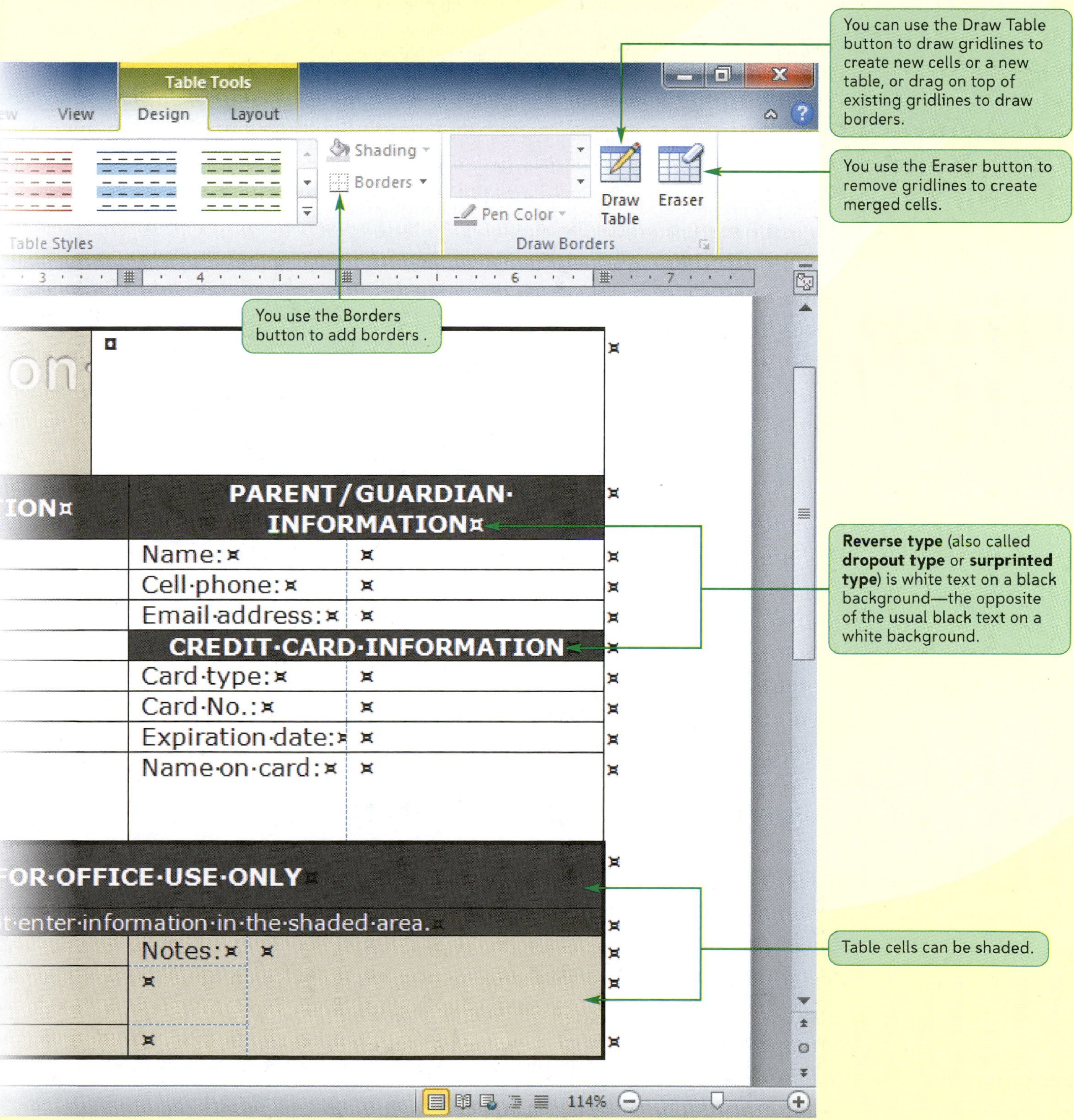

Table Tools
View
Design
Layout
Shading
Borders
Pen Color
Draw Table
Eraser
Table Styles
Draw Borders
You can use the Draw Table button to draw gridlines to create new cells or a new table, or drag on top of existing gridlines to draw borders.
You use the Eraser button to remove gridlines to create merged cells.
You use the Borders button to add borders .
PARENT/GUARDIAN·INFORMATION¤
Name:¤
Cell·phone:¤
Email·address:¤
CREDIT·CARD·INFORMATION
Card·type:¤
Card·No.:¤
Expiration·date:¤
Name·on·card:¤
Reverse type (also called **dropout type** or **surprinted type**) is white text on a black background—the opposite of the usual black text on a white background.
FOR·OFFICE·USE·ONLY
t·enter·information·in·the·shaded·area.
Notes:¤
Table cells can be shaded.
114%

Creating and Using Online Forms

An **online form** is a document that contains labels and corresponding blank areas in which a user electronically enters the information requested. When you create an online form using Word, it's a good idea to use a template file rather than a regular Word file so that users can't change the form itself when entering their information. In addition to the usual template elements (text, graphics, theme, styles, and placeholder text), an online form template can contain content controls that you create. You have used content controls that display information about a document, such as the document title or the author name. When a content control is linked to information in a document, that information is inserted by Word wherever that control appears in a document. Content controls in a form are areas that can contain only the type of information that you specify, such as text or a date. You can also specify a format for the information stored in a control and create rules that determine what kind of information the control will accept. For example, Figure 9-1 shows a form with different types of information, including text, a date, and a value selected from a list.

Figure 9-1 Portion of an online form

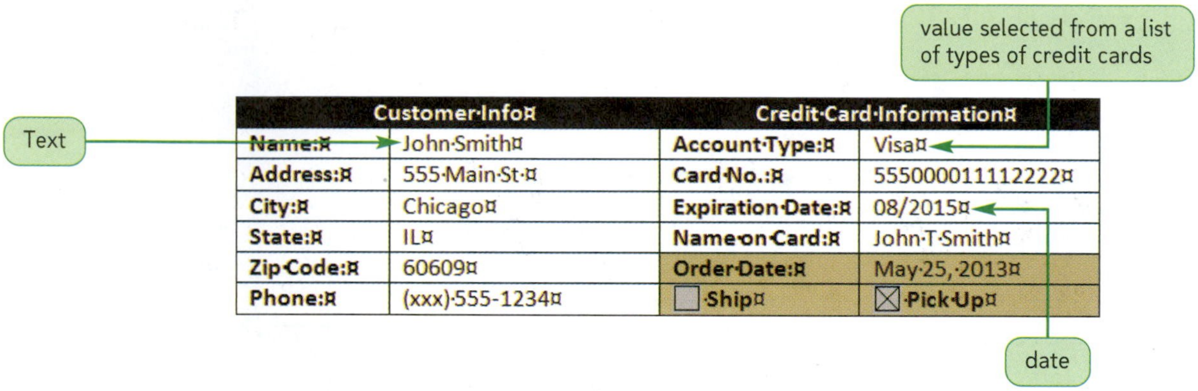

value selected from a list of types of credit cards

Text

Customer·Info¤		Credit·Card·Information¤	
Name:¤	John·Smith¤	Account·Type:¤	Visa¤
Address:¤	555·Main·St·¤	Card·No.:¤	555000011112222¤
City:¤	Chicago¤	Expiration·Date:¤	08/2015¤
State:¤	IL¤	Name·on·Card:¤	John·T·Smith¤
Zip·Code:¤	60609¤	Order·Date:¤	May·25,·2013¤
Phone:¤	(xxx)·555-1234¤	☐ Ship¤	☒ ·Pick·Up¤

date

The fact that you can specify the type of information that appears in a control and thereby allow only certain types of data helps prevent users from entering incorrect information. Placeholder text in each control tells the user what information is required for that particular part of the form.

Planning and Designing the Form

The online registration form you'll create for Pete will consist of a Word table that the parents of new students will use to enter the following information:

- **Photo:** A photo of the child taken during the registration process
- **Contact information for the child and the parent or guardian:** Name, address, phone numbers, and email address
- **Child's date of birth:** Entered using a calendar the user can click
- **Credit card information:** Account type, card number, expiration date, and name on card
- **Note whether the child needs a uniform:** Yes/No response
- **Studio information:** The class the child will be taking, the weekly class cost, and the cost for an 8-week session

The form should contain clear directions, and it should be easy to read and understand.

Figure 9-2 shows Pete's sketch for the online form. He decided to use a table as the structure for the form.

Figure 9-2 Sketch of the structure of the online form

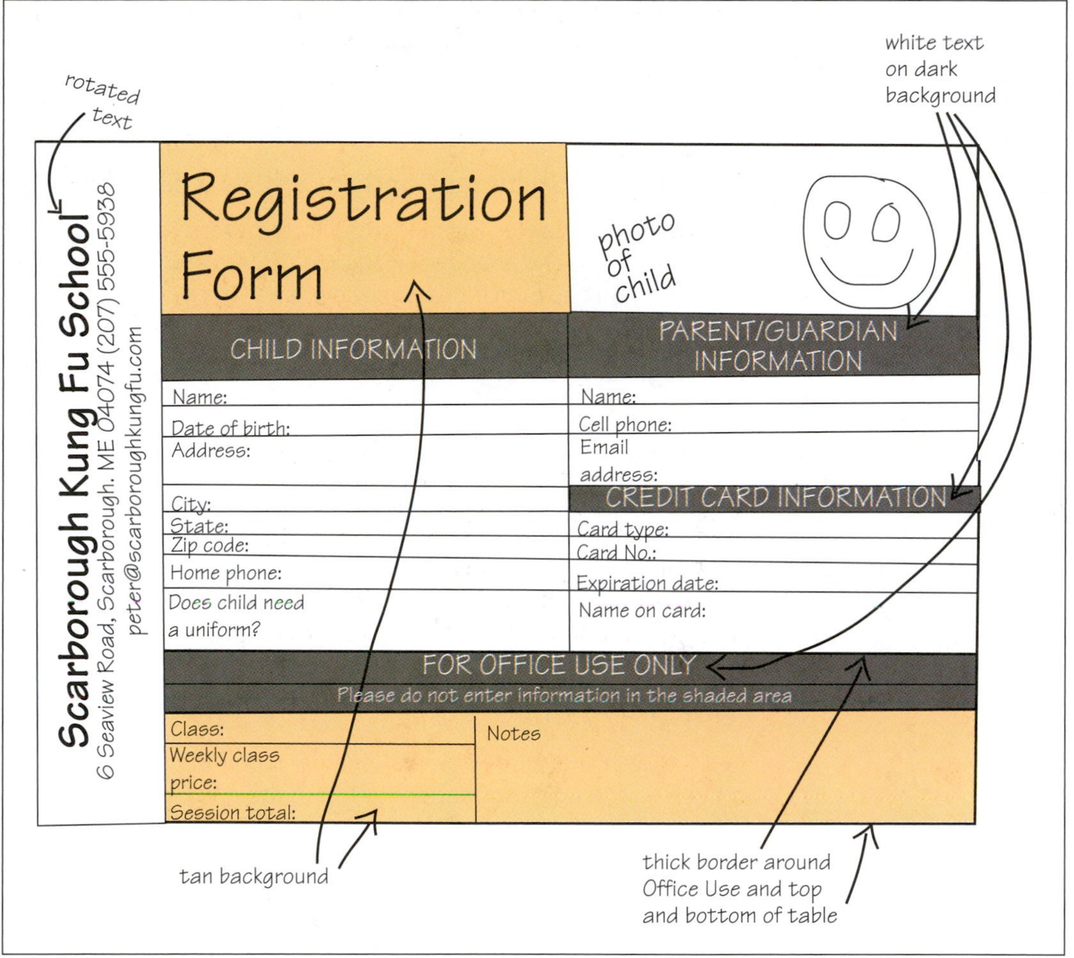

Pete designed the form with the following characteristics:

- The table uses font styles to visually organize the form sections.
- The table has border lines of different weights (½ point and 2¼ points) and cells with different shading (none or white, tan, and dark gray).
- The table has cells of different heights and widths.
- The table contains cells with different types of content (labels, text, dates, numbers, and a photo).

PROSKILLS

Decision Making: Using a Table as the Structure for a Form

Planning the layout of a form is important. If you just start typing, you could end up with a form that is so confusing for the user that they miss filling out important sections. You want the labels and areas in which the user enters the data to be clear and easy to understand. A table is an easy way to organize a form in a logical way. The rows and columns provide a natural organization for labels and areas where the user fills in information. You can add shading and formatting to specific cells to make certain parts of the table stand out or to divide the form into sections. Taking the time to plan and make decisions about how data should appear in a form will result in a form that is easy to build and easy for someone to fill out.

Creating a Custom Table for a Form

Pete already began creating the table for the online form. You'll open his document, save it as a template, and then customize the table based on Pete's form design shown earlier in Figure 9-2.

To open the document and save it as a template:

1. Open the file **RegForm** located in the Word9\Tutorial folder included with your Data Files, and then make sure the rulers and nonprinting characters are visible, that Word is in Print Layout view, and that your zoom is set to Page Width.
2. Save the file as a Word template in the same folder, using the filename **Registration Form**. You will not be including any macros in this template.

   Trouble? Remember that to save a document as a template, you open the Save As dialog box, and then change the file type to Word Template.

Pete's table already has the necessary text for the registration form. He also changed the font, font sizes, and font style of the text in the first row so that it stands out. He wants you to format the rest of the table to match his sketch. First, you need to insert a new column on the left side of the table for the company name.

Merging Cells

Pete's sketch shows the company name appearing in the first column of the table, and rotated so it reads from bottom to top in the column. To create this column and format the company name as Pete has requested, you need to insert a new blank column as the first column in the table. Then, you will need to merge the cells of the new column to form one long cell. You can merge cells in the same row, the same column, or the same rectangular block of rows and columns. When you merge cells, you can create cells that span more than one column. Merging cells is especially useful when you need to enter large amounts of information into a single cell or when you want to add a heading that spans more than one column. You can merge cells using either the Merge Cells button, located in the Merge group on the Table Tools Layout tab, or by using the Eraser button in the Draw Borders group on the Table Tools Design tab, to erase the gridlines between two or more adjacent cells.

To insert a new column and merge cells in the table:

1. Click anywhere in the first cell in the first row, if necessary, and then click the **Table Tools Layout** tab.
2. In the Rows & Columns group, click the **Insert Left** button. A blank column is inserted to the left of the current cell, and all the cells of the new column are selected. See Figure 9-3. Next, you will merge all the cells in the new column.

Figure 9-3 New column inserted to the left of the first column in the table

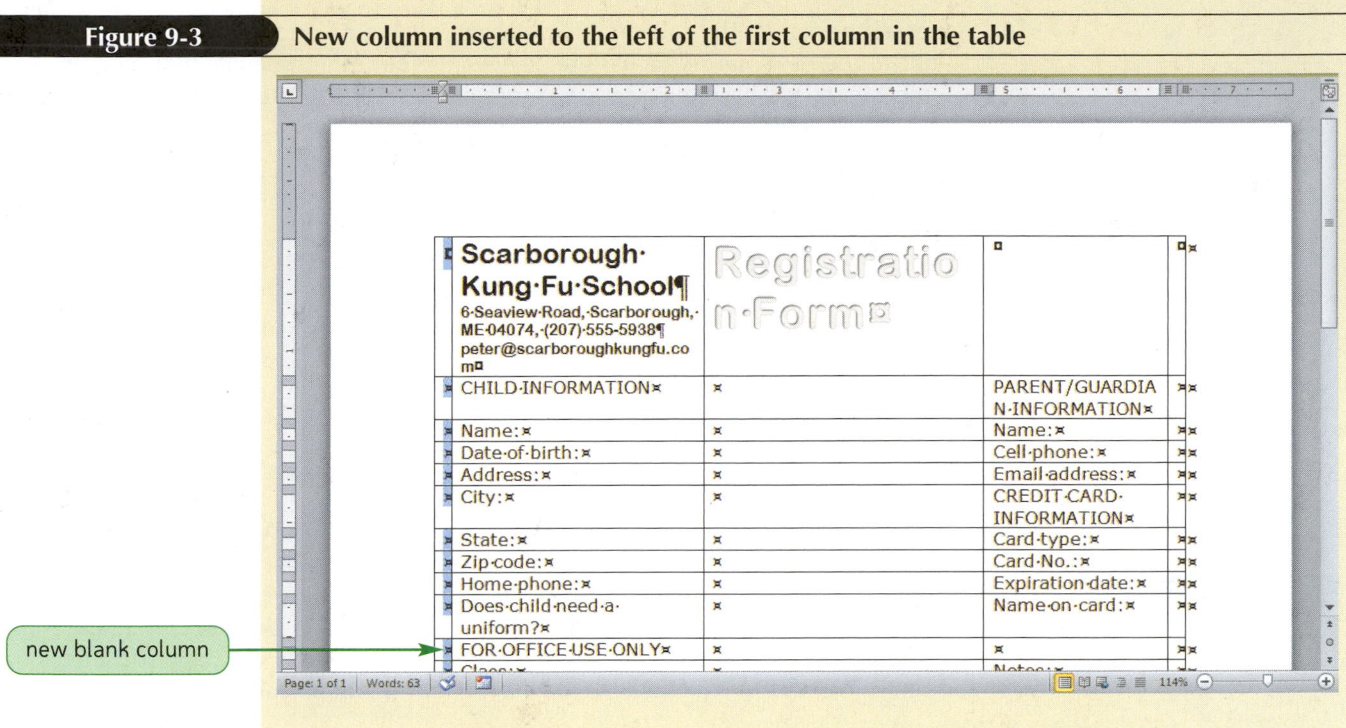

3. In the Merge group, click the **Merge Cells** button. The new column is now one cell. See Figure 9-4. Next, you need to move the address information to the new merged cell.

Figure 9-4 Column merged into one cell

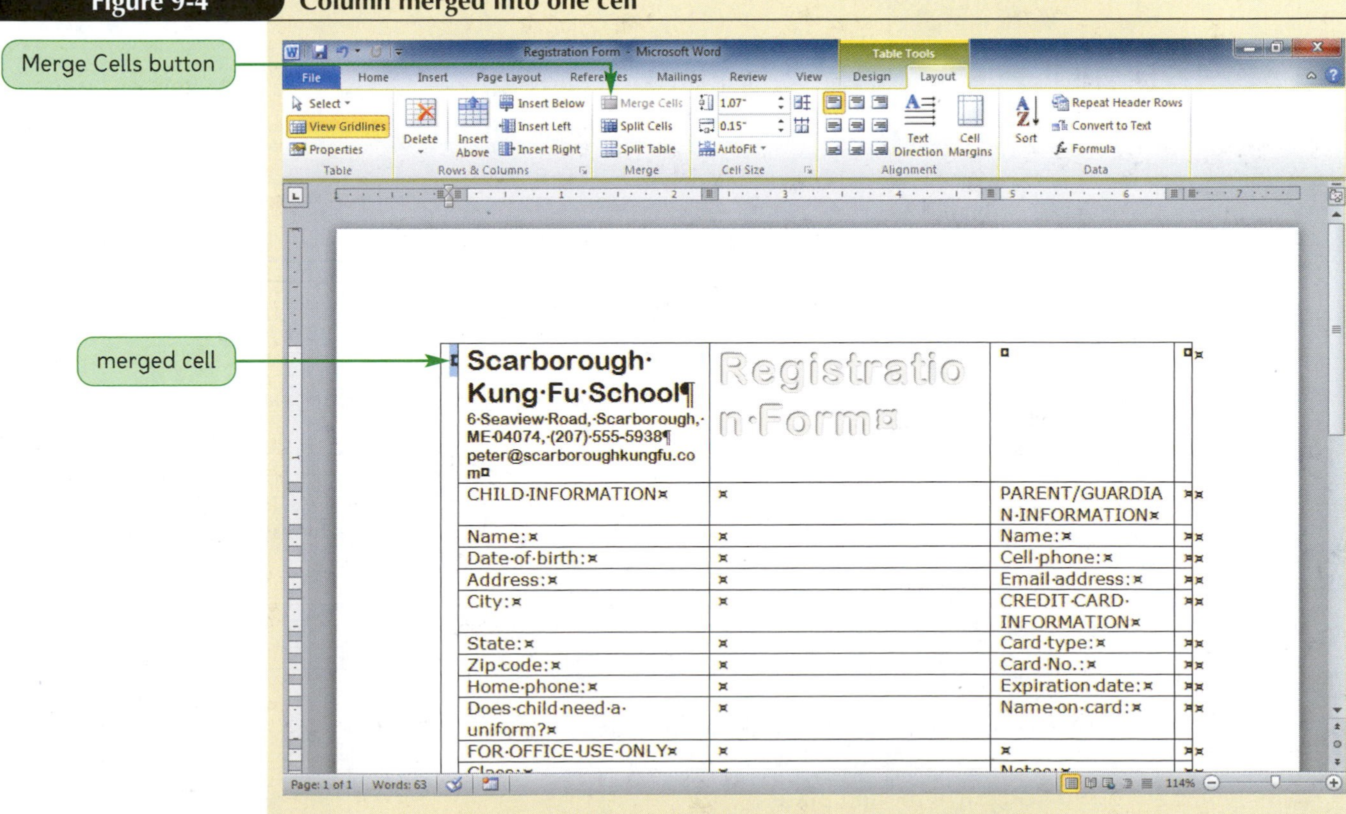

4. Select all the text in the cell containing the studio name and address, and then drag it to the new merged cell. Pete also wants to merge the cells that contain the column headings of the form so they more clearly label the sections of the table. You will use the Eraser tool to merge these cells.
5. Click the **Table Tools Design** tab.
6. In the Draw Borders group, click the **Eraser** button, and then move the pointer on top of the document. The pointer changes to an eraser. You can click a gridline or drag over several gridlines to merge cells.
7. Click the left border of the cell containing "Registration Form." The "Registration Form" cell and the empty cell to its left merge into one cell. You also need to merge the last two cells in the first row in preparation for inserting a photo of the child who is registering.
8. Click the border between the two empty cells in the first row.
9. In the Draw Borders group, click the **Eraser** button to deselect it. Next, you'll merge cells to create section headings in the form.

TIP

If you use the Eraser tool on a border on the edge of the table, the border is erased, but the gridline is not and no cells are merged.

10. Using either the Merge Cells button or the Eraser tool, merge the cell containing "CHILD INFORMATION" and the blank cell to its right, the cell containing "PARENT/GUARDIAN INFORMATION" and the blank cell to its right, and the cell containing "CREDIT CARD INFORMATION" and the blank cell to its right.
11. Merge the cell to the right of "Notes" with the two cells beneath it, and then deselect the cell. See Figure 9-5.

Figure 9-5 Merged cells in table

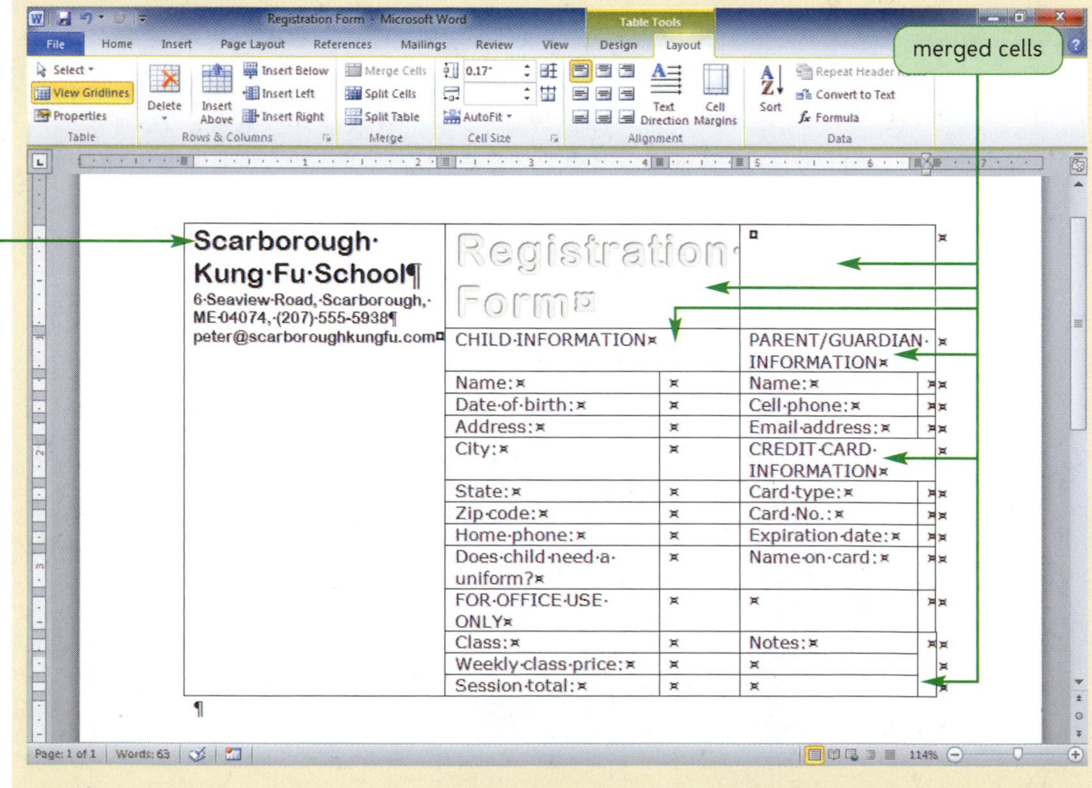

12. Save the template.

Just as you can merge cells, you can also split cells.

INSIGHT

Understanding AutoFit Behavior in Tables

The default setting for tables in Word is for the columns to automatically resize as you enter text. If you want to create a table without the columns resizing, use the Insert Table dialog box to create the new table. (To open the Insert Table dialog box, click the Insert tab, then in the Tables group, click the Table button, and then click Insert Table.) After you set the number of columns and rows, you can click an option button to set the AutoFit behavior. The default is Fixed column width set to Auto. This means that the column widths will change as you enter text, but Word will allow the text to wrap in a cell so that one column does not get unreasonably wide. To set the column widths to a constant value, type the value (in inches) in the box to the right of the Fixed column width option button. If you do not want the text to wrap in a cell and you want the columns to resize as you enter text, click the AutoFit to contents option button. Each column will increase in width so that text does not wrap in a cell; this occurs until the table becomes wider than the page margins, and then the text in the cells will start to wrap, sometimes in unexpected ways. If you are creating a table for a Web page, select the AutoFit to window option button. The table resizes to fit in the window in which it is being displayed.

Splitting Cells

You can split cells vertically (to increase the number of columns in a row) or horizontally (to increase the number of rows in a column). If you select multiple adjacent cells, when you split them, you can specify whether you want to first merge the selected cells into one cell before the split, or whether you want each cell split individually.

REFERENCE

Splitting Cells

- Select the cell or cells that you want to split.
- Click the Table Tools Layout tab, and then click the Split Cells button in the Merge group.
- In the Split Cells dialog box, set the number of columns and rows into which you want to split the current cell or cells.
- If you selected multiple cells, check the Merge cells before split check box if you want the cell contents to merge into one cell before they split into more columns or rows; or uncheck the Merge cells before split check box if you want the cell contents to split into columns and rows without merging first.
- Click the OK button.

or

- Click the Table Tools Design tab. In the Draw Borders group, click the Draw Table button, and then drag the Draw Table pointer to draw a new vertical or horizontal gridline.

In Pete's sketch, he indicated that he wants a row under the row containing "FOR OFFICE USE ONLY," but this row is not included in the table he created. You could insert a row using one of the Insert commands in the Rows & Columns group on the Table Tools Layout tab. But because you need to merge the cell containing "FOR OFFICE USE ONLY" with the cells to its right, you'll use the Split Cells button to merge the cells in this row into one cell and then split the row into two rows.

To split the "FOR OFFICE USE ONLY" cell into two rows:

1. Select the cell containing "FOR OFFICE USE ONLY" and the three blank cells to its right, and then click the **Table Tools Layout** tab if necessary.
2. In the Merge group, click the **Split Cells** button. The Split Cells dialog box opens. See Figure 9-6.

Figure 9-6 Split Cells dialog box

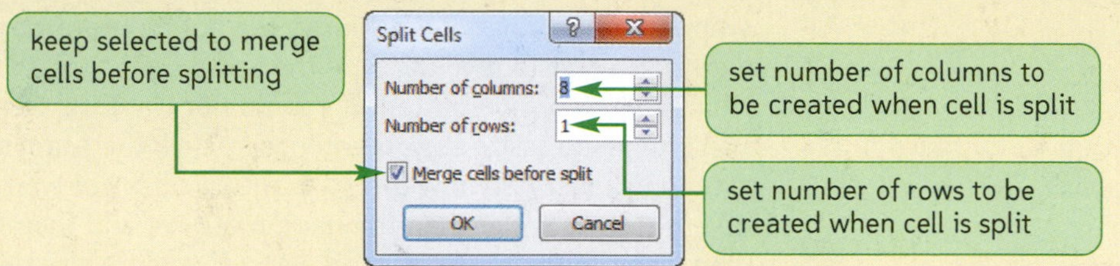

3. In the Number of columns box, type **1**, press the **Tab** key to move to the Number of rows box, type **2**, and then make sure that the Merge cells before split check box is selected. Selecting this check box will merge these cells before splitting them into two rows.
4. Click the **OK** button. The selected cells merge into one cell and then split into two rows.
5. Click in the new blank cell below "FOR OFFICE USE ONLY", change the font size to **10**, and then type **Please do not enter information in the shaded area.** You'll add the shading later in the tutorial.
6. Save the template.

TIP

If you get unexpected results when you merge cells before splitting them, undo the split, and then try splitting the cells without merging them first.

Now you can turn your attention back to the text in the cell in the first column. According to Pete's sketch, he wants the text formatted so it reads from the bottom of the page up to the top. You'll do this next.

Rotating Text in a Cell

Rotating text in tables allows you to fit long phrases or numbers into narrow cells. For example, if a table has many columns containing three- and four-digit numbers, you could rotate the numbers in each cell to keep the columns narrow. Rotating the studio name and address will allow the first column to be narrower and keep the text readable.

To rotate the studio name and address in the first column:

1. Click in the cell containing the studio name and address, and then click the **Table Tools Layout** tab. You don't need to select any text because the command applies to all the text in the cell.
2. In the Alignment group, click the **Text Direction** button. The text in the first column rotates so that it reads from top to bottom. Note that the icon on the Text Direction button changed to reflect this.
3. Click the **Text Direction** button again. The text in the cell and the arrows on the button change to show the text reading from bottom to top. If you clicked the button again, the text would read from left to right again. See Figure 9-7.

Figure 9-7 Table with rotated text

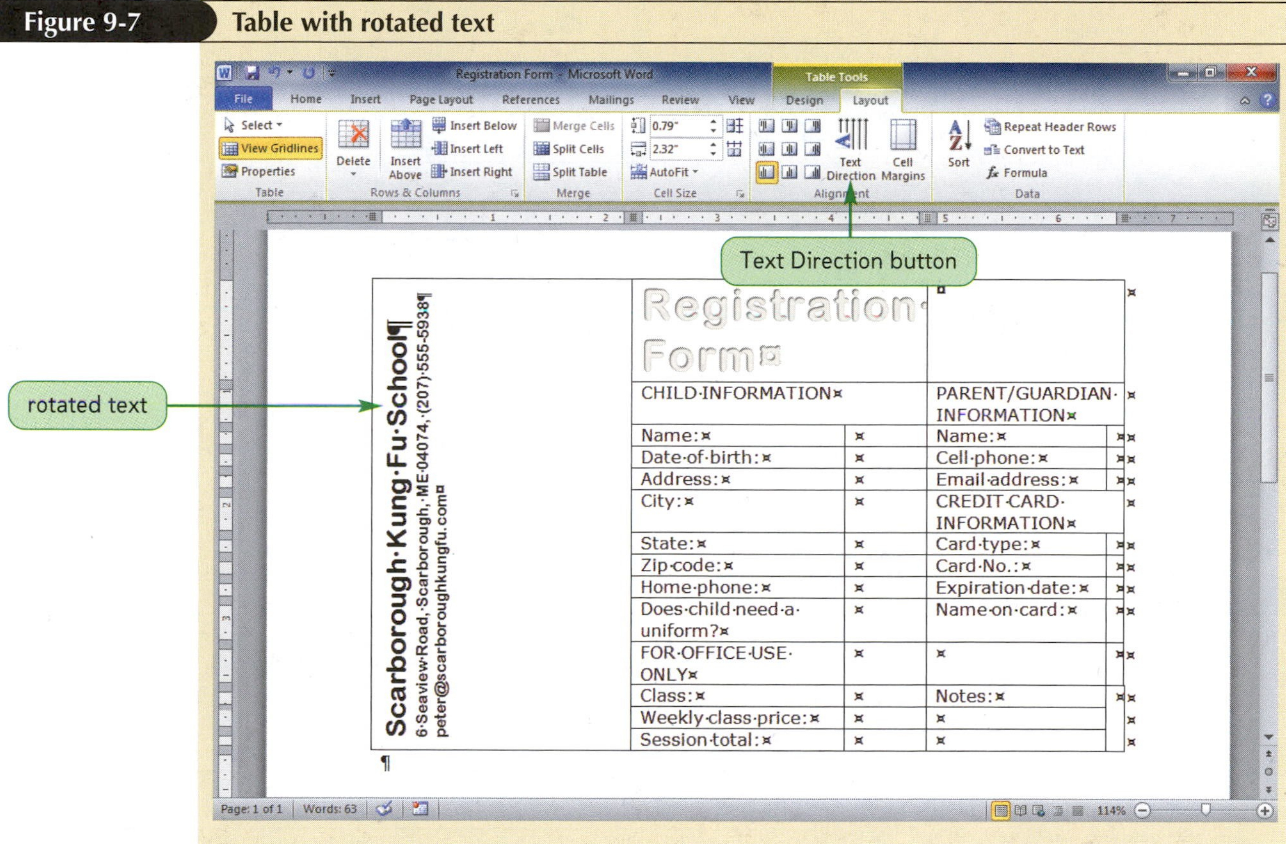

You'll adjust the column widths and row heights next by moving the gridlines.

Moving Gridlines

Until now, the table columns have been automatically resizing to accommodate the widest entry in the column. For many tables, this is what you want. For this form, however, you want to control the column widths, because Word doesn't always format the columns as you would expect; for example, the first column is still over two inches wide, and it doesn't need to be. You can specify exact column widths and row heights in the boxes in the Cell Size group on the Table Tools Layout tab, or you can drag the gridlines. Dragging the gridlines allows you to see the text or graphics you want to fit in your cell.

Before you change the column widths and row heights in the table, you should change the table property that causes the columns to automatically resize so that after you set the column widths, they stay the same width you specify.

To turn off automatic resizing in the table's properties:

1. On the Table Tools Layout tab, click the **Properties** button in the Table group to open the Table Properties dialog box with the Table tab selected, and then click the **Options** button. The Table Options dialog box opens. See Figure 9-8.

Figure 9-8 Table Options dialog box

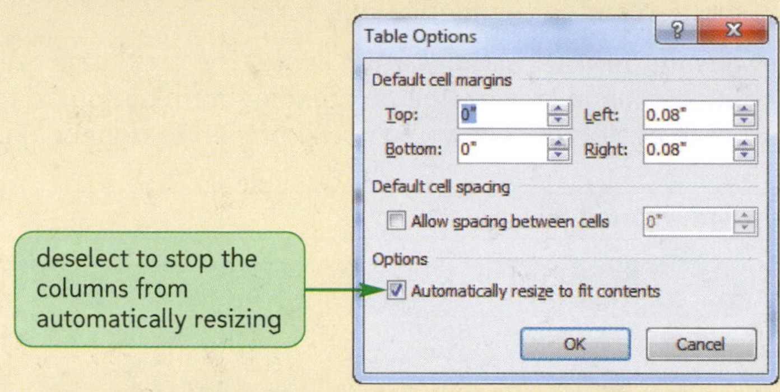

2. Click the **Automatically resize to fit contents** check box to deselect it. This will stop the columns from automatically resizing.
3. Click the **OK** button, and then click the **OK** button in the Table Properties dialog box.

Now you can move the table's gridlines. First you'll make the first column and the cells that contain the labels narrower. It would also be helpful if the cells that will contain the user's data could be a little wider. The widths Pete wants are shown in Figure 9-9.

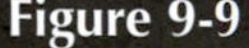

Figure 9-9 New column widths

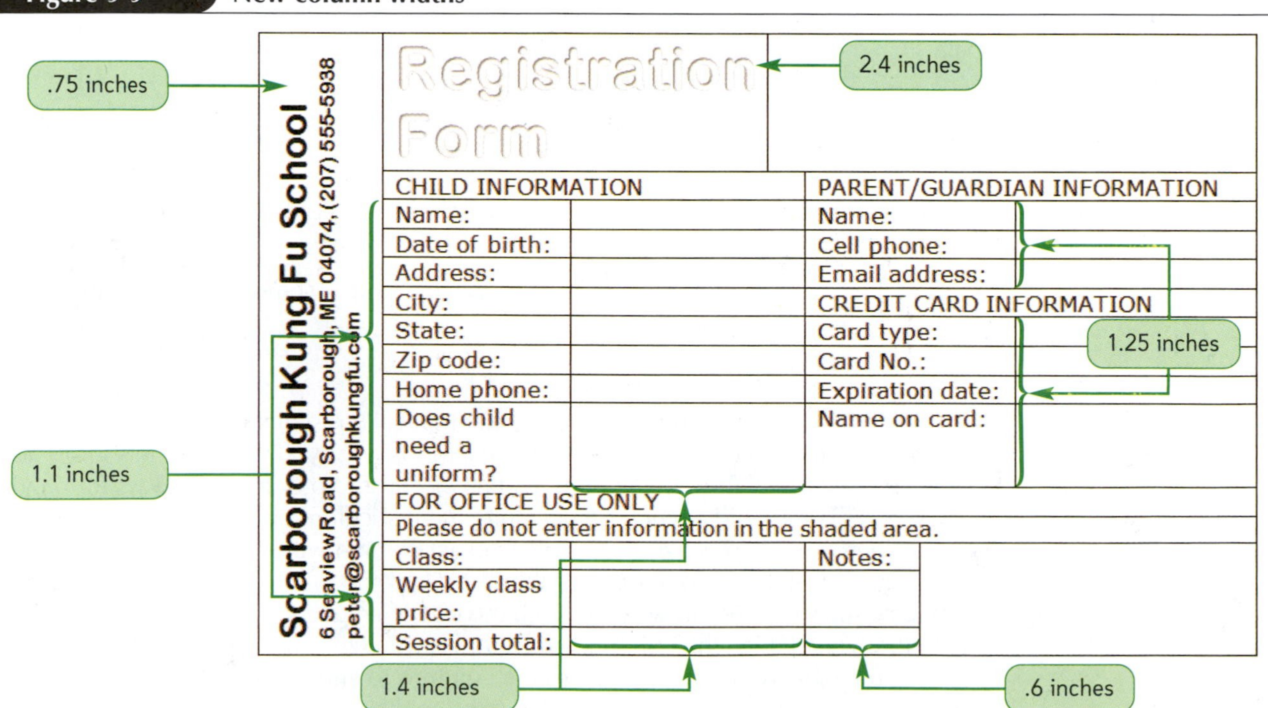

TIP

To change the width of an individual cell or group of cells, select the cell or cells, and then drag the gridlines to a new location.

To change the width of cells by moving gridlines:

1. Click in the first column. On the ruler, notice that the Move Table Column marker between the first two columns is positioned approximately at the 2.25-inch mark.
2. Position the pointer over the gridline between the first two columns so that the pointer changes to +||+, press and hold the mouse button, drag the gridline to the left until the Move Table Column marker is at the **.75-inch** mark on the ruler, and then release the mouse button. See Figure 9-10. Some of the text in the first column is not visible. Don't worry about this for now. Notice that when you resized the first column, the width of the second column increased, but the width of the cells in the last column decreased and the overall width of the table remained the same. You'll reduce the width of the second column now.

Figure 9-10 Resized column

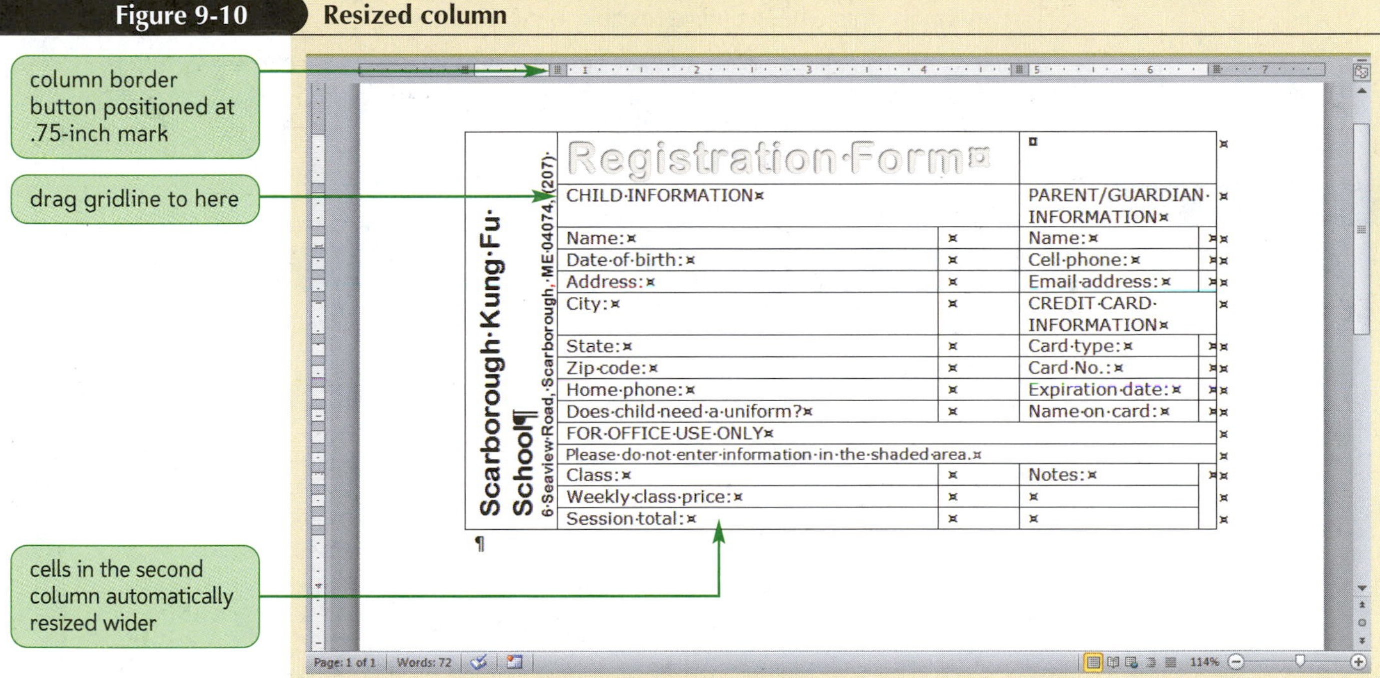

Trouble? If you dragged the Move Table Column marker on the ruler instead of dragging the gridline in the table, the whole table became narrower, not just the first column. Click the Undo button, and then repeat Step 2, this time making sure that you drag the gridline in the table.

3. Select the cells below the "CHILD INFORMATION" heading (from the cell containing "Name" to the cell containing "Does child need a uniform?").

4. Press and hold the **Alt** key, position the pointer over the gridline at the right side of the selected cells so that it changes to +||+, and then press and hold the mouse button. Notice that the ruler changed to indicate the exact widths of the columns. If you keep the Alt key pressed while dragging the gridlines, you can see the precise width of the selected column on the ruler.

   Trouble? When you press the Alt key, the Key Tips appear on the Ribbon. You can ignore this while you are resizing the column.

5. Using the ruler as a guide and keeping the Alt key pressed, drag the gridline left until the width of the selected cells in the second column is approximately **1.1** inches, as shown in Figure 9-11.

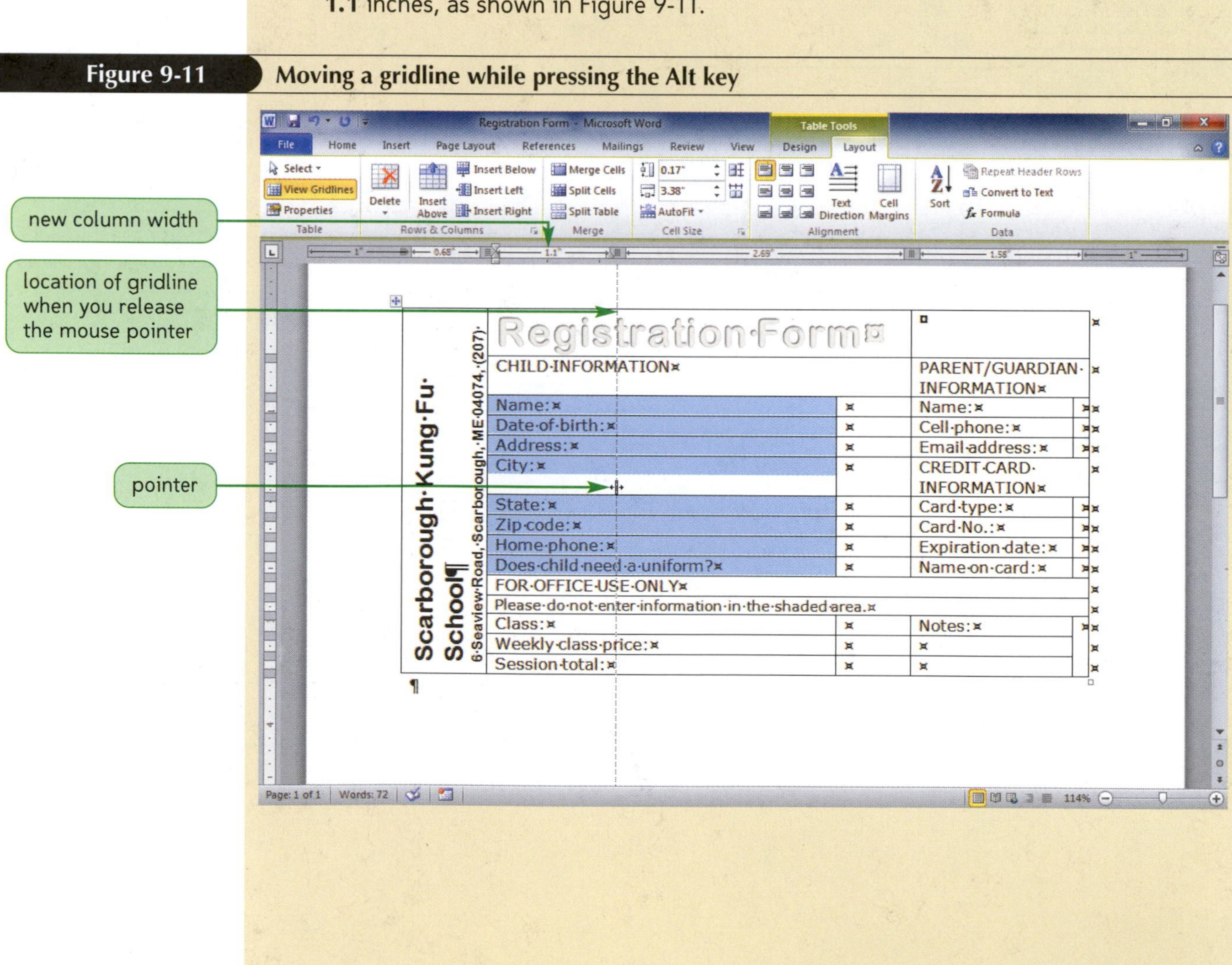

Figure 9-11 Moving a gridline while pressing the Alt key

6. Release the **Alt** key and the mouse button.

7. Decrease the width of the cells in the second column in the last three rows (the cell containing "Class" through the cell containing "Session total") to approximately **1.1** inches. Now you can resize the next column. The right edge of the cell containing the section heading "CHILD INFORMATION" aligns with the right edge of the third column. You want the section heading to remain above the second and third columns, so you need to select this cell when you resize the cells in the third column.

8. Select the cell containing "CHILD INFORMATION," and then drag down in the third column through the cell to the right of the cell containing "Does child need a uniform?". See Figure 9-12.

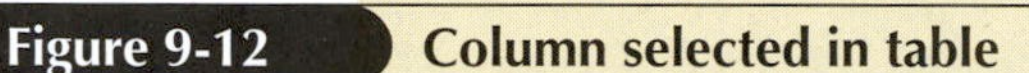
Figure 9-12 Column selected in table

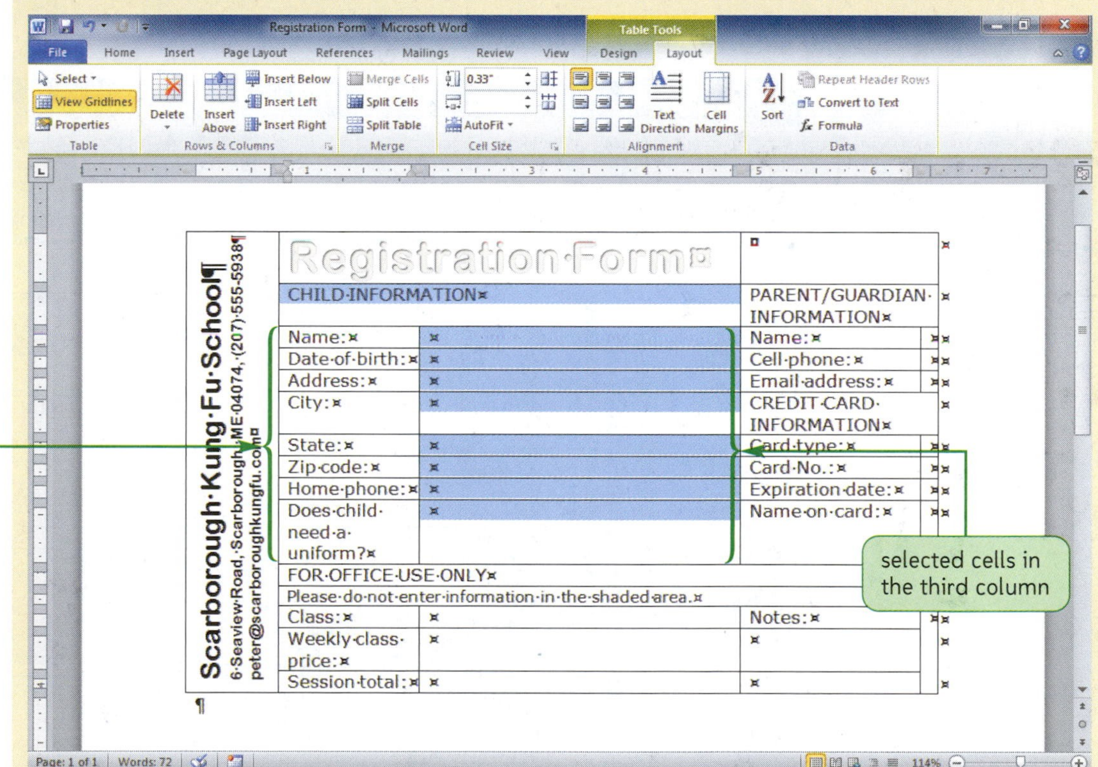

9. Press and hold the **Alt** key, and then drag the right border of the selected cells so that the cells in the third column are approximately **1.4 inches** wide.

Trouble? If the third column is much too narrow even though the measurement on the ruler indicates that it is 1.4 inches wide, reposition the pointer over the border anywhere except the right border of the cell containing "CHILD INFORMATION."

10. Resize the cells to the right of the cell containing "Class" through the cell to the right of the cell containing "Session total" to approximately **1.4 inches**.

11. Resize the cells below the "PARENT/GUARDIAN INFORMATION" heading and above the "CREDIT CARD INFORMATION" heading to approximately **1.25 inches**, and then do the same for the cells below the cell containing "CREDIT CARD INFORMATION" and above the merged cell containing "FOR OFFICE USE ONLY." Now that you've resized the cells to the left of the last column, the width of the last column in the upper half of the table is fine. Next you need to resize the cell containing the label "Notes" and the cells below it.
12. Resize the cell containing "Notes" and the two cells beneath it to approximately **.6** inches.
13. Click in the cell containing "Registration Form," and then drag the right border to the left until it is positioned to the right of the "n" in "Registration." The column should be approximately 2.4 inches wide. Compare your table to the one shown in Figure 9-13.

Figure 9-13 **Table with resized columns**

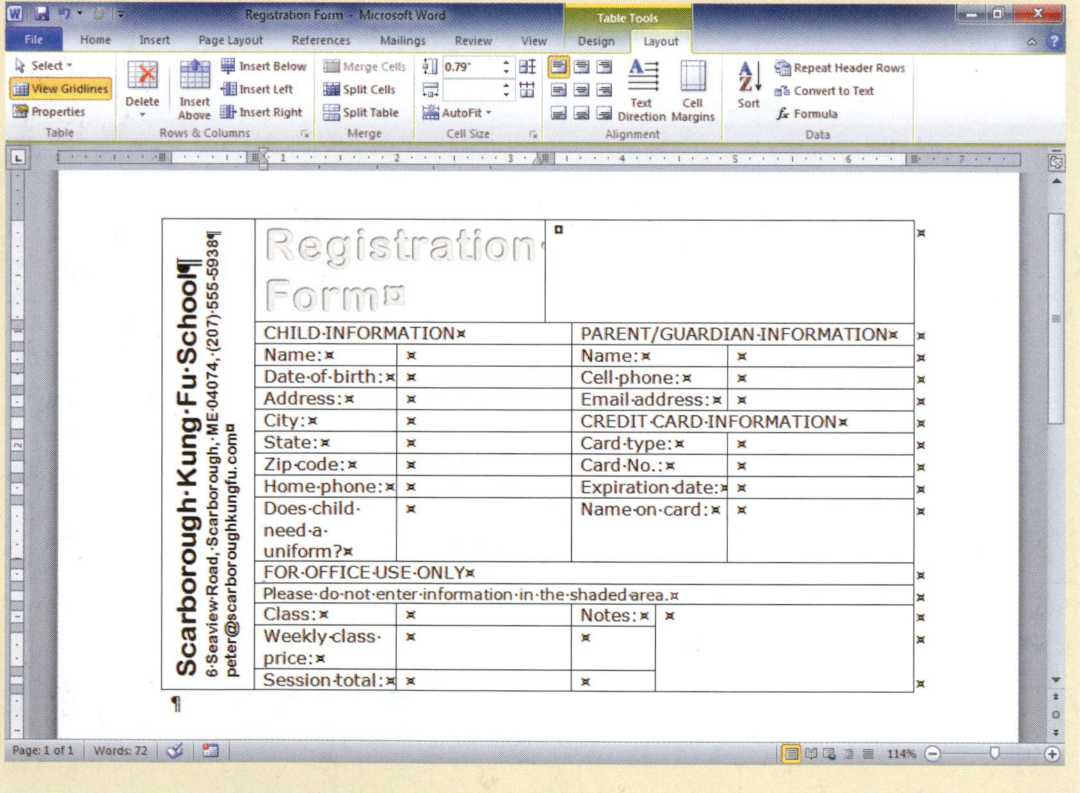

You can also adjust the height of rows. To visually separate the various sections of the form, you'll increase the height of the section heading rows.

To change the height of the section heading cells by moving the gridlines:

1. Click anywhere in the table, making sure that no text is selected, and then position the pointer over the bottom border of the second row so that it changes to ╪.
2. Drag the bottom border of one of the cells in the second row down until the row is approximately double its original height.
3. Drag the bottom border of the row containing "FOR OFFICE USE ONLY" down so that it is approximately double its original height. See Figure 9-14.

Figure 9-14 **Rows resized in table**

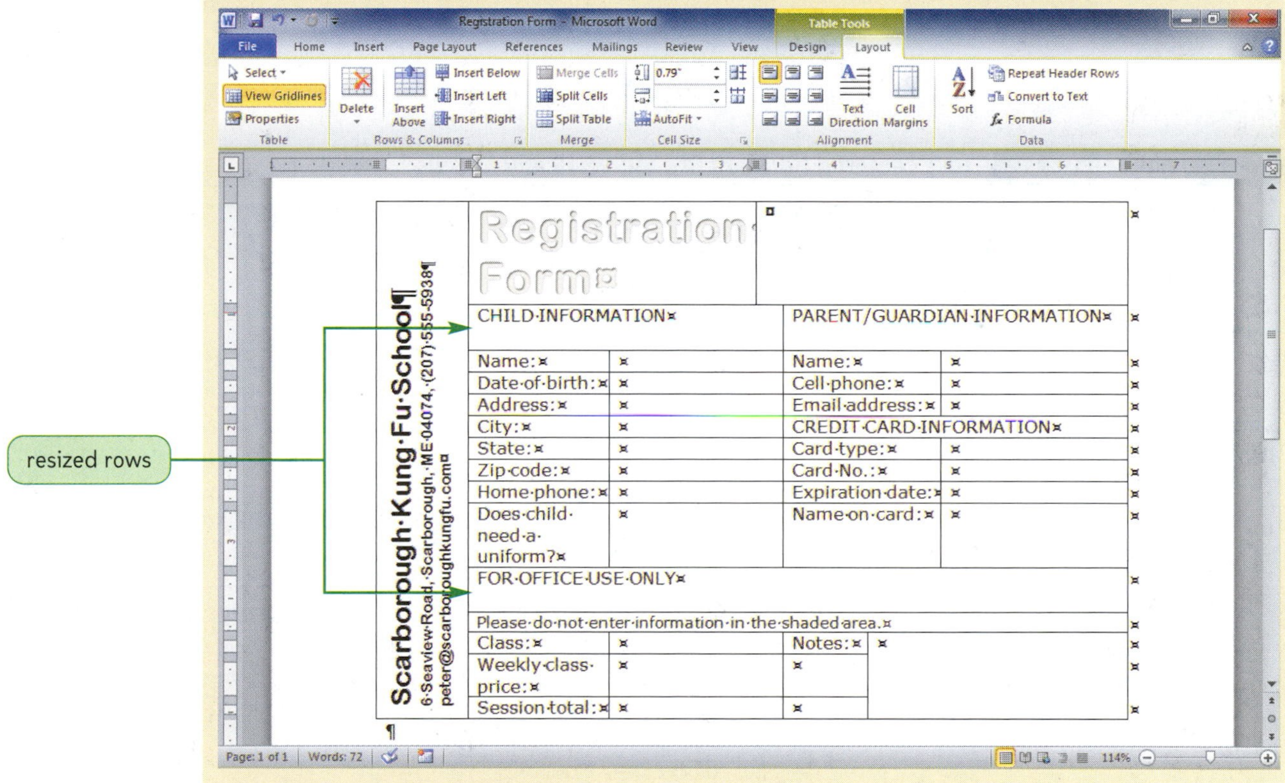

4. Save the template.

You don't want to change the height of the row containing the section heading "CREDIT CARD INFORMATION" because it is part of the Parent/Guardian Information section, and because the row also contains ordinary labels and content. Changing the height of the row would make the height of these cells too large.

Now that you've sized the rows and columns appropriately, you can align the text within cells.

Aligning Text in Cells

The text in the cells of a table is, by default, left aligned and positioned at the top of the cell. To make the registration form more attractive and easier to read, you'll center the text for the section headings horizontally and vertically. On the Table Tools Layout tab, in the Alignment group, there are nine buttons you can use to align text in a cell. You can align text at the left and right edges of the cell, and you can center align it. You can also position the text at the top, middle, or bottom of the cell.

To center the section headings horizontally and vertically:

1. Select the cells containing "CHILD INFORMATION" and "PARENT/GUARDIAN INFORMATION."
2. Click the **Table Tools Layout** tab if necessary, and then click the **Align Center** button in the Alignment group. The text is centered horizontally and vertically in the cell. See Figure 9-15.

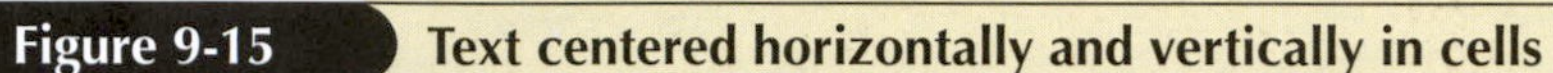
Figure 9-15 Text centered horizontally and vertically in cells

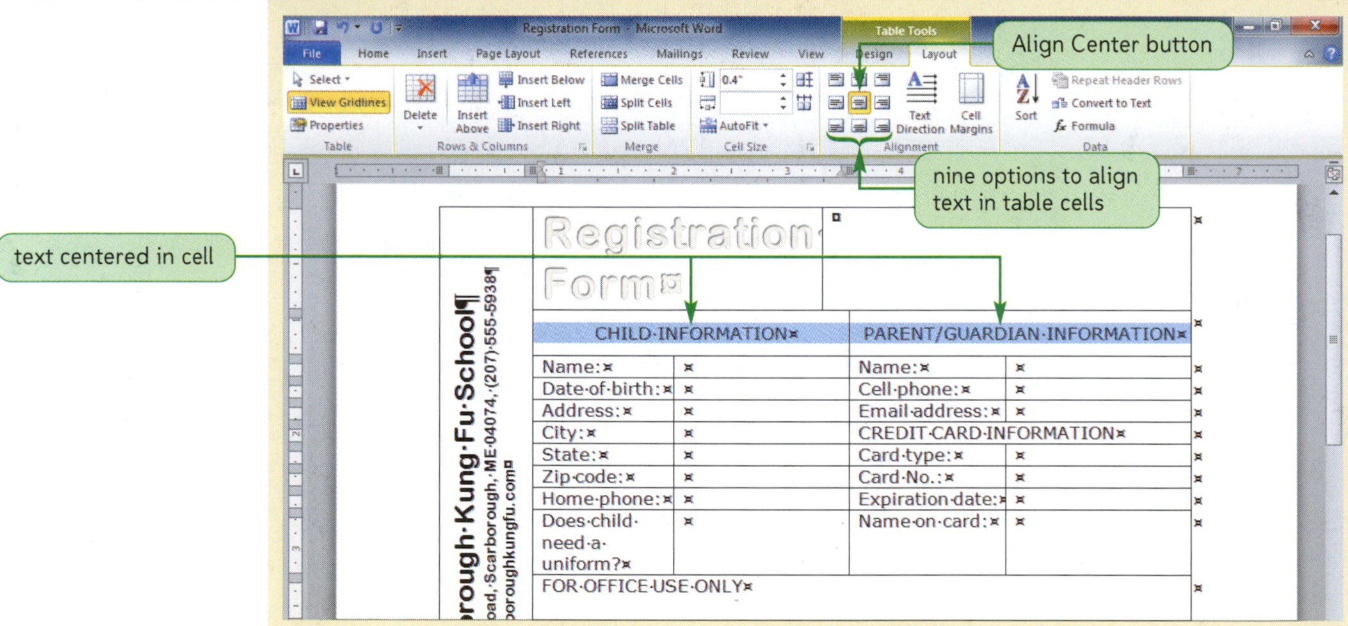

3. Click in the first column. The nine alignment buttons in the Alignment group change so the lines are vertical instead of horizontal.
4. In the Alignment group, click the **Align Center** button. The text in the first column is centered.
5. Format the cells containing "Registration Form," "CREDIT CARD INFORMATION," "FOR OFFICE USE ONLY," and "Please do not enter…" so that the text is centered horizontally and vertically in the cells.
6. Save the template.

Next, you'll add shading to several cells to make the table more attractive and readable.

Shading Cells

Pete thinks the text effect applied to the "Registration Form" heading makes it a little hard to read, so he suggests you add shading to it. Also, according to Pete's sketch, he wants you to add shading to the cells in the "FOR OFFICE USE ONLY" section.

To shade cells in the table:

1. Click the cell containing "Registration Form," and then click the **Table Tools Design** tab.
2. In the Table Styles group, click the **Shading button arrow** to open the color palette, and then click the **Tan, Background 2** color in the top row, third column from the left. The "Registration Form" cell becomes shaded with a light tan color.
3. Select the cell containing "FOR OFFICE USE ONLY" and all the cells below it except the last cell in the table, and then, on the Quick Access Toolbar, click the **Repeat Shading Color** button. Your previous action is repeated, so the selected cells are shaded with the same light tan color.
4. Click in the last cell in the table, and then click **Repeat Shading Color** button again. See Figure 9-16.

Figure 9-16 **Form with shaded cells**

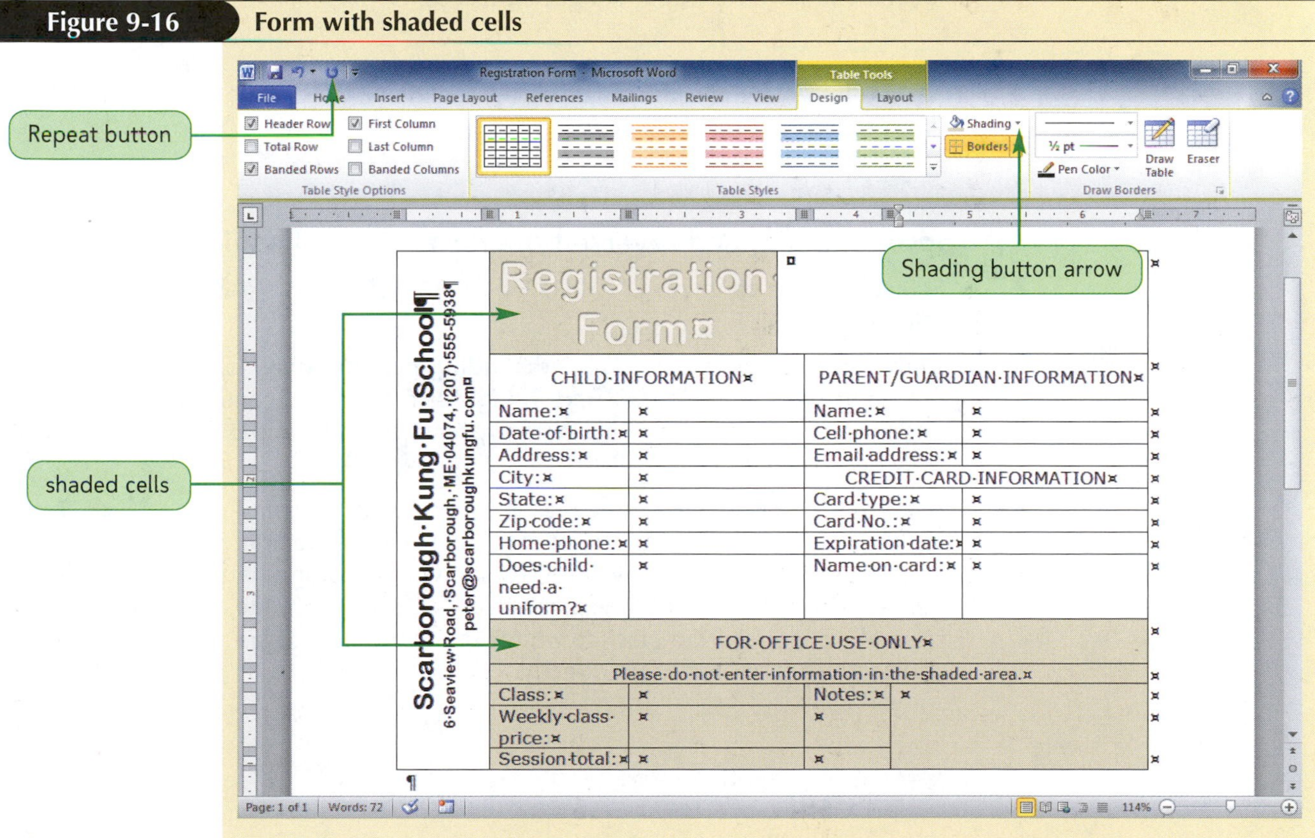

Pete also wants the cells with the section headings to be formatted so they are more prominent. You'll format those cells next.

Formatting Text as Reverse Type

To make the section headings stand out, Pete next wants you to shade those cells with a dark color. However, the text needs to be readable on the dark shading. Pete suggests you format the text in these cells in reverse type, so that the text appears in white, or a light color, making it more readable on the dark background. Reverse type is effective for making a line of text or a title attract the reader's eye; however, large amounts of reverse type can be difficult to read.

REFERENCE

Creating Reverse (Light on Dark) Type in Table Cells

- Select the table cell or the text you want to set in reverse type.
- On the Home tab in the Paragraph group or on the Mini toolbar, click the Shading button arrow; or, on the Table Tools Design tab, click the Shading button arrow.
- Click a dark-colored tile in the color palette.
- If the text is not automatically reformatted as white text, select it, and then, in the Font group on the Home tab or on the Mini toolbar, click the Font Color arrow, and then click the White (or any light color) tile.

First, you'll format the cells containing the section headings with shading, and then format the text so it is readable.

To apply shading and reverse type for the table headings:

1. Select the cells containing "CHILD INFORMATION" and "PARENT/GUARDIAN INFORMATION."
2. In the Table Styles group, click the **Shading button arrow**, and then point to—but do not click—the **Black, Text 1, Lighter 50%** tile (second row, second column under Theme Colors). The Live Preview shows the cells in the table shaded with a gray background.
3. Point to each of the next three tiles in that column, stopping at the **Black, Text 1, Lighter 15%** color (second to last row under Theme Colors). See Figure 9-17. As you point to each tile, Live Preview shows the shading getting progressively darker. When you point to the Black, Text 1, Lighter 15% tile, the text color automatically changes from black to white. This is one way to create reverse type. But you can also format the text directly.

Figure 9-17 Using Live Preview to choose a shading color

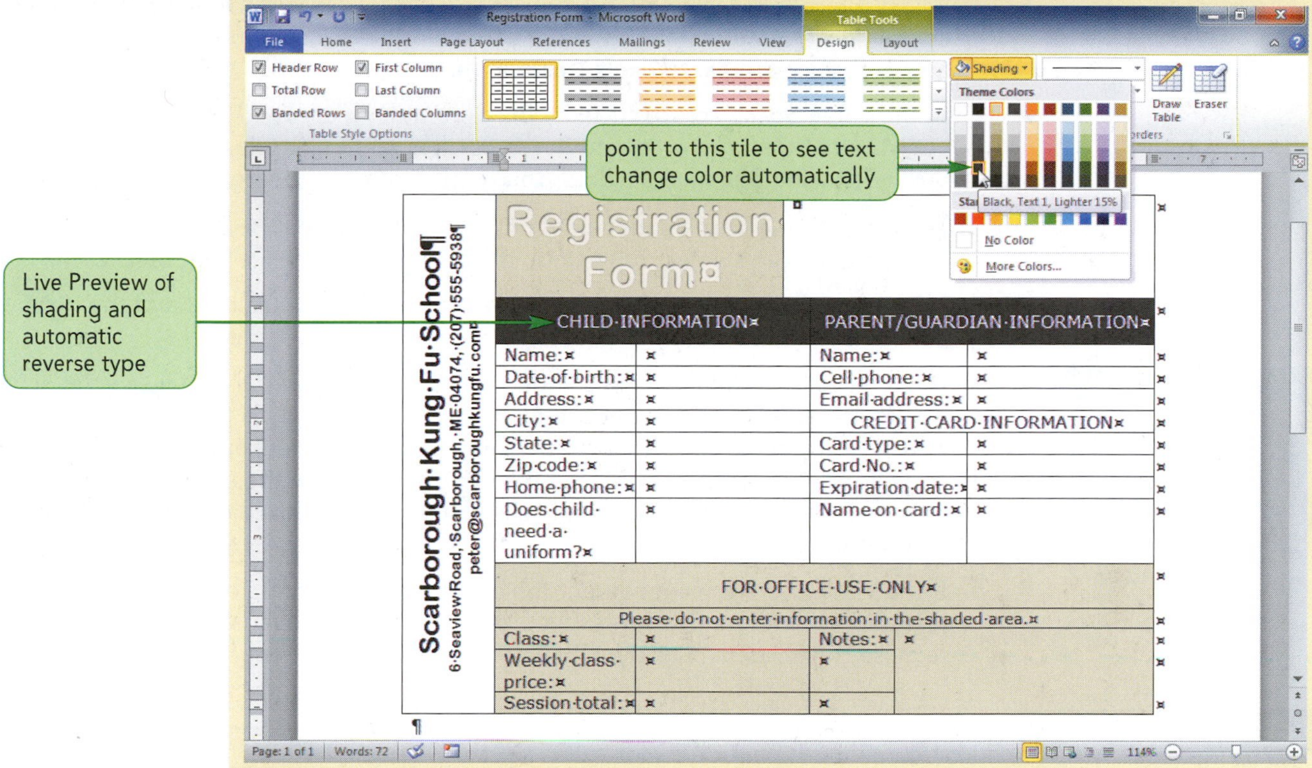

4. Move back up one tile and click the **Black, Text 1, Lighter 25%** tile, and then deselect the cells. The cells are shaded with dark gray; the black text is barely visible.
5. Select the cells containing "CHILD INFORMATION" and "PARENT/GUARDIAN INFORMATION" again, and then click the **Home** tab.
6. In the Font group, click the **Font Color button arrow**, click the **White, Background 1** color (first column, first row under Theme Colors), click the **Bold** button, and then deselect the cells.
7. Format the cells containing "CREDIT CARD INFORMATION" and "FOR OFFICE USE ONLY" with **Black, Text 1, Lighter 25%** shading and **bold**, **white** text.
8. Format the cell containing "Please do not enter…" with **Black, Text 1, Lighter 25%** shading and **white** text. (Do not add bold formatting to the text in this cell.)
9. Save the template.

TIP

Both the Shading button and the Font Color button change to reflect the most recent selection, so you can simply click them to apply the current settings to the new set of selected cells.

Referring again to Pete's sketch in Figure 9-2, you notice that in his design there are no borders between the cells with labels and the cells where users enter information. You will remove the borders from between these cells next.

Drawing and Erasing Borders

You can display or hide gridlines while you are working; but even when hidden, the gridlines still define the table's structure. Table borders, on the other hand, do print. When you create a table, ½-point borders appear along all the gridlines by default.

You'll modify Pete's table by removing the borders between the labels and empty cells next to them. You'll begin by removing the right border of cells that contain labels.

To remove borders from a group of cells using the Borders button:

1. Select the cells containing labels under "CHILD INFORMATION" (from the cell containing "Name" through the cell containing "Does child need a uniform?"), and then click the **Table Tools Design** tab.
2. In the Table Styles group, click the **Borders button arrow**. The Borders menu opens. All of the border options in the Borders menu are selected except No Border and the Diagonal borders. You want to remove the right border.

   Trouble? If the Borders menu did not open, you clicked the Borders button instead of the arrow next to it. Undo the change, and then repeat Step 2.
3. Click **Right Border**, and then deselect the cells. The menu closes and the right border is removed from the selected cells.
4. With the cells containing labels under "CHILD INFORMATION" still selected, click the **Borders button arrow** again. Note that now, not only is the Right Border option deselected, but the All Borders and Outside Borders options are deselected as well. Even though you removed the right border from these cells, the gridline that defines the structure of these cells is still there. If the gridlines are visible, you will see a dotted blue line.
5. If the View Gridlines command at the bottom of the Borders button menu is *not* selected, click **View Gridlines**; if it *is* selected, click a blank area of the document to close the Borders button menu without making any changes. See Figure 9-18.

TIP

You can also click the View Gridlines button in the Table group on the Table Tools Layout tab to display or hide gridlines.

Figure 9-18 Form after border between columns is removed

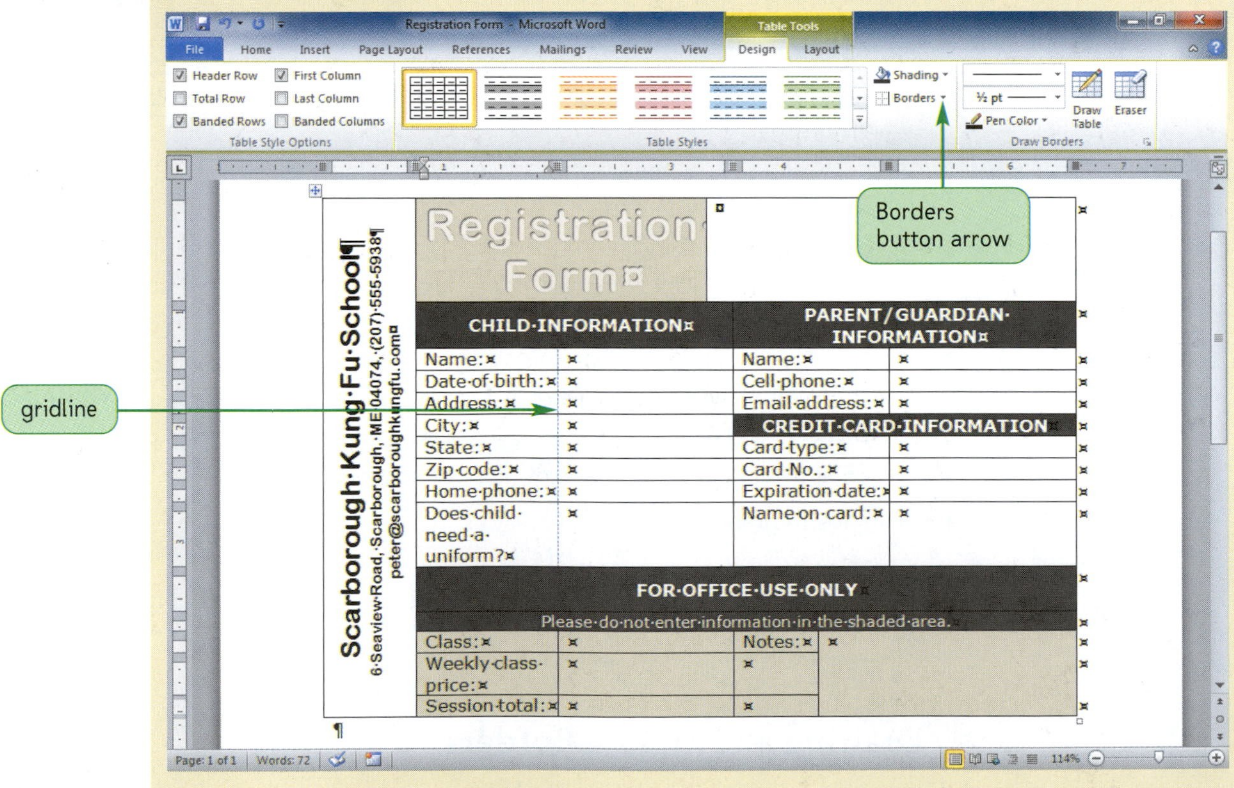

TIP

Remember that using the Eraser button on the Design tab merges cells because you erase the gridline.

Sometimes it's hard to figure out exactly which commands on the Borders menu should be selected or deselected, so you might find it easier to use the Borders and Shading dialog box to modify or remove borders. You'll use this method for the other borders that Pete wants you to remove.

To remove borders using the Borders and Shading dialog box:

1. Select the cells containing labels under PARENT/GUARDIAN INFORMATION (from the cell containing "Name" through the cell containing "Email address").
2. In the Table Styles group on the Table Tools Design tab, click the **Borders button arrow**, and then click **Borders and Shading**. The Borders and Shading dialog box opens with the Borders tab on top. See Figure 9-19. In the Apply to box at the bottom of the Preview section, note that "Cell" is selected. The Preview section illustrates the borders on the selected cells.

Figure 9-19 Borders tab in the Borders and Shading dialog box

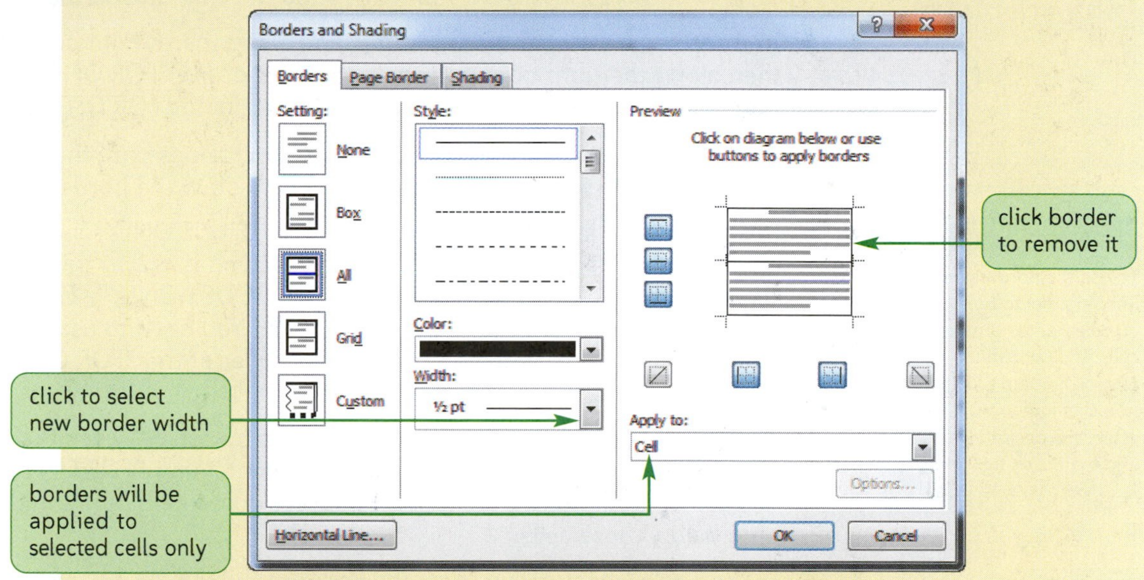

3. In the Preview section, click the **right border**. The border disappears.

   Trouble? If one of the other borders disappeared instead, click that border to make it reappear, then repeat Step 3.
4. Click the **OK** button, and then click a blank area of the table to deselect the cells. The dialog box closes, and the right border of the cells you had selected is removed.
5. Remove the right border of the cells containing labels under "CREDIT CARD INFORMATION," the cells containing "Class," "Weekly class price," and "Session total," and the cell containing "Notes" and the two cells below it. Now you need to remove the bottom borders of the two cells below the cell containing "Notes."
6. With the cell containing "Notes" and the two cells below it still selected, click the **Borders button arrow**, and then click **Inside Horizontal Border**.
7. Save the template.

Next, you'll use the Draw Table tool to draw thicker borders at the top and bottom of the table and around the For Office Use Only area of the table.

To draw thicker borders at the top and bottom of the table and around the Office Use section:

1. On the Table Tools Design tab, click the **Draw Table** button in the Draw Borders group to select it, and then position the pointer on the document. The pointer changes to ✎.
2. In the Draw Borders group, click the **Line Weight button arrow** [½ pt], and then click **2 ¼ pt**. Now any borders you insert will be 2¼ points thick rather than the default ½ point.
3. Drag along the top line of the table, above the first row of the table. As you drag, make sure the line that you draw is a thick gray line, not a dotted rectangle, so that you don't insert a new row above the first row in the table.

   Trouble? If you inserted a new row, undo the change and then repeat Step 3.
4. In three separate operations, drag ✎ first along the bottom border of the table, then along the right border of the right edge of the "FOR OFFICE USE ONLY" section, and finally along the top of the cell containing "FOR OFFICE USE ONLY."

   Trouble? If you make a mistake, undo your changes until the new border disappears, and then repeat the necessary steps to draw the borders correctly.
5. Drag along the left border of the "FOR OFFICE USE ONLY" section. The border all along the entire right edge of the first column is drawn thicker. This is because the left border of the cells in the "FOR OFFICE USE ONLY" section is also the right border of the merged cell in the first column. You need to use the Borders and Shading dialog box to customize the left border of the "FOR OFFICE USE ONLY" section.
6. On the Quick Access Toolbar, click the **Undo** button, click the **Draw Table** button to deselect it, and then select the cells containing "FOR OFFICE USE ONLY," "Please do not enter...," and the three cells containing labels in the second column below those cells.
7. In the Table Styles group, click the **Borders button arrow**, and then click **Borders and Shading**.
8. In the middle pane in the dialog box, click the **Width** arrow, and then click **2 ¼ pt**.
9. Verify that **Cell** is selected in the Apply to box below the Preview section, and then in the Preview section, click the **left border** of the cell in the preview. A thick border is added.
10. Click the **OK** button, and then deselect the cells. The dialog box closes, and the thick border is added to the left of the "FOR OFFICE USE ONLY" section.
11. Deselect the cells, and then compare your table to Figure 9-20.

TIP

To use the Borders and Shading dialog box to place a border around cells, click Box in the Setting column on the left, click the Width arrow, select the desired width, and then click the Apply to arrow and select Cell.

Figure 9-20 Final structure of the table

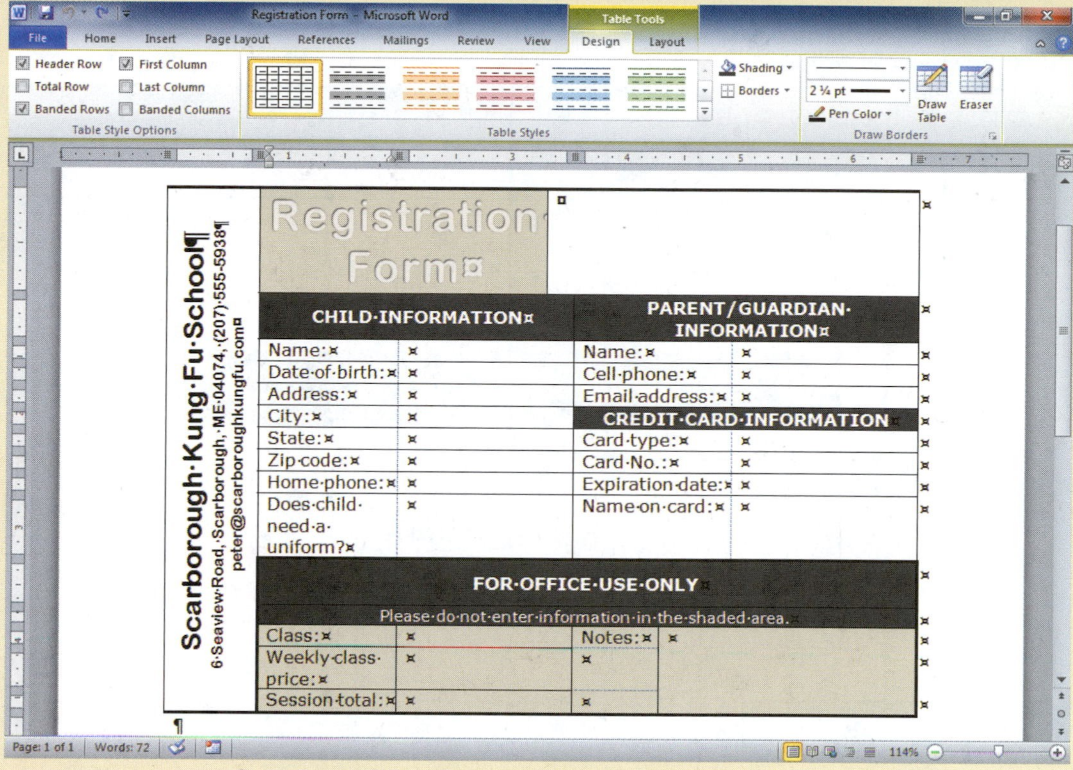

12. Save your changes, click the **File** tab, and then click **Close** in the navigation bar to close the template without exiting Word.

Pete will examine the completed table structure for the form. In the next session, you'll add content controls to the registration form.

REVIEW

Session 9.1 Quick Check

1. What is an online form?
2. What does it mean to merge cells in a table?
3. What does it mean to split cells in a table?
4. How do you rotate text in a table cell?
5. In a table, what is a border? How does it differ from a gridline?
6. How do you align text in a cell?
7. How do you add shading to a cell?
8. What is reverse type?

SESSION 9.2 VISUAL OVERVIEW

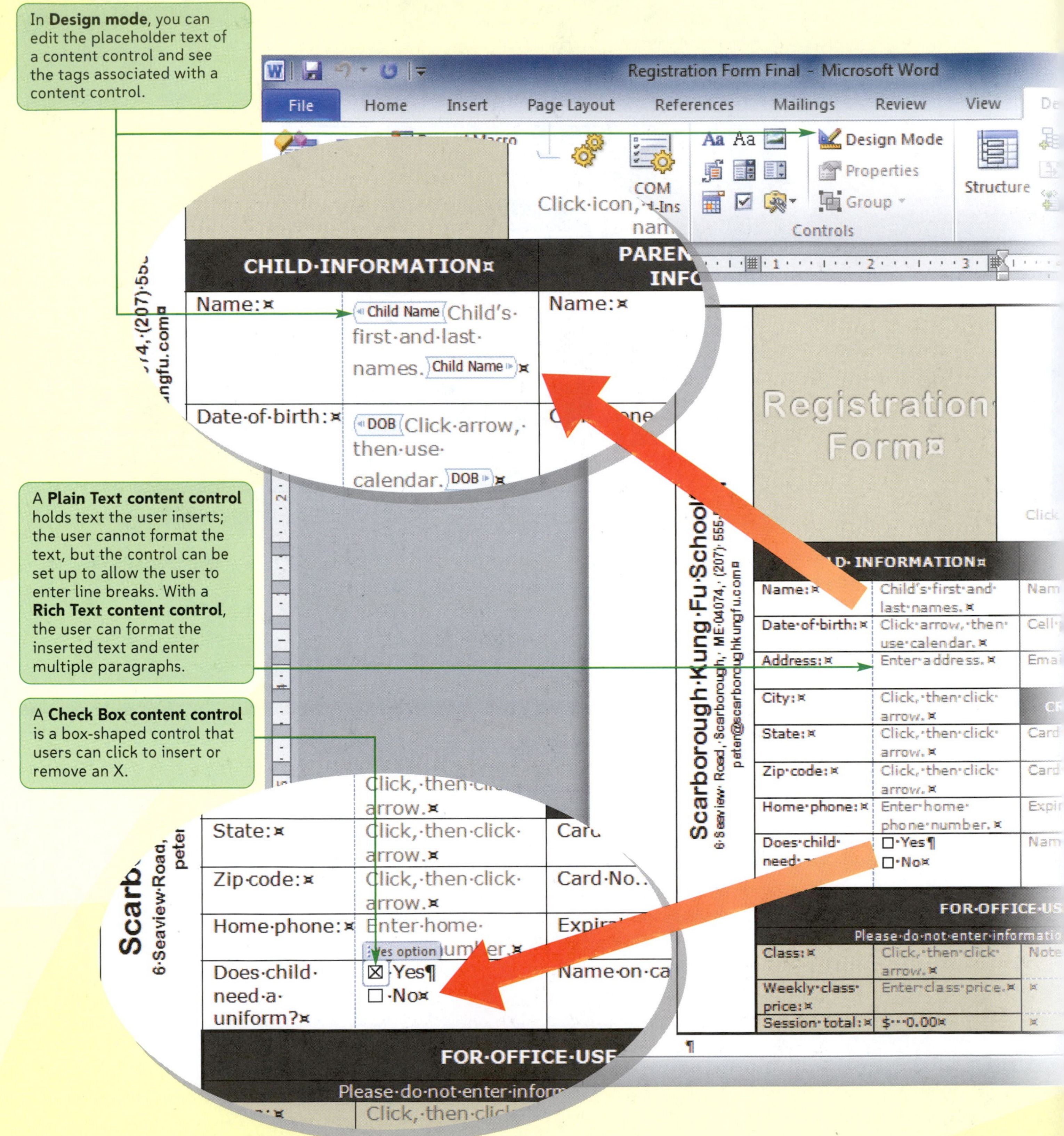
In **Design mode**, you can edit the placeholder text of a content control and see the tags associated with a content control.
A **Plain Text content control** holds text the user inserts; the user cannot format the text, but the control can be set up to allow the user to enter line breaks. With a **Rich Text content control**, the user can format the inserted text and enter multiple paragraphs.
A **Check Box content control** is a box-shaped control that users can click to insert or remove an X.
Registration Form Final - Microsoft Word
File
Home
Insert
Page Layout
References
Mailings
Review
View
Design Mode
Properties
Group
Structure
Controls
CHILD·INFORMATION
Name:
Child Name
Child's·first·and·last·names.
Date·of·birth:
DOB
Click·arrow,·then·use·calendar.
Registration·Form
Scarborough·Kung·Fu·School
State:
Click,·then·click·arrow.
Zip·code:
Home·phone:
Enter·home·phone·number.
Does·child·need·a·uniform?
Yes option
Yes
No
FOR·OFFICE·USE
Please·do·not·enter·information
Address:
Enter·address.
City:
Class:
Weekly·class·price:
Enter·class·price.
Session·total:
$···0.00

CONTENT CONTROLS

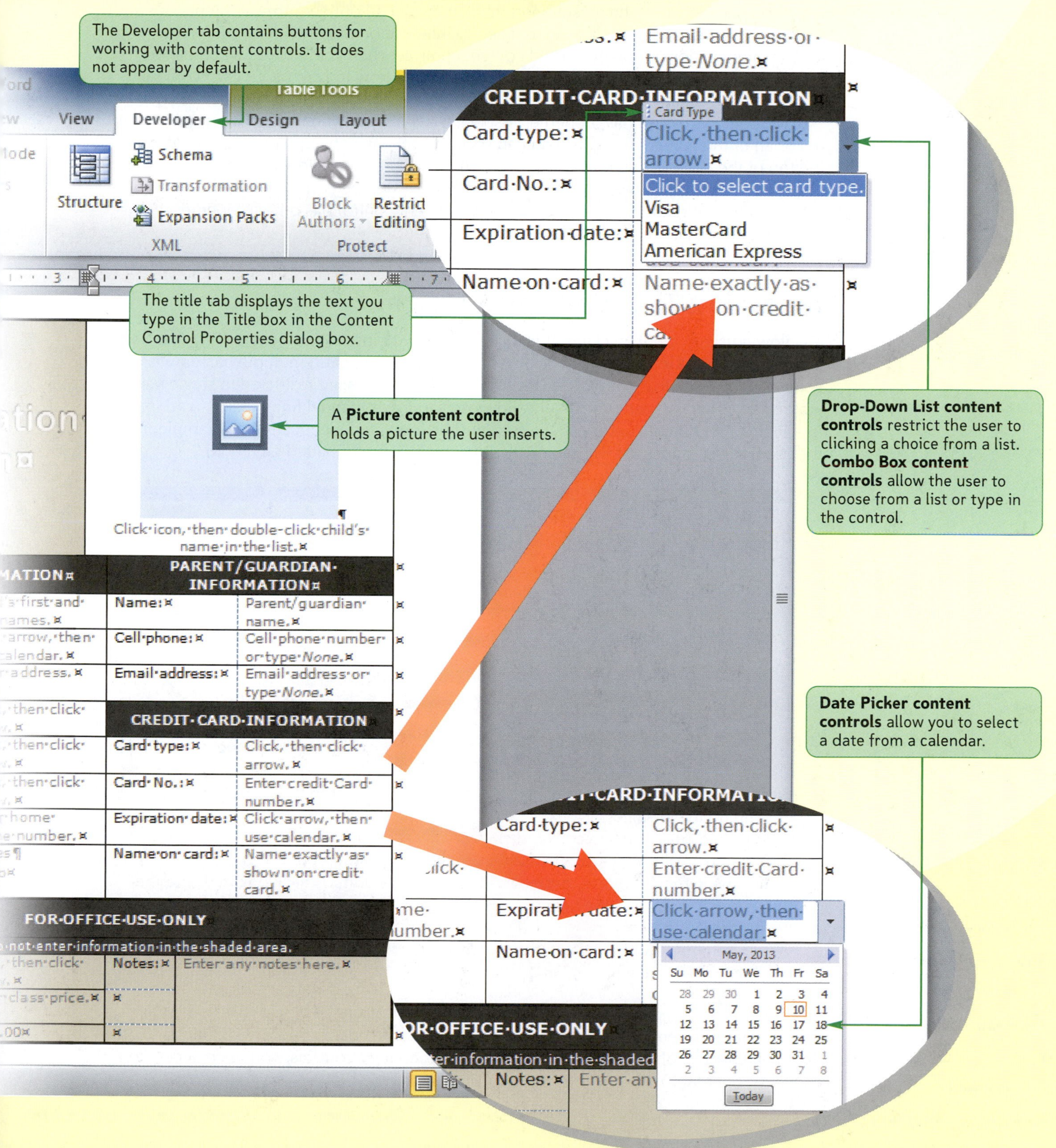

Understanding Content Controls

You have formatted the Registration Form template to make it attractive and easy to read. Now you need to insert the most important elements of an online form—content controls. The content controls will help users enter information into the registration form quickly and efficiently. You have used content controls when you worked with headers, footers, and cover pages. In this session, you will learn how to insert your own content controls, rather than just inserting information into content controls that are already there.

Each content control has properties associated with it that you specify when you insert it. For all of the content controls, you can specify a title, which appears in a title tab at the top of the content control. You can also choose whether to allow the content control to be deleted and to allow the user to edit the contents of the control after they have entered information. In addition, each type of content control has other properties that you can adjust that are specific to that control.

Inserting Text Content Controls

To allow a user to input any kind of text into a form, you insert Plain Text or Rich Text content controls. **Rich Text content controls** allow the user to add multiple paragraphs of text and format the text normally. **Plain Text content controls** are restricted to single paragraphs, although you can specifically allow users to insert manual line breaks. In addition, in a Plain Text content control, all the text must be formatted identically; for example, if the user formats one word with bold, all of the text will be formatted with bold.

REFERENCE

Inserting a Plain Text or a Rich Text Content Control

- Click the Developer tab, and then click the Design Mode button in the Controls group.
- In the Controls group, click the Plain Text Content Control or the Rich Text Content Control button.
- In the Controls group, click the Properties button.
- In the Title box, type the control title.
- If you want the text to be formatted differently than the default format, click the Use a style to format contents check box, and then click the Style arrow and select a style, or click New Style to define a new style.
- Click the Content control cannot be deleted check box if you want to prevent users from deleting the content control.
- Click the Contents cannot be edited check box if you want to prevent the user from changing the placeholder text.
- For a Plain Text content control, click the Allow carriage returns (multiple paragraphs) check box to allow the user to insert more than one paragraph.
- Click the Remove content control when contents are edited check box to delete the content control and leave only the text the user inserts.
- Click the OK button.
- If desired, replace the default placeholder text with specific instructions to the user.

Pete already entered several Plain Text content controls in the form so the parents of new students can enter their information. He asks you to add a couple of additional Plain Text content controls to the form. In order to enter content controls, you need access to the Developer tab. You'll display the Developer tab now.

To display the Developer tab on the Ribbon:

1. Open the file **RegForm2**, located in the Word9\Tutorial folder included with your Data Files, save it as a template named **Registration Form Final** in the same folder, and then make sure the rulers and nonprinting characters are visible, that Word is in Print Layout view, and that your zoom is set to Page Width. Note that you cannot double-click the RegForm2 template in a Windows Explorer window to open it as a template; if you do open it from an Explorer window, it will open as a new document. The options for inserting content controls are located on the Developer tab.
2. Click the **File** tab, and then click the **Options** button in the navigation bar. The Word Options dialog box opens with General selected in the left pane.
3. In the list in the left pane, click **Customize Ribbon**. The right pane of the dialog box changes to show two lists—one listing Word commands and the other listing Ribbon tabs.
4. In the Customize the Ribbon list on the right, click the **Developer** check box to select it, if necessary. See Figure 9-21.

Figure 9-21 Word Options dialog box with Customize Ribbon selected

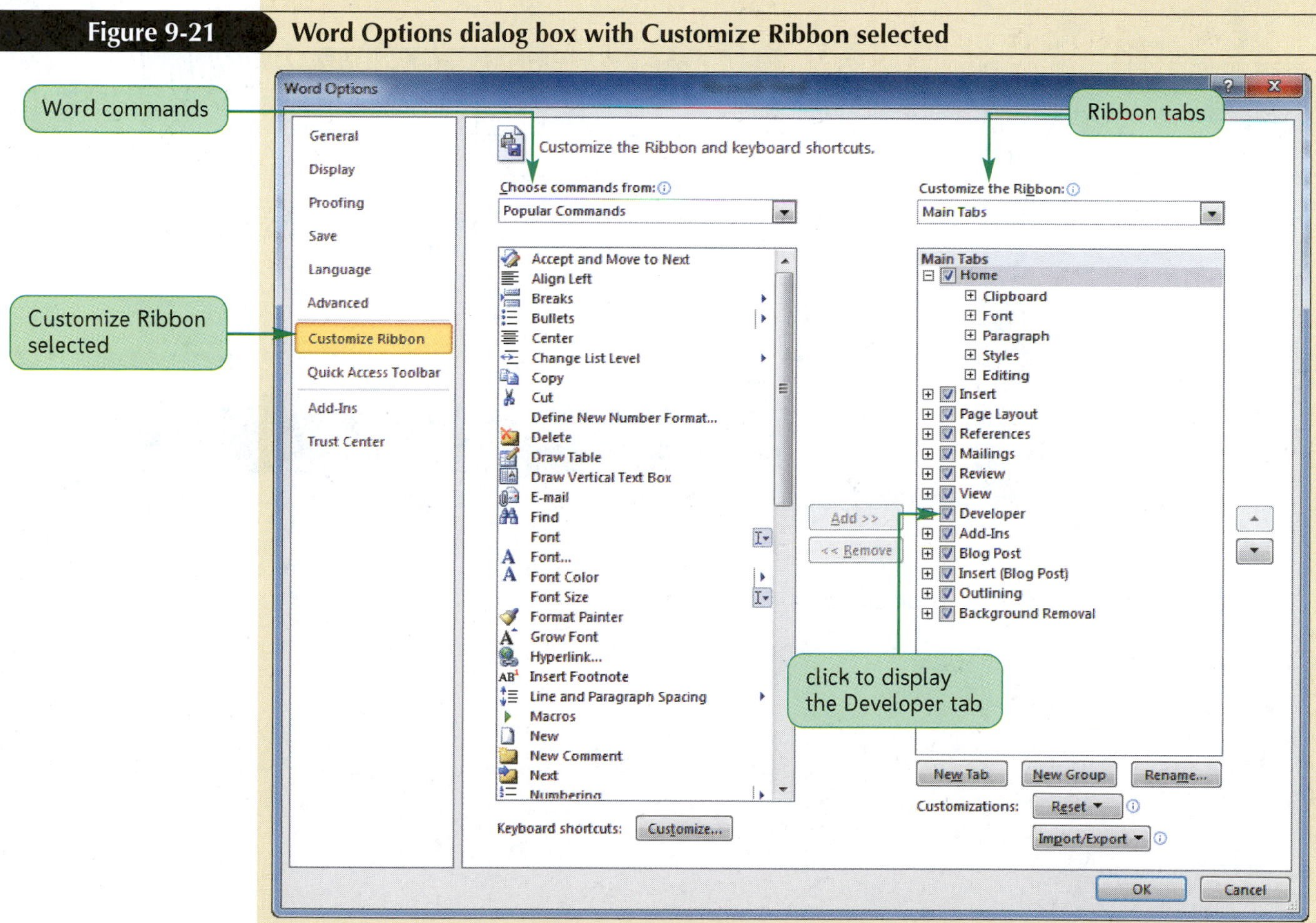

5. Click the **OK** button. The dialog box closes and the Developer tab appears on the Ribbon to the right of the View tab.

Now you can insert content controls in the form. As you can see, Peter already entered content controls in several of the cells. You need to insert a Plain Text content control for the child's name.

To insert a Plain Text content control for the child's name and set the control's properties:

1. In the "CHILD INFORMATION" section, click in the cell to the right of the cell containing "Name," and then click the **Developer** tab.
2. In the Controls group, click the **Plain Text Content Control** button Aa. A Plain Text content control is inserted in the cell. See Figure 9-22. Now you can set the properties for the new Plain Text content control.

Figure 9-22 Plain Text content control inserted

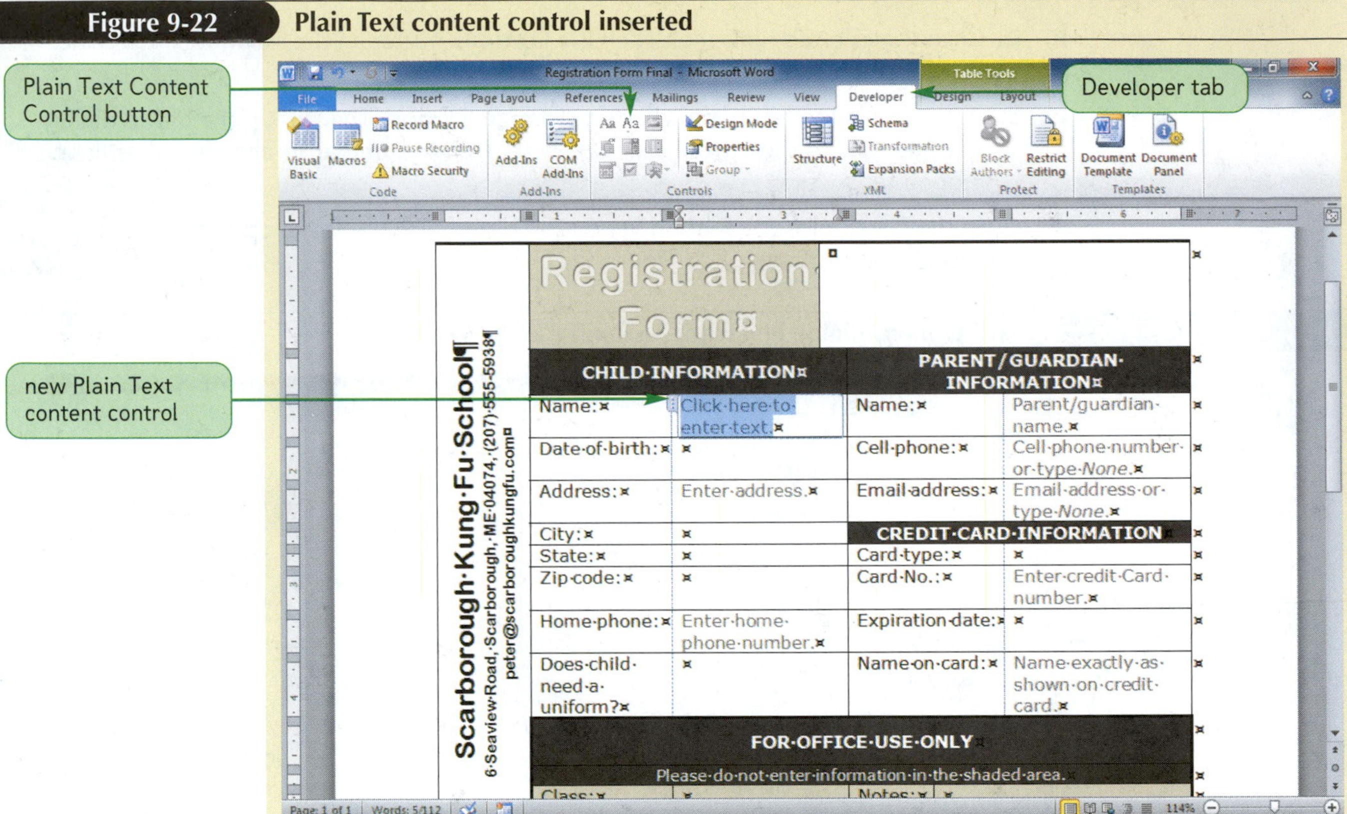

3. In the Controls group, click the **Properties** button. The Content Control Properties dialog box opens. See Figure 9-23.

Figure 9-23 **Content Control Properties dialog box for a Text content control**

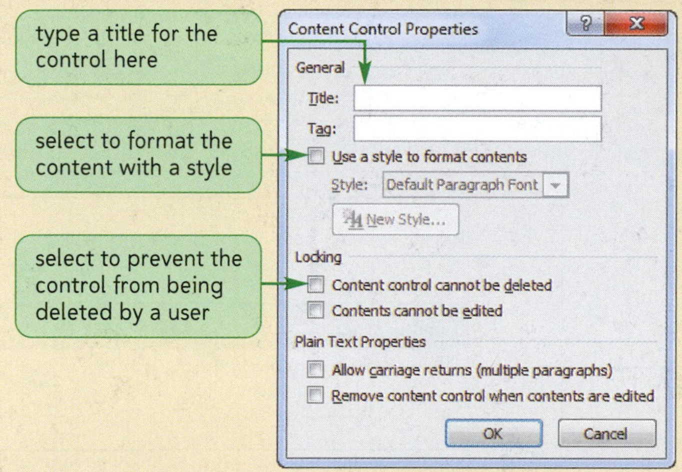

TIP

If the user will need to enter multiple paragraphs in a Text control, click the Allow carriage returns (multiple paragraphs) check box in the Content Control Properties dialog box.

4. Type **Child Name** in the Title box. This is the text that will appear in the tab at the top of the control in the form. To make the child's name stand out, you will format it with the Strong style.
5. Click the **Use a style to format contents** check box, click the **Style** arrow, and then click **Strong**. Next, you'll set a property in the control so users won't be able to delete the content control.
6. Click the **Content control cannot be deleted** check box, and then click the **OK** button. The Content Control Properties dialog box closes. Notice that the title "Child Name" now appears on the title tab of the content control.
7. Click a blank area of the table to deselect the content control.

Usually, the user knows what information to enter into a control just by looking at the title. However, someone using the form for the first time might need instructions, and both new and experienced users sometimes need clarification regarding how to enter information into special controls, such as the Date Picker. To assist in answering user questions, you can customize the placeholder text to provide specific instructions for each control.

Pete wants you to include instructions for the people who will be filling out the form. You decide to modify the placeholder text to include instructions. To change the placeholder text, you need to switch to Design mode. If you are not in Design mode, you will enter information into the control instead of editing the control.

To change the placeholder text in the Child Name control:

1. In the Controls group, click the **Design Mode** button. The button is selected, and tags appear at the beginning and end of the Plain Text content control that you inserted. Tags mark the location of the control in the document. Tags are useful when you plan to use your form in another program. Because you didn't type anything in the Tag box in the Content Control Properties dialog box, the tag is the same as the Title property. The Title property identifies the content control for the person creating the form. See Figure 9-24.

Figure 9-24 Form in Design mode

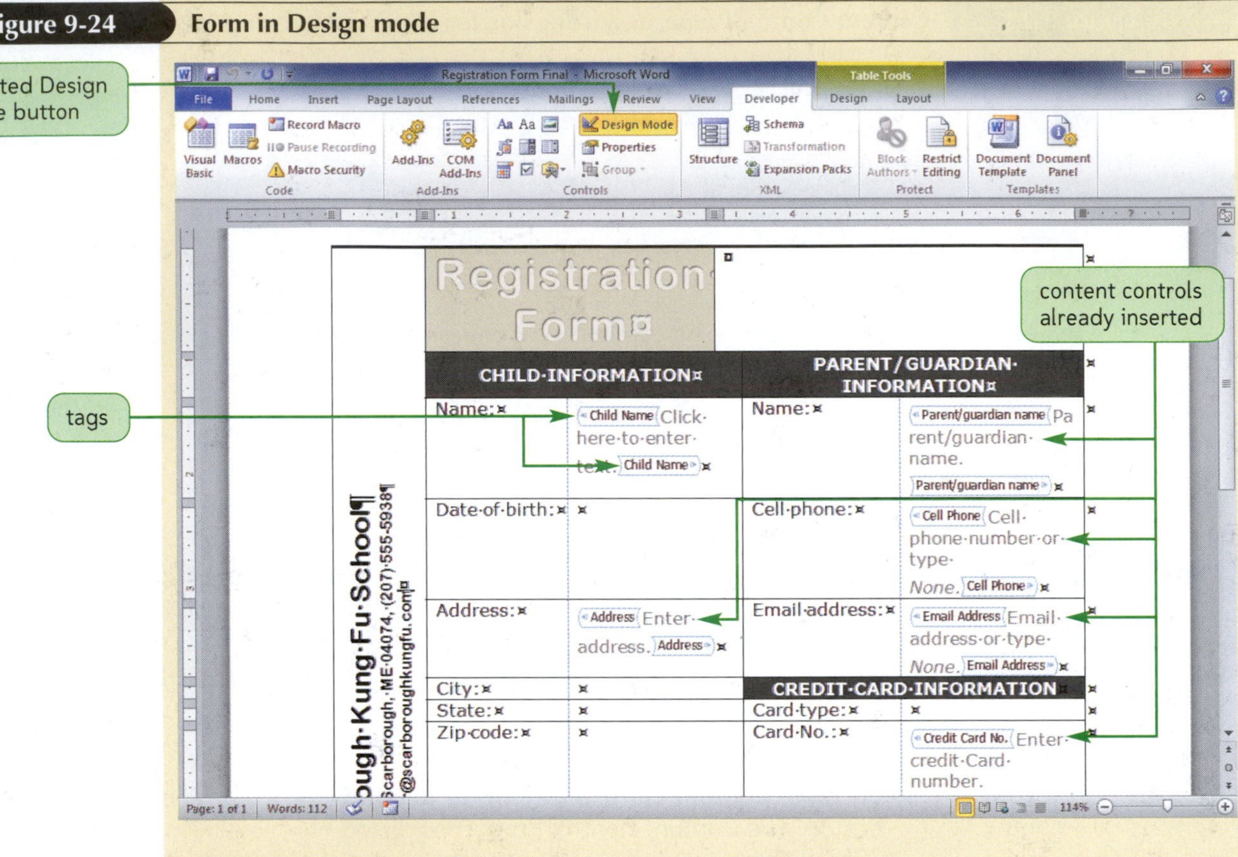

2. In the cell containing the Child Name content control, drag to select the placeholder text, "Click here to enter text."

3. Type **Child's first and last names.**

Trouble? If any of the text you type is black instead of gray, undo your change, carefully select just the current placeholder text, and then type the new placeholder text in Step 3.

You can remain in Design Mode to add additional content controls. You need to add a Plain Text content control in the cell to the right of "Notes."

To enter an additional Plain Text content control:

1. Click in the cell to the right of the cell containing "Notes," and then click the **Plain Text Content Control** button Aa in the Controls group.
2. In the Controls group, click the **Properties** button.
3. Type **Notes** in the Title box, click the **Content control cannot be deleted** check box, and then click the **OK** button.
4. Change the placeholder text for the content control to **Enter any notes here**.
5. Save the template.

TIP

To delete a control, make sure the form is in Design mode, right-click the control, and then click Remove Content Control on the shortcut menu.

All the text content controls are now inserted in the registration form template. It's a good idea to test content controls after you insert them. First you need to turn off Design mode.

To turn off Design mode and test the content controls:

1. In the Controls group, click the **Design Mode** button to deselect it.
2. Click in the cell containing the Child Name content control (the cell to the right of the cell containing "Name" in the "CHILD INFORMATION" section). The content control is selected and you see the title tab with the name of the content control on it.
3. Type **Jane Doe**. The text you typed replaces the placeholder text, and it is formatted with the Strong style as you specified in the Properties dialog box when you inserted this content control.
4. Click in the cell to the right of the cell containing "Name" in the "PARENT/GUARDIAN INFORMATION" section. The placeholder text in this cell is selected and the title tab appears. This is one of the text content controls that Peter inserted.
5. Type **John Doe**. The name replaces the placeholder text. This text is not formatted with a style. The text content controls work as expected. Now you should delete the text you typed to reset the content controls so that they display the placeholder text.
6. Press the **Backspace** key as many times as necessary to delete the name from the cell.
7. Click in the cell containing "Jane Doe." The placeholder text reappears in the cell to the right of "Name" in the "PARENT/GUARDIAN INFORMATION" section.
8. Press the **Backspace** or **Delete** key as needed to delete the name, and then click in any other cell in the table. The placeholder text reappears in the cell.
9. Save your changes.

Pete wants you to insert a content control that allows only a date to be entered for the cell containing the child's date of birth and the cell containing the credit card expiration date. You can use a Date Picker content control for this purpose.

Inserting Date Picker Content Controls

To create a content control that contains a date, you use the **Date Picker content control**. When you insert a Date Picker content control, you can specify what the date will look like in the completed form. To do this, you can select a format from a list, or you can create your own **date-time picture**, which is a pattern of letters indicating a specific format for the date. For example, the date-time picture d-MMM-yy displays the date January 7, 2013, as 7-Jan-13, and the date-time picture dddd, MMMM dd, yyyy displays the date as Wednesday, January 07, 2014.

REFERENCE

Inserting a Date Picker Content Control

- Switch to Design mode, click the Date Picker button in the Controls group, and then click the Properties button.
- In the Title box, type the control title.
- If you want the text to be formatted differently than the default format, click the Use a style to format contents check box, and then click the Style arrow and select a style, or click New Style to define a new style.
- Click the Content control cannot be deleted check box if you want to prevent the user from deleting the content control.
- Click the Contents cannot be edited check box if you want to prevent the user from changing the placeholder text.
- In the Display the date like this list, click a format in the list for the date, or replace the text in the text box with a date-time picture.
- Click the OK button.
- If desired, replace the default placeholder text with specific instructions to the user.

Now Pete asks you to insert Date Picker content controls in the cells that will contain the student's date of birth and the credit card expiration date.

To insert a Date Picker content control in the registration form:

1. Click in the blank cell to the right of the cell containing "Date of birth," and then click the **Date Picker Content Control** button in the Controls group. A Date Picker content control is entered in the cell.
2. In the Controls group, click the **Properties** button. The Content Control Properties dialog box for a Date Picker control opens. The top of this dialog box is the same as the Content Control Properties dialog box for a Text control. See Figure 9-25.

Figure 9-25 Content Control Properties dialog box for a Date Picker content control

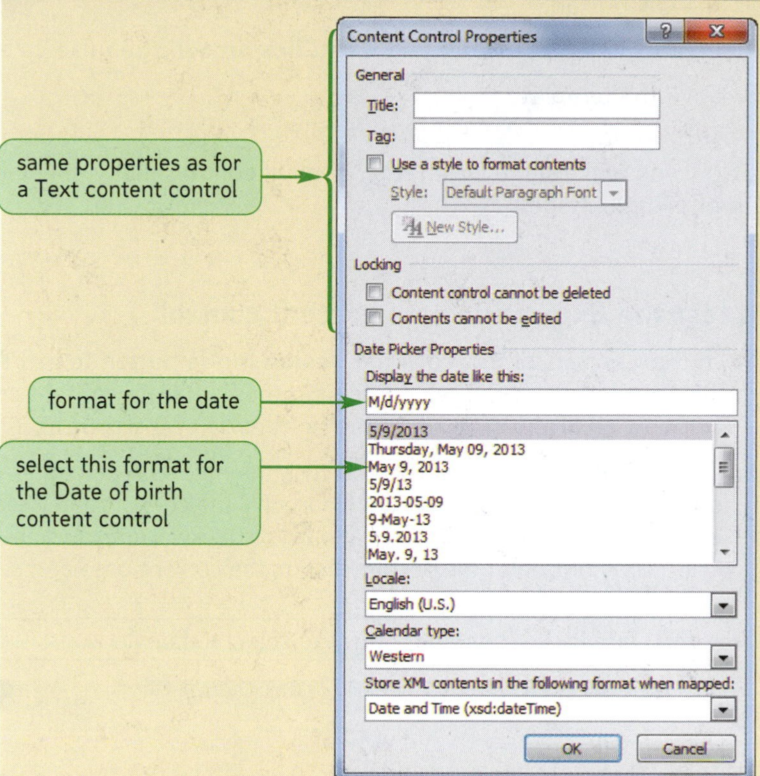

3. Type **DOB** in the Title box, and then click the **Content control cannot be deleted** check box. Now you need to select the format of the date.
4. In the list in the Date Picker Properties section of the dialog box, click the third date format. The Display the date like this box changes to MMMM d, yyyy.
5. Click the **OK** button. Now you need to change the placeholder text.
6. Replace the placeholder text in the cell containing the DOB Date Picker content control with **Click arrow, then use calendar.**

You also need to add a Date Picker control in the cell to the right of the cell containing "Expiration Date." You want this to show just the month and year. That format does not exist in the list in the Content Control Properties dialog box, so you will create a custom date-time picture.

To insert a Date Picker control with a custom date-time picture for the expiration date:

1. Click in the blank cell to the right of "Expiration date," insert a **Date Picker Content Control**, and then, in the Controls group, click the **Properties** button.
2. Type **Exp. Date** as the Title, and then click the **Content control cannot be deleted** check box. You want the month to display as two digits and the year to display as four digits; for example, if a card expires in June 2014, it would appear as 06/2014.

3. Change the text in the Display the date like this box to **MM/yyyy**, and then click the **OK** button.
4. Replace the placeholder text with **Click arrow, then use calendar.**
5. Save the template.

Now you will test the Date Picker content controls that you entered. First, you must turn off Design mode.

To test the Expiration date content control:

1. In the Controls group, click the **Design Mode** button to exit Design mode. The content control in the cell containing the Exp. Date content control is still selected, but now an arrow appears at the right edge of the control.
2. On the Exp. Date content control, click the **arrow**. A calendar appears showing the current month with an orange box around the current date. See Figure 9-26. To change the date, you click the forward or backward arrows next to the month name. The Today button at the bottom inserts the current date and closes the calendar.

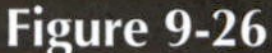

Figure 9-26 Using the Date Picker content control to select a date

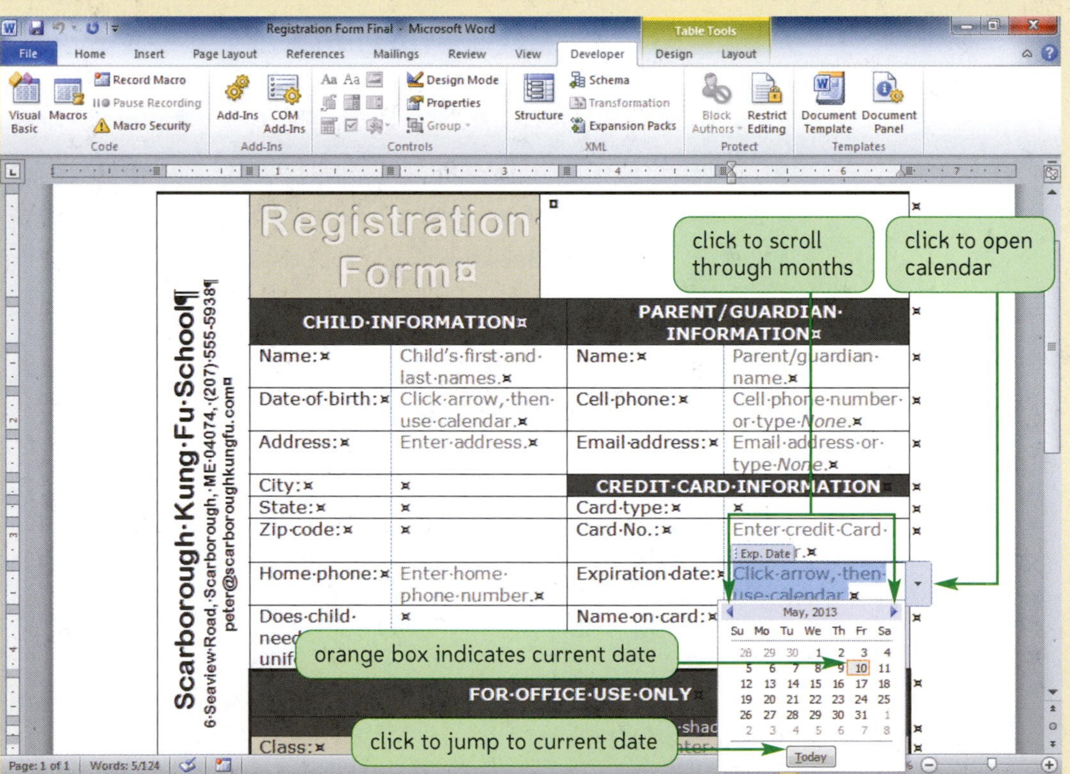

3. Click the **forward** arrow ▶ several times to scroll to any month in the future, and then click **1**. The calendar closes and the date you chose appears in the cell in the format you specified when you inserted the content control—in this case, a two-digit number for the month and year. For example, if you clicked a date in February 2014, it will appear as 02/2014. Because this format shows only the month and year, you can click any date in the month.

4. Drag to select the date in the cell, and then press the **Delete** key. The date you selected is removed from the content control.
5. Click in the cell to the right of the cell containing "Date of birth," click the arrow that appears on the content control, and then click any date. The date you chose appears in the form May 14, 2013.
6. Delete the date you just entered, and then click in any other cell in the table. The placeholder text reappears in the cell to the right of "Date of birth."

Your Date Picker content controls work as they should. You have now specified the content controls that will be used to store text or a date. Next, you need to enter the content controls that offer the user a list of choices.

Inserting List Content Controls

When the information required in a form is limited to specific entries, you can use content controls that offer the user a list of choices. You create the list and the user clicks one of the choices in the list. This type of content control makes it possible to complete a form faster and without making any spelling errors. Word offers three types of list content controls: Drop-Down List, Combo Box, and Building Block Gallery.

Inserting Drop-Down List Content Controls

Drop-Down List content controls restrict the user to clicking a choice from a list. When you insert the control, you add items to the list, and arrange them in an order that suits you. When users complete the form, they are allowed to choose only one item from the list. They cannot type anything else in the control.

REFERENCE

Inserting a Drop-Down List or Combo Box Content Control

- Switch to Design mode, click the Drop-Down List button or the Combo Box button in the Controls group, and then click the Properties button.
- In the Title box, type the control title.
- If you want the text to be formatted differently than the default format, click the Use a style to format contents check box, and then click the Style arrow and select a style, or click New Style to define a new style.
- Click the Content control cannot be deleted check box if you want to prevent the user from deleting the content control.
- Click the Contents cannot be edited check box if you want to prevent the user from changing the placeholder text.
- Click the Add button, then in the Display Name box of the Add Choice dialog box, type an entry for the list, and then click the OK button. Repeat for each entry you want to include in the list.
- To change the wording of an entry, click the entry in the list, click the Modify button, replace the text in the Display Name box in the Modify Choice dialog box with specific instructions to the user, and then click the OK button.
- To move an entry up or down in the list, click it, and then click the Move Up or Move Down buttons.
- To remove an entry from the list, click it, and then click the Remove button.
- Click the OK button.
- Replace the default placeholder text with specific instructions to the user.

Because Pete accepts only certain credit cards, he wants you to insert a Drop-Down List control that includes these cards in the list.

To insert a Drop-Down List control for the credit card type:

1. Click in the blank cell to the right of "Card Type."
2. In the Controls group, click the **Drop-Down List Content Control** button, and then click the **Properties** button. The Content Control Properties dialog box for a Drop-Down List appears. See Figure 9-27.

Figure 9-27 Content Control Properties dialog box for a Drop-Down List control

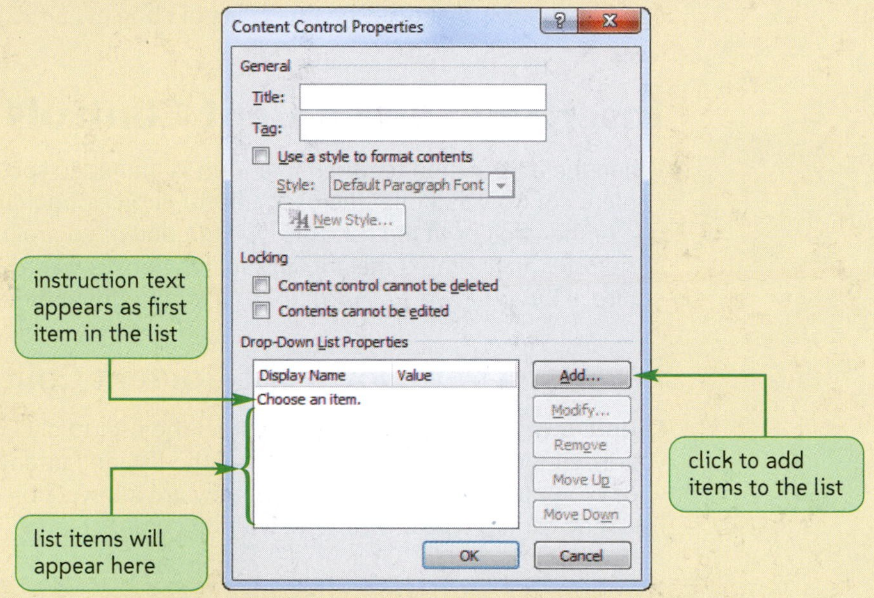

TIP

To set properties for several controls at once, select the controls, click the Group button in the Controls group on the Developer tab, click Group, and then open the Properties dialog box.

3. Type **Card Type** in the Title box, and then click the **Content control cannot be deleted** check box. Now you need to add the items that will appear in the drop-down list below the instruction text.
4. Click the **Add** button to open the Add Choice dialog box, type **MasterCard** in the Display Name box, and then click the **OK** button. As you typed in the Display Name box, the same text appeared in the Value box. You can connect a form to an Access database, and if you do, the contents of the Value field is entered into the database. You can ignore this for now. The Add Choice dialog box closes and "MasterCard" appears as the first item in the list.
5. Add **American Express**, **Discover**, and **Visa** to the list. Pete reminds you that he does not accept the Discover card.
6. In the list, click **Discover**, and then click the **Remove** button. Now you want to move "Visa" up so it is the first item in the list below the "Choose an item" instruction text.
7. In the list, click **Visa**, and then click the **Move Up** button twice. "Visa" is now the first item in the list below the instruction text. Now you want to modify the instruction text.
8. Click **Choose an item.**, and then click the **Modify** button. The Modify Choice dialog box opens. It's identical to the Add Choice dialog box.
9. Replace the text in the Display Name box with **Click to select card type.**, and then click the **OK** button. See Figure 9-28.

Figure 9-28 List items added to Drop-Down List control

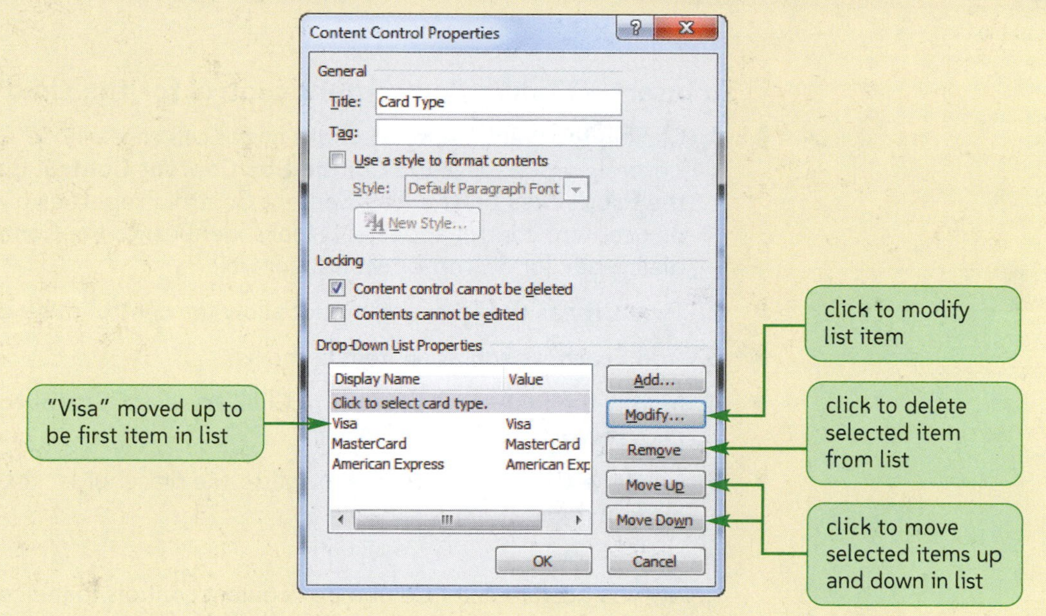

10. Click the **OK** button to close the dialog box.
11. Turn on Design mode, select the placeholder text in the Card Type content control, if necessary, and then type **Click, then click arrow.**
12. Save the template.

Pete asks you to add one more Drop-Down List content control—the control for the class the student will be taking.

To insert a Drop-Down List control for the class:

1. Click in the blank cell to the right of the cell containing "Class," in the Controls group, click the **Drop-Down List Content Control** button, and then click the **Properties** button.
2. Type **Class** in the Title box, click the **Content control cannot be deleted** check box, and then add the following to the list: **Tiny Tots**, **Preschool/Kindergarten**, **Youth**, **Teen**, and **Advanced Teen**.
3. Modify the first item in the list to **Click to select class.**, and then click the **OK** button.
4. Replace the placeholder text with **Click, then click arrow.**
5. Save the template.

Next, you will insert content controls that allow a user to either click an option in a list or to type their own content.

Inserting a Combo Box Content Control

Because the school is located in Scarborough, Maine, most of Pete's students live in that town, but some live in other communities. Pete also gets a few children who visit only in the summer. Instead of using Drop-Down List controls for the child's city, state, and zip code, you can use **Combo Box content controls**, which offer a list of the most likely choices but also allow users to type their own information if it's not in the list you provide.

To insert a Combo Box content control for the child's city:

1. Click in the blank cell to the right of the cell containing "City," in the Controls group, click the **Combo Box Content Control** button, and then click the **Properties** button. The Content Control Properties dialog box for a Combo Box content control appears. It looks identical to the Content Control Properties dialog box for a Drop-Down List control.
2. Type **City** as the Title, and do not allow the control to be deleted.
3. Add **Scarborough** as an item in the list.
4. Modify the first item in the list to **Click to select Scarborough or type your city/town.**
5. Click the **OK** button, and then replace the placeholder text with **Click, then click arrow.**

Now you need to enter Combo Box content controls in the cells to the right of State and Zip.

To insert Combo Box content controls for the child's state and zip code:

1. In the empty cell to the right of "State," insert a **Combo Box Content Control** with **State** as the title, and do not allow the control to be deleted.
2. Replace the first item in the list with **Click to select ME or type your two-letter state abbreviation.**
3. Add **ME** as the second item in the list.
4. Click the **OK** button to close the dialog box, and then replace the placeholder text with **Click, then click arrow.**
5. In the blank cell to the right of the cell containing "Zip code," insert a **Combo Box Content Control** with **Zip Code** as the title, and do not allow the control to be deleted.
6. Replace the first item in the list with **Click to select zip code or enter by typing**. Scarborough has two zip codes, so you will enter them both in the list.
7. Click the **Add** button, type **04074** in the Display Name box, click the **OK** button, and then add **04070** to the list.
8. Click the **OK** button to close the dialog box, and then replace the placeholder text with **Click, then click arrow.**
9. Save the template.

Now you'll test the list content controls.

To test the Combo Box and Drop-Down List content controls:

1. Turn off Design mode, and then click the **City** Combo Box content control. The placeholder text is highlighted and an arrow appears on the right edge of the control.

2. Click the **arrow** for the City control. See Figure 9-29.

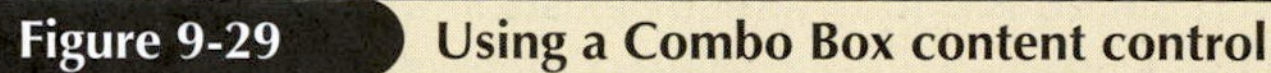

Figure 9-29 Using a Combo Box content control

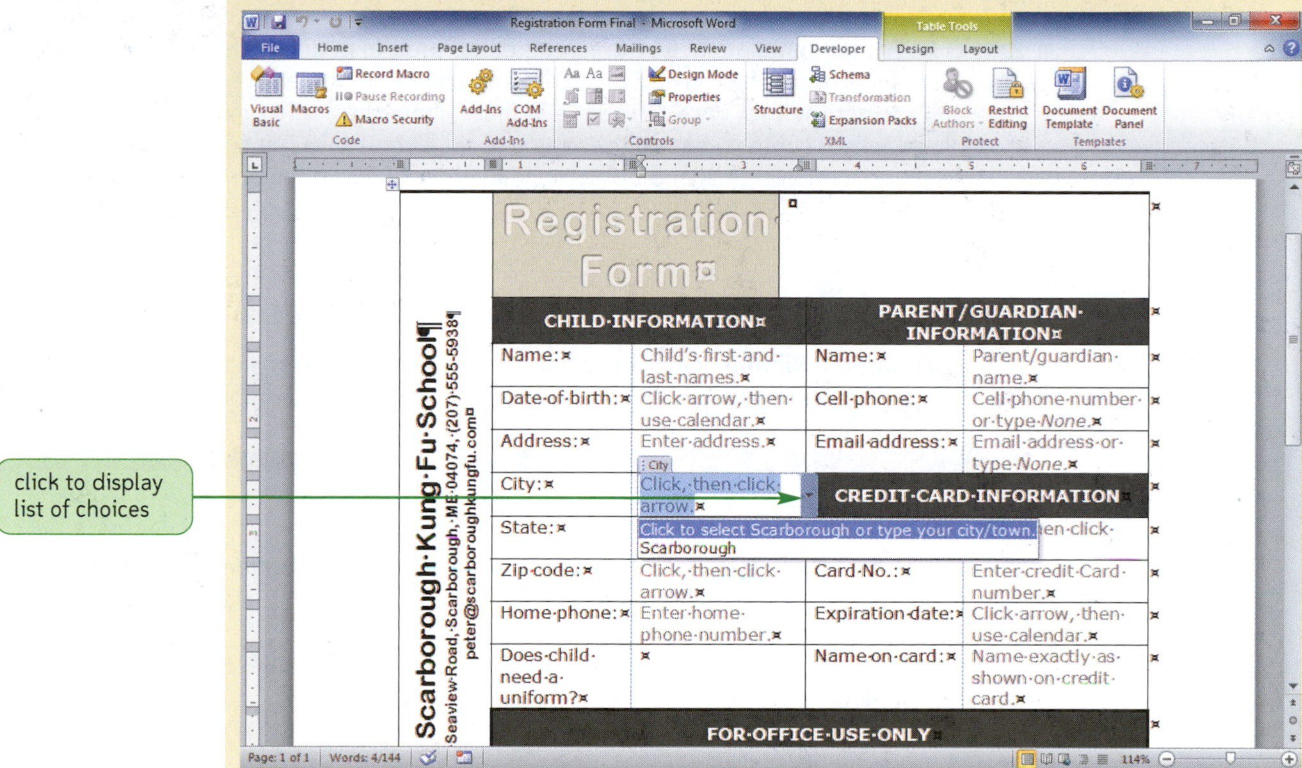

3. In the list, click **Scarborough**. "Scarborough" appears in the cell.
4. Press and hold the **Shift** key, and then press the → key as many times as necessary to select Scarborough.
5. Type **Portsmouth**. "Portsmouth" replaces "Scarborough" in the control. This control works as it should.
6. Click the **State** content control, and then type **NH**. The text you typed replaces the placeholder text.
7. Click the **Card Type** content control, click the **arrow** that appears, and then click **Visa**. "Visa" appears in the control.
8. Click the **arrow** again, and then click **American Express**. Your selection replaces "Visa" in the control.
9. Type any character. Nothing changes because this is a Drop-Down List control and not a Combo Box content control; you cannot type anything into the control.
10. Click the **arrow** for the Card Type control again, click the first item in the list (the instruction text), and then do the same with the **City** and **State** content controls. The placeholder text reappears in the controls.

The list content controls you added to the form work as you expected. Next you will insert a Picture content control at the top of the form.

INSIGHT

Inserting Building Block Gallery Content Controls

Sometimes the information required in a form already exists in Quick Parts that you created. In this case, you can use a Building Block Gallery content control. **Building Block Gallery content controls** are similar to Drop-Down List content controls, but building blocks in the template or on the computer are used to populate the list from which the user can choose. You can also create building blocks that are saved with the template and restrict the user to selecting one of those. From the user's point of view, the Building Block Gallery content control is the same as the Drop-Down List control. The user must select an item in the list and cannot type to enter different text.

Inserting a Picture Content Control

You can insert a **Picture content control** so that users can insert pictures into a form. Users can choose a picture from any accessible folder on the computer.

REFERENCE

Inserting a Picture Content Control

- Switch to Design mode, click the Picture Content Control button in the Controls group, and then click the Properties button.
- In the Title box, type the control title.
- Click the Content control cannot be deleted check box if you want to prevent the user from deleting the content control.
- Click the Contents cannot be edited check box if you want to prevent the user from changing the placeholder text.
- Click the OK button.
- If you want to include instruction text for the user, position the insertion point to the right or left of the content control, and then type the instruction text; use the Format Painter or format the instruction text directly to match the color and font of the placeholder text in other cells.

Pete wants to include a photo of each child with his or her registration form. His staff will photograph the child at the start of the registration process, and they will store the photo on the computer on which the parent or guardian will be completing the online registration form.

To insert a Picture content control in the form and test it:

1. Scroll up to the top of the document, if necessary, and then click in the blank cell to the right of the cell containing "Registration Form."
2. In the Controls group, click the **Picture Content Control** button, and then click the **Properties** button. The Content Control Properties dialog box for Picture content controls opens.
3. Type **Child Photo** in the Title box, click the **Content control cannot be deleted** check box, and then click the **OK** button. You want the picture to be centered in the cell.
4. Click the **Child Photo** title tab on the content control to select the entire control. The control is highlighted.

5. Click the **Table Tools Layout** tab, and then click the **Align Top Center** button in the Alignment group. Notice that there is no placeholder text for this content control. You will include instructions below the content control.
6. Click in a blank area of the cell containing the Picture content control to deselect the control, press the → key to move the insertion point to the right of the picture control, and then press the **Enter** key to insert a blank line below the picture control.
7. Type **Click icon, then double-click child's name in the list.** Next, you'll format the instruction text in this cell to look the same as the placeholder text in the other cells.
8. Select all the text in the cell, change the font to **Verdana (Body)**, change the font color to **White, Background 1, Darker 50%** (the last color in the first column under Theme Colors), and then deselect the text.
9. Make sure Design mode is turned off, and then point to the icon in the middle of the Picture content control. A ScreenTip appears telling you to click the icon to insert a picture. See Figure 9-30.

Figure 9-30 Using a Picture content control

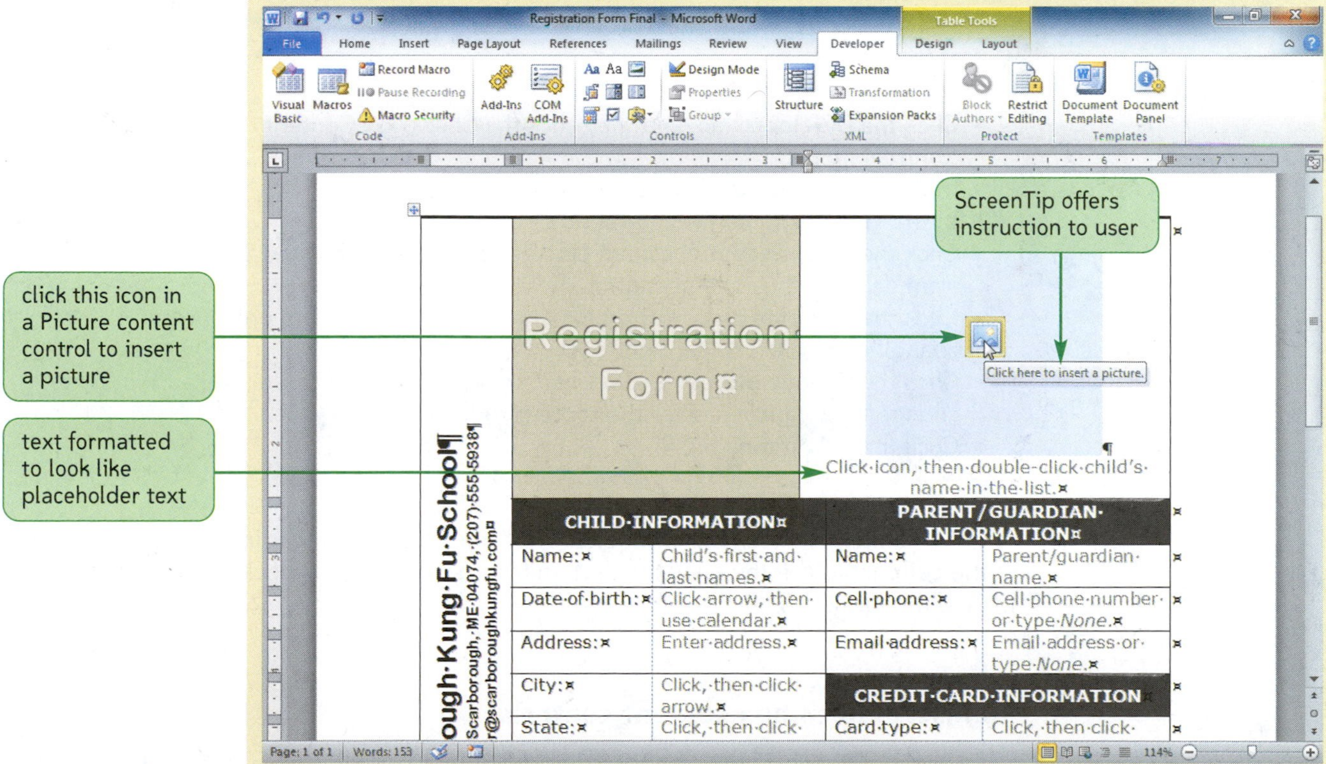

10. Click . The Insert Picture dialog box opens. When the form is saved on the computer the new students will be using, Pete will make sure the photos are stored in the default folder, but for now, you need to locate the photo you will insert as you test the control.
11. Navigate to the Word9\Tutorial folder, and then double-click **Child**. A photo appears in the Picture content control.

TIP

You can insert a graphic into a table cell in the same way you insert a graphic any place in a document—click the Insert tab, and then click one of the buttons in the Illustrations group.

12. Press the **Delete** key to delete the photo you inserted, click a blank area of the document to return the Picture content control back to its original state, and then click a blank area again to deselect any selected text. The picture control works as it should.
13. Save the template.

Next, you will add a check box content control.

Inserting Check Box Content Controls

Many dialog boxes you have used in Word and in other programs include check boxes that you can click to display or remove a check mark to select and deselect items. Similarly, a **Check Box content control** is a box-shaped control that users can click to insert or remove an X. If you want to allow users to select any number of options in a list, you can provide each option as text in the appropriate cell of the template, and then place a check box content control to the left of each item. You might include check box content controls in an online survey form for questions such as, "Which of the following items do you plan to purchase in the next six months?"

REFERENCE

Inserting a Check Box Content Control

- Click the Developer tab, and then click the Check Box Content Control button in the Controls group.
- In the Controls group, click the Properties button.
- In the Title box, type the control title.
- Click the Content control cannot be deleted check box if you want to prevent users from deleting the content control.
- Click the Contents cannot be edited check box if you want to prevent the user from changing the placeholder text.
- Click the Change button next to Checked symbol or next to Unchecked symbol to change the symbol used for the content control.
- Click the OK button.

Pete would like check boxes labeled "Yes" and "No" to appear in the cell to the right of the cell that asks if the child needs a uniform, so you'll add check box content controls to the form.

To insert check box content controls:

1. Click in the cell to the right of "Does child need a uniform?", and then click the **Developer** tab, if necessary.
2. In the Controls group, click the **Check Box Content Control** button ☑. A Check Box content control is inserted in the cell. See Figure 9-31.

Figure 9-31 Check Box content control inserted in form

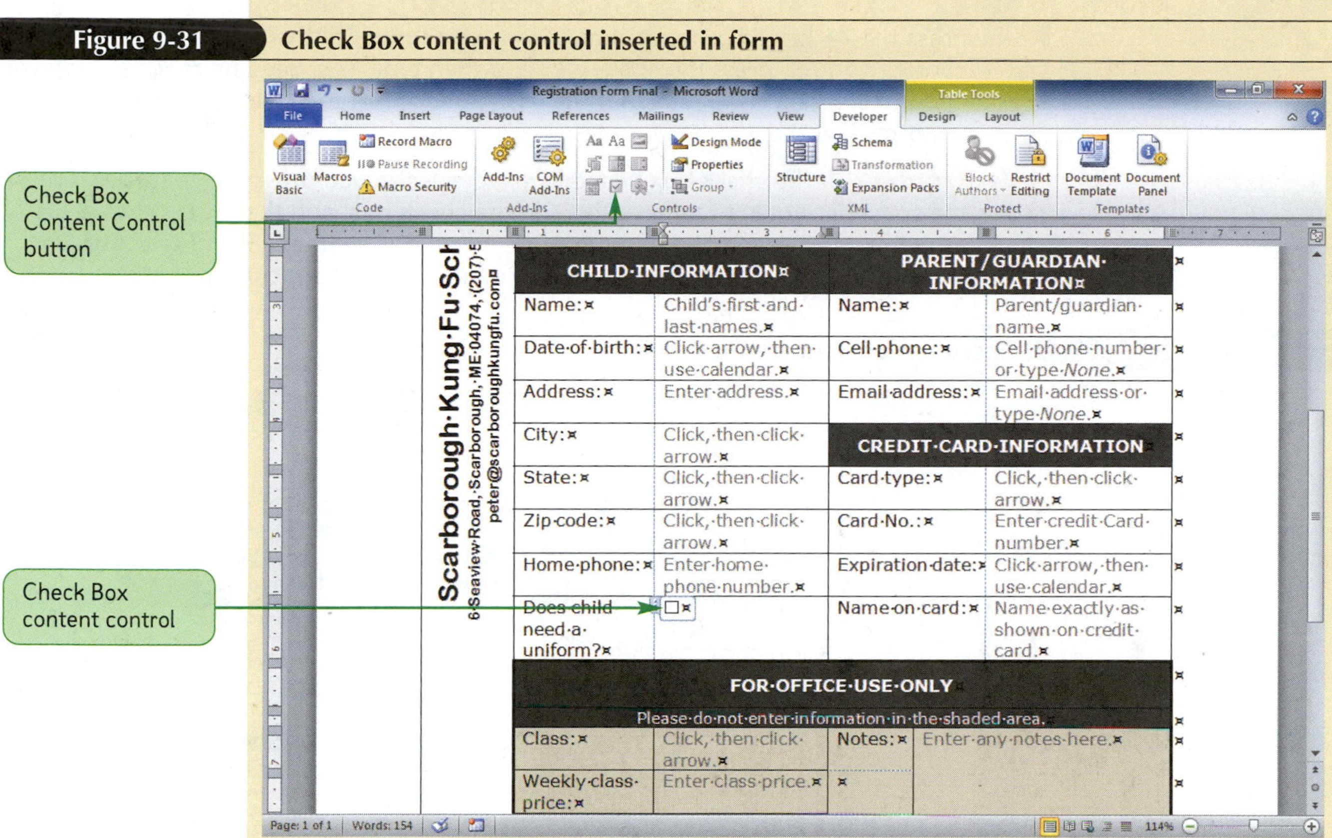

3. In the Controls group, click the **Properties** button to open the Content Control Properties dialog box for a check box content control. See Figure 9-32.

Figure 9-32 Content Control Properties dialog box for a Check Box content control

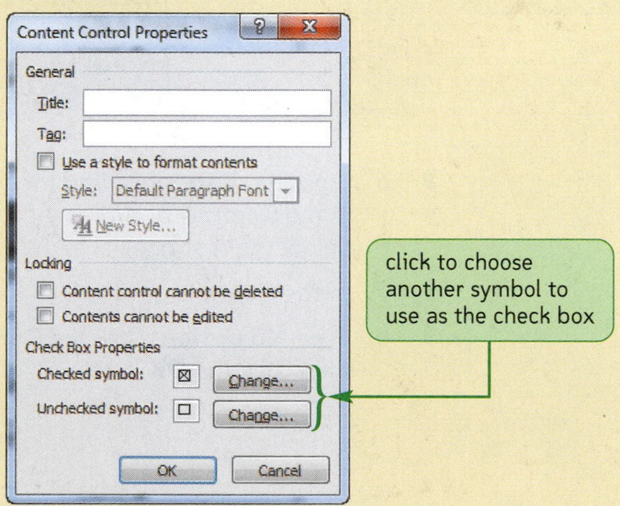

4. In the Title box, type **Yes option**, click the **Content control cannot be deleted** check box to select it, and then click the **OK** button. The dialog box closes and the insertion point is blinking in the content control in the cell.

5. Press the → key twice to position the insertion point to the right of the check box content control, press the **spacebar**, and then type **Yes**. See Figure 9-33. Now you need to create a check box that the user can check if the child does not need a uniform.

   Trouble? If the check box becomes selected after you press the spacebar, press the spacebar again to remove the X in the check box, and then press the → key as many times as needed to remove the check box content control selection box and position the insertion point to the right of the content control.

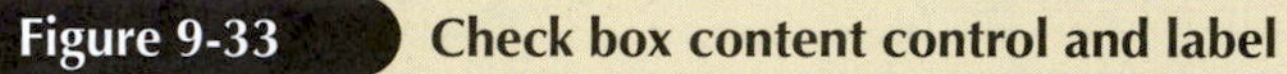

Figure 9-33 Check box content control and label

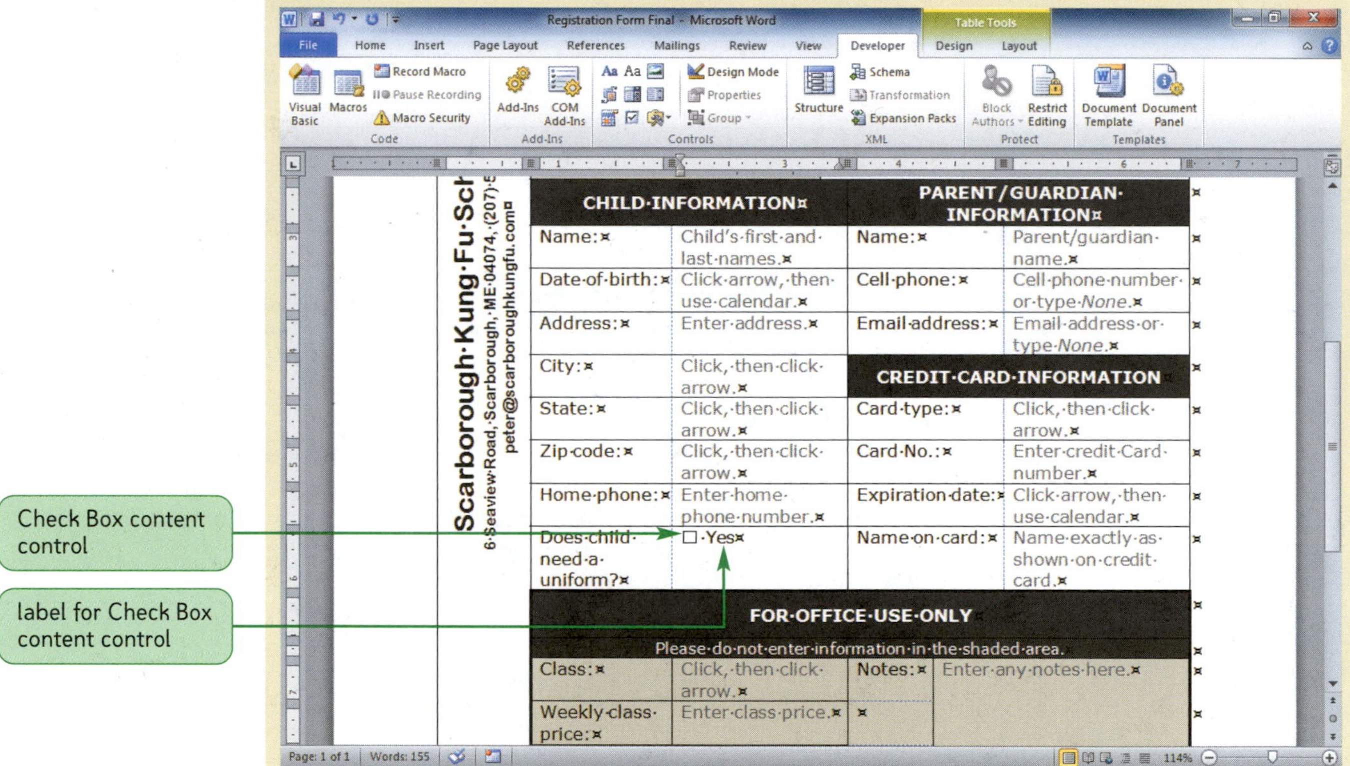

6. Press the **Enter** key, and then click the **Check Box Content Control** button ☑ in the Controls group. A second check box content control is inserted in the line below the first one.
7. In the Controls group, click the **Properties** button.
8. Type **No option**, click the **Content control cannot be deleted** check box, and then click the **OK** button.

9. Press the → key twice to position the insertion point to the right of the check box content control, press the **spacebar**, and then type **No**. Now you can test the check box controls.
10. Click the **Yes** check box. An "X" appears in the check box.
11. Click the **Yes** check box again. The "X" is removed.
12. Save the template.

The form is now mostly complete. In the next session you'll finish the form by inserting a formula in the cell next to "Session total" to calculate the total fee for the session, and then you will learn about protecting the form so users can only enter information using the content controls.

REVIEW

Session 9.2 Quick Check

1. What is the difference between a Plain Text content control and a Rich Text content control?
2. How do you provide instructions for using a content control to a user?
3. Does a form that contains content controls need to be protected in order to test it?
4. True or False. The date-time picture MM/dd/YYYY displays the date in the form 03 February 2010.
5. Name a situation in which you would use a Combo Box content control instead of a Drop-Down List content control.
6. What type of content is included in the list for a Building Block Gallery content control?

SESSION 9.3 VISUAL OVERVIEW

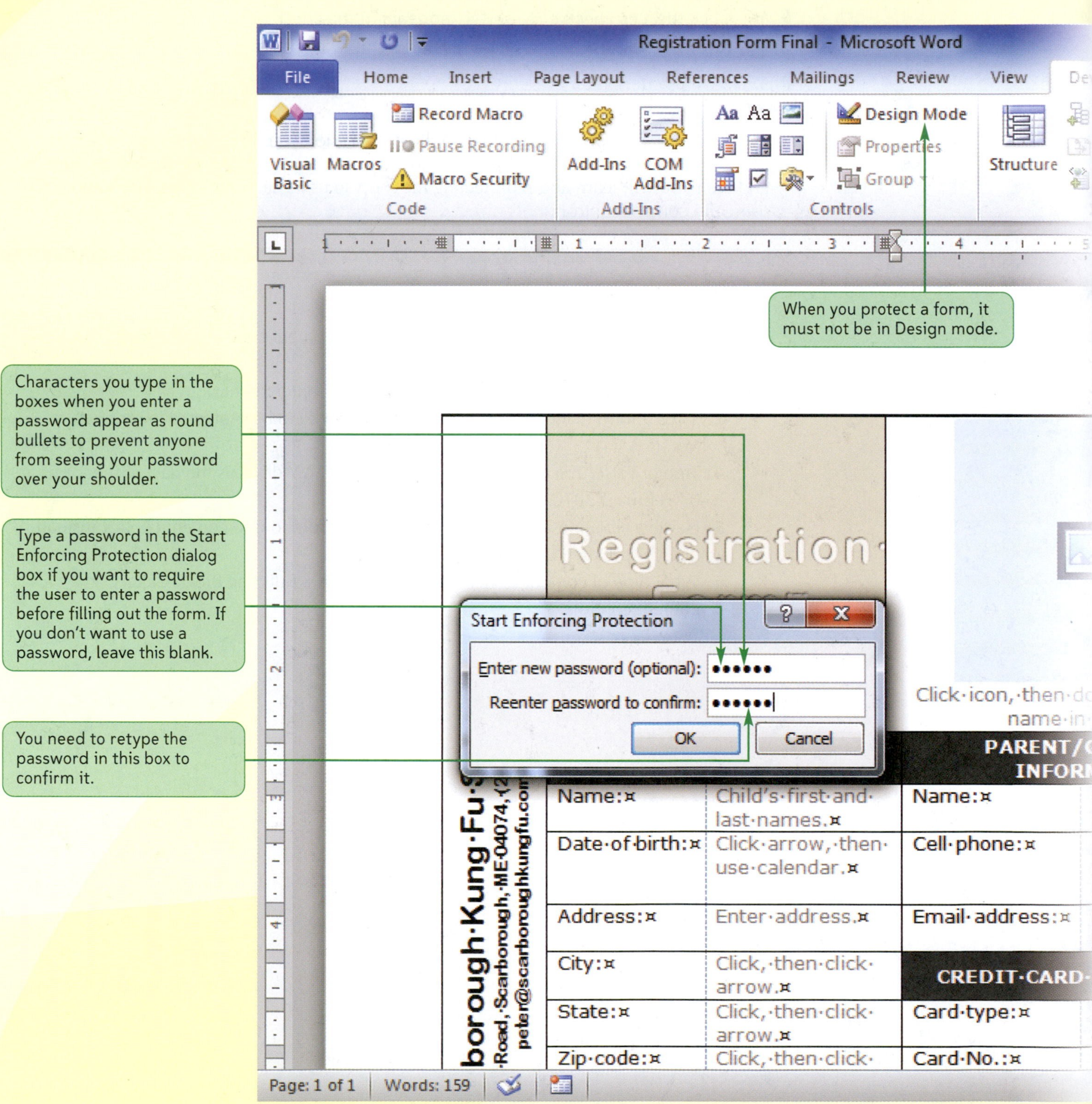

PROTECTING A DOCUMENT

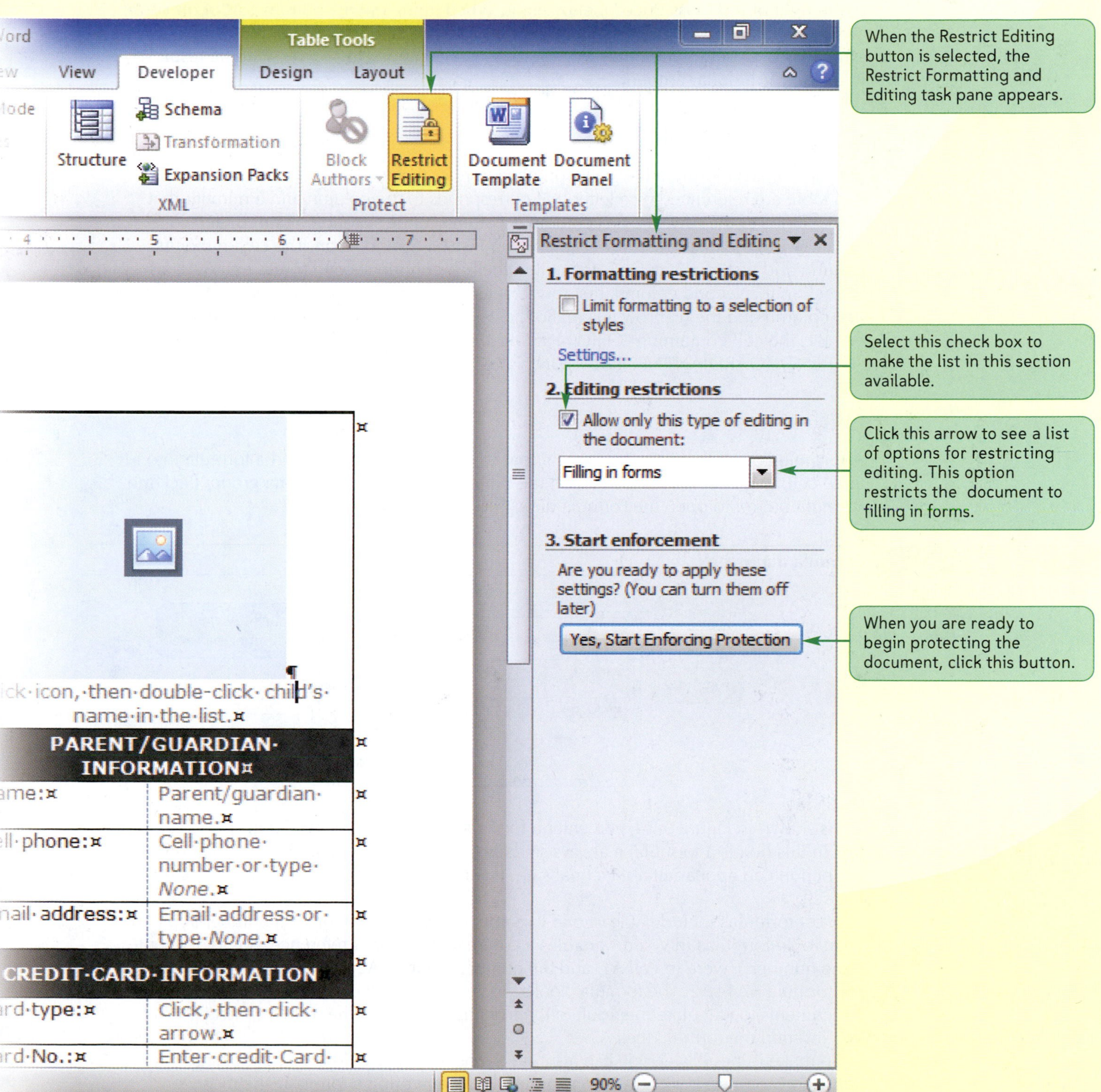

Using Formulas in a Table

The "FOR OFFICE USE ONLY" section of the registration form contains the fields for entering the price of a class and the total for a session. There are eight weeks per session, so this total can be calculated by multiplying the number the employee enters in the cell to the right of the Class Price label by eight. When filling out the bottom part of the form, an employee could do this calculation in his or her head, but to avoid any mathematical errors, you can set up a formula to perform the calculation. You can format the result so it appears as a dollar amount.

Referencing Table Cells

In order to use a formula in a cell, you need to refer to specific cells in the table. Cells in a table are referenced by a letter that corresponds to the column and a number that corresponds to the row. The first column is column A, the second column B, and so on; likewise, the first row is row 1, the second is row 2, and so on. The cell in the first column and first row is cell A1, the cell in the first column second row is cell A2, and the cell in the second column, first row is cell B1. A merged cell is referenced by the first column and the first row it is in. So the cell that contains "Registration Form" is cell B1, the cell containing "CHILD INFORMATION" is cell B2, and the cell containing "PARENT/GUARDIAN INFORMATION" is cell C2.

Understanding Formulas

A **formula** is a mathematical statement that calculates a value. To insert a formula into a table cell, you click the Layout tab on the Ribbon, and then, in the Data group, click the Formula button to open the Formula dialog box. See Figure 9-34.

Figure 9-34 Formula dialog box

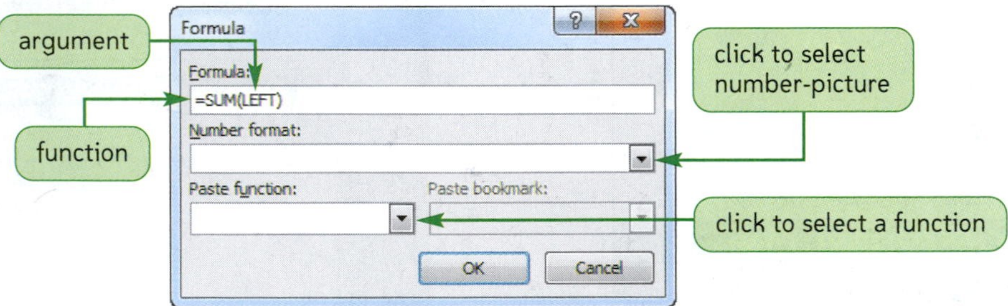

As shown in Figure 9-34, you enter a formula in the Formula box. To indicate that the text in this box is a formula, it always starts with an equal sign. Numbers, variables, or a function can appear after the equal sign. If you type =1+2, the result 3 will appear in the cell.

Most formulas include at least one **variable**, which is a symbol for a number that can change. In formulas in Word, variables are named by the cell reference. So, for example, if the number 1 were in cell A1, and the number 2 in cell A2, you could type into cell A3 the formula =A1+A2. The formula "looks" in the referenced cells (A1 and A2) and uses the contents to calculate the result of the formula. It displays the result in the cell where you inserted the formula (cell A3).

To make things easier, you can also use a function. A **function** is a relationship between variables; basically, it's a shorthand way of writing a formula. The most commonly used function is the SUM function, which adds numbers, usually stored in adjacent cells. All functions take arguments; an **argument** is a value that the function needs in order to calculate its result. Arguments appear between parentheses immediately after the name of the function. In our example—with 1 in cell A1, 2 in cell A2, and the formula in cell A3—you could use the SUM function to add the contents of cells A1 and A2. To do this, you would type =SUM(A1,A2) in cell A3. Finally, because tables are grids, and functions such as SUM are frequently used at the bottom of a column or the end of a row, you can use LEFT, RIGHT, ABOVE, and BELOW as the argument and SUM will add the contents of all the cells in that direction. So the formula in our cell A3 could be =SUM(LEFT).

Word provides 18 basic functions to use in tables. If you plan to do complex calculations, Word is not the best tool to use, but for simple calculations, the Formula dialog box works well.

Inserting a Formula in a Table Cell

A formula in a table cell is a field that can be updated when you change the data used in the formula calculation. Like any field, when you insert a formula, you can specify how the result will be formatted in the document. The key to controlling the content and format of a number is selecting an appropriate numeric picture. Similar to a date-time picture, a **numeric picture** is a pattern of digits and symbols, such as $#,###,### or 00.00, that describes how the number will look. When you assign a numeric picture to a formula, Word takes the number entered by the user and formats it in a certain way. In some cases, Word also prevents the user from entering incorrect characters. For example, you could use a numeric picture that would take a single digit entered by the user and display it with a decimal point and a trailing zero. (That is, if the user entered "5," Word would display "5.0" in the cell.) The numeric picture doesn't change the number itself (provided you enter an appropriate number), but only how it is displayed.

To understand numeric pictures, you first need to understand the symbols used in them. Figure 9-35 shows the most commonly used numeric picture symbols.

Figure 9-35 **Numeric picture symbols**

Symbol	Purpose	Example
0 (zero)	Displays a digit in place of the zero in the field result. If the result doesn't include a digit in that place, the field displays a zero.	Numeric picture "00.0" displays "05.0" Numeric picture "0" displays an integer of any number of digits
#	Displays a digit in place of the # only if the result requires it. If the result doesn't include a digit in that place, the field displays a space.	Numeric picture "$##.00" displays "$ 5.00"
. (decimal point)	Determines the decimal point position.	See examples above
, (comma)	Separates a series of three digits.	Numeric picture "$#,###,###" displays "$3,450,000"
- (hyphen)	Includes a minus sign if the number is negative or a space if the number is positive.	Numeric picture "-0" displays an integer as " 5" or "-5"
; (semicolon)	Separates the positive and negative numeric picture.	Numeric picture "$##0.00;-$##0.00" displays "$ 55.50" if positive, "-$ 55.50" if negative
(parentheses around negative number)	Puts parentheses around a negative result.	Numeric picture ""$##0.00;($##0.00)" displays "$ 55.50" if positive, "($ 55.50)" if negative
$, %, etc.	Displays a special character in the result.	Numeric picture "0.0%" displays "5.0%"

Pete looks over the form, and asks you to add a formula to the last row in the table so that the session total will be calculated in the cell to the right of "Session total." This cell is in the third column, so it is column C, and is in the last row of the table, row 15. To calculate the session total, you will multiply the value in the cell above C15—cell C14—by eight (the number of weeks in a session).

To insert a formula for the session total:

1. If you took a break after the previous session, open the **Registration Form Final** file as a template, make sure the rulers and nonprinting characters are visible, table gridlines are displayed, Word is in Print Layout view, and your zoom is set to Page Width.
2. Click in the cell to the right of the label "Session total" (cell C15), click the **Table Tools Layout** tab, and then click the **Formula** button in the Data group. The Formula dialog box opens. Because there are cells to the left of the current cell, the default function =SUM(LEFT) appears in the Formula text box. You need to change this function to multiply the value in cell C14 by eight.
3. Delete all the text in the Formula box except the equal sign, click the **Paste function** arrow, scroll down the alphabetical list, and then click **PRODUCT**. The function is inserted in the Formula box, followed by parentheses, and the insertion point is blinking inside the parentheses so that you can enter the arguments.
4. Type **C14,8**. You want the result to be displayed with a $.
5. Click the **Number format** arrow, and then click **$#,##0.00;($#,##0.00)** to set the number format as a dollar amount.
6. Click the **OK** button. The dialog box closes. The result of the calculation—"$ 0.00"—appears in the cell to the right of the Session total label. The result is $0 because there is no value in cell C14. Recall that fields update when the document is opened, when you click the Update Field command on the shortcut menu, or when you press the F9 key. Now test the formula.
7. Click in cell **C14** ("Enter class price"), type **15**, right-click the formula field in cell **C15**, and then click **Update Field** on the shortcut menu. The field updates to $ 120.00. See Figure 9-36.

Figure 9-36 Result of a formula displayed in a cell

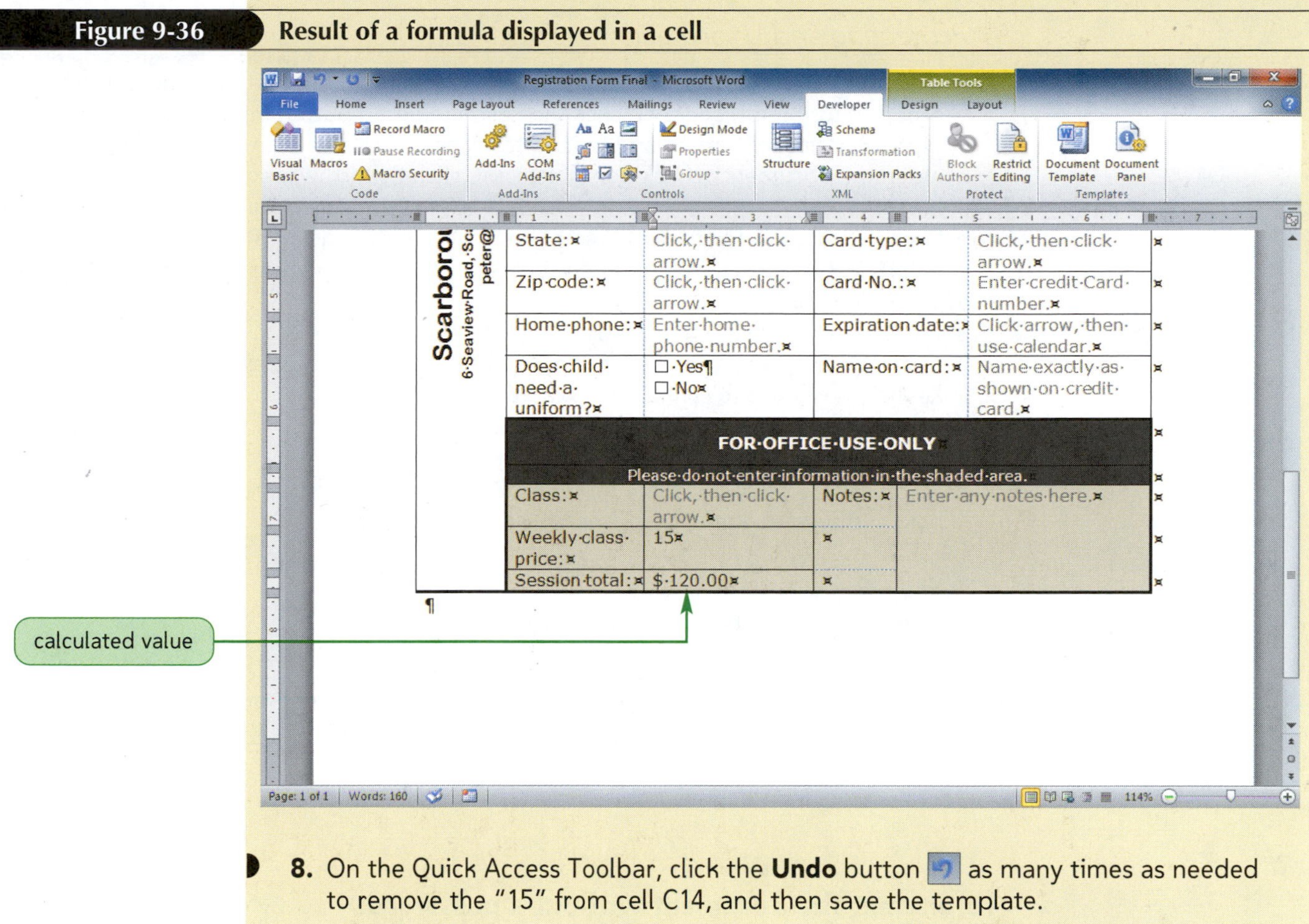

8. On the Quick Access Toolbar, click the **Undo** button as many times as needed to remove the "15" from cell C14, and then save the template.

Protecting the Document for Filling in Forms

Protecting a form means that any changes to the text or structure of the form are prohibited. Protecting a form in order for someone to enter text into a content control is not mandatory; however, it is a good idea if you don't want any of the other text or the table structure to be altered. To protect a form, you use the Restrict Editing command. When you protect the document, you can specify that the document is read-only, meaning a user can open and view it, but not make any changes to it. You can also give restricted access to users for either making tracked changes or adding comments. Finally, for a form, you want users to be able to enter content in the content controls, so you can give limited access to fill in the form. Refer to the Session 9.3 Visual Overview for more information about protecting a document.

Because a form that is protected only allows the user to enter data content controls, make sure you do not set the properties so that the content controls are removed when the contents are edited. Otherwise, as soon as the user types one character in a control, the control will be deleted and the user will not be able to enter any more data.

REFERENCE

Protecting and Unprotecting a Form

- Click the Developer tab, if necessary click the Design Mode button in the Controls group to turn it off, and then click the Restrict Editing button in the Protect group.
- In the Restrict Formatting and Editing task pane, click the "Allow only this type of editing in the document" check box to select it, click the arrow, and then click Filling in forms.
- Click the Yes, Start Enforcing Protection button. If the button is grayed out (not available), click the Design Mode button in the Controls group on the Developer tab to turn off Design mode.
- If you want to use a password, in the Start Enforcing Protection dialog box, type a password in the Enter new password (optional) box, type the same password in the Reenter password to confirm box, and then click the OK button; or, if you do not want to use a password, just click the OK button.
- To turn off protection, click the Stop Protection button at the bottom of the task pane.
- If you used a password, type it in the Password box in the Unprotect Document dialog box, and then click the OK button.

Protecting a Form without a Password

If you add a password when you protect the document, users would need to enter that password to remove the protection. You can protect the form without using a password, and then anyone could open the document and simply click the button to stop protecting the document.

You'll protect the document now.

To protect the document without a password:

1. Click the **Developer** tab. To protect the form, it must not be in Design mode.
2. In the Controls group, make sure the **Design Mode** button is deselected, and then in the Protect group, click the **Restrict Editing** button. The Restrict Formatting and Editing task pane opens to the right of the document window.
3. In section 2. Editing restrictions, click the **Allow only this type of editing in the document** check box to select it. The box below that check box becomes active, and the section expands to include the Exceptions (optional) section.
4. Click the **section 2** arrow, and then click **Filling in forms**. The button in section 3. Start enforcement becomes active.
5. Click the **Yes, Start Enforcing Protection** button. The Start Enforcing Protection dialog box opens, in which you can enter a password. You're just testing the form, so you won't enter a password now.
6. In the dialog box, click the **OK** button. The dialog box closes, the task pane changes to inform you that the document is protected from unintentional editing, and a Stop Protection button appears at the bottom of the task pane. See Figure 9-37. Because you can't edit the form now, most of the buttons on the Ribbon are unavailable (dimmed).

Figure 9-37 Protecting a document for filling in forms

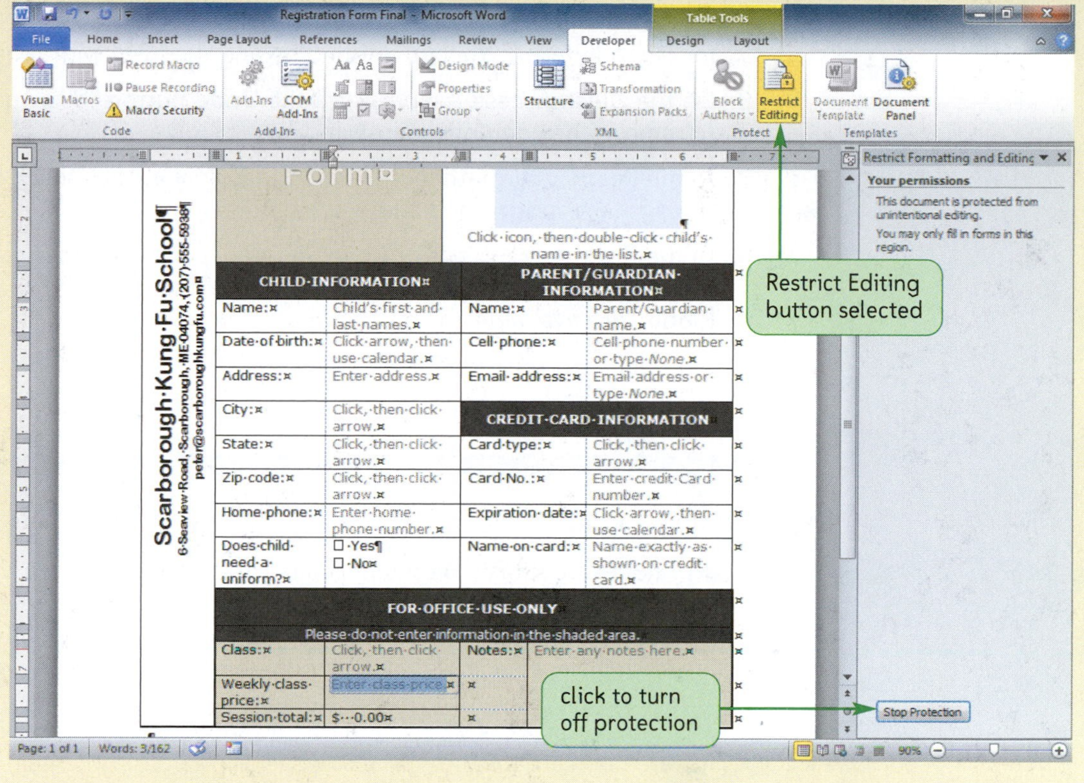

Now you'll test some of the content controls in the protected form to make sure they still work as expected.

To test the content controls in the form:

1. Click in the cell to the right of the "Name" cell in the "CHILD INFORMATION" section, and then type **Jane Doe**. The text you typed replaces the placeholder text.
2. Click in the "Name" cell in the "PARENT/GUARDIAN INFORMATION" section. The next content control, the control in the cell to the right of the cell you clicked, is selected. When the form is protected, if you click anywhere in the document except within a content control, the insertion point moves to the next content control after the location where you clicked. Now you'll test the Picture content control.
3. Click the icon in the Picture content control at the top of the form, navigate to the Word9\Tutorial folder, and then double-click **Child**. A photo of a child appears in the content control. Next, you'll test a list content control.
4. Click in the cell to the right of the "Zip code" label, click the arrow that appears, and then **04074**. The zip code you selected appears in the cell. Now, you'll test the check box content control.
5. In cell to the right of the "Does the child need a uniform?" label, click the **Yes check box**. An "X" appears in the check box. Next, you should make sure the field is calculated correctly when the form is protected.
6. Click in the cell to the right of the "Weekly class price" label, and then type **15**.

7. Right-click cell **C15** (the cell containing the formula), and then click **Update Field** on the shortcut menu. The field updates to show the results of the formula. Note that you cannot press the F9 key to update a field when the document is protected for filling in forms. You are finished testing the form with protection turned on.
8. On the Quick Access Toolbar, click the **Undo** button as many times as needed to remove the content you inserted.
9. In the Restrict Formatting and Editing task pane, click the **Stop Protection** button. Protection is turned off.
10. In the Protect group on the Developer tab, click the **Restrict Editing** button. The button is deselected and the task pane closes. Notice that the buttons on the Ribbon are available again.
11. Save your changes to the template.

INSIGHT

Using Legacy Form Fields

Form fields are similar to content controls; they are spaces in a document that contain a specific type of information and are able to be filled in by a user when a document is protected. Form fields are one of the legacy tools available to Word 2010 users. In computer terminology, *legacy* refers to hardware or software that existed in an older version and is still available in the new version, but is retained only for "backward compatibility." This allows the new software or hardware to work with an older version, or for the software to create something the older version can use. Therefore, **legacy tools** are tools that were available in previous versions of Word.

With legacy form fields, you can add help text—instructions for the user—so that when the user's insertion point is in the form field, the text appears in the status bar or when the user presses the F1 key. To do this, click the Add Help Text button in the Form Field Options dialog box to open the Form Field Help Text dialog box. Click the Type your own option button, and then type help text in the box. This provides help that is similar to the placeholder text displayed for a content control.

Protecting the Online Form with a Password

The registration form for the school is now completed. Because this is the final version of the form, you'll add a password so that no one accidentally turns off protection.

To protect the form with a password:

1. Click the **Developer** tab, make sure Design mode is turned off, and then in the Protect group, click the **Restrict Editing** button. The Restrict Formatting and Editing task pane opens with the check box in section 2 selected and Filling in forms selected in the box in that section.
2. Click the **Yes, Start Enforcing Protection** button. The Start Enforcing Protection dialog box opens.
3. In the Enter new password (optional) box, type **peterd**. The characters you typed appear as round bullets.

TIP

Make a note of your password for future reference.

TIP

Passwords are case sensitive, so *PeterD* is not the same as *peterd*.

4. Press the **Tab** key, type **peterd** in the Reenter password to confirm box, and then click the **OK** button. The dialog box closes, and the Stop Protection button appears in the task pane.
5. Close the task pane, and then save the final, password-protected template.
6. Click the **View** tab, and then click the **One Page** button in the Zoom group. The final registration form template is shown in Figure 9-38.

Figure 9-38 **Final registration form in One Page view**

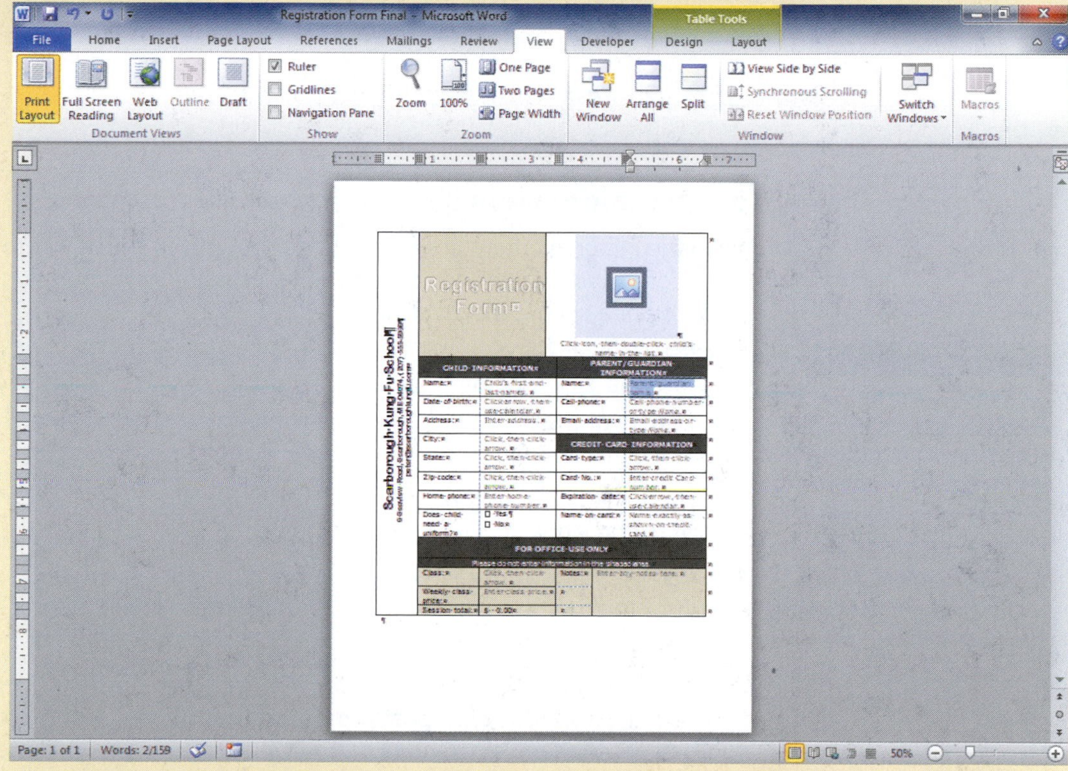

7. Click the **File** tab, and then click **Close** in the navigation bar to close the template but leave Word running.

You have finished protecting the form. Now you are ready to test the completed form as if you were registering a new student at Scarborough Kung Fu School.

Filling in the Online Form

So far you have been acting as a form designer and creator. Now it's time to try out the form from the user's point of view to make sure there are no unexpected glitches. You can do this by filling in the form just as a user would.

To open a new registration form from the template:

1. Click the **File** tab, and then click the **New** tab in the navigation bar. The commands on the New tab appear in Backstage view.
2. In the center pane, click the **New from existing** button to open the New from Existing Document dialog box, and then navigate to the Word9\Tutorial folder.
3. Click **Registration Form Final**, and then click the **Create New** button. The registration form opens in a new document window.
4. Scroll up to the top of the document. The Picture content control in the top row is selected.

Now you will enter some information in the form.

TIP

If the current content control is a Rich Text control, pressing the Tab key inserts a Tab space in the control; it does not move the insertion point to the next control.

To enter information into the form:

1. In the Picture content control in the top row, click [icon], navigate to the Word9\Tutorial folder included with your Data Files, if necessary, and then double-click **Child**. The photo of a child is inserted into the document.
2. Click the cell to the right of the first "Name" label, type **Greg Dunstan**, and then press the **Tab** key. The text you typed appears in the cell and is formatted in bold because of the Properties settings you entered earlier, and the next cell containing a content control is the current cell.
3. Type **Patricia Dunstan**, and then press the **Tab** key. The content control in the cell to the right of "Date of birth" is selected.
4. Click the **arrow** at the right of the cell, click the **backward** scroll arrow to the left of the month name in the calendar as many times as necessary to scroll to **December 2008**, and then click **12**. December 12, 2008 appears in the cell.
5. Press the **Tab** key, type **207-555-3920**, press the **Tab** key, type **12 Birch Lane**, press the **Tab** key, type **patty@dunstanfamily.name**, and then press the **Tab** key. The content control to the right of "City" is selected. This is one of the Combo Box content controls. The next content control, the cell to the right of State, is also a Combo Box. You'll enter text in one and select from the list in the other.
6. Type **South Portland**, and then press the **Tab** key. The State content control is selected.
7. Click the arrow that appears in the content control to the right of the "State" label, click **ME**, and then press the **Tab** key. The content control to the right of "Card type" is a Drop-Down List control.
8. Click the **arrow**, click **Visa**, press the **Tab** key, type **04106**, press the **Tab** key, type **1234 5678 9012**, press the **Tab** key, type **207-555-3112**, and then press the **Tab** key. The Expiration date content control is selected.
9. Use the calendar to select any date in **February 2015** as the expiration date, and then press the **Tab** key. The expiration date for the credit card appears as 02/2015, and the No check box content control in the cell to the right of "Does child need a uniform?" is highlighted.
10. In the cell to the right of "Does child need a uniform?", click the **Yes** check box. An "X" appears in the Yes check box, and the No check box is still highlighted.

11. Press the **Tab** key. Nothing happens. Pressing the Tab key when a check box content control is highlighted doesn't do anything, so you need to click the next content control.
12. Click the content control next to the cell containing "Name on card," type **Patricia E Dunstan**, and then press the **Tab** key. The content control next to "Class" is selected and the arrow appears. This is in the section of the form that only employees will be using.
13. Click the **arrow**, click **Preschool/Kindergarten**, press the **Tab** key, type **Call cell phone number first.**, and then press the **Tab** key. The content control in the cell that will contain the weekly class price is selected.
14. Type **14**, and then press the **Tab** key. The insertion point does not move. Pressing the Tab key moves the insertion point to the next content control, and there are no more content controls in the form. Recall that cell C15, the cell next to "Session total," contains a field. To update the field, you need to right-click in this cell and select the Update Field command on the shortcut menu.
15. Right-click cell **C15** (the cell to the right of the "Session total" label) and then click **Update Field** on the shortcut menu. $ 112.00 appears in cell C15.
16. Drag the **Zoom slider** to the left to change the zoom to 80%. Your completed form should look like the one shown in Figure 9-39.

Figure 9-39 **Completed test form**

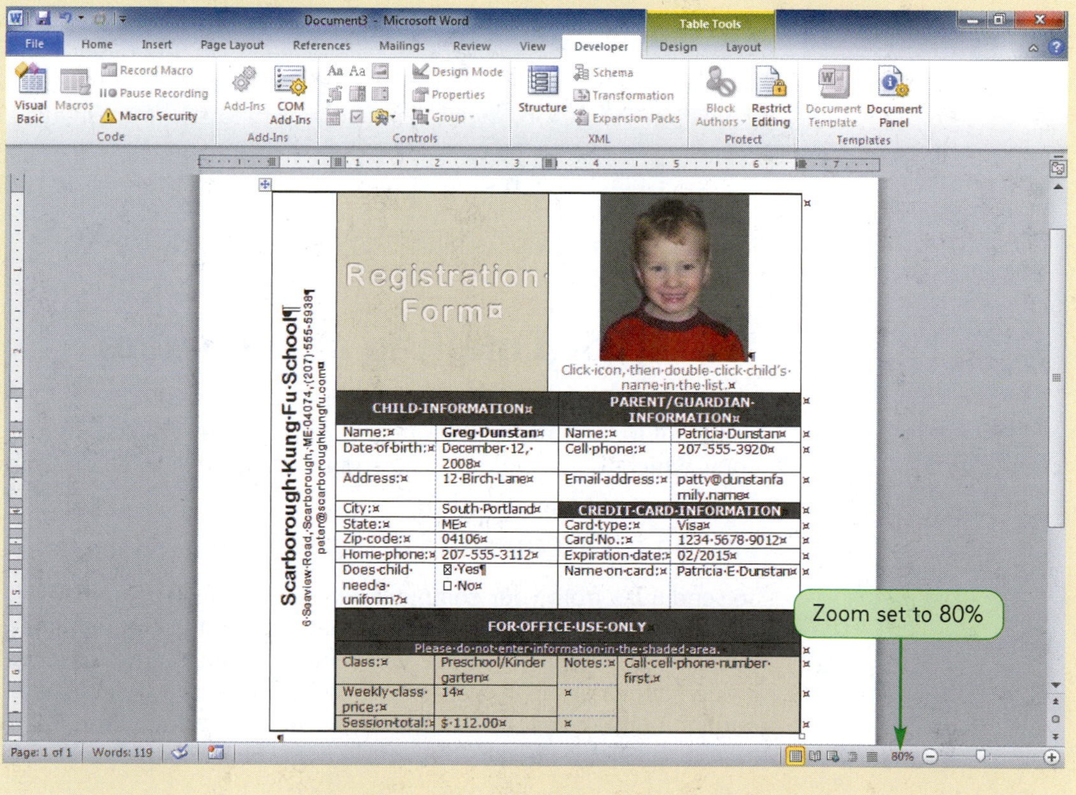

Now that the form is completed, you will save it, and remove the Developer tab from the Ribbon.

To save the form and remove the Developer tab from the Ribbon:

1. On the Quick Access Toolbar, click the **Save** button, navigate to the Word9\Tutorial folder included with your Data Files, replace the text in the File name box with **Test Form**, and then click the **Save** button.
2. If the Developer tab was not displayed when you started working with content controls, hide it by clicking the **File** tab, clicking **Options**, clicking **Customize Ribbon**, clicking the **Developer** tab to deselect its check box, and then clicking the **OK** button.
3. Close the **Test Form** document.

Now that you've finished filling in the form, you can be satisfied that it works as Pete planned. The last thing Pete wants you to do is to look into how he can get copies of the completed registration forms to the parents or guardians of the children they've enrolled.

PROSKILLS

Problem Solving: Organizing a Form

The form you created in this tutorial contains information organized in a logical way for the person who needs to create and store the form. However, as you might have noticed when you entered the information in the form, it is not set up in the most logical way for the user who is pressing the Tab key to move from one control or field to the next. When you design a form, keep the Tab key behavior in mind and try to come up with a design that works for both the person entering the data and the person who will be reading the form. For example, for this form, you could fill all the cells that the user needs to fill out with a color to draw the user's attention to those cells. You could also consider redesigning the table so that pressing the Tab key moves the user through the form in a more logical order. If you keep the end user—the person who will be filling out the form—in mind, you will be able to create a form that is easy for that person to fill out without missing any of the content controls.

Faxing or Emailing a Document

After completing a registration form, the employee at the Kung Fu school needs to give a copy of it to the student's parent or guardian. They would like to either fax or email the copy, which they can do using the options on the Save & Send tab in Backstage view.

Faxing a Document Directly from Word

To send a fax from your computer without having to print first and then send the paper through a fax machine, you need to have either a fax modem that you can set up as a printer, or you need to have subscribed to a fax Internet service. If you have a fax modem, you can open the Print tab in Backstage view, click the button under Printer, and then click Fax in the list. After you click the Print button, the Fax Setup Wizard starts.

Click Connect to a fax modem, and then follow the steps in the wizard. You'll need to have administrative rights on your computer to complete the wizard. When you're finished, the New Fax message box opens for you to type a fax number in the To box. This message box looks similar to a new email message box. Just like an email message, you can type a Subject in the Subject box. The fax is a graphic attachment to a New Fax message. See Figure 9-40. When you're ready, click the Send button on the toolbar.

Figure 9-40 New Fax message box

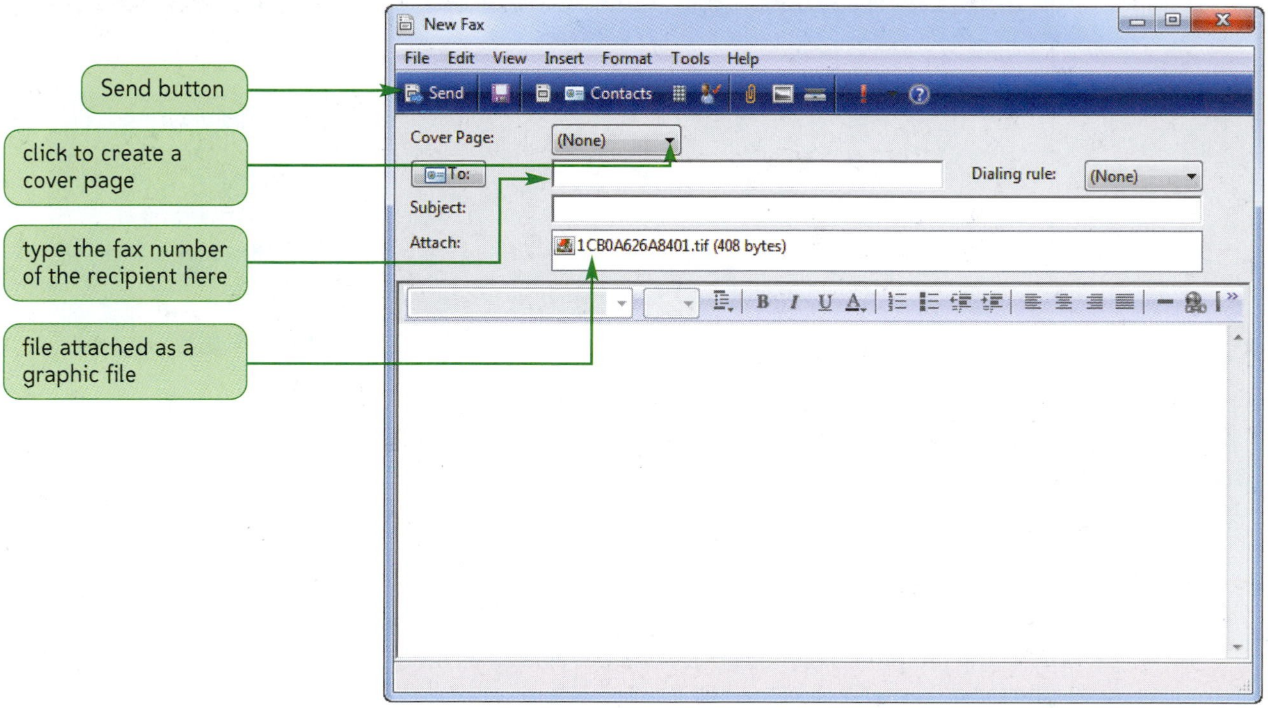

To subscribe to an Internet fax service from within Word, open the Save & Send tab in Backstage view, click Send Using E-mail, and then click Send as Internet Fax. If you have not subscribed to an Internet fax service yet, a dialog box opens stating that you need to sign up with a fax service provider. If you click the OK button in this dialog box, your browser starts and a Web page on the Office.com site opens listing the available fax services that work with Word and links to sign up with the services. See Figure 9-41.

Figure 9-41 Available Fax Services Web page on the Microsoft Office Web site

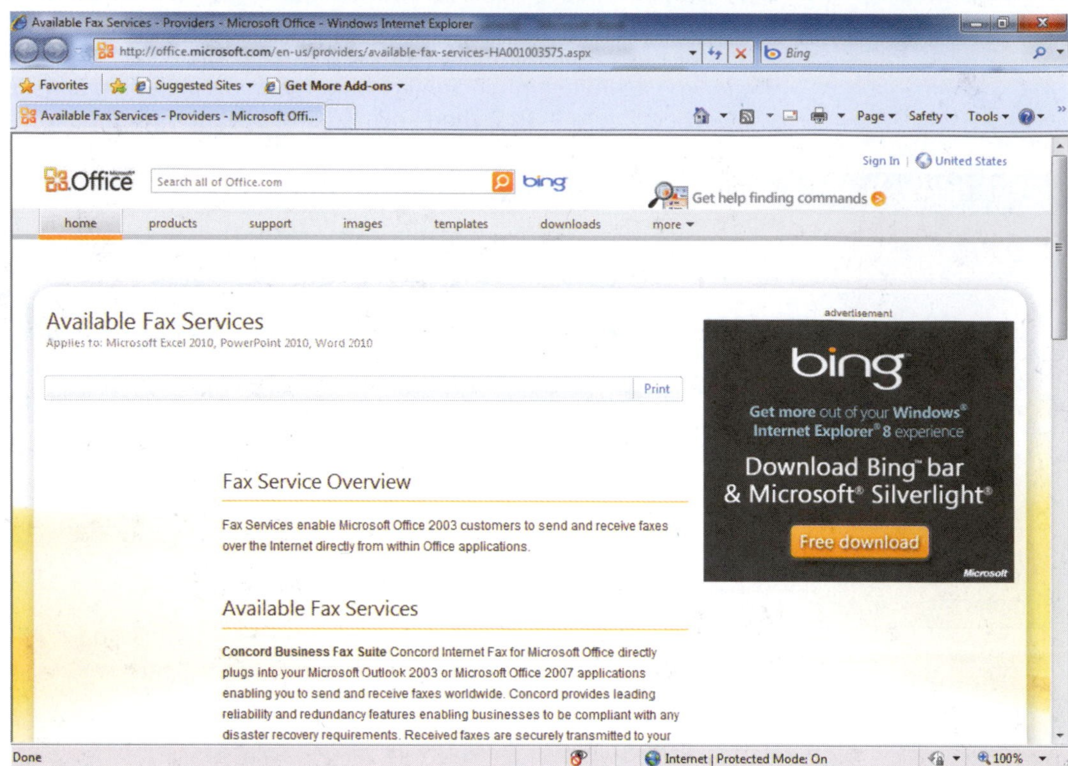

Once you've signed up with a fax service, clicking the Internet Fax command opens a new email message window in Outlook or opens the fax service's interface. You can type the recipient's name and fax number as well as the subject of the fax, and then send the fax.

Sending a Document as an Email Attachment Directly from Word

If you want to share a document with a group of people who have access to email, and if you want to accumulate comments and corrections from members of the workgroup, then you might want to route the document instead of faxing it. When you **route** a document, you send it as an attachment to an email message; the message (with the document attached) then travels to a group of people, from one person to another. The recipients of the e-mail are specified in a **routing slip**. After each person reads the document and makes comments and corrections, he or she sends it to the next recipient on the routing slip. Each recipient then has the benefit of seeing all the comments and corrections of previous reviewers. When the document returns to you, it will have accumulated comments and corrections from all the reviewers.

To understand another use of routing, suppose that Scarborough Kung Fu Studio is preparing to host a special series of classes for women on self-defense. Each time a person signs up for the class, an employee prepares a registration form that can include some information about the woman's fitness level. The employee can then route the order form to Pete so that he can track the number of women taking the courses and assign the woman to a class level. The order form would then be routed to the course coordinator who arranges accommodations for the class participants, then to the class teacher, and so on. If any person in the routing doesn't approve the form, it doesn't go on to the subsequent members of the workgroup. Whether the form is approved or not, it returns to the originator of the routed document.

To email a document as an attachment to an email message, open the Save & Send tab in Backstage view, click Send Using E-mail, and then click the Send as Attachment button. An email message window opens with the document attached. You can then address it and send it as usual.

Pete is pleased with the appearance of the form you created and with how well it works. He's sure it will make the process for enrolling new students more efficient and will improve the accuracy of the records kept at the studio.

REVIEW

Session 9.3 Quick Check

1. What happens when you protect a form?
2. What is a formula?
3. What is a variable?
4. What is an argument?
5. How does the number 34 appear if the numeric picture is $##0.00;($##0.00)?
6. What is always the first character in a formula in a Word table?

Practice the skills you learned in the tutorial using the same case scenario.

PRACTICE

Review Assignments

Data Files needed for the Review Assignments: AppForm.docx, Teen.jpg

Peter Dietz, owner of Scarborough Kung Fu Studios, wants to hire more staff. He asked you to develop an online form that potential employees can fill out. He created a basic table. You need to format the table, insert content controls and a formula, and test the form. Complete the following steps:

1. Open the file **AppForm** from the Word9\Review folder included with your Data Files, and then save it in the same folder as a document template with the filename **Application Form**.
2. Select all the cells in the first row, and then split the selected cells into one column and two rows, merging the cells before you split them. Move the text "Application for Employment" into the first cell in the new second row.
3. Merge the following cells:
   a. the three cells to the right of the cell containing "Photo" (cells B3 through D3)
   b. the cell containing "Gender" and the cell beneath it (cells C4 and C5)
   c. the cell containing "Previous Work Experience" and the three cells to its right (cells A7 through D7)
   d. the cell containing "Dates Employed" and the cell to its right (cells A8 and B8)
   e. the cell containing "Employer Address" and the cell beneath it (cells C9 and C10)
   f. the cells to the right of the merged "Employer Address" cell (cells D9 and D10)
   g. the last four cells in column D (cells D11 through D14)
4. Select the four cells in row 6 (cells A6 through D6), and then split them into six columns and one row, merging the cells before you split them.
5. Drag "Zip:" one cell to the right, drag "ME" one cell to the right, and then drag "State:" one cell to the right.
6. Split the cells containing "Male" and "Female" (cells D4 and D5) into two columns, deselecting the Merge cells before split check box (this will keep the same number of rows). Repeat this for the last four cells in column A (cells A11 through A14). Drag the contents of the last four cells in column A to the cells in the same row in column B. Merge the last four cells in column A, and then type **Office Use Only** in the new merged cell (cell A11).
7. Rotate the text in the merged cell containing "Office Use Only" (cell A11) so that it reads from bottom to top.
8. Turn off automatic column resizing, and then resize the columns as shown in the table below. Make sure you resize the columns in the order they are listed. Note that after you resize cells C11 through C14 in the last step, the width of cells D11 through D14 changes to approximately .6 inches.

Cell	Width (in inches)
A3 ("Photo")	.35
A4 and A5, and then A6 ("Name" through "City")	.9
B4 and B5 (blank cells to the right of "Name" and "Address")	2.75
C4 ("Gender")	.8
D4 and D5 ("Male" and "Female")	.6
A9 and A10 ("From" and "To")	.6
A8 through B10 ("Dates Employed" through cell to the right of "To")	1.35
C8 through C9 ("Employer Name" through "Employer Address")	1.15
A11 ("Office Use Only")	.5
B11 through B14 ("Position Applied For" through "Overtime Rate")	1.2
D11 through D14 ("Notes" and cells beneath it)	1.25
C11 through C14 (to the right of "Position Applied For" through "Overtime Rate")	1.75

9. In row 6, drag the left borders of the cells after you select each of them to change the widths as follows: resize cell E6 ("Zip") to .3 inches, cell D6 (cell to the left of "Zip") to .8 inches, and cell C6 ("State") to .5 inches.
10. Resize row 7 ("Previous Work Experience") so it is approximately twice its original height.
11. Center the text in the cell containing "Scarborough Kung Fu" (cell A1) and the cell containing "Application for Employment" (cell A2) horizontally and vertically. Align the text in the cell containing "Previous Work Experience" (cell A7) so it is left-aligned horizontally and centered vertically.
12. Shade the cells containing "Previous Work Experience" (cell A7), "Office Use Only" (cell A11), and all the cells to the right of the cell containing "Office Use Only" with the light blue color in the second row, fifth column, under Theme Colors in the Shading button color palette (Blue, Accent 1, Lighter 80%). Fill the cell containing "Application for Employment" (cell A2) with the dark blue color in the fifth row, fifth column, under Theme Colors in the Shading button color palette (Blue, Accent 1, Darker 25%), and format the text as reverse type.
13. Add a 2¼ -point border above the cell containing "Scarborough Kung Fu" (cell A1), below the cell containing "Application for Employment" (cell A2), and above the cell containing "Previous Work Experience" (cell A7). Add a 2¼-point border around the shaded "Office Use Only" section at the bottom of the table.
14. Remove the borders (but do not erase the gridlines) from the right of the following cells:
    - A3 ("Photo")
    - A4 ("Name") through A6 ("City")
    - C4 ("Gender")
    - D4 ("Male") through D5 ("Female")
    - C6 ("State")
    - E6 ("Zip")
    - C8 ("Employer Name") through C9 ("Employer Address")
    - A9 ("From") through A10 ("To")
    - B11 ("Position Applied For") through B14 ("Overtime Rate")
    - D11 ("Notes") through D14

15. Remove the bottom border (but do not erase the gridlines) from the following cells: D4 through E4 ("Male" and the cell to its right), A8 ("Dates Employed"), A9 ("From") and B9, D11 ("Notes"), D12, and D13. (*Hint*: If a bottom border doesn't disappear, try selecting the cell below it and remove the top border from that cell.)
16. Display the Developer tab, if necessary, and then insert Plain Text content controls in the cells listed below. Do not allow the controls to be deleted. Use the contents of the cell to the left of the content control as the title of the control. Revise the placeholder text as indicated below.

Cell	Located to the right of	Placeholder text
B4	"Name"	Enter your name.
B5	"Address"	Enter your street address.
D8	"Employer Name"	Enter the name of your former employer.
D9	"Employer Address"	Enter the address of your former employer.
E11	"Notes"	Enter notes.

17. Change the properties of the Name content control (cell B4) so that it uses the Strong style. Change the properties of the Employer Address content control (cell D9) and the Notes content control (cell E11) to allow carriage returns (multiple paragraphs).
18. Insert Date Picker content controls in the cell to the right of "From" (cell B9) and the cell to the right of "To" (cell B10). Use **Start Date** as the title of the control in cell B9 and **End Date** as the title of the control in cell B10. Do not allow the controls to be deleted, and use M/YYYY as the date format. (*Hint*: You have to create a custom date picture.) Change the placeholder text in both cells to **Click arrow to select month and year.**
19. Insert a Drop-Down List content control in the cell to the right of "Position Applied For" (cell C11). Use **Position** as the title, do not allow the control to be deleted, and add **Assistant**, **Lead Assistant**, **Receptionist**, and **Teacher** as the choices in the list. Change the instruction text at the top of the list and the placeholder text to **Select position applied for**.
20. Insert a Drop-Down List content control in the cell to the right of "Decision" (cell C12). Use **Decision** as the title, and do not allow the control to be deleted. Add **Deferred**, **Hired**, and **Not hired** as the choices in the list. Move Deferred so it is the last choice in the list. Change the instruction text at the top of the list and the placeholder text in the control to **Choose hiring status**.
21. Insert a Combo Box content control in the cell to the right of "City" (cell B6). Use **City** as the title, do not allow the control to be deleted, add **Scarborough** as the only item in the list, and change the instruction text at the top of the list and the placeholder text in the control to **Click Scarborough or type your city/town**.
22. Insert a Combo Box content control in the cell to the right of "Zip" (cell F6). Use **Zip Code** as the title, do not allow the control to be deleted, add **04074** and **04070** as the items in the list, and change the instruction text at the top of the list and the placeholder text in the control to **Click zip code or type yours if different.**
23. Insert a Picture content control in cell B3 (to the right of "Photo"). Align the control at the top center of the cell. Insert **Click icon to insert your photo.** under the control in the cell, and format it as dark gray using the White, Background 1, Darker 50% tile in the Font Color palette. (You do not need to set any properties for this control.) Rotate the text in cell A3 so it reads from bottom to top, and center the text horizontally and vertically in the cell.
24. Insert check box content controls in the cells to the right of "Male" and "Female" (cells E4 and E5). Do not allow them to be deleted. Insert **(click box to select)** under

"Gender:" in cell D4, and format the text you inserted as dark gray using the White, Background 1, Darker 50% tile in the Font Color palette.

25. Insert a Plain Text content control in the cell to the right of "Hourly Wage" (cell C13) with the title **Hourly Wage**. Do not allow the content control to be deleted, and change the placeholder text to **Enter hourly wage.**
26. Insert a formula in the cell containing "Overtime Rate" (cell C14) to multiply the hourly wage by 1.5. Change the format to show currency.
27. Protect the template for filling in a form with the password **peterd**, and then save and close the completed template form to the Word9\Review folder. Hide the Developer tab if it was hidden at the beginning of the Review Assignments.
28. Open a new document based on this form. Fill in the form using the name **Olivia Johnson** and fictitious (but reasonable) information for the rest of the controls. Insert your name in the cell to the right of "Notes." Use **Teen.jpg**, located in the Word9\Review folder, as the photo.
29. Save the completed form as **Test Application Form** to the Word9\Review folder included with your Data Files. Submit the final documents to your instructor in electronic or printed form, as requested. Close all open documents.

Apply the skills you learned to create a new template form.

APPLY

Case Problem 1

Data Files needed for this Case Problem: NewStudent.docx, Toddler.jpg

Sanborn Preschool Michelle Naughton owns Sanborn Preschool in Sanborn, Illinois. Every year, when new students register, she and her assistant spend hours retyping the information parents entered on paper forms into the computer. She wants to automate this process and have the parents enter information in an online form. She asks you to help her by preparing the form. She does not want any of the content controls to be deleted as people use the form. Complete the following steps:

1. Open the file **NewStudent** from the Word9\Case1 folder included with your Data Files, and then save it in the same folder as a template with the filename **New Student Registration Form**.
2. Insert a new column A, and then merge the cells in the new column A so it becomes one cell. Fill the cell with Dark Red, Accent 6, Lighter 40%.
3. Merge the two cells to the right of the cell containing "Address" (cells C2 through D2).
4. Select all the cells in the third row (cell B3, which contains "City," through cell E3, which contains "StateIL"), and then split them into six columns and one row, merging them first. Drag "IL" one cell to the right (to cell E3), and then drag "State" one cell to the right (to cell D3). Type **Zip:** in the second to last cell in the third row (cell F3).
5. Merge the last two cells in the last row (cells D5 and E5).
6. Resize the first column A to be approximately .4 inches wide, and then resize the rest of the cells containing labels so they just fit. (*Hint*: If you're having trouble resizing individual cells, select all the text and the end-of-cell mark in the cell you are trying to resize, and then drag the gridline.) Finally, resize the cell to the right of "Photo Date" (cell C6) to be approximately 1-inch wide.

EXPLORE

7. Use the Draw Table button to draw a new row with ½-point borders at the top of the table. After making the Draw Table pointer active, drag a rectangle above the top row of the table, starting approximately one-quarter of an inch above the upper-left corner of the table and ending at the upper-right corner of the table. Type **Sanborn Preschool** in the new cell A1, format the text as 16-point Berlin Sans FB, and center-align the text in the cell. Fill the cell with Dark Red, Accent 6, Lighter 80%.

8. Change the top border of the table and the border above the cells in row 6 (from cell B6, which contains "Photo Date" through cell D6, which is the merged cell in the last row) so they are 2¼ points thick.
9. Insert a Plain Text content control in cell A2 (the merged cell shaded red to the left of the main part of the table) with a title of Last Name. Change the placeholder text to **Type child's last name.** Center the control in the cell.

EXPLORE

10. Create a new style for the control in cell A2 (the merged cell at the left side of the table). In the Content Control Properties dialog box, click the New Style button to open the Create New Style from Formatting dialog box. In the Name box, type **Last Name**. At the bottom of the dialog box, click the New documents based on this template option button. Click the Format button, and then click Font to open the Font dialog box. In the Font style list, click Bold. In the Size list, click 16. In the Effects section, click the Small caps check box. Click the OK button three times.
11. Rotate the contents in cell A2 so they read from bottom to top.
12. Insert Plain Text content controls in the cell to the right of the cells containing "Name" (cell C2) and "Parent/Guardian Name" (cell D2) and in the cell to the right of the cell containing "Address" (cell C3) with appropriate titles and placeholder text.
13. Insert a Date Picker content control in the cell to the right of "Photo Date" (cell C6) with the title **Photo Date** and the placeholder text **Date photo was taken.** Use the format M/d/yyyy.
14. Insert a Picture content control in the last cell in the last row (cell D6) with the title **Current Photo**. Center the content control in the cell.
15. Insert Combo Box content controls with appropriate titles in the cells to the right of "City" (cell C4) and to the right of "Zip" (cell G4). Add **Sanborn** as an item in the City Combo Box list, and **60222** and **60223** as items in the zip code list. Modify the instruction item in the list and the placeholder text to let the user know that he or she can select an item in the list or type different information.
16. Insert a Drop-Down List content control in the cell to the right of "Program" (cell E5) with **Program** as the title and **Choose a program.** as the instruction and placeholder text. Add **Preschool, Toddler**, **Nursery**, and **Kindergarten Prep** as the items in the list. Change the order of these items so that "Preschool" is the third item in the list.
17. Insert five check box form fields in the cell to the right of "Allergies" (cell C5) to the left of each item. In the same cell, add the following above the list: **Select all that apply, or select None.**
18. Protect the form, save your changes, and then close the form without exiting Word. Create a new document based on the New Student Registration Form and save it as **Preschool Test Form** to the Word9\Case1 folder.
19. In the Preschool Test Form document, test the form by inserting sample data. Use the file **Toddler.jpg**, located in the Word9\Case1 folder as the picture to insert. Save the final, filled-in form.
20. Submit the final documents to your instructor in electronic or printed form, as requested. Close all open documents.

Create a form for a mobile pet grooming company using the skills you learned in this tutorial.

CREATE

Case Problem 2

Data File needed for this Case Problem: Dog.jpg

Minneapolis Mobile Pet Minneapolis Mobile Pet is a mobile pet-grooming service owned by Karl Fahlstrom. Karl has a fleet of eight vans that are kept busy with his full schedule. He recently equipped all the vans with laptop computers so his groomers can input information at their appointments. This way they won't have to spend time at the office transferring data from paper to the computer. He asked you to create a simple form for his groomers to use. To complete this case problem, you'll create and test the form shown in Figure 9-42.

Figure 9-42 Grooming Form

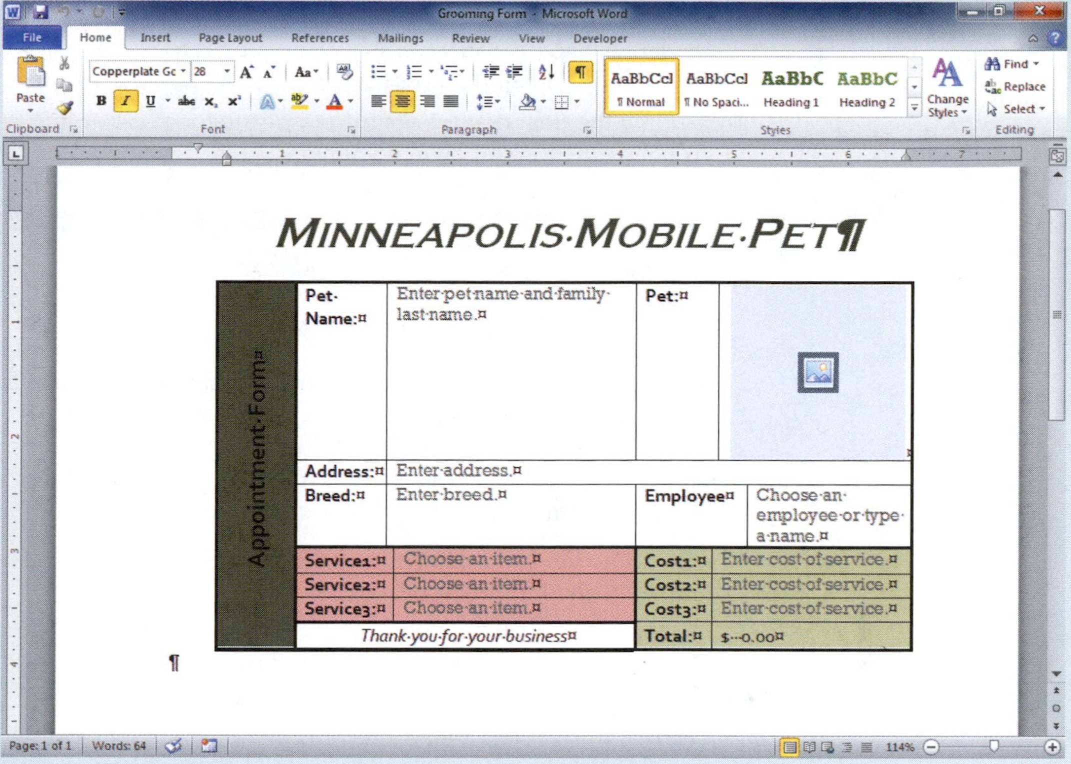

To help you create the form, use the following guidelines:

1. The form uses the Foundry theme, but the font used in the table is 12-point Corbel. Bold is applied to the labels in the cells containing the labels. The text in cell A1 is 16-point bold.
2. The thick border used around sections in the form is 2¼ points wide.
3. The shading in cell A1 is Olive Green, Text 2; the shading in cells D4 through E7 is Tan, Background 2, Darker 10%; and the shading in cells B4 through C6 is Rose, Accent 6.
4. The format of "Minneapolis Mobile Pet" above the table is 28-point Copperplate Gothic Bold set in italics in Olive Green, Text 2, Darker 25% with the small caps effect.
5. Cells C1, C2, and C3 contain Text content controls. The control in cell C2 allows the user to press the Enter key to insert hard line breaks.
6. Cell E1 contains a picture content control.
7. Cell E3 contains a Combo Box content control with **Mark**, **Jack**, and **Marissa** as the values in the list.
8. Cells C4, C5, and C6 contain Drop-Down List controls with **Bath**, **Trim**, and **Nail clipping** as the list values in each control.
9. Cells E4, E5, and E6 contain Plain Text content controls. The function used to calculate the result in E7 is =SUM(ABOVE).
10. The font for the placeholder text in all the cells with content controls is 11-point Rockwell, and it is colored White, Background 1, Darker 50%.

After you have created the form template, complete the following steps:

11. Protect the document for filling in forms using **PET** as the password, and then save it as a template named **Grooming Form** in the Word9\Case2 folder.
12. Create a new document based on this form. Use the file **Dog.jpg**, located in the Word9\Case2 folder, to insert a picture in cell E1, and type **Retriever** as the breed.

Type any name you want for the Pet Name and then type your last name. In the Combo box in cell E3, type your first and last names, and use your address in the Address cell. Select a different service in each of the three service lists in cells C4, C5, and C6. The cost of a bath for a retriever is $50, the trim is $18, and nail clipping is $12.

13. Save the completed form as **Retriever Form** in the Word9\Case2 folder.
14. Submit the final documents to your instructor in electronic or printed form, as requested. Close all open documents.

Apply the skills you learned in the tutorial to create an order form for a landscaping company.

APPLY

Case Problem 3

Data File needed for this Case Problem: Landscaping.docx

Lakeville Landscaping You have recently been asked to design a customer form for Lakeville Landscaping. Mario Ramirez, the owner, has started selling plants directly to his customers. He wants his office staff to be able to input plant orders directly into the computer. He created a table with the information he wants included in the form. You'll design and create a form to allow employees to take plant orders. Complete the following steps:

1. Open the file **Landscaping** from the Word9\Case3 folder. Save it as a Word template named **Landscaping Order** to the same folder.
2. Create a new column consisting of only one cell to the left of the table. Move the name of the company to this cell and rotate it so it reads from bottom to top.
3. In the top row, merge the cells in columns B, C, and D.
4. Format the text in the new merged cell in the first row with bold, and then format the labels in column B and the label in the last cell in the second row (cell D2) with bold.
5. Format the name of the company in cell A1 so it is 14 points and bold.
6. Fill cell A1 with a dark green and reverse type. Fill cell B1 with a light green.
7. Change the width of column A to approximately .57 inches and column B to approximately 1.5 inches.
8. Right-align the labels in the cells in column B in rows 2 through 7 (cells B2 through B7), and then remove the vertical border between the cells in columns B and C.
9. Remove the border below the cell containing "Delivery Date" (cell D2), and then remove the horizontal borders between the last four cells in column D (cells D4, D5, D6, and D7). Fill the last four cells in column D with the same green that you used in cell B1.
10. Draw a 3-point border around the outside of the table.
11. Insert a Text content control in the cell to the right of the cell containing "Type of plant:" (cell C2) with the title **Type of plant** and formatted with the Intense Emphasis style. Change the placeholder text to **Enter type of plant.**
12. Insert a Combo Box content control in the cell to the right of the cell containing "Employee:" (cell C3) with the title **Employee**. Include **Sonia**, **Sun**, and **Leah** as the names in the list. Reorder them in alphabetical order. Change the first item in the list and the placeholder text to **Click an employee name or type your name.**
13. Insert a Date Picker content control in the cell below the cell containing "Delivery Date" (cell D3) with the title **Delivery Date** and the format Fri, June 4, 2013. (*Hint*: Choose a format in the list and then modify the date-time picture. Note that the day of the week is abbreviated, and only one number appears for a single-digit date.)
14. Insert a Plain Text content control in the cell to the right of the cell containing "Cost:" (cell C4) with the title **Cost**. Change the placeholder text to **Enter plant cost.**
15. Insert a Plain Text content control in the cell to the right of the cell containing "Shipping:" (cell C5) with the title of **Shipping**. Change the placeholder text to **Enter shipping cost.**

16. Insert a formula in the cell to the right of the cell containing "Tax:" (cell C6) to add the values in the cells to the right of the "Cost" and "Shipping" cells, and then multiply the result by 7%. Format the result as currency.
17. Insert a formula in the cell to the right of the cell containing "Total:" (cell C7) that adds the values in the cells above it. Format the result as currency.
18. Protect the document using the password **PLANT**, and then save and close the document, but do not exit Word.
19. Create a new document based on the newly created form. Fill in the information for the form using real or fictitious (but reasonable) information. For the employee name, use your own name.
20. Save the completed form as **Completed Order** in the Word9\Case3 folder.
21. Submit the completed documents to your instructor in electronic or printed form, as requested. Close all open documents.

Expand the skills you learned in the tutorial to create a form that asks permission to use a photo in a Web site for a dance studio.

CHALLENGE

Case Problem 4

Data Files needed for this Case Problem: Dance.dotx, Dancer.jpg

Donna Vasquez Dance Donna Vasquez owns and operates a dance studio. Her students perform in competitions and recitals throughout the year. The studio has a Web site, and Donna posts photos of some of her students on it. She always gets permission from the students' parents or guardians first. She asked you to create an online permission form that the parents or guardians can sign. An employee will fill out the form and then send the form via email to the parent or guardian. Design an online fill-in form by completing the following steps:

1. Read through each step for this entire Case Problem. Then, using paper and pencil, design an online fill-in form with the features mentioned in the following steps. As you plan, make function and appearance your main focus.
2. Open the template **Dance** located in the Word9\Case4 folder included with your Data Files. Save it as a template named **Photo Permission** in the same folder. This template appears blank but it contains Quick Parts. Choose the theme, color scheme, and fonts that you want to use.
3. Create a table at the top of the document. Start with one that is four columns and six rows. You can modify it if necessary.
4. Modify the table so that the first row includes the name of the form, and the first column has the name of the dance studio (Donna Vasquez Dance). The cell in the first row should span the width of the table, and the cell in the first column should span the table height (except for the first row). Shade these cells with different, complementary colors. Use an attractive, interesting font for the name of the dance studio.
5. The second row should include a place for the student's name and a place for the photo the studio wants to post on the Web site.
6. Include a label and content control that allows the employee to select the style of dance from a list. The dance styles are ballet, tap, jazz, lyric, modern, and hip-hop.
7. Include a content control that allows the employee to select the student's teacher from a list or type the name of teacher not included in the list (such as teachers who teach only one or two classes.) The full-time teachers at the studio are Miss Julie, Miss Helen, Miss Paula, and Mr. Karl.

EXPLORE

8. Include a Building Block Gallery content control that allows the employee to select the dancer's level from a Quick Part stored with the template. (*Hint*: Click the Insert tab, and then in the Text group, click the Quick Parts button to see the Quick Parts stored with the template.)

9. Include a control for selecting the date of the photo and another control for the date the parent or guardian is contacted. Include a control for typing the parent or guardian's name.
10. Do not allow any of the content controls to be deleted.
11. Modify placeholder text to give helpful instructions, and add any shading and formatting you think will make your form attractive and easy to read. Use thicker border lines if appropriate, and remove any border lines that are distracting.
12. Below the table, type the following: **By signing this document, you give permission for Donna Vasquez Studio to publish the above photo on our Web site.** Below this text, type a line that is long enough to hold a signature.
13. Save and close the template, and then create a new document based on the template. Save the document as **Photo Signature Form** in the Word9\Case4 folder included with your Data Files.
14. Fill out the form using real or fictitious (but reasonable) information. Use your name as the teacher's name. Use the photo **Dancer.jpg**, located in the Word9\Case4 folder included with your Data Files. Save the completed form.
15. **EXPLORE** Display the Save & Send tab in Backstage view, click Send Using E-mail, and then click the Send as Attachment button. In the To box in the new email message window that opens, type your email address.
16. **EXPLORE** Start your email program and retrieve your messages. Open the Photo Signature Form document attached to the message you sent to yourself. If you were filling out this form for a real dance studio, you would sign the form and mail it back to the dance studio.
17. Close your email program.
18. Submit the final documents to your instructor in electronic or printed form, as requested. Close all open documents.

ASSESS

SAM: Skills Assessment Manager

For current SAM information, including versions and content details, visit SAM Central (http://samcentral.course.com). If you have a SAM user profile, you may have access to hands-on instruction, practice, and assessment of the skills covered in this tutorial. Since various versions of SAM are supported throughout the life of this text, check with your instructor for the correct instructions and URL/Web site for accessing assignments.

ENDING DATA FILES

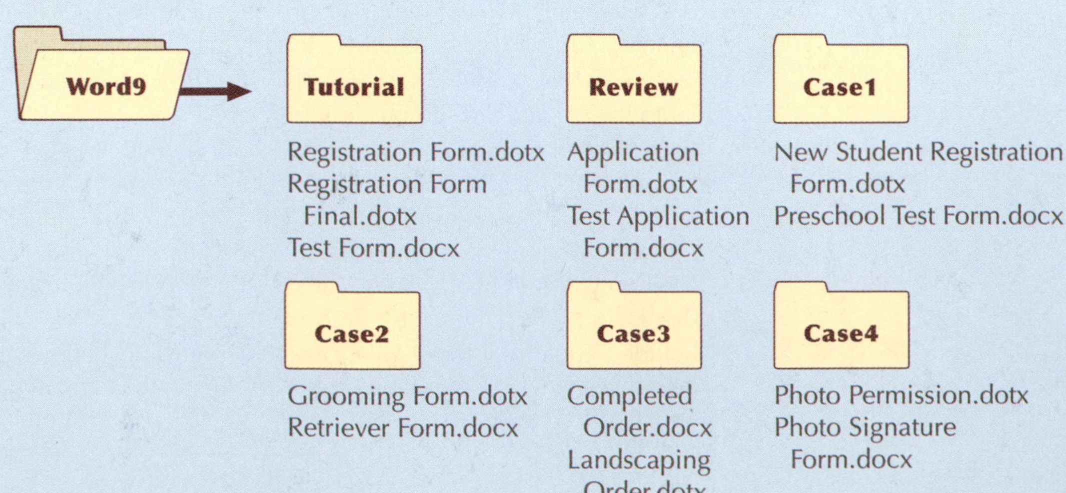

TUTORIAL 10

Managing Long Documents

Creating a Broadband Subscriber Survey Report

WORD

OBJECTIVES

Session 10.1
- Insert subdocuments
- Create subdocuments from text in a master document
- Split, merge, and unlink subdocuments
- Control text flow
- Insert nonbreaking hyphens

Session 10.2
- Add automatic heading numbers and numbered captions
- Create an Excel chart from within a document
- Create cross-references
- Protect a document with editing and formatting restrictions
- Check a document for hidden data
- Check a document for accessibility
- Use synchronous scrolling to compare documents
- Add highlighting to text

Session 10.3
- Use advanced page numbering techniques and style references
- Create and update an index and a table of figures
- Add an entry to a table of contents using a field
- Update fields before printing
- Check compatibility to earlier versions of Word
- Protect a document with encryption
- Mark a document as final

Case | *Continental Broadband Association*

The Continental Broadband Association (CBA) is a consortium of broadband suppliers headquartered in Cambridge, Massachusetts. The companies belonging to CBA supply high-speed Internet access to residential customers as well as to small and large businesses. Recently, CBA contracted with a market research company named Market Data Now, Inc. (MDNI) to obtain information about the needs and concerns of typical broadband subscribers. MDNI's research included an extensive subscriber survey and a series of focus groups.

Three of MDNI's market researchers, Michael Balczak, Katarina Thao, and Lori Tollefson, have been assigned to the research team for this project. Michael will oversee the entire project, and has asked for your help in creating the report on the team's findings. The report will include **front matter** (title page, table of contents, and list of figures) and an index as well as numbered figures and cross-references. The team will set up the report to print on both sides of the paper, so it will require different formats and footers for even and odd pages. When you are finished with the report, you will safeguard against unauthorized edits by encrypting it, and then you will mark it as final.

STARTING DATA FILES

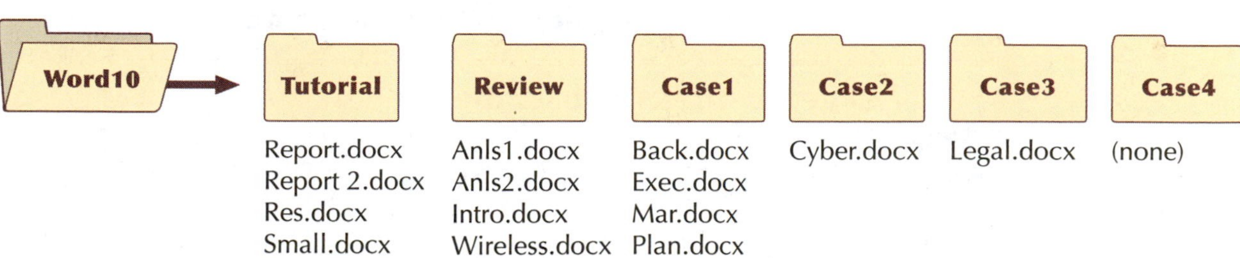

Tutorial	Review	Case1	Case2	Case3	Case4
Report.docx	Anls1.docx	Back.docx	Cyber.docx	Legal.docx	(none)
Report 2.docx	Anls2.docx	Exec.docx			
Res.docx	Intro.docx	Mar.docx			
Small.docx	Wireless.docx	Plan.docx			

SESSION 10.1 VISUAL OVERVIEW

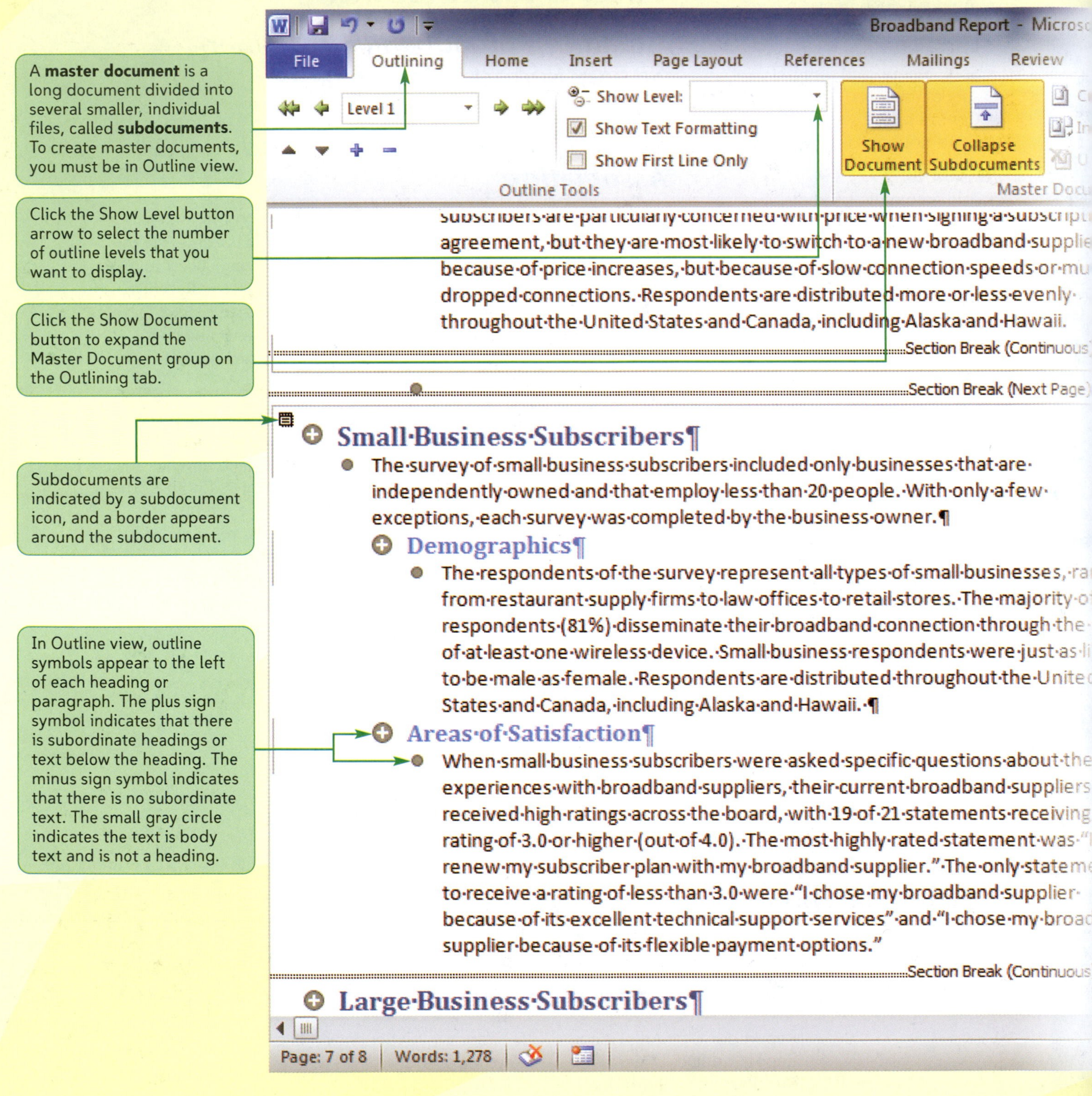

A **master document** is a long document divided into several smaller, individual files, called **subdocuments**. To create master documents, you must be in Outline view.
Click the Show Level button arrow to select the number of outline levels that you want to display.
Click the Show Document button to expand the Master Document group on the Outlining tab.
Subdocuments are indicated by a subdocument icon, and a border appears around the subdocument.
In Outline view, outline symbols appear to the left of each heading or paragraph. The plus sign symbol indicates that there is subordinate headings or text below the heading. The minus sign symbol indicates that there is no subordinate text. The small gray circle indicates the text is body text and is not a heading.
Broadband Report -
File
Outlining
Home
Insert
Page Layout
References
Mailings
Review
Level 1
Show Level:
Show Text Formatting
Show First Line Only
Show Document
Collapse Subdocuments
Outline Tools
agreement, but they are most likely to switch to a new broadband
because of price increases, but because of slow connection speeds or
dropped connections. Respondents are distributed more or less evenly
throughout the United States and Canada, including Alaska and Hawaii.
Section Break (Next Page)
Small Business Subscribers¶
The survey of small business subscribers included only businesses that are independently owned and that employ less than 20 people. With only a few exceptions, each survey was completed by the business owner.¶
Demographics¶
The respondents of the survey represent all types of small businesses,
from restaurant supply firms to law offices to retail stores. The
respondents (81%) disseminate their broadband connection through the
of at least one wireless device. Small business respondents were just as
to be male as female. Respondents are distributed throughout the
States and Canada, including Alaska and Hawaii. ¶
Areas of Satisfaction¶
When small business subscribers were asked specific questions about
experiences with broadband suppliers, their current broadband
received high ratings across the board, with 19 of 21 statements
rating of 3.0 or higher (out of 4.0). The most highly rated statement
renew my subscriber plan with my broadband supplier." The only
to receive a rating of less than 3.0 were "I chose my broadband supplier
because of its excellent technical support services" and "I chose my
supplier because of its flexible payment options."
Large Business Subscribers¶
Page: 7 of 8
Words: 1,278

MASTER DOCUMENTS

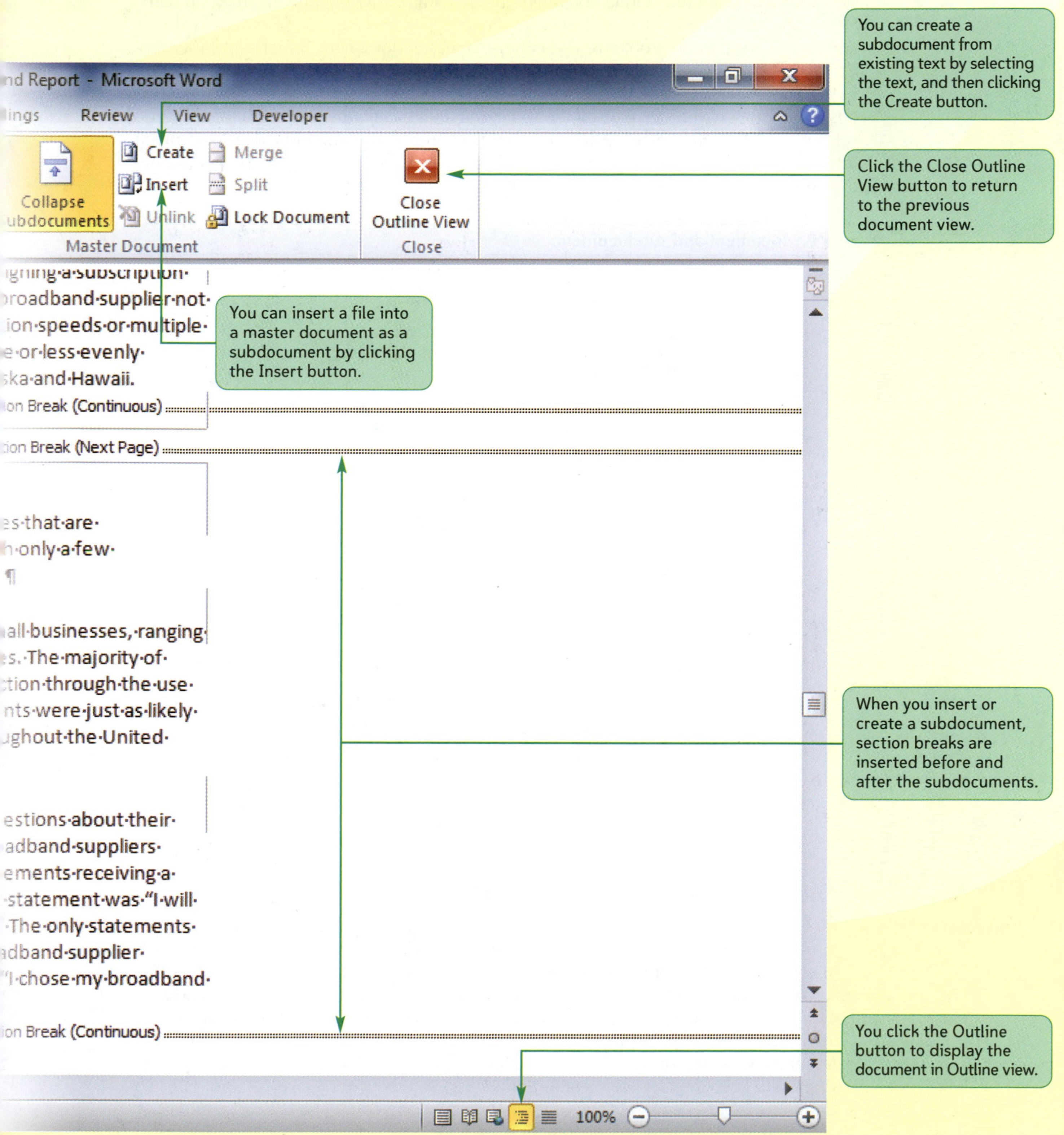
nd Report - Microsoft Word
ings
Review
View
Developer
Create
Merge
Insert
Split
Collapse
ubdocuments
Unlink
Lock Document
Master Document
Close
Outline View
Close
ighing·a·subscription·
roadband·supplier·not·
ion·speeds·or·multiple·
e·or·less·evenly·
ska·and·Hawaii.
on Break (Continuous)
ion Break (Next Page)
es·that·are·
n·only·a·few·
all·businesses,·ranging·
s.·The·majority·of·
tion·through·the·use·
nts·were·just·as·likely·
ghout·the·United·
estions·about·their·
adband·suppliers·
ements·receiving·a·
statement·was·"I·will·
The·only·statements·
adband·supplier·
"I·chose·my·broadband·
on Break (Continuous)
100%
You can create a subdocument from existing text by selecting the text, and then clicking the Create button.
Click the Close Outline View button to return to the previous document view.
You can insert a file into a master document as a subdocument by clicking the Insert button.
When you insert or create a subdocument, section breaks are inserted before and after the subdocuments.
You click the Outline button to display the document in Outline view.

Working with Master Documents

Manipulating pages in a long document can be cumbersome and time-consuming. On the other hand, splitting a long document into several shorter documents makes it hard to keep formatting consistent and to ensure that section and page numbering are always correct. To avoid these problems, you can use a master document, which combines the benefits of splitting documents into separate files with the advantages of working with a single document. A master document is also helpful when several people are simultaneously working on different parts of the same document. Each member of the team can submit a separate document; you can then quickly organize these individual documents into a single, complete document by creating a master document. Figure 10-1 illustrates the relationship between master documents and subdocuments.

Figure 10-1 **Master document and subdocument**

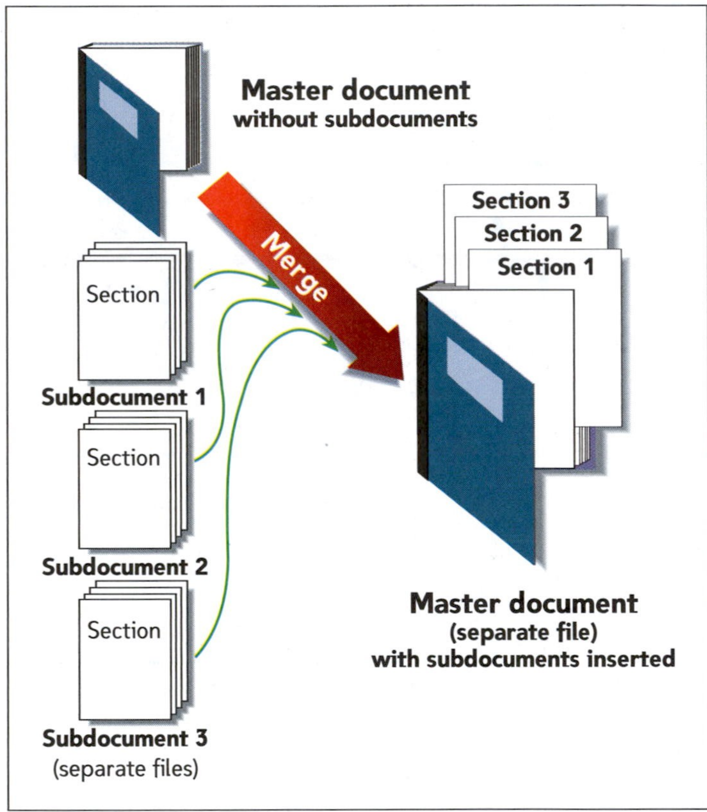

Working with a master document has several advantages:

- **Consistent formatting across elements**—You set up styles, headers, footers, and other formatting elements in only the master document; any subdocuments you create or insert will have the same formatting.
- **Accurate numbering**—You can number the master document, including all subdocuments, with consecutive page numbers, heading numbers, and figure numbers. If you rearrange, delete, or add material, Word updates the numbers to reflect your changes.
- **Accurate cross-referencing**—You can refer to figures or tables in subdocuments and Word will keep the cross-references updated.
- **Complete table of contents and index**—You can easily compile a table of contents and create an index for a master document.
- **Faster editing**—You can edit the master document all at once, or you can edit each subdocument individually. Any changes in the master document automatically take effect and are saved into the subdocument files, and vice versa.

The various workgroups at MDNI often use master documents to combine multiple files into one long document.

Before you begin working with a master document, you must make sure your document contains headings formatted with the built-in headings styles, and you must switch to Outline view.

Working in Outline View

Outline view displays the various heading levels in a document as an outline. You can either create an outline in Outline view, and the built-in heading styles are applied automatically, or you can apply heading styles in Print Layout view, and then display the outline in Outline view.

You can display and work with as many as nine levels of headings in Outline view. The top level heading (the Heading 1 style) is Level 1, with subheadings (Heading 2, Heading 3, etc.) labeled as Level 2, Level 3, and so on. This is similar to viewing the structure of a document in the Navigation pane. One difference between viewing a document in Outline view and viewing the headings in the Navigation pane is that you can see body text below the headings in Outline view.

Outline view has several symbols and buttons that you use in viewing and reorganizing your document. Refer to the Session 10.1 Visual Overview for information on these symbols and buttons. To select an entire section, you click the outline symbol next to that section's heading. To move a section after you select it, you can drag it or click the Move Up or Move Down button on the Outlining tab, which is visible only in Outline view. You can also use buttons on the Outlining tab to change the level of a heading. For instance, you might want to change a Level 1 heading to a Level 2 heading, or to change a Level 3 heading to a Level 1 heading.

REFERENCE

Creating an Outline in Outline View

- On the status bar, click the Outline view button.
- Type the first Level 1 heading, and then press the Enter key.
- To demote a heading, click the Demote button in the Outline Tools group on the Outlining tab; *or* press the Tab key.
- To promote a heading, click the Promote button in the Outline Tools group on the Outlining tab, *or* press the Shift + Tab keys.
- To change text to body text, click the Demote to Body Text button in the Outline Tools group on the Outlining tab.

Michael asks you to create the outline for his report. You'll start working on this in Outline view.

To create an outline in Outline view:

1. Start Word, display nonprinting characters and the ruler, and then save the blank document as **Report Draft** in the Word10\Tutorial folder included with your Data Files.

2. On the status bar, click the **Outline** button. The document switches to Outline view, and a new tab, Outlining, appears on the Ribbon and is selected. The outline level of the current paragraph is Level 1. See Figure 10-2.

   Trouble? If the document is not set to 100% zoom, change the zoom setting now.

Figure 10-2 Outline view

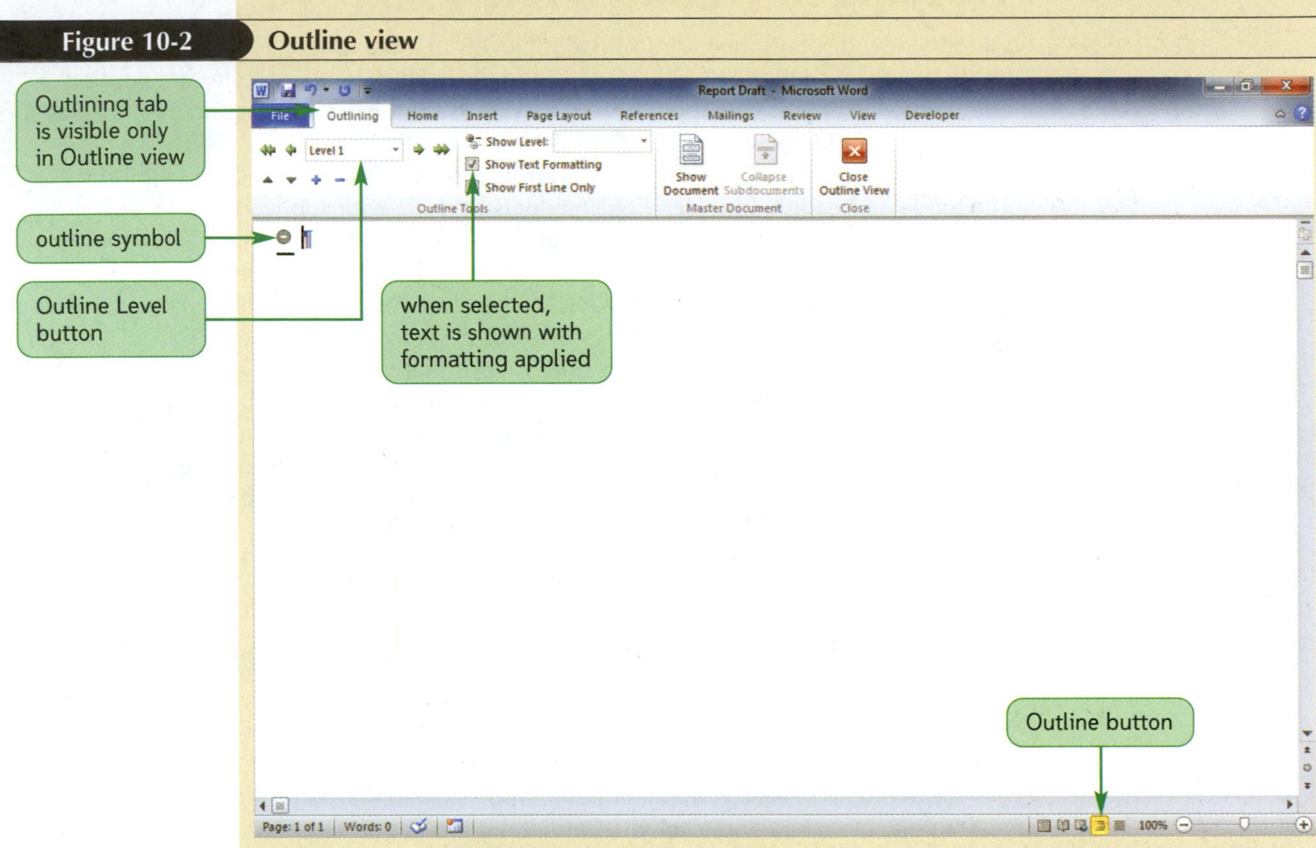

3. Type **Rationale**, and then press the **Enter** key. The text you typed is formatted with the Heading 1 style. You want to change the next heading to a Level 2 heading.

4. In the Outline Tools group, click the **Demote** button. The second paragraph indents, the outline symbol next to the first line changes to a plus sign, and the Outline Level button in the Outline Tools group changes to indicate that this paragraph is now Level 2.

TIP

You can also click the Outline Level button arrow, and then select an outline level, including Body Text, in the list.

5. Type **Personnel**, press the **Enter** key, type **Survey Goals**, and then press the **Enter** key again. The next heading is a Level 1 heading.

6. In the Outline Tools group, click the **Promote** button, and then type **Large Business Subscribers**.

Next, Michael wants you to add body text under the "Rationale" heading. To do this, you'll need to demote the paragraph to body text.

To add body text to an outline:

1. In the first line of the outline, click after "Rationale" and then press the **Enter** key. A new paragraph is created at Level 1. Notice that the outline symbol next to "Rationale" changes to a minus sign, and the outline symbol next to the new paragraph is a plus sign.
2. In the Outline Tools group, click the **Demote to Body Text** button. The paragraph is indented, and the outline symbol changes to a small gray circle that indicates body text. The outline symbol next to the first line changes back to a plus sign.
3. Type **The Continental Broadband Association (CBA), a consortium of broadband suppliers in North America, continually monitors trends in the broadband market.** See Figure 10-3.

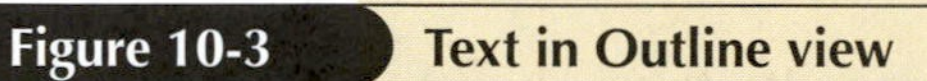

Text in Outline view

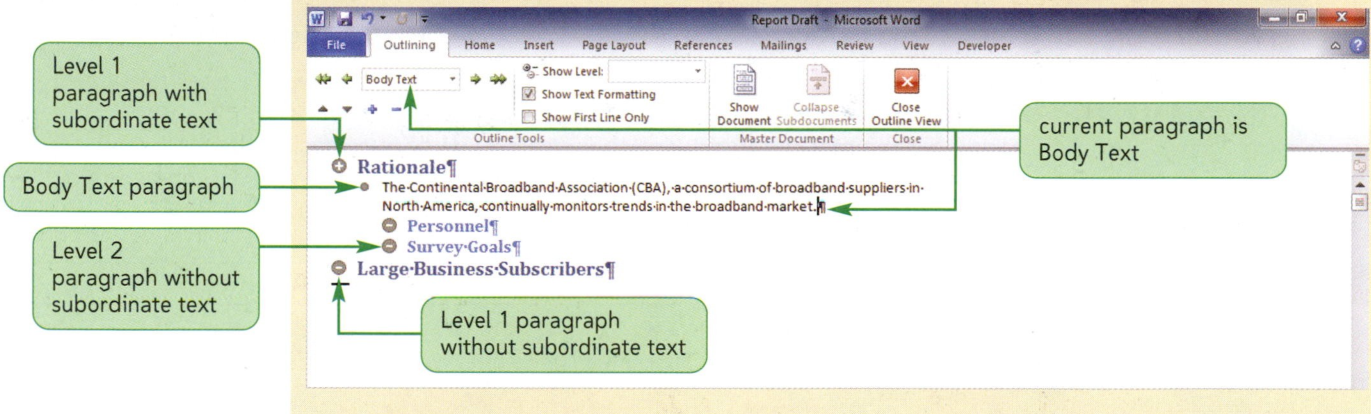

4. Save your changes, and then close the document (but do not exit Word).

Michael took your document and then wrote additional content. He asks you to continue editing the document. First, you'll open his report and save it with a new name.

To open the report and view different levels in Outline view:

1. Open the file **Report**, located in the Word10\Tutorial folder, and then save it to the same folder as **Broadband Report**.
2. On the status bar, click the **Outline** button. The document appears in Outline view with All Levels listed in the Show Level box in the Outline Tools group.

   Trouble? If the document is not set to 100% zoom in Outline view, change the zoom setting now.
3. In the Outline Tools group, click the **Show Level button arrow**, and then click **Level 3**. The document changes to hide all the text at the Body Text level and display only the headings at Level 1 and Level 2. There are no Level 3 headings in the document.
4. Click anywhere in the **Rationale** heading, and then click the **Expand** button in the Outline Tools group. The Rationale heading, which currently displays the next level of headings—the Level 2 headings—expands to show the next available level. In this case, because there are no Level 3 headings, the body text is displayed.

5. In the Outline Tools group, click the **Collapse** button to collapse the Rationale headings back to show only Level 2 headings.

You can easily move sections in the document while working in Outline view. When you move a heading in Outline view, you also move the entire section; that is, you move the heading and its subordinate text. Note that it's customary to refer to a part of a document that begins with a heading as a "section." Don't confuse this use of the word "section" with the more technical use of the term—as in a document that is divided into sections by section breaks.

Michael wants the Survey Goals section to be the first section in the Rationale section. He also wants the Large Business Subscribers section to come after the Executive Summary section. You'll move these sections next.

To move sections in the outline:

1. Next to the Level 2 heading "Survey Goals," click the **plus sign outline symbol**. The heading is selected.
2. Position the pointer over the Survey Goals **plus sign outline symbol**, press and hold the mouse button, and then drag up without releasing the mouse button. As you drag, a horizontal line appears indicating the position of the heading as you drag. See Figure 10-4.

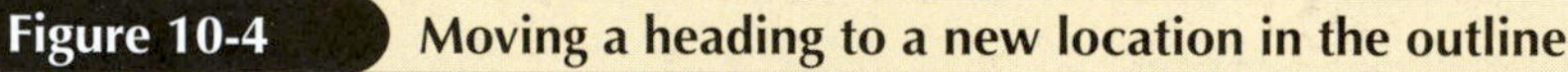

Figure 10-4 Moving a heading to a new location in the outline

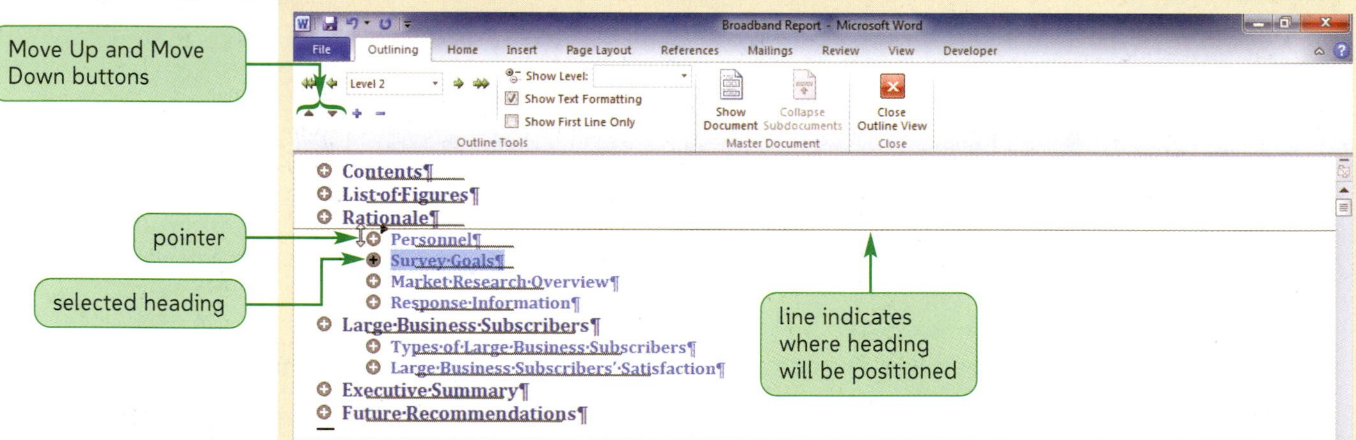

TIP

You can also click the Move Up and Move Down buttons in the Outline Tools group to move selected headings in an outline.

3. When the horizontal line is above the Personnel heading, release the mouse button. "Survey Goals" now appears above "Personnel."
4. Next to "Large Business Subscribers," click the **plus sign outline symbol**. The heading you selected as well as the subordinate headings for this heading are selected.
5. Drag the Large Business Subscribers heading and its subordinate headings down below the "Executive Summary" heading.
6. In the Outline Tools group, click the **Show Level button arrow**, and then click **All Levels**. The headings expand to display the body text beneath them. See Figure 10-5.

Figure 10-5 **Headings expanded in Outline view**

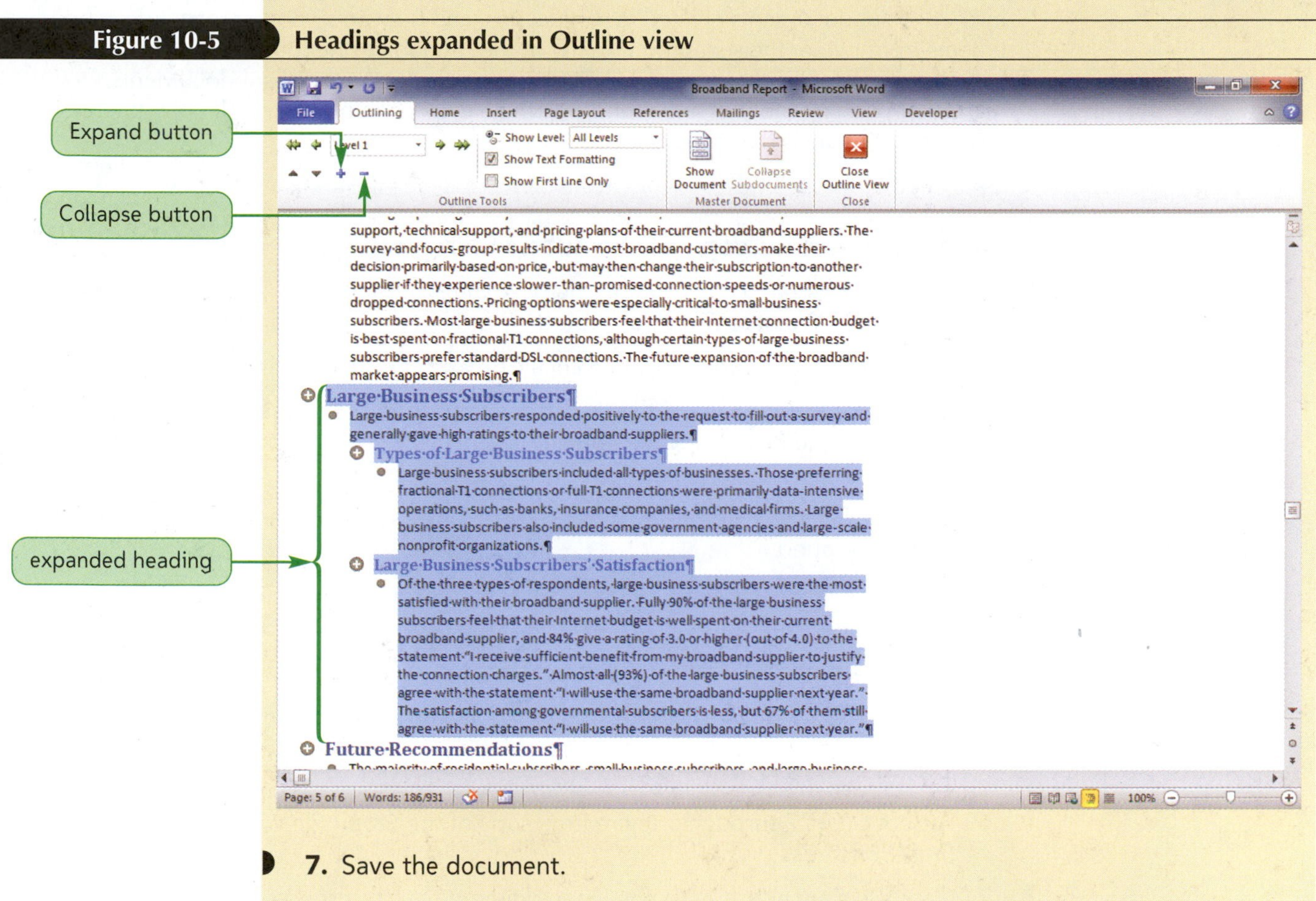

7. Save the document.

Now that you modified the outline, you're ready to create the master document.

Creating a Master Document

To create a master document, you can convert parts of a document into subdocuments, or you can also insert existing files as subdocuments. As soon as you add a subdocument to or create a subdocument from text in a document, the document becomes a master document. After you create a master document, you can open, edit, and print the subdocuments individually; or you can open, edit, and print the entire master document as a single unit. When you save a master document, Word saves each subdocument as a separate file. The master document contains links to the subdocuments, but not their text and objects (such as graphics).

To convert parts of a document into subdocuments, you first apply the built-in heading styles (Heading 1, Heading 2, and so forth) to the headings in the document, and then divide the document into subdocuments at the location of a heading level you select. For example, if you divide a master document into subdocuments at the Heading 1 style, each Heading 1 and its accompanying text are saved as a separate subdocument.

To create a master document by using existing files as subdocuments, you insert the files as subdocuments. Word converts the inserted files into subdocuments by creating a link between the master document and the inserted files. If the subdocuments do not begin with a built-in heading style, the text is incorporated into the master document as body text. Inserting subdocuments into a master document is different from inserting Word files into a document. Inserted Word files become part of the document in which they're inserted, whereas the subdocument file remain separate from the master document in which they're inserted.

Michael's master document is the Broadband Report document. He wants you to insert two subdocuments created by colleagues, and he wants you to create two subdocuments from two of the sections currently in the Broadband Report.

Before you do this, however, first you'll make a backup copy of subdocuments. Instead of opening the files and then using the Save As command, you'll copy the files directly in the Open dialog box.

To make a backup copy of the subdocuments:

1. Click the **File** tab, click **Open** in the navigation bar, and then, if necessary, navigate to the **Word10\Tutorial** folder.
2. Right-click the file **Res**, and then click **Copy** on the shortcut menu.
3. Right-click a blank area of the dialog box, and then click **Paste** on the shortcut menu. The file Res - Copy appears in the file list in the Open dialog box and is selected.
4. Click the selected file **Res – Copy**. The filename is selected and a black border appears around it.

   Trouble? If you have trouble selecting the filename, right-click the file instead, click Rename on the shortcut menu, and then continue with Step 5.
5. Type **Residential**, and then press the **Enter** key. The file is renamed.

   Trouble? If an error message appears indicating that you're trying to change the filename extension, click the No button, and use the filename "Residential.docx" (with the .docx filename extension).
6. Repeat Steps 2 through 5 to create a copy of the **Small** file with the filename **Small Business**.
7. Click the **Cancel** button in the Open dialog box to return to the report without opening a document.

Now you can insert the copies of the two subdocuments into the master document.

Inserting Subdocuments

When you insert a subdocument into a master document, a link is created in the master document to the subdocument, and the text of the subdocument appears within the master document at the location of the insertion point. As shown in the Session 10.1 Visual Overview, the subdocument appears in a box marked with a Subdocument icon. Word inserts section breaks at the beginning and end of the subdocument.

Sometimes a Lock icon appears near the Subdocument icon to indicate that the subdocument is locked. You can't edit locked subdocuments, and all Ribbon options are unavailable when the insertion point is positioned in a locked subdocument. The Lock feature is important when more than one person is working on a master document, because it allows only one person at a time to edit a subdocument.

Michael asks you to insert the document named Residential (written by Katarina) into the master document, and then insert the document named Small Business (written by Lori). You'll start with Katarina's document. To insert a subdocument, you first need to expand the Master Document group on the Outlining tab.

To insert subdocuments into the master document:

1. In the Master Document group on the Outlining tab, click the **Show Document** button to select it. The Master Document group expands to display six additional buttons that you can use to create and work with master documents. See Figure 10-6.

Figure 10-6 Master Document group expanded in Outline view

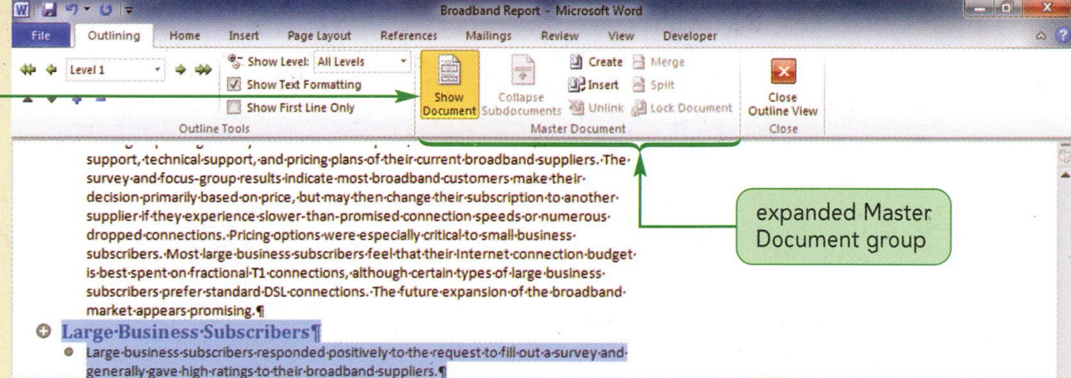

2. In the Level 1 heading "Large Business Subscribers," click to the left of the "L" in "Large." This is where you'll insert the first subdocument.
3. In the Master Document group on the Outlining tab, click the **Insert** button. The Insert Subdocument dialog box opens, which is similar to the Open dialog box.
4. Double-click the file **Residential**, located in the Word10\Tutorial folder. The file is inserted as a subdocument at the location of the insertion point (just above the heading "Large Business Subscribers"). See Figure 10-7. Note that Word inserts a Next Page section break before the newly inserted subdocument and a Continuous section break after the newly inserted subdocument. The Subdocument icon is visible above and to the left of the heading "Residential Subscribers." A box appears around the subdocument, although the sides of the box are broken in places. Now you'll insert the document written by Lori.

   Trouble? If you don't see the "Residential Subscribers" heading, scroll up in the document.

Figure 10-7 Subdocument inserted into master document

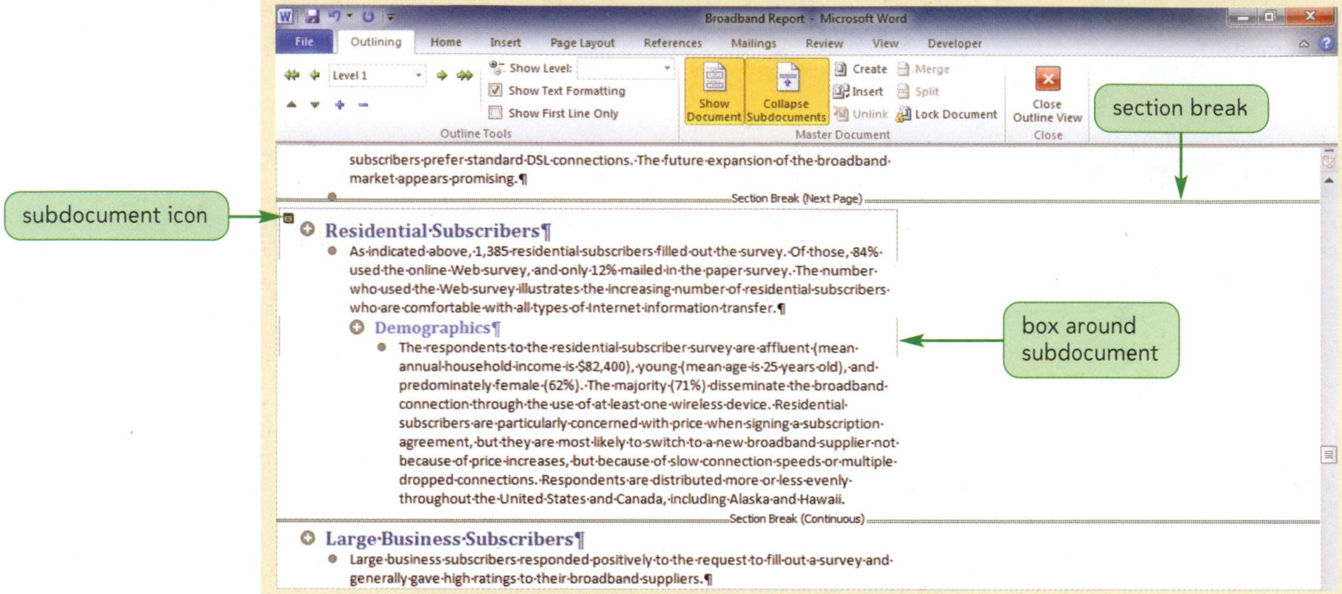

section break

subdocument icon

box around subdocument

5. With the insertion point to the left of the heading "Large Business Subscribers," repeat Steps 3 and 4 to insert the second subdocument, **Small Business**, located in the Word10\Tutorial folder. The Small Business subdocument is inserted after the Residential document and before the heading "Large Business Subscribers." See Figure 10-8. Next you will save the master document with the subdocuments.

Figure 10-8 Second subdocument inserted and expanded

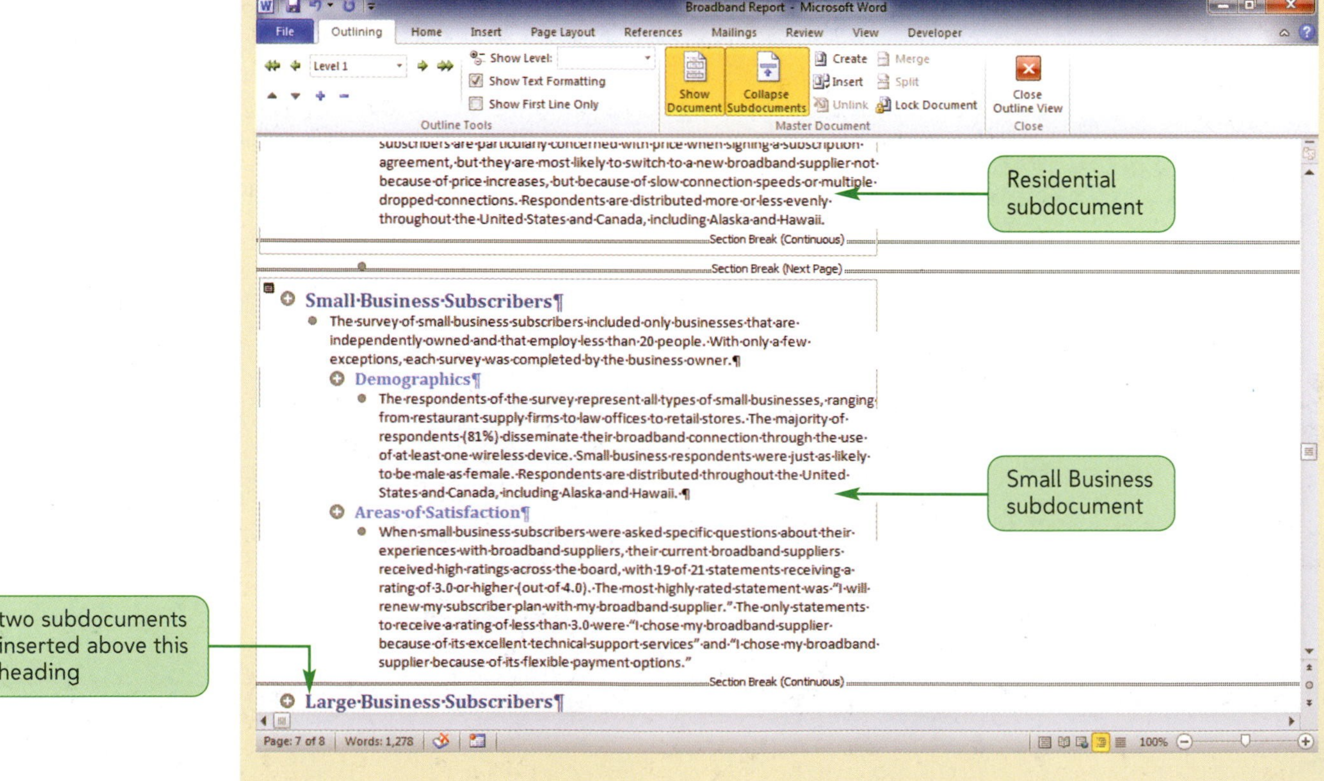

6. On the Quick Access Toolbar, click the **Save** button. The Broadband Report file is now saved as a master document with two subdocuments.

The master document Broadband Report now contains two subdocuments, or more properly, links to two subdocuments. Even though you can manipulate the subdocuments in the master document, the text of these subdocuments continues to be stored in the files Residential and Small Business, and not in the Broadband Report file.

Note that because the subdocuments are linked to the master document, you cannot rename or move the subdocument files. If you do, the link between the master and sub documents will be broken.

Creating a Subdocument

When you create a subdocument by converting a part of the master document, Word creates a new subdocument file using the name of the subdocument's first heading (that is, the first paragraph that is formatted with a heading style). The new subdocument file is saved in the same folder as the master document, and the text of the new subdocument is no longer saved in the master document file.

Now Michael wants you to convert the "Large Business Subscribers" section into a subdocument.

To create a subdocument by converting text in the master document:

1. Scroll down so that you can see all of the subordinate text under the heading "Large Business Subscribers," click the **plus sign outline symbol** next to "Large Business Subscribers" to select the heading and its subordinate text. This is the text that will be converted to a subdocument.
2. In the Master Document group on the Outlining tab, click the **Create** button. Word puts a box around the Large Business Subscribers section, inserts section breaks before and after the Large Business Subscribers section, and displays the Subdocument icon at the beginning of the new subdocument.
3. Save the **Broadband Report** file with the new subdocument. When you save your changes, Word creates a new file named "Large Business Subscribers," using the subdocument's first heading for the filename. The subdocument is saved in the same folder as the master document.

The master document now has three subdocuments. Next, you'll split an existing subdocument into two separate subdocuments.

Splitting Subdocuments

If one subdocument becomes too long and unwieldy, or if you want two people to work on what is currently one subdocument, you can split the subdocument by dividing it into two subdocument files.

Michael wants to split the "Residential Subscribers" subdocument. After the split, the original "Residential Subscribers" subdocument will consist of the Level 1 heading "Residential Subscribers." The new, second subdocument will have the filename "Demographics," and will consist of the Level 2 heading "Demographics." The "Residential Subscribers" subdocument will retain its original filename, "Residential."

To split the Residential Subscribers subdocument:

1. Scroll up to see the Level 1 heading "Residential Subscribers," and then click the **plus sign outline symbol** next to the Level 2 heading "Demographics." (Note that there are two "Demographics" headings in the master document, and you want the one under "Residential Subscribers," not the one under "Small Business Subscribers.")
2. In the Master Document group on the Outlining tab, click the **Split** button. A box appears around the new subdocument and a Continuous section break is inserted to separate it from the subdocument above it.
3. Save the report with the new subdocument. Word creates a new file named "Demographics" and modifies the subdocument named "Residential" so that it no longer includes the "Demographics" paragraph.
4. Click the **File** tab, click **Open** in the navigation bar, and then navigate to the **Word10\Tutorial** folder, if necessary. In addition to the two subdocuments that you inserted, Residential and Small Business, you see the two subdocuments that you created from within the master document, Demographics and Large Business Subscribers. See Figure 10-9.

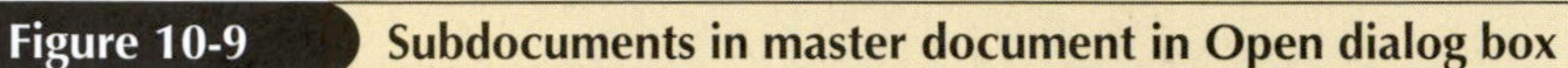
Figure 10-9 Subdocuments in master document in Open dialog box

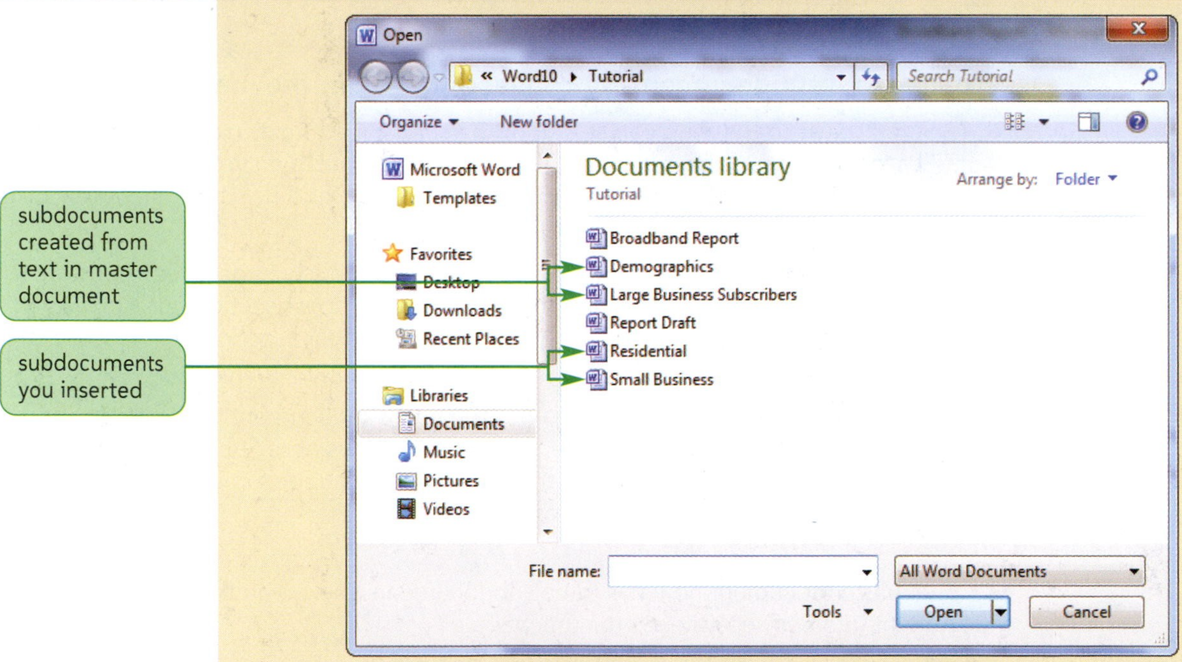

5. Click the **Cancel** button in the Open dialog box to return to the master document.

TIP

You should merge only subdocuments that will be edited by the same person. If two subdocuments will be edited by different people, it makes more sense to keep them separate, no matter how short they are.

Merging Subdocuments

If your master document contains adjacent subdocuments that are fairly short and simple with few graphics or tables, it's sometimes helpful to merge the subdocuments. When you merge subdocuments, Word inserts the contents of the second subdocument into the first one, so that when you save the master document, the first subdocument file contains the contents of both subdocuments. The second subdocument file remains on your disk, but is no longer used by the master document. You could delete this file without affecting your master document.

Michael asks Lori to edit both the Small Business subdocument and the Large Business subdocument. These subdocuments are adjacent to each other in the master document, so you will merge them for Lori.

To merge the Small Business and Large Business subdocuments into one:

1. Scroll so that you can see both the Level 1 heading "Small Business Subscribers" and the Level 1 heading "Large Business Subscribers."
2. Next to the Level 1 heading "Small Business Subscribers," click the **Subdocument** icon. The entire Small Business subdocument is selected.
3. Press and hold the **Shift** key, click the **Subdocument** icon next to the Level 1 heading "Large Business Subscribers," and then release the **Shift** key. With both subdocuments selected, you can now merge them.
4. In the Master Document group on the Outlining tab, click the **Merge** button, and then click anywhere in the master document to deselect the text. The two subdocuments become one. See Figure 10-10. You can see that the Subdocument icon no longer appears next to the "Large Business Subscribers" heading.

Figure 10-10 Two subdocuments merged into one

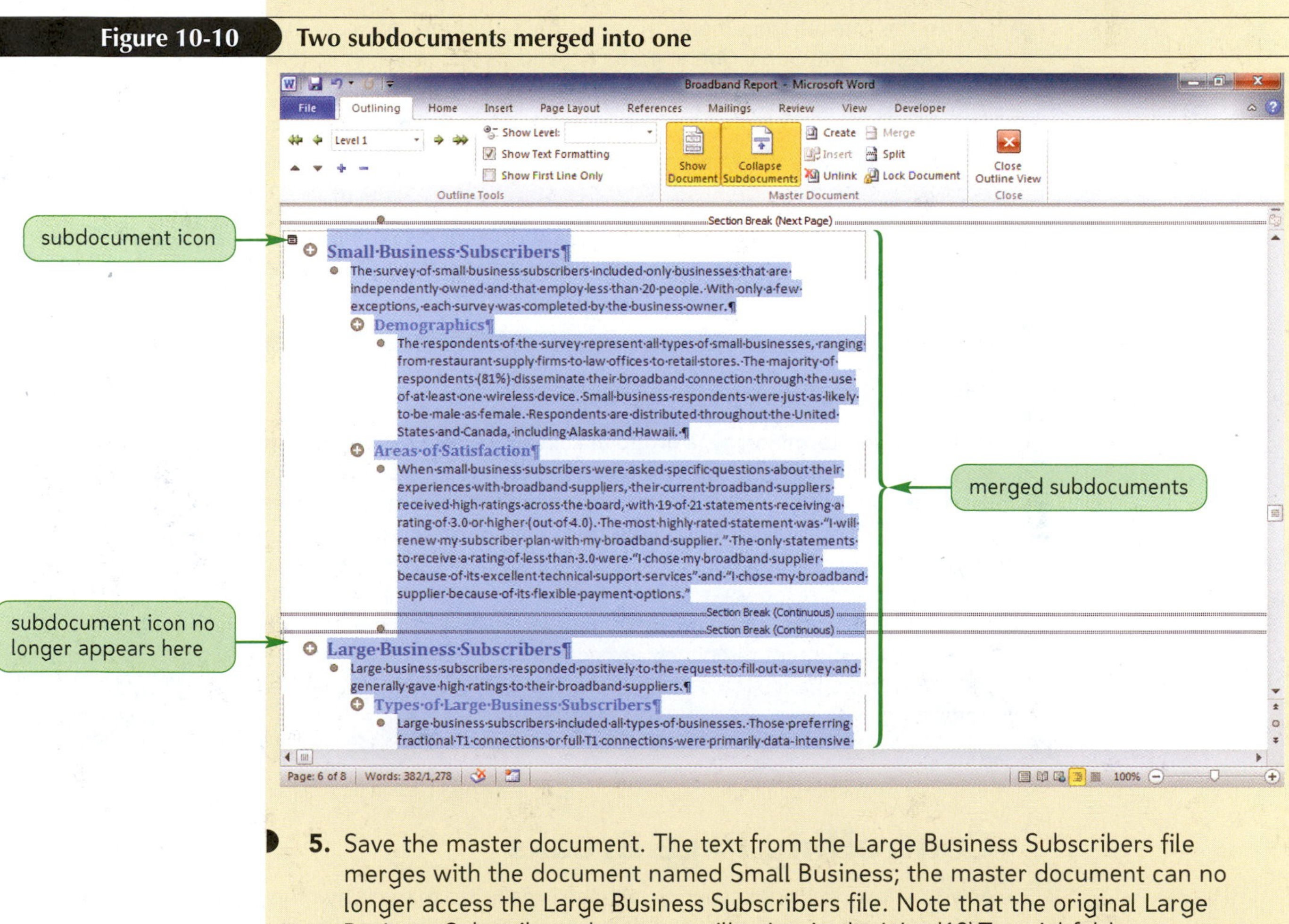

5. Save the master document. The text from the Large Business Subscribers file merges with the document named Small Business; the master document can no longer access the Large Business Subscribers file. Note that the original Large Business Subscribers document still exists in the Word10\Tutorial folder.

The master document now has three subdocuments—Residential, Demographics, and Small Business.

Unlinking a Subdocument

It's also possible to unlink a subdocument and incorporate the content into the master document. This decreases the number of subdocuments but increases the size of the master document. The removed subdocument file still exists, but the master document file can no longer access it. You can delete this unused subdocument file without affecting the master document.

Michael decides that the short "Residential" subdocument (which includes only one heading followed by one paragraph) doesn't have to be a subdocument. He asks you to unlink this content so it is stored in the master document rather than in the subdocument.

To remove the Residential subdocument:

1. Scroll up so you can see the Level 1 heading "Residential Subscribers" in the Residential subdocument, and then click the **Subdocument** icon for the "Residential" subdocument to select all the text in it.
2. In the Master Document group on the Outlining tab, click the **Unlink** button. The "Residential Subscribers" heading and its accompanying text become part of the master document.
3. Click anywhere in the document to deselect the Residential Subscribers section, and then save the master document.

You have learned how to manipulate subdocuments within a master document. Next, you'll deal with issues that arise from undesirable page and line breaks.

PROSKILLS

Teamwork: Leading a Workgroup

In networking terminology, a group of colleagues who have access to the same network server and work together on a common project is called a **workgroup**. The person who oversees a workgroup must build trust among the team members, figure out how best to facilitate communication among the team members, and give the team members a chance to get to know one another. Often a workgroup is charged with creating a document, and each member is responsible for writing at least one part of the document. If you are the leader of this type of workgroup, it's your job to make sure that each team member has the correct document templates and access to the same styles so that when you combine the subdocuments to create the final master document, it will have a consistent style and formatting.

Controlling Page Breaks

As you know, in Print Layout view, page breaks are marked by blue space between the bottom of one page and the top of the next page. If the page break is also a section break, the double-line section break appears below the last line of text on the page, with the text "Section Break (Next Page)." You'll now look at the location of page breaks in the Broadband Report document to make sure the breaks are in reasonable places. As you have seen, when you insert a new subdocument in a master document, Word inserts a

Next Page section break (that is, a section break that also starts a new page) before the new subdocument and a Continuous section break after the subdocument. If you then merge a subdocument with the master document, the Continuous section breaks remain.

You will now switch to Print Layout view and examine the report's page and section breaks.

To view the page and section breaks in the report:

1. In the Close group on the Outlining tab, click the **Close Outline View** button. The master document appears in Print Layout view.
2. Press the **Ctrl+Home** keys to move the insertion point to the beginning of the document, and then scroll through the document, noting the manual page breaks after the text on page 1, after the table of contents on page 2, and after the text (List of Figures) on page 3, and note the Next Page section breaks on pages 5 and 6, and the three Continuous section breaks on pages 6 and 7. (You might see only the dotted lines and not the label for the last Continuous section break on page 7.)
3. Click the **View** tab, click the **Two Pages** button in the Zoom group, and then scroll so that you can see pages 5 and 6 in the program window. The shortness of page 5 is a result of the Next Page section break before the Residential subdocument, which begins on page 6. This Next Page section break on page 5 became unnecessary after you merged the Residential subdocument with the rest of the document, so you will delete this.
4. Change the Zoom to **Page Width**, scroll until you can see the "Executive Summary" heading and its subordinate paragraph on page 5, and then click to the left of the section break line so that the insertion point is positioned just to the right of the paragraph mark. See Figure 10-11. When deleting section breaks or page breaks, it's important to position the insertion point correctly, so that you don't accidentally delete a paragraph mark, which might in turn affect the formatting of subsequent paragraphs.

Figure 10-11 Insertion point positioned to delete the Next Page section break

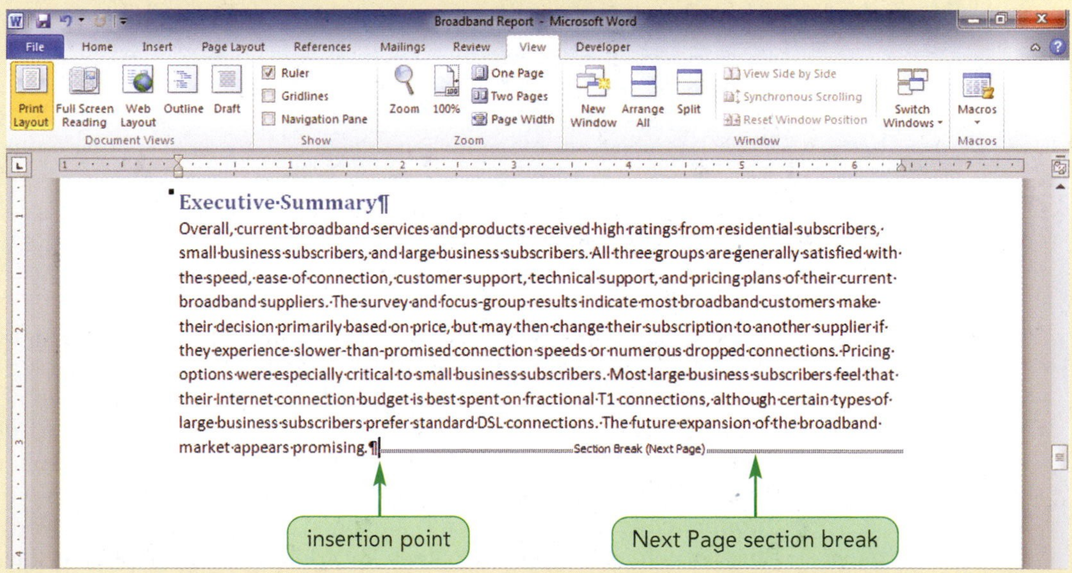

5. Press the **Delete** key. The Next Page section break is deleted, and the "Residential Subscribers" heading moves from page 6 to the current page.

6. Display the document in **Two Pages** zoom again, and then scroll so you can see pages 5 and 6. Lori plans to add more text to the Demographics subdocument in the "Residential Subscribers" section on page 5, so for now you'll leave that subdocument and its accompanying Next Page section break as is.

INSIGHT

Controlling Text Flow

When working on a long document with multiple writers, you need to check the page and section breaks in the document to make sure text flows properly from one page to another. In particular, scan the pages for widows and orphans. A **widow** is the last line of a paragraph that appears alone at the top of a page. A widow looks out of place and can be hard to read. An **orphan** is the first line of a paragraph isolated at the bottom of a page. A reader can easily miss an orphan, jumping instead to the next page. Isolated headings that are stranded at the bottom of a page, with the paragraph following it on the next page, are similar to orphans.

By default, Word documents are set up to prevent widows and orphans. Also, Word's default heading styles prevent headings from being stranded on the bottom of a page. However, when you are working with a group of writers, or if you are working with a document that does not include Word's default heading styles, you might inadvertently incorporate some material into your document that includes these problematic elements. To get rid of a widow or orphan in a document, you could insert a page break. However, this usually creates more problems than it solves. For example, you could insert a page break just before an orphan—that is, just before the first line of a paragraph that is stranded on the bottom of a page—so that the line moves to the next page, joining the rest of its paragraph. But if you then added more text above the page break, and that text spilled over to another page, the page break you added would shift, possibly resulting in a nearly blank page. As you can see, you would have to continually insert and delete hard page breaks to fix widows and orphans as you edit a document.

A better option, as you saw in Tutorial 2, is to use the Keep with next option in the Line and Page Breaks tab of the Paragraph dialog box to tell Word you want to keep a paragraph on the same page as the following paragraph. These check boxes in the Line and Page Breaks tab of the Paragraph dialog box give you even more control over text flow and page breaks:

- Widow/Orphan control—Selected by default, this prevents widows and orphans.
- Keep lines together—When selected, all the lines of a paragraph stay on the same page. A small black dot appears in the left margin when this option is selected.
- Page break before—When selected, a manual page break is inserted before the paragraph. A small black dot appears in the left margin when this option is selected.

In addition to page breaks, you should also look through your document for awkward line breaks. For example, the last paragraph of the document (on page 7) contains two hyphenated words, "e-businesses" and "high-speed." You would not want these words split between two lines. Although this isn't a serious problem, readers might be confused to see "e-" at the end of a line if the word "e-businesses" was split over two lines. To prevent Word from breaking a hyphenated word over two lines, you need to use a hard **nonbreaking hyphen**, which is a hyphen that won't allow the word or phrase containing it to break between two lines. By contrast, a **soft hyphen** is a hyphen that allows the word containing it to appear on different lines. To insert a soft hyphen, you simply press the hyphen key on your keyboard. You insert the nonbreaking hyphen using the Special Characters tab of the Symbol dialog box.

Next, you'll replace the soft hyphen in the words "e-businesses" and "high-speed" with a nonbreaking hyphen.

To insert nonbreaking hyphens in "e-businesses" and "high-speed":

1. Display the document at **Page Width** zoom, scroll to page 7, and then click immediately to the left of the hyphen in "e-businesses" in the last sentence.
2. Press the **Delete** key to delete the soft hyphen. The "e" becomes joined to "businesses," and, as a result, "ebusinesses" appears on the next line. Now you'll insert the nonbreaking hyphen.
3. Click the **Insert** tab, click the **Symbol** button in the Symbols group, and then click **More Symbols**. The Symbol dialog box opens with the Symbols tab selected.
4. Click the **Special Characters** tab. A list of special symbols appears.
5. Click **Nonbreaking Hyphen**, and then click the **Insert** button to insert the hyphen into the document at the location of the insertion point.
6. Click the **Close** button in the Symbol dialog box. The Symbol dialog box closes, and the word "e-businesses" now contains a nonbreaking hyphen.
7. In the last sentence of the paragraph, replace the soft hyphen in "high-speed" with a nonbreaking hyphen.
8. Save your changes, and then close the master document without exiting Word.

TIP

You can also press the Ctrl+Shift+_ keys to insert a nonbreaking hyphen.

Another important special character is the nonbreaking space. A **nonbreaking space** is a space that won't allow the words on either side of it to break over two lines. For example, the phrase "10 KB" (where KB stands for kilobytes, as in a 10 KB file) might be hard to read or distracting if the "10" appears at the end of one line and "KB" appears at the beginning of the next line. To avoid this problem, you can insert a nonbreaking space between the "10" and the "KB." You can insert the nonbreaking space by using the Special Characters tab in the Symbol dialog box or by pressing the Ctrl+Shift+Spacebar keys. The Broadband Report doesn't contain any words that require a nonbreaking space.

You have completed setting up MDNI's Broadband Report using Word's master document feature. In the next session, you'll use Word features to number sections and figures, and then you'll edit the report.

REVIEW

Session 10.1 Quick Check

1. Define the following terms:
   a. master document
   b. subdocument
   c. widow
   d. orphan
2. Describe how to split a subdocument, how to merge subdocuments, and how to remove a subdocument from a master document.
3. What are three advantages of using a master document to manage long documents, rather than working with separate, smaller documents?
4. True or False. After you create a subdocument from text in a master document, Word creates a new file that contains the subdocument.
5. What are the two methods for creating a master document?
6. Define the terms "nonbreaking hyphen" and "nonbreaking space."
7. Why would you use a nonbreaking hyphen or a nonbreaking space in a document?

SESSION 10.2 VISUAL OVERVIEW

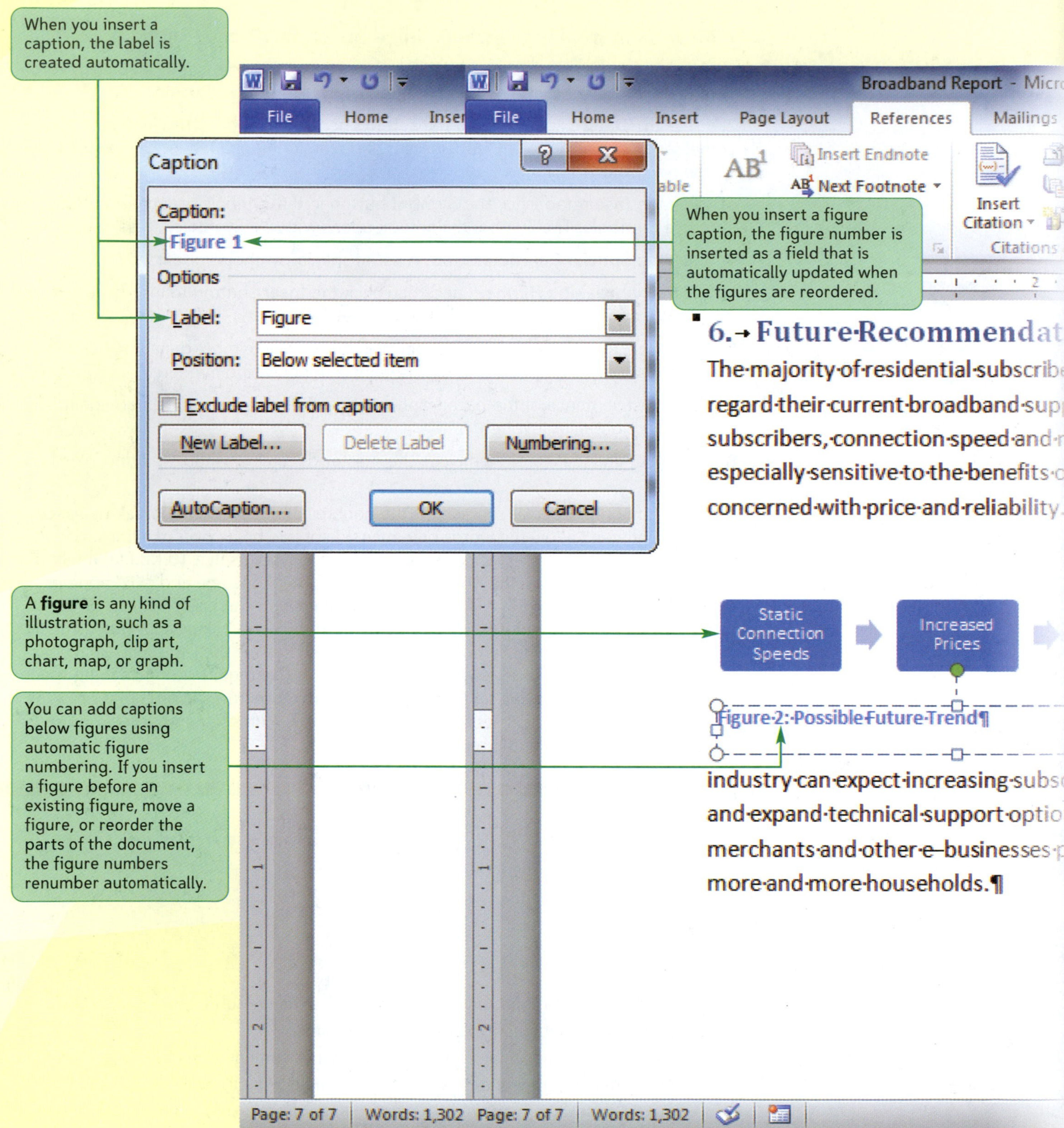
When you insert a caption, the label is created automatically.
When you insert a figure caption, the figure number is inserted as a field that is automatically updated when the figures are reordered.
A **figure** is any kind of illustration, such as a photograph, clip art, chart, map, or graph.
You can add captions below figures using automatic figure numbering. If you insert a figure before an existing figure, move a figure, or reorder the parts of the document, the figure numbers renumber automatically.
Broadband Report - Micro
File
Home
Insert
Page Layout
References
Mailings
Insert Endnote
Next Footnote
Insert Citation
Citations
Caption
Caption:
Figure 1
Options
Label:
Figure
Position:
Below selected item
Exclude label from caption
New Label...
Delete Label
Numbering...
AutoCaption...
OK
Cancel
6.→ Future·Recommendat
The·majority·of·residential·subscribe
regard·their·current·broadband·sup
subscribers,·connection·speed·and·
especially·sensitive·to·the·benefits·o
concerned·with·price·and·reliability.
Static Connection Speeds
Increased Prices
Figure·2:·Possible·Future·Trend¶
industry·can·expect·increasing·subsc
and·expand·technical·support·optio
merchants·and·other·e–businesses·p
more·and·more·households.¶
Page: 7 of 7
Words: 1,302

CAPTIONS AND CROSS-REFERENCES

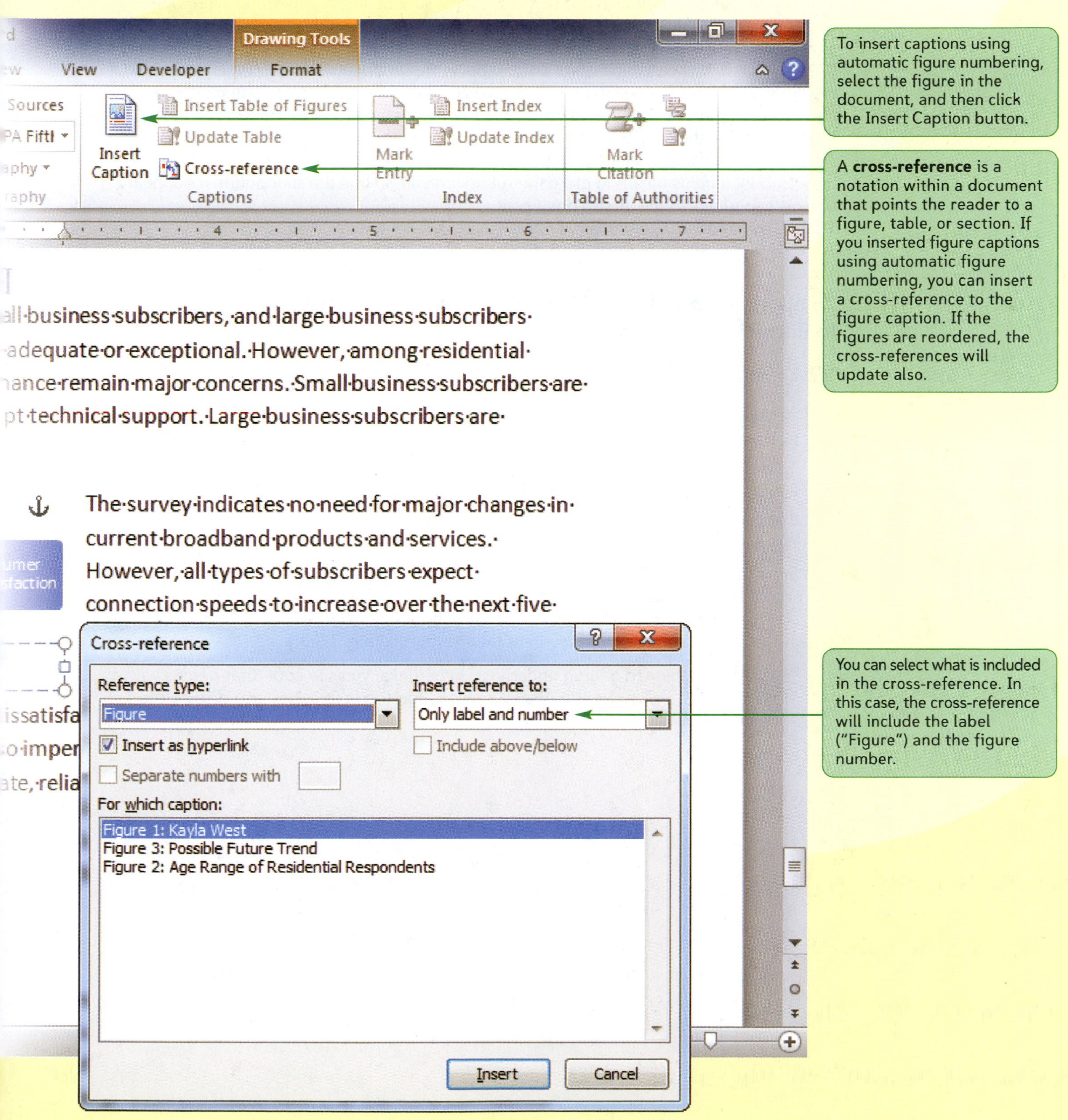

To insert captions using automatic figure numbering, select the figure in the document, and then click the Insert Caption button.

A **cross-reference** is a notation within a document that points the reader to a figure, table, or section. If you inserted figure captions using automatic figure numbering, you can insert a cross-reference to the figure caption. If the figures are reordered, the cross-references will update also.

You can select what is included in the cross-reference. In this case, the cross-reference will include the label ("Figure") and the figure number.

Reopening a Master Document

When you open a master document that has one or more subdocuments, Word doesn't open the subdocuments, but rather displays their filenames as hyperlinks in underlined blue text and enclosed in a rectangular outline. The Subdocument icon and the Lock icon appear next to the link. When you click a subdocument hyperlink, Word opens the subdocument file in another document window; it does not display the text in the master document.

However, in this case, you don't want to open the subdocuments into other document windows. You want to open them into the master document so that you can read and edit the text of the subdocuments within the master document. This process is referred to as expanding the subdocuments. When you expand the subdocuments, the Lock icon disappears, indicating that the text is now available to be modified. Conversely, to collapse subdocuments means to close the subdocuments so that the subdocuments appear only as hyperlinks in the master document.

You'll open the master document and expand subdocuments now.

To open the Broadband Report master document using the Recent tab in Backstage view:

1. If you took a break after the last session, make sure Word is running, close any open documents, and then click the **File** tab on the Ribbon. Backstage view opens with the Recent tab selected in the navigation bar.
2. In the Recent Documents list, click **Broadband Report**. The Broadband Report master document opens.

   Trouble? If the Broadband Report document is not in the Recent Documents list, use the Open dialog box to open the Broadband Report document, located in the Word10\Tutorial folder included with your Data Files.
3. Scroll down until the "Residential Subscribers" heading on page 5 appears at the top of the window. Instead of the text in the Demographics and Small Business subdocuments, you see hyperlinks to the subdocuments. See Figure 10-12. Notice in the status bar that the document is currently six pages long.

   Trouble? If, instead of blue underlined hyperlinks, you see code that begins with "{HYPERLINK . . .," press the Alt+F9 keys to hide the field codes and display the actual hyperlinks.

Figure 10-12 Master Document with hyperlinks to the subdocuments

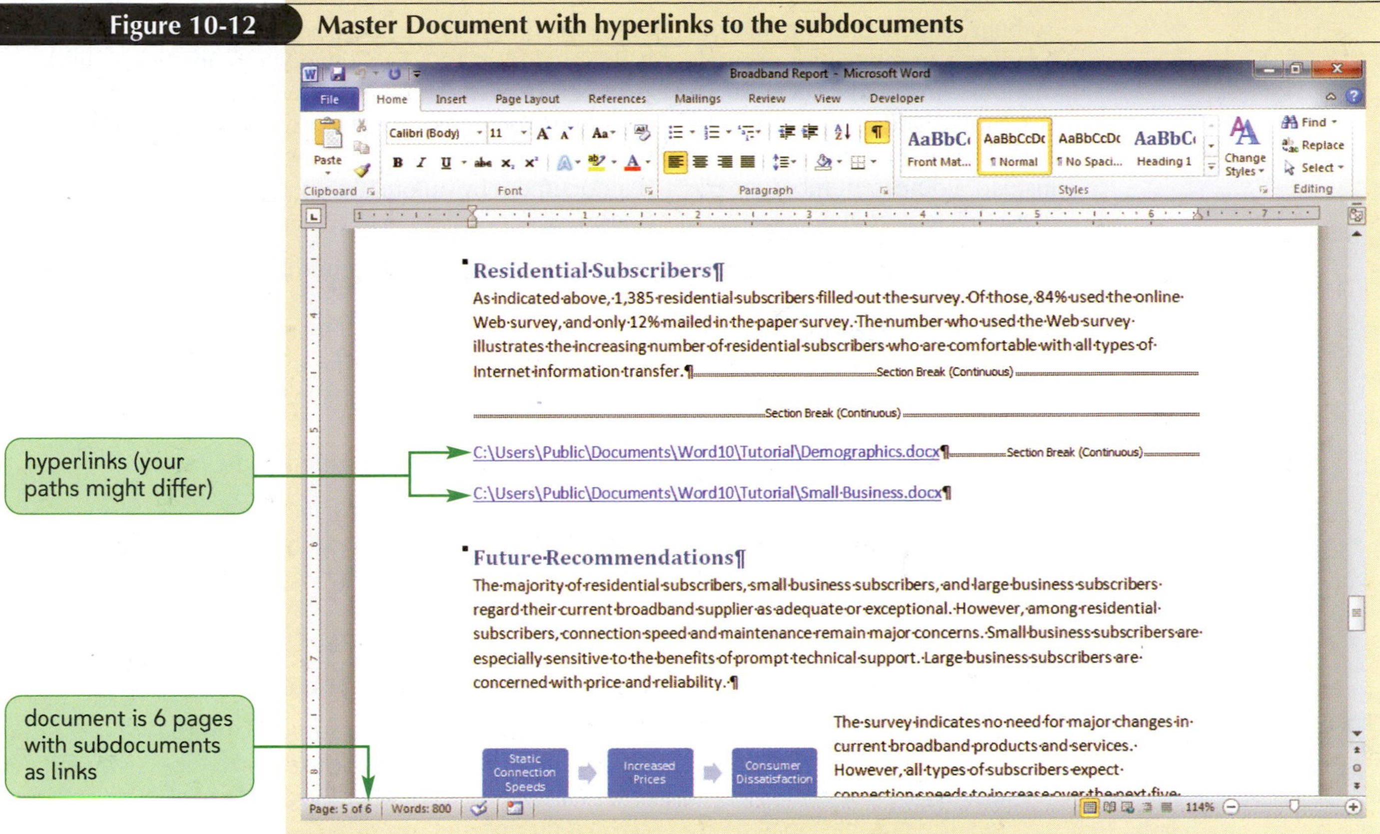

Now that you have opened the master document, you need to expand the subdocuments. As with all the master document commands, to expand subdocuments you must be in Outline view.

To expand subdocuments:

1. Switch to Outline view, and then click the **Show Document** button in the Master Document group on the Outlining tab.
2. In the Master Document group on the Outlining tab, click the **Expand Subdocuments** button, and then scroll down until you can see the Demographics and Small Business subdocument. Word replaced the hyperlinks with the text of the subdocuments, and the document is now seven pages long.
3. Scroll back to the top of the outline, and then click anywhere in the Contents heading.

Now that you have expanded the subdocuments in the master document, you can read and modify the subdocument text.

Adding Section Numbers to Headings

To help readers find the information they need, Michael asks you to give each major heading a number—for example, "1. Rationale" and "2. Executive Summary." You could manually insert text such as "Section 1" before each heading, but what would happen if you had to add, reorder, or delete a heading? You would need to review every heading and change the numbers—a time-consuming process, especially in a long document. Instead, you can number the parts of a document by automatically numbering the headings. This feature has several advantages:

- **Automatic sequential numbering**—Word keeps the heading numbers consecutive even if you add, delete, or move a section.
- **Numbering across subdocuments**—Word numbers the same-level headings of all the subdocuments in the master document consecutively. Then the members of a writing team don't need to know the number of each heading as they write their own subdocuments.
- **Consistent style**—Subdocuments have the number style specified in the master document.

Note that when you use automatic numbering in a master document, the subdocuments must be expanded in order for the headings to be numbered properly.

To number headings automatically in the master document:

TIP

When you add numbers to the headings in a document, Word actually modifies the heading styles to include the numbers.

1. Click the **Home** tab, and then click the **Multilevel List** button in the Paragraph group. The Multilevel List menu opens. See Figure 10-13. The List Library contains four list styles that can be used with headings. Michael wants to use the numbering style that shows a number followed by "Heading 1." This style is sometimes called the legal paragraph numbering style.

Figure 10-13 Multilevel list styles

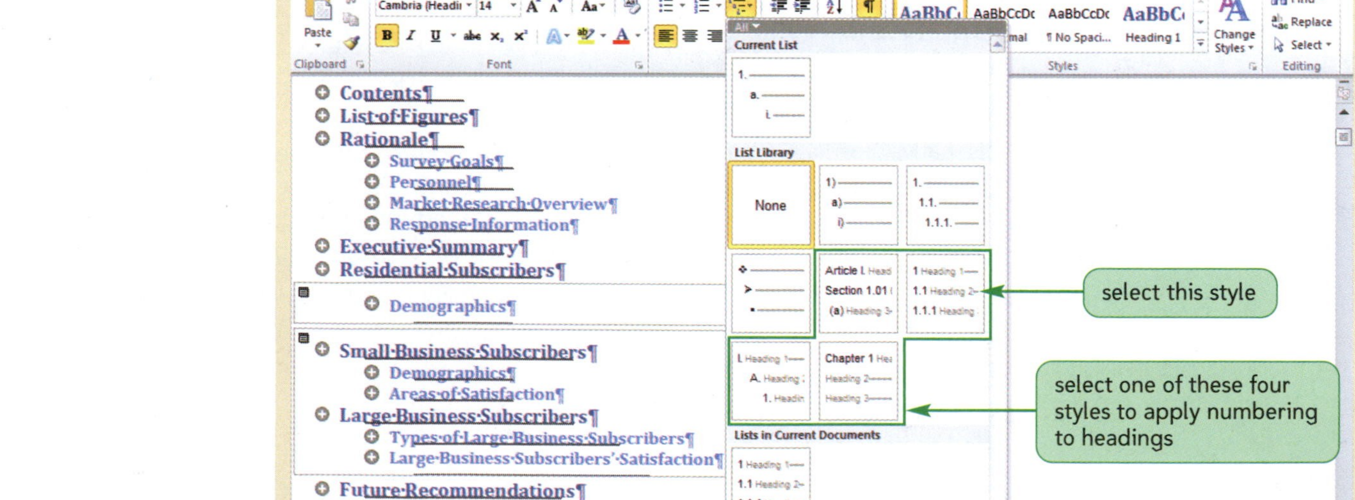

2. Click the last style in the second row of the List Library. The numbers are applied to the document headings, and a sample of the numbering style is now included as part of the heading styles in the Quick Styles gallery. See Figure 10-14. Each Level 1 heading (that is, each heading formatted in the Heading 1 style) has a single number. The numbers assigned to the Level 2 headings consist of the number of the Level 1 heading just above it, followed by a period, and then a sequential number. Michael wants you to customize the numbering format so that each number is followed by a period.

Figure 10-14 **Master document in Outline view showing numbered Level 1 and 2 headings**

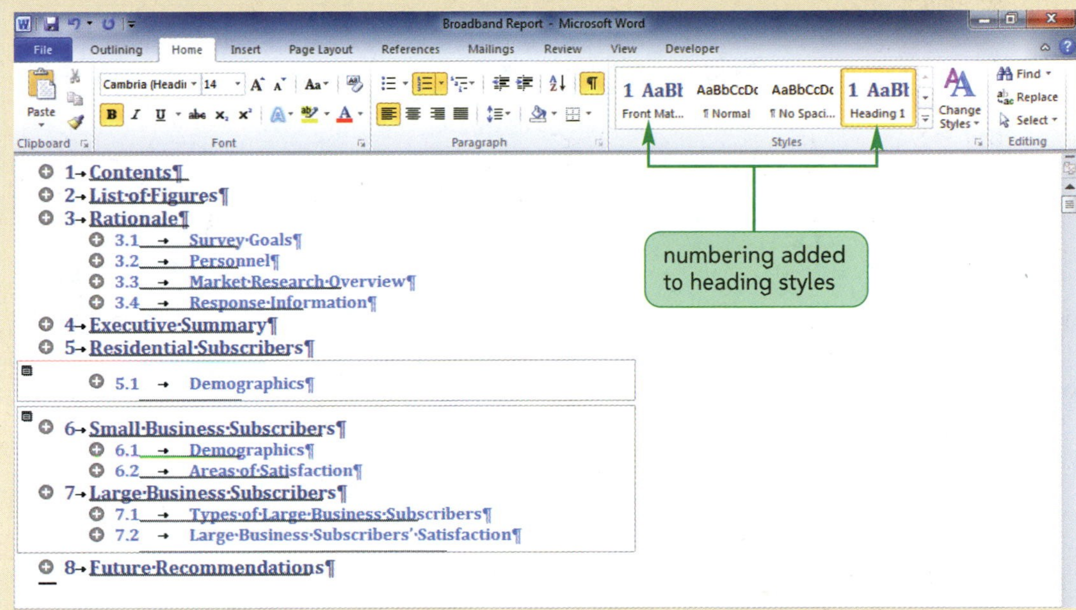

3. Click the **Multilevel List** button, and then click **Define New Multilevel List**. The Define New Multilevel list dialog box opens. See Figure 10-15. You want to change the default setting "1" for Heading 1 styles to "1." (with a period following the number) and Heading 2 styles to "1.1." (with a period following the second number).

Figure 10-15 **Define new Multilevel list dialog box**

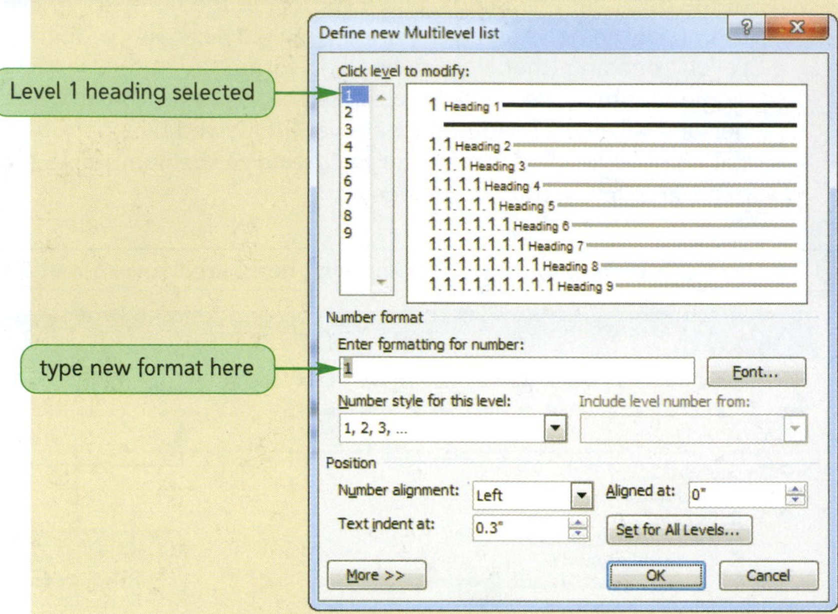

4. In the Click level to modify list, make sure **1** is selected.
5. In the **Enter formatting for number** box, click to the right of the number 1, and then type a period.
6. In the **Click level to modify** list, click **2**, click to the right of the second number 1 in the Enter formatting for number box, and then type a period after "1.1".
7. Click the **OK** button, and then save your changes. The numbers next to the headings change to include periods after each number. Notice the Heading 1 style in the Quick Styles Gallery in the Styles group on the Home tab has been updated to reflect the new number style.

There is one problem, however. When Michael created his version of the report document, he created a style named Front Matter Heading that he applied to the headings "Contents" and "List of Figures." He based this style on the Heading 1 style, but he created the new style so that when he created the table of contents, he used the Table of Contents Options dialog box to specify that the Front Matter Heading should not be included in the table of contents headings. He does not want these headings to be numbered with the rest of the headings in the document as they are not really part of the document outline. To fix this, you will modify the Front Matter Heading style definition so that the numbering is not applied.

To modify the Front Matter Heading style definition:

1. Click the **Home** tab, right-click the **Front Matter Heading** style (it appears as "Front Mat...") in the Quick Styles gallery in the Styles group, and then click **Modify** on the shortcut menu. The Modify Style dialog box opens.
2. At the bottom of the dialog box, click the **Format** button, and then click **Numbering**. The Numbering and Bullets dialog box opens with the Numbering tab selected.
3. If necessary, click the **None** style.
4. Click the **OK** button, and then click the **OK** button in the Modify Style dialog box. The Front Matter Heading style has been modified so that it does not include a number. (You can see this in the Quick Styles gallery on the Home tab.) In the outline, the Contents and the List of Figures headings no longer are numbered, and only the document content has numbered headings. See Figure 10-16.

   Trouble? If the Contents heading still includes a number, click in the Contents heading, and then click the Front Matter Heading style in the Quick Styles gallery.

Figure 10-16 Numbering removed from Contents and List of Figures headings

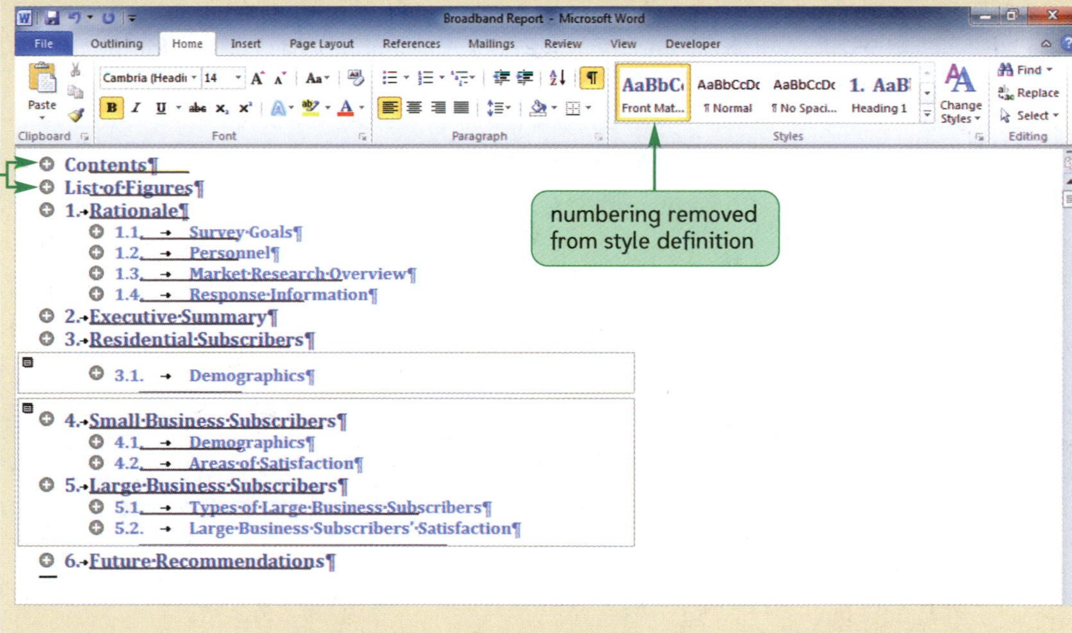

5. Switch to Print Layout view, and then save the document.

Note that as you edit a document that contains numbered headings, heading numbers might sometimes disappear from some headings. If that happens, select the affected heading, and then apply the correct heading style from the Quick Style gallery.

Inserting Numbered Captions

Michael included figures to illustrate key points in the report. Specifically, in section "1.2. Personnel," he inserted a picture of Kayla West, the liaison between Market Research Now, Inc. and the Continental Broadband Association. Also, in section "6. Future Recommendations," he added a SmartArt graphic illustrating one possible future trend. Michael wants to include captions for each figure so the text can refer to them.

You can add captions under figures in a document to number and label the figures. If you use the Insert Caption command, the figure numbers are inserted as fields that are automatically renumbered if you insert new figures or move the figures around. Michael asks you to insert captions with automatic figure numbering.

REFERENCE

Creating Captions

- Select the table or figure to which you want to apply a caption.
- Click the References tab, and then click the Insert Caption button in the Captions group.
- Click the Label arrow, and then click the type of object to which you're applying the caption (for example, figure or table).
- Use the Position arrow to specify whether you want the caption to appear above or below the figure.
- To use double-numbering that includes the number of the preceding Heading 1 heading, click the Numbering button, select the Include chapter number check box in the Caption Numbering dialog box, and then click the OK button.
- Click after the number in the Caption box, and then type a caption.
- Click the OK button in the Caption dialog box.

Now you are ready to create a numbered caption for the figures in the document.

To create a numbered caption:

1. Scroll until you can see the heading "1.2 Personnel" on page 4 and the photo of Kayla West. The picture is below the heading "1.2. Personnel" and the text wraps around it, as shown in Figure 10-17.

   Trouble? If the photo in your document is not positioned as shown in Figure 10-17, drag the photo so it is below the heading and to the left of the body text in the section.

Figure 10-17 **Document with a picture below a heading**

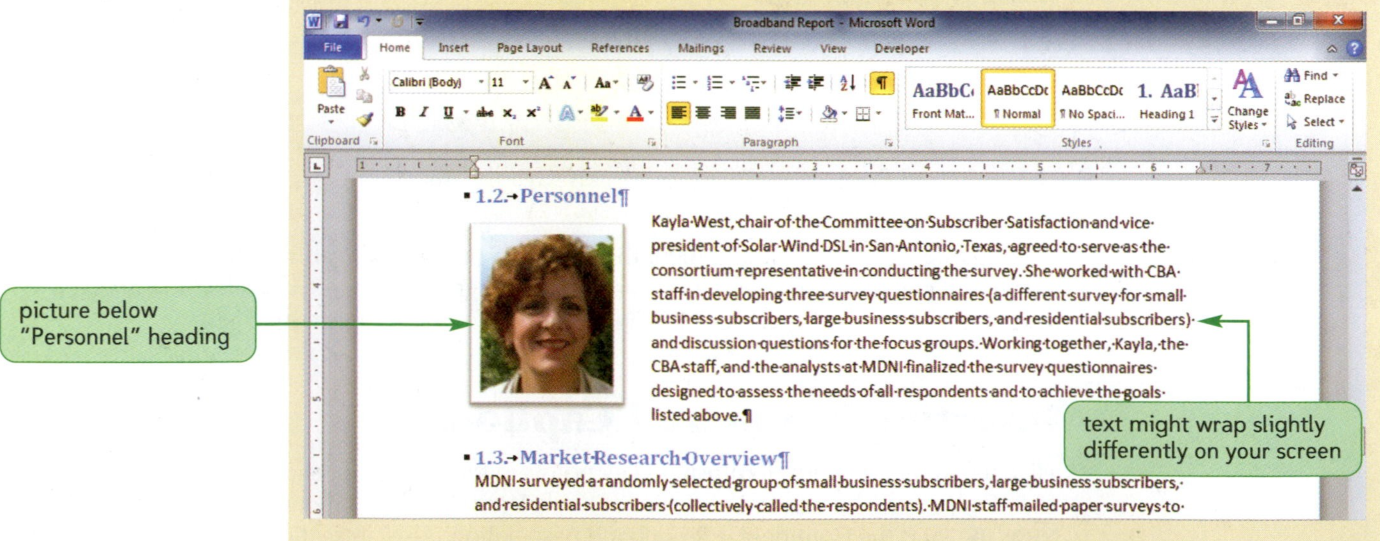

TIP

To change the format of the caption number, such as to Figure 1-1, click the Numbering button in the Caption dialog box.

2. Click the picture of Kayla to select it, click the **References** tab on the Ribbon, and then click the **Insert Caption** button in the Captions group. The Caption dialog box opens. See Figure 10-18. The insertion point is blinking to the right of "Figure 1" in the Caption box.

Figure 10-18 **Caption dialog box**

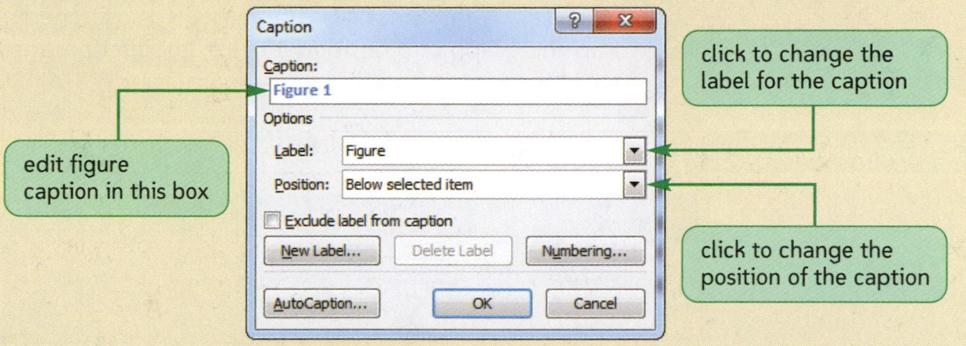

3. Type **:** (a colon), press the **Spacebar**, and then type **Kayla West** in the Caption box.
4. Click the **OK** button. The numbered caption is inserted below the figure as a floating text box with a border. See Figure 10-19.

   Trouble? If the heading "1.3. Market Research Overview" is not positioned below the caption and aligned at the left margin, as shown in Figure 10-19, adjust the position of the picture and the caption box until the heading is aligned at the left margin, below the caption.

Figure 10-19 **Caption inserted under photo**

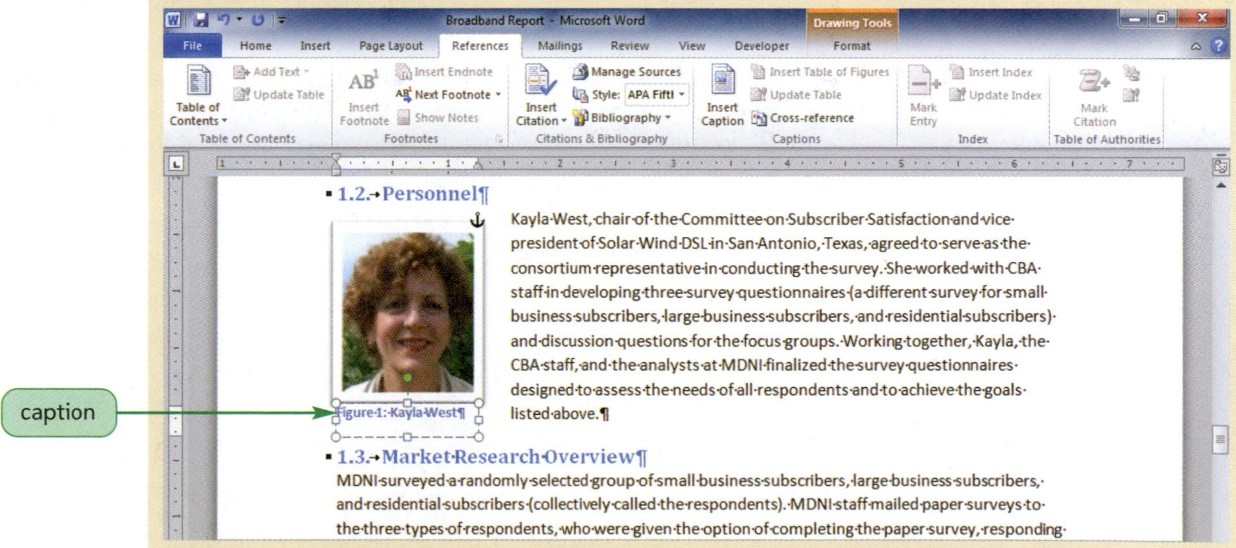

5. In the figure caption, right-click **1**, and then click **Toggle Field Codes** on the shortcut menu. The field code for the number 1 in the caption appears.
6. Right-click the field code, and then click **Toggle Field Codes** to toggle the field codes off.

Now, using the same procedure, you'll insert another numbered caption under a SmartArt graphic illustrating one possible future trend in the broadband industry.

To insert a numbered caption under the SmartArt graphic:

1. Press the **Ctrl+End** keys to move to the end of the document, and then scroll up so that you can see the heading "6. Future Recommendations." See Figure 10-20.

   Trouble? If the SmartArt graphic is not positioned as shown in Figure 10-20, drag the graphic to position it below the first paragraph in the section and to the left of the top part of the second paragraph.

Figure 10-20 SmartArt graphic

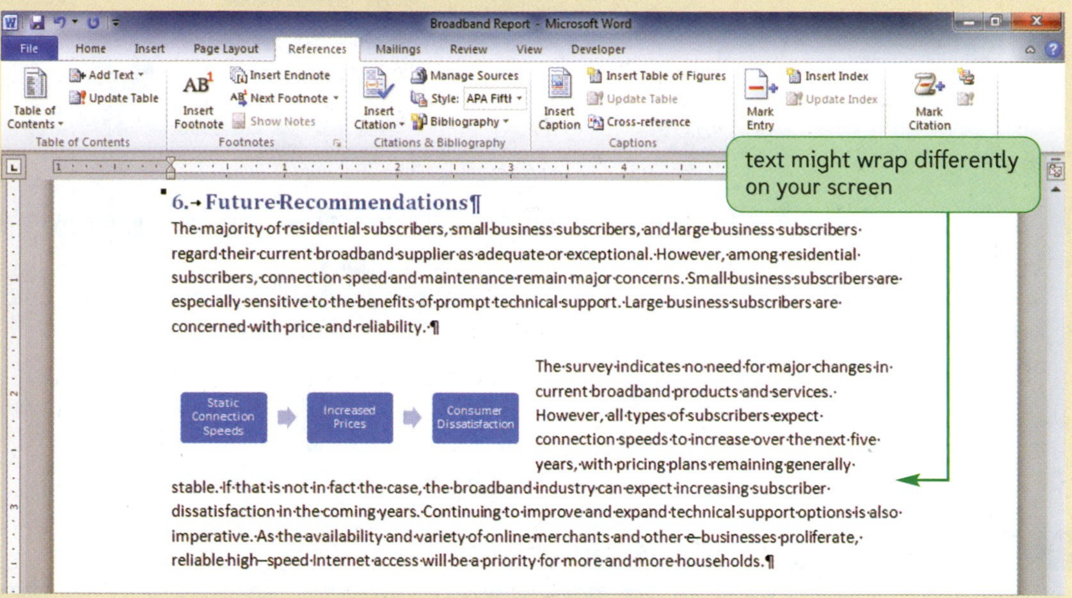

2. Click the SmartArt graphic to select, it, and then click the **Insert Caption** button in the Captions group on the References tab. The Caption dialog box opens with "Figure 2" in the Caption box because this will be the second figure with a caption in the document.

3. Edit the caption in the Caption box to read **Figure 2: Possible Future Trend**, and then click the **OK** button. Compare your screen to Figure 10-21.

Figure 10-21 Figure with new caption

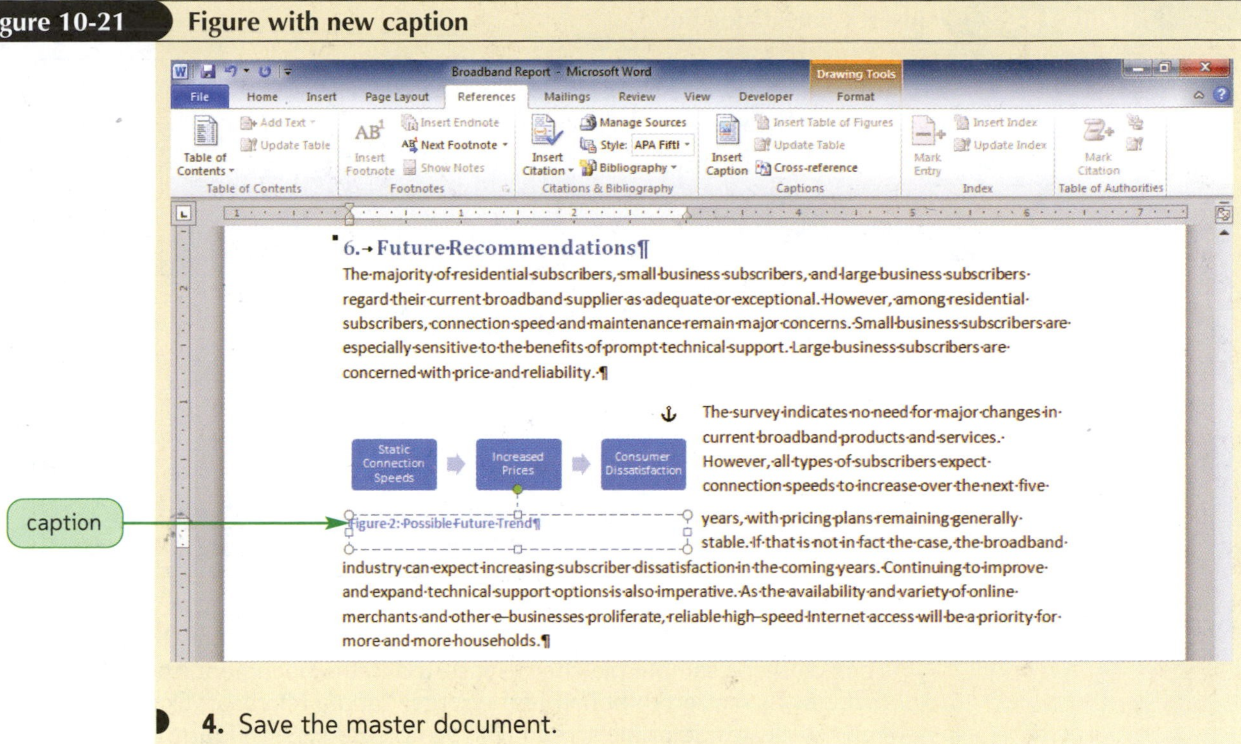

4. Save the master document.

When creating a caption, you can choose to number the captions sequentially as they appear in the document (1, 2, 3, etc.) or you can include the number of the first heading above the caption that is formatted with the Heading 1 style. For example, you could use 1-1 for the first caption under the heading "1. Rationale," 1-2 for the second caption under the heading "1. Rationale," and so on. The captions for figures in the "2. Executive Summary" section would then be numbered 2-1, 2-2, and so on. This type of numbering is sometimes called double-numbering.

Inserting a Chart

As you learned in Tutorial 7, you can insert a chart created in Microsoft Excel into any Word document. Note that you can also create a chart using Excel from within a Word document by clicking the Chart button in the Illustrations group on the Insert tab. This inserts a sample column chart in the document and opens an Excel worksheet.

Michael would like you to add a pie chart in section "3.1. Demographics" to show the age range among residential subscribers.

TIP

You can also insert a chart by clicking the Object button in the Text group on the Insert tab, and then clicking Microsoft Graph Chart on the Create New tab in the Object dialog box.

To create the pie chart in Microsoft Excel:

1. Scroll to page 5, and then click at the beginning of the paragraph just below the heading "3.1. Demographics."
2. Click the **Insert** tab, and then click the **Chart** button. The Insert Chart dialog box opens with Column selected in the category list on the left. See Figure 10-22.

Figure 10-22 Insert Chart dialog box

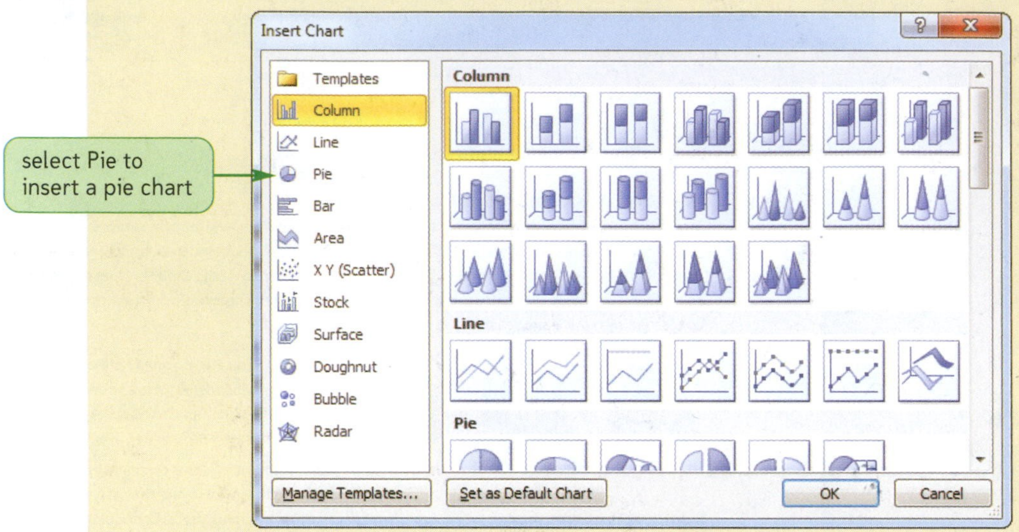

3. In the category list on the left, click **Pie**, and then click the **OK** button. The dialog box closes, a sample pie chart is inserted in the document, the Word program window is resized to fit half of the screen, and a Microsoft Excel worksheet opens on the right side of the screen with sample data. See Figure 10-23. Notice that some of the groups on the active tab on the Ribbon in both windows are collapsed into buttons.

Figure 10-23 Excel worksheet with sample data for pie chart

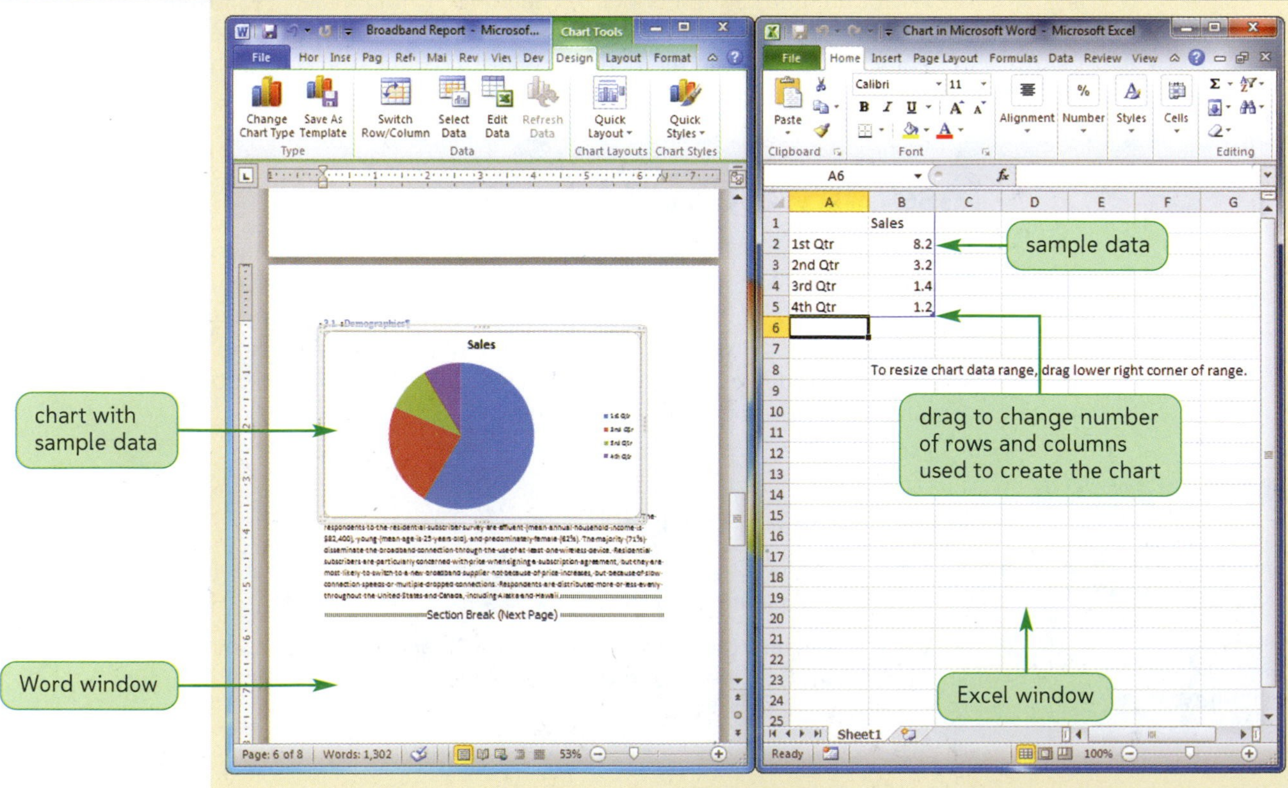

To create the chart for Michael's report, you simply edit the information in the sample worksheet in the Excel window. When you work with a worksheet, the cell in which you are entering data is the active cell. The active cell has a thick black border around it.

To modify the data used to create the chart:

1. In the Excel window, click cell **A2**. This is now the active cell.
2. Type **18 to 29**, and then press the **Enter** key. The first item in the legend in the pie chart in the document changes to reflect the new data that you just typed, and cell A3 is now the active cell.
3. Type **30 to 49**, press the **Enter** key, type **Over 50** in cell A4, and then press the **Enter** key.
4. Click cell **B2**, type **60%**, press the **Enter** key, type **25%** in cell B3, press the **Enter** key, type **15%** in cell B4, and then press the **Enter** key. The pie chart in the document changes to reflect the new data. There are only three categories in this chart, so you need to exclude the last row of data in the worksheet.
5. In the Excel worksheet, click cell **A1**, and then position the point over the small blue shape at the bottom-right corner of the data so that the pointer changes to ↘.
6. Drag the corner up to the bottom of row 4 so that row 5 is left outside of the blue border around the data. The pie chart in the document now includes only three pieces.
7. In the Excel window title bar, click the **Close** button. The Excel window closes, the Excel data is saved in the Word document, and the Word window expands to fill the full screen. The new chart is selected in the document, as shown in Figure 10-24, and three Chart Tools contextual tabs appear on the Ribbon.

Figure 10-24 **Pie chart in the Word document**

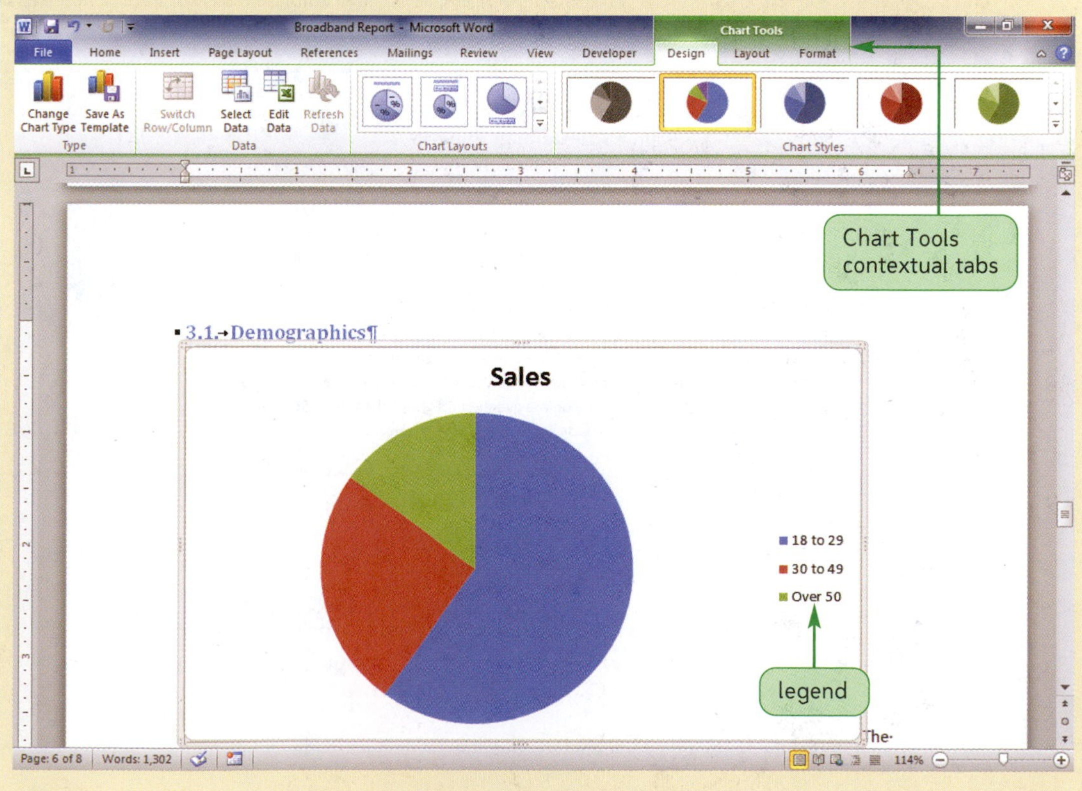

Once the chart is in the document, you can modify it by changing or formatting the various elements of the chart. For example, you can apply a chart style to your chart to change its look. You can also edit or remove the title of a chart. Michael wants you to modify the chart by deleting the title, applying a style, and adding labels.

To modify the chart:

1. Click the **Chart Tools Layout** tab, click the **Chart Title** button in the Labels group, and then click **None**. The title is removed from the chart.
2. In the Labels group, click the **Data Labels** button, and then click **Best Fit**.
3. Click the **Chart Tools Design** tab, click the **More** button in the Chart Styles group, and then click **Style 11** (second row, third column). The chart is reformatted with the Style 11 style.
4. Drag the lower-right corner of the chart up and to the left to resize the chart so it is approximately two-and-one-half inches square.
5. Click the **Chart Tools Format** tab, click the **Wrap Text** button in the Arrange group, and then click **Square**.
6. Drag the chart to the right, and then position it so that the text in the paragraph wraps around it on the left. See Figure 10-25.

Figure 10-25 **Formatted, resized, and repositioned pie chart**

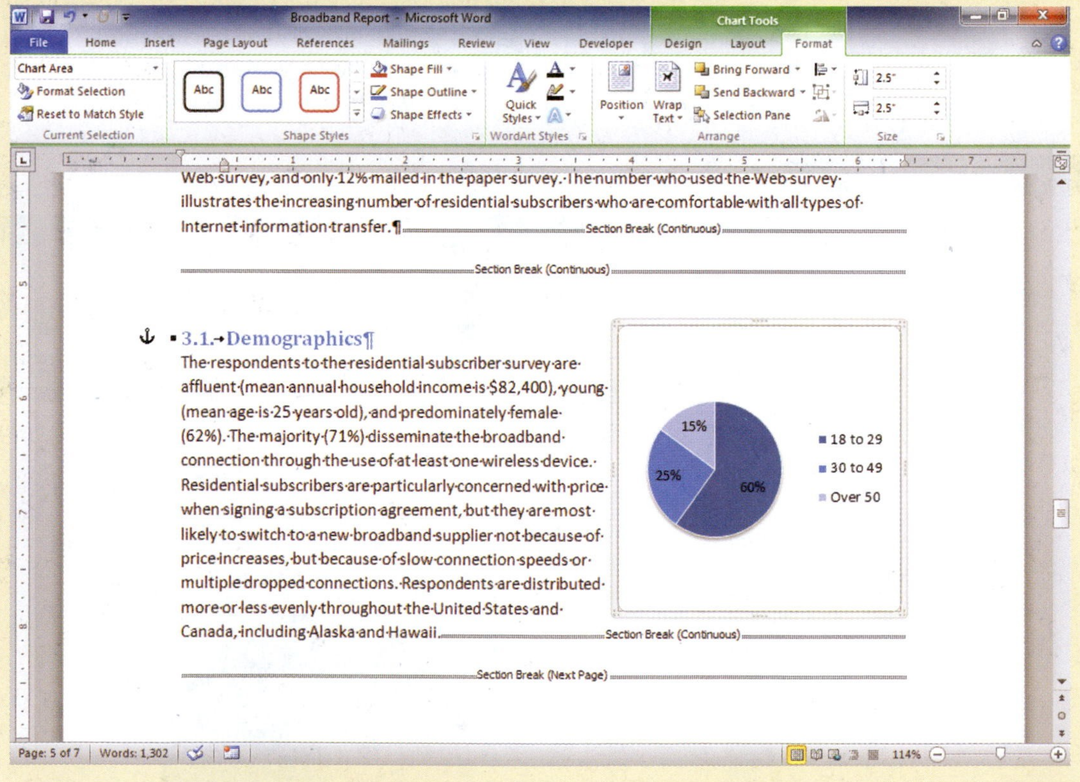
Broadband Report - Microsoft Word
Chart Tools
File
Home
Insert
Page Layout
References
Mailings
Review
View
Developer
Design
Layout
Format
Chart Area
Format Selection
Reset to Match Style
Current Selection
Abc
Shape Fill
Shape Outline
Shape Effects
Shape Styles
Quick Styles
WordArt Styles
Position
Wrap Text
Bring Forward
Send Backward
Selection Pane
Arrange
2.5"
2.5"
Size
Web·survey,·and·only·12%·mailed·in·the·paper·survey.·The·number·who·used·the·Web·survey·illustrates·the·increasing·number·of·residential·subscribers·who·are·comfortable·with·all·types·of·Internet·information·transfer.¶
Section Break (Continuous)
Section Break (Continuous)
3.1.→Demographics¶
The·respondents·to·the·residential·subscriber·survey·are·affluent·(mean·annual·household·income·is·$82,400),·young·(mean·age·is·25·years·old),·and·predominately·female·(62%).·The·majority·(71%)·disseminate·the·broadband·connection·through·the·use·of·at·least·one·wireless·device.·Residential·subscribers·are·particularly·concerned·with·price·when·signing·a·subscription·agreement,·but·they·are·most·likely·to·switch·to·a·new·broadband·supplier·not·because·of·price·increases,·but·because·of·slow·connection·speeds·or·multiple·dropped·connections.·Respondents·are·distributed·more·or·less·evenly·throughout·the·United·States·and·Canada,·including·Alaska·and·Hawaii.
Section Break (Continuous)
Section Break (Next Page)
15%
25%
60%
18 to 29
30 to 49
Over 50
Page: 5 of 7
Words: 1,302
114%

Now you need to insert a caption under the pie chart.

To insert a figure caption under the pie chart:

1. With the pie chart selected, click the **References** tab, and then click the **Insert Caption** button in the Captions group. The Caption dialog box opens. "Figure 2" appears in the Caption box. Word automatically numbers this Figure 2 because you are inserting it before the previously numbered Figure 2. The old Figure 2 is renumbered Figure 3.
2. Change the figure caption to **Figure 2: Age Range of Residential Respondents**, and then click the **OK** button.

   Trouble? If there is extra space above the last line in the paragraph that wraps around the graphic, make the graphic a little shorter.
3. Scroll to page 7 to see that the caption under the SmartArt graphic has been renumbered as Figure 3.
4. Save the document.

Now that you have inserted figure captions for each illustration in the document, you need to refer to each of them in the text. For that, you'll use cross-references.

Creating Cross-References

If you refer to figures within the text—for example, "See Figure 2"—you need to make sure the cross-references change if the figure numbers change. This might be necessary if you add or delete figures or reorganize a document. Word updates cross-references automatically, just as it updates the heading numbering and figure captions.

REFERENCE

Creating Cross-References

- Move the insertion point to the location where you want to insert the cross-reference.
- Type the text preceding the cross-reference, such as "See" and a space.
- Click the References tab, and then click the Cross-reference button in the Captions group.
- Click the Reference type arrow, and then select the item you want to reference.
- Click the Insert reference to arrow, and then select the amount of information from the reference to appear in the cross-reference.
- In the For which numbered item list, click the item you want to reference.
- Click the Insert button to insert the cross-reference.
- Click the Close button to close the dialog box.

Michael wants the figures in the report referenced within the text, so you'll insert cross-references to the three figures.

To insert a cross-reference to Figure 1:

1. Scroll up to page 4 so that you can see the heading "1.2. Personnel," click to the right of "Kayla West" in the first line in the paragraph (not in the figure caption), press the **Spacebar**, type **(see** and then press the **Spacebar** again. The beginning of the edited sentence is now "Kayla West (see , chair of the...". Now you're ready to insert the automatically numbered cross-reference.
2. In the Captions group on the References tab, click the **Cross-reference** button. The Cross-reference dialog box opens. See Figure 10-26. Notice the Insert as hyperlink check box is selected by default. This means you can press and hold the Ctrl key, and then click the cross-reference to jump to the item referenced.

Figure 10-26 **Cross-reference dialog box showing numbered items**

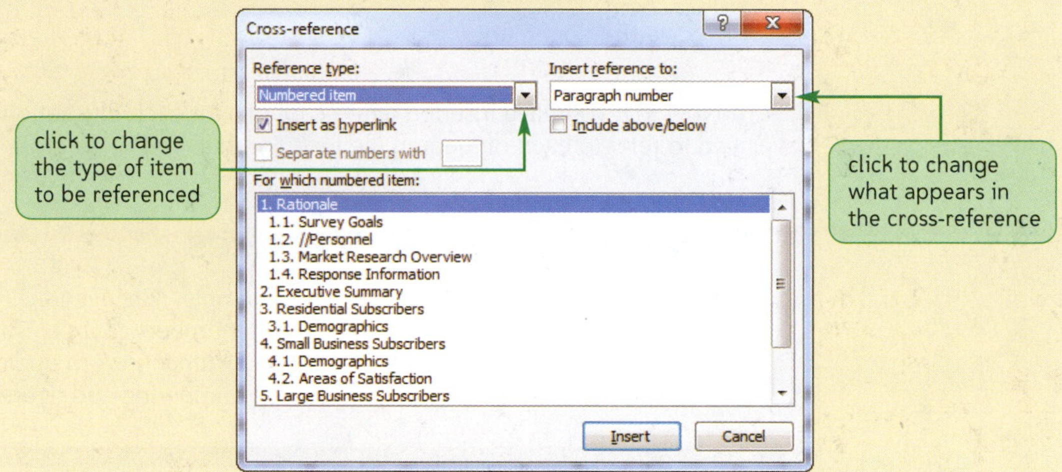

3. Click the **Reference type** arrow, scroll down, and then click **Figure**. The bottom part of the dialog box changes to display the three figure captions in the document, and the Insert reference to box changes to Entire caption. You want the reference to the figure to list only the label "Figure" and the figure number, not the entire caption.
4. Click the **Insert reference to** arrow, and then click **Only label and number**. The first reference is to Figure 1, and this is already selected in the For which caption list. See Figure 10-27.

Figure 10-27 Cross-reference dialog box showing figure captions

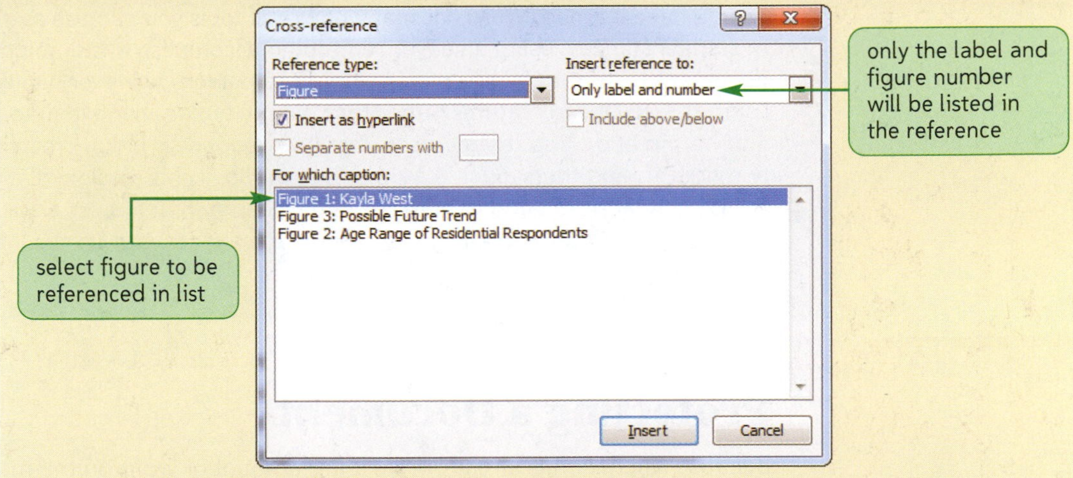

5. Click the **Insert** button to insert this cross-reference, click the **Close** button to close the dialog box, and then type **)** after the cross-reference to close the parentheses. The phrase "(see Figure 1)" appears in the report, so that the sentence reads "Kayla West (see Figure 1), chair of the...." Notice that the cross-reference you created is automatically numbered to match the figure caption number.

The power of all automatic numbering features in Word—heading numbering, caption numbering, and cross-references—becomes evident when you edit a long document with many figures. Now you'll add cross-references to the other two figures.

To insert additional cross-references:

1. Scroll down to page 5 so that you can see the section that begins with the heading "3.1. Demographics," click at the end of the first sentence below that heading, and then, using a cross-reference, insert the sentence **See Figure 2**.
2. Scroll down to page 7, click after the sentence that begins "If that is not in fact the case..." in the second paragraph, and then using a cross-reference, insert the sentence (**See Figure 3**.)
3. Save the master document.

Next, you'll help Michael control the kinds of changes the other team members at MDNI can make to the Broadband Report.

PROSKILLS

Decision Making: Using Advanced Tools in Word

As you have learned, Word has many powerful tools you can use as you create documents. In some instances, using an advanced tool to accomplish a task might not make sense if the document is short or will be used by only one person. However, you should always consider using the advanced features rather than simply typing. For example, using automatic figure numbering and cross-references is usually a good idea. If you create a document with just two figures, and then you add a third, as you did in this session, it is easy to forget to check the document at the end to make sure that the figure numbers are still in the correct order. By using Word's caption and cross-reference tools, you can be sure that the figures will always appear in the correct numeric order.

Protecting a Document

Because Michael has already done a fair amount of work on the master document, he'd like to retain some control over the kinds of changes the other writers make to it, so he decides to protect the document. When you **protect** a document, you restrict the kinds of formatting changes and edits that Word will allow in the document. When specifying formatting restrictions, you can limit formatting in the document to a specific list of styles. You can also block certain formatting changes, such as selecting a new theme.

When specifying editing restrictions, you can choose from the following options:

- **Tracked changes**—Allows users to make any editing changes and the formatting changes allowed by the formatting restrictions, but all changes are marked with revision marks.
- **Comments**—Allows users to insert comments, but not to make any other changes.
- **Filling in forms**—Allows users to fill in forms only; you used this option in Tutorial 9 to protect a form.
- **No changes (Read only)**—Allows users to read the document but not to make changes.

As you learned in Tutorial 9, when you protect a document you can choose to require a password in order to turn off protection. If you are protecting a document because you are concerned that someone might make unauthorized changes to the document, then you should definitely use a password. However, if you are protecting a document that will be shared among a small group of colleagues, and you are using the protect feature simply to ensure that all changes are tracked with revision marks, then a password typically isn't necessary.

REFERENCE

Protecting a Document

- Click the Review tab, and then click the Restrict Editing button in the Protect group to open the Restrict Formatting and Editing task pane.
- To restrict formatting changes, under "1. Formatting restrictions", select the "Limit formatting to a selection of styles" check box, click Settings to open the Formatting Restrictions dialog box, select the restrictions you want, and then click the OK button.
- To specify editing restrictions, under "2. Editing restrictions", select the "Allow only this type of editing in the document" check box, click the arrow, and then click the editing restriction you want.
- Under "3. Start enforcement", click the Yes, Start Enforcing Protection button.
- If desired, type a password in the "Enter new password (optional)" box and in the "Reenter password to confirm" box.
- Click the OK button.

Because Michael wants to be able to see exactly what changes the other team members make to the report, he decides to protect the master document by applying the Tracked changes editing restriction. You already have some experience working with the Track Changes feature, which marks additions, deletions, moved text, and formatting changes with revision marks. Once you protect a document for tracked changes, you should keep in mind the following:

- When a document is protected for tracked changes, you can't turn off the Tracked Changes feature by toggling off the Track Changes button, unless you remove the restrictions first.
- Protecting a master document doesn't protect the separate subdocument files. When you protect a master document for tracked changes, Word creates revision marks for any change made in the master document text or in the subdocuments that are expanded in the master document. However, if you open the subdocuments in separate document windows, you can edit the separate subdocument files without tracking the revisions.

In addition to protecting the master document for tracked changes, Michael wants to apply one formatting restriction—in particular, he wants to block any user from changing the document theme. You're ready to protect the Broadband Report document.

TIP

You can also click the Protect Document button on the Info tab in Backstage view, and then click Restrict Editing.

To apply formatting and editing restrictions to the document and then protect it:

1. Click the **Review** tab, and then click the **Restrict Editing** button in the Protect group. The Restrict Formatting and Editing task pane opens. Michael doesn't care whether the other team members apply new styles to the document, so you can leave the "Limit formatting to a selection of styles" check box in the "1. Formatting restrictions" section deselected. Michael does, however, want to block users from changing the document theme.
2. In the "1. Formatting restrictions" section, click the **Settings** link to open the Formatting Restrictions dialog box. See Figure 10-28.

Figure 10-28 Restricting formatting changes

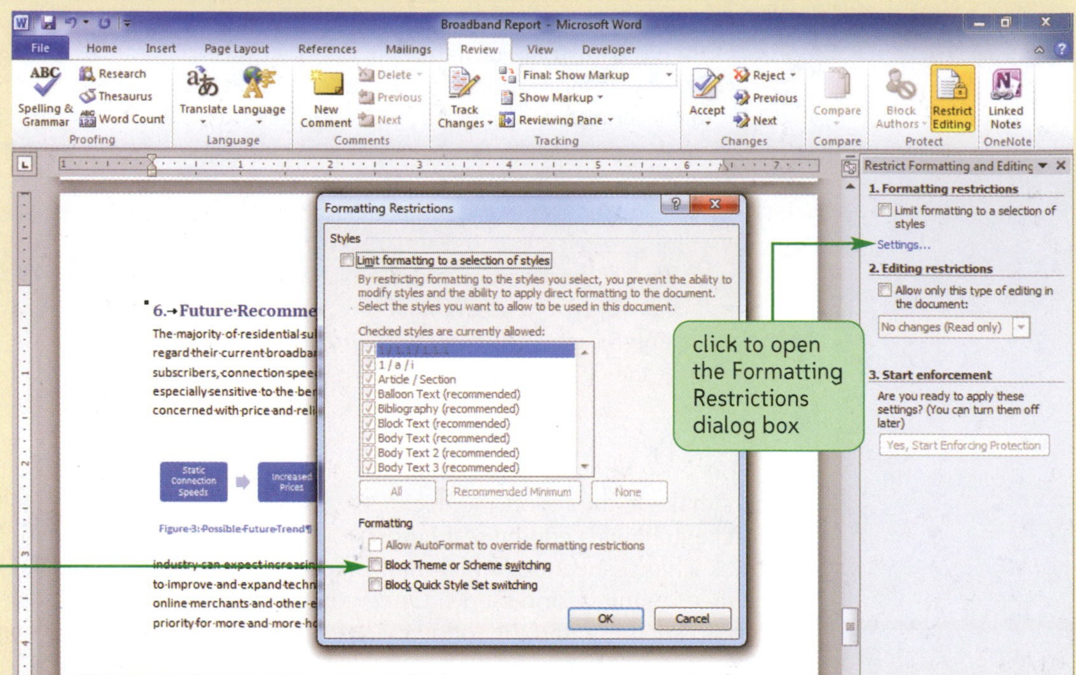

select this check box to prevent users from changing the theme

click to open the Formatting Restrictions dialog box

3. Near the bottom of the dialog box, click the **Block Theme or Scheme switching** check box to select it, and then click the **OK** button. The Formatting Restrictions dialog box closes.
4. In the "2. Editing restrictions" section of the task pane, click the **Allow only this type of editing in the document** check box. A new section of the task pane, labeled "Exceptions (optional)," appears, where you can specify exceptions to the editing restrictions.
5. Click the **arrow** in the 2. Editing restrictions section—which by default is set to No changes (Read only)—and then click **Tracked changes**. The Exceptions (optional) section of the task pane closes because when Tracked changes is selected, no exceptions apply.
6. In the "3. Start enforcement" section of the task pane, click the **Yes, Start Enforcing Protection** button. The Start Enforcing Protection dialog box opens, where you have the opportunity to specify a password.
7. Click the **OK** button to close the dialog box without entering a password.
8. In the task pane, click the **Close** button ✕, and then save the document.

INSIGHT

Choosing When to Protect a Document

It's not convenient or useful to protect every document you create. But most people don't use this feature as much as they should. If you plan to send a document around to colleagues for their comments, you should definitely take the time to protect the document first, so that your colleagues' changes are tracked with revision marks. Otherwise, you might encounter surprises in documents after they are published, mailed, or emailed. For example, a colleague might introduce an error by changing an important sales figure using outdated sales information, and then forget to tell you later. You can prevent this by protecting your shared documents for tracked changes.

Now that the document is protected for revisions, neither you nor anyone else can make changes without having the changes tracked with revision marks.

Michael asks you to revise the Executive Summary section. Because you restricted editing, your changes will be tracked.

To edit the protected document:

1. Scroll up to page 5 so that you can see the heading "2. Executive Summary." Michael realizes that the word "generally" in the second sentence is unnecessary, so he asks you to delete it.
2. In the second sentence below the heading "2. Executive Summary," double-click the word **generally**, and then press the **Delete** key. Because the document is protected for tracked changes, Word marks the word for deletion and adds a revision line in the margin.
3. Click the **Page Layout** tab. The buttons in the Themes group are unavailable. You blocked all users from changing the document theme, so Word prevents you from using these options. See Figure 10-29.

   Trouble? The deletion on your screen might be marked with a balloon in the right margin.

Figure 10-29 **Editing a protected document**

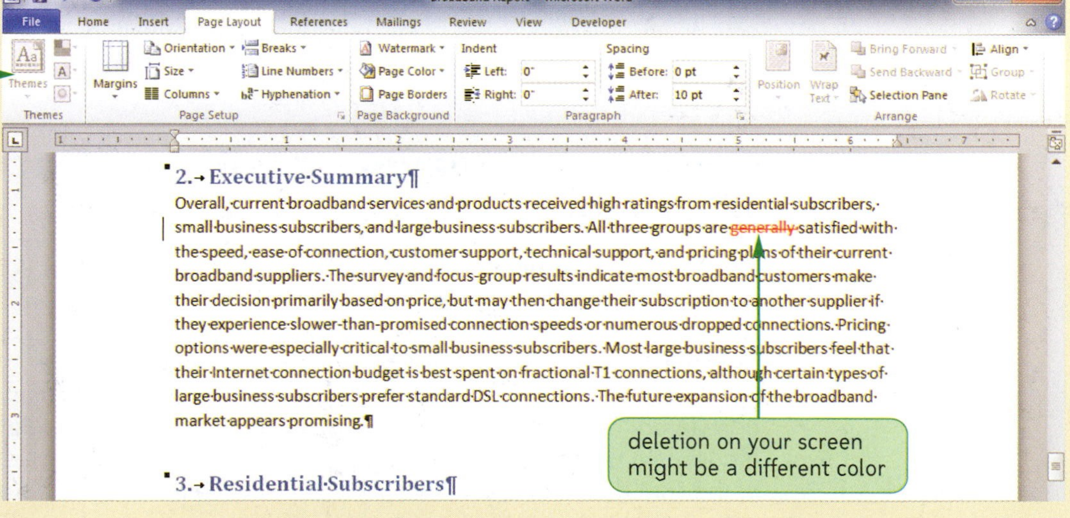

Now you'll turn off the document protection and remove the formatting restriction.

To unprotect the document and turn off the formatting restriction:

1. Click the **Review** tab on the Ribbon, and then click the **Restrict Editing** button in the Protect group. The Restrict Formatting and Editing task pane opens.
2. At the bottom of the task pane, click the **Stop Protection** button. The task pane changes to show the restriction options. From this point on, Word will no longer mark changes with revision marks.
3. In the "1. Formatting restrictions" section of the task pane, click the **Settings** link to open the Formatting Restrictions dialog box, click the **Block Theme or Scheme switching** check box to deselect it, and then click the **OK** button to close the dialog box.
4. In the "2. Editing restrictions" section of the task pane, click the **Allow only this type of editing in the document** check box to remove the check mark, and then close the task pane.

You'll now see what the document would look like if you accepted the revision—that is, if no revision marks appeared in the document.

To review the document with changes accepted:

1. In the Tracking group, click the **Display for Review** arrow (which is currently set to Final: Show Markup), and then click **Final**. The document now appears as it would if you accepted the revision.
2. Save the document. At this point, the document still contains your deletion of the word "generally" marked with revision marks, although you can't see the revision marks.

It's often helpful to use the Final setting to display the document as if all the revision marks have been accepted or rejected, without actually accepting or rejecting the revision marks. However, after you review the document using the Final setting, it's easy to forget to go back and accept or reject the revision marks. If you do forget, you might then accidentally send out a document that contains revision marks to a client or to your manager. Such a mistake could make you look unprofessional, or, even worse, depending on the nature of your revisions, inadvertently reveal sensitive information. To make sure a document doesn't contain any revision marks, or any other types of information that you don't want to reveal to readers of your document, you can use the Document Inspector.

Checking a Document with the Document Inspector

The **Document Inspector** automatically checks a document for comments and revision marks. If it finds any, it gives you the opportunity to remove them. When you remove revision marks with the Document Inspector, all changes are accepted, as if you had used the Accept button in the Changes group on the Review tab.

You can also use the Document Inspector to check a document for personal information stored in the document properties, headers, or footers. In addition, it can search for hidden text (text that is hidden from display using the Hidden check box on the Font tab of the Font dialog box) and for special types of data that can be stored along with the document. You'll use the Document Inspector now to check for revision marks.

To check the document using the Document Inspector:

1. Click the **File** tab to display Backstage view with the Info tab selected.
2. In the Prepare for Sharing section, click the **Check for Issues** button, and then click **Inspect Document**. The Document Inspector dialog box opens. See Figure 10-30.

   Trouble? If a dialog box opens indicating that the file has not been saved, click the Yes button.

Figure 10-30 Document Inspector dialog box

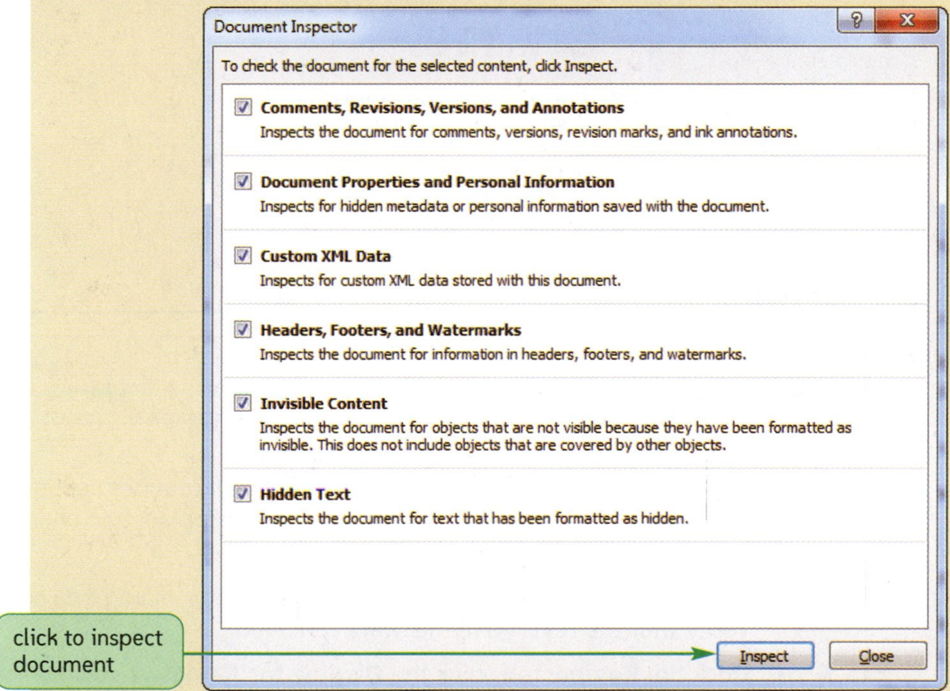

3. Click the **Inspect** button. The Document Inspector dialog box changes to indicate that revision marks, document properties, and custom XML data was found in the document. See Figure 10-31. You only want to remove the revision marks.

Figure 10-31 Document Inspector dialog box after inspecting document

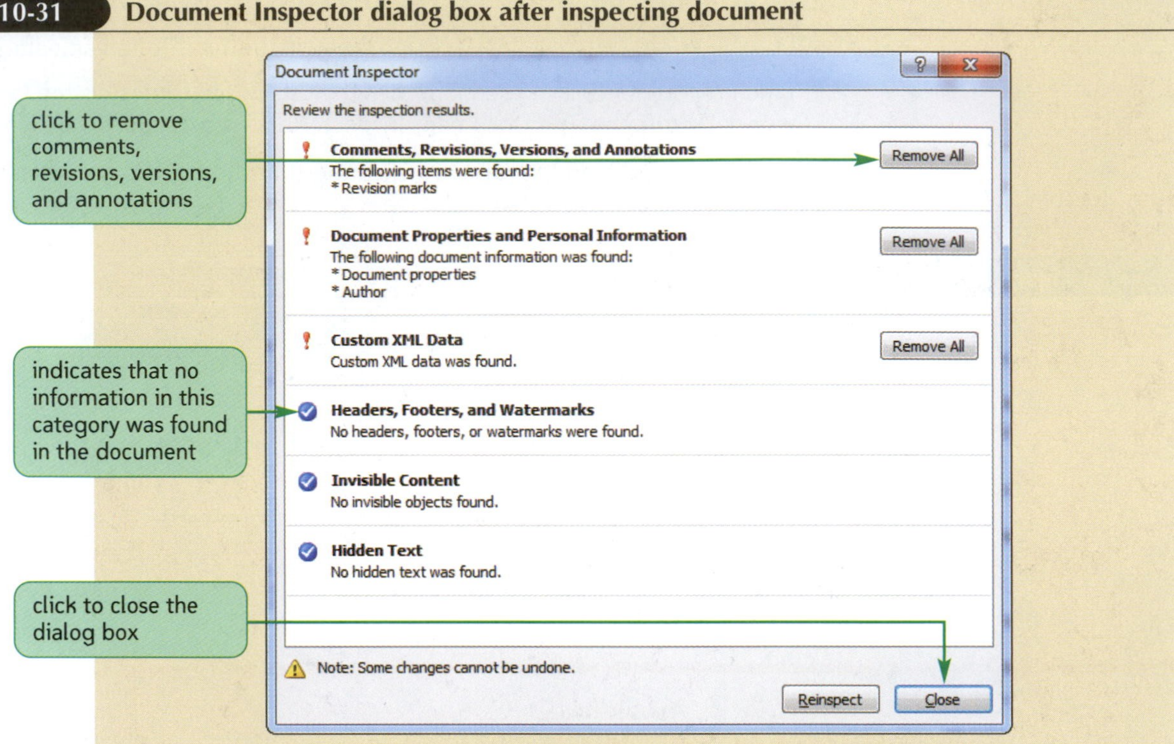

4. In the Comments, Revisions, Versions, and Annotations section at the top of the dialog box, click the **Remove All** button. The top section changes to show that all items were successfully removed.
5. Click the **Close** button. The Document Inspector dialog box closes. Next, you'll verify that the revision marks were removed.
6. Click the **Review** tab, click the **Display for Review** arrow (which currently displays "Final") in the Tracking group, and then click **Final: Show Markup**. If the document did contain revision marks, you would see them now. Because you used the Document Inspector to remove all revision marks, the change you made has been accepted and the word "generally" has been deleted.
7. Save the document.

Checking Documents for Accessibility

If you are planning on distributing your document to a wide audience, you should check your document to make sure it's accessible to as many people as possible. You can use the Check Accessibility command to identify parts of the document that might be problematic for people with vision disabilities who need to use assistive technologies such as a screen reader. The Accessibility Checker classifies potential problems into three categories: errors, warnings, and tips. An error is content that is difficult-to-impossible for people with disabilities to access. Content that is flagged with a warning is content that sometimes makes it difficult for people with disabilities to access. And content flagged with a tip shouldn't be impossible for people with disabilities to access, but could possibly be organized in a way that would make it easier to access.

A common problem in documents is an image or other object that is not text and therefore cannot be converted from text to audio by assistive technologies such as a screen reader. To overcome this, you can add alternative text—commonly called **Alt text**—which is text that describes the object.

Another common problem is when objects are floating in the document instead of being inline in the text. Floating objects might be difficult to navigate to and might not be accessible to people with vision disabilities. Floating objects can be changed to inline objects, but then you run the risk of the document not looking the way you want it to.

To check the document for accessibility issues:

1. Click the **File** tab to display Backstage view with the Info tab selected.
2. In the Prepare for Sharing section, click the **Check for Issues** button, and then click **Check Accessibility**. Backstage view closes, and the Accessibility Checker task pane appears to the right of the document window.
3. In the Errors section of the Accessibility Checker task pane, click the item that starts with **Chart**. A number follows "Chart" in the item name in the task pane. The document scrolls to the pie chart that you inserted. See Figure 10-32. At the bottom of the task pane, an explanation of the problem and suggestions on how to fix it appear. In this case, you can add Alt text to the chart to describe it.

Figure 10-32 Chart selected in the Errors section of the Accessibility Checker task pane

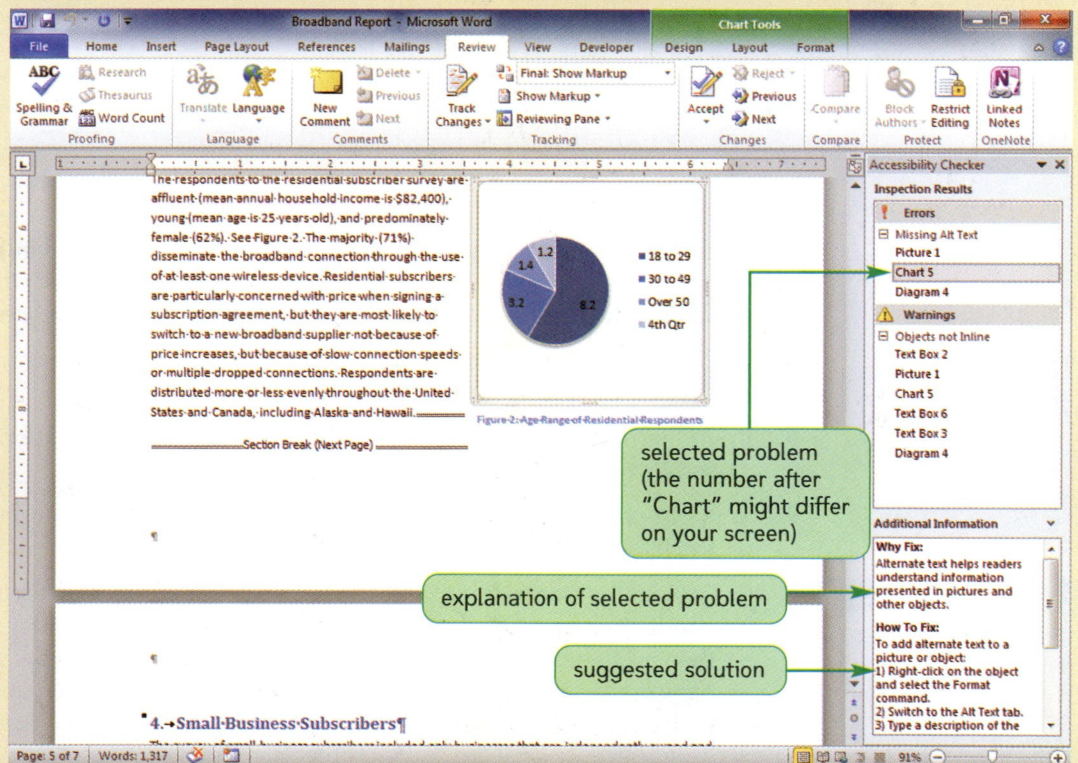

4. In the document, right-click the chart, and then click **Format Chart Area**. The Format Chart Area dialog box opens.
5. In the list on the left, click **Alt Text**. The dialog box changes to display Alt Text options. See Figure 10-33. Only text in the Description box is saved as Alt text if you convert the document to a Web page, so generally, you want to type the Alt text there.

Figure 10-33 **Alt Text selected in the Format Chart Area dialog box**

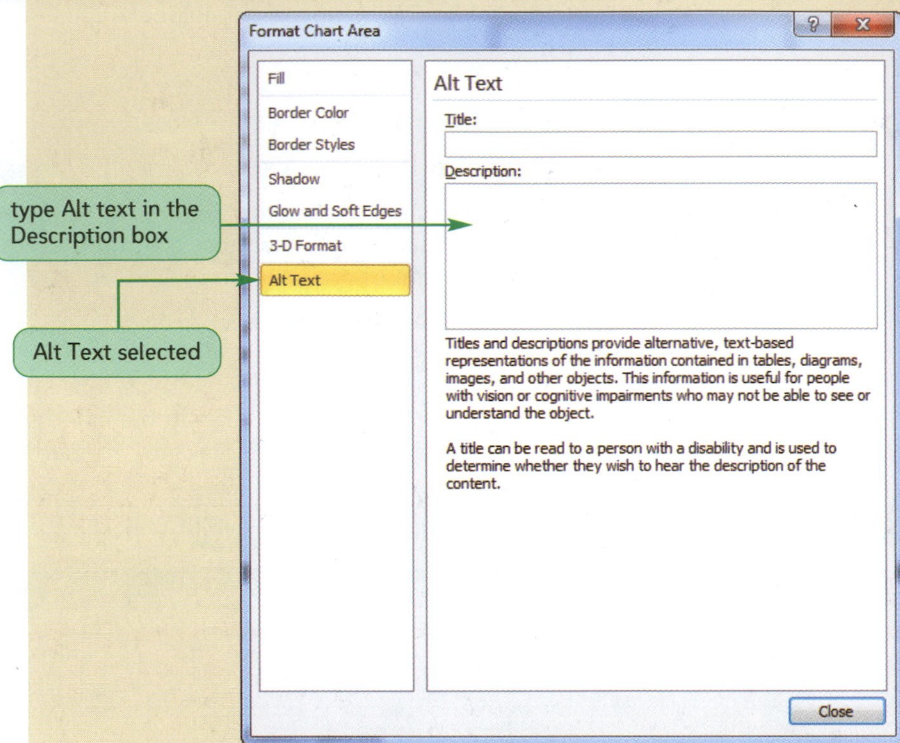

6. Click in the **Description** box, and then type **Pie chart showing the distribution of age ranges of residential respondents. 60% of the respondents are 18 to 29, 25% of the respondents are 30 to 49, and 15% of the respondents are over 50.**
7. Click the **Close** button. The dialog box closes and the Chart item is removed from the list of errors in the Accessibility Checker task pane.
8. In the task pane, click the **Diagram** item in the Errors section. The document scrolls and the SmartArt diagram appears.
9. Right-click the SmartArt diagram, click **Format Object**, and then click **Alt Text** in the list on the left.
10. Click in the **Description** box, and then type **Diagram illustrating that static connection speeds plus increased prices leads to customer dissatisfaction.**, and then click the **Close** button. The other item listed in the Errors section of the task pane is the photo of Kayla. Because this photo has a caption and Kayla is described in the text, you don't need to add Alt text to it. The items in the Warnings section are listed because they are floating objects in the document. Michael tells you that the floating objects do not need to be changed to inline objects.
11. Close the task pane, and then save the document.

TIP

If you were going to convert the document to a Web page, you should add Alt text to all photos and objects.

Managing Multiple Documents Simultaneously with Synchronous Scrolling

One of the hardest parts about collaborating on a document with other people is keeping track of which copy of the file is the correct one, and making sure that all the intended edits are entered into the correct file. Using the Master Document feature can go a long way toward ensuring that all edits are made in the correct file. But if confusion does arise, you can open up both documents, display them side-by-side, and then scroll through both documents at the same time. Scrolling two documents at once—a process known as **synchronous scrolling**—allows you to quickly assess the overall structure of two documents. If this side-by-side comparison suggests numerous differences between the documents, you can then use the Compare feature (as explained in Tutorial 7) to examine, in detail, the differences between the two documents.

While Michael was out of the office, Katarina made a copy of the Broadband Report document, and then edited the chart in the "3.1. Demographics" section. Michael first wants you to examine that section in his document, and then he asks you to use synchronous scrolling to compare Katarina's new copy of the document, which is named Report 2, with his Broadband Report document. You'll start by scrolling to the top of the Broadband Report document and examining two sections of the report at the same time using a split window. Then you will open the Report 2 document and use synchronous scrolling to pinpoint the differences in the two documents.

To examine two sections of the document in one window:

1. Press the **Ctrl+Home** keys to move the insertion point to the beginning of the Broadband Report document.
2. Click the **View** tab. The Window group on the View tab contains several buttons that you can use to manipulate the document window for one or more documents. The Split button allows you to divide the current document window in two, so you can display two different parts of the same document at once.
3. In the Window group, click the **Split** button. A gray horizontal line appears in the document window with the mouse pointer, which changed to ÷, positioned on the line.
4. Without clicking the mouse button, move the pointer up and down in the window. The line moves with the pointer.
5. Move the pointer to the middle of the document window, and then click. The window is split into two, with two separate vertical scroll bars that you can use to scroll to different parts of the document.
6. In the bottom window, scroll down to display the chart in the "3.1. Demographics" heading and the pie chart. See Figure 10-34. Note that what you see in the bottom window is part of the same document that you see in the top window.

TIP

You can also click the New Window button in the Window group on the View tab to open a new window showing the same document. You can then edit this document from either window.

Figure 10-34 **Document window split into two sections**

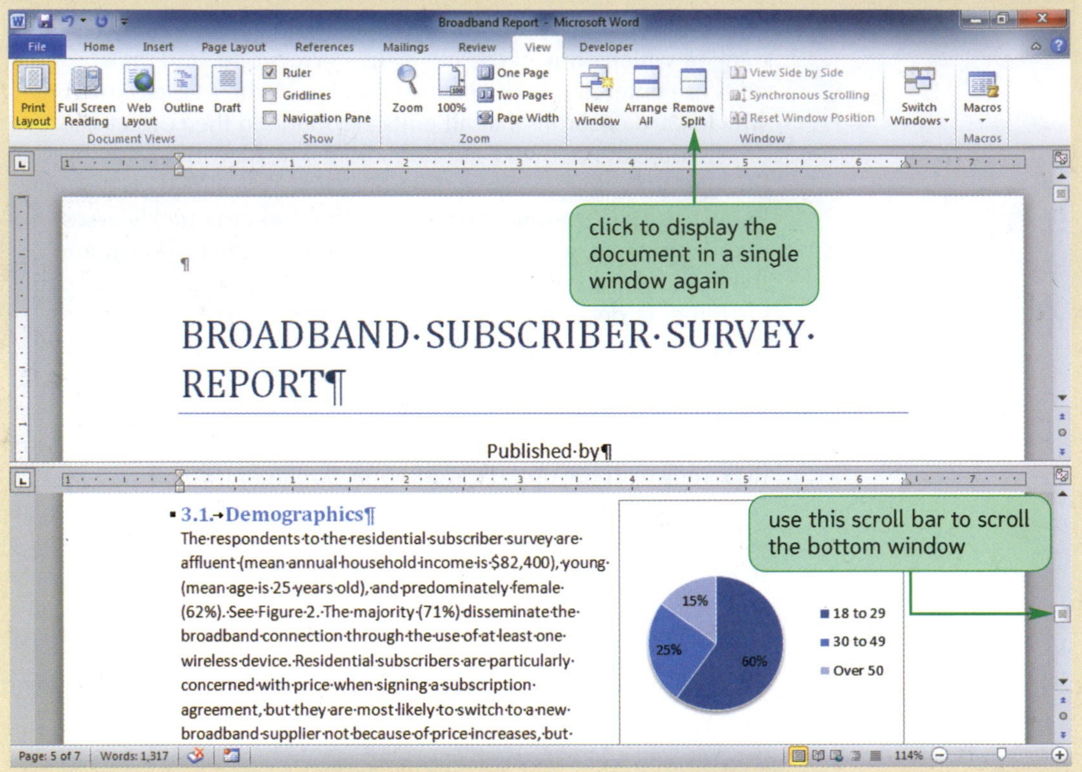

7. In the Window group on the View tab, click the **Remove Split** button to display the document in a single window again.

Synchronous scrolling is turned on by default when you display documents side by side. When the document windows are displayed side by side, you see one larger button for each group on the Ribbon, except for the Document Views group. To access the buttons in a group, click the group's button.

To display the two documents side-by-side and use synchronous scrolling:

1. Open the document **Report 2** from the Word10\Tutorial folder included with your Data Files.
2. In the Report 2 document window, click the **View** tab, and then click the **View Side by Side** button in the Window group. The documents are displayed side by side. See Figure 10-35.

   Trouble? If the documents are displayed one on top of the other, click the Reset Window Position button in the Window group on the View tab.

Figure 10-35 Two documents displayed side by side

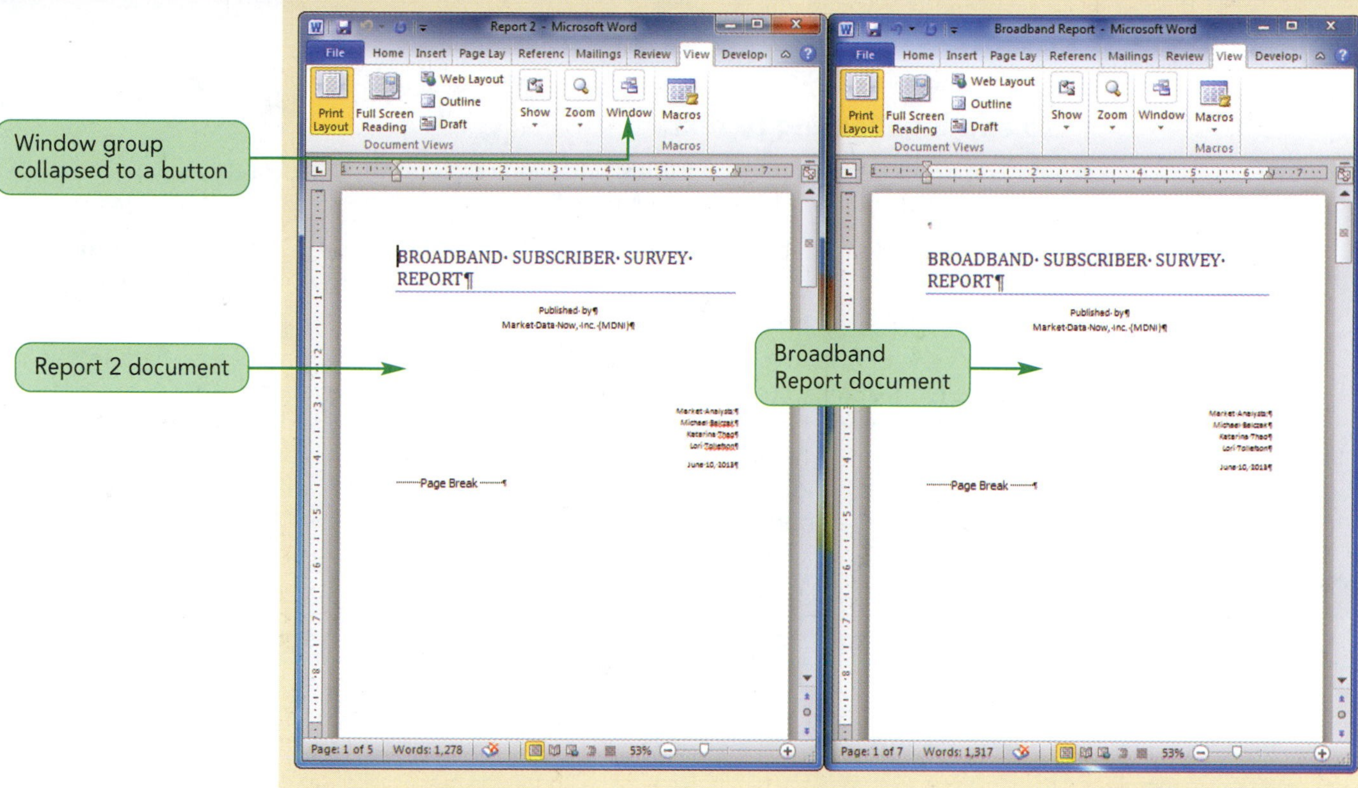

3. In the Report 2 window, drag the scroll box in the vertical scroll bar to scroll down to the "3.1. Demographics" section on page 3. Because synchronous scrolling is turned on, both documents scroll simultaneously. The text is a little small to read easily.
4. In the Report 2 window, increase the zoom to 80%. The zoom level increases in the Broadband Report window as well. In order to see the chart and the text next to it at the same time, you can stack, or tile, the document windows on top of each other.
5. In the Report 2 window, click the **Window** button to display the Window group. Notice that the Synchronous Scrolling button is selected.
6. Click the **Arrange All** button. The windows change so that one is stacked horizontally on top of the other.
7. Scroll the Report 2 document so that you can see the heading "3.1 Demographics" in both windows.
8. In the Report 2 window title bar, click the **Close** button [X]. The Report 2 document closes, and the Broadband Report document window is maximized again.

TIP

If more than two documents are open when you click the View Side by Side button, the Compare Side by Side dialog box opens so you can select the document you want to compare.

Michael does not want to change the pie chart in his document to a column chart, but he wants you to add color to this section so he remembers to check the data in the chart. He asks you to add **highlighting**—that is, a bar of color that looks as if you drew a line over the text with a highlighting pen.

To add highlighting to text:

1. Change the zoom to Page Width, and then scroll down, if necessary, so you can see the section "3.1 Demographics."
2. Click the **Home** tab, click the **Text Highlight Color** button in the Font group, and then move the pointer into the document window anywhere over the text. The pointer changes to .
3. Drag the pointer over the heading **Demographics** and the paragraph mark in this line. Notice that you can't drag the highlighting pointer over the number in front of the heading because it is added automatically; it is not text that you typed into the document. The heading is highlighted in yellow. See Figure 10-36. Michael decides to highlight the figure reference instead because that's what he wants to check, not the entire section.

Figure 10-36 Text highlighted in yellow

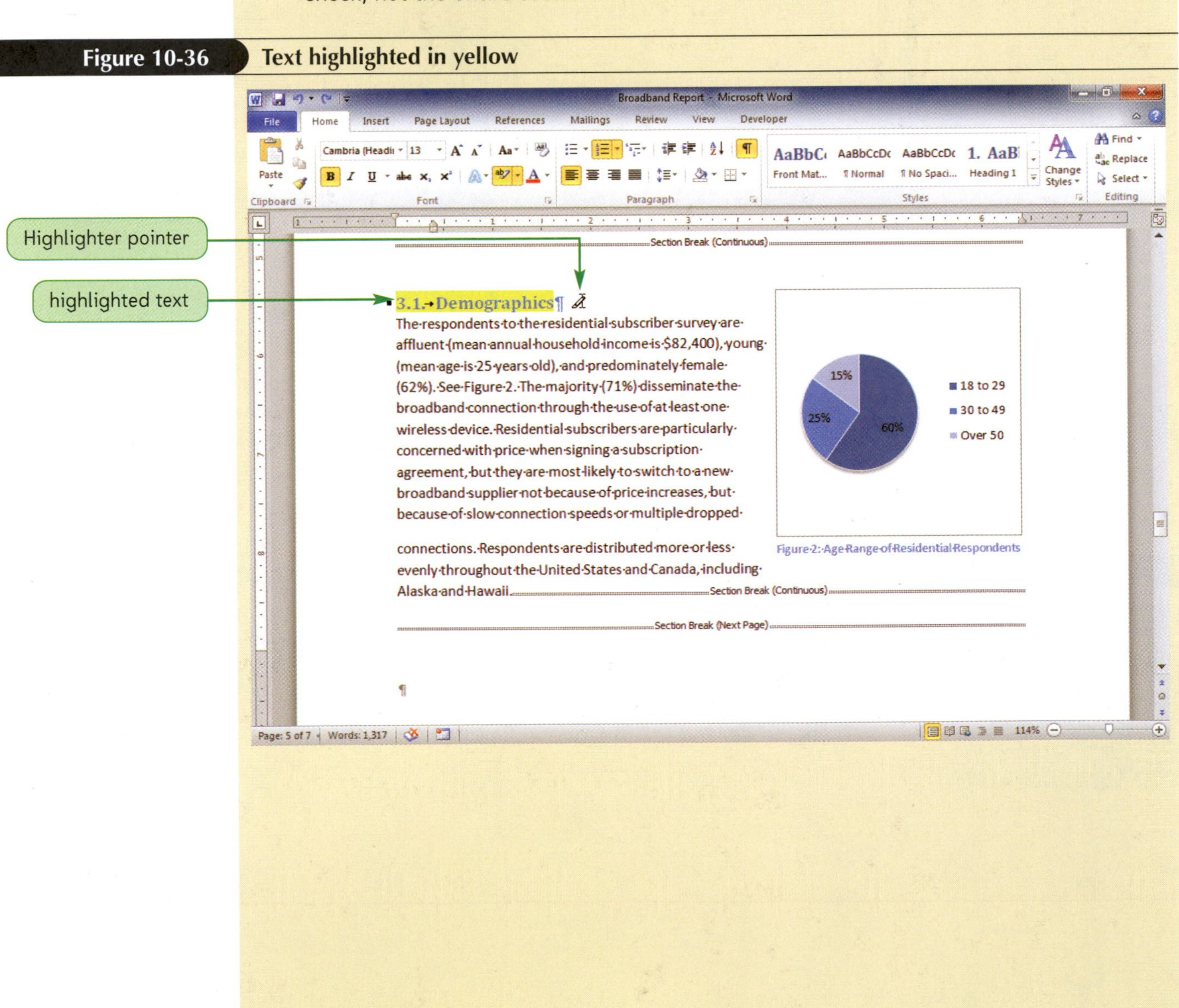
Broadband Report - Microsoft Word
File
Home
Insert
Page Layout
References
Mailings
Review
View
Developer
Highlighter pointer
highlighted text
Section Break (Continuous)
3.1. Demographics
The respondents to the residential subscriber survey are affluent (mean annual household income is $82,400), young (mean age is 25 years old), and predominately female (62%). See Figure 2. The majority (71%) disseminate the broadband connection through the use of at least one wireless device. Residential subscribers are particularly concerned with price when signing a subscription agreement, but they are most likely to switch to a new broadband supplier not because of price increases, but because of slow connection speeds or multiple dropped connections. Respondents are distributed more or less evenly throughout the United States and Canada, including Alaska and Hawaii.
15%
25%
60%
18 to 29
30 to 49
Over 50
Figure 2: Age Range of Residential Respondents
Section Break (Continuous)
Section Break (Next Page)
Page: 5 of 7
Words: 1,317
114%

4. In the paragraph below the heading "3.1. Demographics," drag the pointer over the sentence **See Figure 2** to highlight it in yellow. Now you can remove the highlighting from the heading.
5. In the Font group, click the **Text Highlight Color button arrow** to open a palette of highlight colors, and then click **No Color**.
6. Drag over the heading **Demographics** and the paragraph mark in this line. The highlighting is removed from the heading. Now you can turn off the highlighting tool.
7. In the Font group, click the **Text Highlight Color** button. The button becomes deselected and the pointer changes back to its usual shape.
8. Save the document.

In this session, you added advanced elements to a document, including automatically numbered headings and figure captions and cross-references. You also created an Excel chart from within the document, and then you protected the document and checked it to make sure it is accessible to all readers. Finally, you examined two similar documents side by side using synchronous scrolling. In the next session, you will modify a table of contents, create a table of figures, and create an index. You will also check it for compatibility with earlier versions of Word, encrypt the document, and mark it as final.

REVIEW

Session 10.2 Quick Check

1. True or False. When you open a master document that has one or more subdocuments, Word also displays the subdocuments within the master document.
2. Explain how to add automatic numbering to section titles in a master document.
3. What button do you use to insert a figure caption?
4. True or False. When you use the Chart button in the Illustrations group on the Insert tab to create a chart, you can create only pie charts.
5. Suppose you want to include the text "(See Figure 3)" in a report and you want to make sure the figure number is automatically renumbered, if necessary, to reflect additions or deletions of figures in the document. What should you do?
6. What kind of editing restrictions can you specify when protecting a document?
7. Explain how to start the Document Inspector.

SESSION 10.3 VISUAL OVERVIEW

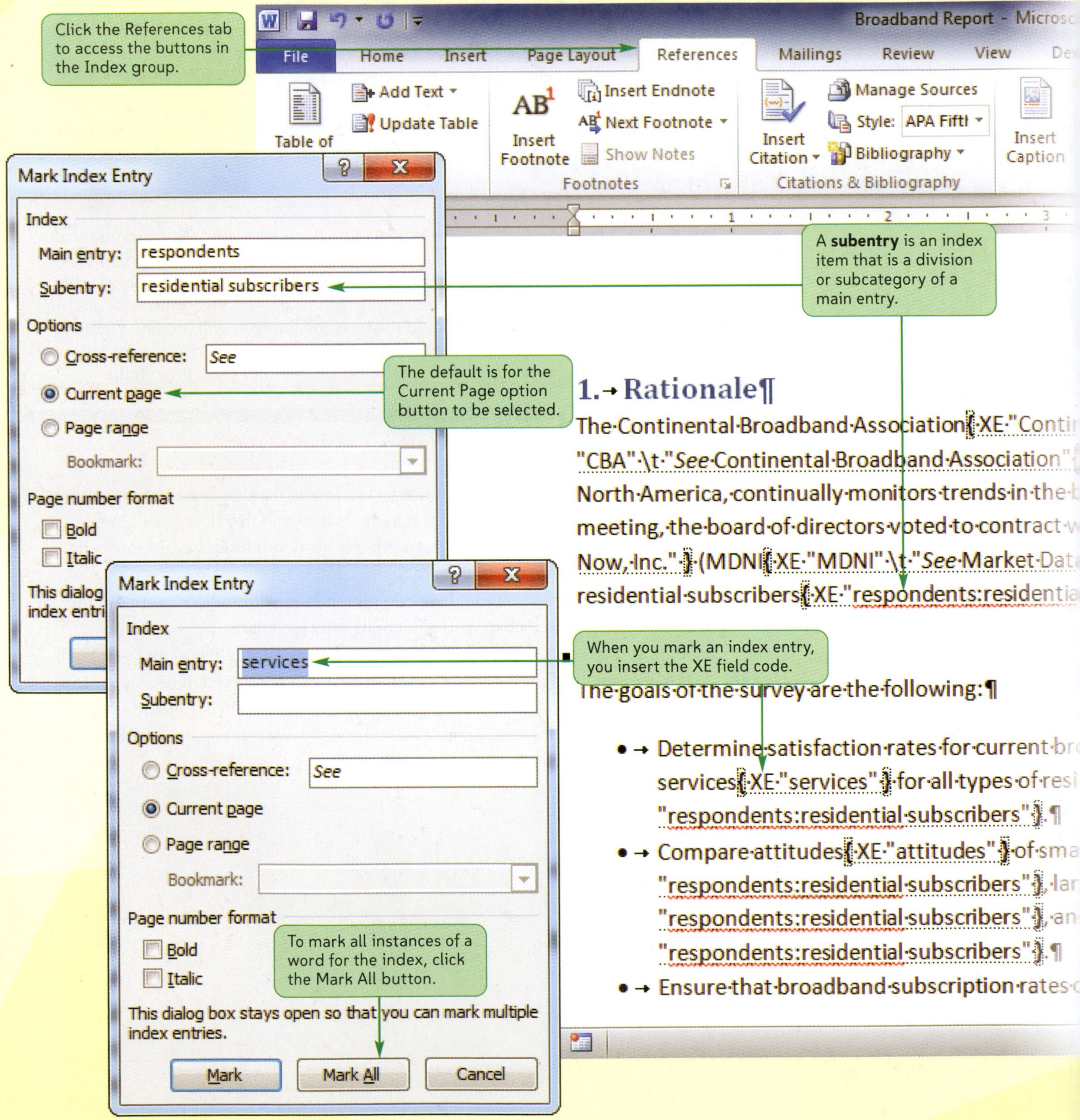

Click the References tab to access the buttons in the Index group.
A subentry is an index item that is a division or subcategory of a main entry.
The default is for the Current Page option button to be selected.
When you mark an index entry, you insert the XE field code.
To mark all instances of a word for the index, click the Mark All button.
Mark Index Entry
Main entry: respondents
Subentry: residential subscribers
Main entry: services
This dialog box stays open so that you can mark multiple index entries.
Mark
Mark All
Cancel
1. Rationale
The goals of the survey are the following:

INDEXING A DOCUMENT

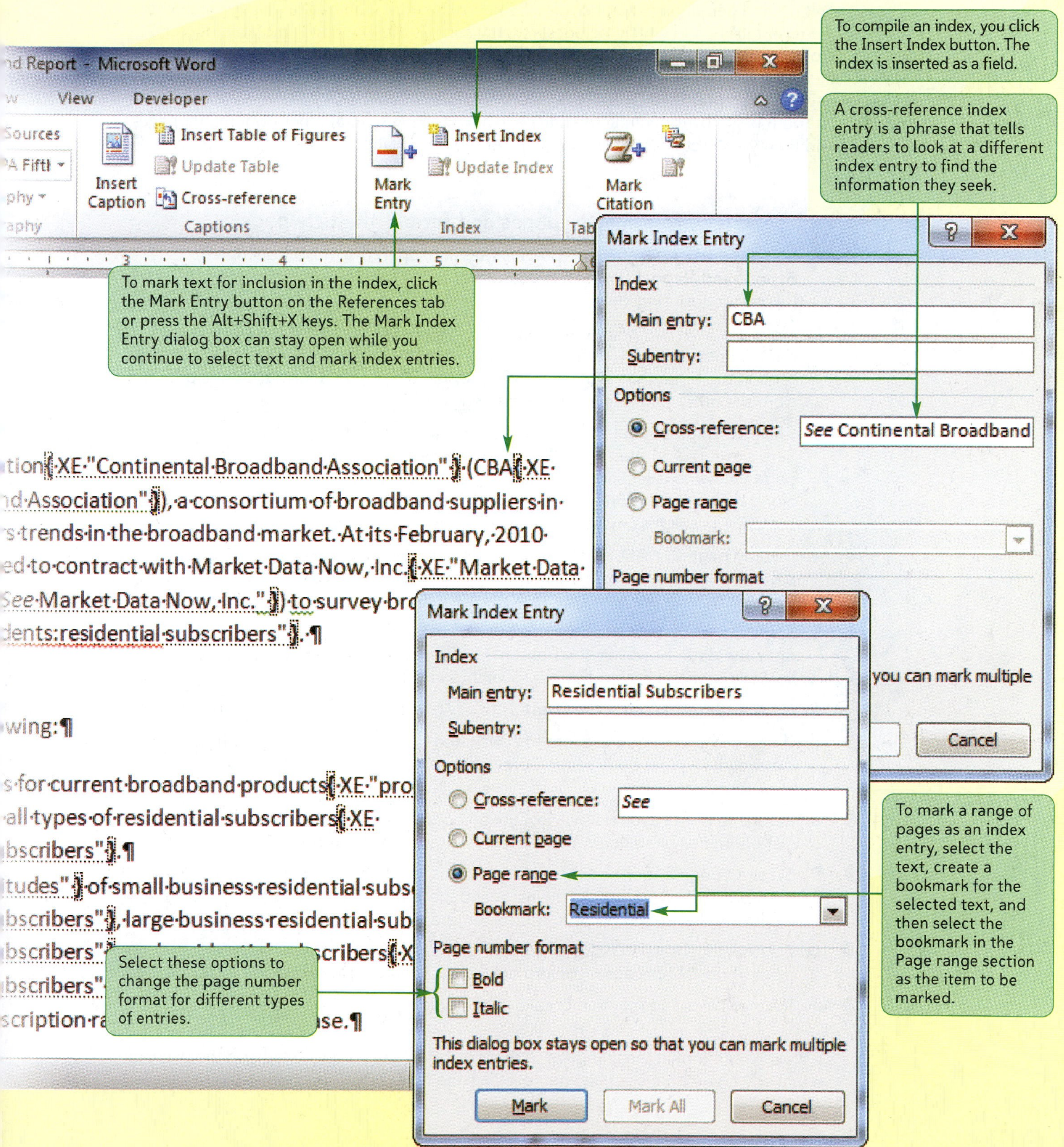

To compile an index, you click the Insert Index button. The index is inserted as a field.
A cross-reference index entry is a phrase that tells readers to look at a different index entry to find the information they seek.
To mark text for inclusion in the index, click the Mark Entry button on the References tab or press the Alt+Shift+X keys. The Mark Index Entry dialog box can stay open while you continue to select text and mark index entries.
To mark a range of pages as an index entry, select the text, create a bookmark for the selected text, and then select the bookmark in the Page range section as the item to be marked.
Select these options to change the page number format for different types of entries.
Mark Index Entry
Index
Main entry: CBA
Subentry:
Options
Cross-reference: See Continental Broadband
Current page
Page range
Bookmark:
Page number format
Mark Index Entry
Main entry: Residential Subscribers
Cross-reference: See
Page range
Bookmark: Residential
Bold
Italic
This dialog box stays open so that you can mark multiple index entries.
Mark
Mark All
Cancel
Insert Table of Figures
Update Table
Cross-reference
Insert Caption
Captions
Mark Entry
Insert Index
Update Index
Index
Mark Citation

Numbering Pages with Number Formats

Michael wants to add footers to the Broadband Report that include the name of the section and page numbers. Like most books, reports, and other long documents, the report will use a different page-numbering scheme for the front matter—the pages preceding the report itself, and which includes material such as the title page and table of contents. Front matter is usually numbered with lowercase Roman numerals (i, ii, iii,...), whereas the main sections of a report are numbered with Arabic numerals (1, 2, 3,...). The first page of the report itself typically begins with page number 1.

You'll begin by formatting the title page and creating several other front matter pages, and then you'll set up the page numbers for the front matter.

To insert new front matter pages and format the title page:

1. If you took a break after the previous session, open the master document **Broadband Report**, expand the subdocuments, switch to Print Layout view, and display nonprinting characters.
2. Move the insertion point to the end of page 1, immediately to the right of the date "June 10, 2013." Here you will delete the page break and insert a next page section break, so that you can format the title page with a format that is different from the other pages in the front matter.
3. Click the **Page Layout** tab on the Ribbon, click the **Breaks** button in the Page Setup group, and then click **Next Page** under Section Breaks. Word inserts a new page following a section break, and the insertion point moves to the new page, along with the Page Break line that was originally on page 1. Next, you will delete the page break that moved to page 2.
4. Display **page 2**, make sure the insertion point is in the blank, right-aligned paragraph at the top of the page, and then press the **Delete** key three times. The page break and the blank paragraphs are deleted.
5. Scroll up to see the date on page 1. It doesn't look like there is a section break after the date. However, the Contents heading appears on page 2. You can verify that the section break is there by switching to Draft view.
6. On the status bar, click the **Draft** button. The document appears in Draft view.
7. If necessary, change the zoom to 100%, and then scroll to the top of the document. A Next Page section break appears below the date and above the "Contents" heading.
8. Return to Print Layout view. Now you need to change the page break after the List of Figures heading on page 3 to a Next Page section break.
9. Scroll to page 3, position the insertion point in front of the Page Break, and then press the **Delete** key. The manual page break is deleted, and the heading "1. Rationale" moves up onto the current page.
10. Position the insertion point in front of "Rationale." You will not be able to click in front of the "1" because it is formatted as a numbered list.
11. Insert a Next Page section break.

Next, you'll format the title page so that the text is centered vertically on the page and so that when you do insert page numbers, a page number will not appear on this page.

To center the title page text vertically on the page and set the first page to hide page numbers:

1. Press the **Ctrl+Home** keys to position the insertion point on page 1 (the title page).
2. In the Page Setup group on the Page Layout tab, click the **Dialog Box Launcher**. The Page Setup dialog box opens.
3. Click the **Layout** tab, click the **Vertical alignment** arrow, and then click **Center**. Notice that "This section" appears in the Apply to box in the Preview section of the dialog box. This tells Word that you want the text in this section (which consists only of the title page) to be centered between the top and bottom margins. Now you need to specify that the first page in this section (that is, the title page) will not include a page number later, when you add page numbers to the rest of the document.
4. Under "Headers and footers," click the **Different first page** check box to select it. See Figure 10-37.

TIP

You can also click the Different First Page check box in the Options group on the Header & Footer Tools Design tab.

Figure 10-37 Layout tab in the Page Setup dialog box set to align text vertically on the page

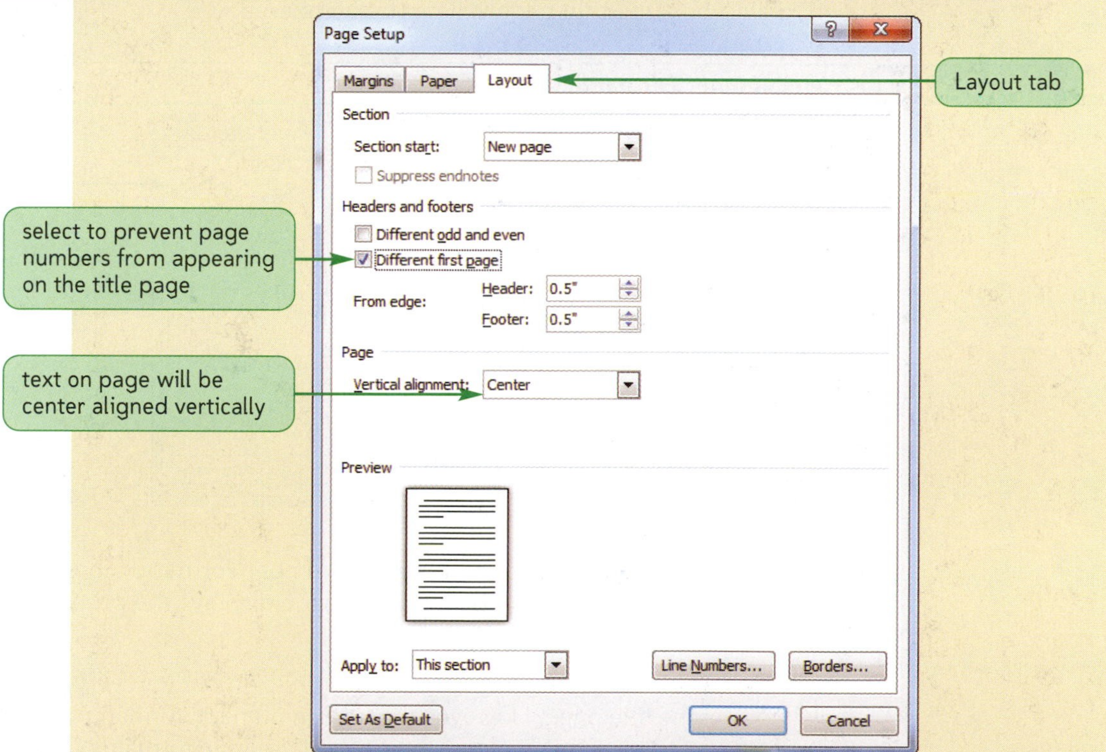

5. Click the **OK** button, and then change the zoom to **One Page**. The text on the title page is centered vertically on the page.

Now you're ready to set up the page numbering for the front matter (that is, the title page, table of contents, and list of figures). You'll start by inserting a page number using one of the default page number styles. Then you will format the page numbers as lowercase Roman numerals (i, ii, iii, etc.).

To set up page numbers for the front matter:

1. Switch back to Page Width view, scroll to page 2, and then position the insertion point to the left of the "Contents" heading.
2. Click the **Insert** tab on the Ribbon, click the **Page Number** button in the Header & Footer group, point to **Bottom of Page**, and then click **Plain Number 3**. The document switches to Header and Footer view, the Header & Footer Tools Design tab is displayed, and a page number field is inserted on the right side of the footer.
3. In the Header & Footer group, click the **Page Number** button, and then click **Format Page Numbers**. The Page Number Format dialog box opens. You want to change the format of the page numbers in this section to lowercase Roman numerals.
4. Click the **Number format** arrow, and then click **i, ii, iii, ...** . You want the page numbering to start at 1 (or i).
5. In the Page numbering section, click the **Start at** option button. The Roman numeral one (i) is displayed in the Start at box. See Figure 10-38. Because you clicked the Different first page check box on the Layout tab in the Page Setup dialog box, the title page will not be numbered.

Figure 10-38 Page Number Format dialog box

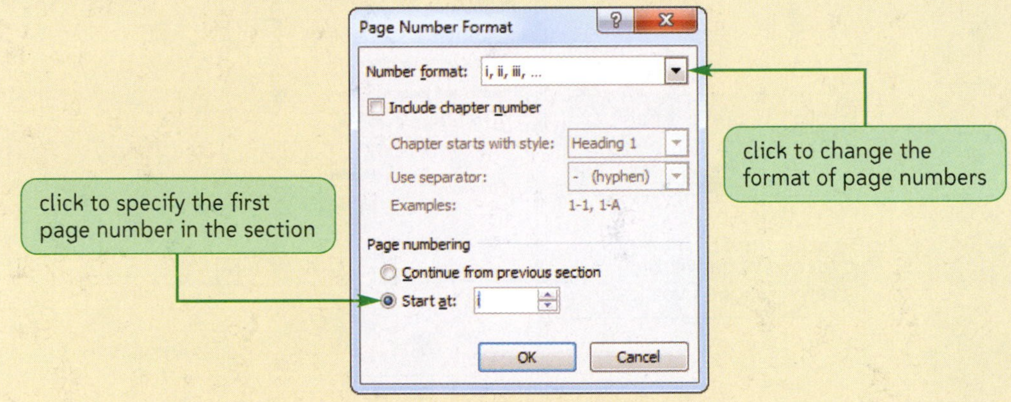

6. Click the **OK** button to close the Page Number Format dialog box. The page number field in the footer on the Contents page displays the page number "i."

The page numbers you just inserted appear in the footer of every page in the document except the title page. However, the Roman numeral format was only applied to the current section. The page numbers in the report itself are formatted to use Arabic numerals (1, 2, 3). The first page of the report (which contains the heading "1. Rationale") is currently numbered as page 3. In the next steps, you will set up the page number so the page is numbered page 1.

To set up the page numbers for the second section to begin with 1:

1. While still in Header and Footer view, scroll down until you can see the page numbered 3, in the footer for Section 3. This is the first page of the report itself.
2. Click the **3** page number to select the page number field, and then, in the Navigation group, click the **Link to Previous** button to deselect it.

3. In the Header & Footer group, click the **Page Number** button, and then click **Format Page Numbers** to open the Page Number Format dialog box. In the Number format list, "1, 2, 3, ..." is selected. Next, you need to indicate that you want this section to begin with page number 1.
4. Click the **Start at** option button in the Page numbering section to select it. The Arabic numeral one (1) appears in the Start at box.
5. Click the **OK** button to close the dialog box, and then scroll down to view the footers in the rest of the document. The numbering starts with page 1 on the page containing the heading "1. Rationale" and proceeds consecutively through the document.
6. Close Header and Footer view, and save the document.

You have set up the page numbering for the master document. Next you will work on the footer for the document.

Changing the Footer and Page Layout for Odd and Even Pages

Most professionally produced books and reports are printed on both sides of the paper and then bound. The blank space on the inside of each page, where the pages are bound together, is called the **gutter**. When you open a bound book or report, odd-numbered pages appear on the right, and even-numbered pages appear on the left. Often, the headers and footers for odd-numbered pages have text that is different from the headers or footers for the even-numbered pages.

Michael wants to follow these standards in the Broadband Report. Specifically, he wants you to use the page layouts shown in Figure 10-39.

Figure 10-39 **Page setup for odd and even pages**

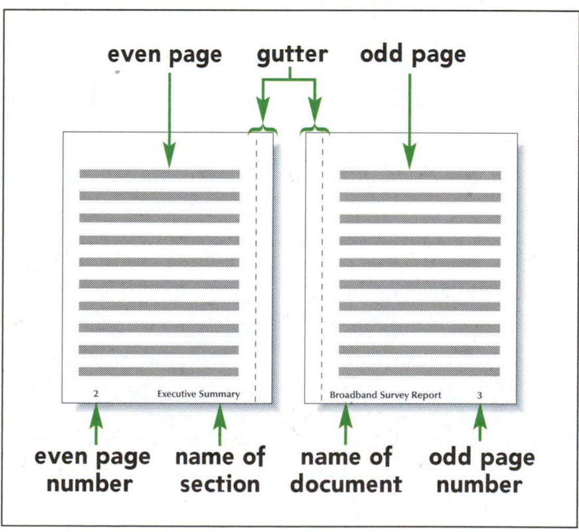

To do this, you'll use the following guidelines:

- Set the gutter to one-half inch. This will cause Word to shift the text on odd pages to the right (one-half inch in this case), leaving a wider margin on the left, and to shift the text on even pages to the left (again, one-half inch), leaving a wider margin on the right. When the even and odd pages are printed back-to-back (in a printing format called **two-sided printing**), the gutters line up on the same edge of the paper, thus leaving room for the binding.
- Change the location for page numbers so it's different on odd and even pages. In a page layout that distinguishes between odd and even pages, the page numbers are usually printed near the outside edge of the page rather than near the gutter to make them easier to see in a bound copy. On odd pages, the page numbers appear on the right; on even pages, the numbers appear on the left.
- Enter different text for the footers on odd and even pages. In many books, the section title is included in the header or footer of odd pages; at the same time, the book or chapter title is included in the header or footer of even pages. Sometimes this text is shifted toward the gutter (just as page numbers are shifted toward the outer edge). MDNI's standard style is for the odd-page footers to include the document title (for example, "Broadband Report") and the even-page footers to include the section title (for example, "Residential") closer to the gutter.

First, you'll change the page setup in the master document to distinguish between odd and even page footers, and then you'll increase the size of the gutter to allow enough room to bind the report without obscuring any text. To make these changes, you'll use the Page Setup dialog box.

To change the page setup in the report for printing odd and even pages:

1. On the second page of the document (numbered page i, with the heading "Contents"), position the insertion point before the heading "Contents," click the **Page Layout** tab, and then click the **Dialog Box Launcher** in the Page Setup group to open the Page Setup dialog box.
2. Click the **Margins** tab, and then change the setting in the Gutter box to **0.5"**.
3. Click the **Layout** tab, and then click the **Different odd and even** check box in the Headers and footers section. This allows you to enter page numbers and text differently in odd and even pages.
4. Click the **Apply to** arrow, and then click **This point forward**. Now, these options apply to the remainder of the report.
5. Click the **OK** button. The Page Setup dialog box closes. Now the footers on the odd pages of the document will differ from those on the even pages. This change doesn't affect the title page, however, because you selected "This point forward" in Step 4. Because you set the gutter to .5-inch with odd and even pages formatted differently, the body text on each page has shifted.
6. Scroll through the document to see that the body text on odd pages (for example, the Contents page) is shifted to the right; in other words, the left margin has increased in width, but the right margin remains the same. Conversely, on the even pages (for example, the List of Figures page) the body is shifted to the left; in other words, the left margin remains the same, and the right margin has increased. You no longer see the page number on the even page. You will fix this problem next, when you edit the footers.
7. Change the zoom to **Two Pages**, and then scroll so you can see pages 1 and 2.

TIP

The page number in the status bar reflects the total number of consecutive pages in the document, not the page number schemes created for document sections.

The title page appears on the left side of the window, and the Contents page appears on the right. The title page is the first page in the document, but the second page is numbered i. The title page can't be an even page (a left page)—the first page of a report formatted for odd and even pages is always a left page. However, you do not need to adjust this, as Word fixes it automatically. To see this, you'll look at the document in the preview that appears on the Print tab in Backstage view.

To examine the document on the Print tab in Backstage view:

1. Click anywhere on page 1 (the title page), click the **File** tab, and then click the **Print** tab in the navigation bar. The title page of the document appears in the preview area of the Print tab.
2. Use the Zoom slider to zoom out until you can see the first three pages of the document. See Figure 10-40.

Figure 10-40 Blank page automatically added after title page

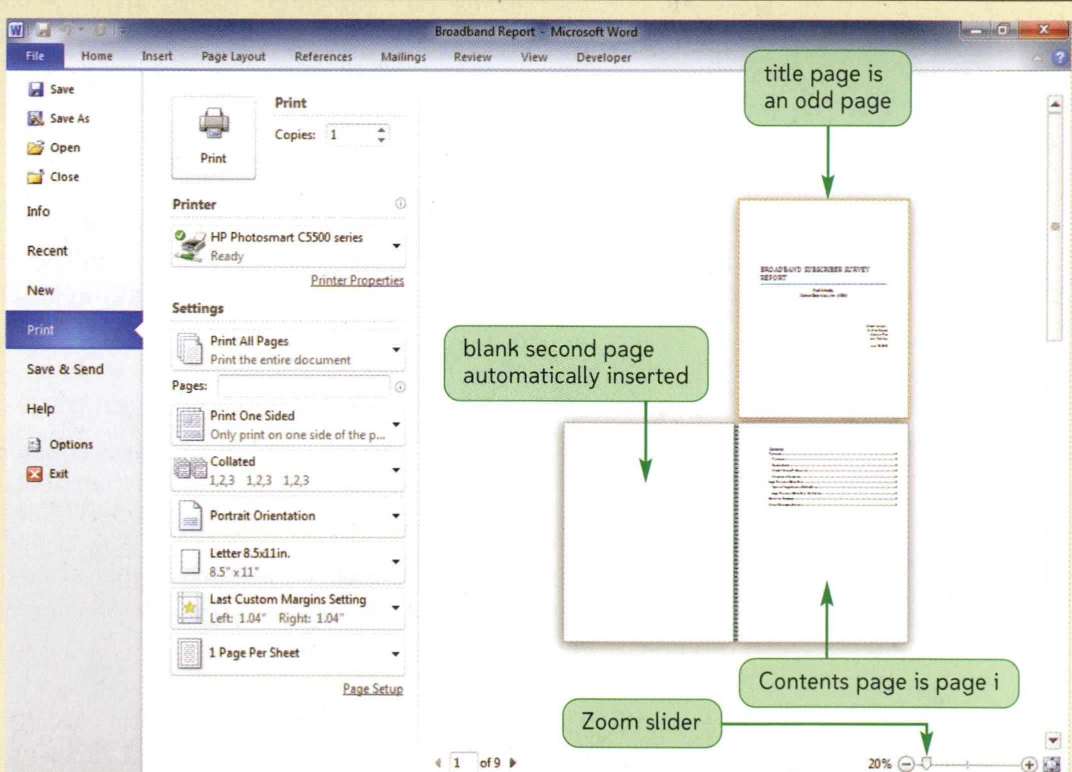

The title page appears on the right side of the first row of pages. This is because the title page is an odd-numbered page, belonging on the right. In the second row, a blank page appears on the left side and the Contents (page i) appears on the right. This is because you set up the document for different odd and even pages, and then you set up the Contents page to be numbered with the odd number i. The title page, which isn't numbered, is still the first page in the document, and so is considered by Word to be an odd page. However, you can't have two odd-numbered pages in a row (the margins, gutter spacing, and footer text would be off), so Word inserted a blank, even-numbered page between the title page and the Contents page. Note that you can't see this blank page in Print Layout view, but the total page count in the status bar includes this blank page.

3. Click the **File** tab to close Backstage view, and then click anywhere on the page containing the Contents heading. The page count in the lower-left corner of the document window tells you that this is page 3 of the document.
4. Click anywhere in the title page of the document. The page count in the lower-left corner of the document window tells you that this is page 1 of the document.

INSIGHT

Reviewing Your Document on the Print tab in Backstage View

The blank page after the title page, which you saw on the Print tab in Backstage view, is not visible in Print Layout view. Nevertheless, it is part of the document, and when you print the document your printer will include a blank page after the title page. This is exactly what you want in a document that will be printed on both sides of each page; the blank page ensures that the back of the title page remains blank. If the document did not include this blank page, then the Contents page would be printed on the back of the title page, turning the Contents page (which is set up to be an odd page) into an even page. The remaining odd and even pages would also be reversed. This significant difference between the appearance of the document on the Print tab in Backstage view and Print Layout view underscores the importance of reviewing your documents occasionally on the Print tab to make sure they will look the way you want when printed.

Now that you have specified that odd and even pages will be set up differently, you can add footer text and format page numbering differently in the odd and even footers.

To format footers differently for odd and even pages:

1. Change the zoom to **Page Width**, scroll to display the footer area of the second page in the document—the Contents page—and then double-click the footer area to open Header and Footer view. The label "Odd Page Footer –Section 2–" appears on the left side of the footer area, and the insertion point is to the left of the page number. This is the odd page footer in the second section of the document. In the right margin, the footer contains the page number "i." Because this is an odd page, you'll leave the page number at the right and insert the document name at the left.
2. Press the **Backspace** key twice to move the insertion point to the left margin. The page number field moves with the insertion point. You'll move it back to the right margin after you enter the document name.
3. With the insertion point at the left edge of the footer area, type **Broadband Report**, and then press the **Tab** key twice to move the page number field back to the right margin, where it is aligned at a right tab stop.
4. Scroll down to the next page until you can see the footer text box labeled "Even Page Footer -Section 2-". When you set up the document for even and odd pages, the page numbers on the even pages were removed. You'll reinsert the page number in this footer now.
5. Click the blank paragraph on the left side of the footer, click the **Page Number** button in the Header & Footer group, point to **Bottom of Page**, and then click **Plain Number 1**. A page number field appears above the blank paragraph, displaying the page number "ii."

6. In the Navigation group on the Header & Footer Tools Design tab, click the **Next** button to move the insertion point to the footer labeled "Odd Page Footer – Section 3," verify that the insertion point is located to the left of the page number field, press the **Backspace** key twice to move the insertion point to the left margin, type **Broadband Report**, press the **Tab** key twice to move the page number field back to the right margin, and then scroll down until you can see the even page footer at the bottom of the page containing the chart.

Next, you'll add the section titles to the even page footers.

Inserting a Style Reference into a Footer

In long reports, it's customary to have the even page footers display the section title on that page. For example, in an even page that includes the heading "2. Executive Summary," you would insert the heading "Executive Summary" in the footer. Rather than manually entering a heading in each footer, it's easier to have Word insert the proper text automatically using a style reference. A **style reference** is a field code that inserts text formatted with a particular style. Like many of the Word features you've used in this tutorial, style references are useful because they allow Word to update information automatically in one part of a document to reflect changes made in another part of a document.

Michael wants you to format the footer on each even page so it includes the Level 1 heading. To do this, you'll insert a style reference to the Heading 1 style. As a result of this style reference, the footer on each page will include the text of the first heading on a page that is formatted with the Heading 1 style. As the heading text for the various parts of the document changes only from one page to another, the heading text in the footer will change accordingly. Furthermore, if Michael changes a heading, the text in the footer will change as well.

To insert a style reference to the section title into the footer:

1. In the footer for the Even Page Footer –Section 3, click to the right of the page number field, if necessary, and then press the **Tab** key twice to position the insertion point at the right margin.
2. Click the **Insert** tab, click the **Quick Parts** button in the Text group, click **Field** to open the Field dialog box, click the **Categories** arrow, and then click **Links and References**.
3. In the Field names box, click **StyleRef** (an abbreviation of "style reference"). Next, you'll indicate the style to which the StyleRef field code should refer.
4. In the Style name box, click **Heading 1** (the style applied to the main headings in the document). See Figure 10-41.

Figure 10-41 Inserting a style reference to the Heading 1 style

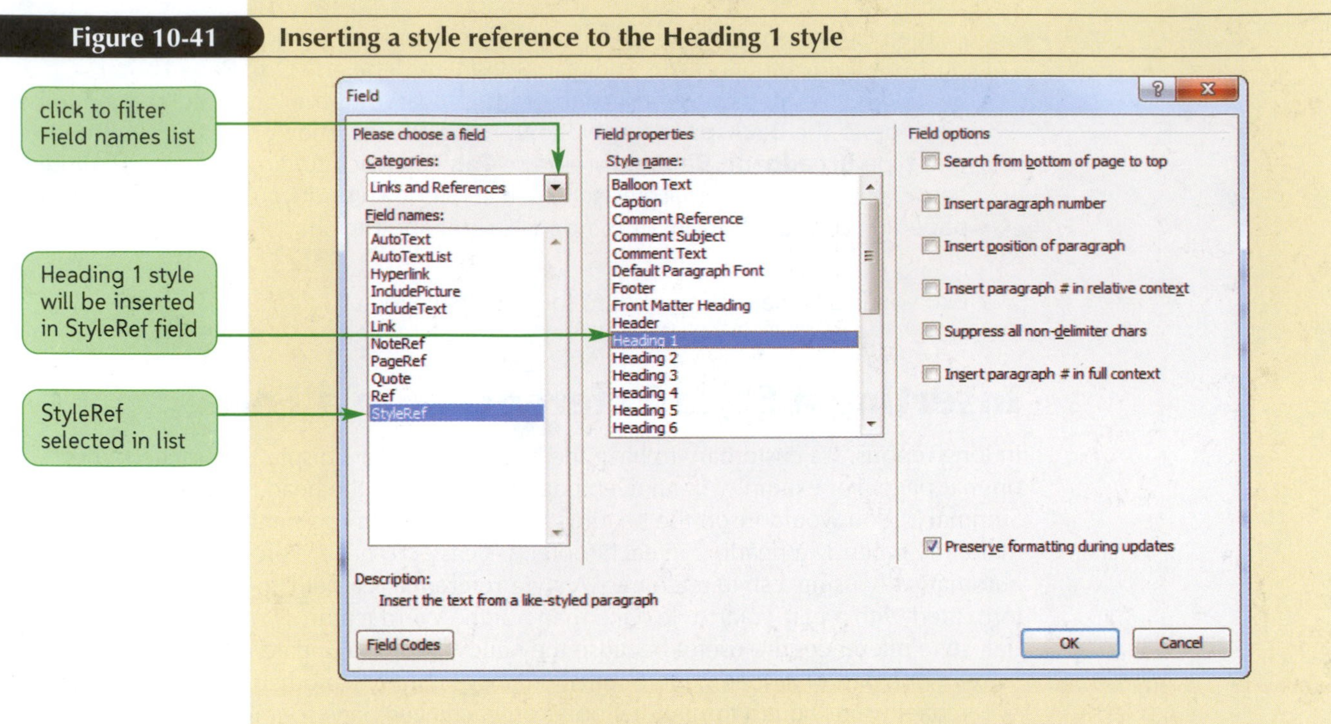

5. Click the **OK** button. The Field dialog box closes. The text "Executive Summary" appears in the footer, because that is the first heading on the page that is formatted with the Heading 1 style.
6. Scroll to the next even numbered page, which is numbered page 4, view the footer, and then scroll to page 6 to view the footer on that page.
7. Close Header and Footer view, and then save the document.

The report is now set up so Michael can print the document on both sides of the page. Next, you will create an index.

Creating an Index

TIP

It's a good idea to spend some time thinking about which topics and terms must be in your index before you start creating it.

Michael wants you to create an index to help readers locate specific information in the report. As you probably know, an index is a list of words and phrases (called entries) accompanied by the page numbers on which they appear in a printed document. For example, if customers want information on "competition," they should be able to look in the index and find a list of all the pages on which the entry "competition" appears in the report.

Compiling an index by hand is tedious, time-consuming, and error-prone. It's also inefficient because if you insert, delete, or move text from one part of the document after you create the index, the page numbers might change. You would then have to go through the entire index again, making any necessary page number changes. On the other hand, once you set up an index using the Word Index feature, the page numbering is automatic, no matter how much you reorganize the document.

When you create an index with Word, you generate entries in one of three ways:

- Select a word or phrase and have Word mark every occurrence of that entry. This is fast, efficient, and accurate. It isn't, however, foolproof. For example, sometimes a portion of the document contains a particular topic that doesn't use the exact phrase you selected for the topic.

- Move the insertion point to the location where you want an entry, and insert an index entry.
- Select a range of pages, assign it a bookmark, and then mark the bookmarked pages as an index entry. This would result in an entry such as "business subscribers, 4–6" (where the 4–6 refers to the bookmarked range of pages).

You'll use all these methods as you create the index for the Broadband Report.

Marking Index Entries

When you mark an index entry, you select the word or phrase you want to appear in the index, and then use the Mark Index Entry dialog box to refine the entry. For example, you can specify that the text appears as the main entry, and then provide subentries related to it. That way, the index includes a main topic, such as "Broadband connections," with an indented list of associated subtopics, such as "cable modem" and "DSL." When you mark an index entry in your document, Word inserts a field code that appears if you display nonprinting characters. You can hide these codes if necessary after you finish marking entries.

To create the index for the Broadband Report, you'll start by marking the main entries for the index.

REFERENCE

Marking Index Entries and Subentries

- Select the word or phrase you want to mark as an index entry.
- Click the References tab, and then click the Mark Entry button in the Index group to open the Mark Index Entry dialog box; *or* press the Alt+Shift+X keys to open the Mark Index Entry dialog box.
- If necessary, type an index entry in the Main entry text box, and then, if desired, type an entry in the Subentry text box.
- Make sure the Current page option button in the Options section is selected.
- Click the Mark button to mark this occurrence, or click the Mark All button to mark every occurrence in the document.
- Click the Close button.

You'll start creating the index by selecting the first occurrence of a word or phrase that you want as a main index entry, and then telling Word to mark every occurrence of it throughout the document. The first entry you'll mark is "Canada."

To mark every occurrence of a main index entry:

1. Change the zoom to **Page Width**, use the Navigation pane to find the first occurrence of the word "Canada," select it, and then close the Navigation pane. The word "Canada" should be selected at the bottom of page 2 (page 6 in the Word document according to the status bar). Now you can add this word to the index.
2. Click the **References** tab, and then click the **Mark Entry** button in the Index group. The word you selected, "Canada," appears in the Main entry box of the Mark Index Entry dialog box, and the **Current page** option button is selected in the Options section of the dialog box. This ensures that the current page of this entry will appear in the index.
3. Click the **Mark All** button. Word searches your document for every occurrence of "Canada" and marks each as an index entry. In the document, you can see that Word has inserted the field code {XE "Canada"} next to the word "Canada." See Figure 10-42.

Figure 10-42 Marking an index entry

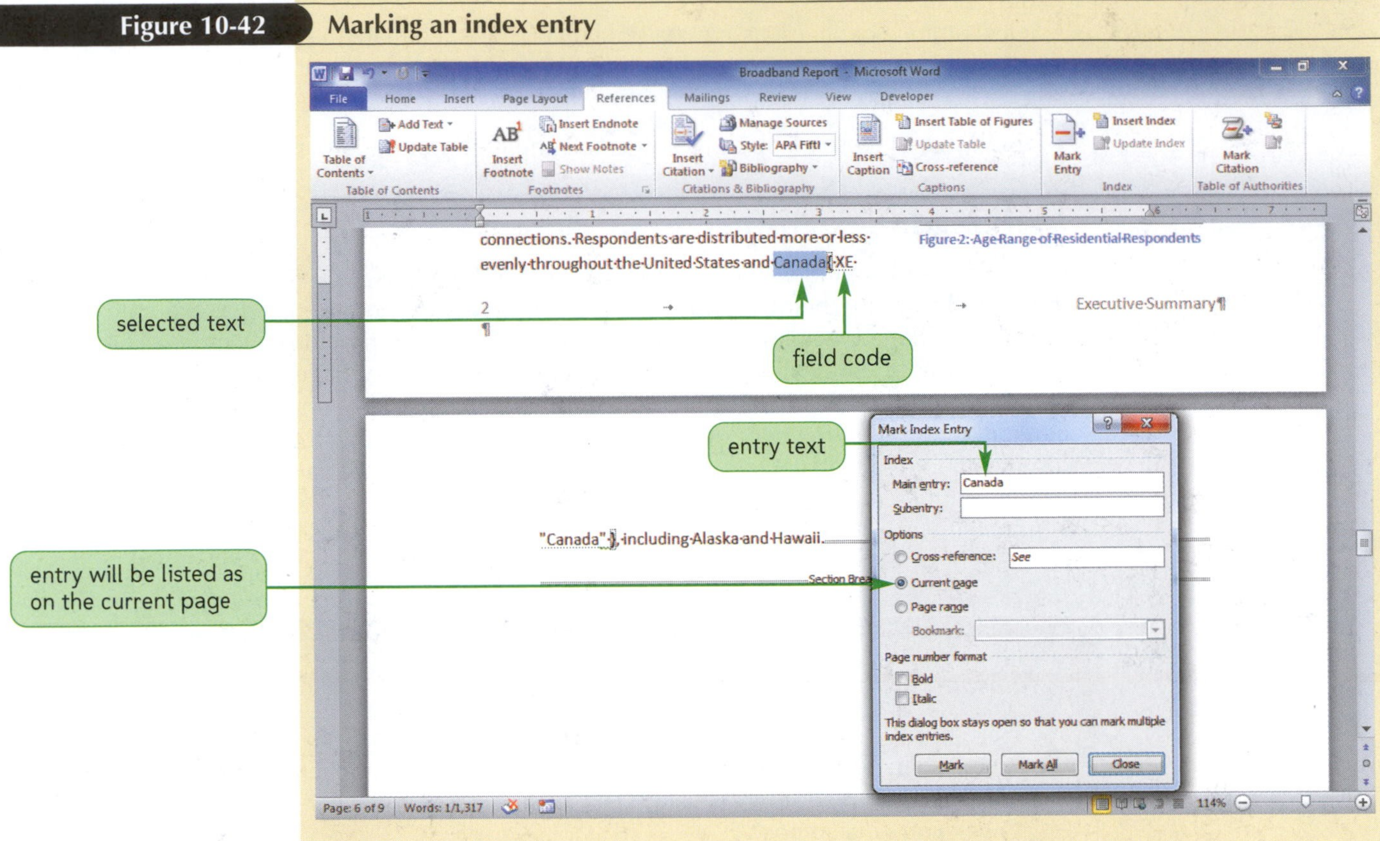

4. Close the Mark Index Entry dialog box to return to the document window.
5. Scroll down to the paragraph below the heading "4.1. Demographics." You see the field code {XE "Canada"} to the right of the word "Canada" in this paragraph.

Throughout the report, Word has marked "Canada" as an index entry. You'll mark a few more index entries now.

To mark additional index entries in the report:

1. Scroll up to display the first paragraph below the heading "1. Rationale."
2. In the first sentence of the paragraph, select the phrase **Continental Broadband Association**.
3. Press the **Alt+Shift+X** keys to open the Mark Index Entry dialog box, and then click the **Mark All** button. Word marks every occurrence of Continental Broadband Association with the XE field code.
4. Without closing the Mark Index Entry dialog box, click in the document window, and then select the phrase **Market Data Now, Inc.** in the same paragraph. If necessary, drag the dialog box out of the way to see the phrase, but don't close the dialog box.
5. Click the **Mark All** button in the Mark Index Entry dialog box. Even though the button was dimmed (because the document window is active, rather than the dialog box), Word immediately activates the dialog box and the button when you click the button, and marks the highlighted phrase throughout the report. The highlighted phrase now appears in the Main entry text box.

TIP

Entries marked for inclusion in an index are case sensitive, so if you mark "products" the word "Products" will not be included unless you mark it separately.

6. In the first bulleted item below the heading "1.1. Survey Goals," select the word **products**, and then click the **Mark All** button in the Mark Index Entry dialog box.
7. Repeat this procedure for the words **services** in the first bulleted item and **attitudes** in the second bulleted item. Leave the Mark Index Entry dialog box open.

Your index contains six entries so far, which is sufficient to demonstrate the power of this feature. If you were creating a full index for a complete document, you would continue to mark words and phrases as index entries. Instead, you'll add some subentries to the index.

Marking Subentries

A high-quality index contains subentries as well as main entries. In the Broadband Report, you'll create a main entry for "respondents" and subentries for "Residential Subscribers," "Small Business Subscribers," and "Large Business Subscribers."

To create subentries in an index:

1. Scroll down until you see the heading "1.3. Market Research Overview," and then select the phrase **small business subscribers** in the first sentence.
2. Click the **title bar** of the Mark Index Entry dialog box to make it active without marking an index entry.
3. Select the text in the **Main entry** box, type **respondents**, click in the **Subentry** box, and then type **small business subscribers**. This creates a main entry "respondents" with the subentry "small business subscribers."
4. Click the **Mark All** button. Word marks all occurrences of "small business subscribers" with the entry "respondents" and the subentry "small business subscribers."
5. Repeat Steps 1 through 4, except select the phrases **large business subscribers** and **residential subscribers** and create the index entries with "respondents" as the main entry and "large business subscribers" and "residential subscribers" as the subentries.
6. In the middle of the paragraph, select the word **respondents** in the phrase "to the three types of respondents," and then mark it as a main entry, without a subentry, for all occurrences of the word throughout the text. Do not close the Mark Index Entry dialog box.

You have marked several subentries for a main index entry. Next, you'll create a cross-reference index entry.

Creating Cross-Reference Index Entries

You can also create cross-reference index entries. For example, you've already marked "Continental Broadband Association" as an index entry, but what if someone looks up CBA? You'd want the index to read: *"CBA. See* Continental Broadband Association." The index you're creating for the Broadband Report includes two cross-references. You'll create them now.

To create a cross-reference index entry:

1. Scroll up to display the paragraph below the heading "1. Rationale" and then select the abbreviation **CBA**, located in parentheses in the first line of the paragraph.
2. In the Mark Index Entry dialog box, click the **title bar**.
3. With "CBA" as the main entry, click the **Cross-reference** option button in the Options section of the dialog box, click to the right of the word *See* in the box, if necessary, and then type **Continental Broadband Association**.
4. Click the **Mark** button. You can't click the Mark All button, because a cross-reference entry appears only once in the index and doesn't carry a page number. Now you'll create the "MDNI" cross-reference that tells readers to look up "Market Data Now, Inc." in the index.
5. In the paragraph below the heading "1. Rationale," select **MDNI** (in parentheses in the second-to-last line of the paragraph), and then mark it with a cross-reference to **Market Data Now, Inc.** Don't close the Mark Index Entry dialog box.

Next, you'll add an index entry that refers to a range of pages.

Creating an Index Entry for a Page Range

In addition to main entries and subentries that list individual pages, sometimes you'll want to include an index entry that refers to a range of pages, such as the range of pages for the Small Business section. In a case such as this, you need to insert a bookmark to the section you want to index.

REFERENCE

Creating a Page Range Index Entry

- Select a range of pages.
- Click the Insert tab, and then click the Bookmark button in the Links group.
- Type the name of the bookmark, and then click the Add button. The Bookmark dialog box closes.
- Make sure the Mark Index Entry dialog box is open, click the Page range option button, click the Bookmark arrow, and then click the bookmark name.
- Click the Mark button.

You need to create an index entry for the section "Residential Subscribers." This entry will span a range of pages.

To create an index entry with a reference to a range of pages:

1. Scroll until you see the heading "3. Residential Subscribers."
2. Switch to Outline view, select the entire "Residential Subscribers" section, including the "3.1 Demographics" subsection, and then show all outline levels.
3. Click the **Insert** tab, and then click the **Bookmark** button in the Links group to open the Bookmark dialog box.
4. Type **Residential** as the bookmark name, and then click the **Add** button to create a bookmark for the selected range of pages.
5. With the text still selected, click the **Page range** option button in the Mark Index Entry dialog box, click the **Bookmark** list arrow, and then click **Residential**.
6. Verify that **Residential Subscribers** appears in the Main entry box.
7. Click the **Mark** button to mark this index entry.
8. Select the entire section titled "4. Small Business Subscribers," including its subsections; assign it the bookmark **SmallBusiness** (all one word, no spaces), and then create a page range index entry with the main entry **Small Business Subscribers**.
9. Assign the section titled "Large Business Subscribers" the bookmark **LargeBusiness**, and then create a page range index entry with the main entry **Large Business Subscribers**. These sections don't span multiple pages now, but they will eventually, after Lori and Katarina add more text to them.
10. Close the Mark Index Entry dialog box, close Outline view, and then save the document.

Compiling an Index

After you mark all the desired index entries, subentries, cross-references, and page-range references, you're ready to **compile** the index—that is, you're ready to tell Word to generate the index using the marked entries. Most often, indexes appear at the end of books, reports, or long documents.

REFERENCE

Compiling an Index

- Move the insertion point to the location where you want to insert the index.
- Hide the field codes.
- Click the References tab, and then click the Insert Index button in the Index group.
- Select the desired options for controlling the appearance of the index.
- Click the OK button.

You'll compile the index on a new page at the end of the Broadband Report.

To compile the index:

1. Press the **Ctrl+End** keys, and then press the **Ctrl+Enter** keys to insert a page break below the last paragraph in the document.
2. Type **Index**, and then press the **Enter** key.
3. Format the Index heading with the **Front Matter Heading** style. Before you compile the index, you need to hide the field codes because by displaying them, the page count is changed.
4. Click the **Home** tab, if necessary, and then click the **Show/Hide** button ¶ in the Paragraph group to hide nonprinting characters and the field codes. You're ready to compile the index.

   Trouble? If the field codes remain visible, click the File tab, click Options, click Display, deselect the Hidden text check box, and then click OK.
5. Position the insertion point in the blank line below the Index heading, click the **References** tab, and then click the **Insert Index** button in the Index group to open the Index dialog box with the Index tab selected. "From template" appears in the Formats box, indicating that the index will be formatted using the document's template styles, and 2 appears in the Columns box, indicating that the index will be arranged in two columns.
6. Click the **OK** button. The dialog box closes and the index is compiled. See Figure 10-43.

Figure 10-43 Index for the Broadband Report document

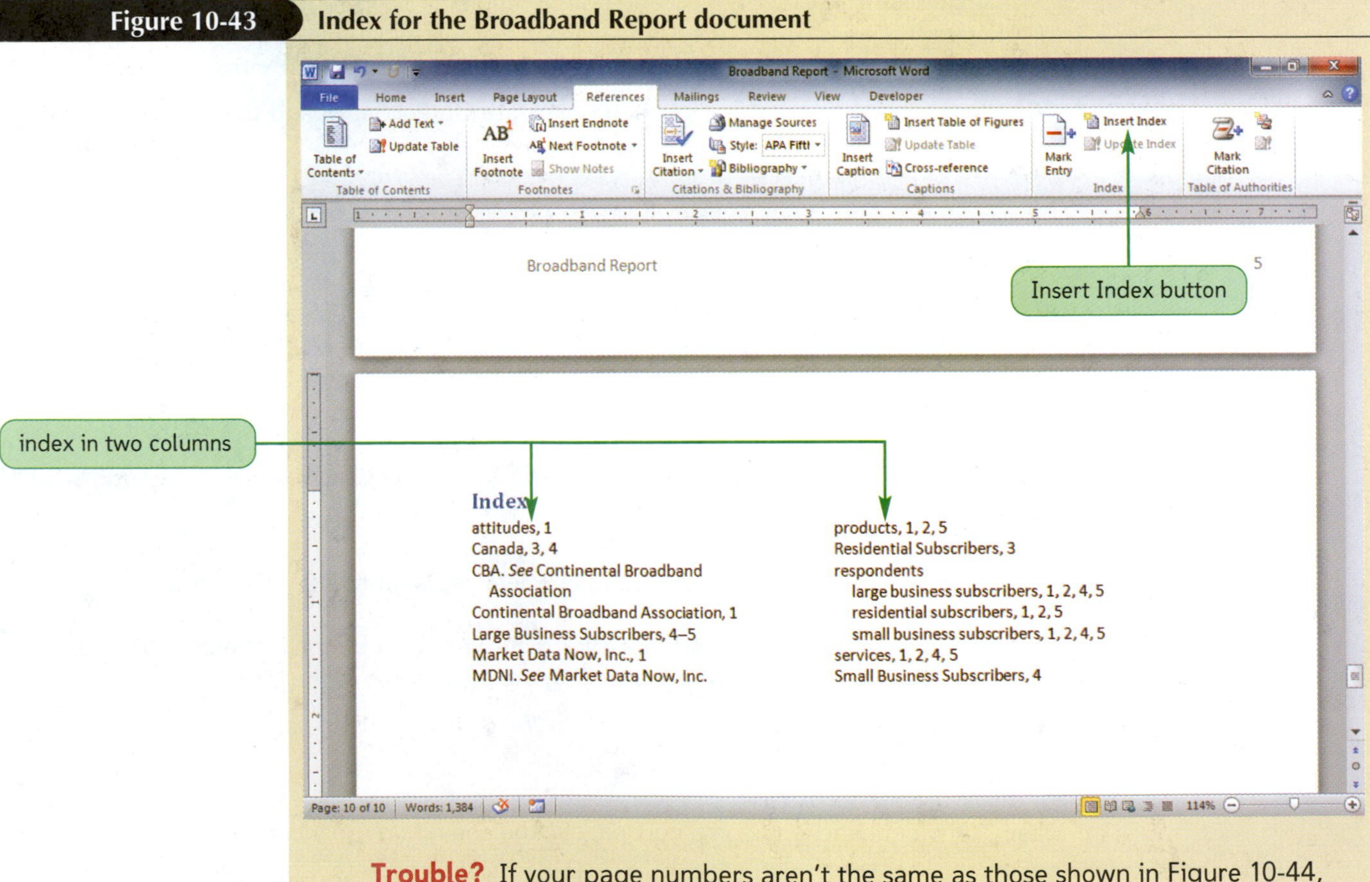

Trouble? If your page numbers aren't the same as those shown in Figure 10-44, don't worry—differences in printers can cause page numbering differences.

Your index is short but representative of the entries that would appear in a full index.

Updating an Index

After an index is compiled, you can still make changes to it, including adding new entries. Michael asks you to add one more entry to the index. You'll mark the entry, and then update the index to include the new entry.

To create a new index entry and then update the index:

1. Scroll up to see the last paragraph of the document, just above the index, select the term **e-businesses** in the last sentence, and then mark all occurrences of "e-businesses" as main index entries.
2. Close the Mark Index Entry dialog box, and then scroll down to display the index on the last page of the document.
3. Hide nonprinting characters, click anywhere in the index, click the **References** tab, and then click the **Update Index** button in the Index group. The e-businesses entry is added to the index.

Now you need to update the table of contents.

To update the table of contents:

1. Scroll up to page 2 in the document so that you can see the table of contents.
2. Click anywhere in the table of contents, and then click the **Update Table** button in the Table of Contents group on the References tab. The Update Table of Contents dialog box opens.
3. Click the **Update entire table** option button, and then click the **OK** button. The table of contents is updated to include the numbered headings and all of the other changes to headings that you made as you worked on the document.

Notice that the table of contents does not include the "Index" heading. When Michael created the table of contents using the Table of Contents Options dialog box, he specified that the text formatted with the Front Matter Heading style should not be included in the table of contents. Michael asks you to add a line below the table of contents that looks like it is part of the table of contents, but is really made up of the text "Index," a dot leader, and a page number field that displays the page number on which the "Index" heading is currently located.

To add an entry below the table of contents with a page field:

1. Scroll down to the "Index" heading on the last page of the document, select the **Index** heading, and then create a bookmark named **Index**.
2. Scroll back up to the table of contents, position the insertion point in the blank paragraph below the table of contents, and then type **Index**. Now you will insert a right tab stop with a dot leader that will align the page number for the Index section below the other page numbers in the table of contents.
3. Click the **Home** tab, and then in the Paragraph group, click the **Dialog Box Launcher** to open the Paragraph dialog box.
4. Click the **Tabs** button, and then type **5.9** in the Tab stop position box. This is the position of the page numbers in the table of contents. Now you need to specify that the tab stop is a right tab stop and that the dotted line leader appears.

5. In the Alignment section, click the **Right** option button, and then click the **2...** option button in the Leader section.
6. Click the **OK** button. The dialog box closes.
7. Press the **Tab** key. The insertion point moves to the right margin, and a row of dots appears to the right of the word "Index." Now you need to insert a page number field to display the page number of the Index bookmark.
8. Click the **Insert** tab on the Ribbon, click the **Quick Parts** button in the Text group, and then click **Field** to open the Field dialog box.
9. In the Field names list, click **PageRef**, click **Index** in the Bookmark name list, and then click the **OK** button. The dialog box closes and the page number field for the Index bookmark is inserted at the insertion point. The "Index" heading now appears to be included in the table of contents. See Figure 10-44.

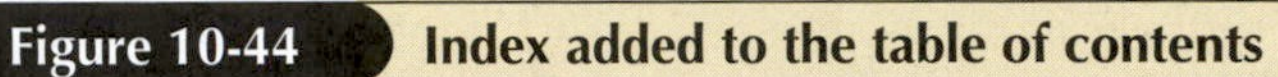

Figure 10-44 Index added to the table of contents

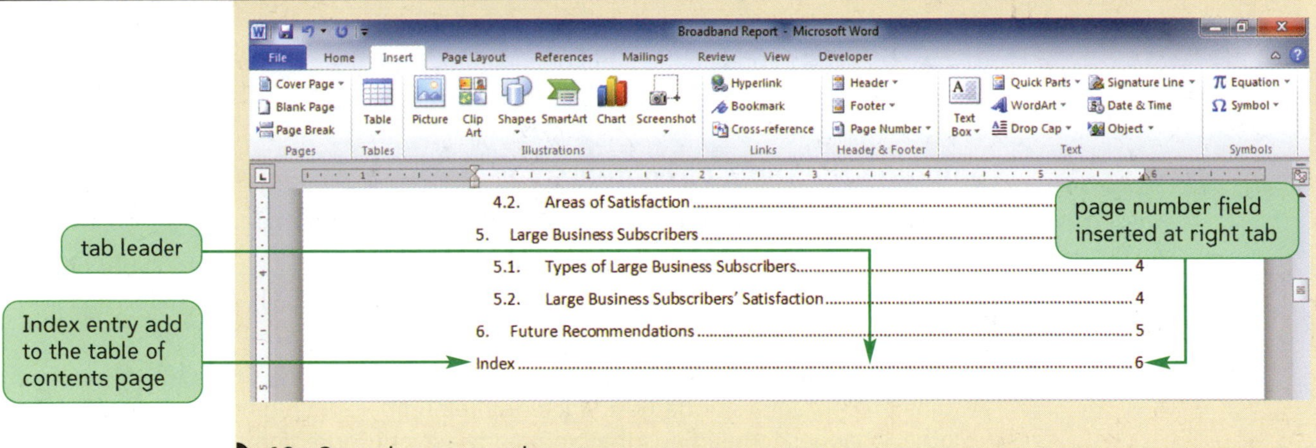

10. Save the master document.

Keep in mind that, if the page flow in the report changes as a result of editing and revisions, and Michael has to update the table of contents later using the Update Table button in the Table of Contents group on the References tab, the page field in the "Index" line would not be updated. Instead, Michael would have to update the page number field by right-clicking it, and then clicking Update Field on the shortcut menu.

Creating a Table of Figures

A **table of figures** is a list of the captions for all the pictures, charts, graphs, slides, or other illustrations in a document, along with the page number for each. As with a table of contents, the entries in a table of figures are links to the captions to which they refer. You can click an entry in a table of figures to jump to that caption in the document.

To create a table of figures:

1. Scroll to page ii, display nonprinting characters, and then position the insertion point in the first blank paragraph below the heading "List of Figures."
2. Click the **References** tab on the Ribbon, and then click the **Insert Table of Figures** button in the Captions group. The Table of Figures dialog box opens with the Table of Figures tab selected. The selected options are the same as in the Table of Contents dialog box so the table of figures will be formatted the same as the table of contents. Notice that Figure appears in the Caption label box.

3. Click the **OK** button. The dialog box closes and a table of figures is generated, as shown in Figure 10-45.

Figure 10-45 **Table of figures inserted in document**

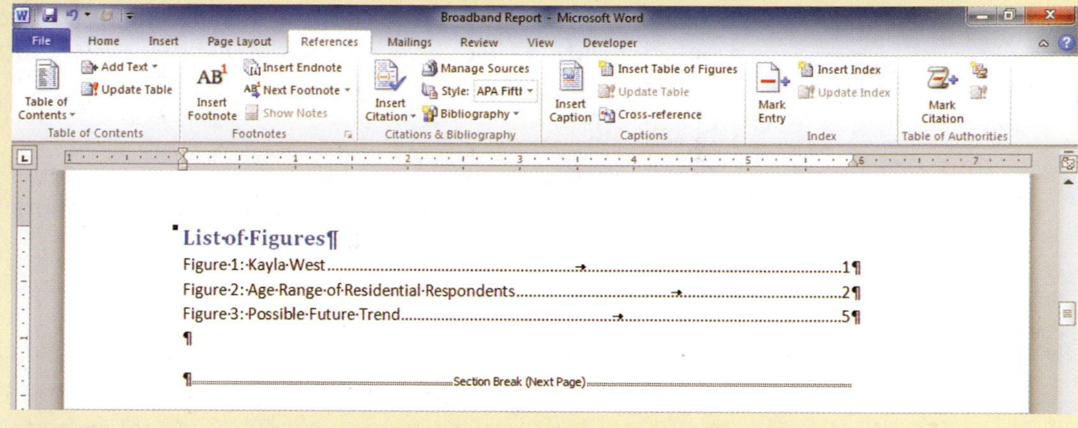

4. Scroll up to the title page, and then add your name in a new line after "Lori Tollefson."
5. Save the document.

INSIGHT

Creating a Table of Authorities

Besides tables of contents and lists of figures, Word can also generate other lists. When creating legal documents, you may have to create a **table of authorities**, which is a list of references to cases, statutes, or rules. Similar to other Word-generated lists, a table of authorities includes the page numbers on which the references appear. To create a table of authorities, first mark all the citations (references) by clicking the References tab, clicking the Mark Citation button in the Table of Authorities group to display the Mark Citation dialog box, select the appropriate category (Cases, Statutes, Rules, Treatises, and so forth), and then click the Mark or Mark All button. Then you can generate the table of authorities by clicking the Insert Table of Authorities button in the Table of Authorities group on the References tab. To update a table of authorities after adding more citations to a document, click the Update Table of Authorities button in the Table of Authorities group on the References tab.

You're now ready to print the Broadband Report document.

Updating Fields Before Printing

Many of the elements you have added to the Broadband Report, such as the cross-references and the table of contents, include fields. As you know, you should always update fields in a document before printing, to ensure you are printing the most current information in the document. Instead of manually updating the fields, you can set Word to automatically update fields before printing. By default, the option to update fields before printing is turned off.

Michael wants you to print the document. Before you do, you'll set the option to update the fields before printing.

To change the options to update fields before printing and print the document:

> **TIP**
> You can also press the Ctrl+A keys to select everything in the document, and then press the F9 key to update all fields.

1. Click the **File** tab, and then click **Options** in the navigation bar. The Word Options dialog box opens.
2. In the list on the left, click the **Display** tab, and then click the **Update fields before printing** check box under "Printing options" to select it, if necessary.

   Trouble? If the Update fields before printing check box is already selected, do not click it.
3. Click the **OK** button to close the dialog box. Now you will print the document. Because the fields will be updated, you need to hide nonprinting characters again so the index is updated correctly.
4. Hide nonprinting characters, and then print the Broadband Report document. The Update Table of Contents dialog box opens prompting you to update the table of contents. The Update page numbers only option button is selected.
5. Click the **OK** button. The dialog box closes and the Update Table of Figures dialog box opens with the Update page numbers only option button selected.
6. Click the **OK** button. The dialog box closes and the document prints. Next, you should turn off Update fields before printing so you leave Word in the same state you found it when you started this tutorial.
7. Click the **File** tab, click **Options** in the navigation bar, click the **Display** tab, click the **Update fields before printing** check box under "Printing options" to deselect it, and then click the **OK** button.

Next, you'll check the document for compatibility with earlier versions of Word.

Checking Compatibility

Michael plans to post the final version of the survey report file on his company's network. He asks you to check the document for features that are not compatible with earlier versions of Word.

To check compatibility with earlier versions of Word:

1. Click the **File** tab. Backstage view appears with the Info tab selected.
2. In the Prepare for Sharing section, click the **Check for Issues** button, and then click **Check Compatibility**. The Microsoft Word Compatibility Checker dialog box opens.
3. Click the **Select versions to show** button. In the menu that opens, Word 2007 has a check mark next to it. You want to check the document for compatibility with both Word 2007 and earlier versions of Word.
4. If there is no check mark next to Word 97-2003, click **Word 97-2003**; otherwise, click a blank area of the dialog box. The list closes and the document is rechecked. Several issues were found. See Figure 10-46. Look over the features in the dialog box. Most of the incompatible features would probably show up properly; you just wouldn't be able to edit them. You inform Michael of these incompatibilities so he can decide later if he wants to save the document in an earlier format.

Figure 10-46 Microsoft Word Compatibility Checker dialog box with compatibility issues listed

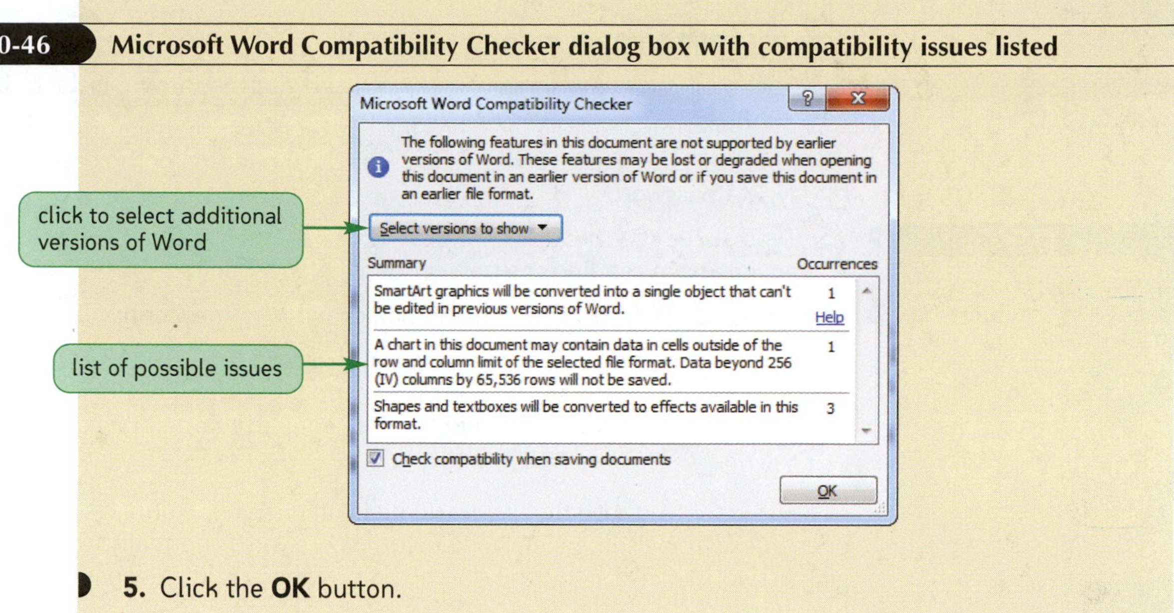

5. Click the **OK** button.

Next, you'll encrypt the document and mark it as final.

Encrypting a Document

To **encrypt** a file is to modify the data structure to make the information unreadable to unauthorized people. When you encrypt a Word document, you assign a password to the file. The only way to open the file is by entering the password. When you create passwords, keep in mind that they are case-sensitive; this means that "PASSWORD" is different from "password." Also, you need to be able to remember your password. This might seem obvious, but if you forget the password you assign to a document, you won't be able to open it.

Michael has asked you to encrypt the master document.

REFERENCE

Encrypting a Document

- Click the File tab to open Backstage view with the Info tab selected.
- In the Permissions section, click the Protect Document button, and then click Encrypt with Password.
- In the Encrypt Document dialog box, type a password in the Password box, and then click the OK button to open the Confirm Password dialog box.
- Retype the password in the Reenter password box, and then click the OK button.

Michael asks you to prevent any unauthorized readers from opening the report by encrypting it.

To encrypt the document:

1. Click the **File** tab to open Backstage view with the Info tab selected.
2. In the Permissions section, click the **Protect Document** button, and then click **Encrypt with Password**. The Encrypt Document dialog box opens. Here you'll type a password.
3. Type **survey** in the Password box. The characters appear as black dots to prevent anyone from reading the password over your shoulder.
4. Click the **OK** button. The dialog box changes to the Confirm Password dialog box.
5. Type **survey** again to verify the password, and then click the **OK** button again. The dialog box closes and a message appears in the Permissions section on the Info tab telling you that a password is required to open this document.

TIP

To remove the password, delete the password in the Encrypt Document dialog box, and then click the OK button.

Now, when you save the file, it will be in an encrypted format, so that it can't be opened except by someone who knows the password. (Normally, you would use a stronger password than "survey," but for the purpose here, you'll keep it simple and easy to remember.)

PROSKILLS

Decision Making: Creating Strong Passwords You Can Easily Remember

In a world where sharing digital information electronically is an everyday occurrence, a password used to encrypt a document is just one more password to remember. When deciding on a password, you should consider a strong password that consists of at least eight characters using a combination of uppercase and lowercase letters, numbers, and symbols. However, this type of password can be difficult to remember, especially if you have to remember multiple passwords. Some people use the same password for everything. This is not a good idea because if someone ever discovered your password, they would have access to all of the data or information protected by that password. Instead, it is a good idea to come up with a plan for creating passwords. For example, you could choose a short word that you can easily remember for one part of the password. The second part of the password could be the name of the file, Web site, or account, but instead of typing it directly, type it backwards, or use the characters in the row above or below the characters that would spell out the name. Or you could split the name of the site and put your short word in the middle of the name. Other possibilities are to combine your standard short word and the site or account name, but replace certain letters with symbols—for example, replace every letter "E" with "#" or memorize a short phrase from a poem or story and use it with some of the substitutions described above. Establishing a process for creating a password means that you will be able to create strong passwords for all of your accounts and documents that you can easily remember.

Marking a Document as Final

Encryption is designed to help make your documents secure against unauthorized changes. If security isn't a vital concern—perhaps because you will only be sharing a document among a few colleagues—consider using the Mark as Final feature instead. When you mark a document as final, all editing features are turned off and the document file becomes a read-only file. Also, the Marked as Final icon appears in the status bar. Note that anyone can turn off the Mark as Final feature, so it does not provide actual security. However, in an informal setting, it offers a convenient way to alert readers that you are not expecting any changes to a document.

Michael asks you to mark the document as final so that anyone viewing it knows that he does not want any changes made to it.

To mark a document as final:

1. On the Info tab in Backstage view, click the **Protect Document** button in the Permissions section, and then click **Mark as Final**. A dialog box opens telling you that the document will be saved and marked as final.
2. Click the **OK** button. The dialog box closes and another dialog box opens telling you that the document was marked as final.
3. Click the **OK** button. The dialog box closes and a message is added to the Permissions section of the Info tab telling you that the document has been marked as final.
4. Click the **File** tab to exit Backstage view. A yellow Marked as Final bar appears at the top of the window. See Figure 10-47.

Figure 10-47 Document marked as final

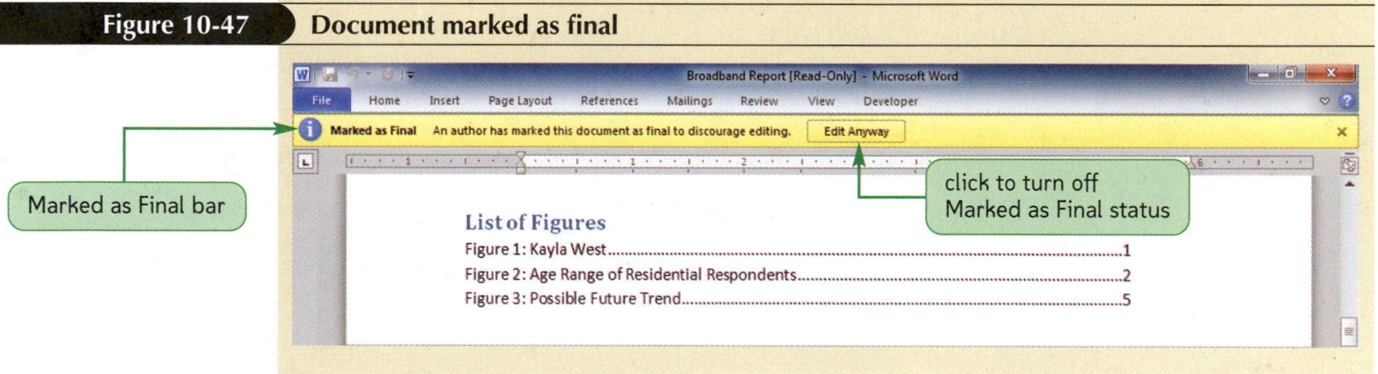

If you want to edit a document that is marked as final, click the Edit Anyway button in the yellow Marked as Final bar to remove the Marked as Final status.

INSIGHT

Adding a Digital Signature to a Document File

A **digital signature** is an electronic attachment, not visible within the contents of the document, that verifies the authenticity of the author or the version of the document by comparing the digital signature to a digital certificate. You can obtain a digital certificate from a certification authority, or you can create one yourself on your computer that can only be used to validate a document on the same computer. Only a certification authority can provide legitimate, certifiable digital signatures. When you digitally sign a document, the document is automatically marked as final to protect it from changes. If you remove the Marked as Final status so that you can make changes to the document, the signature is marked as invalid (because it is no longer the same document the signatory signed). When you open a Word document containing a digital signature that you haven't verified, the Signatures task pane opens to the right of the document window, informing you that the document contains an invalid digital signature. You can then click the warning bar and validate the signature, after which other documents with that digital signature will not be flagged as invalid. To add a digital signature to a document, click the Protect Document button on the Info tab in Backstage view, click Add a Digital Signature, and then click the OK button. If the Get a Digital ID dialog box opens, that means no digital certificate is stored on the computer you are using. You could click the Create your own digital ID option button and create your own digital certificate, but then others can't verify your digital signature, and you can verify it only on the current computer. If you click the OK button with the Get a digital ID from a Microsoft partner option button selected, your browser starts and a Web page opens listing certificate authorities from whom you can purchase a digital certificate. Note that you cannot add a digital signature to a master document; you must unlink all the subdocuments first.

You have completed the Broadband Report for Michael and his team. The skills you learned in this tutorial will be extremely useful as you create long documents for school and in the workplace.

REVIEW

Session 10.3 Quick Check

1. What type of page numbers are typically used in front matter?
2. How do you format page numbers in a document?
3. Define "gutter" and explain how to change the size of a document's gutter.
4. Define "style reference."
5. What are the basic steps in creating an index?
6. True or False. When a document is digitally signed, you can no longer edit it or add comments to it.

Practice skills you learned in the tutorial using the same case scenario.

PRACTICE

Review Assignments

Data Files needed for the Review Assignments: Anls1.docx, Anls2.docx, Intro.docx, Wireless.docx

The Market Data Now, Inc. (MDNI) team of Michael Balczak, Katarina Thao, and Lori Tollefson asks for your help with another project. The team has to prepare a report for the new Wireless Services Committee (WSC). The WSC was formed to study attitudes about citywide wireless networks and the Internet access they provide. The MDNI team developed, administered, and analyzed print and Web surveys of wireless users to determine their attitudes about wireless technology and what they want from it. Each member of the team wrote a section of the report. It's your job to compile the report as a master document and to perform the necessary revisions such as creating an index. Complete the following steps:

1. Start Word, switch to Outline view, and then save the document as **New Report** to the Word10\Review folder included with your Data Files.
2. Type the following as Level 1 and Level 2 headings as an outline:
   Subscription Rates
   - **Broadband Subscription Rates**
   - **Wireless Subscription Rates**

   Survey Results and Analysis
   - **Requested Wireless Services**
   - **Current Wireless Services**
3. Move the Level 1 heading "Survey Results and Analysis" with its subordinate text up above the "Subscription Rates" heading, and then move the Level 2 heading "Current Wireless Services" above the Level 2 heading "Requested Wireless Services."
4. Insert the following as body text under the Level 1 heading "Survey Results and Analysis": **The survey included 75 items.** Save your changes.
5. Open the file **Wireless** from the Word10\Review folder included with your Data Files, and save it in the same folder using the filename **Wireless Report**.
6. In the Word10\Review folder, make copies of the three files **Anls1**, **Anls2**, and **Intro** and rename the copies **Analysis 1**, **Analysis 2**, and **Introduction**, respectively.
7. Display nonprinting characters, switch to Outline view, move the insertion point to page 4 (which is blank), and then insert the **Introduction** file as a subdocument in the Wireless Report. Next, immediately after the first subdocument, insert the files **Analysis 1** and **Analysis 2** as additional subdocuments. Save the master document.
8. Merge the Analysis 1 subdocument (which begins with the heading "Survey Results and Analysis") with the Analysis 2 subdocument (which begins with "Subscription Rates"). Save your changes to the master document.
9. Split the first subdocument (which begins with the heading "Background") into two subdocuments. The second subdocument should begin with the Level 1 heading "Demographics of Respondents" and include the "Executive Summary" section. Save your changes to the master document.
10. Unlink the first subdocument (which begins with the heading "Background") so it becomes part of the master document. Save your changes to the master document.
11. Convert the heading "Personnel and Organization" into a subdocument. Save your changes to the master document.
12. Use the Show Level button to display the first three levels of headings, and then, using the legal paragraph numbering format, add automatic numbering to all the section headings. Add a period after each heading number. (In the Define New Multilevel List dialog box, keep in mind that the document contains Level 3 headings in addition to Level 2 and Level 1 headings.)

13. There is a Next Page section break on page 6, and another one on page 7. On page 6, delete the Next Page section break. (Make sure you do not delete the Next Page section break on the empty page 7.)
14. On page 5, insert a caption below the table that reads "Figure 1," and then on page 7, insert a caption below the SmartArt graphic that reads "Figure 2."
15. On page 8, delete the placeholder "[INSERT PIE CHART]," and in its place insert a pie chart that illustrates the following data:
    High 70%
    Average 19%
    Low 11%
16. Resize the pie chart so it's about 3 inches wide and 2 inches tall, wrap text around the chart using the Square option, and then position it on the left side of the paragraph below the heading "4.4.1. Project Managers," with the paragraph text wrapping to the right. Format the chart so that the title does not appear and so that the percentage of each pie slice appears on the slice.
17. Insert a caption below the pie chart that reads "Figure 3."
18. Create cross-references to the table, the SmartArt graphic, and the pie chart, replacing the highlighted cross-placeholder reference near each object.
19. Protect the document by blocking changes to the theme and allowing only changes marked with tracked changes. Do not require a password. Save and close the document.
20. Reopen the **Wireless Report** document and expand its subdocuments.
21. Center the title page between its top and bottom margins, and select the Different first page check box in the Layout tab of the Page Setup dialog box.
22. Open the **Wireless** document from the Word10\Review folder, display it side-by-side with the Wireless Report document, and use synchronous scrolling to see how much you have added to the Wireless Report document. Close the **Wireless** document.
23. On the title page (page 1), below "Lori Tollefson" in the list of market analysts, insert a new paragraph, and then type your name. Remove the editing and formatting restrictions.
24. In the front matter of the **Wireless Report** document, insert lowercase Roman numeral page numbers on the right side of the footer, with page i starting on the Contents page. (You might need to drag the right tab stop to the right edge of the margin.)
25. Insert Arabic numerals as page numbers on the rest of the report, with page 1 starting on the page containing the heading "Background."
26. Set up the pages for two-sided printing, with a 0.5-inch gutter.
27. Set up footers so that the odd-page footers include the document title **Wireless Subscriber Committee Report** at the left margin and the page number at the right margin, and the even-page footers in the section of the document numbered with Arabic numerals have the page number at the left margin and the Heading 1 text at the right margin. (*Hint*: After inserting the Heading 1 text, click in the first even page footer numbered with Arabic numerals, click Link to Previous in the Navigation group on the Header & Footer Tools Design tab, scroll up to the even page footer in the front matter, and then then delete the Level 1 heading in that footer.) Adjust the right tab stop in the footers so it is at the right margin.
28. Create the following index entries:
    a. Mark every occurrence of "Market Data Now, Inc.," and "WiFi" as index entries.
    b. Create a cross-reference index entry for the abbreviation "MDNI" to "Market Data Now, Inc."
    c. Mark the section "4. Survey Results and Analysis" with a bookmark named **ResultsAndAnalysis**, but do not include the Index heading in this bookmark, and then mark the bookmark as the index entry **Survey Results and Analysis**.
29. Hide nonprinting characters, move the insertion point to the end of the document, below the heading "Index," and then generate the index.

30. Mark every occurrence of "wireless services" and "broadband services" as index subentries under the main entry **services**. Hide nonprinting characters, and then update the index.
31. Below the "List of Figures" heading in the front matter, insert a table of figures.
32. Update the table of contents, and then add the "Index" heading to the table of contents using a combination of text, a dot tab leader, and the PageRef field.
33. Check the document for hidden information, and then remove all tracked changes.
34. Check the document for accessibility, and then add **Diagram illustrating the connection between training, communication, and promotion.** as Alt text in the SmartArt diagram.
35. Encrypt the document using the password **MDNI**, mark the document as final, and then submit the completed documents to your instructor in printed or electronic form, as requested.

Apply your skills to help create a business plan for a promotional products company.

APPLY

Case Problem 1

Data Files needed for this Case Problem: Back.docx, Exec.docx, Mar.docx, Plan.docx

Big Picture Products Loren Stravusky of Eugene, Oregon, has recently started a business named Big Picture Products. The company will produce and market mugs printed with color photographs, which can be used by businesses as promotional items. She and her three partners have written the various parts of a business plan. She asks you to help her put the document together, format it, and add the remaining sections. Complete the following steps:

1. Open the file **Plan** from the Word10\Case1 folder included with your Data Files, and then save it in the same folder using the filename **Business Plan**.
2. On the title page (page 1), below Loren Stravusky's name, type your name.
3. In the Word10\Case1 folder, make copies of the three files **Back**, **Exec**, and **Mar**, and rename the copies **Background**, **Executive**, and **Market**, respectively.
4. On the blank page 4 of the Business Plan document, insert the document named **Executive** as a subdocument. If you see a dialog box indicating that a Heading 1 style exists in the Executive document and the Master Document, click Yes. (When incorporating documents from multiple writers, it's common to encounter some style inconsistencies. In that case, it's best to click Yes in this dialog box to use the styles of the master document.)
5. Immediately after the first subdocument, insert **Background** as a subdocument, and then insert **Market** as a subdocument.
6. Merge the subdocuments named **Executive** and **Background**, and then delete one of the section breaks above the heading "Background."
7. Split the new, larger subdocument named **Executive** at the heading "The Company" to create a new subdocument.
8. Add legal style automatic numbering to all the section headings, and then modify the heading numbers to add a period after each heading number.
9. In the second paragraph below the heading "1. Executive Summary," replace the hyphens in "high-quality" and "low-priced" with nonbreaking hyphens.
10. (EXPLORE) Add captions to the two tables using the label "Table" where indicated in the master document by the highlighted placeholder text.
11. Insert cross-references to the two tables where indicated in the master document by the highlighted placeholder text. (*Hint:* In the Cross-reference dialog box, select Table in the Reference type box.)
12. (EXPLORE) Below the "List of Tables" heading in the front matter, insert a list of all the tables.

13. On page 8, insert an Excel clustered column chart where indicated by the highlighted placeholder text. Use the data in Table 2 in your document as the data for the chart. Do not wrap text around the chart. Remove the chart title and the Legend.
14. Add a figure caption below the chart, and then add a cross-reference to this figure where indicated by the highlighted placeholder text.
15. Center the text on the title page between its top and bottom margins, and set the first page so it won't show a page number.
16. Set the page numbering of the front matter to centered, lowercase Roman numerals, with page i starting on the "Contents" page, and then start Arabic numeral numbering with page 1 on the "Executive Summary" page.
17. Set up the pages (except the title page) for two-sided printing, with a 0.5-inch gutter.
18. Set up the footers for the section numbered with Arabic numerals so that the odd-page footers (starting on page 1, which is Section 3) include the text "BPP Business Plan" at the left margin and the page number at the right margin, and the even-page footers have the page number at the left margin and the Heading 1 text at the right margin.
19. Create an index with entries for every occurrence of "mugs" and "Big Picture Products." (*Hint*: Use the instance of "Big Picture Products" under the heading "1. Executive Summary" to mark that entry.)
20. Mark the abbreviation "BPP" as a cross-reference in the index to "Big Picture Products."
21. Switch to Outline view, show All Levels, and then drag to select the "6. Sales Forecast" section (without selecting the INDEX heading). Mark the selected text with the bookmark **SalesForecast**, and then mark that section with the index entry **Sales Forecast**.
22. Move the insertion point to the end of the document (the insertion point should be in the paragraph below the INDEX heading), and then compile the index using the default settings.
23. Update the table of contents, and then add the Index to the table of contents.
24. Mark the document as final, and then submit the completed report to your instructor in printed or electronic form, as requested. Close any open files.

Expand your skills by exploring Word features to help create an informational cyber security report for a consulting firm.

CHALLENGE

Case Problem 2

Data File needed for this Case Problem: Cyber.docx

Cronkite Security Consulting Terrell Prassad is a computer security consultant at Cronkite Security Consulting (CSC). He is working on an informational report for CSC's clients. The report summarizes the essential elements of an effective cyber security policy for large and small organizations. He asks you to prepare front and back matter for the report and to create two subdocuments within the master document so his staff can review each section individually. You'll help Terrell manage the various sections of the report, format the document, and prepare it for printing. Complete the following steps:

1. Open the file **Cyber** from the Word10\Case2 folder included with your Data Files, and save it in the same folder using the filename **Cyber Security**. Review the document—notice the comment and that the document contains two levels of headings.
2. Check the document with the Document Inspector and remove any comments, revisions, versions, or annotations.
3. Convert the "Modern Threats" and the "Modern Solution" sections into subdocuments, and then save the master document so the subdocuments are saved as separate documents.

4. Return to Print Layout view, open the **Cyber** document from the Word10\Case2 folder, display the two documents side-by-side, and scroll through them using synchronous scrolling. Close the **Cyber** document.
5. Create a single subdocument from the two subdocuments you created in step 3, and then save your changes to the master document.
6. Protect the document against changes to its theme and for tracked changes.
7. In the first paragraph under "Rationale," delete the words "the following" so the phrase reads "...of this report are:" and then, in the first line below the bulleted list, delete the word "specifically."
8. Remove the editing and formatting restrictions, and then encrypt document with the password **4Security**.
9. Save the document, and then close it.
10. Re-open the **Cyber Security** document, and then expand its subdocuments.
11. In the "Location Security" section, insert a figure caption below the SmartArt graphic, and then insert cross-references to the figure at both locations indicated by highlighted placeholder text.
12. Set up the first page of the document so the text is centered vertically on the page and so the title page will not have a header or page number when you add one to the rest of the document.
13. Set up a gutter of 0.5 inches.
14. **EXPLORE** Use the appropriate check box in the Options group on the Header & Footer Tools Design tab to set up the document for different even and odd pages.
15. **EXPLORE** In the first even header, insert a header using the Motion Even Page header style. In the first odd header, insert a header using the Motion Odd Page header style.
16. **EXPLORE** House style at Cronkite Security requires "e-mail" to be spelled with a hyphen. Use the Replace command to replace all occurrences of "e-mail" (with a hyphen) with "e-mail" (with a nonbreaking hyphen). (*Hint*: In the Find and Replace dialog box, click the More button, and then click Special.)
17. Mark all occurrences of "password", "Password", "passwords", "Passwords", and "Information Technology" as index entries.
18. Mark "IT" as a cross-reference index entry to "Information Technology."
19. Compile the index on a new page at the end of the document. Add the heading **Index**.
20. Check the document for accessibility, and then add **SmartArt graphic that illustrates recommendations for protecting the server.** as Alt text for the SmartArt graphic.
21. Check the document for compatibility with earlier versions of Word.
22. Save the document, and then submit your documents to your instructor in electronic or printed form, as requested.

Compile a table of authorities for a legal brief and create a document with the headings shown in Figure 10-49.

CREATE

Case Problem 3

Data Files needed for this Case Problem: Legal.docx

Kekoanui and Lee LLP Naomi Kamei is a paralegal at the law offices of Kekoanui and Lee, in Honolulu, Hawaii. The firm is handling a lawsuit filed by Peli Promotions, an advertising company, against a competitor. It's your job to help generate a table of authorities for a legal brief. Naomi also needs your help in preparing the structure of a report she is preparing for the law firm's partners. The report summarizes the firm's pro bono activities (that is, legal work donated for free) on behalf of nonprofit agencies, government agencies, and individuals over the past five years. The report will be presented to the firm's board of directors. Naomi has not written the report yet, but she would like you to set up the document with the appropriate title page, headers, footers, page numbers, and so on. Complete the following steps:

1. Open the file named **Legal** from the Word10\Case3 folder included with your Data Files and save it as **Legal Brief**. This document includes the beginning of a 30-page legal brief, and several citations.

EXPLORE

2. Move the insertion point to the blank paragraph below the heading "Table of Authorities" on page 2, and then generate a table of authorities using the default settings.
3. Save your changes, and then close the file.
4. Create a new, blank document, and then save it as **Pro Bono Report** in the Word10\Case3 folder included with your Data Files.
5. Add the headings shown in Figure 10-48. Make sure you include one blank Body Text paragraph after each heading.

Figure 10-48 **Outline for Pro Bono Report**

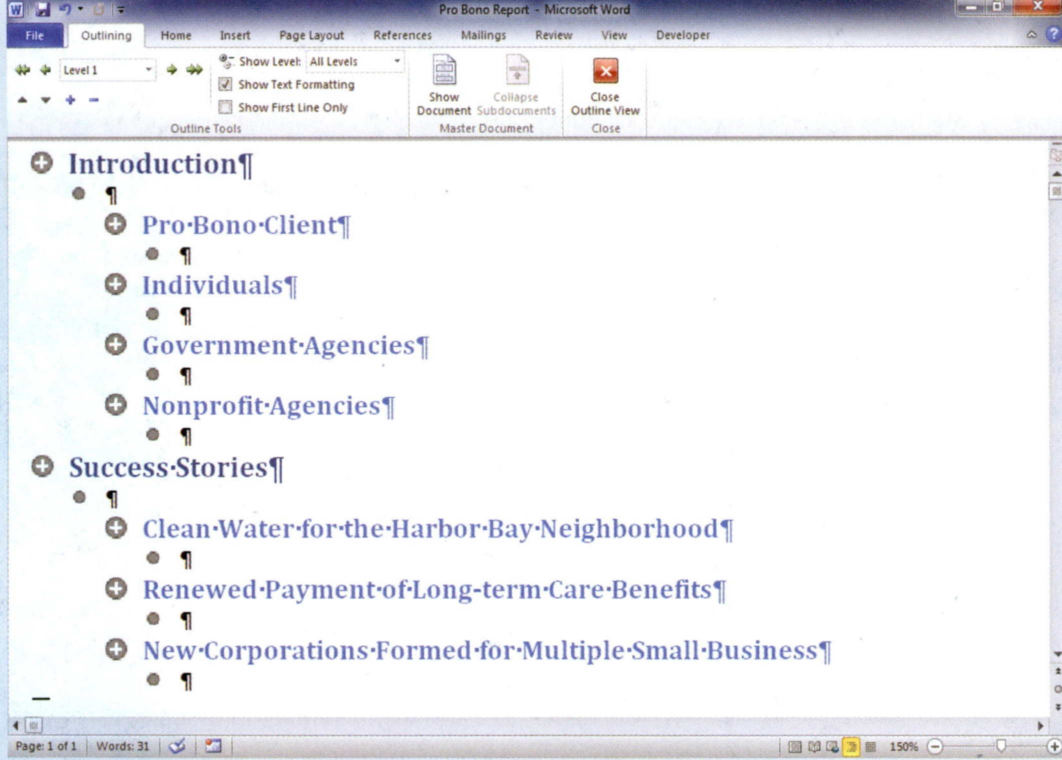

EXPLORE

6. Use the legal style of automatic numbering to add heading numbers, formatting the Level 1 numbers as uppercase letters (A, B, C, etc.) and the Level 2 numbers as uppercase letters followed by a period and then a number and a period.
7. Convert the "Introduction" and "Success Stories" sections into subdocuments. Make sure there is one blank Body Text paragraph between the last heading in the document and the last section break.

EXPLORE

8. In Print Layout view, click in the blank paragraph after the "A. Introduction" heading, type **=rand()** and press the Enter key to insert three paragraphs of random text in the document so that you can see what the finished document will look like. Insert random text after each heading, and then remove any blank paragraphs.
9. Insert a cover page using the Pinstripes cover page style. Enter **Pro Bono Report** as the title, **2009–2013 Activities** as the subtitle, and your name as the author. Include the current date, and enter **Law Offices of Kekoanui and Lee** as the company name.

10. Set up the document for two-sided printing, with a 0.5-inch gutter and odd and even pages. Insert the Accent Bar 1 page number style in the even page footers, and the Accent Bar 2 page number style in the odd page footers. Scroll through the document and make sure the page numbers appear on all the pages except the first page. Insert them on any additional pages as needed.
11. Encrypt the document using the password **ProBono**.
12. Change the theme to the Opulent theme, and then save your changes. Open the two subdocument files, and note that they are still formatted in the Office theme.
13. Submit your documents to your instructor in electronic or printed form, as requested. Close all open documents.

Use the Internet and other sources to collect information about preparing a guided tour.

RESEARCH

Case Problem 4

There are no Data Files needed for this Case Problem.

Preparing a Guided-Tour Brochure Your instructor will divide your class into workgroups of three to six students and appoint a workgroup leader or have each workgroup select one. Each workgroup will collaborate to prepare a document that provides a guided tour of a real or imaginary place. Your goal is to create a brochure like you might receive from a chamber of commerce that introduces you to a city or county. You might want to select a place in which most of your workgroup has some interest and at least one member of the group has expertise, such as your school campus or your city. Alternatively, you could select an unfamiliar place and then conduct the necessary research to learn about your chosen location. Another approach is to create a guided tour of the landscape in your favorite online role-playing game or of the geographical area discussed in a favorite novel. Working together, your group should complete the following steps:

1. Discuss in a planning meeting how the workgroup will accomplish its goals and how it can make all the chapters consistent in style and format.
2. Create a detailed outline for the guided tour brochure. Plan to divide the brochure into chapters and to include numerous figures, so the brochure is well-illustrated. You can include digital photographs, drawings, or other types of illustrations.

3. If you are writing about an online role-playing game, include screenshots of selected locations. (*Hint*: Use the Screenshot button in the Illustrations group on the Insert tab.)
4. Plan the brochure's overall formatting. Pick an appropriate theme as well as theme fonts, colors, and effects. Decide if you want to use the default heading styles or modify the heading styles. Also, decide how you want to format figures and tables, including how you want text to wrap around these elements. You will use two-sided printing, so plan the headers and footers accordingly.
5. Write the chapters, dividing them up so each workgroup member writes at least one. Each workgroup member should base his or her chapter on research or personal knowledge. Include illustrations, but do not include captions or cross-references at this point. Format the chapter according to the formatting plan created in Step 3, and then protect the chapter for tracked changes (without a password).
6. Each group member should review each of the chapters written by the other members of your workgroup. Review the chapters electronically. Make at least one edit per document (the changes should be marked with revision marks) and include at least one comment, and then pass each document file along to the next group member, so that all of the group's changes are made in a single copy of each document file. When you are finished, each workgroup member should have a copy of his or her document file that contains edits and comments from all the members of the workgroup.
7. Retrieve the file for your chapter or chapters, unprotect the document, and accept or reject the edits made by the other workgroup members. Delete any comments. Discuss the chapter with the other group members as necessary until you all agree on the final status of all the chapters.

For the remaining steps, you have two options: 1) Perform the remaining steps as a group; or 2) Perform the remaining steps individually, so that each member of the workgroup creates his or her own copy of the guided tour brochure. Ask your instructor if you should work alone or as a group.

8. Create a new document to be used as the master document for the brochure, save it as **Guided Tour** in the Tutorial.10\Case4 folder included with your Data Files, insert a title page, write a brief preface or introduction, and set up headings for the table of contents, for the list of figures and/or list of tables, and for the index.
9. Insert the various chapter files as subdocuments, and then format the document consistently according to the formatting plan you agreed on in Step 3. Add figure captions and cross-references.
10. Set up the brochure for two-sided printing. Create appropriate headers or footers for the odd and even pages. Make sure you include page numbers, the brochure title, and chapter names in the headers or footers.
11. Insert the table of contents.
12. Mark appropriate index entries and then insert the index.
13. Review the document on the Print tab in Backstage view, and make any necessary changes to ensure that your brochure looks polished and professional.
14. Change the setting to update fields before printing, and then print the document. Print on both sides of the document pages if possible.
15. Submit your documents to your instructor in electronic or printed form, as requested.

ASSESS

SAM: Skills Assessment Manager

For current SAM information, including versions and content details, visit SAM Central (http://samcentral.course.com). If you have a SAM user profile, you may have access to hands-on instruction, practice, and assessment of the skills covered in this tutorial. Since various versions of SAM are supported throughout the life of this text, check with your instructor for the correct instructions and URL/Web site for accessing assignments.

ENDING DATA FILES

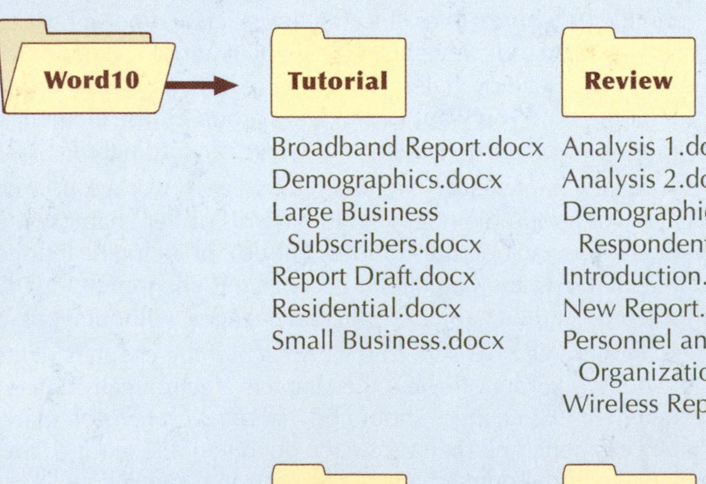

Tutorial
Broadband Report.docx
Demographics.docx
Large Business Subscribers.docx
Report Draft.docx
Residential.docx
Small Business.docx

Review
Analysis 1.docx
Analysis 2.docx
Demographics of Respondents.docx
Introduction.docx
New Report.docx
Personnel and Organization.docx
Wireless Report.docx

Case1
Background.docx
Business Plan.docx
Executive.docx
Market.docx
The Company.docx

Case2
Cyber Security.docx
Modern Solution.docx
Modern Threats.docx

Case3
Introduction.docx
Legal Brief.docx
Pro Bono Report.docx
Success Stories.docx

Case4
Guided Tour.docx
various subdocument files

ProSkills

Decision Making

Maximizing Your Time

All professions require you to manage your time so that you can complete the most quality work in the shortest amount of time. To accomplish this, you need to decide which skills and tools to use and consider how your choices will impact the quality of the outcome and the speed with which you can accomplish the outcome. For example, in many professions, you need to manage many documents. Some will be created from templates; others will be ones you create from scratch. Some professions require you to create and manage very long documents or work on or manage documents created by a team. Word provides many tools for creating and working with documents. Spending the time to learn how to harness the power of these tools can save you time and energy and help you minimize errors. This time investment can pay off large dividends in the end.

Before you can decide which skills and tools you need to use, you need to have a firm understanding of what your goal is. Once you have identified the goal—or outcome—you need to decide if it can be accomplished in one sitting or if you need to break it down into tasks, possibly assigning some of these tasks to others. If you decide that you need to work with a team, then you must develop and manage an action plan and determine key milestones so that you can track the completion of each task. Occasionally, even the best-laid plans veer off-course. In this case, the project manager must be able to determine why, when, and where the tasks fell behind schedule to help set them back on course.

Often, the most challenging part of implementing your decisions is dealing with the human and behavioral ramifications. For larger projects that take longer to complete, your action plan should include regular communication with all affected parties, including weekly project status updates, scheduled training sessions and mechanisms for handling inquiries, feedback, or opposition.

When you have achieved your goal, you might be asked to document your experiences to serve as a reference model for other groups or teams who might face similar decision or tasks. You should be prepared to discuss what went right and how your decisions helped create a successful outcome. You should also be able to identify anything that went wrong, as this can serve a useful purpose for future implementation efforts. By reflecting on the decision process and its implementation, the entire organization can learn from the experience, which can then inform better decision making down the road.

PROSKILLS

Using Word Tools to Manage Your Documents Effectively

This book has taught you many advanced skills for working with Word, including ways to work more efficiently. For example, if you need to frequently review documents and insert comments, you can create a keyboard shortcut for inserting comments. Or if you are responsible for compiling long documents, including master documents, from a variety of documents submitted by colleagues, you can create a template that includes styles and placeholder text to ensure that the final document contains all the information needed and to ensure that you don't need to spend valuable time reformatting the submissions to match the document style. Using these skills, you can add more complexity to documents you may have already created for work, school, or home, and you can create new, complex documents from scratch. In

ProSkills

the following exercise, you'll create or revise a number of documents by using the Word skills and features presented in Tutorials 8 through 10.

Note: Please be sure *not* to include any personal information of a sensitive nature in the documents you create to be submitted to your instructor for this exercise. Later on, you can update the documents with such information for your own personal use.

1. Collect the Word documents you use regularly, and add document properties to help you keep your files organized.
2. If you are working on your own computer, customize the Quick Access Toolbar by adding buttons that you use frequently.
3. Open a new document. If you are working on your own computer, create Quick Parts that you save to the Building Blocks template that you can use for a future report for school or work. If you are not working on your own computer, save the document as a template, and then save the Quick Parts in the template.
4. Take a long report that you have already created for school or work, and pick out text in the document that you want to draw attention to with special, character-level formatting. For example, you might choose to format a company name that is used repeatedly in a different font and font color. Record a macro that applies the formatting you want, and then use the macro throughout the document to apply the formatting.
5. Add a text or picture watermark to the report.
6. Create a form that collects information that you can include in your report from colleagues or friends. Format the form attractively. Use the Picture content control if appropriate.
7. Include a pull quote or sidebar somewhere in the report. Change the format so it looks attractive in the document.
8. Expand the report by adding figures with captions. Include cross-references to the figures within the report text. Format the pictures with picture styles.
9. Check the document for accessibility, and then add Alt text to describe any objects.
10. Insert additional material in the report as one or more subdocuments, or consider creating a subdocument from text in the report.
11. Add a table of contents and a table of figures.
12. Set the document up for two-sided printing, with appropriate headers and footers. Don't forget to include page numbers, with a different style of page number for the front matter.
13. Create a useful index that includes all the important terms and concepts in your document.
14. Check the document for hidden or personal data and remove that data.
15. Mark the document as final.
16. Submit your documents to your instructor in electronic or printed form, as requested.

ADDITIONAL CASE 1

Creating a Form Letter and a Program

WORD

OBJECTIVES

- Insert, resize, and position a graphic
- Insert and format a Word date field
- Change the theme and the theme fonts
- Update a style
- Use mail merge to create a form letter
- Use mail merge to create a directory
- Format text using styles
- Create tab stops with and without dot leaders
- Change the font size
- Insert a colored page background
- Center text vertically on a page
- Add page and paragraph borders

Case | *Washington Engineers Society*

Angela Notraga is an engineer and is active in the Washington Engineers Society, which annually awards scholarships to students. Angela needs to send a letter to this year's winning students inviting them to the Society's annual banquet. She also needs to prepare a program for the banquet. Complete the following steps:

1. Open the file **Engineer** from the AddCases folder included with your Data Files, and save the file as **Engineer Form Letter** in the same folder.
2. At the top of main document, insert the picture file **Logo**, which is stored in the AddCases folder. Change the scale of the height of the picture to 1.85 inches without changing the width. (*Hint*: To make sure the width doesn't change, click the dialog box launcher in the Size group on the Picture Tools Format tab to open the Layout dialog box with the Size tab selected, and then deselect the Lock aspect ratio check box.)
3. Change the theme to Essential, and then change the theme fonts to Median.
4. Select any paragraph, change the font size to 12 points, change the line spacing to single spacing, and then update the Normal style to match the selected text.
5. Replace the [Date] placeholder with a date field in the "11 February 2013" format.
6. Begin a mail merge using Engineer Form Letter as the main document. Use the file **Engineer Data** from the AddCases folder as the data source.
7. Replace the bracketed highlighted text with merge field codes from the Engineer Data data source. Use the format "Joshua Randall Jr." in the Address Block merge field, and format the paragraph appropriately. Format the Greeting Line merge field as "Dear Joshua Randall Jr.". Replace the [Your name] placeholder with your name.
8. Save the document.

STARTING DATA FILES

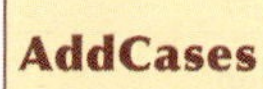

Engineer.docx
Engineer Data.mdb
Logo.jpg

9. Preview the merge, correct any errors, and then merge the Engineer Form Letter main document with all records of the data source to a new document. Save the merged document as **Engineer Award Letters** in the AddCases folder.
10. Print the last letter of the merged document, and then close all the documents. Do not save changes to the Engineer Form Letter document.
11. Open a new document, save it as **Program Main** to the AddCases folder, and then begin a Directory mail merge using the **Engineer Data** from the AddCases folder as the data source.
12. Insert the following merge fields: First_Name and Last_Name separated by a space. Press the Tab key, and then insert the School_Name, Award_Name, and Award_Amount fields separated by tabs. Press the Enter key, and then save your changes.
13. Merge all the records to a new document. Save the document as **Dinner Program** to the AddCases folder.
14. Create the document shown in Figure 1-1. The theme is Horizon. All the text is formatted with styles available in the Styles gallery on the Home tab. The list of student names is 12-point, and the tabs in that list are set at 1.5", 3.75", and 5.5". The page background color is Gold, Background 2, Lighter 80%. The text is centered vertically on the page. Save your changes.

Figure 1-1 **Dinner Program**

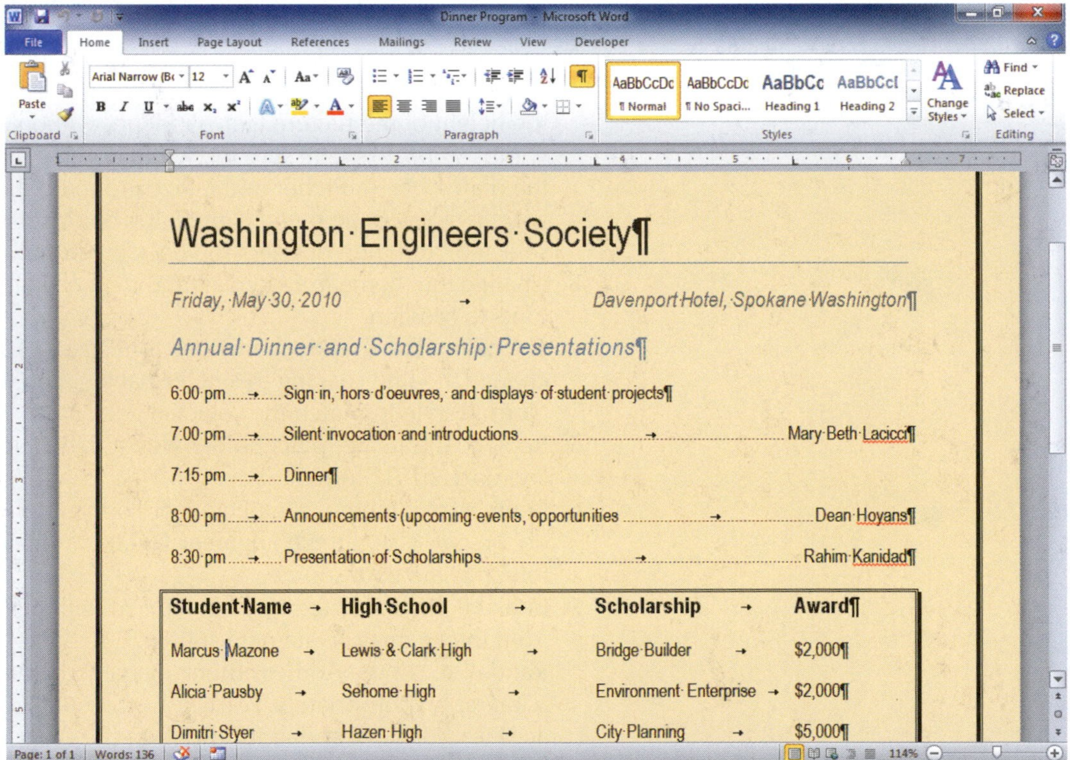

15. Close all open documents without saving changes. Submit the completed documents in electronic or printed form, as requested.

ENDING DATA FILES

Dinner Program.docx
Engineer Award Letters.docx
Engineer Form Letter.docx
Program Main.docx

ADDITIONAL CASE 2

Creating a Promotional Flyer

WORD

OBJECTIVES

- Adjust the margins of a document
- Sort a table
- Import pictures
- Resize graphics
- Apply a table style
- Adjust table column widths
- Change the text font, size, color, and effect
- Set text wrapping options
- Remove the background of a photo
- Modify the style set of the document
- Remove space after paragraphs
- Create and modify a SmartArt graphic

Case | *PersonalRec*

Bruno Lambert owns and operates a small business in Portland, Maine, called PersonalRec, which coordinates and sponsors active recreational trips to destinations in the United States and Europe. Bruno rents or ships equipment so that travelers can sail, ski, surf, and enjoy other forms of recreation as soon as they arrive. His signature service is to provide clients with a hot-air balloon ride at the end of their trip. Bruno asks you to help him create an appealing and informational flyer that he can distribute at athletic meets and recreational events to advertise his business. Complete the following steps:

1. Open the file **RecFlyer** from the AddCases folder included with your Data Files, and then save the document in the same folder using the filename **PersonalRec Flyer**.
2. Change the page setup so that the top and bottom margins are 0.5 inch and the left and right margins are 1 inch.
3. Sort the rows of the table so that the categories in column 2 appear in alphabetical order.
4. In the first cell in the second row delete the text "RecGolf" and then insert the graphics file **RecGolf**—that is, the file whose name you just deleted. Repeat this procedure for the rest of the cells in the first column—that is, delete the name of the graphics file and then insert the graphics file into the cell. All the image files are located in the AddCases folder included with your Data Files. Adjust the height (with the aspect ratio fixed) of each of the pictures to 1.0 inch.
5. Apply the Table Colorful 1 table style to the table.

STARTING DATA FILES

AddCases

RecBal.jpg
RecFlyer.docx
RecGolf.jpg
RecLogo.jpg
RecSail.jpg
RecSki.jpg
RecSnow.jpg
RecSurf.jpg

6. Adjust the cell margins of the first column so they are zero. (*Hint*: Click the Cell Margins button in the Alignment group on the Table Tools Layout tab.) Adjust the width of the first column so it's just wide enough to fit the contents, and then adjust the width of the Description column so that the table spans the width of the page.
7. Modify the font style of the text in the column headings for the second and third columns by removing the italics and increasing the size to 14-points.
8. At the top of the flyer, insert the PersonalRec logo, **RecLogo.jpg**, located in the AddCases folder.
9. Set the size of the logo to 1.0 inch in height (keeping the aspect ratio locked), and then position the logo in the top right with the text wrapping set to Square.
10. Remove the background of the logo. You will need to use the Mark Areas to Keep and Mark Areas to Remove buttons.
11. Change the font of the company name ("PersonalRec") to 28-point Trebuchet MS.
12. Change the font color of the company name to Blue, Accent 1, and then apply the Offset Diagonal Top Left Shadow effect. (If the logo background changes color, undo your changes, and then repeat this step, making sure you do not select the paragraph mark after the company name.)
13. Apply the Perspective style set. Delete any extra blank paragraphs. Remove the space after the two lines containing the address.
14. At the end of the document, insert the Circle Arrow Process SmartArt graphic from the Cycle category. In the top shape, insert **Achieve your personal best!**; in the middle shape, insert **Adventure recreation travel!**; and in the bottom shape, insert **PersonalRec!** Modify the font size of the text in the bottom shape to 12 points.
15. Change the colors of the SmartArt graphic to Colorful Range – Accent Colors 2 to 3, and then change the style to the 3-D Cartoon style.
16. Save the file, and then submit the completed document to your instructor in printed or electronic form, as requested. Close all open documents.

ENDING DATA FILES

AddCases

PersonalRec Flyer.docx

ADDITIONAL CASE **3**

Creating a Confirmation Order Form

WORD

OBJECTIVES

- Create WordArt
- Format text with styles
- Change the color of text
- Redefine a style
- Insert a date field
- Create tables and use advanced table formatting
- Create a footer
- Cut, copy, and paste text and objects
- Modify a document property
- Create a form template with content controls
- Use formulas in tables
- Protect a form
- Use a document template to create a report

Case | *Pictures!*

Miranda Lajoie is the owner of Pictures! in Lafayette, Kentucky. Pictures! puts customers' photos and messages on mugs, plates, and t-shirts. Miranda asks you to create an order form for the customers to fill out by hand that an employee can then enter into the computer. The employee will scan or store the customer's photo at the same time and include the photo in the onscreen form. This completed form can be confirmed as correct by the customer and will follow the item through the whole process so that the employees who put the photos on the items can double-check that they are putting the correct photo on the correct item. You will prepare these forms by completing the following steps:

1. Open the document **Order** from the AddCases folder included with your Data Files, and then save it as **Order Request** in the same folder.
2. Convert the text **Pictures!** at the top of the document to WordArt using the Fill – Orange, Accent 6, Warm Matte Bevel style. Center the WordArt in the line. (*Hint*: Use the Distribute Horizontally command on the Align button menu in the Arrange group on the Drawing Tools Format tab.)
3. Format the label "Name:" using the Strong style in the Styles gallery on the Home tab, and then change the color to Orange, Accent 5, Darker 25%. Redefine the Strong style to match this format, and then apply the redefined format to the other labels above the [INSERT DATE] placeholder and to the text "Photo description:" at the end of the document.
4. Replace the [INSERT DATE] placeholder text with a date field in the format 8/10/2013.
5. Format the table with any table style that looks attractive in the document.

STARTING DATA FILES

Tutorial

Boys.jpg
Order.docx

6. Merge the cells in the last row into one cell. Change the font size of the text in the last row to 10 points, italicize it, and then align the text in this cell to the right.
7. Cut the last line of text in the document, and then paste it as a footer, centered.
8. Add your name as the author property. Save your changes.
9. Open a new, blank Word document. Save it as a Word template named **Order Confirmation** in the AddCases folder.
10. Copy the WordArt logo, customer contact labels, date field, and the footer from the Order Request document to this document.
11. Modify the Normal style so the font size is 12 points.
12. In the paragraph below the date field, type: **Please confirm that the photo and the items ordered are correct. If you have any corrections, please let your sales representative know. Your items will be ready in approximately one hour.**
13. Adjust the tab stops in the line that begins with "City" to 2" and 3", and then adjust the tab stop in the next line to 2".
14. Insert a Plain Text content control after each label in the customer contact section. Add an appropriate title to each control, and do not allow the controls to be deleted. Select the control, remove bold, and change the font color to Black, Text 1 (or Automatic).
15. In the line containing the date field, insert a Right tab stop at 6.5".
16. Position the insertion point after the date field, press the Tab key, and then insert the time in the format 1:36 PM to be updated automatically. Format the time as 14 points and bold.
17. Create a 6×7 table below the last paragraph. Type **Item**, **Quantity**, **Price**, and **Total** as column labels, skip the fifth column, and then type **Personalization** as the last column label.
18. Copy the items and their prices from the Order Request document to the second through fourth rows in the table in the form. Match the destination formatting.
19. Insert a Plain Text content control in the first three rows under Quantity. Use appropriate titles and do not allow the content control to be deleted.
20. Insert formulas in the first three rows under "Total" to calculate the total price for each item. (*Hint*: Use the PRODUCT formula and use cell references for the argument. If you use LEFT, you will get an incorrect result if no quantity is entered in the Quantity column.)
21. Merge the six cells in the last three rows and the first two columns. In this cell, type: **Items left for more than 30 days will be discarded or resold.** Format this in bold.
22. In the last three cells in the "Price" column, type **Subtotal**, **Tax**, and **Total**.
23. In the cell to the right of "Subtotal," insert a formula to add the numbers above it. In the cell to the right of "Tax," insert a formula that multiplies the amount in the cell to the right of Subtotal by .06 (sales tax in Kentucky is 6%). (*Hint:* The Subtotal value is in cell C5.) Format the tax as currency.
24. In the cell to the right of Total, insert a formula that adds the amounts in the two cells above it. Format this number as currency.
25. Merge all the cells in the second-to-last column, and then insert a Photo content control in the merged cell. Merge the six cells below the "Personalization" heading in the last column, and then insert a Plain Text content control. Add appropriate titles and do not allow the content controls to be deleted.
26. Format the table attractively. Format at least one cell so it is filled with black and uses reverse type. (Reapply the bold formatting to the merged cell at the bottom of the first two columns, if necessary.)
27. Protect the template for filling in forms, save your changes, and then close the document.

28. Create a new document based on the Order Confirmation template. Insert your own information in the content controls in the customer contact section. Enter **5** as the number of mugs sold, **3** as the number of plates, and **2** as the number of t-shirts. Insert the photo **Boys**, located in the AddCases folder, in the Photo content control. Update the fields in the Total column.
29. Open a new document, type "Happy Birthday Grandma!" and then translate it into Swedish. Copy the translated text, and then paste it into the content control under Personalization in the form. Close the translation document without saving changes.
30. Save the completed form as **Order Test** to the AddCases folder.
31. Submit the completed documents in electronic or printed form, as requested.

ENDING DATA FILES

AddCases

Order Confirmation.dotx
Order Request.docx
Order Test.docx

Creating an On-Screen Order Form

OBJECTIVES

- Change page orientation
- Design and create an on-screen form
- Merge and split cells and change column widths in a table
- Shade cells in a table
- Change font effects and colors
- Insert form fields for text, drop-down lists, and check boxes
- Set up a form for automatic calculations
- Protect a document

Case | *Cardenas Transcription, LLC*

Shiana Cardenas is the owner of Cardenas Transcription, LLC, located in Phoenix, Arizona. She and her employees type transcriptions of legal and medical notes. Shiana asks you to help her design an online order form so that as her employees receive requests for services, they can fill out a standard form. Complete the following steps:

1. Open the template file **Cardenas** from the AddCases folder included with your Data Files, and then save it as a document template in the same folder using the filename **Cardenas Form**.
2. Change the page orientation from portrait to landscape, and set the top and bottom margins to 0.7 inch.
3. Increase the width of the second column until the right edge of the table is at 9 inches on the ruler, and then decrease the width of the first column to 2.25 inches.
4. Change the theme to Verve, but select the Slipstream theme colors.
5. In the first cell in the second column, format the company name as 20-points and bold, format the company address, telephone number, and email address in the Heading 2 style, and then remove the space before the text formatted as Heading 2.
6. Center all the text in the cell containing the company name horizontally and vertically, and then shade this cell with Green, Accent 3, Lighter 80%.
7. In the first cell in the first column, insert clip art of a woman in a purple shirt sitting in front of a computer. Resize the image so it is 1.5 inches high, and then center it horizontally and vertically in the cell.

STARTING DATA FILES

Cardenas.dotx

8. Merge the cells containing the text "Order Information," "Legal Services," and "Medical Services" with the cells to their right.
9. In the merged cell containing "Order Information," change the font size to 14-point bold, apply Blue, Accent 1, Lighter 80% as shading, and center the text between the left and right borders. Use the Format Painter to copy this formatting to the other two merged cells, and then apply the same blue shading to those cells.
10. Split the blank cell next to "Dictation Method" in the "Legal Services" section into two columns. In the new middle cell, insert a Check Box content control. To the right of the check box, insert a space and then the text **Telephone**. In the third cell in that row, insert another Check Box content control. To the right of the check box, insert space and then the text **Digital Recorder**.
11. Split cell B20 (the blank cell next to "Dictation Method" in the "Medical Services" section) and then copy the check boxes and labels you just created to these new cells.
12. Insert a date/time field in the cell to the right of "Date" (below "Order Information"), so that the date and time automatically appear in the form 8/16/2013 4:42 PM.
13. Insert Combo Box content controls for the city, state, and ZIP code with the following list values: for the city and state, use Phoenix, AZ, and for the zip code, use 85003.
14. In the cell to the right of "Type of document", add a Drop-Down List content control with the values **None**, **Letter**, **Contract**, **Brief**, **Report**, **Speech**, and **Other**.
15. In the cell to the right of "Specialty", insert a Drop-Down List content control with the values **General Practitioner**, **Dermatology**, **Oncology**, **Pediatric Medicine**, **Surgery**, and **Other**.
16. In the cell to the right of "Approx cost (in dollars)", add a formula to calculate the number of hours (cell B23) multiplied by $65, and format it as currency. Insert a Plain Text content control in cell B23 and change the placeholder text to **Click here to enter duration (in hours).**
17. Insert Date content controls in the cells to the right of "Due date" in both the Legal Services and the Medical Services sections, and to the right of "Date of patient appointment" in the Medical Services section.
18. Insert Plain Text content controls in the rest of the cells in the second column.
19. Protect the completed document template form for filling in forms, and then save and close it.
20. Create a new document based on **Cardenas Form** in the AddCases folder. Fill in the report using the information shown in Figure 4-1.

Figure 4-1 **Completed form**

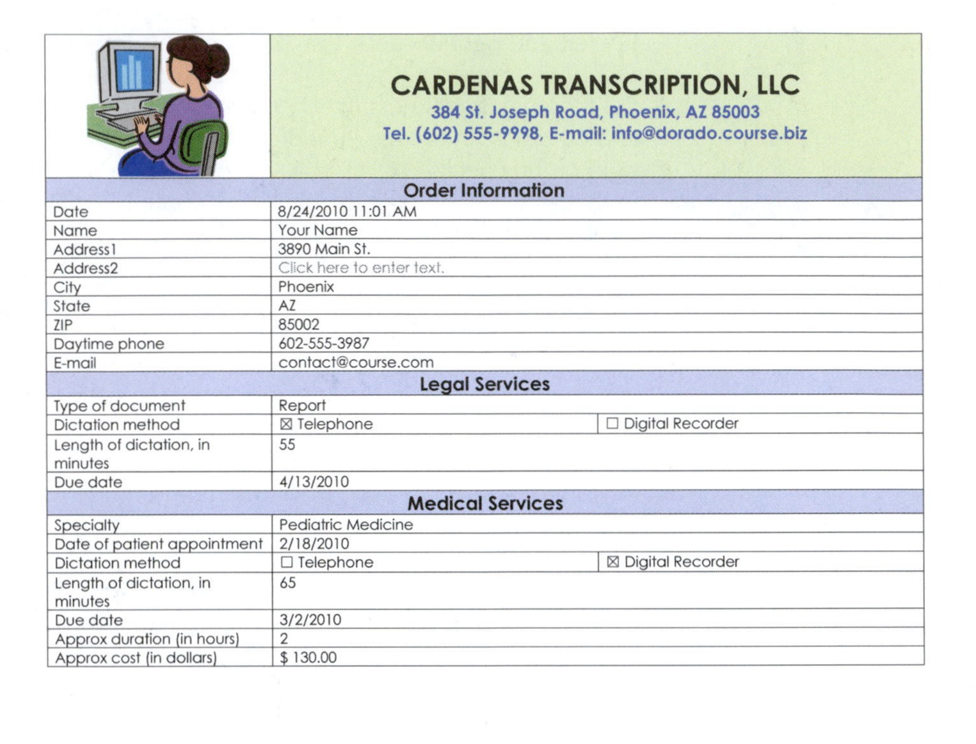

CARDENAS TRANSCRIPTION, LLC
384 St. Joseph Road, Phoenix, AZ 85003
Tel. (602) 555-9998, E-mail: info@dorado.course.biz

Order Information		
Date	8/24/2010 11:01 AM	
Name	Your Name	
Address1	3890 Main St.	
Address2	Click here to enter text.	
City	Phoenix	
State	AZ	
ZIP	85002	
Daytime phone	602-555-3987	
E-mail	contact@course.com	
Legal Services		
Type of document	Report	
Dictation method	☒ Telephone	☐ Digital Recorder
Length of dictation, in minutes	55	
Due date	4/13/2010	
Medical Services		
Specialty	Pediatric Medicine	
Date of patient appointment	2/18/2010	
Dictation method	☐ Telephone	☒ Digital Recorder
Length of dictation, in minutes	65	
Due date	3/2/2010	
Approx duration (in hours)	2	
Approx cost (in dollars)	$ 130.00	

21. Save the filled-in form as a Word document named **Cardenas Order** in the AddCases folder.
22. Submit the completed documents in printed or electronic form, as requested.

ENDING DATA FILES

Cardenas Form.dotx
Cardenas Order.docx

APPENDIX A

Microsoft Office Specialist Certification Skills

WORD

OBJECTIVES

- Learn about the Microsoft Office Specialist certification program
- Manage document versions
- Share documents and create a blog post
- Use advanced Save options
- Work with a table of contents
- Hyphenate a document
- Insert and format text boxes
- Format comments, footnotes, and endnotes
- Set spelling and grammar checking options
- Apply character attributes
- Break links between text boxes
- Save Quick Parts to the global Building Blocks template
- Save a chart as a template
- Apply a template to an existing document
- Use the Style Organizer
- Apply styles to an index, specify columns, and specify language
- Create a table of authorities
- Complete a mail merge to email
- Create envelope forms
- Apply merge rules in a mail merge
- Create a custom macro button
- Add Help content to form fields
- Link a form to a database

This appendix provides information about the Microsoft Office Specialist certification program and the benefits of achieving certification. The appendix also presents coverage of additional skills related to the Microsoft Office Specialist Expert exam for Microsoft Word 2010 that are not covered in the main tutorials of this text. Finally, the appendix includes a grid showing where the skills for both the Word 2010 Specialist (Core) exam and the Word 2010 Expert exam are covered in this text.

STARTING DATA FILES

WordA

MDNI.docx
MDNI Styles.dotx
MDNI Template.dotx
Results.docx

What Is Microsoft Office Specialist Certification?

Certification is a growing trend in the Information Technology industry whereby a software or hardware company devises and administers exams for users that enable them to demonstrate their ability to use the software or hardware effectively. By passing a certification exam, users prove their competence and knowledge of the software or hardware to prospective employers and colleagues.

The Microsoft Office Specialist program is the only comprehensive, performance-based certification program approved by Microsoft to validate desktop computer skills using the Microsoft Office 2010 programs, including Microsoft Word. The program provides computer program literacy, measures proficiency, and identifies opportunities for skill enhancement. Successful candidates receive a certificate that sets them apart from their peers in the competitive job market. The certificate is a valuable credential, recognized worldwide as proof that an individual has the desktop computing skills needed to work productively and efficiently. Certification is a valuable asset to individuals who want to begin or advance their computer careers.

The Microsoft Office Specialist exams are developed, marketed, and administered by Certiport, Inc., a company that has an exclusive license from Microsoft. Exams must be taken at an authorized Certiport Center, which administers exams in a quiet room with the proper hardware and software and has trained personnel to manage and proctor the exams.

Go to www.microsoft.com/learning/en/us/certification/mos.aspx#certifications to access the Microsoft Office Specialist Certification page, as shown in Figure A-1.

Figure A-1 Microsoft Office Specialist Certification page

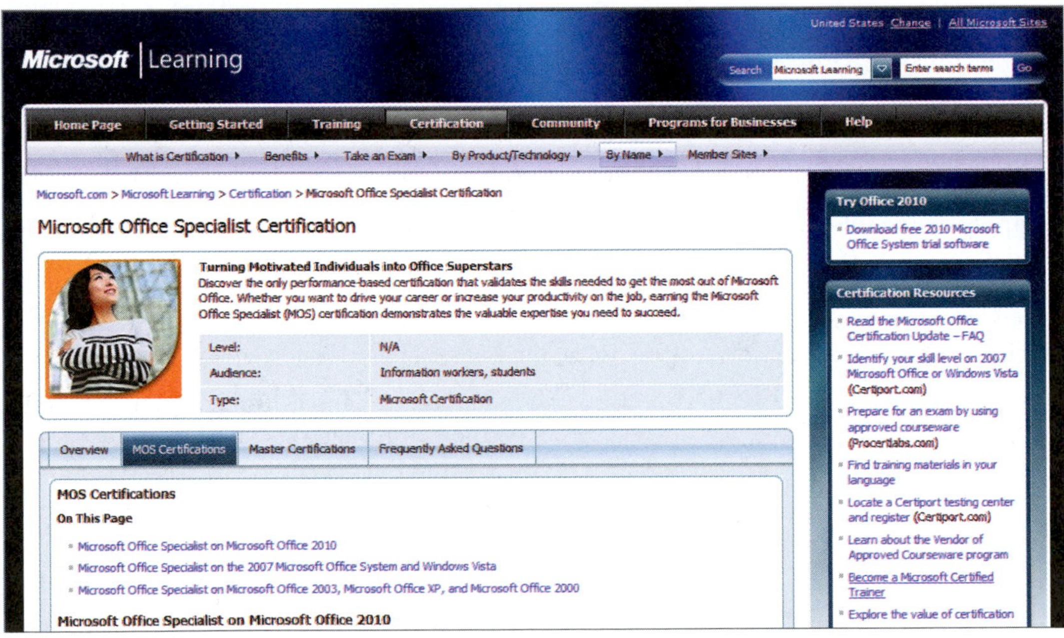

Used with permission from Microsoft.

> **TIP**
> For more information about the exams, view the FAQ documents at www.microsoft.com/certification or www.certiport.com/portal.

Benefits of Achieving Certification

Achieving Microsoft Office Specialist certification in one or several of the Microsoft Office 2010 programs can be beneficial to you and your current or prospective employer. Earning certification acknowledges that you have the expertise to work with Microsoft Office programs. Individuals who are Microsoft Office Specialist certified report increased competence and productivity with Microsoft Office programs, as well as increased credibility with their employers, coworkers, and clients. Certification sets you apart in today's competitive job market, bringing employment opportunities, greater earning potential and career advancement, and increased job satisfaction.

Certification can help you increase your productivity within your current job and is a great way to enhance your skills without taking courses to obtain a new degree. Another benefit of Microsoft certification is that you gain access to a member website, career-building tools, and training. More information about the certification series can be located on the Certiport web site at www.certiport.com/portal, as shown in Figure A-2.

Figure A-2 **Certification information on the Certiport site**

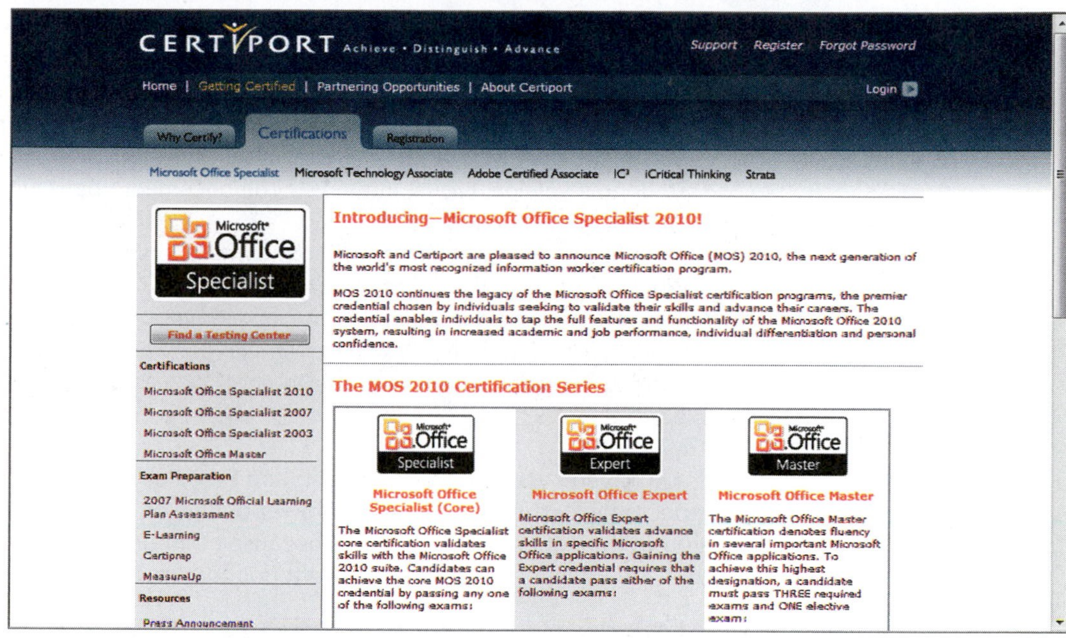

Courtesy of Certiport, Inc. www.certiport.com

Certification Process

> **TIP**
>
> Course Technology publishes a multitude of Microsoft Office 2010 products that you can use for self-study. Visit www.cengagebrain.com to view the options. You can also purchase the texts directly from this site.

The steps to successfully completing Microsoft Office Specialist Expert Certification for Microsoft Word are outlined below. The expert-level user should be able to perform many of the advanced skills in the program. Note that the Web addresses shown throughout might change. If you cannot find what you're looking for, go to the main site (www.microsoft.com or www.certiport.com) to search for a topic.

1. Find an authorized testing center near you using the Certiport Center locator at www.certiport.com/Portal/Pages/LocatorView.aspx.
2. Prepare for the exam by selecting the method that is appropriate for you, including taking a class or purchasing self-study materials.
3. Take a practice test (recommended) before taking the exam. To view the practice tests available, go to www.certiport.com/portal. Follow the online instructions for purchasing a voucher and taking the practice test.
4. Contact the Certiport Center and make an appointment for the exam you want to take. Check the organization's payment and exam policies. Purchase an exam voucher at www.certiport.com/portal. Go to the Certiport Center to take the test, and bring a printout of the exam voucher, your Certiport username and password, and a valid picture ID.
5. You will find out your results immediately. If you pass, you will receive your certificate two to three weeks after the date of the exam.

If you do not pass, refunds will not be given. But keep in mind that the exams are challenging and do not become discouraged. If you purchased a voucher with a retake, a second chance to take the exam might be all you need to pass. Check your Certiport Center's exam retake policies for more information.

Managing Document Versions

After you save a document for the first time, Word automatically saves your documents at regular intervals. Each instance of an automatically saved document is known as a **version**. If your computer crashes, or you make a change to a document that you later decide to reverse, you can sometimes return to an earlier version of your document.

REFERENCE

Managing Document Versions

- Open the document for which you want to manage versions.
- Click the File tab to display the Info tab in Backstage view. If previous versions of the document exist, you see them listed under "Versions."
- To open a version, click it in the list. The document opens with an orange Autosaved Version bar at the top.
- To save the open version as the new, current version of the document, click the Restore button in the Autosaved Version bar.
- To compare the open version to the current version of the document, click the Compare button in the Autosaved Version bar, then use the Track Changes features to accept or reject changes in the document.

If you haven't yet saved a document, and Word or your entire computer shuts down unexpectedly, perhaps because of a power outage or hardware failure, Word saves a version of the document. Files saved because of an unexpected or improper shut down might have unexpected names, or might not contain all of your latest edits.

REFERENCE

Recovering and Deleting Versions

- To recover a version of a document that you have not yet saved, click the File tab to display the Info tab in Backstage view, click the Manage Versions button, and then click Recover Unsaved Documents.
- In the Open dialog box, select the file you want to recover, click the Open button, and then save the document to a new location.
- To delete versions automatically saved by Word, click the File tab to open the Info tab in Backstage view, click the Manage Versions button, click Delete All Unsaved Documents, and then click the Yes button.

Sharing Documents

The Save & Send tab in Backstage view provides numerous options for sharing documents with other people.

Sending Documents via Internet Fax

Sometimes you will want to send documents via a fax sent over the Internet. You can do this from the Save & Send tab in Backstage view.

To send a document via Internet fax, you do the following:

1. Sign up for an account with an Internet fax service provider.
2. Open the document you want to fax, click the File tab to open Backstage view, and then click the Save & Send tab in the navigation bar. Send Using E-mail is selected in the Save & Send section.
3. Click the Send as Internet Fax button, and then follow the directions that appear on the screen.

Creating and Publishing a Blog Post

You can create and update blog posts in Word. Before you can publish them, though, you need to register for a blog account with an Internet blog provider that is compatible with Microsoft Word 2010.

To create and publish a blog post:

1. Start Word, click the **File** tab to open Backstage view, and then click the **New** tab in the navigation bar.
2. In the top row under "Available Templates," click the **Blog post** button, and then click the **Create** button. A blank blog post opens, and the Blog Post tab and the Insert tab are the only tabs on the Ribbon. If you have not previously registered for a blog account, you also see the Register a Blog Account dialog box. To register a blog account, you could click the Register Now button to open the New Blog Account dialog box. From there, you could follow the prompts to register your blog account.
3. Click the **Register Later** button in the Register a Blog Account dialog box to close the dialog box.
4. At the top of the blog post, click the **[Enter Post Title Here]** placeholder text, type **My New Blog**, click in the blank paragraph below the blog title, and type **This is the first entry in my new blog.** At this point, you could use the tools on the Insert tab to add tables, WordArt, photos, or other graphics to your blog post.
5. Save the blog post as **Sample Blog Post** in the WordA folder included with your Data Files. Now that you've written your first blog post, you can publish it.
6. On the Blog Post tab, click the **Publish** button in the Blog group. If you have not previously registered for a blog account, you see the Register a Blog Account dialog box again. At this point, you could click the Register an Account button and then follow the on-screen instructions to register a blog account and publish your blog.
7. Click the **Cancel** button to close the Register a Blog Account dialog box, and then click the **OK** button in the Microsoft Word dialog box.
8. Click the **File** tab and then click **Close** in the navigation bar to close the blog post.

TIP

To add, remove, or change blog accounts, click the Manage Accounts button in the Blog group on the Blog Post tab.

Changing File Types, File Modes, and Save As Options

Sometimes it's helpful to change a Word document to a different file type before sharing it with another person. You can either save a file with a different file type by specifying a file type in the Save as type box in the Save As dialog box, or you can convert any open Word document to a different file type from the Save & Send tab in Backstage view. In the File Types section of this tab, you can click the Change File Type option to access a list of available file types, such as:

- Word 97-2003 Document – Uses the Word 97-2003 document format compatible with previous versions of Word
- OpenDocument Text – Uses the OpenDocument text format compatible with other word-processing programs
- Template – Creates a Word template from the file
- Plain Text – Uses a format that contains only the text of the document without any formatting

- Rich Text Format – Uses a format that contains the text and the formatting of your document
- Single File Web Page – Uses a format of a single file Web page

Once you select one of these file type options, you click the Save As button, the Save As dialog box opens, and you can rename the file and select a save location.

Understanding Compatibility Mode

When you use Word 2010 to open a document created in an earlier version of Word, the document opens in Word 2007 Compatibility Mode or Word 97-2003 Compatibility Mode, whichever is appropriate. In these modes, Word 2010 disables any features incompatible with older file types and displays "Compatibility Mode" after the file name in the title bar. You can check for compatibility issues by using the Compatibility Checker:

1. With the file open in the document window, click the File tab to open Backstage view and display the Info tab.
2. In the Prepare for Sharing section, click the Check for Issues button, and then click Check Compatibility to open the Microsoft Word Compatibility Checker dialog box.
3. Click the Select versions to show button to display a menu listing Word 97-2003 and Word 2007. See Figure A-3. By default, check marks appear next to both versions of Word. If you need to check for compatibility with only one version of Word, click the other version to remove the check mark. If compatibility issues are found, these will be listed in the Summary box. Review these before you convert the file to the newest Word file format as they explain what changes will occur in the formatting and appearance of the document once the file is converted to the updated format.

Figure A-3 **Microsoft Word Compatibility Checker dialog box**

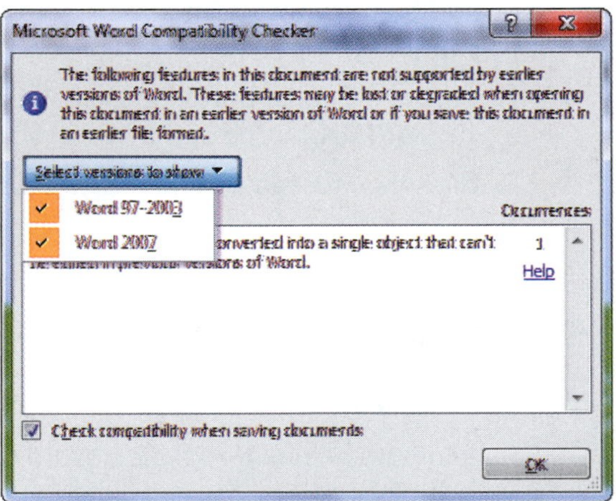

4. To convert the file to the file format that is compatible with Word 97-2003, click the Save as type arrow in the Save As dialog box, and then select Word 97-2003 Document, or click the Save & Send tab in Backstage view, click Change File Type, and then click Word 97-2003 Document in the right pane.

Managing Default Save Options

In the Word Options dialog box, you can change the default setting for the file type used for a newly saved document. You can also change the default save location and how often a file is saved automatically.

REFERENCE

Managing Save Options

- Click the File tab to open Backstage view, click the Options command, and then click Save in the left pane of the Word Options dialog box.
- To change the default file type, click the Save files in this format arrow in the right pane, and then click the file type you want from the list.
- To change the default location for newly saved files, click the Browse button to the right of the Default file location box to open the Modify Location dialog box, browse to and select the folder you want, and then click the OK button to close the Modify Location dialog box.
- To change how often a file is automatically saved, change the number in the box for saving AutoRecover information.
- Click the OK button to close the Word Options dialog box.

Navigating and Searching Through a Document

You can use the Find and Replace dialog box to search for non-printing and other special characters.

To search for non-printing paragraph marks:

1. Open the document **MDNI** located in the WordA folder included with your Data Files, and then save the document as **MDNI Report** in the same folder. Make sure non-printing characters are displayed.
2. Click the **Home** tab, click the **Find button arrow** in the Editing group, and then click **Advanced Find**. The Find and Replace dialog box opens, with the Find tab displayed.
3. If you see the More button in the Find and Replace dialog box, click the **More** button to expand the dialog box. You can search for non-printing characters indicating paragraphs, tabs, or line breaks.
4. Click the **Special** button to open a menu of special document elements that you can search for, and then click **Paragraph Mark**. A caret symbol (^) and the letter "p" appear in the Find what box in the Find and Replace dialog box. This code tells Word that you want to search for the non-printing paragraph character.
5. Click the **Find Next** button. The next paragraph mark in the document (immediately after the photo) is selected. (You might need to drag the Find and Replace dialog box by its title bar to move it if you can't see the selected paragraph mark.)
6. Click the **Cancel** button to close the Find and Replace dialog box.

TIP

To display only the document text, without page breaks, headers, footers, and certain other elements, click the Draft button in the status bar.

Using the Go To Command

The Go To command on the Find menu allows you to go to a specific page, section, heading, or other location in a document.

To use the Go To command to go to specific locations in a document:

1. In the Editing group on the Home tab, click the **Find button arrow** and then click **Go To**. The Find and Replace dialog box opens with the Go To tab displayed. "Page" is selected in the Go to what box by default, but you can select other options to go to.
2. Click the **Next** button to move the insertion point to the top of page 2 of the MDNI Report document.
3. Click in the **Enter page number** box, and then type **4**. The Next button in the dialog box changes to the Go To button.
4. Click the **Go To** button to move the insertion point to the top of page 4.
5. In the Go to what box, click **Section**, and then use the Previous and Next buttons to move among the various sections in the document.
6. Click the **Close** button to close the Find and Replace dialog box, and then press the **Ctrl+Home** keys to move to the beginning of the document.

Browsing by Text, Page, or Other Object

There are three buttons at the bottom of the vertical scroll bar that can be used to navigate through a document—the Previous and Next buttons, and the Select Browse Object button. The Select Browse Object button allows you to search the document for specific objects or in a specific manner. For example, you can choose to browse your document by edits, headings, graphics, tables, fields, endnotes, footnotes, comments, and sections. The Next button and Previous button at the bottom of the vertical scroll bar change to reflect the most recently selected item using the Select Browse Object button. The default is Next Page and Previous Page. You can also access the Find and Replace dialog box from this menu.

To use the Select Browse Object button:

1. Click the **Select Browse Object** button near the bottom of the vertical scroll bar. The Select Browse Object menu opens.
2. Move the mouse pointer over the **Browse by Page** button. The name of this button appears at the top of the menu.
3. Click the **Browse by Page** button. The menu closes and the insertion point moves to the beginning of the next page.
4. Point to the **Next Page** button to see the ScreenTip that identifies this button as the Next Page button, and then click. The insertion point moves to the beginning of the next page.
5. Click the **Select Browse Object** button, and then click the **Browse by Heading** button. The insertion point moves to the left of the next heading in the document.
6. Point to the **Next Heading** button. The ScreenTip indicates that the button is now the Next Heading button.
7. Click the **Select Browse Object** button, and then click the **Find** button. The Find and Replace dialog box opens with the Find tab displayed.
8. Click the **Cancel** button to close the Find and Replace dialog box.

Working with a Table of Contents

You already know how to use the Table of Contents button on the References tab to insert a table of contents in a document. When you insert a table of contents, you can adjust the default table of contents settings. For example, you can select a tab leader to separate each heading from its page number. You can also change the formatting applied to each heading in the table of contents.

To insert and modify a table of contents:

1. Move the insertion point to the beginning of page 2 of the MDNI Report document (to the left of the "R" in "Rationale"), click the **Insert** tab, click the **Blank Page** button in the Pages group, and then scroll up and click at the beginning of the new blank page 2 (above the page break). This is where you will insert the table of contents.
2. Click the **References** tab on the Ribbon, click the **Table of Contents** button in the Table of Contents group, and then click **Insert Table of Contents** near the bottom of the menu to open the Table of Contents dialog box. In the Print Preview and Web Preview boxes in the Table of Contents dialog box, you can review how your table of contents will appear, and make adjustments if you want to.
3. Click the **Modify** button to open the Style dialog box. See Figure A-4. Each heading within the table of contents is formatted with a style. Level 1 headings are formatted with the TOC 1 style, Level 2 headings are formatted with the TOC 2 style, and so on. You can modify these TOC styles to make the table of contents headings look any way you want.

Figure A-4 Style dialog box

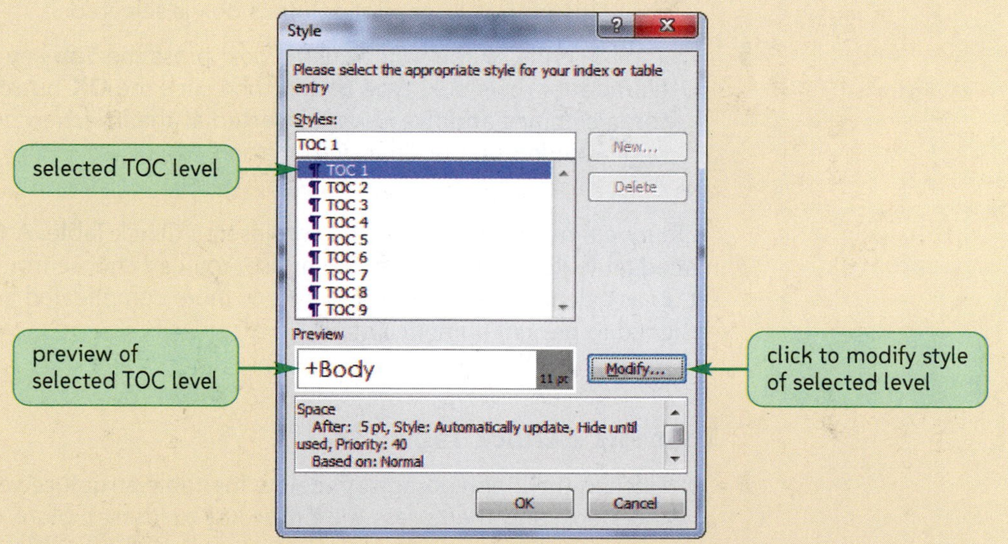

4. Verify that TOC 1 is selected in the Styles box, and then click the **Modify** button to open the Modify Style dialog box. In this dialog box, you can make a variety of formatting changes.
5. Click the **Font Color** arrow (the box currently contains "Automatic"), click the **Green, Accent1, Darker 50%** tile (fifth from the left in the bottom row of the Theme Colors section), and then click the **OK** button to close the Modify Style dialog box and return to the Style dialog box. The Preview of the selected TOC 1 style in the Preview box is now green.

6. Click the **OK** button to close the Style dialog box. You return to the Table of Contents dialog box. In the Print Preview box, the Heading 1 entry is now green.
7. Click the **Tab leader** arrow, and then click the straight line option (third option in the menu). The tab leaders in the Print Preview box are now solid lines.
8. Click the **OK** button to close the Table of Contents dialog box. The new table of contents, with green text for the Heading 1 level and a solid line tab leader, is inserted in the document.

TIP

You can deselect the Right align page numbers check box to remove the tab leader lines and shift the page numbers to the left.

Inserting Tables

The fastest way to insert a table in a document is to use the Table button in the Tables group on the Insert tab, which allows you to drag the mouse pointer to select the desired number of rows and columns. In some situations, however, you might prefer to use the Insert Table dialog box, the Quick Tables option, or the Draw Table pointer.

To use the Insert Table dialog box to insert a table:

1. Press the **Ctrl+End** keys to move to the end of the MDNI Report document, click the **Insert** tab on the Ribbon, and then click the **Page Break** button in the Pages group.
2. In the Tables group on the Insert tab, click the **Table** button to display the menu.
3. Click **Insert Table** to open the Insert Table dialog box. The Number of columns and Number of rows boxes display a default number of rows and columns, and the value in the Number of columns box is selected.
4. Type **3** in the Number of columns box, press the **Tab** key to select the value in the Number of rows box, type **5**, and then click the **OK** button. A blank table with three columns and five rows is inserted at the insertion point, ready for you to begin adding text or other information.

To save time on formatting, you can insert a Quick Table. A **Quick Table** is a preformatted table designed for a particular use. You can choose from Quick Tables that are set up as calendars, simple tabbed lists, or more complicated grids, called matrices, designed to present numeric data.

To insert a Quick Table:

1. Click in the blank paragraph below the table structure you inserted in the preceding steps, and then press the **Enter** key to insert a blank paragraph.
2. Click the **Insert** tab on the Ribbon, click the **Table** button in the Tables group, and then point to **Quick Tables**. A gallery of Quick Tables appears.
3. Scroll to the bottom of the Quick Tables gallery, and then click **With Subheads 2**. A table containing placeholder text with a formatted header row and formatted second and eighth rows for subheadings is inserted in the document. A sample heading for the Quick Table, "Enrollment in local colleges, 2005," is also inserted. The insertion point is in the first cell in the table, and the Table Tools Design tab is the active tab on the Ribbon.

TIP

To move rows or columns, you select the rows or columns, and then drag them to a new location.

Inserting Symbol and Picture Bullets

The default bullet symbol is a round, black circle. The Bullet Library, which appears when you click the Bullets button in the paragraph group on the Home tab, offers some additional bullet styles. You can also define your own bullet style using symbols or pictures as bullets.

To use symbols as bullets:

1. Scroll up to page 3, and then select the bulleted list below the heading "Survey Goals." This list is currently formatted with the default bullet style.
2. Click the **Bullets button arrow** in the Paragraph group on the Home tab, and then click **Define New Bullet**. The Define New Bullet dialog box opens.
3. Click the **Symbol** button. The Symbol dialog box opens, displaying a gallery of symbols you can use as bullets.
4. Click the **clubs** symbol in the top row, click the **OK** button to close the Symbol dialog box, and then click the **OK** button to close the Define New Bullet dialog box. The bullets in the document are now formatted as clubs.

Now you'll reformat the same list using picture bullets.

To use pictures as bullets:

1. Verify that the bulleted list is still selected.
2. Click the **Bullets button arrow** in the Paragraph group, click **Define New Bullet**, and then click the **Picture** button in the Define New Bullet dialog box. The Picture Bullet dialog box opens allowing you to select from a number of predefined picture bullets installed with Microsoft Office.
3. Scroll down and click the dark red X (just below the green square) to select it.
4. Click the **OK** button to close the Picture Bullet dialog box, and then click the **OK** button to close the Define New Bullet dialog box. The list is now formatted with red Xs as the bullets.

TIP

To use a picture stored on your computer as a bullet, click the Import button and select the picture you want.

Hyphenating a Document

Hyphenation is turned off by default in a new Word document. However, you can easily turn it on, and then adjust settings related to hyphenating a document.

To turn on hyphenation in a document:

1. Scroll down so the heading "Market Research Overview" on page 3 is at the top of the screen. Notice that no lines on this page end with a hyphenated word.
2. Click the **Page Layout** tab on the Ribbon, click the **Hyphenation** button in the Page Setup group, and then click **Automatic**. The Hyphenation menu closes, and the text layout shifts to account for the insertion of hyphens in words that break near the end of a line. By default, any word that ends within .25 inches of the end of a line is hyphenated.

Inserting Text Boxes

A **text box** is an object that contains text and that you can treat as an inline object or a floating object. Word offers an assortment of predesigned text boxes as building blocks. Text boxes that contain text copied from the document are called **pull quotes**, because they contain text "pulled" from the document. Pull quotes offer an opportunity to reiterate an important point and provide relief from unbroken text. A variation on pull quotes is **sidebars**, which are text boxes that contain additional, related information that is not contained in the main document.

TIP

You can also click the Draw Text Box option below the gallery, and then click and drag the crosshair pointer to draw a text box in the document.

TIP

To format the text in a text box vertically instead of horizontally, select the text box, click the Text Direction button in the Text group on the Drawing Tools Format tab, and then click the desired text direction.

To insert a building block text box containing a pull quote:

1. Scroll down to page 5 in the MDNI Report document, and then click anywhere in the paragraph under the heading "Future Recommendations."
2. Click the **Insert** tab on the Ribbon, and then click the **Text Box** button in the Text group. A gallery of text boxes opens. Some of the text boxes include "Quote" in their names and some include "Sidebar." There is no difference as far as Word is concerned; clicking any of the options in the gallery inserts a floating object with formatted placeholder text that you can change.
3. In the gallery, scroll down and then click the **Austin Pull Quote** text box. A text box with green bars on the top and bottom is inserted on the left side of the page. The Drawing Tools Format tab is the active tab on the Ribbon, and the placeholder text in a content control in the text box is selected.
4. Type **The survey indicates no need for major changes in current broadband products.** You will change the font color of this pull quote text to make the text easier to read.
5. Drag the mouse pointer to select the text in the text box, click the **Text Fill button arrow** in the WordArt Styles group on the Drawing Tools Format tab, and then click the **Green, Accent1, Darker 50%** tile (fifth color from the left in the bottom row of the Theme Colors section).
6. With the text box still selected, click the **More** button in the Shape Styles group to open the Shape Styles Gallery, and then click the **Subtle Effect – Green, Accent 1** style (fourth row, second option from the left).
7. With the text box still selected, click the **Shape Effects** button in the Shape Styles group, point to **Shadow**, and then click the **Offset Diagonal Top Right** shadow option (first option in the third row in the Outer section of the gallery). You can also apply effects that combine shadow and 3-D effects to text boxes.
8. With the text box still selected, click the **Shape Effects** button in the Shape Styles group, point to **3-D**, and then click **Oblique Top Right** (second option under Oblique) to apply a 3-D effect to the text box.
9. Position the pointer on the text box border so that the pointer changes to ✥, and then drag the text box to position it below the heading "Future Recommendations" as shown in Figure A-5.

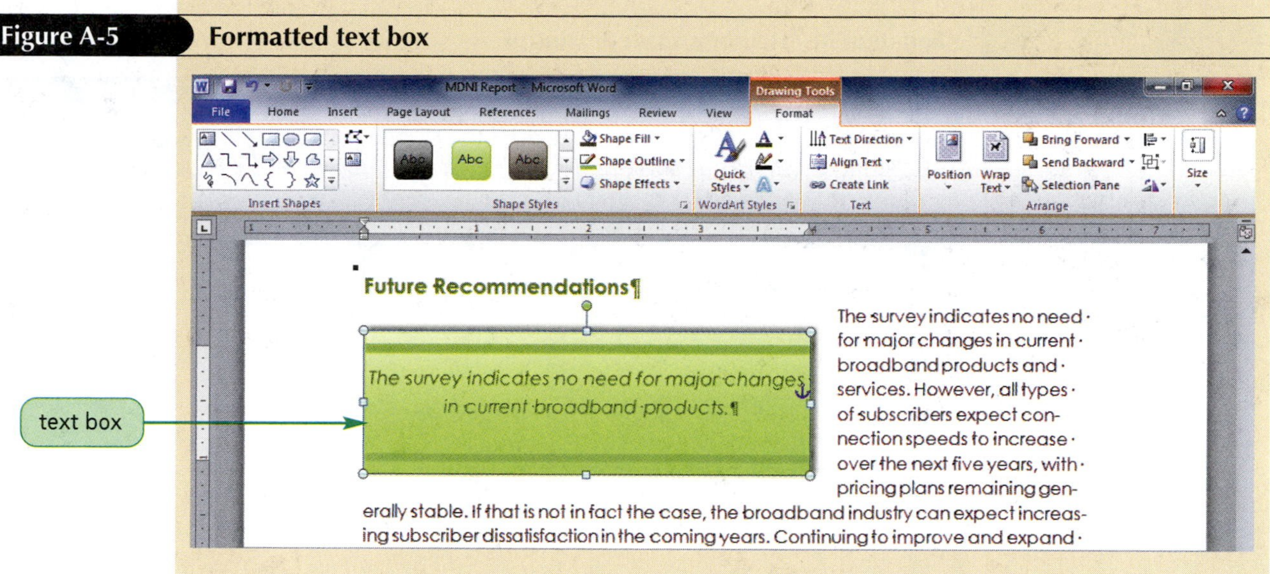

Figure A-5 Formatted text box

Inserting an Equation

To insert one of several standard equations in a Word document, you can use the Equation gallery, which you open by clicking the Equation button arrow in the Symbols group on the Insert tab. To create your own equation, you can click the Equation button to open a content control, and then use the options on the Equation Tools Design tab to build your equation.

To insert an equation into the document:

1. Press the **Ctrl+End** keys to move the insertion point to the end of the document, and then press the **Ctrl+Enter** keys to start a new page.
2. Click the **Insert** tab on the Ribbon, and then click the **Equation button arrow** in the Symbols group to display the Equation gallery.
3. Scroll down through the gallery to review the various equations, and then scroll back up and click the **Area of Circle** equation. The equation is inserted in the document within a content control. It is formatted as an inline object, so if you type text before it, it will move right to accommodate the new text. See Figure A-6.

TIP

Click the Insert New Equation option below the Equation gallery to insert a blank content control in which you can type your own custom equation.

Figure A-6 Equation inserted in a content control

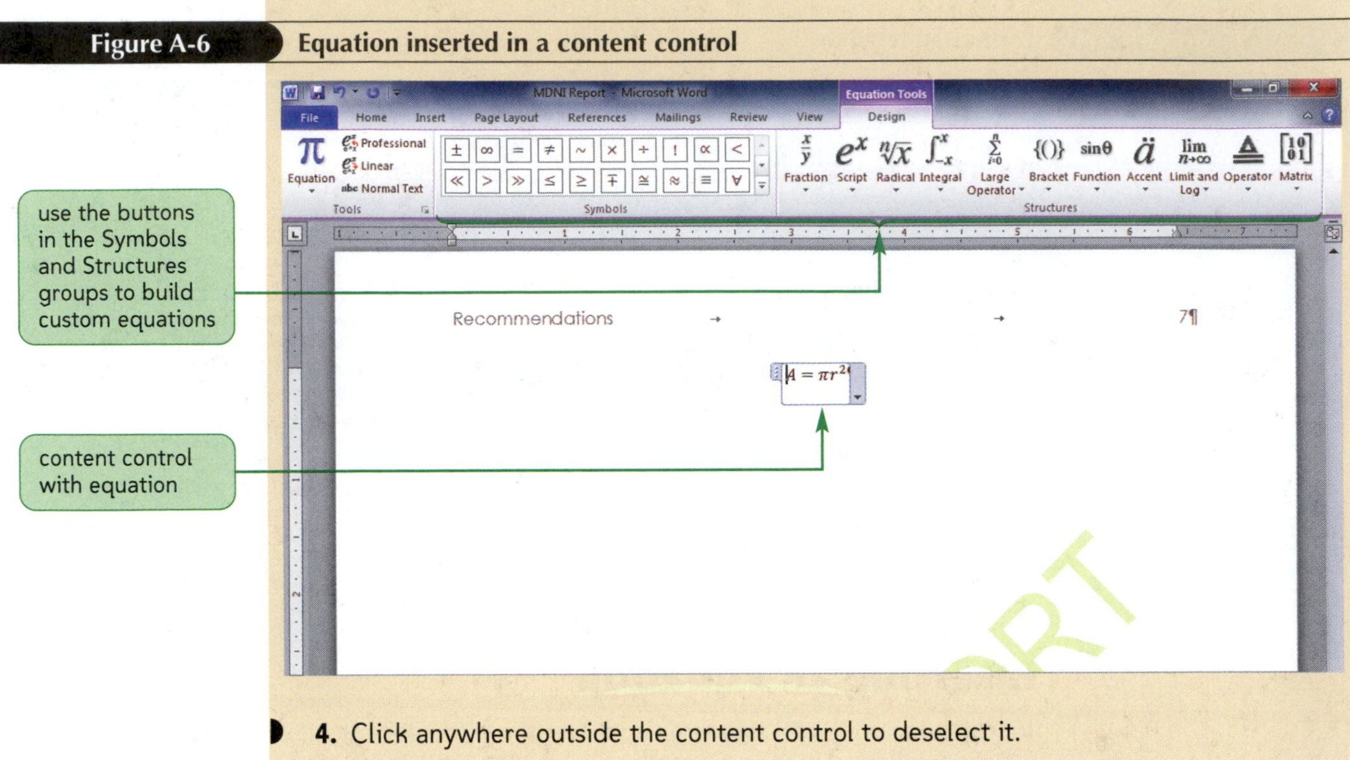

4. Click anywhere outside the content control to deselect it.

Inserting a Screenshot

A **screenshot** is an image of a screen open in Windows. Using the Screenshot button in the Illustrations group on the Insert tab, you can quickly capture a screenshot of an open window and insert it into a document.

To capture a screenshot of the MDNI Report document:

1. With the MDNI Report document still open, open a new, blank document, and save it as **Screenshot** in the WordA folder included with your Data Files.
2. Click the **Insert** tab on the Ribbon, and then click the **Screenshot** button in the Illustrations group. A menu opens with thumbnail images of all the windows currently open on your computer, including other Office applications, browsers, email programs, and so on. The only window that does not appear in this menu is the current document, Screenshot.
3. Click the thumbnail image for the MDNI Report document. A screenshot of the Word window, with the MDNI Report document displayed, is inserted in the Screenshot document.
4. Save and close the Screenshot document. You return to the MDNI Report document.

TIP

To capture only part of a window as a screenshot, click the Insert tab, click the Screenshot button, click Screen Clipping, and then drag the pointer to select part of the window.

Using Microsoft Clip Organizer

Microsoft Clip Organizer is a separate Office utility that you can use to store and manage your collection of clip art images, animations, photos, videos, and other media.

To start Microsoft Clip Organizer:

1. Click the **Start** button, click **All Programs**, scroll down the list of programs if necessary, click **Microsoft Office**, click **Microsoft Office 2010 Tools**, and then click **Microsoft Clip Organizer**. The Microsoft Clip Organizer window opens, with a list of clip art collections in the left pane. The Office Collections contain clip art installed on your computer as part of Microsoft Office. The Web Collections give you access to clip art available from Office.com.
2. Double-click the **Office Collections** folder to expand the list of folders, double-click the **Animals** folder to expand the list of folders, and then click the **Wild** folder. The only image of a wild animal installed as part of Office, a tiger, appears in the right pane.
3. Move the mouse pointer over the tiger image, and then click the arrow that appears on the right side of the image. A menu of options opens. See Figure A-7.

Figure A-7 Image displayed in Microsoft Clip Organizer

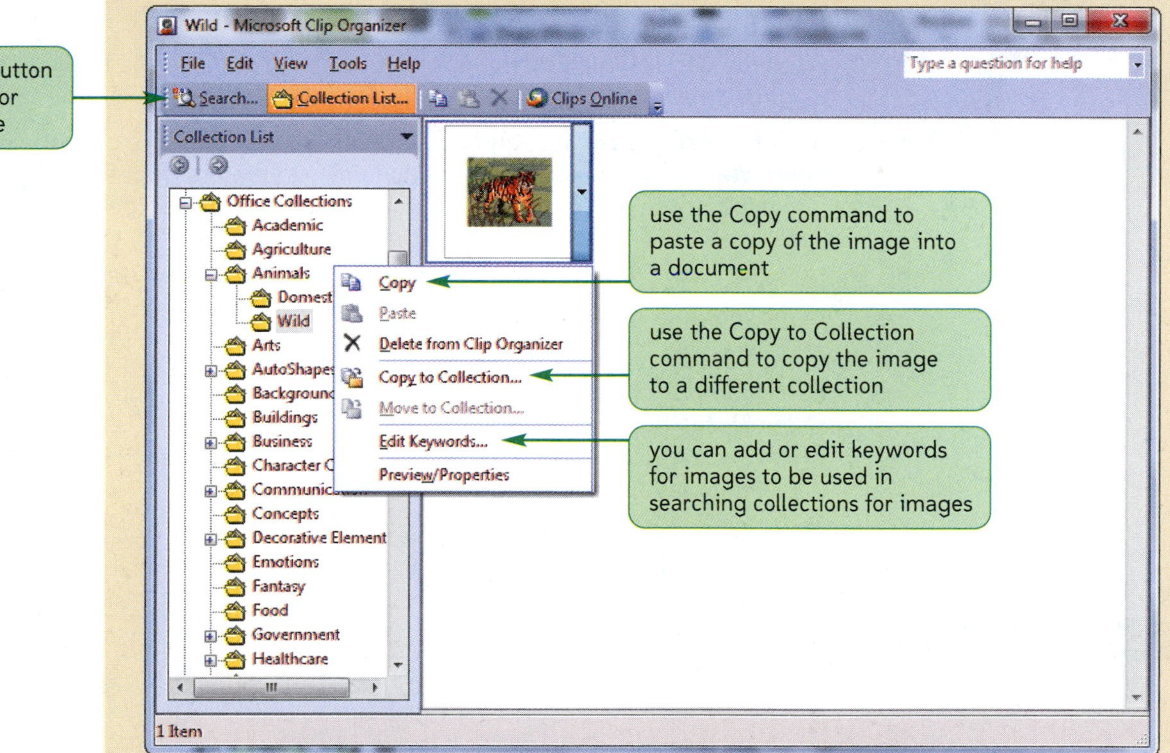

4. Click the **Close** button to close the Microsoft Clip Organizer window and return to the MDNI Report document in Word.

Working with Comments

By default, Word displays comments in bubbles in a document's margin. Comments displayed this way are easy to edit—you just click in the margin bubble and edit it like regular text. You can delete or insert comment text, or format it to add emphasis. If you are working on a small monitor, however, you might find it helpful to display comments inline instead. Inline comments are indicated by a color highlight on the commented text, along with the initials of the user who made the comments and the comment number. To display comments inline, you do the following:

1. Click the Review tab, click the Show Markup button in the Tracking group, point to Balloons, and then click Show All Revisions Inline.
2. To display an inline comment in a floating window, position the mouse pointer over the colored highlight.
3. To revert to Word's default setting, click the Show Markup button in the Tracking group, point to Balloons, and then click Show Only Comments and Formatting in Balloons.

TIP

You can adjust the margin above a header and below a footer by changing the settings in the Header from Top or the Footer from Bottom boxes in the Position group on the Header & Footer Tools Design tab.

Working with Footnotes and Endnotes

The options in the Footnote and Endnote dialog box allow you to format and manage footnotes and endnotes.

To manage footnotes in the MDNI Report document:

1. Press the **Ctrl+Home** keys to move the insertion point to the beginning of the document.
2. Click the **References** tab, and then, in the Footnotes group, click the **Next Footnote** button to move the insertion point to the first footnote number, 1, which is located at the end of the first sentence in the paragraph below the "Market Research Overview" paragraph on page 3.
3. In the Footnotes group, click the **Show Notes** button to move the insertion point to the footnote itself, at the bottom of page 3.
4. In the Footnotes group, click the **Next Footnote** button twice to move to the third footnote in the document, at the bottom of page 5, and then click the **Show Notes** button to toggle back to footnote number "3" in the document, which is located at the end of the first paragraph under the heading "Future Recommendations" on page 5.
5. Click the **dialog box launcher** in the Footnotes group to open the Footnote and Endnote dialog box. See Figure A-8.

Figure A-8 Footnote and Endnote dialog box

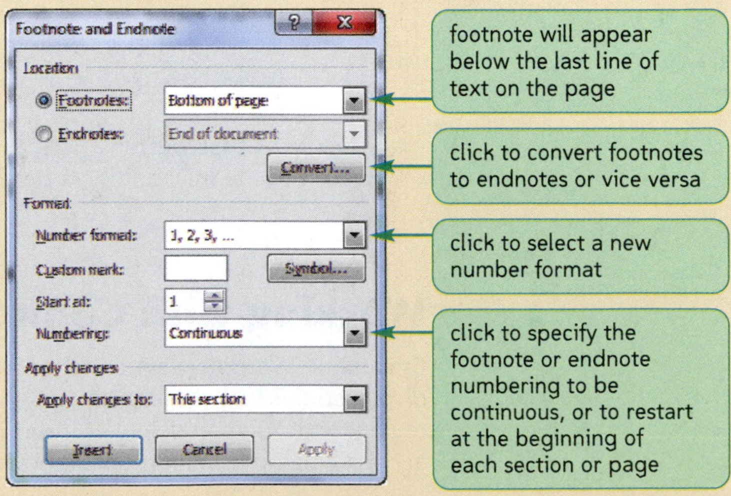

6. In the Location section, click the arrow on the box next to "Footnotes," and then click **Below text**.
7. In the Format section, click the **Number format** arrow, and then click the fourth numbering option of lowercase Roman numerals.
8. Click the **Apply changes to** arrow, click **Whole document**, and then click the **Apply** button. The Footnote and Endnote dialog box closes, and the footnote on page 5 is numbered "iii".
9. Save the document and close it.

Using Auto Check for Errors in Mail Merge

A mistake in a large mail merge can be expensive, because it could result in misprinted envelopes or letterhead, as well as wasted printer toner. Mistakes typically result from a data source that lacks the necessary merge fields, or that has the wrong kind of data stored in the merge fields (for example, text in a numeric field). To prevent such errors, you can click the Auto Check for Errors button in the Preview Results group on the Mailings tab before completing the merge. This opens the Checking and Reporting Errors dialog box shown in Figure A-9.

Figure A-9 Checking and Reporting Errors dialog box

In this dialog box, you can keep the default option for completing the merge while you are monitoring it, so you can check for errors as the merge happens. Or, you can choose one of the other two options, which enable you to complete the merge without monitoring it and then check the resulting error report. You could then correct any mistakes before printing the merged documents.

Setting Spelling and Grammar Options

You already know how to use the spelling and grammar checker to check a document for errors, and how to take advantage of the automatic corrections performed by AutoCorrect. The Proofing tab in the Word Options dialog box includes advanced settings for the Grammar Checker and AutoCorrect. You will open a document and configure these settings.

To configure Grammar Checker options:

1. Open the **Results** document located in the WordA folder included with your Data Files, and save it with the name **Survey Results** in the same folder. Make sure that non-printing characters are displayed.

TIP

To turn off AutoCorrect, click the AutoCorrect Options button, deselect the Replace text as you type check box on the AutoCorrect tab, and then click the OK button.

2. Click the **File** tab on the Ribbon, click **Options** in the navigation bar to open the Word Options dialog box, and then click **Proofing** in the left pane. See Figure A-10. You can deselect and select the check boxes in the "When correcting spelling in Microsoft Office programs" and "When correcting spelling and grammar in Word" sections in the right pane to modify the spelling and grammar checker. For example, to hide errors in the document rather than marking them with wavy underlines, you could deselect the Check spelling as you type and Mark grammar errors as you type check boxes. To check only spelling when you use the Spelling and Grammar dialog box, deselect the Check grammar with spelling check box.

Figure A-10 Proofing options in the Word Options dialog box

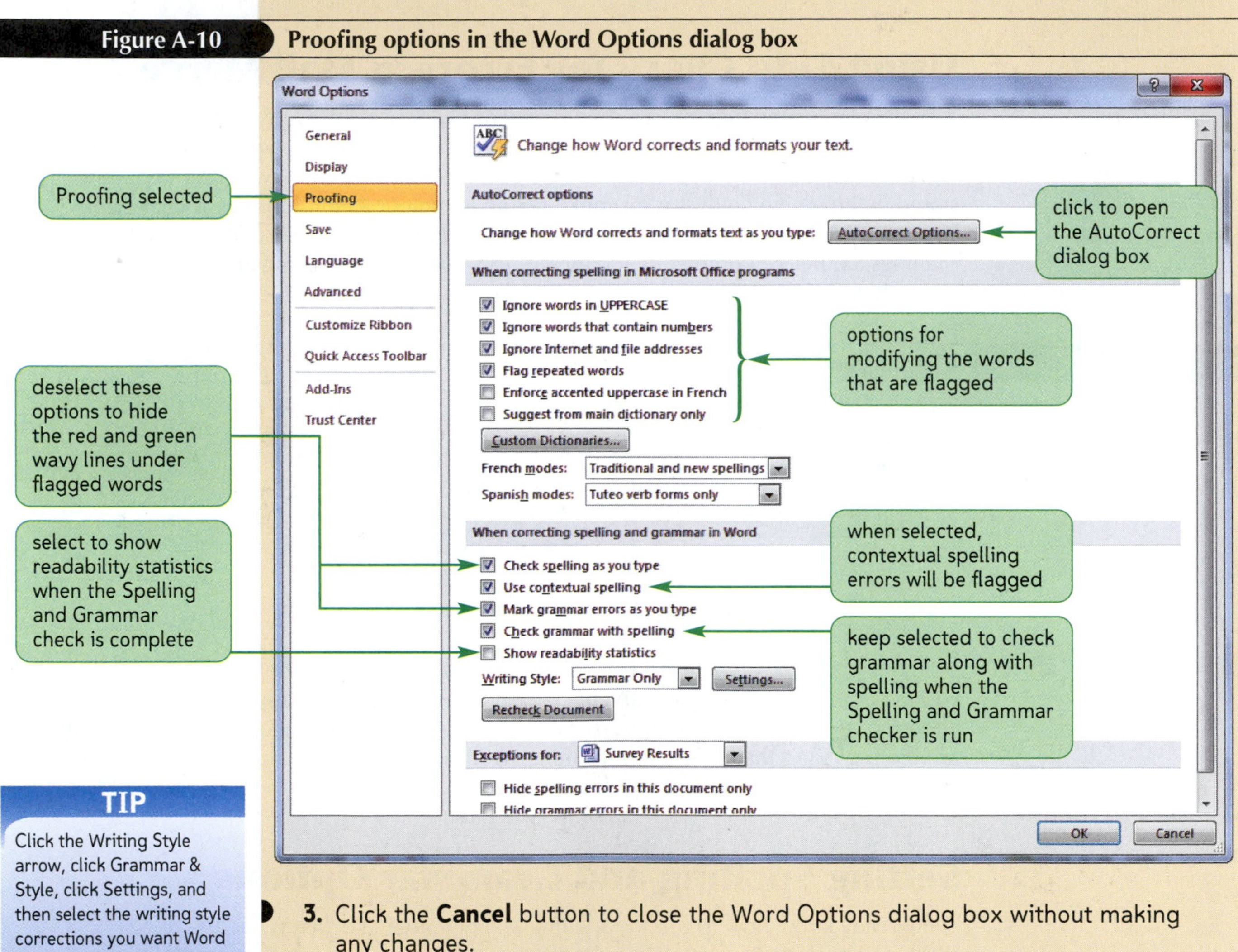

TIP

Click the Writing Style arrow, click Grammar & Style, click Settings, and then select the writing style corrections you want Word to make automatically.

3. Click the **Cancel** button to close the Word Options dialog box without making any changes.

Applying Character Attributes

You already know how to format text using the options in the Font group on the Home tab. To apply additional attributes to characters, do the following:

1. Click the Dialog Box Launcher in the Font group to open the Font dialog box.
2. On the Font tab, click the check boxes in the Effects section to apply different font effects such as Strikethrough, Double strikethrough, Superscript, Subscript, Small caps, and All caps.
3. Click the OK button to close the dialog box and apply the attributes you selected.

Breaking Links Between Text Boxes

In Tutorial 8 you learned that you can link two text boxes so that text flows from the first one to the second one automatically. To unlink text boxes, click in the first text box, and then click the Break Link button in the Text group on the Drawing Tools Format tab. The text in the second text box is removed, and again appears in the original text box.

Working with Templates

Templates are very useful for formatting documents with consistent styles. As you work with documents, you can save custom building blocks to the Building Blocks template, you can save a chart as a template, and you can attach a new template to a document.

Saving Quick Parts to the Building Blocks Template

In Tutorial 8 you learned that you can save a Quick Part to a template, so that any time someone uses the template, they can access that Quick Part. However, when you save Quick Parts to the global Building Blocks template that is stored on your computer, they are available to all documents you create on that computer. If you choose to save a Quick Part to the global Building Blocks template, when you exit Word, a message box will open telling you that you have made changes to the Normal.dotm template, and asking you to confirm and save these changes. See Figure A-11. You need to click the Save button to save the Quick Parts; if you click the Don't Save button, the Quick Parts will not be saved and will not be available to you the next time you use Word on that computer.

Figure A-11 **Message box asking you to confirm saving changes to the Building Blocks template**

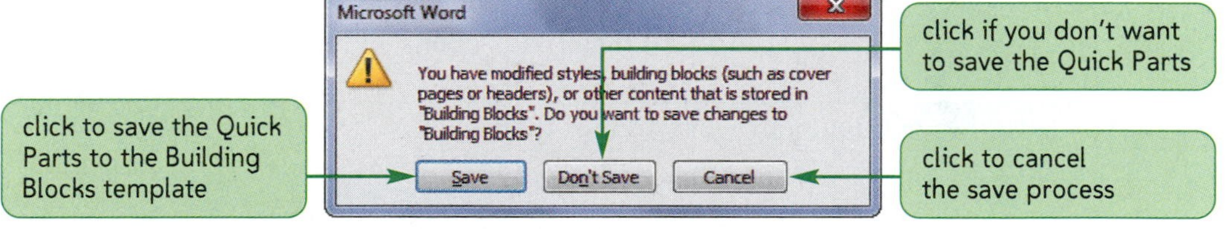

Saving a Chart as a Template

You can save a chart created in a Word document as a template. This is useful if you have a chart layout and style you want to use in other documents.

To save the pie chart as a template:

1. Go to page 5, and then click the pie chart. The Chart Tools contextual tabs appear on the Ribbon.
2. Click the **Design** tab, and then click the **Save As Template** button in the Type group. The Save Chart Template dialog box opens. This dialog box is similar to the Save As dialog box. Notice that the file type in the Save as type box is "Chart Template Files" and the default location is C:\Users\<user name>\AppData\Roaming\Microsoft\Templates\Charts. To be able to use the chart template, you need to save it to this location. For this appendix, you'll save it to the WordA folder.
3. Type **Chart Template** in the File name box, navigate to the WordA folder included with your Data Files, and then click the **Save** button.

To use the chart template, click the Chart button in the Illustrations group on the Insert tab to open the Insert Chart dialog box, and then click Templates at the top of the list. Any templates you have saved to the default location appear in the dialog box. Select the template you want to use, and then click the OK button.

Attaching a New Template to a Document

You can attach a different template to a document. You will not see any changes to the document, but anything stored with the new template—for example, macros, building blocks (sometimes called customized Quick Parts)—are now available to the document.

To attach a new template to a document:

1. Open the **MDNI Template** document located in the WordA folder included with your Data Files, and then save it as a template file with the new name **MDNI Template Attached** in the same location. The MDNI Template Attached file does not need to remain open to be attached to a document. You will close it.
2. Close the **MDNI Template Attached** file.
3. On page 5 of the Survey Results document, click anywhere in the level one heading "3. Residential Subscribers." In the Styles group on the Home tab, notice that the Heading 1 style is selected. Text formatted with the Heading 1 style is dark orange and bold.
4. Click the **File** tab, click **Options** in the navigation bar to open the Word Options dialog box, and then click **Add-Ins** in the left pane.
5. At the bottom of the right pane, click the **Manage** arrow, click **Templates**, and then click the **Go** button. The Word Options dialog box closes, and the Templates and Add-ins dialog box opens with the Templates tab selected. See Figure A-12.

TIP

You can also display the Developer tab, and then in the Templates group, click the Document Template button to open the Templates and Add-ins dialog box.

Figure A-12 Templates and Add-ins dialog box

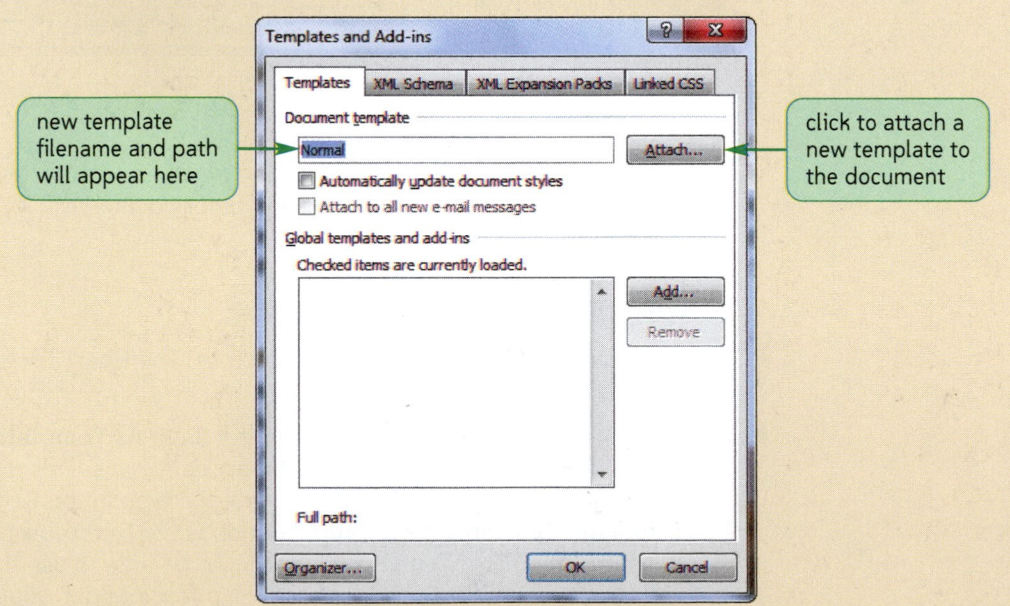

6. Click the **Attach** button to open the Attach Template dialog box.

7. Navigate to the WordA folder included with your Data Files, click the **MDNI Template Attached** template file, and then click the **Open** button. The Attach Template dialog box closes, and the template and its path are listed in the Document template box. The MDNI Template Attached file includes style definitions for the Heading 1 style that are different from the style definitions in the original template. You want the current document to be updated with the new template's style definitions.
8. Click the **Automatically update document styles** check box to select it.
9. Click the **OK** button. The dialog box closes. Notice that the "3. Residential Subscribers" heading is now formatted as dark gray, bold, and underlined. The Heading 1 style is still selected in the Styles group. This style was updated with the style definition in the new template you attached.

Using the Style Organizer

The Style Organizer is a list of all the styles in the current document and template. You can use it to copy styles from one document or template to another.

To use the Style Organizer:

1. Click anywhere in the paragraph below the heading "3. Residential Subscribers." In the Styles group, notice that the Report Text button is selected. The definition of the Report Text style in the template that was applied to this document is 11-point Verdana, with 1.15 line spacing and 10 points of space after paragraphs.
2. In the Styles group on the Home tab, click the **Dialog Box Launcher** to open the Styles task pane.
3. At the bottom of the task pane, click the **Manage Styles** button to open the Manage Styles dialog box.
4. At the bottom of the Manage Styles dialog box, click the **Import/Export** button. The Manage Styles dialog box closes and the Organizer dialog box opens. See Figure A-13. The list on the left shows styles in the current document. The list on the right includes styles defined in the default Normal template. None of the three buttons between the two lists are available. You want to redefine the Report Text style in the Survey Results document so it is the same as the Report Text style in another MDNI template.

TIP

You can also click the Organizer button in the Templates and Add-ins dialog box to open the Organizer dialog box.

Figure A-13 Organizer dialog box

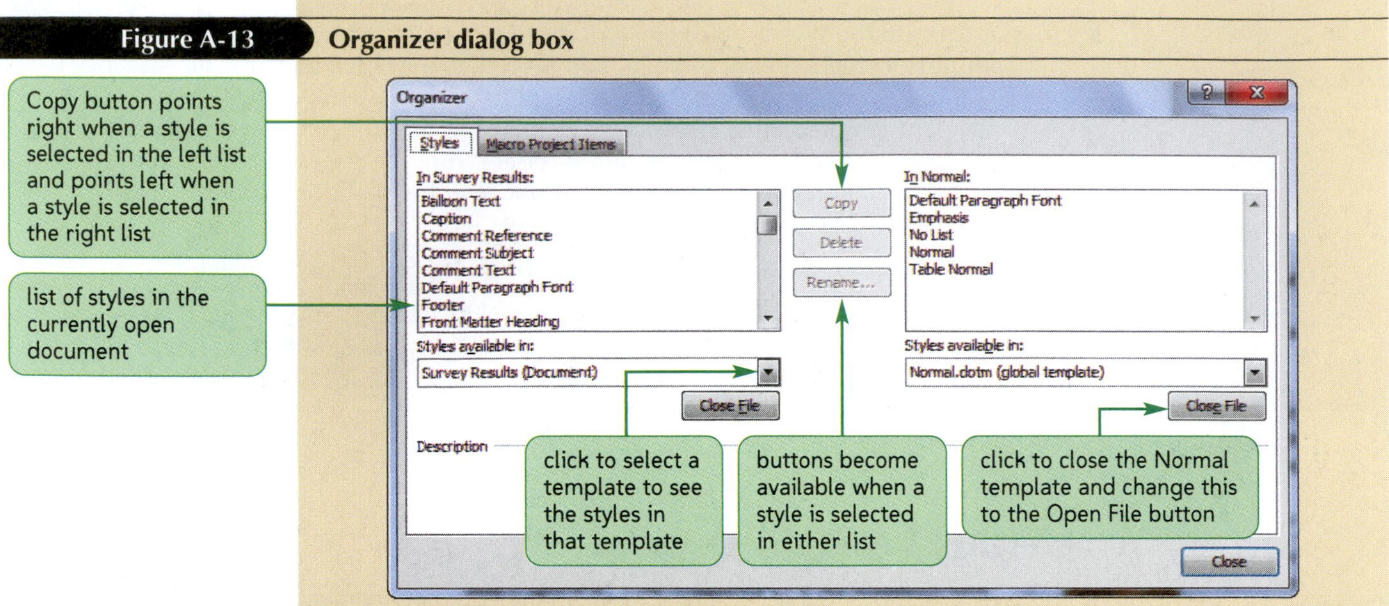

5. On the right side of the dialog box, click the **Close File** button. The Normal.dotm template is closed on the right, and the button you clicked changes to the Open File button.
6. Click the **Open File** button to open the Open dialog box, navigate to the WordA folder, click the **MDNI Styles** template, and then click the **Open** button. The Open dialog box closes, MDNI Styles (Template) appears in the Styles available in box on the right side of the Organizer dialog box, and the list of styles available in that template appears in the list on the right in alphabetical order. Notice that the first style in the list on the left is selected, and the three buttons in the middle are now available. Because a style in the list on the left is selected, the Copy button contains an arrow pointing from left to right.
7. Scroll down the list on the right, and then click **Report Text**. The Report Text style is selected, the style in the list on the left is no longer selected, and the arrow on the Copy button changes so that it points from right to left.
8. Click the **Copy** button. Because the Report Text style already exists in the Survey Results Document (the list of styles on the left), a dialog box opens asking if you want to overwrite the existing style entry.
9. Click the **Yes** button. The dialog box closes and the selected style definition is copied to the Survey Results document.
10. Click the **Close** button. The Organizer dialog box closes.
11. In the Styles task pane, click the **Close** button ✕. The current paragraph, which is formatted with the Report Text style, reflects the new style definition of 12-point Arial, 1.5 line spacing, and 6 points of space after the paragraph.

Working with an Index

In Tutorial 10, you learned how to mark entries and create an index of those entries. There are several ways you can customize an index to suit your needs using the options in the Index dialog box.

To customize the index in the document:

1. Press the **Ctrl+End** keys to move to page 9, right-click anywhere in the index, and then click **Edit Field** on the shortcut menu. The Field dialog box opens with Index selected in the Field names list.
2. On the right side of the dialog box, click the **Index** button. The Field dialog box closes, and the Index dialog box opens with the Index tab selected. See Figure A-14. This is the same dialog box that opens when you create an index. In this dialog box, you can select a new format, change page number alignment, set the number of columns for the entries, or change the language.

Figure A-14 Index dialog box

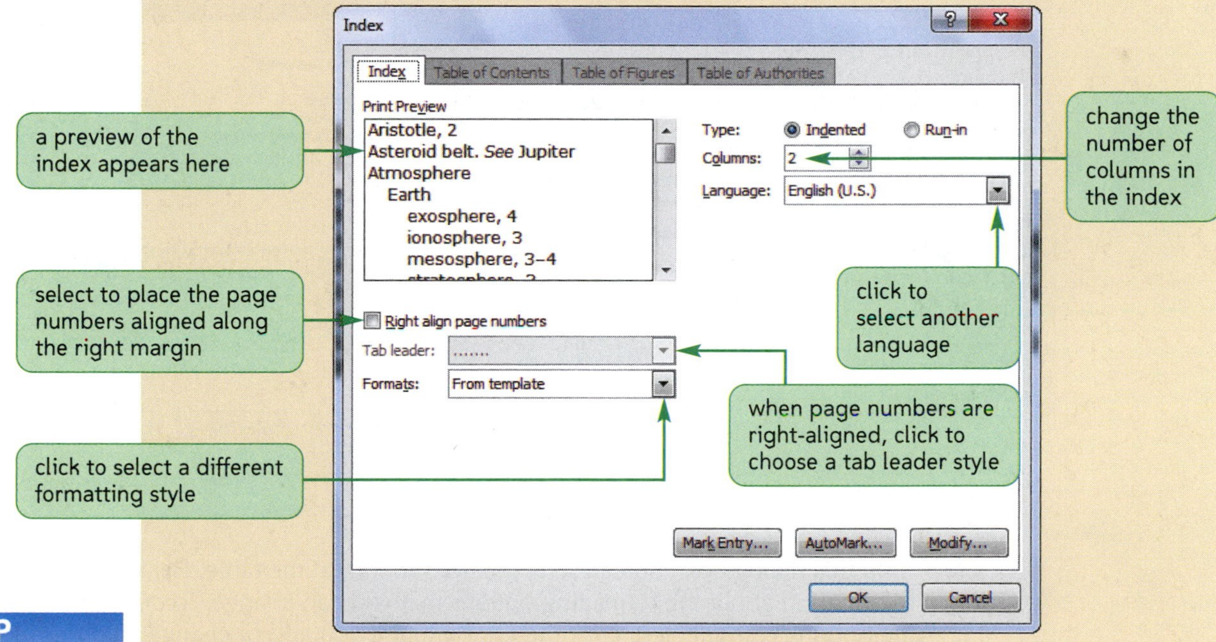

TIP

If additional languages are installed, you can change the language used by clicking the Language arrow, and then selecting the language you want to use.

3. Click the **Formats** arrow, and then click **Modern**. The preview in the Print Preview changes to show the index in the Modern style.
4. In the Columns box, change the number to **1**.
5. Click the **OK** button. A dialog box opens asking if you want to replace the selected index.
6. Click the **OK** button. The dialog box closes and the original index is replaced with the index with the new formatting.
7. Save the document.

Creating a Table of Authorities

Besides tables of contents and lists of figures, Word can also generate a table of authorities. A **table of authorities** is a list of references to cases, statutes, or rules in a legal document. Similar to other Word-generated lists, a table of authorities includes the page numbers on which the references appear. To create a table of authorities, first mark all the citations (references) by clicking the References tab, clicking the Mark Citation button in the Table of Authorities group to display the Mark Citation dialog box, selecting the appropriate category (Cases, Statutes, Rules, Treatises, Regulations, or Other Authorities), and then, similar to the way you mark index entries, clicking the Mark or Mark All button. Once you have finished marking citations, you can generate the table of authorities by clicking the Insert Table of Authorities button in the Table of Authorities group on the References tab to open the Table of Authorities dialog box (see Figure A-15).

Figure A-15 Table of Authorities dialog box

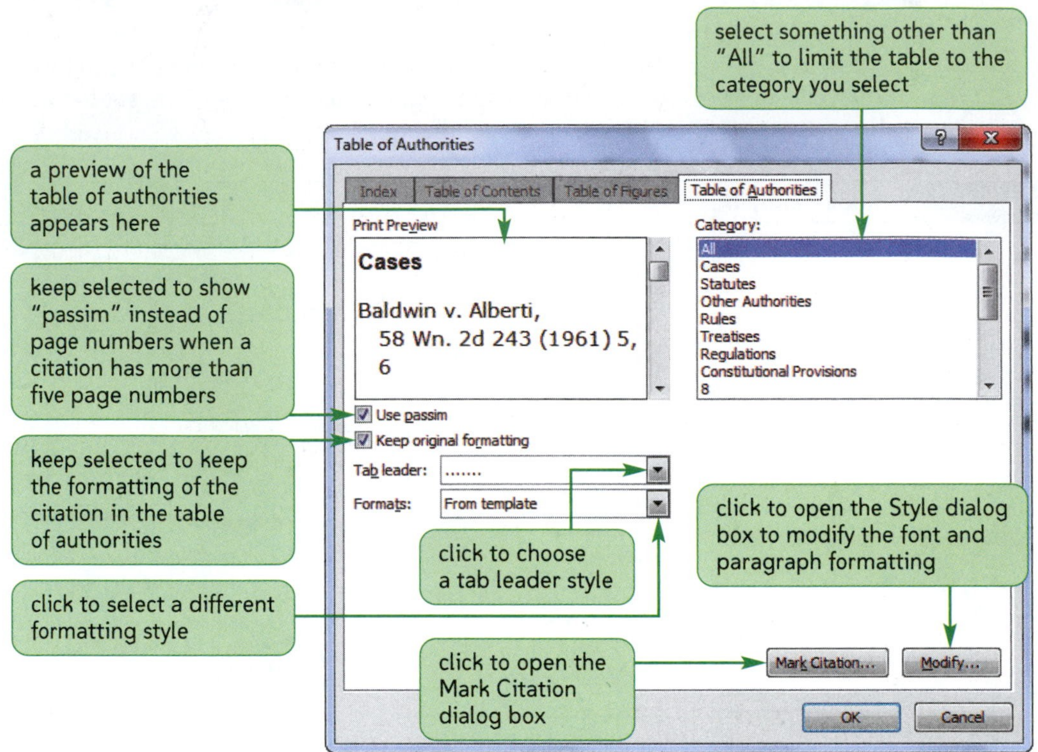

In this dialog box you can select options to format the table. Refer to Figure A-15 for information about the formatting options that you can change. To create the table with the options you selected, click the OK button. If you add or change citations in the document after you create the table of authorities, you can update it by clicking the Update Table of Authorities button in the Table of Authorities group on the References tab.

Using Advanced Mail Merge Options

In addition to the several types of mail merges you learned about in Tutorials 4 and 6, you can also perform a mail merge to email recipients, and you can create envelope forms.

Using Mail Merge to Send Email to Multiple Recipients

If you need to send the same message to multiple recipients via email, you can use the Mail Merge feature to do this.

REFERENCE

Performing a Mail Merge to Email Recipients

- With the email message main document open in Word, click the Mailings tab on the Ribbon, click the Start Mail Merge button in the Start Mail Merge group, and then click E-mail Messages.
- In the Start Mail Merge group, click the Select Recipients button, and then click the appropriate option based upon the location of your recipient list. If you click the Select from Outlook Contacts option, follow the prompts in the series of dialog boxes that open to select the appropriate contacts from your Outlook Contacts.
- Insert the appropriate merge fields in the email message main document using the buttons in the Write & Insert Fields group on the Mailings tab.
- In the Preview Results group on the Mailings tab, click the Preview Results button to preview the email messages in the merge.
- In the Preview Results group on the Mailings tab, click the Auto Check for Errors button, and then respond to any dialog boxes as needed.
- On the Mailings tab, click the Finish & Merge button in the Finish group, and then click Send E-Mail Messages.
- In the Merge to E-mail dialog box, click the To arrow, click Email_Address, enter an appropriate subject in the Subject line box, click the Mail format arrow to specify the format for the email message (HTML, Attachment, or Plain text), and then click the OK button.

Using Mail Merge to Create Envelopes

You learned how to create a single envelope in Tutorial 1. You can also use Mail Merge to create envelopes for multiple recipients.

To create envelope forms in a mail merge, do the following:

1. Click the Mailings tab on the Ribbon, click the Start Mail Merge button in the Start Mail Merge Group, and then click Envelopes to open the Envelopes Options dialog box shown in Figure A-16.

Figure A-16 **Envelope Options dialog box**

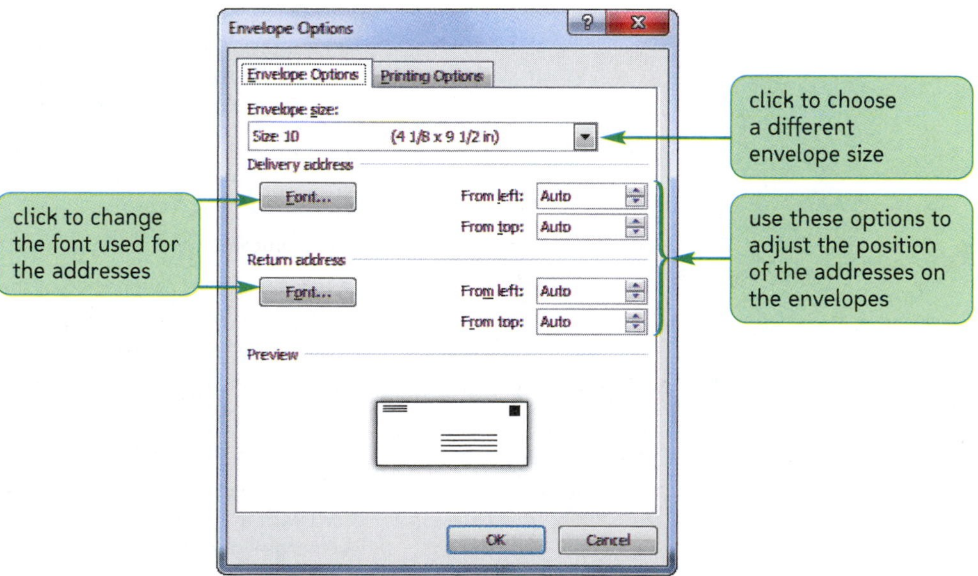

2. In the Envelopes Options dialog box, click the Envelope size arrow, and then select the size of the envelope you are using.
3. Use the options in the Delivery address and Return address sections to change the format and the position of each address, and then click the OK button. The dialog

box closes and the document is sized with the dimensions of the envelope. Paragraph markers appear in the upper-left corner of the document where the return address will appear and in the middle of the document where the recipient's address will appear. The insertion point is in the paragraph marking the return address position.

4. Type the return address, and then click the paragraph marker marking the recipient's address position. A dotted line border appears around the area where the recipient's address will appear.
5. In the Start Mail Merge group on the Mailings tab, click the Select Recipients button, select the option corresponding to your data source containing the list of recipients, and then complete the steps to select the data source (the same as for a letter mail merge).
6. In the Write & Insert Fields group, click the Address Block button to open the Insert Address Block dialog box, make sure the default options are acceptable, if necessary, click the Match Fields button to match fields, and then click the OK button.
7. In the Preview Results group on the Mailings tab, click the Preview Results button, and then scroll through the results.
8. In the Finish group, click the Finish & Merge button, click Print Documents, and then click the OK button in the Merge to Printer dialog box to print the envelope forms.

Creating Rules for Mail Merges

For any type of mail merge you perform, the Rules button in the Write & Insert fields group of the Mailings tab allows you to add specialized fields that apply rules to further customize your mail merge. For example, suppose you are a teacher sending letters introducing yourself to the parents of new students, and inviting the parents to a one-on-one conference prior to the start of classes. When you set up the merge, you can insert the Fill-in field in the main document letter to prompt you as each data record is merged to enter the specific date and time of that recipient's parent-teacher conference. The options on the Rules menu are described in Figure A-17.

Figure A-17 Options on the Rules menu on the Mailings tab

Rule	Function
Ask	Displays a prompt as Word merges each data record with the main document, and your response to the prompt appears in the resulting merge document for that record. Insert the Ask field when you want to repeat the same information more than once in the same document.
Fill-in	Displays a prompt as Word merges each data record with the main document, and your response to the prompt appears in the resulting merge document for that record.
If...Then...Else	Displays information based upon specific conditions you set.
Merge Record #	Displays the numerical position of the current data record in the data source at the time of the merge, taking into account any sort or filter options you set on the data source prior to the merge.
Merge Sequence #	Numbers each record in the merge, and displays this number only after the merge is complete.
Next Record	Merges all the data records into one merged document.
Next Record If	Based upon a condition you set, Word either merges the current data record with the merged document, or merges the next data record into a new merged document.
Set Bookmark	Enables you to specify a number or specific text to a bookmark, and then you insert a REF field in the main merged document. When the REF field is processed in the mail merge, the contents of the bookmark are inserted.
Skip Record If	Based upon a condition you set, if the condition is met, Word will skip the current data record and with the next data record, start a new merge document.

Creating a Custom Macro Button on the Quick Access Toolbar

In Tutorial 8 you learned how to record and run macros. You also learned how to customize the Quick Access Toolbar. To make it easier to run a macro, you can assign a button to it when you create it. The default location for a button you assign to a macro is the Quick Access Toolbar.

To create a macro and assign it to a button on the Quick Access Toolbar:

1. Click the **View** tab on the Ribbon, click the **Macros button arrow** in the Macros group, and then click **Record Macro**. The Record Macro dialog box opens. You will record a macro to add the company name to the header.
2. In the Macro name box, type **CompanyHeader**.
3. Click the **Store macro in** arrow, and then click **Survey Results (document)** to store the macro in just this document.
4. Click in the **Description** box, and then type **Add the company name to the header**.
5. In the Assign macro to section, click the **Button** button. The Record Macro dialog box closes, and the Word Options dialog box opens with Quick Access Toolbar selected in the left pane and the Customize Quick Access Toolbar options displayed in the right pane. In the Choose commands from list, Macros is selected, and the name of the macro preceded by "Project.NewMacros." appears in the list.
6. In the list on the left, click **Project.NewMacros.CompanyHeader**, and then click the **Add** button. The macro is added to the Customize Quick Access Toolbar list on the right.
7. Click the **OK** button. The dialog box closes, the pointer changes to , and the Stop Recording button appears on the status bar. Note also that a new button appears on the Quick Access Toolbar.
8. Click the **Insert** tab on the Ribbon, click the **Header** button in the Header & Footer group, and then click **Edit Header**. The insertion point appears in the header on the current page. The Header & Footer Tools Design tab is the active tab on the Ribbon.
9. Type **Market Data Now, Inc.**, and then click the **Close Header and Footer** button in the Close group on the Design tab.
10. On the status bar, click the **Stop Recording** button . The macro stops recording and the pointer changes back to the normal pointer.

Now you can test the macro using the button on the Quick Access Toolbar. First you will delete the header you added as you recorded the macro.

To run the macro using the custom macro button on the Quick Access Toolbar:

1. Click the **Insert** tab, click the **Header** button in the Header & Footer group, and then click **Remove Header**.
2. On the Quick Access Toolbar, point to the **CompanyHeader** button . The whole name for the macro, Project.NewMacros.CompanyHeader, appears as the ScreenTip.

3. Click the **CompanyHeader** button. The macro runs and the company name appears in the header.
4. Save the document as a macro-enabled document named **Survey Results with Macro** in the WordA folder, and then close the document.

Working with Forms

You learned how to create a form by adding content controls in Tutorial 9. You can also use form fields to create a form, and if you use form fields, you can then extract the data from a form so that you can import it into an Access table.

Working with Form Fields

In Tutorial 9, an InSight box describes form fields, which are legacy tools that are similar to content controls. If you want to add a form field to a document, display the Developer tab, click the Legacy Tools button in the Controls group, click the Text Form Field button, the Check Box Form Field button, or the Drop-Down Form Field button, and then click in the document. To customize a form field, select it, and then click the Properties button in the Controls group to display the Form Field Options dialog box for that specific type of form field. Because form fields do not have placeholder text like content controls, you can click the Add Help Text button, and then type text that will appear in the status bar or when you press the F1 key.

If you need to delete a form field from a form, make sure the form is not protected, click the form field to select it, and then press the Delete key.

Linking a Form to a Database

If you create a form using legacy form fields, you can link that form to an Access database so that you can import the data collected in the form into a table in the database. Unfortunately, you cannot extract data from a form using this method if the form was created with content controls instead of form fields. To extract data so that you can import it into an Access table, after a form containing legacy form fields has been filled out, do the following:

1. Click the File tab on the Ribbon, click Options in the navigation bar to open the Word Options dialog box, and then click Advanced in the list on the left.
2. Scroll down to the Preserve fidelity when sharing this document section, and then click the "Save form data as delimited text file" check box to select it. See Figure A-18. Now when you save the form, only the form data will be saved to a new file.

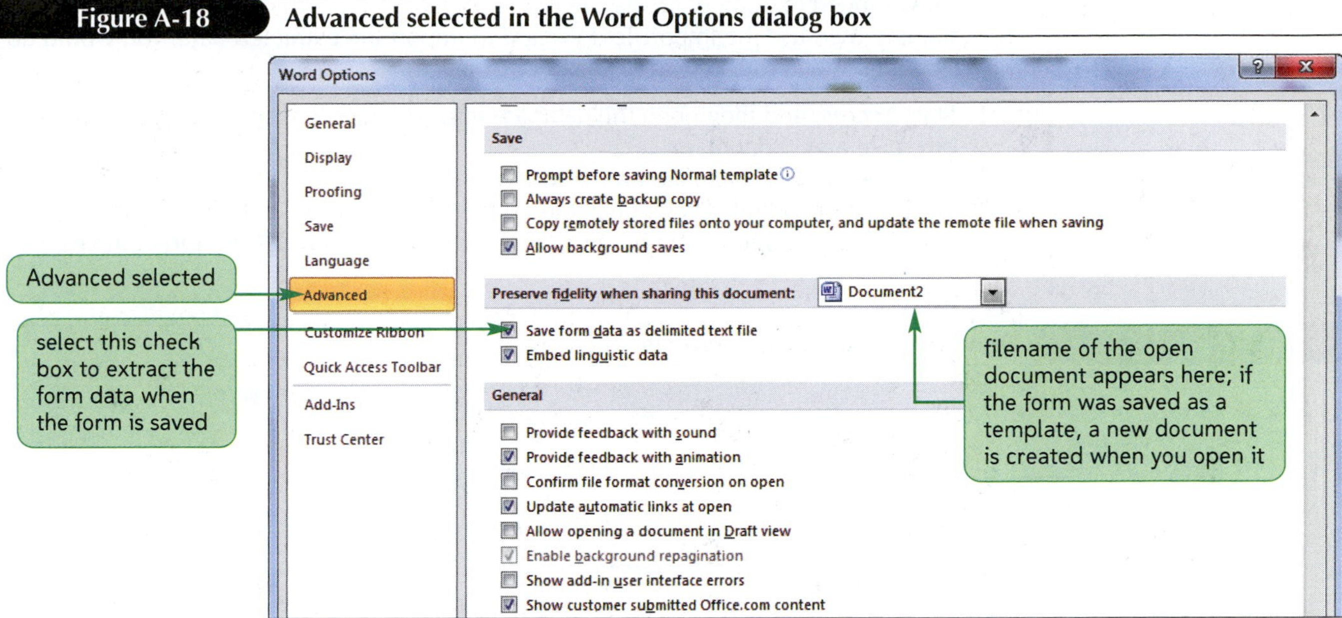

Figure A-18 Advanced selected in the Word Options dialog box

3. Click the OK button to close the Word Options dialog box, and then click the Save button on the Quick Access Toolbar. The Save As dialog box opens. Plain Text appears in the Save as type box.
4. Type a new filename in the File name box, if desired, and then click the Save button. The File Conversion dialog box opens showing a preview of the data extracted from the form in the Preview box. Each piece of data is between quotation marks and separated from the subsequent piece of data by a comma. See Figure A-19. The comma is a delimiter, which is a character that signals that another piece of data follows. Other common delimiters are tabs and paragraph marks.

Figure A-19 File Conversion dialog box

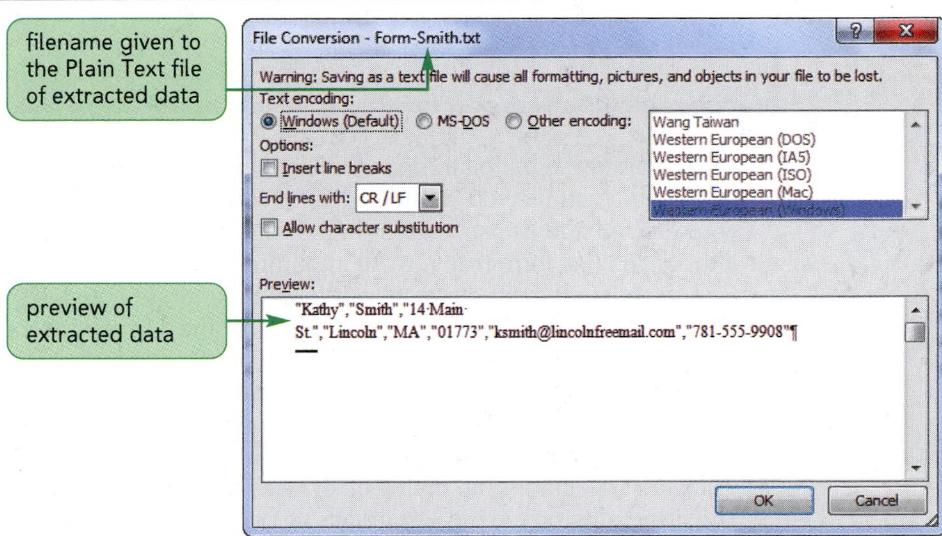

5. Click the OK button. The dialog box closes. The original form is still open with its original name.

Because you selected the "Save form data as delimited text file" check box, you created a new Plain Text file consisting only of the data from the open form. If you want to save the original form with a new name, deselect the "Save form data as delimited text file" check box, and then use the Save As command.

Next, you need to open or create the Access database into which you want to import the data, and then use the Import Text Wizard to import the extracted data. You would do the following:

1. Start Access, and then open the database into which you want to import the data, or create a new database.
2. Click the External Data tab on the Ribbon.
3. In the Import & Link group, click the Text File button. The Get External Data – Text File dialog box opens with the title "Select the source and destination of the data." See Figure A-20.

Figure A-20 First Get External Data – Text File dialog box

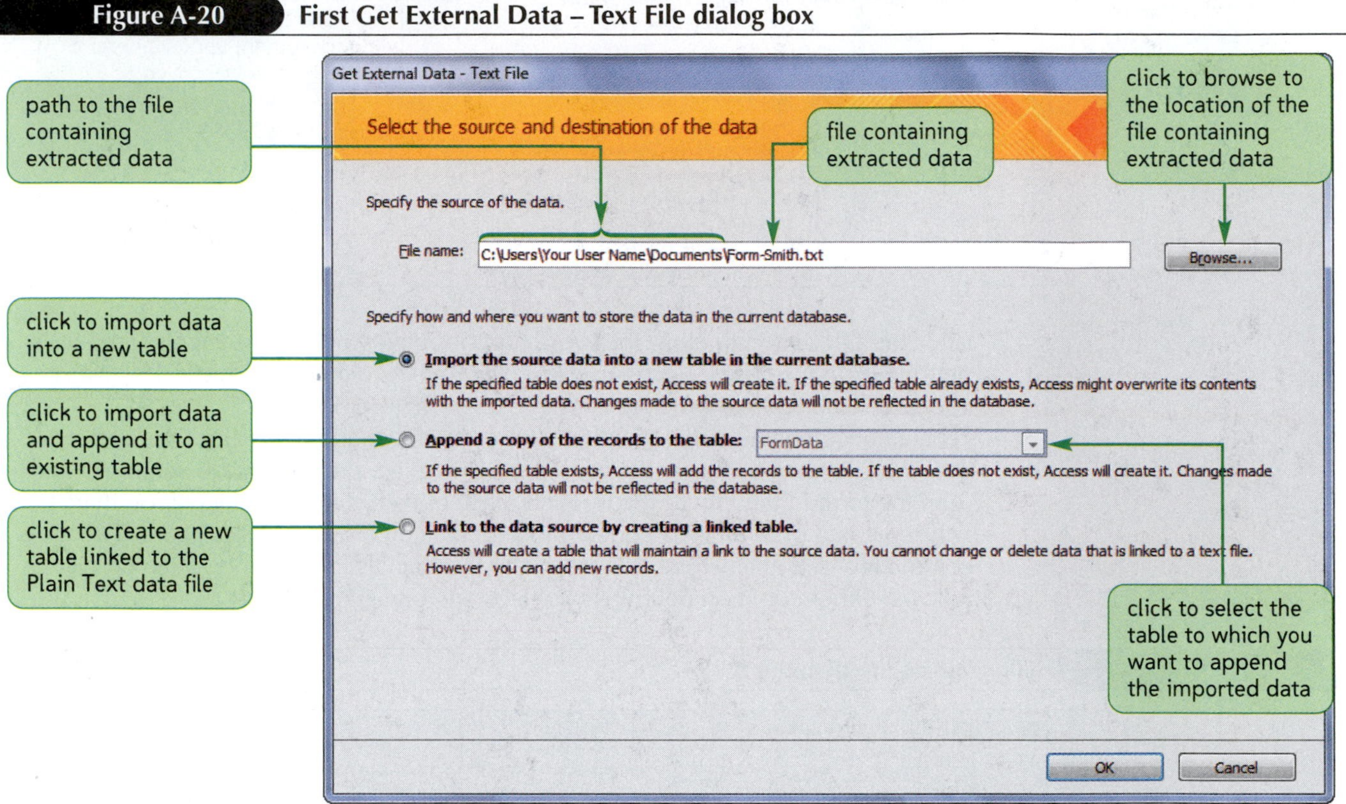

4. Click the Browse button to open the File Open dialog box, navigate to the location of the plain text file you created, click it, and then click the Open button. The file you selected and its path appear in the File name box.
5. If this is the first form that you are importing, keep the "Import the source data into a new table in the current database" option button selected. If you already created the table by importing data from a form, click the "Append a copy of the records to the table" option button, and then click the box arrow and select the table name. Note that if you want to append the data to an existing table, that table must be closed. If you want to link the data to a new table, click the "Link to the data source by creating a linked table" option button.
6. Click the OK button. The dialog box closes and the Import Text Wizard starts. The first dialog box in the wizard lets you choose the format of the data. See Figure A-21. The Delimited option button is selected by default, and this is correct.

Figure A-21 First Import Text Wizard dialog box

Import Text Wizard

Your data seems to be in a 'Delimited' format. If it isn't, choose the format that more correctly describes your data.

Delimited - Characters such as comma or tab separate each field

Fixed Width - Fields are aligned in columns with spaces between each field

Sample data from file: \\KITTY-WORK\PUBLIC\MCAS\FORM-SMITH.TXT.

1"Kathy","Smith","14 Main St.","Lincoln","MA","01773","ksmith@lincolnfreemail.com","781-

select this option when the data is separated by delimiters

preview of data being imported

7. Click the Next button. The next dialog box asks which delimiter separates the fields. The Comma option button is selected by default and this is correct because when you extracted the data, Word separated the fields with commas.
8. Click the Next button. If you chose to create a new table when importing the data or link to a new table, in the third dialog box, you can name and type the fields. (If you chose to append the data to an existing table, this dialog box is skipped.) You can also wait and do this after the table is created in Access. If you want to name the fields at this point, click a field column in the large preview area, type the new field name in the Field Name box, and then click the Data Type arrow to select a data type. You can also click the Do not import field (Skip) check box if you do not want to import the selected field.
9. Click the Next button. If you chose to create a new table when importing the data, in the fourth dialog box in the wizard, you can decide how to handle the primary key. (If you chose to append the data to an existing table or link to a new table, this dialog box is skipped.) The default selection, the Let Access add primary key option button, is usually the best option.
10. Click the Next button. If you chose to create a new table or link to a new table when importing the data, in the fifth and last dialog box of the wizard, a temporary table name is selected in the Import to Table box, and you can type the new table name in the Import to Table box. If you chose to append the data to an existing table, the table name appears in the Import to Table box.
11. Click the Finish button. The table is created, the Import Text Wizard dialog box closes, and the Get External Data – Text File dialog box appears again with the title Save Import Steps. If you click the Save import steps check box, the series of choices you made will be saved and you can choose this set of steps another time to import data.
12. Click the Close button. The dialog box closes and the table is listed in the Navigation Pane in the Access window.

Note that if you created a linked table, you cannot edit the data in the table because it is linked to the original Word file.

ENDING DATA FILES

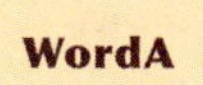

Chart Template.crtx
MDNI Report.docx
MDNI Template Attached.dotx
Sample Blog Post.docx
Screenshot.docx
Survey Results with Macro.docm
Survey Results.docx

Microsoft Office Specialist: Word 2010 Core Certification Skills Reference

Sharing and Maintaining Documents

Skill	Pages Where Covered
Sharing and Maintaining Documents	
Apply different views to a document	WD 3, WD 367
Select zoom options	WD 3-WD 4
Split windows	WD 575
Arrange windows	
View Side by Side	WD 576
Synchronous Scrolling	WD 576
Arrange document views	
Reorganize a document outline	WD 112-WD 116, WD 534-WD 536
Master documents	WD 530-WD 532, WD 537-WD 551
Subdocuments	WD 537-WD 551
Web layout	WD 369
Draft	WD A7
Switch between windows	OFF 7, WD 345
Open a document in a new window	WD 575
Apply protection to a document	
Apply protection by using the Microsoft Office Backstage view commands	
Apply controls and restrictions to document access	WD 566-WD 569
Password-protect a document	WD 566-WD 569
Mark as Final	WD 603
Applying protection by using Ribbon commands	WD 510-WD 512
Manage document versions	
Recover draft versions	WD A4
Delete all draft versions	WD A4
Share documents	
Send documents via E-mail	WD 354, WD 360
Send documents via SkyDrive	WD 354-WD 361
Send documents via Internet fax	WD A4
Change file types	WD A5-WD A6
Create PDF documents	WD 360
Create a blog post	WD A5
Publish a blog post	WD A5
Register a blog account	WD A5
Save a document	
Use compatibility mode	WD A6
Use protected mode	OFF 23, WD 28
Use Save As options	WD A6-WD A7

Skill	Pages Where Covered
Apply a template to a document	
Find templates	WD 23, WD 51, WD 220-WD 225, WD 259-WD 262
Locate a template on your disk	WD 51, WD 220-WD 225
Find templates on the Web	WD 221, WD 224

Formatting Content

Skill	Pages Where Covered
Apply font and paragraph attributes	
Apply character attributes	WD 31-WD 36, WD 233, WD A18
Apply styles	WD 55, WD 73-WD 76
Use Format Painter	WD 26, WD 34-WD 36
Navigate and search through a document	
Use the Navigation Pane	
Headings	WD 112-WD 116
Pages	WD 113
Results	WD 54-WD 55, WD 67-WD 71
Use Go To	WD A7-WD A8
Use Browse by button	WD A8
Use Highlight features	WD 54-WD 55, WD 67-WD 71
Set Find and Replace options	
Format	WD 71
Special	WD A7
Apply indentation and tab settings to paragraphs	
Apply indents	
First line	WD 83-WD 86
Hanging	WD 83-WD 86
Set tabs	WD 132-WD 135
Use the Tabs dialog box	WD 132, WD 305-WD 306
Set tabs on the ruler	WD 132-WD 135
Clear tab	WD 133
Set tab stops	WD 132-WD 135
Move tab stops	WD 132-WD 133
Apply spacing settings to text and paragraphs	
Set line spacing	WD 15-WD 18
Set paragraph spacing	WD 15-WD 18, WD 238-WD 239
Create tables	
Use the Insert Table dialog box	WD A10
Use Draw Table	WD 159
Insert a Quick Table	WD A10
Convert text to table	WD 311
Use a table to control page layout	WD 159

Skill	Pages Where Covered
Manipulate tables in a document	
Sort content	WD 111
Add a row to a table	WD 119, WD 123
Add a column to a table	WD 123
Manipulate rows	
Split	WD 466
Merge	WD 158, WD 462
Move	WD A10
Resize	WD 125
Delete	WD 124
Manipulate columns	
Split	WD 466
Merge	WD 462
Move	WD A10
Resize	WD 125
Delete	WD 124
Define the header row	WD 128
Convert tables to text	WD 311
View gridlines	WD 478
Apply bullets to a document	
Apply bullets	WD 54, WD 58-WD 60
Select a symbol format	WD A11
Define a picture to be used as a bullet	WD A11
Use AutoFormat	WD 312
Promote and demote bullet levels	WD 312

Applying Page Layout and Usable Content

Skill	Pages Where Covered
Apply and manipulate page setup settings	
Set margins	WD 2, WD 19-WD 21
Insert non-breaking spaces	WD 547
Add hyphenation	WD A11
Add columns	WD 164-WD 168
Remove a break	WD 139
Force a page break	WD 117
Insert a section break	
Continuous	WD 138-WD 140
Next Page	WD 138-WD 140
Next Odd	WD 585-WD 586
Next Even	WD 585-WD 586
Insert a blank page into a document	WD 95

Skill	Pages Where Covered
Apply themes	
Use a theme to apply formatting	WD 54-WD 55, WD 76-WD 79
Customize a theme	WD 223, WD 228-WD 230
Construct content in a document by using the Quick Parts tool	
Add built-in building blocks	
Quotes	WD 399-WD 402
Text boxes	WD 399-WD 402
Header	WD 144-WD 150, WD 406
Footer	WD 144-WD 150, WD 406
Cover page	WD 150-WD 153
Watermark	WD 396
Equations	WD A13-WD A14
Create and manipulate page backgrounds	
Format a document's background	WD 369-WD 370
Set a colored background	WD 369-WD 370
Add a watermark	WD 396
Set page borders	WD 163, WD 196-WD 197
Create and modify headers and footers	
Insert page numbers	WD 86-WD 88
Format page numbers	WD 146
Insert the current date and time	WD 198
Insert a built-in header or footer	WD 144-WD 150
Add content to a header or footer	
Custom dialog box	WD 410
Manual entry	WD 146
Delete a header or footer	WD 434
Change margins	WD A16
Apply a different first page attribute	WD 147-WD 148

Including Illustrations and Graphics in a Document

Skill	Pages Where Covered
Insert and format pictures in a document	
Add captions	WD A26
Apply artistic effects	WD 389
Apply picture styles	WD 196-WD 197
Compress pictures	WD 390
Modify a shape	WD 160, WD 393
Adjust position and size	WD 40-WD 41
Insert screenshots	WD A14

Skill	Pages Where Covered
Insert and format shapes, WordArt, and SmartArt	
Add text to a shape	WD 392
Modify text on a shape	WD 394
Add captions	WD 555-WD 559
Set shape styles	WD 175
Border	WD 393
Text	WD 392
Adjust position and size	WD 393
Insert and format Clip Art	
Organize Clip Art	WD A14-WD A15
Add captions	WD 555-WD 559
Apply artistic effects	WD 389
Compress pictures	WD 390
Adjust position and size	WD 178-WD 185
Apply and manipulate text boxes	
Format text boxes	WD A12-WD A13
Save a selection to the text box gallery	WD A12-WD A13
Apply text box styles	WD A12-WD A13
Change Text direction	WD A12-WD A13
Apply shadow effects	WD A12-WD A13
Apply 3-D effects	WD A12-WD A13

Proofreading Documents

Skill	Pages Where Covered
Validate content by using spelling and grammar checking options	
Set grammar	WD A17-WD A18
Set style options	WD A18
Configure AutoCorrect settings	
Add or remove exceptions	WD A17-WD A18
Turn on and off AutoCorrect	WD A18
Insert and modify comments in a document	
Insert a comment	WD 324-WD 325, WD 329-WD 330
Edit a comment	WD A15-WD A16
Delete a comment	WD 339
View a comment	
View comments from another user	WD 330, WD 335-WD 336
View comments inline	WD A15-WD A16
View comments as balloons	WD 330, WD 335-WD 336

Applying References and Hyperlinks

Skill	Pages Where Covered
Apply a hyperlink	
Apply a hyperlink to text or graphic	WD 361-WD 365
Use a hyperlink as a bookmark	WD 361-WD 365
Link a hyperlink to an e-mail address	WD 106, WD 361
Create endnotes and footnotes in a document	
Demonstrate difference between Endnotes and Footnotes	WD 135, WD 138
Manage footnote and endnote locations	WD A16-WD A17
Configure footnote and endnote format	WD A16-WD A17
Presentation	WD A16-WD A17
Change footnote and endnote numbering	WD A16-WD A17
Create a Table of Contents in a document	
Use default formats	WD 247-WD 251
Set levels	WD A9-WD A10
Set alignment	WD A9-WD A10
Set tab leader	WD A9-WD A10
Modify styles	WD A9-WD A10
Update a table of contents	
Page numbers	WD 251-WD 252
Entire table	WD 251-WD 252

Performing Mail Merge Operations

Skill	Pages Where Covered
Set up mail merge	
Perform a mail merge using the Mail Merge Wizard	WD 198-206
Perform a mail merge manually	WD 270-WD 289
Use Auto Check for Errors	WD A17
Execute mail merge	
Preview and print a mail merge operation	WD 204-205, WD 285-WD 287

Microsoft Office Specialist: Word 2010 Expert Certification Skills Reference

Sharing and Maintaining Documents

Skill	Pages Where Covered
Configure Word options	
Change default program options	WD 236, WD 390, WD 412, WD 427, WD 440-WD 444, WD 446, WD 485, WD 600
Change spelling options	WD A17-WD A18
Change grammar checking options	WD A17-WD A18
Apply protection to a document	
Restrict editing	WD 505, WD 510, WD 512
Apply controls or restrictions to document access	WD 567
Apply a template to a document	
Modify an existing template	WD 259-WD 262
Create a new template	WD 224-WD 226
Apply a template to an existing document	WD A19-WD A21
Manage templates by using the Organizer	WD A19-WD A22

Formatting Content

Skill	Pages Where Covered
Apply advanced font and paragraph attributes	
Use character attributes	WD A18
Use character-specific styles	WD 73-WD 74, WD 240
Create tables and charts	
Insert tables by using Microsoft Excel data in tables	WD 340-WD 346
Apply formulas or calculations in a table	WD 506-WD 509
Modify chart data	WD 350
Save a chart as a template	WD A19-WD A20
Modify chart layout	WD 562
Construct reusable content in a document	
Create customized building blocks	WD 404-WD 405, WD 406-WD 409
Save a selection as a quick part	WD 404-WD 405, WD 408-WD 409
Save quick parts after a document is saved	WD A19
Insert text as a quick part	WD 404-WD 405, WD 409
Add content to a header or footer	WD 130-WD 131, WD 144-WD 150
Link sections	
Link text boxes	WD 403
Break links between text boxes	WD A19
Link different sections	WD 147, WD 584

Tracking and Referencing Documents

Skill	Pages Where Covered
Review, compare, and combine documents	
Apply tracking	WD 324-WD 329
Merge different versions of a document	WD 332-WD 336
Track changes in a combined document	WD 333-WD 336
Review comments in a combined document	WD 338
Create a reference page	
Add citations	WD 89-WD 95
Manage sources	WD 97
Compile a bibliography	WD 95-WD 97
Apply cross references	WD 549, WD 564
Create a Table of Authorities in a document	
Apply default formats	WD A23-WD A24
Adjust alignment	WD A23-WD A24
Apply a tab leader	WD A23-WD A24
Modify styles	WD A23-WD A24
Mark citations	WD A23-WD A24
Use passim (short form)	WD A23-WD A24
Create an index in a document	
Specify index type	WD A22-WD A23
Specify columns	WD A22-WD A23
Specify language	WD A22-WD A23
Modify an index	WD 597
Mark index entries	WD 580-WD 581, WD 591-WD 595

Performing Mail Merge Operations

Skill	Pages Where Covered
Execute a Mail Merge	
Merge rules	WD A24-WD A26
Send personalized email messages to multiple recipients	WD A24-WD A26
Create a Mail Merge by using other data sources	
Use Microsoft Outlook tables as data source for a mail merge operation	WD 273, WD A24-WD A26
Use Access tables as data source for a mail merge operation	WD 310
Use Excel tables as data source for a mail merge operation	WD 319
Use Word tables as data source for a mail merge operation	WD 305-WD 307

Skill	Pages Where Covered
Create labels and forms	
Prepare data	WD 295-WD 299, WD 307-WD 311
Create mailing labels	WD 299-WD 304
Create envelope forms	WD A24-WD A26
Create label forms	WD 295-WD 304

Managing Macros and Forms

Skill	Pages Where Covered
Apply and manipulate macros	
Record a macro	WD 424, WD 429
Run a macro	WD 431, WD 437
Apply macro security	WD 427
Apply and manipulate macro options	
Run macros when a document is opened	WD 439-WD 440
Run macros when a button is clicked	WD 431, WD A27-WD A28
Assign a macro to a command button	WD 431, WD A27-WD A28
Create a custom macro button on the Quick Access Toolbar	WD 431, WD A27-WD A28
Create forms	
Use the Controls group	WD 482-WD 483, WD 484-WD 503
Add Help content to form fields	WD 512, WD A28
Link a form to a database	WD A28-WD A31
Lock a form	WD 504-WD 505, WD 510, WD 512
Manipulate forms	
Unlock a form	WD 512
Add fields to a form	WD 482-WD 483, WD 484-WD 503, WD 512
Remove fields from a form	WD 488, WD A28

GLOSSARY/INDEX

Note: Boldface entries include definitions.

SPECIAL CHARACTERS

A

B

C

G

H

N

T

U

V

W

Z

TASK REFERENCE

TASK	PAGE #	RECOMMENDED METHOD
Action, redo	WD 10	Click
Action, undo	WD 10	Click
AutoCorrect, customize	WD 412	*See* Reference box: Customizing AutoCorrect
AutoMacro, record	WD 439	Click View tab, click Macros button arrow in Macros group, click Record Macro, an AutoMacro name (AutoExec, AutoNew, AutoOpen, AutoClose, or AutoExit), click Store macro in arrow, click desired template, click OK, record macro, click View tab, click Macros button arrow in Macros group, click Stop Recording
Bibliography, convert to static text	WD 99	Click bibliography, click in bibliography content control, click Convert bibliography to static text
Bibliography, insert	WD 95	Create citations, click desired location for bibliography, click Bibliography button in Citations & Bibliography group on References tab, click bibliography style
Bibliography, select a style for	WD 90	Click References tab, click Style arrow in Citations & Bibliography group, click style
Bibliography source, edit	WD 97	Click citation, click , click Edit Source, edit source information, click OK
Bibliography, update	WD 98	Click bibliography, click Update Citations and Bibliography on bibliography content control tab
Bold, apply to text	WD 33	Select text, click **B** in Font group on Home tab
Bookmark, create	WD 361	Select text, click Insert tab, click Bookmark button in Links group, type bookmark name, click Add
Border, add custom	WD 394	Click Border button arrow in Paragraph group on Home tab, click Borders and Shading, click Custom, select Style, Color, and Width, click border position in Preview section, click OK
Border, insert around page	WD 196	Click Page Layout tab, click Page Borders button in Page Background group, click Page Border tab, click Box, click OK
Building blocks, create category	WD 411	Select text, click Insert tab, click Quick Parts button in Text group, click Save Selection to Quick Part gallery, click Category arrow, click Create New Category, type category name, click OK, click OK
Building blocks, delete	WD 410	Click Insert tab, click Quick Parts button in Text group, click Building Blocks Organizer, select Quick Part, click Delete, click Yes, click Close
Building blocks, edit properties	WD 410	Click Insert tab, click Quick Parts button in Text group, click Building Blocks Organizer, select Quick Part, click Edit Properties, change properties as desired, click OK, click Yes, click Close
Bullets, add to paragraph	WD 58	Select paragraph, click in Paragraph group on Home tab
Captions, create	WD 556	*See* Reference box: Creating Captions
Character spacing, adjust	WD 232	Select text, click Dialog Box Launcher in Font group on Home tab, click Advanced tab, click Spacing arrow, select spacing option, type point measurement in By box, click OK
Chart, create	WD 559	Click Insert tab, click Chart button in Illustrations group, select chart type, click OK
Citations, create	WD 90	*See* Reference box: Creating Citations

TASK	PAGE #	RECOMMENDED METHOD
Citation, edit	WD 90	*See* Reference box: Creating Citations
Clip art, align to margin	WD 184	Wrap text around clip art, click clip art, click [button] in the Arrange group on the Picture Tools Format tab, click Align to Margin, click [button] again, click alignment option
Clip art, crop	WD 180	Click clip art, click Picture Tools Format tab, click Crop button in Size group, drag picture border
Clip art, crop to shape	WD 182	Click clip art, click Picture Tools Format tab, click Crop button arrow in Size group, point to Crop to Shape, click shape
Clip art, insert	WD 178	Click Insert tab, click Clip Art button in Illustrations group, type keywords in Search for box, click Go, click image in Clip Art task pane
Clip art, resize	WD 180	Click clip art, drag sizing handle
Clip art, wrap text around	WD 171	Click clip art, click Picture Tools Format tab, click Wrap Text button in Arrange group, click text wrapping option
Clipboard, use to cut, copy, and paste	WD 63	*See* Reference box: Cutting (or Copying) and Pasting Text
Clipboard task pane, open	WD 64	In Clipboard group on Home tab, click Dialog Box Launcher
Column, insert in table	WD 123	Click column, click Table Tools Layout tab, click Insert Right or Insert Left button in Rows & Columns group
Column width, change in table	WD 125	Double-click or drag border between columns
Columns, balance text in	WD 195	Click end of rightmost column, click Page Layout tab, click Breaks button in Page Setup group, click Continuous
Columns, create different widths	WD 397	Click Page Layout tab, click Columns button in Page Setup group, click Left or Right
Columns, customize widths	WD 397	Click Page Layout tab, click Columns button in Page Setup group, click More Columns, deselect Equal column width check box, set widths in Width boxes, click OK
Columns, format text in	WD 164	Click where you want columns to begin, click Page Layout tab, click Columns button in Page Setup group, click More Columns, select options, click OK
Comment, delete single	WD 336	Click in comment balloon, click Review tab, click Delete button in Comments group
Comments, delete all in document	WD 336	Click in comment balloon, click Review tab, click Delete button arrow in Comments group, click Delete All Comments in Document
Comments, insert	WD 330	*See* Reference box: Inserting Comments
Compatibility, check	WD 600	Click File tab, click Info tab, click Check for Issues button, click Check Compatibility, click Select version to show, click option without a check mark
Compressed folder, create	FM 18	In folder window, select files and folders to be compressed, right-click selection, point to Send to on shortcut menu, click Compressed (zipped) folder, type folder name, press Enter
Compressed folder, extract all files and folders from	FM 19	Right-click compressed folder, click Extract All on shortcut menu
Compressed folder, open	FM 18	Double-click compressed folder
Content control, Building Block Gallery, insert	WD 498	Click Building Block Gallery Content Control button in Controls group on Developer tab

TASK	PAGE #	RECOMMENDED METHOD
Content control, Check Box, insert	WD 500	*See* Reference box: Inserting a Check Box Content Control
Content control, Date Picker, insert	WD 490	*See* Reference box: Inserting a Date Picker Content Control
Content control, Drop-Down List or Combo Box Content, insert	WD 493	*See* Reference box: Inserting a Drop-Down List or Combo Box Content Control
Content control, Picture, insert	WD 498	*See* Reference box: Inserting a Picture Content Control
Content control, Plain Text or Rich Text, insert	WD 484	*See* Reference box: Inserting a Plain Text or a Rich Text Content Control
Cover page, insert	WD 150	Click Insert tab, click Cover Page button in Pages group, click cover page
Cover page, delete	WD 152	Click Insert tab, click Cover Page button in Pages group, click Remove Current Cover Page
Cross-references, create	WD 563	*See* Reference box: Creating Cross-References
Date, insert current as updateable field	WD 198	Click Insert tab, click Date & Time button in Text group, click date option, select Update automatically checkbox if necessary, click OK
Date, insert with AutoComplete	WD 6	Start typing date, press Enter
Definition, look up in dictionary	WD 253	Right-click word or selected text, point to Look Up, click Encarta Dictionary: English (North America)
Developer tab, show	WD 435	Click File tab, click Options, click Customize Ribbon, click Developer check box in list on right to select it, click OK
Document, check for accessibility	WD 573	Click File tab, click Info tab, click Check for Issues button, click Check Accessibility, click objects in Accessibility Checker task pane
Document, close	WD 43	Click File tab, click Close
Document, create new	WD 23	Click File tab, click New tab, click Create
Document, email, send via	WD 519	Click File tab, click Save & Send tab, click Send Using E-mail, click Send as Attachment, address email message, send message as usual
Document, encrypt	WD 601	*See* Reference box: Encrypting a Document
Document, fax from Word	WD 517	Click File tab, click Save & Send tab, click Send Using E-mail, click Send as Internet Fax, click OK, click Connect to a fax modem, follow steps in Fax Setup Wizard, type fax number in To box, type Subject, click Send
Document, inspect	WD 571	Click File tab, click Info tab, click Check for Issues button, click Inspect Document, click Inspect, click Remove All as needed, click Close
Document, mark as final	WD 603	Click File tab, click Info tab, click Protect Document button, click Mark as Final, click OK, click OK
Document, open	WD 28	Click File tab, click Open, select drive and folder, click filename, click Open
Document, print	WD 21	Click File tab, click Print tab, click Print button
Document, preview printed page	WD 21	Click File tab, click Print
Document, protect	WD 567	*See* Reference box: Protecting a Document
Document, save with same name	WD 9	On Quick Access Toolbar, click
Documents, compare or combine	WD 333	*See* Reference box: Comparing and Combining Documents
Documents, scroll synchronously	WD 576	Open two documents, click View tab, click View Side by Side button in Window group

TASK	PAGE #	RECOMMENDED METHOD
Drop cap, insert	WD 166	Click in paragraph, click Insert tab, click Drop Cap button in Text group, select options
Embedded object, modify	WD 345	Double-click object, use commands and tools of source program to modify object, click outside embedded object
Endnotes, create	WD 136	*See* Reference box: Inserting a Footnote or an Endnote
Envelope, create	WD 23	*See* Reference box: Creating an Envelope
Field codes, view	WD 420	Right-click field, click Toggle Field Codes
Field, edit	WD 420	Right-click field, click Edit Field, make changes, click OK
Field, update	WD 420	Right-click field, click Update Field
Fields, update before printing	WD 600	Click File tab, click Options, click Display tab, click Update fields before printing check box, click OK
File, close	OFF 22	Click File tab, click Close
File, copy	FM 14	*See* Reference box: Copying a File or Folder in a Folder Window
File, delete	FM 17	Right-click file, click Delete
File, insert into a Word document	WD 225	Click Insert tab, click Object button arrow in Text group, click Text from File, click file, click Insert
File, move	FM 13	*See* Reference box: Moving a File or Folder in a Folder Window
File, open	OFF 23	*See* Reference box: Opening an Existing File
File, print	OFF 29	*See* Reference box: Printing a File
File, rename	FM 16	Right-click file, click Rename on shortcut menu, type new filename, press Enter
File, save	OFF 19	*See* Reference box: Saving a File
File, save to SkyDrive	OFF 25	*See* Reference box: Saving a File to SkyDrive
File, switch between open	OFF 7	Point to program button on taskbar, click thumbnail of file to make active
Files, select multiple	FM 14	Hold down Ctrl key and click files
Files, view in Large Icons view	FM 10	Click , click Large Icons
Folder window, return to a previously visited location	FM 7	Click , click location in list
Folder window, return to previous location	FM 14	Click
Folder, copy	FM 14	*See* Reference box: Copying a File or Folder in a Folder Window
Folder, create	FM 11	*See* Reference box: Creating a Folder in a Folder Window
Folder, move	FM 13	*See* Reference box: Moving a File or Folder in a Folder Window
Font, change	WD 31	Select text, click Font arrow in Font group on Home tab, click font
Font color, change	WD 34	Select text, click in Font group on Home tab, click color
Font size, change	WD 31	Select text, click Font Size arrow in Font group on Home tab, click point size
Footer, add	WD 146	Double-click in bottom margin, type footer text, select options on Header & Footer Tools Design tab
Footnotes, create	WD 136	*See* Reference box: Inserting a Footnote or an Endnote
Form, protect and unprotect	WD 510	*See* Reference box: Protecting and Unprotecting a Form

TASK	PAGE #	RECOMMENDED METHOD
Format, copy	WD 34	Select text whose format you want to copy, click [button] in Clipboard group on Home tab, use Format Painter pointer to select text
Formula, insert in a table cell	WD 508	Click in cell, click Table Tools Layout tab, click Formula button in Data group, delete text in Formula box, click Paste function arrow, select function, type arguments separated by a comma, click OK
Header, add	WD 144	Double-click top margin, type header text, select options on Header & Footer Tools Design tab
Headings, browse by	WD 112	Click [button] in Editing group on Home tab, click [button] in Navigation pane
Headings, reorganize in Navigation Pane	WD 112	Click [button] in Editing group on Home tab, click [button] in Navigation pane, drag heading to new location in outline
Help, get in Office	OFF 26	*See* Reference box: Getting Help
Highlighting, add to text	WD 578	Click Text Highlight Color button in Font group on Home tab, drag over text
Horizontal line, insert	WD 371	Click Borders and Shading button arrow on Home tab in Paragraph group, click Borders and Shading, click Horizontal Line, click a line style, click OK
Hyperlink, edit	WD 373	Right-click hyperlink, click Edit Hyperlink, select options, click OK
Hyperlink, insert in document	WD 137	Type email address or URL, press spacebar or Enter
Hyperlink, remove	WD 137	Right-click hyperlink, click Remove Hyperlink
Hyperlink, use	WD 137	Press and hold Ctrl and click the hyperlink
Hyperlink to a location in the same document, create	WD 362	*See* Reference box: Creating a Hyperlink to a Location in the Same Document
Hyperlink to another file or Web page, create	WD 364	*See* Reference box: Creating a Hyperlink to Another Document
Index entries and subentries, mark	WD 591	*See* Reference box: Marking Index Entries and Subentries
Index entry, cross-reference, create	WD 594	Select text, click Mark Entry button in Index group on References tab, click Cross-reference option button, type text to reference, click Mark
Index entry, page range, create	WD 594	*See* Reference box: Creating a Page Range Index Entry
Index, compile	WD 595	*See* Reference box: Compiling an Index
Index, update	WD 597	Click References tab, click Update Index button in Index group
Italics, apply	WD 34	Select text, click *I* in Font group on Home tab
Line spacing, change	WD 15	Select text to change, click [button] in Paragraph group on Home tab, click spacing option
Link, break	WD 351–352	*See* Reference box: Breaking a Link to a Source File
Macro, edit	WD 432	Click View tab, click Macros button in Macros group, select macro, click Edit, make changes, close Visual Basic window
Macro, import	WD 436	Click Developer tab, click Visual Basic in Code group, click project name, click File, click Import File, navigate to location of file, click desired file, click Open, close Visual Basic window
Macro, record	WD 429	*See* Reference box: Recording a Macro
Macro, run	WD 432	Click View tab, click Macros button in Macros group, select macro, click Run

TASK	PAGE #	RECOMMENDED METHOD
Macro, save a document or template with	WD 434	Click File tab, click Save As, click Save as type arrow, click Word Macro-Enabled Document or Word Macro-Enabled Template, click Save
Macro, security settings, change	WD 427	Click File tab, click Options, click Trust Center, click Trust Center Settings, click Macro Settings, click desired option, click OK, click OK
Mail merge data source, create	WD 275	*See* Reference box: Creating A Data Source for a Mail Merge
Mail merge data source, edit in Word	WD 293	*See* Reference box: Editing a Data Source in Word
Mail merge data source, filter	WD 297–298	Select type of main document, select or create data source, click Edit Recipient List button in Start Mail Merge group on Mailings tab, click arrow button in column header for field you want to filter by, click field entry, click OK
Mail merge data source, sort	WD 296	*See* Reference box: Sorting a Data Source by Multiple Fields
Mail merge main document, select type of	WD 272–273	Click Mailings tab, click Start Mail Merge button in the Start Mail Merge group, click type of main document
Mail merge, finish by merging to new document	WD 287	Click Mailings tab, click Finish & Merge button in Finish group, click Edit Individual Documents, click OK
Mail merge, finish by merging to printer	WD 287	Click Mailings tab, click Finish & Merge button in Finish group, click Print Documents, click OK
Mail merge, insert merge fields in main document for	WD 281–282	Click Mailings tab, click Insert Merge Field button arrow in Write & Insert Fields group, click merge field
Mail merge, preview merged document for	WD 285	Click Mailings tab, click Preview Results button in Preview Results group
Mailing labels, create	WD 299–300	Click Mailings tab, click Start Mail Merge button in Start Mail Merge group, click Labels, click Label vendors arrow, click vendor, click option in Product number box, click OK, select data source, insert merge fields, click Update Labels in the Write & Insert Fields group, finish merge
Margins, change	WD 19	Click Margins button in Page Setup group on Page Layout tab, click margins option
Mini Translator, display	WD 261	Click Review tab, select translation languages, click Translate button in Language group, click Mini Translator, select text, point to selected text, move mouse pointer over Mini Translator
Multilevel list style, apply	WD 312	Format text as bulleted or numbered list, select list, click [button], click style
My Documents folder, open	FM 8	In folder window, click ▷ next to Libraries, click ▷ next to Documents, click My Documents
Navigation Pane, open	WD 70	Click [button] in Editing group on Home tab
Nonbreaking hyphen, insert	WD 547	Click Insert tab, click Symbol button in Symbols group, click More Symbols, click Special Characters tab, click Nonbreaking Hyphen, click Insert, click Close
Nonbreaking space, insert	WD 547	Click Insert tab, click Symbol button in Symbols group, click More Symbols, click Special Characters tab, click Nonbreaking Space, click Insert, click Close
Nonprinting characters, show	WD 4	Click ¶ in Paragraph group on Home tab,
Numbered headings, create	WD 552	In Outline view, display headings only, click Home tab, click Multilevel List button in Paragraph group, click desired numbering style

TASK	PAGE #	RECOMMENDED METHOD
Numbering, add to paragraphs	WD 60	Select paragraphs, click [icon] in Paragraph group on Home tab
Object, embed in Word document	WD 343	Select and copy object in source program, return to Word, click destination location, click Paste button arrow in Clipboard group on Home tab, click Paste Special, in As list box select option that will paste object as an Object, click OK
Object, link to Word document	WD 346–347	Select and copy object in source program, return to Word, click destination location, click Paste button arrow in Clipboard group on Home tab, click Use Destination Theme & Link Data or click Keep Source Formatting & Link Data
Office program, exit	OFF 30	Click [icon]
Office program, start	OFF 5	*See* Reference box: Starting an Office Program
Office program, switch between open	OFF 7	Click program button on taskbar to make active
Options, customize	WD 441	Click File tab, click Options, change options as desired, click OK
Outline, create in Outline view	WD 533	*See* Reference box: Creating an Outline in Outline View
Page break, insert	WD 95	Click where you want to break page, click Insert tab, click Page Break button in Pages group
Page Color gradient, add	WD 369–370	Click Page Layout tab, click Page Color button in Page Background group, click Fill Effects, click Gradient tab, click One color or Two colors, select colors and shading style, click OK
Page Color, add	WD 369–370	Click Page Layout tab, click Page Color button in Page Background group, click color
Page number, insert	WD 86	Click Insert tab, click Page Number button in Header & Footer group, select options from menu
Page numbers, format	WD 584	Insert page numbers, click Page Number button in Header & Footer group on Header & Footer Tools Design tab, click Format Page Numbers, click Number format arrow, click format, click Start at option button, set start number, click OK
Page orientation, change	WD 30	Click Page Layout tab, click Orientation button in Page Setup group, click orientation
Page Width zoom, select	WD 4	Click View tab, click Page Width button in Zoom group
Pages, browse by	WD 113	Click [icon] in Editing group on Home tab, click [icon] in Navigation pane
Paragraph, decrease indent	WD 84	Click [icon] in Paragraph group on Home tab
Paragraph, increase indent	WD 84	Click [icon] in Paragraph group on Home tab
Paragraph spacing, add or remove default	WD 15	Click paragraph, click [icon] in Paragraph group on Home tab, click options to add or remove space before or after paragraphs
Paragraph spacing, select specific setting	WD 16	Click paragraph, click Page Layout tab, adjust settings in Spacing Before and After boxes in Paragraph group
Paste Options, select	WD 66	Paste text or graphic in document, click [icon], click paste option
Photo, change color	WD 389	Select photo, click Picture Tools Format tab, click Color button in Adjust group, click options
Photo, correct color	WD 389	Select photo, click Picture Tools Format tab, click Corrections button in Adjust group, click options

TASK	PAGE #	RECOMMENDED METHOD
Photo or other picture, apply style to	WD 193	Click picture, click Picture Tools Format tab, click More button in Picture Styles group, click style
Photo or other picture, crop	WD 180	Click picture, click Picture Tools Format tab, click Crop button in Size group, drag graphic border to crop
Photo or other picture, crop to shape	WD 182	Click picture, click Picture Tools Format tab, click Crop button arrow in Size group, point to Crop to Shape, click shape
Photo or other picture, insert	WD 41	Click Insert tab, click Picture button in Illustrations group, select picture file, click Insert button
Photo or other picture, remove background	WD 190	*See* Reference box: Removing a Photo's Background
Photo or other picture, rotate	WD 188	Click picture, click Picture Tools Format tab, click [icon] in Arrange group, click rotation option
Photo or other picture, resize	WD 180	Click picture, drag sizing handle
Photo or other picture, wrap text around	WD 171	Click picture, click Picture Tools Format tab, click Wrap Text button in Arrange group, click text wrapping option
Picture, compression options, change	WD 390	Click File tab, click Options, click Advanced, click Set default target output to arrow, select compression setting
Preview pane, open	FM 17	In folder window, click [icon]
Print Layout view, select	WD 4	Click [icon]
Program window, maximize	OFF 8	Click [icon]
Program window, minimize	OFF 8	Click [icon]
Program window, restore down	OFF 8	Click [icon]
Properties, add to document	WD 415	Click File tab, click Info tab, click in boxes on right, type new property, to add additional properties, click Properties, click Advanced Properties, click Custom tab, select property, click in Value box, type value, click OK
Property, insert as a field	WD 419	Click Insert tab, click Quick Parts button in Text group, click Field, click DocProperty in Field names list, click property in Property list, click OK
Property, insert as Quick Part	WD 417	Click Insert tab, click Quick Parts in Text group, point to Document Property, click desired property
Quick Access Toolbar, customize	WD 443	*See* Reference box: Adding a Button to the Quick Access Toolbar
Quick Part, create	WD 406	*See* Reference box: Creating a Quick Part
Research task pane, open	WD 253	Right-click text in document, point to Look up, click option; or, click Review tab, click Research button in Proofing group
Reveal Formatting pane, open	WD 245	Click [icon] at bottom of Styles pane, click [icon] in Style Inspector
Ribbon, customize	WD 444	Click File tab, click Options, click Customize Ribbon, click New Tab, click New Tab (Custom), click Rename, type tab name, click OK, click New Group (Custom), click Rename, type group name, click OK, select commands in list on left, click Add, click OK
Row, delete from table	WD 124	Click in row, click Delete button in Rows & Columns group on Table Tools Layout tab, click Delete Rows
Row height, change in table	WD 125	Drag divider between rows

TASK	PAGE #	RECOMMENDED METHOD
Rulers, display	WD 4	Click View tab, click Ruler checkbox in Show group
Section, insert in document	WD 138	Click where you want to insert section break, click Page Layout tab, click Breaks button in Page Setup group, click section break type
Shading, apply to paragraph	WD 38	Click in paragraph, click [button] in Paragraph group on Home tab, click color
Shape with text, add	WD 392	*See* Reference box: Adding a Shape with Text
SkyDrive, access files on	WD 358	*See* Reference box: Accessing Files Stored on Sky Drive
SkyDrive, create shared folder on	WD 358	Start Internet Explorer, sign into Windows Live, display your Sky Drive folders, click New, click Folder, type a name for new folder, click Change, select sharing options, click Next, click Add files, click select documents from your computer to begin uploading document you want to share
SkyDrive, email URL of file saved in Public folder	WD 358	Start Internet Explorer, sign into Windows Live, display document on your SkyDrive, right-click URL in browser's Address bar, click Copy, open email program and paste URL into a new email
SkyDrive, save document to	WD 356–357	Click File tab, click Save & Send tab, click Save to Web, click Sign In button and sign into Windows Live if necessary, click SkyDrive folder you want to save document to, click Save As, type file name in Save As dialog box, click Save
SmartArt, create	WD 140	Click Insert tab, click SmartArt button in Illustrations group, in left pane of the Choose a SmartArt Graphic dialog box click a category, in middle pane click a SmartArt style, click OK, replace placeholder text with new text
Special character, insert	WD 168	*See* Reference box: Inserting Symbols and Special Characters
Spelling, correct individual word	WD 11	Right-click word marked with wavy red underline, click correctly spelled word
Spelling and grammar, check	WD 71	*See* Reference box: Checking a Document for Spelling and Grammar Errors
Style, apply	WD 73	Select text, click style in Styles group on Home tab or click [button] in Styles group on Home tab and click a style
Style, create a new	WD 242	*See* Reference box: Creating a New Style
Style, modify	WD 226	*See* Reference box: Modifying Styles Using the Style pane
Style Inspector, open	WD 245–246	Click [button] at bottom of Styles pane
Style Set, select	WD 231	Click Home tab, click Change Styles button in Styles group, point to Style Set, click style set
Styles pane, change way styles are displayed in	WD 237	Click Options in bottom-right corner of the Styles pane, select style pane options, click OK
Styles pane, open	WD 236	In Styles group on Home tab, click Styles Dialog Box Launcher
Subdocument, create	WD 541	In Outline view, select text to convert to subdocument, click Create button in Master Document group on Outlining tab
Subdocument, expand	WD 551	In Outline view, click Expand Subdocuments button in Master Document group
Subdocument, insert	WD 539	In Outline view, on Outlining tab, click Insert button in Master Document group, select file, click Open

TASK	PAGE #	RECOMMENDED METHOD
Subdocument, merge	WD 543	In Outline view, click subdocument icon next to first subdocument, press and hold Shift, click subdocument icon next to second subdocument, click Merge button in Master Document group on Outlining tab
Subdocument, split	WD 542	In Outline view, click outline symbol next to piece of subdocument you want to split, click Split button in Master Document group on Outlining tab
Subdocument, unlink	WD 544	In Outline view, click subdocument icon next to subdocument you want to unlink, click Unlink button in Master Document group on Outlining tab
Symbol, insert	WD 168	*See* Reference box: Inserting Symbols and Special Characters
Synonym, replace selected word or text with	WD 254	Right-click word or selected text, point to Synonyms, click synonym
Tab stop, set	WD 133	*See* Reference box: Setting and Clearing Tab Stops
Table, convert to text	WD 311	Select table, click Table Tools Layout tab, click Convert to Text in Data group, select separator character, click OK
Table, delete	WD 118	Select table, right-click table, click Cut
Table, insert	WD 117	Click Insert tab, click Table button in Tables group, drag pointer to select columns and rows
Table, sort	WD 121	*See* Reference box: Sorting the Rows of a Table
Table, turn off automatic resizing	WD 468	Click table, click Table Tools Layout tab, click Properties button in Table group, click Options, click Automatically resize to fit content check box to deselect it, click OK, click OK
Table borders, draw	WD 480	Select table, click Table Tools Design tab, click Draw Table button in Draw Borders group, click Line Style button arrow and select desired line style, click Line Weight button arrow and select desired weight, click Pen Color button arrow and select desired color, drag on table to draw border
Table borders, erase	WD 464	Select table, click Table Tools Design tab, click Eraser button in Draw Borders group, drag over border
Table cells, create reverse type	WD 476	*See* Reference box: Creating Reverse (Light on Dark) Type in Table Cells
Table cells, merge	WD 462	Select cells, click Table Tools Layout tab, click Merge Cells button in Merge group
Table cells, split	WD 465	*See* Reference box: Splitting Cells
Table of Authorities	WD 599	Click References tab, click Insert Table of Authorities button in Table of Authorities group, click OK
Table of Contents, add text to	WD 251	Select text, click References tab, click Add Text button in Table of Contents group, click level
Table of Contents, create	WD 248	*See* Reference box: Creating a Table of Contents
Table of Contents, update	WD 252	Click References tab, click Update Table button in Table of Contents group, click Update entire table option button, click OK
Table of figures, create	WD 598	Click References tab, click Insert Table of Figures button in Captions group, click OK
Table style, apply	WD 126	*See* Reference box: Formatting a Table with a Table Style
Tabs, clear all from document	WD 305	Click Dialog Box Launcher in Paragraph group on Home tab, click Tabs, click Clear All, click OK

TASK	PAGE #	RECOMMENDED METHOD
Template from Office.com, create a new document from	WD 224	Click File tab, click New tab, click option under "Office.com Tempates," click template, click Download
Template installed with Word, create a new document from	WD 224	Click File tab, click New tab, click Sample templates, click template, click Create
Template saved to folder other than Templates folder, create new document from	WD 262	Click File tab, click New tab, click New from existing, navigate to correct location, click template, click Create New
Template saved to Templates folder, create new document from	WD 262	Click File tab, click New tab, click My templates, click template, click OK
Template, saving a document as	WD 259	*See* Reference box: Saving a Document as a Template
Text, align	WD 36	Select text, click [icon], [icon], [icon], or [icon] in Paragraph group on Home tab
Text, center vertically on page	WD 583	Click Page Layout tab, click Dialog Box Launcher in Page Setup group, click Layout tab, click Vertical alignment arrow, click Center, click OK
Text, convert to table	WD 307–308	Set up text with consistent separator characters, select text, click Insert tab, click Table button in Tables group, click Convert Text to Table, click appropriate option button under "Separate text at," click OK
Text, copy and paste	WD 63	*See* Reference box: Cutting (or Copying) and Pasting Text
Text, find and replace	WD 68	*See* Reference box: Finding and Replacing Text
Text, rotate in table cell	WD 467	Click cell, click Table Tools Layout tab, click Text Direction button in Alignment group as needed to achieve desired rotation
Text, select entire document	WD 37	Press Ctrl+A
Text, select multiple adjacent lines	WD 18	Click and drag in margin to left of text
Text, select multiple nonadjacent lines	WD 18	Select text, press and hold Ctrl, select additional lines of text
Text, select multiple paragraphs	WD 18	Click and drag in margin to left of text
Text box, insert	WD 399	Click Insert tab, click Text Box button in Text group, click Draw Text Box, click in document, type text
Text box, insert formatted	WD 400	Click Insert tab, click Text Box button in Text group, click desired style, click in document, type text
Text boxes, link	WD 402	Select text you want to link, click Insert tab, click Text Box button in Text group, click Draw Text Box, click outside the text box, click Text Box button in Text group, click Draw Text Box, drag to draw second text box, click in text box containing the content, click Text Box Tools Format tab, click Create Link button in Text group, and then click in the empty text box
Text Effects, apply	WD 33	Select text, click [icon] in Font group on Home tab, click text effect
Theme, select new	WD 77	Click Page Layout tab, click Themes button in Themes group, click theme
Theme colors, customize	WD 229	Click Page Layout tab, click [icon] in Themes group, click Create New Theme Colors, select theme colors, type theme name in Name box, click Save
Theme colors, select	WD 227	Click Page Layout tab, click [icon] in Themes group, click set of theme colors
Theme fonts, customize	WD 229	Click Page Layout tab, click [icon] in Themes group, click Create New Theme Fonts, select heading and body font, type name for theme fonts in Name box, click Save
Theme fonts, display	WD 78	Click Page Layout tab, point to [icon] in Themes group

TASK	PAGE #	RECOMMENDED METHOD
Theme fonts, select	WD 228	Click Page Layout tab, click [button] in Themes group, click set of theme fonts
Theme, create a custom	WD 229	Click Page Layout tab, click Themes button in Themes group, click Save Current Theme, navigate to new location if necessary, type theme name in File name box, click Save
Track Changes, accept and reject	WD 337	*See* Reference box: Accepting and Rejecting Changes
Track Changes, turn on or off	WD 326	Click Review tab, click Track Changes button in Tracking group
Translation languages, select	WD 256–257	Click Review tab, click Translate button in Language group, click Choose Translation Language, select language for Mini Translator and document translation, click OK
Translation of current document, display	WD 258	Click Review tab, select translation languages, click Translate button in Language group, click Translate Document
User name and initials, change	WD 326	Click Review tab, click Track Changes button arrow in Tracking group, click Change User Name, type new user name and initials, click OK
Watermark, create	WD 396	Click Page Layout, click Watermark button in Page Background group, click desired text watermark or click Custom Watermark, in Printed Watermark dialog box, click Picture watermark option button and then select picture or click Text watermark and type text in Text box, click OK
Web page, open in Internet Explorer	WD 373	Start Internet Explorer, right-click blank area of Favorites bar and click Menu Bar to insert a check if necessary, click File, click Open, select Web page, click OK
Web page, save document as	WD 367	*See* Reference box: Saving a Word Document as a Web Page
Window, split	WD 575	Click View tab, click Split button in Window group
Windows Explorer, open	FM 28	Click [button] on taskbar
Word, start	WD 4	Click [button], click All Programs, click Microsoft Office, click Microsoft Word 2010
WordArt, apply transform effect	WD 175	Click WordArt, click [button] in WordArt Styles group on Drawing Tools Format tab, click Transform, click transform effect
WordArt, change color	WD 175	Click WordArt, click [button] in WordArt Styles group on Drawing Tools Format tab, click color
WordArt, change shape	WD 176	Click WordArt, click [button] in WordArt Styles group on Drawing Tools Format tab, click Transform, click transform effect
WordArt, insert	WD 169	Click Insert tab, click WordArt button in Text group, click WordArt style, type text
WordArt, resize	WD 173	Click WordArt, drag corner handle, or, in Size Group on Drawing Tools Format tab, click Size button and change Height and Width settings
WordArt, wrap text around	WD 171	Click WordArt, click Drawing Tools Format tab, click Wrap Text button in Arrange group, click text wrap option
Workspace, scroll	OFF 9	Click arrow button on scroll bar or drag scroll box
Workspace, zoom	OFF 9	Drag Zoom slider
Zoom setting, change	WD 3	Drag Zoom slider